The Palgrave Handbook of Management History

Bradley Bowden • Jeffrey Muldoon •
Anthony M. Gould • Adela J. McMurray
Editors

The Palgrave Handbook of Management History

Volume 2

With 65 Figures and 6 Tables

Editors
Bradley Bowden
Griffith University
Nathan, QLD, Australia

Jeffrey Muldoon
Emporia State University
Emporia, KS, USA

Anthony M. Gould
Département des relations industrielles
Université Laval
Québec, QC, Canada

Adela J. McMurray
School of Management
RMIT University
Melbourne, VIC, Australia

ISBN 978-3-319-62113-5   ISBN 978-3-319-62114-2 (eBook)
ISBN 978-3-319-62115-9 (print and electronic bundle)
https://doi.org/10.1007/978-3-319-62114-2

© Springer Nature Switzerland AG 2020
This work is subject to copyright. All rights are reserved by the Publisher, whether the whole or part of the material is concerned, specifically the rights of translation, reprinting, reuse of illustrations, recitation, broadcasting, reproduction on microfilms or in any other physical way, and transmission or information storage and retrieval, electronic adaptation, computer software, or by similar or dissimilar methodology now known or hereafter developed.
The use of general descriptive names, registered names, trademarks, service marks, etc. in this publication does not imply, even in the absence of a specific statement, that such names are exempt from the relevant protective laws and regulations and therefore free for general use.
The publisher, the authors, and the editors are safe to assume that the advice and information in this book are believed to be true and accurate at the date of publication. Neither the publisher nor the authors or the editors give a warranty, expressed or implied, with respect to the material contained herein or for any errors or omissions that may have been made. The publisher remains neutral with regard to jurisdictional claims in published maps and institutional affiliations.

This Palgrave Macmillan imprint is published by the registered company Springer Nature Switzerland AG.
The registered company address is: Gewerbestrasse 11, 6330 Cham, Switzerland

This book is dedicated to the founding figures of management history:
- *Sidney Pollard (1925–1998)*
- *Dan Wren (1932–)*
- *Art Bedeian (1946–)*

As management historians, we stand on the shoulders of giants.

Preface

The *Palgrave Handbook of Management History* is going to press in a time of crisis as the effects of the Coronavirus and its aftermath cause the most profound economic, social, and managerial challenge since World War II. For a management historian who has a profound faith in the extraordinary resilience and strength of liberal, democratic free-market societies, this crisis brings to the fore the most fundamental issues of management – how do societies innovate, create value and wealth, provide sustainable employment, and raise the living standards of the ordinary citizen? In recent times, these issues – which have remained *the* fundamental challenges of *every* society – have taken second place behind concerns as to the environment, inequality, and the detrimental effects of globalization. As we move forward out of this crisis, these secondary problems still deserve attention, most particularly those relating to the detrimental effects of globalization, a process of economic integration that has stripped too many societies of their painfully constructed manufacturing capabilities, managerial expertise, labor skills, and employment opportunities. However, as we move forward, we need to remind ourselves of the gains that have been made across the decades and centuries rather than sink into a misinformed state of despair. On almost every front, the world is better placed to handle economic, social, and medical crises than what it was even 30 years ago. On every front, gains have been extraordinary. Poverty has been curtailed in every region on the planet. Literacy and education have increased massively. The supportive structures of the state in terms of welfare programs, medical advances, and educational experiences now provide a far more significant safety net than that which existed 30 or 40 years ago. In the USA, for example, in 2019 the *percentage* of Gross Domestic Product spent on social support services (e.g., education, health, welfare, etc.) was double what it was in 1960 and 50% higher than what it was in 1990 (OECD 2019). In absolute terms, the gains have been even more significant, given the massive increases in the American economy's overall capacity.

In considering the problems and possibilities before us, we need to remind ourselves how management has become one of the central institutions of modern civilisation. Whereas once the world of business was dominated by the activities of small-scale, family-owned enterprises, today the bulk of the goods and services produced within market economies are generated by corporate entities, each staffed by a bevy of managers and associated professionals (e.g., accountants, human resource staff, marketing and information technology personnel, etc.). Yes, it is true that small-scale entrepreneurs and start-ups still generate much of a modern economy's innovative drive, inventing new technologies and more efficient work practices. It is also true that small firms have similar managerial problems to large ones: they need to marshal resources effectively, motivate staff, and sell into competitive markets. Increasingly, however, innovation is only economically meaningful to the extent that new ideas are taken up by corporate behemoths and transformed into goods and services produced *en masse*. Numerically as well as economically, small-scale entrepreneurs find themselves overshadowed by an ever-growing class of professional managers. An Organisation for Economic Co-operation and Development (OECD) survey, for example, estimated that in 2014 only 15.8% of OECD labor force participants were self-employed. In 26 of the 37 OECD countries, moreover, self-employment declined between 2000 and 2014, often by significant margins (Peetz 2019: 163–164). In the case of the USA, labor force statistics suggest that only 10% of the workfroce were self-employed in 2014 (Desilver 2019). By contrast, the most recent US labor force statistics indicate that 11.38% of the workforce, some 14.8 million people, were employed in "management occupations." If we extend our estimates to include those in associated "business and financial occupations" the figure grows to 22 million, or 14.8% of the labor force (United States Bureau of Labor Statistics 2020).

The extraordinary rise of management as a profession and a discipline confronts us with fundamental questions that are central to the modern experience. What is management and in what ways do modern forms of management – as found in democratic market societies – differ from those found in both pre-industrial and totalitarian societies, if indeed there is a difference at all? Is the advance of modern forms of management a positive or negative historical phenomenon? Do the forms of management that emerged in the North Atlantic littoral during the eighteenth and nineteenth centuries have a universal application? Has there been a convergence or a divergence of global managerial practices across the last 50–100 years? It is to these questions that the *Palgrave Handbook of Management History* speaks.

In both the opening chapter (1, "Management History in the Modern World") and the introductory section of the *Handbook* (What is Management and Management History), we begin our exploration of these questions with a consideration of the deep divides that now characterize management history, a battle that has seen understandings of management itself become contested terrain. In reflecting upon current divisions within the discipline in our opening section, my Co-Editor, Jeffrey Muldoon (Chap. 5, "Conflicting Visions: A Recap About the Debates Within Management History"), makes a noteworthy point that I can only but endorse:

> My perception is that the field is very different from the one I entered into about 10 years ago. In some ways, the field is worse. Although the Journal of Management History remains a well-regarded journal, we no longer see history articles published in higher-level journals such as the Journal of Management. Although we have new perceptions, the clarity and precision that I believe characterized the field during the period of ascendancy and domination by the University of Oklahoma (Dan Wren) and the Louisiana State University ascendancy is increasingly gone. Yet, at the same time, we also have witnessed increased debates that are furthering the field. No matter one's perspective, these current debates about

traditional history versus the new postmodernist history can only benefit the field, as it moves us beyond single studies with little connection to each other to rigorous debates that may advance the discipline. Although I am a critic of much of the new history, I am respectful of the talents of the postmodernist side, their intellectual contributions, and mostly, because it is inspiring debate.

As I observe in the *Handbook*'s introductory Chap. 1, "Management History in the Modern World: An Overview," the contested field of management history today witnesses three different understandings of not only management but also its historical evolution. Long dominant is the tradition to which Muldoon is a proud exponent, one historically associated with the Management History Division of the Academy of Management in general and Dan Wren (University of Oklahoma) and Art Bedeian (Louisiana State University) in particular. Unabashed enthusiasts for free market capitalism, this US tradition has been primarily concerned with the ideas that have shaped management and how management has dealt with human problems of alienation and disengagement even as it pursued greater efficiencies. Existing alongside this American tradition is another school of thought of equally long standing, one associated with the Austrian-born English management historian Sidney Pollard – a tradition to which I subscribe. Although the differences between the American and Pollardian traditions are modest in the broad scheme of things, Pollard differed from his US counterparts in placing greater emphasis on the rupture that occurred in managerial practices with the Industrial Revolution. In Pollard's opinion, any resemblance between pre-industrial and modern forms of management – as they exist in market economies – are more apparent than real. As Pollard (1965: 7) explained it, modern managers are "unlike the builders of the pyramids" in that they have to "not only show absolute results in terms of certain products of their efforts, but to relate them to costs, and sell them competitively." Long ascendant, both the American and Pollardian traditions of management history are now under challenge from a new "critical" or "postmodernist" tradition that perceives management in universally hostile terms, as a source of oppression and degradation. As Roy Jacques and Gabrielle Durepos (2015: 101) expressed it in the *Routledge Companion to Management and Organizational History*, management "emerges from several major forces related to American industrialization beginning in the 1870s and largely completed by 1920"; changes initially associated with "an American 'Reign of Terror'" during the late nineteenth century, a time when capitalism and management "effectively silences the fight that was going on between labour and employers for authority within the factory." The problem with "management history," Jacques and Durepos (2015: 102) continue, is that "stories" about worker experiences from outside management "disciplines" (i.e., labor history, sociology, etc.) have typically been ignored by management history – a point that has undoubted merit.

In essence, the first half of the *Palgrave Handbook of Management History* is largely theoretical in purpose, as we explore both the debates that currently define the field *and* the historical origin of the concepts and understandings that underpin these debates. It is with these debates that we begin the *Handbook* with our first section,

What is Management and Management History? Edited by Jeffrey Muldoon, this section begins with a discussion as to the nature of management and concludes with Muldoon's Chap. 5, "Conflicting Visions: a Recap About the Debates Within Management History."

Although the first half of the *Handbook* is largely theoretical in nature, we would be negligent in our duties if we failed to locate current debates and understandings within a long-term perspective. This explanation necessarily entails two interrelated but distinct undertakings. One involves an exploration of the deep intellectual and organizational roots of management in the human experience. The other is an examination of the rupture that I believe occurred in managerial and work practices during the closing decades of the eighteenth century and the opening decades of the nineteenth century in the economies located around the North Atlantic littoral. It is to this issue that we turn in the *Handbook's* second part: Work, Management, and Economic Organization in the Pre-modern World. In doing so, this part emphasizes rather than downplays the transformation that occurred during the Industrial Revolution. In terms of transport, for example, the tonnage of a single modern bulk freighter easily surpasses that put to sea by the *combined* fleets of Genoa and Venice in the thirteenth century – fleets whose size and complexity were among the wonders of the late medieval world. In such circumstances, long-distance maritime trade was largely restricted to luxury items of high value (silks, spices, dyed woolen cloth, etc.) and durable necessities (grain, timber, wine). On land, transport problems were even more apparent. Only items of considerable value would bear the cost of transport that exceeded ten miles or more, an outcome that restricted the great bulk of pre-industrial production to strictly local needs. In turn, the gearing of production to local wants curtailed the need for innovation. Everywhere in the pre-modern world, a lack of smelted metal – which only became a common commodity from the 1780s – resulted in "capital" goods lacking in durability. In the absence of durable capital goods, productivity remained low. Across the globe, every society found itself bound within a Malthusian trap, a world in which temporary gains in population and output invariably hit what appeared an unbreakable resource ceiling. Even in England, the most dynamic European society, per capita living standards in the early 1700s were little different to those experienced in the early 1300s (Phelps Brown and Hopkins 1956). The Industrial Revolution thus heralded more than a new age of managerial endeavor. It also marked the dawn of a new era in the human experience, one where material plenty rather than privation became the lived experience of the typical citizen.

Both the Industrial Revolution and the revolution in ideas that preceded it (the European Enlightenment) entailed new ways in looking at the world, a transformation associated with not only new intellectual concepts but also new intellectual disciplines: most notably economics and management. Accordingly, in the third part of the *Handbook* (The Foundations of Knowledge and Management: An Introduction), Kaylee Boccalatte and I explore the epistemological and economic understandings that came to define the modern world. In doing so, we also investigate the oppositional currents – some grounded in socialism and Marxism and others in English Romanticism and German and Italian philosophic idealism – that emerged in contradiction to these dominant understandings. Following on from this, my fellow Editor, Jeffrey Muldoon, examines how the discipline of management emerged in the century and a half prior to World War II in a section entitled The Classic Age of Management Thought: Mid-nineteenth Century Until 1939. In this part, Muldoon investigates, among other things, the intellectual and practical contributions of Frederick Taylor, Henry Ford, Elton Mayo, Kurt Lewin, and those associated with Britain's Tavistock School, contributions that remain seminal not only to the managerial endeavors of the modern world but also to the disciplines of management, management history and organizational psychology. In the Handbook's fifth section, Postmodernism, I conclude the first half of the *Palgrave Handbook of Management History* by returning to the debates that currently divide management history through an exploration of the lives, ideas, and intellectual influence of the three most significant postmodernist thinkers: Jacques Derrida, Michel Foucault, and Hayden White. In considering the ideas of these three philosophers as well as postmodernism more generally, it is argued (Chap. 27, "Postmodernism: An Introduction" by Bowden) that "In the final analysis ... the fundamental differences between postmodernist and non-postmodernist historians revolves more around different understandings of freedom rather than different epistemologies." As disciples of Friedrich Nietzsche, Martin Heidegger, or Benedetto Croce, leading postmodernist philosophers have advocated a complete freedom of individual will and being. In considering this call for absolute freedom, I echo Albert Camus's (1951/1978: 296–297) belief that absolute freedom is always tyrannical, just as absolute virtue is always homicidal.

In the second volume of the *Palgrave Handbook of Management History*, we move from a consideration of the theoretical principles and debates that have both underpinned and divided management history to an estimation of how management has developed since World War II and how managerial practices have manifested themselves in various geographical locations. In the first section of this half of the Handbook, entitled Management in the Age of Prosperity, 1940s to 1980, Kevin Tennent has brought together seven chapters, penned by nine authors, covering themes such as Keynesianism, Peter Drucker, Michael Porter, Alfred Chandler, industrial relations, the rise of marketing and organizational psychology, as well as British management more generally. In summing up the transformation that occurred between 1945 and 1980, Tennent (Chap. 32, "Management in the Age of Prosperity, c. 1940–1990: Section Introduction") makes the pertinent point that these years represented a,

> ... third era of globalization, with an increasing emphasis on cross border trade in intermediate products and horizontal FDI with the expansion of multinational enterprises across borders, in the capitalist world at least. This impetus created new opportunities for managers and the overarching ideology of managerialism based around the planning and coordination of economic activity by dispassionate administrators, people who were ideally separated from the ownership of capital.

The post-1945 transformation in managerial ideas and practices is continued in Anthony Gould's section, Management in an Age of Crisis, which brings together seven single-authored chapters. In introducing this section, Gould (Chap. 40,

"Introduction: Public Policy Failure, the Demise of Experts, and the Dawn of a New Era") speaks to the central dilemmas of the modern world, observing how

> The story of the 45th U.S President's political ascendancy embodies the paradox of the last 50 years. Experts have let down the public... they have often been wrong... Wallowing in the intellectual debris of post-industrialism, more experts used more theory and logic to misread who was to be the President of the United States in 2016... the decimated middle-class and those worse-off... were fed-up with the experts, and not without justification. A new and dystopic era had emerged. It was post-neoliberalism – post-industrialism.

In the final two sections of the *Palgrave Handbook of Management History,* we turn our attention towards a consideration of how management has manifested itself geographically. In doing so, the question that we have constantly before us is the following: are we witnessing at a national or a regional level a continued application of Western models of management that largely emerged from the Anglosphere, or are we now witnessing something fundamentally different in Asia, Africa, Latin America, and Continental Europe? In short, has there been a convergence or divergence of managerial practices? To answer this fundamental question our penultimate section – Different Experiences: Europe, Africa, and the Middle East – examines the history of management in Africa (four chapters), the Middle East (one chapter), and Europe (chapters on France, Denmark, and the Orthodox East, i.e., Byzantium and Russia). In summary, this section points to the following conclusion: that in Africa and the Middle East, a Western model of capitalism and management has prevailed within the formal economy, as it has continued to do in Western Europe. By contrast, the historical experiences of Byzantium and Russia – each of which acted as the militarized eastern sentinels of European culture – proved infertile soil for Western models of capitalism and management. In our final section, we continue this geographical exploration through a consideration of the experiences of India, China (two chapters), Latin America, Australia, and New Zealand as well as Asia more generally. In doing so, we are led towards similar conclusions to that found in our penultimate section, namely that a Western model of capitalism and management has largely prevailed. The key exception to this rule, we suggest, has been China. As Elly Leung's (Chaps. 59, "The Making of a Docile Working Class in Pre-reform China," and 60, "Governmentality and the Chinese Workers in China's Contemporary Thought Management System") two chapters indicate, in China a new system of social and workplace despotism has emerged, a system of oppression based upon a fusion of traditional confucian beliefs and an updated variation of Mao Zedong's model of Marxism. Achieving extraordinary economic successes in the closing decades of the twentieth century and the opening decades of the twenty-first century, the long-term viability of this peculiar Chinese system of management now appears questionable. As mass uprisings in Hong Kong have indicated, Western models of freedom are hardly alien to modern Chinese aspiration. Such outcomes point to the fact that the Western model of management has been successful in large part because it has been associated with individual freedom. As Sidney Pollard (1965: 6–7) observed in *The Genesis of Modern Management,* "the absence of legal enforcement of unfree work was not only one of the marked characteristics of the new capitalism, but one of its seminal ideas, underlying its ultimate power to create a more civilized society."

In exploring the genesis and history of management the *Palgrave Handbook of Management History* owes a debt to many people, most particularly to the 27 authors who have contributed to our 63 chapters. A special debt is owed to our Section Editors, most particularly Kevin Tennent (University of York, UK), Anthony Gould (Laval University, Quebec), and Jeffrey Muldoon (Emporia State University, USA). As friends, collaborators, fellow authors, and editors, they have carried an often-heavy burden over the last 2 years. I would also like to acknowledge the efforts of Adela McMurray in initiating this project and in helping us through the project's initial travails. Finally, I would like to extend a special thanks to the staff of Palgrave's London office. In doing so, I – as well as all the editors and authors involved in this project – am particularly in the debt of Ruth Lefreve. Without her efforts and encouragement, this work would not have been possible.

Brisbane   Bradley Bowden
March 2020

References

Camus A (1951/1978) The rebel(trans: Bower A). Alfred A Knopf, New York

Desilver D (2019) Ten facts about American workers. Pew Research Centre, Washington DC. https://www.pewresearch.org/fact-tank/2019/08/29/facts-about-american-workers/

Jacques R, Durepos G (2015) A history of management histories: does the story of our past and the way we tell it matter. In: McLaren PG, Mills AJ, Weatherbee TG (eds) The Routledge companion to management and organizational history. Routledge, London/New York, pp 96–111

Organisation for Economic Co-operation and Development (2019) Social expenditure update 2019: Public social spending is high in many OECD countries. Organisation for Economic Co-operation and Development, Paris. http://www.oecd.org/els/soc/OECD2019-Social-Expenditure-Update.pdf

Peetz D (2019) The realities and futures of work. Australian National University Press, Canberra

Phelps Brown EH, Hopkins SV (1956) Seven centuries of the prices of consumables, compared with builders' wage rates. Economica 23(92):296–314

Pollard S (1965) The genesis of modern management: a study of the Industrial Revolution in Great Britain. Edward Arnold, London

United States Bureau of Labor Statistics (2020) Economic news release, Table 3 – union affiliation of employed wage and salary workers by occupation and industry. United States Bureau of Labor Statistics, Washington DC. https://www.bls.gov/news.release/union2.t03.htm

Contents

Volume 1

Part I Introduction 1

1 Management History in the Modern World: An Overview 3
   Bradley Bowden

Part II What Is Management and Management History? 23

2 What Is Management? 25
   Bradley Bowden

3 Debates Within Management History 45
   Jeffrey Muldoon

4 Methodologies Within Management History 67
   Jeffrey Muldoon

5 Conflicting Visions: A Recap About the Debates Within
   Management History 87
   Jeffrey Muldoon

**Part III Work, Management, and Economic Organization in
the Pre-modern World** 111

6 The Pre-modern World and Management: An Introduction 113
   Bradley Bowden

7 Management in Antiquity: Part 1 – The Binds of Geography 131
   Bradley Bowden

8 Management in Antiquity: Part 2 – Success and Failure in the
   Hellenic and Roman Worlds 153
   Bradley Bowden

9 From Feudalism to Modernity, Part I: Management, Technology, and Work, AD 450–1750 183
Bradley Bowden

10 From Feudalism to Modernity, Part 2: The Revolution in Ideas, AD 450–1750 215
Bradley Bowden

11 The Origins of Robust Supply Chain Management and Logistics in the Caribbean: Spanish Silver and Gold in the New World (1492–1700) 245
Oliver W. Aho and Robert A. Lloyd

12 Transformation: The First Global Economy, 1750–1914 271
Bradley Bowden

Part IV The Foundations of Knowledge and Management: An Introduction **307**

13 The Foundations of Knowledge and Management: An Introduction 309
Bradley Bowden and Kaylee Boccalatte

14 Intellectual Enlightenment: The Epistemological Foundations of Business Endeavor 321
Bradley Bowden

15 Economic Foundations: Adam Smith and the Classical School of Economics 345
Bradley Bowden

16 Neo-Classical Thought: Alfred Marshall and Utilitarianism 367
Kaylee Boccalatte

17 Foundations: The Roots of Idealist and Romantic Opposition to Capitalism and Management 387
Bradley Bowden

18 The Marxist Opposition to Capitalism and Business 411
Kaylee Boccalatte

19 Conflicting Understandings of the Industrial Revolution and Its Consequences: The Founding Figures of British Management History 435
Bradley Bowden

Part V The Classic Age of Management Thought (Mid-Nineteenth Century Until 1939) 473

20 Certain Victory, Uncertain Time: The Limitations of Nineteenth-Century Management Thought 475
    Jeffrey Muldoon

21 Taylor Made Management 499
    Jeffrey Muldoon

22 Henry Ford and His Legacy: An American Prometheus 521
    Jeffrey Muldoon

23 Spontaneity Is the Spice of Management: Elton Mayo's Hunt for Cooperation 545
    Jeffrey Muldoon

24 Organizational Psychology and the Rise of Human Resource Management 565
    Jeffrey Muldoon

25 To the Tavistock Institute: British Management in the Early Twentieth Century 593
    Jeffrey Muldoon

26 Kurt Lewin: Organizational Change 615
    Jeffrey Muldoon

Part VI Postmodernism 633

27 Postmodernism: An Introduction 635
    Bradley Bowden

28 The Intellectual Origins of Postmodernism 645
    Bradley Bowden

29 Paul-Michel Foucault: Prophet and Paradox 671
    Bradley Bowden

30 Jacques Derrida: Cosmopolitan Critic 699
    Bradley Bowden

31 Hayden White and His Influence 723
    Bradley Bowden

Volume 2

Part VII Management in the Age of Prosperity (1940s to 1980) 747

32 Management in the Age of Prosperity, c. 1940–1990: Section Introduction 749
Kevin D. Tennent

33 Keynesianism: Origins, Principles, and Keynes's Debate with Hayek 755
Kaylee Boccalatte and Bradley Bowden

34 The Age of Strategy: From Drucker and Design to Planning and Porter 781
Kevin D. Tennent

35 Chandler and the Visible Hand of Management 801
Kevin D. Tennent

36 Industrial Relations in the "Golden Age" in the UK and the USA, 1945–1980 823
Jim Phillips

37 The Rise of Marketing 841
Alex G. Gillett and Kevin D. Tennent

38 Organizational Psychology's Golden Age, 1940–1970 859
Alice White

39 British Management 1950–1980 873
John Quail

Part VIII Management in an Age of Crisis 887

40 Introduction: Public Policy Failure, the Demise of Experts, and the Dawn of a New Era 889
Anthony M. Gould

41 Labor and Employment Practices: The Rise and Fall of the New Managerialism 913
John Godard

42 A Return to the Good Old Days: Populism, Fake News, Yellow Journalism, and the Unparalleled Virtue of Business People 935
Mark Balnaves

43 Why did the Great Recession Fail to Produce a *New* New Deal in the USA? 951
Jon D. Wisman

44	Trade Union Decline and Transformation: Where to for Employment Relations? Bradley Bowden	971
45	The New Executive: Interconnected Yet Isolated and Uninformed – Leadership Challenges in the Digital Pandemic Epoch Kathleen Marshall Park	1011
46	Conclusion: Management Theory in Crisis Jean-Etienne Joullié	1047

Part IX Different Experiences: Europe, Africa, and the Middle East **1071**

47	Different Experiences: Europe, Africa, and the Middle East – An Introduction Bradley Bowden	1073
48	Management in the Middle East Anthony M. Gould	1081
49	Work and Society in the Orthodox East: Byzantium and Russia, AD 450–1861 Bradley Bowden	1105
50	Changing Corporate Governance in France in the Late Twentieth Century Peter Wirtz	1141
51	Flexicurity: The Danish Model Jørgen Burchardt	1163
52	Pre-colonial Africa: Diversity in Organization and Management of Economy and Society Grietjie Verhoef	1185
53	Africa and the Firm: Management in Africa Through a Century of Contestation Grietjie Verhoef	1207
54	Managing Africa's Strongest Economy: The History of Management in South Africa, 1920–2018 Grietjie Verhoef	1239
55	Why Entrepreneurship Failed to Emerge in "Developing Countries": The Case of Colonial Africa (1952–1972) Michele Akoorie, Jonathan M. Scott, Paresha Sinha, and Jenny Gibb	1269

Part X Different Experiences: Asia, Latin America, and the Pacific **1287**

56 Introduction: Management Heterogeneity in Asia 1289
    Anthony M. Gould

57 The Perfect Natural Experiment: Asia and the Convergence
    Debate 1317
    Anthony M. Gould

58 Indian Management (?): A Modernization Experiment 1331
    Nimruji Jammulamadaka

59 The Making of a Docile Working Class in Pre-reform China 1351
    Elly Leung

60 Governmentality and the Chinese Workers in China's
    Contemporary Thought Management System 1367
    Elly Leung

61 In Search of the Traces of the History of Management in
    Latin America, 1870–2020 1387
    Carlos Dávila

62 Think Big and Privatize Every Thing That Moves:
    The Impact of Political Reform on the Practice of Management
    in New Zealand 1411
    Andrew Cardow and William Wilson

63 Management in Australia – The Case of Australia's Wealthiest
    Valley: The Hunter 1431
    Bradley Bowden

Index 1465

About the Editors

Professor Bradley Bowden is an Australian academic and management historian. He is currently Editor-in-Chief of the *Journal of Management History* and Co-Editor in the Palgrave Macmillan Debates in Business History Series. He has twice won the Academy of Management's John F Mee Award for Outstanding Contribution to Management History. Between 2016 and 2017, he also served as Chair of the Management History Division of the Academy of Management.

Professor Jeffrey Muldoon is Associate Professor and Baehr Distinguished Professor at Emporia State University. His research interests include management history (with special emphasis on the Hawthorne studies and the career of George Homans), social exchange, entrepreneurship, and leadership. His research has appeared in such journals as *Stress and Health*, *Leadership and Organization Development Journal*, *Personnel Review*, *Career Development International*, and the *Journal of Management History*. His research in history had won the Best Student Paper at the Academy of Management in 2009 and the Most Outstanding Paper Award for the *Journal of Management History* in 2013 for his paper on The Hawthorne Legacy. Professor Muldoon is on numerous editorial boards, including Associate Editor of *Journal of Management History*. He also won the John F Mee award.

Professor Anthony M. Gould is *Professeur titulaire* (full professor) of Employment Relations at Laval University, Canada, and Chief Editor of *Relations industrielles/Industrial Relations*, the oldest journal of its kind in the world. Concurrently, he is a Visiting Research Professor at Griffith University in Brisbane, Australia, and sits on the International Advisory Committee of Macquarie University's Centre for Workforce Futures in Sydney, Australia, and the International Advisory Committee for the University of NSW Business School's *Economic and Labour Relations Review* also in Sydney. Professor Gould has served on the editorial committees of well-known scholarly journals including the highly respected *Journal of Management History*, a role for which he was awarded *Emerald Publishing*'s Best Reviewer Prize in 2017. With aide and encouragement from talented and generous colleagues, since 2010 Professor Gould has authored more than 20 peer-reviewed articles (often with others) concerning labor and economic history, industrial sociology, management strategy, and research methods. This *corpus* is published mostly in elite scholarly journals (as measured by *impact factor* and *Cite-Score, etc.*) and has been cited multiple times.

Professor Gould has held professional jobs in six countries while maintaining consulting and governance-based relationships with individuals and institutions in the Middle East and Asia. Prior to entering academia in 2007, he was a Senior Executive in large government agencies in Australia and the UK.

Professor Adela J. McMurray has extensive research experience in public and private sectors and has published over 280 refereed publications. Her research is internationally recognized and she is the recipient of four Australian Research Council grants, two Cooperative Research Centre grants, and various other competitive grants totaling over $5 million. Professor McMurray is Associate Editor of the *Journal of Management History*, has chaired the USA Academy of Management's International Theme Committee, and is a member of the Management History Division and a number of editorial advisory boards. She is the recipient of national and international awards for best research papers, teaching, and supervision excellence.

Contributors

Oliver W. Aho Department of Economics, Management, and Project Management, Western Carolina University, Cullowhee, NC, USA

Michele Akoorie ICL Graduate Business School, Auckland, New Zealand

Mark Balnaves Gulf University for Science and Technology, Kuwait City, Kuwait
University of Newcastle, Newcastle, NSW, Australia

Kaylee Boccalatte James Cook University, Douglas, QLD, Australia

Bradley Bowden Griffith Business School, Griffith University, Nathan, QLD, Australia

Jørgen Burchardt Museum Vestfyn, Assens, Denmark

Andrew Cardow School of Management, Massey University, Albany, New Zealand

Carlos Dávila School of Management, Universidad de los Andes, Bogotá, Colombia

Jenny Gibb School of Management and Marketing, University of Waikato, Hamilton, New Zealand

Alex G. Gillett The York Management School, University of York, York, UK

John Godard University of Manitoba, Winnipeg, MB, Canada

Anthony M. Gould Département des relations industrielles, Université Laval, Québec, QC, Canada

Nimruji Jammulamadaka Indian Institute of Management Calcutta, Kolkata, India

Jean-Etienne Joullié Gulf University for Science and Technology, Hawally, Kuwait
Université Laval, Québec, QC, Canada

Elly Leung Business School, University of Western Australia, Perth, WA, Australia

Robert A. Lloyd Fort Hays State University, Hays, KS, USA

Jeffrey Muldoon Emporia State University, Emporia, KS, USA

Kathleen Marshall Park Department of Administrative Sciences, Metropolitan College, Boston University, Boston, MA, USA

MIT Sloan School of Management, Cambridge, MA, USA

Jim Phillips Economic and Social History, University of Glasgow, Glasgow, UK

John Quail York Management School, University of York, York, UK

Jonathan M. Scott School of Management and Marketing, University of Waikato Tauranga CBD Campus, Tauranga, New Zealand

Paresha Sinha School of Management and Marketing, University of Waikato, Hamilton, New Zealand

Kevin D. Tennent The York Management School, University of York, York, UK

Grietjie Verhoef College of Business and Economics, University of Johannesburg, Johannesburg, South Africa

College of Global Business, Monash University, Melbourne, VIC, Australia

Alice White Wellcome Trust, London, UK

William Wilson School of Economics and Finance, Massey University, Albany, New Zealand

Peter Wirtz IAE Lyon School of Management, Magellan Research Center, University of Lyon, Lyon, France

Jon D. Wisman Professor of Economics, American University, Washington, DC, USA

Part VII

Management in the Age of Prosperity (1940s to 1980)

Management in the Age of Prosperity, c. 1940–1990: Section Introduction

32

Kevin D. Tennent

Contents

Introduction	749
Planning and Managerialism	750
The Fall of Planning	752
References	753

Abstract

Welcome to this section of the handbook, which focuses on the history and development of management in an intellectual and practical sense between the 1940s and the 1980s. The introduction provides a brief overview of the themes of the period which the chapters in the section go on to explore in more detail.

Keywords

Planning · Managerialism · Keynesianism · Post-War World

Introduction

When Bradley Bowden, the overall editor of this handbook, approached me to edit this section, based on the management history of the 1940–1990 period, I jumped at the chance. Growing up in its aftermath, in the 1980s and 1990s, the contradictions and challenges the post-war period threw up for economies and societies around the world have long fascinated me. As a graduate student in the late 2000s as the global financial crisis of 2007–2008 played out, I had the opportunity to teach on a module focusing on Britain's economic and business history from 1945 to 2000. The

K. D. Tennent (✉)
The York Management School, University of York, York, UK
e-mail: kevin.tennent@york.ac.uk

© The Author(s), under exclusive licence to Springer Nature Switzerland AG 2020
B. Bowden et al. (eds.), *The Palgrave Handbook of Management History*,
https://doi.org/10.1007/978-3-319-62114-2_111

complexity even of this story was both intriguing and gripping, and the phenomena within it set the subtext of many expectations, whether economic, social, political, legal, technological, environmental, or cultural that continues to play out in the twenty-first century. To meet these many opportunities, challenges, and contrasts, the discipline and practice of management also came of age in some ways, defining itself, and arguably perhaps even reaching the apogee of its powers. This section of the volume attempts to give a flavor of some of these opportunities, challenges, and contrasts. To some extent, it is centered on the experience of Western economies, particularly the USA and UK, and I accept that this is an inherent weakness, but these economies were in some ways dominant of the global discourse in this period, both positively and negatively, particularly in terms of the practice and ideology of management and this in itself makes them worthy of our study. I hope that you enjoy the chapters of this section and find them useful in your own work.

Planning and Managerialism

The era opened with the cataclysm that was World War II, fought globally between 1939 and 1945. Two regional conflicts in Europe and on the Pacific Rim essentially combined through the overlapping involvement of the lingering European empires, particularly the British, French and Dutch, together with the emerging global powers of the Soviet Union and the United States. As well as representing a triumph against the fascism of the Axis powers, Germany, Italy, and Japan, the war represented something of a re-arrangement of international geopolitics. The remaining European empires were fatally weakened through a complex process involving both the re-assertion of the rights of aboriginal peoples around the world and the subversion of their metropoles to the wider needs of the Cold War which would emerge between the United States and the Soviet Union. A new system of international relations and economic governance was put in place through the foundation of the United Nations and following the 1944 Bretton Woods conference, which aimed to establish a stable gold-based system for world currency, together with the introduction of the Global Agreement for Tariffs and Trade. The war had brought with it its own challenges of mass organization, creating a need to assess the suitability of potential leaders and train them, and Alice White's ► Chap. 38, "Organizational Psychology's Golden Age, 1940–1970" looks at the rise of organizational psychology, which emerged from the military in allied countries to become a major tool for management selection and training.

This new global system encouraged the emergence of what Jones (2009, p. 144) has described as the third era of globalization, with an increasing emphasis on cross border trade in intermediate products and horizontal FDI with the expansion of multinational enterprises across borders, in the capitalist world at least. This impetus created new opportunities for managers and the overarching ideology of managerialism based around the planning and coordination of economic activity by dispassionate administrators, people who were ideally separated from the ownership of capital. This will be the starting point for Kevin D. Tennent's

▶ Chap. 34, "The Age of Strategy: From Drucker and Design to Planning and Porter" on the development of the strategic management discipline. It is worth noting at this point, however, that this mid-twentieth century phenomenon was an inheritance from an earlier era, the Second Industrial Revolution, characterized by the emergence of scientific management (Taylor 1911) together with M-form structures (1962, 1977), and was then amplified in importance by thinkers such as Adolf Berle in the search for solutions to the Great Depression of the early 1930s. Berle and Means (1932) championed the concept of managerialism as an opportunity to allow the dispassionate redistribution of corporate profits; this idea was, to some extent, accepted in the mainstream of American corporate thinking until the 1970s (Smith et al. 2018, 2019) and further advocated by thinkers such as Peter Drucker in his many works (e.g., 1946, 1955, 1967, 1974), a selected few of which are considered by Tennent in his chapter. This organizational turn, based upon large-scale hierarchy and administrative bureaucracy, was not just confined to the United States, and critical conservative authors such as Burnham (1942) noted its similarity to the systems of political and economic coordination used in totalitarian fascist and communist states, and thus identified it as a potential threat to western democracy (McLaren 2011; Mollan 2019). These organizations, identified as the "modern industrial enterprise" by Alfred D. Chandler (1962), were easily conflated with the broader growth of government intervention in capitalist economies since the 1930s and which picked up in speed in the 1940s and 1950s, largely allied with demand-side stimulus economics inspired by the ideas of John Maynard Keynes (1936). Chandler's historical work, at first intended to "diagnose the present" more than the past, is the subject of ▶ Chap. 35, "Chandler and the Visible Hand of Management" by Kevin D. Tennent, while chapter "Keynesianism and it's Social and Political Influence" will investigate the hegemony of Keynesian thinking in the period.

The immediate aftermath of World War II, through to the early 1970s, was marked by a period of recovery then an age of untrammelled prosperity previously unknown, yet a series of new challenges and contradictions emerged. The industries of the Second Industrial Revolution reached their apogee in America and Europe, fuelled by the Cold War, rising consumerism and motorization, further encouraging the rise of the service sector. Wages reached record levels and living conditions improved dramatically, together with an expectation of full employment, while unionization reached new heights. Jim Philips' ▶ Chap. 36, "Industrial Relations in the "Golden Age" in the UK and the USA, 1945–1980" on industrial relations in the "golden age" investigates this phenomenon further. Medical breakthroughs such as antibiotics improved infant mortality dramatically, meaning that the post-war "baby boom" generation came to have a substantial economic, political, and cultural impact throughout their lives which is still playing out today, and which remains to be fully known as they enter old age. The economies of West Germany and Japan bounced back dramatically after the war, creating a sense of insecurity in English-speaking countries around the competitiveness of industry. Perhaps the impacts of these trends were most apparent in Britain, which saw continued economic growth and full employment based on service sector expansion in the London area at the same time as industrial decline in the North, Midlands, and Scotland, while seeing the loss of sterling as an exchange currency. John Quail will concentrate on attempts to introduce new management ideas into British industry in his ▶ Chap. 39, "British Management 1950–1980." Undoubtedly the age of high managerialism, coupled with large-scale political and economic planning, the 1950s and 1960s saw considerable prosperity and progress. Alongside the planning came consumerism and an increasing need to orient strategy toward the market, a phenomenon which Alex G. Gillett investigates in his ▶ Chap. 37, "The Rise of Marketing."

Conversely as the 1960s wore on and turned to the 1970s, there was considerable evidence that managerialism and the related discipline of rationalized strategic planning seemed to be failing both society and the economy, and was having a destructive impact on relations between the west and the rest of the world. One of the most high profile failures of strategic planning was the American escalation of the Vietnam War, led by Defense Secretary Robert McNamara, hired from Ford by President Kennedy to apply data-driven techniques (McCann 2017, p. 495). As the war continued and the Vietcong successfully engaged the American forces using guerrilla tactics, McNamara got caught up in a deadly feedback loop of planning for larger and larger direct applications of air and land forces. Meanwhile, in the economic sphere, the failure of the Penn Central Railroad in 1970 was blamed upon bureaucratic managerialism (Daughen and Binzen 1971). In the UK, the 1964–1970 Wilson government assumed the problem was that British industry was falling behind those of America, West Germany, and Japan due to a lack of scale, pumped money into the modernization of industry built new plants in declining industries, and forced companies to merge together, but ultimately failed to arrest the relative decline of the country's manufacturing sector (Owen 1999). Some of the trends investigated by Quail fall into this broader theme. This contrasted with the West German system of Ordoliberalism introduced after World War II in which the state had not interfered in the allocation of resources within industry, encouraging the relatively small firms of the *Mittelstand* to concentrate on consolidating technological advantage while introducing workplace co-determination in which workers were given seats on boards in 1952 (Bonefeld 2012; Kuntz 2018).

The Fall of Planning

The increasing confidence of postcolonial states who had acted to nationalize and expropriate western assets was to some extent exemplified by the 1973 oil crisis in which a group of Middle Eastern countries successfully exploited their position as oil exporters to send an inflationary shockwave through the western world. This unforeseen ripple destabilized economies though increasing inflation and unemployment such that Keynesianism was seen as unable to provide an effective response, and to a large extent hastened the turn away from planning that characterized the late 1970s and 1980s. Ironically, the crisis benefitted the Soviet Union, then expanding oil exploration, which was able to increase its lending to developing countries as the west was forced to retreat (Painter 2014). These shocks caused great impetus for change in management studies, with a Friedmanite (1962) view of the role of the corporation taking over, and encouraging management theory to narrow also, not just dropping planning, but with a confinement of the role of management to the economic sphere. The dogma of competition inspired by supply-side neoclassical economics replaced Keynesianism by the mid-1980s. This trend was perhaps best symbolized by the role of the work of Michael Porter (1979, 1980, 1985, 1990) who characterized corporate strategy as being oriented to the suppression of mobility barriers, but also a reduction in the role of labor unions, particularly in English-speaking counties. Once the Berlin Wall fell in 1989 and the Cold War ended, competition-based capitalism was assumed to have triumphed, despite the relative resurgence of China following reforms in 1979.

By the end of the period considered by this volume, a new form of stability had emerged. World War II remained important in social consciousness, but the sense of economic communalism and grand-scale corporatist planning for a progressive future it had engendered had evaporated as the need to rebuild had disappeared. The oil shocks themselves had reduced the faith of business in planning, together with a concern that management's time and effort was becoming tied up in unproductive processes. The state too tried to turn away from large-scale bureaucracy to an extent turning to the "New Public Management" in an attempt to run its organizations more efficiently (McLaughlin et al. 2002), partly placing an emphasis on relational working, a theme which Gillett's chapter addresses. The discipline was refocused, shorn of its societal role, but yet in this form found new relevance with the entry of the business or management school to the traditional university around the world. Managerialism, though more often at the time known as "administration" had been all powerful in the 1950s and 1960s, but had ultimately not succeeded in creating the progressive, enlightened society that its adherents from Berle to Drucker and Andrews had hoped for. This credo would be overtaken by a financialized form of management in which resources were allocated to production only to satisfy the needs of shareholders for a return, in both manufacturing and the newly risen service (and professional services) industries. The state and the allied force of industry in the form of professional managers were therefore easily portrayed as having failed in the post-war decades, ironically encouraging the rise of a new form of management more narrowly concerned with economic outputs. This "neoliberal view" would turn out to be perhaps more hegemonic in the 40 years following 1980 than managerialism and Keynesianism had been between 1940 and 1980. This was a fascinating period of contradiction and change indeed, both in management and the contested spaces of its activity, and I hope that the collection of chapters we present here goes some way toward satisfying the need for an explanation of its evolution and development.

References

Berle A, Means G (1932) The modern corporation and private property. Macmillan, New York
Bonefeld W (2012) Freedom and the strong state: on German Ordoliberalism. New Polit Econ 17(5):633–656

Burnham J (1942) The managerial revolution, or, what is happening in the world now. Putnam, London

Chandler AD (1962) Strategy and structure: chapters in the history of the American industrial enterprise. M.I.T. Press, Cambridge

Chandler AD (1977) The visible hand: the managerial revolution in American business. Harvard University Press, Cambridge, MA

Daughen JR, Binzen P (1971) The wreck of the Penn central. Little, Brown, Boston

Drucker P (1946) Concept of the corporation. The John Day Company, New York

Drucker PF (1955) The practice of management. Butterworth-Heinemann, Oxford

Drucker PF (1967) The effective executive. Butterworth-Heinemann, Oxford

Drucker PF (1974) Management: tasks, responsibilities, practices. Butterworth-Heinemann, Oxford

Friedman M (1962) Capitalism and freedom. University of Chicago Press, Chicago

Jones GG (2009) Globalization. In: The Oxford handbook of business history. Oxford University Press, Oxford

Keynes JM (1936) The general theory of employment, interest and money. Macmillan & Co, London

Kuntz T (2018) German corporate law in the twentieth century. In: Wells H (ed) Research handbook on the history of corporate and company law. Edward Elgar, Cheltenham

McCann L (2017) 'Killing is our business and business is good': the evolution of 'war managerialism' from body counts to counterinsurgency. Organization 24(4):491–515. https://doi.org/10.1177/1350508417693852

McLaren PG (2011) James Burnham, the managerial revolution, and the development of management theory in post-war America. Manag Organ Hist 6(4):411–423. https://doi.org/10.1177/1744935911425824

McLaughlin K, Osbourne SP, Ferlie E (2002) New public management: current trends and future prospects. Routledge, London

Mollan S (2019) Writing the right into management theory: from James Burnham to Samuel T. Francis. Inequality, Justice and Ethics Seminar Series, University of York Management School

Owen G (1999) From empire to Europe: the decline and revival of British industry since the second world war. Harper Collins, London

Painter DS (2014) Oil and geopolitics: the oil crises of the 1970s and the cold war. Hist Soc Res 39(4):186–208. https://doi.org/10.12759/hsr.39.2014.4

Porter M (1979) How competitive forces shape strategy. Harv Bus Rev 57(2):137–145. https://doi.org/10.1097/00006534-199804050-00042

Porter ME (1980) Competitive strategy: techniques for analyzing industries and competitors. Free Press, New York

Porter ME (1985) Competitive advantage: creating and sustaining superior performance. Free Press, New York

Porter ME (1990) The competitive advantage of nations. Free Press, New York

Smith A, Tennent KD, Russell J (2018) Berle and Means' the modern corporation and private property: the military roots of a stakeholder model of corporate governance. Seattle Univ Law Rev 1–25 (still online first)

Smith A, Tennent K, Russell J (2019) The rejection of industrial democracy by Berle and Means and the emergence of the ideology of managerialism. Econ Ind Democr. https://doi.org/10.1177/0143831X19883683

Taylor FW (1911) The principles of scientific management. Harper & Brothers, New York

Keynesianism: Origins, Principles, and Keynes's Debate with Hayek

33

Kaylee Boccalatte and Bradley Bowden

Contents

Introduction	756
The Economic Consequences of the Peace: Diplomat and Economic Critic	759
Richard Kahn and the Origins of Keynesianism	765
Keynes: Towards a General Theory	769
Keynes and Hayek: The Debate	773
Conclusion	776
Cross-References	778
References	778

Abstract

The son of a Cambridge economist and a student of Alfred Marshall, Keynes was raised to believe in the benefits of market forces and competition. Yet, Keynes went on to become *the* great exponent of state intervention in the economy. In arguing in favor of state intervention, however, Keynes also contended that the profit-motive provided "social and psychological justification for significant inequalities of income and wealth." A paradoxical figure, Keynes lived a life of wealth and privilege while always showing concern for the social effects of capitalism. In exploring Keynes's ideas, we trace his intellectual development from his first public work *The Economic Consequences of the Peace* through to his seminal work *The General Theory of Employment Interest and Money*. In doing so, we also explore how Keynes's work stimulated a powerful anti-Keynesian tradition through the rebuttals penned by Friedrich August Hayek,

---

K. Boccalatte (✉)
James Cook University, Douglas, QLD, Australia
e-mail: kaylee@btfarms.com.au

B. Bowden
Griffith Business School, Griffith University, Nathan, QLD, Australia
e-mail: b.bowden@griffith.edu.au

© The Author(s), under exclusive licence to Springer Nature Switzerland AG 2020
B. Bowden et al. (eds.), *The Palgrave Handbook of Management History*,
https://doi.org/10.1007/978-3-319-62114-2_33

an author who believed that government intervention always led to adverse long-term consequences by causing a misallocation of resources. As management historians, we suggest, a proper understanding of our craft can only be achieved if our ideas are grounded in an awareness of this debate.

Keywords

Keynes · Keynesian · Economics · Kahn · Hayek · Wealth creation · Investment · Employment

Introduction

Keynes changed the world. More specifically, his economic policies shaped the post-war global economy. By 1950, he was "the world's most celebrated economist" (Moss and Schumpeter 1996). Despite earning worldwide recognition and a place in history with the publication of his *The Economic Consequences of the Peace*, John Maynard Keynes achieved even greater fame with *The General Theory of Employment, Interest and Money* (Keynes 1919/2005, 1936/1964; Dimand 2019). With this book, Keynes believed that he would "largely revolutionise...the way the world thinks about economic problems" (Skousen 2007). Keynes was right. Having an acute understanding of the "economic theory of his time" Keynes was able to develop the "reasoned challenge to the reigning orthodoxy" of economics, a challenge embodied in *The General Theory* (Krugman 2018). Perhaps his exposure to sophisticated economics and the inner works of politics during his early years contributed to his "revolutionary" mind (Skousen 2007). An intellectual rebel, Keynes nevertheless grew up in privileged circles and was raised to "believe that free trade promoted peace" (Markwell and Oxford University Press 2006). His father was "an economics professor at Cambridge University" and a friend of Alfred Marshall – who would go on to be "described as a supreme" authority "among the economists of the English speaking world" (Davenport 1935/1965; Skousen 2007; ▶ Chap. 16, "Neo-classical Thought: Alfred Marshall and Utilitarianism" by K. Boccalatte). Keynes's mother bore an equally impressive figure as the "first woman mayor" of Cambridge (Skousen 2007). Despite receiving no "formal training" in economics (for his degree was in mathematics), Keynes, after only a "single course from Marshall," developed an acumen for the subject, "quickly" becoming proficient enough to begin teaching (Skousen 2007). Keynes's unique economic prowess would go on to flourish during some of the worst times in the history of the Western world. From the depths of destruction and devastation caused by World War I and its aftermath, Keynes became an economist – undeterred by the challenges of re-shaping an economy and purposed to better the lives of the people at their time of need. Keynes was not a socialist, for "he came to save capitalism, not to bury it" (Skousen 2007; Krugman 2018). He did, however, go on to become *the* great exponent of state intervention in the economy. This chapter examines Keynesianism and its social and political influence.

Keynes's early frustrations with economic management arose during the peace negotiations following World War I. During the war, Keynes was part of the "British Treasury" and later appointed as their "official representative" at the "Paris Peace Conference" where the *Treaty of Versailles* – the "Treaty of Peace with Germany" – would be negotiated (Keynes 1919/2005, 1936/2017; Treaty of Peace with Germany (Treaty of Versailles) 1919). Much to the disappointment of Keynes, the economic implications of negotiations were overlooked. The Paris Peace conference had centered its objectives on punishing those perceived by the war's victors as responsible for war rather than establishing a workable "peace" (Sharp 2010). Little attention was paid to economic stability. Rather, attention focused on detailing what Keynes deemed, a Carthaginian Peace. When it became clear that "hope could no longer be entertained of substantial modification" to the harsh terms of the treaty, Keynes "resigned" from his delegate position and made public his case against the treaty (Keynes 1919/2005). By this stage, Keynes was already an experienced economist. He saw that the development of the *Treaty of Versailles*, a "deliberately cruel settlement," as one constructed by the self-interest of a few that would have a steep cost to many (Sharp 2010). The strength of *The Economic Consequences of the Peace* is found in Keynes's ability to critically evaluate the conditions of Europe both before and after World War I in ways that highlight the interconnected nature of the European and global economy. Significantly, Keynes not only identified failings in the adopted terms of peace but also provided logical economic remedies to the issues being faced by Europe during this time. In order to understand Keynesianism and its social and political influence, therefore, it is necessary that we commence our analysis with the book that initially earned Keynes "a place in...history" (Dimand 2019). Accordingly, the first section of this chapter involves a discussion of Keynes's critique of the Versailles Treaty.

While Keynes's reputation as a "famous" economist had his roots in war, his ideas developed during the ensuing peace (Janes 2014). Returning to Cambridge following the war, Keynes met Richard Kahn. Kahn would go on to play a significant role not only in the development of Keynes's economic thought but in his life. After meeting Keynes, Kahn wrote his fellowship dissertation titled, *The Economics of the Short Period* (Aslanbeigui and Oakes 2011). The contents of this dissertation made "a remarkable contribution to the then-emerging theory of imperfect competition" and went on to influence "Keynes in his development of the appropriate framework for the economics of underemployment equilibrium" (Harcourt 1992/2003). While Kahn's dissertation was not published at the time, his next piece of work, an article entitled *The Relation of Home Investment to Unemployment*, was published only 1 year later (Aslanbeigui and Oakes 2011). Within this article, Kahn conceptualized the principle of the "multiplier," a theory later adopted and propounded by Keynes, allowing investors to "shape investment behaviour...the economy...and impact the lives of everyone in society" (Wolff and Resnick 2012). Kahn's contribution to economic development was, therefore, highly significant. Geoffrey Harcourt stated that had Kahn's dissertation "been published closer to the time when it was first written, it and his 1931 multiplier article together would surely have meant the subsequent receipt of the Nobel Prize" (Kent 2007; Harcourt 1994). Despite not receiving a Nobel Prize, Kahn's contribution to economics did not go unnoticed. In 1946 Kahn was appointed as a Commander "of the Civil Division of the Most Excellent Order" of the British Empire (Supplement. 37598: Central Chancery of the Orders of Knighthood 1946). And in 1965, he was presented with the prestigious title of "Barony of the United Kingdom" for life, thereby causing him to be known as "Baron Kahn" (Issue. 43708: Crown Office Corrigendum 1965). While the degree of Kahn's influence on Keynes is much debated, it is "fair to say that, without the crucial influence of Kahn, Keynes would not have reached...the particular insights that he did" (Harcourt 1994).

If the extent of Keynes's debt to Kahn is unclear, what is nevertheless obvious is the profound revolution in economic thought that Keynes initiated (Dimand et al. 2010). He not only developed a new theory – *The General Theory* – but also successfully exposed the "fallacy of composition" of traditional economics (Krugman 2018). Within his book, *The General Theory of Employment Interest and Money*, Keynes explores the economic foundations upon which society is built. In doing so, Keynes not only sought to understand the relationships between key factors of the economy but ultimately to "discover what determines the volume of employment" (Keynes 1936/2017). By the early 1930s such concerns were more than academic interest as the global economic slipped into a deep recession amid closing businesses and soaring unemployment. While there existed proposals for "long-run" solutions, as Keynes famously observed, "*In the long run* we are all dead" (Keynes 1929). Keynes took a novel approach to remedy this situation. Rather than investigating how and why the economy was depressed, Keynes looked to answer a critical question: "given that overall demand is depressed – never mind why – how can we create more employment?" (Krugman 2018).

The substance of Keynes's work was at a time embroiled in the "most famous" debate "in the history of contemporary economic thought" as Keynes exchanged intellectual blows with the Austro-English economist, Friedrich August Hayek (Bas 2011). Hayek's debate with Keynes confronts us with an alternate view on the consequences of interfering with the economy. An exponent for a measured external intervention in managing (i.e., stabilizing) the economy, Keynes's concepts presented within *The Treatise of Money* were challenged by Hayek in a series of published articles. Hayek was a supporter of "laissez-fair" economics (Facchini 2016), believing that interventionist tactics upset the natural state of the economy. Hayek argued, for example, that artificially improving the supply of money through lowering interest rates would have negative long-term economic consequences (Ebenstein 2003). Central to these adverse consequences, in Hayek's estimation, was an imbalance in the economy. For stimulating demand in the short term, Hayek believed that government intervention redirects capital away from long-term market needs and in consequence discourages "real investment" (Ebenstein 2003). Hayek published two lengthy articles, namely: *Reflections on the Pure Theory of Money of Mr. J. M. Keynes* and *Reflections on the Pure Theory of Money of Mr. J. M. Keynes (continued)* (along with one *Erratum* by the same name) criticizing elements of Keynes book (Hayek 1931a, b, 1932). Within his sole reply titled, *The Pure Theory of Money. A Reply to Dr. Hayek*, Keynes asserted that Hayek had misinterpreted his work, and even where Hayek's critique was correct, the matters he identified were inconsequential in terms of his overall conclusions (Keynes 1931). It can be thus surmised that the debate with Hayek contributed in part to the development and articulation of the ideas found within Keynes's later work in *The General Theory*.

Keynes's work revolutionized economic management. Living at a time that bore witness to some of the most volatile economic events experienced by the Western world (i.e., World War I, the Great Depression, and World War II), Keynes was determined to do what he could to make the world better for the people of this time, namely: improving the economy in the short term. Examining Keynes's contribution to management history is the core purpose of this chapter. In doing so, it is not possible to review all facets of his work. Instead, every effort will be made to do justice to those elements of his work which pertain to the central theme of this chapter. We will, therefore, commence this chapter with an examination of Keynes's first famed book *The Economic Consequences of the Peace* and trace the development of his models and concepts through to the publication of his seminal work *The General Theory of Employment, Interest and Money*.

The Economic Consequences of the Peace: Diplomat and Economic Critic

World War I shattered the global economy that had emerged during the nineteenth century (see ▶ Chap. 12, "Transformation: The First Global Economy, 1750–1914," for discussion of this economy). As Keynes expressed it, Germany "and her allies . . . imposed war" upon "the Allied and Associated Governments," and as a result "overturned the foundations on which" society "lived and built" (Keynes 1919/ 2005; Treaty of Peace with Germany (Treaty of Versailles) 1919). While an Armistice brought the war to an end in November 1918, the fight for peace was far from over (Henig 1995). Georges Clemenceau famously stated at the time, "we have won the war: now we need to win the peace, and it may be more difficult" (Henig 1995). In the wake of war, "the leaders of thirty-two countries" ("representing between them some three-quarters of the world's population") were responsible for negotiating the terms of peace, terms which would establish order, "make the world safe for democracy," and most importantly, "ensure that 1914–1918" was the "war to end all wars" (Sharp 2010). Five (original) Peace Treaties were signed for this purpose (Sharp 2010). Ending the war between Germany and the Allied and Associated Powers was the "Treaty of Peace with Germany" or the *Treaty of Versailles* (Keynes 1919/2005; Treaty of Peace with Germany (Treaty of Versailles) 1919).

Keynes predicted that the "terms of peace" contained within the *Treaty of Versailles* would have dire political and economic consequences for Europe (Keynes 1936/2017, 1919/2005; Sharp 2010). As the "British delegation's Treasury representative at the Paris Peace Conference," Keynes attended many conference sessions where the *Treaty of Versailles* was "negotiated" (Keynes 1936/2017; Janes 2014). He was displeased with their outcome. Germany was held responsible for imposing "war" and thus for the resultant "loss and damage" incurred by all those they subjected to war (Treaty of Peace with Germany (Treaty of Versailles) 1919). As such, it was believed that Germany should pay. Keynes was dissatisfied with the resulting "vindictive and unworkable settlement" (Sharp 2010). Aiming to overcome these issues diplomatically, Keynes expressed his concerns to "Foreign Secretary Sir Austen Chamberlain" writing, "We have presented a Draft treaty to the Germans which contains in it much that is unjust and much more that is inexpedient" (Graebner and Bennett 2011; Harrod 1982). Keynes was not alone in this belief. James Headlam-Morley, the British Political Intelligence Department's "effective leader," was quoted as saying on the eve of signing that, "I have not found one single person here who approves of" the treaty "as a whole." Headlam-Morley went on to say, the treaty is "quite indefensible and in fact is, I think, quite unworkable" (Sharp 2010; Graebner and Bennett 2011). Despite the growing "doubts and warnings" as to the long-term viability of the treaty permeating "the entire conference," no immediate revisions were made (Graebner and Bennett 2011).

Dissatisfied with the direction and likely "longevity" of the treaty, Keynes "resigned from the British delegation" in June of 1919 and took "his case against the Treaty from closed meeting rooms to the reading public" (Keynes 1936/2017; Sharp 2010; Keynes and Hutchison 1973). Keynes publicly objected to the "Allied leaders'" proposed "terms of peace" within his publication of *The Economic Consequences of the Peace* (Keynes 1936/2017, 1919/2005; Sharp 2010). It was with this book that Keynes found himself transformed from diplomat to economic critic. Publication of *The Economic Consequences of the Peace* also commenced Keynes's "public life," which saw him go on to become one of the "most important economic" thinkers of the "twentieth century" (Keynes 1936/2017). Contrasting post-war economic circumstances with the comparative prosperity that existed on the eve of hostilities, Keynes's study paints post-1918 Europe as a land of stark inequality. On the one hand, the people of England appeared "a great deal richer than" they were before the war. They were looking not only to replace what had been taken by the war but to "broaden and intensify" their lifestyle "comforts" (Keynes 1919/2005). Of England Keynes comments: "All classes alike...build their plans, the rich to spend more and save less, the poor to spend more and work less" (Keynes 1919/2005). On the other hand, the citizens of "continental Europe" were struggling to survive (Keynes 1919/2005). Central and Eastern Europe alike were destitute. Their citizens – "allied and enemy alike" – Keynes states, were engaged in a battle of "life and death, of starvation and existence"(Keynes 1919/2005, 1936/2017). Before the war, by contrast, the continent of Europe had prospered in apparent unity. Benefiting from advancing technologies in industry, transport, and communication, "the greater part of" European society was "reasonably contented" with its "standard of comfort" (Keynes 1919/2005). Of this pre-war European era, Keynes painted a picture of what was outwardly a veritable "economic Utopia" in which, for some, the world was their "oyster" (Keynes 1919/2005). Providing an example of this prosperity, Keynes states that an "inhabitant of London could order by telephone, sipping his morning tea in bed, the various products of the whole earth, in such quantity as he might see fit, and reasonably expect their early delivery upon his doorstep" (Keynes 1919/2005). Significantly, Keynes says, this same Londoner, considered "this state of affairs as normal, certain and permanent, except in the direction of further improvement" (Keynes 1919/2005). On the surface, Europe prospered. Under the surface of Europe's pre-war economy, however, was an unstable, untenable, and "unnatural reality" (Keynes 1936/2017). Four specific "economic peculiarities" contributed to this instability. According to Keynes, these included: "the instability of an excessive population dependent for its livelihood on a complicated and artificial organization, the psychological instability of the laboring and capitalist classes, and the instability of Europe's claim, coupled with the completeness of her dependence, on the food supplies of the New World" (Keynes 1919/2005). Running on an increasingly precarious foundation, the subsequent war shook the European economy to the core. With war, the "extraordinary" age of "economic progress" had come to an abrupt halt (Keynes 1919/2005). Life for the Europeans had changed, a "great part of the Continent" was now "sick and dying" (Keynes 1919/2005). After the war, hope for a better future, a future with "justice" satisfied and "life" re-established, hinged on the outcome of the Paris Peace Conference (Keynes 1919/2005).

The conference and the *Treaty of Versailles* were central to Keynes's critique. Four political leaders – David Lloyd George (Prime Minister of the United Kingdom), Georges Clemenceau (President of France), Thomas Woodrow Wilson (President of the United States of America) and to a lesser extent, Vittorio Emanuele Orlando (Prime Minister of Italy) – dominated negotiations for the *Treaty of Versailles* (Dimand 2019; Janes 2014). Each member of this "Council of Four," Keynes says, brought to the negotiations different characteristics and different agendas (MacMillan 2001; Keynes 1919/2005). Clemenceau, described as by "far the most eminent member of the Council," sought "to weaken and destroy Germany in every possible way" (Keynes 1919/2005). Preoccupied with "French interests" and an associated intention of subjecting Germany to a "Carthaginian Peace," Clemenceau paid little attention to the ways in which the stifling Germany's "commercial activity" would have a negative effect on Europe's economy (Keynes 1919/2005). Lloyd George was more cautious and perceptive by nature (Keynes 1919/2005). Outlining his approach to treaty terms, he stated: "I do not want ... to pursue any policy of vengeance, but we have got so to act that men in future who feel tempted to follow the example of the rulers who plunged the world into this war will know what is waiting for them at the end of it" (Sharp 2010). Lloyd George doubted Germany had the capacity to pay the "astronomical" cost of war. However, he succumbed to public demands for precisely this, winning the 1918 British election by effectively pledging to "extract the full cost of the war from Germany" (Dimand 2019; Keynes 1919/2005; Sharp 2010). Although Keynes considered Orlando a "minor player," Italian interests were often aligned with those of France. Thus, where treaty rights contrasted the interests of "French and Italian Industry" against "German industry," the united "French and Italian case" possessed "great force" in negotiations (Keynes 1919/2005, 1936/2017). Wilson, on the other hand, was a "major player" but lacked the political prowess necessary to influence the other members of the council (Keynes 1919/2005, 1936/2017). In describing Wilson, Keynes stated, he is someone who "would do nothing that was not honourable...nothing that was not just and right" (Keynes 1919/2005). In elaborating on this description, however, Keynes declared that the "President was not a hero or a prophet." Instead, he was "but a generously intentioned man... lacking that dominating intellectual equipment ... necessary to cope with the subtle and dangerous spellbinders ... in the swift game of give and take, face to face in Council – a game of which he had no experience at all" (Keynes 1919/2005). It was with this combination of men and their ability to develop a suitable treaty with Germany that the hopes of Europe's future rested.

The *Treaty of Versailles* would outline the reparations demanded of Germany for their role in initiating hostilities (Dimand 2019). Left seething by the terms of what they deemed "the Peace of shame," the German's did not have the capacity to pay the reparations demanded of them, reparations that were moreover outside the scope of the terms of the initial truce (Dimand 2019; Kershaw 2009; MacMillan 2001). For in requesting an armistice, Germany did so on the basis of "the Fourteen Points" outlined by United States President, Thomas Woodrow Wilson, during his "speech before Congress" in February 1918 (MacMillan 2001; Keynes 1936/2017, 1919/2005). Significantly, however, the major European victors (i.e., France, Britain, and Italy) were never prepared to accept Wilson's fourteen terms "without modification" (MacMillan 2001). For, Wilson's fourteen points provided reparation only for "invaded territory" and failed to account for the lives lost and damage done at sea and by air (Keynes 1919/2005). The cost of war had certainly been high. Soldiers' blood was spilled in battle, civilian lives were lost, and economies deteriorated. Accordingly, for the "victorious" Europeans, it was felt that Germany must pay for "*all... damage*" (Keynes 1919/2005). In summing up the conflicting agendas, Keynes stated that "Two rival schemes for the future polity of the world took the field – the Fourteen Points of the President, and the Carthaginian Peace of M. Clemenceau." Mutually opposed, Keynes went on to note that in the final analysis, "only one of these [plans] was entitled to take the field" (Keynes 1919/2005).

Keynes likened the *Treaty of Versailles* to the Carthaginian Peace: a peace which saw the "harsh...terms" imposed by Rome with the intent of disabling its ancient enemy, Carthage, to such a degree that there was no "possibility" of the city "recovering power" (Dimand 2019). Within the *Treaty of Versailles*, the Allies were seeking "compensation" from Germany for "all damage done to the civilian population of the Allies and to their property by the aggression of Germany by land, by sea, and from the air" (Keynes 1919/2005). Using a "strict interpretation" of these terms, Keynes calculated what damages could "be claimed from the enemy" (Keynes 1919/2005). France, according to Keynes, would have "the greatest claim" (Keynes 1919/2005). For losses incurred, to "*physical and material* damage" ($2.5b) and for losses at sea ($1.5b), Keynes calculated France was owed a figure amounting to approximately four billion dollars ($4b) (Keynes 1919/2005). Adding this figure to the cost of damages incurred by Great Britain, Belgium, and "Other Allies," Keynes surmised that the amount owing by Germany to her enemies, for damages incurred in war, totaled $10.6b. He believed that had the Allies requested the sum of $10b from the "German Government at the Peace Negotiations ... an immediate and certain solution" would have been achieved – a fair and *realistic* solution (Keynes 1919/2005). However, practicability was not a cornerstone of

Peace negotiations. Providing an example of the exorbitant amounts demanded of Germany, Keynes says the "French Minister for Finance" (M. Klotz) estimated his country's total "claims for damage to property" to be $26.8b. Klotz's figure, "more than six times" of Keynes's "estimate" could "never have been justified" (Keynes 1919/2005). In total, Keynes estimated that the *Treaty of Versailles* demanded of Germany approximately $40b in reparations (Keynes 1919/2005). This figure was more than 80 times greater than her annual "trade balance" adjusted for "the rise in pre-war prices" ($500,000,000) (Keynes 1919/2005). As such, the figure indebted Germany to reparation payments in excess of 30 years (the initial timeframe examined for reparation payments at the conference) (Dimand 2019). Keynes concludes his discussion on reparations by stating:

> The policy of reducing Germany to servitude for a generation, of degrading the lives of millions of human beings, and of depriving a whole nation of happiness should be abhorrent and detestable, – abhorrent and detestable, even if it were possible, even if it enriched ourselves, even if it did not sow the decay of the whole civilized life of Europe. Some preach it in the name of Justice. In the great events of man's history, in the unwinding of the complex fates of nations Justice is not so simple. And if it were, nations are not authorized, by religion or by natural morals, to visit on the children of their enemies the misdoings of parents or of rulers. (Keynes 1919/2005)

Keynes's main "purpose" in his book *The Economic Consequences of the Peace* was to "show that the Carthaginian Peace is not *practically* right or possible," nor was it a means to securing enduring peace (Keynes 1919/2005). The consequences of this treaty were nevertheless felt throughout Europe.

Europe immediately after the Treaty was in large part a place of misery. Economically stunted by the loss of domestic and international trade, a depression so severe as to mean "actual starvation for some" was feared to be on the horizon (Keynes 1919/2005). The "Council of Four" had paid "no attention" to the "economic rehabilitation of Europe" (Keynes 1919/2005). Three key facets of the European economy were perceived by Keynes as failing: "internal productivity," the ability to "transport and exchange" what was produced, and an "inability" to import the resources necessary for domestic production (Keynes 1919/2005). Moreover, domestic production was unable to feed and maintain the population. According to Mr. Hoover, "the population of Europe" was "at least [100 million] greater than" could "be supported without imports" (Keynes 1919/2005). Governments needed to intervene. However, in an unfortunate effort to "secure the resources...required" for domestic use, the European governments – "unable, or too timid or too short-sighted" to increase taxes or acquire loans – "printed notes for the balance" (Keynes 1919/2005). That is, they printed money in order to purchase necessary goods. Keynes aptly demonstrates that "this process" causes inflation and reduces the value of that country's currency. In severe cases (as had occurred in "Russia and Austria-Hungary"), the value of currency is rendered, "for the purposes of foreign trade...practically valueless" (Keynes 1919/2005). In these situations, without some form of "regulation," "essential commodities soon attain a level of price out of reach of all but the rich" (Keynes 1919/2005). For, as Keynes stated, "The price of imported commodities, when converted at the current rate of exchange" is far higher than the "local price" (Keynes 1919/2005). This means that "many essential goods will not be imported at all by private agency, and must be purchased by the government" and sold to citizens "below cost price" (Keynes 1919/2005). While this practice fends off society's starvation, it pushes a government towards "insolvency" (Keynes 1919/2005). Despite the country's currency retaining "a measure of purchasing power over some commodities" in domestic markets, inflation detrimentally affects the currencies ability to accurately represent the real value of any given commodity (Keynes 1919/2005). Keynes provides an example of the impact:

> If a man is compelled to exchange the fruits of his labors for paper which, as experience soon teaches him, he cannot use to purchase what he requires at a price comparable to that which he has received for his own products, he will keep his produce for himself, dispose of it to his friends and neighbors as a favor, or relax his efforts in producing it. A system of compelling the exchange of commodities at what is not their real relative value not only relaxes production, but leads finally to the waste and inefficiency of barter. (Keynes 1919/2005)

Inflation, Keynes says, is "not merely a product of the war, of which peace begins the cure. It is a continuing phenomenon" (Keynes 1919/2005).

Peace had failed to restore what war had destroyed. Keynes had remedies; proposals that he believed would create economic policies for the promotion and "re-establishment of prosperity and order" in Europe (Keynes 1919/2005). Past decisions such as those made by the Council of Four at the Paris Peace Conference could not be changed. The direction Europe took into the future, however, could be. Keynes outlined a plan for remedying Europe through four divisible yet interconnected areas, namely: "The revision of the treaty," "The settlement of inter-Ally indebtedness," "An international loan and the reform of the currency," and finally, reviewing the "the relations of Central Europe to Russia" (Keynes 1919/2005). Central to Keynes's proposed revision of the treaty was the modification of the reparations demanded of Germany, a revision that would see the cost of claims limited to a much reduced $10 billion and a feasible means – one proposed by Keynes – of extracting this payment over a 30-year period (Keynes 1919/2005). Inter-ally loans also required revision. War left many Allies (e.g., United Kingdom, France, Italy, Russia) with "a network of heavy" debts; debts that imposed significant economic strain upon countries financially struggling in the wake of war (Keynes 1919/2005). In proposing widespread changes to free these countries from the chains of this liability, Keynes stated:

> The war has ended with every one owing every one else immense sums of money. Germany owes a large sum to the Allies; the Allies owe a large sum to Great Britain; and Great Britain owes a large sum to the United States. The holders of war loans in every country are owed a large sum by the State; and the State in its turn is owed a large sum by these and other taxpayers. The whole position is in the highest degree artificial, misleading, and vexatious. We shall never be able to move again, unless we can free our limbs from these paper shackles. (Keynes 1919/2005)

Fiscal changes, however, formed only part of Keynes' plan. Many factors of European life required inter-country connectedness (i.e., transport, trade), and

Keynes believed that supporting Germany to "take up again her place in Europe as a creator and organizer of wealth for her Eastern and Southern neighbours" would benefit the European economy (Keynes 1919/2005). Recognizing that "many persons" would oppose these proposals, Keynes reminded his readers that when opposing a "German or Russian economic recovery" because of a "national...hatred for the populations or their Governments," society must be "prepared to face the consequences" of such actions. For, "Even if there is no moral solidarity between the races...of Europe, there is an economic solidarity which we cannot disregard" (Keynes 1919/2005). Accordingly, Keynes believed that the European public could build a stronger economic future for their country "by setting in motion those forces of instruction and imagination which change *opinion*" (Keynes 1919/2005). It was "to the formation of the general opinion of the future" that his book *The Economic Consequences of the Peace* was dedicated (Keynes 1919/2005).

Richard Kahn and the Origins of Keynesianism

After the war, Keynes returned to lecture at Cambridge. It was during this time that Keynes acumen for "making money" and "managing it" developed into an interest in monetary theory (Keynes 1936/2017). It was also during this time that he met Richard Kahn. Under the tutelage of Keynes, Kahn (influenced by "Marshall's *Principles*") began writing his Fellowship Dissertation on *The Economics of the Short Period* (Harcourt 1994; Kahn 1984). It was this topic choice that inadvertently stimulated the "radical restructuring of the shape of Keynes" work (Kahn 1984). Conceiving links between various factors of the economy (e.g., wages rates and prices or interest and employment), Kahn's dissertation not only displayed "considerable originality" but also developed concepts that would be utilized by others (including Keynes) in the study of economics (Aslanbeigui and Oakes 2011). Many of the concepts identified by Kahn were also "central concerns in the development of Keynesian theory" as evident in Keynes "short-period theory," *The General Theory* (O'Shaughnessy 1994; Kahn 1989).

If Kahn's fellowship dissertation had an enduring impact on Keynes's thinking, it was however not until the publication of Kahn's "multiplier" article in 1931 that a marked shift became evident in Keynes's public work (Kahn 1984). Published in the *Economic Journal* in June 1931, Kahn's article, entitled *The Relation of Home Investment to Unemployment*, not only introduced "the multiplier" into economic theory, it also "opened up" a realm of "possibilities" for which the "new technique" could be used (Wright 1956; Kahn 1984).

Kahn's "multiplier theory" is founded on the "fact that a net increase in the demand for any commodity, provided it is not offset by a decline in the demand for any other commodity, sets in motion a process of expansion which is eventually transmitted throughout the entire economic system" (Wright 1956). Taken independently, this definition is similar to Malthus or Lauderdale's "formulations of this type of theory of effective demand" which, according to Professor Paglin, "were on the right track, but...lacked precision" (Wright 1956; Spiegel 1971/1991).

Distinguishing Kahn's "multiplier theory" was its ability to demonstrate "*quantitatively* the related changes in income and (investment) demand" (Wright 1956). Despite Kahn never using the term "multiplier" within the article – instead employing the name "ratio" – by 1933 the term "multiplier" as a means to describe Kahn's theory had been "adopted in professional circles" (Wright 1956). Keynes applied the term (i.e., multiplier) within his work soon thereafter, first in his publication *The Means to Prosperity* and then again within a follow-up article, aptly named "The Multiplier" (Wright 1956).

It is evident that Richard Kahn played a marked role in Keynes's life. This is undisputed. What is debated in economic circles is "the nature of Kahn's contribution to Keynes's thinking" and the degree to which Kahn influenced Keynes' ideas (Marcuzzo 2002; Samuelson 1994).

Kahn was an understated economist. Combining "empirical investigation and theoretical innovation," Kahn's *The Economics of the Short Period* made a "substantial" contribution to economic theory, at the time of writing (i.e., 1930) (Aslanbeigui and Oakes 2011; Kahn 1989; O'Shaughnessy 1994). Inspiring Kahn's work was Marshall's "concept of the 'short period'" (Kahn 1989). However, while Marshall introduced "the element of Time as a factor in economic analysis," he did not explore its significance in-depth (Kahn 1989; Aslanbeigui and Oakes 2011). In economics, moreover, time is inherently difficult to measure when "there is no hard and sharp line of divisions between "long" and "short" periods" (Kahn 1989). Markets fluctuate. There are periods of "fairly continual expansions" and periods of "sub-normal activity" (Kahn 1989). Typically, periods of "sub-normal activity" do "not deviate from the long-period norm" (Kahn 1989). However, it is when these periods of "sub-normal activity" (e.g., decreased trade) extend persistently beyond "a year or two" and industries "approach a static state, as opposed to a state of progress," that the importance of action in the "short period" becomes readily apparent (Kahn 1989). The purpose of Kahn's dissertation was to "trace the factors that combine to determine the price and output of the product of an industry in such a short period" (Kahn 1989). Before Kahn, Marshall, like "other economists," "devoted...little space to the short period," treating "short-period effects, for the most part, as mere modifications of long-period tendencies" (Kahn 1989). Kahn, however, recognized that "the short period is not the same at both ends – and never has been" (Kahn 1989; O'Shaughnessy 1994). According to O'Shaughnessy, Kahn's "development of Marshall's concept of the short period" gave Keynes an important tool which was used to great effect in *The General Theory* (O'Shaughnessy 1994). He states:

> Rejecting Marshall's emphasis on a relatively quick adjustment to a position of long-period equilibrium, Kahn stressed the empirical relevance of the concept of short-period equilibrium, especially when the required adjustment was in a downwards direction. Since, in the short period, the quantity of labour required to produce a given output is mainly determined by technical considerations, there is no question of factor substitution. (O'Shaughnessy 1994)

According to Pigou, Kahn's dissertation, written post-World War I, had accomplished something "much harder than answering questions," for Kahn had "found the right questions to ask" (Aslanbeigui and Oakes 2011). There is thus little doubt that Keynes' prominent work, *The General Theory*, was influenced by the work of his former student, Kahn.

Both Kahn and Keynes had an interest in Britain's post-war economy. Specifically, the issue of unemployment. For post-war Britain was riddled with "workers, able and eager to work" but "denied the opportunity" to do so (Party 1929). Each political party vying for electoral success had a "solution" (Party 1929). Of the competing agendas, one proved more important for the development of Kahn's ideas than any others, namely the assertion by Lloyd George during his 1929 election campaign that the Liberal Party could reduce unemployment by funding public works (e.g., building "road and bridges") without increasing "national or local taxation" (Kahn 1931, 1984; Party 1929). The ability to finance such proposals was, however, "a key concern for...opponents and proponents during the election campaign" (Kent 2007). It was in determining the viability of Lloyd Georges' proposal that Keynes (a life-long Liberal supporter) and Henderson were inspired to publish *Can Lloyd George do it?* It was also central to Kahn's study, "The Relation of Home Investment to Unemployment" (Kahn 1984). In describing the effect of the former work, Kahn (1984) later recalled that Keynes and Henderson's work within *Can Lloyd George do it?* "marked a milestone in the development of thought." It also inspired Kahn himself to examine Lloyd George's proposal, primarily "because of" the "arithmetical and logical problems which it raised" (Kahn 1984).

Central to Lloyd George's campaign was employment, it being argued that the gainful employment of the country's "unemployed" population would have a positive and cumulative effect on economic progress. The "unemployment fund," at the time, paid a "cash disbursement of" £50 million per year in benefits to those without work (Keynes and Henderson 1929). Accordingly, if the government's proposed work program decreased the number of "unemployed," "relief" payments – including "the dole" – would "no longer be payable" to those members of society who had found work (Kent 2007). According to Keynes, this saving "alone would furnish between a quarter and a third of the total cost" of the government's proposals (Kent 2007). Further economic benefit, so it was predicted, would be found in the effects of increased consumption. For, a person "employed" spends more than a person "unemployed" (Kent 2007). Therefore, government "spending on public works" not only increases employment (decreasing unemployment payments), it also stimulates "greater trade activity" by increasing "domestic spending" and market "confidence" (Kent 2007). Government spending on public works would thus create a "cumulative effect." For "the greater trade activity" stimulated by the Government's initial investment in "public works" would go on to "make for further trade activity" (Kahn 1984; Keynes and Henderson 1929). Those directly employed by "public works" (i.e., primary employment) through increased spending and trade would stimulate a secondary wave of new employment (i.e., secondary employment).

Despite acknowledging this phenomenon, Keynes and Henderson, within their article, *Can Lloyd George do it?*, made "no attempt ... to separate out the ratio of secondary to primary employment" (Kahn 1984). Despite believing the correlative relationship between government spending employment was "of immense importance," they did not believe it was "not possible to measure the effects of" spending "with any sort of precision" (Kahn 1989). Keynes and Henderson, therefore, "so far as is known," "made no estimate of the 'multiplier' – the ratio of the total additional employment (primary and secondary) to the primary employment" within their publication (Kahn 1984).

For Kahn, the "superficially obvious object" of his article was to estimate the "multiplier" (Kahn 1984). Kahn's publication of "The Relation of Home Investment to Unemployment" thus both follows on from Keynes and Henderson's *Can Lloyd George Do It?* and acts as a corrective to its obvious failings. The scope of Kahn's publication, however, while examining the implications of Lloyd George's proposal for reducing unemployment by funding "public works," is restricted to the "arithmetical question" proposed by Lloyd's Georges claims (Kahn 1931, 1984). Distinguishing between "primary" and "secondary" forms of employment (terms later adopted by Keynes in *General Theory*), Kahn set the foundation from which he was able to calculate the changes in employment resulting from government investment (as proposed by Lloyd George) (Kahn 1984). In determining how "Government investment" influences the "ratio of secondary employment to primary employment," Kahn developed what became known as the "multiplier theory" (Kent 2007). Kahn's "multiplier" demonstrates how "exogenous" investment can stimulate a cycle of increased income and consumption within a society (Meade 1993). For, increased employment stimulates favorably "the state of confidence" for consumer and "entrepreneurs" alike (Kahn 1984). Significantly, Kahn (1984) later noted, no "account of the large increase in employment everywhere resulting indirectly from the addition to the national purchasing power represented by the wages of the workers directly employed in this way" had been attempted by economists (Kahn 1984). In seeking to remedy this failing, Kahn's theory was "designed to evaluate the amount of 'secondary' employment (in the ordinary consumption goods industries of a country) brought about by a given amount of 'primary' employment (in the production of capital goods)" (Kent 2007).

In reflecting upon the significance of "The Relation of Home Investment to Unemployment," Keynes subsequently observed that Kahn's,

> ... argument in this article depended on the fundamental notion that, if the propensity to consume in various hypothetical circumstances is (together with certain other conditions) taken as given and we conceive the monetary or other public authority to take steps to stimulate or to retard investment, the change in the amount of employment will be a function of the net change in the amount of investment; and it aimed at laying down general principles by which to estimate the actual quantitative relationship between an increment of net investment and the increment of aggregate employment which will be associated with it. (Keynes 1936/2017)

According to Keynes, "in given circumstances a definite ratio, to be called the *Multiplier*, can be established between income and investment and, subject to certain simplifications, between the total employment and the employment directly employed on investment" (i.e., "primary employment") (Keynes 1936/2017). In other words, the "value of the *multiplier*" is the "rate at which 'every dollar spent by the government...create[s] several dollars of income'" (Scheall 2015). As a result, governments working to close the gap between "current spending and the level of spending ... would ensure both zero inflation and zero unemployment" (Scheall 2015).

By establishing a "precise relationship...between aggregate employment and income and the rate of investment," we can thus see how Kahn's work was "integral" to the development of Keynes's "theory of employment" (Keynes 1936/2017). While the degree to which Kahn's work influences Keynes's is debatable, there is no doubt that Kahn – as both his "favourite pupil" and "Executor to Keynes' estate" as well as a close colleague – played a significant role in Keynes's life and the development of his economic theories (Fantacci et al. 2012; Kerr and Harcourt 2020).

Keynes: Towards a General Theory

The Great Depression of the 1930s was a "major turning point" in economic history (Crafts and Fearon 2013). Production rates fell, banks began to fail, and unemployment soared (Skousen 2007). Existing economic models (at the time) centered on "'long run' solutions" to the problem, solutions that did nothing to alleviate the troubles of financial strain imposed upon the people of the time (Keynes 1936/2017). Keynes believed economists "ought to... do better," do more to "alleviate some of that suffering," and more to aid the recuperation of the economy in the short term (Keynes 1936/2017). For, as he had famously stated in *A Tract on Monetary Reform*, "*In the long run* we are all dead" (Keynes 1929). Keynes acknowledged the failings of the capitalist or "free market" economy, specifically its inherent instability and its natural deterrence from full employment (Keynes 1936/2017; Skousen 2007). However, he also "argued that these failures had surprisingly narrow, technical causes" (Krugman 2018). As Keynes (1964: 379) expressed it,

> I see no reason to suppose that the existing system seriously misemploys the factors of production which are in use ... It is determining the volumes, not the direction, of actual employment that the existing system has broken down.

To redress the economy's perceived faults, Keynes proposed a solution: a "revolutionary" solution (Keynes 1936/2017). Within *The General Theory of Employment, Interest and Money*, Keynes proposed that governments "deliberately running federal deficit and spending money on public works...would expand "aggregate demand" and restore confidence" (Skousen 2007). His reasoning was simple: "mass unemployment has a simple cause, inadequate demand, and an easy solution, expansionary fiscal policy" (Krugman 2018). In summing up his views on fiscal expansion, Keynes (1964: 129) provided a famous if somewhat flippant example:

> If the Treasury were to fill old bottles with bank-notes, bury them at suitable depths in disused coal-mines ... and leave it to private enterprise on well-tried principles of **laissez-faire** to dig the notes up again (the right to do so being obtained, of course, by the tendering for leases of the note-bearing territory), there need be not more unemployment and ... the real income of the community, and its capital wealth also, would probably become a good deal greater.

Keynes's *The General Theory* was not the cause of the world's subsequent recovery from the depression. Where governments pursued policies of fiscal expansion – as with Franklin Roosevelt's New Deal – it was typically done without guidance from Keynes's *General Theory*, which was not published until 1936. Nor did "Keynesian" policies bring about the end of the Great Depression. It was World War II that "restored full employment" (Krugman 2018). Keynesian economics is, however, credited with aiding governments in their fight to ensure "the postwar world" did not "slip back into depression" (Krugman 2018).

Keynes's *The General Theory* rethinks economics. In introducing his theory, Keynes informed his "fellow economists" that escaping from the "habitual modes of thought and expression" is difficult (Keynes 1936/2017). However, he goes on to say that such an escape is necessary in order to open the mind and accept the "new" and "extremely simple" ideas presented in his book (Keynes 1936/2017). While Malthus had previously recognized "failures of demand were possible," in the 1930s there existed no "model" to support such a line of examination (Krugman 2018). For Keynes, "classical" economic models are applicable for explaining economic behavior only in a "special case" – not the "general case." They are thus inapplicable to "the economic society in which we actually live" (Keynes 1936/2017; Skousen 2007). By way of illustrating this, Keynes convincingly refuted the "then conventional" understanding of the relationship between wages and labor (Krugman 2018; Keynes 1936/2017). Classical economic theory, Keynes says, bases its "theory of employment" on two "fundamentally wrong" "postulates": (1) "The wage is equal to the marginal produce of labour"; (2) "The utility of the wage when a given volume of labour is employed is equal to the marginal disutility of that amount of employment" (Keynes 1936/2017). Diverging from classical thought, Keynes conceived that:

> When employment increases aggregate real income is increased. The psychology of the community is such that when aggregate real income is increased aggregate consumption is increased, but not by so much as income. Hence employers would make a loss if the whole of the increased employment were to be devoted to satisfying the increased demand for immediate consumption. Thus, to justify any given amount of employment there must be an amount of current investment sufficient to absorb the excess of total output over what the community chooses to consume when employment is at the given level. For unless there is this amount of investment, the receipts of the entrepreneurs will be less than is required to induce them to offer the given amount of employment. (Keynes 1936/2017)

By examining the *actual* behavior of the economy – forgoing "the way in which we should like our Economy to behave," as is characteristic of classical economists – Keynes was able to propose a relatively "simple" solution to overcoming economically depressed markets (Keynes 1936/2017; Krugman 2018). For in his model, increased demand not only stimulated increased production, it also produced an increase in investment as employer's put in orders for new machines, factories, and transport.

Constructing an alternative theory, detached from the models of classical economy requires sophisticated thought. According to Keynes, the "real classical model" could be described as "model of a barter economy, in which money and nominal prices don't matter" (Krugman 2018). Guided by Say's law (i.e., "supply automatically creates its own demand, because income must be spent"), and denying interest rates play a significant role in managing the economy, Keynes argued that traditional economics was fundamentally misguided (Krugman 2018; Keynes 1936/2017). Central to Keynes's alternative model was an attempt to "discover what determines the volume of employment" (Keynes 1936/2017). To begin explaining his theory, Keynes provided an overview of the factors comprising a business cycle, notably income, investment, and employment. Of these three factors, Keynes argued that demand is key to this cycle (Keynes 1936/2017). Reinforcing the significance of demand, Keynes states, "All production" (and thus all employment necessary to facilitate production) "is for the purpose of ultimately satisfying a consumer" (Keynes 1936/2017). Identifying what factors influence a consumer's "propensity to consume" is, therefore, central to demand (Keynes 1936/2017). Accordingly, stimulation of these demand factors – including, the wage-unit, income, and capital-values (i.e., the value of one's home) – has the ability to influence the level of aggregate demand (Keynes 1936/2017). According to Keynes, "the propensity to consume is a fairly stable function" and "as a rule, the amount of aggregate consumption mainly depends on the amount of aggregate income" (Keynes 1936/2017). This insight is significant to understanding of employment. For it leads Keynes to conclude that "employment can only increase *pari passu* with an increase in investment; unless, indeed, there is a change in the propensity to consume" (Keynes 1936/2017). Furthermore, by establishing a "ratio" (i.e., multiplier) "between income and investment and… between the total employment and the employment directly employed on investment," Keynes was able to determine "the precise relationship, given a propensity to consume, between aggregate employment and income and the rate of investment" (Keynes 1936/2017). This "step is an integral part" of Keynes's "theory on employment" (Keynes 1936/2017).

What factors influence investment? This deceptively simple question requires a highly complex response. Prior to examining the question, Keynes outlined *why* a person may invest, noting that when a person "buys an investment or capital asset," they purchase "the right to the series of prospective returns, which" they expect "to obtain from selling its output, after deducting the running expenses of obtaining that output, during the life of the asset" (Keynes 1936/2017). In other words, people invest with the expectation of being better off than they would otherwise have been. By calculating the *marginal efficiency of capital,* investors are able to determine the net return they can expect to receive from a capital investment (Keynes 1936/2017; Krugman 2018). Keynes defined the *marginal efficiency of capital* as "being equal to that rate of discount which would make the present value of the series of annuities given by the returns expected from the capital-asset during its life just equal to its supply price" (Keynes 1936/2017). There exists, therefore, a relationship between "the marginal efficiency of capital" and "the rate of investment" (Krugman 2018; Keynes 1936/2017). Keynes, however, expanded on this finding, stating that "the rate of investment will be pushed the point on the investment demand-schedule where the marginal efficiency of capital, in general, is equal to the market rate of interest (Keynes 1936/2017). From this accurate insight, Keynes concluded that it is the "investment demand-schedule" (i.e., the depreciation or wearing out of past investment) and the "rate of interest" that influences investment (Keynes 1936/2017). In tying this insight with the volume of employment, it can be concluded that "employment is determined by the point at which the value of output is equal to the sum of investment and consumer spending" (Krugman 2018). Consumer spending is thus central to employment, spurring not only direct production but also increased investment. As Keynes stated, "since the expectation of consumption is the only *raison d'être* of employment, there should be nothing paradoxical in the conclusion that a diminished propensity to consume has" all things being equal, "a depressing effect on employment" (Keynes 1936/2017).

Wages and price have an important relationship in the economy. In exploring their relationship, Keynes posed two questions: (a) "Does a reduction in money-wages have a direct tendency...to increase employment?" (b) "does a reduction in money-wages have a certain or probable tendency to affect employment in a particular direction" (Keynes 1936/2017)? Keynes not only looked toward his theory in order to answer these questions but, characteristically, also outlined how his theory filled the gap left by classical thought. Classical economics, specifically "Professor Pigou's *Theory of Unemployment*" says Keynes, has "no method of analysis" through which these questions are able to be answered (Keynes 1936/2017). For, classical theory "has nothing to offer, when it is applied to the problem of what determines the volume of actual employment as a whole" (Keynes 1936/2017). Keynes's theory on the other hand does. According to Keynes, a reduction in wages does *not* correlate with an increase in employment (Keynes 1936/2017). Instead, changes in employment levels are influenced by changes in aggregate demand (Keynes 1936/2017). Keynes nevertheless identified that there are various methods through which demand may be increased – each with varying degrees of success. In summary, Keynes observed that, "If, for example, the increased demand is largely directed towards products which have a high elasticity of employment, the aggregate increase in employment will be greater than if it is largely directed towards products which have a low elasticity of employment" (Keynes 1936/2017). If investment cultivates demand, it must therefore follow that money influences demand. It also follows that money primarily influences demand through the "rate of interest" (Keynes 1936/2017). However, this conclusion "presents a deceptive simplicity" (Keynes 1936/2017). For, the rate of interest is quantitatively affected by "the schedule of liquidity-preference," "the schedule of marginal efficiencies" and "the investment multiplier," each of which is individually defined by a further layer of factors, including wages (Keynes 1936/2017). Given these complexities, Keynes concluded that Government intervention is vital to ensuring a stable economic future.

A free market, free from any form of government intervention is inevitably subject to severe fluctuations in trade cycles. Free markets, therefore, in Keynes's estimation, typically fail to "provide for full employment" or an equitable distribution of "wealth and incomes" (Keynes 1936/2017). Accordingly, in summing up the need for government intervention in the economy, Keynes (2019) stated

> In conditions of *laissez-faire* the avoidance of wide fluctuations in employment may...prove impossible without a far-reaching change in the psychology of investment markets such as there is no reason to expect. I conclude that the duty of ordering the current volume of investment cannot safely be left in private hands.

Unlike traditional economists, Keynes also recognized the importance of interest rates in managing an economy (Keynes 1936/2017). For the "rate of interest" has the direct ability to influence economic activity (Keynes 1936/2017). Acknowledging that in a free market, "the rate of interest is not self-adjusting at a level best suited to the social advantage," Keynes asserted that government intervention in managing interest rates aids not only the alleviation of the "booms" and "slumps" of the market. It also has the ability to keep the economy in a "quasi-boom" state (Keynes 1936/2017). As Keynes stated:

> ...the remedy for the boom is not a higher rate of interest but a lower rate of interest! For that may enable the so-called boom to last. The right remedy for the trade cycle is not to be found in abolishing booms and thus keeping us permanently in a semi-slump; but in abolishing slumps and thus keeping us permanently in a quasi-boom.

In calling for increased state intervention, Keynes was not, however, a proponent for socialism. Instead, he aimed to "save capitalism" from its own failings (Krugman 2018). In doing so, he believed that incentives such as "money-making" and "private wealth-ownership" were critical to ensuring that certain "activities" reach their full potential (Keynes 1936/2017). Keynes's remedy to a depressed economy, unlike "many of his contemporaries" (i.e., socialists, communists, fascists, etc.) vying for "government takeover," involved the government introducing policies to stimulate "effective demand" and revitalize the market in the relatively short term (Krugman 2018). For Keynes, the problem of mass unemployment was, in fact, relatively easy to solve (Krugman 2018).

Keynes and Hayek: The Debate

Keynes did not develop his revolutionary theory without controversy. Party to the "most famous" debate "in the history of contemporary economic thought" was John Maynard Keynes and "rival" economist, Friedrich August Hayek, who would later win a Nobel Prize in Economics (Bas 2011). Supporting "doctrines...in direct opposition to Keynes," it was Hayek who initiated the debate with a critical review of Keynes's work in *A Treatise on Money* (Bas 2011; Facchini 2016; Kahn 1984). In doing so, Hayek set out to "show up" Keynes's *Treatise* "as a theoretical dead end"

(Hayek 1935/2008). The debate that ensued spanned 2 years (1931–1932) and centered primarily on the interpretation of the content of Keynes book, and more specifically their differing views on the "nature of a free market economy" (Bas 2011; Facchini 2016). At the time of this debate, the global economy was already failing, evidence in Keynes's estimation that the "self-regulating" free market was *not* "self-regulating" (Keynes 1936/2017). As an exponent for "interventionism" (Facchini 2016), Keynes believed that markets could be stabilized by government policies without any detrimental effect on a nation's long-term productive capacities (Facchini 2016). Hayek, on the other hand, was a supporter of "laissez-fair" economics (Facchini 2016).

The debate between Keynes and Hayek was important not only in itself but also in terms of the theoretical conclusions that occurred as a result of their interaction (Bas 2011). The most obvious effect of the debate is found in Keynes's reaction, Keynes subsequently declaring that a desire to "re-shape and improve" his "central position" was behind his early withdrawal from the debate (Bas 2011). The main result of this reshaping of ideas is found in Keynes's publication of *The General Theory*, a work that displayed a "new elaboration of his model" when compared to that found within his previously published *The Treatise on Money* (Bas 2011). While the debate between the two economists ended, for the followers of their respective disciplines it was – and is – "indeed, ongoing" (Scheall 2015).

Hayek is renowned for his "profound and enduring" contribution to economic thought, most specifically his work on macroeconomics. In his first major work, *Prices and Production* – a study that was originally presented across four lectures at the University of London in 1930–1931 – Hayek outlined a novel theoretical proposal: that "industrial fluctuations" are caused by a "misalignment" between real loan interest rates and the "natural rate of interest" (Scheall 2015; Hayek 1935/2008). For, in Hayek's estimation, when real loan interest rates are "below" the "natural rate," economic instability – a precursor to economic collapse – ensues (Scheall 2015; Keynes 1936/2017). As Hayek observed, "unnaturally low interest rates lead in the short run to what appear to be positive effects that are inexorably reversed in the longer run: boom is eventually and unavoidably followed by bust" (Scheall 2015).

Hayek's solution to stimulating the trade cycle in depressed markets was markedly different to that of Keynes's. Keynes argued that by increasing consumer demand and elevating consumption levels (i.e., spending), economic "breakdown" could be curtailed (McNerney 2016). Thus, government intervention plays an important role in controlling market fluctuations. For Hayek, however, disrupting the *natural* order of the market had long-term consequences. Artificially "lowering interest rates," for example, manipulates monetary supply, thereby distorting the "structure of production by encouraging [the] production of temporarily early capital goods" (Ebenstein 2003). In times of depression, third-party management of interest rates thus creates an imbalance in the economy (Ebenstein 2003). For, "in the short run, increase in the demand for consumer goods can redirect production from longer temporal capital processes to the quick production of consumer goods, thereby entailing less capital investment in the longer temporal process" (Ebenstein 2003).

Hayek's point was that unnatural intervention "would discourage real investment," i.e., investment that usefully serves the long-term needs of the economy (Ebenstein 2003).

Hayek's critical review of Keynes's *The Treatise on Money* ignited a debate that would outlive both parties. Central to the debate was Hayek's criticism of Keynes's incomplete analysis of a "capital theory" (Scheall 2015; Facchini 2016). While Keynes acknowledged that a more thorough analysis would have improved his study, he was of the opinion that publication of the work was "too pressing to wait for an adequate theoretical analysis" (Scheall 2015; Facchini 2016). According to Hayek, Keynes's "fallacious theory of capital" was the root of many problems within his work. For, from this theory stemmed an "obscure analysis of investment" and an "unsatisfactory account of profits" – central factors of an economy (Hayek 1931b; Zouache 2008). While Hayek agreed "perfectly" with Keynes's assertion that the profits achieved by "entrepreneurs" has a direct influence on an entrepreneur's business, he also sensibly observed that there exists a correlation between profits and the level of investment undertaken by entrepreneurs (Hayek 1931b). As a result, Hayek disagreed with Keynes's account of "why profits arise" and "with his implication that only changes in 'total profits' ... can lead to an expansion or curtailment" in production (Hayek 1931b). According to Hayek, Keynes's assessment led one to believe "that *any* change in the amount of capital per head of working population is equivalent to a change in the average length of the roundabout process of production" (Hayek 1932). He went on to say:

> ... his [Keynes] exclusive insistence on new investment and his neglect of the process of re-investment makes him overlook the all-important fact that an increase in the demand for consumers' goods will not only tend to stop new investment, but may make a complete reorganisation of the existing structure of production inevitable-which would involve considerable disturbances and would render it impossible, temporarily, to employ all labour. (Hayek 1932)

What Keynes is ultimately discussing within his *Treatise on Money*, according to Hayek, are "shifts in the money streams and the consequent changes in price levels" (Hayek 1932). He goes on to say that "It seems never to have occurred to him that the artificial stimulus to investment, which makes it exceed current saving, may cause dis-equilibrium in the real structure of production which, sooner or later, must lead to a reaction" (Hayek 1932). Ultimately, Hayek says, Keynes's explanation of a trade cycle dictates that the central factor influencing an economic "boom" is *not* "the increase in investment, but the consequent increase in the prices of consumer's goods and the profit which is" subsequently gained (Hayek 1932). He goes on to provide three key reasons why Keynes's proposal would consequently fail in practice, namely: the stimulus is not able to be maintained indefinitely, increased consumer demand may lead to a "decrease in investment," and finally it may "produce a decrease" in "general activity and employment" (Hayek 1932).

Keynes's response to Hayek's critique is surmised in a relatively short article, *The Pure Theory of Money. A Reply to Dr. Hayek* (Keynes 1931). Within this paper, Keynes surmised that many of the faults identified and examined by Hayek were in fact misinterpretations of his work. Moreover, Keynes suggested, where Hayek's criticisms were true they did not detract from the fundamental concepts that Keynes had outlined. Referencing the content of Hayek's publication *Prices and Production* throughout, Keynes's reply evolves to become in part a review of Hayek's book. Careful to emphasis what he perceived to be a fundamental failing of Hayek's work in his response to Hayek, Keynes reviews the concepts within *Prices and Production* stating:

> This book as it stands, seems to me to be one of the most frightful muddles I have ever read, with scarcely a sound proposition in it beginning with page 45, and yet it remains a book of some interest, which is likely to leave its mark on the mind of the reader. It is an extraordinary example of how, starting with a mistake, a remorseless logician can end up in Bedlam. Yet Dr. Hayek has seen a vision, and though when he work up he has made nonsense of his story by giving the wrong names to the objects which occur in it, his Khubla Kahn is not without inspiration and must set the reader thinking with the germs of an idea in his head. (Keynes 1931)

Following the publication of his response, Keynes withdrew from the "debate" (Bas 2011).

As a result of the three articles Hayek authored in *Economica* "reflecting" upon Keynes's work in the *Treatise on Money* – and Keynes's response to this intellectual assault – Hayek's critique "dominated" the academic journal (i.e., *Economica*) "for a full year" (Ebenstein 2003; Hayek 1931b, 1932). Several generations on, the questions that emerged from the debate still inform and divide economists, managers, business leaders, politicians, and governments. What is the best response to a slowing economy? Is it government intervention, directed towards full employment and increased demand? Or, should instead, society seek instead to bolster the supply-side factors in the economic equation: profits, higher productivity, greater efficiencies? As in the time of Hayek and Keynes, these questions remain deeply divisive.

Conclusion

Across his academic career, Keynes spoke to the central issues of his time, creating insights and debates that remain central to our time. A member of the British delegation responsible for the drafting of the *Treaty of Versailles*, Keynes vehemently opposed to the harsh peace terms. The purpose of his first major book *The Economic Consequences of the Peace* was "to show that the Carthaginian Peace is not *practically* right or possible" (Keynes 1919/2005). The "Germans could not pay what they had not got," nor was it in the best interests of Europe for Germany to be transformed into an "inefficient, unemployed" nation with no hope of economic recovery (Dimand 2019; Keynes 1919/2005).

Evident within the final chapters of *The Economic Consequences of the Peace* is a clear interest in macroeconomic factors, and the relationship between political decisions and economic outcomes. In pursuing these themes, Keynes's ideas were influenced by his one-time student, Richard Kahn, an economist who conceived the "Multiplier Theory," i.e., the "rate at which 'every dollar spent by the government...create[s] several dollars of income" (Scheall 2015). In building upon Kahn's insights in his *The General Theory*, Keynes transformed not only economics but also politics through his attack on the "reigning orthodoxy of classical economics" (Krugman 2018). Unlike his classical counterparts, Keynes recognized that within a free market, decreased demand can lead to not only "involuntary unemployment" but also a vicious economic circle whereby falling consumer demand led to further reductions in both demand and production (Krugman 2018). Arguing that a free market is – if left to itself – often incapable of providing "full employment," Keynes' proposed a theory that would "save capitalism" rather than destroy it (Keynes 1936/2017; Krugman 2018). In doing so, Keynes proposed that government intervention in the form of "policies" aimed at regulating "effective demand" (Krugman 2018; Keynes 1936/2017). In aiming to increase consumer demand, Keynes argued, the main short-term objective is not increased levels of individual wealth but rather a greater *inducement* to invest. For, as Keynes (1936/1964: 31–32) explained in his *General Theory*,

> If in a potentially wealthy community the inducement to invest is weak, then, in spite of its potential wealth, the working of the principle of effective demand will compel it is reduce its actual output, until, in spite of its potential wealth, it has become so poor that its surplus over its consumption is sufficiently diminished to correspond to the weakness of the inducement to invest.

Although Keynes was no socialist, his ideas nevertheless represented a profound questioning of the role of market competition in liberal democratic societies. No one recognized this with greater clarity than Hayek, one of the twentieth century's greater defenders of competition and free markets. In critiquing Keynes's work in 1931–1932, Hayek observed that Keynes was trying to steer economic thought in a relatively new direction, attempting to "amalgamate" his "new ideas with the monetary teaching tradition in Cambridge" (Hayek 1931b). According to Hayek, this attempt was unsuccessful. His thoughts on the matter were communicated within three articles (two with written substance) written in response to Keynes publication, *The Treatise on Money*. Despite referring to Keynes works as "undeniably...magnificent," Hayek is largely critical of the publication, finding faults in many key elements including, prices, investment, and capital (Hayek 1931b, 1932). In providing his criticisms of Keynes, Hayek was not only giving voice to what became a powerful anti-Keynesian tradition during the closing decades of the twentieth century, he also provided a spur to Keynes, forcing him into a thorough reconsideration of his own principles; a reconsideration that found fruit in Keynes's *General Theory*.

As management historians, we still live in the shadow of the Keynes-Hayek debate. Divisive as this debate has been, we can nevertheless hardly pursue our own analysis without an understanding of economics in general and this debate in particular. For, as Keynes once said:

...the ideas of economists and political philosophers, both when they are right and when they are wrong, are more powerful than is commonly understood. Indeed, the world is ruled by little else. Practical men, who believe themselves to be quite exempt from any intellectual influences, are usually the slaves of some defunct economist.

Cross-References

► Conflicting Understandings of the Industrial Revolution and Its Consequences: The Founding Figures of British Management History
► Economic Foundations: Adam Smith and the Classical School of Economics
► Intellectual Enlightenment: The Epistemological Foundations of Business Endeavor
► Neo-classical Thought: Alfred Marshall and Utilitarianism
► The Marxist Opposition to Capitalism and Business

References

Aslanbeigui N, Oakes G (2011) Richard Kahn's fellowship dissertation: the fate of 'the economics of the short period'. Eur J Hist Econ Thought 18(3):381–405. https://doi.org/10.1080/09672560903552629
Bas DS (2011) Hayek's critique of the general theory: a new view of the debate between Hayek and Keynes. Q J Austrian Econ 14(3):288–310
Crafts NFR, Fearon P (2013) The great depression of the 1930s: lessons for today, 1st edn. Oxford University Press, Oxford. https://doi.org/10.1093/acprof:oso/9780199663187.001.0001
Davenport HJ (1935/1965) The economics of Alfred Marshall. Cornell University Press, New York
Dimand RW (2019) One hundred years ago: John Maynard Keynes's the economic consequences of the peace: edited by John Maynard Keynes, London: Macmillan, 1919; New York: Harcourt, Brace and Howe, 1920, 298 pp. Hist Econ Rev 73(1):1–13. https://doi.org/10.1080/10370196.2019.1656080
Dimand RW, Mundell RA, Vercelli A, International Economic Association (2010) Keynes's general theory after seventy years, vol 147. Palgrave Macmillan, New York/Basingstoke
Ebenstein A (2003) Friedrich Hayek: a biography. The University of Chicago Press, Chicago
Facchini F (2016) The Hayek-Keynes macro debate continues. J Écon Étud Hum 22(1):1–13. https://doi.org/10.1515/jeeh-2016-0012
Fantacci L, Marcuzzo MC, Rosselli A, Sanfilippo E (2012) Speculation and buffer stocks: the legacy of Keynes and Kahn. Eur J Hist Econ Thought 19(3):453–473. https://doi.org/10.1080/09672567.2010.501109
Graebner NA, Bennett EM (2011) The Versailles Treaty and its legacy: the failure of the Wilsonian vision. Cambridge University Press, New York. https://doi.org/10.1017/CBO9780511835162
Harcourt GC (1992/2003) On political economists and modern political economy. Routledge, London
Harcourt GC (1994) Kahn and Keynes and the making of "the general theory". Camb J Econ 18(1):11–23. https://doi.org/10.1093/oxfordjournals.cje.a035256
Harrod RFS (1982) The life of John Maynard Keynes. Norton, New York
Henig RB (1995) Versailles and after, 1919–1933, 2nd edn. Routledge, London/New York. https://doi.org/10.4324/9780203134306
Issue. 43708: Crown Office Corrigendum (1965) The London Gazette, July 9

Janes D (2014) Eminent Victorians, Bloomsbury Queerness and John Maynard Keynes' the economic consequences of the peace (1919). Lit Hist 23(1):19–32. https://doi.org/10.7227/LH.23.1.2

Kahn RF (1931) The relation of home investment to unemployment. Econ J 41(162):173–198. https://doi.org/10.2307/2223697

Kahn RF (1984) The making of Keynes' general theory. Press Syndicate of the University of Cambridge, Cambridge

Kahn R (1989) The economics of the short period. Palgrave Macmillan, New York

Kent RJ (2007) A 1929 application of multiplier analysis by Keynes. Hist Polit Econ 39(3):529–543. https://doi.org/10.1215/00182702-2007-021

Kerr P, Harcourt GC (2020) Joan Robinson: critical assessments of leading economists, vol 1. Routledge, London

Kershaw I (2009) Hitler. Penguin Books, London

Keynes JM (1919/2005) The economic consequences of the peace. Harcourt, Brace and Howe, New York

Keynes JM (1929) A tract on monetary reform. Macmillan, London

Keynes JM (1931) The pure theory of money. A reply to Dr. Hayek. Economica 34:387–397. https://doi.org/10.2307/2549192

Keynes JM (1936/1964) The general theory of employment, interest, and money. Harcourt Brace Jovanovich, New York/London

Keynes JM (1936/2017) The general theory of employment, interest, and money. Wordsworth Editions, Hertfordshire

Keynes JM, Henderson HD (1929) Can Lloyd George do it? The Nation and Athenaeum, London

Keynes JM, Hutchison TW (1973) The collected writings of John Maynard Keynes, volumes I–VI and XV–XVI. Econ Hist Rev 26(1):141–152. https://doi.org/10.2307/2594765

Krugman P (2018) Introduction to the general theory of employment, interest, and money, vol 2020. Springer Nature Switzerland AG, Switzerland

MacMillan M (2001) Peacemakers six months that changed the world. John Murray, Hachette

Marcuzzo MC (2002) The collaboration between J. M. Keynes and R. F. Kahn from the treatise to the general theory. Hist Polit Econ 34(2):421–447. https://doi.org/10.1215/00182702-34-2-421

Markwell D, Oxford University Press (2006) John Maynard Keynes and international relations: economic paths to war and peace. Oxford University Press, New York/Oxford. https://doi.org/10.1093/acprof:oso/9780198292364.001.0001

McNerney J (2016) Wealth of persons: economics with a human face. Cascade Books, Eugene

Meade J (1993) The relation of Meade relation to Kahn multiplier. Econ J 103(418):664–665

Moss LS, Schumpeter JA (1996) Joseph A. Schumpeter, historian of economics. Routledge, London/New York

O'Shaughnessy TJ (1994) Kahn on the economics of the short period. Camb J Econ 18(1):41–54. https://doi.org/10.1093/oxfordjournals.cje.a035260

Party L (1929) We can conquer unemployment: Mr. Lloyd George's Pledge. Cassell and Company, La Belle Sauvage, London

Samuelson PA (1994) Richard Kahn: his welfare economics and lifetime achievement. Camb J Econ 18(1):55–72. https://doi.org/10.1093/oxfordjournals.cje.a035261

Scheall S (2015) Slaves of the defunct: the epistemic intractability of the Hayek-Keynes debate. J Econ Methodol 22(2):215–234. https://doi.org/10.1080/1350178X.2015.1024875

Sharp A (2010) Consequences of peace: the Versailles settlement: Aftermath and legacy, 1919–2010. Haus Pub, London

Skousen M (2007) The big three in economics: Adam Smith, Karl Marx, and John Maynard Keynes. M.E. Sharpe, Armonk. https://doi.org/10.4324/9781315700229

Spiegel HW (1971/1991) The growth of economic thought, 3rd edn. Duke University Press, London

Supplement. 37598: Central Chancery of the Orders of Knighthood (1946) The London Gazette (Supplement), June 13

Treaty of Peace with Germany (Treaty of Versailles) (1919) Library of Congress

von Hayek FA (1931a) Erratum: reflections on the pure theory of money of Mr. J. M. Keynes. Economica 34. https://doi.org/10.2307/2549191

von Hayek FA (1931b) Reflections on the pure theory of money of Mr. J. M. Keynes. Economica (33):270–295. https://doi.org/10.2307/2548035

von Hayek FA (1932) Reflections on the pure theory of money of Mr. J. M. Keynes (continued). Economica (35):22–44. https://doi.org/10.2307/2548974

von Hayek FA (1935/2008) Prices and production and other works. Ludwig von Mises Institute, Auburn

Wolff RD, Resnick SA (2012) Contending economic theories: neoclassical, Keynesian, and Marxian. MIT Press, Cambridge, MA

Wright AL (1956) The genesis of the multiplier theory. Oxf Econ Pap 8(2):181–193

Zouache A (2008) On the microeconomic foundations of macroeconomics in the Hayek-Keynes controversy. Eur J Hist Econ Thought 15(1):105–127. https://doi.org/10.1080/09672560701858707

The Age of Strategy: From Drucker and Design to Planning and Porter

34

Kevin D. Tennent

Contents

Introduction	782
Proto-strategy: Organizational Statesmanship and Managerialism	784
The Golden Age of the Design and Planning Schools	788
Positioning Strategy: The Impact of Michael Porter	793
Concluding Remarks	796
References	797

Abstract

By the 1990s, Strategic Management had emerged and consolidated itself as a "capstone" element of many business and management school degree programs, most notably on MBA courses. This chapter follows the development of the strategic management discipline from the late 1930s to the early 1990s by considering some of the most important works in the field, demonstrating how strategy detached itself from the broader managerial and societal concern of organizational purpose reflected in the works of authors in the field before 1975. It narrowed in focus to become a purely economic construct, with the effect of hiving off governance and leadership as entirely separate academic subfields.

Keywords

Strategic management · Drucker · Porter · Mintzberg · Design school · Positioning school

K. D. Tennent (✉)
The York Management School, University of York, York, UK
e-mail: kevin.tennent@york.ac.uk

© The Author(s), under exclusive licence to Springer Nature Switzerland AG 2020
B. Bowden et al. (eds.), *The Palgrave Handbook of Management History*,
https://doi.org/10.1007/978-3-319-62114-2_36

Introduction

The period from the Second World War until the 1980s was one in which the developed world grew more comfortable with the concept of the large organization as an integral part of the economy and society. It was, to a large extent, the dominant mechanism for the organization of the capital-intensive second industrial revolution industries then in their heyday as well as the emerging organizations of the third, as well as some of the increasingly important service industries. Scale was felt through the factors of capital, land, and labor as organizations had evolved to subsume and organize their own supply chains and distribution channels. Industrial and commercial organizations, typologized by Alfred D. Chandler (1962) as the "modern industrial enterprise," were therefore becoming increasingly complicated, employing many more people than before, and typically developed hierarchies and managerial structures that involved a mix of decentralization and centralized authority, often with chains of managers or administrators who were increasingly removed from the shop floor. The modern industrial enterprise together with other large-scale corporate organizations was enjoying an increasing amount of authority over the everyday lives of the populace in western countries and gradually in the wider world too. This behemoth is needed to be controlled and directed in some way (although for whose benefit remained contested ground). The academic disciplines of administrative science, business policy, and then eventually strategic management emerged to rise to the challenge of providing theories and prescriptions to first make sense of and then provide instruction for this challenge. Generally speaking, this involved deliberate and conscious forward thinking of some form as to how best to direct and deploy these resources, through some rationalizing process.

This chapter aims therefore to discuss some of the major themes emerging from this cache of writers who attempted to provide schemas for the rationalization and control of the modern industrial enterprise, which undoubtedly involved the evolution of a business progressive paradigm with quasi-militarist overtones. The strategic management discipline, with its inherent disagreements and competing schools of understanding as it emerged from the 1950s and 1960s onward, has been heavily chronicled and critiqued by recent authors with an interest in the field including Mintzberg and Waters (1985), Mintzberg (1978, 1990, 1994, 2004), Mintzberg et al. (1998), Carter et al. (2008), as well as Chia and Holt (2009). The related acceleration of business school activity has been critiqued in the works of authors such as Kharuna (2007) and McDonald (2017). This account aims to be sympathetic and complimentary to the works of these authors and the themes they bring forward but also aims to broaden the discussion somewhat. It is difficult to escape the oeuvre of Mintzberg, perhaps the discipline's most effective historian because of the reflexive character of his work. Mintzberg et al.'s (1998) work is an extremely valuable work as it charts the battles around what strategy ought to be, what we might consider the planning, position, and perspective wars. Mintzberg's earlier work (1990; Mintzberg and Waters 1985) focused on a critique of the normative understandings of the design and planning schools (and the assumptions that later schools identified by Mintzberg, including the positioning and cultural inherited) that forward thinking around the deployment of resources was a necessity, showing that strategy could also be developed on the hoof or even retrospectively, and his thinking ultimately culminated in a critique of MBA education that suggested that strategic management had culminated in an empty process of strategic programming detached from the reality of running a large organization, with the consequence that strategy, rather than the success of the organization, became the overriding aim (2004). Segal-Horn (1998) and later Carter et al. (2008) follow in a similar mold, focusing on the military origins of the very notion of strategy as traceable back to antiquity in the warring city states of Greece, the very term deriving from "Strategia," a subunit of Greek soldiers and their commander, a "Strategios." This is then mapped through the work of Machiavelli (1515) and Clausewitz and Rapoport (1982) to demonstrate that strategy is ultimately about the projection of power in society, a characteristic often overlooked or underplayed by economically theorized approaches, perhaps most notoriously, but not exclusively, those of Michael Porter (1980, 1985, 1990). Chia and Holt (2009) further focus on the notion of deliberacy and strategic action as the projection of power, even suggesting that direct projection of power can ultimately end up having the opposite effect to that originally intended.

Nonetheless, this chapter would like to contribute the idea that there is more to this story than the mis-adaption and application of rationalistic and militaristic ideology to complex business environments. In particular it would like to contribute the idea that managerialism is a "missing" school of strategic management from the normative classification put forward by Mintzberg et al. (1998). Mintzberg is right that the period running from the 1940s to the 1980s, and especially between the 1940s and 1970s when the influence of the Second World War was at its height, was the golden age of strategic planning. There was, further, a progressive obsession with political and economic planning as well as of urban space (see Jacobs (1962) for a contemporary critique of this), which spilled over into corporate strategy. An important part of the story to consider is that as the discipline defined itself, it gradually narrowed in scope and ambition, perhaps with destructive consequences – starting firstly through the work of pioneering authors such as Barnard (1938), Drucker (1946, 1955, 1967, 1974), and Selznick (1948, 1957) who incorporated strategy within the mid-century concept of managerialism (Doran 2016; Klikauer 2015), a broad concept of the corporation and organizational statesmanship in early attempts to define it, to a plan for the corporation under planning and design school authors such as Christensen et al. (1978) and Ansoff (1965), to an economically deterministic choice for the corporation by the time that we reach Porter (1979, 1980, 1985, 1990) and his resource-based view critics (Barney 1991; Dierickx and Cool 1989; Grant 1991; Prahalad and Hamel 1990; Wernerfelt 1984). By the 1980s "strategic management" had emerged as a distinct discipline out of "business administration" or "business policy," but in its mainstream it had become almost entirely concerned with the holy grail of "sustained competitive advantage," a relatively narrow conceptualization in which the aim of a successful firm was to create long-term economic rents for itself. These views assumed that there were no costs associated with cooperation and organization itself and that organizations were essentially malleable to the creation of strategy. This shift was to a large extent the consequence of a perceived need to remold managerialism to a Friedman (1962) style purpose of making a profit within the law, something furthered by Jensen and Meckling (1976), escaping both the Druckerian model and the design and planning-based approaches to strategic management. This chapter therefore begins with a discussion of some of the early authors who conceived strategy very differently to later authors, in a much more holistic fashion, before tracking the contraction down through design and planning to positioning and resources.

Proto-strategy: Organizational Statesmanship and Managerialism

In the USA of the 1920s and 1930s, a paradigm had emerged that the complex modern organization was becoming an increasingly hegemonic entity in society. The Great Depression following the Wall Street Crash of 1929 reinforced this Zeitgeist. Berle and Means (1932) identified the power gap created by the increasing control over American society's resources enjoyed by large corporations. These corporations were increasingly characterized by the separation of ownership and control, and a major point of dispute following the Dodge v Ford case had been the extent to which management were obliged to run a corporation in the interests of creating a surplus for shareholders (Henderson 2007). This phenomenon spilled over into foreign policy, partly driving the US expansionary relations with Latin American states until the introduction of the "Good Neighbour" policy by Roosevelt in 1933. Adolf Berle was partly inspired by his experience of serving in the US military during the country's occupation of the Dominican Republic, which was encouraged by corporations in the fruit industry (Russell et al. 2017). Nonetheless Berle, who had served in the military with his co-author Gardiner Means, saw value in the dispassionate character of military service as an entity of itself and viewed the separation of ownership and control in the large corporation as an opportunity to reorient management toward a similar ideology of dispassionate service in favor of the public good (Smith et al. 2018). This was expressed as a claim that "neither the claims of ownership nor those of control can stand against the paramount interests of the community" (Berle and Means 1932, p. 356), creating the expectation that the moral duty of senior management should be to provide stable and fair employment together with a steadiness and continuity of business itself. This arguably subverted the idea of shareholder primacy toward some form of stakeholder primacy. Berle and Means assigned an ideological, moral duty to the corporation to serve all its stakeholders equally but also, and critically, felt that this duty should be reserved to the manager as the professional (and perhaps university trained) expert rather than workers themselves (Smith et al. 2019, pp. 15–19). The Berle and Means book went through numerous reprints and had a significant and deep influence over American business culture for the next half a century or so (Bratton 2000; Bratton and Wachter 2009; North 1983; Pepper 2019; Thompson 2019; Tsuk 2005).

The expectation that managers should provide moral leadership capable of furthering the complex organization as a societal as well as economic entity was then taken up by early writers including Chester Barnard (1938), Philip Selznick (1948, 1957), and, perhaps most famously, Peter Drucker (1946, 1955, 1967, 1974) who attempted to consider how this synthesis could be achieved for the whole organization, rather than its individual functions. Barnard, a former president of the Rockefeller Foundation and the New Jersey Bell Telephone Company, used *The Functions of the Executive* to set out a theory of human cooperation and organization in the round, before discussing in more depth what the role of the executive might be in directing and shaping such systems. Barnard covered all forms of formal organization, not just the profit making (1938, p. 7), and made important contributions around the nature of decision-making in complex environments (1938, pp. 197–205) as well as in terms of the barriers to cooperation which he considered could be overcome through common purpose and communication achieved through efficiency (1938, pp. 82–92), essentially a continued communal enthusiasm for contributing to the organization (McMahon and Carr 1999). The essence of Barnard's theorization was that increasing human cooperation required increased moral complexity with many different codes of morals (e.g., family, religious, social, organizational, and professional) coming together within individuals, which also necessitated an equivalent technical proficiency. Within this maze Barnard identified leadership or a high personal aptitude for both technical attainment (understanding of the technological basis for the business) and moral complexity as the "strategic factor" affecting the organization; thus to combine the two vectors successfully required a form of "moral creativeness" expressed in a dynamic process (1938, pp. 288–289).

Moral creativeness was not just the ability to reconcile conflicting ethical codes with each other but also the ability to design codes of ethics for others, which would hold the organization together (1938, pp. 272–284). This was difficult to do or properly comprehend in a complex organization, and ultimately Barnard suggests that while much prescriptive knowledge is known of the technical and functional sides of business, including accounting, finance, and personnel work (of the types already elaborated by people like Taylor (1911) and Mayo (1924)), what was required was a more general theory of organizational behavior. This would allow the five million or so people that Barnard estimated were involved in a form of executive work in the USA to share knowledge and ideas more readily (1938, pp. 288–290). Barnard saw organizations as complex institutions which meshed together many different priorities for individuals, and that strategy was about creating a shared, cooperative code or purpose that could consolidate these claims together. Barnard's legacy and his focus on the character of cooperation and decision-making influenced by competing moral codes and priorities would go on to be further influential in the organizational behavior field (Mahoney 2005). This was not least in the works of Herbert Simon (March and Simon 1958; Simon 1947, 1982), who established the related field of organizational behavior by exploring the rationality of humans as decision-makers, leading to the idea that organizational context was so powerful that it could encourage bounded rationality.

Selznick's (1948, 1957) writing would continue to struggle with the moral problem of organizational complexity in a similar vein, by pointing to the essential challenge of unifying leadership in what were increasingly habitually ingrained and routine-bounded organizations. Selznick's response, best developed in his pithy 1957 book, was the concept of *institutional statesmanship* creatively transcending everyday aims of efficiency and organization by instead using relationships between the stakeholders within and without the organization to direct it, realizing that these interactions were the potential sources of strength for the organization. The term "resources and capabilities," later a central fixture of the resource based or cultural school, appears for perhaps the first time in a strategic management text, and certainly 2 years before its credited origin in Penrose (1959), as for Selznick the role of the institutional statesman is to create a unity of purpose to best use these existing facets of the organization (1957, p. 149). But again there remained a sense of moral purpose, or "institutional integrity," that an organization should retain a "sense of security" and that the statesman's role was to identify change that would only further contribute to the organization's agreed and desired purpose through the building of cogent myth, not to radically reshape or contravene it (1957, pp. 150–153). Selznick thus continued to conceptualize strategy as a problem of social cooperation, arguing that leadership involved reshaping the social structure of an organization itself to achieve excellence. Thus his work could be applied to both for profit and not for profit organizations. Selznick's contribution, which sees the organization as both an inelastic and intangible entity, would be underrated by later strategy writers, his book having only 95 citations on Google Scholar at the time of writing, but it clearly inspired the thinking of Alfred D. Chandler (1962) who based his research on the concept of seeking an explanation for the rise of the modern industrial enterprise as an institution. Chandler is a critically important early writer who spans the bridge between the organizational statesmanship and the design school, ▶ Chap. 35, "Chandler and the Visible Hand of Management," I do not deal with him explicitly here. But Selznick through Chandler would go on to inspire the institutional school of organizational analysis (Fligstein 1990; Gillett and Tennent 2018; Scott 2001; Skelcher and Smith 2015; Thornton and Ocasio 2008), which has become increasingly influential in the twenty-first century.

Barnard and Selznick both saw the organization and thus management as an isolated unit of analysis, with social purpose beyond the organization remaining more implicit, but the intellectual contribution of Peter Drucker, at least within his works on strategy, would be to more explicitly connect the purpose of management and the organization to broader societal purpose. Mintzberg et al. (1998, pp. 13–14) say relatively little about Drucker, concentrating mainly on his 1970 paper on entrepreneurship and a 1994 summary in Harvard Business Review (Drucker 1970, 1994), but do identify that his view was one compatible with the Minzbergian view of "strategy as perspective" or "an organization's fundamental way of doing things" (Mintzberg et al. 1998, pp. 13–14). Perspective was inward looking not just to resources and capabilities but also upward looking, considering also the view of the organization held by the strategy makers. But this to some extent undersells Drucker's strongest work on strategy, which was to essentially argue that the duty of management was to use its perspective to identify how best it could profit by serving the needs of society. Drucker thus prescribed strategy content to some extent, as well as process. This was a stream of research started with his ethnographic work on General Motors, *The Concept of the Corporation*, which focused on the internal structure and workings of the company more than the market side, suggesting that the company would be more productive if it further decentralized its management style (1946, pp. 120–125). So controversial was Drucker's view that he saw the GM CEO, Alfred P. Sloan's memoir *My Years with General Motors* (1967), as a rebuttal. But this book was merely the start of Drucker's project to reform American business by consolidating and building the managerialist project.

Drucker's *Practice of Management* (1955) is perhaps the most relevant of his works which touch on corporate strategy; while some of the ideas of the book may seem self-evident to modern practitioners, they may not have been so in the 1950s. Both prescriptive and philosophical, the book builds an egalitarian and progressive portrait of the potential of management as an open *practice* that anyone with new and innovative ideas should enter rather than a *profession* with entry to be closed by degree or certification. Its primary purpose was to manage a business, prioritizing economic performance (1955, pp. 7–9) and building a productive enterprise which "transmuted" human and material resources into something greater than their constituent parts. Critically for strategists, this was a process which was lengthening due to the technological sophistication of new plants and products (1955, pp. 11–15). A longitudinal case study of Sears (a company also later examined by Chandler) as it evolved from mail order firm to an out of town "big box" store through the early twentieth century is used to develop one of the earliest points of the book – that the role of management is essentially to adapt the organization to face the market, but this required a conscious adjustment of perspective to carefully consider what business the firm should be in (1955, pp. 25–41). Interestingly for the later thinking of Porter, this entailed some horizon scanning and thought around concepts of value together with the structure of the market and likely future changes within it and a broad belief that investment in marketing would deliver results as it was the defining constitutive factor which made a profit seeking business a business, leading Drucker (1955, p. 36) to make the startling claim that European industry was struggling compared to American industry because it was not market oriented enough. A similar claim was made for the American railroad and coal industries that had declined because managements had not thought carefully about what business they were in (Drucker 1955, pp. 48–49), which seems perhaps to naively overlook the concerns of long-term capital investment and sunk costs which could make switching the means of production costly. The idea that value was constituted from what the customer seeks would prove to be critical for the future development of the strategic management discipline. More broadly, a sense emerges that though Drucker saw the corporation as a social system, he did not conceptualize it as a slow evolving dogmatic institution in the way that Selznick did; enlightened managers would operate in concert to build and adapt the bureaucracy to the needs of the economy.

Drucker then moves on through a discussion of managerial objective setting to square the idea of corporate value creation with social contribution, which in his view should be the essential strategic objective of management. Here, Berle's ideas are extended. Drucker argues for a broader focus of strategy than just profit making and, ultimately, that companies as the primary engine of wealth creation and indeed resource concentration had a broader responsibility to society. Modern industrial society was unable to exist without the legal personality of the company, and hinting at the influence of Adam Smith's (1776) concept of self-interest, he argues that self-interest alone on the part of property owners was insufficient to further the public good. Thus, in an almost Millsian conception of liberty (1863), it was down to management to ensure the public good by using their powers to act within ethical standards in order not to infringe upon either the common weal or individual freedom (Drucker 1955, pp. 375–377). Echoing yet attempting to turn the famous quote of the General Motors President Charles E. Wilson on its head, Drucker maintained instead that it was business' role to make itself good for the country or at least to combine the private and public good together by making the common good the same thing as self-interest. Thus Berle's disinterested service was not enough; the ultimate aim point of managerial strategy should be that the public good determined the self-interest of capital, which we can interpret as manifesting itself in the provision of high-quality goods and services, in employment conditions, and in a general consideration for the wider community in the pursuit of business activity. For Drucker, this ethical synthesis was ultimately only achievable through management skill and improved practice, the shortcoming being perhaps being the implicit assumption that all managers should come to share Drucker's vision.

Drucker continued to pursue this mission throughout his many publications until his death in 2005; *The Effective Executive* (1967) was a slimline volume which took a critical view of the challenge of organizational statesmanship, honing in on the problem of executive work, and specifically the idea that executives had to manage their time correctly to actually achieve their objectives, as much time was spent (or wasted?) on symbolic duties. This book, and his later tome *Management: Tasks, Responsibilities, Practices* (1974) which underlined and expanded many of the ideas of *The Practice of Management*, demonstrated an increased practitioner focus in Drucker's work. Both books are written in fairly short, readable paragraphs designed for busy readers, with frequent (but sometimes quite oblique in terms of how they were put together) historical vignettes, and intensify his thesis around the ultimate social mission of management as a public good to be achieved through a sequence of objectives. To some extent Drucker's work, as it became more concerned with functionalist areas, then veered away from strategic management in the pure sense, but his work remained concerned with management skill and its linkage to the overall ethical direction of management. Strategic management scholars have perhaps been poorer for neglecting Drucker as well as other strategic thinkers of the managerialist era.

The Golden Age of the Design and Planning Schools

One of the characteristics of the development of management studies in the USA in the 1950s was a split in approach between the two leading institutions – the Carnegie Institute of Technology's Graduate School of Industrial Administration (which employed Herbert Simon among others), which favored a research-based approach, and the experience-based approach favored by the Harvard Business School (HBS) (Mintzberg 2004, pp. 22–26). HBS had developed a distinctive applied intellectual style based around the principle of "problem-based learning," in which business practitioners were invited into the class to pose strategic problems for students to devise policies to solve. This approach was introduced in HBS's Business Policy course in 1912 and proved popular with students such that it was rolled out onto the school's other modules. By the 1960s, HBS was in a golden age of expansion and growth; a 14-week "Advanced Management Program" (AMP) aimed at senior executives aged between 30 and 50 had been introduced in 1945 and continued to succeed, cross funding the growth of the school's MBA program and allowing for the construction of dedicated classrooms, dormitories, and "executive facilities." By 1967 the AMP could boast 460 past or present chairmen or presidents of American companies among its alumni (McDonald 2017, p. 152). This teaching environment encouraged the development of a new rationalistic "strategy as process" approach embodied by the pervasive and influential textbook by Christensen, Andrews, and Bower (1978), *Business Policy: Text and Cases*, first published in 1965. This foundational text emphasized that strategy or policy as it was more properly conceived at the time should be made through a rational design process. Further, and in a major difference from the more theoretical thinking of the organizational statesmanship school, content was de-emphasized in favor of process, with the consequence that leadership was not something to be reflected on in itself but something to be developed through a process of "strategic analysis" (Christensen et al. 1978, pp. 9–11).

Transferability of experience and skill came from analysis (1978, pp. 247–259) while still involving explicit engagement with the moralities of organization (1978, pp. 524–533). The central concept was that the teaching of decision-making had to involve an awareness of the context so that learners could reach an informed judgment, however superficial an understanding this might be. Therefore *Business Policy* consisted mainly of a series of empirical case studies, intended to fully immerse students into context, but linked together by short theoretical chapters authored by Kenneth Andrews that emphasize strategic design rather than strategy content. Content was context specific, and the design of strategy considered more an art than science (1978, pp. 10–11). As Freedman (2013) notes, the strategist's role was to bring the rationality of generalism to the table and to follow a sequential framework of external and internal analysis, strategic decision-making, and implementation, guiding the design of a strategy. This generalist and rationalist step-by-step approach would make it possible for strategists to foresee, intervene, and construct the future direction of an organization, perhaps for many years to come (1978, pp. 125–142). The case method attempted to bring reality into the classroom, enhanced by Andrews' focus on SWOT analysis (1978, pp. 247–259), originally intended to be a sort of "look before you leap" organizing framework than a matrix in itself, which Hill and Westbrook (1997) would later deride as a mere list-making process. Rather the idea was for the strategist to use the SWOT analysis to inform their decision-making process (though the mechanics for this were left somewhat vague) as to how the company's existing attributes could best be melded to "design" an appropriate "choice of products and markets" (1978, p. 258) and, echoing

Chandler, a structure to support and deliver it. A design metaphor was used with Andrews calling the CEO or company president the "Architect of Organizational Purpose" (1978, pp. 19–21), who had the skill to choose both the optimal activities for a firm and the force of personality to see them carried through. Mintzberg (2004; Mintzberg et al. 1998) has long been sharply critical of the unreflexive character of the case method enshrined in this book, pointing out that a mere explanatory article on a company is not sufficient for students unfamiliar with its products, processes, or people to truly understand it and thus that it encourages "disconnected" decision-making among graduates when they move into the real world.

The Christensen, Andrews, and Bower (1978) textbook has fallen out of use in management teaching and learning since the 1970s, but an overall processual and thus design view of strategy remains dominant in pedagogy today, despite its implicitly paternalistic view of the strategist. Stakeholder management was a part of the process to be visited on the pathway between design and implementation. Christensen, Andrews, and Bower (1978) continued to some extent emphasize the moralistic concerns of the managerialists and clearly understood the political role of strategy yet at the same time assume strategy making to be entirely the role of the CEO. The book does include some consideration of "fit" in terms of the strategy's relevance to the potentially unaligned aspiration of individual managers and the company's potential contribution to society (Christensen et al. 1978, pp. 448–454, 524–533). However, while McDonald (2017, p. 260) suggests that this evidences Andrews' ethical focus, there was a difference in approach from Drucker for whom societal contribution was not optional; for Andrews, it was an element of strategy to be judged and chosen in itself and most relevant to the CEO's ethical compass. Further, these stages of the process came after a strategy had been chosen in relation to the SWOT analysis, somewhat closing the door to political discussion. The implication was a power relation granted to the CEO, not the strategy of statesmanship as skill alluded to by Barnard and Selznick. This perhaps has the dangerous implication that managers may take less seriously the need to embrace a process of coalition building, reducing the building of support to a box ticking exercise, before attempting to change an organization's strategy.

The concept of processuality and thus the envelope of perceived rationality remains an almost taken-for-granted part of much strategic management pedagogy in the twenty-first century, perpetuated by mass market textbooks including Pettigrew (1988) and perhaps most pervasively Johnson and Scholes (1993). The Pettigrew book is conceptually underpinned by the concepts of context, process, and change, while Johnson and Scholes present strategy as a linear process of analysis, choice, and implementation. While using a Venn diagram to display the three concepts, rebranded in recent editions as "Strategic Position," "Strategic Choices," and "Strategy in Action" in an attempt to show that these concepts should not become a linear pathway, as choices may have to be reinterpreted in light of recent events, the chapters of *Exploring Strategy*, now in its twelfth edition (Whittington et al. 2019), still proceed in a manner which would be recognized by Andrews. While Mintzberg et al. (1998) present strategy as a conflict of interpretation between ten schools with very different and not always compatible intellectual assumptions and heritages, the *Exploring Strategy* series shoehorns concepts and frameworks almost shorn of context into parts of the process, so Porter's Five Forces (1980) becomes an external analysis tool, while Barney's VRIN (1991) becomes an internal analysis tool, facilitating an essential SWOT construction process, while Porter's Generic Strategies (1985) are introduced as a tool for strategic choice. This structure bears a remarkable resemblance to Mintzberg et al.'s visual interpretation of the design school model (1998, p. 26), and with the textbook claiming sales of over a million cumulatively, it seems likely that repackaged versions of the Andrews model will continue to have impact in practice for a long time to come.

The danger inherent in strategy process was that the process would become an end in itself, an outcome most clearly fulfilled by the related, but different, planning school – different because it insisted on the explicit statement of objectives as a future outcome of the process rather than relying on implicit managerial values and judgment (Mintzberg 1994, p. 40). The planning school probably represented the apex of managerialism in practice; it took the assumption that rationalization rested on process from the design school and extended this premise considerably. Strategy formation was not to be a loose activity based around one CEO but now a mass activity involving the entire cohort of senior managers in the modern industrial enterprise, together with a staff of dedicated planners. These managers were expected to engage in strategy formation as a formal process, broken down into steps, and complimented by rigorous analysis techniques. This process would mean that new strategies emerged fully planned and cogent to the overall organizational purpose and objectives, often to be implemented through systems of budgetary control and objective setting (Mintzberg 1994, p. 42).

The planning school's foremost proponent was H. Igor Ansoff, who's text *Corporate Strategy: An Analytic Approach to Business Policy for Growth and Expansion* (1965, 1988) sets out perhaps the most extensively detailed manual for corporate expansion and diversification. Building on the ideas of Chandler around capabilities, and Drucker around objectives, as well as sharing Drucker's essential paradigm that management was a skill to be learned, the book is far more precise and systematizing than the *Business Policy* series. Written in a very "matter of fact" style with the positivist epistemological feeling of an engineering manual, the book is proudly prescriptive and is paradoxically both broad and narrow in scope all at once; Ansoff claims that strategic decisions are almost entirely related to growing the firm and how this will be achieved, either through present products or markets or through diversification (1988, p. 24). This focus has had the ironic impact that the most widely diffused and replicated element of Ansoff's work has been the "growth vector components" matrix which illustrates these choices (1988, p. 109), but this diagram was only part of a much broader series of steps intended to engineer firms to bridge the "impedance match" between firm and environment. A range of schematics and flow diagrams, breaking everything into steps, choices, and classifications, are provided, including, for instance, a "Decision Schematic in Strategy Formulation" which pathed the strategist through a consideration of whether capabilities suited diversification or organic growth, which was intended to help the reader analyze the "gap" between firm and objectives (1988, p. 46). One of the most complicated was the 19-point "Decision Flow in Project Selection" intended to appraise strategic projects for synergy (identifying and measuring this being another key concept of the book) and portfolio fit, which proposed 16 decision points in itself (1988, p. 186)! These planning schematics may have encouraged managers to think more carefully about what they were doing and certainly provided the enveloping security of recipes and methods. Ansoff was followed by other authors in proposing frameworks for forward strategic planning, most notably Steiner (1969).

From a historical perspective, it is hard to escape the conclusion that the foremost weakness of the planning school, and indeed by extension the design school, was that the future rarely works out in exactly the way we intend. Mintzberg and Waters (1985) were foremost in critiquing the limits of "deliberate" strategy, suggesting that the consistency in patterns of decision and intraorganizational cooperation were insufficient to deliver intended strategy if it was blown off course by the emergence of unforeseen environmental conditions. Empirically, the challenge of emergence overtook corporate as well as social and political planners as the 1960s turned to the 1970s, as competition from Asian economies started to threaten the viability of second industrial revolution manufacturing in North America and Europe, and the 1973–1974 oil crisis caused a general inflationary shock. Planners evolved techniques such as scenario planning, in which a number of different futures were designed to attempt to cope with uncertainty, most famously at Shell, where it was claimed that the scenario planners had foreseen the oil crisis as a possibility, allowing the company to turn the crisis to its relative advantage (Cornelius et al. 2005). One of the most high-profile failures of planning was outside the corporate sphere. The US Secretary of Defense and HBS graduate Robert McNamara mismanaged the Vietnam War, based on the assumption that the planned maximum application of force, including the rational calculation of "kill ratios," would win out in the end over the Vietcong, a force using more spontaneous, emergent guerrilla tactics which suited the local landscape (McCann 2017; Summers 1981). The McNamara case also emphasizes the detachment between planner or strategist and on the ground events or implementation, inherent in planning-based approaches, with a dangerous disconnect coming into effect which may blind the strategist to the ineffectiveness of direct action.

In its creation of rationalizing roles for managers, design and planning can be seen as stage at which managerialism was at its foremost influence in strategic management, but it also had more pernicious effects. Core among them was the Ansoffian assumption that growth was the normative objective of all firms and that no other outcome was worthy of being considered a sufficiently great "engineering" problem in business policy. Thus while Ansoff took on Drucker's interest in objectives, he dropped out the broader sense of aligning corporate purpose with society's needs and even to some extent neglects the profit making and value creating potential of business. At its worst, in terms of corporate policy, the soft diffusion of planning school ideas perhaps exacerbated an obsession with increasing corporate size and diversification in the later 1960s and early 1970s, leading to the formation of conglomerate firms with an increasingly blurred sense of core capability. In 1970, 430 out of the 500 largest US industrial companies had three or more product divisions with forms of decentralized management; even as early as 1966, 46 of the largest 500 industrial companies had eight or more divisions (Blackford 2008, pp. 197–198). Despite the best intentions of theoreticians such as Ansoff, this forced the initiative toward what generalized managers could control, the financial side of companies, and thus a focus on economization and operational efficiency over innovation. In some ways, this last phase of corporatist managerialism may have hastened the rise of its antithesis, financialization. Not surprisingly, the 1970s and especially the 1980s saw an attempt to refocus strategy around the unitary business unit with specific competencies.

Positioning Strategy: The Impact of Michael Porter

The strategy academic who would lead the change toward the refocusing of strategy around the unitary business unit was Michael Porter. Porter took the rationalist and analytical apparatus of the design and planning schools and completely subverted it by introducing a new concentration on market logics and prescriptive strategy content. Porter achieved a genuinely transformational paradigm shift, successfully rebranding the discipline from "business policy" to "strategic management" or even just "strategy," one which has also been credited with establishing the field as a serious space for rigorous scholarly endeavor (McDonald 2017, pp. 414–415; Mintzberg 2004, p. 35). Indeed, one of the biggest critics of Porter's theories, Jay Barney (2011, p. 25), credits Porter with defining the academic field in several ways – he defined the "appropriate dependent variable" (and in the process shifted it toward quantitative analysis), with establishing theoretical frameworks, defining the correct unit of analysis, defining the role of social issues to the field, and generally with taking a field defined by loose and uncertain frameworks into a serious academic discipline but one still able to influence the work of managers. Further, Porter respectfully encouraged a conversation with his critics in the aim of more properly establishing the discipline (Barney 2011, pp. 30–31).

Like Christensen, Andrews, and Bower, Porter's scholarship emerged in the executive education dominated environment of HBS, where he completed an MBA in 1971. In redefining the field, he took inspiration from the field of industrial economics, or more properly "industrial organization," completing his PhD in Harvard's economics department under Professor Richard Caves, who was influenced by the work of Joe Bain (McDonald 2017, pp. 411–413). Differing starkly from authors such as Barnard, Selznick, Drucker, Penrose, and Chandler who took the organization as a starting point, Bain (1956) took a neoclassical black box view of the firm, assuming away the idea that they could internalize transactions, and saw markets as the main unit of analysis. Bain thence argued that in the long run, the return on capital in all sectors should converge, because excess profits in any one industry would naturally cause an inflow of capital and competition into it, bidding down prices as supply increased. Bain's interest was informing competition policy, to attempt to rectify monopolism in markets, but Porter was intellectually entrepreneurial, taking the idea back to HBS and reversing it (McDonald 2017, pp. 412–413). The essential direction of Porter's scholarship would be that the aim of firm strategy was to identify markets or positions within markets where the forces of competition were weak and then exploit them to generate monopoly rents. This elegant simplicity of purpose provided intellectual compatibility with the claim of Jensen and Meckling (1976) that firms were essentially legal fictions while proving extremely popular with HBS's practice focused students. This reconceptualization would allow Porter to eclipse the design and planning school scholars while adapting the "frameworks as tools" approach, both inside and outside the walls of HBS.

Porter's first "blockbuster" framework, generally known as the "Five Forces," first appeared in a *Harvard Business Review* article in 1979, essentially acting as a preview for his first major book, *Competitive Strategy: Techniques for Analyzing Industries and Competitors* (1980), which centers around the concept, introducing it as early as page 4. This all-enveloping framework was designed to facilitate a structural analysis of a target industry to help strategists understand the fundamental characteristics which affected the supply and demand economics of the industry and thus to identify possible "defensible" and "offensive" strategies within that industry. The most important insight was to broaden the focus from simply thinking about the firms competing within an industry to more broadly factor in the impact of buyers, suppliers, and the threat of substitutes and barriers to potential new entry. Thus some industries, such as the provision of oil tankers, might be characterized by high buyer power as there were only a limited number of buyers (the large oil companies), while others, such as steel manufacturing, might see more acute competitive pressure from other industries producing a substitute product (Porter 1980, p. 6). This was not necessarily a new ground for strategy; both Drucker (1955, pp. 53–54) and Chandler (1962, pp. 9–11), for instance, have drawn attention to careful analysis of the industry and market structure, but Porter centered his thesis on it and avoided lengthy case studies, keeping real-world examples very pithy.

The second major framework introduced in *Competitive Strategy* was the three generic strategies (Porter 1980, pp. 35–44), a somewhat militaristic framework which claimed there were only three truly viable firm strategies, whether offensive or defensive – overall cost leadership, differentiation, and focus – any firm trying to mix them would fail in the long term, as it would be "stuck in the middle," unable to defend its position, and thus "almost guaranteed low profitability" (Porter 1980, p. 41). Thus the task of management was to decide how value could be created and exploited based around the cost and price interplay of the market and to occupy that part of the market by erecting mobility barriers such that no one else could compete. While the book goes into considerable detail as to how these competitive positions might be achieved, the character and structural rigidity of the organization itself are assumed away; it is assumed that everything a manager needs to do is achievable without any process of organizational statesmanship or broader thought around implementation using the resources of the firm itself. This is a consequence of the re-imagination of the firm as merely an economic person. The very empirical basis of the framework, which claims that only one firm can successfully hold each position in a given industry, has been attacked by Speed (1989, p. 10). Speed points out that Porter provides only two examples of the U-shaped relationship between market share and profitability that underpins the concept (1980, pp. 43–44), while D'Aveni (1994) claimed that companies would simply be unable to resist eroding the optimal positions of the generic strategies, leading to a destructive phenomenon known as "hypercompetition" in which any rents would be competed away.

Porter's second volume, *Competitive Advantage: Creating and Sustaining Superior Performance* (1985), continues in a similar vein and indeed repeats the five forces and generic strategies frameworks in the first few pages (1985, pp. 7, 12). What was new in the book was a deeper delve inside the firm in which Porter considered the organizational basis for competitive advantage, although this remained exclusively a matter of economic optimization. A new framework, the Value Chain (1985, pp. 46–47), was proposed which allowed for the analysis of industry and market to be extended to the economic configuration of activities inside the firm, with the proposition that economically alike activities and functions ought to be placed together to optimize the linkages between them, driving the firm's chosen generic strategy. Thus the firm-level implementation question left open by *Competitive Advantage* was answered, and a profound point was made around implementation – competitive advantage did not just come from the production activity of a firm but was a fully fledged project involving all functions and support activities, such as logistics, procurement, human resource management, and research and development (1985, pp. 113–115). This opened up the potential for outsourcing or economization outside of noncore activities, though again the assumption appears to be that these activities could be costlessly reshaped to meet the needs of the organization. By the mid-1980s, political leaders such as US President Ronald Reagan had picked up on the compatibility of Porter's ideas with the "neoliberal" project to make western economies more "competitive," appointing Porter to a President's Commission on Industrial Competitiveness in 1985 (McDonald 2017, p. 419). This created the opportunity for his vision to be further expanded through a third volume, *The Competitive Advantage of Nations* (1990). This book attempted to expand the unit of analysis to the national level, by introducing another new framework, "The Determinants of National Advantage" (often known as "Porter's diamond") (1990, p. 72), which became influential in the international business sub-discipline, essentially that a competitive and dynamic market within a country in a given industry would make it easier for firms from that country to establish a global competitive advantage in the same industry. For Porter, the world truly could be described in terms of neoclassical supply-demand economics.

The Porterian view of the world is one that is attractive to practitioners in the form of senior managers and policy-makers alike in that it offers a fairly straightforward and simple to understand set of prescriptions about the state of the world. Porter sets out his mission to go beyond the design school in offering strategy content in the introduction to *Competitive Strategy*, pointing out that the emphasis of formal strategic planning processes had been about asking questions of industry analysis in the right way, rather than answering them (1980, p. xxii). This he had certainly done while appropriating the formal mechanics of strategy. His "outside-in" approach, however, in borrowing from neoclassical economics, inherited the ahistorical assumption of the gnomic present (McCloskey 1998), building in the assumption that the past culture and heritage of a firm did not matter when setting its future direction. This assumption was challenged to some extent by the scholars of the resource-based view (Barney 1991; Dierickx and Cool 1989; Grant 1991; Prahalad and Hamel 1990; Wernerfelt 1984), who argued for a different version of competitive advantage – firm resources, both tangible and intangible, were valuable and inimitable since their exact configuration was impossible for others to replicate – Porter, of course seeking to set out an economically optimal configuration. Teece et al. (1997) would later seek to meld the two views together into a "dynamic capabilities" approach, suggesting that unique firm resources were themselves vital in building competitive advantage. Porter himself attempted to answer his critics in an article in which he claimed that "operational effectiveness is not strategy" (1996, p. 61), defending the idea that competitive advantage was achieved through a conscious process of value creation, not by falling back on resources inherent within the firm. His response was essentially that firms were not sticking to his prescriptions closely enough. None of this refocusing and consequential disciplinary narrowing of strategic management around the economic determinants of firm advantage would have developed without Porter's contribution.

Concluding Remarks

The history of strategic management into the 1980s and 1990s saw a narrowing of focus, from a managerialist paradigm of the manager as a "renaissance man" (and they were usually men) directing productive resources for societal and organizational good to a much tighter definition around the achievement of "sustained competitive advantage." This shift has encouraged the academic growth of the discipline, bringing it closer to economics, yet at the same time has made it more specific, ignoring the relationships between strategy and governance and strategy and leadership. It also to some extent echoed the growing sociopolitical interest in economic competition for its own sake after around 1975. This vision has been perpetuated and implanted into the consciousness of business people and perhaps to some extent mainstream culture not just by university teaching but also by management consultants (McKenna 2006), including Porter's own company, Monitor (McDonald 2017, p. 420). The work of Porter and the RBV scholars, in particular, has ironically given its militaristic antecedence, ceded the field of governance to the intellectually compatible sub-discipline headed by the "law and finance" view scholars (La Porta et al. 2000; La Porta and Lopez-De-Silanes 1998), while leadership has been taken over by a field of scholars following the work of Burns (1978) and Bass (1985). This narrowing has undoubtedly been problematic; it has led to a progressive and unreflexive denial that strategy involves power relations at all.

This is not to contest that thinking about market position and the unique creation of value is a desirable thing for business or indeed perhaps for not for profit contexts too – it clearly is, and it is important for managers to think carefully about what their organization can offer that others cannot. As so often with ideology, it is the extreme view that becomes damaging – the narrow focus upon competitive advantage and thence the creation of monopoly rents to the exclusion of all else. This approach is justified through the neoclassical economic belief that wealth created by firms would trickle down to all of society, but this is incompatible with Bain's original concern with the monopoly problem which was that monopolies appropriate excessive resources from consumers and thence society, as well as potentially stymying resources. This concern has to some extent been echoed by critical governance scholars arguing for a return to some form of managerialism (Lazonick 2013; Lazonick and O'Sullivan 2000; Stout 2002, 2012), who have pointed to increasing inequality in society since 1980 caused by an overconcentration on shareholder value. Severing the explicit link between strategy and governance first identified by Berle and Means in the 1930s has created the intellectual space for the strategic activities of managers to be subverted to this ideology. Focusing on one's core activities, for instance, creates the perfect justification for downsizing and outsourcing, both drivers of economic and thence political instability in the west.

One final caveat – despite the broader focus on the strategy of the organization and its role within society of Barnard, Selznick, Drucker, and Andrews, this has as a whole been a very narrow story. Space has to some extent precluded a broader treatment of other authors, but I have tried to deal with the authors that I consider the most important, particularly those who influence the pedagogy of strategic management most. This has been a very white, male, essentially paternalist and American story, with most of the protagonists based within the (north eastern) USA and a particular focus on HBS. It is clear that a more "gestalt" approach to strategic management is required, echoing the broad focus of the work of Drucker to some extent, rather than the narrow focus of Porter, but a twenty-first-century approach drawing upon a broader and more diverse range of perspectives could be more profitable for both organizations and society as we move forward.

References

Ansoff HI (1965) Corporate strategy. An analytic approach to business policy for growth and expansion. McGraw Hill, New York
Ansoff HI (1988) Corporate strategy, Revised edn. Penguin Business, London
Bain JS (1956) Barriers to new competition: their character and consequences in manufacturing industries. Harvard University Press, Cambridge, MA
Barnard CI (1938) The functions of the executive. Harvard University Press, Cambridge, MA
Barney J (1991) Firm resources and sustained competitive advantage. J Manag 17(1):99–120. https://doi.org/10.1177/014920639101700108
Barney J (2011) Establishing strategic management as an academic discipline. In: Competition, competitive advantage, and clusters: the ideas of Michael Porter. Oxford University Press, Oxford
Bass BM (1985) Leadership and performance beyond expectations. Free Press, New York
Berle A, Means G (1932) The modern corporation and private property. Macmillan, New York
Blackford MG (2008) The rise of modern business: great Britain, the United States, Germany, Japan and China. The University of North Carolina Press, Chapel Hill
Bratton WW (2000) Berle and Means reconsidered at the century's turn. J Corp Law 26:737–770
Bratton WW, Wachter ML (2009) Tracking Berle's footsteps: the trial of the modern corporation's last chapter. Seattle Univ Law Rev 33:849–875

Burns JM (1978) Leadership. Harper & Row, New York
Carter C, Clegg SR, Kornberger M (2008) A very short, fairly interesting and reasonably cheap book about studying strategy. Sage, London
Chandler AD (1962) Strategy and structure: chapters in the history of the American industrial enterprise. M.I.T. Press, Cambridge
Chia RCH, Holt R (2009) Strategy without design: the silent efficacy of indirect action. Cambridge University Press, Cambridge
Christensen CR, Andrews KR, Bower JL (1978) Business policy: text and cases. Richard D. Irwin, Homewood
Clausewitz C, Rapoport A (1982) On war: Carl von Clauewitz: edited with An introduction by Anatol Rapoport. Penguin, Harmondsworth
Cornelius P, Van De Putte A, Romani M (2005) Three decades of scenario planning in Shell. Calif Manag Rev 48(1):92–109
D'Aveni RA (1994) Hypercompetition: managing the dynamics of strategic maneuvering. Free Press, New York
Dierickx I, Cool K (1989) Asset stock accumulation and sustainability of competitive advantage. Manag Sci 35(12):1504–1511
Doran C (2016) Managerialism: an ideology and its evolution. Int J Manag Knowl Learn 1:81–97
Drucker PF (1946) Concept of the corporation. The John Day Company, New York
Drucker PF (1955) The practice of management. Butterworth-Heinemann, Oxford
Drucker PF (1967) The effective executive. Butterworth-Heinemann, Oxford
Drucker PF (1970) Entrepreneurship in business enterprise. J Bus Policy 1(1):3–12
Drucker PF (1974) Management: tasks, responsibilities, practices. Butterworth-Heinemann, Oxford
Drucker PF (1994) The theory of the business. Harv Bus Rev Sept-Oct:72:95–104
Fligstein N (1990) The transformation of corporate control. Harvard University Press, Cambridge, MA
Freedman L (2013) Strategy: a history. Oxford University Press, Oxford
Friedman M (1962) Capitalism and freedom. University of Chicago Press, Chicago
Gillett AG, Tennent KD (2018) Shadow hybridity and the institutional logic of professional sport: perpetuating a sporting business in times of rapid social and economic change. J Manag Hist 24 (2). https://doi.org/10.1108/JMH-11-2017-0060
Grant RM (1991) The resource-based theory of competitive advantage: implications for strategy formulation. Calif Manag Rev 33(3):114–135
Henderson MT (2007) Everything old is new again: lessons from Dodge v. Ford Motor Company. John M. Olin Law & Economics Working Paper (2D Series). https://doi.org/10.2139/ssrn.1070224
Hill T, Westbrook R (1997) SWOT analysis: it's time for a product recall. Long Range Plan 30 (1):46–52. https://doi.org/10.1016/S0024-6301(96)00095-7
Jacobs J (1962) The death and life of great American cities. Jonathon Cape, London
Jensen MC, Meckling WH (1976) Theory of the firm: managerial behavior, agency costs and ownership structure. J Financ Econ 3(4):305–360. https://doi.org/10.1016/0304-405X(76)90026-X
Johnson G, Scholes K (1993) Exploring corporate strategy. Prentice-Hall, Englewood Cliffs
Khurana R (2007) From higher aims to hired hands. Princeton University Press, Princeton
Klikauer T (2015) What is managerialism? Crit Sociol 41(7–8):1103–1119. https://doi.org/10.1177/0896920513501351
La Porta R, Lopez-De-Silanes F (1998) Copyright ©1999. All rights reserved. J Polit Econ 24 (3):273–274. https://doi.org/10.1016/S0099-1767(98)90076-9
La Porta R, Lopez-de-Silanes F, Shleifer A, Vishny R (2000) Investor protection and corporate governance. J Financ Econ 58(1–2):3–27. https://doi.org/10.1016/S0304-405X(00)00065-9
Lazonick W (2013) From innovation to financialization: how shareholder value ideology is destroying the US economy. In: Wolfson MH, Epstein GA (eds) The handbook of the political economy of financial crises. Oxford University Press, Oxford

Lazonick W, O'Sullivan M (2000) Maximizing shareholder value: a new ideology for corporate governance. Econ Soc 29(1):13–35. https://doi.org/10.1080/030851400360541

Machiavelli N (1515) The prince. Translator Mariott, W. K. Available online at http://www.gutenberg.org/files/1232/1232-h/1232-h.htm

Mahoney JT (2005) Economic foundations of strategy. Sage, Thousand Oaks

March JG, Simon HA (1958) Organizations. Wiley, New York

Mayo E (1924) The basis of industrial psychology. Bull Taylor Soc 9:249–259

McCann L (2017) 'Killing is our business and business is good': the evolution of 'war managerialism' from body counts to counterinsurgency. Organization 24(4):491–515. https://doi.org/10.1177/1350508417693852

McCloskey DN (1998) The rhetoric of economics. University of Wisconsin Press, Madison

McDonald D (2017) The golden passport: Harvard Business School, the limits of capitalism and the moral failure of the MBA elite. Harper Collins, New York

McKenna CD (2006) The world's newest profession: management consulting in the twentieth century. Cambridge University Press, Cambridge

McMahon D, Carr JC (1999) The contributions of Chester Barnard to strategic management theory. J Manag Hist (Arch) 5(5):228–240. https://doi.org/10.1108/13552529910282222

Mill JS (1863) Utilitarianism. Parker, Son and Bourn, London

Mintzberg H (1978) Patterns in strategy formation. Manag Sci 24(9):934–948

Mintzberg H (1990) The design school: reconsidering the basic premises of strategic management. Strateg Manag J 11(3):171–195

Mintzberg H (1994) The rise and fall of strategic planning. Prentice Hall, Hemel Hempstead

Mintzberg H (2004) Managers not MBAs: a hard look at the soft practice of managing and management development. Berrett-Koehler Publishers, San Francisco

Mintzberg H, Waters JA (1985) Of strategies, deliberate and emergent. Strateg Manag J 6(3):257–272

Mintzberg H, Ahlstrand B, Lampel J (1998) Strategy safari: the complete guide through the wilds of strategic management. Financial Times, Harlow

North DC (1983) Comment on Stigler and Friedland's' the literature of economics: the case of Berle and Means. J Law Econ 26(2):269–271

Penrose E (1959) The theory of the growth of the firm. Sharpe, New York

Pepper A (2019) Agency theory and executive pay. Palgrave Macmillan, New York

Pettigrew A (1988) The management of strategic change. Blackwell, Oxford

Porter ME (1979) How competitive forces shape strategy. Harv Bus Rev 57(2):137–145. https://doi.org/10.1097/00006534-199804050-00042

Porter ME (1980) Competitive strategy: techniques for analyzing industries and competitors. Free Press, New York

Porter ME (1985) Competitive advantage: creating and sustaining superior performance. Free Press, New York

Porter ME (1990) The competitive advantage of nations. Free Press, New York

Porter ME (1996) What is strategy? Harv Bus Rev 74(6):61–78

Prahalad CK, Hamel G (1990) The core competence of the corporation. Harv Bus Rev 68(3):79–91. https://doi.org/10.1007/3-540-30763-X_14

Russell J, Smith A, Tennent KD (2017) Adolf Berle's critique of US corporate interests in the Carribbean Basn. In: Pettigrew WA, Chan D (eds) A history of socially responsible business, c. Palgrave Macmillan, New York, pp 1600–1950

Scott WR (2001) Institutions and organizations. Sage, London

Segal-Horn S (1998) The development of strategic management thought. In: The strategy reader. Wiley-Blackwell, Hoboken

Selznick P (1948) Foundations of the theory of organization. Am Sociol Rev 13(1):25–35

Selznick P (1957) Leadership in administration. Haprer & Row, Publishers, New York

Simon HA (1947) Administrative behavior: a study of decision-making processes in administrative organization. Macmillan, New York

Simon HA (1982) Models of bounded rationality, vols 1 and 2. MIT Press, Cambridge, MA

Skelcher C, Smith SR (2015) Theorizing hybridity: institutional logics, complex organizations, and actor identities: the case of nonprofits. Public Adm 93(2):433–448. https://doi.org/10.1111/padm.12105

Sloan AP (1967) In: McDonald J, Stevens C (eds) My years with General Motors. Pan, London

Smith A (1776) An inquiry into the nature and causes of the wealth of nations. George Routledge and Sons, London

Smith A, Tennent KD, Russell J (2018) Berle and Means' the modern corporation and private property: the military roots of a stakeholder model of corporate governance. Seattle Univ Law Rev. 42(2):535–563

Smith A, Tennent K, Russell J (2019) The rejection of industrial democracy by Berle and Means and the emergence of the ideology of managerialism. Econ Ind Democr. https://doi.org/10.1177/0143831X19883683

Speed RJ (1989) Oh mr porter! A re-appraisal of competitive strategy. Mark Intell Plan 7(5–6):8–11. https://doi.org/10.1108/EUM0000000001043

Steiner G (1969) Top management planning. Macmillan, New York

Stout L (2002) Bad and not-so-bad arguments for shareholder primacy. Calif Law Rev 75:1189–1209. https://doi.org/10.3868/s050-004-015-0003-8

Stout L (2012) The shareholder value myth. Berrett-Koehler Publishers, Inc., San Francisco

Summers HG (1981) On strategy: the Vietnam war in context. Strategic Studies Institute, US Army War College, Carlisle Barracks

Taylor FW (1911) The principles of scientific management. Harper & Brothers, New York

Teece DJ, Pisano G, Shuen A (1997) Dynamic capabilities and strategic management. Strateg Manag J 18(7):509–533. https://doi.org/10.1002/(SICI)1097-0266(199708)18:7<509::AID-SMJ882>3.0.CO;2-Z

Thompson RB (2019) Adolf Berle during the new deal: the brain truster as an intellectual jobber. Seattle Univ Law Rev 42(2):663–695

Thornton PH, Ocasio W (2008) Institutional logics. In: Green R, Oliver C, Lawrence TB, Meyer RE (eds) The sage handbook of organizational institutionalism. Sage, London, pp 99–128

Tsuk D (2005) From pluralism to individualism: Berle and Means and 20th-century American legal thought. Law Soc Inq 30(1):179–225

Wernerfelt B (1984) A resource-based view of the firm. Strateg Manag J 5(2):171–180

Whittington R, Regnér P, Angwin D, Johnson G, Scholes K (2019) Exploring strategy, 12th edn. Pearson, New York

Chandler and the Visible Hand of Management

35

Kevin D. Tennent

Contents

Introduction	802
Positives About Chandler	804
Critiques	809
Conclusion	817
Cross-References	818
References	819

Abstract

The work of Alfred D. Chandler Jr. (1918–2007) was undoubtedly path breaking as well as paradigm building. His corpus of work can claim foundational relevance to at least two separate subfields of the management studies discipline – strategic management, and management/business history, together with theory sets such as transaction cost economics and historical institutionalism. Chandler's career was profoundly important in building the management studies discipline in both theoretical and empirical terms, seeking to explain the rise of the "modern industrial enterprise," yet it requires understanding within its own historical context. Chandler's work remains resonant today, and this chapter aims to critically explore the implications of this phenomenon, both interrogating the affirmative impacts of his writing and the contemporary world it reflected as well as that of his critics.

K. D. Tennent (✉)
The York Management School, University of York, York, UK
e-mail: kevin.tennent@york.ac.uk

Keywords

Alfred D. Chandler · Business history · Strategic management · Institutional theory · Managerialism

Introduction

The work of Alfred D. Chandler Jr. (1918–2007) was undoubtedly path breaking as well as paradigm building. His considerable corpus of work (Chandler 1954, 1956, 1962, 1977; Chandler and Daems 1979; Chandler and Hikino 1990) can claim foundational relevance to at least two separate subfields of the management studies discipline – strategic management (Mintzberg 1990; Mintzberg et al. 1998), and management/business history (Lamoreaux et al. 2004; Hannah 2009), as well as attracting more widespread attention for its impactfulness (The Economist 2009). Chandler's career, stretching from the 1950s to the early 2000s, was undoubtedly profoundly important in building the discipline in both theoretical and empirical terms, seeking as it did to explain the rise of the "modern industrial enterprise," yet in itself it requires understanding within its own historical context. The role of this section of the book is to explore the development of management theory and practice between c. 1940 and c. 1990, a period which might be considered, in North America, Western Europe, Australasia, and perhaps Japan at least, one of "high modernity" – or that period in which western business and thus managerial activity, operating as a powerful institution, essentially seemed to have completed its development. But a major function of modernity's Faustian Pact is its vulnerability to change (Berman 1982), and this period of hegemony, based around the modern industrial enterprise, seemed to ebb away, partly due to the re-assertion of financial capitalism and partly due to the rise of emerging markets where capitalism was often based around what Chandler might himself have termed "personal capitalism." Yet Chandler's work remains resonant today, and this chapter aims to critically explore the implications of this phenomenon, both interrogating the affirmative impacts of his writing and the contemporary world it reflected as well as that of his critics.

This chapter will therefore trace Chandler's career from the 1950s to the 1990s, critically evaluating the intellectual propositions and impact of his three major books, *Strategy and Structure* (1962), *The Visible Hand* (1977), and *Scale and Scope* (1990), as well as the influence of his work with Alfred Sloan (1967), before considering some of the challenges to the primacy of his work that have emerged from strategic management scholars (Mintzberg 1990; Mintzberg et al. 1998; Chia and Holt 2009), business historians (John 1997; Langlois 2003, 2004; Lamoreaux et al. 2004; Hannah 2009), and critical management scholars (Cooke 2003; Cummings et al. 2017) alike. Yet, critically, Chandler's work remains influential, almost "hard wired" into business and management knowledge, and despite the emergence of whole new schools of thought, no new paradigm has succeeded in supplanting him or rendering his writing fully obsolete. Many social scientists (and perhaps some who would not consider themselves social scientists) continue to acknowledge his work, at least in a superficial sense – according to Google Scholar, at the time of writing *Strategy and Structure* has well over 20,000 citations, *The Visible Hand* more than 9,000 and *Scale and Scope* more than 7,000 though perhaps fewer today are intimately familiar with its contents. Some broader theoretical bodies of work owe Chandler a distinct intellectual debt, including transaction cost theory (Williamson 1981, 1989, 1998; Leiblein and Miller 2003; Jacobides and Winter 2005), institutional theory (Scott 2001; Thornton and Ocasio 2008), the resource-based view of strategy together with its descendent dynamic capabilities theory (Mahoney and Pandian 1992; Hart 1995; Teece et al. 1997; Teece 2007), and international business history (Wilkins 1970, 1988, 1989, 1998; Jones 2005; Tennent 2009).

Chandler began his academic career in the 1950s, earning his doctorate from Harvard in 1952, a formative period for the management studies discipline. The discipline as a whole was re-gaining respect within the American university, led by the Graduate School of Industrial Administration (GSIA) at the Carnegie Institute of Technology, in Pittsburgh, Pennsylvania, which began taking a social science research approach to the subject from the late 1940s, after a period in which the more established business schools at Harvard, Wharton, Stanford, and Columbia had experienced a "dark age," retrenching into narrow case study-based pedagogy (Mintzberg 2004, pp. 21–29). The more broadly based GSIA model, which drew from a range of subjects including economics, sociology, political science, psychology, and mathematics among others to create a concept of management studies as a "compound discipline," would be the one which two influential reports published by the Carnegie and Ford Foundations recommended propagating at the end of the 1950s (Mintzberg 2004; Khurana 2007, pp. 268–273; Cummings et al. 2017, pp. 9–12). Though Chandler was working within the history department at MIT, *Strategy and Structure* was ideally placed to satisfy the emerging market for management textbooks, and within this, the need for management to legitimate itself as a discipline with sufficient intellectual rigor to be taught within the research-intensive university. Cummings et al. (2017) identify *Strategy and Structure* as being the first of four key texts which performed this function by pointing to the "noble origins" of the field, the others being Pollard (1965), George (1968), and Wren (1972). These histories continue to be drawn upon by textbook writers including Bateman and Snell (2009) and Rue and Byars (2009) to form "chapter 2" histories which function to provide a brief (and perhaps triumphal) background of the origin of the field before progressing onto the more gnomic areas of knowledge (Cummings et al. 2017, pp. 10–11).

Chandler's intellectual influence is thus pervasive, not just in terms of the types of knowledge dealt with by researchers, but also in terms of shaping the knowledge assimilated by learners who go on to become practitioners. Chandler is deserving of his own chapter in this collection because as we will discover, his critics have identified that his work was subject to a degree of finalism (though one he gradually retreated from across his career), reflecting the concern of Cummings and Bridgman (2011) that our view of the past is often shaped by the concerns of our own time, rather than consisting of a purely empiricist operation. This foundational power reinforces Chandler's continued legacy and resonance, which takes on increased relevance if we are to understand the post-1945 period appropriately, given the emerging critiques that American managerialist practices and ideologies justified by "chapter 2 history" were weaponized during the cold war and thus formed a key element of the neo-colonialist discourse (Cooke et al. 2005a, b; Kelley et al. 2006; Genoe McLaren and Mills 2008; Spector 2006, 2008; Mollan 2018). Chandler's work continues to pervade the business and management history disciplines, but it has had a deeper political significance, being co-opted into a model of Americanized economic and managerialist development. Through its titular usurpation of Smith, Chandler's most conventionally empirical and chronological book *The Visible Hand* not only stakes history's claim to primacy in the management discipline but seeks to establish professional management as the driving force in the modern industrial economy, a model for all aspiring industrialisers to follow.

Chandler's dominance of the business history field chimed somewhat uncomfortably with me as a PhD student when I came into business history from a humanities history background in the mid-2000s. As a humanities historian schooled in the empiricist tradition of von Ranke (1973) and Elton (1978), and from a sphere in which historians tended to pick their own patch of temporal turf to occupy, the idea that history should be subjected to a broad, central unifying narrative that tied it to a theoretical paradigm seemed unsettling. Chandler's work seemed to me to be doing exactly what history should not do, set out presentist and finalist judgments about the past. Mysteriously empirical and yet nonempirical at once, Chandler's work is epistemologically and ontologically interesting as it provides a model of how theory might be built from history. The inherent danger in this, though, is that the historian might lose objectivity and begin to build history from the theory; something Chandler's critics have accused him of. But yet, as I eased my way into my PhD, I found that his work and the allied (and not subsidiary) work of Mira Wilkins provided an intellectual structure that I could attach my research onto and even attempt to refine in a modest way. This theoretical element gave me legitimacy in a physical space then contested with cliometrically driven economic historians. The enigmatic quality, at once finalist yet structurally malleable, of the Chandlerian paradigm surely makes it worthy of discussion in itself.

Positives About Chandler

The work of Alfred D. Chandler is infused with a wonderful logic, which permeates the design of the books. Each of the three books has a structure that allows it to be used flexibly, both as a history to be read through from start to finish and secondly as a reference book. Each paragraph is masterfully constructed, the first sentence often unlocking the supplementary information below. The first book, *Strategy and Structure*, is perhaps the most elegant in this pattern, setting out a series of general propositions around the development and growth of the large industrial enterprise which then dominated the American economic landscape, before laying out a basic history constructed by the use of secondary sources, then magnifying outwards into four comparative large scale case studies of American Corporations, based upon archival research – E. I. du Pont de Nemours & Co., General Motors Corporation, Standard Oil Company (New York), and Sears, Roebuck and Company. This is then wrapped by an analytical conclusion that consolidates together the theory which emerges from the four case studies, evaluating the emergence of the modern industrial enterprise as a capability building and consolidating organization based upon a cadre of professional managers, whose main role was the administrative coordination and planning of the enterprise. So powerful is this analysis, which extrapolates theoretical insights from the empirics, that Rowlinson et al. (2014, pp. 263–264) argue that it is an "exemplar" of analytically structured history, superseding the genre of "corporate history" because concepts are given importance over individual business entities. This was the core of the thesis of modern industrial enterprise which Chandler would then expand outwards in *The Visible Hand* by considering the longer term history of the modern industrial enterprise and how it rose in tandem with the profession of management. *Scale and Scope* eventually took this theme "global," seeking to cast the rise of the modern industrial enterprise and the profession of management as broader explainers of the fate of entire national economies. Chandler's vision does not stay exactly constant through these three volumes but rather evolves and refines his logic, introducing new theoretical constructs and also re-defining some concepts, probably inspired by the work of other historians as the business history field expanded. The extrapolation of theory from comparative archival research, thus establishing a basis for the comparison of otherwise esoteric case studies, was undoubtedly Chandler's biggest single methodological contribution to the business and management history field.

The most important theoretical contribution emerging from *Strategy and Structure* was that of the M-Form, or multidivisional, organization. A secondary, but interrelated, contribution was the differentiation between "strategic decisions," which were taken for the long-term health of the enterprise, and "tactical decisions" which were of day-to-day importance. Building on Chandler (1956), in which the contemporary popularity of the "de-centralized structure" among the 50 largest American industrial corporations had been established, the four firms studied in *Strategy and Structure* were chosen because they appeared to have innovated the multidivisional form of organization to administer the increasing scale and scope of their operations. As the corporations expanded to serve the rapidly industrializing and urbanizing American markets in the years between about 1870 and 1950, they both vertically and horizontally integrated, expanding vertically to gain access to raw materials and distribution channels, and horizontally to take advantage of opportunities for related diversification. This required an inter-related logical system of dispersed responsibility throughout the organization, which Chandler claimed his four main case studies had creatively innovated independently as required, without outside influence (3). Specialist administrators were required, who generally did not perform any "functional work" (9) who coordinated, planned, and appraised the work of those below them as well as allocating the resources of the firm to productive uses. Administrators themselves formed a hierarchy; the highest would often be involved in administering the work of other administrators, rather than having direct involvement with operations. The hierarchy divided into four units (9–11) – the

General Office which coordinated and administered major functions at the heart of the company, taking purely strategic decisions with regard to resource allocation. A series of *Division Central Offices* would sit below the *General Office*, having strategic control of functions relating to individual product lines. Below this sat the *Departmental Headquarters* which coordinated, appraised, and planned the activities of a number of *Field Units* which actually carried out the activities of the firm, be it manufacturing, retailing, or research, or even a support function such as engineering or accounting. Management in the *Field Units* was expected to be an almost entirely tactical concern taking place within the parameters and resource constrains set down by the *General Office*.

The identification of this hierarchical split led Chandler to the titular demarcation between *Strategy* and *Structure*. Room for strategy, and thus strategic design and planning, was created by the strategy/tactics split. Strategy, or the allocation of available resources towards the growth of the enterprise, was considered an "entrepreneurial" activity by Chandler, who considered it the economic (and perhaps societal) duty of such executives to take a long term outlook for their firms (12). Strategies for growth required implementation, which was supported by the "the design of organization through which the enterprise is administered." (14) Administration within the structure was the role of mere managers, who coordinated, appraised, and planned within the resources allocated to them. Thus, Chandler constructed a purely strategic history, differentiating his work from the later, more functionally orientated histories of Pollard, George, and Wren, which concerned themselves more closely with the management of operations and human resources within enterprises, rather than the enterprise as a whole. This created a domain for a business history which concerned itself with the history of whole enterprises and less so the functional knowledge within them. But perhaps even more influentially, by positing that structure must follow strategy for an enterprise to be successful Chandler played an important role in creating the emerging discipline of strategic management, complementing the work of Selznick (1957) who had already identified some notional ideas of policy implementation (Mintzberg 1990; Mintzberg et al. 1998). The focus on design perhaps influenced the ideas of Kenneth Andrews in the textbook most heavily associated with the design school, first published by a team of Harvard authors in 1965 (Christensen et al. 1978).

Other strategic management concepts appeared in *Strategy and Structure* in nascent form, notably elements of positioning school and resource-based view thinking, although prescriptive strategy content was not developed in the way that Porter (1979, 1980, 1985) would later develop it. By emphasizing the planning role of the *General Office*, Chandler had intellectually created the space for strategy, but also emphasized the role of the executive in allocating resources to the demands of the external market as driven by changes in customers, supply, technology, and actions of competitors, a sort of precursor of Porter's (1979) pervasive "Five Forces" framework. In a curious note tucked away at the very end of the book (453), Chandler claims that his findings relating to the diversification of firms across product and industry boundaries support those of Penrose (1959), which he admits he had not read until after he had completed his own manuscript. Penrose, however, was arguing something subtly different – she agreed in that managers drove growth, but this was an internal impulse based upon unique firm resources that provided the opportunity to exploit market imperfections, rather than a process designed by management to exploit market growth (Burgelman 1983, p. 62). Penrose's book directly inspired the resource-based view of strategic management (Mintzberg et al. 1998, pp. 276–278; Carter et al. 2008), which argues that competitive advantage evolves from the unique bundle of tangible and intangible resources and capabilities held by a firm (Wernerfelt 1984; Dierickx and Cool 1989; Prahalad and Hamel 1990; Grant 1991; Barney 1991). The resource-based view scholars generally ignored Chandler despite his evidence that firms combine tangible resources such as plants, machinery, offices, warehouses, and other marketing and purchasing facilities, sources of raw materials, research and engineering labs with the intangible, and most valuable "technical, marketing, and administrative skills of personnel" over time (14). Teece et al. (1997) in seeking to re-establish the linkage between internal and externally derived competencies cited both *Strategy and Structure* and the more recent *Scale and Scope*, as they sought to move the resource-based and positioning views closer together. Chandler had already identified that dynamic processes of resource adoption and adaptation were in play within the modern industrial enterprise, concluding that:

> If the need to use resources provided the dynamic force that changed structure and strategy, the nature of the investment in these resources helped to determine the course and direction of growth and of subsequent structural change. (384).

Professional managers were therefore the people best placed to understand the need to direct resources in a dynamic fashion as the economy changed and evolved; they were the people who oversaw the accumulation of resources, their rationalization where necessary, and their continued growth, a process considered critical within the modern post second industrial revolution economy.

Chandler's dynamic view of the history of the enterprise as a dynamic process resting upon the judgment of professional managers continued into *The Visible Hand*. This volume was more ambitious than *Strategy and Structure*, throwing the start date back to 1790, the very beginnings of recognizable modern industrial enterprise in the USA. Chandler aimed to usurp Smith's (1776) concept of the "invisible hand" of the market by demonstrating that while the market remained the generator of demand, it had since about 1840 lost its ability to coordinate supply to the very visible institution of managerial capitalism. Chandler felt that neoclassical economists had not dealt with the reasons for the existence of the corporation in sufficient detail, instead assuming it away as an aberration aiming to pursue the notion that enterprises existed only to pursue monopoly power and prevent perfect competition from taking its natural course (4). The book was essentially an exercise in die-hard transaction cost economics in the mold of Coase (1937), but with the refination that administrative coordination of the production and distribution process by salaried managers in itself had outstripped the savings from lower information and transactions costs. The internalization of many different business activities within a single enterprise under a managerial hierarchy had allowed for greater productivity, lower costs, and higher profits than mere market mechanisms allowed, and further, managerial promotion had come to be about training, experience and performance rather than kinship or money. The propositions of the book place further faith in managerialism, arguing that career managers preferred long-term stability and growth rather than aiming for short-term profitability (6–12). Chandler was moving closer to Berle and Means (1932) and Drucker (1946) in orientation, though Chandler's focus clearly remained on the economic domain, and he stops short of a Keynesian viewpoint, retaining a belief that the market would provide demand. Indeed, the concept of profit had entered the discussion much more visibly than in *Strategy and Structure*, as did the opportunities presented by the introduction of mass production and distribution in a sweeping narrative that took the reader through the development of the US railroads and manufacturing industry to reach the triumphal endpoint of the modern industrial corporation around 1920. In doing this Chandler had also provided one of the standard texts on the administrative development of the railroad and the distributive and retailing industries. While focusing on developments in the 1840–1920 era, there remained a confident sense that the book explained the rise of mid–/late twentieth-century modernity.

Chandler's final volume, *Scale and Scope,* very much represented the final affirmation and refination of both his theoretical and empirical contributions. It is also, perhaps, the most impressive in terms of academic scope, bringing a comparative angle to his discussion of managerial capitalism by considering the rise of the modern industrial enterprise in Britain and Germany also, processes characterized as being embodied by "personal capitalism" and "cooperative capitalism," respectively. As we will see in more depth below, this focus would prove controversial as the British were portrayed as relative losers in the development race, having failed to properly exploit the opportunities that a separation of ownership and control could open up, including the recruitment of professional managers and the development of advanced organizational capabilities required to compete in the second industrial revolution (12). Chandler's main theoretical nuances, some of which had been major themes throughout, were now more clearly signposted. Multiple use of a single asset or resource, which had previously been termed "economies of joint production," could now following Teece (1980) be rebranded as the more catchy "economies of scope" alongside "economies of scale." Economies arising from downstream vertical integration were now also repackaged into a "three-pronged investment in production, distribution and management," which were all necessary to ensure the success of the modern industrial corporation. Despite some acceptance of the possibility of the fallibility of corporations to financialized imperatives (11), managerial incompetence, or attempts to exploit their workforces, the book presents a kind of historically motivated recipe for success in business. All at once *Scale and Scope* is more about strategy content than its predecessors, but not quite in the prescriptive sense developed by Porter; it also demonstrates a commitment to comparative history and suggests that Chandler had moved closer to the economic and business history community that had embraced his chronologically oriented work.

Yet *Scale and Scope* also returned to *Strategy and Structure's* original prototheorization around dynamic capabilities and seems to have decisively influenced the thinking of David Teece (1993), who wrote a length review essay of the book. The first section of the conclusion was devoted to "Organizational Dynamics as the Core Dynamic" (594), stressing that organizations had to create and maintain their own capabilities, which then provided both the source and dynamic for the continuing growth of the firm. A conscious process of maintenance was necessary if the organization was to avoid atrophy of skill and the depreciation of the physical plant – some of the earnings of the firm had to be pumped into maintaining this. Teece (1993) praised *Scale and Scope* for highlighting these nonmarket features of firms, thus contributing alongside the work of to an evolutionary theory of the firm overall, for instance, highlighting that the scale and scope economies of the second industrial revolution were not available to all, but only those with the organizational capabilities to take advantage of them, namely, the three prongs of investment in production, distribution, and management. Such expansion was also not limited to the size of the market, as neoclassical economics would assume, but by the administrative capabilities of the M-Form organization. For Teece et al. (1997) and Teece (2007, 2010), this belief that organizations would be able to use their capabilities to shape future market opportunities among as yet unforeseen economic disruptions would be crucial in his future work, which remains influential in strategic management.

Critiques

One of the most intriguing features of *Scale and Scope*, written right at the end of the period of study of this section of the Handbook (c. 1940–1990), was the very last few pages (621–628) of the conclusion, which give the distinct sense that even Alfred D. Chandler Jr. was forced to admit that the world he had documented and theorized with such Herculean effort had already started to ebb away. The modern industrial enterprise had, it seemed, enjoyed its heyday in the 1960s, not just in the US, but in Germany, Britain, and Japan (which had adopted managerial enterprise even more enthusiastically since 1945 than the west), though M-Form American firms had continued to dominate the scene; as late as 1973, 211 out of 401 non-Communist industrial enterprises employing more than 20,000 people globally had been US owned (19). Having attempted to explain the present through the past in 1962 and 1977, Chandler now retreated into history claiming that a historian was not in a good position to analyze or evaluate the unprecedented developments that he was at least in a position to diagnose. Corporations seemed to be unable to maintain their institutional power, partly because they were becoming themselves subject to a new "market for corporate control" in which they and their constituent parts were being sold on the open market, with many corporations buying new subsidiaries in industries that they had no capabilities to compete in. This process also seemed to be distancing the *General Office* from its divisional parts as portfolio managers asserted their power over corporations as stockholders, with the assumption that managerial specialism was not required for a firm to make a profit (621).

These new trends were symptomatic of a period where a new generation of academics and practitioners were attempting to overturn established orthodoxies around managerialism and the closely related orthodoxy of strategic planning. The turbulent environment of the 1960s and 1970s, characterized by the Cold War, the gradual slowdown of industrial growth in the west, and the challenge of decolonization in Africa and Asia threw up a series of events including the Vietnam War and the 1973 Oil Crisis which eroded confidence in the postwar consensus which had been based around rational economic and social planning, a related rational concept to managerial planning. The work of Henry Mintzberg (1978, 1990, 1994; Mintzberg and Waters 1985), who studied the actual implementation of strategies by organizations from the early 1970s onwards, actively started to challenge design and planning school notions of strategy by demonstrating that strategies could be *emergent* as well as *planned.* Mintzberg (1978, p. 935) directly compared Chandler's definition of strategy with those of game theory and military strategy, demonstrating that all had in common the assumptions that strategy was explicit, developed consciously and purposefully, and made in advance of the specific decisions to which it applied. Yet by focusing on the experiences of Volkswagen and the US state in the Vietnam War, Mintzberg was able to suggest that these things were not automatically interdependent, and that planning and strategy were not the same thing; indeed, all that strategy implied was a consistency, or pattern in decision making over time. For instance, in Vietnam, President Johnson had ended up being swept along by rapidly emerging environmental conditions to follow a pattern of escalation of the conflict through direct US intervention (involving 500,000 ground troops), despite the earlier stated and planned strategy set by President Kennedy to indirectly intervene by providing military advisors to the South Vietnamese (1978, pp. 938–941). But yet it would be difficult to argue that Johnson's actions in Vietnam were not strategic. Closer to Chandler's immediate world, General Electric's CEO Reginald Jones (1972–81) continued to place his company's faith in strategic planning, using an impressive range of techniques to plan the allocation of resources within the firm and maintain, devise, and revise its structure to support the allocation but yet suffered almost nonexistent growth in stock prices through the 1970s with declining profit/equity ratio, a stagnant state of affairs which legitimated the company's employment of the notoriously pro-shareholder value Jack Welch as Jones's successor (Mintzberg 1994, pp. 101–104). Essentially, Chandler had assumed that the modern industrial enterprise had the power to hold environmental conditions stable or perhaps even shape them, through the time interval between planning and realization. Further, as seemed to have happened in the General Electric case, planning could actually distract managers from opportunities for innovation that might arise from more creative approaches to implementation, or simply tie up managerial time that might be better spent elsewhere, and thus act as a break on effective strategic management.

In his concern with implementation, Mintzberg (1990) also raised questions about the link between strategy and structure, which lies at the heart of the Chandler (1962) thesis, though also forming part of a broader critique of the design school. This appeared to play on a contradiction within Chandler's own theorization which drew attention to the importance of managing resources and capabilities; Mintzberg (1990) essentially argued that assuming that managers could act freely, remolding firms into the M-Form did a disservice to the organization's existing capabilities, which were housed by its structure. Organizations were going concerns and could not delete the past, nor their existing capabilities – but claiming that these things could be remolded was tantamount to claiming that strategy must altogether take precedence over these existing capabilities. Mintzberg thus revised the theory to claim that strategy and structure had a symbiotic relationship, following each other "as the left foot follows the right in walking" (Mintzberg 1990). Burgelman (1983) had already proposed that strategy may at least in some cases follow structure, even suggesting that it did so in Chandler's own case data on du Pont, which seemed to suggest that multiple layers of the hierarchy were involved in re-organization, and that before re-organization the center of the firm had very little influence over strategic formulation, which resided with department heads. Indeed, parts of both Chandler's du Pont and General Motors case studies seemed to involve the management imposing structure post hoc to consolidate administrative control over diversifications that had already taken place to take advantage of opportunities in rapidly growing industries (91–113; 130–142). Chandler's theorization seemed to have been post hoc, the adoption of a new structure only putting the *General Office* at the center of strategy formulation after it had been put in place (Burgelman 1983, p. 63). Chandler had extrapolated his theory perhaps not from the experience of the re-organization itself, which was an attempt to catch up with the organizational chaos generated by the rapid growth of the firm, but the structure that had been put in place to impose order and attempt to contain future growth within the organization's boundaries. The real world is messy, and the revisionary approaches of Mintzberg and Burgelman illustrate that strategy formulation and implementation are not always distinct things; while Chandler does not go as far as Christensen et al. (1978) and Ansoff (1965) in prescribing a rational planning process, his extrapolation of one from his cases is subject to question.

An inter-related tendency was the drive away from managerialism towards shareholder value ideology, actively furthered by the Chicago School and their allies, which was happening even as Chandler was writing *The Visible Hand*. This perhaps reveals a further weakness in Chandler's work – the lack of any substantive engagement with questions of governance, purpose, and mission beyond the idea that the modern industrial corporation existed to build the economy. Indeed, some important intellectual legitimations of shareholder value ideology had already been published by 1977, perhaps most notably Jensen and Meckling (1976) who neatly sidestepped Coasean theories of the firm by claiming that firms were a legal fiction-based nexus of contracts, the most important of which was that held with the stockholders. This rendered the boundaries of firms and indeed managerial authority irrelevant, and indeed Jensen and Meckling purported to demonstrate that managers in firms would always choose activities which suppressed the total value of the firm below that achievable if they were the sole owners (what Chandler would have described as the inferior form of personal capitalism). The high profile failure of the Penn Central Transportation Corporation, an unwieldy merger between two railroad companies in 1970, affected a broad sweep of sectors across the American economy and society. While it is undoubtedly true that the agency of American railroads to reallocate their resources to more profitable activities was heavily regulated by the Interstate Commerce Commission until the 1980 Staggers Act, revelations that personal differences between Penn's President, Chairman, and Finance Chairman had impeded decision making together with a record of unsuccessful diversifications outside of the rail industry brought the fallibility of professional managers as guardians of the nation's wealth into stark focus (Daughen and Binzen 1971). The ensuing rush for shareholder value as financial institutions and markets reasserted their primacy over the corporation, encouraging the stripping of assets, downsizing and offshoring of workforces, and the dismantlement of much of the managerial hierarchy of corporations (Lazonick and O'Sullivan 2000; Stout 2002, 2007), has unleashed a number of calls for a return to a broader managerialism in which the interests of a broader group of stakeholders are considered (Lazonick 2013; Stout 2012).

It is tempting therefore to see parallels between Chandler and other progressive managerialist authors, particularly the path breaking work of Berle and Means (1932), who initially drew attention to the domination of the American economy by large corporations and the resulting implications of the separation of ownership and control. Nevertheless, Berle and Means argued that if managers are to have the most powerful claim over the allocation of the firm's resources, then this implied a broader responsibility to society of the corporation which was as much a social mechanism as an economic one (Smith et al. 2018). Chandler avoids this, assuming the moral triumph of managers over the economy is to be taken for granted and complete, with the *General Office* having ultimate claim over the direction of the firm's resources, including the reinvestment of profit. Chandler was comfortable with this finality, but in his insistence that managers were heroic he misses the opportunity to interrogate the onset of financialization more closely in *Scale and Scope*. If the modern industrial enterprise was such a strong institution, why did it corrode away so readily?

Perhaps the answer lies within critiques that the rise of the modern industrial enterprise was not an economic phenomenon based on economies of scale and scope at all, but more of a sociological or institutional one. Thus, its existence was more of a mirage designed to legitimate American capitalism. Fligstein (1990, 2008) argues that Chandler's own evidence can simply be read another way. Chandler takes great pains to avoid the assertion that the growth of the firm was based on the exploitation of monopoly rights, but Fligstein (2008, pp. 247–248) points to contemporary testimony to characterize the vertical and horizontal merger wave between 1895 and 1904 as an attempt to preserve the possibilities of cartelization after the 1890 Sherman Act. Managers claimed to be combining firms because it would reduce competition, not because they would be able to exploit scale or scope economies to deliver better products to consumers. This mean firms were able to defend themselves on the basis of monopoly power, not efficiency; certainly high margins were generated through the creation of national or international scale firms, but this was the result of supply not demand side dynamics. Khurana (2007, pp. 27–28) shows that Chandler ignored two other important factors – firstly, the changing social order in the late nineteenth-century USA, which saw large scale increases in literacy as well as population growth and urbanization. Literacy meant there was suddenly a cadre of people with the clerical skills to carry out the planning, co-ordination, and monitoring of the work and performance of others. Secondly, Khurana drew on DiMaggio (1988, pp. 14–15) to show that the role of agency was important; corporations provided "institutional entrepreneurs" with an opportunity to build environments that they found amenable. Managers were seeking to create sympathetic conditions for the organizations that they were expanding, to the exclusion of alternative political, social, and cultural interests. Freeland (2001) shows that power contests were imperative in the evolution of the M-Form; in the case of General Motors, the structure was used by Alfred Sloan to maintain power over his subordinates by claiming that it protected them from DuPont's claims for more direct control over the company, while on the other hand allowing division heads to maintain operational power. Thus, the M-Form was at least as much about political compromise and the maintenance of goodwill in the hierarchy as it was about the administrative coordination of a multiproduct business.

Chandler appears guilty of (perhaps willfully) ignoring the political and social aspects of the growth of large corporations. This suited the weaponization of his work as an account of the socially benign forces of capitalism creating growth, together with opportunities to stabilize the middle classes through managerial jobs, within the Cold War context. The United States Information Service donated copies of *Strategy and Structure* to European universities (The University of York's (UK) copy has a 'donated by USIS' stamp inside the front cover), while the UK House of Commons held a copy in its library for the use of Members of Parliament (The British Library's present copy was transferred from the House of Commons Library, which had originally acquired it in 1968). If *Strategy and Structure* was politically influential, Cooke (2003) provides evidence of another political undertone in *The Visible Hand* – just a few years after the civil rights struggle, Chandler seemed to be ignoring or denying the possibility that modern management had emerged as a mechanism to control the 4 million slaves in the ante-bellum south, in the same period that railroads were supposedly bringing it into being. *The Visible Hand* featured three pages on slavery, conceding that at least 18,859 "overseers" had been employed on plantations in 1850 and that there was some evidence that plantation owners had needed "full-time assistance to carry out their managerial function" (65). Yet at the same time Chandler actively denied that the plantations fitted within modern industrial capitalism, defining them as "an ancient form of large scale production," because he claimed there was no meaningful separation of ownership and control, on the grounds that most plantations were smaller than New England's cotton mills in terms of labor force and that overseers were mainly concerned with the supervision of slaves rather than forward planning, while accounting was a task usually carried out by plantation owners (64–65). Cooke (1906–1910) provides evidence that considerable division of labor and sophisticated proto-Taylorist managerial activity using hierarchy, teamwork, and resource allocation through the agricultural cycle did exist on plantations, to the extent that slaves themselves may have been co-opted as lower-level managers. Even Chandler's figure of 18,859 "overseers" had been open to challenge; it was unclear why 1850 had been chosen, when Chandler's own source, Scarborough (1966, p. 11), had shown that the number had more than doubled by 1860 – nor indeed did Chandler provide a comparative figure of overseers or managers for the railroads. It is hard to see how 18,859 "overseers" could have controlled 4 million people without considerable coordinative and administrative skill. The plantation industry and its use of slavery simply did not fit into Chandler's finalist narrative, perhaps because it appeared to have ended with the civil war, or because it was intellectually incompatible with the idea of a benign, technically progressive modern capitalism.

Chandler's progressive finality of vision opened up another line of critique emerging from the intellectual tradition that perhaps most closely derived its key ideas from his work. This was the broad sense that American economic development, and particularly the development of the heroic modern industrial enterprise within this paradigm, was in some way an inevitable driver of progress, a phenomenon Leslie Hannah (2009) has called "Hollywood History." John (2008) identifies Chandler as a historian emerging from a particular American intellectual tradition of "progressive historians," particularly Frederick Jackson Turner (1861–1932) and Charles A. Beard (1874–1948). Turner was a historian of the American West who drew attention to the importance of the expanding frontier for American economic development; his thesis claimed that the frontier's expansion had absorbed the nation's resources, and slowed the onset of modern industrial enterprise but had created the ingredients of a successful democracy. Chandler's PhD supervisor had been Frederick Merk, a "loyal disciple" of Turner at Harvard, who introduced Chandler to the "frontier thesis," which Chandler perpetuated to some extent, particularly in the claim that trans-Appalachian railways required managerial synthesis and that the eventual scattering of population in the west had impeded the growth of distribution networks to the extent that the corporations of the second industrial revolution were required to coordinate them (232–233). From Beard, as well as his great-grandfather Henry Varnum Poor, he took a disdain for financiers and investors, sensing that financiers had too short term an interest in an organization to invest its resources in building long-term competences (235–236). John argues that these influences made Chandler into a progressive in a similar mold to the New Dealers of the 1930s, and an endorser of Keynesian economics, as well as someone who had a genuine belief in the power of the human spirit, developing an interest in human capital towards the end of his career (238–239) and, despite the challenge of Mintzberg, retaining a faith in planning in his final two books *Inventing the Electronic Century* (2001) and *Shaping the Industrial Century* (2005).

Yet this commitment to progressive politics coupled with a distrust of finance may have led Chandler into the trap of writing what Lameroux et al. (2004), while criticizing the attempts of Langlois (2003, 2004) to envelop Chandler's work into a broader neo-classical paradigm, have termed "Whiggish History." Among historians, Chandler's work on Britain in *Scale and Scope* has been especially controversial. Chandler essentially argued that British capitalism lost competitiveness in the long run because British firms did not invest sufficiently in renewing their capabilities, and further, because they were too small, only really separating ownership from control and generating anything approximating the M-Form too late, often in the post-World War II period (1990, pp. 389–392). Hannah (2009) presents compelling evidence that Chandler became less critical about his comparative perspectives, inadvertently bending the data to suit the narrative that British firms were less successful because they were less managerially advanced than their US and German counterparts. This was part of a broader agenda that saw personal or family capitalists (or indeed any nonmanagerial form) as archaic predecessors or even enemies of modernity, much in the same way as plantations in the Ante-Bellum South. Hannah does not disagree that Britain suffered an economic slowdown in the twentieth century and that British businessmen sometimes followed quite conservative strategies, especially where accounting standards were poor, mergers were often defensive, and traditionalist managers were often supported by complacent owning families (16–17). Yet it appeared that Chandler had ignored elements of the American and German stories that did not suit his endpoint, most notably elements of family or personal ownership, for instance, in the copper industry or the *Mittelstand* (19, 34), the persistence of some inefficient holding companies such as US Leather while devoting three pages to the British Calico Printers Association (33), and even glossing over the extremes of the fascist period in Germany after 1933 (35). Case studies of the copper industry and the tobacco industry were also used to show that Chandler overstated American dominance in these industries in the early years of the 1900s, characterizing Rio Tinto, the largest copper company in the world in 1900 as a family owned firm whose failure to invest in vertical integration (it owned its own smelting works in Spain as well as mining!) had locked the British out of copper forever (19–20). Rio Tinto had of course also persisted as a global leader where many of the American and German firms lionized by Chandler, such as Anaconda, had failed, despite the nationalization of its Spanish assets in the 1950s (21). Chandler had also underplayed the extent to which British companies had frustrated the attempts of James B. Duke to build a global tobacco empire, forcing his interests into a merger instead, known as British American Tobacco (22–30). A extremely skilled business historian himself, Hannah was adept at diagnosing Chandler's faults in constructing a comparative history, which concedes is a difficult thing to do, but the problem arose in that Chandler was still extrapolating theory from history but without testing it against larger samples of leading firms, as he had done in *Strategy and Structure*. This led him not just to be more subjective and thus distort his treatment of some industries, but also "led to grotesque missclassifications of supposed casual determinants" (32). Chandler was convinced that he had discovered the "magic ingredient" necessary to ensure not just sustained competitive advantage but the key to modernity and indeed economic growth itself.

Chandler's legacy to the business history discipline then was a double edged sword. At once his work gave it structure but also bound it to a progressive ideology that assumed economic growth based around the visible hand of management and large-scale industry was the normative mode of development. Even by the time that *Scale and Scope* (and perhaps even *The Visible Hand*) was published, it was clear this was not the case, but the weight of the Chandlerian paradigm crushed the potential for innovation and thus a more questioning attitude to the new paradigms of shareholder value and financialization out of the discipline. *The Visible Hand* blatantly closes off legitimate business history enquiry to earlier periods of business or family forms of it, or even to small and medium sized businesses, which are deemed to be "un-professional" or "un-modern." There is a sense that nothing is to be gained from studying other discourses or paradigms and an unquestioning uncritical attitude set in.

This leads to miscategeorizations and misunderstandings based around the Chandlerian and Williamsonian assumption that the boundaries of a firm are coterminous with its legal boundaries. Salient alternatives, such as network (n-form) and project forms (p-forms) of organization, have been marginalized in business history because it assumed that they do not have capabilities worth studying. This was exemplified by the controversy around Mira Wilkins' concept of the free-standing company (1986, 1988, 1998), a prolific category of British proto-multinational firm often developed by networks of businessmen, which, because they tended to invest in property- or project-based assets abroad and have a minimal headquarters which only seemed to satisfy the requirements of company law (Casson 1998), could not possibly develop recognizable strategic management capabilities. Yet this was not a disablement to companies which would arguably fit the free-standing label such as the New Zealand and Australia Land Company, which operated a chain of professionally managed sheep and cattle stations in Britain's Antipodean colonies from a small office in Edinburgh, vertically integrated into dairy manufacturing, and survived for 102 years, from 1866 to 1968 (Tennent 2009, 2013)! This confusion arose from Wilkins' Chandlerian quest to discover the origins of the contemporary multinational business landscape; because free-standing companies were now less visible, or had changed their strategies to avoid dual taxation (Mollan and Tennent 2015), she assumed they were a retrograde model of capitalism (Mollan 2018).

The P-form organization has suffered similar neglect; project management scholars note the relevance of Chandler's work in explaining the growth of the large corporation but are also in search of ways to break out of it to embrace the whole breadth and scope of project forms (Söderlund and Lenfle 2013). As Scranton (1998, 2014) notes, project forms and organizations can embrace a broad range of industrial settings, from the construction and transport to aerospace and shipbuilding sectors as well as in specialty manufacturing – and arguably constitute the "other side" of the second industrial revolution. Project management clearly lends itself to historical examination as well as each project has a different genesis and temporal development pathway yet clearly possesses relevant knowledge on process which can be transferred to other projects. Gillett and Tennent (2017) apply the concepts of Flyvbjerg (2014) and Morris and Geraldi (2011) to their Swarm model (Tennent and Gillett 2016, pp. 166–169), in order to explain why England hosted the 1966 FIFA World Cup, an enterprise which from the perspective of Chandlerian business history would appear unsuited or irrelevant to management analysis as a temporary, small scale event – yet elite sport is clearly a salient feature of modernity (Gillett and Tennent 2018), and surely requires analysis from the perspective of management history?

The theoretical dominance of Chandler over business history may therefore not just have impeded innovation but also have furthered the sense of isolation, referred to by Taylor et al. (2009), that the field has felt from other more "mainstream" management topics, such as strategy. Business historians have tended to rely on Chandler (and to a lesser extent Williamson) for theorization despite the development of newer theories in the strategy field, including the work of Mintzberg. This means that the scope of business history work for theoretical refination has been limited. For instance, Higgins and Toms (2011) carry out a systematic review of British Public Limited Companies between 1949 and 1984 to establish the extent to which the sustained competitive advantage (SCA) of British firms was determined by organizational structure, but despite successfully challenging Chandler by demonstrating the weakness of this link, they remain entirely within a Chandlerian paradigm, concluding that "structure follows strategy" (109). They flirt briefly with the work of Barney (1991) as an alternative theorization, accepting that the resource-based view might have relevance for their conceptualization of SCA, but do not pursue it, despite the opportunities it might open up for their analysis. Yet to genuinely challenge the work of Alfred D. Chandler, business historians surely need to find alternative, less teleological explanations of management phenomena in order to attain the sort of dual integrity required of contemporary historical organization studies (Maclean et al. 2016). The very strength of Chandler's work was that it attained this dual integrity within itself, by speaking to contemporary theoretical concerns at a time in which there was a demand for "chapter 2 history." This may partly explain why scholars in fields such as strategic management, transaction cost economics, and institutional theory have continued to cite Chandler (but perhaps not actually read him) while under-utilizing much of the output of more recent business historians.

Conclusion

The work of Alfred D. Chandler was monumental in scale and remains undoubtedly of critical import to this day. The danger, however, was that Chandler took a finalist approach to history, seeking to explain the success of his times and making the perhaps fatal mistake that more of the same was needed to sustain it. This was a whiggish history for a whiggish period of history, in which everything was growth. Decline happened to industries and firms that had failed to invest in scale, scope, and managerial capabilities and therefore was unmodern. Chandler had few answers to an economic decline perhaps already setting in the western world as he was writing. Certainly there was great uncertainty around the future direction of the US economy by the 1970s that led to calls for new forms of leadership to be brought forward (Spector 2014). This whiggishness, from which Chandler's work derives its theoretical import, is perhaps its very undoing also. The long-range field of historical enquiry spanning multiple periods together with the search for underlying theoretical structures in *The Visible Hand* perhaps invites comparisons to Braudel's *longue durée* approach (1972), which was controversial to many empiricist historians (Green and Troup 1999, p. 94), yet Braudel remained committed to understanding historical actors within their temporal and spatial contexts. Braudel, of course, did not seek to explain his present. Chandler fell into McCloskey's trap of gnomic presentism (1998), building a four-dimensional model of industrial growth rooted in 1962's context, based around the vectors of volume, geographic, functional, and product lines. This was a static model or at least one grounded in its context, a growing and globally hegemonic postwar economy, not in actuality suitable for all time. This gnomic mode of determinism casts doubt onto the theoretical half-life of Chandler's work, one of the foundational texts in the management studies discipline, because it may undermine the theoretical foundations upon which thousands of studies rely.

By 1990 and in the publication of *Scale and Scope,* Chandler had noted with bewilderment that the global economy, startled by the Japanese and South Korean challenge together with the oil crises of the 1970s and macroeconomic impact of the Chicago School, was no longer developing in the fashion described in his earlier books. In the introduction and conclusion of the book, he eschews conscious explanation of the present to a large extent, retreating into the history discipline, claiming that the history of the enterprise cannot explain its present as competition, both inter-company and inter-country had intensified (despite his defense of the Rhine model in *Scale and Scope*). Chandler's retreat into history as his ability to explain empirical reality diminished was intellectually damaging for the business and management history subject area it encouraged scholars to forget the powerful linkages made to some contemporarily important research areas, including institutional logics and dynamic capabilities thinking. These schools of thought were rising in the early 1990s yet clearly to some extent inspired by the arguments of *Scale and Scope*.

Yet the notion of the managerial enterprise may continue to hold some relevance in the early twenty-first-century era of entrepreneurship and firm building which rests on the internet and information technology. Some firms not even established at the time of Chandler have grown into perhaps neo-Chandlerian enterprises based apparently on the construction of managerial logics and capabilities with relatively little concern to distribute profits to their shareholders. As they grew through the late 2000s and into the 2010s expanding firms such as Amazon, Apple, Google, and Facebook seemed to prioritize long-term growth at the expense of shareholders and resisted overt financialization (though they do accept the outsourcing of capabilities). In periods of expansionism, the visible hand may have an important role to play. Chandler told us how capabilities were built and perhaps therefore how they might be built. Maintaining them when the process of expansion was ended was a different matter. Chandler's work may therefore have enduring relevance in the twenty-first century.

Cross-References

- ▶ The Age of Strategy: From Drucker and Design to Planning and Porter
- ▶ Debates Within Management History
- ▶ The Intellectual Origins of Postmodernism

References

Ansoff HI (1965) Corporate strategy. An analytic approach to business policy for growth and expansion. McGraw Hill, New York

Barney J (1991) Firm resources and sustained competitive advantage anonymous. J Manag 17(1):99–120

Bateman TS, Snell SS (2009) Management: leading and collaborating in a competitive World. McGraw Hill, Boston

Berle A, Means G (1932) The modern corporation and private property. Macmillan, New York

Berman M (1982) All that is solid melts into air: the experience of modernity. Simon and Schuster, New York

Braudel F (1972) In: Reynolds S (ed) The mediterranean and the Mediterranean world in the age of Philip II. Collins, London

Bridgman T, Cummings S (2011) The relevant past : why the history of management should be critical for our future. Acad Manag Learn Educ 10(1):77–93

Burgelman RA (1983) A model of the interaction of strategic behavior, corporate context, and the concept of strategy. Acad Manag Rev 8(1):61

Carter C, Clegg SR, Kornberger M (2008) A very short, fairly interesting and reasonably cheap book about studying strategy. Sage Publications, London

Casson M (1998) An economic theory of the free-standing company. In: Wilkins M, Schröter H (eds) The free standing company in the world economy, 1830–1996. Oxford University Press, Oxford

Chandler A (1954) Patterns of American railroad finance, 1830–50. Bus Hist Rev 28(3):248–263

Chandler AD (1956) Management decentralization: an historical analysis. Bus Hist Rev 30(2):111–174

Chandler AD (1962) Strategy and structure : chapters in the history of the American industrial enterprise. M.I.T. Press, Cambridge

Chandler AD (1977) The visible hand: the managerial revolution in American business. Belknap Press, Cambridge, Mass

Chandler AD (2001) Inventing the electronic century: the epic story of the consumer electronics and computer industries. Free Press, New York

Chandler AD (2005) Shaping the industrial century: the remarkable story of the modern chemical and pharmaceutical industries. Harvard University Press, Cambridge, MA

Chandler AD, Daems H (1979) Administrative coordination, allocation and monitoring: a comparative analysis of the emergence of accounting and organization in the U.S.A. and Europe. Acc Organ Soc 4(1–2):3–20

Chandler AD, Hikino T (1990) Scale and scope : the dynamics of industrial capitalism repr. 1990. Belknap Press, Cambridge, MA

Chia RCH, Holt R (2009) Strategy without design: the silent efficacy of indirect action. Cambridge University Press, Cambridge

Christensen CR, Andrews KR, Bower JL (1978) Business policy: text and cases. Richard D. Irwin, Inc, Homewood

Coase R (1937) The nature of the firm. Economica 4(16):386–405

Cooke B (2003) The denial of slavery in management studies. J Manag Stud 40(8):1895–1918

Cooke B, Mills AJ, Kelley ES (2005a) Situating maslow in cold war America. Group Org Manag 30(2):129–152

Cooke B, Mills AJ, Kelley ES (2005b) Situating maslow in cold war America: a recontextualization of management theory. Group Org Manag 30(2):129–152

Cummings S et al (2017) A new history of management. Cambridge University Press, Cambridge

Daughen JR, Binzen P (1971) The wreck of the Penn central. Little, Brown, Boston

Dierickx I, Cool K (1989) Asset stock accumulation and sustainability of competitive advantage. Manag Sci 35(12):1504–1511

DiMaggio PJ (1988) Interest and agency in insititutional theory. In: Zucker LG (ed) Institutional patterns and organizations: culture and environment. Ballinger Publishing, Cambridge, MA

Drucker P (1946) Concept of the corporation. The John Day Company, New York
Elton GR (1978) The practice of history. Collins, London
Fligstein N (1990) The transformation of corporate control. Harvard University Press, Cambridge, MA
Fligstein N (2008) Chandler and the sociology of organizations. Bus Hist Rev 82(2):241–250
Flyvbjerg B (2014) What you should know about megaprojects and why: an overview. Proj Manag J 45(2):6–19
Freeland RF (2001) The struggle for control of the modern corporation. Cambridge University Press, Cambridge
Genoe McLaren P, Mills AJ (2008) A product of "his" time? Exploring the construct of the ideal manager in the Cold War era. J Manag Hist 14(4):386–403
George CS (1968) The history of management thought. Prentice-Hall, Englewood Cliffs
Gillett AG, Tennent KD (2017) Dynamic sublimes, changing plans, and the legacy of a megaproject: the case of the 1966 Soccer World Cup. Proj Manag J 48(6):93–116
Gillett AG, Tennent KD (2018) Shadow hybridity and the institutional logic of professional sport: perpetuating a sporting business in times of rapid social and economic change. J Manag Hist 24(2):228–259
Grant RM (1991) The resource-based theory of competitive advantage: implications for strategy formulation. Calif Manag Rev 33(3):114–135
Green A, Troup K (1999) The houses of history: a critical reader in twentieth-centry history and theory. Manchester University Press, Manchester
Hannah L (2009) Strategic games, scale and efficiency, or chandler goes to hollywood. In: Coopey R, Lyth P (eds) Business in Britian in the twentieth century. Oxford University Press, Oxford, pp 15–47
Hart SL (1995) A natural-resource-based view of the firm. Acad Manag Rev 20(4):986–1014. URL: http://www.jstor.org/stable/258963
Higgins DM, Toms S (2011) Explaining corporate success: the structure and performance of British firms, 1950–84. Bus Hist 53(1):85–118
Jacobides MG, Winter SG (2005) The co-evolution of capabilities and transaction costs: explaining the institutional structure of production. Strateg Manag J 26(5):395–413
Jensen MC, Meckling WH (1976) Theory of the firm: managerial behavior, agency costs and ownership structure. J Financ Econ 3(4):305–360
John RR (1997) Elaborations, revisions, dissents: Alfred D. Chandler, Jr.'s, "the visible hand" after twenty years. Bus Hist Rev 71(2):151–200
John RR (2008) Turner, beard, chandler: progressive historians. Bus Hist Rev 82(2):227–240
Jones G (2005) Multinationals and global capitalism: from the nineteenth to the twenty-first century. Oxford University Press, Oxford
Kelley ES, Mills AJ, Cooke B (2006) Management as a cold war phenomenon? Hum Relat 59(5):603–610
Khurana R (2007) From higher aims to hired hands. Princeton University Press, Princeton
Lamoreaux NR, Raff DMG, Temin P (2004) Against whig history. Enterp Soc 5(3):376–387
Langlois RN (2003) The vanishing hand: the changing dynamics of industrial capitalism. Ind Corp Chang 12(2):351–385
Langlois RN (2004) Chandler in a larger frame: markets, transaction costs, and organizational form in history. Enterp Soc 5(3):355–375
Lazonick W (2013) From innovation to financialization: how shareholder value ideology is destroying the US economy. In: Wolfson MH, Epstein GA (eds) The handbook of the political economy of financial crises. Oxford University Press, Oxford
Lazonick W, O'Sullivan M (2000) Maximizing shareholder value: a new ideology for corporate governance. Econ Soc 29(1):13–35
Leiblein MJ, Miller DJ (2003) An empirical examination of transaction-and firm-level influences on the vertical boundaries of the firm. Strateg Manag J 24(9):839–859

Maclean M, Harvey C, Clegg SR (2016) Conceptualizing historical organization studies. Acad Manag Rev 41(4):609–632

Mahoney JT, Pandian JR (1992) The resource-based view within the conversation of strategic management. Strateg Manag J 13(5):363–380

McCloskey DN (1998) The rhetoric of economics. Univ of Wisconsin Press, Madison

Mintzberg H (1978) Patterns in strategy formation. Manag Sci 24(9):934–948

Mintzberg H (1990) The design school : reconsidering the basic premises of strategic management. Strateg Manag J 11(3):171–195

Mintzberg H (1994) The rise and fall of strategic planning. Prentice Hall, Hemel Hempstead

Mintzberg H (2004) Managers not MBAs: a hard look at the soft practice of managing and management development. Berrett-Koehler Publishers, Inc, San Francisco

Mintzberg H, Waters JA (1985) Of strategies, deliberate and emergent. Strateg Manag J 6(3):257–272

Mintzberg H, Ahlstrand B, Lampel J (1998) Strategy safari: the complete guide through the wilds of strategic management. Financial Times, Harlow

Mollan S (2018) The free-standing company: a "zombie" theory of international business history. J Manag Hist 22(2):156–173

Mollan S, Tennent KD (2015) International taxation and corporate strategy: evidence from British overseas business, circa 1900–1965. Bus Hist 57(7):1054–1081

Morris PWG, Geraldi J (2011) Managing the institutional context for projects. Proj Manag J 42(6):20–32

Penrose E (1959) The theory of the growth of the firm. Sharpe, New York

Pollard S (1965) The genesis of modern management: a study of the industrial revolution in Great Britian. Harvard University Press, Cambridge, MA

Porter M (1979) How competitive forces shape strategy. Harv Bus Rev 57(2):137–145

Porter ME (1980) Competitive strategy: techniques for analyzing industries and competitors. Free Press, New York

Porter ME (1985) Competitive advantage: creating and sustaining superior performance. Free Press, New York

Prahalad CK, Hamel G (1990) The core competence of the corporation. Harv Bus Rev 68(3):79–91. Hahn D, Taylor B (eds)

Rowlinson M, Hassard J, Decker S (2014) Research strategies for organizational history: a dialogue between historical theory and organization theory. Acad Manag Rev 39(3):250–274

Rue LW, Byars LL (2009) Management: skills and applications. McGraw Hill, Boston

Scarborough WK (1966) The overseer: plantation management in the Old South. Louisiana State University Press, Baton Rouge

Scott WR (2001) Institutions and organizations. Sage Publications, London

Scranton P (1998) Endless novelty: speciailty production and American industrialization, 1865-1925. Princeton University Press, Princeton

Scranton P (2014) Projects as a focus for historical analysis: surveying the landscape. Hist Technol 30(4):354–373

Selznick P (1957) Leadership in administration. Haprer & Row, Publishers, Inc, New York

Sloan AP (1967) In: McDonald J, Stevens C (eds) My years with general motors. Pan, London

Smith A (1776) An inquiry into the nature and causes of the wealth of nations. George Routledge and Sons, London

Smith A, Tennent KD, Russell J (2018) Berle and means' the modern corporation and private property: the military roots of a stakeholder model of corporate governance. Seattle Univ Law Rev 42(2) (forthcoming)

Söderlund J, Lenfle S (2013) Making project history: revisiting the past, creating the future. Int J Proj Manag 31(5):653–662

Spector B (2006) The harvard business review goes to war. Manag Organ Hist 1(3):273–295

Spector B (2008) "Business responsibilities in a divided world": the cold war roots of the corporate social responsibility movement. Enterp Soc 9(2):314–336

Spector B (2014) Flawed from the "Get-Go": Lee Iacocca and the origins of transformational leadership. Leadership 10(3):361–379

Stout L (2002) Bad and Not-so-Bad arguments for shareholder primacy. Calif Law Rev 75:1189–1209

Stout LA (2007) The mythical benefits of shareholder control. Va Law Rev 93(3):789–809

Stout L (2012) The shareholder value myth. Berrett-Koehler Publishers, Inc, San Francisco

Taylor S, Bell E, Cooke B (2009) Business history and the historiographical operation. (February 2015), 37–41

Teece DJ (1980) Economies of scope and the scope of the enterprise. J Econ Behav Organ 1(3):223–247

Teece DJ (1993) The dynamics of industrial capitalism: perspectives on Alfred Chandler's scale and scope. J Econ Lit 31(1):199–225

Teece DJ (2007) Explicating dynamic capabilities: the nature and microfoundations of (sustainable) enterprise performance. Strateg Manag J 1350:1319–1350. NE Al (ed)

Teece DJ (2010) Business models, business strategy and innovation. Long Range Plan 43(2–3):172–194

Teece DJ, Pisano G, Shuen A (1997) Dynamic capabilities and strategic management. Strateg Manag J 18(7):509–533. Dosi G, Nelson RR, Winter SG (eds)

Tennent KD (2009) Owned, monitored, but not always controlled: understanding the success and failure of Scottish free-standing companies, 1862–1910. Unpublished PhD Thesis, LSE, London

Tennent KD (2013) Management and the free-standing company: the New Zealand and Australia land company c. 1866–1900. J Imp Commonw Hist 41(1):81–97

Tennent KD, Gillett AG (2016) Foundations of managing sporting events. Routledge, New York

The Economist (2009) Guru: Alfred Chandler. https://www.economist.com/news/2009/04/09/alfred-chandler. Accessed 21 Dec 2018

Thornton PH, Ocasio W (2008) Institutional Logics. In: Green R et al (eds) The sage handbook of organizational institutionalism. Sage Publications, London, pp 99–128

von Ranke L (1973) In: Iggers GG, von Moltke K (eds) The theory and practice of history 1973 repri. The Bobs-Merrill Company, Indianapolis

Wernerfelt B (1984) A resource-based view of the firm. Strateg Manag J 5(2):171–180

Wilkins M (1970) The emergence of multinational enterprise: American business abroad from the colonial era to 1914. Harvard University Press, Cambridge, MA

Wilkins M (1986) Defining a firm: history and theory. In: Hertner P, Jones G (eds) Multinationals: theory and history. Ashgate, Aldershot

Wilkins M (1988) The free-standing company, 1870–1914: an important type of British foreign direct investment. Econ Hist Rev 41(2):259–282

Wilkins M (1989) The history of foreign investment in the United States to 1914. Harvard University Press, Cambridge, MA

Wilkins M (1998) The free-standing company revisited. In: Wilkins M, Schröter H (eds) The free-standing company in the World economy, 1830–1996. Oxford University Press, Oxford

Williamson OE (1981) The economics of organization : the transaction cost approach. De Economist 87(3):548–577

Williamson OE (1989) Transaction cost economics. In: Armstrong M, Porter R (eds) Handbook of industrial organization vol 3. Elsevier B.V, Amsterdam, pp 135–182

Williamson OE (1998) Transaction cost economics: how it works; where it is headed. De Economist 146(1):23–58

Wren D (1972) The evolution of management thought. The Ronald Press Company, New York

36. Industrial Relations in the "Golden Age" in the UK and the USA, 1945–1980

Jim Phillips

Contents

Economy	825
Society	829
Workplaces and Authority	833
Conclusion	836
References	837

Abstract

The dominant interpretation of industrial relations in the UK and USA from 1945 to 1980 emphasizes the "power" of trade unions and manual workers, which narrowed the agency of employers and managers. This involves a linear "rise and fall" narrative, where stable economic growth provided trade unions with an advantage which they exploited and then squandered. Such narrative is shown in this chapter to be inaccurate. Many workers encountered substantial reversals in the 1950s and 1960s. The 1970s, by comparison, often characterized as beset by industrial and social chaos, was for many workers a decade of progress. Labor's bargaining power was constrained by deindustrialization from the late 1950s onward. The linear narrative of general improvement is further qualified by the experiences of female and ethnic minority employees, who struggled to secure justice in the workplace. Class also remained a key fault line. Collective bargaining was retarded in most manual and many white-collar settings by employer objections to sharing control over the organization of work. Business power, not union power, was the chief characteristic of industrial relations in both the USA and the UK from 1945 to 1980.

J. Phillips (✉)
Economic and Social History, University of Glasgow, Glasgow, UK
e-mail: James.Phillips@glasgow.ac.uk

Keywords

Industrial relations · Deindustrialization · Trade unions · Business power

"Industrial relations" has a variety of meanings and applications. In this chapter it is used to analyze two sets of relationships: those in the workplace, between employers and workers, and those within the broader realm of collective bargaining, where the wages and conditions of work were negotiated, generally between employers and the union representatives of employees, although state officials and government ministers were often involved too.

The chapter focuses on the UK and USA from 1945 to 1980. In each country industrial relations were dynamic and sometimes conflictual. The chapter takes issue with the dominant interpretation of industrial relations in this period in both historical literature and popular or politicized memory. This interpretation emphasizes the "power" of trade unions and manual workers, which supposedly narrowed the agency of employers and managers. It relies on a linear "rise and fall" narrative, where the unusual contingencies of the "golden age" of stable economic growth provided trade unions with an advantage which they exploited and then squandered. The "rise" from the 1940s to the 1970s of entrenched collective bargaining, stable employment, economic security, and growing real wages was followed in the 1980s and 1990s by the "fall" of declining union influence, lost industrial jobs, and employment precariousness (Phelps Brown 1986, pp. 1–23, 151–97). Such narrative is shown in this chapter to be inaccurate. Within a general pattern of economic improvement, many workers encountered substantial reversals in the 1950s and 1960s. The 1970s, by comparison, often characterized by "establishment" journalists and anti-trade union politicians as beset by industrial and social chaos (Marr 2008, pp. 337–40, 373–7; Thatcher 1995, pp. 397–403, 419–30), was for many workers a decade of welcome progress. The experiences of coal miners in the UK illustrate this alternative interpretation. They lost ground with their industry's contraction in the 1950s and 1960s but regained it in the 1970s through concerted activism and coal's improving competitive position in energy markets. In the 1980s miners then encountered a second and more profound reverse, targeted by a hostile UK government for political and industrial obliteration in the 1980s (Arnold 2016).

The chapter sets out the analysis of industrial relations in three parts. First, there is an examination of developments in the economy, where labor's bargaining power was ostensibly strengthened by high levels of employment. In both the UK and the USA, there was substantial growth of real wages in the 1950s and 1960s. This was attained through union-negotiated improvements in pay, but progress was punctured by the periodically fractious nature of industrial relations. Strikes and other forms of industrial protest drew much political attention. Narratives of industrial decline developed in the UK, linking the falling share of global manufacturing and comparatively slow growth in international terms in the UK and USA with allegedly high levels of industrial unrest (Joseph 1975). There were similar critiques in the USA, accompanied by hostile Cold War claims that trade unions were unpatriotic and even traitorous (Faue 2018, pp. 123–29). The emphasis on decline was, however, highly problematic and in more recent literature has been challenged by accounts that emphasize an alternative meta-narrative of deindustrialization. This was a major destabilizing factor in industrial relations in both countries from the 1950s onward, as the case of the UK miners indicates, belying the linear narrative of progress for all.

In the second part of the chapter, the impact on industrial relations of social change is examined, focusing on gender and race. Developments in these areas further qualify the linear progress narrative. One criticism of collective bargaining is that unions privileged their disproportionately white and male members in manual sectors. It would be unfair, however, and probably wrong, to portray unions in either the USA or the UK as institutionally racist and sexist. Women and minority workers were often highly critical of their unions, but positive improvements were secured through many collective actions that were designed to equip female and ethnic minority employees with greater justice in the workplace.

Class remained a key fault line, as the third and final section of the chapter demonstrates, exploring power and authority in workplaces. In the UK members of the Amalgamated Engineering Union wore badges – "buttons" in US vocabulary – bearing the three words "EDUCATE, ORGANISE, CONTROL." The latter, arguably, was the keynote in many workplaces. Collective bargaining was retarded in most manual and many white-collar settings by employer objections to sharing control over the organization of work. In the USA employers seeking to strengthen such control lobbied for an increase in the "right to work," a euphemism for the enforcement of non-union contracts with their employees. In the UK, in similar vein, employers resisted the introduction of union-channel worker directors in large manufacturing companies. In each country employers worked hard to prevent a broadening of the collective bargaining agenda, compelling unions to focus their bargaining effort on wages and other contractual issues.

Economy

In the golden age that followed the Second World War, there was stable economic growth in most advanced industrial countries, the UK and USA included. In the UK real wages grew at an annual average rate of 2.7 per cent from 1951 to 1973, meaning that living standards grew by almost 50 per cent in these 22 years (Gazely 2014, p. 153). In the USA real wages increased even faster, by 70 per cent from 1950 to 1970 (Zieger 1994, p. 138). Unemployment was measured in different ways in the USA and the UK, and precision in its measurement is difficult to establish. But by any measure it was historically low in each economy, although slowly growing before a marked acceleration from around 1980. In the UK out-of-work benefit-claimants represented less than 3 per cent of the economically active throughout the 1950s and 1960s, rising to between 4 and 6 per cent in the 1970s. In the new economic environment of the 1980s, this measure of unemployment jumped and was rarely below ten per cent per annum (Tomlinson 2017, p. 146). The same pattern was observable in the USA, where unemployment from 1950 to 1969 averaged 4.8 per cent per annum but 6.7 per cent per annum from 1970 to 1993 (French 1997, p. 83).

Real wage improvements in the 1950s and 1960s resulted from trade union activism. In the USA "workplace contractualism" was embedded in many industrial sectors. Industrial relations were rules-based and predictable. Jobs were defined in writing, with corresponding wage rates negotiated and agreed. There were grievance procedures for either party to follow where disagreements arose. This stability suited employers and managers, as did the related spread of so-called pattern bargaining in automobile manufacturing, steel, coal mining, meat processing, rubber, electrical products, oil, and trucking. Pattern bargaining within a sector involved small- and medium-sized enterprises adopting the wages and conditions agreed by managers and union negotiators in leading firms. The economies of scale and reduced opportunity costs associated with this patterning suited labor representatives as well as employers (French 1997, pp. 98–99). Agreements in various industries followed the precedent established in automobile manufacturing, with cost of living agreements and annual improvement factors (Zieger 1994, pp. 147–48).

In the UK industrial relations were less predictable in the 1950s and 1960s. Harold Wilson's Labour government elected in 1964 was concerned that instability in this area was damaging economic performance more broadly and established the Royal Commission on Trade Unions and Employers' Associations, chaired by Lord Donovan, an English high court judge. This concluded in 1968 that prolonged low unemployment had moved pay bargaining from industry level to workplace level. Inflationary pressures had developed because local deals often supplemented national agreements and were sometimes established only after unofficial strikes. Stronger workplace union organization was needed along with greater education to help employees understand the harmful aggregate effects of frequent stoppages (Ackers 2014). Business organizations and the Conservative opposition disagreed with Donovan's emphasis on voluntary reforms, favoring statutory enforcement of agreements between employers and unions and making unofficial strikes illegal. The Labour government was pushed into proposing fines for unofficial strikers, membership ballots before official strikes, and government-imposed solutions to interunion disputes that intermittently disrupted production, particularly in motor manufacturing. The relationship between the Labour Party and the trade unions in the UK was close. Unions helped to fund the party. This invited accusations that Labour was "controlled" by the unions. In fact the relationship between party and unions was more subtle than its critics admitted. A set of informal "rules" applied, meaning that unions rarely intervened in questions of Labour government policy where this did not directly bear on matters of employment. The draft reform of industrial relations breached these rules, however, encroaching on what unions considered to be their domain (Minkin 1992, pp. 114–16). Unions duly mobilized against the proposals, which were dropped. The issue of industrial relations had nevertheless become highly politicized (Smith 2011).

This politicization reflected a significant turn in debates about economic life in the 1950s and the 1960s. Despite rising living standards, the dominant tone emphasized regression. Growth was faster in other advanced economies, notably the Federal

Republic of Germany (FRG) and Italy. A political preoccupation with decline emerged in the UK, permeating and even dominating historical literature on economic life from the 1960s until well into the twenty-first century. The decline narrative was central to the election and governance of Margaret Thatcher, who became Prime Minister of the UK in 1979. A parallel discourse developed in the USA, with faithful adherents among followers of Ronald Reagan, elected in 1980 as President. "Declinism" encompassed significant blame apportionment. Social democratic policy-makers and consensus-seeking managers and business leaders attracted much criticism, but those deemed especially culpable were trade unionists and manual workers, who allegedly exploited unusually favorable labor market conditions to obtain wage increases that were not accompanied by commensurate productivity increases. This was a core tenet of the linear industrial relations narrative, shaping changes in the law instituted in the USA and UK in the 1980s to limit union freedoms, but it was based on an exaggerated reading of worker behavior, including the scale and impact of strikes. Annual average working days lost to strikes per thousand employees in the USA and the UK are midrange in the table of mature economies from the 1950s to the 1980s, higher than in the FRG but significantly lower than in Italy (van der Velden 2016), where economic growth and industrial production were expanding rapidly (Pizzolato 2013a, pp. 47–58).

These broader comparisons underline the growing impression that the emphasis on decline was and is misdirection. A more meaningful framework for understanding economic developments in both the UK and the USA is deindustrialization (Tomlinson 2016). In each of these national economies, there was a gradual move away from "traditional" industries – coal, metals, shipbuilding, and textiles – from the late 1950s onward, and into lighter manufacturing, with an emphasis on higher value-added consumer goods along with services which were seen as promoting faster growth. Coal miners in Kentucky migrated north in the 1950s to work in the consumer goods factories of Chicago, Cleveland, Columbus, and Detroit (Portelli 2011, pp. 255–59). In the UK economic restructuring was managed at central government level. In Scotland employment in coal mining was reduced from a post-1945 peak of 86,000 in 1957 to 36,000 in 1967, at least in part to release workers for deployment in other sectors (Phillips 2013).

This shift in the distribution of employment greatly qualifies the linear narrative. The economic leverage of coal miners in the UK was diminished and only retrieved from the late 1960s. Various factors were involved in the miners' fightback, but the emergence of a new generation of union leaders was important. Determined action in pursuit of wages included large-scale unofficial strikes in 1969 and 1970 in Scotland, Yorkshire, and South Wales. This activism then produced national strikes across the UK coalfields in 1972 and 1974 that went some way to restoring the relative position of miners' wages in the "league table" of manual workers, which had fallen significantly as a result of deindustrialization. By the late 1960s, miners on average were earning 50 per cent less than workers employed in car assembly. It was this broader question, the fall in coal industry employment, which underpinned the miners' mobilization. In Scotland the miners also secured a marked stabilization of employment from the late 1960s until the late 1970s, helped by the sudden escalation in the price of oil, coal's main competitor (Phillips 2017). After cruel fortunes in the "high" golden age decades of the 1950s and the 1960s, coal miners in the UK duly experienced the 1970s as a period of optimism. Strong hopes for a better future were then confounded by large-scale pit closures and mass redundancies following defeat in the great but doomed strike for jobs in 1984–1985 (Arnold 2016).

Industrial change contributed to similar fluctuations in the USA. An instructive case is the Radio Corporation of America (RCA), which incrementally shifted manufacture of radio transmitters and receivers from Camden, New Jersey, in search of cheaper labor. In 1940 production of receiving equipment was transferred west, to a giant facility at Bloomington, Indiana, where in the early 1960s wage rates in electrical work were still 13 per cent below the US average. RCA was among hundreds of manufacturing firms that relocated across state and then international frontiers during the golden age. In RCA "green" workers in newly industrialized territories gradually acquired class consciousness from their engagement in assembly line manufacturing. Labor conditions were duly bargained upward over time, sometimes after recurrent strike action. But the linear narrative of progress is again qualified. Where workers gained enough organizational capacity to win a greater share of the value created by their labor, a further movement of capital often ensued. RCA retained a presence in Indiana but shifted a growing share of production to Memphis, Tennessee, in 1957 and then, from 1964, to Ciudad Juárez, just south of the international frontier in Mexico (Cowie 1999).

These developments were part of a broader trend, encouraged by "boosterism" in US southern and western "sunrise" states, where policy-makers sought economic diversification. Inward investment by industrial employers was stimulated by "business-friendly" measures such as low-tax incentives plus "right-to-work" laws. These made provision for the employment of non-union members, even in unionized workplaces. This accelerated deindustrialization in northern and eastern states and consolidated the southward and westward regional redistribution of industry. The process has been characterized as the "Dixification of America," with workers in the north and east obliged to temper their wage demands for fear of losing employment to start-up businesses in the south (Cummings 1998). Meat-packing in Chicago exemplified these trends, with job insecurity and falling real wages becoming the new labor "normal" for workers in Packingtown from the late 1950s onward as leading firms in the sector moved operations west and south (Halpern 1997). Dixification contributed to the loss of union membership across the USA. Among the nonfarm workforce, trade union density – union members as a portion of all employees – decreased after the Second World War from a 1945 peak of 35.5 per cent to 31.4 per cent in 1960. Union density then dropped to 27.4 per cent in 1970 and 24.7 per cent in 1980 (French 1997, pp. 94–5).

In the UK union density was jeopardized by deindustrialization. Employment in manufacturing peaked in the late 1960s, although in foreign-owned factories in Scotland not until 1975 (Hood and Young 1982, pp. 5–6, 30–7). At Timex in Dundee, the US-owned producer of watches and then sub-assembly electronics, average employment fell from over 6000 in 1975 to 4000 in 1982 before falling away to 2000 in 1983, 1000 in 1985, and 500 in 1991 before eventual closure in

1993 (Knox and McKinlay 2011). Union density across the UK nevertheless stabilized and then actually increased, exceeding 50 per cent only after the peak of industrial employment, around 1970, and rising to 54.5 per cent by 1980. Growth reflected a recruitment effort undertaken among tertiary sector workers, especially those in public services, meaning that union membership was growing faster among female than male employees. Union density among women workers rose from 31.2 per cent in 1970 to 39.9 per cent in 1980 (Wrigley 2002, pp. 18–19). This effort had lasting effects. In 2018 in the UK, union density overall was only around 23 per cent, but among public sector workers, it was just over 51 per cent (Roper 2018). Women and public sector workers in the 1970s were seeking union protection against government counter-inflationary pay controls which they considered unjust, especially when set against less restrictive measures on dividends and profits (Tomlinson 2017, pp. 189–90). The public sector was also the fastest area of union growth in the USA in the 1960s and 1970s. Female and ethnic minority employees likewise attained a greater share of overall membership. There was continued expansion of female union membership in private sector manufacturing too. Forty per cent of employees in the US automobile industry were women by the 1970s. Members of the United Automobile Workers (UAW) were central to the establishment of the Coalition of Labor Union Women in 1973, which promoted female voice in the labor movement (Faue 2018, pp. 146–48, 158–60).

Society

The growth of female union membership in the UK signaled the presence in industrial relations of broader social movements, where identities of race and gender intersected with class. Trade unions in both the USA and the UK are sometimes understood as being indifferent or even hostile to the interests of female and black workers. But unions were dynamic, slowly accommodating the interests of African Americans in the USA and African Caribbean, African, and Asian immigrants in the UK (Lunn 1999). Industrial bargaining was an important element in reducing inequalities of gender as well as race, perhaps having a greater impact even than the policy-based civil rights agenda which developed impetus in the 1960s. This tended to privilege individual rights, and the "equal pay for equal work" model, ignoring the structural barriers confronting women and minority workers collectively (Cowie 2010, pp. 68–72).

Racism was a major problem in the UK from the 1950s to the 1970s. Authoritative studies in the late 1960s illuminated the discrimination encountered by workers from African Caribbean, African, and South Asian immigrant traditions. African Caribbean workers often found themselves in employment of lower status than their pre-migration education and experience warranted (Daniel 1968). South Asian workers also faced entrenched difficulties. An illuminating case is that of Sikh bus drivers in the English Midlands city of Wolverhampton. One of these workers in 1967 was sent home for wearing a turban, contravening a dress code agreed by the employer and the local trade union. The driver was supported by other Sikhs. Local

Transport and General Workers' Union (TGWU) officials and non-Sikh colleagues were initially unsympathetic. Sikh community leaders and Labour Party members pushed the TGWU to support a lengthy community-based campaign that eventually produced a change of policy in 1969, allowing bus company employees to wear turbans while on duty. The victimized bus driver had relatives who worked at the large Goodyear tyre factory in Wolverhampton. Their mobilization of factory workmates intensified the campaign (Seifert and Hambler 2016).

The confluence of class and community in labor struggles was frequently evident also in the USA. The broader dynamics of social change and the emergent civil rights agenda were prominent too. African Americans were plainly discriminated against in the labor market. Unemployment among black men averaged 8.5 per cent per annum and among black women averaged 8.8 per cent between 1950 and 1969, almost twice the whole economy average (French 1997, p. 83). African Americans in employment also tended to occupy lower-status positions. Labor organization coalesced with civil rights activism to fight against this injustice. A key episode was the 1968 action by sanitation workers in Memphis. Garbage in the city was collected more or less entirely by African American male workers, who sought alleviation of dangerous and dehumanizing conditions through Local 133 of the American Federation of State, County and Municipal Employees (AFSCME). The authorities, marshaled by the mayor of Memphis, Henry Loeb, refused to recognize the union. Two workers were killed in February 1968, crushed when sheltering inside a garbage truck during torrential rain. About 1300 sanitation workers responded by pushing the AFSCME into citywide strike action. Pickets demonstrated with placards stating "I AM A MAN," these words freighted with enormous meaning in southern US society emerging fitfully and violently from racial segregation. The strikers were supported by the National Association for the Advancement of Coloured People and the Southern Christian Leadership Conference, including its president, Dr. Martin Luther King Jr., who addressed three separate strike rallies. On 3 April Dr. King delivered one of his best-known speeches, "I have been to the Mountaintop," at one of these rallies, to a big crowd of strikers, trade unionists, and civil rights activists. He was assassinated in Memphis by a white supremacist sniper the following evening. Mayor Loeb had declared the strike illegal, but the city's position shifted because of the furious uprising of African American youth that followed Dr. King's murder. Union recognition was conceded, and further struggles by the garbage collectors produced significant improvements in wages and working conditions (Cosgrove 2017, pp. 39–47, 98–100, 161).

The flavor of social justice combined with the politics of class and race was also evident in the waterfront activism of dock workers in San Francisco from the 1950s to the 1970s. Local 10 of the International Longshore and Warehouse Union (ILWU) showcased the determination of African American workers to improve their position through collective action and defend the rights of other exploited black workers. Paul Robeson, the African American singer, union campaigner, and civil rights activist, was an honorary member of Local 10, and so was Dr. King. Action included expressions of international solidarity. The Local organized recurrent boycotts of ships carrying goods from and to South Africa. These raised awareness about the racist nature of the Apartheid regime. Black trade unionists in South Africa drew moral strength from these boycotts and communicated their thanks to the San Francisco longshoremen. This transmission of international solidarity was two-way, with the San Francisco workers further emboldened to act in defense of themselves and others by contacts with their union brothers in South Africa. Local 10 maintained boycotts of South African ships in the 1980s. In 1978 it also refused to load military equipment onto a vessel bound for Chile, where the military dictator Augusto Pinochet had killed thousands of trade unionists along with communists, socialists, liberals, and other opponents since seizing power in 1973 (Cole 2013).

Movements involving the intersection of class with gender were likewise increasingly observable from the 1960s. A notable point of departure in the UK was the 3-week strike at the Ford car plant in Dagenham, Essex, by 187 female sewing machinists in the summer of 1968. Their action was joined by 195 female sewing machinists at Ford's other major works in England, Halewood, Merseyside, and led to the temporary laying-off of 9000 or so other workers across the company (Torode 1968). Union representatives constructed the sewing machinists' grievances in gender and equal pay terms, in negotiations with Ford and then, as the action gradually shut down the entire plant, with Barbara Castle, the Labour government's secretary of state for employment. But for the machinists, gender pay inequality was not the real issue. They were disputing their pay-grading in class terms by calling for a recalibration exercise, seeking acknowledgment of the skill and value embedded in their work. The interpretation of their demands in the language of equal pay obscured the class connotations of the dispute, as the women challenged the authority of their multinational employer by calling its occupational grading scheme into question (Cohen 2012).

The legal environment changed after the Ford strike in the UK. Castle introduced the 1970 Equal Pay Act, and this was followed in 1975 by the Sex Discrimination Act. The shifting legal terrain was illustrated by a further important dispute involving female employees in car manufacturing. Trico Folberth was a US multinational, producing windscreen wipers and other accessories in Brentford, West London. Castle's legislative pursuit of equal pay for equal work was complicated by practices in most workplaces that made it difficult to compare the value of different tasks undertaken by female and male employees. At Trico men generally worked on nightshifts and women on day shifts. But after short notice cancellation of a night shift in the spring of 1976, a small number of men were redeployed on day shift. This exposed the injustice of the firm's rewards system to the 400 women who worked in the factory. After a strike lasting 21 weeks, they won equal pay on the basis of the illegitimacy and possible illegality of their employer's practices under the Equal Pay and Sex Discrimination Acts (Groves and Merritt 2018). Wider economic and social factors influenced this positive outcome. As with the sewing machinists' action at Ford in 1968, the strike of the Trico women interrupted a complex supply chain, triggering a wider cessation of production which placed their employer in a difficult position. And as with Ford, the Trico strike was founded on a strong sense of working class consciousness: the women were demanding equality of treatment as workers (Stevenson 2016).

The Trico strike overlapped with a longer dispute at the Grunwick photo-processing plant just several miles to the north in London's outer urban-industrial belt. A large majority of Grunwick's 450 workers were women of South Asian origin. Earnings across the Grunwick workforce were well below the London average rates for manual employment. The action started as a protest in the hot summer of 1976 against compulsory overtime and morphed into a 2-year campaign for union recognition. The strikers did not win their case, and most were sacked. The strike was important nevertheless in signaling the greater confluence in industrial relations of race, gender, and class. Like the Sikh bus drivers' action in Wolverhampton, the Grunwick strikers challenged the union movement to pursue workplace justice for all workers, irrespective of ethnic and racial origin (McDowell et al. 2014). They also challenged the gender and class authority of their male employer, demanding greater voice in the workplace. There were also periodic picket-line confrontations as a replacement workforce was bussed through a blockade mounted by the sacked Grunwick employees and their trade unionist supporters from many other workplaces, including coal miners from Scotland and South Wales as well as Yorkshire (McGowan 2008).

The Grunwick strike, incubating tensions of class and social authority, duly contributed to the further politicization of industrial relations in the UK, strengthening the emergent Thatcherite anti-union narrative. Legal and policy changes followed in the 1980s, designed to curtail union privileges and restore the "right of management to manage" (Dorey 2014). The anti-union narrative developed traction during the 1978–1979 "Winter of Discontent," when the Labour government's anti-inflationary strategy of wage controls was challenged by strikes involving manual workers in public services and private sector manufacturing. Hostile critiques of workers and unions developed "in real time" and were central to the election of Thatcher's Conservative government in May 1979. Forgotten in this dominant anti-union narrative is the extreme low pay which public sector employees, many of them women, were seeking to improve (Martin 2009). Thatcherites unjustly "othered" the low paid as a subversive and illegitimate menace to society and wilfully exaggerated the impact of their strikes (Hay 2015).

There was a parallel rise of anti-union politics in the USA in the 1970s. This involved lobbying organizations like Business Roundtable, founded in 1972, claiming that workers' pay demands were the main source of inflation and economic slowdown. Democrats in the House of Representatives and Senate attempted to introduce a Full Employment Bill in the mid-1970s. One of its advocates, Representative Augustus Hawkins of California, an African American, argued that civil rights were meaningless unless accompanied by the right to work. It was the duty of the Federal government to provide citizens with employment where the market failed to do so. The Bill was remorselessly criticized by business campaigners and orthodox financial thinkers, including Alan Greenspan, future head of the US Federal Reserve and then chair of the President's Council of Economic Advisers. Legislation eventually passed in 1978 was an expression of aspiration rather than a concrete economic and social project. Instead, greater labor market discipline was accepted as the central policy goal by both Republicans and Democrats. De-recognition of unions was called for, and the movement of capital to union-free labor markets in southern states was further promoted (Cowie 2010, pp. 224–36, 266–84). The process intensified with the election of Reagan as President in 1980, which was followed by a nationwide strike of 13,000 air traffic controllers in 1981. Their union, the Professional Air Traffic Controllers Organization, was ostracized from the civil aviation industry, and the strikers barred for life from future federal employment (Zieger 1994, pp. 194–98).

Workplaces and Authority

The anti-union activism of Business Roundtable in the USA qualified the linear progress narrative. It was also a reminder of the structural influence of class conflict on industrial relations. The English sociologist Alan Fox examined this question in a research paper for the Donovan Royal Commission in 1966. Fox argued that perceptions of industrial relations were shaped by the frame of reference adopted. Most employers and mangers rejected a pluralist conceptualization of their firms as coalitions of competing interests. They saw businesses instead in unitary terms, with members bound by shared values and goals. The participation of employers in collective bargaining was compatible with their unitary frame of reference because of a vital distinction between *market relations*, defined by Fox as the "terms and conditions on which labour is hired," and *managerial relations*, "what management seeks to do with its labour having hired it." Employers generally accepted the legitimacy of settling market relations collectively rather than individually but still opposed trade union influence in managerial relations (Fox 1966).

The broad rejection by UK employers of pluralism in workplaces was illustrated by their opposition in the 1970s to union-channel worker directors in manufacturing firms with 2000 or more employees. This innovation was recommended in 1977 by a commission of inquiry established by the Labour government in 1975, chaired by Alan Bullock of the University of Oxford, and was already an embedded feature of corporate governance in the Federal Republic of Germany. Many unions favored worker directors as a means of arresting disinvestment and deindustrialization. The Confederation of British Industry (CBI), representing small- and medium-sized businesses, and the major multinationals of Courtaulds, ICI, Shell UK, Unilever, and United Biscuits united with Conservative politicians to resist the initiative, even threatening an investment "strike" that would greatly have destabilized economic life in the UK. The episode indicated that real power in industrial relations during the golden age resided with employers and their organizations rather than with workers and trade unions. Their victory consolidated managerial sovereignty over workplaces and also incentivized pay conflict in the years that followed, including that of the 1978–1979 Winter of Discontent. Unions were compelled to defend their members on the terrain of cash outcomes rather than the design of production (Phillips 2011).

A narrow focus in on market relations also contributed to unstable collective bargaining in US car manufacturing. The UAW tried unsuccessfully to widen the scope of dialogue with employers to encompass "entry into the realm of managerial prerogative relating to planning of production" (Zieger 1994, p. 148). Rebuffed, the union concentrated instead on maximizing monetary returns, including wages, benefits, pensions, and holiday entitlements. In exchange management insisted on the ever-tighter maintenance of an unappetizing labor regime which required endless routine and repetition. This was classic Fordism, but entering its "twilight" by the late 1960s (Pizzolato 2013b), its legitimacy weakened in part by generational change. Younger workers had increased expectations arising from improved living standards and the extension of education which clashed with the physical and mental tortures of the assembly line (Cowie 2010, pp. 44–49). The evolving civil rights struggle also held weight. Younger working class African Americans had a distinct critique of the alienating labor regime as they experienced it. They resented the limited opportunities for promotion and their supervision by older white employees. They likened auto-assembly factories to the slavery-era cotton plantations. In 1968, a year of global revolutions of class, race, gender, and youth, African American workers formed the Dodge Revolutionary Union Movement (DRUM) in Chrysler's largest factory in Detroit. DRUM members established contacts with protagonists in other car factories, in the steel industry, and in the postal service. A pan-industry alliance, the League of Revolutionary Black Workers, had a short but eventful existence with an influential legacy in the subsequent development of African American activism (Pizzolato 2013a, pp. 144–60).

Social authority was also contested in UK workplaces. A key structural element was the shift in the distribution of industrial employment noted in the first part of this chapter. The value of government regional aid was substantially increased from the late 1950s, with more grants and loans persuading private firms to locate their businesses in areas of shrinking "traditional" industry where there was surplus labor. Many inward investors, including US firms across engineering and other manufacturing sectors, seized these opportunities (Gibbs and Tomlinson 2016). The UK location provided access to markets in the European Free Trade Area and then in the European Economic Community, which the UK joined in 1973. Workplace industrial relations in the regional aid districts were often tense. The existence of a "culture clash" was identified by employers and employees alike, and resentments were multilayered. Employers expected disciplined workers, willing to accept wages above local market rates but below national industry averages. US firms in particular wanted to capitalize on the cost advantage of moving production from their higher-wage home environment by minimizing union influence in their new factories. Employees accepted their transfer from established local industry – coal, metals, and ships – but in Scotland at least only on the promise of greater economic security and employment stability. Disputes were triggered where union and skilled traditions were offended by the US production regime (Knox and McKinlay 1999).

A typical Scottish case was the earthmoving equipment factory owned and operated by the US multinational Caterpillar, at Uddingston in Lanarkshire. This opened in 1956 on the cleared site of a mining village, Tannochside, and was Scotland's largest single factory in the 1960s and 1970s. The premises covered 65 acres, with employment peaking at around 2500 in 1968. Caterpillar initially resisted union recognition, which the workers won after a 9-week strike in the winter of 1960–1961. Caterpillar fought a rearguard action, accepting the presence of full-time union officers but not workplace stewards. This was unsuccessful. Emboldened, the stewards incrementally exerted a foothold in the factory, securing bargaining rights on a variety of organizational questions (Knox and McKinlay 2003). The victorious recognition strike was long remembered by workers as an indicator of the employer's hostility to collective bargaining and the fundamental importance of activism in pursuit of trade union voice and improved working conditions (Gibbs and Phillips 2018).

A second instructive Scottish case is the car plant at Linwood in Renfrewshire, 10 miles west of Glasgow. This was one of several motor industry initiatives funded by the UK government as a means of diversifying regional economies in South Wales, Merseyside, and Central Scotland. Linwood opened in 1963, initially owned and operated by Rootes and then from 1967 by Chrysler. The labor regime ran counter to the experiences of workers drawn to Linwood from marine engineering, shipbuilding, and coal mining backgrounds. There were frequent short stoppages in the 1960s, followed in the 1970s by major confrontations where control of production was a larger issue than wages. Managers were under mounting pressure to exert control of costs in an increasingly competitive global market. In trying to assert authority, they merely alienated many employees. In 1975 Chrysler obtained fresh investment from the Labour government in return for establishing a form of industrial partnership across its English and Scottish holdings. But the firm's commitment to employee involvement was superficial. The promised introduction in 1976 of new models at Linwood was abandoned, and Chrysler sold its UK operations altogether in 1978 to Peugeot-Citroen, without consulting the workforce. Popular understanding of these various issues at Linwood – including lost local influence over economic and industrial assets – contributed to the longer-term growth of support in Scotland for political-constitutional changes, including "Home Rule" within the UK and then independence (Phillips et al. 2019).

These details of conflict and insecurity are important. Car manufacturing is associated with the "affluent worker," a significant theme in debates about golden age economic improvement in the UK, identified and developed in a sequence of sociological studies in the 1960s (Goldthorpe et al. 1969). Recent re-evaluation has emphasized the extent to which working class affluence was highly conditional, qualified for some by long and arduous hours, and for others by the opposite difficulty of intermittent redundancy and unemployment. Material gains in many sectors had to be squeezed from the hands of grudging employers (Savage 2005; Todd 2008). A pioneering study of car assembly workers at Ford's Halewood factory included two important findings that are relevant here. First, large corporate employers in the industry cultivated competition between their employees at different factories. Internal working class divisions resulted, undermining union efforts to enhance pay and conditions across the industry. Second, the labor process was strenuous and alienating. "Affluent" workers did not easily come by their earnings (Beynon 1973). At Linwood cyclical employment peaks of 9000 were interspersed with heavy redundancies: more than 2000 were "released" in 1975 alone (Phillips et al. 2019). This aggravated industrial relations in a way that strongly qualifies the linear progress narrative. Workers at Linwood and many other industrial sites were protecting their economic security rather than imposing their will illegitimately on society, as political critics of trade unions often claim (Whiting 2008).

Conclusion

Industrial relations in the USA and the UK in the golden age were not characterized by high levels of trade union power. This chapter has shown that there was no linear narrative either in the conduct of collective bargaining. There was a significant growth of real wages in both countries in the 1950s and 1960s arising from two related factors: the relatively low levels, historically, of unemployment, which provided labor with an unusual degree of market advantage, and the ability of trade union negotiators to secure improved terms through bargaining with employers who could afford to meet demands in an era of continuous expansion.

Union power was nevertheless highly circumscribed by structural economic change in both the USA and the UK. From the late 1950s onward, there was a marked shrinkage of industrial sectors where union density had been comparatively high: in coal mining, metals, heavy engineering, and shipbuilding. In the UK this was by government design, with the aim of growing the economy more quickly by shifting capital resources and labor into consumer goods manufacturing. This contributed to improved living standards generally, but union bargaining strength was diminished in the shrinking sectors. The fall in coal industry employment, for example, eroded the relative position of miners' earnings in the manual wages league. Deindustrialization is often assumed to have commenced no earlier than the late 1960s, after the peak of employment in all manufacturing sectors. But in the coalfields and elsewhere, it was a basic fact of economic life from the 1950s onward, conditioning worker dissatisfaction and slowly preparing the ground for the miners' fightback in the 1970s. "Early-onset" deindustrialization indicates that the fruits of economic progress and collective bargaining were not shared equally by all workers.

The partial and nonlinear nature of progress is additionally demonstrated by the contested nature of industrial relations on gender and ethnic lines. In the UK immigrant workers from African Caribbean, African, and South Asian countries experienced discrimination in encounters with employers, unions, and white workmates. The same was true, with even greater force, of African American workers in the USA. In both countries there were serious barriers to the advancement of women. Protests in the sphere of industrial relations by female and ethnic minority workers challenged the authority of employers and sometimes trade union officialdom also. These workers were asserting their right to access greater justice and did so partly in class terms. Unions were slow to recognize the distinct problems of gender and race. But collective action, usually through established labor organizations, helped to narrow inequalities of this type along with changes in the law.

Workers and their unions were ultimately less influential than their employers, even in the unusual circumstances of low unemployment and stable growth. This is clear from the capacity of employers to prevent wider scope collective bargaining after the Second World War in both the USA and the UK. They accepted dialogue on "market relations" issues such as wages, hours, overtime, breaks, and holidays but refused to discuss "managerial relations" questions like investment, product development, and the organization of work. This business opposition to broader scope dialogue was arguably dysfunctional. It incentivized wage conflict because in bargaining terms employees and unions were given no alternative other than to focus on extracting greater financial reward from the employment relationship. The problem was fundamentally ideological: employers were over-committed to protecting their own workplace and organizational sovereignty. The blocking of worker company directors by UK employers in the 1970s demonstrates the power of this ideology, as does the US Business Roundtable's promotion of union-free work environments while vetoing effective full employment legislation. Business power, not union power, was the chief characteristic of industrial relations in both the USA and the UK from 1945 to 1980.

References

Ackers P (2014) Game changer: Hugh Clegg's role in drafting the 1968 Donovan report and redefining the British industrial relations policy-problem. Hist Stud Ind Relat 35:63–88

Arnold J (2016) Vom Verlierer zum Gewinner – und zurück. Der Coal Miners als Schlüsselfigure der Britishen Zeitgeschichte. *Geschichte und Gesellschaft* 42:266–297

Beynon H (1973) Working for Ford: men, masculinity, mass production and militancy. Allen Lane, London

Cohen S (2012) Equal pay – or what? Economics, politics and the 1968 Ford sewing machinists' strike. Lab Hist 53(1):51–68

Cole P (2013) No justice, no ships get loaded: political boycotts on the San Francisco and Durban waterfronts. Int Rev Soc Hist 58:185–217

Cosgrove S (2017) Memphis 68: the tragedy of Southern Soul. Polygon, Edinburgh

Cowie J (1999) Capital moves: RCA's seventy-year quest for cheap labor. Cornell University Press, Ithaca

Cowie J (2010) Stayin' alive: the 1970s and the last days of the working class. The New Press, New York/London

Cummings SD (1998) The dixification of America: The American Odyssey into the conservative economic trap. Praeger, Westport

Daniel WW (1968) Racial discrimination in England: based on the PEP report. Penguin, Harmondsworth

Dorey P (2014) The stepping stones programme: the conservative party's struggle to develop a trade union policy, 1975–79. Hist Stud Ind Relat 35:89–116

Faue E (2018) Rethinking the American labor movement. Routledge, New York/London

Fox A (1966) Industrial sociology and industrial relations. Royal Commission on Trade Unions and Employers' Associations, Research Paper 3. HMSO, London

French MJ (1997) US economic history since 1945. Manchester University Press, Manchester

Gazely I (2014) Income and living standards, 1870–2010. In: Floud R, Humphries J, Johnson P (eds) The Cambridge economic history of modern Britain, Vol. II, 1870 to the present. Cambridge University Press, Cambridge, pp 151–180

Gibbs E, Phillips J (2018) Who owns a factory?: Caterpillar Tractors in Uddingston, 1956–1987. Hist Stud Ind Relat 39:111–138

Gibbs E, Tomlinson J (2016) Planning the new industrial nation: Scotland, 1931–1979. Contemp Br Hist 30(4):585–606

Goldthorpe J, Lockwood D, Bechhofer F, Platt J (1969) The affluent worker: industrial attitudes and behaviour. Cambridge University Press, Cambridge

Groves S, Merritt V (2018) Trico: the longest equal pay strike. Lawrence & Wishart, London

Halpern R (1997) Down on the killing floor. Black and white workers in Chicago's packinghouses, 1904–54. University of Illinois Press, Urbana/Chicago

Hay C (2015) The trade unions and the "winter of discontent": a case of myth-taken identity. Hist Stud Ind Relat 36:181–203

Hood N, Young S (1982) Multinationals in retreat: the Scottish experience. Edinburgh University Press, Edinburgh

Joseph K (1975) Reversing the trend. Barry Rose Law Publishers, London

Knox WW, McKinlay A (1999) Working For the Yankee Dollar: American inward investment and Scottish labour, 1945–1970. Hist Stud Ind Relat 7:1–26

Knox WW, McKinlay A (2003) "Organizing the unorganized": union recruitment strategies in American transnationals, c. 1945–1977. In: Gall G (ed) Union organizing: campaigning for trade union recognition. Routledge, London, pp 19–38

Knox WW, McKinlay A (2011) The union makes us strong? Work and trade unionism in Timex, 1946–83. In: Tomlinson J, Whatley CA (eds) Jute no more: transforming Dundee. University of Dundee Press, Dundee, pp 266–290

Lunn K (1999) Complex encounters: trade unions, immigration and racism. In: Campbell A, Fishman N, McIlroy J (eds) British trade unions and industrial politics, Vol. Two: the high tide of trade unionism, 1964–79. Ashgate, Aldershot, pp 70–90

Marr A (2008) A history of modern Britain. Pan, London

Martin T (2009) The beginning of labour's end? Britain's "winter of discontent" and working-class women's activism. Int Lab Work Class Hist 75(1):49–67

McDowell L, Sundari A, Pearson R (2014) Striking narratives: class, gender and ethnicity in the "Great Grunwick Strike", London, UK, 1976–1978. Women's Hist Rev 23(4):595–619

McGowan J (2008) "Dispute", "Battle", "Siege", "Farce"? – Grunwick 30 years on. Contemp Br Hist 22:383–406

Minkin L (1992) The contentious alliance. Trade unions and the labour party. Edinburgh University Press, Edinburgh

Phelps Brown H (1986) The origins of trade union power. Oxford University Press, Oxford

Phillips J (2011) UK business power and opposition to the bullock committee's 1977 proposals for worker directors. Hist Stud Ind Relat 31(32):1–30

Phillips J (2013) The moral economy and deindustrialization in the Scottish coalfields, 1947–1991. Int Lab Work Class Hist 84:99–115

Phillips J (2017) Economic direction and generational change in twentieth century Britain: the case of the Scottish coalfields. Engl Hist Rev 132:885–911

Phillips J, Wright V, Tomlinson J (2019) Industrial restructuring, the Linwood car plant and Scotland's political divergence from England in the 1960s and 1970s. Twentieth Century British History, forthcoming

Pizzolato N (2013a) Challenging global capitalism: labor migration, radical struggle, and urban change in Detroit and Turin. Palgrave Macmillan, London

Pizzolato N (2013b) The American worker and the Forze Nuove: Detroit and Turin at the twilight of fordism, *Viewpoint Magazine*, 25 Sept 2013

Portelli A (2011) They say in Harlan county. Oxford University Press, Oxford

Roper, C. (2018) 'Trade union membership is growing, but there's still work to do.', Trades Union Congress Blog, https://www.tuc.org.uk/blogs/trade-union-membership-growing-there's-still-work-do; Accessed 4 Jan 2019

Savage M (2005) Working class identities in the 1960s: revisiting the affluent worker studies. Sociology 34:929–96

Seifert R, Hambler A (2016) 'Wearing the Turban: the 1967–1969 Sikh bus drivers' dispute in Wolverhampton. Hist Stud Ind Relat 37:83–111

Smith P (2011) Order in British industrial relations: from Donovan to neoliberalism. Hist Stud Ind Relat 31–32:115–154

Stevenson G (2016) The forgotten strike: equality, gender, and class in the trico equal pay strike. Lab Hist Rev 81(2):141–168

Thatcher M (1995) The path to power. Harper Collins, London

Todd S (2008) Affluence, class and crown street: reinvestigating the post-war working class. Contemp Br Hist 22:501–518

Tomlinson J (2016) De-industrialization not decline: a new meta-narrative for post-war British history. Twentieth Century Br Hist 27(1):76–99

Tomlinson J (2017) Managing the economy, managing the people. Narratives of economic life in Britain from Beveridge to Brexit. Oxford University Press, Oxford

Torode J (1968) Ford women machinists go back to work on a promise. The Guardian, 1 July 1968, p. 16

van der Velden S (2016) Global conflicts dataverse. International Institute of Social History. https://datasets.socialhistory.org/dataverse/labourconflicts. Accessed 4 Jan 2019

Whiting R (2008) Affluence and industrial relations. Contemp Br Hist 22:519–536

Wrigley C (2002) British trade unions since 1933. Cambridge University Press, Cambridge

Zieger RH (1994) American workers, American Unions, 2nd edn. John Hopkins University Press, Baltimore and London

The Rise of Marketing

Alex G. Gillett and Kevin D. Tennent

Contents

Introduction	842
In the Beginning	843
After the Wars	846
Marketing and Management Education	847
Purpose of Business and Management Education	847
End of the Century: Broadening the Scope of Markets and Marketing	849
Summary	854
Cross-References	854
References	855

Abstract

Marketing and sales have existed in some form for centuries, but it was in the twentieth century that modern marketing management emerged as a distinct field of study and profession. This chapter narrates that development with reference to marketing practice, academic research, and education, to show how ideas about the scope of marketing broadened, particularly during the decades after World War II. In particular, this chapter examines the ideas from services and relationship marketing that first emerged during and before the 1980s.

Keywords

Marketing · Sales · Education · Textbook theory · Professionalization · Brands · Services · Relationships · Customers

---

A. G. Gillett (✉) · K. D. Tennent
The York Management School, University of York, York, UK
e-mail: Alex.gillett@york.ac.uk; Kevin.tennent@york.ac.uk

© The Author(s), under exclusive licence to Springer Nature Switzerland AG 2020
B. Bowden et al. (eds.), *The Palgrave Handbook of Management History*,
https://doi.org/10.1007/978-3-319-62114-2_92

Introduction

Marketing can be defined in numerous ways – many definitions exist, and the various textbooks and professional bodies each have their own explanation. To understand what marketing means for managers, this chapter shall use one of the most up-to-date (at the time of writing) definitions by a professional body:

> Marketing is the activity, set of institutions, and processes for creating, communicating, delivering, and exchanging offerings that have value for customers, clients, partners, and society at large. (American Marketing Organization 2017)

Most academic interpretations make a similar point (understandably as good academic research both reflects and informs marketing management practices, as highlighted later in this chapter). Thus, the modern-day understanding of marketing is of a management process and is about exchanges with customers and other stakeholders (individuals and organizations) internal and external to the organization, including regulators, affiliates and strategic partners, suppliers, competitors, residents, employees and internal departments ("internal marketing"), and others relevant to the context of the organization concerned (Buttle 1996; Godson 2009).

This chapter summarizes the history of marketing, synthesizing some of the key literature. The theory has evolved toward a multi-stakeholder perspective in which service and relationships are given as much significance as product design and advertising. Marketing can be considered as a heterogeneous and nuanced subject and that there is still much to be discovered. As with other areas of management history, temporalities and geographies are very important, as are firms, their customers, and other stakeholders. Unlike some papers on the history of marketing, this chapter does not attempt to box off distinct "eras of the economy." Readers wishing for such a temporal framework should see, for example, the papers by Keith (1960) who identified distinct paradigms firms had gone through up to that point – the production era, the sales era, and the marketing era – or by Bartels (1988) who charts the twentieth century into seven distinct marketing "periods," from "discovery" to "socialization." Gilbert and Bailey (2001) looked back even further to identify four eras: Antecedents (1500–1750), Origins (1750–1850), Institutional Development (1850–1930), and Refinement and Formalization (1930–present). Jones and Shaw (2002) also produced a detailed synthesis of the history of marketing thought which is also useful and based on a much looser framework, but is from the perspective of US economic history, rather than management history more generally. Indeed, Hollander et al. (2005) compare 28 attempts at periodizing marketing history, and although they offer suggestions to how to periodize research in marketing, their paper highlights the limitations and complexities of such an approach. This chapter thus presents a narrative of the marketing history that has clearer links to management history and less emphasis on trying to define distinct eras.

In the Beginning

Selling and buying, markets, and commerce can of course be traced back to ancient history. Archaeologists, anthropologists, historians, and sociologists have all studied these things in different contexts and documented their findings. Trade and war are a fundamental part of the story of human beings from prehistory to the present day. The Vikings traveled by sea to discover new lands, and evidence shows that their settlements contained not only items originating locally and from Scandinavia but also contact with Africa and Asia. Similarly, it is known that the Roman Empire stretched across countries and continents. They built roads to transport their military and had clear lines of supply, such as in England where there were many such roads – in particular along the length of the country stretching from the South Coast up to the Scottish border. Significantly, this linked major cities in a fairly direct line heading north to Hadrian's Wall, where the Army had Forts across the breadth of the country to protect its hostile border with Scotland. As well as allowing efficient mobilization of military resources and travel for those with the means to do so, evidence suggests that supplies may have been transported and some trade would presumably also occur en route. Elsewhere, the Silk Road, stretching from Asia to Europe, was a major network of trade routes that enabled interactions between cultures that would influence cultural, social, and religious life.

Other concepts such as brands and branding can be traced to antecedents "stretching back millennia" (Duguid et al. 2010, p. 9), but "it is only in the nineteenth century that a defensible property right in marks sufficient for the task of modern marketing emerges" (Ibid.). Egan (2011) goes back further to identify eighteenth-century entrepreneurs such as Wedgwood as an example of a brand from the 1700s which to this day enjoys a market-leading reputation among consumers and in its industry (cf. Lane 2019). Other examples could include the hallmarks and emblems of metal smiths. However, Ambler (2006) distinguishes "modern marketing" as an independent discipline and career path for marketing "specialists" which really begins in the twentieth century, particularly in the USA. Tadajewski and Jones (2012), for example, postulate a link between scientific management and marketing ideas in the early twentieth century as being consistent with ideas of customer centricity and social benefit. Their findings challenge some subsequent interpretations of scientific management.

Considering marketing as something which began to professionalize in the twentieth century leads naturally to discuss the formation of its professional and industry bodies. Today, several major sales and marketing bodies exist in the UK, including (but not limited to) *The Chartered Institute of Marketing*, the *Institute of Sales Management, Institute of Direct and Digital Marketing*, and the *Advertising Association*, and in the USA, the *American Marketing Association*. In the UK the story begins before the term "marketing" was in such use as it is today, with the formation of the Sales Managers, Association in 1911, which stated its mission as:

> To promote, encourage and coordinate the study and advancement of sales management in all its branches, both home and overseas. To initiate and maintain investigation and research

into the best methods of sales management, to safeguard the interests of sales managers, to extend, increase and disseminate knowledge, to exchange information and ideas with regard to all matters concerned therewith, and to assist and further, in all practicable ways, the development and improvement of sales management, market research, advertising and the conduct and handling of all sales of commodities, goods and service in the higher interest of the British people. Chartered Institute of Marketing (n.d.)

By the 1920s this organization was evolving fast and over the next few years broadened its network globally when it affiliated with the *American National Association of Sales Managers*, the *Associated Advertising Clubs of the World*, and also the *Advertising Association*. Formative to professionalization, annual examinations were introduced and certifications were awarded for the first time in 1928, and by the middle of the next decade, a 3-year syllabus was introduced, emphasizing the importance weighted on education. However, in 1931 the organization had symbolically changed the name of its magazine to *Marketing* – this is significant because a group of members were apparently disgruntled by what they perceived to be a shift in emphasis away from sales and selling, toward the relatively newer, broader (and arguably less direct but more ambiguous) field of *Marketing* (The Chartered Institute of Marketing n.d.; Institute of Sales Management n.d.).

Meanwhile, in the USA, the National Association of Teachers of Advertising (NATA) had formed in 1915 but, similarly, over the next few years broadened its interests to include economics and accounting and changed its name several times but by 1933 had settled on the *National Association of Marketing Teachers (NAMT)*. In around 1930 the American Marketing Association was founded separately, but the two organizations soon joined forces, publishing the *Journal of Marketing* in 1936 and merging into a single entity in 1937 (Agnew 1941). Today, the journal is still a leading publication of research of marketing over 80 years later.

The first half of the twentieth century was of course defined by two world wars.

This had significant implications for firms involved with industries such as financial services, mining, manufacturing, foodstuffs, and shipping, in participating nations such as Britain, France, Germany, Japan, China, and the USA, as well as in neutral countries. Sudden and dramatic changes in the geopolitical environment affected everyday life, globally (Smith et al. 2016). As priorities changed, so did demands: The need for munitions and equipment to fuel the war effort was given priority over the manufacturing of other items, such as confectionary. Supply was also disrupted; Domestic agriculture was realigned to produce particular crops, rationing was enforced, and imported items and ingredients became more difficult to obtain, as shipping became more dangerous. Furthermore, methods of communication familiar to advertising, sales, and marketing people were also used by governments, military, and departments of the civil service to encourage or discourage certain behaviors: Posters were displayed at public places encouraging citizens to join the army, grow vegetables, not gossip, and to reduce waste. Indeed, the German and Italian fascist regimes of World War II (WW2) had made a significant use of propaganda in an attempt to legitimize their regimes before and during hostilities. From carefully designed aesthetics – including large infrastructure and construction projects such as stadiums, and even hosting global sporting events such as the FIFA (soccer) World Cup and Olympic Games to publicize their alleged physical supremacy as athletes, as well as technological and operational might. All of this was part of an effort to carefully manage the regimes' public image as perceived by their domestic populations and also the rest of the world (Tennent and Gillett 2016, 2017, 2019).

Additionally, there were efforts to carefully manage populations using personal data. Hitler's regime gathered statistics by census and segmented populations along lines of nationality, ethnicity, disability, and so on. The resulting data was computed using advanced punch-card technology to identify, Segment, stratify and control the population. The oppressive and often terminal outcome for citizens was based upon how socially or biologically wanted or unwanted their designated segment was deemed to be (Aly et al. 2004).

Although it is an extreme political example of the application of statistically driven social segmentation, the acts of the German Reich, together with the subsequent population control and management applied by the USSR, appear to have raised fears, particularly in the UK. Social control by grouping, stratification, and hierarchy based on political regimes is fundamental to the dystopian science fiction of Orwell (1945, 1949) published in the aftermath of war and which became bestselling novels and cultural reference points in the UK and USA. However, there are similarities to Huxley's (1932) *Brave New World* influenced by his earlier perceptions of twentieth-century industrialization and advances in science and engineering, which he had experienced during his time at Brunner and Mond (later part of *Industrial Chemical Industries [ICI]*) (Northern Echo 2005).

Through the first half of the twentieth century, business management thinking had also become more engaged with data-driven approaches to planning and decision-making and advances in statistics and behavioral sciences. Although far less extreme than Orwell or Huxley's visions of a fictional dystopian future (and certainly less so than Hitler's political misuse of population data), there are nevertheless ethical dimensions to data-driven marketing which, while visibly addressed through various Data Protection Acts in the twenty-first century, were still relatively unregulated for much of the twentieth century. Robinson's (2012) account of mail-order "quack" doctors and their market research at the turn of the twentieth century shows how it led to innovative approaches in advertising and direct mail based upon social science techniques using statistical correlation and quota sampling. On the one hand, this enabled companies to more accurately target prospective customers than by blanket advertising but which arguably can be seen as forbears of modern-day telesales scams. Lauer (2012) identifies the use of retail sales ledgers in the 1930s in America as a significant forerunner to what is today known as data mining, as systematic analysis known as customer control using records of credit information was used to identify current and lapsed customers to target through direct-mail techniques. Today, these efforts would be referred to as "win back and save" (as managers understood it was easier to reclaim old customers than to find completely new ones) as well as cross- and up-selling (i.e., encouraging grocery customers to purchase furnishings or to increase the price points of products they purchased in an existing category). Although seemingly more ethical than Robinson's case, in contrast to the modern consumer, the customers in Lauer's findings still apparently had no option to opt out of such promotions nor control of who had access to their credit data.

The inter-war years had been significant for the origins of efforts which transformed "luxury" items into "necessities" for many families in Britain, as producers and retailers succeeded in creating mass markets for items such as radios and furniture. Although not everything succeeded immediately, for example, firms such as Hoover advertised its vacuum cleaners as a time- and labor-saving innovation, targeting maids and housewives and augmenting its efforts with door-to-door salesmen. Although popular in America, it took longer for Hoover to establish itself in Britain, and the reputation of door-to-door selling was sometimes negative. Similarly, cars and telephones also took longer to diffuse to British consumers relative to the USA (Scott 2017).

After the Wars

Recalibration of society and industry after WW2 meant that European economies began to improve. Quick growth in living standards and demand (despite rationing for some items which lasted into the 1950s) coupled with increased opportunities for consumer credit and mortgages, and the growth in advertising due to the growth of television, meant that the mid-twentieth century was characterized by mass marketing and a rise in consumerism which mirrored the USA (Aveyard et al. 2018; Egan 2011). New conceptual and methodological perspectives from behavioral sciences on management decisions and statistical and customer behavior analysis were leveraged due to advances in computing technology, and scientific approaches to marketing were popular. For example, continued interest in the profiling of society by wealth, births, and migrations led to frameworks that could be used by marketers for demographic profiling (Egan 2011).

McCarthy (1960) and Borden (1964) are often credited as introducing and refining the idea of a marketing mix – an analogous list of ingredients that marketers could adjust to meet the tastes of customers, calibrated into the 4Ps of marketing (product, price, place/distribution, and promotion). With mass markets and advertising opportunities more available than ever before, the idea of brand and product management was becoming more strategic. The introduction in 1968 of the "growth-share matrix" (Boston Consulting Group n.d.) provided a tool by which managers could prioritize focus on specific markets and products, by organizing their portfolio by market growth and share relative to competitors. Thus, investment could be targeted based upon the strategy and objectives of the organization, although the tool would become misunderstood and misapplied in later years (McKeown 2016).

An illustrative and influential case of the growth of branding and merchandising during the mid-twentieth century is its introduction to global sporting events. For the FIFA (soccer) World Cup 1966, hosted by England, an opportunity was identified for branding, merchandising, and product development on a scale not previously associated with such a sporting event. A variety of products were licensed including clothing, ash trays, pottery, a World Cup ale, and themed music in different genres (Tennent and Gillett 2016, 2018). It was intended by the FA Organizing Committee that these products, mostly emblazoned with a cartoon mascot *World Cup Willie*, would help to cross-promote the tournament and, indeed, each other. This very deliberate commercial strategy did not really pay off as hoped, but these entrepreneurial efforts had a legacy; merchandizing was a theme that future World Cups – and other sporting events such as the Olympic Games – would develop much further.

The increasingly strategic approach to marketing management often required a varied skill set, encompassing technical as well as business knowledge. For context, we now consider the history and role of business and marketing education for twentieth-century managers, before rejoining our historical narrative of marketing in the late twentieth century.

Marketing and Management Education

The academic research, education, and practice of marketing (and related topics such as sales and strategy) can be explained metaphorically as being three cogs of the same machine, which interdependently drive each other; academic research is based on what is practiced, for example, to explain what is happening and why and to make suggestions for improving marketing (e.g., by being more ethical, more effective, or more efficient). In turn, this research synthesized from academic study is used to inform the various textbooks and curricula applied in business education from schools to universities, as well as professional training. The interlocking relationship between the practice and academic tripartite is shown in Fig. 1, although this interdependent view has not always been evident in academia, which at times adopted a "top-down" view (with academic research at the top) mentioned below. It is in this context that this chapter now gives a very brief explanation of post-WW2 marketing and business education.

Purpose of Business and Management Education

Since WW2 there has been a concentration in some schools, affecting both the research and teaching fields, on functional sub-disciplines and statistical analysis driven by economics and quantitative sociology – identified by Mintzberg (2004) as rescuing the business school from a purely vocational focus. Bonet (2015, p. 1) counters this approach by arguing that management is also "an art whose education has to include humanities." This humanities approach was inherent in the other main school of management education, led by the Harvard Business School (Bonet 2015; Mintzberg 2004). This emphasis was led by the military-inspired teaching of business policy (Hoskin and MacVe 1986, 1988; Carter et al. 2008) later known as *strategic management* (Mintzberg 2004) which integrated an understanding of the various business functions together.

Fig. 1 The cog metaphor of the academic and practice tripartite relationship

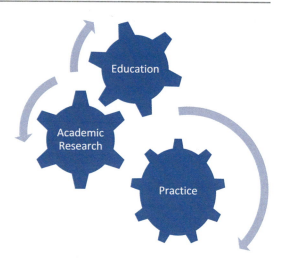

Harking back to the influence of Sun Tzu (2015, but originally c. 500 BCE), the humanities basis was indicated by the emphasis on "war stories" or case studies based on empirical research. Strategy was a rationalizing construct to be applied across different contexts and cases, an approach epitomized by the work of Chandler (1962, 1977, 1990) which attempted to create generalizable theory from historical cases (▶ Chap. 35, "Chandler and the Visible Hand of Management") and Ansoff's *Corporate Strategies Matrix* (1965). Ansoff's work emphasized strategic direction on a two-dimensional plain as if the organization was an army, an approach later echoed by Porter in his *Generic Strategies Matrix* (1980) and later considered by Mintzberg et al. (1998) to be the strategy of *Position* (see also ▶ Chap. 34, "The Age of Strategy: From Drucker and Design to Planning and Porter").

Military ideas and analogies and thus the case method were welcomed enthusiastically by other sub-disciplines such as marketing and sales, as epitomized by Ries and Trout's *Marketing Warfare* (2006) which is inspired by General von Clausewitz's *On War* (1832). The reduction of management studies to frameworks based on rationalism has facilitated the union of the quantitative school with the case study school. This emerged from the late 1970s onward in tandem with neoliberalism which encouraged enterprise culture and thus the growth of the business school initially built on the provision of Master of Business Administration (MBA) courses (Kanter 2005).

The expansion of scientifically, analytically, and econometrically casted theories (Kanter 2005) which attempt to "discover patterns and laws" was based on a "firm belief in causal determinism for explaining all aspects of corporate performance" (Ghoshal 2005, p. 77), excluding the role of human intentionality (Bailey and Ford 1996). These theories, supported by influential reports and financial investment, came to dominate business school teachings (Clegg and Ross-Smith 2003). Kanter (2005) identifies the popularity of these theories among the businesses sponsoring and hiring MBA candidates as reaching a nadir during the 1980s, as American-style one-sided shareholder capitalism "was considered the very model of a modern economic system" (p. 93), a demand that business schools and management professors were willing to supply.

The weakness of these theories and their underlying positivist and economically [neo]liberal ideology (Friedman 2002) is highlighted by Ghoshal (2005) who argues "it is an error to pretend that the methods of the physical sciences can be indiscriminately applied to business studies because such a pretension ignores some fundamental differences that exist between the academic disciplines" (p. 77). Emphasis on neoliberalism means that neoliberal economics is considered normative by business schools – but suppresses the history of ideas in the field because anything that doesn't fit is ignored.

However, some critical and alternative ideas did emerge from the marketing thinking that evolved toward the end of the 1980s and through the 1990s, with more emphasis placed on service, on relationships and networks, and on business ethics, to which we now turn.

End of the Century: Broadening the Scope of Markets and Marketing

In the Western Hemisphere at least, the 1980s may be remembered as a decade in which politically conservative governments led the UK and USA. Consistent with the neoliberal approach, market-based approaches were in favor and introduced quite rapidly into the public sector. An ideology based upon private sector business management became dominant, and the academic study of public administration and political science became the domain of business schools (Lynn 2007). Indeed, the work of management "gurus" such as Peters and Waterman and Michael Porter had a great influence on government thinking.

This new era of in-depth restructuring of the public sector (Pollitt 1990; Hood 1991; Ferlie 1998) has been labeled *New Public Management* (NPM), an expression attributed to Hood (1991, 1995). Although "there is some doubt as to what NPM is, and if there is a single NPM" (Lapsley 2008, p. 91), it has been defined as being based upon the core values of value for money, efficiency, performance measurement and management, transparency, and contestability (Hood 1991; Ferlie 2007).

Whereas some national governments (e.g., USA and New Zealand) sought to encourage a local government culture of competition (Domberger and Hall 1996), NPM in Britain was initially typified by an even stronger emphasis on market forces. This involved the privatization of some public services, and the requirement for the Compulsory Competitive Tendering (CCT) of others, meaning that the role of local authorities would now be more of a commissioning agent than a direct service provider (Coulson 2004).

CCT was first introduced in 1980 with the Local Government, Planning and Land Act (1980) for construction, highways, and maintenance work and in 1982 extended to health authorities for support activities such as catering, cleaning, maintenance of estates, and portering services. By the late 1980s, the Local Government Act (1988) was introduced, and CCT was extended even further to public services such as refuse collection, public libraries, and arts centers and, by the end of the decade, eventually also to sports and leisure management services (The Guardian 2011).

Notwithstanding governmental approaches, some academics believed that at around the same time there was a reconceptualization in the orientation of marketing as a field of study and practice, from transactions to relationships (Berry 1983; Bund-Jackson 1985; Webster 1992). This was because of broader thinking and application by managers, consultants, and academics as to the scope and purpose of marketing throughout the latter decades of the twentieth century, particularly in industrial, business-to-business contexts and services markets (Mattsson and Johanson 2004; Palmer et al. 2005; Gummesson 2008).

> Marketing is so basic that it cannot be considered a separate function within the business. Marketing requires separate work...but it is, first, a central dimension of the entire business. It is the whole business seen from the point of view of its final result, that is, from the customer's point of view...concern and responsibility for marketing must, therefore, permeate all areas of the enterprise. Drucker (1973 cited by Doyle 1995 p. 33)

The above quotation, attributed to Peter Drucker (who believed in a vocational definition of *management* in which its function and broader responsibilities held a social purpose), shows that the centrality of the customer should be paramount to marketers and that marketing activities and customer perspective should be the responsibility of everyone within an organization, not just its sales team or people with "marketing" in their job title. For example, from the management practice and academic field of operations management, Terry Hill categorized operational capabilities which can lead to competitive advantage and market success. Published in academic literature in the mid-1980s (Hill 1985), his simple yet insightful typology enabled managers to consider the client's perspective by identifying two things: (a) what drives customers in buying the products manufactured by a company at all (*order qualifiers*) and (b) what makes customers purchase a certain product instead of a similar one manufactured by a competitor (*order winners*). Operations Management was explicitly identifying customer preference as a key variable, and that this should require coordination across the firm to deliver on "order winners" that are based on realistic sales promises that the organization can fulfill practically, to meet customer expectations. This customer preference seems significant because the Operations Management disciple is sometimes (perhaps unfairly) thought of as inward looking and dominated by a logic of engineering or technology that could on occasion put it at odds with Sales departments.

Such observations led Gummesson to distinguish between *full-time marketers* (FTMs) and *part-time marketers* (PTMs) and to identify that in many situations, the impact of PTMs is more important to long-term success in the marketplace than that of FTMs (Gummesson 1991). Furthermore, it is suggested that because interaction and co-production occur between service providers and customers, and that customers might also interact with one another, even the customers themselves can be viewed as PTMs (Gummesson 1991). Marketing is therefore seen more as market-oriented management and an overall process rather than a separate function of the organization (Grönroos 1996).

Indeed, Ames (1970) and Webster (1978) identified how planning in the industrial setting (as distinct from the consumer goods sector) requires more working relationships across functions and a tighter link to corporate strategy, because evolving client demands could imply changes throughout the supplier firm, such as to capital commitments for equipment, shifts in development activities, or adapting (or even innovating) engineering and manufacturing approaches. Thus, strong interdependencies exist between an organizations' marketing function (i.e., departments or job titles along the lines of business development, sales, proposals, public relations, advertising, or simply called "marketers") and other functional units, such as research and development, logistics, and so on. Sales and marketing professionals may then have an account management role involving coordinating between their employer (the supplier organization) and the client organization – a boundary position integrative across functions (Day 1992). As such, marketing (and sales) departments were perhaps taking on a broader remit, in some scenarios having (or at least attempting) increasing influence over other business functions within their organizations, so as to ingrain client needs into activities throughout the firm. Negotiation and diplomacy are thus important interpersonal skills for sales and marketing professionals. In this context there is less emphasis on "marketing" as a transaction or something that a seller does to a target and more emphasis on leveraging interdependencies and striving for mutually agreeable outcomes, perhaps over a long-term arrangement – "win-win" scenarios that retain customers (Hutt and Speh 1984). The firm-wide and strategic nature of this interpretation of "marketing" was consistent with ideas elsewhere, for business strategists were by the next decade using terms such as *co-opetition* (e.g., Nalebuff et al. 1996).

Research on marketing published throughout the 1980s suggested that other members of an organization's environment should be acknowledged as being a form of customer (Håkansson 1982), that the philosophy of marketing should be given greater consideration (Deshpande 1983), that broader consideration should be given to what a "general theory" of marketing might need to include (Hunt 1983), and, reminiscent of Hutt and Speh (1984), that marketers should consider long-term interactive relationships, rather than just maximizing transactions for short-term gain (Gummesson 1987). This thinking was consistent with earlier work emanating from Northern Europe emanating from the studies of the Industrial Marketing and Purchasing (IMP) Group in which it was proposed that business transactions be viewed as part of a continual stream of engagement, not isolated events (IMP Group 1982).

Contrary to Fig. 1 which depicted a balanced and interdependent relationship between academia and practice, the mainstream view in management science around this time had suggested gaps between science and practice as being due to the irrationality of managers who should be controlled so as to be brought in line with theory. Network researchers challenged this stance, approaching gaps between science and practice as being gaps in theory to be explored and met

(Johanson and Mattson 1994 cited by McLoughlin and Horan 2002, p. 540). The IMP Group and others such as Gummesson appear to have been critical of marketing thinking as being dated, as global markets emerged and the US internal market faced fresh competition as economies and industry developed around the world and supply could increasingly be sourced from Asia or Europe. Thus, buyers and suppliers should strive to differentiate on good service and meeting consumer needs as the ratio or balance of buyers to suppliers shifted.

However, the most fashionable ideas of the day appear to have been based on simple diagrams that lent themselves to "brainstorming exercises" at corporate away days: 2x2 boxes such as SWOT analysis or Porter's generic strategies: These were about identifying a firm's "strengths," "weaknesses," "opportunities," and "threats" which could be determined by other compatible analyses, for example, by considering the scopes of cost or differentiation to find a position within a market that could be dominated or niched (Porter 1980). The focus tended to be based around market share, and how much should be sought, as a primary performance measure. The measurement of the profit impact of marketing was popular through the 1960s, 1970s, and 1980s as firms sought to demonstrate accountability to shareholders (Buzzell and Gale 1987), and military-like strategies for achieving "competitive advantage" through analyzing a firm's position in an industry or market to identify barriers to entry, achieving "first mover advantage," and avoiding the middle ground also gained favor and became staples of marketing and strategy texts during this time (e.g., Porter 1979, 1980).

While useful and popular, there seems to have been a tendency for these approaches and tools to be interpreted as short-termism – as a "quick fix" and a way to manipulate or "beat" the customer – and that it led to a mindset that other firms should all be seen as hostile competitors. It is from observations such as this that led researchers to study the nature of networks, interactions, and relationships as described above.

Concern for processes and service relationships was not the preserve of business-to-business marketers or Northern Europeans. A corpus of research on service processes and services management was simultaneously emerging and included the work of many US scholars who were interested in service operations and processes from a marketing perspective, such as balancing efficiency and effectiveness to achieve excellent customer experiences and customer retention in a way that was also practical and profitable for the service provider. For example, Parasuraman et al. (1985) identified barriers to customer-perceived quality which can be summarized as follows:

1. Misconceptions of what the customer actually wants, leading to an inappropriate or incomplete service "product"
2. Inadequate resources, for example, under-staffing to achieve short-term, transactional cost efficiencies
3. Inadequate delivery, for example, resulting from lack of training or poor recruitment leading to lack of knowledge or lack of interest in the customer

Parasuraman et al. (1985, 1988, 1991) developed criteria for assessing service quality and developed a survey mechanism known as SERVQUAL for collecting and measuring customer perception data, thus providing an insight to the service orientation of organizations from the perception of service customers. The original model is based on the assumption that service experience from the customer's point of view can be covered by ten criteria, namely, access, reliability, credibility, security, understanding the customer, responsiveness, courtesy, competence, communication, and tangibles. Since then, researchers and business people (particularly in the hospitality and hotel sectors) have adapted the scale by omitting or adding to the list of statements to measure service quality in their specific context (Wirtz and Lovelock 2016). Elsewhere, service marketing scholars provided various reiterations of the marketing mix, extending it to incorporate more "Ps" (such as process, physical evidence, and people) Chartered Institute of Marketing (2015). Ideas from engineering and manufacturing were also adapted, such as fishbone diagrams and other cause and effect analyses, flowcharting and blueprinting, and the Gap Model – a tool used for designing or analyzing and redesigning service processes to highlight potential service failure points and opportunities to optimize the offering. A key point to all of these tools was that they were intended to be customer-centric, with processes designed around meeting or exceeding customer expectations with the objective of customer satisfaction, retention, and positive word-of-mouth effects to build reputation, all of which could reduce the reliance on advertising, discounts, or other promotional efforts (these ideas have been proposed and developed by various authors, but a comprehensive overview is provided by Wirtz and Lovelock 2016).

In the related field of sales, customer centricity with an emphasis on identifying and providing solution to needs was also considered as an important step forward: Rackham's (1987) SPIN selling method offered an evidence-based formula for sales approaches based on probing to understand clients' explicit needs so as to offer valued solutions and capabilities to clients, particularly for high-value and industrial settings, and was positioned as a progression beyond the dated "door-to-door salesman" approaches which had developed around low-value and transactional consumer goods sales techniques from earlier in the century.

Ideas such as those presented above indicate that marketing as an academic discipline was moving closer to strategy, at times overlapping. Perhaps this was to fulfill an apparent void, as the field of strategic theory was itself perceived to be moving away from customer centricity and toward ideas of capturing economic rents in one form or another (▶ Chap. 34, "The Age of Strategy: From Drucker and Design to Planning and Porter"). The broadening of marketing thought corresponded with acknowledgment of marketing as a profession, and by the turn of the decade, textbooks in the fields of marketing (e.g., Kotler 1988) and sales management (e.g., Lancaster and Jobber 1990) demonstrate a broad, firm-wide, customer-centric, and service-/relationally based approach to the subjects. Significantly, in the UK, the professional body The Chartered Institute of Marketing received external validation when it was awarded *Royal Charter* in 1989.

Summary

This chapter follows the suggestions of Gillett (2014a) that management and business historians may find it rewarding to investigate historical cases using the lens of marketing, particularly in the broader sense explicated by the industrial, services, and relationship marketing scholars to research supply networks and brand relationships. In particular, relationships involving organizations from different sectors offer opportunities to explore institutional logics, differences, and complexities through history (Gillett and Tennent 2018). Additional opportunities might be to explore historical examples of the evolution of marketing practices aimed at *decreasing* consumption, as suggested by Gillett (2014b).

It is acknowledged that the ideas presented very much reflect the Western perspective of the authors, and the sources used are limited to those published in the English language and predominantly emanate from Northern and Western Europe and the USA. Tennent et al. (2019) advise that it is important for researchers to be reflexive and aware of their own perspectives, paradigm, and biases and also those of the sources upon which they base their findings. In this spirit readers are encouraged to consider these things for their own research and to use the knowledge presented here as a point of departure for their own research.

Along these lines it is also acknowledged that other economies are worthy of investigation. For example, other geographic economies require more research. Jones and Tadajewski (2017) provide insight as to the influence of German historical thinking. Other literature also exists, for example, in Asia, Africa, South America, and Southern Europe. Different geographies and temporalities of course have their own concepts and cases, and Jones and Tadajewski (2016) provide a useful cross section of research on this. Furthermore, phenomena such as Guanxi in China and the Keiretsu of Japan indicate that Western ideas of relationship marketing appear related but sufficiently different to warrant caution when applying them for explanatory power (e.g., Wang 2007). The formerly communist "Iron Curtain" countries of Europe offer further opportunities to examine attitudes and toward marketing and purchasing in centrally planned, or newly "opened," economies during the twentieth century (e.g., Patterson 2012; Afanassieva 2015). Furthermore, the illicit, illegal economies which have existed throughout history all over the world, including in Western European contexts (e.g., Jones 2016), are also worthy of additional research.

Cross-References

▶ Chandler and the Visible Hand of Management
▶ The Age of Strategy: From Drucker and Design to Planning and Porter

References

Afanassieva M (2015) Survival through networks: the 'grip' of the administrative links in the Russian post-Soviet context. Public Manag Rev 17(9):1261–1281. https://doi.org/10.1080/14719037.2014.906964

Agnew HE (1941) The history of the American marketing association. J Mark 5(4):374–379. https://doi.org/10.1177/002224294100500408

Aly G, Roth KH, Black E, Oksiloff A (2004) The Nazi census: identification and control in the Third Reich. Temple University Press, Philadelphia

Ambler T (2006) The new dominant logic of marketing: views of the elephant. In: Lusch RF, Vargo SL (eds) The service-dominant logic of marketing. Armonk, New York, pp 286–296

American Marketing Organization (2017) Definitions of marketing. Retrieved from https://www.ama.org/the-definition-of-marketing-what-is-marketing/. Accessed 15 Jan 2020

Ames BC (1970) Trappings vs. substance in industrial marketing. Harv Bus Rev 48:95–96

Ansoff HI (1965) Corporate strategy: an analytic approach to business policy for growth and expansion. McGraw-Hill Companies, New York

Aveyard S, Corthorn P, O'Connell S (2018) The politics of consumer credit in the UK, 1938–1992. Oxford University Press, Oxford

Bailey J, Ford C (1996) Management as science versus management as practice in postgraduate business education. Bus Strateg Rev 7(4):7–12. https://doi.org/10.1111/j.1467-8616.1996.tb00136.x

Bartels R (1988) The history of marketing thought, 3rd edn. Publishing Horizons, Columbus

Berry LL (1983) Relationship marketing. In: Berry LL, Shostack GL, Upah G (eds) Emerging perspectives on services marketing. American Marketing Association, Chicago, pp 25–28

Bonet E (2015) Educating managers for the 21st century. Paper presented at the 4th EDAMBA-EIASM consortium on doctoral supervision and the New Global Research Landscape, ESADE Universitat Ramon Llull, Barcelona, 26–29 Jan

Borden NH (1964) The concept of the marketing mix. J Advert Res 4: 2–7.

Boston Consulting Group (n.d.) What is the growth share matrix? Retrieved from https://www.bcg.com/en-gb/about/our-history/growth-share-matrix.aspx. Accessed 15 Jan 2020

Buttle F (1996) Relationship marketing. In: Buttle F (ed) Relationship marketing: theory and practice. Paul Chapman Publishing/Sage, London, pp 1–16

Buzzell RD, Gale BT (1987) The PIMS principles: linking strategy to performance. Simon and Schuster, New York

Carter C, Clegg SR, Kornberger M (2008) A very short, fairly interesting and reasonably cheap book about studying strategy. Sage, London

Chandler AD (1962) Strategy and structure: chapters in the history of the American industrial enterprise. MIT Press, Cambridge

Chandler AD (1977) The visible hand: the managerial revolution in American business. Belknap Press, Cambridge

Chandler AD (1990) Scale and scope: the dynamics of industrial capitalism. Belknap Press, Cambridge

Chartered Institute of Marketing (2015) 7 Ps: a brief summary of marketing and how it works. Retrieved from https://www.cim.co.uk/media/4772/7ps.pdf. Accessed 15 Jan 2020

Chartered Institute of Marketing (n.d.) Our history. Retrieved from https://www.cim.co.uk/about-cim/our-history/. Accessed 15 Jan 2020

Clausewitz CV (18321976 reprint). On war. Princeton University Press, Princeton

Clegg SR, Ross-Smith A (2003) Revising the boundaries: management education and learning in a postpositivist world. Acad Manag Learn Educ 2(1):85–98. https://doi.org/10.5465/amle.2003.9324049

Coulson A (2004) Local politics, central power: the future of representative local government in England. Local Gov Stud 30(4):467–480. https://doi.org/10.1080/0300393042000318941

Day GS (1992) Marketing's contribution to strategic dialogue. J Acad Mark Sci 20:323–329. https://doi.org/10.1177/0092070392204006

Deshpande R (1983) Paradigms lost: on theory and method in research in marketing. J Mark 47(4):101–110. https://doi.org/10.1177/002224298304700411

Domberger S, Hall C (1996) Contracting for public services: a review of the antipodean experience. Public Admin 74(1):129–147. https://doi.org/10.1111/j.1467-9299.1996.tb00861.x

Doyle P (1995) Marketing in the new millennium. Eur J Mark 29(13):23–41. https://doi.org/10.1108/03090569510147712

Duguid P, Lopes TDS, Mercer J (2010) Reading registrations: an overview of 100 years of trademark registrations in France, the United Kingdom, and the United States. In: Lopes TDS, Duguid P (eds) Trademarks, brands, and competitiveness. Routledge, New York, pp 27–48

Egan J (2011) Relationship marketing: exploring relational strategies in marketing, 4th edn. Pearson Education, London

Ferlie E (1998) The new public management in the United Kingdom: origins, implementation and prospects. Managerial reform of the State International seminar, The Ministry of Administration and State Reform, Brasil, 17–18 November 1998

Ferlie E (2007) The new public management: an overview. Retrieved from http://www.uk.cbs.dk/content/download/61555/847751/file/The%20New%20Public%20Management-1.pdf. Accessed 14 Sep 2007

Friedman M (2002) Capitalism and freedom, 40th Anniversary edition. The University of Chicago Press, Chicago

Ghoshal S (2005) Bad management theories are destroying good management practices. Acad Manag Learn Educ 4(1):75–91. https://doi.org/10.5465/amle.2005.16132558

Gilbert D, Bailey N (2001) The development of marketing-A compendium of historical approaches. In: Baker M (ed) Marketing: critical perspectives on business and management. Routledge, New York, pp 75–91

Gillett AG (2014a) Trademarks, brands, and competitiveness. Bus Hist 56(4):677–678. https://doi.org/10.1080/00076791.2013.763660

Gillett AG (2014b) The rise of marketing and market research. Bus Hist 56(8):1381–1382. https://doi.org/10.1080/00076791.2013.828437

Gillett AG, Tennent KD (2017) Dynamic sublimes, changing plans, and the legacy of a megaproject: the case of the 1966 soccer World Cup. Proj Manag J 48(6):93–116. https://doi.org/10.1177/875697281704800608

Gillett AG, Tennent KD (2018) Shadow hybridity and the institutional logic of professional sport: perpetuating a sporting business in times of rapid social and economic change. J Manag Hist 24(2):228–259. https://doi.org/10.1108/JMH-11-2017-0060

Gillett AG, Tennent KD (2019) 'Filip' or flop? Managing public relations and the Latin American reaction to the 1966 FIFA World Cup. Sociol Soc 20(7–8):923–935. https://doi.org/10.1080/14660970.2019.1680493

Godson M (2009) Relationship marketing. Oxford University Press, Oxford

Grönroos C (1996) Relationship marketing: strategic and tactical implications. Manag Decis 34(3):5–14. https://doi.org/10.1108/00251749610113613

Gummesson E (1987) The new marketing – developing long term interactive relationships. Long Range Plan 20(4):10–20. https://doi.org/10.1016/0024-6301(87)90151-8

Gummesson E (1991) Marketing-orientation revisited: the crucial role of the part-time marketer. Eur J Mark 25(2):60–75. https://doi.org/10.1108/03090569110139166

Gummesson E (2008) Total relationship marketing, 3rd edn. Butterworth-Heinemann, Oxford

Håkansson H (ed) (1982) International marketing and purchasing of industrial goods: an interaction approach. Wiley, London

Hill T (1985) Manufacturing strategy. Macmillan Education Ltd, London

Hollander SC, Rassuli KM, Jones DB, Dix LF (2005) Periodization in marketing history. J Macroecon 25(1):32–41. https://doi.org/10.1177/0276146705274982

Hood C (1991) A public management for all seasons? Public Admin 69(Spring):3–19. https://doi.org/10.1111/j.1467-9299.1991.tb00779.x

Hood C (1995) The "new public management" in the 1980s: variations on a theme. Acc Organ Soc 20(2/3):93–109. https://doi.org/10.1016/0361-3682(93)E0001-W

Hoskin KW, Macve RH (1986) Accounting and the examination: a genealogy of disciplinary power. Acc Organ Soc 11(2):105–136. https://doi.org/10.1016/0361-3682(86)90027-9

Hoskin KW, Macve RH (1988) The genesis of accountability: the west point connections. Acc Organ Soc 13(1):37–73. https://doi.org/10.1016/0361-3682(88)90025-6

Hunt SD (1983) General theories and the fundamental explananda of marketing. J Mark 47(4):9–17. https://doi.org/10.1177/002224298304700402

Hutt MD, Speh TW (1984) The marketing strategy center: diagnosing the industrial marketer's interdisciplinary role. J Mark 48(Fall):53–56. https://doi.org/10.1177/002224298404800406

Huxley A (1932) Brave new world. Chatto & Windus, London

IMP Group (1982) An interaction approach. In: Håkansson H (ed) International marketing and purchasing of industrial goods. Wiley, Chichester, pp 10–27

Institute of Sales Management (n.d.) History of the institute of sales management. Retrieved from https://www.ismprofessional.com/heritage/. Accessed 15 Jan 2020

Jackson BB (1985) Winning and keeping industrial consumers: the dynamics of customer relationships. Lexington, DC Heath

Jones ET (2016) Inside the illicit economy: reconstructing the smugglers' trade of sixteenth century Bristol. Routledge, New York

Jones DB, Shaw EH (2002) A history of marketing thought. In: Weitz BA, Wensley R (eds) Handbook of marketing. Sage, London, pp 39–65

Jones DB, Tadajewski M (eds) (2016) The Routledge companion to marketing history. Routledge, New York

Jones DB, Tadajewski M (2017) Foundations of marketing thought: the influence of the German historical school. Routledge, New York

Kanter RM (2005) What theories do audiences want? Exploring the demand side. Acad Manag Learn Educ 4(1):93–95. https://doi.org/10.5465/amle.2005.16132566

Keith RJ (1960) The marketing revolution. J Mark 24(3):35–38. https://doi.org/10.1177/002224296002400306

Kotler P (1988) Marketing management: analysis, planning, implementation and control, 6th edn. Prentice-Hall, New Jersey

Lancaster G, Jobber D (1990) Sales technique & management, 2nd edn. Pitman, London

Lane J (2019) Secrets for sale? Innovation and the nature of knowledge in an early industrial district: the potteries, 1750–1851. Enterp Soc 20(4):861–906. https://doi.org/10.1017/eso.2019.8

Lapsley I (2008) The NPM agenda: back to the future. J Financ Account Manag 24(1):77–96. https://doi.org/10.1111/j.1468-0408.2008.00444.x

Lauer J (2012) Making the ledgers talk: customer control and the origins of retail data mining, 1920–1940. In: Berghoff H, Scranton P, Spiekermann U (eds) The rise of marketing and market research. Palgrave Macmillan, New York, pp 153–169

Lynn LE Jr (2007) Public management: a concise history of the field. In: Ferlie E, Lynn LE Jr, Pollitt C (eds) The oxford handbook of public management. Oxford University Press, Oxford, pp 27–50

Mattsson L-G, Johanson J (2004) Discovering market networks. Eur J Mark 40(3/4):259–274. https://doi.org/10.1108/03090560610648048

McCarthy EJ (1960) Basic marketing. Irwin, Homewood

McKeown M (2016) The strategy book, 2nd edn. FT Prentice Hall, London

McLoughlin D, Horan C (2002) Markets-as-networks: notes on a unique understanding. J Bus Res 55(7):535–543. https://doi.org/10.1016/S0148-2963(00)00193-4

Mintzberg H (2004) Managers, not MBAs: a hard look at the soft practice of managing and management development. Berrett-Koehler Publishers, San Francisco

Mintzberg H, Ahlstrand B, Lampel J (1998) Strategy safari: a guided tour through the wilds of strategic management. Free Press, New York

Nalebuff BJ, Brandenburger A, Maulana A (1996) Co-opetition. Harper Collins Business, London

Northern Echo (2005) Brave new world of Billingham. Retrieved from https://www.thenorthernecho.co.uk/news/6964479.brave-new-world-of-billingham/ Accessed 15 Jan 2020

Orwell G (1945) Animal farm: a fairy story. Secker and Warburg, London

Orwell G (1949) Nineteen-eighty four. Penguin, Harmondsworth

Palmer R, Lindgreen A, Vanhamme J (2005) Relationship marketing: schools of thought and future research directions. Mark Intell Plan 23(3):313–330. https://doi.org/10.1108/02634500510597337

Parasuraman A, Zeithaml VA, Berry LL (1985) A conceptual model of service quality and its implications for future research. J Mark 49(4):41–50. https://doi.org/10.1177/002224298504900403

Parasuraman A, Zeithaml VA, Berry LL (1988) SERVQUAL: a multiple-item scale for measuring consumer perceptions of service quality. J Retail 64(1):12–40

Parasuraman A, Berry LL, Zeithaml VA (1991) Refinement and reassessment of the SERVQUAL scale. J Retail 67(4):420–450

Patterson PH (2012) The bad science and the black arts: the reception of marketing in socialist Europe. In: Berghoff H, Scranton P, Spiekermann U (eds) The rise of marketing and market research. Palgrave Macmillan, New York, pp 269–293

Pollitt C (1989) Performance indicators in the longer term. Public Money Manag 9(3):51–53. https://doi.org/10.1080/09540968909387558

Pollitt C (1990) The new managerialism and the public services – the Anglo American experience. Basil Blackwell, Oxford

Porter ME (1979) How competitive forces shape strategy. Harv Bus Rev 57(2):137–145

Porter ME (1980) Competitive strategy: techniques for analyzing industries and competitors. The Free Press, New York

Rackham N (1987) Making major sales. Gower Publishing Company Limited, London

Ries A, Trout J (2006) Marketing warfare: authors' annotated edition. McGraw Hill Professional, New York

Robinson DJ (2012) Mail-order doctors and market research, 1890–1930. In: Berghoff H, Scranton P, Spiekermann U (eds) The rise of marketing and market research. Palgrave Macmillan, New York, pp 73–93

Scott P (2017) The market makers: creating mass markets for consumer durables in inter-war Britain. Oxford University Press, Oxford

Smith A, Tennent KD, Mollan S (eds) (2016) The impact of the First World War on international business. Routledge, New York

Tadajewski M, Jones DB (2012) Scientific marketing management and the emergence of the ethical marketing concept. J Mark Manag 28(1–2):37–61. https://doi.org/10.1080/0267257X.2011.619072

Tennent KD, Gillett AG (2016) Foundations of managing sporting events. Routledge, New York

Tennent KD, Gillett AG (2018) Opportunities for all the team: entrepreneurship and the 1966 and 1994 soccer world cups. Int J Hist Sport 35(7–8):767–788. https://doi.org/10.1080/09523367.2018.1544555

Tennent KD, Gillett AG, Foster WM (2019) Developing historical consciousness in management learners. Manag Learn. https://doi.org/10.1177/1350507619869669

The Guardian (2011) Timeline: outsourcing and the public sector. Retrieved from https://www.theguardian.com/society/microsite/outsourcing_/story/0,13230,933819,00.html. Accessed 11 Jan 2020

Tzu S (2015) The art of war. Sheba Blake Publishing, New York

Wang CL (2007) Guanxi vs. relationship marketing: exploring underlying differences. Ind Mark Manag 36(1):81–86. https://doi.org/10.1016/j.indmarman.2005.08.002

Webster FE Jr (1978) Management science in industrial marketing. J Mark 42(January):21–27. https://doi.org/10.1177/002224297804200106

Webster FE Jr (1992) The changing role of marketing in the corporation. J Mark 56(4):1–17. https://doi.org/10.1177/002224299205600402

Wirtz J, Lovelock C (2016) Services marketing: people, technology, strategy, 8th edn. World Scientific Publishing Company, Singapore

Organizational Psychology's Golden Age, 1940–1970

38

Alice White

Contents

Introduction	860
What Is Organizational Psychology?	860
The Early Years: Applied Psychology Before the Second World War	861
Organizational Psychology at War	862
Selection in the Services	863
Planning for Demobilization	864
Patronage and the Professionalization of Organizational Psychology	866
Publicizing New Work in Organizational Psychology	868
Conclusion	868
Cross-References	870
References	870

Abstract

The purpose of this chapter is to discuss organizational psychology in the mid-twentieth century Britain. This chapter explores why organizational psychology flourished between 1940 and 1970 by tracing the influence of war, social, and cultural factors that made organizations more receptive to the efforts of psychologists to extend their expertise and professionalize the field. It focuses on the work of psychologists for the British military and the Tavistock Institute of Human Relations, which was the most notable group applying psychological theories and methods to the study of organizations in Britain at the time.

Keywords

British management · Great Britain · Military · Selection · Leadership · Tavistock Institute

A. White (✉)
Wellcome Trust, London, UK
e-mail: a.white@wellcome.ac.uk

© The Author(s), under exclusive licence to Springer Nature Switzerland AG 2020
B. Bowden et al. (eds.), *The Palgrave Handbook of Management History*,
https://doi.org/10.1007/978-3-319-62114-2_35

Introduction

Was the period from 1940 to 1970 a "golden age" for organizational psychology? There was certainly a boom in the sort of work we would identify as organizational psychology during this era, and many see this period as a time when significant developments took place (Featherman and Vinovskis 2001; House 2008). But why? What was it about this form of management that was so appealing at the time?

This time was a time of "Big Science," characterized by large-scale projects, often supported by governments or international agencies, with research conducted by teams that often bringing together different forms of scientific expertise (Dennis 2015). Organizational psychology shares some of these characteristics (House 2008). The people who have worked and who currently work in the field of organizational psychology consider that they approach the problems and questions of organizations scientifically: Viteles, considered one of the earliest organizational psychologists, was quoted as saying "If it isn't scientific, it's not good practice, and if it isn't practical, it's not good science" (Katzell and Austin 1992). This chapter thus approaches the history of organizational psychology from a history of science perspective.

Analyzing the development of the field in terms of theories, methods, and professionalization enables us to trace the problems and opportunities that gave rise to new ways of managing people. Looking at who engaged with organizational psychology (whether as practitioners, patrons, workers and unions, and funders), and why, demonstrates what people hoped to get from the application of these methods. Understanding what organizational psychology consisted of, and the structures and cultures within which it operated, helps us to make sense of what made this approach particularly appealing, leading to a seeming "golden age."

What Is Organizational Psychology?

Organizational psychology, simply defined, is "psychology applied to work" (Takooshian 2012). It encompasses topics such as employee selection, job analysis, motivation and morale, leadership, and relations between and within groups and teams. It was initially known as industrial psychology in many places because work focused on factories before the growth of service work and corporations in the postwar period.

The term organizational or industrial-organizational (I-O) psychology is more commonly used in America than elsewhere; in the UK, the field came to be known as occupational psychology, and Peter Warr observes that in continental Europe, the term work psychology is traditionally used (Warr 2014). The terms psychotechnics and applied psychology have also been applied to the same set of concepts and methods. To keep things simple, though, this chapter will refer to organizational psychology.

As this list of terms and places indicates, there is no single history of organizational psychology. It has proceeded with varying focuses and been received differently in different times and places. The history of psychology in American management is discussed in detail elsewhere in this volume (▶ Chap. 24, "Organizational Psychology and the Rise of Human Resource Management" by J. Muldoon) and has been written about in many other places: most histories of organizational psychology give accounts of organizational psychology in America (The Editors of Encyclopaedia Britannica 2016), or "the United States and abroad," as illustrated by the US-focused summaries in timelines (Jex 2002; Takooshian 2012; Koppes Bryan 2012).

Recent histories of organizational psychology discuss the reception and growth of the field other parts of the world, and many recent national histories of psychology discuss organizational psychology in a local context. Accounts that center upon countries such as Canada, India, Australia, and New Zealand note significant Anglo-American influence on the development of ideas and practices from the Second World War onwards (Webster 1988; Bhawuk 2008; Haig and Marie 2012; Nixon and Taft 2013; Warr 2014; Carpintero 2017). Moreover, while some have suggested that American psychology was "parochial" until relatively recently (Triandis 1994 as cited in Warr, p. 82), recent historical research indicates that organizational psychology was shaped by new ideas and practices from Britain during the Second World War and postwar era (Burnes and Cooke 2013; Warr 2014; White 2016). This chapter thus covers the history of organizational psychology in the UK, which offers lessons in its own right and will enable the reader to trace its influence in other places in future reading and research.

The Early Years: Applied Psychology Before the Second World War

The application of psychological analysis and methods to the workplace has a long history. Some histories of organizational psychology locate the roots of the field in the studies of individual differences arising from Darwin and Galton's work and the studies of fatigue that were influenced by the concept of entropy and the laws of thermodynamics (Rabinbach 1992; Kozlowski 2012; Vinchur 2018). Carpintero's history of organizational psychology situates the foundations of organizational psychology in the scientific study of work organizations in the late nineteenth century (Carpintero 2017). Vinchur's account of the early years covers the period from the late 1800s to the early 1930s, and likewise, the chapter in Koppes' book discusses influential figures such as Walter Dill Scott, Hugo Münsterberg, and Walter Van Dyke Bingham, whose work took place before the 1930s (Koppes 2014; Vinchur 2018). In 1932, in what is often considered the first organizational psychology textbook, Morris S. Viteles wrote about the history of the field. He discussed factors such as social trends, an economic emphasis on efficiency in industry, and the growth of interest in experiments and individual differences that gave rise to the field (Viteles 1932).

Specific focuses within organizational psychology have had their roots traced back to the first half of the twentieth century. In terms of research into individual differences, one of the largest-scale early applications was that of the Alpha and Beta tests administered by Robert Yerkes and colleagues during the First World War (Carson 1993; Koppes Bryan 2012; Carpintero 2017). The Hawthorne Studies into attitudes and motivations of workers took place in the 1920s and early 1930s, and have been mythologized in many histories of management since then (Gillespie 1993; Gale 2004). They are one of the best-known examples of organizational psychology research and are discussed elsewhere in this volume (▶ Chap. 23, "Spontaneity is the Spice of Management: Elton Mayo's Hunt for Cooperation" in the chapter by J. Muldoon).

In Britain, notable efforts to apply psychology to organizations included studies of morale and employee attitudes at the Cadbury and Rowntree works, led by psychologists such as Charles Myers, who founded the National Institute of Industrial Psychology in 1921 (Bunn 2001). The Industrial Fatigue Research Board was created in 1918 and followed by the Industrial Health Research Board. Figures such as Lyndall Urwick, Frank Watts, and Clarence Northcott all researched and published works in the field of human relations before the Second World War (Guillén 1994; Ussishkin 2011; Weatherburn 2019).

So, with these developments taking place in the first half of the twentieth century, why might the "golden age" of organizational psychology span the 1940s–1970s? Koppes explains that by the end of the 1930s, "psychologists had developed the basic infrastructure for applications in business and industry" and that "the groundwork had been laid for greater concern with employees' place in the workplace" (Koppes 2014, p. 30). The period that followed was one in which psychologists built upon these foundations, staking their claims to expertise and increasing the remit of their field.

Organizational Psychology at War

The Second World War provided opportunities to make significant inroads in this regard. As the nation mobilized to engage in total war, British psychologists sought new outlets for their expertise. Though there was little demand for psychologists' services initially, it was not long before the success of German Blitzkrieg caused alarm and a sense that, for Britain to survive, it would need to ensure that its human resources were used in the most efficient possible way (1942). There was a sense that, during the First World War, many technically able men and potential leaders had wasted their time or been killed while in roles that did not utilize their skills (Bruton 2013; ▶ Chap. 24, "Organizational Psychology and the Rise of Human Resource Management" by J. Muldoon, this volume) and there was a fear that this was beginning to happen again in the Second World War. *The Times* published an article decrying that "weapons and equipment are wasted [because] sufficient corresponding attention has not been paid to the best methods of attaining an equal standard in the human component of the Army" (1941) and William Beveridge was charged with investigating how efficiently the nation was deploying its people.

Influential up-and-coming leaders in the British military, such as Sir Ronald Adam, sought out experts to help with efficiency and also to enable them to say that they were doing something to remedy shortcomings (Crang 2000; French 2001; Field 2011a). In this context, psychologists from different backgrounds justified their entry into new spheres of work. Initially, their work concentrated on selection, testing, and dealing with problem individuals.

Selection in the Services

Frederick Bartlett headed the psychology program at the University of Cambridge, and he and his staff were chosen to assist the most prestigious of the forces, the Royal Air Force (RAF), with solving various personnel problems such as fatigue, personnel selection, and training. Bartlett's prewar work had been predominantly laboratory-based, testing for cognition and perception. This made his group well-suited to the task of assessing whether potential airmen would be capable of performing specific tasks required of them under specific circumstances, such as under the influence of amphetamines. In 1941, Bartlett resigned after the Air Ministry demanded proof of the military usefulness of his work, which he took as a personal insult. He was replaced by Edward Alexander Bott, who came from Canada to lead psychological research in the RAF (English 1992).

Psychologists from the NIIP such as Alec Rodger and J.G.W. Davies became consultants for the British Navy and built upon their prewar work in career counselling and aptitude-testing by creating tests to allocate servicemen and women to appropriate roles (Vernon and Parry 1949). A general selection scheme based on their methods was rolled out in the Army too, where a Directorate for the Selection of Personnel was created to oversee testing for specific capabilities for qualities such as intelligence, agility, following instructions, mechanical, mathematical, and verbal aptitude (1944; Crang 1999). Specific tests were devised for roles such as Morse-code operators, where the ability to perceive the differences between sounds was vitally important. This form of selection, which focused on the rank-and-file soldier and allocating people to jobs they might not have tried before, built on prewar work, where the NIIP had been involved in selecting machine-operators based on their dexterity and mechanical aptitude and helping school-leavers who did not yet have workplace experience.

Psychological methods for selecting people for specific technical roles were swiftly put into place but one significant personnel challenge to the British military remained well into 1942: the selection of officers. The popular perception was that Army officers were chosen from those who wore the correct "old school tie" and had attended elite private schools. The supply of competent men from this source was running low and capable men from other backgrounds were overlooked or had been put off from applying for commissions. The scientific approach of psychology offered hopes of a way to remedy this, promising to select based on potential and merit rather than class.

Most British psychologists were busy selecting rank-and-file soldiers, sailors, and airmen though; they had no tests ready to deploy to measure leadership ability and reputations to lose (Vernon and Parry 1949; Ahrenfeldt 1958). So remarkably, it was psychiatrists who played a significant role in investigating what made someone "officer material." Psychiatrists who had specialized in maladjustment investigated "problem" officers who were failing to perform as expected in leadership roles. Many of the people conducting this work were affiliated with the Tavistock Clinic, such as John Bowlby and Wilfred Bion. They began by making suggestions about managing or reallocating these difficult cases before moving on to test new methods for selecting potential leaders to avoid ill-suited people being chosen in the first place (Thalassis 2004; White 2016). Psychologists such as Eric Trist, Isabel Menzies Lyth, and Harold Bridger did play a key role though, developing tests specially adapted to select the most intelligent people rather than merely filter out those at the bottom of the scale.

The work of the Army's psychological staff resulted in the creation of War Office Selection Boards (WOSBs), which featured intelligence tests, personality "pointer" tests, group tasks, and discussions (which became known as Leaderless Group tests) (Vinden 1977; Crang 2000; White 2016). WOSBs were tested by being used on people about to complete officer training, whose "officer potential" had already been established by Army leadership to use as a yardstick by which to measure the new methods, which they considered a success because they met expectations about what made a good officer. Similarly, Bartlett noted that the RAF liked the tests he provided them because they achieved the same results as were already being achieved but "in less time and with less difficulty" (Bartlett 1942). The candidates themselves also approved of WOSBs; they felt they received useful advice on their abilities and potential even if they did not pass.

With War Office approval following the successful pilot, the WOSBs scheme very rapidly expanded, with boards established around the UK for men and for women, and then around the world to select leaders in British Army units positioned overseas. Bott adopted similar selection methods in the RAF, and Boards were set up for what were seen to be special cases in the Army, such as selecting young men to attend accelerated university courses that would lead to commission on graduation, selecting artillery officers, and selecting repatriated prisoners of war (POWs) who might be able to return to service (White 2016).

Planning for Demobilization

Though its application was popular with Army modernizers, the press, and the common soldier, some people had concerns about the increasing influence of organizational psychology. The psychological basis selection that made it an appealing solution to the Army's problems led to criticism from other psychologists, who questioned the WOSBs' scientific validity and the competence of the staff administering them (Vernon and Parry 1949; Ungerson 1950; Field 2011b). However, the same critics tended to acknowledge that the WOSBs were tremendously successful in changing perceptions of the organization, helping the Army to appear more modern and forward-thinking, and that they solved the most pressing "officer problem" by significantly increasing the number and quality of officer candidates available.

If psychologists were concerned about what applied psychology might do to the reputation of their discipline, Prime Minister Winston Churchill was aghast at the thought of what psychologists might be doing to his armed forces. He initiated an Expert Committee on the Work of Psychologists and Psychiatrists to investigate their work, with the hopes that it would prevent them from asking inappropriate or probing questions. Ronald Adam, who sought to modernize the British forces, saw to it that people amenable to social science methods such as Stafford Cripps participated, and soon the committee vindicated the psychologists work. The committee then began to look to future applications of psychology. They divided the spoils of war by agreeing that laboratory studies were Bartlett's domain, that any future technical selection and counselling work should be the remit of the NIIP psychologists and that selecting managers was best suited to the Army psychologists and psychiatrists.

Only 6 months after the Expert committee was established, representatives from the Ministry of Labour and the Civil Service were being invited to see the new techniques of selection in action and appreciate the potential value of psychology to employers. Various influential figures were also invited from companies such as Unilever. The minutes of this committee offer insight into the way that organizational psychologists explained and justified their practices, carved out niches for their work, and established connections with organization leaders who could employ them and sustain them in their new roles after the war (White 2016).

Psychologists had the ideal opportunity to demonstrate their ability to apply their military experience on demobilization via their work with returning POWs. They argued that these men would need assistance in returning to democratic society and that society would need assistance in accepting them back. The military was already experiencing difficulties with some returning POWs, and psychologists warned heads of industry that returning men who did not adjust well would be difficult employees to manage who could potentially direct their dissatisfaction into revolutionary fervor or disruptive, criminal acts. The Army sanctioned the creation of a psychological scheme to manage the POWs' return, and numerous industries agreed to participate. The resulting collaboration was Civil Resettlement Units (CRUs), which brought together experts and practices from selection, social work, counselling, and career guidance. Like the Expert Committee, the CRUs functioned as a bridge to take organizational psychology beyond the military and into peacetime contexts.

As the variety and scale of military psychology projects indicate, war acted as a turning point for psychologists and enabled them to apply their ideas not just on a new scale but also in new ways. Military historians have described the influx of psychological experts into the Second World War British military as a move on the part of new leaders looking to modernize the organizations, especially in the case of the Army (Crang 2000; French 2001; Field 2011a). What is often overlooked is why the military opted for psychologists rather than other forms of expertise, and why psychologists might want to do this sort of work. Psychologists offered the appearance of a scientific new approach, even when held to produce the same sort of results as older systems, just on a different scale. They proved their practical credentials by working with and within large organizations to develop large-scale programs that built on existing methods and expertise. Hundreds of thousands of men and women underwent psychological testing to be allocated to a suitable role. Even just to operate the various schemes, a great number of people had to be trained in psychological principles and methods to administer the testing programs. Previously, most psychologists in Britain had been confined to often short-term investigations of specific problems that organizations faced, "problem" people or groups, school-leavers, and factory hands. With the need to mobilize the entire country under conditions of total war, psychologists were able to select people for many different roles, and even investigate leaders and question what made a good manager. Moreover, they took every opportunity to ensure that business leaders were aware of their work. Organizational psychology had begun its boom.

Patronage and the Professionalization of Organizational Psychology

At the end of the war, one psychologist explained in wonder that the psychologists who had gone to work with the military "may have no profound grasp of psychopathology, but they can teach us something in the way of practical psychology... in the practical handling of negotiations" (King 1989). This epitomizes both the advances that had been made by organizational psychology and the skepticism with which it was still viewed by academics. After the war, organizational psychologists in Britain flung them into establishing their organizational work as a respectable field of scientific endeavor by establishing research institutes and groups, ensuring that their work could be published, and securing funding.

The Tavistock Institute of Human Relations (TIHR) was officially founded in 1947 with the support of a grant from the Rockefeller Foundation. The TIHR was created by psychologists and psychiatrists who had worked with the British military and who were keen to continue their organizational studies. Long before the war, Tavistock staff had expended lots of time and effort in seeking Rockefeller funding, competing with the psychiatrists at the Maudsley for patronage (Jones and Rahman 2009). It was the interdisciplinary and organization-focused approach they developed during the war that finally enabled them to secure it. External funding for research most often supported projects that were interdisciplinary and problem-focused (House 2008). Organizational psychology benefitted from this funding because its foundations lay in practical problem-solving involving teams of experts working with organizations. The 1945 funding proposal to the Rockefeller contains the first proposal bringing together all of the components that would come to be defined as organization development (Burnes and Cooke 2013), which would later be popularized by the group surrounding Kurt Lewin.

The relationships established with industry leaders and influencers during the war provided valuable sources of income and projects for research after the war beyond Rockefeller too, which was crucial to the TIHR's survival. Right away, the Post Office asked for help with personnel problems and asked for help with selection and training, and Unilever asked Bridger to help them develop a WOSB-like program to select managers (Trahair 2015). Soon afterwards, Stafford Cripps formed a Productivity Committee with a Human Factors Panel administered by the Medical Research Council, which funded several projects led by psychologists who had worked on WOSBs, including the Glacier Project and the Longwall Coal Mining Project (Trist 2008).

Elliott Jaques headed the project at Glacier Metals, where he and his team studied psychological factors in group morale, productivity, stress, and attitudes. With this project, as with the military work and the subsequent TIHR research, an "action research" technique was used that involved collaboration with the people in the organization that has requested the consultation on everything from what the problems are that exist, how problems might be resolved, and even how this should be written about afterwards. Significant findings from the Glacier Project were that people become frustrated when their roles and status are unclear, and people in managing positions sometimes avoid responsibility and exercising their authority by delegating too much (Hickson and Pugh 2012; Jaques 2013). Jaques also went on to theorize about the relationship between time-periods that people were trusted to work independently and how their pay should correspond (Hickson and Pugh 2012).

The Mining Project run by Eric Trist was much more difficult to establish than the Glacier Project. The Coal Board was perplexed that, despite having brought in expensive new technology that had significantly increased production in America, productivity was not increasing in British mines: in fact, the opposite was true as absenteeism and group rivalries arose. One of Trist's research fellows, Ken Bamforth, had been a miner and was able to get his former pit in Yorkshire to agree to participate in a study of a mine using the new technology. They found that social systems were considered completely separately from technical systems and argued instead for a socio-technical approach that incorporated the ways that people liked to work and found rewarding with methods that enabled them to operate new machinery (Karwowski 2006). They created smaller groups of workers using a variety of skills and allowed workers to select their team members. The Divisional Board soon shutdown the project because of concerns about publicizing the information that some pits had autonomous working groups. The same thing happened in the East Midlands. Finally, James Nimmo (a Pembroke alumnus, like Trist) agreed for them to conduct research in Durham, where they also had the support of the National Union of Mineworkers (1955; Guillén 1994; Trist 2008).

Keen to establish whether the socio-technical system would be applicable in other places, Trist agreed that he and his colleague Kenneth Rice would work for Gautam Sarabhai to resolve issues at his Ahmedabad calico mills (Trahair 2015). Trist worked on the selection of executives in London and Rice went to India to investigate whether implementing autonomous groups would improve performance. The groups involved in the study from the outset agreed to the experiment and performance increased, but some managers in other locations and newly appointed managers refused to implement the autonomous working groups (Miller 1975).

Whether or not you agree with their findings, these studies have had a significant impact on the field of organizational psychology, introducing new research focuses on attitudes to periodicity and the relationships of people to technology.

Publicizing New Work in Organizational Psychology

As Muldoon explains elsewhere in this handbook, the academic spread of human relations was limited in the 1930s because there were very few academic jobs and journals to maintain the research (▶ Chap. 23, "Spontaneity is the Spice of Management: Elton Mayo's Hunt for Cooperation" by J. Muldoon, this volume). By the late 1940s, the practitioners of human relations and organizational psychology had learned from these prewar difficulties and did all they could to publish papers on their work and establish a respectable scientific reputation among their peers as well as among the businesses and organizations who used their consultancy services.

In 1947, Tavistock Publications was founded to publicize the research of the Institute and in the same year, the TIHR and the Research Center for Group Dynamics (initially based at MIT and then at the University of Michigan) collaborated to produce *Human Relations*, which became "the leading journal in the field of organizations for almost two decades" (Guillén 1994). Eric Trist described the journal as one of the actions that the group took "to get a reputable name for the Tavistock Institute" because their articles "wouldn't have been accepted by any of the other British psychological journals" (Trist 2008). Paul Edwards' recent analysis of the journal's early contents seem to bear this out, noting that the majority of articles had very few citations and only half had any discussion of research methods (Edwards 2016). Cooke and Banerjee go so far as to argue that rather than simply being an outcome of the relationship between the TIHR and the Research Center, the journal was the boundary object around which they formed their alliance (Banerjee and Cooke 2012).

Despite the existence of the journal, the psychologists still often found it difficult to publish their work because of the nature of their consultancy projects. Rice was blamed by Jaques for the discontinuation of the Glacier Project because Rice wrote about the work without clearing his publication with the trade union (Trahair 2015). Similarly, even after moving around three different coal mines to find one amenable to their work, Trist and his colleagues could not get them to agree to them publishing about the autonomous working groups (Trist 2008).

Conclusion

The path to professionalizing organizational psychology in Britain was not a smooth one. For the TIHR, which applied psychology and therefore lay beyond academia, there were numerous challenges: organizations broke off consultations, collaborators and other psychologists blocked the publication of findings, and funding was a continual source of concern. Nonetheless, organizational psychology grew enormously in scale and influence from the 1940s to 1970. Those working in the psychological sciences today are still concerned about how to efficiently collaborate on a large scale (Diener 2006) and the consultation projects of this earlier era offer valuable insights.

The war provided opportunities for psychologists to apply their ideas on an unprecedented scale. Their scientific approach appeared to offer something new and promising when people despaired of traditional methods to solve personnel problems such as selection and leadership. As well as offering a solution to the British military's organizational challenges, wartime work drew together thinkers that had a significant impact on organizational psychology and gave them opportunities for connections and research. The Tavistock Institute was founded out of the group who created the WOSBs. Canadians Edward Bott, Brock Chisholm, and Eliot Jaques also worked on the WOSBs and went on to make substantial contributions to organizational psychology. Thousands of others were trained in psychological principles and methods to carry out psychological testing, and hundreds of thousands underwent the testing, experiencing applied psychological methods for the first time and demonstrating that people were willing to be subjected to the psychological gaze (Rose and Miller 2008).

The selection methods have also provided remarkably enduring. The Army Officer Selection Board still in place today builds upon WOSBs methods and Civil Service Selection Boards were established on the same model. Other organizations and other nations adopted WOSBs practices too. During the war, British psychologists worked with colleagues in America to share their methods with the Office for Strategic Services (Banks 1995) and WOSB methods were adopted in Commonwealth nations including Canada and India (Copp and McAndrew 1990). Organizations ranging from fire services to consumer goods firms like Unilever adopted WOSBs approaches to selecting people for management roles (Trist and Murray 1990).

CRUs transformed how people thought about the psychology of POWs and drew more psychologists and industrial leaders into organizational psychology. These and the work of the Expert Committee showcased the possibilities of organizational psychology to people in a position to commission such projects and resulted in various consultations, projects and opportunities for the TIHR specifically and for organizational psychology more broadly over the next few decades.

The resulting postwar work is perhaps not as well-known as the iconic Hawthorne Studies but has shaped management and organizational psychology thinking. Peter Drucker has called Jaques' work at Glacier "the most extensive study of actual worker behavior in large-scale industry" (Drucker 2016). The socio-technical approach which developed from the postwar projects that ran in the 1950s and early 1960s was influential in its time and had a subsequent impact on Swedish initiatives to humanize work in the late 1960s and early 1970s, and the Quality of Working Life approach (Yousuf 1995). It has been described as "one of the most enduring products of the human relations movement" and continues to be widely used by industry into the twenty-first century (Midgley 2001; Latham 2007).

Work to establish publishing outlets, and the nature of funding in this era, from places such as the Ford Foundation, Rockefeller Foundation, the Industrial Productivity Committee, and the Department of Scientific and Industrial Research helped to support and legitimize organizational psychology (Guillén 1994) in a way that had not been possible in Mayo's era.

The development of these new theories, methods, organizations, publishing outlets, and funding opportunities from 1940 to 1970 resulted in a "golden era" for organizational psychology.

Cross-References

▶ Kurt Lewin: Organizational Change
▶ Organizational Psychology and the Rise of Human Resource Management
▶ Spontaneity is the Spice of Management: Elton Mayo's Hunt for Cooperation

References

(1941) Army misfits. The Times 2
(1942) House of commons debate: captain Margesson's Statement, Hansard, Volume 377, London. https://hansard.parliament.uk/Commons/1942-02-19/debates/51bf3636-3e17-4a1a-82fe-9149621de363/CaptainMargessonSStatement
(1944) Personnel selection in the British Army: recruits. Ministry of information. UKY 591, Imperial War Museum, London. https://www.iwm.org.uk/collections/item/object/1060005150
(1955) Tavistock Institute: comparative study of three mining systems. Wellcome Library SATIH/B/2/3/1/5, London
Ahrenfeldt RH (1958) Psychiatry in the British Army in the second world war. Routledge & K. Paul, London
Banerjee A, Cooke B (2012) How human relations got its name: the journal as boundary object. Tavistock Institute of Human Relations, London
Banks LMI (1995) The office of strategic services psychological selection program. U.S. Army Command and General Staff College, Fort Leavenworth
Bartlett FC (1942) Memorandum for the expert committee on the work of psychologists and psychiatrists in the services: an experiment in validation, CAB 89/25, The National Archives, Kew
Bhawuk DPS (2008) Towards an Indian organizational psychology. In: Dalal AK, Paranjpe A, Rao KR (eds) Handbook of Indian psychology. Cambridge University, New Delhi, pp 471–491. Foundation Books
Bruton E (2013) "Sacrifice of a genius": Henry Moseley's role as a signals officer in world war one. Royal Society Television. http://royalsociety.tv/rsPlayer.aspx?presentationid=1145. Accessed 21 Oct 2013
Bunn G (2001) Charlie and the chocolate factory: C.S. Myers Memorial Lecture. Psychologist 14:576–579
Burnes B, Cooke B (2013) The Tavistock's 1945 invention of organization development: early British business and management applications of social psychiatry. Bus Hist 55:768–789
Carpintero H (2017) History of organizational psychology. Oxf Res Encycl Psychol. https://doi.org/10.1093/acrefore/9780190236557.013.39
Carson J (1993) Army alpha, army brass, and the search for army intelligence. Isis 84:278–309

Copp T, McAndrew B (1990) Battle exhaustion: soldiers and psychiatrists in the Canadian Army, 1939–1945. McGill-Queen's Press – MQUP, Montreal

Crang JA (1999) Square pegs and round holes: other rank selection in the British Army, 1939–45. J Soc Army Hist Res 77:293–298

Crang JA (2000) The British Army and the People's war, 1939–1945. Manchester University Press, Manchester

Dennis MA (2015) Big science. Encyclopædia Britannica. Online edition, https://www.britannica.com/science/Big-Science-science

Diener E (2006) Introduction to the special section: professional issues in psychological science and a discussion of collaboration indicators. Perspect Psychol Sci 1:312–315

Drucker P (2016) People and performance. Taylor & Francis Group, Routledge, London

Edwards P (2016) Human relations: the first 10 years, 1947–1956. Hum Relat. https://doi.org/10.1177/0018726716635058

English A (1992) Canadian psychologists and the aerodrome of democracy. Can Psychol 33:663–674

Featherman DL, Vinovskis MA (eds) (2001) Social science and policy-making: a search for relevance in the twentieth century. University of Michigan Press, Ann Arbor

Field GG (2011a) Blood, sweat, and toil: remaking the British working class, 1939–1945. Oxford University Press, Oxford

Field GG (2011b) A citizens' Army. In: Remaking the British working class, 1939–1945. Oxford University Press, Oxford, pp 251–297

French D (2001) Raising Churchill's army. Oxford University Press, Oxford

Gale EAM (2004) The Hawthorne studies – a fable for our times? QJM 97:439–449. https://doi.org/10.1093/qjmed/hch070

Gillespie R (1993) Manufacturing knowledge: a history of the Hawthorne experiments. Cambridge University Press, Cambridge

Guillén MF (1994) Models of management: work, authority and organization in a comparative perspective. University of Chicago Press, Chicago

Haig BD, Marie D (2012) New Zealand. In: Baker DB (ed) The Oxford handbook of the history of psychology: global perspectives. Oxford University Press, Oxford, pp 377–394

Hickson PDJ, Pugh PDS (2012) Great writers on organizations, 3rd Omnibus edition. Gower Publishing, Ashgate – Aldershot

House JS (2008) Social psychology, social science, and economics: twentieth century progress and problems, twenty-first century prospects. Soc Psychol Q 71:232–256

Jaques E (2013) The changing culture of a factory. Routledge, London

Jex SM (2002) Organizational psychology: a scientist-practitioner approach. Wiley, Hoboken

Jones E, Rahman S (2009) The Maudsley Hospital and the Rockefeller Foundation: the impact of philanthropy on research and training. J Hist Med Allied Sci 64:273–299

Karwowski W (2006) International encyclopedia of ergonomics and human factors, 2nd edn, 3 volume set. CRC Press, Boca Raton

Katzell RA, Austin JT (1992) From then to now: the development of industrial-organizational psychology in the United States. J Appl Psychol 77:803–835. https://doi.org/10.1037/0021-9010.77.6.803

King P (1989) Activities of British psychoanalysts during the second world war and the influence of their inter-disciplinary collaboration on the development of psychoanalysis in Great Britain. Int Rev Hist Psychanal 16:14–33

Koppes LL (2014) Historical perspectives in industrial and organizational psychology. Psychology Press, New York

Koppes Bryan LL (2012) A history of industrial and organizational psychology. In: Kozlowski SWJ (ed) The Oxford handbook of organizational psychology. Oxford University Press, New York, pp 22–76

Kozlowski SWJ (2012) The Oxford handbook of organizational psychology. Oxford University Press, New York

Latham GP (2007) Work motivation: history, theory, research, and practice. Sage, Thousand Oaks

Midgley G (2001) Systemic intervention: philosophy, methodology, and practice. Springer Science & Business Media, New York

Miller EJ (1975) Socio-technical systems in weaving, 1953–1970: a follow-up study. Hum Relat 28:349–386. https://doi.org/10.1177/001872677502800403

Nixon M, Taft R (2013) Psychology in Australia: achievements & prospects. Elsevier, Sydney

Rabinbach A (1992) The human motor: energy, fatigue, and the origins of modernity. University of California Press, Berkeley

Rose N, Miller P (2008) Governing the present: administering economic, social and personal life. Polity, Cambridge, UK

Takooshian H (2012) Industrial-organizational psychology. In: Rieber RW (ed) Encyclopedia of the history of psychological theories. Springer US, New York, pp 563–566

Thalassis N (2004) Treating and preventing trauma: British military psychiatry during the second world war. University of Salford

The Editors of Encyclopaedia Britannica (2016) Industrial-organizational psychology. Encyclopædia Britannica

Trahair R (2015) Behavior, technology, and organizational development: Eric Trist and the Tavistock Institute. Transaction Publishers, New Brunswick

Triandis HC (1994) Cross-cultural industrial and organizational psychology. In: Dunnette MD, Hough LM, Triandis HC (eds) Handbook of industrial and organizational psychology. Consulting Psychologists Press, Palo Alto, pp 103–172

Trist E (2008) "Guilty of Enthusiasm", from management laureates. In: Bedeian AG (ed) The modern times workplace, vol 3. Jai Press, Greenwich 1993. http://www.moderntimesworkplace.com/archives/ericbio/ericbio.html. Accessed 24 Oct 2012

Trist EL, Murray DH (1990) The social engagement of social science: the socio-psychological perspective. Free Association Books, London

Ungerson B (1950) Mr Morris on officer selection. Occup Psychol 24:54–57

Ussishkin D (2011) The 'will to work': industrial management and the question of conduct in interwar Britain. In: Beers L, Thomas G (eds) Brave new world. School of Advanced Study, University of London, London, pp 91–108

Vernon PE, Parry JB (1949) Personnel selection in the British forces. University of London Press, London

Vinchur AJ (2018) The early years of industrial and organizational psychology. Cambridge University Press, Cambridge

Vinden FH (1977) The introduction of war office selection boards in the British Army: a personal recollection. In: Bond B, Roy I (eds) War and society: a yearbook of military history. Routledge, London

Viteles MS (1932) Industrial psychology. W.W. Norton, New York

Warr P (2014) Some historical developments in I-O psychology outside the United States. In: Koppes LL (ed) Historical perspectives in industrial and organizational psychology. Psychology Press, New York, pp 81–110

Weatherburn M (2019) Human relations' invented traditions: sociotechnical research and worker motivation at the interwar Rowntree cocoa works. Hum Relat. https://doi.org/10.1177/0018726719846647

Webster EC (1988) I/O psychology in Canada: from birth to Couchiching. Can Psychol 29:4–10. https://doi.org/10.1037/h0079757

White A (2016) From the science of selection to psychologising civvy street: the Tavistock Group, 1939–1948. PhD, University of Kent, Canterbury

Yousuf SMA (1995) Quality of working life as a function of socio-technical system. Mittal Publications, New Delhi

British Management 1950–1980

John Quail

Contents

General Business Context at 1950	874
Business Management: Structure and Performance 1950–80	879
Managerial Capacity in UK Companies 1950–80	883
References	885

Abstract

The governance, managerial structures, and functional performance of large British companies at the end of World War II had preserved intact that in existence before the War: proprietorial governance (Quail 1996, 2000), sparse or nonexistent top management, poor financial planning and control, functional silos, and weak coordination of production and marketing. The nature of and changes in British management over the period to 1980 were conditioned by the slow changes in the preexisting company culture and structure, foreign competition, the role of the State, and the resurgent City of London and finance capital leading to a merger boom and great increases in the size of businesses. The general story is of a slowly increasing managerial professionalization and capability emerging during an escalating crisis of competitiveness into the 1970s and beyond. At the same time developments in company law, state regulation and intervention, and activist finance began to create a new environment within which managements had to operate and which conditioned managerial structures, skills, and priorities. In short by 1980 a managerial revolution of a kind was emerging within the firm but operation remained constrained by tradition and the external forces of financialization and global competition. The chapter starts with a general description of the business context within which management operated including a brief

J. Quail (✉)
York Management School, University of York, York, UK
e-mail: jq504@york.ac.uk

© The Author(s), under exclusive licence to Springer Nature Switzerland AG 2020
B. Bowden et al. (eds.), *The Palgrave Handbook of Management History*,
https://doi.org/10.1007/978-3-319-62114-2_38

analysis of the prewar "inheritance" in terms of firm governance, organizational structures and recruitment, and the relative performance of UK business in an international context. There then follows a more detailed account of UK governance and management structure recruitment and performance. The general conclusion is that by 1980 preconditions for a possible managerialist transformation of UK business were being established.

Keywords

UK management structures · Proprietorial management · Managerial capacity · Slow management change

General Business Context at 1950

The position and prospects for UK management and managers in 1950 did not look immediately promising. The 1939–45 War had seen immense efforts in production, in technological innovation, and in mass production. Yet in the process it laid bare huge deficits across UK industry in capacity, skill, and organization. Barnett, for example, gives numerous examples of poor performance, poor quality management, and poor management of quality, frequently quoting UK government sources (Barnett 1986). The organizational incapacity revealed does not come as a particular surprise, however, if one considers the governance, organizational structures, and skill sets of the overwhelming majority of UK companies in the interwar years. The problems stemmed primarily from UK company governance structures which were based on the requirements of UK company law which originated in a strict separation of office holders/employees from the board – designed as an elected committee of shareholders working for the interests of the body of shareholders as a whole. As firms grew and became more complex, committees of directors were formed to oversee parts of the business with departmental officers in attendance as when required. Boards were generally part time though the Chair would often be in more frequent attendance, sometimes even full-time. The 1908 Companies Act permitted the appointment of managing directors who were also not required to be full time. The result was that there was generally no full-time professional top management below the board and interdepartmental coordination was largely ad hoc. As the scale and scope of business expanded in the interwar years the internal organizational responses to the imperatives of complexity and growth were grudging and minimal (Quail 1996, 2000). With a few – a very few – exceptions, Scientific Management was not adopted by UK industry. Smith and Boyns conclude that in the great majority of cases British managements applied piecework systems rather than planning systems, organization design, and management task definition and ignored planning with objectives and targets (Smith and Boyns 2005). Marketing in the interwar years became cumulatively managed by Trade Associations, cartels, or other restrictive agreements (Mercer 1995, passim).

Recruitment of managers in the interwar years, and indeed after the war, was nepotistic and, where it was not, largely privileged public school boys. The Acton Society Trust found in 1956 that less than 10% of managers born before 1895 were public school educated but this increased to 30% of managers born between 1920 and 1924 who would have started work aged 16 or so around 1940. Once recruited, the same source says, public schoolboys were more likely to achieve promotion and rise to top management than entrants from other types of schools (Acton Society Trust 1956). There is a not inconsiderable literature boosting the leadership qualities and moral character of the public schoolboy for industrial management despite considerable evidence raising serious doubts on their commitment and ability (Quail 1998). International economic rivals like Germany or the United States recruited relevantly qualified graduates for industrial posts. That public schoolboys were considered suitable managerial material after what has been called a "Cook's Tour" of the firms various departments followed, if lucky, by a personal assistant appointment to a manager (Keeble 1992, p. 141) is as much a statement about the limited amount of knowledge and experience apparently considered necessary as it is about patronage-based recruitment.

A partially and then fully protected and cartelized economy in the 1920s and 1930s followed by the closed economy of World War II left UK business with rather less than optimal managerial resources and a maladaptive business culture as it faced an evolving and competitive global economy after the war. Nevertheless "[a]t midcentury, and after the catastrophic disruption of World War II, Britain accounted for 25 percent of world manufactured exports compared to 27 percent for the United States, 9 percent for Germany and 3 percent for Japan..." (Jones 1997, 112ff). Figures for overall UK Gross Domestic Product per hour worked show that while the UK had fallen behind the USA by 1900 it was not until 1970 "that the other large European economies reached British levels...." But while "(d)uring the 1950s and 1960s British productivity grew at a much faster rate than for decades... it grew much faster still in in most of Western Europe and Japan [who between the 1950s and 1973] narrowed the large technological gap which had existed between themselves and the United States" (Jones 1997, pp. 112, 113). The consequence was that by 1975 Britain's share of world exports was 9% (Jones 1997, p. 113), resulting in increased import penetration. "In 1983 for the first time since the Industrial Revolution, Britain imported more manufactured goods in value than it exported" (Jones 1997, p. 113). The fate of some sectors was striking: cotton textiles lost most of their export markets and faced great import penetration. In 1950 the UK produced one-third of world shipping output "but 30 years later British shipbuilding was a marginal force in the world industry." In 1950 "the country was the world's greatest car exporter ... But over the next decade export markets were steadily lost" imports began to grow – 5% in 1965, 33% by 1975 (Jones 1997, p. 114). British passenger car production fell from 1.9 million to 880,000 between 1972 and 1982 (Jones 1997, pp. 112–117).

The reasons advanced for this reverse were generally poor management, labor recalcitrance, or foreign competition. Management performance will be a central theme in later sections but during the years 1950–80 labor was a particularly popular object of criticism. The US ambassador to London in the late 1940s opined that "the only answer to Britain's problems is to work harder and, I fear, for less." A historian of the Marshall Plan comments: "In subsequent years popular discussion of productivity in British industry rarely rose much above this level. During the 1950s British employers would join the chorus and, with considerable success, lay the charge of sloth at the door of organised labour" (Carew 1987, p. 136). By the 1960s and 1970s this charge, it is persuasively argued, provided deep cover for bad management policies, decisions, and practices (Williams et al. 1983, pp. 251–258).

The use of productivity – GDP per labor hour – as the key measure of industrial efficiency can tend to privilege a labor-centric focus and ignore other highly relevant structural and institutional factors. A wider and rather more convincing analysis of British industrial failings is given by Williams et al. in their "Why Are the British Bad at Manufacturing?" A loose summary of their approach would that the problem of foreign competition faced by British firms was compounded by difficulties in accessing investment and a takeover boom in our period but were largely the consequence of the failings of management. The "distraction effect of bad working practices and labour disputes is less important than commonly supposed. Ineffectual management is immediately responsible for the non-price deficiencies of British manufactures" (Williams et al. 1983, p. 46). The areas of weakness are identified as the absence of "enterprise calculation" (essentially a combination of research, strategy, and planning), a lack of understanding of the nature of the changing national and international "composition of demand," and the consequential failure to design, produce, and market saleable goods. On top of the "problems of differentiated national demand" UK enterprise faced "problems of international distribution" (Williams et al. 1983, p. 48). British shipbuilding declined because, with the exception of one company (sic!), British shipbuilders continued building relatively small bespoke vessels for British shipping companies while developing world demand was for much larger standardized and mass produced vessels. UK overseas car sales were undermined by poor distribution, marketing, and servicing (ibid., pp. 49–58). These internal deficiencies were compounded by difficulties in accessing investment and the disruption caused by a merger boom starting in the 1960s. Meanwhile it is asserted that "after our review of the evidence and arguments about labour productivity and costs we could conclude that British industry's workplace performance is quite reasonable. The evidence shows that [UK] labour productivity performance is respectable in relative international terms" (Willams et al., p. 41).

The Chandler argument that the failures in UK enterprise stemmed from the failure to build multidivisional organizations with a top strategic management making investment decisions is considered overly simplistic and rigid by Williams et al. Citing Kantor, they say it is essential to have improvisation and innovation at middle management levels which provides the strategic options, appraises them, and proceeds to manufacture and marketing those that are approved by a top management exercising "enterprise calculation" (Kantor 1982). These are the necessary precondition for success. "The quality and marketing of UK manufacturing products has nothing to do with labour disputes and is the province of senior management."

The "distraction effect of bad working practices and labour disputes is less important than commonly supposed. Ineffectual management is immediately responsible for the non-price deficiencies of British manufactures" (Williams et al., p. 46).

The role of the UK government in the postwar economy was initially spectacular with the Labour government's program of nationalizations. But more generally the postwar Labour and Conservative governments did not pursue an activist industrial policy "except those considered essential for national security and national prestige: aircraft and computers. Apart from Rolls Royce (jet engines) US companies with huge domestic markets largely overwhelmed the UK aircraft and computer industries...there was no industrial policy" (Owen 2009, p. 50). The British state did however take a more activist role in competition policy. The post–World War II boom engaged an industry structurally indistinguishable from the prewar years. Indeed the War had strengthened the power of the already pervasive trade associations which had acted as intermediaries between government and industry during the war. Retail Price Maintenance had effectively stopped price competition in many areas of activity (Mercer 1995, p. 141). The British government became concerned and it was a wartime coalition government's 1944 White Paper that put down a marker that "Employers... must seek in larger output rather than higher prices the reward of enterprise and good management. There has in recent years been a growing tendency towards combines and toward agreements, both national and international, by which manufacturers have sought to control prices and output, to divide markets and fix conditions of sale. Such agreements or combines do not necessarily operate against the public interest; but the power to do so is there. The Government will therefore seek power to inform themselves of the extent and effect of restrictive agreements, and of the activities of combines; and to take appropriate action to check practices which may bring advantages to sectional producing interests but work to the detriment of the country as a whole (BPP 1943–44, quoted Mercer 1995, p. 54). The responsibility to see this through passed to a Labour government in 1945 given extra impulsion "when the incoming Attlee administration found itself with the urgent necessity of increasing productivity to close the post-war dollar gap and ensure economic survival" (Francis 1992, p. 1). As Mercer puts it: "[b]y 1945...the tenacity of potentially price-fixing and output-restricting trade associations presented a contradictory force in an expansionist world economy, while the trade associations themselves formed a formidable *political* barrier..." (Mercer 1995, p. 35).

Legislation was inevitable, the more so as the US pressure grew to remove national and international cartels in its postwar sphere of influence. The result, the 1948 Monopolies and Restrictive Practices Act did not work well; the outcome was muffled and ineffective due to industrial resistance and minimal powers in the Act to gain information and enforce compliance. Further legislation by the successor Conservative government, the Restrictive Trade Practices Act 1956, was more successful and required "the registration of all agreements between two or more persons producing, supplying or processing manufactured goods which fixed prices and discounts, allocated quotas and markets, or stipulated methods of manufacture" (Mercer 1995, p. 126). The Registrar was empowered to refer such agreements to a powerful Restrictive Practices Court. If the Court found agreements restrictive they became automatically void. However, the Act in practice only affected cartels while large firms "in monopolistic positions or using monopolistic practices [were] often specially exempted from legislation" (Mercer 1995, p. 127). The result was that the Act did not "create a paradise of free atomistic competition" (which may have been initially intended) "but, in the long run ... contribute[d] to the overall tendency of twentieth-century British business towards concentration and oligopoly" (Mercer 1995, p. 125) through anticompetitive mergers.

It was not the only force easing the path toward concentration. A clause in the 1948 Companies Act, whose wider potential appears little noticed at the time, stated that any director could be removed by an ordinary resolution of the shareholders. Directors had hitherto generally been subject to periodic re-election at company Annual General Meetings of shareholders but this new power for shareholders meant that the balance of power between shareholders now effectively presented as "owners" and directors as their "employees" had shifted very significantly: it enabled hostile takeovers that could immediately remove sitting directors and insert others (Segrestin et al. 2018). Previously, outsiders intending to acquire a majority of voting shares would have had considerable difficulty in doing so and, if successful, would have been involved in protracted trench warfare with sitting directors. As the City of London recovered after wartime restrictions were lifted and the quantity of ordinary stock in circulation and in the hands of financial institutions increased, the enhanced power of shareholders allowed hostile takeover to flourish, further increasing the tendency toward concentration and the growth of firms.

Before consideration of the spectacular growth of firms in the period 1950–80 it is prudent to first set out the particular – and peculiar – make-up of UK companies' capital and revenue structure in this period. Unlike European and US companies that relied heavily on bank lending to finance current capital expenditure, UK companies had much less access to this source because the security required was based on a liquidation approach, namely fixed assets. European, Japanese, and US banks used a more liberal going-concern approach monitored via a series of liquidity and gearing ratios (Williams et al. 1983, p. 69). "To a remarkable degree British companies have financed investment out of internally generated funds, [the Wilson Committee] showed that from 1964 to 1975 retained earnings averaged 70 per cent of total funds available" while "the banks and the stock exchange supplied roughly equal proportions of the 25 per cent of available funds that were externally provided." The stock exchange finance was debt (debentures) rather than equity (Williams et al., p. 59). "British companies did emerge from the Second World War flush with liquid assets, and reserves were considerable through the 1950s... But by the mid 1960s this liquidity reserve was exhausted... From the early 1960s onwards therefore, the sustainable rate of expansion in the corporate sector depended on profit, or the surplus earned on existing assets" (Williams et al., p. 61). However, the average rate of profit in British manufacturing dropped from approximately 13% in 1960 to 3% in 1978 (Williams et al. 1983, p. 63). The implications were emphatically restrictive. However, in the particular circumstances of UK enterprise calculation "assets double as production and financial assets. Enterprises may therefore pursue trading profit or growth through the purchase of assets as well, or instead of, using those assets to produce final products" (Williams et al., p. 77). The lack of liquid funds from profits led to takeovers financed more or less entirely by new issues of shares by acquiring companies. This enabled a great increase in firm concentration; Prais shows that by 1970, 100 firms were responsible for half of UK manufacturing output – in 1958 this had taken 420 firms (Prais 1976).

Whether from the perspective of efficiency and rationalization of production or increased profits the results were disappointing. Meeks' study of approximately 1000 firms shows that the profitability in the 7 years after merger in the majority of cases was below the sum of that achieved separately by the premerger firms in the 3 years before merger (Meeks 1977).

The end of the 1970s, therefore, presents a landscape of much larger firms, performing less well financially, faced with difficulties in raising finance and the task of optimizing the structure and performance of their companies in a world made more difficult by the depressed economic situation following the dramatic rise in oil prices in 1974 following the formation of a cartel of Oil Producing and Exporting Countries (OPEC). An influential 1970s management history literature, however, accentuates the positive picture of the ownership, strategy, and structure of UK firms finding it closer to the American than any other European economy in terms of company size, separation between ownership and control, and adoption of the multidivisional structure (Channon 1973; Hannah 1976). The actual capacity and performance of the new greatly enlarged firms to perform like the large US multidivisional companies is very questionable, however, as Meeks' study suggests, and requires further examination of the relation of firm structure to firm performance.

Business Management: Structure and Performance 1950–80

In general terms the physical and ideological structure of UK companies at the beginning of the postwar period was, as we have seen, that the directors and managers of a company were sharply different in status, and there was no top management structure below the Board, coordination of departments being the responsibility of a managing director or through board functional or departmental committees. Contemporary early postwar commentary from members of the small UK-managerialist avant-garde is helpful in identifying both the scope for and limits to change. Lyndal Urwick's 1954 pamphlet, *The Load on Top Management – Can It Be Reduced?*, asserts that the size and complexity of companies has grown immensely. The consequences for the "top manager" are the increasingly difficult requirement to coordinate/reconcile the managers of different and growing number of specialisms involved, together with relations with employees, customers, and government as well as ensuring smooth production and disruptive innovation. (This reference to a "top manager" is interesting because it easily applies to the US CEO or European structures but points an accusatory finger by implication at the UK managing director or chairman/proprietor and the more diffuse command structure of UK companies).

There follows a set of recommendations for adapting the organization for the new circumstances:

- Adopt a formal organization pattern with exact definitions of jobs and functions
- Divorce policy making (the Board) from execution (the Management)
- Separate research on policy making from policy execution
- Unify ultimate responsibility in a single chief executive
- Provide specialist assistance for industrial relations
- Provide specialist assistance for public relations
- Provide expert general staff assistance to the CEO

Finally the "separate businesses" within the firm should be decentralized – a reference is made to General Motors, implying a divisional structure.

This list would appear to encompass everything the great majority of large UK. Businesses were **not** doing with the exception of the separation of the board from management which was endemic and not noticeably accompanied by synergy. The assumption that UK boards generally had the capacity to develop policy in a form that was executable by management was optimistic. Nevertheless it was not impossible. A notable case is the United Steel Companies. The company published an admirably professional and clear series of lectures by its senior staff to the Engineering School at Cambridge in 1953 complete with organization charts, investment and financial planning systems, budgetary control, company structure – originating in a merger of four companies which had evolved into a decentralized structure somewhere between the functional and divisional form – and research, staff recruitment, and training (United Steel Companies Limited 1953).

The kind of practical problems of growth and complexity where expansion is rapid and innovative are addressed by Charles Renold in his pamphlet *The Organizational Structure of Large Undertakings – Management Problems* (Renold 1949). Renold, an owner/employer and a pioneer in management practice and management education, addresses the growth of his company involving an increasing diversity of specialisms and markets and dispersed operating units. The consequence is a growing difficulty of centralized management particularly when "several levels of authority have to be recognised and you have a multi-tier structure." One major difficulty is the communication of the "feel of the situation" from the units to the top. Another is establishing that the delegated powers from the top to the unit are being used correctly. The internal functional hierarchies must not be turned into spies. The choice appears to be between a new body of internal advisors or commissars, and is not resolved. These rapid changes are taking place in an organization which had emerged from a merger of three firms before the War to form what appears to have been a true M-form but which rapid development now appeared to be disrupting. The paper is of particular interest because of its uncertainty given that Renold had established a high-quality budgetary control system between the wars which would have seemed adaptable as company-wide corporate plan and out-turn method subject to audit. In any case the firm survived and prospered.

It would be wrong therefore to conclude that British Management was trapped entirely without options by its historic legacy. Indeed at board level there were shifts in perspective. *The Director*, the journal of the Institute of Directors, suggested that the composition of company boards and the role of the director were shifting to a merging of director and managerial roles to some degree. In a discussion on the appointment of a replacement when a part-time director retires, it is stated that full-time executive directors expect the "place to be filled from inside by a full time executive" and that there "is a noticeable tendency, particularly in manufacturing industry for the proportion of of full-time members of company boards to increase" (Copeman 1952a). The proprietorial standing of a directorship and the necessity for a new director to take up "a large holding" of shares was questioned: "If this were done it would limit the scope of appointments. Many suitable candidates had very little capital" (Copeman 1952b). A manufacturing employer wrote "If trend there be today, surely it is toward a board composed perhaps a majority of executive directors, with a number of non-executive directors who can bring not only other and perhaps wider experience but also a measure of detachment" (Tyzac 1960). There was also some anecdotal evidence of increased mobility up managerial hierarchies and from senior management to the board (G H Copeman, *The Director,* Vol 4 No.1, Oct 1952).

This is consistent with other evidence on the declining role of inherited positions in British companies: the proportion of founders and inheritors among chairmen decreased from 21% in 1907 to 4% in 1989, and for managing directors from 34% to 2%. Eight percent of the top 100 industrial companies were under personal ownership in 1983 and 4% in 1993. But social mobility did not ensue: business leaders, in the nineteenth and even more so in the twentieth century, were in their overwhelming majority (around 80%) recruited from the upper and upper middle classes – landowners, businessmen, senior civil servants, and professionals, and in the 1960s, more than half were themselves sons of businessmen. By the 1990s, however, there was "a sharp increase in the proportion of business leaders originating from a working class and lower middle class background: 39% for the generation active 1989" (All, p. 87). By 1998 25% of the top 100 directors in 1998 had come from a lower middle and 11% from a lower class background. So the "possibility of reaching the top appears to have increased by about 10–15% for individuals coming from a less privileged background" (Cassis 2009, pp. 86–88).

The discussion so far has largely considered the governance structure of large UK companies, and the changing recruitment to senior positions within it over time. However, the environment within which UK companies were operating was particularly stormy in the 1960s and 1970s not least the growth of firms in as a result of the merger boom where the span of control lengthened considerably. It is sensible to approach the nature of the resulting organizations holistically. It is not enough to concentrate on firm structure, or to ascribe aspirational modernity to a particular organizational form like the M-form and award points for adopting it. Companies need to survive and prosper. Their resources in manpower, technical expertise, marketing skills, and the specifics of their existing management structure and quality govern their options. The literature is not short of surveys and studies which are generally critical in our period, particularly where comparisons are made with the capabilities of US firms.

A number of studies and surveys of this literature are usefully gathered in Wilson and Thomson (2006) and give a very downbeat picture. Firstly there was a wide variation in investment in machinery and its efficient usage, with performance generally below that of US manufacturers whose managements were superior at all levels. The variation in UK management quality is identified as the reason for the variation in productivity levels in UK firms. Management quality manifested itself in the use of budgetary control and long term planning, in greater capital investment, in production based on sales requirements rather than production dominating sales, on work study, and so on. US subsidiaries in the UK earned close to double the profits than UK companies in the period 1950–64. British top management did not coordinate or control the activities of their separate units or functions effectively, the result of a deliberate strategy of decentralization, and a reluctance to create middle level jobs with wide responsibility. This was the consequence of the holding company form favored in mergers combined with a proprietorial tradition of an aloof board membership of "'practical men' and gentlemanly amateurs" (Coleman 1973, p. 113) which was not prepared to dilute its sovereignty by significant delegations to functional or middle management (Quail 2002).

However, a rather different picture emerges from a study by Higgins and Toms of 200 UK quoted companies between 1950 and 1984 (Higgins and Toms 2012). Their aim is to "present an empirically rigorous analysis of the relationship between organisational structure and long run financial performance of British companies" using a sample of 200 companies (p. 108). The rather hectic environment in this period is illustrated by the survival rate of firms: of 3011 quoted companies trading in 1950 only 6% were still trading as independent organizations in 1984. The sample of 200 companies represents the survivors and their study supplies information on the "relationship between firms in the same industry, pursuing similar strategies but using different organisational structures and their financial performance can be examined." The study therefore gives a richer mix and wider appraisal of management performance, company form, and company survival and success. "Profit, unlike size, is more readily compared through time and is more easily related to changes in economic conditions and strategy. As a measure of success, profitability does not rule out the large number of smaller firms that may represent the more dynamic sectors of the economy [and] may include the family firms and networked organisations highlighted as alternatives to Chandler's big business dominated paradigm" (pp. 86–87).

Higgins and Toms find that firms in their sample were more likely to restructure and to adopt the multidivisional form in the 1950s and 1960s than in the 1970s but this was associated with underperformance and failure. Greater success in this period came with the adoption of the holding company. Post 1970 proportions were reversed: greater than 60% of structural changes were associated with top performers and the change most associated with success was change from functional to holding company structures. The multidivision firms in the 1984 sample were a minority "being associated with poor performance as often as superior performance" (p. 109).

An international survey of firms in France, Germany, and the UK by Horovitz allows a more detailed appraisal of a sample of large UK firms in the late 1970s (Horovitz 1980). Horovitz studied 18 companies describing most of them as holding companies where a "small central staff overlooks from twenty to fifty subsidiaries, each headed by a managing director, each having its own products, brands and markets and the necessary logistics to operate (administration, accounting, personnel etc.) Many decisions are decentralised to the subsidiary level while central office staff and directors shape policy decisions at the group level [and] act as bankers for the subsidiaries" (Horovitz 1980, p. 54). There is some prospect of development but it is muted: of the 18 UK companies studied 6 were "holding structure with divisional domains," the latter described as "much more areas of interest than managerial centres" each domain having a chairman, "not always a full-time executive" who sits on the subsidiaries boards and the main board. A further step to order and consolidate diversification is taken in 2 of the 18 companies described as "holding structures with divisions" These are "reinforcing central staff (group services, chief of planning....)" and their divisions now have chief executives with their own small staffs. Note however that "subsidiaries remain the basic product market unit." This view taken together with the findings of Higgins and Toms appears to confirm that by the end of our period the multidivisional structure was not yet a reliable option for many large companies whether from the view that existing examples had not shown promise or that the leap from holding company to multidivisional form required particular management skills that were not available internally or externally except via consultants which carried considerable risks post restructure. The absence of a recruitable body of relevantly experienced managers could well be a significant factor in the lack of success in attempts at the M-form in Higgins and Tom's survey and the tentative explorations in divisional structures found in two companies in Horovitz's sample.

The discussion so far has emphasized the limited organizational capacity of UK management structures looking particularly at their adaptability in changing circumstances. The rigidity of the proprietorial structure of the firm, somewhat modified as our period has proceeded, has shown considerable lack of flexibility and capacity for change. The question must arise as to the organizational and management skills deployed within these structures and the capacity of the managers themselves carry out in day-to-day operations and administration and to adapt and change as external circumstances to ensure survival and hopefully continued survival. The next section will consider the capacity of the managerial hierarchies within the firm.

Managerial Capacity in UK Companies 1950–80

The governance and organizational structures we have discussed so far have shown themselves to be to a minor degree adaptable, demonstrated perhaps by a modest advance in managerial recruitment and career advancement to the board and a toe in the water of divisional structures. Expectations must be therefore also modest in considering managerial organization and operational technique and their managerial performance. A number of studies and surveys give a mixed picture usefully gathered in Wilson and Thomson (2006).

Firstly there was a wide variation in investment in machinery and its efficient usage, with performance below that of US manufacturers where "the greatest single factor in American industrial supremacy over British industry is the effectiveness of its management at all levels" (AACP report quoted, p. 110). The variation in UK management quality is identified as the reason for the variation in productivity levels in UK firms. Management quality manifested itself in the use of budgetary control and long-term planning, in greater capital investment, in production based on sales requirements rather than production dominating sales, on work study, and so on. It is noted that US companies' subsidiaries earned an average after-tax profit of 15.4% while UK companies earned 8.7% in a large sample of companies in the period 1950–64.

There had been considerable efforts to use American mass production techniques in the UK after World War II which were "generally unsuccessful." The reason for this is suggested to be "because few firms had a sufficiently professional management cadre to make them operate efficiently" (Wilson & Thomson (2006), p. 112, ref to Tiratsoo et al. 2003). Granick's (1962) survey of four countries' processes of planning and control concluded that the "American advantage lay in the presence of substantial functional staffs at headquarters, whereas in Britain managerial practice did not require such staffs..." [quoted Wilson & Thomson, p. 112]. British top management "did not coordinate or control the activities of the separate units or functions effectively." This was a deliberate strategy of decentralization and a reluctance "to create middle level jobs with wide responsibility" This was the consequence of the holding company form favored in mergers combined with a proprietorial tradition of an aloof board membership of "'practical men' and gentlemanly amateurs" (Coleman 1973, p. 113) which was not prepared to dilute its sovereignty by significant delegations to functional or middle management (Quail 2002).

The development of trained professional management cadres in depth within the UK firm was therefore a key constituent of improved performance at both enterprise and national economy level. We have seen the structural impediments to this development working within the firm. It useful to note that government was concerned and encouraged management studies degree courses and supported the creation of two business schools in London and Manchester in the 1960s. These schools struggled to establish themselves as institutions and survived largely on foreign students (Wilson 1995, pp. 219–222) is stated elsewhere that the qualifications they produced up to 1981 tended to be used to add a credentialist gloss to more traditional patterns and privileges derived from public school and Oxbridge. Alternatively graduates moved into the developing and lucrative field of consultancy (Whitley et al. 1981). The number of undergraduates taking business courses was tiny in our period – 621 in 1970 rising to 1309 in 1980 (Quail 1999).

The numbers would accelerate rapidly in the 1980s and 1990s, however. This is a factor to add to other observations in this chapter on the increasing presence of senior managers and the decreasing presence of hereditary recruits on the boards of companies, the beginnings of divisionalization out of opportunist and loose holding companies leading to something approaching a managerial revolution in the 1990s. This story I leave to others.

References

Acton Society Trust (1956) Management succession. Acton Society Trust, London
Barnett C (1986) The audit of war. Macmillan, London
BPP (British Parliamentary Papers) (1943–44) Employment policy, vol viii Cmd. 6527 para 54
Carew A (1987) Labour under the Marshall Plan. Manchester University Press, Manchester
Cassis Y (2009) Elites, Entrepreneurs, and British business in the twentieth century. In: Coopey R, Lyth P (eds) Business in Britain in the twentieth century. Oxford University Press, Oxford
Channon D (1973) Strategy & structure of British enterprise. Macmillan, London
Coleman D C (1973) Gentlemen and Players, Economic History Review 2/2
Copeman GH (1952a) The Director, vol 3, no 8, May 1952
Copeman GH (1952b) The Director, vol 3, no 9, June 1952
Francis M (1992) Labour's industrial policies and plans from 1931 to 1965. In: Labour: the party of industrial modernisation? vol 3. Business History Unit LSE, London
Granick D (1962) The European Executive, London: Wiedenfeld & Nicholson
Hannah L (1976) Rise of the corporate economy. Methuen, London
Higgins DM, Toms S (2012) Explaining corporate success: the structure and performance of British firms 1950–84. In: Colli A, de Jong A, Iverson MJ (eds) Mapping European corporations: strategy, structure, ownership and performance. Routledge, Abingdon
Horovitz JH (1980) Top management control in Europe. Macmillan, London
Jones G (1997) Great Britain: big business, management and competitiveness in twentieth century Britain. In: Chandler AD Jr, Amatori F, Hikino T (eds) Big business and the wealth of nations. Cambridge University Press, Cambridge, p 104
Kantor R (1982) The middle manager as innovator. Harv Bus Rev 60(4):95–105
Keeble S (1992) The ability to manage. Manchester University Press, Manchester
Meeks G (1977) Disappointing marriage: a study of the gains from merger. Cambridge University Press, Cambridge
Mercer H (1995) Constructing a competitive order. Cambridge University Press, Cambridge
Owen G (2009) Industrial policy in twentieth century Britain. In: Coopey R, Lyth P (eds) Business in Britain in the twentieth century. Oxford University Press, Oxford
Prais SJ (1976) The evolution of giant firms in Britain 1909–70. Cambridge University Press, Cambridge
Quail J (1996) Proprietors and managers: structure and technique in large British enterprise 1890 to 1939. PhD thesis, University of Leeds
Quail J (1998) From personal patronage to public school privilege: social closure in the recruitment of managers from the late nineteenth century to 1930. In: Kidd A, Nichols D (eds) The making of the British middle class? Sutton, Stroud
Quail J (1999) Mapping the managerial revolution in the UK. Centre for Business History in Scotland, Glasgow
Quail J (2000) The proprietorial theory of the firm and its consequences. J Ind Hist 3(1):1–28
Quail J (2002) Visible hands and visible handles: understanding the managerial revolution in the UK. J Ind Hist 5(2):2002
Renold C (1949) The organizational structure of large undertakings – management problems. British Institute of Management, London
Segrestin B, Johnston A, Hatchuel A (2018) The separation of directors and managers: a historical examination of the legal status of managers. Acad Manag Proc 2018(1):12831. https://doi.org/10.5465/AMBPP.2018.134. hal-01885773

Smith I, Boyns T (2005) Scientific management and the pursuit of control in Britain to c.1960. Account Bus Financ Hist 15(2):187–216

The United Steel Companies Limited (1953) Industrial management – a course of lectures given at Cambridge University for the Faculty Board of Engineering. The United Steel Companies Limited, Sheffield

Tiratsoo N, Edwards R, Wilson JF (2003) Shaping the Content of Business Education in Great Britain, 1945-1990: Production Engineers, Accountants and Shifting Definitions of Relevance. In: Amdan RP, Kevalshagen R, Larsen E (eds) Inside the Business Schools, The Content of European Business Education, Copenhagen Business School Press

Tyzac JET (1960) Letter from J. E.V. Tyzac. The Director, vol 12, no 8, February 1960

Urwick L (1954) The load on top management – can it be reduced? Urwick Orr and Partners, London

Whitley R, Thomas A, Marceau J (1981) Masters of business – the making of a new elite? Tavistock Publications, London

Williams K, Williams J, Thomas D (1983) Why are the British bad at manufacturing? Routledge, London

Wilson JF (1995) British business history. Manchester University Press, Manchester

Wilson JF, Thomson A (2006) The making of modern management. Oxford University Press, Oxford

Part VIII

Management in an Age of Crisis

Introduction: Public Policy Failure, the Demise of Experts, and the Dawn of a New Era

40

Anthony M. Gould

Contents

The Lead-Up to the Age of Crisis: From the New Deal Consensus to Neoliberalism to the Calamity-Ridden Contemporary World	894
Management in an Age of Crisis: Trump, *Brexit* and Those Incompetent and Co-opted Experts	904
Cross-References	909
References	910

Abstract

Throughout the twentieth century, there have been distinctive public policy eras. Much demarcation between epochs arose because of tipping-point moments of change in overarching theory/philosophy about societal values and conjecture concerning how to instantiate such values with rules and regulation. In the contemporary era, public policy development is visceral in nature and largely undertaken based on consensus about what "feels" right. A reason for this change in emphasis concerns the long-term failure of experts and decision makers to deliver results for ordinary people; failure exacerbated by abrupt moments of crises. This book explores aspects of how the new approach to public policy creation influences management as a discipline. The first chapter is contextual. It argues that – largely because of widespread skepticism about the worth of specialists and theory and suspicion that expertise has been co-opted by moneyed interests – public policy is no longer done as it once was.

A. M. Gould (✉)
Département des relations industrielles, Université Laval, Québec, QC, Canada
e-mail: anthony.gould@rlt.ulaval.ca

© The Author(s), under exclusive licence to Springer Nature Switzerland AG 2020
B. Bowden et al. (eds.), *The Palgrave Handbook of Management History*,
https://doi.org/10.1007/978-3-319-62114-2_40

Keywords

Industrial-age · Post-industrial · Crisis · Fordism · Neoliberalism · Theoretical · Trump · *Brexit* · Management

There is no shortage of opinion about how to characterize the modern world and distinguish it from preceding epochs. Conjecture about this matter is invariably influenced by the training, theoretical orientations, preconceptions, and biases of scholars themselves and relatedly what gets established as an object of analytic interest. Of course, beyond academia there are the bewildered and alienated ordinary souls who must make their way on the postindustrial landscape. Incredible as it may seem to the wealthy and powerful, these people – of no particular importance and increasingly estranged from the forces that shape their lives – do think about things. Although they may not know about managing hedge funds or how to trade derivatives, they are acutely aware that for at least several decades it has been becoming harder to get ahead. Indeed, within our collective consciousness, there is the idea that although our forebears may have had it tougher than us in many ways, unlike us, they had something to look forward to. Hence, a distinguishing feature of modernity is that, for the majority, conditions are declining. The content of public policy – as well as the process by which it gets done – impacts this trend. It is axiomatic that the way Western law makers and regulators approach their craft has altered over several decades. There are conventional means of assessing such change as well as off the wall approaches. In the spirit of iconoclasm – and as something of a protest against the smart ones who have in various ways failed us – I prefer the latter type. I start therefore by discussing late night television. As strange as it might seem, the tonight show guys are saying something profound about what has happened to public policy in the West.

From 1962 until 1992, TV legend Johnny Carson was an American institution. It was hard to find anyone who had not heard of him. Indeed, with accolades including six Emmys, the Governor's Award (1980), a Peabody award (1985), induction into the Television Academy's Hall of Fame (1987), the Presidential Medal of Freedom (1992), a Kennedy Centre Honour (1993), and a posthumous star on Hollywood Boulevard's Walk of Fame, it was probably hard to find any baby boomer who had not seen his tonight show which was broadcast weekly across the United States by NBC at 11.30 p.m.

Much like his modern-era equivalents, Carson's format relied heavily on political satire. He would typically open with a monologue about the protagonists of his day, an era spanning seven Presidential administrations: Kennedy, Johnson, Nixon, Ford, Carter, Reagan, and Bush, 41. Carson was as talented and engaging as any of his successors. Indeed, the likes of Jay Leno, and David Letterman have magnanimously acknowledged his influence on themselves personally as well as on their shows' formats (Luippold 2012). However, a careful comparative analysis of Carson's style reveals a key difference between the substance of his humor and that of those who followed him. Carson's one-liners were typically about matters of personal eccentricity, perhaps with a focus on a target's misdeeds, appearance, and displays of physical incompetence. Here, in chronological order, are a few of his trinkets still doing the rounds on the Internet: "*Did you know Richard Nixon is the only President whose formal portrait was painted by a police sketch artist?*" "*That would have been a great ticket, Reagan and Ford. An actor and a stuntman*" (a reference to Gerald Ford's clumsiness and an incident in which he fell down the steps while alighting from Air Force One). "*Ronald Reagan just signed the new tax law. But I think he was in Hollywood too long. He signed it, 'Best wishes, Ronald Reagan.'*" "*Nancy Reagan fell down on the Whitehouse lawn and broke her hair.*"

Carson rarely drew on disembodied consideration of public policy for inspiration. Public policy is dry, bookish, based – at least partly – on a depersonalized understanding of abstract notions about how and why variables are related. When done in a sophisticated way, it applies a methodology. For example, typically from a well-defended construct about the way the world is, it progresses to a protocol resembling Descartes's scientific method and associated conjecture (constrained by principles of logic) about how to interpret research output and which output to interpret. Looking beyond the needs analysis, and research and development stages, regulation is drafted, moves through iterations, becomes authoritative, and is evaluated. This process is the antithesis of entertaining and contains little scope to be funny. If it were to be turned into a Vaudeville routine, it would require a certain spectator sophistication. After all, even the funniest joke about the relative merits of Monetarism versus Keynesianism will fall flat in the absence of a threshold understanding of what these terms mean. Even if this hurdle can be surmounted, public policy is not quirky. Rather cerebral and impersonal. As comedic subject matter, it is a stillborn, to use a Hollywood insider term.

Fast-forward to 2018. Modern era tonight show hosts do not overlook haircuts, sexual escapades, or general stupidity in their never-ending quest to get a laugh. The personal weirdness factor is alive and well as a source of inspiration. However, in the post-*Brexit* era – an era when the world waits in anticipation for a wall to emerge between the United States and Mexico (a wall that Mexico is going to pay for and to the other side of which illegal immigrants will soon be deported) – a new *genre* of humor has emerged. For example, here is part of a skit performed by Irish comedians, Foil, Arms, and Hog (broadcast 30 June, 2016) entitled "*WTF is Brexit*" in which two guys are talking with each other at a urinal....

Guy 1: *Okay, so the UK is in Europe – right?*
Guy 2: *Yeah*
Guy 1: *So they have the Euro?*
Guy 2: *No*
Guy 1: *Oh, so they are not part of the EU?*
Guy 2: *No, they are part of the EU.*
Guy 1: *What?*
Guy 2: *Yeah, for now.*
Guy 1: *What do you mean for now?*
Guy 2: *Brexit!*

Guy 1:	*What is Brexit?*
Guy 2:	*It's the British exit from the EU.*
Guy 1:	*So Britain wants to leave the EU? When?*
Guy 2:	*According to the EU, ASAP! Well actually, just Wales and England want to leave the EU.*
Guy 1:	*What about the other two? That's not fair.*
Guy 2:	*Well, when the UK leaves the EU, then Scotland's going to leave the UK – and then join the EU!*
Guy 1:	*And what about England?*
Guy 2:	*Oh well, they are going to reconnect with the Commonwealth.*
Guy 1:	*What's the Commonwealth?*
Guy 2:	*The former territories of the British Empire.*
Guy 1:	*So now they have an empire again?*
Guy 2:	*Look, all you need to remember is that the UK is leaving Europe.*
Guy 1:	*Well where the hell are they going to go, Asia?*

The above exchange has nothing to do with politicians or public figures. Rather, it is a reference to the befuddlement surrounding *Brexit*. If it is funny, it is so because the whole plan seems ill conceived and a paranoid reaction to unspecified problems that may not even exist.

Another contemporary era window on emerging comedic content concerns modern America's disquieting rise in mass murder on school and university campuses. For example, on the 20th of February 2018, following the Valentine's day shooting at Marjorie Stoneman Douglas High school in Florida in which an alienated young man with a tragic recent past killed 17 people, US President Trump floated the idea of issuing firearms to teachers as a public policy initiative. He said, *"up to 20 percent of teachers should be armed to stop the maniacs from attacking students."* The following day he described *"a gun-free school as a magnet for criminals."* On the 23rd February, late night comedian Steven Colbert had this to say about the President's suggestion.

"Yes – just arm the teachers! I'm sure it's in the school budget. Sorry your school can't afford enough copies of 'To kill a Mockingbird' but good news! We're giving you something that can kill any bird."... *"Now Trump's idea of arming teachers did not go over well with law enforcement officials or teachers or people who are children.......or others."* In commenting on Trump's tweet that *"if a potential sicko shooter has a large number of 'very weapons talented' teachers and others who will be instantly shooting, the sicko will never attack that school,"* Colbert said *"Yeah, that's what sickos are known for – logical reasoning."* Colbert then said *"what does he mean by 'weapons-talented?' That's not a phrase I want to associate with teachers...wow Earl, you sure are handy with guns. Have you thought about working with children?"*

In the above monologue, Colbert obviously mentions the President. Perhaps to enhance the comedic potential of the skit, it is helpful to know something about the kind of man Donald Trump is. However, the joke here is really about ideas. As such, it is the proposal not the person that steals the comedic limelight.

So what is underlying change in tonight-show fodder? One hypothesis is that what people find funny has altered. This does not seem likely in any profound way. A competing hypothesis is more compelling: the proposition that contemporary ideas about how society should be organized are approaching the absurd; or at least have crossed a line such that they are now in a zone that renders them literally laughable. Perhaps part of the problem is that the policy wonks have been marginalized. They no longer are setting the course. It could be that there are justifiable reasons for banishing the experts, or at least admonishing them. Maybe they have failed, or just not done well enough. Alternatively, maybe – somewhere along the line – they were co-opted to do the bidding of the wealthy and those with special interests.

Aside from the reference to Carson *vis-à-vis* his modern equivalents, there is a more conventional way to examine what has happened to Western civic society since the 1960s. Since the end of the Second World War, there have been three eras of thought about public sector governance. The first has been variously characterized as the epoch of the New Deal consensus or regulated state capitalism, umbrella terms for Fordism, broadly conceived (Williams et al. 1992). The second is often referred to as the era of Neoliberalism. The third is still taking shape and hard to characterize. However, it is distinctive in two related respects. First, it emerges from the ruins of public policy that has been chronically failing for decades as well as economic and governance crises that know no modern precedent. Second, it represents a mostly visceral reaction on the part of ordinary people against theory and experts. In this latter respect, contemporary era decision makers often present themselves as skeptical of evidence-informed reasoning or even openly disdainful of it. The emerging epoch is henceforth referred to as the "age of crisis."

The contemporary-era nascent social and political landscape is especially intriguing. To the extent that it is possible to make historical judgments about its causes and correlates, it was born from the long-term failure of policy to deliver results for ordinary people and, more recently, global calamities for which no one in authority seems to have answers, the 2008 financial crisis being the most notable case in point. It seems that in the aftermath of all that has gone wrong – the creeping malaise as well as the abrupt moments of unexpected catastrophe – thinkers have letdown the populous. As noted, it is not entirely clear whether their disappointing performance pertains more to failure of imagination or being, in various ways, "bought." Whatever the case, if theory is now a thing of the past, what is to be its replacement? A starting point here is to attempt to conceive of its opposite. One solution – possibly the new orthodoxy – is to posit a mishmash of notions that feel right, or make large numbers of people feel good. The key word here is "feel." Concisely, feeling is antithetical to thinking. Unburdened by a need for rationale, feelings have a life of their own. Hence, reasoning and argumentation does little to change the way they are subjectively experienced. However, context influences them. For example, consider anger. For the mentally adjusted, rage and resentment is manifest following a real or imagined injustice. It is possible that having unfairness put-right (or misconceptions corrected) assuages passion however, even in such relatively rare circumstances the preinjustice state is not recaptured and emotion not cognition invariably continues to inform actions. Furthermore, unlike theorizing, feelings are subjectively negative or positive and mostly untameable through voluntary acts of will. This is largely why to feel bad is, in principle, harmful; it is difficult to come back from. In this sense, it is noncomparable to its "thinking" equivalent, which would be something merely akin to theory requiring adjustment or jettisoning, or a null-hypothesis being unable to be rejected. For current purposes, the query of the moment is how does it arise that a society devises its governing principles based on feelings rather than theorizing? This is a thorny but nonetheless inescapable question in the modern world. At least part of the answer emerges from understanding how theory has failed; and failed in such a way as to disenfranchise – indeed harm – large numbers of people. It is from such an historical examination that this book begins. The date is around 1980 for most OECD countries; but for the people of Chile, came 7 years earlier in the aftermath of Augusto Pinochet's military *coup d'état* which overthrew the democratically elected socialist government of Salvador Allende.

The Lead-Up to the Age of Crisis: From the New Deal Consensus to Neoliberalism to the Calamity-Ridden Contemporary World

Sometime around the late 1970s, a different orientation towards public policy entered the mainstream in Western countries. In certain jurisdictions including the United States and the UK, the change was relatively abrupt. In others such as Australia, New Zealand, and Canada, it was incremental (Katz and Darbishire 2000; Gould 2010). The details about why there was a departure from the postwar prescription for societal betterment create much of this book's context and merit attention. For example, it appears that the Fordist-based paradigm and Fordist-based Kaldorian economic growth as the West's dominant mode of production was by the mid-1970s not as effective as it had been or at least could be portrayed as such (Mead 2004; Koch 2006). Several decades earlier theorists such as Italian socialist philosopher Antonio Gramsci (1934, reprinted in 1971), in reinterpreting Marx's notion of economic determinism argued that Fordism, by virtue of the moment in history when it took root and its subsequent ubiquity, is archetypal of Western-style capitalism (Antonio and Bonanno 2000). In his short essay, *Americanism and Fordism* he argued that Fordism embodies a sophisticated mix of *bourgeois* strategy and manipulation, classical Marxist-style exploitative elements, and a State-based response which stabilizes conditions that would otherwise culminate in a proletariat revolution. Whatever the case, the approach became, at least in relative terms, a practical and ultimately broadly beneficial theory about how to manage private capital while accommodating disparate interests of various actors in the process.

Fordism supplied business people with key theory that allowed the promise of industrialism to be realized. For 150 years before the beginning of the twentieth century, conjecture about workforce management was piecemeal and no orthodoxy was hegemonic. In a sense, creation of a universal blueprint for employee superintendence lagged behind philosophizing about the role and relevance of macrolevel elements of the new capitalist system as espoused by, on the one hand, its proponents such as Adam Smith and, on the other, its critics such as Marx and Engels. With some exceptions such as with Scottish textile mill owner Robert Owen (1771–1858) who provided counsel on how to motivate employees thus establishing his reputation as the first management theorist (Joullié and Spillane 2015), prior to the twentieth century, there was a paucity of practical advice. Indeed, until the twentieth century, what passed for ideas about administrative science are often better interpreted as sympathetic philosophy concerning the importance of the new management class. An example of such proselytizing is seen in the work of Alexander Hamilton (1771–1804) who put flesh on the bones of Adam Smith's *Wealth of Nations* treatise (1776). Hamilton produced a report on the subject of manufactures that extolled the transformative potential of management. However, the nearest he came to providing down-to-earth advice concerning governance was to reiterate Smith's counsel that factory efficiency is mostly achieved through division of labor and job specialization (Joullié and Spillane 2015; Gould et al. 2017).

It was not until the early 1900s that an integrated set of tenets concerning how to run large enterprises for profit and provide stewardship of private capital arose and abruptly became *zeitgeist* (Wren and Greenwood 1998; Scheiber 2012). Hence, Fordism was born as a panacea for the problem that had bedeviled business people since the advent of steam-powered technology. The dilemma was this: how could capital, in the form of increasingly differentiated and sophisticated machines, be integrated with labor to optimize investor return in the new industrial world? The solution entailed using semi-skilled workers deployed on an automated assembly line to do specialized tasks with dedicated apparatuses. In the early 20th century – an economic setting where key industrial and consumer markets were unsaturated and therefore demand invariably equaled supply – the perennially elusive ideal of optimal investor return was mostly a secondary consequence of something less abstract, output of standardized products.

A conspicuous feature of Fordism is that it emerges from theory. Scholarly opinion differs about whether it was a derivative of, or strongly influenced by, Taylorism (e.g., Hounshell 1984; Sorensen 1956; Doray and Macy 1988). However, unambiguously it belongs to the family of approaches that today are frequently derided as being in the scientific management tradition. Imperfect as these strategies now seem, *a-theoretical* they were not. They can be defended using logic that, in many cases, is informed by data obtained from the shop floor. Indeed, data kept scientific management theory alive and ultimately brought it – at least partially – to heal with the Hawthorne studies and ensuing human relations revolution of the 1930s (Wren and Greenwood 1998; Taneja et al. 2011; Joullié and Spillane 2015). In this sense, Taylor's *magnum opus*, the *Principles of Scientific Management* (1911) is technically impressive due to the author's commitment to using mathematical theorems in particular to present a view of how variables are related and his concern about empirical confirmation.

Another key characteristic of Fordism is that, as Gramsci made clear in what he wrote in his diary whilst imprisoned under the Mussolini Fascist regime, the term itself came to denote more than an approach to factory management. As the twentieth century progressed, the construct expanded and took on at least five divergent meanings that, taken together, define – not just a management blueprint – but a public policy era. First, Fordism is a label applied to a particular mode of economic growth that entails a virtuous cycle of mass production and consumption (Koch 2006). In a sense, it instantiates Adam Smith's conception of the trajectory of modernity as outlined in landmark works such as Max Weber's *The Protestant Work Ethic and the Spirit of Capitalism* (1905). Second, Fordism symbolizes something of a capitalist concession. Ironically, in spite of Henry Ford's unitarist inclinations and legendary hatred of unions, the term now embraces begrudging employer recognition that they should tolerate organized labor as a broadly beneficial component of their forfeiture in the twentieth century's new social contract. Relatedly, it signifies that workers should accept management perogative in return for rising wages (Watts 2005; Baca 2004). Third, Fordism is widely allied with the distinctively industrial-age notion that Western industries mature into inefficient but broadly accommodative structures of monopolistic competition where cost-plus rather than market consensus determines pricing (Watts 2005). Fourth, Fordism is associated with legitimization of deficit financing and credit-fuelled consumption (McDermott 1992; Tylecote 1995). In the New Deal era, its imperfections formed much of the rationale for State intervention in economic matters including, in particular, the establishment of a welfare state and state regulated capitalism. Fifth, Fordism has also become a research paradigm, used for example to analyze the proliferation of mass media, transportation, and politics (Wren and Greenwood 1998; Roobeek 1987). To gain perspective on how Fordism and its inextricable historical link with regulated entrepreneurship was woven into the fabric of American – and Western – industrial life, one need only reflect on the recently established hard-won legitimacy of organized labor in the middle decades of the twentieth century. For example, in 1952 General Dwight Eisenhower, Republican Presidential nominee and archetypal tough-guy said about labor unions.

> I have no use for those, regardless of their political party, who hold some foolish dream of spinning the clock back to days when unorganized labor was a huddled, almost helpless, mass. Today in America, unions have a secure place in our industrial life. Only a handful of unreconstructed reactionaries harbor the ugly thought of breaking unions. Only a fool would want to deprive working men and woman of the right to join the union of their choice. (Speech to the American Federation of Labor in New York City. 17 September, 1952 (cited in Newton, 2011))

And so it was. During the 1950s under a Republican administration, the New Deal consensus was hegemonic. Whatever the inadequacies of Fordism, the theory as it applies to production – in combination with its institutional employer concessions and attendant state-based softening strategies to halt what Marxists saw as the natural course of dialectical materialism – was working and doing so for most people. For example, the decades of the 1930s to the 1960s saw inequality diminish to an unprecedented level (Gould et al. 2017; Moody 2007). During the era, the top 20% of wealthy people in the USA never held more than 65% of private capital. By contrast, since 1990 this figure has always been above 70% (Wisman 2013; Gould et al. 2017; Appleby 2011). From 1950 until 1972, real average weekly wages rose in the United States by 48%, from $212 to their highest point on record, $315. Over the same period, real income growth for families increased even more dramatically. For example, the poorest 20% of American households more than doubled (116%) their disposable income in the period 1947–1973 (Moody 2007; Mishel et al. 2005; Piketty 2014).

In the 1970s, postwar growth associated with Fordism began to decline and commentators speculated that the model itself needed re-examination. In the worst economic slump since the great depression, the US gross domestic product dropped by 1% from 1973 to 1975 and industrial output fell by 10% (Moody 2007). Over the same period, the world's 25 riches countries saw their economic growth rate fall from 5% to 0 (Harrison and Bluestone 1988; Lichtenstein 2002). In the lead-up to the 1975 world recession, inflation was rising steeply in Western countries. However, it was the external shock of the 1973 OPEC crisis in which Arabian Gulf States acting as a cartel unprecedentedly quadrupled the price they were charging the West for oil, that seemed to herald the beginning of a new era. The OPEC crisis, as an extraordinary – as opposed to a cyclical – phenomenon, was a convenient whipping post for contemporary-era economists trying to make sense of what was happening (Moody 2007; Issawi 1979; Kolm 1977). Indeed, although much contemporaneous literature attached importance to it as the principal cause of the epoch's malaise, more systemic elements were undermining prosperity from as early as the 1960s. Moody (2007), for example, provides a nuanced thesis about why the long-boom was abating from the mid-1960s. He argues that return on capital deployed in Western industries was falling from around this time. A reason for this was that from approximately the early 1960s, international competition was encroaching on domestic market share in circumstances of near market saturation. In economic parlance, Western industries were moving towards structures of perfect competition in which output settles at a point where, for any particular firm, marginal cost equals marginal revenue, and for practical purposes, return on capital diminishes to an international norm. To the extent that "harder working" capital was responsible for reduced surpluses, conditions for workers started to attenuate. Specifically, from the early 1970s onwards, their wage growth stagnated. In fact, over the next 20 years (from 1972 until the beginning of the Clinton administration), average real weekly wages in the United States fell (almost) every year (Moody 2007). Adding to the problem was the scourge of inflation, which was out of control in the late 1970s period of stagflation (Brenner 2002; Mandel 1978). However, this era was relatively short-lived. What was really happening was real wage growth was slowing because of shrinking growth in surpluses and insidious employer recalcitrance concerning the perennial wage/profit share. Whatever the case, by the 1990s American workers had 1960s purchasing power. In a vain attempt to address the problem, they toiled more. In the 1970s and 1980s, the nation's employees put in an average of 3 h per week in overtime. In the 1990s, the figure was 4.2 h. By the early 2000s (2000–2004), during the period of slower economic growth and consequent rising unemployment, it was 5.4 h (Moody 2007; Harrison and Bluestone 1988). Life in the West had been getting difficult for ordinary people. It seemed that, with the rise of Japan and the Asia Tiger economies, more of the world was sharing capitalism's benefits; Fordist-era industry structures of monopolistic competition were outmoded, or at least appeared so.

If, in the 1970s, conditions were turning against Western workers, it is equally true that a hitherto marginal strain of thought was entering the mainstream. It is likely that worsening economic circumstances made it easier to argue that the world needed a fresh approach. The new prescription was ready to be implemented and well-articulated. It came largely courtesy of Austrian-school theorists such as Friedrich Hayek and later his acolytes, the *anti-Keynesian/Monetarist* Milton Friedman and James Buchanan with his conception of public choice theory (Buchanan 2003). The alternative way of thinking was, at least according to certain commentators, a return to the common sense of the enlightenment and the ideas of eighteenth- and nineteenth-century thinkers such as Jean Baptiste Say (1767–1832), and Alexander de Toqueville (1805–1859), each interested in understanding America's uniqueness in the new industrial world and, in various ways, influenced by Adam Smith's (1773–1790) belief in natural law, utilitarianism and the inevitability of progress (Ebenstein 2002, 2003; Combe 1996). Another inspiration for the new liberals came from even earlier thinkers. For example, there was John Locke (1632–1704) who had argued persuasively that people are inherently selfish and, from this, it follows that they have a natural right to defend their life, health, liberty, and possessions. This doctrine ultimately worked its way into the American Declaration of Independence with the expression "life, liberty, and pursuit of happiness." However, in spite of such an apparently impressive intellectual pedigree, the prescription that was to come from Friedman and his ilk in the 1970s is arguably a radical variant of earlier liberalism. It was, at its core, the notion that government and governance are largely pernicious influences or at least more intrusive than should be the case and its corollary thesis, that *laissez-faire* capitalism is inclined to remedy both economic and social problems. The world was soon to enter the era of neoliberalism, a shorthand term for what is often thought of in North America as free-market conservatism.

In summary therefore, it was under the twin influences of increasingly lackluster results that beset the plight of Western countries in the 1970s combined with the persuasive skill of scholars and some earlier politicians such as 1964 Republican Presidential nominee Barry Goldwater that much of the world haltingly entered the neoliberal era. Somewhat like the Keynesian pump-priming intellectual foundations of New-Dealism, neoliberalism is not *a-theoretical*. Indeed, as a cursory reading of Freidrich Hayek's *Road-to-Serfdom* (1945) or even Ayn Rand's *Atlas Shrugged* (1992), originally published in 1957 (which proposes as virtuous through its exposition of the so-called philosophy of objectivism unchecked ego and ruthless pursuance of self-interest) reveals, part of its problem has turned out to be that it preferences dogma over data. In other words, its unyielding and dispassionate adherence to ideology has guided its implementation.

Neoliberalism's proponents assert that application of the market principle should be expanded in at least five related ways. First, policy should allow private sector entities to compete to provide services that hitherto have been the preserve of the public sector. In most OECD countries, this project is applied in arenas such as the administration of prisons, hospitals, and schools. It manifests as privatization of national airlines, telecommunications, and welfare systems (Combe 1996;

Connell 2010). There is a partially disguised agenda here; if someone wants something, indeed needs it, they should pay for it. The fact that they may not be able to is a short-run impediment and one that reflects negatively on the needy person's character; the logic being that it is they, through their choices, who placed themselves in the dependent situation (Dean 2009; Cooper 2012). Second, the market solution should be the default option to remedy social – as opposed to economic – problems (Brady 2008; Harvey 2005). Hence, it should not be viewed narrowly as merely a means of enhancing commercial performance as classically occurs when firm managers make choices concerning lease or buy, vertical or horizontal integration, or outsourcing. Third, policy makers should be creative in finding ways to apply the market solution; in other words, they must proactively conceive of new functions and speculate about how an unfettered private sector will fulfill them for profit. In this regard, it is only in the last 35 years that there has emerged in the Western World conceptions of supply and demand for drinking water, body parts, and outer space (Connell 2010). Fourth, the Schumpeterian phenomenon of industry creative destruction is not to be disparaged but rather is ultimately beneficial for myriad actors, including those who lose their jobs when an economic sector becomes defunct (Harvey 2006). Apparently, the idea here is that laid-off workers, irrespective of their age or other circumstances, are presented with retraining opportunities that – if they are responsible citizens – they will have budgeted for during the period when they were employed. Fifth, labor markets, because they are markets, are not exempt from deregulation. This aspect of the agenda is multifaceted. Perhaps its most contentious element concerns antiunionism. Neoliberalists propose that unions create competitive distortions (Braedley and Luxton 2010). They bid up the cost of labor beyond its market value. They are incompatible with the principle of merit-based promotion and appointment. They are a cause of indolence and inefficiency. For these reasons, they are typically a key initial target in implementing the neoliberal agenda. An example of this phenomenon is the case of Augusto Pinochet's assault on Chilean unions in 1973 which came almost immediately after he seized power. Similarly, there was Reagan's defeat of air traffic controllers in 1981, Thatcher's dismantling of the miners' union in 1984 and, in Australia, the Howard government's entanglement with dock workers in its first term (1997) and later, after it gained control of the nation's upper house of parliament, its *WorkChoices* agenda (2005).

A key upside of neoliberalism for the public is, in principle, the promise of reduced taxes and an ensuing downward pressure on prices. For example, in the United States, the passing of Proposition 13 in California in 1978, a referendum to cap property tax, has historical significance. It is heralded as the commencement of a new policy direction for Western governments (Connell 2010; Chapman 1998). However, in reflecting on changing taxation regimes over the last 40 years, authors such as Connell (2010) argue that although in the USA and other OECD countries tax-cuts have been an animating theme of both conservative and liberal electoral campaigns, government receipts have fallen very little. Rather, there has been a conspicuous shift from direct to indirect taxations arrangements, a circumstance that unambiguously discriminates against low-income earners in favor of wealthy people. In short, neoliberalism in practice promotes regressive tax regimes.

As noted, in the Western world, an emphasis on supply-side economics, the more technical description of much of the tax-related ideology that informs neoliberalism, is mostly associated in an applied sense with the modern-era governments of Reagan and Thatcher in the 1980s (Gould and Robert 2013; Gwartney 2008). The theory had not broken into the mainstream prior to this time, but perhaps came close to doing so during the failed 1964 US Presidential campaign of Barry Goldwater, a man whose time had not yet come. However, history has a way of being Western-centric. In particular, the first real test-run of resurrected liberalism came in 1973 following Augusto Pinochet's military *coup* in Chile. The historical importance of Chile in this area cannot be overstated and is eloquently summed-up by Robert Packenham and William Ratliff (2007 p. 9) from the Hoover Institute who note...

> The first country in the world to make that momentous break with the past – away from socialism and extreme state capitalism toward more market-orientated structures and polices – was not Deng Xiaoping's China or Margaret Thatcher's Britain in the late 1970s, Ronald Reagan's United States in 1981, or any other country in Latin America or elsewhere. It was Pinochet's Chile in 1975.

In decisively rebuking his socialist predecessor Allende, Pinochet brought in the "Chicago-boys," mostly Chilean economic consultants who had spent time at the University of Chicago under the tutelage of ideologues such as Milton Friedman. The job of the advisers was to recast the old order. Henceforth, the market solution was to be the guiding maxim for addressing the nation's economic and social problems. To support the approach, the regime removed trade barriers, privatized key state-owned industries, created a central bank with authority to set interest and exchange rates independently, cut wages, and privatized social security. In foreshadowing what was to come soon in the United States, William Simon, Secretary of the Treasury, described the new South American dictator as having brought economic freedom to his country (Asen 2009). In fact, despite the USA's official position that it merely approved of – or at most tacitly supported – the Pinochet regime, several scholars have argued that America proactively paved the way for him through undermining the Allende government using the CIA to stage destabilization initiatives and covert trade-related interventions such as an "invisible blockade." Authors such as Peter Kornbluh in his book *the Pinochet File* (2003), Tim Weiner in, *Legacy of Ashes* (2007), and Christopher Hitchens's, *The Trial of Henry Kissinger* (2001) have proposed slightly differing theses concerning US manipulation of South-American politics during the 1970s.

The Chilean dalliance with neoliberalism did not go as planned. In 1986, the Indian economist Amartya Sen provided a postmortem of the experiment. His conclusions were gloomy. In what ended-up being known as the "Chicago road to socialism," he noted that, by the early 1980s, the new approach had been disastrous, prompting a wholesale buy-back of public assets in an effort to restore the *status-quo*. Ironically, the State ended-up owning and running more of the economy than it had during the Allende administration, including industries focusing on manufacturing and exporting as well as the banking sector.

The rest of the world's enthusiasm for neoliberalism was not dampened in the wake of the Chilean experiment. However, even before factoring-in the impacts of, for example, the 2008 global financial crisis, the new way was not delivering its promised benefits or at least not doing so for the majority of people living in OECD countries. For example, in the early 2000s, the "great moderation" in the business cycle was unmistakable on graphs (Summers 2005). The postindustrial more tempered boom-bust sequence seemed to be attributable to certain of neoliberalism's peripheral elements. These included increased central bank independence, application of the "Taylor Rule" (which specifies that in the long run, an independently operated central bank will raise interest rates by more than one percent for each 1% rise in the inflation rate) in monetary policy and greater within-sector flexibility including elements such as "just-in-time" inventory management but, more particularly, increasingly flexible labor markets (to use the vernacular). At that time, proponents of rationale expectations and efficient markets theory held the intellectual high ground. The market solution was working, but for whom? Analysts such as Mark Weissbrot and Rebecca Ray (2011) had the temerity to compare the period 1960–1980 with the period 1980–2005. They focused on indicators including economic growth and social/psychological measures within low and middle-income countries which, according to at least one variant of the theory (e.g., Moody 2007), should have been first in-line to receive neoliberalism's advantages. They concluded that, far from such nations being the beneficiaries of a so-called rising-bottom, they had in fact declined on key financial indices. Within the United States – a country that was likely to be at risk of setback when measured in narrow economic terms – it is conspicuous that even social justice indicators have it in 2015 at number 25 out of 31 OECD countries, just above Turkey, Greece, and Chile (Kauder and Potrafke 2015). When further scrutinized, it seems that some sectors of the US population were hit particularly hard by the new social and economic order. For example, researchers such as Case and Coates (2017) and Case and Deaton (2017) have been tracking the aggregate fate of middle-aged white Americans (particularly white American males) without college-level degrees since 1999. They note that the mean mortality-rate for this cohort was declining steadily throughout the twentieth century but in the twenty-first century, in contrast to other wealthy countries, began to rise precipitously. They further conclude that the trend-reversal is mostly attributable to elements such as suicide and drug overdose that, in turn, come from lost status arising principally from job insecurity and career disruption in the age of neoliberalism. Such research is a bombshell. It indexes a larger phenomenon that turns out to be a colossal blind spot for those espousing neoliberalism in theory. For example, in their book *The Spirit-Level: Why Inequality Matters*, Wilkinson and Pickett (2010) provide evidence that any mode of production – even if it produces across the board rising levels of prosperity – will have adverse aggregate psychological impacts if it also exacerbates wealth inequality. A thought experiment (not taken from the book) serves to underscore this point. Imagine a boss arrives at work and randomly summons one of their employees to tell them that they are to receive a salary increase of, say, 20%. The employee feels elated. Imagine, the same boss subsequently announces to all other equivalent-level employees that they will receive a pay rise of 25%. Now, the first employee feels worse than they did before the boss arrived.

In 2000, once again before the 2008 crisis, Crotty undertook a postmortem on the global economic effects of Neoliberalism. His conclusions were dismal. He wrote (p. 10).

> The evidence to date supports neoliberalism's critics. The promised benefits of neoliberalism have yet to materialize. Global income growth has slowed as has the rate of global capital accumulation, at least for the majority of the world's people. Productivity growth has deteriorated, real wage growth has declined, inequality has risen in most Western countries, real interest rates are higher, financial crises erupt with increasing regularity, the less developed nations outside East-Asia have fallen even further behind the more advanced and average unemployment has risen.

Hence, over-reliance on the market solution was not delivering its assured dividends even before 2008. In the wake of the new approach, the US middle-class was being decimated and the twentieth century's promise of social-mobility was now a pipedream. Following the global financial crisis – an event for which it seems likely that no party with skin in the game foresaw – government, the private sector, and an increasingly beaten-down public were unmistakably in reaction-mode. Initially within the United States and elsewhere there was a fleeting return to Keynesian-style pump priming, even by the hard-line *Neocons* (Stewart 2009). When the postcrisis mess was handed from the Bush to the Obama administration pump-priming and prop-up measures continued, for a brief time, and mostly only for corporate America. For example, following the collapse of merchant bankers Lehman Brothers (LB) and the takeover of Merrill Lynch (ML) by the Bank of America (BofA), the new Federal government invested 85 billion dollars to ensure that merchant bank AIG remained solvent (Boyer 2009). Overall, the US Federal Reserve sponsored massive – although less than recommended – stimulatory initiatives (*Institut économique de Montréal*, 2009; Boyer 2009). In Europe in 2008, the EU Commission recommended a 200 billion euros stimulus package (about 1.5% of the aggregate GDP of the countries being targeted).

However, in 2010, the G20 summit held in Toronto marked the beginning of a fresh global financial policy orientation of governments struggling to manage the aftermath of the crisis (Le Queux and Peetz 2013; Lo Duca and Stracca 2014). Because the bailouts were now threatening the solvency and credit-ratings of countries around the world, stringency was the new *ordre du jour*. The plan devised in Toronto was to reduce public debt within G20 nations by 50% by 2013 (Le Queux and Peetz 2013). Long-term austerity had begun. Once again, the State was the standard-bearer for free-market orthodoxy and it was ordinary people who were to take another body blow.

In his book *Failed* (2015), Mark Weissbrot presents a subversive thesis about the strategic orientation of governments following the 2008 crisis. Weissbrot examined the minutes of regular IMF consultations with member governments (covering 27 countries) for the years 2008–2011. He concludes that participants viewed spending cuts to the public sector and reduced public services as indispensable. This finding is perhaps unremarkable. However, Weissbrot observed something more insidious. Specifically, austerity measures are typically implemented in parallel with an agenda to limit democratic participation. For example, in Europe there has been an emphasis on transferring decision making to unelected bodies and, insofar as possible, to lessen the influence of national governments. In a similar vein, in the United States the lower 70% of those eligible to vote never do and therefore elected representatives disregard their preferences (Kiesa and Levine 2016). Such recent precipitous decline in electoral participation has provided impetus for theorists such as Ferguson to extend his investment theory of party competition to the arena of congressional elections. Ferguson notes that, since approximately 1980, campaign spending is a near perfect predictor of electoral outcomes (Ferguson 1995).

There is a fuzzy boundary between the end of the period of neoliberalism and the emergence of the next – current – era, described here as the "age of crisis." As Ferguson (1995) notes, there is no special reason to believe that much of the neoliberal agenda is being jettisoned. On the contrary, it has made people who were always very rich and who make electoral donations, even more so. However, what distinguishes the new era is two elements. First, the most conspicuous of the contemporary Western-style public policy makers are, at least overtly, contemptuous of experts and disdainful of approaches that seem based on theory and philosophy. As noted, in the modern-era, the way a strategy makes one feel mostly eclipses consideration of whether theory predicts that it will work. Second, despite a now more disguised but still hard-core continued preoccupation with the substance of neoliberalism, the contemporary epoch's approach to governance resurrects some elements of New-Dealism, or at least pays lip-service to their value. Such elements include isolationism, protectionism, and xenophobia. In the very recent past, President Trump's preoccupation with building a wall between Mexico and the USA, *Brexit*, the rise of the *alt-right* and resurrected plans to reinstate bygone era tariffs and trade embargos are evidence of a widespread popular yearning for the good-old-days. Despite some aggressive rhetoric, it is unclear whether these agendas will be implemented or even if they could be. It is also not clear whether contemporary-era leaders have commitment to their implementation. Indeed, it seems likely that they do not. After all, as argued, compared to their predecessors, the leaders and decision makers of 2018 are mostly not theory-driven and as such unmoored from ideological allegiance.

To prosecute the case that contempt for theory and superficial preoccupation with good-old-days socialist-style protectionist elements (at least for those in the in-group) are distinctive hallmarks of the new era, it is instructive to examine two recent Western-World phenomena. First, there is the celebration of the nonexpert as a panacea for complex problems. The key word here is "celebration." Modern history is replete with examples of politicians who were not technically competent. Indeed, in the case of the USA at least, this was part of the original vision of the founding fathers with their conception of the citizen-statesman (Gould et al. 2017). What delineates the new epoch however is lauding ignorance as a virtue. An early sign of the change came just before the 2008 US Presidential election when Republican nominee Senator John McCain chose as his running mate then Alaskan governor Sarah Palin. Ms Palin was chosen according to McCain because although not an expert in anything vaguely relevant to the most pressing problems faced by the country, she does not parse words and has common sense (Dunn 2011). For example, during the 2008 Vice-Presidential debate held on the 2nd of October when she was asked which of her side's policy plans would have to be scaled-down due to the global financial crisis, Palin did not miss a beat. She said ...."*How long have I been at this – like five weeks?*" In an effort to show that she related to ordinary people, the same Ms Palin, inquired confidently, "*What is it that a V-P actually does?*" when asked on the 25th of June 2008 by Larry Kudlow of CNBC about the role. Second, there has been the rise of populist fringe movements that manifest anger and resentment but have few creative, well-defended public policy suggestions. This is not a partisan matter and occurs on the left and right of the political spectrum as in the case, on the one hand, with Occupy Wall Street and, on the other, with the Obama-era Tea Party movement.

Management in an Age of Crisis: Trump, *Brexit* and Those Incompetent and Co-opted Experts

Donald Trump was never going to win the 2016 American Presidential election. He was not even going to throw his hat in the ring. Prior to his official announcement made in Trump Tower on 16 June 2015, he certainly gave indications that he would run. However, he was really just an overly indulged carnival-barker with a twitter account. His US-Mexico wall idea was comparable to mid-twentieth-century eccentric millionaire Howard Hughes's *H-4 Hercules* concept. The showy *Spruce Goose*, as it was better known, was an enormous but useless seaplane that was originally trumpeted as the ultimate solution for Axis-power submarines sinking US supply ships in the Atlantic after the country entered the Second World War. Members of Roosevelt's War Cabinet were unimpressed with the idea, but ultimately Hughes Aircraft Corporation secured a development contract with the Department of the Navy to build three prototypes (McDonald 1981). The Wall was to be Trump's *Spruce Goose,* expensive and inefficient, flamboyant and headline grabbing, but in the end, more about style than substance.

It was not that Trump did not have marketing skill and the sectional appeal that inevitably comes from hard-hitting rhetoric, an ostensible real-estate empire and a list of authored books with menacing titles like *Think Like a Champion* (2009), *Time to get Tough* (2011), *Think Big and Kick Ass* (2007), and *the Art of the Deal* (1987). Undeniably, his capacity to manipulate the media was impressive. It was reminiscent of actor Orson Wells who, in 1938, created mass panic in the tristate area when he read aloud on a wireless broadcast H.G. Well's *War of the Worlds*; announcing that Martians had landed in a carpark at Grover's Mill New Jersey and 7000 US servicemen had been deployed to face them down. Orson Well's career took off following this incident. Similarly, Trump's posturing about being President aimed merely to secure a fifteenth series of the *Apprentice* with NBC, to promote brand Trump, and to fire a warning shot across the bow of the real contenders who, according to him, were losers and needed to lift their game. At 68, Trump was too old, lacked discipline, knew nothing about bureaucracy, championed ridiculous and impractical ideas, and had no experience with elected office. Besides, Trump could not run because he could not allow his tax returns to be released or certain of his disreputable business dealings to be scrutinized. In declaring Chap. 5 bankruptcy, he had walked away from the *Taj-Mahal* Casino in Atlantic City with debt owing to ordinary people; dishwashers, painters, carpenters, plumbers, glaziers, and drapery installers (and this was not the first time). He had a class action against him by former Trump University students. Depending on one's political sympathies, he was either a branding genius or a shameless narcissistic self-promoter. Either way, the idea of him being a candidate was Barnumesque, an off-the-wall publicity stunt but nonetheless patently absurd as a matter of practice. This was what the experts said. They were wrong.

When Trump did announce his candidacy, it was clear he could not win the primaries. He was competing in a field of 17, which included experienced State governors, Senators, and credible business people. There had not been such a large showing on the Republican side since the Lincoln-Douglas election of 1860. Moreover, Trump had no background in the GOP, no debate experience, no *SuperPac*, and continued to say things that embodied simultaneously incoherence and viciousness. He made crude and offensive remarks about women and seemed to have an adolescent's preoccupation with their weight and appearance. He ridiculed and insulted people who were unable to respond. He showed limited engagement with complex issues and an unyielding preference for the glib and superficial over the scholarly and analytic. Perhaps most offputtingly, he crossed a sacred line by casting aspersions on the bravery and patriotism of Senator John McCain. During the Vietnam War, McCain, then a Navy pilot serving on the U.S.S. Forestall was captured and horrendously tortured for 6 years by the Vietcong in circumstances where he ultimately could have secured his freedom but refused to do so unless every prisoner being held alongside him was also released. Trump said about the Senator on 18 July 2015 at a campaign event at the Family Leadership Summit in Ames, Iowa...

> He's not a hero. He's a hero because he was captured. I like people who weren't captured.

Once again, the experts said Trump would not – could not – become the Republican standard-bearer. They were wrong – for the second time.

Following Trump's nomination on May 3, 2016, he was not going to beat Hilary Clinton in the general election. This could not happen because the whole of America participates, or at least has the right to participate, in deciding who will be their nation's President. The influence of the lunatic fringe was now diluted. The polls were showing that there would be regression towards the mean, attenuation. The Electoral College system, while not perfect, had been conceived by the wise founding fathers and thoughtfully refined after the Civil War. It invariably produces an optimal solution. Although the Democratic nominee was not especially inspiring and came with baggage, survey data indicated that she would naturally fall into the role. It was not even necessary for her to campaign much, hold press conferences, or go to red states. All she needed to do was what she was already doing and was comfortable with; stay mostly in New York and California and appear on shows that appealed mainly to liberal-minded women such as *The View* and *Ellen*. In the second Presidential debate held on the 16 of September, during a clash about the causes of poor quality public schools and ageing infrastructure, Trump seemed to wear it as a badge of honor that he does not pay his share of tax. "*That makes me smart,*" he said. Expert commentators on CNN denounced this utterance as unprecedentedly injudicious (e.g., Diaz 2016 27 September). It defied logic and reason. Trump had forgotten that the bulk of people who would soon vote were taxpayers. In asking why they – the battlers – should be subsidizing a millionaire at tax time, they would join the dots about what sort of man Trump was. However, this was all prologue. Later his candidacy would fall off a cliff. On October 7, when the tawdry *Access-Hollywood* tape came out which revealed an exchange in which Trump shamelessly boasted that his fame gave him the green light to sexually assault women as and when he felt like it, he was undoubtedly finished. Now it was a matter of the iron-law of arithmetic. His base of voters was, from that moment forward, to be only some percentage of males, 50% of those who would be casting a ballot. Boolean logic predicted he would soon be rendered a historical footnote. He was about to become the twenty-first-century's Gary Hart, the 1988 Democratic party frontrunner who was forced to drop out in favor of Michael Dukakis when it was revealed that he had a girlfriend, Donna Rice, while he was married. Inductive reasoning was relevant here. Hart was a former diplomat. He was an intelligent and attractive man. However, what he did or was alleged to have done, despite being comparatively trifling, finished him. *Ipso facto*, 28 years later the star of *the Apprentice* was soon to get an ignominious dose of his own medicine; he would be fired. This was, once again, the consensus of experts offering narrowly focused analyses. They were wrong – for a third time. Zero out of three for the *intelligencia* concerning their analysis of the rise of Trump.

The story of the 45th US President's political ascendancy embodies the paradox of the last 50 years. Experts have let down the public – at least most of them – with their prescriptions for societal betterment. Whether well intentioned or disingenuously attempting to create a pretext which allows the wealthy to further enrich themselves at the expense of everyone else, they have often been wrong. Their remedies and proselytizing have seemingly arisen from disciplined analysis. Wallowing in the intellectual debris of postindustrialism, more experts used more theory and logic to misread who was to be the President of the United States in 2016. Despite the risk of throwing the baby out with the bathwater, the decimated middle-class and those worse-off who would never likely get to be part of it were fed-up with the experts, and not without justification. A new and dystopic era had emerged. It was post-neoliberalism – postindustrialism. For the first time since Henry Ford worked out how to combine capital with labor and the state thoughtfully responded to make sure that no one was left behind, the world was a-theoretical. Philosophy was no longer to undergird public policy. The airplane was being built as it was being flown and the way people felt was more important than ideas defended using evidence-informed application of reasoning. Action without theory may have haltingly started with the emergence of Sarah Palin but had now reached its crescendo with the election of Trump. The rise of the brazenly brash and overtly anti-intellectual American politician was a manifestation of a larger phenomenon. Theory and ideological commitment was being cast asunder everywhere. Consider the UK's Justice Secretary, Michael Gove's comment about *Brexit,* made on June 6, 2016, before the Presidential election. In refusing to name any European economist who thought Britain's exit from the Union was a good idea, Gove said in an interview with *Faisal-Islam*...

I think that the people of this country have had enough of experts with organizations with acronyms – saying that they know what is best and getting it consistently wrong, because these people – these people – are the same ones who got consistently wrong (quote reproduced verbatim).

The population sided with him. Throughout the Western World, the public was giving experts the salutatory message that they are not as good as they think they are, a missive for which even the most enlightened person of reason should have sympathy. Indisputably, there is abundant evidence that the clever ones have not done very well. In their mediocrity, they have contributed to the dawning of the new era, both through their bad advice and elitist and condescending way of conveying it. It may even be worse than just a case of incompetence, a case well laid out in economist Thomas Sowell's book, *Intellectuals and Society* (2010) wherein the author argues that much social commentary and public policy development work is substandard because, unlike when running a business, for example, those who produce theory or instantiate it through regulation mostly have nothing at stake if they get it wrong. Indeed, a more pernicious thesis also exists, the possibility that experts are being manipulative, clandestinely working, for example, for those with money and power. In Kurt Andersen's recent book *Fantasyland: How America went Haywire* (2017), this theme is developed and its relationship with conspiracy theories, the blurring of the boundary between news and entertainment and the rise of populist fringe movements well explored. Whatever the case, the new era of public policy is skeptical, indeed disdainful, of ideas. Hence, the age of crisis is also the age of the eschewing of the pointy-heads. Insofar as actual policy manifestation is concerned, it is a disjointed and decontextualized patchwork of nineteenth-century notions about the value of *laissez-faire* capitalism, industrial age forms of protectionism and attendant xenophobia and *ad hoc* economic winner-picking. How long this will last or what will be its results could not be less clear.

From the beginning of the twentieth century, there have been attempts to periodize approaches to management philosophy, public administration, and the shifting economic *milieu*. Each such effort has typically focused on a slightly different object of analysis. Elements established as analytically consequential have included approaches to people management (e.g., Barley and Kunda 1992), the beginning and end-points of economic long waves (e.g., Kondratieff and Stolper 1935; Schumpeter and Nichol 1934; Rostow 1978; Sterman 1986), and recently the moral and ethical legitimacy of the public versus private sector (e.g. Park and Gould 2017; Gould et al. 2017). Some proposed frameworks have been deterministic. These embed within them the notion that human endeavor advances the development of theory and, at key tipping-points, the framework being applied is unrecognizable. When such thresholds are reached, a new era is commenced. For example, there is Barley and Kunda's (1992) classification of management ideologies: industrial betterment (1870–1900), scientific management (1900–1923), welfare capitalism/human relations (1923–1955), systems rationalization (1955–1980), and organizational culture (1980–1995). In a similar vein, there is Gantman's (2005) typology of the nineteenth-century's liberal capitalism, the early and mid-twentieth-century's organized capitalism and the disorganized capitalism from the late twentieth century. In this chapter, several of the key frameworks for understanding management and public-policy recent history have been collapsed together and summarized as the late industrial-age era of Fordism broadly conceived and the epoch of neoliberalism. Each of these eras, although an approach to public policy, has had a symbiotic relationship with philosophy concerning the management of private capital. In other words, the way the State handles matters of public administration has invariably created something of a template for people management generally; or perhaps it is the other way around. Indeed, the causal direction of this relationship remains unclear and will not be addressed here. Rather, for present purposes, what is noteworthy is that historically there has been synergy between public policy and approaches to private-sector governance and each such endeavor has typically been theory-driven.

An understanding that the rupture between industrialism and postindustrialism has much to do with insidious long-term public policy failure and unexpected moments of crisis is a solid starting point for coming to grips with the nature of modernity. But it is only a starting point. Indeed, the road ahead for the sense-makers is tough and the scholarly agenda plagued by unique challenges. Some of these pertain to interpreting what is happening. Others concern drawing conclusions about how – apparently shambolic elements – will stabilize, if they will stabilize, and/or whether they are best viewed as transitional. Another research agenda is about the indirect impacts of public policy. For example, how does its substance and process of creation impact management more broadly and the management of private capital? These are arguably pressing issues. They are dealt with – head-on – in the pages that follow.

In this section, outstanding business and management scholars explore aspects of the contemporary world of work and governance in circumstances where the context is shaped by long-term public policy failure, moments of economic and social catastrophe, and community skepticism. Authors delve into facets of the lead-up to the present epoch as well as its more consequential current manifestations. The section has six more chapters (▶ Chaps. 41, "Labor and Employment Practices: The Rise and Fall of the New Managerialism," ▶ 42, "A Return to the Good Old Days: Populism, Fake News, Yellow Journalism, and the Unparalleled Virtue of Business People," ▶ 43, "Why did the Great Recession Fail to Produce a *New* New Deal in the USA?," ▶ 44, "Trade Union Decline and Transformation: Where to for Employment Relations?," ▶ 45, "The New Executive: Interconnected Yet Isolated and Uninformed – Leadership Challenges in the Digital Pandemic Epoch," and ▶ 46, "Conclusion: Management Theory in Crisis"). ▶ Chapter 41, "Labor and Employment Practices: The Rise and Fall of the New Managerialism" by Professor John Godard from the Asper School of Business at the University of Manitoba, is an expose of the rise and fall of the new managerialism which examines, since the 1950s Golden Age, supervisory practices in Western – mostly USA – workplaces and details their consequences, too many of which have been largely unforeseen. ▶ Chapter 42, "A Return to the Good Old Days: Populism, Fake News, Yellow Journalism, and the Unparalleled Virtue of Business People" authored by Professor Mark Belnaves from Kuwait's Gulf University of Science and Technology, addresses one aspect of technology's role, the rise of the digital persona. Belnaves argues that this rise is a somewhat overlooked but undoubtedly sinister cause of (so-called) trusted sources no longer being as advertised. ▶ Chapter 43, "Why did the Great Recession Fail to Produce a *New* New Deal in the USA?" by

Professor Jon D Wisman from American University (Washington, D.C.), explores how and why a wealthy elite's command over ideology was significantly delegitimized during the Great Depression, but remained essentially unchallenged during the Great Recession, with the consequence that whereas a levelling of income, wealth, and privilege occurred in the wake of the earlier crisis, its widening has characterized the later one. Professor Bradley Bowden, from Griffith University, in ▶ Chap. 44, "Trade Union Decline and Transformation: Where to for Employment Relations?" writes a focused piece about the marginalization of unions and organized labor over the last 50 years. In this piece, Bowden shines a light on a key myth about the phenomenon. Specifically, he argues that it is not so much union decline which should be our analytic focus but rather how the construct of unionization has become largely the preserve of high-paid professionals; now well serving the interests of this cohort and neglecting organizational labor's traditional constituency, the low-skilled/low-paid. In ▶ Chap. 45, "The New Executive: Interconnected Yet Isolated and Uninformed – Leadership Challenges in the Digital Pandemic Epoch" by Professor Kathleen M. Park (Boston University and Research Fellow at MIT's Sloan School of Business) describes and interprets recent shifts in executive thinking. Her thesis on this topic explores the theme of the paradox of decline in ethical action in combination with a rise in ethics education. It also highlights the problem of an increasingly narrow focus in management thinking and priorities in the lead-up to the age of crisis. The conclusion of this section (▶ Chap. 46, "Conclusion: Management Theory in Crisis"), written by Professor Jean-Etienne Joullié, from the Gulf University for Science and Technology and Laval University, argues that in tandem with public policy failure, there has been failure on the part of management theorists to position their discipline in an appropriate epistemological framework. Joullié argues that their pretentions to establish management as science, on the same footing, for example, as physics, have fallen short. To the extent that the practice of management influences – and is influenced by – public policy, Joullié's chapter represents an appropriate conclusion to this section. Indeed, it reveals something about the systemic, and to an extent, exponential nature of decline. Insofar as the world of work and employment is concerned, it also sheds light on another aspect of how experts have failed to deliver.

Cross-References

- ▶ A Return to the Good Old Days: Populism, Fake News, Yellow Journalism, and the Unparalleled Virtue of Business People
- ▶ Conclusion: Management Theory in Crisis
- ▶ Labor and Employment Practices: The Rise and Fall of the New Managerialism
- ▶ Management History in the Modern World: An Overview
- ▶ The New Executive: Interconnected Yet Isolated and Uninformed – Leadership Challenges in the Digital Pandemic Epoch
- ▶ Trade Union Declinc and Transformation: Where to for Employment Relations?
- ▶ What Is Management?
- ▶ Why did the Great Recession Fail to Produce a *New* New Deal in the USA?

References

Andersen K (2017) Fantasyland: how America went Haywire: a 500-year history. Penguin Random House, New York

Antonio RJ, Bonanno A (2000) A new global capitalism? From 'Americanism and Fordism' to 'Americanization-globalization'. Am Stud 41(2–3):33–77

Appleby, J. (2011). The relentless revolution: a history of capitalism, Reprint edition. W. W. Norton & Company, New York.

Asen R (2009) Ideology, materiality, and counterpublicity: William E. Simon and the rise of a conservative counterintelligentsia. Q J Speech 95(3):263–288

Baca G (2004) Legends of Fordism. Soc Anal 48:171–180

Barley SR, Kunda G (1992) Design and devotion: surges of rational and normative ideologies of control in managerial discourse. Adm Sci Q 37(3):363–399

Boyer M (2009) La crise économique et ses conséquences sur l'emploi. Les cahiers de l'institut économique de Montréal, Montreal

Brady D (2008) Rich democracies, poor people: how politics explain poverty. Oxford University Press, New York

Braedley S, Luxton M (2010) Neoliberalism and everyday life. McGill-Queens University Press, Montreal

Brenner R (2002) The boom and the bubble: the US in the world economy. Verso, New York

Buchanan J (2003) Center for study of public choice at George Mason University, Fairfax

Case A, Coates TN (2017) Fear and despair: Consequences of inequity. Chapter 1 in knowledge to action. Oxford University Press, New York

Case A, Deaton A (2017) Suicide, age, and wellbeing: an empirical investigation. NBER working paper 21279, chapter 10. In: Insights in the economics of aging. University of Chicago Press, Chicago, pp 307–334

Chapman JI (1998) Proposition 13: some unintended consequences. Public Policy Institute of California, San Francisco

Combe E (1996) Précis d'économie. Presses universitaires de France, Paris

Connell R (2010) Understanding neoliberalism. In: Braedley S, Luxton M (eds) Neoliberalism and everyday life. McGill-Queens University Press, Montreal

Cooper M (2012) Family values: between neoliberalism and the new social conservatism. Zone Books, New York

Dean J (2009) Democracy and other neoliberal fantasies: communicative capitalism and left politics. Duke University Press, Durham

Diaz D (2016) https://www.cnn.com/2016/09/26/politics/donald-trump-federal-income-taxes-smart-debate/index.html

Doray B, Macy D (1988) From Taylorism to Fordism: a rational madness. Free Association Books, New York

Dunn G (2011) The lies of Sarah Palin: the untold story behind her relentless quest for power. St Martin's Press, New York

Ebenstein AO (2002) Hayek's journey: the mind of Freidrich Hayek. Palgrave-McMillan, New York

Ebenstein AO (2003) Friedrich Hayek: a biography. University of Chicago Press, Chicago

Eisenhower DD (1952) Speech to the American federation of labor made in New York City. 17 Sept 1952 (cited in Newton J (2011) Eisenhower: the Whitehouse Years. Doubleday, New York)

Ferguson T (1995) Golden rule: the investment theory of party competition and the logic of money-driven political systems. University of Chicago Press, Chicago

Gantman ER (2005) Capitalism, social privilege and managerial ideologies. Ashgate, Hampshire

Gould AM (2010) The Americanisation of Australian workplaces. Labor Hist 51(3):363–388

Gould AM, Robert M (2013) The neoliberal peas and thimble trick: changing rhetoric of neoliberal champions of across two periods of economic history and two messages about why the message is less sanguine. Adv Appl Sociol 3:79–84

Gould AM, Bourk MJ, Joullié JE (2017) From the industrial revolution to trump: six periods of changing perceptions of American business managers. J Manag Hist 23(4):471–488

Gramsci A (1971) Selections from the prison notebooks. International Publishers, New York
Gwartney JD (2008) Supply-side economics. In: Henderson DR (ed) Concise encyclopedia of economics, 2nd edn. Liberty Fund, Indianapolis
Harrison B, Bluestone B (1988) The great U-turn: corporate restructuring and the polarising of America. Basic Books Inc, New York
Harvey D (2005) A brief history of neoliberalism. Oxford University Press, Oxford
Harvey D (2006) Neoliberalism as creative destruction. Geogr Ann Series B Hum Geogr Geogr Power Power Geogr 88(2):145–158
Hayek F(2001). The road to serfdom, Routledge Classics edition. Routledge, New York.
Hitchens C (2001) The trial of Henry Kissinger. Verso, New York
Hounshell DA (1984) From the American system to mass production, 1800–1932: the development of manufacturing technology in the United States. Johns Hopkins University Press, Baltimore
Issawi C (1979) The 1973 oil crisis and after. J Post Keynesian Econ 1(2):3–26
Joullié JE, Spillane R (2015) The philosophical foundations of management thought. Lexington Books, London
Katz H, Darbishire O (2000) Converging divergences: worldwide changes in employment relations systems. ILR Press, Ithaca
Kauder B, Potrafke N (2015) Globalization and social justice in OECD countries (27 Feb 2015). CESifo working paper series no. 5210. Available at SSRN: https://ssrn.com/abstract=2576127
Kiesa A, Levine P (2016) Do we actually want higher youth voter turnout? Stanf Soc Innov Rev 14:2–6
Koch M (2006) Roads to post-Fordism: labour markets and social structures in Europe. Routledge/Taylor and Francis Group, New York/London
Kolm SC (1977) La grande crise de 1974. Ann Écon Soc Civil 32(4):815–823
Kondratieff ND, Stolper WF (1935) The long waves of economic life. Rev Econ Stat 17(6):105–115
Kornbluh P (2003) The Pinochet file: a declassified dossier on atrocity and accountability. The New Press, New York
Le Queux S, Peetz D (2013) Between "too big to fail" and "too small to matter": the borderless financial crisis and unions. Int J Manpow 34(3):198–212
Lichtenstein N (2002) State of the union: a century of American labor. Princeton University Press, Princeton
Lo Duca M, Stracca L (2014) The effect of G20 summits on global financial markets. Working paper series for the European Central Bank. Paper N° 1668
Luippold R (2012) Why Johnny Carson matters 20 years after "tonight show" finale. The Huffington Post, May 22
Mandel E (1978) The second slump. A Marxist analysis of recession in the seventies. New Left Books, London
McDermott J (1992) History in the present: contemporary debates about capitalism. Sci Soc 56(3):291–323
McDonald JJ (1981) Howard Hughes and the Spruce Goose. Tab Books, Blue Ridge Summit
Mead WR (2004) The decline of Fordism and the challenge to American power. N Perspect Q 21(3):53–61
Mishel L, Bernstein J, Allegretto S (2005) The state of working America, 2004/2005. Cornell University Press, Ithaca
Moody K (2007) U.S. labor in trouble and transition: The failure of reform from above, the promise of revival from below. New York, Verso
Pakenham R, Ratliff W (2007) Available from the Hoover Press is Law and economics in developing countries, by Edgardo Buscaglia and William Ratliff. www.hooverpress.org
Park KM, Gould AM (2017) The overlooked influence of personality, idiosyncrasy and eccentricity in corporate mergers and acquisitions: 120 years and six distinct waves. J Manag Hist 23(1):7–31
Piketty T (2014) Capital in the 21st century. Harvard University Press, Cambridge, MA
Rand A (1992) Atlas Shrugged, 35th anniversary edn. Dutton, New York
Roobeek AJM (1987) The crisis in fordism and the rise of a new technological paradigm. Futures 19(2):129–154

Rostow WW (1978) The world economy: history and prospect. University of Texas Press, Austin
Scheiber L (2012) Next Taylorism: a calculus of knowledge work. Peter Lang, Frankfurt am Main
Schumpeter JA, Nichol AJ (1934) Review of Robinson's economics of imperfect competition. J Polit Econ Univ Chicago Press 42(2):249–259
Sen A (1986) Chapter 22 social choice theory. In: Handbook of mathematical economics, vol 3. Elsevier ScienceDirect, New York, pp 1073–1181
Sorensen CE (with Williamson ST) (1956) My forty years with Ford. Norton, New York
Sowell T (2010) Intellectuals and society. Basic Books, New York
Sterman JD (1986) The economic long wave: theory and evidence. Syst Dyn Rev 2(2):87–125
Stewart JB (2009) Eight days: the battle to save the American financial system. The New Yorker Magazine, September 21
Summers PM (2005) What caused the great moderation? Some cross-country evidence. Federal Reserve Bank Kansas City Econ Rev 3:5–32
Taneja S, Pryor MG, Humpheries JH, Toombs LA (2011) Where are the new organization theories? Evolution, development and theoretical debate. Int J Manag 28(3):959–978
Taylor FW (1911) The principles of scientific management. Harper & Brothers, New York/London
Trump D (1987) The art of the deal. Random House, New York
Trump D (2007) Think big and kick ass. Harper-Collins, New York
Trump D (2009) Think like a champion: an informal education in business and life. Vanguard Press, New York
Trump D (2011) Time to get tough: making America #1 again. Regency Publishing, New York
Tylecote A (1995) Technological and economic long waves and their implications for employment. N Technol Work Employ 10(1):3–18
Watts S (2005) The people's tycoon: Henry Ford and the American century. Random House, New York
Weber M (1905) The protestant ethic and the spirit of capitalism (trans: Baehr P, Wells GC). Penguin Books, London, ed., 2002
Weiner T (2007) Legacy of ashes: the history of the CIA. Anchor Books, New York
Weissbrot M (2015) Failed: what the experts got wrong about the global economy. Oxford University Press, New York
Weissbrot M, Ray R (2011) The scorecard on development, 1960–2010: closing the gap. Center for Economic and Policy Development, Washington D.C
Wilkinson R, Pickett K (2010) The spirit level: why equality is better for everyone. Penguin Books, London
Williams K, Haslam C, Williams J (1992) Ford versus Fordism: the beginning of mass production? Work Employ Soc 6(4):517–555
Wisman JD (2013) Wage stagnation, rising inequality and the financial crisis of 2008. Camb J Econ 37(4):921–945
Wren D, Greenwood R (1998) Management innovators: the people and ideas that have shaped modern business. Oxford University Press, New York

Labor and Employment Practices: The Rise and Fall of the New Managerialism

41

John Godard

Contents

The Golden Age and Industrial Pluralism	914
The Demise of the Golden Age	917
Managerialism Redux	919
The Limits to the New Managerialism: Ideology vs. Practice.	922
The End of the New Managerialism?	927
Cross-References	930
References	930

Abstract

Since the beginning of industrial capitalism, labor resistance and control have been central problems for management. Yet these problems have varied considerably, in large part depending on the context within which the employment relation is embedded and particularly the broader political economy characterizing it. Workplace and management practices have tended to develop in reflection of this context, while forming an important component of it, with social as well as economic consequences. This chapter addresses these practices, the conditions under which they have developed from the 1950s to present, and what some of their consequences have been.

Keywords

management history · work · employment · HRM · managerialism

J. Godard (✉)
University of Manitoba, Winnipeg, MB, Canada
e-mail: john.godard@umanitoba.ca

Since the beginning of industrial capitalism, labor resistance and control have been central problems for management (Bendix 1956) and ultimately states. These problems arise largely from the nature of the capitalist employment relation, yet have varied in large part depending on the context within which this relation has been embedded and particularly the broader political economy characterizing it. Labor and employment practices have tended to develop in reflection of this context, while forming an important component of it, with important social as well as economic consequences. In this chapter, I address these practices, the conditions under which they have developed since the so-called "golden age" of the post-World War II era, and what some of their consequences have been. A problem with any such analysis is that management practices have varied extensively within and across nations. I focus on practices dominant in the USA, but refer to this variation where relevant (see Godard 2019 for a comparative analysis).

The Golden Age and Industrial Pluralism

There is perhaps no better example of the importance of the broader political economy in which labor and employment practices are embedded than the "golden age" of the 1950s and 1960s. During this period, unemployment was at historically low levels and productivity, GDP, and income growth rates at historically high ones throughout the developed world. These conditions were associated with the growth of large scale work organizations, characterized by mass production technologies and operating in largely stable, concentrated markets. At risk of oversimplification, increased economies of scale achieved by these firms fuelled productivity increases that were shared with workers, thus enabling them to purchase more goods and services, and in turn generating increased demand and hence further expansions of productive capacity and the economies of scale deriving from them. A "virtuous circle" is thus said to have existed.

Of central importance to this circle were so-called labor-capital accords in most developed nations. These accords were often implicit, and many had begun to emerge prior to the Second World War. They also varied substantially from one nation to the next. But at minimum, they entailed economic policies designed to smooth economic cycles and minimize unemployment, coupled with social and labor market policies designed to ensure some minimum quality of life for those both in and out of employment.

In industrial relations and (what is now known as) human resource management, these accords meant improved rights and protections at work, including (in theory, if not always in practice) the right to meaningful collective representation and bargaining. This was especially true in the United States, where they also meant the adoption of bureaucratic workplace practices, including extensive job descriptions specifying what could be expected of employees, and seniority-based rules for determining promotion and layoff. They also entailed employer recognition and accommodation of what were seen to be distinctive employee interests and provision of wage and benefit gains commensurate with productivity gains and inflation. The expectation was that, in return, workers would come to accept their positions of subordination and that labor unions would play an important role in ensuring that they did so. In this regard, unions would address worker discontent through collective bargaining and representation, thereby helping to "institutionalize" and control conflict in the workplace and beyond. In effect, they were to serve as "managers of discontent," essentially playing an important if often contentious role for management (Mills 1948).

These practices were especially characteristic of large US employers located in what came to be labeled the "core" of the economy (Averitt 1968). State social and labor market programs were weakest in this nation, creating a condition under which workers remained highly dependent on employers for their economic and social welfare. Core employers typically provided an array of benefits, essentially ensuring that this would be the case, and workers came to enjoy the various rights and protections associated with union coverage. These firms were typically characterized by well-developed personnel and IR departments, which, in addition to performing basic personnel administration, were responsible for negotiating collective agreements and administering the various rights and benefits arising from them.

In an era characterized by low unemployment and rapid growth, and limited if any skill requirements for entry-level jobs, employee selection largely amounted to ensuring that applicants possessed minimum educational qualifications and capabilities. Once hired, new employees might be subject to some formal training, but for the most part the expectation was that they would develop firm-specific skill sets and experience over time. As they did so, they could expect to move up a "job ladder," into jobs characterized by higher pay and greater responsibility. Coupled with seniority-based benefits (e.g., vacation entitlements), workers had a strong incentive to conform to managerial expectations and remain "loyal" to their employer (Edwards 1979). Workers also came to expect regular, after inflation, improvements in pay and benefits, largely in reflection of ongoing improvements in productivity and ultimately their employers' ability to pay.

Although these arrangements were subject to criticisms that they favored more senior male and white workers, and although they fell far short of fully "democratizing" the workplace, they were in many respects much more consistent with democratic values than either the welfare capitalist practices that often preceded (and continued to compete with: Jacoby 1997) them or the new managerialist practices that were eventually to (in theory) supersede them. Clear work rules limited the range and amount of work that workers could be required to do, providing them with some measure of "concrete freedom on the job" (Perlman 1949). Workers could not be arbitrarily disciplined and had a right to due process should they be. Promotion was based not on currying favor with supervisors or with willingness to "rate bust," but rather on largely objective seniority criteria that could reasonably be associated with ability and experience. Workers could expect to receive decent pay and benefits, enabling them to participate as equals in civil society. They also enjoyed substantial job and income security, protecting them from the exigencies – and coercion of market forces. Finally, through their union, they could develop a true sense of fraternity and empowerment at work, and even meaningful voice in their political system.

These arrangements were in considerable measure a product of the times. It would appear, for example, that the willingness of US employers to accept and work with labor unions was largely pragmatic. Labor stability and acquiescence were essential if these employers were to take advantage of expanding markets and achieve ongoing productivity gains, providing unions with substantial power at the bargaining table, and rendering employers dependent on union ability and willingness to manage discontent in the workplace – in return for substantial concessions and acceptance of the union as a legitimate entity. Many of the rights and protections granted at the bargaining table were also consistent with the orderly management of human resources and largely complementary to the bureaucratic organizational structures that had become predominant in large employers – structures that were in turn conducive to relatively high levels of market stability and high levels of market concentration. Indeed, most large nonunion employers adopted similar policies and practices, in part as a "union substitution" strategy, but also because they were consistent with efficiency interests. Finally, this was the cold war era, in which a central tenet of the dominant ideology (especially in the USA) was that only capitalism could be expected to deliver steadily improving jobs and living standards. This tenet became central to worker expectations and, in the USA, the "American way."

These arrangements were also limited in both coverage and effectiveness. There continued to be a large economic periphery characterized by relatively low pay and largely autocratic employment practices (Averitt 1968; Galbraith 1973). Employers in this sector tended to be small or intermediate in size and to operate in more competitive markets than their counterparts in the economic core. They also tended to be more labor intensive and less subject to the kinds of productivity gains enjoyed by these employers. Most important, they were typically not just nonunion, but aggressively antiunion.

Even in the economic core, however, a number of employers managed to remain nonunion, and groups and associations backed by many core employers continued to mount substantial attacks on 'Big Labor' (Jacoby 1997; Godard 2009). There also continued to be substantial resistance on the shop floor (see Fairris 1994). Although workers and their leaders had come to largely accept management's right to manage, they still found themselves in positions of subordination, often in dehumanizing, Taylorized jobs (O'Toole et al. 1973: 29–38). But because they had substantial rights and protections, they could engage in acts of resistance with less fear of retribution. It is little coincidence that the study of "organizational behavior," with its focus on problems of motivation, leadership, and group norms, flourished in the 1950s and 1960s – even if this field has failed to ever grasp how the nature and context of the employment relation gives rise to these problems.

There were also important differences between the archetypical US "core" model and the dominant management models in other developed countries (see Marsden 1999). For example, British workplaces during this period were characterized by less formal structures and hence by greater reliance on worker discretion and good will than in the USA (e.g., Burawoy 1985: 139–40). Union recognition by employers was also voluntary, yet with density much higher than in the USA, and formal bargaining tended to be at the industry level, yet supplemented by on-going, informal bargaining at the workplace level. Personnel management and industrial relations would seem to have been largely undeveloped (Guest and Bryson 2009: 124).

In Germany, the combination of a strong state, a strong vocational training system, very high union density, industry-wide bargaining, worker representation on supervisory boards, mandatory works councils, and ultimately an alternative variety of capitalism, made for a substantially different management context. Although German workplaces may have been bureaucratic in design, workplace rules were jointly determined and hence differed substantially from those of US workplaces. Moreover, US-style internal labor markets were unsuited to the German workplace, where training and advancement were based on the German vocational skill system and depended much less on informal, on-the-job learning and seniority (Marsden 1999: 119–28). Finally, decision making was not just accommodative, it came to be largely collaborative (see Adams 1995: 142–49).

Despite these differences, it can be reasonably concluded that, indeed, bureaucratic work organization in some form came to be omnipresent, and accommodation of worker interests and organizations (i.e., unions) central to managerial policies in the core of major developed economies. In this regard, the term "industrial pluralism" was popularized to refer to the widespread belief that workers and management had distinctively different and often conflicting interests and that accommodation of these differences was not only essential to the maintenance of industrial stability but was also a hallmark of modern democracy. The practical realization of this belief may have varied, but it was made possible by the ability of employers to grant bureaucratic terms and conditions of employment and continual improvements in incomes. It was also accompanied by a culture of entitlement, under which workers came to believe that they had a right to expect fair and just treatment at work and steadily improving living standards in return for their subordination.

The Demise of the Golden Age

The preconditions for the post-World War II model began to break down in the mid-1960s, as the economies associated with large scale mass production (aka "Fordism") began to diminish (see Harvey 1989: 141–72; Arrighi 2007:123–30; Glyn 2006). Not only did productivity growth and profitability begin to decline, price inflation began to increase, largely in reflection of massive US-government spending on the Vietnam War but also the inability of firms to provide the steady wage increases central to postwar accord without having to raise prices. Where the former made it increasingly difficult for employers to grant the kinds of increases in real income that had been central to the postwar accord, the latter threatened to undermine living standards and increased cost uncertainty for employers. Labor unrest also began to increase, as employers attempted to reduce annual wage increases, workers rebelled against often boring and even dehumanizing work, and employers increasingly sought productivity gains by intensification of work processes rather than efficiency gains. These problems continued throughout much of the 1970s and into the early 1980s. Inflation was further fuelled by OPEC oil price increases in 1973 and then 1979. International competition, particularly from Japanese producers in the automobile and electronics sectors, also became increasingly intense, putting pressure on employers to enhance quality and output levels.

By the end of the 1970s, the political climate had also begun to shift considerably. Economic liberalism, which many thought had been fully discredited half a century earlier, was resurrected and reborn under the nomenclature of "neoliberalism." The postwar accord and the government policies associated with it came under increasing attack from politicians and pundits adhering to this dogma, supported by a network of privately financed "think tanks" and institutes (e.g., Harvey 2005).

These developments were most pronounced in the UK, the USA, and to a lesser extent Canada. The postwar accords in these countries were always relatively weak, especially in comparison with those in their more corporatist European and Scandinavian counterparts, where worker rights and protections were stronger, labor unions represented a large majority of workers, and institutional conditions induced employers to adopt more of a "stakeholder" orientation. These differences, coupled with different political traditions and more "coordinated," social market economies, meant that employers, labor unions, and governments found it to be in their interests and capacities to achieve consensus as to how to address the new economic "realities" they confronted. This was reflected in strike activity. Although there was some increase in labor unrest in these countries, strike activity remained almost trivial compared to levels in the USA, Canada, and the UK (Godard 2011), where there was little foundation for such consensus.

These differences were stark with regard to the USA, which had a long history of institutional norms favoring strong property rights, weak labor rights, and weak government (e.g., Godard 2009), and a political system with only weak checks and balances against corporate interests (Jacoby 1991). As a result, commitment to the postwar accord had always been pragmatic, but the "new deal" labor laws and policies supporting it had always been fragile. Indeed, laws supporting the right to form a union were virtually gutted within only a few years after the conclusion of the Second World War, if not earlier, and union density had begun to slowly decline before the end of the 1950s (Godard 2009).

Combined with the rise of the political right and the election of Ronald Reagan, the result was a shift to neoliberal state policies, characterized by weak rights and protections for workers, government and corporate attacks on labor unions, deregulation, privatization, liberalization of international capital markets, and harsh monetary and fiscal policies. There was an ensuing substantial weakening (or even gutting) of the postwar accord, creating a more hostile environment for both workers and their unions. This was accompanied by the growing "financialization" of the economy, as financial interests gained enhanced control over firms, and decision making came to be increasingly emphasize short term financial gain over longer term growth, productivity, and even profitability (Harvey 1989; Ho 2009). Repeated acts of "downsizing" and plant closures, coupled with high levels of unemployment and a substantial weakening of labor unions, essentially created a more submissive and insecure workforce, achieving labor "peace" in considerable measure through coercion rather than consent.

In contrast to the US case, governments in Canada and the UK made some effort to forge a new consensus, in reflection of their more paternalistic and hence accommodative political traditions. But these efforts ultimately failed. In the UK, a Labor government's efforts at a corporatist settlement collapsed during the "winter of discontent" in 1978–1979, helping to create the conditions for the election of Margaret Thatcher and a dramatic shift towards neoliberalism in the 1980s. In Canada, an effort to cure inflation with wage and price controls in the late 1970s failed, ushering in a conservative government and a turn towards neoliberalism, albeit one that was more gradual and less dramatic than in the UK.

Although it varied in specifics, the shift to neoliberalism came to be largely institutionalized in western countries. It also came to dominate elite economic and political thought, giving rise to the "Washington Consensus" and the neoliberal trade policies and agreements associated with it. Growing hyperbole over globalization, along with enhanced competition from newly industrializing economies, only served to further cow workers and their leaders. The culture of entitlement that had developed during the golden age gradually gave rise to one of compliance. Within this culture, it was no longer appropriate to expect more, or even to expect either states or employers to provide the rights and protections that could be taken-for-granted in the postwar era. There was to be no quid pro quo for subordination – other than a permanent, full-time job if one was lucky, and decent pay and benefits if one was very lucky.

Managerialism Redux

The developments of the 1970s and 1980s created the conditions for the emergence of new managerial ideologies. Pundits argued that the postwar model of management was obsolete and that there was need for corporations to eliminate bureaucratic hierarchies and replace them with more organic, "clan" forms of organization (e.g., Ouchi 1980, 1982). These were sold as consistent with Japanese management practices, which were to become a fad in business schools throughout the 1980s.[1] As promoted by business school academics, there was need to return to a more unitary, managerialist approach, albeit under a new and more sophisticated guise than in the past (Godard and Delaney 2000). Under this approach, workers would in theory be viewed not as "costs" or "problems" to be managed, but rather as resources to be developed and deployed so as to unleash their potential. A critical underlying

---

[1] Arguably, much of the management literature on Japanese practices was based on a fundamental misunderstanding of how and why the Japanese system actually appeared to work The Japanese system has traditionally been characterized by a collectivist (almost feudal) orientation, with strong norms privileging worker ("member") interests over those of shareholders, a strong belief in relative equality, and noncompetitive (within Japan) markets. This could not be more different than the US case, yet is something that business school academics seemed unable (or unwilling) to process (e.g., Dore 2000).

assumption was that worker attitudes and behavior could be readily molded to suit managerial goals.

This argument was both facilitated by and facilitative of the continuing shift towards neoliberalism and the culture of compliance it generated. Both made it increasingly possible and profitable to discard the more pluralistic, accommodative practices of the postwar era. In particular, compliant workers, faced with a growing scarcity of good jobs and constant threats of job loss should their performance be unsatisfactory, coupled with weak employment laws and weakened labor unions, meant that employers virtually had a green light to either ignore or radically reshape the post-World War II accord as they saw fit. Emergent managerial ideologies provided both the justification and the motivation for doing so. Although they overlapped, there were three such ideologies: (1) the "new" HRM (aka "strategic" HRM), (2) the high performance paradigm, and (3) the flexible firm thesis.

The new HRM was perhaps the most central to the new managerialism. Although there were initially different variants of this new paradigm (see Legge 1995b; Strauss 2001), all were predicated on the argument that the management of "human resources" is of key strategic importance and can serve as an inimitable source of competitive advantage if only the appropriate policies and practices are adopted (Tichy et al. 1982). Under the new HRM, selection is to become more "scientific" and based on values and social skills as much as technical acumen or general ability. The implicit assumption is that workers should be hired only if they are likely to buy into management goals and be good "team" players. Training and development are to be enhanced, but more so as to further inculcate management values and skills than so as to develop technical abilities. Workers are to be subjected to regular performance appraisals, based on "scientific" supervisory assessments, and on specific performance criteria against which employees can be evaluated and compared. In turn, pay and promotion are to be linked to performance rather than to seniority. Finally, firms should engage in strategic HR planning, and HR conisderations should play a key role in strategic management decision processes.

Proponents of the new HRM typically had little to say about worker rights or labor unions, at most tending to advocate nonunion communication and "justice" systems.[2] In effect, where the traditional model assumed that workers were distinctive stakeholders and hence that there was need to accommodate their interests and values, proponents of the new HRM assumed that worker perceptions of their interests could be altered so as to conform to managerial goals. Unions were considered to be both unnecessary and undesirable unless they were willing to discard their traditional, adversarial approach and collaborate with the employer.

There were also a number of variants of the high performance paradigm (e.g., Godard 2004). But as conceived by the "MIT school," this paradigm focused more

---

[2] I need to emphasize "typically." The so-called "Harvard" version (Beer et al. 1984, 1985) did pay attention to labor-management relations, as did an "MIT" version (Kochan and Barocci 1985). Yet these variants seem to have been rapidly eclipsed by a more unitary, performance driven version, dominated by psychologists with little concept of labor unions or why they exist (Godard 2014; Beer et al. 2015).

on the design of work and on workplace participation systems than did the new HRM (see Kochan and Osterman 1994; Pfeffer 1994). Under the postwar model, workers tended to be assigned to clearly defined, individualized jobs and had little input into decisions that might affect how they performed these jobs. In effect, they were hired into a job and simply expected to do it. The high performance paradigm instead advocated more flexible job designs, with multiskilling, job rotation, and, most important, team-based work systems, where workers could perform a wider variety of tasks in conjunction with their fellow team members. In the ideal, teams would be self-directed or "autonomous," controlling the pace at which they worked and how they did their work, and with limited if any direct supervision. They would also have responsibility for a measurable output, with bonuses based on team rather than individual performance. Accompanying these teams would be various participation and communication systems, including labor-management "steering committees," "quality circles," team "briefings" (information sessions), periodic "town-hall" meetings, and a variety of added information sources (e.g., newsletters) on developments in the workplace.

In theory, these practices were most effective at enhancing performance if implemented in conjunction with lean production and total quality management systems (Lawler 1986) and if fully accompanied by complementary HRM practices (Pfeffer 1994). The HRM practices advocated were largely consistent with the new HRM, although they also entailed promises of job security and efforts to work with unions under the guise of a win-win "mutual gains" approach (Pfeffer 1994; Kochan and Osterman 1994). In theory, both helped to create the levels of loyalty and "buy-in" necessary for the effectiveness of high performance systems. They also facilitated flexibility in the allocation and use of human resources.

The major difference between the new HRM and the high performance paradigm was that the former typically assumed an entirely unitary model of the firm, under which workers can be selected, indoctrinated, and "incentivized" to identify with employer interests, while the latter viewed workers as distinctive stakeholders. The latter, however, may also be labeled as "managerialist," as it also assumed that loyalty and commitment can be maximized, and conflict minimized, if management only adopts and correctly implements the appropriate policies and practices (Godard and Delaney 2000). It was also predicated on the existence of a compliant labor force, with only weak rights and protections in the labor market, and largely compliant labor unions. Again, neoliberal government policies largely created these conditions.

The third ideology emergent during this era was the "flexible firm thesis" (Atkinson 1984; see Legge 1995b: 139–73). This thesis included more flexible job descriptions, multiskilling, job rotation, and team-working, all of which are part-and-parcel of the high performance model but do not require implementation in conjunction with it. It also included, however, increased use of temporary and part-time employees, increased "outsourcing," and an increased willingness to lay-off workers, none of which is consistent with the high performance model. These practices were argued to have been increasingly adopted by employers in order to adjust to fluctuations in demand in a more uncertain and competitive economic environment. In this regard, the flexible firm thesis may have been somewhat less normative than its other two counterparts, although a clear implication was that firms would and *should* become increasingly flexible over time.

Again, the assumption underlying the flexible firm thesis was of a largely neoliberal environment, under which management was subject to few meaningful constraints from either governments or unions and could count on a largely compliant labor force, with few options other than to take whatever jobs were on offer. It became commonplace for management pundits to proclaim that the full-time, permanent jobs of the postwar era were largely dead, except perhaps for a privileged group of essential workers, and that workers must expect to constantly "remake" themselves as they moved from one job to another. More important, this thesis became central to the argument that problems of economic growth were caused by unduly rigid labor markets and that there was a need to further weaken labor rights and protections in order address them. This thesis became especially prominent in European economies and provided the justification for a variety of neoliberal reforms (Thelen 2014).

The Limits to the New Managerialism: Ideology vs. Practice.

The new managerialism, and particularly the new HRM, became very much the rage in business schools within but also beyond the USA, spawning the newly formulated (or reformulated) area of study, Human Resources Management, and gradually eclipsing the field of industrial relations in both academia and management practice. The practices associated with it also generated considerable controversy. Although proponents typically assumed that these practices were "win-win," improving both job quality and performance, more critical scholars argued either that they involved work intensification and management by stress (Graham 1993), or that they largely amounted to ideological justifications for undermining the quality of employment (Legge 1995a, b), or that they represented a new and more insidious form of control, characterized by hidden forms of power and domination and designed to alter worker norms and consciousness (Townley 1994), or that they simply did not generate the promised "payoffs" in most contexts (Godard 2004; Kaufman 2015).

The available empirical evidence, however, calls into question just how widely the sets of practices associated with the new managerialism ever came to be adopted (Godard 2004) or how much of a difference they have made where adopted. To begin, increases to part-time and temporary employment have been relatively limited and highly variable across nations. For example, in the USA, only 4 percent of labor market participants were in temporary positions as of the mid-2010s, and although part-time work accounted for 13 percent of the labor force, this was little changed from the 1970s (OECD 2017; Bernhardt 2014: 5). In the UK, the equivalent statistics were 6 and 24 percent, respectively, with the latter having increased by only 6 percentage points from the early 1980s. Moreover, those increases that did occur in the UK and elsewhere may have been in large measure attributable less to employer practices in large firms than to the expanding share of jobs in the retail and accommodation sectors. Although larger, "core" sector employers may have made increased use of these practices, it would seem to have been indirectly, through the contracting out of subsidiary functions (e.g., food services, security, janitorial; see Bernhardt 2014: 8–13; Bernhardt et al. 2016: 27).

Moreover, evidence as to job stability suggests that, if anything, there has been an increase in average job tenure in most developed nations (at least, since 1992: OECD StatExtracts 2017). This is not consistent with arguments that employers have become quicker to lay off workers than in the past. Indeed, even in the USA, where restrictions on layoffs are perhaps the lowest in the developed world, it appears that, at least since 1984, those changes that occurred largely tracked changes in unemployment levels and in this sense suggest little major shift in employer practices (Bernhardt 2014; Farber 2015). UK data also suggest a long term decline in both voluntary and involuntary separations since at least the mid-1990s (Bewley 2013).

Similarly, as of the early 2000s, large scale government surveys revealed that fewer than one in ten employers in the USA, UK, and Canada had adopted autonomous teams for their core workers (e.g., Blasi and Kruse 2006; Kersley et al. 2006; Godard 2017: 137), even though these are central to the high performance model. It would appear that some of the practices (e.g., appraisals) associated with this model and with the new HRM have been widely adopted (Godard 2004; Wood and Bryson 2009: 160); my own surveys of workers in the USA, UK, Canada, and Germany in 2003 and 2009 tend to bear this out as well (see Godard 2019: appendix). But the adoption of these practices does not appear to reflect any widespread fundamental change in management regimes (e.g., see Boudreau and Lawler III 2014). In most cases, their adoption seems to have been piecemeal and grafted on to more traditional (albeit perhaps weakened) bureaucratic practices (Godard 2004; Godard 2019: appendix), involving what Legge has labeled "thinking pragmatism" (1995b: 330) and Boudreau and Lawler III (2014) as "stubborn traditionalism."

This is not to suggest that there have been no substantive changes in management practices over the past three or more decades. In actuality, available data on the former are almost nonexistent for the period prior to the mid-1990s, which is when these practices were most heavily promoted. The best available (UK) data do suggest, however, that the level of real change in work and HRM practices would appear to have been limited to a few "new" practices (e.g., information sharing and briefings) and to have been gradual (e.g., Wood and Bryson 2009: 159).

How much of an actual difference these practices have made to labor and employment relations is also not clear. There has in this regard been a virtual cottage industry of studies attempting to establish that both high performance and new HRM practices have meaningful effects. Yet reviews of the most carefully conducted studies have concluded that these studies have typically yielded either weak or readily contestable results (Delaney and Godard 2001; Godard 2004; Wall and Wood 2006; Marsden and Canibano 2010; Kaufman 2015). The most widely cited meta-analysis of the research (Combs et al. 2006) finds a modest positive effect, but to obtain this effect, it lumped together all manner of practices, including those associated with the traditional, postwar model (Kaufman 2015). It also found little association for performance appraisal systems, teams, and information sharing, all of which are central to the literature. A subsequent meta-analysis (Jiang et al. 2012) is also unconvincing.[3]

A particular problem has been that employers may adopt some or many of these practices in some form, but just how extensively they do so, or whether they even represent anything new, may vary considerably. For example, the organization of work in groups or small departments has always been widespread, and so it is possible that the word "team," which seems to have become widespread (e.g., Kersely et al. 2006: 90), often entails more of a semantic than a substantive change to how work is performed. This is especially so given the limited implementation of "self-directed" teams noted above. In addition, however, appraisal systems would seem too often be largely bureaucratic exercises with little purpose other than to placate HR departments and create the appearance of professional management.

The research does seem to show that some professional HRM and "new work" practices have, on average, positive performance effects (e.g., training, performance pay, profit sharing), and it may be that some of these practices (e.g., in the UK, appraisals: see Bewley 2013) have continued to diffuse across employers. But even if so, this may simply reflect the adoption of more formally rational management techniques, made more possible by a neoliberal context and a more compliant workforce, rather than a magic elixir associated with these techniques or some Foucauldian spell they cast over workers. Employers adopting such practices may be more sophisticated than those that do not do so, but how much of a change in workplace relations or even in the employment experience their adoption has entailed remains uncertain in view of the existing research. This is especially true if one compares their implications to those of more traditional bureaucratic practices. It is in this respect quite likely that the latter may indeed have been weakened somewhat, especially in nonunion workplaces in the private sector, but they would still appear to be prevalent and, indeed, judging by much of the research on high performance work systems, many of them (e.g., seniority rules, internal "justice" systems) now seem to be considered as part-and-parcel of "best practice" (Godard 2004; Kaufman 2015).

This conclusion is reinforced by research into the effects of new HRM and work practices on workers, which suggests that only limited effects for various new work and HRM practices (see Bockerman et al. 2012; Godard 2010). In this regard, a particularly striking finding from a more recent (2009) survey of US workers is that more traditional bureaucratic practices have far more positive implications for

---

[3]It suggests positive effects for various categories of work and HRM practices, and for a combined overall measure labeled as "high performance work systems" – which now seems to have become a generic term that includes any and all HRM and nonbureaucratic work practices rather than those associated with the high performance paradigm as initially formulated. As for other meta-analyses, however, this analysis included such a potpourri of measures, from studies of such varying quality that it is difficult to know what the authors really found. It also suffered from a number of the problems associated with these sorts analysis (see Jiang et al. 2012: 1278–79).

various dimensions of job quality than do their more recent "new" counterparts (Frege and Godard 2014). Thus, to the extent that the former have replaced by the latter, the net outcome is likely to be worsened. But the available evidence suggests that this has not, in any case, generally happened, and that "old" and "new" practices bear quite strong positive associations (Frege and Godard 2014: 961). So it would seem that "new" practices may have altered the experience of work somewhat in the USA, but not in any fundamental way.

Again, however, it is difficult to generalize across nations, as much may depend on the institutional context within which various practices are implemented. For example, drawing on the European Working Conditions Survey, Lorenz and Valeyre (2005) found that the adoption of new work practices tended to be much more consistent with a learning model in Germany and the Scandanavian countries than in Britain and Ireland, likely in reflection of better employment protection and vocational training systems in the former. In their study of US and German workers, Frege and Godard (2014) found that the frequency with which individual "new" practices have been adopted varied considerably between the USA and Germany, likely because German institutions allow a much greater role for worker interests in the determination of these practices than is the case for the USA, but also because the problem of control is addressed through national institutions rather than employer practices, thereby altering both their purpose and their design. It also found that the "effects" of these practices on workers are far more positive in Germany than in the USA; in turn bureaucratic practices had much smaller effects than in the USA, likely because institutions ensure less need for the various protections these practices provide in the latter. So, again, it would appear that the practices adopted and their apparent effects depend very much on the institutional environment in which they are adopted. Perhaps paradoxically, a neoliberal context may make it easier to implement these practices, but it may also mean that they are less effective for management (Godard 2004).

It would also be a mistake to assume that these practices have remained static and hence that their effects on labor and employment relations have not strengthened over time. As for any "innovative" practices, there has likely been substantial learning and adjustment, as employers determine what seems to work and what does not and as new iterations emerge. For example, the term "talent management" has become increasingly predominant in the HRM literature, suggesting a stronger human capital development orientation than initially found in the new HRM literature (Dundon and Rafferty 2018). It would also appear, partly in reflection of this orientation, that employers have begun to rely somewhat more on external labor markets than in the past and are more likely to focus on (and reward) "core" employees at the expense of their more peripheral counterparts.

In addition, the "subjects" of "new" work and HRM practices may adjust to them over time in ways that either enhance or diminish any effects that they do have, or they may develop ways to alter or undermine them depending on their orientations and opportunities to do so (see Vallas 2006). Alternatively, many of these practices (e.g., appraisal, performance pay) may remain in name only, as managers seek to avoid discord and hence only go through the motions (e.g., give everyone the same bonus). My own (Canadian) research finds, for example, that although high performance work practices appeared to have had both positive and negative effects for workers as of the 1990s, their negative effects seem to have declined a decade later, and any positive effects they still had were limited to participative practices in union workplaces (Godard 2010).

More important, the effects of these practices on workplace relations may have been altered over time as complementary information and communications technologies have become more sophisticated. This may be the case if the latter enhance access to knowledge and facilitate learning through various feedback systems (Martin 2017). It may also be the case if they facilitate the constant surveillance of workers, through secondary listening devices, automatic customer feedback surveys, remote tracking systems, and performance metric systems (Green 2004).

These caveats notwithstanding, the available evidence just does not suggest that the practices associated with the new managerialism have in themselves had particularly strong effects on labor and employment relations Their main effect would seem to have been to help HRM practitioners elevate their stature and hence influence in organizations, adopting various credentialing systems and promoting themselves as "professionals" (Guest and Bryson 2009: 124). These practitioners would in the process also seemed to have undergone an ideological shift, under which they are less likely to recognize that workers may have distinctive interests and more likely to try to legitimate themselves as essential to the "strategic" interests of the employer (Kochan 2007). This shift has been accompanied by an Orwellian change in language-in-use, designed to create the impression of a unity of interests (e.g., "team" instead of "group," "unit," or "department"), and an implied expectation that workers will behave accordingly.

Underpinning much of this change has been the emergence of a new and (initially) burgeoning area for business school academics with a vested interest in establishing the performance effects of new work and HRM practices (Legge 1995b: 319–21; Kaufman 2015) and in developing seemingly new "innovations" for management (e.g., Gittell 2016). Often, this research has been highly instrumentalist, promoting an objectified view of workers (and employees in general), not as *human* resources, but rather as simply resources (Godard 2014). This may in turn be transmitted to HRM practitioners and students, ultimately hardening managerial orientations towards workers.

Overall, the primary effect of the new managerialism may have been to alter how managers think about workers, and what they expect from them, rather than to alter the actual work and HRM the practices adopted. To be sure, both popular accounts and the available research point to an intensification of the labour process (Green 2004, 2006) and a lowering of job quality (Green 2004, 2006). But these developments have been largely made possible by the rhetoric and the realities of neoliberalism, the culture of compliance that they have generated, and the application of new technologies of control. To the extent that the new managerialism has played a role, it has been mainly to reinforce and help to obfuscate these developments through its introduction of a unitary ideology and language-in use.

The End of the New Managerialism?

Although its overall implications may be debated, it would now appear that the era of the new managerialism is coming to an end (if it has not already done so). For a significant portion of the economy, we may even be witnessing the decline if not the end of the HRM function and even management as it has come to be understood.[4] This may be especially so in liberal market economies, where the new managerialism (and neoliberalism) has been most prominent.

First, even if new work and HRM practices do make some difference to performance, their overall success has proven to be limited, and any contributions that they have made are likely to have already been realized (e.g., in the UK: see van Wanrooy et al. 2013). It would appear in particular that HRM has failed as a "strategic" area (Boudreau and Lawler III 2014) and that those employed in it are once again perceived to be performing a largely bureaucratized, secondary function – one that may actually do more to frustrate than to facilitate performance. In larger, more "responsible" employers, there has been a proliferation of various family friendly, diversity, "wellness," and "respectful workplace" initiatives, but these are just sticking plaster for problems largely created by the more coercive and stressful environments (both at work and outside of it) in which workers find themselves. Although they may help to advance employer scores on various "best employer" rankings and may have positive implications for subsets of workers, they are a long way off from the strategic role promised by proponents of the new managerialism.

The HRM function itself may also be increasingly falling victim to outsourcing to third parties specializing in selection, appraisal design, training, and pay systems (Greer et al. 1999), thereby hollowing out HR departments and rendering them little more than clearing houses for the selection and monitoring of these parties and their programs. There seem to be no strong data on the extent to which this has occurred, but in an environment in which most labor market participants are desperate to get a "good" job, there is in any case rarely much need for elaborate search, selection, and indoctrination processes. Again, this may be especially true of the USA, where workers have very little by way of rights and protections both within and outside of the employment relationship.

New technologies may also have significantly altered the HRM function. The application of these technologies can reduce selection, monitoring, and evaluation processes to little more than the use of elaborate online score-cards, essentially eliminating the need for judgement or expertise (Head 2014: 66-71). Of particular

---

[4]This section is largely speculative and calls for a more thorough analysis than is possible here. Such analysis would likely be most effectively informed by some variant of regulation theory and couched in terms of the end of neoliberal globalization as a "regime of accumulation," drawing parallels with the end of "Fordism." However, I am struck by just how much the analysis in this and the preceding section is consistent with Karen Legge's analysis more than two decades ago (Legge 1995a, b, esp. 286–340). I had not read this carefully until putting the final touches on the present chapter.

note has been a corresponding growth in consulting firms selling sophisticated information systems with the potential to marginalize or even eliminate HR departments.

The ability to continuously monitor employees and track their performance would appear to have become widespread, in effect leading to the "robotization" of much work if not the replacement of workers with actual robots. These systems would appear to be especially characteristic of major employers emergent during the neoliberal era (e.g., WalMart, Amazon: see Head 2014: 30–40) and have implications not just for the function of HRM but also for the practices to which workers are subject. These employers are generally intensely antiunion, provide workers with few if any meaningful rights or benefits, pay low wages, and rely extensively on temporary and part-time workers. They also outsource extensively, relying either on "temp" firms for a portion of their labor force or on "offshoring" for a sizeable portion of their production. To an extent, these practices may be viewed as an extension of the flexible firm thesis, although they appear to be motivated entirely by cost considerations and not by any need for flexibility per se. Where they are adopted, the employment relationship tends to be both autocratic and exploitive, with HRM departments playing, at most, a legal monitoring role.

The growth of so-called "platform work" and the "gig" economy would appear to take the application of new technologies to an even further level. These jobs give rise to highly controlled, autonomized conditions, in which workers have very little task discretion and limited if any interaction with co-workers. Rather than adopting practices that are merely facilitated by a neoliberal environment, these jobs actually internalize this environment, with workers treated as independent contractors and expected to perceive themselves as such, yet subject to employer rules and monitoring. New technologies, and the firms that control them, have been the handmaidens for these developments, essentially playing a mediating role between employers on the one hand and workers on the other (Katz and Krueger 2017), and effectively obfuscating the employment relationship through a technological variant of Marx and Engels' "cash nexus" (1848). Although these jobs would appear to account for a minute portion of the labor force as of this writing, the evidence suggests that they have been growing rapidly over the past decade.[5]

Overall, these developments suggest that the era of the new managerialism is at an end. This is not because the traditional employment relationship is no longer prevalent; indeed, the overwhelming majority of jobs continue to fit this characterization or some variant of it. But notions of self-directed teams and employee consultation now seem to be almost quaint, and the elaborate selection, socialization, and performance management practices of the new HRM just another set of bureaucratic rituals, designed mainly to bolster management's belief in its own

---

[5] Although it would appear that the so-called gig economy amounts to only a tiny percentage of jobs (in the USA, less than 1.0%: Hall and Krueger 2018: 708), the available evidence suggests that roughly one in six workers in the USA is now either an independent contractor, an on-call worker, a temporary help agency worker, or a contract firm worker. It further suggests that these jobs have accelerated since the mid-2000s, increasing by from 60 to 70 percent between 2005 and 2015 (Katz and Krueger 2016).

professionalism. Not only does HRM for-the-most-part fail to deliver much "strategic" payoff, even its basic functions seem to be increasingly obsolete or at best highly routinized and threatened by outsourcing.

Of equal or even greater importance, the conditions that initially gave rise to the new managerialism may also be coming to an end. To begin, it would appear that the compliant worker has been giving way to the calculative worker of neoliberal theory, where workers are characterized by low levels of engagement and motivated largely by carrots and sticks, à la Taylor's scientific management. To the extent that it is possible to continuously monitor behavior and performance, this augurs well for employers, in effect providing the basis for a new regime of control. Yet the ability to do so would, despite the application of new technologies, seem to be inherently limited in most sectors. This has left many employers having to face a "crisis" of engagement. Their workers may still be highly compliant, but this compliance is contradicted by low levels of loyalty and, more important, hidden forms of resistance (e.g., Paulsen 2014: 1–16). Within such an environment, "new" HRM practices and their high performance counterparts are even more futile, especially if their objective is to develop high levels of commitment or involvement rather than to merely intensify the work process or exact greater compliance.

More important, substantial declines in unemployment, coupled with a growing awareness of inequality, a lack of meaningful income growth, inadequate pensions, increasingly precarious health coverage, and a hollowing out of democratic institutions (e.g., labor unions) may create a complementary yet broader culture of generalized hostility. There has been an expectation of eventual reciprocity and hence reward after many, many years of compliance, only to be met with continued degradation. This has been substantially worsened by the great recession of 2008, which reversed any gains that workers were beginning to enjoy at the turn of the century, and subsequently reinforced the perception that the system is rigged against the "average" citizen.

In the post-World War II era, the workplace was in many respects the outlet not just for discontent at work, but also for broader sources thereof. Labor and employment practices, and particularly the willingness to accommodate the distinctive interests of workers, coupled with effective union representation and regular income gains, played an important role in lessening not just economic instability, but political and social instability as well. Neither would appear any longer to be so. Instead, discontent has come to pervade civil society. This discontent is not just a reflection of labor market and work experiences. It also reflects the broader failure of neoliberalism, and especially neoliberal globalization, to deliver on its promises.

Yet, again, the extent to which this has been the case varies within, and more important, across nations, depending on occupational location but also broader institutional conditions and cultural traditions. These problems would appear to be most pervasive in neoliberal economies, and this would indeed appear to have been the case, especially if one judges by the management literature, but also if one judges by political developments in the USA (Trumpism) and the UK (Brexit) at the time of this writing. These developments will likely only lead to even greater public anger and frustration once the populist promises driving them have proven to be false. Yet even if not, they portend an end to the era of neoliberal globalization, the limitations *to* which, and consequences *of* which, have in any case been increasingly exposed since the 2008 crisis.

The great question is not so much one of whether these developments will usher in a new political economic era, but rather one of what this era will look like. The answer to this question will have major implications for labor markets and ultimately labor and employment practices. Whether it will entail a further neo-liberalization and intensification of work and employment, or whether it will entail some sort of "new" new deal, in which genuinely democratic values and principles predominate (e.g., Frege and Godard 2014) remains to be seen. The answer will likely vary by sector and nation, and be substantially influenced by the ways in which emergent technologies are deployed. But either way, it would seem that the new managerialism is now, or will soon become, yesterday's news.

Cross-References

▶ A Return to the Good Old Days: Populism, Fake News, Yellow Journalism, and the Unparalleled Virtue of Business People
▶ Conclusion: Management Theory in Crisis
▶ Introduction: Public Policy Failure, the Demise of Experts, and the Dawn of a New Era
▶ Management History in the Modern World: An Overview
▶ The New Executive: Interconnected Yet Isolated and Uninformed – Leadership Challenges in the Digital Pandemic Epoch
▶ Trade Union Decline and Transformation: Where to for Employment Relations?
▶ What Is Management?
▶ Why did the Great Recession Fail to Produce a *New* New Deal in the USA?

References

Adams R (1995) Industrial relations under liberal democracy. University of South Carolina Press, Columbia
Arrighi G (2007) Adam Smith in Beijing. Verso, London
Atkinson J (1984) Management strategies for a flexible organization. Pers Manag 16(8):28–31
Averitt RT (1968) The dual economy: the dynamics of American industry structure. WW Norton, New York
Beer M, Spector B, Lawrence PR, Quinn Mills D, Walton RE (1984) Managing human assets. The Free Press, New York
Beer M, Spector B, Lawrence PR, Quinn Mills D, Walton RE (1985) Human resource management: a general manager's perspective. Text and cases. The Free Press, New York
Beer M, Bosalie P, Brewster C (2015) Implications for the field of HRM of the multi-stakeholder perspective proposed thirty years ago. J Hum Resource Manage 54(3):427–438
Bendix R (1956) Work and authority in industry. Wiley, New York
Bernhardt A (2014) Labour standards and the organization of work: gaps in data and research. Institute for Research on Labor and Employment, UC Berkeley. http://www.irle.berkeley.edu/files/2014/Labor-Standards-and-the-Reorganization-of-Work.pdf

Bernhardt A, Batt R , Houseman S, Appelbaum E (2016) Domestic outsourcing in the U.S.: a research agenda to assess trends and effects on job quality. Prepared for the future of work symposium, U.S. Department of Labor, Washington, DC, Dec 2015

Bewley H (2013) "Changes in the institutions and practice of workplace employment relations" presentation to the British Academy, Nov 2013

Blasi J, Kruse D (2006) U.S. high performance work practices at century's end. Ind Relat 45:457–478

Bockerman P, Bryson A, Ilmakunnas P (2012) Does high involvement management improve worker well-being? J Econ Behav Organ 84:660–680

Boudreau J, Lawler EE III (2014) Stubborn traditionalism in HRM: causes and consequences. Hum Resour Manag Rev 24(3):232–244

Burawoy M (1985) The politics of production. Verso, London

Combs J, Hall A, Liu Y, Ketchen D (2006) Do high performance work practices matter? A meta-analysis of their effects on organizational performance. Pers Psychol 59:501–528

Delaney J, Godard J (2001) An industrial relations perspective on the high performance paradigm. Hum Resour Manage Rev 11:395–429

Dore R (2000) Stock market capitalism: welfare capitalism. Oxford University Press, Oxford

Dundon T, Rafferty A (2018) The (potential) demise of HRM? Hum Resour Manag J 28:1–15

Edwards Richard (1979) Contested Terrain. New York: Basic Books

Fairris D (1994) Shopfloor relations in the postwar capital-labor accord. In: Kotz D, McDonough T, Reich M (eds) Social structures of accumulation. Cambridge University Press, Cambridge

Farber H (2015) Job loss in the great recession and it aftermath: U.S. evidence from the displaced workers survey, Working paper #589. Princeton University Industrial Relations Section

Frege C, Godard J (2014) Varieties of capitalism and job quality: the attainment of civic principles at work in the USA and Germany. Am Sociol Rev 79(5):942–965

Galbraith JK (1973) Economics and the public purpose. Houghton Mifflin, Boston

Gittell JH (2016) Transforming relationships for high performance: the power of relational coordination. Stanford Business Books/Stanford University Press, Stanford

Glyn A (2006) Capitalism unleashed. Oxford University Press, Oxford

Godard J (2004) A critical assessment of the high performance paradigm. Br J Ind Relat 42-2:349–378

Godard J (2009) The exceptional decline of the American labor movement. Ind Labor Relat Rev 63(1):81–107

Godard J (2010) What's best for workers? The implications of work and human resource practices revisited. Ind Relat 49(3):465–487

Godard J (2011) Whatever happened to strikes? Br J Ind Relat 49-2:282–303

Godard J (2014) The psychologisation of employment relations? Hum Resour Manag J 24(1):1–18

Godard J (2017) Industrial relations, the economy, and society, 5th edn. Captus Press, Toronto

Godard J (2019) Work and Employment Practices in Comparative Perspective. forthcoming in C Frege and J Kelly (eds.) Comparative Employment Relations, 2nd edn. London: Routledge

Godard J, Delaney J (2000) Reflections on the 'high performance' paradigm's implications for industrial relations as a field. Ind Labor Relat Rev 53(3):482–502

Graham L (1993) Inside a Japanese transplant: a critical perspective. Work Occup 20(2):174–193

Green F (2004) Why has work effort become more intense? Ind Relat 43(4):709–741

Green F (2006) Demanding work. Princeton University Press, Princeton

Greer CR, Youngblood SA, Gray DA (1999) Human resource management outsourcing: the make or buy decision. Acad Manag Exec 13(3):86–96

Guest D, Bryson A (2009) From industrial relations to human resource management: the changing role of the personnel function. In: Brown W, Bryson A, Forth J, Whitfield K (eds) The evolution of the modern workplace. Cambridge University Press, Cambridge

Hall J, Krueger A (2018) An analysis of the labor market for uber's driver partners in the United States. Ind Labor Relat Rev 71(3):705–732

Harvey D (1989) The condition of modernity. Blackwell, Oxford

Harvey D (2005) A brief history of neoliberalism. Oxford University Press, Oxford, UK

Head S (2014) Mindless: why smarter machines are making dumber humans. Basic Books, New York

Ho K (2009) Liquidated: an ethnography of wall street. Duke University Press, Durham

Jacoby S (1991) American exceptionalism revisited. In: Jacoby S (ed) Masters to managers: historical and comparative perspectives on American employers. Columbia University Press, New York, pp 173–200

Jacoby S (1997) Modern Manors: welfare capitalism since the new deal. Princeton University Press, Princeton

Jiang K, Lepak D, Hu J, Baer J (2012) How does human resource management influence organizational outcomes: a meta-analytic investigation of mediating mechanisms? Acad Manag J 55(6):1264–1294

Katz LF, Krueger AB (2016) The rise and nature of alternative work arrangements in the United States, 1995–2015, NBER working paper 22667

Katz LF, Krueger AB (2017) The role of unemployment in the rise of alternative work arrangements. Am Econ Rev 107(5):388–392

Kaufman BE (2015) Market competition, HRM, and firm performance: the conventional paradigm critiqued and reformulated. Hum Resour Manag Rev 25:107–125

Kersely, Barbara, Carmen Alpin, John Forth et al. (2006) Inside the Workplace. London: Routledge

Kersley B et al (2006) Inside the workplace: findings from the 2004 worplace employment relations survey. Routledge, London

Kochan TA (2007) Social legitimacy of the HRM profession: a U.S. perspective. In: Boxall P, Purcell J, Wright P (eds) The Oxford handbook of human resource management. Oxford University Press, Oxford

Kochan TA, Barocci TA (1985) Industrial relations and human resource management. Little Brown, Boston

Kochan T, Osterman P (1994) The mutual gains enterprise. Harvard University Press, Boston

Lawler EEIII (1986) High involvement management. Josey Bass, San Francisco

Legge K (1995a) Rhetoric, reality, and hidden agendas. In: Sotrey J (ed) Human resource management: a critical text. Routledge, London, pp 33–59

Legge K (1995b) Human resource management: rhetorics and realities. Macmillan, Basingstoke

Lorenz E, Valeyre A (2005) Organizational innovation, HRM, and labour market structure: a comparison of the EU-15. J Ind Relat 47(4):424–442

Marsden D (1999) A theory of employment systems. Oxford University Press, Oxford

Marsden D, Canibano A (2010) An economic perspective4 on employee participation. In: Wilkinson A, Gollan P, Marchington M, Lewin D (eds) The Oxford handbook of participation in organizations. OUP, Oxford, pp 130–163

Martin L (2017) Do innovative work practices and use of information and communications technologies motivate employees? Ind Relat 56(2):263–292

Mills CW (1948) The new men of power. Harcourt Brace, Englewood Cliffs

OECD (2017) StatExtracts. OECD, Geneva. https://stats.oecd.org/

O'Toole J et al (1973) Work in America. Report of a task force to the secretary of health, education, and welfare. MIT Press, Cambridge

Ouchi W (1980) Markets, bureaucracies, and clans. Adm Sci Q 25(1):129–141

Ouchi W (1982) Theory Z. Basic Books, New York

Paulsen R (2014) Empty labor. Cambridge University Press, Cambridge

Perlman S (1949 [1928]) A theory of the labour movement. Augustus Kelly, New York

Pfeffer J (1994) Competitive advantage through people. Harvard University Press, Boston

Strauss G (2001) HRM in the USA: correcting some British impressions. Int J Hum Resour Manag 12(6):873–897

Thelen Kathleen (2014) Varieties of Liberalization. Cambridge: Cambridge University Press

Tichy N, Fombrun C, Devanna M (1982) Strategic human resource management. Sloan Manag Rev 23(2):47–61

Townley B (1994) Reframing human resource management: power, ethics, and the subject of work. Sage, London

Vallas SP (2006) Empowerment redux: structure, agency, and the remaking of managerial authority. Am J Sociol 111(6):1677–1717

Wall T, Wood S (2006) The romance of human resource management and business performance: the case for big science. Hum Relat 58(4):429–462

Wanrooy V, Bewley H, Bryson A et al (2013) Employment relations in the shadow of recession. Palgrave Macmillan, Houndsmills

Wood S, Bryson A (2009) High involvement management. In: Brown W, Bryson A, Forth J, Whitfield K (eds) The evolution of the modern workplace. Cambridge University Press, Cambridge

A Return to the Good Old Days: Populism, Fake News, Yellow Journalism, and the Unparalleled Virtue of Business People

42

Mark Balnaves

Contents

The Hypergiants (Super Aggregators), Doxing and Swarms	939
Social Presence, Social Proof, and the Social Distribution of Knowledge	944
Conclusion	946
Cross-References	947
References	948

Abstract

Primo Levi, a victim of Auschwitz, warned in an interview to The New Republic in 1986 that empathy in contemporary industrial societies can disappear without warning and replaced with a new fascism, which "with its trail of intolerance, abuse, and servitude, can be born outside our country and imported into it, walking on tiptoe and calling itself by other names; or it can loose itself from within with such violence that it routs all defenses." Professor Anthony Gould in his introductory chapter provides a timely reminder, and warning, that public policy and management theory are not necessarily simply a matter of clinical, scientifically constructed, models, but a part of genuine human forces, historical and otherwise, that have led to an age of crisis. Levi's point is that events in the contemporary moment can move far faster than we recognize and trusted sources disappear even faster. In this chapter, the author provides a brief overview of the rise of digital personae in the context of intentionality and the trusted source.

M. Balnaves (✉)
Gulf University for Science and Technology, Kuwait City, Kuwait

University of Newcastle, Newcastle, NSW, Australia
e-mail: Balnaves.M@gust.edu.kw; mark.balnaves@newcastle.edu.au

© The Author(s), under exclusive licence to Springer Nature Switzerland AG 2020
B. Bowden et al. (eds.), *The Palgrave Handbook of Management History*,
https://doi.org/10.1007/978-3-319-62114-2_45

Keywords

Digital persona · Trusted news source · Internet privacy · Electronic markets · Persona studies

High frequency trading algorithms got a shock in 2013 when an AP tweet claimed that Barack Obama had been hurt in an explosion. Over USD $130 billion in stock value was wiped in minutes. AP said its Twitter account had been hacked and the stock prices recovered quickly. Social media, clearly, affected the stock market. Bad news, good news, false news, true news, public opinion are all part of the mix of markets in the good old days and in the contemporary moment of fake news. However, fake news has introduced a new element in the reign of President Donald Trump that affects the checking of facts in the business of media and the business of business. The trusted source is no longer trusted. The rise of active and passive digital personae, swarms and doxing, have amplified gossip, rumor, populism, and confused the checking of trusted sources.

Of course, businesses can make money by delivering false news, as did William Randolph Hearst when he realized that manufacturing facts about the Spanish-American war increased circulation. Hearst, like Trump, also felt that "other people existed mainly to gratify his own desires" (Proctor 1998, p. 14). Indeed, the expression *yellow journalism* comes from the Hearst era with the yellow referring to the character *yellow kid* in the comic *Hogan's Alley*, a favorite reading of Hearst. However, there is a dramatic qualitative difference between the Hearst era and today because it is often very difficult to work out whether a human or nonhuman is responsible for news. President Donald Trump's Tweets are an interesting exception, like Hearst, because the assumption is, even in satire like *Saturday Night Live*, that Trump is the genuine author of his own Tweets for most of the time and in real time. But how influence works on the Internet is no simple matter. Reddit built its company by starting with fake followers and President Trump learnt the lesson. Figure 1 is a screenshot of Trump's Twitter audit accessed on November 5, 2018, by the author showing 5,450,240 fake followers.

What Donald Trump has recognized is that there is no newshole that limits his creation of news. The newshole is the amount of space available to a news organization to devote to a publication after advertising revenue for an edition has been calculated. In print newspapers, only a certain amount of physical space can be allocated to news before it becomes uneconomical in print production and circulation. Online news, of course, has changed the business models around newsholes.

But Donald Trump's fake followers raise the problem of what counts as an "agent" or an "actor" in contemporary online news cycles. An agent in digital media can extend beyond human sentient beings. This is precisely why people get upset when they are misrepresented online, trying to work out whether actions are intentional or not. For instance, when Bettina Wulff, wife of former German president Christian Wulff, found that a Google search of her name came up "prostitute," she sued Google, successfully. Bettina had a digital persona she did not want,

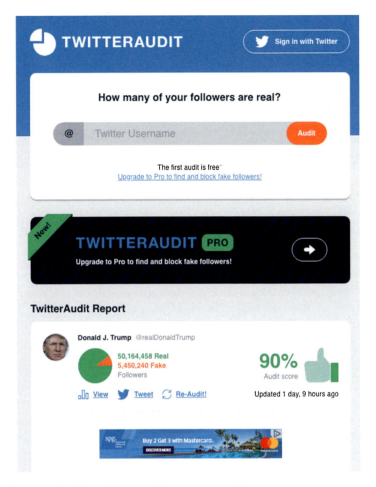

Fig. 1 Twitter audit of Donald Trump's followers, real and fake

projected into the minds of human agents but passively constructed by nonhuman agents, the Autocomplete feature in Google. In 2012 a Japanese man took Google to Court over its Autocomplete (Instant) that returned up to 10,000 results implicating him in crimes. Tokyo Courts ruled that Google suspend its Autocomplete and Google replied, "no," that it would not obey Japanese law (Boxall 2012).

Debates about agency in philosophy, psychology, and sociology are complex. Barry Hindess (1988) in his critique of rational choice theory advanced a minimal concept of the agent as a site of decision and action, where the action is in some sense a consequence of the agent's – actor's decision. "Actors do things as a result of their decisions. We call those things actions, and the actor's decisions play a part in their explanation. Actors may also do things that do not result from their decisions, and their explanation has a different form" (Hindess 1988, p. 44–45). Hindess argued that a capacity to make decisions is an integral part of anything that might be called an agent. For Hindess, therefore, state agencies, political parties, football clubs, churches are all examples of actors in his minimal sense. "They all have means of reaching decisions and of acting on at least some of them" (Hindess 1988, p. 46). The actions of Google's Autocomplete feature, an organizational agent, is, of course, always dependent upon the actions of others such as managers, elected officers, employees, and other organizations.

Digital personae raise key issues in control and the extent to which an agent can intentionally interfere with the creation and maintenance of a digital persona. Businesses, governments, and individuals attempt to manipulate digital personae to make them attractive, by mimicking human behavior or providing visual and other cues that enhance the possibility of trust, precisely the concern in the United States about Russian interference in its elections. Never before has the role of nonhuman agents in this way been possible or their impact so far reaching.

In the case of normal everyday affairs, of course, there is a range of databases and many organizations involved in collecting information on individuals and creating profiles of them. There have been a number of terms to try to describe these profiles, such as Dividual, epers, shadow order, data double, capta shadow, databased self, and Cyber-I (Clarke 2013). However, *digital persona* best captures what happened to Bettina Wulff because it focuses clearly on the very idea of the person, of how we present our self and our identity to others. Roger Clarke coined the term digital persona in 1992 and continues to explore it (Clarke 2014). His original motivation was that "we need the construct as an element in our understanding of the emerging network-enhanced world" (Clarke 2014, p. 82). Internet robots, agents, who can act and interact with other agents, human and nonhuman, now account for over 60 percent of Internet activity (Madrigal 2013) and understanding the behavior of human and nonhuman agents is now essential in a democratic society that values autonomy.

Clarke (2001) further distinguished between active and passive digital personae. An active persona, in a digital context, is an agent that acts on behalf of the individual and runs in the individual's workstation or elsewhere in the Internet. A simple implementation of this idea is in the vacation feature in email servers, which returns a message such as "I am away on holidays until <date>." Where the sender is a mailing list, this may result in broadcast of the message to hundreds or thousands of list-members. A passive digital persona does not involve projection of the persona into the online world. Figure 2, adapted from Roger Clarke (2001), shows the operation of a passive digital persona. A Visa card transaction is an obvious example of part of the creation of a passive digital persona within the Visa system.

Projected active digital personae include mail filterers, news, and knowbots (intelligent searches of networks). Active digital persona can be projected by the individual or imposed by others. The difference between active and passive is in the degree to which control can be exercised over what is happening to the persona. If the individual is projecting their persona, they may wish to create filters around themselves and restrict the bombardment of information through the networked world. Clarke (2013) distinguishes between passive digital persona as superficial digital representations of a person or people and formal digital personae as structured

Fig. 2 Passive digital personae

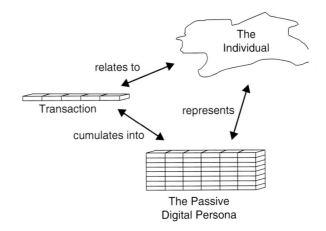

data representations that occur as the result of physical online transactions of data. If someone has illegal access to someone's computerized health data, for example, then they could construct a persona based on that structured data. Informal digital personae are, by contrast, based on people's perceptions. Clarke (2013) also distinguishes between projected personae, a persona that a person wants to project and imposed personae, an image created by someone else. In the 15 or so years since Clarke introduced the construct, there has been a range of developments in information technology, not least the increasing use of sophistication in social media networks and associated algorithmic nonhuman agents that can have their own personalities, represent or gather information about real personalities, or impose personalities online. While how at a theoretical level, "all the layers of digital personae are simultaneously woven in a complex situation remains obscure," there can be little doubt that the hypergiant, superaggregators, are well aware of the impact of digital personae (de Kerckhove and de Almeida 2013, p. 277).

The Hypergiants (Super Aggregators), Doxing and Swarms

> We're building toward a web where the default is social. Every application and product will be redesigned from the ground up to use a person's real identity and friends. Mark Zuckerberg, CEO Facebook (Hongladarom 2011).
> There is something innately threatening about a persona, constructed from data and used as a proxy for the real person. It is reminiscent of the popular image of the voodoo doll (Gibson 1984, p. 97).

We now know that Facebook failed to compel British political consulting firm *Cambridge Analytica t*o delete all traces of data from its servers after acquiring details of 87 million Facebook users. These data enabled the company to retain predictive models drawn from social media profiles during the Clinton-Trump US presidential election (Lewis et al. 2018). A person's ability to control their own persona is, of course, compromised when their data is sold to others without their knowledge. But third party sales are not the only problem facing the modern digital persona. Personal dataveillance, low data quality decisions, lack of subject knowledge of, and consent to, data flows, blacklisting, denial of redemption, arbitrariness, acontextual data merger, and complexity and incomprehensibility of data, among many others affect the degree of agency of any one of us. It is not within the compass of this chapter to cover all the possible variations in technical control, but the major Internet aggregators are well aware of the impact of various technical matters on business and others. In its 2012 regulatory filing, for example, Facebook identified over 83 million "fake" accounts, – impersonations, fake people, real pets, fake pets, "undesirable accounts" (undefined by Facebook), and others. Facebook understands these sites as agents, potentially damaging to other agents and their own users. A person's Facebook identity is not simply a page but a network where people either feel more or less in control of what they do on that network. Over 11 million teenagers left Facebook to other sites, such as Instagram, WeChat, and other platforms, not only because of "cool" but precisely because of issues of control and importantly the "right to forget" (Kampmark 2015; Rosen 2012).

While Facebook seeks to control fake personalities, including fake and real pets, this does not extend to every nonhuman. Grumpy Cat (Fig. 3), Boo the Dog, and the popular Hatsune Miku (Vocaloid) are good examples. In 2013 Grumpy Cat won Webby's Meme of the Year. Grumpy Cat, who has his own "reps," is a highly successful nonhuman, nonanimal, active digital persona, which at the time of writing had 8.6 million followers on its Facebook page. Grumpy Cat's owner made 24 million pounds from Grumpy Cat's first two years as a digital persona (Goldhill 2014). Adweek in 2013 provided a summary of Grumpy Cat's competition on the Internet. Tabatha Bundesen and her brother first posted pictures of the cat on Reddit after which the Internet community started to create memes. Grumpy Cat the business has

Fig. 3 Grumpy Cat (the official picture). (Source: Grumpy Cat used under Fair Use)

monetized into fan sites, T-shirts, books, and wall calendars, among many other merchandise.

Facebook calls Grumpy Cat and other digital personae making money on the Internet, like Boo the Dog, "public figures" in order to get around the problem of calling them "fake sites" in reporting to the US government (Sneed 2013). It is not surprising that nonhuman digital personae get status as public figures. Vocaloid 3-D projections came into public physical spaces in 2010 and have become as popular as Facebook-based animal celebrities. Vocaloid is a singing voice synthesizer created by a joint university and Yamaha project. Hatsuni Miku has become one of its nonhuman stars. She is a singing digital avatar created by Crypton Future Media. People can buy her and then program her to perform any song on a computer. But in 2010 she also went on tour as a 3-D hologram http://www.mikufan.com/). Miku would appear to breach the author's definition of digital personae as "running in" computers. Miku, however, is still tied to computers and networks, even when she is a projection. What is important is that she is a nonhuman active digital personae not as a "one off" but, like Grumpycat, as a personality in a relationship with fans.

Readers might stop, at this point, and ask what Grumpy Cat has to do with management in crisis or with the title of this chapter. All of the examples so far touch on *identity* and *trusted sources*. The "good old days" of yellow journalism, its early days, have returned but with a twist. Public opinion and market information can be manipulated by nonhuman agents. Grumpy Cat is a fairly transparent digital persona, supervised by a human agent. President Trump is an active digital persona, a "doxing" President, with 5 million or more fake followers, exaggerating his impact on public opinion.

Communities can also combine to create digital personae. #Gamergate is a good example where a gaming community used its skill to dox others, that is, create a crowd persona that dramatically affects individuals. In August 2014, Eron Gjoni, a programmer, wrote posts about Zoe Quinn, a game developer for controversial *Depression Quest*, accusing her of sleeping with a video game journalist Nathan Grayson (https://thezoepost.wordpress.com/). Gioni had been in a relationship with Quinn (Dockterman 2014). Anita Sarkeesian, a high profile critic of sexism in games, with others, became the target of abuse, with one person even creating a computer game in which players were invited to abuse her (Dockterman 2014).

There were approximately 1.8 million users of the #gamergate between September 25, and October 25,, 2014, according to the analytics group Topsy.com. It is not surprising that terms such as "sealioning" and "swarm" have emerged precisely to describe the #gamergate phenomenon. Digital personae were not just individuals, but groups formed as crowd digital personae. "Gamers" with doxing skills of a high order demonstrated how quickly personal information that most people could not access can be deployed. Sarkeesian's own digital persona, @femfreq, Feminist Frequency, was able to rapidly mobilize opposition to those in the gamer community who were using gamergate as a misogyny vehicle.

Andy Balow (2014) worked with the chief data scientist at Betaworks in the USA and took all the social graphs of everyone in the dataset of 316,669 tweets associated with #gamergate in order to visualize the different personae using open-source package Gephi. Figure 4 shows all the hundreds of small communities that fall

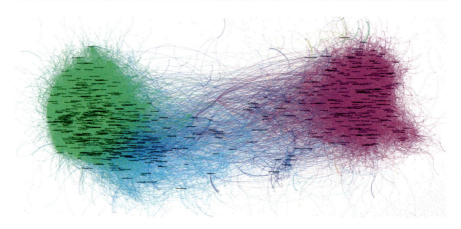

Fig. 4 #gamergate Swarm. (Source: Betaworks)

into two major poles antigamergate on the right-hand side and pro-gamergate on the left-hand side, with little to not intersection between them.

Trolls and others, of course, and unlike the #gamergate controversy, do not necessarily disclose who they are or, alternatively, create fake versions of other people. Chuck Norris, the US celebrity, fell victim to sites pretending to be him and leading to the famous Chucknorris facts site, providing humorous comments about Norris. Norris decided not to sue, appreciating that he had an expanded set of fans who were not using their sites maliciously. "I know there are a lot of fake Chuck Norris pages on places like Facebook & Myspace. To cut down on confusion, this is the only page I personally have on Facebook & I don't have a page on Myspace. If you ever want to find out if a page is really mine, you can visit my website link [...]. Sincerely your friend, Chuck Norris (Norris 2011).

The terrorist group Islamic State, or ISIS, was adept at being malicious and, as a comprehensive Bookings Institute study demonstrated, technically proficient at creating Twitter swarms and mass producing Twitter account to influence perceptions of ISIS size. Figure 5 is a representation of different accounts, but also the degree of reciprocity obvious among them.

The sophistication of online collection of data about individuals is now well known. Acxiom perhaps is the largest of these aggregators. It works on a global scale and on-sells data about individuals to whoever can pay for those data. Many people have not heard about Acxiom. Most people though would have flash cookies on their computers that collect data for aggregators like Acxiom (flash cookies are normally undetectable, except now for Firefox browsers). Acxiom has in its database approximately 1500 facts about half a billion people worldwide. It works behind the scenes for Google and many other major Internet companies (Mason 2009). Acxiom holds passive digital personae.

We are now in a position to provide some clarity on the differences between active and passive digital personae and supervised and nonsupervised contexts in which they operate. Table 1 distinguishes between contexts where humans are

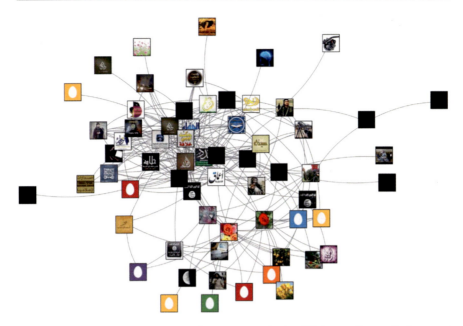

Fig. 5 ISIS Twitter. (Source: Berger and Morgan (2015) *The ISIS Twitter Census: Defining and describing the population of ISIS supports on Twitter*)

Table 1 Human and nonhuman digital personae and human agency

	Human	Nonhuman
Supervised	Digital persona activity actively created by a human agent (e.g., President Donald Trump Tweets; ISIS Twitter swarms; #gamgergate)	A digital persona of a nonhuman agent created by a human agent (e.g., Grumpy Cat, Boo the Dog, Hatsune Miku)
Unsupervised	A false digital persona of a human agent created by a human agent (e.g., Chuck Norris fake sites)	A passive digital persona of a real human agent created by a nonhuman agent (e.g., Visa Card, Google Autocomplete)

directly involved in the activities of a persona and those where they are not. Donald Trump's Tweets have a human agent behind them as far as we know. They are "supervised" in a general sense. Chuck Norris fake sites, while generated by humans, are not supervised by him (although they now have his imprimatur). Grumpy Cat, however, is fully nonhuman, although supervised. Data collected by the hypergiants and other major aggregation sources are not supervised by the human agents from which the data are collected.

"Control," like constructs such as "power," involves a range of other constructs in any conceptualization or measurement (Lukes 1974). Table 1 therefore is not intended as a final clarification of the complexity surrounding contemporary digital personae. However, there can be little doubt that crowd or individual digital personae can and do influence activity on the Internet and human perceptions based on that activity. There is also a level of technical complexity in generating persona that is beyond many people's competencies and for many it is difficult to know when hypergiants are manipulating our personae.

Individuals wanting to control their own sites have its correlate in super aggregators, like Google and Comcast, wanting to control its spaces. Super aggregators can and do decide to bias one form of traffic over another. This is no minor issue and has led, of course, to Net Neutrality debates. The aggregators in all their forms have become more concentrated and more influential as well as more complicated. Google, for instance, purchased the currency platform, Jambool, to help developers manage and monetize their virtual economies across the globe (Takahashi 2010). Google, like Comcast, has vested interests in where traffic goes and a banking platform would no doubt affect the nature of traffic flows. Google could, for example, limit an aspiring creative artist's digital persona by exercising what is called "ramp control" (Leaver et al. 2012, p. 2), slowing down the service in order to stop the artist uploading broadband materials that exemplify their work or even potentially affecting banking service. The individual might never know that it was the super aggregator limiting their activities, of course, left probably to think that they need a new service provider in order to increase bandwidth.

Social Presence, Social Proof, and the Social Distribution of Knowledge

Which brings us back to President Trump's Tweets. He is not seen as a fake persona by his followers and his Tweets are perceived to be directly from him. In the language of theory, Trump has achieved social presence, trust, and social proof. These three dimensions have become important constructs in explaining the behavior of human agents in the study of digital personae. Social presence is conceived as the extent to which "the medium permits users to experience others as being psychologically present" (Fulk et al. 1987, p. 531). Since the construction of a digital persona is necessarily mediated through digital media, social presence plays a key role for actively created digital personae of human agents. Previous research found that displaying human photos (Cyr et al. 2009) or avatars (Teubner et al. 2014) on a Web site can increase a person's perceived social presence. Similarly, many agents use human photos and avatars in the process of actively creating their digital persona. Importantly, an increase in social presence positively influences a person's level of trust towards a platform (Gefen and Straub 2003). Trust is a key construct in technology-mediated transactions. In electronic commerce, it is conceived as "an expectation that others one chooses to trust will not behave opportunistically by taking advantage of the situation" (Gefen et al. 2003, p. 54). In the context of digital persona, trust has to be understood as a broader concept, because it does not only involve possible future decisions, but more subtle dimensions of trust, such as engagement and public opinion (Balnaves et al. 2014). This also becomes evident in the terminology "follower" used in the prominent social networks primarily used for creating digital personae.

Another reason why social presence and trust play a critical role for digital persona is that the purpose for actively (and often also for passively) creating a digital persona is – directly and indirectly – related to marketing activities in the broadest possible sense. A key construct in this context is social proof, that is, "the fact that people tend to believe that decisions and actions taken by the majority reflect the correct behaviour in a given situation" (Vastola et al. 2014).

> The tendency to see an action as more appropriate when others are doing it normally works quite well. As a rule, we will make fewer mistakes by acting in accord with social evidence than contrary to it. Usually, when a lot of people are doing something, it is the right thing to do. This feature of the principle of *social proof* is simultaneously its major strength and its major weakness. Like the other weapons of influence, it provides a convenient shortcut for determining how to behave but, at the same time, makes one who uses the shortcut vulnerable to the attacks of profiteers who lie in wait along its path. (Cialdini 1983, 1994).

While social interactions have evolutionarily been dominated by human-human, and for most of human history even face-to-face interactions, advances in digital media have turned the domain of social interaction into a "mixed zone" in which sentient human beings and computerized agents interact (Riedl et al. 2014; Teubner et al. 2014). Agents in the digital society form beliefs about the agency of digital personae they encounter, and these beliefs in turn affect their intentions.

It can be reasonably argued, therefore, that Donald Trump has established social presence and social proof with his digital persona. Trump's followers also by extension see his news as part of what Alfred Schutz (1946) would call their common intrinsic interests. Alfred Schutz's (1946) work on zones of relevance and interest within social phenomenology fits well here. A person's place in the social distribution of knowledge for Schutz is defined by the type of knowledge that they possess and the social role that they have at any particular point in time. There are, for him, four regions, or zones, of decreasing relevance of knowledge. There is knowledge and activity of primary relevance within our reach that can be immediately observed by us and also at least partially dominated by us. The zone of minor relevance is where individuals may be acquainted with knowledge that may contain reference to our chief interests. Zones of knowledge which are relatively irrelevant or absolutely irrelevant are areas of knowledge which people take for granted, but where the "that" and the "how" of things are not essential. For example, no car driver is supposed to be familiar with the laws of mechanics, no radio listener with those of electronics, although there are circumstances where such knowledge might be of primary relevance, such as experts or enthusiasts (Balnaves and Willson 2012, p. 69).

There is a point in society where my competencies allow me to operate either badly or well, especially in a modern society that puts a premium on knowledge. My set of competencies in building and managing my digital persona, therefore, is directly related to the amount of control and the degree of agency that I have over my persona. The more others control my digital persona online, the less capacity I have to change any imposed persona and the more an imposed persona is acting on someone else's behalf. A person might, perhaps, voluntarily surrender their persona to another, and the populism of those like President Trump would fall into that category.

Conclusion

This chapter has not been written as an anti-Donald Trump piece. However, William Randolph Hearst and Donald Trump share similarities not only in their personalities but also in their capacity to generate, purposely, false news. Hearst would never have expected yellow journalism to become standard news, despite his voracious appetite for fake news. Nor would Hearst have expected a President of the United States to occupy the newshole so thoroughly. Hearst no doubt, though, would have done exactly what Donald Trump has done; amplify through Twitter.

In this chapter, the author has attempted to show how digital personae, active and passive, have become a permanent part of how knowledge is distributed and acted upon in contemporary society, affecting individual and business decisions alike, public opinion and markets. Jacques Derrida used the expression "democracy to come" to describe his ideal of democracy. Democracy, for Derrida, welcomes strangers, accepts diversity, and enhances participation (Lucy and Mickler 2006). While this chapter is not strictly about the theory or social constitution of democracy, the role of digital personae in democracy – online citizens-consumers-organizations – is obvious – as is their role in electronic markets. The capacity to swarm has obvious implications for public opinion, the formation of social movements and markets.

When Michel Foucault (1977) wrote about discursive practices as groups of statements that provide a language for talking about a particular topic at a particular historical moment, he did not have in mind nonhuman Internet robots and algorithmic languages (although mathematics, for him, is a discursive practice). Each discursive practice implies a play of prescriptions that designate exclusions and choices. Humans have developed an ability to make inferences about their counterparts' mental states (cf. mentalizing or theory of mind, Frith and Frith 2006). This ability enables humans (i) to assess and predict the intentions, beliefs, and behaviors of others in communicative, collaborative, and competitive social interactions and thus (ii) to increase chances of survival and overall human success.

The idea of "mixed zone" fits well into Alfred Schutz's ideas about our different positions in the social distribution of knowledge. The Internet has provided a system where one's digital persona might be imposed by others, what Schutz would call "imposed interests" compared with "common intrinsic interests." A person is, even without the Internet, dependent on the competencies of others, like doctors and accountants. However, the rise of digital personae changes the processes by which trust, social presence, and social proof operate. Islamic State was able to mobilize 47,000 Twitter accounts to project its digital persona – its knowledge of social media networks operates at technical and strategic levels.

The author has kept to the minimal concept of what counts as a social actor – proposed by Hindess (1988) – as a site of decision and action, where the action is in some sense a consequence of the agent's decision. This conception keeps intentionality in the theoretical picture. Other explanations of the effects of complexity in contemporary society have taken other and different forms. Actor-network theory (ANT) or (AT) is a contemporary example of the attempt to analyze the role of human and nonhuman agents and their impact on society. Donald MacKenzie (2006) is a famous example of the application of the ANT concept of performativity in financial markets. He looked at the relationship between financial models and the actual practices of financial traders and firms, how particular financial technologies are created, and how they affect market structures. For MacKenzie (2006), neo-classical economics is not real until it is *enacted into being* (performativity). Actor network theory (ANT), enrolment theory, or the sociology of translation, created by Bruno Latour, Michel Callon, and John Law, looks at the agency of nonhumans, from animals to machines and links the concepts of actor and network to by-pass the classic distinction between agency and structure. Latour (2006), as a result, discounts traditional models of self, and by extension, intentionality, – "there is no model of (human) actor in AT nor any basic list of competences that have to be set at the beginning because the human, the self and the social actor of traditional social theory is not on its agenda." (2006).

In the literature on persona, there is a wide range of definitions of persona, reflecting differences in the idea of agency. Persona Studies, for example, takes a dramaturgical approach, where "persona, in terms of origins, in and of itself implies performance and display. Jung, for instance, calls persona a mask where one is 'acting a role' ... I have used persona to describe how online culture pushes most people to construct a public identity that resembles what celebrities have had to construct for their livelihood for at least the last century." (Marshall 2014). ANT on the other hand emphasizes digital persona as a "hybrid or quasi-object" "it is a combination of both human creation and technological mediation ... Online persona, in the terminology of ANT, is a constructed, performative presentation of identity. It is constituted through a combination of human action, ongoing mediation of present human action, and the automation, through technological delegation, of previous actions" (Henderson 2014). Sherry Turkle (1997), on the other hand, argued that on-line life selves demonstrate a "de-centering" of the very idea of "self." "What I am saying is that the many manifestations of multiplicity in our culture, including the adoption of multiple on-line personae, are contributing to a general reconsideration of traditional unitary notions of identity."

However, as argued in this chapter, active and passive digital personae, as originally conceived by Roger Clarke (2001), makes a better fit for the highly technical nature of contemporary digital media and how actions follow from actual activities, whether swarms, doxing, or profiling.

Cross-References

▶ Conclusion: Management Theory in Crisis
▶ Introduction: Public Policy Failure, the Demise of Experts, and the Dawn of a New Era

- Labor and Employment Practices: The Rise and Fall of the New Managerialism
- Management History in the Modern World: An Overview
- The New Executive: Interconnected Yet Isolated and Uninformed – Leadership Challenges in the Digital Pandemic Epoch
- Trade Union Decline and Transformation: Where to for Employment Relations?
- What Is Management?
- Why Did the Great Recession Fail to Produce a *New* New Deal in the USA?

References

Balnaves M, Adam M, James M (2014) A theory of digital persona. Unpublished working paper, University of Newcastle.

Balnaves M, Willson M (2011) A new theory of information and the Internet: Public sphere meets protocol. Peter Lang, New York

Balow A (2014) 72 Hours of #Gamergate. Digging through 316,669 tweets from three days of Twitter's Two-Month-old Trainwreck. https://medium.com/message/72-hours-of-gamergate-e00513f7cf5d

Boxall A (2012) Man wins injunction against Google after claiming auto-complete web search ruined his life. Digital Trends, March 26, 2012. http://www.digitaltrends.com/web/man-wins-injunction-against-google-after-claiming-auto-complete-web-search-ruined-his-life/#ixzz3fpiwiUGC

Cialdini RB (1983) Influence: the psychology of persuasion. New York: Harper Collins. p 194

Cialdini RB (1994) Principles and techniques of social influence. In: Tesser A (ed) Advanced social psychology, McGraw-Hill: New York

Clarke R (2001) Roger Clarke's dataveillance and information privacy home-page. http://www.anu.edu.au/people/Roger.Clarke/DV/

Clarke R (2013) Data risks in the cloud. J Theor Appl Electron Commer Res 8(3):59–73

Clarke R (2014) Persona missing, feared drowned: the digital persona concept, two decades later. Inf Technol People 27(2):182–207

Cyr D, Head M, Larios H, Pan B (2009) Exploring human images in website design: a multi-method approach. MIS Q 33(3):539–566

de Kerckhove D, de Almeida CM (2013) What is a digital persona? Technoetic Arts 11(3):277–287

Dockterman E (2014) What is #Gamergate and why are women being threatened by video games. Time, Oct 16. http://time.com/3510381/gamergate-faq/

Frith CD, Frith U (2006) The neural basis of mentalizing. Neuron 50(4):531–534

Fulk J, Steinfield CW, Schmitz J, Power JG (1987) A social information processing model of media use in organizations. Commun Res 14(5):529–552

Gefen D, Straub DW (2003) Managing user trust in B2C e-services. E-Serv J 2(2):7–24

Gefen D, Karahanna E, Straub DW (2003) Trust and TAM in online shopping. MIS Q 27(1):51–90

Gibson M (1984) Neuromancer. Grafton-Collins, London

Goldhill O (2014) How to make millions from your cat: cat videos aren't just the quirky hobby of generation y, but a source of wealth and fame. Could your moggy be a potential cash cow? The Telegraph, December 8. http://www.telegraph.co.uk/men/the-filter/11279907/How-to-make-millions-from-your-cat.html

Henderson NJ (2014) Online persona as hybrid-object: tracing the problems and possibilities of persona in the short film Noah. M/C J 17(3)

Hindess B (1988) Choice, rationality and social theory. Unwin Hyman, London

Hongladarom S (2011) Personal identity and the self in the online and offline world. Mind Mach 21(4):533–548

Kampmark B (2015) To find or be forgotten: global tensions on the right to erasure and internet governance. J Glob Faultlines 2(2):1–18

Latour B (2006) Reassembling the social: an introduction to actor-network theory. Organ Stud 27(10):1553–1557

Leaver T, Willson M, Balnaves M (2012) Transparency and the ubiquity of information filtration? Ctrl-Z: New Media Philos 1(2). http://www.ctrl-z.net.au//journal?slug=leaver-willson-balnaves-transparency-and-the-ubiquity-ofinformation-filtration

Lewis P, Pegg D, Hern A (2018) Cambridge analytica kept Facebook data models through US election. Sunday, 6 May. https://www.theguardian.com/uk-news/2018/may/06/cambridge-analytica-kept-facebook-data-models-through-us-election

Lucy N, Mickler S (2006) The war on democracy: conservative opinion in the Australian press. University of Western Australia Press, Nedlands

Lukes S (1974) Power: a radical view. Macmillan Press, London

MacKenzie D (2006) An engine, not a camera: how financial models shape the markets. MIT Press, Cambridge, MA

Madrigal AC (2013) Welcome to the internet of thingies: 61.5% of web traffic is not human, The Atlantic. http://www.theatlantic.com/technology/archive/2013/12/we

Marshall PD (2014) Seriality and persona. M/C J 17(3). http://journal.media-culture.org.au/index.php/mcjournal/article/view/802

Mason R (2009) Acxiom: the company that knows if you own a cat or if you're right-handed. http://www.telegraph.co.uk/finance/newsbysector/retailandconsumer/...company-that-knows-if-you-own-a-cat-or-if-youre-right-handed.html

Norris C (2011) Facebook, May 27. https://www.facebook.com/officialchucknorrispage/posts/i-know-there-are-a-lot-of-fake-chuck-norris-pages-on-places-like-facebook-myspac/185419061507454/

Proctor B (1998) William Randolph Hearst, the early years, 1863–1910. Oxford University Press, New York

Rosen J (2012) The right to be forgotten. Stanford Law Rev Online 64(2012):88

Riedl R, Davis FD, Hevner AR (2014) Towards a NeuroIS research methodology: intensifying the discussion on methods, tools, and measurement. J Assoc Inf Syst 15(10), Article 4. https://aisel.aisnet.org/jais/vol15/iss10/4

Schonfeld E (2010) Techcrunch. Zuckerberg: "We are building a web where the default is social." https://techcrunch.com/2010/04/21/zuckerbergs-buildin-web-default-social/

Schutz A (1946) The well informed citizen: an essay on the social distribution of knowledge. Soc Res 13(4):463–478

Sneed T (2013) Who is grumpy cat, hollywood's next big star? The feline internet sensation could be getting a movie deal. US News, May 30. http://www.usnews.com/news/articles/2013/05/30/who-is-grumpy-cat-hollywoods-next-big-star

Takashi D (2010) Google confirms acquisition of virtual currency firm Jamboo. Reuters, August 17. http://www.reuters.com/article/idUS118200328620100817

Teubner T, Adam TP, Camacho MS, Hassanein K (2014) Understanding resource sharing in C2C platforms: the role of picture humanization. ACIS 2014 proceedings, Auckland, pp 1–10

Turkle S (1997) Computational technologies and images of the self. Soc Res 64(3):1093–1111

Vastola A, Cataldo A, Mariani A (2014) Social media marketing and wine: naked wines case study. In: Vrontis D, Weber Y, Tsoukatos E (eds) The future of entrepreneurship, refereed proceedings of the 7th annual EuroMed conference of the EuroMed academy of business, September 18–19, Kristiansand, pp 1640–1652

Why did the Great Recession Fail to Produce a *New* New Deal in the USA?

43

Jon D. Wisman

> *A society which reverences the attainment of riches as the supreme felicity will naturally be disposed to regard the poor as damned in the next world, if only to justify itself for making their life a hell in this.*
> *(R. H. Tawney 1926, 222).*
>
> *The class which has the means of material production at its disposal, has control at the same time over the means of mental production, so that... the ideas of those who lack the means of mental production are subject to it.*
> *(Karl Marx 1845, 172).*
>
> *The United States, despite its formally democratic character, is firmly in the hands of a moneyed oligarchy, probably the most powerful ruling class in history.*
> *(Robert McChesney 2014a, 58).*

Contents

A Historical Glance at Laissez-Faire Ideology	953
Inequality and the Dynamics of Ideology	954
Exploding Inequality and the Generation of Severe Crises: Parallels Between the 1920s and the Three Decades Prior to 2008	956
Radically Opposite Reactions	957
Both Political Parties in Harness to Wall Street	961
How Do the Elite, So Few in Number, Win Elections?	963
Final Reflections	965
Cross-References	966
References	966

J. D. Wisman (✉)
Professor of Economics, American University, Washington, DC, USA
e-mail: jdwisma@american.edu

© The Author(s), under exclusive licence to Springer Nature Switzerland AG 2020
B. Bowden et al. (eds.), *The Palgrave Handbook of Management History*,
https://doi.org/10.1007/978-3-319-62114-2_46

Abstract

In a manner remarkably similar to the decade of the 1920s, inequality soared for over three decades prior to the crisis of 2008, provoking in both instances financial crises and severe macroeconomic dysfunction. The 1930s depression witnessed a strong egalitarian political reaction to the laissez-faire ideology that had justified the inequality-generating institutional changes of the 1920s, resulting in a New Deal that launched four decades of institutional change that considerably improved general welfare and lessened inequality. The Grand Recession and its wake, by contrast, has not put that same ideology seriously into question, malaise becoming expressed predominantly in a form of rightwing populism, behind which inequality continues to explode. Why such radically divergent reactions to severe hardship? This chapter explores three foremost reasons for why ideology legitimating inequality survived practically unscathed during the later crisis: First, the crisis beginning in 2008 proved to be less severe, in part due to wiser public policy responses. Second, the welfare net that developed in the wake of the earlier crisis softened the degree of hardship accompanying the later crisis. And third, the elite's command over ideology had become more sophisticated and thus capable of surviving the later crisis essentially intact.

Keywords

Inequality · Ideology · Great Depression · Laissez-faire · Barack Obama

JEL Classification Codes

B · E02 · H1 · N1

In 2008, at the onset of the worst macroeconomic crisis to afflict the United States since the Great Depression, Democrat Barack Obama, promising major change, won the Presidency with a decisive victory over Republican John McCain, commanding 53% to 46% of the popular vote and 365 to 173 in the Electoral College. After his inauguration, he received sky-high public approval ratings. Democrats also commanded majorities in both houses of Congress giving the new President a challenge and opportunity that politicians rarely encounter – a crisis so severe that he could claim legitimacy to rewrite the social contract so as to reverse the soaring inequality that had evolved in the previous 35 years and return the nation to furthering the progressive measures that were instituted during the 40 years following the Great Depression's New Deal. Along with a Democrat-controlled Congress, he faced an opportunity to launch a New New Deal and it was widely expected that he would do so. In the wake of his election, he appeared on the cover of *Time* as FDR with the heading "The New New Deal." Such an opportunity was captured by Milton Friedman's quip that "Only a crisis—actual or perceived—produces real change" (1982, ix). But Obama and Congressional Democrats failed to seize the occasion.

Inequality continues to soar and progressive programs that had been instituted between the mid-1930s and mid-1970s continue to be weakened.

A considerable amount of ink has been spent on explaining why Democrats failed to seize, or were effectively blocked from seizing, their once-in-a-political-career opportunity (e.g., Skocpol et al. 2012; McChesney 2014b). But what has been inadequately recognized is the degree to which all of politics is fundamentally a fight for shares of income, wealth, and privilege, and the overwhelming role that ideology has always played in this struggle. Ideology has always been second only to violence in creating and maintaining inequality.

The Great Depression of the 1930s witnessed a strong egalitarian political reaction to the laissez-faire ideology that had justified the inequality-generating institutional changes of the 1920s, resulting in a New Deal, that launched four decades of progressive institutional change, considerably improving general welfare and substantially lessening inequality. The Grand Recession and its wake, by contrast, has not put that ideology seriously into question, malaise becoming expressed predominantly in a form of rightwing populism that has provided cover behind which inequality continues to explode. Why such radically divergent reactions to severe hardship? This chapter explores three dominant reasons for why the laissez-faire ideology legitimating inequality survived practically unscathed during the later crisis: First, the crisis beginning in 2008 proved to be less severe, in part due to a prompt and wiser public policy response. Second, the welfare net that developed in the wake of the earlier crisis softened the degree of hardship accompanying the later crisis. And third, the elite's command over ideology had become more entrenched and sophisticated and thus capable of surviving the later crisis practically intact.

A Historical Glance at Laissez-Faire Ideology

Whereas religion served the predominant role of legitimizing inequality in pre-modern societies, economics evolved to increasingly do so with the rise of capitalism, and among economic doctrines, laissez-faire has played a dominant role. Laissez-faire ideology has its origins in the struggle of a rising bourgeois class to curb the absolutist state's restrictions on their pursuit of profits. It received its theoretical grounding in the work of Adam Smith and the subsequent Classical School of economics. It has since served to legitimate strictly limiting government's interference in markets, while justifying its enforcement of private property rights.

Although laissez-faire ideology remained dominant throughout the nineteenth century, as industrialization and urbanization accompanying economic growth increased inequality, it also greatly augmented the potential, as Marx anticipated, that the working class could organize and threaten violence against the elites' state for redress. The evolution of an urban industrial working class brought with it organized, at times violent, resistance to long workdays, low wages, child labor, and unhealthy working conditions. To reduce and hopefully eliminate the threat of violence, elites began bribing the working class with various benefits and with the franchise. These strategies for calming working class revolutionary fervor resulted in higher living standards for workers.

The progressively greater democratization at the ballot box decreased the ease with which elites could use the state to violently curb the aspirations of workers, especially in putting down strikes. Retention of their control over the state would depend increasingly on their control over ideology. Always before, excepting severe crises, they had been successful in convincing the producers below that what was more narrowly in the interests of elites was equally in the interests of the workers. But now, because elites could no longer so readily back up their ideology with violence, they had lost their violence-backed monopoly control over the state.

By the end of the nineteenth century and during the first two decades of the twentieth century, workers used the state to politically advance their collective interests on an unprecedented scale. The state was transformed from the executive committee of the ruling class to that social agency that could limit or, in the extreme, eliminate the capturing by elites of disproportionate shares of income, wealth, and privilege. Without revolution, the working class had in principle gained power to rewrite the social script. That they did not fully do so is testament to the power elites retained over ideology.

Elites' command over ideology got a decided boost when a number of forces, most notably the seemingly unpatriotic strikes during World War I and the Bolshevik Revolution, turned public sentiment against worker organizations, enabling a robust form of laissez-faire ideology to recapture the political sphere and generate exploding inequality (Wisman and Pacitti 2004). But laissez-faire ideology's return to dominance was short-lived, becoming significantly delegitimated by the severity of the Great Depression.

However, in the 1970s, a convergence of events, most notably stagflation, dollar devaluation, heightened strike activity, and presumed moral degeneracy, enabled elites to depict government as "the problem." Laissez-faire ideology began returning to the dominance it had commanded in the 1920s. It retains that dominance to this day.

Inequality and the Dynamics of Ideology

Elite control can be maintained by either physical or ideological force, as has been recognized by social thinkers since Machiavelli. Physical force has often been necessary for initially establishing and solidifying a hierarchical social structure. However, brute force is relatively inefficient in that it generates strong resentment and the constant threat of insurrection. It is also costly in terms of policing resources. A far more efficient and effective long-term strategy – one that decreases the costs of resentment and physical repression – is for elites to generate an ideological system that convinces not only themselves but all beneath them of the moral and functional appropriateness of the existing social order. Those below are led to believe that their lesser status in terms of income, wealth, and privilege is as it must be.

During the greater part of history since the rise of the state and civilization, an aristocracy controlled access to land and the dominant ideology legitimated their privileged position. With the rise of capitalism, the owners of capital came to control access to the means of production and an ideology rose to dominance that legitimates the institutions and practices of capitalism. It is this control of ideology, backed when necessary by state violence, that has enabled the continual exploitation of producers since the rise of civilization 5500 years ago. It is also control of ideology that permits exploitation to continue, even when the exploited have gained the franchise and thus possess in principal the political means to bring it to an end. Beyond violence, ideology has always been elites' most powerful political weapon.

Ideology is deception, although not usually conscious deception. It is a form of mystification that serves specific interests. It promotes a mistaken view of aspects of reality, most importantly, social aspects and social relations. In doing so, it has always been a powerful instrument for creating and maintaining inequality (Wisman and Smith 2011).

Ideology is an aspect of legitimation. Legitimation refers to a set of beliefs concerning the nature of reality. It concerns how people mentally experience and understand their world. As such, it is neither positive nor negative. Humans evolved such that they must give meaning to their world (Berger and Luckmann 1967). Ideology, by contrast, refers to the way in which reality is misrepresented to serve special interests. It presents a false view of social relations that enables the exploitation of some by others.

At times, warfare and economic, demographic, ecological, or other natural catastrophes brought on crises severe enough to threaten the elite's ideology and thus their fitness to rule. However, their superior command over ideology always permitted them to eventually reclaim legitimacy and control over labor and thus its exploitation – the expropriation of the surplus workers produced.

Ideological control is generally expressed through the manipulation of social discourse. As Jim Sidanius and Shana Levin put it,

> ...almost all perspectives on legitimizing ideologies suggest that their power is derived from their consensuality.... legitimizing ideologies are believed to be effective in regulating group-based inequality because they are often endorsed by dominants and subordinates alike. All other things being equal, the greater the degree to which both dominants and subordinates agree on the veracity of hierarchy-enhancing legitimizing myths, the less physical violence will be necessary to keep the system of stratification intact (2001, 316).

For subjugation of labor and its exploitation to be efficiently sustainable, workers must be led to believe that their inferior status in terms of income, wealth, and privilege is as it must be. And strikingly, Elizabeth Haines and John Jost find that "people may be more willing to accept relatively illegitimate accounts than is commonly assumed...[and the authors] found that people misremembered the explanations that were given to them as more legitimate than they actually were" (2000, 232).

With the exception of periods of extreme crises, elite control has always been adequately legitimated such that most folks found it acceptable, even when it meant their lives were filled with hardship and misery. This was especially true if all other sufferers remained quiescent. As Tolstoy famously noted, there are "no conditions of life to which a man cannot get accustomed, especially if he sees them accepted by everyone around him" (2017).

Exploding Inequality and the Generation of Severe Crises: Parallels Between the 1920s and the Three Decades Prior to 2008

Since the beginning of the twentieth century, there have been two major explosions in inequality: the first between World War I and the late 1920s and the second since the mid-1970s. Both were facilitated by robust revivals of laissez-faire ideology. Both also set the stage for severe macroeconomic dysfunction, accompanied by economic privation that most afflicted the less-well-off.

The periods leading up to both crises appeared to be highly prosperous. Between 1922 and 1929, GNP grew at an annual rate of 4.7% and unemployment averaged 3.7% (White 1990, 69). Between 1993 and 2007, GNP growth averaged 3.25% (US Department of Commerce n.d.) and unemployment averaged 5.2% ("Current Population Survey (CPS)" n.d.). However, in both periods productivity gains outpaced wages, such that the share of total income received by the richest 5% of the population, for instance, increased from 24.3% in 1919 to 33.5% in 1929. The disposable income of the top 1% of taxpayers rose 63% (Livingston 2009, 38). The real prosperity of the 1920s was reserved for those residing in the top of the income scale (Bernstein 1966; Stricker 1983). Contributing to this heightened inequality were tax "reforms" that reduced corporate taxes and lowered the maximum personal income tax rate from 65% to 32% (Sobel 1968, 52–53).

Similarly, real disposable income declined for wage earners in the three decades leading up to 2008. Average weekly earnings (in 1982 dollars) declined from $331.39 in 1973 to $275.93 in 2005, greatly lagging behind productivity gains (Miringoff and Opdycke 2014, 226). What is especially striking about the two periods is the dramatically larger shares of income and wealth accruing to the ultra-wealthy, especially the top one-hundredth of 1%. Their income shares soared from about 1.7% to 5% in the first period and from about 0.9% to 6% in the second (Saez 2010).

Greater inequality during both of these periods generated three dynamics that heightened risks of financial crises. The first is that holding ever greater income and wealth, an elite flooded financial markets with credit, helping keep interest rates low and encouraging the creation of new credit instruments with higher risk profiles. Stock and real estate markets soared. The second dynamic is that greater inequality meant that individuals were forced to struggle harder to find ways to consume more to maintain their relative social status, with the consequence that they saved less, increased their indebtedness, and worked longer hours. The third dynamic is that, as the rich took larger shares of income and wealth, they gained more command over ideology and hence politics. Reducing the size of government, deregulating the economy, and failing to regulate newly evolving financial instruments flowing out of this ideology. Together, these three dynamics set the stage for the financial crises of 1929 and 2008 (Wisman 2013a, 2014). The Great Depression and Great Recession were the consequences.

Radically Opposite Reactions

The Great Depression's widespread suffering generated worker militancy and called into question the elite's laissez-faire ideology and its political and economic policies.[1] It also challenged the prevailing economic theory that legitimated these policies, making space for the Keynesian revolution. Moreover, as Milton and Rose Friedman wrote, the Depression "discredited [and] shattered the public's confidence in private enterprise" (1988, 458; 462). This delegitimation of the elite's ideology, their most controlling political tool, led to political changes during the subsequent four decades that reduced inequality in income, wealth, and opportunity. These political changes were guided and made possible by economic doctrines that depicted greater equality as positive and active government intervention as essential for a prosperous and fair economy. Only government could guarantee a more equitable society – a "New Deal."

The most significant government measures reducing inequality and improving conditions for the broad population included workers' rights to collectively bargain, minimum wages, Social Security, the G.I. Bill, Medicare, Medicaid, Food Stamps, public housing and rent subsidies, Project Headstart, Job Corps, Occupational Safety and Health Administration, the Consumer Product Safety Commission, the Mine Enforcement and Safety Administration, and the Environmental Protection Agency. Public goods that benefit the general population such as schools, community colleges and state universities, parks, playgrounds, and public transit were vastly expanded in quantity and quality. And the percent of Americans living in poverty declined dramatically from about 30% in 1950 to 10% in 1973 (Appleby 2011, 321). Highly progressive income taxation also reveals the intent of redistribution toward greater equality. The highest marginal income tax rates were: 1942–43: 88%, 1944–45: 94%, and 1946–50: 91%. Top marginal tax rates remained in the upper 80% from 1951 until 1964, and 70% from 1965 until 1981.[2]

---

[1] Melvyn Dubofsky notes that "The Great Depression and the New Deal had wrought a veritable political revolution among American workers. Masses of hitherto politically apathetic workers, especially among first-generation immigrants and their spouses, went to the polls in greater numbers" (1986, 212).

[2] The impact of tax rates on inequality is clear. OECD countries in which taxes have been cut most on high incomes have witnessed the greatest increases in income accruing to the very wealthy (Deaton 2013, 212). Piketty also notes that "...the resurgence of inequality after 1980 is due largely to the political shifts of the past several decades, especially in regard to taxation and finance" (Piketty 2014, 20).

Whereas the top 1% of households in 1929 received 22.5% of all pre-tax income (including capital gains), they received only 9% by the late 1970s (Piketty and Saez 2006). What Arthur Burns termed a "revolutionary leveling" (Williamson 1991, 11), and Claudia Goldin and Robert Margo, the "Great Compression" (1992) between the 1930s and mid-1970s, seemed to confirm Simon Kuznets' conjecture that inequality would decrease in the later stages of economic development (1955). Thanks to the relative delegitimation of the elites' laissez-faire ideology and thus political power, relative wealth distribution returned to levels that had disappeared in the decades after the Civil War.

However, by the mid-1970s, ideology began turning against the active government intervention that had benefited the broad population for four decades. Due to the elites' wealth, superior education, and influence over the political sphere, this ideological reversal was destined to happen eventually (Wisman 2013b), but in the 1970s specific events hurried it along.

Stagflation delegitimated Keynesian economics,[3] setting the stage for a strong rejection of government intervention in the economy. Liberal policies were alleged to be at the root of what pundits claimed was the decline of the American century. Evidence included loss of gold backing of the dollar and its devaluation; loss of the Vietnam War; and with the widespread use of recreational drugs and sexual promiscuity, alleged rising moral degeneracy; and leftist extremism.[4] Welfare, union power, and labor legislation were claimed to have sapped work incentives. High taxes, especially on the rich, allegedly reduced entrepreneurial energies and the incentives to save and invest, resulting in stagnation and anemic tax revenues (the infamous "Laffer Curve").

Legislation flowing out of the rising discontent with activist government reversed the trend toward greater equality. This shift of income, wealth, and privilege toward the rich set in motion a self-reinforcing process since it meant that they commanded yet more resources with which to influence public opinion and policy. And research reveals that their expenditures on creating and disseminating ideology yield high returns (Glaeser and Raven 2006). The consequence is that inequality has reached levels of the 1920s. The elite, thanks to their recapture of ideology that guided political policy to change the economic rules of the game, recaptured more than they had lost during the four decades of the "great compression" (Wisman and Pacitti 2015).

But why did the onset of the Great Recession in 2008 not follow, at least in part, the script written during the Great Depression? Whereas the Great Depression witnessed a strong egalitarian political reaction to the laissez-faire ideology that had justified the inequality-generating institutional changes of the 1920s, the Grand

---

[3]As Chicago School economist John Cochrane has put it, "When inflation came in the nineteen-seventies, that was a major failure of Keynesian economics" (Cassidy 2010, 31). As early as 1980, Robert Lucas wrote that "At research seminars, people don't take Keynesian theorizing seriously anymore; the audience starts to whisper and giggle to one another" (Lucas 1980, 19).

[4]Home-grown domestic terrorism also characterized this period. In 1972, there were 1900 domestic bombings. Notable terrorist groups included the Weathermen, the Black Liberation Army, and the Symbionese Liberation Army (Burrough 2015).

Recession did not put seriously into question that same ideology that had legitimated the previous 40 years of exploding inequality. Instead, the widespread malaise has been largely channeled into an expression of populism that enables the rules of the game to continue to be reformulated to direct yet more income, wealth, and privilege to an elite. Indeed, since 2008, inequality has continued to explode.

Why such radically divergent reactions to systemic dysfunction and severe hardship? Why did the ideology legitimating inequality survive practically unscathed during the later crisis? Three reasons stand out: First, the crisis beginning in 2008 proved to be less severe, in part due to wiser public policy responses. Second, the welfare net that developed in the wake of the earlier crisis softened the degree of hardship accompanying the later crisis. And third, the elite's command over ideology had become more entrenched and sophisticated and thus capable of surviving the later crisis practically intact.

Two calamitous public policy mistakes followed the stock market crash of 1929: The Federal Reserve System permitted the money supply to contract, creating a liquidity crisis, bank failure, deflation, and massive bankruptcies. Second, blaming unfair foreign competition for the crisis, Congress passed the Smoot-Hawley Tariff Act of 1930, the most protectionist in US history. Both helped magnify a financial crisis into a full-blown depression. The immediate response to the severe crisis that began in 2008 was radically wiser. The Federal Reserve massively injected liquidity into the banking system and bailed out banks, precluding a collapse of the financial system, deflation, and the massive bankruptcies that had characterized the early 1930s.[5] A rush to protectionism was also precluded. At the G20 meeting in London in 2009, world leaders committed to avoid the mistakes of the early 1930s by coordinating fiscal and monetary expansion and eschewing protectionism. Only when the threat of depression seemed averted did increasing voices insist on fiscal austerity.

The Great Depression was far harsher for the general population than would be the case during the Great Recession. Whereas unemployment reached 25% in the former, it attained only 10% in the latter.[6] Moreover, no public safety net existed during the Great Depression, whereas a considerable public support system limited suffering during the Great Recession.

Although laissez-faire ideology legitimated public policies that enabled explosions in inequality prior to both crises, its uninterrupted reign was only slightly more than a decade prior to 1929, whereas its dominance spanned three decades prior to 2008. Thus, in this later period, it had time to become far more deeply entrenched in politics and social attitudes, supported by social institutions such as education, media, think tanks, and popular entertainment. Further, whereas in the

---

[5]Relative success appears not to have been due to the lesser severity of the 2008 financial crisis. Ben Bernanke avowed at the Financial Crisis Inquiry Commission hearing: "As a scholar of the Great Depression, I honestly believe that September and October of 2008 was the worst financial crisis in global history, including the Great Depression" (*Financial Crisis Inquiry Commission* 2011, 354).

[6]Although official unemployment reached 25% in 1933, more recent estimates claim it was closer to 50% (Gans 2014, 56).

1930s, socialism was broadly entertained as a more just alternative to dysfunctional capitalism, the 1991 collapse of the Soviet Union all but eliminated it from political discourse.

In his first inaugural Presidential address in 1981, Ronald Reagan declared that "Government is not the solution to our problem; government is the problem." And in fact, until workers acquired the franchise, although government provided for defense and a degree of social stability, it enabled elites to extract as much surplus as possible from the working population, so for the latter it was indeed a problem. Workers, whether slaves, serfs, indentured servants, or wage workers generally retained merely the wherewithal to survive. Yet, while government served to enable the exploitation of the producers, its goodness was rarely in doubt. Ideology, crafted and controlled by elites, depicted the state as sacred, its rulers chosen by gods, or gods themselves. Government was part of the sacred order of things. Even when the state came to be legitimated in secular terms (as a *social contract*), elites continued to use the state to insure that they could capture most of the workers' output beyond the latter's survival needs.

However, since the late eighteenth century, laissez-faire ideology has served to cultivate a distrust of government, and the elite's need for this distrust became especially necessary after workers gained the franchise. The vote gave workers the power to peacefully claim a fairer share of society's income, wealth, and privilege. The role of the state was in principle reversed from a social agency that enabled elites to capture virtually all income beyond subsistence, to one that could impede them from doing so. If the state were to become truly democratically controlled, then for elites, government would indeed become "the problem." Thus, a winning ideological strategy for elites would be to convince the electorate that government is not to be trusted. And since the late 1970s, this strategy has worked. Whereas in the 1970s, 70% of Americans had "trust and confidence" that the government could successfully deal with domestic problems, only 22% held the same view in 2011 (Ford 2012).[7] The consequence has been massive tax cuts (incidentally mostly benefitting the rich) to "starve the beast," shredded welfare for the poor (depicted as lazy free-loaders), and deregulation. And as government programs that benefit the larger population have been cut, their quality has worsened, thereby giving credence to the view that government is incompetent. To check the power of those who do not buy into this ideology, more measures have been taken to restrict the right to vote.

---

[7] The ideology of "government as the problem" has been so successful that a huge percent of Americans do not even recognize very substantial benefits they receive from government. For instance, Paul Krugman points out that 40% to 44% of those who receive Social Security, unemployment benefits, and Medicare claim that they "have never used a government program" (2012).

During the three decades prior to the crisis of 2008, the majority of Americans witnessed a decline in the quality of their lives. Their wages stagnated and their jobs became less secure as freer international trade forced them to compete with low-wage foreign workers and new technology rendered their skills obsolete.[8] For many, neighborhoods decayed, as did public services such as schools for their children (Putnam 2016). And then the crisis of 2008 made everything so much worse. The victims' response had been ideologically conditioned to blame a government controlled by intellectual elites and Wall Street.

Both Political Parties in Harness to Wall Street

Obama's initial measures prompted progressives quickly to conclude that he had betrayed his campaign promises. He brought in Wall Street foxes (e.g., Timothy Geithner and Lawrence Summers) who had raided and devastated the hen house to fix it. Rather than nationalize mega banks, he bailed them out, saving their wealthy owners from massive losses, while letting poor homeowners go bankrupt on loans they were fraudulently sold.[9] The failing auto industry was bailed out at a final taxpayer loss of $10 billion.[10] Absent a massive jobs program, unemployed workers were left idle and discouraged, many dropping out of the job market to which some have yet to return.[11] Consequently, corporate balance sheets recovered quickly, while mainstreet small businesses and American households floundered. It is true that although Democrats held majorities in both houses during his first two years, Obama faced the threat of filibusters in the Senate. But rather than attempting to end-run Congress by appealing directly to voters with a strategy such as FDR's

---

[8] Production workers earned $9.26 an hour in inflation-adjusted dollars in 1972. Forty-four years later, in 2016, they earned $9.20 (Cassidy 2017).

[9] No mortgage executives were held accountable and mortgage companies were permitted to foreclose on homeowners instead of being forced to modify loans or reduce balances. About nine million households lost their homes. At the end of Obama's presidency, 63.7% of households owned their own homes, the lowest since 1965 (the peak was 69.2 in 2004) (Jackson 2017). Black households were especially impacted. By 2014, almost half of their wealth had vanished (Heideman 2017), a crushing blow given that net median white household wealth is 13 times higher than for blacks (*The Economist* 2016).

[10] The wealthy were generally spared the pain of the crisis. By the end of Obama's second year, the S&P 500 stock index had risen almost 60%, recovering most of its losses after its 2007 peak. By the end of his second term, it had gained 166%.

[11] The labor-force participation fell from 65.7% to 62.8% (half of the decline due to demographics) during the Obama years, the lowest in four decades, while the median jobless rate was 7.7%, higher than during any post-World War Two administration (Jackson 2017).

fireside chats, he futilely tried to appease Republican opposition.[12] The fact that Obama ended up embracing the same politics that had generated inequality over the preceding 35 years was the straw that broke the camel's back. Many of his supporters wound up supporting Trump.[13]

The Democrats' disappointing response to their unique opportunity to put American society back onto a progressive track is symptomatic of the extent to which a wealthy elite has captured government. Whether Democrats or Republicans have controlled the White House or Congress has made relatively little difference in who is winning in America. Since Jimmy Carter, income, wealth, and privilege have continued to shift toward an elite no matter which party has been in power.[14] The only difference is that Republican policies have been more clearly crafted to benefit the elite. Government under both parties had let down a majority of Americans and many were ready for anything but more of the same. Donald Trump's appeal was that he appeared and professed to not be a part of that establishment that had betrayed everyday Americans.[15] And although the Republican Party is seen as part of the establishment, due to its support of cultural stances that are anathema to the Democratic Party, it was stronger at the end of the Obama administration than at any time since 1928 (Time 2017). Incidentally, inequality as measured by the Gini

---

[12] Obama did not engage in reaching out to Americans through television (as had Ronald Reagan) to draw support for his policies and thereby skirt-around and bring pressure upon Congressional members. It should be noted that a conservative coalition opposing Roosevelt's projects formed in 1934. However, Roosevelt became increasingly supportive of workers as the Depression dragged on. In his presidential campaign of 1936, he advocated a wealth tax. He also advocated marginal income tax rates as high as 79%, stiffer inheritance taxes, and greater taxes on corporate profits. He attempted, unsuccessfully, to make guaranteed employment a part of the Social Security Act. He was also not reticent in his attacks on the rich, referring to them in his presidential address of 1936 as "economic royalists," an "autocracy" that sought "power for themselves, enslavement for the public" (Kennedy 2001, 227–82).

[13] During the 2016 election campaign, Donald Trump received the greatest support in those counties with the highest levels of economic distress, as well as where the mortality rates were highest from alcohol, drug abuse and suicide (Burns 2018).

[14] The election of Jimmy Carter in 1976 shifted the Democratic Party rightward, where it has since stayed, despite Bernie Sanders' attempt to take it back to the politics of FDR, Harry Truman, JFK and Lyndon Johnson, during whose administrations, wealth inequality decreased. It was especially Bill Clinton who dragged the party further to the right with his campaign pledge to end welfare "as we know it." During the administrations of Carter, Clinton, and Obama, wealth inequality increased (Studebaker 2016).

[15] Ganesh Sitaraman writes that "The defining feature of the 2016 election was the strength of anti-establishment candidates who channeled popular discontent with elites and with the current functioning of American politics. In the primaries, Senator Bernie Sanders received more than 12 million votes, Donald Trump received more than 13 million votes, and Senator Ted Cruz won more than seven-and-a-half-million votes. Together, explicitly anti-establishment candidates took more than 30 million primary votes, out of around fifty-six million cast" (Sitaraman 2017, 271).The Public Religion Research Institute conducted a poll in June 2016 and found that 49 percent of voters agreed with the statement "Because things have gotten so far off track in this country, we need a leader who is willing to break some rules if that's what it takes to set things right" (cited in Galston 2018, 74).

coefficient rose more during the Obama years than during any other administration over the past forty years (Regalia 2015). Obama failed to push hard for his campaign promise to permit the expiration of George W. Bush's tax breaks for the richest Americans, even though he enjoyed Democratic majorities in both Houses in 2009 and 2010. Emmanuel Saez reports that 52% of income gains since the financial crisis and up to 2016 had accrued to the wealthiest 1% of households, while average household's income remains at about the same as in 1999 (Ehrenfreund 2017).

The fact that both parties have become beholden and in service to monied interests is a direct outcome of surging inequality which has provided elites with ever-greater resources with which to purchase candidates and control government policies. Since election campaigns are funded by private money and organized labor has been busted, candidates in need of massive amounts of money to run for office are trapped. They must appeal to wealthy interests to get and stay elected.[16] There have been exceptions such as Bernie Sanders, and a more recent number of candidates for the Presidential election of 2020, but they prove the rule.

How Do the Elite, So Few in Number, Win Elections?

Although both parties have been substantially captured by monied interests, the Republican Party is generally the party to which the elite gravitate. But how could they ever rally sufficient support to get their candidates elected, given that the elite not only constitute but a very small fraction of the voting public, but also officially embrace political programs that blatantly are to their own benefit? For instance, the Republican Party has long advocated slashing funds for programs that benefit lower income households, such as food stamps, unemployment benefits, funding for public education, and publicly provided health care. And proving their allegiance to the rich elite, they have ever advocated cutting taxes for the wealthy. So how do they get their candidates elected?

It should first be noted that the GOP has a long history of demonizing the least privileged as lazy and handicapped by dependency on welfare, or as a Tea Party bumper sticker puts it, "Keep Working. Millions on Welfare are Counting on You."[17]

---

[16] Democrats as well as Republicans are dependent on the rich and the corporations they own. In the 2014 elections, for example, about 32,000 individuals — 0.01 percent of the population — accounted for 30 percent of all political contributions (Olsen-Phillips et al. 2015). With few exceptions, contributions from individual firms are given equally to Republicans and Democrats. Corporations hedge their bets, investing in politicians of all stripes to ensure that, no matter who is elected, they will have access. Politicians almost always respond to the will of their contributors, not constituents (Bonica et al. 2013).

[17] In an infamous 2012 campaign speech, Mitt Romney claimed that 47% of the country constitutes a "taker class," paying little or nothing in taxes, but expecting taxes on the productive classes for free health care, food, housing, etc. Many workers buy into this view. Catherine Rampell reports that "Across rural America, the Rust Best, Coal Country and other hotbeds of Trumpism, voters have repeatedly expressed frustration that the lazy and less deserving are getting a bigger chunk of government cheese" (2016).

The least privileged are told to buck up and go fend for themselves as earlier Americans always did. American society is presented as providing exceptional opportunity for vertical mobility. Anyone by dint of persistence and hard work can make it to the very top, making Americans far more ambivalent than Western Europeans about fairness.[18]

Neoclassical economics' claim that all economic actors get their just desserts reinforces the view that by working diligently, anyone can make it in America. This idea of fluid vertical mobility has deep roots in US culture. For much of its history, thanks to abundant land and emigrants fleeing Europe's rigid class structure, there was greater social mobility in America than anywhere else on Earth, making Americans more prone to internalize responsibility for their successes or failures. The rich have earned it and the poor are responsible for their poverty.

Europeans, by contrast, are less ready to find the poor at fault. For instance, a World Values Survey found that 71% of Americans versus 40% of Europeans believe that the poor could work their way out of poverty. "…54 percent of Europeans believe that the poor are unlucky, whereas only 30 percent of Americans share that belief." And "Sixty percent of American respondents, but only 26 percent of Europeans say that the poor are lazy" (Alesina et al. 2001, 237, 242, 243).[19]

Americans also greatly underestimate the magnitude of inequality. Whereas people on average believe that the richest 20% own almost 60% of all wealth, they in fact own about 85%. More striking, whereas they believe that the bottom 40% own 8% to 10% of wealth, they in fact hold only 0.3% (Norton and Ariely 2011).

The GOP also exploits the fact that for many people, cultural issues trump economic ones.[20] This is in part because economic issues are complex and hotly contested. Elites find support from some professional economists that tax cuts for the rich and corporations, cuts in welfare, and deregulation will generate economic dynamism, increase employment, and raise wages. So even when the economic consequences of this platform are unclear, voters find reason to support a political party that also happens to endorse their hot cultural stances on issues such as abortion, gay rights, race, immigration, gun control, and creationism. Moreover, these cultural issues are laden with an emotional energy that economic issues lack.[21]

---

[18]Some conservatives have attempted to propagate a view that fairness is "hostile to capitalism, destructive of national security, and dangerous to liberty" (Woodward 2012, B6).

[19]Other evidence also suggests the greater extent to which Americans hold individuals responsible for their own fates. For instance, Alesina, Glaeser, and Sacerdote have found "an extremely strong relationship in the United States between supporting capital punishment and opposing welfare" (2001b, 242).

[20]Matt O'Brien writes that today's Republican Party is composed of three different wings. The first is Wall Street that puts up the money to get their leaders elected. The second wing is middle-class professionals who are attracted to tax cuts. The third wing is the white working class who are sold the argument that their woes are due to immigrants, free trade, welfare cheats, and many of whom are attached to cultural issues such as right to life, etc. (O'Brien 2017).

[21]Behavioral economists are finding that people systematically make decisions that are against their own interests, driven more by emotions than economic reason. In *What's the Matter with Kansas?* (2005), Thomas Frank provides wide-ranging evidence for this view.

The manner in which racism has played this role was extensively addressed by W. E. B. Du Bois (1935), and it has been alleged to have played an important role in the election of Donald Trump (Zeitz 2017).

Final Reflections

The sustained 40-year period of declining inequality between the 1930s and 1970s appears to have been a modern historical anomaly, if not a singularity. The reason is to be found in the elite's greater potential for crafting ideology that is widely persuasive and thus can be expected to reverse any setbacks. Not only do their greater material assets enable them to essentially purchase elections, they have the best educations, the most gifted friends and acquaintances, all of which make them on average more astute and successful in identifying and attaining their interests than less-privileged citizens. They are not evil or behaving in bad faith, but sincerely believe that the doctrines and policies they support, and which make them ever richer, are in fact the best for everyone.

What hope, then, remains for greater equality? By crafting their self-interested ideology to be ever more convincing to the larger population, elites have managed over the past 45 years to appropriate ever larger shares of national income, wealth, and privilege. This ideology has become deeply entrenched in the American psyche. It is plausible that the legitimacy of such ideology can only be effectively challenged by an extremely severe crisis – one that greatly reduces living standards and security – an event as extreme as the Great Depression. But what if elites who control the state by purchasing politicians and controlling ideology have learnt how to limit the damage of severe crises? This appears to have been the case with the crisis of 2008. Relatively limited suffering enabled the entrenched ideology to survive intact, deflecting blame from the wealthy elite to Wall Street and establishment politicians (not clearly realizing that they are agents of the elite!), immigrants, free trade, and welfare dependents.

The future could be one in which gradually, under an ideological umbrella, more and more measures will be launched that further increase the elites' capacity to capture ever more income, wealth, and privilege, continuing the explosive rise in inequality of the past 45 years. Indeed, as this is being written, under the Trump administration and a Republican Congress, precisely this is happening, at yet greater speed.

Or might elites come to realize that great inequality is not in fact in their best interest? Jared Diamond suggests that this is unlikely. He notes that in past civilizations elites pursued their own immediate self-interest even when they had before them the evidence of severe environmental decline, their civilization's decay, and thus the long-run ruin of the foundations upon which their own privileges and livelihoods depended (Diamond 2011). Diamond's investigations suggest that elites do not manage to recognize and act upon their enlightened long-run self-interests, even when their policies are leading to their own ruin. Similarly, according to Bos van Bavel (2016), capitalist classes brought forth robust economic growth in Iraq in the fifth to seventh century, Italy in the tenth to twelfth century, and the Low Countries in the eleventh to thirteenth century. However, the increasing political power of their ever-wealthier capitalist classes led to institutional changes that permitted them to massively rent seek as opposed to investing in productive capital, bringing that robust economic dynamism to an end and propelling their societies into first stagnation and then long-run decline. Moreover, in his magisterial study of inequality levelling, Walter Scheidel finds "little solid evidence for leveling by peaceful means" (2017, 377).

Could the US become a failed state? Daron Acemoglu and James Robinson remind us that "Countries become failed states... because of the legacy of extractive institutions, which concentrate power and wealth in the hands of those controlling the state, opening the way for unrest, strife, and civil war" (2012, 376).

Cross-References

- ▶ A Return to the Good Old Days: Populism, Fake News, Yellow Journalism, and the Unparalleled Virtue of Business People
- ▶ Conclusion: Management Theory in Crisis
- ▶ Economic Foundations: Adam Smith and the Classical School of Economics
- ▶ Intellectual Enlightenment: The Epistemological Foundations of Business Endeavor
- ▶ Introduction: Public Policy Failure, the Demise of Experts, and the Dawn of a New Era
- ▶ Keynesianism: Origins, Principles, and Keynes's Debate with Hayek
- ▶ Labor and Employment Practices: The Rise and Fall of the New Managerialism
- ▶ Management History in the Modern World: An Overview
- ▶ Neo-classical Thought: Alfred Marshall and Utilitarianism
- ▶ The New Executive: Interconnected Yet Isolated and Uninformed – Leadership Challenges in the Digital Pandemic Epoch
- ▶ Trade Union Decline and Transformation: Where to for Employment Relations?
- ▶ What Is Management?

References

Acemoglu D, Robinson JA (2012) Why nations fail: the origins of power, prosperity and poverty, 1st edn. Crown Publishers, New York

Alesina A, Glaeser E, Sacerdote B (2001) Why doesn't the United States have a European-style welfare state? Brook Pap Econ Act 32(2):187–278

Appleby J (2011) The relentless revolution: a history of capitalism. Reprint edition. W. W. Norton & Company, New York

Bavel, Bas van. 2016. *The Invisible Hand?: How Market Economies Have Emerged and Declined since AD 500*. Oxford: Oxford University Press.

Berger PL, Luckmann T (1967) The social construction of reality: a treatise in the sociology of knowledge. Anchor, New York

Bernstein I (1966) The lean years: a history of the American worker. Penguin Books, Boston, pp 1920–1933

Burns, Harry. 2018. "How Well GDP Measures the Well-Being of Society". Khan Academy. March 21, 2018. https://www.khanacademy.org/economics-finance-domain/macroeconomics/macro-economic-indicators-and-the-business-cycle/macro-limitations-of-gdp/a/how-well-gdp-measures-the-well-being-of-society-cnx

Bonica, Adam, Nolan McCarty, Keith T Poole, and Howard Rosenthal. 2013. "Why Hasn't Democracy Slowed Rising Inequality?" Journal of Economic Perspectives 27 (3): 103–24.

Burrough B (2015) Days of rage: America's radical underground, the FBI, and the forgotten age of revolutionary violence. Penguin Press, New York

Cassidy J (2010) After the blowup. In: The New Yorker, 11 Jan 2010. http://www.newyorker.com/reporting/2010/01/11/100111fa_fact_cassidy

Cassidy J (2017) Obama's economic record: an assessment|The New Yorker, 9 Jan 2017. https://www.newyorker.com/news/john-cassidy/obamas-economic-record-an-assessment

Current Population Survey (CPS) n.d. Accessed 9 Sept 2017. https://www.bls.gov/cps/

Deaton A (2013) The great escape: health, wealth, and the origins of inequality. Princeton University Press, Princeton

Diamond J (2011) Collapse: how societies choose to fail or succeed. Revised edition. Penguin Books, New York

Du Bois WEB (1935) Black reconstruction in America (The Oxford W. E. B. Du Bois): an essay toward a history of the part which Black Folk played in the attempt to reconstruct democracy in America, 1860–1880. Edited by Henry Louis Gates, 1 edn. Oxford University Press

Dubofsky M (1986) Not so 'turbulent years': a new look at the 1930s. In: Stephenson C, Asher R (eds) Life and labor: dimensions of American working-class history. State University of New York Press, Albany, pp 205–223

Ehrenfreund M (2017) At the world economic forum, talk of equitable capitalism, 20 Jan 2017. https://www.abqjournal.com/931747/at-the-world-economic-forum-talk-of-equitable-capitalism.html

Financial Crisis Inquiry Commission (2011) The financial crisis inquiry report. Government Printing Press, Washington, DC

Ford M (2012) '5 Myths about the American Dream.' The Washington Post., 8 Jan 2012

Frank T (2005) What's the matter with Kansas?: how conservatives won the heart of America. Reprint edition. Holt Paperbacks, New York

Friedman M (1982) Capitalism and freedom. University of Chicago Press, Chicago

Friedman M, Friedman RD (1988) The tide in the Affairs of men. In: Anderson A, Bark DL (eds) Thinking about America: the United States in the 1990s. Hoover Institution Press, Stanford, Calif

Galston, William A. 2018. *Anti-Pluralism: The Populist Threat to Liberal Democracy*. New Haven, CT: Yale University Press. https://doi.org/10.2307/j.ctt21668rd.

Gans HJ (2014) Seeking a political solution to the economy's problems. Challenge 57(5):53–64. https://doi.org/10.2753/0577-5132570504

Glaeser EL, Raven RE (2006) Corruption in America. J Public Econ 90(6–7):1053–1072

Goldin C, Margo RA (1992) The great compression: the wage structure in the United States at mid-century. Q J Econ 107(1):1–34. https://doi.org/10.2307/2118322

Haines EL, Jost JT (2000) Placating the powerless: effects of legitimate and illegitimate explanation on affect, memory, and stereotyping. Soc Justice Res 13(3):219–236. https://doi.org/10.1023/A:1026481205719

Heideman P (2017) Assessing Obama. 20 Jan 2017. http://jacobinmag.com/2017/01/barack-obama-presidency-trump-inauguration

Jackson B (2017) Obama's final numbers. FactCheckOrg https://www.factcheck.org/2017/09/obamas-final-numbers/

Kennedy DM (2001) Freedom from fear: the American people in depression and war. Reprint edition. Oxford University Press, New York, pp 1929–1945

Krugman P (2012) Romney's closet. International Herald Tribune, 25 Feb 2012
Kuznets S (1955) Economic Growth and Income Inequality. Am Econ Rev 45(1):1–28
Livingston J (2009) Their great depression and ours. Challenge 52(3):34–51
Lucas RE (1980) The death of Keynesian economics. Issues and Ideas:18–19
Marx K (1845) The German ideology. In: Tucker RC (ed) The Marx-Engels reader, 2nd edn. Norton & Co., New York, pp 146–202
McChesney RW (2014a) A new new deal under Obama? In: McChesney RW (ed) Blowing the roof off the twenty-first century: media, politics, and the struggle for post-capitalist democracy. NYU Press, pp 51–61. http://www.jstor.org.proxyau.wrlc.org/stable/j.ctt1287jtm.6
McChesney RW (2014b) Blowing the roof off the twenty-first century: media, politics, and the struggle for post-capitalist democracy. Monthly Review Press, New York
Miringoff M-L, Opdycke S (2014) America's social health: putting social issues back on the public agenda. Routledge, Armonk
Norton MI, Ariely D (2011) Building a better America—one wealth quintile at a time. Perspect Psychol Sci 6(1):9–12. https://doi.org/10.1177/1745691610393524
O'Brien M (2017) Perspective|Trump's tax plan gives wall street everything it wants—and that's bad news for them. Washington Post, 6 Oct 2017. https://www.washingtonpost.com/news/wonk/wp/2017/10/06/trumps-tax-plan-gives-wall-street-everything-it-wants-and-thats-bad-news-for-them/
Olsen-Phillips, Peter, Russ Choma, Sarah Bryner, and Doug Weber. 2015. "The Political One Percent of the One Percent in 2014: Mega Donors Fuel Rising Cost of Elections". OpenSecrets Blog. April 30, 2015. https://www.opensecrets.org/news/2015/04/the-political-one-percent-of-the-one-percent-in-2014-mega-donors-fuel-rising-cost-of-elections/
Piketty T (2014) Capital in the twenty-first century. Harvard University Press, Cambridge
Piketty T, E Saez (2006) The evolution of top incomes: a historical and international perspective. Working paper 11955. National Bureau of Economic Research. http://www.nber.org/papers/w11955
Putnam RD (2016) Our kids: the American dream in crisis. Reprint edition. Simon & Schuster, New York
Rampell C (2016) Why the white working class votes against itself. The Washington Post, 22 Dec 2016. https://www.washingtonpost.com/opinions/why-the-white-working-class-votes-against-itself/2016/12/22/3aa65c04-c88b-11e6-8bee-54e800ef2a63_story.html?utm_term=.a40097aa3311
Regalia M (2015) Obama's Economic Legacy: & 'Just the Facts.' U.S. Chamber of Commerce, 11 Sept 2015. https://www.uschamber.com/above-the-fold/obama-s-economic-legacy-just-the-facts
Saez E (2010) Striking it richer: the evolution of top incomes in the United States (Updated with 2008 Estimates). http://elsa.berkeley.edu/~saez/saez-UStopincomes-2008.pdf
Scheidel W (2017) The great leveler: violence and the history of inequality from the stone age to the twenty-first century. Princeton University Press, Princeton
Sidanius J, Levin S (2001) Legitimizing ideologies: the social dominance approach. In: Jost JT, Major B (eds) The psychology of legitimacy: emerging perspectives on ideology, justice, and intergroup relations. Cambridge University Press, Cambridge, pp 307–331
Sitaraman G (2017) The crisis of the middle-class constitution why income inequality threatens our republic. Alfred A. Knopf, New York
Skocpol T, Carpenter D, Bartels LM, Edwards M, Mettler S (2012) Obama and America's political future. Sew edition. Harvard University Press, Cambridge
Sobel R (1968) The great bull market: wall street in the 1920s. W. W. Norton & Company, New York
Stricker F (1983) Affluence for whom – another look at prosperity and the working classes in the 1920s. In: Leab DJ (ed) The labor history reader. University of Illinois Press, Urbana
Studebaker, Benjamin. 2016. "Why Bernie vs Hillary Matters More Than People Think". February 5, 2016. https://benjaminstudebaker.com/2016/02/05/why-bernie-vs-hillary-matters-more-than-people-think/

Tawney RH (1926) Religion and the rise of capitalism. Harcourt, Brace & World, New York

The Economist (2016) A reflection on Barack Obama's presidency, 24 Dec 2016. https://www.economist.com/news/christmas-specials/21712062-barack-obamas-presidency-lurched-between-idealism-and-acrimony-some-his

Time (2017) 10 historians on what will be said about President Obama's legacy. Time 20 Jan 2017. http://time.com/4632190/historians-obamas-legacy/

Tolstoy L (2017) A quote from Anna Karenina. Goodreads 2017. http://www.goodreads.com/quotes/74806-there-are-no-conditions-to-which-a-person-cannot-grow

US Department of Commerce, B. E. A (n.d.) Bureau of economic analysis. Accessed 9 Sept 2017. https://www.bea.gov/itable/error_NIPA.cfm

White EN (1990) The stock market boom and crash of 1929 revisited. J Econ Perspect 4(2):67–83. J Econ Perspect 4(2):57–83

Williamson JG (1991) Inequality, poverty, and history: the Kuznets memorial lectures. Blackwell, Cambridge

Wisman JD (2013a) Wage stagnation, rising inequality and the financial crisis of 2008. Camb J Econ 37(4):921–945

Wisman JD (2013b) Government is whose problem? J Econ Issues 47(4):911–938. https://doi.org/10.2753/JEI0021-3624470406

Wisman JD (2014) The financial crisis of 1929 reexamined: the role of soaring inequality. Rev Polit Econ 26(3):372–391

Wisman JD, Pacitti A (2004) U.S. labor reexamined: 1880–1930: success, ideology, and reversal. In: Champlin DP, Knoedler JT (eds) The institutionalist tradition in labor economics. M.E. Sharpe, Armonk, pp 88–102

Wisman JD, Pacitti A (2015) What the American elite won over the past 35 years and what all other Americans lost. Challenge 58(3):1–25

Wisman JD, Smith JF (2011) Legitimating inequality: fooling Most of the people all of the time. Am J Econ Sociol 70(4):974–1013

Woodward C (2012) To understand America, look at New Zealand. Washington Post, 19 Feb 2012

Zeitz J (2017) Does the white working class really vote against its own interests? POLITICO magazine, 31 Dec 2017. http://politi.co/2Cfymeg

Trade Union Decline and Transformation: Where to for Employment Relations?

44

Bradley Bowden

Contents

Introduction	972
Union Decline and Changing Academic Explanations	981
Union Transformation: Australia, the United States, and Canada	988
Where to for Unions and Employment Relations?	998
Conclusion	1003
Cross-References	1005
References	1006

Abstract

One of the central social institutions of the late nineteenth and early twentieth centuries, trade union, is a diminished force in most Western societies. In the United States, only 6.5% of private sector workers were in a union in 2018. In Australia, where 64.9% of the workforce belonged in 1948, only 14.5% of the nation's employees held a union card. Across the last three decades, a variety of factors have been identified as supposedly causal: higher productivity in non-union workplaces, lacklustre organizing, and neoliberal governments. In most of the literature, union decline has been associated with a growth in precarious employment and independent contracting. In exploring both union decline and employment transformation, this chapter pays particular attention to circumstances in the United States, Australia, and Canada. In doing so, it argues that most current academic understandings are based on myth and error. In the last 40 years, it is high-paid professional and managerial work that has grown in leaps and bounds, not low-paid service work. In all Western societies, self-employment and independent contracting are inconsequential. Despite expressed concern for the poor, unions in America, Australia, and Canada are today dominated by high-

B. Bowden (✉)
Griffith Business School, Griffith University, Nathan, QLD, Australia
e-mail: b.bowden@griffith.edu.au

© The Author(s), under exclusive licence to Springer Nature Switzerland AG 2020
B. Bowden et al. (eds.), *The Palgrave Handbook of Management History*,
https://doi.org/10.1007/978-3-319-62114-2_116

paid workers employed in health, education, and the public sector; a cohort that makes up around 60% of the union membership in all three countries.

Keywords

Unions · Gig economy · Uber · Precarious employment · Outsourcing · Neo-liberal · Self-employment

Introduction

The primary purpose of this chapter is one of charting the fate of trade unions and employment relations more generally over the last few decades. Once seminal institutions in Western society, trade unions have in most countries become a numerically insignificant force, at least in the private sector. In my home country, Australia, where an extraordinary 64.9% of the workforce belonged to a union in 1948, only 14.5% of workers held a union ticket in 2016 (Bowden et al. 2009: Appendix 19; ABS 2019a). Even in Canada, a nation where unions operate within a comparatively benign legal environment, only 14.3% of private sector workers were unionized in 2018 (Statistics Canada 2019). In the United States in 2018, private sector union density stood at a woeful 6.5% (United States Bureau of Labor Statistics 2019a). What explains such outcomes? Are unions themselves the cause of the problem, having become bureaucratized and insensitive to worker needs? Or is it, as many suggest, the product of "neo-liberal" policies and employer hostility? Are unions victim of a general, retrograde shift in employment towards increased outsourcing and casualization? Or is it simply that unions, a product of an industrialized past, are now a bygone institution? If the latter is the case, then why is union density still high among public sector workers? In exploring these questions, we are, as historians, not seeking answers simply due to idle curiosity. Rather, we look to the past, to various patterns of past change and to the validity (or otherwise) of past explanations, to better understand the present. Yet in looking to the past our starting point *must* be a reasonably accurate view of the present. For if our analysis of present circumstances is profoundly in error, then it is likely we will pursue erroneous or misleading lines of historical inquiry to explain things that are, in truth, not significant.

In this author's opinion, a good example of how best to proceed is found in John Godard's chapter in this section of the *Palgrave Handbook of Management History*, entitled "Labor and Employment Practices: The Rise and Fall of the New Managerialism" (Chap. 41). In this, Godard brings to his analysis a cautious, considered judgment that is, unfortunately, increasingly rare in the field of labor relations. Unlike many others whom we will cite below, Godard frames his discussions of precarious and nonstandard employment by noting that these remain minority experiences that show little evidence of increasing. As Godard (▶ Chap. 41, "Labor and Employment Practices: The Rise and Fall of the New Managerialism") expresses it,

...increases to part-time and temporary employment have been relatively limited and highly variable across nations ... in the USA, only 4 percent of labor market participants were in temporary positions as of the mid-2010s, and although part-time work accounted for 13 percent of the labor force, this was little changed from the 1970s ... UK data also suggest a long term decline in both voluntary and involuntary separations, since at least the mid-1990s.

In contradiction to the cautious assessment of Godard, where the levels of precarious employment are carefully quantified, a reverse tendency seems to be now the norm in both management history and labor relations, where academics often appear intent on depicting changes in employment in ever more dire and catastrophic terms. In a chapter in the recent *Routledge Companion to Management and Organizational History*, Mir and Mir (2015: 256), for example, speak of how the labor market in modern societies is characterized by "the growth of inequality," "insecurities caused by layoffs," and, "trade policies ... that forced labour to take pay cuts." Similarly, in her *Globalization and Labour in the Twenty-First Century*, Burgmann (2016: 5) advises us that "From the 1970s onwards states rolled out abundant new rules ... [of] a neoliberal kind" as part of a "conscious strategy on the part of capital to increase exploitation of labour." Elsewhere, we read how the very relevance of social democratic and labor parties has been undercut by a "crisis of equality," a calamity in which the "economic inequality" of capitalism "has been exacerbated by ...the impact of neoliberalist ideology ... the substantial expansion of equality issues ... including issues of gender, racial, ethnic and sexual equality" (Johnson 2019: 1). Lindy Edwards (2019: 1–2) – an academic who has served as economic advisor to Australia's Department of Prime Minister and Cabinet – similarly informs us that "Anyone looking at the reality of worker exploitation ... knows it is not a separate issue to gender equality and radical equality ... We see it in the Labour hire companies and the growth of the gig economy." There also appears widespread acceptance of the opinion that the transformation of employees into "independent contractors" devoid of normal work rights, and an associated "Uberization" of work, is the new norm. Thus, according to Healy et al. (2017: 236), the growth of "the gig economy" reveals the "potential for accelerating 'fragmentation': breaking down once-whole jobs into discrete task elements, each of which is then auctioned off to the lowest bidder."

Often, advocates of a "catastrophic" view of modern employment appear to mistake the visibility of a problem for its prevalence. The Uber automobile driver and food deliverer are today, for example, a ubiquitous feature of urban life in any large Western city. When I leave my apartment in inner-city Brisbane – Australia's third largest town – it often appears that an Uber driver operates every second car. However, I often ask myself: have I really seen 10 Uber drivers or 1 Uber driver 10 times? For, despite all the attention that it has attracted, the "gig economy" and the Uber phenomenon are distinctively minority trends. A recent United Kingdom survey, conducted by the Chartered Institute of Personnel and Development in December 2016 and cited by Peetz (2019: 170), found that only 4% of adults had worked in the "gig" economy "at some time in the previous 12 months." Moreover, of those who did work in the "gig economy," a clear majority (58%) had permanent jobs elsewhere, only performing "gig" work to supplement their main income. Nor was it the case that "gig" workers universally experienced a feeling of social oppression. Instead, 49% reported that they were "living comfortably" or "doing alright" (cited Peetz 2019: 172–173). As for food delivery workers, a class of worker engaged in more precarious and dangerous work, an Australian survey confirmed the suspicions I garnered from observing such individuals. Of the 58 food delivery riders interviewed, an overwhelming majority (47 of the 58) "were in Australia on a temporary work, student or working holiday visa" (Goods et al. 2019: 510). In summing up what they believed to be the occupational norm, one rider advised Goods et al. (2019: 517), "Yeah it's only for backpackers." To thus extrapolate general conclusions as to the state of the labor market from the experiences of a comparative handful of workers – many of whom appear to be performing these jobs as a temporary supplement while studying or travelling – is intellectually indefensible. Similarly, no one would deny that discrimination based on gender, race, or sexual orientation still occurs. Nevertheless, one would never know from the writings of Johnson (2019), Edwards (2019), and the like that discrimination because of gender, race, or sexual orientation is illegal in virtually every advanced economy. Nor is one reminded that minority groups benefit from positive discrimination due to affirmative action policies, or that female workforce participation is – in virtually every society – at or close to historic highs.

Central to the "catastrophic" labor relations scholarship is the view that Western societies have witnessed the large-scale displacement of employees – enjoying the benefits of union membership, regulated employment, annual leave, sick pay, etc. – by independent contractors, a trend supposedly driven by a dominant "neo-liberal ideology" (see, for example, Perry 1997; Hall 2000; Peetz 2006; Gall et al. 2011). Historically, however, discussions as to the extent of the contracting phenomenon have suffered from a lack of reliable data. There is also the difficulty of distinguishing not only independent contractors from employees but also in differentiating them from independent businesses, that is, the self-employed plumber who does work at their own volition (see Vandenheuvel and Wooden 1995, for a discussion on these points).

A recent labor force survey conducted by the Australian Bureau of Statistics (ABS) in August 2019, and released in December 2019, provides what is probably a reasonably accurate insight into the extent of "standard" employment, independent contracting, and self-employment. In order to avoid presentation of this ABS data in a too compressed a form, the results of the ABS (2019b: Table 10.1) survey are presented in two figures. Figure 1 examines the prevalence of independent contracting and self-employment in blue-collar and low-wage service industries (agriculture, mining, manufacturing, utilities, wholesale, retail, hospitality, and transport). Figure 2 examines circumstances in white-collar and professional industries (information technology, finance, real estate, professional and scientific work, private-sector administration, public-sector administration and defense, education, health, art and recreation, and "other" services). As is self-evident, in blue-collar and low-wage service industries, independent contracting is only a significant factor in

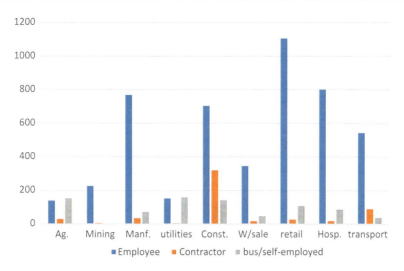

Fig. 1 Australian workforce, Aug. 2019 – Employees, contractors, self-employed: blue-collar and low-wage service industries (in thousands). (Source: Australian Bureau of Statistics, Characteristics of Employment, August 2019, Table 10.1)

construction, where the subcontracting of work is an age-old practice. Self-employment, by comparison, is significant in agriculture (the family farm), utilities (the self-employed plumber, electrician, etc.), construction, and – to a much lesser degree – retail (the family shop), hospitality (the family restaurant), and transport (the self-employed truck driver and, more recently, Uber driver). There is nothing in these figures to suggest some fundamental and malevolent alternation in employment circumstances. One suspects a similar survey undertaken 100 years ago would have detected even higher levels of self-employment.

In Fig. 2, the only industry where independent contracting and self-employment rival standard employee forms of engagement is in real estate, an industry that employs few people. Once more, one suspects a survey undertaken 100 years ago would have detected similar patterns. Outside of real estate, the most significant cohorts of independent contractors and self-employed are found among professional and scientific workers. Most of these people, one suspects, would be consultants, not a category of employment that one normally associates with misery and exploitation. In health care, one also suspects that most of the 88,400 independent contractors and 85,900 self-employed workers would be people like my daughter: consulting medical specialists. From my observations, this group also does not appear sunk in misery and degradation.

Australian circumstances – which point to the continuing importance of the employee-employer relationship and the comparative unimportance of independent contracting – do not appear atypical among advanced economies. In his recent *The Realities and Futures of Work*, Peetz (2019: 163–164) points to an Organisation for Economic Co-operation and Development (OECD) survey that indicates that "self-employment" is "not growing." Indeed, in 26 of the

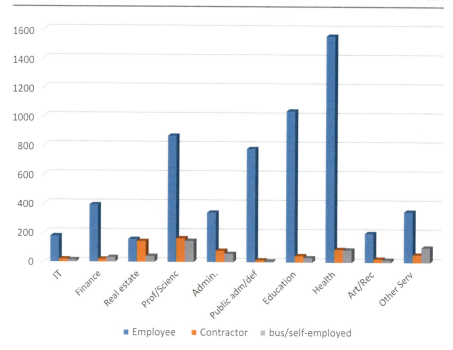

Fig. 2 Australian workforce, Aug. 2019 – Employees, contractors, self-employed: white-collar and professionals (in thousands). (Source: Australian Bureau of Statistics, Characteristics of Employment, August 2019, Table 10.1)

37 countries surveyed by the OECD, the level of "self-employment" fell between 2000 and 2014, often by significant percentages. Across the OECD as a whole, only 15.8% of employed labor force participants were self-employed in 2014. Now, in presenting these figures, Peetz conflates two very different things, namely, the genuinely self-employed business operator who works at their own volition (i.e., the independent farmer) and the independent contractor who works at someone else's behest (i.e., the contract harvester on a farm). Nevertheless, what is clear from the figures that Peetz cites is that self-employment *and* independent contracting are inconsequential in most Western societies. In France and Germany, self-employment in 2014 amounted to 9.7% and 11%, respectively. Self-employment in the American republic is of a similar dimension, i.e., approximately 10% (Desilver 2019). It should be noted in passing that Peetz's concession that self-employment and contracting is *not* a major factor in Western economies represents a significant (and commendable) reassessment on his behalf. Previously, Peetz (2002, 2006; Peetz and Bailey 2011, 2012) had long argued that the use of contractors and subcontractors *was* a major factor in both union decline and a generally more precarious work environment.

If we need to discount the idea that union decline can be explained by a general shift towards outsourcing and precarious forms of self-employment, we also need to dispense with the idea that 30 years of "neo-liberal" policies have seen a steady advance of insecure forms of low-paid employment at the expense of better-paid jobs. In fact, the reverse is true. Western societies have seen an increase of higher-paid professional employment at the expense of low-paid jobs – most particularly in agriculture and menial forms of manual labor (domestic work, laboring as navvies, carters, etc.) – and, to a lesser degree, medium-waged jobs (most particularly in manufacturing). This is evident in Fig. 3, where I allocate Australian workers into three broad categories, based on ABS (2019b) data on employment and hourly wage rates. These categories are high-paid (mining, utilities, construction, finance, professional and scientific work, public-sector administration and defense, education and health), medium-paid (agriculture, manufacturing, wholesale, transport, information technology, real estate, private-sector administration), and low-paid (hospitality, retail, and arts and recreation). Now, some will, no doubt, argue that this is an arbitrary allocation and that there are low-paid workers (i.e., defined as those employed in industries where an hourly rate of less than $30 per hour and part-time work is the norm) in education just as there are high-paid in retail. This is undoubtedly true. Nevertheless, the *norm* in industries such as construction (mean wage of $38.70), health ($41.10), education ($49), and public administration ($49.60) is a wage that is high by past standards, providing employees with a standard of life unique in the human experience. It should be noted that in assigning an industry "high-wage" status I am mindful as to the prospect of secure or full-time work in addition to the possession of a mean hourly wage approximating $40 an hour or more.

It should be noted that the Australian situation is hardly unique. Although differences in collating employment by "industry" rule out a direct comparison of Australia and the United States on a like-for-like basis, if we look to "occupational"

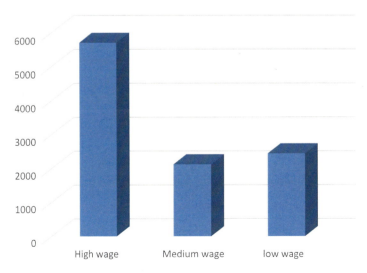

Fig. 3 Australian workforce, August 2019 – High-paid, medium-paid, low-paid (in thousands). (Source: Australian Bureau of Statistics, Characteristics of Employment, August 2019, Table 3.2)

employment in the United States in 2018, it is evident that almost half the United States workforce is employed in high-wage occupations (management, professional, construction, protective services such as firefighters). By comparison, 29% were employed in medium-waged jobs in either private-sector administration or "blue-collar" work (minus construction). Only 22.7% were employed in low-paid service and retail work (United States Department of Labor 2019a). What is therefore evident – in both the United States and Australia – is that the *most* significant change in the workforce is not the expansion of low-paid retail and service work. Rather, it is the growth of high paid work, most particularly in managerial and professional jobs, the latter two groups now comprising 43.5% of the United States workforce.

Is this sociological transformation reflected in terms of union membership, that is, has there been a displacement of "traditional," "medium-paid" workers by high-paid professionals? We explore this question in Fig. 4, which looks at the occupational distribution of trade union members in Australia in 2018, and the United States and Canada for 2017, according to four broad occupational categories (public sector, education, health; blue-collar; retail, wholesale, hospitality, art, and recreation; and private-sector professionals in finance, business services, science, etc.). As is self-evident, the fact that the United States, Australia, and Canada have markedly different labor relations laws – those in the United States regarded as the least sympathetic to union organization and those in Canada viewed as the most favorable – makes virtually no difference to where unions recruit. In the United States, 61% of union members are employed in the public sector or in private-sector jobs in

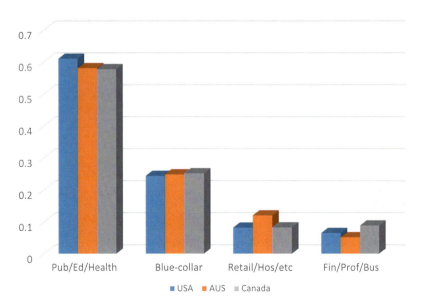

Fig. 4 Union membership by occupational categories, 2017–2018: United States, Australia, and Canada (in percent). (Source: Australian Bureau of Statistics, Characteristics of Employment, August 2018, Table 3; United States Bureau of Labor Statistics, "Economic News Release, 18 January 2019 – Table 3"; Statistics Canada, "Union Status by Industry, 2016–2018")

education or health (United States Bureau of Labor Statistics 2019a). In Australia and Canada, the comparable figures are 58% and 57.7%, respectively (ABS 2019a; Statistics Canada).

The fact that trade unions – at least in the case of the United States, Canada, and Australia – have become institutions dominated by one occupational cohort (i.e., comparatively well-paid workers in the public sector, education, and health) means it is not enough to explain union *decline*. One also needs to explain the process of *sociological transformation* that changed unions from being institutions that represented unskilled laborers, factory workers, and the like into organizations dominated by professionals who work in a restricted area of the economy, *and* the relationship between this transformation and the process of union decline. The fact that union membership is today strongest in the public sector also makes it hard to explain union decline in terms of "neo-liberalism," policies that Peetz (2019: 33) argues are commonly manifest in the "privatisation of public services or assets ... and the running of public sector agencies along 'corporate' lines." For if government-implemented policies of "neo-liberalism" are the primary cause of union decline, why is it that those most directly exposed to "neo-liberalism" (i.e., those employed by "neo-liberal" governments) have witnessed continuing high levels of unionization? This trend, it should be noted, is most pronounced in Canada, where the nation's comparatively high union density (28.9% in 2018) is largely a public-sector phenomenon, the public sector boasting an extraordinary density rate of 67.1% (2,722,200 members) that contrasts markedly with Canada's pitiful private-sector density of 14.3% (1,715,300 members) (Statistics Canada 2019). The fact there is also very little difference in the pattern of membership in the United States, Australia, and Canada also suggests that the "sustained institutional protections" (i.e., laws, supportive government agencies, etc.) identified by Bruce Western (1995) are not seminal to union decline and survival. Differences in union organization strategies, to the extent that they exist, must also be ruled out as a significant factor in union decline and survival. Neither in the United States nor Australia, nor Canada, has union organizing been able to avert the marginalization of union membership in most areas of private-sector employment.

In exploring *both* the process of union decline *and* its changing social composition, this chapter argues that the *only* proposition that can explain outcomes in the three countries we consider (United States, Australia, and Canada) is that they are the product of the far-reaching sociological changes evident in all Western societies since World War II. In the United States, for example, union density peaked at 35% in 1953, at a time when 50.2% of the nonagricultural workforce were engaged in industrial occupations (mining, construction, manufacturing, transport, etc.). By 2017, at a time when union density stood at only 10.7%, only 17.5% of the American workforce were in industrial occupations (Bowden 2018: 281). A similar pattern is obvious in Australia. Here, union density peaked at 64.9% in 1947–1948, a time when some 60.1% of the workforce were engaged in industrial occupations. By August 2016, when barely one-fifth of the Australian workers were found in industrial occupations, union density stood at a derisory 14.5% (Bowden 2018: 281). What makes the process of union decline and transformation a complex rather than a simple matter is that, everywhere across the Western world, union decline was mitigated during the 1960s and 1970s by the unionization of white-collar and professional workers in the public sector, education, and health. In the case of Australia, as Fig. 5 indicates, between 1971 and 1996, union decline occurred at a slower rate than the fall in blue-collar employment. After 1996, however, it happened at a much faster rate. Similar trends, as we shall discuss below, were also evident in the United States, Canada, and other advanced economies.

Why was it that the influx of new types of workers in the 1960s and 1970s only provided a temporary reprieve for unions, eventually ending in a precipitous decline in membership among what remained of the labor movement's "traditional" blue-collar base? No doubt, the answer to this question is complex. However, one thing that we can *infer* – although not *prove* – is that the influx of middle-class professionals eventually proved a double-edged sword as public-sector and professionally dominated unions pursued policies that proved unattractive to other workers. Traditionally in the academic literature the concept of "social unionism" (i.e., the pursuit of nontraditional objectives such as equality, racial and gender inclusiveness, climate change, etc.) has also been portrayed as a way of building support among younger and "marginalized" workers (see, for example, Schenk 2003; Burgmann and Burgmann 2017). However, in his recent book, *Getting the Blues: The Future of Australian Labor*, Nick Dyrenfurth – a long-time labor activist and head of the union-aligned Curtin Research Centre – suggests the reverse. In Dyrenfurth's (2019: 6) opinion, the increasingly middle-class composition of organized labor has seen it transformed from one articulating a "social-democratic" ethos concerned with "bread-and-butter" issues (jobs, wages, welfare) to a "progressive" movement

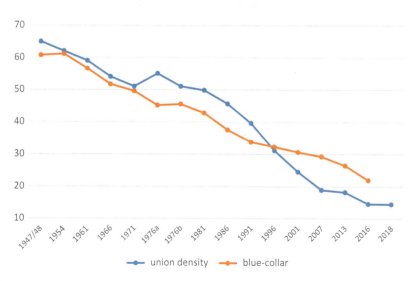

Fig. 5 Union density and blue-collar workforce share, Australia, 1947/48–2018*. ((Sources: Bowden et al., Work & Strife in Paradise, Appendix 19, 21). Note: Two different figures produced for 1976 under two different data series, the older of which was discontinued)

"championing" such issues as "diversity," "inclusivity," and "climate change." Rather than building support, Dyrenfurth (2019: 4) suggests that such policies have reduced its appeal among those for whom work, family, national identity, and patriotism are issues of defining importance. That the fracturing of the social-democratic/progressive coalition – evidenced in Brexit, the election of Donald Trump, the reelection of a conservative government in Australia in 2019, the resounding victory of the British Conservative party in December 2019 – is *one* factor in the dismal support that unions currently enjoy among blue-collar and low-paid service-sector (see Fig. 3) is probable. That it is now a *central* factor in the continued decline of trade unionism is at least possible.

Union Decline and Changing Academic Explanations

Like most areas of research, those who publish on trade unions invariably do so with some "agenda" in mind. Rarely are unions portrayed as a good in and by themselves. Rather, their beneficial role is found in the provision of some greater "good": industrial peace, increased productivity, amelioration of social inequality, fermenting revolution. In the Preface to the 1902 edition of their famed study, *The History of Trade Unionism*, Sidney and Beatrice Webb (1902: xix) argued, for example, that trade unions only succeeded – and only play a socially-beneficial role – when they associate the interests of members with "the utmost possible stimulus to speed and productivity." Conversely, they suggested, any union "struggle against ... maximising productivity ... must necessarily fail" (Webb and Webb 1902: xviii). The association of trade unionism with efficient markets and productive workplaces also characterized the work of John Commons and the so-called Wisconsin school in the late nineteenth and early twentieth centuries. In Commons' (1905: 11) opinion, union-enforced collective agreements, by "taking wages out of competition," forced employers to improve profitability by more efficient work practices rather than by cutting wages. By contrast, the Russian Marxist, Vladimir Lenin (1902/1946: 216) believed that unions only played a useful role when they were turned into training grounds for revolution, a process in which the activist "intervenes in every sphere and in every question of social and political life ...rousing political discontent."

Never totally dormant, the tension between these fundamentally different understandings of unionism – one associating it with increased productivity and market efficiency and the other with far-reaching social change – re-emerged in the 1960s and 1970s. On one side were the industrial relations "pluralists" – John Dunlop (1958), Hugh Clegg (1975), Allan Flanders, and Alan Fox (1969) – who, concerned by rising levels of industrial disputation, saw in trade unions a necessary social glue. As Clegg (1975: 310, 316) explained, unions played an essential societal role when they share with management a set of "rules," "a moral doctrine" that puts boundaries around "greed and social division." In opposition to such "pluralist" beliefs, and benefiting from a rising tide of student and worker militancy, emerged alternative understandings largely founded upon Marxism. In famously rejecting "pluralist" assumptions, the British Marxist, Richard Hyman (1978: 32), declared that "trade unionism" was only useful to the extent that it acted "as an effective means of pursuing interests which differ significantly from those of the employer." In a similar vein, Ian Turner (1965: xvii) declared the "labor movement" to be "the institutional method by which the masses transform themselves from ... weights to be pushed around to social levers in their own right." Alongside these "pluralist" and "radical" schools of thought, there also emerged another tradition that emphasized the pragmatic, largely nonideological viewpoint of the typical union member. In Australia, this "pragmatic" tradition was personified in the work of James Seymour (Jim) Hagan, an academic responsible for the training of a generation of industrial relations academics and labor historians at the University of Wollongong (including me). As Hagan (1966: 22, 1) expressed it in his *Printers and Politics*, the typical craft unionist "was essentially conservative," happy to work within the confines of capitalism and seeing in their unions a "means of preserving a privileged position" within the workforce. In arguing in favor of this "pragmatic" view of unionism, Hagan was of course pursuing an agenda of his own, in which trade unionism was perceived as an essential platform for a social-democratic state, based upon acceptance of capitalism and piece-meal "bread-and-butter" reforms (see Hagan, 1981: i–xii, for his core concept of "laborism").

During the 1980s, a profound alteration occurred in the academic literature on trade unions. Whereas in the previous decade the literature depicted unions as important agents for either social stability or far-reaching change, now the very survival of trade unions appeared at stake as traditional blue-collar unions in manufacturing and mining suffered from mass layoffs in the global recession of 1981–1983. In Canada, for example, the United Steelworkers Union – historically one of the nation's most powerful – lost almost a third of its membership in the early 1980s, membership falling from 180,000 to 125,000 (Yates 2003: 223). Writing of United States circumstances, Kochan et al. (1986/1988): 110, 114) observed in the most influential study of the era that "the 1980s stand out as a period of fundamental structural change," a time in which unionized workforces suffered "intensified competition from either international or domestic nonunion competitors." Echoing the Webbs' earlier opinion, Kochan et al. (1986/1988: 103–104) argued that unions had erred in focusing on "job control" and higher wages at the expense of productivity maximization. In the opinion of not only Kochan, Katz, and McKersie but of a host of renowned academics (Sabel 1982; Piore and Sabel 1984; Enderwick 1984; Mathews 1989), union survival was now dependent upon its unconditional embrace of new forms of work organization, variously described as "post-Fordist," "flexible specialization," "lean production," or "flexible-volume production." In an oft-cited book – *What do Unions do?* – Freeman and Medoff (1984: 169) claimed that, "most studies of productivity find that unionized establishments are more productive than otherwise comparable non-union establishments," although they did add the proviso that "unionized labor costs are also higher." So pervasive did the "post-Fordist" literature become that many, if not most, senior union officials deluded themselves that structural changes in the economy actually favored a revitalization of unionism. Heralding a major shift in official Australian union attitudes, an Australian Council of Trade Union (ACTU) study, *Australia Reconstructed*, asserted in 1987:

> Previously, industry and production proceeded largely under authoritarian supervision ... The conditions and imperatives of production now asserting themselves in Western civilized countries are qualitatively different. Maximum productivity cannot be achieved through the old methods. (ACTU/TDC 1987: 135)

Convinced that in the new "post-Fordist" world we would see a simultaneous advance in union membership, productivity, and real wages, the ACTU actively (and successfully) sought the dismantling of Australia's centralized system of wage-fixation, premised on economic need, in favor of a system of enterprise-based bargaining in which wages were linked to skill levels and productivity increases.

In retrospect, the trade union and academic interest in workplace productivity represents an important recognition that nominal wage increases are meaningless in the medium-to-long term unless they correspond to a per capita increase in the society's goods and services. It is also true, however, that most of the "post-Fordist" literature of the time was simplistic, typically involving grandiose predictions that had little correspondence to the actual course of subsequent events. Manufacturing, retail, and fast-food continued to be dominated by traditional "Fordist" or "Taylorist" work methods. Where productivity gains were made, they did little to offset the long-term, secular decline of manufacturing in most Western societies. In the United States, for example, factory employment continued to fall in *absolute* terms, job numbers declining from a peak of 17.2 million in 1953 to 14.7 million in 2017 before modestly rebounding to 14.9 million in 2018 under the Trump administration's protectionist policies (Bowden 2018: 281; United States Department of Labor 2019a). In Australia as well, manufacturing employment in August 2019 (886,100) was well down on the peak (1.2 million) recorded in 1954 (ABS 2019b). Claims that unionized workplaces, by allowing workers a "collective voice" in decision-making, were inherently more productive than their nonunion firms – a claim never made by the Webbs – were always implausible. To the extent that union firms *were* more productive than their nonunion counter-parts, Hirsch and Addison (1986: 207) observed that such gains typically followed a union-induced wage "shock" (i.e., higher wages) as management sought efficiencies to offset higher labor costs. Rarely, however, were efficiencies sufficient to offset the higher costs of unionized labor, Hirsch and Addison (1986: 198) concluding that, "all the available evidence suggests that unionism reduces profitability."

By the early 1990s, it was obvious to all-and-sundry that the unionized embrace of work reform and productivity had done little to offset a loss of private-sector members in "traditional" blue-collar callings. Writing of the dire circumstances that prevailed in the United States in the mid-1990s, Juravich and Bronfenbrenner (1998: 262) lamented the fact private-sector membership was in "free fall." It was, Juravich and Bronfenbrenner (1998: 262) continued, only an increase in public-sector members – who by then comprised one-third of the unionists affiliated with the American

Federation of Labor/ Confederation of Industrial Organizations (AFL/CIO) – that "prevented the wholesale hemorrhaging of the labor movement." Such circumstances were the new norm across the English-speaking world and beyond. In Canada, union density fell from 39.2% to 32.6% across the course of the 1990s. Once more, only an increase in public-sector membership avoided a collapse in overall density rates, Kumar and Murray (2003: 204) recording that, at that time, "Just under half of all union members in Canada (48.3 per cent) can be found in just three sectors: education, health and social services, or public administration." Similarly, in Australia, union density among manufacturing workers, the historic backbone of the nation's unionized sector, fell from 51.2% in 1986 – when unions decided to link wage increases to productivity – to 38.7% a decade later. By 2007, union density in manufacturing stood at a feeble 21.3%. Across the private sector as a whole, union membership fell from 1.36 million in 1992 to 1.21 million in 2000. During the same period, the number of nonunionists in the private sector rose from 3.2 million to almost five million (ABS 2007).

Amid a collapse in private-sector membership, industrial relations academics and senior union officials both embraced a new fad as they searched for a magic elixir to revive sagging union fortunes: the so-called "Organizing Model."

In terms of origins, the "Organizing Model" was a peculiarly American invention, inspired by the belief that the combination of grass-roots activism and social mobilization that had been so effective on university campuses during the anti-Vietnam war and Civil Rights movements was also applicable to union revitalization (Voss and Sherman 2003: 65–66; Bronfenbrenner 2003: 32). The fundamental (stated) premise of the "Organizing Model," as articulated by Kate Bronfenbrenner (the leading advocate of the new strategy) and her co-authors in 1998, was that "Unions themselves bear significant responsibility for the decline in unionization" (Bronfenbrenner et al. 1998: 5). According to advocates of the "Organizing Model," unions suffered from bureaucratization and a loss of organizing and reforming zeal. The supposed result of this malady was a short-sighted "Servicing Model," in which unions serviced the needs of largely passive existing members (i.e., wage bargaining, dispute resolution, etc.). The recommended solution to this "problem" was to "empower" workers "to solve problems themselves, as opposed to having the union office – away from the workplace – solve it for them" (Peetz 2006: 164). In the process, organizing was to be redirected away from traditional activities (recruitment, bargaining, etc.) towards the fostering of networks of rank-and-file activists. Almost from the start, the concept of the "Organizing Model" was linked to the idea of "social movement unionism," in which union organizing and bargaining would supposedly become part of "community coalitions active in struggles for change." Accordingly, issues such as environmental action, greater racial, and sexual equality would become a core part of a new, transformative union agenda (Schenk 2003; Voss and Sherman 2003). As Charlotte Yates (2002: 39, 33) expressed it in relation to Canadian circumstance, central to the "Organizing Model" was an extension of unionism from a "privileged section of the working class" so as to "build membership among women and ethnically and racially diverse groups of workers," many of whom possessed a precarious hold on their jobs.

Enthusiastically embraced in the United States by a new AFL/CIO leadership (John Sweeney, Richard Trumka, Linda Chavez-Thompson), in 1995 American workers were promised organizing campaigns "at an unprecedented pace and scale" (Bronfenbrenner et al. 1998: 1). The summer of 1996 was declared a "Union Summer." One thousand college students and youth workers were mobilized for organizing drives. Spreading with religious-like fervor from the United States, the "Organizing Model" became the official policy of the Australian and New Zealand union movements in 1993–1994. British unions also embraced the concept (Bowden 2009: 138). Although no overarching peak council endorsed the "Organizing Model" in Canada, by 1999 it was nevertheless core to the revitalization strategies of broad sections of organized labor, including such unions as the Canadian Union of Public Employees, the United Steelworkers, and the United Brotherhood of Carpenters and Joiners (Yates 2002). Across the late 1990s and early 2000s, one constantly read academic articles pointing to the "Organizing Model's" successes. "In 1998," Bronfenbrenner (2003: 32) reported, "for the first time in decades, American unions organized as many new workers as were lost from lay-offs, plant closings, decertifications, and contracting out." Across the border in Canada, Yates (2003: 234, 221) pointed to the organization of Pinkerton security guards, and "more than 50 Kentucky Fried Chicken outlets in British Columbia," as "evidence that industrial unions are adapting successfully to new economic conditions." Similarly, in New Zealand, Sarah Oxenbridge (2003) reported how the Services and Food Workers Union had exploited the "Organizing Model" to rebuild its membership among some of the nation's worst-paid workers. Across the Tasman Sea in Australia, Rae Cooper (2002: 249) declared that recent statistics on union membership "were cause for celebration," unions having added "an extra 23,500 new recruits." As late as 2006, Peetz (2006: 163) was still arguing that, due to the "Organizing Model," the "tide that had seemed to swamping unions had somehow been held back ... By 2004, in trend terms, union membership had stabilised."

The fundamental premise behind the "Organizing Model" – that workers, preoccupied with countless other concerns (shopping, meal preparation, football practice, medical concerns, etc.), would enthusiastically embrace the role of union activist – was always impracticable. Writing in 2009, I (Bowden 2009: 140) observed in relation to the Australian situation that, "Empirically, there is no evidence to suggest that ...the organizing model has had any meaningful effect." More than a decade later, the merit of this conclusion is even more obvious. In 1992, a few years prior to the adoption of the "Organizing Model," Australia boasted 2.5 million union members and a union density of almost 40%. By 2016, however, barely 1.5 million Australian workers held a union ticket. Union density had collapsed, falling to 14.6% (ABS 2006, 2017: Table 18). In Canada, where Kumar and Murray (2003: 202–204) had fretted over the fact that – with union density at 32.6% in 2000 – unions had become too reliant on membership in 3 sectors (education, health, and public administration), union density stood at 28.1% in 2018. Of the Canadian total,

58.5% were in education, health, and public administration, compared to 48.3% in 2000. In the United States, union density stood at 10.5% in 2018, a third less than the figure recorded in 1993 (15.7%). Despite vaunted local successes, the attempt to build support among racial minorities ended in ignominious failure. Whereas in 1993, 20.8% of African-American workers were union members, by 2018 only 12.5% were unionized. Among Hispanics and Latinos, union density fell from 14.8% in 1993 to 9.1% in 2018 (United States Bureau of Labor Statistics 2019b).

As evidence as to the failure of the "Organizing Model" became obvious the proffered explanations as to union decline increasingly emphasized the "neo-liberal" policies of governments and employers. In other words, the blame shifted from the unions themselves to cultural and political trends in the wider society. Thus, we are advised that "in Anglo-Saxon countries" both "governments and employers" have attacked "unions through neo-liberal legislation" (Ibsen and Tapia 2017: 179), that "privatization, marketization, liberalization, deregulation, and reductions in state funding" had curtailed union strength (Gall et al. 2011: 2), and that unions and the "working poor" are subject to "the policies of unmitigated – oppressive – neo-liberalism" (McManus 2018: 1).

Now, no one would deny that there *was* a greater emphasis on market economics and free trade between the 1980s and the late 2010s. It is also undoubtedly the case that in broad areas of the economy this was *one* undoubted factor in union decline. The problem with the neo-liberal "explanation," however, is that it has become an excuse for lazy thinking, in which a complex phenomenon that played out differently in different countries – and in different areas of the economy – is treated as if it was an all-destructive hurricane that obliterated the previous Keynesian and pre-Keynesian landscape. Should we, for example, treat the Rudd-Gillard governments that ruled Australia between 2007 and 2013, bringing in the more union-friendly *Fair Work Act 2009*, as a "neo-liberal" administration? Was Barack Obama, with his policies for extended health care, a "neo-liberal"? Is Donald Trump, with his protectionist trade policies, an example of "neo-liberalist globalism"? Indeed, on a number of key fronts – American protectionism, Brexit, etc. – market liberalization and globalization appears to be in retreat. Nowhere, moreover, can we see evidence of a society where long-established institutions of the welfare state have been destroyed. Even in the United States, as Fig. 4 suggests, the various levels of government continue to employ the bulk of the nation's teachers, nurses, and emergency service workers. Across the OECD the share of GDP going to taxes has risen not fallen, typically consuming around a third of the total. Of this total, 26% on average comprises contributions to social security (OECD 2019a). That the state remains a significant factor in the Australian economy is ascertained by the fact that in August 2018 almost a third of Australian workers were employed in either health care and social assistance (1.53 million), education (968,000) or public administration (811,600), areas that now comprise the great bulk of Australian union members (ABS 2019a). The benevolence of the supposed "neo-liberal" state is even more vital to Canadian union survival, where the public sector employs – as we have previously noted – 58.5% of the unionized workforce.

If we look to both the academic literature on both the "Organizing Model" and "neo-liberalism," we can ascertain a confusion of purpose or, rather, a conflating of two very different strategic objectives – union revitalization and radical social change in the pursuit of environmental action, greater levels of gender, racial and sexual equality – as if they were one. This conflating of two separate objectives as one begs the question: what is the *primary* objective? Is it rebuilding trade union numbers and union density? If this were the primary objective, then unions would be better off directing their attention at the large cohorts of comparatively well-paid professionals in finance, scientific and technical research, business services at the like. Not only are such workers a significant and growing part of the workforce, they also have attributes – job security, comparatively high wages – that make the payment of union dues a less onerous financial burden than it is for the casual fast food worker or office janitor. If, on the other hand, social change is the key objective – addressing the plight of the marginalized – then unions need to transform themselves into the organizations that Lenin (1902/1946: 216) envisaged, in which the union activist "intervenes in every sphere and in every question of social and political life ...rousing political discontent." Accordingly, traditional industrial objectives (wage bargaining, dispute resolution, recruitment) should take second fiddle behind social mobilization. Admittedly, advocates of transformative "social movement unionism" (Yates 2002; Bronfenbrenner 2003; Peetz 2019) would argue that union involvement in community, environmental, and social equality campaigns attracts members who would not otherwise be favorably inclined towards unionism. The historical record, however, contradicts this view. Nowhere has the pursuit of "social movement unionism" resulted in a statistically significant increase in union membership among racial minorities or among low-paid retail and hospitality workers. For the fact of the matter is that the pursuit of traditional union objectives – wage increases, job security, etc. – are things that most workers can readily identify as in their self-interest. By contrast, the pursuit of "social objectives" is inherently divisive. It will attract some. However, it will also alienate others who believe that such objectives represent a misallocation of their membership dues. It is certainly a mistake to assume that the working class voter still identifies with social democratic or "progressive" party politics. A YouGov survey of voters in the December 2019 British election, for example, found that 50% of those drawn from the poorest quartile composed of less skilled workers, and those outside the workforce, voted for either the Conservatives or the Brexit Party. Support for the Conservatives and the Brexit Party among those from the quartile above them, comprising skilled workers, was even higher, 52% voting for one of these two parties. By comparison, only 34% of those in the poorest quartile voted Labor. In the second poorest quartile, support for Labor was even lower at 31% (McDonnell and Curtis 2019).

The capacity of "social movement unionism" to erode rather than enhance union strength is evidenced in my home state of Queensland, Australia, where the Queensland Nurses Union (QNU) has long been one of the state's largest, proudly boasting a commitment to "positive and sustainable social change" (QNU 2016: 21). In recent years, however, the QNU has faced a nonunion rival, the Nurses Professional

Association of Queensland (NPAQ), which provides workers with indemnity insurance and representation in any personal employment matter. In explaining how the NPAQ came into existence, the association's website states that it resulted from the action of "a group of nurses" annoyed at the QNU's "use of membership money to battle for political causes which quite possibly at least half of their members disagree with" (NPAQ 2019). Strictly nonpolitical, the NPAQ recruited 5000 members in quick order, presumably at the QNU's expense. In explaining why nurses should join this association rather than the established union, the NPAQ's (2019) website, which operates under the slogan, "Protection without Politics," declares:

> Not one cent of your hard-earned membership money goes to any political party or cause. 100% goes to providing protection and advancement to you and your profession.

At one level, the NPAQ's 5000 odd members are inconsequential. In 2018, the Australian health sector boasted an estimated 328,500 unionists, a larger total than found in any other industry. However, as is the case with other highly unionized professional industries in Australia (public administration, education), an increasing numeric strength disguises a steady decline in union density. Whereas 34.5% of Australia's health workers were union members in 1996, by 2018 only 22.6% of the workforce was unionized (ABS 2019b). Thus, while we cannot be sure of how many health workers were alienated – or attracted – by the "social movement unionism" of organizations such as the Nurses Union, we *can* conclude it has been ineffective in actually building union density within the sector.

Union Transformation: Australia, the United States, and Canada

If we look at the *process* of union decline – *and* the debates associated with that decline – we can ascertain that in the United States, Australia, Canada, and elsewhere the *initial* fall in union density (i.e., prior to 1980) was primarily associated with structural changes in the economy as well as a growing employer propensity to relocate work to nonunion locales. These developments eroded organized labor's strength among "traditional" unionists in areas such as manufacturing, mining, and transport. The large-scale loss of unionized blue-collar jobs in the global recession of the early 1980s appeared to confirm the prognosis that the crisis of union membership was primarily one of productivity and workplace efficiency; problems that both unions and industrial relations academics believed could be reversed if union members became more productive and efficient. In retrospect, the "productivity" agenda pursued between the late 1970s and the early 1990s needs to be seen as a failed attempt to rebuild unionism on its traditional sociological base of blue-collar workers. With the failure of this revitalization campaign obvious by the early 1990s, the numerical and intellectual leadership of organized labor passed to a different type of unionist. Increasingly university educated – and drawing strength from the unionized membership in areas such as education, health, and the public sector – this new generation of activists and theorists typically believed that union salvation lay in the "Organizing Model," "social movement unionism," and in ideological and cultural campaigns against "neo-liberalism" and social inequality in all its manifestations.

One of the paradoxes caused by both the shift in the center of union gravity (i.e., from blue-collar to professionally based unions) and the growing emphasis on a "progressive" union agenda (i.e., working to redress social, gender, and racial inequalities) is that the union movement has become well represented among comparatively well-paid professionals and poorly represented among the less affluent and the marginalized. There is thus a gulf between stated intent – to transform unionism from a force representing a "privileged section of the working class" into one with a strong "membership among women and ethnically and racially diverse groups of workers" (Yates 2002: 39, 33) – and actual outcome.

This paradoxical effect is evident in Figs. 6, 7, 8, 9, and 10, which record the areas where union membership was located in the United States and Canada in 2017 and in Australia in 2018. The most significant caution that needs to be given in presenting this data is to note that the United States differs from Australia and Canada in recording public sector teachers, nurses, and the like under the level of government that employs them (i.e., local government, state government, etc.) rather than under the occupational industry (i.e., education, health, etc.). The implications of this

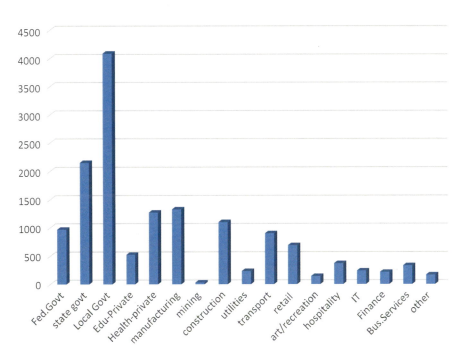

Fig. 6 United States union membership by industry, 2017 (in thousands). (Source: US Bureau of Labor Statistics, Table 3: Union Affiliation of Wage and Salary Earners, 2017–2018)

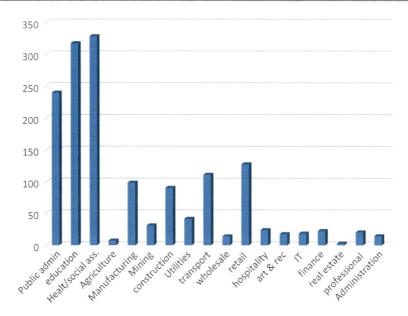

Fig. 7 Australian union membership by industry, 2018 (in thousands). (Source: ABS, Characteristics of Employment, Aug. 2018, Table 3.1)

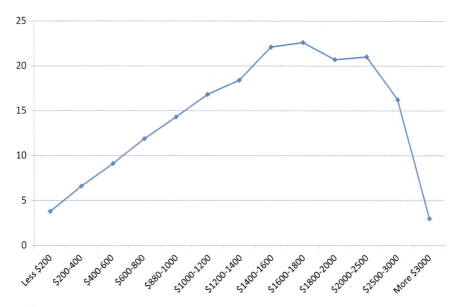

Fig. 8 Australian union density according to wage bands, 2016. (Source: ABS, Characteristics of Employment, Australia, August 2016)

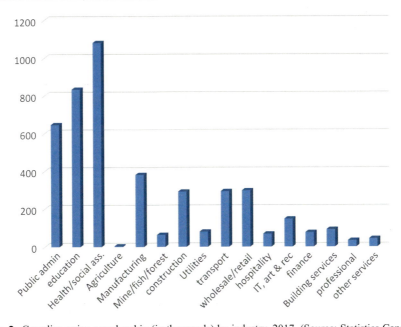

Fig. 9 Canadian union membership (in thousands) by industry, 2017. (Source: Statistics Canada, Union Status by Industry, 2014–2018 – Employees who are union members)

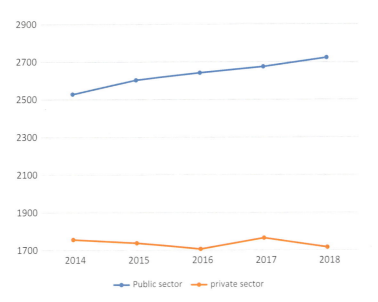

Fig. 10 Canadian private and public sector union membership (in thousands), 2014–2018. (Source: Statistics Canada, Union Status by Industry, 2014–2018 – Employees who are union members)

difference in data presentation are, as noted below, most significant with regards our understandings of Canadian circumstance.

In looking at the United States context, it is evident that local and state government employment (i.e., teachers, health workers, social workers, police, firefighters, etc.) is today the great bastion of American union strength. Together, unions in local government (4.1 million) and state government (2.2 million) are responsible for 42.2% of United States union membership. Density is also higher in these two sectors than elsewhere. In local government, 40.7% of the workforce are unionized. Among state government workers, union density stood at 30.9% in 2017. When the 972,000 unionists employed by the federal government – where union density stood at 26.5% in 2017 – are added, we can ascertain that almost half of American unionists (48.8%) are directly employed by the state, an outcome that belies the supposed hostility of the "neo-liberal" state to union membership. Yes, it is true, that in certain regions – most particularly the South and the Mid-West – there is an aversion to unions among governments in the so-called "Right to Work" states. However, this aversion should not be seen as the national norm. Public-sector unionism would not survive if this were the case. Meanwhile, membership in the most significant areas of "traditional" blue-collar work in the United States – manufacturing (1.3 million unionists), construction (1.1 million) and transport (903,000) – provided a total of 3.3 million unionists in 2017; a figure overshadowed 7.2 million government-employed union members. It is also the case that the number of private-sector unionists in professionally dominated health care (1.3 million) rivaled that found in manufacturing. Private-sector unionists in education (526,000) also easily outnumbered those found in hospitality (374,000). Collectively, as we previously noted in Figs. 4, 61% of union members in 2017 either were government employees or employed in private-sector jobs in education and health. By contrast, union membership in the industries most associated with casual and insecure work – retail (692,000 unionists), hospitality (364,000 unionists), and art and recreation (144,000) – collectively boasted 1.2 million members. This represented only 8.2% of United States union membership in 2017. What is thus evident is that the pattern of American union membership in 2017 was atypical of that of the wider workforce. Strong in the public sector, it was weak in the private sector. In the low-paid, industries where racial minorities are concentrated, unionism has proved unattractive. The same conclusion applies to the fast-growing areas of private-sector professional employment (business services, information technology, etc.)

In Australia, where overall union density (14.6% in 2018) is higher than in the United States (10.5% in 2018), the association of unionism with a comparatively small – and comparatively privileged – section of the workforce is even more apparent. As is evident in Fig. 7, health care and social assistance (328,500 union members in 2018) and education (317,500 members) are the two great bastions of Australian union strength. Together, these two sectors were responsible for 42.3% of Australia's total union membership. The reliance of organized labor on these two groups can also be ascertained by the fact that, considered alone, union membership in health care and education rivals the combined total (379,000) found in *all* blue-collar callings (agriculture, mining, construction, utilities, manufacturing, and transport). Although unionists in Australian education are slightly less numerous than those found in health care and social assistance, it is education that boasts the highest density rate (34.4%). Outside of education, only public administration (30.8%), utilities (31.6%), health care and social assistance (22.6%), and transport (21.9%) exceed the national average (ABS 2019a: Table 18). As is the case in education and health care, where many are employed in state-owned schools, universities and hospitals, the union strength in utilities and transport is associated with state ownership and/or regulation (i.e., government-owned power stations, bus companies, railroads). Far from suffering economic disadvantage, workers in the education sector also boast some of the highest wages in Australia, the mean hourly rate in education standing at $49.00 per hour in 2018. Although the mean hourly wage rate in health care and social assistance ($41.10) in 2018 was significantly less than education, it could hardly be considered a low-wage sector (ABS 2019b: Table 3.2).

If the three principal sources of Australian union strength (health care and asocial assistance, education, and public administration) are associated with comparatively high-paid professional work, it was also the case in 2018 that the largest cohort of *private-sector* unionists (127,200) were in the low-paid retail sector. Significantly, union density in this sector (12.4%) was almost the same as that found in manufacturing (12.6%), an area of historic union strength (ABS 2019a: Table 18). It was also far superior to the union density obtained in the retail sector in the United States (4.5%).

What explains the comparative strength of Australian unionism in retail and, to lesser degree, hospitality, when compared to the United States and Canada? Significantly, it owes nothing to either the "Organizing Model" or "social movement unionism," strategies that have proved largely ineffective in spreading support for unionism among low-paid workers. Instead, it rests on the "social partnership" fostered between Australia's largest union – the Shop, Distributive and Allied Trades Association (SDA) – and large employers in retailing and fast food. In essence, the SDA has negotiated "enterprise agreements" with employers that allow them to avoid the otherwise compulsory provisions of Australia's system of judicially determined "awards" (i.e., the *General Retail Industry Award*, the *Fast Food Industry Award*). The nature of this "social partnership" is apparent in the Agreement that currently applies to McDonald's workers – the *McDonalds' Australia Enterprise Agreement 2013* – where the only penalty rate (i.e., additional allowance) that applies is a 10% loading between the hours of 1 AM and 5 AM. Accordingly, if a 21-year-old employed as a Level 2 worker (the most common designation) worked an 8-h shift on a Saturday under the union-negotiated Agreement they would have received $172.88 in June 2018. The same worker, if engaged under the *Fast Food Industry Award*, would have received $212.90; an outcome that leaves those on "union conditions" $40.02 worse off. In return for such benefits, under s.43 of the Agreement, employers agreed to invite SDA officials to inductions and "crew meetings" at each store (SDA 2013/2018). Similarly, under the *KFC Team Members Enterprise Agreement (Queensland and Tweed Heads 2014–2017)*, the SDA agreed to a "buy-out" of penalty provisions in return for a 9% increase in base rates.

Consequently, in June 2018 a KFC worker – employed under "union conditions" – who undertook an 8-h shift was $28.33 worse off on Saturdays, and $72.31 worse off on Sundays, than if they had been employed under the award. Once more the SDA gained a suite of concessions relating to membership recruitment, concessions embodied in s.15 of the Agreement under the heading, "Union Related Matters and Union Encouragement" (Fair Work Commission 2014). [Note: federal "enterprise agreements" in Australia remain in force after their "expiry" date unless formally repealed by the Commonwealth Fair Work Commission].

Without the "social partnership" between the SDA and large employers, it is probable that Australian unions would boast few members in retail and hospitality. In 2018, union membership in these two sectors (151,100 members) represented 9.9% of Australia's total union strength. Nevertheless, despite this significant addition, it is apparent that, in modern Australia, people with high incomes are far more likely to be a union member than those with low incomes. As Fig. 8 indicates, which summarizes the results of an Australian Bureau of Statistics (2017) survey, of those earning $1600–$1800 per week in August 2016, 22.6% were unionized. Among those paid $2500–$3000 per week – the second highest wage cohort that the ABS reports – 16.2% were union members. By contrast, among those earning $600–$800 per week only 11.9% were union members. Among the ABS's worst paid cohort – those earning less than $200 per week – only 3.8% were union members. Now, historically, the higher wages obtained by union workers vis-à-vis their nonunion workers have been attributed to union bargaining success (see, Freeman and Medoff 1984; Peetz 2006). In other words, union membership *causes* a higher subsequent wage. There is, however, reason for concluding that the circumstances revealed in Fig. 8 results from the reverse, that is, it is the *prior* possession of a high wage that causes union membership. Accordingly, the decision not to join a union by low wage earners is, one suspects, informed in large part by the belief that union fees are an unaffordable luxury. Union membership can thus be seen as something akin to private medical insurance: a luxury enjoyed by society's more prosperous to protect them against unforeseen and adverse outcomes.

Invariably, Canada is a nation linked to what Bruce Western (1995: 12) refers to as "sustained institutional protections" that supposedly support both union organizing and bargaining. In the International Trade Union Federation's (ITUF) *Global Rights Index, 2018*, for example, Canada received the second highest ranking (Level 2 in a 6-level index), alongside nations such as Israel, Japan and Switzerland. By comparison, Australia ranked at Level 3 ("Regular Violations of Rights"). The United States obtained a rank of 4 ("Systematic Violation of Rights"), a score that supposedly puts it in a par with Haiti, Botswana, and Vietnam (ITUF 2018: 10–11). At first glance, this emphasis on "institutional" factors – largely associated with the greater ease with which Canadian unions can gain recognition as the official "bargaining agent" for a workplace – appears to be borne out by the nation's comparatively high union density (28.9% in 2018), a rate that has declined only modestly in recent years. However, as we have previously noted, since the mid-1990s, the strength of Canadian unionism has been increasingly associated with "just three sectors: education, health and social services, or public administration" (Kumar and Murray 2003: 204). The comparatively narrow base of Canadian unionism – as well as its extraordinary strength in it bastions of support – is also indicated in Fig. 9, which looks at membership by industry in 2017. At first glance, the similarities between Australian circumstances as revealed in Fig. 7 appear striking. Where Canada differs from Australia, however, is not in where its membership is concentrated but rather in the union densities obtained in areas of strength. Whereas union density in education in Australia stood at 34.4% in 2018, in Canada in 2017 an extraordinary 69% of educational workers were unionized. Densities were also far higher in public administration (67.3%) and health care and social assistance (52.4%). When we turn our attention to "traditional" blue-collar areas of union strength, we also once again find that density is much higher in Canada than Australia or the United States. In construction in 2017, 28.7% of the Canadian workforce was unionized. In Australia, by comparison, only 13% of the construction workforce was unionized in 2018. Similarly, in transport the density recorded in Canada in 2017 (38.1%) was much higher than in Australia, where only 21.9% of the transport workforce was unionized (Statistics Canada 2019; ABS 2019a). Canadian public sector unions have also avoided the long-term decline in support that has characterized Australia, where public sector density fell from 67.1% in 1992 to 38.9% in 2016 (ABS 2007, 2017).

The supposition that Canadian unions enjoy considerable support in both the private and the public sector – a conclusion easily garnered by a cursory consideration of union density across a range of industries – is contradicted by the trends evident in Fig. 10, which records changes in private and public sector membership. As is evident, private-sector membership is not only much lower than public sector membership, it is also trending downwards even as public-sector membership trends upwards. How can we therefore explain the comparatively high density rates in industries such as transport (36.9%), construction (28.7%), and manufacturing (23.3) given the fact that private-sector density (14.8% in 2017) is so low?

To explain the Canadian paradox of residual strength in "traditional" blue-collar industries – in the context of low private-sector membership – some basic mathematics and logic is required.

In 2017, there were 1,764,400 private-sector unionists in Canada (Statistics Canada 2019). If we look to union membership by industry, we can assume that nearly all of the unionists employed in finance and real estate (76,500), in business services (91,800), wholesale and retail (294,600), accommodation and food services (68,600), professional and technical services (33,800), and nonpublic "other services" (43,600) are employed in the private-sector – a total that comes to 608,900. If we (conservatively) assume that half of the 147,300 unionists employed in information, culture and recreation are in the private-sector than we have 687,550 private-sector service workers. Let us now (conservatively) assume that only 25% of unionists in health and education (1,915,100) are engaged in the private sector. On this assumption, our private-sector total rises to 1,166,325. We can also safely assume that nearly all of the unionists employed in agriculture, mining and forestry (68,100) are also in the private sector. This gives us a likely 1,234,425 private-sector unionists, outside of utilities, construction, manufacturing, and transportation, leaving space for 529,975 union members in these four industries. However, the total union strength in utilities (80,400), construction (292,300), manufacturing (381,600), and transportation (294,600) in 2017 came to 970,500. This would suggest that as many as 440,525 – or 45.4% – of the unionists employed in these four sectors work in the public sector. Even if my estimations of private sector membership in other industries is astray by several hundred thousand, it is nevertheless evident that public sector employment *must* be acting as a union refuge even for industries such as utilities, transportation, construction and manufacturing.

The manufacturing sector's experiences exemplify the experiences of Canadian private-sector union membership. Writing of the situation that prevailed in Canada in 2008, Bernard (2009: 11) lamented the fact that, "From 2004 to 2008, more than one in seven manufacturing jobs (322,000) disappeared in Canada." In Ontario, and in Newfoundland and Labrador, almost one-fifth of all manufacturing jobs were lost across this 5-year period. Significantly, unionized jobs in manufacturing had a greater propensity to be lost than nonunionized ones, Bernard (2009: 9) observed that, "From 1998 to 2008, unionized jobs in manufacturing disappeared twice as quickly as non-unionized ones." The circumstances that caused Bernard's lamentations were associated with a loss of 321,800 factory jobs between 2004 and 2008, losses that caused manufacturing employment to fall from 2.3 million in 2004 to 1,970,300 in 2008 (Bernard 2009: 9). By 2018, however, Canadian manufacturing had shed a further 318,068 jobs, leaving Canada with only 1,652,232 factory workers. In other words, Canada has lost 639,898 manufacturing jobs since 2004, losses which one suspects were particularly acute among private-sector unionized workplaces.

If private-sector employment – and hence union membership – is worse in Canada than the headline figures on union density would suggest, it is nevertheless also the case that public sector unionism enjoys unusual health. Two factors explain the unusually high level of union membership among Canadian public-sector workers. First, unlike the situation in Australia, Canadian collective agreements invariably contain clauses that enforce de facto compulsory unionism, an outcome that Canadian labor law expressly encourages. Thus, if we look to a typical public sector collective agreement, in the form of the *Collective Agreement between the Toronto District School Board and the Elementary Teachers' Federation of Ontario 2014–2019*, we find two clauses of particular significance. First, in Clause A.2.1, the Agreement grants the Elementary Teachers' Federation of Ontario recognition as "the sole and exclusive Bargaining Agent" for the teaching workforce. Even more significantly, Clause B.13.1 states that, "The Board shall deduct from each Teacher's pay and from each Continuing Education Teacher's Pay the regular union dues pursuant to the *Labour Relations Act*." In addition, Clause B.13.3 of the Agreement required the "Board" to "deduct from the pay of each Teacher" any levy authorized by the Elementary Teachers' Federation (see Elementary Teachers' Federation of Ontario 2017: 51, 37). In other words, the individual teacher who is covered by the Collective Agreement has little discretion as to whether or not they will be a financial member of the relevant union. This is a very different situation than that which prevails in Australia, where compulsory unionism is expressly prohibited by

Section 336 (1)(b)(i) of the *Fair Work Act*, which declares that workers are "free to become, or not become, members of industrial associations" (Australian Government 2009).

The second factor that has benefited Canadian public sector unions is the comparative benevolence of all sectors of government when it comes to both union bargaining *and* the provision of employment. In describing the experiences of public sector employees since the Global Financial Crisis of 2007–2009, J.B. Rose (2016: 101) declares it a period of "consolidation," characterized by a "sustained" increase in "public employment" that contrasted markedly with earlier recessions, when governments had cut public sector employment. Rather than cut jobs, Canadian governments increased employment as part of "fiscal stimulus programs" (Rose 2016: 102). Canada's federal government also increased spending in areas such as the National Child Benefit, affordable housing, health care, public transport, and postsecondary education (Fodor 2013). Overall, public sector employment grew from 3.4 million in 2008 to almost 3.8 million in 2018 (Rose 2016; Statistics Canada 2019). With unionized collective agreements continuing to cover around three-quarters of the public sector workforce (Rose 2016: 102), most of these additional 379,265 public sector workers ended up swelling the ranks of organized labor, given the prevalence of the de facto compulsory union membership clauses we noted in the Agreement negotiated by the Elementary Teachers' Federation of Ontario. This unusual propensity to negotiate with organized labor distinguishes Canadian public sector employers from their American counterparts. For while United States collective agreements typically contain "union recognition" and membership clauses similar to those in Canada – and unlike those in Australia – there is nevertheless, as we have previously noted, an aversion to unionized bargaining in the so-called "Right to Work" states in the American South and Mid-West. In consequence, Canadian *public-sector* unions – if not their private-sector counterparts – have benefited from both favorable laws and benevolent governments. As a result, as Rose (2016: 103) observes, Canada's largest union, the Canadian Union of Public Employees (CUPE), grew by 67% between 1998 and 2013. By 2019, the CUPE (2019) claimed 700,000 members in areas as diverse as "emergency services, education, early learning and child care, municipalities, social services, libraries, utilities, transportation, airlines." Other unions to have benefited significantly from the favorable confluence of factors in the Canadian public sector include the National Union of Public and General Employees (390,000 members in 2019) and the Public Service Alliance of Canada (200,000 members in 2019).

The Canadian experience arguably highlights the paradox of unionism in advanced Western economies. Workers in traditional areas of union strength such as manufacturing continue to experience a precarious existence in the face of continuing job losses. In low-paid industries such as retail and hospitality, the near total absence of a union presence belies any claim that unionism has been effective in extending its representation from the comparatively "privileged" (Yates 2002: 39). In the accommodation and food services sector of the Canadian workforce, there were, for example, 1,125,000 workers scrapping a living in 2018 – a total that is equivalent to almost 30% of the entire public sector workforce. However, only 5.6 of these battlers boasted a union ticket, a lower percentage than that obtained 5 years before, when 5.8% belonged to a union (Statistics Canada 2019). Across the private sector as a whole, unionism in Canada – as elsewhere – continues its long retreat.

In summary, we can conclude that rather than having witnessed an expansion of its social base because of the "union revitalization" campaigns pursued with the endorsement of countless academic researchers, unionism has witnessed a further shrinkage, a process that increasingly confines union membership to comparatively privileged sections of the workforce employed in education, health, and the public sector.

Where to for Unions and Employment Relations?

In a recent article, Simon Mollan (2019: 513) criticized my predilection – as demonstrated in my study, *Work, Wealth and Postmodernism* – for viewing "the chief issues of our time ... through the lens of economics" (i.e., productivity, labor force participation, real wage growth, etc.). In doing so, Mollan (2019: 513) argued in favor of "postmodernist concerns with power and its distribution," an orientation that prioritizes "inequality and discrimination in work, pay, and advancement based on gender, ethnicity, race, or sexuality." This emphasis on power and politics also characterizes the conclusions of Jon Wisman's ▶ Chap. 43, "Why did the Great Recession Fail to Produce a *New* New Deal in the USA?" in this section of the *Palgrave Handbook of Management History*. For Wiseman (▶ Chap. 43, "Why did the Great Recession Fail to Produce a *New* New Deal in the USA?"), the central issue of our time is the struggle against "the entrenched" neo-liberal "ideology" that serves to "increase the elites' capacity to capture ever more income, wealth and privilege, continuing the explosive rise in inequality of the past 45 years."

In looking at the issues of employment relations and trade unionism there is thus today – as there always has been – two fundamentally different ways of perceiving these issues. One perspective – grounded in the traditions of Sidney and Beatrice Webb, John Commons, John Dunlop, Allan Flanders, Hugh Clegg, Jim Hagan – accepts the benefits of free market capitalism, believing that employees and their unions can work cooperatively with employers and government to build employment, real national wealth, and a just share for workers. In articulating this viewpoint at the dawn of the twentieth century, Sidney and Beatrice Webb (1902: xviii, xx) condemned as "short-sighted" the tendency of union activists to ignore just employer concerns about productivity and profitability, arguing instead for a balancing of "compatible" worker and employer interests. By contrast, the alterative perspective – informing commenters and activist such as Marx, Lenin, Foucault, Hyman, Bronfenbrenner, Yates, and Peetz – has seen employment relations primarily in terms of power, a battle that sets workers in perpetual opposition to employers and hostile state agencies. As Peetz (2019: 13) expresses it, "Eventually, increases in work intensity or working hours become unsustainable in the face of organized and unorganized resistance by employees."

It is fair to say that among labor relations academics the more radical perspective – emphasizing conflict, power and the incompatibility of employer and employee interests – is today in the ascendancy. At first glance, the ascendancy of the more radical perspective appears paradoxical. Across the Western world, support for social democratic and progressive parties among blue-collar workers and lower-paid white-collar workers has collapsed. As Dyrenfurth (2019: 6) notes in relation to the Australian experience, "Like its social democratic cousins, Australian Labor is increasingly detached from its working-class base of blue-collar and precarious white-collar workers." Similarly, support for unions among poorer blue-collar and service industry workers (i.e., retail, hospitality, recreation, etc.) is lower now than it was during the first decade of the twentieth century.

How can we explain the popularity of a radical perspective, emphasizing power imbalances and inequality, when comparatively well-paid workers who boast jobs in education now dominate the ranks of trade unions, health care, and public administration? Explanation is found in the fact that the working lives of a large section of the workforce – and a much bigger percentage of those who hold a union ticket – are no longer *primarily* shaped by what Adam Smith (1776/1999: Book 1, Chap. V, para. 4) referred to as the "higgling of the market." Rather, if you are employed as a university lecturer in a state-owned or state-funded university, or as a nurse in public or public-funded hospital, your employment is primarily determined by politics rather than economics. Even if the wider market economy is behaving poorly, showing little vitality in terms of either productivity or per capita growth, a government can still increase public sector employment and wages, either by increasing taxes or by borrowing. Moreover, the greater the number of people employed in the public sector – and in firms reliant on government funding rather than market sales – the more likely the government will concede to pressure from the organized blocs which benefit from government largesse (i.e., public-sector unionists, state-funded schools and universities, public hospitals, etc.). Fearing adverse electoral consequences, governments across the Western world have thus shown a proclivity in recent decades to increase taxes, an outcome that tends to advance the interests of the public sector at the private sector's expense. Reflecting this trend, the ratio of taxes to Gross Domestic Product (GDP) across the OECD reached an unprecedented peak in 2016. On average, a sum equivalent to 34.4% of national wealth was extracted from the populace and the private sector in the way of taxes (OECD 2019a: 1). When academics such as Wisman (▶ Chap. 43, "Why did the Great Recession Fail to Produce a *New* New Deal in the USA?") therefore argue against "tax cuts," "cuts in welfare," and "deregulation," we see a happy confluence of genuinely held belief and public-sector self-interest, an outcome that is the exact mirror opposite of the "neo-liberal" argument that tax cuts and less regulation favor the private sector.

If, in the *public sector*, concerns relating to economics, productivity, and profitability can be safely foregone in favor of discourses about power and "neo-liberal" ideology, such matters are less easily overlooked in the private sector, an area of the economy that still employs the great bulk of the workforce. If you are a factory worker, for example, you will probably share the view that greater productivity and profitability are good things, making your continued employment more rather than less likely. Conversely, you are also likely to view falling productivity as a bad thing, likely to lead to a decline in real wages.

Certainly, if we look beyond matters relating to union survival and growth to the wider employment problems of our society, there is just reason to be worried about matters relating to productivity and economic growth. As I (Bowden 2018: 278–279) have noted previously, since 2000 the global economy has suffered from a marked slowdown in productivity (see Fig. 11). Whereas prior to 2000 the world's advanced economies boasted total factor productivity growth rates of 1.5% per annum, between 2000 and 2008 the rate of productivity growth averaged only 0.8% per annum. Since 2008, increases in productivity have slowed even further, often slipping into negative territory. Unsurprisingly, as Fig. 12 indicates, real wage growth across the world's advanced economies has mirrored the downward trend that has characterized productivity. Unable to secure real wage gains in an economy that barely grew in per capita terms many households suffered a range of adverse circumstances: increased indebtedness, a greater likelihood of homelessness, a more precarious job situation. Reflective of this retrograde trend, household indebtedness in the world's advanced economies has risen from – on average – 45.37% of GDP in 2000 to 63.93% of GDP in December 2016. Significantly, the crisis of falling productivity, and hence stagnant or declining real GDP per capita, is not only a

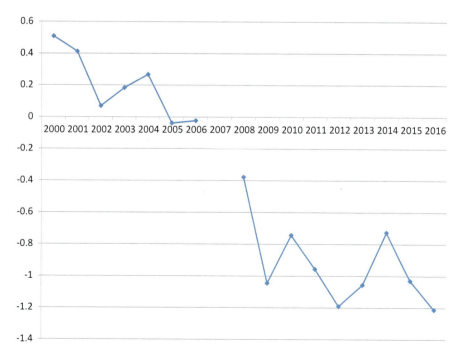

Fig. 11 Annual total productivity growth in percent: Advanced economies, 2000–2016 (2007 = index of 100). (Source: International Monetary Fund, World Economic Outlook, October 2017b, Annex Fig. 2.2.3)

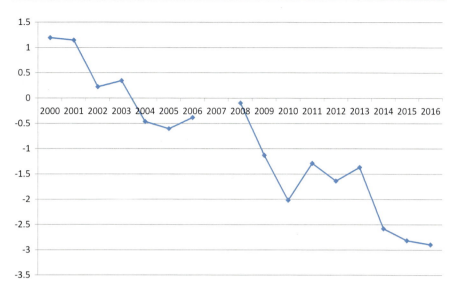

Fig. 12 Changes in annual median wage growth in percent: Advanced economies, 2000–2016 (2007 = index of 100). (Source: International Monetary Fund, World Economic Outlook, October 2017, Annex Fig. 2.2)

problem of advanced economies. It is also manifest in developing economies, where annual productivity growth has more than halved since the Global Financial Crisis, falling from an average of 1.7% prior to the recession to barely 0.7% in the years after the economic crisis (International Monetary Fund 2017a).

If I had, therefore, to identify the principal employment relations problem in the modern world, I would not give pride of place to trade union decline. Since the mid-1990s, unions have maintained only a marginal presence among low-paid service workers and medium-paid blue-collar workers. It is difficult to see the restoration of this long lost presence. Such weaknesses, moreover, do not threaten the long-term survival of trade unions. Indeed, to cite Sidney and Beatrice Webb (1902: xxvii), unions are "a State within our State," boasting their own bureaucratic apparatus and political apparatchiks. Firmly ensconced among public sector workers, and professionals employed in education and health, unions will remain a significant social force into the foreseeable future. Nor would I identify social inequality as the principal problem. There is a considerable difference between inequality in a poor, preindustrial society and that found in modern liberal democracies. As we have noted previously, there is little evidence that the welfare state with its protective safety net is under threat. Rather than decreasing, the percentage of national GDP allocated to public social expenditure is approaching record highs in most OECD countries, averaging slightly more than 20% of GDP. It is also a mistake to believe that the United States is a particular laggard in this regard. Its expenditures as a share of GDP are not only close to the OECD, they are also superior to those of Australia and Canada. United States expenditures on social programs, measured as a share of GDP, are also more than double that obtained in 1960. In 2019, expenditures were also approximately 50% higher than in 1990 (OECD 2019b).

What principally concerns me is the apparent loss of economic dynamism across virtually all advanced societies, a problem that manifests itself in the declining levels of productivity and real wage growth that we identified in Figs. 11 and 12. Such problems have the most severe effect on younger workers yet to gain a secure foothold in the workforce, and poorer workers in the private sector for whom an increase in real wages is typically a more pressing concern than abstract notions of social inequality unrelated to immediate financial benefit.

How can labor relations scholarship and, more particularly, management history, contribute to problems relating to slowing economic growth, lower levels of productivity, and stagnant or declining real wages? In confronting this problem, we need to recognize that the solutions offered by industrial relations academics in the 1970s and 1980s (i.e., Kochan et al. 1986/1988; Sabel 1982; Piore and Sabel 1984, etc.) have little modern relevance, at least in the private sector. As the American labor law specialist, Raymond Holger (2016: 142) recently noted with regret, "the collective bargaining model has run its course." Nevertheless, despite the disappearance of historic patterns of employee representation built around trade unionism, it remains the case that the "human problem" remains core to any long-term improvements in productivity and societal wealth. For, throughout history, even during what we think of as the Industrial Revolution, ingenuity in the organization of work has typically been more important than any productivity-enhancement that resulted from new technologies. Moreover, ingenuity in the organization of work has always come down to relationships between workers and management. One also does not need to be a Marxist to recognize that employers and workers have distinct and different interests, and that in liberal democracies it is only possible to achieve long-term gains in workplace relations by respecting these differences. As the noted management theorist, Chester Barnard (1936: 88) observed during the Great Depression of the 1930s, "Strictly speaking," organizational objectives have "no meaning for the individual." In other words, although employee interests may be compatible with those of the employer, they are never identical. Historically, this difference in interests has resulted in either industrial conflict or (more commonly) employee disengagement. Writing in the 1930s, Elton Mayo (1933: 165, 172) lamented how modern workplaces were often characterized by "social disorganization," "personal maladjustment," and a sense of "personal futility." Similarly, in the mid-1970s, High Clegg (1975: 316) expressed concern as to the "competitive greed" of both workers and employers, a problem he likened to "a disease." Today, few of us would contradict Godard's ▶ Chap. 41, "Labor and Employment Practices: The Rise and Fall of the New Managerialism" update as per style conclusion in his chapter in this *Palgrave Handbook of Management History* that workplaces "face a 'crisis' of engagement," characterized by "low levels of loyalty" and "commitment."

If the problems of productivity, commitment, and engagement are age-old – ones typically confronted by every generation, albeit in different guises – then it is likely that the solutions to modern problems will also share commonalities with past remedies. Both Holger (2016) and Bruce Kaufman (2003, 2008) argue for a return to the system of nonunion representation advocated by John D. Rockefeller, Jr., in the early twentieth century. For in Rockefeller's (1916: 19) estimation, "the soundest industrial policy is that which has constantly in mind the welfare of the employees as well as the making of profits," a policy that Rockefeller associated with "internal bargaining between management and [non-union] worker representatives elected through secret ballot." While there is merit in Kaufman and Holger's proposal, one also suspects that its take-up will be limited. Even more than in the 1920s, there will be a lurking fear among nonunion firms that elected systems of employee representation will act as a Trojan horse through which unionism will re-enter the workplace. What other alternatives are there? My colleague and co-editor, Jeff Muldoon, is a great believer in the continued relevance of Elton Mayo's research into the "human problem" that has always existed at the core of any managerial system. As he argues in his chapter in this *Palgrave Handbook* (▶ Chap. 23, "Spontaneity Is the Spice of Management: Elton Mayo's Hunt for Cooperation"), the great value of Mayo's work is that it looks at "the whole situation" in seeking to foster workplace cooperation, perceiving workers as individuals who seek a complex mix of extrinsic and intrinsic benefits from their job. What is also clear is that not only are problems of employee engagement central to the revitalization of the economy, productivity, and real wages, but that trade unions – now a distinctly minority force in the private sector – will only play a modest role in the necessary process of employee-management re-engagement.

Conclusion

As is the case with many other people, the process of union decline and transformation is for me not only a matter of professional inquiry. It is also intensely personal. My father, a truck driver, served for more than two decades on the Branch Committee of Management of the Transport Workers Union, the Australian equivalent of the International Brotherhood of Teamsters. My mother, a telephonist, served as honorary President of her union, the Australian Telephone and Phonogram Officers Association. Between February 1980 and July 1988, I was a member of one of world's most militant unions, the communist-dominated Seamen's Union of Australia, serving both on and below deck as a rank-and-file seafarer. When, after leaving seafaring, I did my PhD at the University of Wollongong, I studied with the support of a scholarship provided by the Transport Workers Union. A modified version of my PhD thesis, *Driving Force: The History of the Transport Workers Union of Australia, 1883–1992*, was my first significant publication (Bowden 1993). In subsequent years I completed the commissioned histories of two other unions (Bowden 1996, 2008). When I obtained my first permanent academic job at Griffith University, my principal job in 1995 and 1996 was to head a research project into workplace relations in the Queensland coal industry. In the mid-1990s, as is the case today, the coal industry provided the backbone of the state's economy. In 2018–2019, for example, Queensland exported a record 224 million tonnes of coal, almost all of which is high-value metallurgical coal used in steelmaking. Not only is coal the largest single source of foreign exchange earnings in Australia, it is also the case that Queensland exports a greater volume of metallurgical coal than any other region or nation on the planet. Among Australian workers, few have been more stalwart supporters of organized labor than Queensland's coal miners. Between 1944 and 1949, the coalmining vote helped elect the communist lawyer, Fred Patterson, to the Queensland Parliament, the only time a communist was elected to an Australian parliament. When I researched the industry in the mid-1990s, often staying at Dysart in Queensland's Central Highlands, an estimated 75.5% of the coal-mining workforce was unionized. At Dysart, where unionism pervaded every pore of community life, I suspect that union density was close to 100% when I stayed there. At election time, an overwhelming majority voted Labor. As late as 2007, 71.4% of the Dysart electorate voted for the Labor Party (Australian Electoral Commission 2007).

If in the mid-1990s, Dysart was the embodiment of union strength and solidarity, by 2019 it exemplified the deep divisions that have emerged within organized labor, a movement increasingly dominated by urban professionals whose goals and aspirations are profoundly at odds with "traditional" unionists in mining, forestry, power generation, and primary metal processing. For by the time of the May 2019 election the most divisive issue in Australian politics was a new mega-coal project, the so-called Adani mine, adjacent to the existing coal mining town of Clermont, some 100 km from Dysart. For the union representing coal miners, the Construction Forestry Mining & Energy Union (CFMEU), the Adani mine opened up the prospect of tens of thousands of additional unionized jobs, not only at Adani but also at other mines likely to follow its lead into a hitherto unexploited coalfield. Among unions associated with urban professionals, however, opposition to Adani was almost universal. In an article entitled "Adani v Workers: Which Side are You On?" Colin Long (2018: 1–2), the long-serving Victorian Secretary of the National Tertiary Education Union (i.e., the union that covers academic staff) declared, "the movement to stop Adani's Carmichael coalmine" was "of generational significance." Calling for the total cessation of coal mining, Long (2018: 1–2) – who in late 2018 became President of the Victorian Trades Hall Council – declared that every worker and unionist had to decide whether they were "on the side of . . . a future free of environmental devastation" or, alternatively, on the side of "those who support Adani's mine." In the run-up to the federal election, Australia's Green Party organized a 5000 km protest caravan, which took the anti-Adani campaign into the heart of the coalmining districts, terminating in a mass protest at Clermont; a caravan that attracted a counter-protest movement of irate coal miners. In articulating pro-Adani sentiments, the CFMEU's National President, Tony Maher (2019: 3) declared the anti-Adani caravan to be "vainglorious," "absurd," and "deeply traumatizing and polarizing" to "hundreds of thousands" of Queensland workers and their families. When the Australian nation voted in May 2019, the polarizing effect of Adani and climate change became obvious. In the inner city electorates of Melbourne and Sydney, both the Labor Party and the Greens increased their vote. In regional Queensland, Labor was wiped out, losing 25 of the state's 30 electorates. Of the five Queensland electorates that Labor managed to win, all were in the metropolitan capital, Brisbane, and its urban environs. In Dysart, only 26% voted Labor. Almost 40% of Dysart residents voted for a number of populist, nationalist parties (One Nation, United Australia Party, Katter's

Australia Party, Fraser Anning's Conservative National Party), before giving their decisive preference vote to the conservative Liberal National Party. In Clermont, the coalmining town at the epicenter of the anti-Adani protests, only 7.94% voted Labor (Australian Electoral Commission 2019). Alienated from the dominant, urbanized voices in both the Labor Party and the wider union movement, coalmining towns such as Clermont and Dysart are today far removed from the communities among whom I stayed in 1995 and 1996. Union density in coal mining has slipped from 75.5% to less than 38% (Bowden and Barry 2015). Metropolitan unionists and their environmental allies are regarded with suspicion, if not hatred.

The alienation of coal workers and unionists in Dysart from the wider labor movement is hardly unique. It is replicated in the coal mining towns of West Virginia, the steel towns of Indiana and the working class districts of northern England. The all-too evident divisions that now exist between "traditional" blue-collar workers and lower-paid service workers on the one side, and the professionals and skilled workers employed in public administration, education and health on the other, points to a fundamental but easily overlooked fact. The profound process of sociological transformation that has characterized Western societies during the last 70 years has not only resulted in a process of union decline. It has also brought about a transformation of unionism, a process of change that has produced – and will continue to produce – unions and union activists with very different concerns and interests to those of yesteryear. Increasingly, unions focus with ever greater intensity on those issues that Simon Mollan (2019: 513) identifies as being worthy of primary interest: – "postmodernist concerns with power and its distribution . . . inequality and discrimination in work, pay, and advancement based on gender, ethnicity, race, or sexuality." Ideologically opposed to jobs in mining and energy-intensive industries in manufacturing, union activists drawn from professional and semi-professional occupations are also little concerned with the prosaic issues of productivity enhancement that concerned union officials in the 1970s and 1980s. Thus, as the fissures *within* the ranks of organized labor become ever wider, the survival of unions outside of a comparatively small section of the workforce looks increasingly precarious. This leaves a fundamental question: to whom do traditional blue-collar workers, and poor private-sector service workers, concerned with prosaic bread-and-butter issues, now look to for leadership?

Cross-References

- ▶ A Return to the Good Old Days: Populism, Fake News, Yellow Journalism, and the Unparalleled Virtue of Business People
- ▶ Conclusion: Management Theory in Crisis
- ▶ Industrial Relations in the "Golden Age" in the UK and the USA, 1945–1980
- ▶ Introduction: Public Policy Failure, the Demise of Experts, and the Dawn of a New Era
- ▶ Labor and Employment Practices: The Rise and Fall of the New Managerialism
- ▶ Management History in the Modern World: An Overview

▶ The New Executive: Interconnected Yet Isolated and Uninformed – Leadership Challenges in the Digital Pandemic Epoch
▶ To the Tavistock Institute: British Management in the Early Twentieth Century
▶ What Is Management?
▶ Why Did the Great Recession Fail to Produce a *New* New Deal in the USA?

References

Australian Bureau of Statistics (2007) Trade union membership time series, 1990–2006. Cat. No. 63100TS0001. Australian Bureau of Statistics, Canberra

Australian Bureau of Statistics (2017) Characteristics of employment, Australia, August 2016. Cat. 6333.0. Australian Bureau of Statistics, Canberra. https://www.abs.gov.au/AUSSTATS/abs@.nsf/DetailsPage/6333.0August%202016?OpenDocument

Australian Bureau of Statistics (2019a) Characteristics of employment, Australia, August 2018. Cat. 6333.0. Australian Bureau of Statistics, Canberra. https://www.abs.gov.au/AUSSTATS/abs@.nsf/DetailsPage/6333.0August%202018?OpenDocument

Australian Bureau of Statistics (2019b) Characteristics of employment, Australia, August 2019. Cat. 6333.0. Australian Bureau of Statistics, Canberra. https://www.abs.gov.au/ausstats/abs@.nsf/mf/6333.0

Australian Council of Trade Unions/Trade Development Commission (1987) Australia reconstructed. Australian Government Printing Service, Canberra

Australian Electoral Commission (2007) Virtual tally room: federal election result 2007 – QLD division, Capricornia, polling places. Australian Electoral Commission, Canberra. https://results.aec.gov.au/13745/Website/HouseDivisionPollingPlaces-13745-157.htm

Australian Electoral Commission (2019) Virtual tally room: federal election result 2019 – QLD division, Capricornia, polling places. Australian Electoral Commission, Canberra. https://results.aec.gov.au/24310/Website/HouseDivisionPage-24310-157.htm

Australian Government (2009) Fair work act 2009. Commonwealth of Australia, Canberra. https://www.legislation.gov.au/Series/C2009A00028

Barnard C (1936) The functions of the executive. Harvard University Press, Cambridge, MA

Bernard A (2009) Trends in manufacturing employment. Perspectives. Statistics Canada, Cat. No. 75-001-X. https://www150.statcan.gc.ca/n1/en/pub/75-001-x/2009102/pdf/10788-eng.pdf?st=VgErBfOw

Bowden B (1993) Driving force: the history of the transport workers union of Australia, 1883–1992. Allen & Unwin, Sydney

Bowden B (1996) A breed apart: the history of the Bacon factories' Union of Employees 1946–1996. Boolarong Press, Brisbane

Bowden B (2008) Against the odds: the history of the united firefighters union in Queensland, 1917 to 2008. Federation Press, Sydney

Bowden B (2009) The organising model in Australia: a reassessment. Labour Ind 20(2):138–158

Bowden B (2018) Work, wealth and postmodernism: the intellectual conflict at the heart of business endeavour. Palgrave Macmillan, Cham

Bowden B, Barry M (2015) Recasting industrial relations: productivity, place and the Queensland coal industry, 2001–2013. J Ind Relat 57(1):48–71

Bowden B, Blackwood S, Rafferty C, Allan C (eds) (2009) Work & strife in paradise: the history of labour relations in Queensland 1859–2009. Federation Press, Sydney

Bronfenbrenner K (2003) The American labor movement and the resurgence in union organizing. In: Fairbrother P, Yates CAB (eds) Trade unions in renewal. A comparative study. Continuim, London/New York, pp 32–50

Bronfenbrenner K, Friedman S, Hurd R, Oswald RA, Seeber RL (1998) Introduction. In: Bronfenbrenner K, Friedman S, Hurd R, Oswald RA, Seeber RL (eds) Organizing to win: new research on union strategies. IRL Press, Ithaca/London, pp 1–18

Burgmann V (2016) Globalization and labour in the twenty-first century. Routledge, London

Burgmann M, Burgmann V (2017) Green bans, red union: the saving of a city. University of New South Wales Press, Sydney

Canadian Union of Public Employees (2019) About us. Canadian Union of Public Employees, Ottawa. https://cupe.ca/about-us

Clegg H (1975) Pluralism in industrial relations. Br J Ind Relat 13(3):309–316

Commons J (1905) Trade unionism and the labor question. Augustus Kelley, New York

Cooper R (2002) Trade unionism in 2001. J Ind Relat 44(2):247–262

Desilver D (2019) Ten facts about American workers. Pew Research Centre, Washington DC. https://www.pewresearch.org/fact-tank/2019/08/29/facts-about-american-workers/

Dunlop JT (1958) Industrial relations systems. Holt, New York

Dyrenfurth N (2019) Getting the blues: the future of Australian labor. Connor Court, Brisbane

Edwards L (2019) The Left needs to start talking about the long chain economy. Chifley Research Centre. https://www.chifley.org.au/the-left-needs-to-start-talking-about-the-long-chain-economy/

Elementary Teachers' Federation of Ontario (2017) Collective agreement between the Toronto District School Board and the elementary teachers' Federation of Ontario 2014–2019. https://ett.ca/collective-agreement-2014-2019/

Enderwick P (1984) The labour utilisation practices of multinationals and obstacles to multinational collective bargaining. J Ind Relat 26(3):345–364

Fair Work Commission (2014) KFC team members enterprise agreement – Queensland and Tweed Heads (NSW) 2014–2017. https://www.fwc.gov.au/search/document/all?search_api_views_fulltext=KFC%20Team%20Members%20Enterprise%20Agreement%20%E2%80%93%20Queensland%20and%20Tweed%20Heads%20(NSW)%202014-2017%20

Flanders A, Fox A (1969) Collective bargaining: from Donovan to Durkheim. Br J Ind Relat 7(2):151–180

Fodor M (2013) Taxation and the neo-liberal counter-revolution: the Canadian case. In: Himelfarb A, Himelfarb B (eds) Tax is not a four letter word. Winlfred University Press, Waterloo, pp 101–117

Freeman RB, Medoff JL (1984) What do unions do? Basic Books, New York

Gall G, Hurd R, Wilkinson A (2011) Labour unionism and neo-liberalism. In: Gall G, Hurd R, Wilkinson A (eds) The international handbook of labour unions: responses to neo-liberalism. Edward Elgar, London, pp 1–12

Goods C, Veen A, Barratt T (2019) 'Is your gig any good?' Analysing job quality in the Australian platform-based food-delivery sector. J Ind Relat 61(4):502–507

Hagan J (1966) Printers and politics. Australian National University Press, Canberra

Hagan J (1981) The history of the A.C.T.U. Longman Cheshire, Melbourne, AUS.

Hall R (2000) Outsourcing, contracting-out and labour hire: implications for human resource development in Australian organizations. Asia Pac J Hum Resour 38(2):23–41

Healy J, Nicholson D, Pekarek A (2017) Should we take the gig economy seriously? Labour Ind 27(3):232–248

Hirsch BT, Addison JT (1986) The economic analysis of unions: new approaches and evidence. Allen & Unwin, Boston

Holger R (2016) From Ludlow to Chattanooga. A century of employee representation plans and the future of the American labor movement. J Manag Hist 22(2):130–145

Hyman R (1978) Pluralism, procedural consensus and collective bargaining. Br J Ind Relat 16(1):16–60

Ibsen CL, Tapia M (2017) Trade union revitalisation: where are we know? What to next? J Ind Relat 59(2):170–191

International Monetary Fund (2017a) Global financial report, October 2017. International Monetary Fund, Washington, DC

International Monetary Fund (2017b) World economic outlook, October 2017. International Monetary Fund, Washington, DC

International Trade Union Federation's (2018) Global rights index (2018). International Trade Union Confederation, Geneva. https://www.ituc-csi.org/ituc-global-rights-index-2018

Johnson C (2019) Social democracy and the crisis of equality. Springer, Cham

Juravich T, Bronfenbrenner K (1998) Preparing for the worst: organizing and staying organized. In: Bronfenbrenner K, Friedman S, Hurd R, Oswald RA, Seeber RL (eds) Organizing to win: new research on union strategies. IRL Press, Ithaca/London, pp 262–282

Kaufman B (2003) John R. Commons and the Wisconsin school on industrial relations strategy and policy. Ind Labor Relat Rev 57(1):3–30

Kaufman B (2008) Paradigms in industrial relations: original, modern and versions in between. Br J Ind Relat 46(2):313–339

Kochan TA, Katz HC, McKersie RB (1986/1988) The transformation of American industrial relations. Basic Books, New York

Kumar P, Murray G (2003) Strategic dilemma: the state of union revival in Canada. In: Fairbrother P and Yates C A B (eds.) Trade unions in renewal: a comparative study. Continuum, London and New York, pp 200–220

Lenin VI (1902/1946) What is to be done? In: Lenin VI (ed) Selected works, vol 1. Foreign Languages Publishing House, Moscow, pp 142–350

Long C (2018) Adani v workers: which side are you on? Green Left Weekly 1171:1–2. https://www.greenleft.org.au/content/adani-v-workers-which-side-are-you

Maher T (2019) Energy, mining and climate: fact and fiction. Speech to The Sydney Institute, Sydney. https://me.cfmeu.org.au/sites/me.cfmeu.org.au/files/uploads/ResearchSubs/Sydney_Institute_Maher_FINAL4.pdf

Mathews J (1989) Tools of change: new technology and the democratisation of work. Pluto Press, Sydney

Mayo E (1933) The human problems of an industrial civilization. Macmillan, New York

McDonnell A, Curtis C (2019) How Britain voted in the 2019 general election, YouGov. https://yougov.co.uk/topics/politics/articles-reports/2019/12/17/how-britain-voted-2019-general-election

McManus S (2018) Change the rules, Speech to the Australian Press Club, 21 March 2018. Australian Council of Trade Unions, Melbourne. https://www.actu.org.au/actu-media/speeches-and-opinion/sally-mcmanus-press-club-speech-change-the-rules-for-more-secure-jobs-and-fair-pa

Mir A, Mir R (2015) Re-examining 'flexibility'. In: McLaren PG, Mills AJ, Weatherbee TG (eds) The Routledge companion to management and organizational history. Routledge, London/New York, pp 253–264

Mollan S (2019) Phenomenal differences: varieties of historical interpretation in management and organization studies. Qual Res Organ Manag 14(4):495–515

Nurses Professional Association of Queensland (2019) Protection without politics. https://www.npaq.com.au/

Organisation for Economic Co-operation and Development (2019a) Revenue statistics 2019 – Australia. Organisation for Economic Co-operation and Development, Paris. https://www.oecd.org/tax/revenue-statistics-australia.pdf

Organisation for Economic Co-operation and Development (2019b) Social expenditure update 2019: public social spending is high in many OECD countries. Organisation for Economic Co-operation and Development, Paris. http://www.oecd.org/els/soc/OECD2019-Social-Expenditure-Update.pdf

Oxenbridge S (2003) A story of crisis and change: the service and food workers union of Aotearoa. In: Fairbrother P, Yates CAB (eds) Trade unions in renewal. A comparative study. Continuim, London/New York, pp 135–157

Peetz D (2002) Decollectivist strategies in Oceania. Relations Industrielles / Industrial Relations 57(2):252–281

Peetz D (2006) Brave new work place: how individual contracts are changing our jobs. Allen & Unwin, Sydney

Peetz D (2019) The realities and futures of work. Australian National University Press, Canberra

Perry CR (1997) Outsourcing and union power. J Lab Res 18(4):521–534

Peetz D, Bailey J (2011) Neo-liberal evolution and union responses in Australia. In: Gall G, Hurd R, Wilkinson A (eds) The international handbook of labour unions: responses to neo-liberalism. Edward Elgar, London, pp 62–81

Peetz D, Bailey J (2012) Dancing alone? the Australian union movement over three decades. J Ind Relat 54(4):525–541

Piore M, Sabel C (1984) The second industrial divide. Basic Books, New York

Queensland Nurses Union (2016) 2015–16 annual report: report of the Queensland Nurses Union of Employees and Australian Nurses and Midwifery Federation. https://www.qnmu.org.au/DocumentsFolder/NEW%20WEB%20documents/ReportsSubmissions/2016/QNU%20Annual%20Report%202015-2016%20WEB.pdf

Rockefeller JD Jr (1916) Labor and capital – partners. The Atlantic Monthly (July):12–20

Rose JB (2016) Constraints on public sector bargaining in Canada. J Ind Relat 58(1):93–110

Sabel C (1982) Work and politics. Cambridge University Press, Cambridge, UK

Schenk C (2003) Social movement unionism: beyond the organizing model. In: Fairbrother P, Yates CAB (eds) Trade unions in renewal. A comparative study. Continuim, London/New York, pp 244–262

Shop, Distributive and Allied Trades Association (2013/2018) McDonalds' Australia enterprise agreement 2013. Shop, Distributive and Allied Trades Association. https://www.sda.org.au/download/enterprise-agreements/MCDONALDS-AUSTRALIA-ENTERPRISE-AGREEMENT-2013.pdf

Smith A (1776/1999) An inquiry into the nature and causes of the wealth of nations. Penguin Classics, London

Statistics Canada (2019) Union status by industry. Statistics Canada, Ottawa. https://www150.statcan.gc.ca/t1/tbl1/en/tv.action?pid=1410013201

Turner I (1965) Industrial labour and politics. Australian National University Press, Canberra

United States Bureau of Labor Statistics (2019a) Economic news release, 18 January 2019: table 3 – union affiliation of employed wage and salary workers by occupation and industry. United States Bureau of Labor Statistics, Washington, DC. https://www.bls.gov/news.release/union2.t03.htm

United States Bureau of Labor Statistics (2019b) TED: the economics daily, 25 January. United States Bureau of Labor Statistics, Washington, DC. https://www.bls.gov/opub/ted/2019/union-membership-rate-10-point-5-percent-in-2018-down-from-20-point-1-percent-in-1983.htm?view_full

United States Bureau of Labor Statistics (2019c) News release, 6 November 2019: productivity and costs, third quarter 2019. United States Bureau of Labor Statistics, Washington, DC. https://www.bls.gov/news.release/pdf/prod2.pdf

Vandenheuvel A, Wooden M (1995) Self-employed contractors in Australia: how many and who are they? J Ind Relat 37(2):263–280

Voss K, Sherman R (2003) You just can't do it automatically: the transition to social movement unionism in the United States. In: Fairbrother P, Yates CAB (eds) Trade unions in renewal. A comparative study. Continuim, London/New York, pp 51–77

Webb S, Webb B (1902) The history of trade unionism, 2nd edn. Longmans, Green and Co., London

Western B (1995) A comparative study of working-class disorganization: union decline in eighteen advanced capitalist countries. Am Sociol Rev 60(2):179–201

Yates CAB (2002) Expanding labour's horizons: union organizing and strategic change in Canada. Just Labour 1(1):31–40

Yates CAB (2003) The revival of industrial unions in Canada: the extension and adaptation of industrial union practices to the new economy. In: Fairbrother P, Yates CAB (eds) Trade unions in renewal: a comparative study. Continuum, London/New York, pp 221–243

The New Executive: Interconnected Yet Isolated and Uninformed – Leadership Challenges in the Digital Pandemic Epoch

45

Kathleen Marshall Park

Contents

Introduction	1012
Interconnected Yet Isolated and Uninformed?	1013
Tesla: Mall World Meets Green Energy – Upscale Transport and Technological Innovation in the Automobile Industry	1014
Facebook: Profiteering in the Information Age	1017
Trump: Not Just an Individual but an Entire Organization	1021
Leadership Challenges in the Digital Pandemic Epoch	1025
Virtual Worlds and Organizational Directions	1025
Business Models, Intermediation, and the Enduring Importance of Ethical Perspectives	1026
Managing in an Economically, Sociologically, Technologically and Medically Complex Landscape	1027
Disrupting Practice While Venerating Tradition	1028
Technology, Power, and Organizational Context	1029
Conclusion: Connecting, Disconnecting, and Reconnecting in Crises	1030
Cross-References	1031
References	1032

Abstract

This analysis interprets a shift in executive thinking amidst the increasing electronic communication, information abundance, and cyber interconnections of the global digital economy and pandemic. The shift concerns the paradox of a potentially intensifying decline in effective and appropriate managerial action and ethical awareness alongside escalating electronic input from stakeholders worldwide. As leaders of globally impactful companies or countries confront the

---

K. M. Park (✉)
Department of Administrative Sciences, Metropolitan College, Boston University, Boston, MA, USA

MIT Sloan School of Management, Cambridge, MA, USA
e-mail: kmparque@bu.edu

© The Author(s), under exclusive licence to Springer Nature Switzerland AG 2020
B. Bowden et al. (eds.), *The Palgrave Handbook of Management History*,
https://doi.org/10.1007/978-3-319-62114-2_3

dilemma of increased information and interconnection from various sources, in tandem with an increased insularity from the daily challenges of consumer experiences, difficulties ensue due to leadership disconnection from individual stakeholders, organizational objectives, and global health, safety, and wellness imperatives. The following analysis highlights an often increasingly narrow focus in management thinking and priorities in an age of multiple crises.

Keywords

Digital economy · Digital revolution · Internet era · Information age · Technology leadership · Information overabundance · Cyber interconnections · Social media · Inequality · Insularity · Management ethics · Strategic action · COVID-19 · Pandemic · Digital divide

Introduction

Digitally available sources of information and means of interconnection currently abound. In the midst of these influence leadership, as always, has been a topic of considerable attention and debate. Crises continue to recur. Yet it has not been clear if the increasing abundance of information and profusion of interconnectivity – and the ubiquity of various forms of crises – have resulted in more ethical, effective, and appropriate courses of leadership action in the competitive global digital economy. The present analysis examines a shift in executive leadership and management thinking. The shift concerns the paradox of increasing digital interconnections juxtaposed against potentially decreasing ethical awareness and decreasing strategically efficacious efforts by corporate leadership. Corporate leaders can arguably more and more be found to demonstrate tendencies toward being isolated and uninformed despite the barrage of social media, digital communications, and frequent incursions of business news – both factual and sensationalist – into daily life. The Internet/digital/sharing/experience/connection/innovation/global/gig economy has meant increased digitization, technology firms with massive power (Ovide 2020), market capitalizations (Mueller et al. 2017), and multiple new platform business models and online interconnections (Desjardins et al. 2016). This multifaceted economy has also corresponded to increased distance and disaffection between corporate top leadership and global stakeholders, if stakeholder engagement is not managed effectively and with a consistent emphasis on social responsibility (Park et al. 2019). The present analysis first considers some specific exemplars of highly visible corporate leaders confronting challenging situations ranging from quotidian yet widespread vexations to a more far-reaching type of global conundrum (Reeves et al. 2020). The analysis subsequently looks more broadly at leadership challenges in the digital and pandemic epoch, where technology can strengthen leaders and firms while sometimes also endangering individual privacy rights and providing an inadequate informational bulwark and insufficient work-and-study-from-home conditions in times of widespread infectious disease. In conclusion our exploration turns to reflections on corporate leadership evolution amidst digital directions.

Interconnected Yet Isolated and Uninformed?

The modern executive has an unprecedented level of access to information as well as to input from multiple levels of the organization and from stakeholders in the surrounding business environment (Roetzel 2019). The multilayered information inflow occurs through assorted modalities and platforms commonly accessible in the digital economy (Hemp 2009). In the prevailing hierarchies and physical distancing realities, the modern executive has become even further isolated from daily life situations as experienced by those at lower levels inside or outside the organization (Pazzanese 2016). This isolation occurs economically, psychologically, and strategically. Although these concerns are ongoing (Freeman 1996), they have intensified in recent years in tandem with increasing information flows (Marques and Batista 2017) and a pandemic crisis. Compelling examples of 21st century corporate isolation can be found in Elon Musk (Tesla), Mark Zuckerberg (Facebook), and Donald Trump (The Trump Organization) – to associate each of these corporate leaders, entrepreneurs, and, in various ways, transformers, with in some cases just one of their many business endeavors. We argue here for the simultaneous occurrence of digital interconnectedness and multiple forms of market awareness, on the one hand, and disaffection with and isolation from essential realities and effective actions, on the other hand. We propose that the executive interconnectedness and awareness become juxtaposed against a purposeful isolation as a form of executive protection. The isolation serves as protection against bombardment from undesired information – ranging from distracting "noise" to anything contrary to the desired worldview – and lower echelon disillusionment with upper echelons due, for instance, to increasing income polarization. This analysis examines the economic, psychological, and strategic dimensions of modern executive isolation, not as a uniform or universal phenomenon among all business leaders but rather as emblematic of key experiences in the modern digital economic era and pandemic epoch.

The phenomenon of the isolated executive has also become interrelated with the rise of the celebrity executive (Lovelace et al. 2018) and businessperson-as-politician phenomena (Gould et al. 2017), further underscoring that being a network node and in the social media vanguard does not equate with an intensive level of being usefully informed and orientated toward value creation. Such disconnections also have the potential to adversely impact shareholder value or other forms of social or environmental value added by the firm. These issues can arise as part of peak organizational or individual performance as well during performance crises (Hemp and Stewart 2004).

In examining the central themes of being interconnected, isolated, and uninformed, we look at each of the exemplar executives in turn. The central themes are situated against a backdrop of popular maneuvers and cycles within business strategy, such as the occurrence of waves of mergers and acquisitions propelling new business leadership toward heights of both strategic accomplishment and sometimes individual excess (Park 2012). For instance, we are presently in what has been described as the seventh acquisitions wave – and the third acquisitions wave of the globalization era – calling on business leaders to demonstrate an often perplexing combination of both innovative management and protective actions (Park and Gould 2017). The seventh acquisitions wave coincides with the proliferation of information in the digital economic era. Specific events and challenges seemingly unique to each of our exemplar executives further illustrate common themes and lessons concerning the reconciliation of information overload and effective action. We look at Musk, Zuckerberg, and Trump, in turn, as each encounters and resolves – or fails to resolve – leadership and management crises within the broader digital business, economic, and pandemic context of their dilemmas.

Tesla: Mall World Meets Green Energy – Upscale Transport and Technological Innovation in the Automobile Industry

Elon Musk is one of the three exemplars of a digitally interconnected yet arguably strategically, economically, and psychologically disconnected corporate CEO or political leader. Musk presents in worldwide media outlets as a respected, highly visible, hugely financially successful, serial entrepreneur, who has been involved in the founding of numerous companies including PayPal, Tesla, and SpaceX (Baggaley 2018). His digital image and fame have transcended those of virtually as all the other founders of firms in industries where he has a presence (Assis and Shaw 2018). An active cyber communicator, he has over 30 million followers on Twitter, with the number still increasing (Trackalytics 2019). He has repeatedly demonstrated that he knows how to use – and some would say abuse – his social media power (Wheeler 2018). He is not alone among the exemplars showcased in his ability to use social media massively to his advantage.

Affirming the breadth and efficacy of his digital interconnectedness in the form of his millions of followers, Musk has shown no reluctance to engage repeatedly – on seemingly an almost daily basis – with various business and popular media outlets. For instance, whether inadvertently or deliberately, he in July 2018 defamed a rescue diver engaged in a perilous extraction of schoolchildren trapped in an aboveground marine cave in Thailand (Davies 2018). He later retracted these rash musings and apologized. Then, in September 2018, in his attempts to shore up the financial status of Tesla, he prematurely and inappropriately tweeted his plans for the company's privatization (Boudette and Phillips 2018). He subsequently retracted and apologized yet again; but "the tweet that cost him $20 million" resulted in an SEC fine and precipitated his resignation of the chairmanship of Tesla (Telford 2018), gaining him both further infamy and renown. In November 2019 he announced a brief break from Twitter – and returned just days later with even more followers (Trackalytics 2020; Vigdor 2019).

Stripped of the Tesla chairmanship after the inappropriate privatization tweeting during the fall of 2018, Musk continued at Tesla with only the CEO position, in addition to his positions and entrepreneurial pursuits at his other companies (Goldstein 2018). He had already perpetuated his celebrity status to the point that his photo can be widely identified without an accompanying caption and his name needs no qualification as "founder of" or "head of" any organization (Wheeler 2018). Simply the names "Elon" and "Elon Musk" or his widely appearing image on its own generates immediate recognition. Millions of people in the USA and around the world follow his name, his image, his companies, his accomplishments, and even his dating life. Elon Musk the individual/CEO/entrepreneur has become – through electronic media – a digitally enhanced global phenomenon.

Musk's voluminous Twitter output illustrates his conversancy with social media and interest to engage in frequent interaction with his "followers," who may or may not be identical to his employees, shareholders, or broader stakeholders. Notwithstanding his stature and outreach to mount a global social media deluge, Musk has exhibited evidence of a strategic divorcement from the performance realities of at least one of his firms, Tesla, which is worth considering in further detail. During late 2017 through 2018, activist and hedge fund investors began to show signs of unrest and interest to replace Musk in his corporate top leadership position at Tesla due to the long run of negative profits and the riskiness of an over-consolidation of power in the firm (Kopecki 2018). Instead of responding promptly and directly to legitimate strategic performance concerns, Musk continued with his Twitter outbursts unabated. His tweeting of his privatization pipe dream ultimately cost him as much $40 million, due to subsequent fines beyond even the initial $20 million reported (Disparte 2018). As mentioned, Musk had to resign as chairman of the board of Tesla (Mejia 2018) while retaining the still considerable and highly influential responsibilities of CEO (Berger 2018). These types of losses may in one sense humanize him, but in other senses the chairmanship loss and the fine distance him from a spectrum of stakeholders. Through his reported conspicuous consumption and the abundant media coverage of his lavish personal lifestyle – as well as an unrelenting work ethic – he has repeatedly differentiated himself from his generally affluent customer base and loyal global followers (Wood 2014). Although his work ethic and innovativeness could be considered positively, many of his actions exemplify a form of overconfidence consistent with hubris (e.g., Roll 1986), as well as an avid desire for self-promotion and differentiation consistent with the tenets of social identity theory (Bromiley and Rau 2016; Tajfel and Turner 1979).

To their credit, Musk and his fellow founders and colleagues have boldly created a new niche in a relatively traditionalist auto world with the Tesla hybrid vehicles. In a mature and intermittently stagnating industry, the Tesla innovators fueled a momentum not seen since Henry Ford and the Model T (Watts 2005), Ferdinand Porsche and the Volkswagen (Ludvigsen 2009), or the amazing success of the Acura, Infiniti, and Lexus luxury car brands only brief decades after the initial tentative motorcycle manufacturing forays from nuclear-ravaged Japan into global markets (Economist 2014). Whether it is more of an automobile or a battery innovation (McFadden 2018); whether it is due to the mall venues and waiting lists and a calculated absence from the conventional auto advertising and sales techniques (Pruitt 2017); or whether it is the still-startling combination of groundbreaking innovation and breathtaking design (previously the almost exclusive domain of Apple in the technology giant world), Tesla has unquestionably made an impact and established an unprecedented social media outreach in the auto industry (Hawkins 2017). The leadership interconnections with the present, wait-listed, and aspirational consumer base are worldwide, prolific, and strong. Within less than 15 years of its founding, Tesla attained a soaring – although perhaps overstated and ephemeral – market valuation and worldwide brand name recognition requiring up to or over a century by competitors to achieve (Fortune 2017).

Yet the very reasons for the unparalleled interconnectedness of Musk are also giving rise to repeated instances of his own isolation, as can be seen through delving deeper into some of his strategic performance issues. The presently most visible of the many companies of which he has been a founder, Tesla, has, as of this writing, had only four profitable quarters and one overall annual profit – in 2019 (Isidore 2020) – since its publicly traded inception (Harwell 2018) and despite its vaunted market capitalization (Matousek 2018). The founder, Musk, is highly visible; the car is only somewhat less visible and has been appearing more widely starting with increased production rollouts around 2017 and with the 2018 online launch of the more moderately priced Model 3, yet the car still remains an aspirational or entirely unattainable luxury for most consumers (C. Jones 2019). Despite its prized status as environmentally beneficial (or at least not yet known to be harmful), it has been economically (due to price) or practically (due to production levels) out of reach for most car buyers. While Tesla experienced a historic quarter with the 2019 introduction of the Model 3 (Harwell 2018; Wattles 2018), that profitability was not sustained into the next quarter (McCormick 2019), although overall the year ended in the black for the firm. In addition, the most forward-thinking among the environmentally conscious critics have raised questions about the Tesla battery's composition (Westervelt 2016), as well as its longevity and recyclability (Gardiner 2017). Fossil fuels and extractable energy resources are not involved in the rechargeable batteries of Tesla, but the impact of the hard elements present in these long-range batteries winding up in landfill has been a source of concern. The longer-term environmental and health implications of the battery disposal are not yet fully known.

From these perspectives, the isolation of Musk emerges. He has a mass market image but not a mass market product. Tesla the firm has not yet performed consistently in stock price, profitability, or even reputation, as the isolation of the founder simultaneously becomes more apparent. Musk tweeted of IPOs, high-status investment banking, and private equity advisors when none of these relationships or events contractually existed. His imaging, marketing, and social media skills make him widely and deeply interconnected within the digital economy. At the same time, the historically erratic performance of Tesla and Musk's apparent lack of grasp of certain key realities, alongside his own burgeoning personal wealth and hubris, all contribute to his separation and isolation from stakeholder interests and needs and perhaps ultimately even from the leadership of a firm he helped found. He has been perhaps overly concerned with image, brand, and a personal reputation built up through digital interconnection – at the risk of diminishing financial returns and profitability and endangering the chances for a global consumer outreach built at least as much on product performance as on founder personality.

The very strengths that Musk has exhibited as a technology leader and entrepreneur – boldness in thinking, looking to innovative new solutions, willingness to take on and try to defy long odds – have put him on unsettled ground in dealing with the novel coronavirus of 2019, global pandemic (Woodward 2020), which first surfaced near the exotic animal markets of Wuhan, China, in December of that year (Maron 2020). Whether from a business, an innovation, or a philanthropic humanitarian perspective (Higgins 2020), Musk struggled with the pandemic. Accustomed to taking on the long shots and pushing the boundaries of the possible, he initially recklessly downplayed the by now medically and scientifically established risks of the virus, namely, its long incubation period and what has been termed its stealth transmission (Lopez and Matousek 2020). Musk insisted for a month that his factories continue to run (Holmes 2020); continued tweeting voluminously, if not always with clear content and objectives; and committed, waffled over, and then recommitted substantial funds and ventilators toward the treatment of those stricken with the potentially highly dangerous and severe respiratory infection (Coffey 2020). He has also continued to display his innovative characteristics of questioning, networking, and brainstorming (Vance 2017). His approach is not passive (Stewart 2020); it could even sometimes be termed impactful and evolving (Berke and Hartmans 2020); but it demonstrates more of the inchoate thinking of the early-stage innovator and entrepreneur struggling for ideas to coalesce toward viable solutions than of the clear-sighted commander dealing with a sudden and relatively unknown crisis situation.

From the perspective of leadership challenges in the digital era, Elon Musk's futuristic helmsmanship of Tesla, SpaceX, Neuralink, and the literally named Boring Company (for penetrating into the earth for the creation of massive transportation networks), as well as his ownership of Hyperloop, the superfast aboveground transportation brand, has attracted customers, investors, and capitalization. His humanitarian and philanthropic actions in the pandemic, as well as his firms long-term corporate profitability and stock price performance, have been less clear. Global image recognition and millions of Twitter followers do not substitute for a strong business strategy, focused giving, and stakeholder confidence. Musk's track record of risk taking and some positive payoffs, as well as his capabilities for innovation and outreach, can perhaps continue to build areas of strength for him in moving forward in times of crisis.

Facebook: Profiteering in the Information Age

Another of the exemplar CEOs is Mark Zuckerberg, who by the very nature of his central business, Facebook, is highly digitally interconnected and centrally embedded in the social media revolution. Yet he has demonstrated disconnectedness and isolation with respect to ethics, innovation, and what could be termed the seasoned intuition of a battle-hardened corporate strategist. Zuckerberg illustrates additional dimensions of the juxtaposition of interconnectedness with isolation. As CEO of

Facebook, he has been viewed as innovative yet also derivative (Barr 2018), struggling through acquisitions to stay on the leading edge in social media and demonstrating – an again potentially derivative – philanthropy while also exhibiting the challenges of confronting an ethical conundrum. As has now been widely recognized and researched, the Facebook social media phenomenon can be traced back to earlier social media platforms (Arthur 2009) and often complex and conflicted interactions with fellow founders or almost-founders, including Tyler and Cameron Winklevoss and Eduardo Saverin (e.g., Carlson 2012; Kosoff 2016). The Facebook development team interjected new elements increasing the attractiveness of their platform to both extant users of other social media, such as MySpace, and users who had at that point not yet ventured into the online and social media worlds. Additionally, within about 5 years of the Facebook launch in 2004 and IPO in 2012, it became apparent that there were numerous privacy issues and concerns (Senguptanov 2011; Vanian 2018). Initially, Facebook surmounted some of these challenges by introducing further privacy controls and by buying competitors such as Instagram for $1 billion in 2012 and WhatsApp for $19 billion in 2014; the company also purchased assorted smaller and larger firms, including brand-new augmented reality firm Oculus for around $3 billion also in 2014 (Loizos 2017; Toth 2018). The acquisitions count exceeds 75 companies at a cost of over $23 billion and rising (Crunchbase 2019). While Facebook developed a strategy of purging (Barr 2018; Parr 2011; Walden 2011), purchasing (Ramzeen 2019), or dismissing (Jeong 2018) rival founders or firms, Zuckerberg ultimately imperils his own firm and shareholders by pursuing innovation externally through acquisitions and by ignoring social media competitors from emerging markets (Thomas 2018).

The ethical, innovative, and economic disconnections as demonstrated by the Facebook CEO remain (Sanders and Patterson 2019). In the March 2018 post-US presidential election milieu, furor resulted from the disclosure of unwarranted access to personally identifiable information on over 80 million Facebook accounts as a result of data inadvertently or deliberately made available by Facebook to political consulting firm Cambridge Analytica. This firm, Cambridge Analytica, had been hired by the Trump political campaign in 2016 to improve access to amenable or impressionable voters. In the view of many observers and analysts, CEO Zuckerberg could neither adequately defend nor explain the release of such personally identifiable user information to a clearly partisan political consulting firm acting for the Trump campaign as well as other clients (Confessore 2018). Meanwhile Facebook continued shedding users and share value in 2018 while failing to recruit new users as fast as previously (Schneider 2018). The total number of active monthly users continues to climb, but the rate of growth of acquiring new users has consistently fallen particularly among younger demographics (Solon 2018).

While CEO Zuckerberg is the face of a preeminent brand of social media connectivity apparently sanctioning disclosures of user details, he is himself unquestionably protected by his personal wealth and privilege (Frier 2017). While he presides over the brand – Facebook – that heralded the explosion of the global social media phenomenon, he apparently derived rather more inspiration from fellow founders and existing social media than is often acknowledged (Barr 2018). As an apparent icon of innovation, he must now increasingly buy that innovation and usurp the advantages from the competition rather than generating new innovations internally (Parkin 2014). It is not clear how long this strategy can last (Hoium 2018). There is evidence that younger users are increasingly shying away from Facebook (Lang 2015; Sulleyman 2018) in favor of the more recent, innovative, and visual social media such as Snapchat, Twitch (YPulse 2019), and TikTok (Hughes 2020) – although teens also like Instagram and WhatsApp (Moreau 2019), both now owned by Facebook, and reinforcing the point about Facebook buying innovation. As additional risk factors to the waning Facebook social media market dominance, there are ever more offerings from the indefatigable and technologically imperialistic Google (Wagner and Molla 2018); users everywhere express concerns over trust violations and privacy risks (Vanian 2018); and Facebook equivalents from emerging markets tech giants such as Tencent (WeChat) in China and Cardbox in India challenge the global hegemony of a brand previously synonymous with social media (MacBride 2017).

Providing a counterpoint to the strategic blunders, Zuckerberg has ventured into philanthropy. Citing humanitarian concerns – for instance, when he and his wife announced the birth of their first child (Thielman 2015) – he proclaimed his donation of $45 billion in Facebook stock toward using technology for addressing social concerns (Forbes 2017). Rather than creating a charitable foundation, he launched an LLC simultaneously providing himself with substantial tax advantages and far greater latitude in the types of investments that can be made (Eisinger 2015). In essence, the LLC lets him avoid capital gains taxes on stock distributions while not limiting him to strictly philanthropic allocations (Shinal 2017). Zuckerberg seems to lack awareness of the detrimental impact of his token philanthropy, privacy inroads, and innovation appropriation on everyday consumers of social media (The Guardian 2015). As a hyper-wealthy social media mogul in the public eye, he maintains a certain exalted status even as he has come increasingly under fire for his disconnections from stakeholder needs and interests (Entis 2014). Staying attuned to his shareholders and stakeholders may or may not be a strength in his future, as he currently navigates a widening gap between ways in which he has been highly interconnected – through his still massively popular (in terms of sheer numbers of participants) social media platform – and his increasing innovative-ethical-and-economic disconnectedness and isolation (Carman 2017). Author Ben Mezrich has followed Zuckerberg and Facebook for over a decade (Mezrich 2009), and he writes (Mezrich 2019: P1): "From the very beginning, Zuckerberg has shown a pattern of deflecting and discarding things and people that don't conform to his worldview or his ambition." This worldview Mezrich identifies as rooted in repeated betrayals of consumer privacy in pursuit of a business model based on connectivity, where privacy would counteract deep interconnectivity and consequently also profitability. As mentioned, those betrayals have been costly to the firm with continuing reverberations (Isaac and Singer 2019).

There are also interesting interconnections with leadership challenges in the digital economy in the sense of what happens with purported stock market efficiencies – and efficient markets have been upheld as a theoretical ideal for decades – combined with rapid response times in the digital economy. Specifically, when

Facebook encountered – and was alleged to have been involved in – breaches of data and therefore breaches in customer security in March 2018 (Rosenberg et al. 2018), confidence in the senior leadership plummeted (Cadwalladr 2018) and stock prices plunged (Shen 2018). What remains difficult to understand is how both seemingly rebounded, as Zuckerberg and other Facebook top management at least initially were able to reassure analysts and investors – as well as the larger public – that not only had the breaches been addressed but that there would be newer/better/faster/systems implemented to block any such future attempts. After the precipitous plunge, the stock price resurged by May 2018 (Bhardwaj 2018), and the future again looked positive for both the iconic entrepreneurial CEO and the firm. However, if there is one characteristic that is true for top corporate management in the digital economy, it is that nothing stands still. While dinosaurs ruled for millennia, top corporate leaders, also at the top of their metaphorical food chains, typically measure their intervals of dominance in months (CBS 2018).

If the digital economy can mean rapid losses and rapid rejuvenation, it also means rapid losses again. Facebook stock prices rebounded within a few months of the Cambridge Analytica revelations (Mirhaydari 2018) but massively fell by July 2018, as the firm missed projected user increases (Neate 2018) and ended 2018 with undeniable net losses (Rodriguez 2018). In continuation of the privacy and reputational difficulties and in further reification of the financial implications, Facebook in July 2019 received a record-setting $5 billion fine from the FTC for mishandling private consumer data (Fair 2019; Romm 2019). Many industry observers and analysts expressed sentiments that the fine did not go far enough, in part because it did not require acknowledgment by Facebook of intentionality or of any harm resulting to consumers from disclosures of their private data (EPIC 2019; Newcomb 2018; Statt 2019).

If the profiteering and privacy incursions have been issues, the COVID-19 coronavirus has offered something of an opportunity for redemption, or at least for providing further information, if not misinformation, for Zuckerberg and Facebook (Chang and Clegg 2020). Like millions across the USA and around the world, Zuckerberg has been, in his words, housebound, although understandably the term has a somewhat different meaning at billionaire status (Dwoskin 2020). However, the billions have come in handy toward image rehabilitation and redemption, as the Chan Zuckerberg Initiative – the abovementioned flexible philanthropic vehicle founded by Zuckerberg and his wife Priscilla Chan after the birth of their first child (Eisinger 2015) – has dedicated dollars to fighting disease (Shieber 2020). Yet the Facebook algorithms, web server support, and interlocking structure of the social media forum create a tendency toward system overload and misinformation propagation that perhaps cannot be entirely overcome (Paul 2020). In addition, Facebook struggles to deal – in both technology and psychology – with the volume of depressed outpourings from individuals housebound in more straightened circumstances (Newton 2020). It is not clear if the social media platform has the technological or empathetic depth to handle this volume (Durkee 2020). It could come in handy that Zuckerberg's declared concentration – major – at Harvard

(Little 2016), before he left midway through his undergraduate experience, was not computer science but psychology (Barrie 2015; Sanders and Patterson 2019).

Rapid flows of information in the digital epoch are not necessarily about in-depth assimilation of and reflection on that information, but rather about speedy processing, rapid decision-making, and moving quickly on to the next. Facebook has been undeniably fast in ascent (Martineau and Matsakis 2019) and fast in certain aspects of its COVID-19 response (Rodriguez 2020), but whether it has been *right* and just are questions open to interpretation. Where corporate ethicists and even economists have asserted the primacy of *values*-centered leadership (Arrow 1951), Jeff Bezos – founder and leader of tech colossus Amazon – has gone on record to say that he likes to promote leaders and executives who can admit when and where they are wrong (Stillman 2018) but who also have the track record of being predominantly *right* (Welch and Ward 2017). With Bezos as with legendary technology innovator and leader Steve Jobs, *right* exists as a dynamic construct to be repeatedly tested, proved, and improved in the maelstrom of information flows complicating the discernment of clear trends and exalting those with repeatedly revenue-producing insights (Glazer 2018). Stumbling too frequently or dramatically, as Musk and Zuckerberg have both already done and as we will see even further with upcoming exemplar Trump, complicates establishing a legacy of technological, strategic, and also humanitarian success. The digital economy and the challenges of the pandemic have meant abundant, electronic, swiftly accessible information – as well as online interconnections with and viewpoints from millions of stakeholders worldwide – but all leading into decisions made seemingly no less on the bases of hunches and imperfect information now than in preceding eras.

Trump: Not Just an Individual but an Entire Organization

With respect to the previous point of having a seasoned and battle-hardened strategic intuition, our final exemplar occupies an intriguing position as a businessperson politician. By way of background, we examine some upheavals encountered by Donald Trump in his presidency. We further explore his robust stream of social media communications in the context of his economic, psychological, and strategic isolation, counterbalanced by lingering stalwart support.

Donald Trump experienced a turbulent start to his presidency. Heir to and head of the Trump family fortune – known as the Trump Organization – bequeathed to him by his father, he pulled off a stunning political upset in 2016 to attain the highest elected office in the USA. Two years into his term in office, Trump intersected with the Facebook leadership privacy violations, when Zuckerberg was called in 2018 to testify before the US House and Senate due to Facebook user data obtained and unmasked by consulting firm Cambridge Analytica to boost the Trump political campaign prospects (Cadwalladr 2018; Rosenberg et al. 2018). The next year, in 2019, he became enmeshed in impeachment proceedings in the US Congress due to allegations and increasing evidence (Sevastopulo 2019) of his having inappropriately pressured the president of Ukraine to besmirch the standing of former US vice president Joe Biden, a then Trump presidential rival and forthcoming presidential contender (Fedor 2019). Based on similarities to the infamous US Watergate scandal in the 1970s, the pressuring actions have been dubbed "Ukrainegate" and have echoed internationally with adverse consequences for Trump's global reputation (Sevastopulo et al. 2019). Strong partisan lines and deeply held loyalties suggest that the impeachment, regardless of documented evidence or official outcomes, will remain to some extent an irresolvable conundrum on perceptions of wrongdoing.

Born at the start of the US "baby boom" era in 1946, well before the digital revolution, Trump has nevertheless responded to the impeachment proceedings and to previous issues with the social media élan of a much younger millennium-era technology user. Even as numerous individuals testified in high-visibility sessions before Congress, Trump – demonstrating a social media verve bordering on obsession – was simultaneously tweeting ad hominem rebuttals in flawed refutation of already documented credentials and events (P. Baker 2019). Trump has shown himself to be highly adept in his use of social media. Victor in a pyrrhic election and perhaps cognizant of the risks of his position, he has been from the start engaged in Twitter-based outreach with constituents to an extraordinary degree (Jones 2015). These outbursts, among other factors, have been taken in evidence of a degree of overconfidence and self-absorption differentiating Trump from many individuals while also giving him commonality with previous ephemerally powerful and charismatic leaders (Braun 2017; Schyns et al. 2019). His differentiation, which becomes a form of psychological isolation, has also been described as extreme narcissism (e.g., Galvin et al. 2015; Grijalva and Harms 2014). Perhaps not surprisingly given the social media floods and multiple issues, factual and counterfactual contestations, the Trump administration has suffered astonishing internal turmoil and staff departures (Shubber 2019; Tenpas 2019). The imputed levels of presidential narcissism have been implicated in the unusually high levels of Executive Office turnover (Lu and Yourish 2019). Narcissism can produce or reflect a sense of grandiosity and can momentarily inspire followers even while ultimately separating leaders from their realm of influence (Chatterjee and Hambrick 2007; Conway 2019).

Beyond this psychological isolation, we look next at his economic isolation. As a wealthy individual from a wealthy family, Donald Trump has led a relatively insulated life. Nevertheless, he has developed a surprising depth of insight into the lowest common denominators of the mass market psyche and national concerns about economic development, global competitiveness, and personal reassurances for advancement. Perhaps part of this insight stems from stories from the maternal side of the experience of his mother, Mary Anne MacLeod Trump, who was raised in the impoverished setting of an Isle of Lewis croft in Scotland and who worked for several years as a domestic servant in the household of Louise Whitfield Carnegie after initially emigrating from Scotland to the USA (Burleigh 2017; Pilon 2016; Sebak 2018). Donald Trump's Make America Great Again campaign stems at least partly from a broad-based economic malaise, as US consumers have become frightened by job losses and declining real incomes (Stein and Van Damm 2018). While the USA remains the top global economic power in terms of nominal GDP, the USA cedes the first-place ranking to China when GDP becomes adjusted for purchase power parity (Focus Economics 2017). The USA falls even further down the economic rankings in terms of *rate* of economic growth and present as well as predicted contributions to the global economy, compared to the projected ascendancy of the emerging markets (IMF 2017). More recently, global economic shocks such as currency depreciations and trade wars have weakened growth projections from emerging markets while also suggesting the unsustainability of present growth rates in the US economy (Giles 2018).

As president of the USA, Trump has favored tax incentives and policies benefiting the upper half of the top 1% of the income distribution in the country (Stewart 2018). Yet he has maintained the allegiance of many – particularly white female blue collar (Kim 2019), as well as white male blue collar or working-class voters (Lombardo 2018; McAdams 2019). Ironically, in a previous generation, this cohort of voters would typically have been members of another political party and unionized. Trump has bridged the economic isolation of his wealth through an uncanny boundary spanning across the extremes of socioeconomic status. Still, his actions have not always matched his talk. For instance, his reported treatment of undocumented Polish workers building Trump Tower in the 1980s evoked much criticism with respect to secrecy around rule breaking, promises betrayed, and wages unpaid (Bagli 2017). This incident, among others, encapsulated his paradoxical but inherently antithetical intertwining of elite status and common touch (Wigglesworth 2017). He has seemed as if he could combine being both "elite" and relating to "everyman," yet this type of dichotomy cannot be sustained indefinitely (Lubit 2002).

His economic isolation extended to a scientific and intellectual isolation in his failure to respond promptly and effectively to the COVID-19 coronavirus, a subset of the sudden acute respiratory syndrome category of viruses, pandemic (Ho and Dajose 2020). Trump failed to grasp already then widely available data and analytics indicating a super-exponential rate of spread of the highly transmissible virus, and he likewise failed to proactively urge availability of the antibody tests already established as effective in the China, South Korea, and European locations of the earlier penetration of the virus (Abutaleb et al. 2020). In addition, he incorporated elements of xenophobia and hate-mongering into his rhetoric of verbal offense against mainland China (Weiner 2020) while strikingly omitting – until the virus reached a true crisis level in the USA – mention of testing and containing measures the aforementioned countries had found effective in combatting the virus. His scientific and intellectual isolationism and deliberate avoidance of hard truths, in addition to previous issues and transgressions, reinforced an image of the US presidency as social media-inclined, science-averse, and in some manner a laughingstock and buffoon as infection rates in the USA quickly surpassed those reported in China (Pilkington & Pengelly 2020). The delays exacerbated the already flourishing "digital divide" (NTIA 1998; OECD 2000; UNCTAD 2019) – the severely limited access to wired, mobile, Internet, and various other technological resources and the information available from those resources (Roberts 2019) –

experienced by up to 30% of the US population (Schumacher and Kent 2020), including many children (Vick, 2017), as well as over one billion globally, principally the socioeconomically disadvantaged and in emerging market economies (Silver et al. 2019). When quarantine and containment measures finally went into effect in the USA and sent multitudes home to conduct their lives online, many did not have the requisite online access to continue with work, educational, and personal connectivity pursuits (Finley 2020). For the millions in the USA on the wrong side of the digital divide, the delayed responses to COVID-19 have meant not only income deprivation, physical distancing, and sheltering in place but also a scarcity of information, entertainment, and socialization while isolated at home with an inadequate supply of digital devices or insufficient access to Internet connectivity (Ovide and Crawford 2020).

Finally, in the sense of strategic isolation, Trump has been many times mentioned as a successful businessperson and entrepreneur, who forged his own path despite his fortunate wealthy origins. Yet it has also been asserted, with appropriate numerical calculations, that he would have been just as wealthy today not owing to his strategic insights and business acumen but simply by having invested his inherited wealth in an index fund (Levine 2015). If his strategic business sense has not been his key competitive advantage, what did propel Trump forward in the building industry, into the public consciousness, and ultimately into the presidential seat? Although in many respects – economically, psychologically, and strategically – isolated and disconnected, Trump has, as noted, remained in fundamental ways interconnected with his core constituency. This paradox reinforces the juxtaposition of interconnectedness and isolation alongside the rewards that can be reaped from social media outreach on pivotal issues of constituent concern.

Overall, Trump has been a conundrum. His upbringing, his wealth, and even his political stances have isolated him in many ways both nationally and globally (Poushter and Fagan 2018), yet he has also shown a mass market touch sufficient to have propelled him into the Oval Office (Bickart et al. 2017). He has shrewdly deployed social media for maintaining his core voter support. His late-night and early-morning tweets have shared his thinking with his more than 60 million – and still increasing (Trackalytics 2018) – followers in the social media-savvy digitally interconnected world, bringing him closer and closer to his voters and followers through their frequently consulted electronic devices. Staying attuned to his core supporters has enabled Trump to maintain his form of simultaneous interconnectedness and isolation. Demonstrating allegiance, his Republican supporters in Congress have remained at least initially steadfast and responsive to his anti-impeachment Twitter bombardment (Blow 2019; Savage 2019). Trump has retained many voting loyalists who remain supportive of his platform (Brownstein 2019) and seem to be unconcerned with his extreme self-absorption and often dramatic absence of empathy, remorse, or compassion (Gourguechon 2019). An expedient, highly anticipated and welcomed COVID-19 economic assistance bill has also been helpful to his cause, at least in the short term (Werner et al. 2020), while the scope of the pandemic remained uncertain (Werner and DeBonis 2020). Despite flourishing scandals and accusations and multiple instances of his economic, psychological, and strategic isolation, Trump has found ways to navigate those divides, even if only temporarily.

We now turn from our specific exemplars to examining broader implications for leadership opportunities and challenges in the global digital and pandemic epoch.

Leadership Challenges in the Digital Pandemic Epoch

Leadership has been a topic of enduring interest from ancient (Tzu and Giles 1910) through Renaissance (Machiavelli 1513/1992) and modern times (e.g., Pfeffer 2015; Selznick 1957). Moreover, the close interconnections of leadership, influence, and power have been topics of considerable management scholarship (e.g., Zaleznik 1970). The complexity inherent in the inception and implementation of leadership vision has made these topics difficult to understand (Follett 2004), but known when seen (West 2017). That is, people can often struggle to define the essence of leadership or how to be a good leader, but there can be remarkable agreement on who great leaders are. Likewise there has been attention to the dark side of leadership and to leadership gone awry (Higgs 2009; Lubit 2002). What is different now are phenomena such as the social media frenzy and the global-digital-interconnected-sharing-experience-global-gig economy in an epoch dominated by the Internet and the proliferation of information (Isaacson 2014). Leaders must also contend with longer-standing strategic issues involving power dynamics and the juxtaposition of competition and collaboration to thrive in worldwide markets (Park 2016, 2019). In an age of ever more permeable boundaries and faster communications – between individuals as well as across time and space – what are the implications for the modern executive, managing a global consumer base that in the aggregate never sleeps and that has widely shared interests yet also highly diversified tastes and preferences?

Virtual Worlds and Organizational Directions

Modern executives have become their own avatars of innovation, living in virtual worlds (Kohler et al. 2009) in many ways disconnected from the daily reality of their millions of stakeholders worldwide (Fu 2017). Yet these online, cyber, virtual worlds of carefully managed social media outreach and – avowed or disavowed – celebrity status demonstrate the amazingly rapid scaling up of information dissemination alongside the careful crafting of narratives avowing the enhancement of stakeholder interests and minimization of personal interest (Denning 2011). Such statements of community and stakeholder solidarity, belied by personal fortunes increasing at seemingly exponential levels (Rotman 2014), bring us back to classic dilemmas of managerialism and principal-agent conflicts (Berle and Means 1932), and even more fundamentally to the risks of plutocracy (DeSilver 2018). Rule by the rich – whether by elected political office, by inheritance, or from various social media platforms –

may seem laughable, until it is not (Domhoff 1967). These technology and business leaders, whether they are similar to their images or not, exert real impact in real-world organizations.

The impact of leadership encompasses concerns both inside and outside the organization. Inside the organization, leadership in the digital economy involves challenges such as transforming organizational structures, inspiring new projects and product development teams, and maintaining a frontline position in human capital and talent development (Goldberg 2017; Kluz and Firlej 2016).

Looking across organizational boundaries, leadership challenges in the digital economy center on issues such as evolving and enhancing business models, innovation ecosystems, and value chains (Ritter and Ruggero 2017). Outside the organization, the increasingly global array of stakeholders – customers, suppliers, competitors, analysts, and investors – and factors in the macroeconomic business environment concern and challenge corporate leaders. Structures, systems, and stakeholders, whether internal or external, have each become more complex and differentiated – as well as more agile – in the digital economy, spawning additional issues for leaders who must address simultaneously global- and local-level concerns, multiple online and in-person interactions, and products and services for technologically adroit early adopters as well as more traditional and technologically conservative consumers (Gartner 2017). These multiple concerns are broad yet also can be focused along specific lines of issues such as business models and the changing role of intermediation in the context of ethical and sustainable as well as financially remunerative performance.

Business Models, Intermediation, and the Enduring Importance of Ethical Perspectives

There is a range of leadership-in-the-digital-era considerations around business models and stakeholder concerns. For instance, new forms of platform business models reflect the advancement of the digital revolution and the momentum of the sharing economy (Rietveld et al. 2019). These models link customers and suppliers in new ways providing unprecedented avenues for intermediation. That is, connections among different stakeholder groups or between company and customer are not always direct. Some type of agent or intermediary can help forge a connection, bringing together the customer and the asset (Zhao et al. 2019). Sometimes the assets to be brought to the customers are the leaders themselves, as when corporate boards perform searches to find the best leaders for their organizations (Khurana 2002). In the sociological tradition, intermediation and disintermediation had been viewed as alternatives, with the bridging role acknowledged as sometimes valuable but not necessarily desirable or essential (Simmel 2006). In the earlier days of digital connectivity, preferences leaned toward disintermediation to reduce costs and inefficiencies and to get as close to the customer as possible (Jallat and Capek 2001). Now in the days of intensive digital interconnections, intermediation has become highly valued for quickly mobilizing and allocating resources to customers (Porter and Heppelmann 2014). Those leaders with the vision and acumen to contribute to these new business models and momentum – reaching new customers and making money while also safeguarding concerns such as customer privacy, ethical conduct, and care of the natural environment – win accolades as well as ethical and financial results (Desjardins 2018).

The ethical and related perspectives of corporate citizenship, responsibility, and sustainability are key parts of the global strategic leadership outlook. The profit-making and often environmentally sustaining aspects of the new business models and innovation ecosystems involve technology as well as people and values. Technology facilitates new approaches to long-standing dilemmas in developing new products and services – for which people are willing to pay – and getting them quickly to market. The evolving relationship between work and technology centers on *people* – whether as individuals, teams, and organizations – performing tasks simplified by technology but doing so in the context of an increasingly complex and competitive global business environment (Glenn et al. 2017). Multiple cultures, currencies, climates, and differences in consumer tastes and preferences as well as variations in levels of national economic development must all be taken into account (Ghemawat 2001). The escalation in complexity on several dimensions demands increased leadership attention.

Managing in an Economically, Sociologically, Technologically and Medically Complex Landscape

Business leadership requires comprehension of sociologically, economically, technologically, and even scientifically and medically complex scenarios. While technology provides the infrastructure facilitating communications and connections – and can provide the *appearance* of many more connections being in place – digital outreach does not automatically mean a highly functioning business connection has been formed nor that a fast and effective science-based response can be mounted in times of epidemiologic crisis. We consider first the sociological- and technological-driven connections and then implications in situations of medical complexity.

As an example of technologies in interconnection, LinkedIn, the professional connection platform, will suggest connections and then tell users they are connected; but in fact, a vital next step remains to be completed; the initial "congratulations you have made a connection" represents only an *invitation* to connect extended to the person with whom LinkedIn says you have already "made a connection." The invited party must accept to confirm the connection. Then, at even the next level, the connection should function in various ways to add value to the individuals who are connected. If it is a business connection, adding value nowadays in a business sense would typically mean fulfilling the people, planet, and profits triple bottom line – that is, making money (profits), protecting stakeholders (who are different groups of people affected by your business), and safeguarding the environment (planet). This organizational or corporate multidimensional mission comes to the heart of our purpose in reflecting on dilemmas confronting the modern executive.

To be connected in appearance – to have the digital capability and outreach for interconnection – is not the same as to be connected in ways adding real value for business purposes. The modern executive too often fails to recognize the performance risks of being seemingly interconnected but in reality isolated and uninformed (Baker 1990). In this respect we echo the leadership philosophy of Amazon founder Jeff Bezos. Leadership not only draws on networks, connections, and credentials; it also becomes vitally a question of making "the right" (Welch and Ward 2017) decisions for adding value.

The challenges of leadership in the digital economy also concern millennia-old issues of influence and motivation. Digital capabilities facilitate the translation of innovative ideas into business realities. Digital business strategy and technology strategy fundamentally center on communication and collaboration, rallying organizational incumbents and stakeholders toward an articulated vision. Modern digital strategy and the historic art of influence converge in building and sustaining a leadership innovation and performance momentum. As seen with Musk and Trump, mobilizing digitally on Twitter can be either a form of noise or a form of influence. Sometimes the noise dominates, and the medium overrides the message. Knowing when to reach out for a synchronous voice-to-voice conversation "in real time" or "in real life" – and with key impactful individuals – can mean the difference between success and failure. As taught in management communications classes, "you are your own best visual aid" – meaning you, the authentic person, and the key elements of the message, not just the latest in digital sophistication, are the effective means to demonstrate mastery in communication.

Rallying effectively in times of pandemic crisis represents a problematic and untried arena for most leaders, as pandemics tend to be more broadly spaced and not encountered by the same generations of leadership. Typically, business leaders within a generation will encounter cycles or waves of business volatility, usually not concomitant with occurrences of devastating health consequences. Nevertheless, business cycles or waves and pandemic waves can coincide with sometimes intensive economic impact. The convergence between business cycles and national and global health crises can exert extreme blows to the economy such as in the successive flu pandemics and mortality rates of the early twentieth century, the stock market run-up and then crash of the 1920s, and then the global recession of the 1930s. The argument here is not for strict causation but for the recurring coexistence or close sequence of business, health, and economic events. Digital interconnections and modalities allow us to communicate faster to try to address health issues and economic downturns, but we need to provide tactics and solutions to take advantage of these communications particularly during urgent or emergency-level situations.

Disrupting Practice While Venerating Tradition

Digital workplace automation and business models disrupt established practices yet can be seen to venerate leadership traditions (Feser 2016). Trends in artificial intelligence, blockchain, machine learning, robotics, natural language learning, big data, and data science may contribute to workplace automation and cost reduction. However, these innovations also increase the complexity inherent in business management. The need for an overarching understanding and a clear distillation of vision and mission remain leadership imperatives. Human fears concerning loss of employment, status, and income remain the same. These deep-level concerns must be addressed lest they be forgotten. For instance, new business models in the abstract are generally greeted with approval, particularly by end users experiencing enhanced transportation, travel, dining, real estate location, and accommodation – as well as new ways of finding and staying connected to important people in our lives – and by the companies profiting from these business model, product, and service innovations. But what comes between the people and profits? Workplace automation generates huge fears of job loss. Yet the attractive new business models do not necessarily mean workplace innovation, nor do they necessarily imply ultimate job loss. If job loss or job change is involved, clarity is essential. The aphorism that "businesses do not downsize their way to greatness" can be adapted for the digital economy to mean that "businesses do not automate their way to greatness." Fundamental leadership challenges around exercising power and influence, protecting and improving the lives of followers, and maintaining organizational momentum persist (Heifetz and Linsky 2017).

Technology, Power, and Organizational Context

Technology means the possibility that some or all products or services now desired will transform dramatically in upcoming years. For instance, for all the allure of the new Teslas, will autonomous driving and alternative transportation services at some not-too-distant point in time displace our current conceptions of personal vehicles (Naughton and Welch 2019)? Will Facebook tumble to ever newer, trendier – and perhaps more privacy-preserving – forms of social media? The joy of driving, the joy of connecting, and – for some – the joy of power are part of the fundamental needs and desires to which the exemplar leaders speak and are part of why they continue to have influence and interconnections, although the influence may eventually wane as their connections with consumers and other stakeholders become attenuated through the types of economic, psychological, and strategic disconnections we have examined with our exemplars.

Granted, some types of organizations, particularly for-profit enterprises, frequently have limited longevity, but other types of organizations – for instance, not-for-profit entities involving institutions such as higher education, religion, or shared affiliations (e.g., Masons) – have endured for centuries and even millennia. Leaders in the digital economy or any era must recognize their organizational context and decide how best to proceed. Sustaining profit-making momentum may require "creative destruction," dramatically changing and reducing, combining, or otherwise morphing into new organizational forms and identities while preserving the aforementioned fundamentals of connections. Strategic change can transform organizational identities as well as enhance competitive capabilities and outcomes (Park et al. 2018). Carefully selected and implemented strategic actions – whether involving an internal emphasis such as on new product development or an external perspective such as with mergers and acquisitions – provide opportunities for innovation. As illustrated by the many companies purchased by Facebook in order to maintain its competitive advantage in innovative products (Crunchbase 2019; Toth 2018), the connection between acquisitions and innovation clearly exists and has been previously noted (Park and Meglio 2019). Preserving different forms of not-for-profits and key aspects of not-for-profit organizational identity requires paying close attention to not just innovation but also to core values, vision, and mission. The Latin-language ATMs in Vatican City are an example of capturing both the history and the present of language and technology in that setting (Hooper 2012). Technology and automation in the digital economy reinforce the centrality of organizational and leadership ethics and directions and avoiding ethical transgressions (LaForgia et al. 2019).

Conclusion: Connecting, Disconnecting, and Reconnecting in Crises

Returning to the previously mentioned perspectives on leadership, strategy, and recurring waves of business tactics and maneuvers – particularly the premiere business strategy tactic of mergers and acquisitions – as well as of disease cycles and economic impact, in conclusion we position leadership connection and disconnection in the context of successive ages of crisis. We take the global business perspective and the health perspective in turn. From the second (1920s) through the seventh (starting in 2014) merger waves – that is, from the previous century through the turn of the millennium – we have seen a return of income polarization and extreme disparities in access to opportunity and social mobility. In the interim, concomitant with the rise and fall of unions in the USA, income levels converged. The fourth-to-fifth merger waves (1980s and 1990s) heralded the explicit greed-is-good unrestrained opportunism and wealth-building takeovers, followed sometimes by incarceration, ostracism, and stigma for the corporate or investment leaders for illegal maneuvers. The momentum then transitioned to the unbridled overseas expansions, mega-mergers, and mergers-of-equals of the sixth and seventh waves. We have looked at modern business executives, particularly in the upper echelons, being highly digitally interconnected – and often extremely conversant in the use of social media – but at the same time dramatically disconnected from the strategic performance realities of the companies they are leading. These executives may have mass market appeal, but they distance themselves from the social immobility and income compression of what used to be known as the working class. In sum, we apprehend increasing digital interconnectedness juxtaposed against decreasing levels of strategic, economic, and ethical awareness within the ranks of corporate leadership. In addition to strategic, economic, and ethical isolation, the rising volume of information has seemed to paradoxically correspond to lower information uptake.

As revealed in the exemplar cases, this conjunction of circumstances influences digital economy executives being both isolated and uninformed amidst the increasing challenges of leadership.

Intriguingly, business cycles and disease cycles have coincided in the twentieth and twenty-first centuries (Lotterman 2020), a simultaneity that has challenged at least one of our exemplars. Paralleling with even longer-standing history, waves of pandemics have swept nations, regions, and the world (Janus 2020). From the global perspective and beginning with evidence from Bronze Age and even prehistoric times, early forms of smallpox and measles, through the bubonic plague, many variations of flu, polio, cholera, HIV, and then COVID-19, crises of infectious disease have recurred and have challenged scientists, healthcare providers, and organizational leaders in finding solutions (MacArthur 2020). Whether crises involve going viral in an undesired informational sense or in the realm of infectious diseases, pandemics of social disconnection and health and safety distress challenge the modern business leaders in both cyber and physical space. Reconnection can perhaps be accomplished by returning to core communication and ethical values and behaviors transcending yet also addressing these crises.

Cross-References

- ▶ A Return to the Good Old Days: Populism, Fake News, Yellow Journalism, and the Unparalleled Virtue of Business People
- ▶ Conclusion: Management Theory in Crisis
- ▶ Conflicting Understandings of the Industrial Revolution and Its Consequences: The Founding Figures of British Management History
- ▶ Economic Foundations: Adam Smith and the Classical School of Economics
- ▶ Henry Ford and His Legacy: An American Prometheus
- ▶ Introduction: Public Policy Failure, the Demise of Experts, and the Dawn of a New Era
- ▶ Labor and Employment Practices: the Rise and Fall of the New Managerialism
- ▶ Management History in the Modern World: An Overview
- ▶ Trade Union Decline and Transformation: Where to for Employment Relations?
- ▶ What Is Management?
- ▶ Why Did the Great Recession Fail to Produce a *New* New Deal in the USA?

Acknowledgements The author thanks Professors Anthony Gould, Bradley Bowden, and all the editors of the *Palgrave Macmillan Handbook of Management History* and Palgrave senior editor Ruth Lefevre for their guidance and encouragement for this contribution. Professor John Carroll of the MIT Sloan School of Management has consistently inspired my innovative lines of thinking. Special thanks to the Boston University (BU) MET Department of Administrative Sciences and Office of the Dean, as well as to BU graduate students Maxim Tsybanov, Medina Altynbayeva, Yaqiu Guo, and Esteban Lopez for invaluable research support and assistance.

References

Abutaleb Y, Dawsey J, Nakashima E, Miller G (2020) The U.S. was beset by denial and dysfunction as the coronavirus raged, published 4 April 2020 by The Washington Post. Available online at https://www.washingtonpost.com/national-security/2020/04/04/coronavirus-government-dysfunction/. Accessed 10 Apr 2020

Arrow KJ (1951) Social choice and individual values. Wiley, New York

Arthur C (2009) Facebook paid up to $65m to founder Mark Zuckerberg's ex-classmates, published 12 February 2009 by The Guardian. Available online at https://www.theguardian.com/technology/2009/feb/12/facebook-mark-zuckerberg-ex-classmates. Accessed 3 Mar 2019

Assis C, Shaw JM (2018) Elon Musk is more famous than ever, and maybe more dangerous, published 7 September 2018 by MarketWatch. Available online at https://www.marketwatch.com/story/elon-musk-is-more-famous-than-ever-and-maybe-more-dangerous-2018-08-31. Accessed 28 Jan 2019

Baggaley K (2018) Elon Musk's hyperloop dream may come true – and soon, published 11 March 2018 by NBC News. Available online https://www.nbcnews.com/mach/science/elon-musk-s-hyperloop-dream-may-come-true-soon-ncna855041. Accessed 25 Jan 2019

Bagli CV (2017) Trump paid over $1 million in labor settlement, documents reveal, published 27 November 2017 by The New York Times. Available online at https://www.nytimes.com/2017/11/27/nyregion/trump-tower-illegal-immigrant-workers-union-settlement.html. Accessed 7 Mar 2019

Baker WE (1990) Market networks and corporate behavior. Am J Sociol 96:589–625. https://doi.org/10.1086/229573

Baker P (2019) Key Takeaways from Marie Yovanovitch's hearing in the impeachment inquiry: even as Ms. Yovanovitch was testifying about "the smear campaign against me," President Trump hurled insults at her on Twitter, published 15 November 2019 by The New York Times. Available online at https://www.nytimes.com/2019/11/15/us/politics/impeachment-hearings.html. Accessed 25 Nov 2019

Barr S (2018) When did Facebook start? The story behind a company that took over the world: the social media platform currently has more than two billion users worldwide, published 23 August 2018 by The Independent UK. Available online at https://www.independent.co.uk/life-style/gadgets-and-tech/facebook-when-started-how-mark-zuckerberg-history-harvard-eduardo-saverin-a8505151.html. Accessed 3 Mar 2019

Barrie J (2015) The worst-kept secret about Mark Zuckerberg is that he's *not* actually a coding genius, published 5 January 2015 by BusinessInsider. Available online at https://www.businessinsider.com/mark-zuckerberg-is-not-actually-a-coding-genius-2015-1. Accessed 18 Dec 2019

Berger S (2018) Here's what CEOs actually do all day: Tesla's CEO Elon Musk, published by CNBC 20 June 2018. Available online at https://www.cnbc.com/2018/06/20/harvard-study-what-ceos-do-all-day.html. Accessed 25 Jan 2019

Berke J, Hartmans A (2020) Elon Musk says Tesla will make ventilators in case of a shortage caused by the coronavirus – here are all the other humanitarian crises he's tried to fix, published 21 March 2020 by BusinessInsider. Available online at https://www.businessinsider.com/elon-musk-efforts-humanitarian-crises-and-their-status-2018-7. Accessed 8 Apr 2020

Berle AA, Means GC (1932) The modern corporation and private property. Macmillan, New York

Bhardwaj P (2018) Eight weeks after the Cambridge Analytica scandal, Facebook's stock price bounces back to where it was before the controversy, published 11 May 2018 by BusinessInsider. Available online at https://www.businessinsider.com/facebooks-stock-back-up-cambridge-analytica-charts-2018-5. Accessed 15 Feb 2019

Bickart B, Fournier S, Nisenholtz M (2017) What Trump understands about using social media to drive attention, published 1 March 2017. Available online at https://hbr.org/2017/03/what-trump-understands-about-using-social-media-to-drive-attention. Accessed 23 Feb 2019

Blow CM (2019) For Trump, impeachment is a show, published 24 November 2019 in The New York Times. Available online at https://www.nytimes.com/2019/11/24/opinion/trump-impeachment.html. Accessed 25 Nov 2019

Boudette NE, Phillips M (2018) Elon Musk says Tesla may go private, and its Stock Soars, published 7 August 2018 by The New York Times. Available online at https://www.nytimes.com/2018/08/07/business/tesla-stock-elon-musk-private.html?action=click&module=RelatedLinks&pgtype=Article

Braun S (2017) Leader narcissism and outcomes in organizations: a review at multiple levels of analysis and implications for future research. Front Psychol 8:773–773. https://doi.org/10.3389/fpsyg.2017.00773

Bromiley P, Rau D (2016) Social, behavioral, and cognitive influences on upper echelons during strategy process. J Manag 42(1):174–202. https://doi.org/10.1177/0149206315617240

Brownstein R (2019) Will Trump's racist attacks help him? Ask blue-collar white women – his strategy rests on a bet: that these voters will respond just as enthusiastically to his belligerence as working-class white men, published 25 July 2019 by The Atlantic. Available online at https://www.theatlantic.com/politics/archive/2019/07/trumps-go-back-attacks-white-working-class-women/594805/. Accessed 3 Dec 2019

Burleigh N (2017) Donald Trump's mother, Mary Anne MacLeod, is key to understanding the President's deep insecurity, published 28 December 2017 by Newsweek. Available online at https://www.newsweek.com/trump-mom-mary-anne-macleod-insecurity-deep-president-white-house-ivanka-758644. Accessed 25 Nov 2019

Cadwalladr C (2018) The Cambridge Analytica files – 'I made Steve Bannon's psychological warfare tool': meet the data war whistleblower, published 17 March and 18 March 2018 by The Guardian. Available online at https://www.theguardian.com/news/2018/mar/17/data-war-whistleblower-christopher-wylie-faceook-nix-bannon-trump. Accessed 12 Feb 2019

Carlson N (2012) How Mark Zuckerberg booted his co-founder out of the company, published 15 May 2012 by BusinessInsider. Available online at https://www.businessinsider.com/how-mark-zuckerberg-booted-his-co-founder-out-of-the-company-2012-5. Accessed 23 Nov 2019

Carman A (2017) Mark Zuckerberg has a small army of Facebook employees who delete comments on his page, published 18 January 2017 by The Verge. Available online at https://www.theverge.com/2017/1/18/14314872/mark-zuckerberg-personal-facebook-page-comments-team. Accessed 25 Feb 2019

CBS (2018) Can Facebook restore public trust after Cambridge Analytica scandal? Published on 8 April 2018 by CBS News. Available online at https://www.cbsnews.com/news/facebook-cambridge-analytica-restore-public-trust-after-privacy-scandal/. Accessed 10 Feb 2019

Chang A, Clegg N (2020) How Facebook wants to handle misinformation around the coronavirus epidemic, interview of Nick Clegg by Ailsa Change published 25 March 2020 by NPR All Things Considered. Available online at https://www.npr.org/2020/03/25/821591134/how-facebook-wants-to-handle-misinformation-around-the-coronavirus-epidemic. Accessed 10 Apr 2020

Chatterjee A, Hambrick DC (2007) It's all about me: narcissistic chief executive officers and their effects on company strategy and performance. Adm Sci Q 52(3):351–386. https://doi.org/10.2189/asqu.52.3.351

Coffey D (2020) The week that wasn't in COVID-19: Elon Musk, 'pandemic' scientist's cure, proof COVID-19 was not man-made, published 3 April 2020 by MedScape. Available online at https://www.medscape.com/viewarticle/928119. Accessed 8 Apr 2020

Confessore N (2018) Cambridge Analytica and Facebook: the scandal and the fallout so far, published in the New York Times 4 April 2018. Available online at https://www.nytimes.com/2018/04/04/us/politics/cambridge-analytica-scandal-fallout.html. Accessed 24 Jan 2019

Conway GT III (2019) Unfit for office: Donald Trump's narcissism makes it impossible for him to carry out the duties of the presidency in the way the Constitution requires, published 3 October 2019 by The Atlantic. Available online at https://www.theatlantic.com/ideas/archive/2019/10/george-conway-trump-unfit-office/599128/. Accessed 3 Dec 2019

Crunchbase (2019) Democratizing the way innovators access opportunities – Facebook 77 acquisitions as of 8 February 2019. Available online at https://www.crunchbase.com/organization/facebook/acquisitions/acquisitions_list. Accessed 17 Feb 2019

Davies A (2018) A brief history of Elon Musk's market-moving tweets, published 29 August 2018 by Wired. Available online at https://www.wired.com/story/elon-musk-twitter-stock-tweets-libel-suit/. Accessed 28 Jan 2018

Denning S (2011) The leader's guide to storytelling: mastering the art and discipline of business narrative. Revised edition. Wiley, New York

DeSilver D (2018) For most U.S. workers, real wages have barely budged in decades, published 7 August 2018 by Pew Research Center. Available online at http://www.pewresearch.org/fact-tank/2018/08/07/for-most-us-workers-real-wages-have-barely-budged-for-decades/. Accessed 3 Mar 2019

Desjardins J (2018) The eight major forces shaping the future of the global economy, published 4 October 2018 by the Visual Capitalist. Available online at https://worldview.stratfor.com/article/8-major-forces-shaping-future-global-economy and http://www.visualcapitalist.com/the-8-major-forces-shaping-the-future-of-the-global-economy/. Accessed 20 Oct 2018

Desjardins G, Gould AM, Park KM (2016) Something for nothing in the digital age? Strategic management and the manipulation of 'free' in the Information Millennium. In: Delener N, Fuxman L, Lu FV, Rodrigues S (eds) Exceeding the vision: global business and technology association 18th international conference, Dubai, UAE, October 16–20, pp 552–557. ISSN: 2471-6006. Available online at http://gbata.org/journal-of-global-business-and-technology-jgbat/publications/. Accessed 10 Oct 2019

Disparte D (2018) Elon Musk versus the SEC: when a tweet costs $40 million, published 29 September 2018 by Forbes. Available online at https://www.forbes.com/sites/dantedisparte/2018/09/29/elon-musk-versus-the-sec-when-a-tweet-costs-40-million/#6d15a28b1556. Accessed 28 Jan 2019

Domhoff GW (1967) Who rules America? Prentice-Hall, Englewood Cliffs

Durkee A (2020) Even Facebook is struggling under the weight of the coronavirus, published 25 March 2020 by Vanity Fair. Available online at https://www.vanityfair.com/news/2020/03/facebook-coronavirus-surge-struggle-zuckerberg. Accessed 7 Apr 2020

Dwoskin E (2020) Why the coronavirus pandemic is a test Facebook can't afford to fail: as use of the social media giant's services surge, it could prove to be a moment of redemption for chief executive Mark Zuckerberg, published 27 March 2020 by The Washington Post. Available online at https://www.washingtonpost.com/technology/2020/03/27/facebook-zuckerberg-coronavirus-test/. Accessed 10 Apr 2020

Economist (2014) The limits to Infiniti: Japanese luxury cars. The Economist 411(8890):69. Available online at https://www.economist.com/business/2014/06/07/the-limits-to-infiniti

Eisinger J (2015) How Mark Zuckerberg's altruism helps himself, published 3 December and 4 December 2015 by The New York Times. Available online at https://www.nytimes.com/2015/12/04/business/dealbook/how-mark-zuckerbergs-altruism-helps-himself.html. Accessed 3 Mar 2019

Entis L (2014) Why Mark Zuckerberg's $1 salary means nothing, published 1 April 2014 by Entrepreneur.com. Available online at https://www.entrepreneur.com/article/232696. Accessed 12 Feb 2019

EPIC (2019) Facebook privacy, by EPIC Electronic Privacy Information Center. Available online at https://epic.org/privacy/facebook/. Accessed 10 Oct 2019

Fair L (2019) FTC's $5 billion Facebook settlement: record-breaking and history-making, published 24 July 2019 by the FTC and Lesley Fair. Available online at https://www.ftc.gov/news-events/blogs/business-blog/2019/07/ftcs-5-billion-facebook-settlement-record-breaking-history. Accessed 10 Nov 2019

Fedor L (2019) Trump impeachment inquiry enters new public phase – key witnesses to testify in televised hearing on president's actions in Ukraine, published 12 November 2019 by The Financial Times. Available online at https://www.ft.com/content/5f7b744e-057b-11ea-a984-fbbacad9e7dd. Accessed 23 Nov 2019

Feser C (2016) Leading in the digital age, roundtable moderated by Claudio Feser. McKinsey Quarterly, March 2016. Available online https://www.mckinsey.com/featured-insights/leadership/leading-in-the-digital-age. Accessed 30 Dec 2018

Finley K (2020) When school is online, the digital divide grows greater, published 9 April 2020 by Wired. Available online at https://www.wired.com/story/school-online-digital-divide-grows-greater/. Accessed 2020-04-12

Focus Economics (2017) The World's top 10 largest economies, published 30 December 2017 and updated 8 November 2018 by Focus Economics. Available online at https://www.focus-economics.com/blog/the-largest-economies-in-the-world. Accessed 7 Mar 2019

Follett MP (2004) Power. In: Metcalf HC, Urwick LF (eds) Dynamic administration, the collected writings of Mary Parker Follett. Harper, New York, pp 70–95. https://doi.org/10.4324/9780203486214

Forbes (2017) Zuckerberg emphasizes long-term, tech-focused philanthropic strategy in reflection letter, by Kathleen Chaykowski and Forbes Staff, published 13 December 2017. Available online at https://www.forbes.com/sites/kathleenchaykowski/2017/12/13/zuckerberg-emphasizes-long-term-tech-focused-philanthropic-strategy-in-reflection-letter/#acfa541606bc. Accessed 3 Mar 2019

Fortune (2017) Tesla overtakes GM as America's most valuable automaker, published 11 April 2017. Available online at http://fortune.com/2017/04/10/tesla-gm-market-value-stock/ Accessed 25 Feb 2019

Freeman RB (1996) Toward an apartheid economy? Harv Bus Rev 74(5):114–121. Retrieved from https://hbr.org/1996/09/toward-an-apartheid-economy

Frier S (2017) This team runs Mark Zuckerberg's Facebook page – "his image in the digital domain needs to be controlled" – published 18 January 2017 by Bloomberg Businessweek. Available online at https://www.bloomberg.com/news/articles/2017-01-18/this-team-runs-mark-zuckerberg-s-facebook-page

Fu L (2017) The wealth gap in the U.S. is worse than in Russia or Iran, published 1 August 2017 by Fortune. Available online at http://fortune.com/2017/08/01/wealth-gap-america/. Accessed 10 Feb 2019

Galvin BM, Lange D, Ashforth BE (2015) Narcissistic organizational identification: seeing oneself as central to the organization's identity. Acad Manag Rev 40(2):163–181. https://doi.org/10.5465/amr.2013.0103

Gardiner J (2017) The rise of electric cars could leave us with a big battery waste problem, published 10 August 2017 by The Guardian. Available online at https://www.theguardian.com/sustainable-business/2017/aug/10/electric-cars-big-battery-waste-problem-lithium-recycling. Accessed 3 Mar 2019

Gartner (2017) Leadership in the digital age: a Gartner trend insight report. Available online at https://www.gartner.com/en/conferences/content/people-leadership-trends?utm_source=google&utm_medium=cpc&utm_campaign=evt_na_2018_glg%20-%20LG. Accessed 22 Dec 2018

Ghemawat P (2001) Distance still matters: the hard reality of global expansion. Harv Bus Rev 79(8):137–147. Retrieved from https://hbr.org/2001/09/distance-still-matters-the-hard-reality-of-global-expansion

Giles C (2018) Strong global growth conceals emerging market fragility: tiger index points to strains as IMF set to warn against escalating trade conflict, published 6 October 2018 by FT.com. Available online at https://www.ft.com/content/bf8f2c00-c8b3-11e8-ba8f-ee390057b8c9. Accessed 7 Mar 2019

Glazer R (2018) Leadership lesson from Jeff Bezos and Steve Jobs: stop worrying about being right, and focus on this instead, published 20 August 2018 by Inc. Available online at https://www.inc.com/robert-glazer/jeff-bezos-steve-jobs-didnt-need-to-be-right-and-you-dont-either-heres-why.html. Accessed 25 Feb 2019

Glenn JC, Florescu E, Gordon TJ (2017) State of the Future Version 19.1. Millennium Project, Washington, DC

Goldberg J (2017) Trends in leadership and leadership development: the evolution of market needs. Graziadio Bus Rev 20(1). Available online accessed 2019-2012-2007. Retrieved from https://gbr.pepperdine.edu/2017/04/trends-in-leadership-and-leadership-development/

Goldstein M (2018) Elon Musk steps down as chairman in deal with S.E.C. over tweet about Tesla, published 29 September 2018 by The New York Times. Available online at https://www.nytimes.com/2018/09/29/business/tesla-musk-sec-settlement.html?action=click&module=RelatedLinks&pgtype=Article. Accessed 19 Apr 2020

Gould AM, Bourk MJ, Joullié J-E (2017) From the industrial revolution to Trump: six periods of changing perceptions of American business managers. J Manag Hist 23(4):471–488. https://doi.org/10.1108/JMH-04-2017-0018

Gourguechon P (2019) Every leader needs some narcissism, so how do we know when it turns dangerous? Published 6 May 2019 by Forbes-Leadership Strategy-Insights. Available online at https://www.forbes.com/sites/prudygourguechon/2019/05/06/every-leader-needs-some%2D%2Dnarcissism-so-how-do-we-know-when-it-turns-dangerous/#1910343f49c2. Accessed 3 Dec 2019

Grijalva E, Harms PD (2014) Narcissism: an integrative synthesis and dominance complementarity model. Acad Manag Perspect 28(2):108–127. https://doi.org/10.5465/amp.2012.0048

Harwell D (2018) Tesla turns a profit in what Musk calls 'a historic quarter', published 24 October 2018 by The Washington Post. Available online at https://www.washingtonpost.com/technology/2018/10/24/tesla-turns-profit-what-musk-calls-historic-quarter/?noredirect=on&utm_term=.011761233740. Accessed 2 Mar 2019

Hawkins A (2017) How Tesla changed the auto industry forever: autopilot, electrification, and a boot-to-bonnet commitment to technology, published 28 July 2017 by The Verge. Available online at https://www.theverge.com/2017/7/28/16059954/tesla-model-3-2017-auto-industry-influence-elon-musk. Accessed 28 Jan 2019

Heifetz RA, Linsky M (2017) Leadership on the line, with a new preface: staying alive through the dangers of change. Harvard Business Review Press, Boston

Hemp P (2009) Death by information overload. Harv Bus Rev 87(9):82–89. https://hbr.org/2009/09/death-by-information-overload. Accessed 10 Feb 2019

Hemp P, Stewart TA (2004) Leading change when business is good. Harv Bus Rev 82(12):60–72. https://hbr.org/2004/12/leading-change-when-business-is-good. Accessed 25 Apr 2019

Higgins T (2020) Elon Musk's defiance in the time of coronavirus – the Tesla CEO held out for days on suspending U.S. car production, published 20 March 2020 by the Wall Street Journal. Available online at https://www.wsj.com/articles/elon-musks-defiance-in-the-time-of-coronavirus-11584733458. Accessed 3 Apr 2020

Higgs M (2009) The good, the bad and the ugly: leadership and narcissism. J Chang Manag 9(2):165–178. https://doi.org/10.1080/14697010902879111

Ho D, Dajose L (2020) The tip of the iceberg: virologist David Ho speaks about COVID-19, published 20 March 2020 in Caltech Matters by California Institute of Technology. Available online https://www.caltech.edu/about/news/tip-iceberg-virologist-david-ho-bs-74-speaks-about-covid-19. Accessed 29 Mar 2020

Hoium T (2018) Why Facebook's oculus acquisition hasn't paid off... yet, published 31 August 2018 by Motley Fool Investing. Available online at https://www.fool.com/investing/2018/08/31/why-facebooks-oculus-acquisition-hasnt-paid-off-ye.aspx. Accessed 17 Feb 2019

Holmes A (2020) Elon Musk keeps downplaying the severity of coronavirus, and hedged his promise to produce ventilators for hospitals mere minutes after making it, published 19 March 2020 by BusinessInsider. Available online at https://www.businessinsider.com/elon-musk-coronavirus-tesla-promises-experts-ventilators-controversy-2020-3. Accessed 8 Apr 2020

Hooper J (2012) Inside the Vatican bank: silence, secrets and Latin cash machines, by John Hooper in Vatican City, published 28 June 2012 by The Guardian. Available online at https://www.theguardian.com/world/2012/jun/28/inside-vatican-bank-silence-secrets-latin-cash-machines. Accessed 8 Mar 2019

Hughes M (2020) What is TikTok, and why are teens obsessed with it? Published 5 February 2020 by How-To Geek. Available online at https://www.howtogeek.com/536434/what-exactly-is-tiktok-and-why-are-teens-obsessed-with-it/. Accessed 15 Apr 2020

IMF (2017) World economic outlook: a shifting global economic landscape, published 16 January 2017. Available online at https://www.imf.org/external/pubs/ft/weo/2017/update/01/. Accessed 12 Sept 2017

Isaac M, Singer N (2019) Facebook agrees to extensive new oversight as part of $5 billion settlement, published 24 July 2019 by The New York Times. Available online at https://www.nytimes.com/2019/07/24/technology/ftc-facebook-privacy-data.html. Accessed 10 Oct 2019

Isaacson W (2014) The innovators: how a group of hackers, geniuses, and geeks created the digital revolution. Simon & Schuster, New York

Isidore C (2020) Tesla posts first annual profit, published 30 January 2020 by CNN Markets Now. Available online at https://www.cnn.com/2020/01/29/business/tesla-earnings/index.html. Accessed 15 Apr 2020

Jallat F, Capek MJ (2001) Disintermediation in question: new economy, new networks, new middlemen. Bus Horiz 44(2):55–60. https://doi.org/10.1016/S0007-6813(01)80023-9

Janus O (2020) 20 of the worst epidemics and pandemics in history: plagues and epidemics have ravaged humanity throughout its existence, often changing the course of history, published 21 March 2020 by LiveScience. Available online at https://www.livescience.com/worst-epidemics-and-pandemics-in-history.html. Accessed 10 Apr 2020

Jeong S (2018) Zuckerberg struggles to name a single Facebook competitor, published 10 April 2018 by The Verge. Available online at https://www.theverge.com/2018/4/10/17220934/facebook-monopoly-competitor-mark-zuckerberg-senate-hearing-lindsey-graham. Accessed 5 Feb 2019

Jones V (2015) Trump: the social media president? CNN commentary published 26 October 26, 2015. Available online at https://www.cnn.com/2015/10/26/opinions/jones-trump-social-media/index.html. Accessed 25 Feb 2019

Jones C (2019) Wasn't Tesla supposed to make more money as the Model 3 ramped? Published 22 January 2019 by Forbes. Available online at https://www.forbes.com/sites/chuckjones/2019/01/22/wasnt-tesla-supposed-to-make-more-money-as-the-model-3-ramped/#15f7ce72c737. Accessed 28 Feb 2019

Khurana R (2002) Market triads: a theoretical and empirical analysis of market intermediation. J Theory Soc Behav 32(2):239–262

Kim A (2019) Are blue-collar white women Trump's Red Wall? They're the one group whose support for impeachment isn't growing, published 25 October 2019 by Washington Monthly. Available online at https://washingtonmonthly.com/2019/10/25/are-blue-collar-white-women-trumps-red-wall/. Accessed 3 Dec 2019

Kluz A, Firlej M (2016) How to be a leader in the digital age, published 10 May 2016 by The World Economic Forum: Leadership. Retrieved from https://www.weforum.org/agenda/2016/05/how-to-be-a-leader-in-the-digital-age/. Accessed 23 Apr 2019

Kohler T, Matzler K, Füller J (2009) Avatar-based innovation: using virtual worlds for real-world innovation. Technovation 29(6/7):395–407. https://doi.org/10.1016/j.technovation.2008.11.004

Kopecki D (2018) Musk's defiant, rebel CEO persona is putting his company and its investors at risk, say management experts, published 10 September 2018 and updated 11 September 2019 by CNBC News. Available online at https://www.cnbc.com/2018/09/10/musks-rebel-ceo-persona-shows-lack-of-judgment-puts-investors-at-risk.html

Kosoff M (2016) Facebook's ousted co-founder is trying to become the Marc Andreessen of Asia: once part of the founding team of Facebook, Eduardo Saverin disappeared to Southeast Asia, where he's been quietly building a V.C. empire, published 24 February 2016 by Vanity Fair. Available online at https://www.vanityfair.com/news/2016/02/eduardo-saverin-orami-investments-asia. Accessed 23 Nov 2019

LaForgia M, Rosenberg M, Dance GJX (2019) Facebook's data deals are under criminal investigation, published 13 and 14 March 2019 by the New York Times, p A1. Available online at https://www.nytimes.com/2019/03/13/technology/facebook-data-deals-investigation.html. Accessed 8 Mar 2019

Lang N (2015) Why teens are leaving Facebook: it's 'meaningless', published 21 February 2015 by The Daily Dot and The Washington Post. Available online at https://www.washingtonpost.com/

news/the-intersect/wp/2015/02/21/why-teens-are-leaving-facebook-its-meaningless/?utm_term=. 87d91aad5bc5. Accessed 5 Mar 2019

Levine M (2015) Should Trump have indexed? Most people should probably just invest in low-cost index funds – but some people shouldn't, published 3 September 2015 by Bloomberg Businessweek. Available online at https://www.bloomberg.com/opinion/articles/2015-09-03/should-donald-trump-have-indexed. Accessed 8 Mar 2019

Little K (2016) What 10 CEO titans studied in college before making it big, published 25 March 2016 by CNBC. Available online at https://www.cnbc.com/2016/03/24/what-10-ceo-titans-studied-in-college-before-making-it-big.html. Accessed 30 Dec 2019

Loizos C (2017) Facebook agreed to pay a lot more for Oculus than we realized: here's why, published 18 January 2017 by TechCrunch. Available online at https://techcrunch.com/2017/01/18/facebook-agreed-to-pay-a-lot-more-for-oculus-than-we-realized-heres-why/. Accessed 17 Feb 2019

Lombardo TJ (2018) Why white blue-collar voters love President Trump: he has mastered their language, published 16 September 2018 by The Washington Post. Available online at https://www.washingtonpost.com/outlook/2018/09/17/why-white-blue-collar-voters-love-president-trump/. Accessed 3 Dec 2019

Lopez L, Matousek M (2020) Tesla went from high fives at an all-hands meeting to shutting down its factories – Here's how it came to accept the coronavirus, published 1 April 2020 by BusinessInsider. Available online at https://www.businessinsider.com/tesla-coronavirus-response-was-unorganized-and-dangerous-workers-say-2020-4. Accessed 8 Apr 2020

Lotterman E (2020) Real world economics: epidemics are chock full of basic economics, published 15 March 2020 by TwinCities Pioneer Press. Available online at https://www.twincities.com/2020/03/15/real-world-economics-epidemics-are-chock-full-of-basic-economics/ Accessed 8 Apr 2020

Lovelace JB, Bundy J, Hambrick DC, Pollock TG (2018) The shackles of CEO celebrity: sociocognitive and behavioral role constraints on "star" leaders. Acad Manag Rev 43(3):419–444. https://doi.org/10.5465/amr.2016.0064

Lu D, Yourish K (2019) The turnover at the top of the Trump administration is unprecedented, published 8 March 2019 by The New York Times. Available online at https://www.nytimes.com/interactive/2018/03/16/us/politics/all-the-major-firings-and-resignations-in-trump-administration.html. Accessed 8 Mar 2019

Lubit R (2002) The long-term organizational impact of destructively narcissistic managers. Acad Manag Perspect 16(1):127–138. https://doi.org/10.5465/ame.2002.6640218

Ludvigsen K (2009) Ferdinand Porsche – genesis of genius: road, racing and aviation innovation 1900 to 1933. Bentley Publishers, Cambridge, MA

MacArthur S (2020) Outbreak: 10 of the worst pandemics in history, published by MPH Online. Available at https://www.mphonline.org/worst-pandemics-in-history/. Accessed 10 Apr 2020

MacBride E (2017) Facebook's seven largest emerging markets competitors, by Elizabeth MacBride, published 30 September 2017 in Forbes. Available online at https://www.forbes.com/sites/elizabethmacbride/2017/09/30/facebooks-seven-emerging-markets-competitors/#67799bb177db. Accessed 7 Feb 2019

Machiavelli N (1513/1992) The Prince (trans: Marriott WK, Everyman's library ed). Alfred A. Knopf, New York

Maron DF (2020) 'Wet markets' likely launched the coronavirus – here's what you need to know, published 15 April 2020 by National Geographic. Available online at https://www.nationalgeographic.com/animals/2020/04/coronavirus-linked-to-chinese-wet-markets/. Accessed 17 Apr 2020

Marques RPF, Batista JCL (2017) Information and communication overload in the digital age. IGI Global, Hershey

Martineau P, Matsakis L (2019) All the times Facebook moved fast and sometimes broke things, published 6 February 2019 by WIRED. Available online at https://www.wired.com/story/15-years-later-what-is-facebook/. Accessed 10 Oct 2019

Matousek M (2018) Tesla has transformed the car industry – but its biggest strength could become its greatest liability, published 12 February 2018 by BusinessInsider. Available online at https://www.businessinsider.com/teslas-influence-on-the-auto-industry-2018-2. Accessed 29 Jan 2019

McAdams D (2019) A theory for why Trump's base won't budge: the president has followed the predictable course for narcissism in one way, alienating many who have served in his administration, and defied expectations in another, by continuing to attract an adoring core, published 2 December and updated 4 December 2019 by The Atlantic. Available online at https://www.theatlantic.com/ideas/archive/2019/12/how-narcissists-wear-out-their-welcome/602446/. Accessed 5 Dec 2019

McCormick E (2019) Tesla unveils $35,000 standard Model 3, shifts worldwide sales to online-only, published 28 February 2019 by Yahoo Finance. Available online at https://finance.yahoo.com/news/tesla-unveils-35000-standard-model-3-220744734.html. Accessed 27 Feb 2019

McFadden C (2018) 20 greatest innovations and inventions of automobile engineering: from the first engine to today, published 1 May 2018 in Interest Engineering. Available online at https://interestingengineering.com/20-greatest-innovations-and-inventions-of-automobile-engineering-from-the-first-engine-to-today. Accessed 23 Feb 2019

Mejia Z (2018) Tesla CEO Elon Musk resigns as chairman – here's how his role could change, published 2 October 2018 by CNBC. Available online at https://www.cnbc.com/2018/10/02/tesla-ceo-elon-musk-resigns-as-chairman%2D%2Dheres-what-that-really-means.html. Accessed 25 Jan 2019

Mezrich B (2009) The accidental billionaires: the founding of Facebook: a tale of sex, money, genius and betrayal. Knopf Doubleday Publishing Group, New York

Mezrich B (2019) 'I was right about Mark Zuckerberg': the author of the book that inspired 'the social network' reflects on a decade of Mark Zuckerberg's career, published 4 February 2019 by The Atlantic. Available online at https://www.theatlantic.com/technology/archive/2019/02/ben-mezrich-mark-zuckerberg-then-and-facebook-today/581983/ Accessed 24 Nov 2019

Mirhaydari A (2018) Facebook stock recovers all $134B lost after Cambridge Analytica data scandal, published 10 Mary 2018 by CBSNews. Available online at https://www.cbsnews.com/news/facebook-stock-price-recovers-all-134-billion-lost-in-after-cambridge-analytica-datascandal/. Accessed 14 Feb 2019

Moreau E (2019) Hottest social app trends for teens, published and updated 9 January 2019 by Lifewire. Available online at https://www.lifewire.com/hottest-social-app-trends-for-teens-3485940. Accessed 5 Mar 2019

Mueller SC, Bakhirev A, Böhm M, Schröer M, Krcmar H, Welpe IM (2017) Measuring and mapping the emergence of the digital economy: a comparison of the market capitalization in selected countries. Digit Pol Regul Gov 19(5):367–382. https://doi.org/10.1108/DPRG-01-2017-0001

Naughton K, Welch D (2019) This is what peak car looks like – for many people, new forms of mobility are making privately owned vehicles obsolete, published 28 February 2019 by Bloomberg Businessweek. Available online at https://www.bloomberg.com/news/features/2019-02-28/this-is-what-peak-car-looks-like?srnd=businessweek-v2. Accessed 22 Feb 2019

Neate R (2018) Over $119bn wiped off Facebook's market cap after growth shock: shares crash as social network admits user growth fell after Cambridge Analytica breach, published 26 July 2018 by The Guardian. Available online https://www.theguardian.com/technology/2018/jul/26/facebook-market-cap-falls-109bn-dollars-after-growth-shock. Accessed 17 Feb 2019

Newcomb A (2018) A timeline of Facebook's privacy issues – and its responses: Facebook's recent crisis is just one of many privacy issues that company has had to deal with in its relatively short existence, published 24 March 2018 by NBC News. Available online at https://www.nbcnews.com/tech/social-media/timeline-facebook-s-privacy-issues-its-responses-n859651. Accessed 20 Oct 2019

Newton C (2020) How Facebook is preparing for a surge in depressed and anxious users – and why it's Mark Zuckerberg's biggest worry about the user base, published 19 March 2020 by The Verge UK. Available online at https://www.theverge.com/2020/3/19/21185204/facebook-coronavirus-depression-anxiety-content-moderation-mark-zuckerberg-interview. Accessed 7 Apr 2020

NTIA (1998) Falling through the Net II: new data on the digital divide, published 28 July 1998 by the National Telecommunications and Information Administration, US Department of Commerce. Available online at https://www.ntia.doc.gov/report/1998/falling-through-net-ii-new-data-digital-divide. Accessed 5 Apr 2020

OECD (2000) Schooling for tomorrow knowledge base. Available online at https://www.oecd.org/site/schoolingfortomorrowknowledgebase/themes/ict/. Accessed 5 Apr 2020

Ovide S (2020) The pandemic feeds tech companies' power: our online habits are changing, likely for good – this could make tech companies even more muscular, published 8 April 2020 by The New York Times. Available online at https://www.nytimes.com/2020/04/08/technology/coronavirus-big-tech.html. Accessed 14 Apr 2020

Ovide S, Crawford S (2020) Erasing America's digital divide: interview with Susan Crawford, published 14 April 2020 by The New York Times. Available online at https://www.nytimes.com/2020/04/14/technology/coronavirus-digital-divide.html. Accessed 15 Apr 2020

Park KM (2012) Leadership perspectives on the global market for corporate control. In: Delener NJ (ed) Service science research, strategy and innovation: dynamic knowledge management methods. IGI Global Business Science Reference, Hershey, pp 377–399

Park KM (2016) Leadership, power and collaboration in international mergers and acquisitions: conflict and resolution. In: Risberg A, King DR, Meglio O (eds) The Routledge companion to mergers and acquisitions. Routledge, New York, pp 177–195. https://doi.org/10.4324/9780203761885.ch11

Park KM (2019) Through the language looking glass: power and politics in the discourse of mergers and acquisitions. BU MET Department of Administrative Sciences Working Paper 2019-12-08. Boston University, Boston

Park KM, Gould AM (2017) The overlooked influence of personality, idiosyncrasy and eccentricity in corporate mergers and acquisitions: 120 years and six distinct waves. J Manag Hist 23(1):7–31. https://doi.org/10.1108/JMH-09-2016-0056

Park KM, Meglio O (2019) Playing a double game? Pursuing innovation through ambidexterity in an international acquisition program from the Arabian Gulf Region. R&D Manag 49(1):115–135. https://doi.org/10.1111/radm.12361

Park KM, Meglio O, Bauer F, Tarba S (2018) Managing patterns of internationalization, integration, and identity transformation: the post-acquisition metamorphosis of an Arabian Gulf EMNC. J Bus Res 93(May):122–138. https://doi.org/10.1016/j.jbusres.2018.05.019

Park KM, Meglio O, Schriber S (2019) Building a global corporate social responsibility program via mergers and acquisitions: a managerial framework. Bus Horiz 62(3):395–407. https://doi.org/10.1016/j.bushor.2019.01.006

Parkin S (2014) What Zuckerberg sees in oculus rift: Facebook acquired oculus rift because it believes virtual reality could be the next big thing after mobile, published 26 March 2014 in MIT Technology Review. Available online at https://www.technologyreview.com/s/525881/what-zuckerberg-sees-in-oculus-rift/. Accessed 15 Feb 2019

Parr B (2011) Facebook's complicated ownership history explained, published 13 April 2011 by Mashable. Available online at https://mashable.com/2011/04/13/facebooks-complicated-ownership-history-explained/. Accessed 23 Nov 2019

Paul K (2020) As coronavirus misinformation spreads on social media, Facebook removes posts, published 31 January 2020 by Reuters. Available online at https://www.reuters.com/article/us-china-health-facebook/as-coronavirus-misinformation-spreads-on-social-media-facebook-removes-posts-idUSKBN1ZV388. Accessed 7 Apr 2020

Pazzanese C (2016) The costs of inequality: increasingly, it's the rich and the rest, published 8 February 2016 by The Harvard Gazette. Available online at https://news.harvard.edu/gazette/story/2016/02/the-costs-of-inequality-increasingly-its-the-rich-and-the-rest/. Accessed 12 Feb 2019

Pfeffer J (2015) Leadership BS: fixing workplaces and careers one truth at a time. HarperBusiness, New York

Pilkington E, Pengelly M (2020) Trump was warned in January of Covid-19's devastating impact, memos reveal, published 7 April 2020 by The Guardian UK. Available online https://www.theguardian.com/world/2020/apr/07/donald-trump-coronavirus-memos-warning-peter-navarro. Accessed 10 Apr 2020

Pilon M (2016) Donald Trump's immigrant mother: Donald Trump's mother, Mary, was an immigrant – but Trump doesn't often bring up his Scottish ancestry on the campaign trail, published 24 June 2016 by The New Yorker. Available online at https://www.newyorker.com/news/news-desk/donald-trumps-immigrant-mother. Accessed 24 Nov 2019

Porter ME, Heppelmann JE (2014) How smart, connected products are transforming competition. Harv Bus Rev 92(11):64–88. Retrieved from https://hbr.org/2014/11/how-smart-connected-products-are-transforming-competition

Poushter J, Fagan M (2018) On global affairs, Americans have more confidence in other world leaders than in Trump, published 5 November 2018 by Pew Research. Available online at http://www.pewresearch.org/fact-tank/2018/11/05/on-global-affairs-americans-have-more-confidence-in-other-world-leaders-than-in-trump/. Accessed 23 Feb 2019

Pruitt S (2017) Electric innovations drive Tesla to top of U.S. auto industry: this week, luxury electric car maker Tesla surpassed GM as the most valuable automotive company in the country, published 11 April 2017 by History.com. Available online at https://www.history.com/news/electric-innovations-drive-tesla-to-top-of-u-s-auto-industry. Accessed 24 Feb 2019

Ramzeen AV (2019) 72 Facebook acquisitions – the complete list – infographics, published 17 June 2019 by TechWyse. Available online at https://www.techwyse.com/blog/infographics/facebook-acquisitions-the-complete-list-infographic/. Accessed 29 Oct 2019

Reeves M, Lang N, Carlsson-Szlezak P (2020) Lead your business through the coronavirus crisis, published 27 February 2020 by Harvard Business Review. Available online at https://hbr.org/2020/02/lead-your-business-through-the-coronavirus-crisis. Accessed 10 Apr 2020

Rietveld J, Schilling MA, Bellavitis C (2019) Platform strategy: managing ecosystem value through selective promotion of complements. Organ Sci 30(6):1232–1251. https://doi.org/10.1287/orsc.2019.1290

Ritter R, Ruggero E (2017) Leadership in innovation needs innovation in leadership: as businesses face evolving challenges, four aspects of leadership will become dramatically more important: insight, integrity, courage, and agility, published October 2017 by McKinsey & Co. McKinsey Quarterly. Retrieved from https://www.mckinsey.com/business-functions/operations/our-insights/leadership-in-innovation-needs-innovation-in-leadership. Accessed 22 Apr 2019

Roberts E (2019) Digital divide available on the Stanford University Department of Computer Science website 2019–2020. https://cs.stanford.edu/people/eroberts/cs181/projects/digital-divide/start.html. Accessed 2 Apr 2020

Rodriguez S (2018) Here are the scandals and other incidents that have sent Facebook's share price tanking in 2018, published 20 November 2018 by CNBC. Available online at https://www.cnbc.com/2018/11/20/facebooks-scandals-in-2018-effect-on-stock.html. Accessed 15 Feb 2019

Rodriguez S (2020) Facebook has moved fast during coronavirus outbreak, and it could restore the company's reputation, published 21 March 2020 by CNBC. Available online at https://www.cnbc.com/2020/03/20/facebook-coronavirus-moves-could-help-restore-its-reputation.html. Accessed 7 Apr 2020

Roetzel PG (2019) Information overload in the information age: a review of the literature from business administration, business psychology, and related disciplines with a bibliometric approach and framework development. Bus Res 12(2):479–522. https://doi.org/10.1007/s40685-018-0069-z

Roll R (1986) The hubris hypothesis of corporate takeovers. J Bus 59(2):197–216. https://doi.org/10.1086/296325

Romm T (2019) 'Unconstitutional, unlawful and unsupported': how Facebook initially tried to fight a multibillion-dollar U.S. fine, published 30 September 2019 by The Washington Post. Available online at https://www.washingtonpost.com/technology/2019/09/30/unconstitutional-unlawful-unsupported-how-facebook-initially-tried-fight-multi-billion-dollar-us-fine/. Accessed 11 Oct 2019

Rosenberg M, Confessore N, Cadwalladr C (2018) How Trump consultants exploited the Facebook data of millions, published 17 March 2018 by the New York Times. Available online at https://www.nytimes.com/2018/03/17/us/politics/cambridge-analytica-trump-campaign.html. Accessed 12 Feb 2019

Rotman D (2014) Technology and inequality, published 21 October 2014 by The MIT Technology Review. Available online at https://www.technologyreview.com/s/531726/technology-and-inequality/. Accessed 10 Feb 2019

Sanders J, Patterson D (2019) Facebook data privacy scandal: a cheat sheet, published 24 July 2019 by TechRepublic. Available online at https://www.techrepublic.com/article/facebook-data-privacy-scandal-a-cheat-sheet/. Accessed 8 Nov 2019

Savage C (2019) 8 takeaways from the whistle-blower complaint – the whistle-blower's complaint and the inspector general's report have been released. Here's what they say, published 26 September 2019 by The New York Times. Available online at https://www.nytimes.com/2019/09/26/us/politics/whistleblower-declassified-report.html

Schneider A (2018) Facebook's big growth is slowing, sending its stock tumbling, published 26 July 2018 by NPR. Available online at https://www.npr.org/2018/07/26/632653239/facebooks-big-growth-is-slowing-sending-its-stock-tumbling. Accessed 29 Jan 2019

Schumacher S, Kent N (2020) Internet use around the world as countries grapple with COVID-19, published 2 April 2020 by Pew Research Center. Available online at https://www.pewresearch.org/fact-tank/2020/04/02/8-charts-on-internet-use-around-the-world-as-countries-grapple-with-covid-19/. Accessed 5 Apr 2020

Schyns B, Wisse B, Sanders S (2019) Shady strategic behavior: recognizing strategic followership of dark triad followers. Acad Manag Perspect 33(2):234–249. https://doi.org/10.5465/amp.2017.0005

Sebak R (2018) Rick Sebak digs up distant Carnegie-Trump connection – research into Andrew Carnegie's marriage reveals an unlikely, albeit tenuous, connection between the Pittsburgh icon and the 45th President, published 19 March 2018 online and April 2018 in Pittsburgh Magazine. Available online at https://www.pittsburghmagazine.com/rick-sebak-digs-up-distant-carnegie-trump-connection/. Accessed 23 Nov 2019

Selznick P (1957) Leadership in administration. Row, Peterson, Evanston

Senguptanov S (2011) F.T.C. settles privacy issue at Facebook – Mark Zuckerberg, Facebook's chief executive, said in a blog post Tuesday that the company had made "a bunch of mistakes," published 29 November 2011 by The New York Times. Available online at https://www.nytimes.com/2011/11/30/technology/facebook-agrees-to-ftc-settlement-on-privacy.html. Accessed 10 Nov 2019

Sevastopulo D (2019) Impeachment: the facts pile up against Donald Trump – witnesses claim the president pressured Ukraine to investigate his opponents, but there is no sign Republicans will abandon him, published 22 November 2019 by The Financial Times. Available online at https://www.ft.com/content/a33fc32c-0d16-11ea-bb52-34c8d9dc6d84. Accessed 23 Nov 2019

Sevastopulo D, Williams A, Olearchyk R (2019) Ukrainegate: a guide to the US impeachment inquiry: Donald Trump is facing the most perilous crisis of his tenure after becoming only the fourth US president – after Andrew Johnson, Richard Nixon and Bill Clinton – to face an impeachment inquiry in the House of Representatives, published 8 November 2019 by The Financial Times. Available online at https://www.ft.com/content/22bbbeb8-e449-11e9-9743-db5a370481bc. Accessed 25 Nov 2019

Shen L (2018) Why Facebook suddenly Shed $35 billion in value, published 19 March 2018 by Fortune. Available online at http://fortune.com/2018/03/19/facebook-stock-share-price-cambridge-analytica-donald-trump/. Accessed 12 Feb 2019

Shieber J (2020) Zuckerberg details the ways Facebook and Chan Zuckerberg initiative are responding to COVID-19, published 3 March 2020 by TechCrunch. Available online at https://techcrunch.com/2020/03/03/zuckerberg-details-the-ways-facebook-and-chan-zuckerberg-initiative-are-responding-to-covid-19/. Accessed 7 Apr 2020

Shinal J (2017) The corporation Mark Zuckerberg founded to solve big problems is growing like a tech start-up, not a charity, published 18 August 2017 by CNBC. Available online at https://www.cnbc.com/2017/08/18/chan-zuckerberg-initiative-hiring-raising-money-like-a-start-up.html. Accessed 3 Mar 2019

Shubber K (2019) Former Donald Trump aide becomes US president's nemesis – Fiona Hill describes White House push for Ukraine probes as a 'domestic political errand', published 21 November 2019 by The Financial Times. Available online at https://www.ft.com/content/89f1dbde-0c9a-11ea-bb52-34c8d9dc6d84. Accessed 23 Nov 2019

Silver L, Vogels EA, Mordecai M, Cha J, Rasmussen R, Rainie L (2019) Mobile divides in emerging economies, published 20 November 2019 by Pew Research Center, Internet and Technology. Available online at https://www.pewresearch.org/internet/2019/11/20/mobile-divides-in-emerging-economies/. Accessed 3 Apr 2020

Simmel G (2006) Georg Simmel in translation: interdisciplinary border-crossings in culture and modernity (trans: Kim D). Cambridge Scholars Press, Cambridge, UK

Solon O (2018) Does Facebook's plummeting stock spell disaster for the social network? Published 26 July 2018 by The Guardian. Available online at https://www.theguardian.com/technology/2018/jul/26/facebook-stock-price-falling-what-does-it-mean-analysis. Accessed 17 Feb 2019

Statt N (2019) EPIC privacy group sues FTC for letting Facebook off easy – the group wants the FTC to alter the $5 billion settlement terms, published 26 July 2019 by The Verge. Available online at https://www.theverge.com/2019/7/26/8932023/facebook-ftc-privacy-5-billion-settlement-privacy-lawsuit-epic. Accessed 10 Nov 2019

Stein J, Van Damm A (2018) For the biggest group of American workers, wages aren't just flat. They're falling. Published 15 June 2018 by The Washington Post. Available online at https://www.washingtonpost.com/news/wonk/wp/2018/06/15/for-the-biggest-group-of-american-workers-wages-arent-just-flat-theyre-falling/?utm_term=.289d778d8dfd. Accessed 5 Mar 2019

Stewart E (2018) America's getting $10 trillion in tax cuts, and 20% of them are going the richest 1%, published 11 July 2018 by Vox.com. Available online at https://www.vox.com/policy-and-politics/2018/7/11/17560704/tax-cuts-rich-san-francisco-fed. Accessed 8 Mar 2019

Stewart E (2020) Elon Musk's coronavirus journey: a timeline – Elon Musk's reaction to the coronavirus crisis has been, um, less than ideal, but it's improving, published 26 March 2020 by VOX.com. Available online at https://www.vox.com/recode/2020/3/19/21185417/elon-musk-coronavirus-tweets-panic-ventilators-chloroquine-tesla-factory Accessed 8 Apr 2020

Stillman J (2018) This is the number 1 sign of high intelligence, according to Jeff Bezos – this is what the Amazon founder looks for when he wants to know if someone is really smart, published 25 September 2018 by Inc. Available online at https://www.inc.com/jessica-stillman/this-is-number-1-sign-of-high-intelligence-according-to-jeff-bezos.html?cid=sf01001. Accessed 24 Feb 2019

Sulleyman A (2018) Facebook losing its grip on young people, who are quitting the site in millions: social network said to have a 'teen problem', and Snapchat could take advantage, published 12 February 2018 by The Independent UK. Available online at https://www.independent.co.uk/life-style/gadgets-and-tech/news/facebook-quit-young-people-social-media-snapchat-instagram-emarketer-a8206486.html. Accessed 5 Mar 2019

Tajfel H, Turner JC (1979) An integrative theory of intergroup conflict. In: Austin WG, Worchel S (eds) The social psychology of intergroup relations. Brooks/Cole, Monterey, pp 33–47

Telford T (2018) Elon Musk: Tweet that cost $20 million was 'worth it', published 29 October 2018 by The Washington Post. Available online at https://www.washingtonpost.com/business/2018/10/29/musk-tweet-that-cost-million-was-worth-it/?noredirect=on&utm_term=.97ee1553caa1. Accessed 28 Jan 2019

Tenpas KD (2019) Tracking turnover in the Trump administration, published January 2019 and updated 11 March 2019 by the Brookings Institution. Available online at https://www.brookings.edu/research/tracking-turnover-in-the-trump-administration/. Accessed 11 Mar 2019

The Guardian (2015) Internet mocks Mark Zuckerberg's philanthropy in letter to daughter: Twitter dug into the Facebook founder's 2,000-word letter his newborn, which also announced his new charity initiative to combat general global problems, published 1 December 2015 by The Guardian Staff Writers. Available online at https://www.theguardian.com/technology/2015/dec/01/mark-zuckerberg-daughter-charity-internet-reaction. Accessed 3 Mar 2019

Thielman S (2015) Mark Zuckerberg and Priscilla Chan announce baby girl – and $45bn charity initiative: in a Facebook post to newborn child Max, the Facebook CEO says he will administer the initiative himself using 99% of shares in company's stock, published 1 December 2015 by The Guardian. Available online at https://www.theguardian.com/technology/2015/dec/01/mark-zuckerberg-and-priscilla-chan-announce-new-baby-and-massive-charity-initiative. Accessed 4 Mar 2019

Thomas C (2018) Global economic power struggle: emerging vs developed markets, published online April 9, 2018. Available https://www.seeitmarket.com/global-economic-power-struggle-emerging-developed-markets-17829/. Accessed 21 Oct 2018

Toth S (2018) Companies acquired by Facebook – 66 Facebook acquisitions, published 4 January 2018 by Techwyse. Available online at https://www.techwyse.com/blog/infographics/facebook-acquisitions-the-complete-list-infographic/. Accessed 9 Jan 2018

Trackalytics (2018) Twitter profile Trackalytics for Donald J. Trump @realDonaldTrump. Available online at https://www.trackalytics.com/twitter/profile/Realdonaldtrump/. Accessed 22 Dec 2018 and 29 Jan 2019

Trackalytics (2019) Twitter profile Trackalytics for Elon Musk @elonmusk. Available online at https://www.trackalytics.com/twitter/profile/elonmusk/. Accessed 3 Feb 2019 and 7 Mar 2019

Trackalytics (2020) Trackalytics Twitter Statistics@elonmusk (Elon Musk), updated 20 April 2020. Available online at https://www.trackalytics.com/twitter/profile/elonmusk/. Accessed 20 Apr 2020

Tzu S, Giles L (1910) The art of war, by Sun Tzu and translated by Lionel Giles. Available online at http://classics.mit.edu/Tzu/artwar.html and https://web.archive.org/web/20160304063441/http://www.talesofoldchina.com/library/giles-suntzu.php. Accessed 15 Feb 2019

UNCTAD (2019) Digital economy report published by the United Nations Conference on Trade and Development, Division on Technology and Logistics. Available online at https://unctad.org/en/Pages/Publications.aspx and https://unctad.org/en/Pages/DTL/STI_and_ICTs/ICT4D-Report.aspx. Accessed 5 Mar 2020

Vance A (2017) Elon Musk: Tesla, SpaceX, and the quest for a fantastic future. HarperCollins Publishers, New York

Vanian J (2018) Facebook is the least trusted major tech company when it comes to safeguarding personal data, poll finds, published 8 November 8, 2018 by Fortune. Available online at http://fortune.com/2018/11/08/mark-zuckerberg-facebook-reputation/. Accessed 29 Jan 2019

Vick K (2017) The digital divide: a quarter of the nation is without broadband, published 30 March 2017 online and 10 April 2017 in print by Time Inc. Available online at https://time.com/4718032/the-digital-divide/. Accessed 12 Apr 2029

Vigdor N (2019) Elon Musk Bids Twitter farewell – briefly: the Tesla chief executive announced that he was "going offline" and that he was "not sure about good of Twitter," published 1 November and updated 5 November 2019 by The New York Times. Available online at https://www.nytimes.com/2019/11/01/business/elon-musk-twitter.html. Accessed 20 Apr 2020

Wagner K, Molla R (2018) Facebook's user growth has hit a wall – Facebook added 22 million new daily users last quarter, its smallest quarterly jump since at least 2011, published 25 July 2018 by Recode. Available online at https://www.recode.net/2018/7/25/17614426/facebook-fb-earnings-q2-2018-user-growth-troubles. Accessed 29 Jan 2019

Walden C (2011) Unsocial networking: Cameron and Tyler Winklevoss are looking for justice, rather than money, in their feud with Facebook, published 4 March 2011 by Telegraph UK. Available online at https://www.telegraph.co.uk/technology/facebook/8360775/Tyler-and-Cameron-Winklevoss-Facebooks-Mark-Zuckerberg-owes-us-310-million.html. Accessed 23 Nov 2019

Wattles J (2018) Tesla scores a profit, and Elon Musk keeps a promise, published 24 October 2018 by CNN Business. Available online at https://www.cnn.com/2018/10/24/tech/tesla-earnings-profit-elon-musk/index.html. Accessed 2 Mar 2019

Watts S (2005) The People's Tycoon: Henry Ford and the American century. A.A. Knopf, New York

Weiner G (2020) Don't let Trump's cult of personality make Covid-19 worse: the coronavirus crisis has taken the personalized presidency to an insidious new level, published 8 April 8 2020 by The New York Times. Available online at https://www.nytimes.com/2020/04/08/opinion/covid-trump-presidency. Accessed 10 Apr 2020

Welch S, Ward M (2017) The surprising trait Jeff Bezos looks for in successful employees, published 7 November 2017 by CNBC. Available online at https://www.cnbc.com/2017/11/06/the-surprising-trait-jeff-bezos-looks-for-in-successful-employees.html. Accessed 9 Feb 2019

Werner E, DeBonis M (2020) Worried that $2 trillion law wasn't enough, Trump and congressional leaders converge on need for new coronavirus economic package – political leaders say more aid is needed to confront mounting economic problems, published 6 April 2020 by The Washington Post. Available online at https://www.washingtonpost.com/us-policy/2020/04/06/trump-democrats-coronavirus-stimulus-trillion/ Accessed 20 Apr 2020

Werner E, Kane P, DeBonis M (2020) Trump signs $2 trillion coronavirus bill into law as companies and households brace for more economic pain, published 27 March 2020 by The Washington Post. Available online at https://www.washingtonpost.com/us-policy/2020/03/27/congress-coronavirus-house-vote/. Accessed 17 Apr 2020

West G (2017) Scale: the universal Laws of life, growth, and death in organisms, cities, and companies. Penguin, New York

Westervelt A (2016) What do we do with all of Tesla's lithium-ion batteries? Published 22 August 2016 by KUNR Broadcasting Network. Available online at https://www.kunr.org/post/what-do-we-do-all-teslas-lithium-ion-batteries#stream/0

Wheeler DR (2018) Stop worshipping guys like Elon Musk, published 16 July 2018. Available online https://www.cnn.com/2018/07/16/opinions/elon-musk-tweet-tech-billionaire-hubris-wheeler-opinion/index.html. Accessed 28 Jan 2019

Wigglesworth A (2017) Trump defends social media use in tweet, published 30 December 2017 in the LA Times. Available online at https://www.latimes.com/politics/la-pol-updates-everything-president-1514673945-htmlstory.html. Accessed 23 Feb 2019

Wood R (2014) Tax-smart billionaires who work for $1, published 5 April 2014 by Forbes. Available online at https://www.forbes.com/sites/robertwood/2014/04/05/tax-smart-billionaires-who-work-for-1/#e6a27d7dfee8. Accessed 9 Feb 2019

Woodward A (2020) Both the new coronavirus and SARS outbreaks likely started in Chinese 'wet markets'. Published 26 February 2020 by BusinessInsider. Available online at https://www.businessinsider.com/wuhan-coronavirus-chinese-wet-market-photos-2020-1. Accessed 17 Apr 2020

YPulse (2019). TikTok wasn't the only social platform that gained young users this year, Published 24 December 2019 by YPulse – Social Media – Actionable Research on Gen Z and Millennials. Available online at https://www.ypulse.com/article/2019/12/24/tiktok-wasnt-the-only-social-platform-that-gained-young-users-this-year/. Accessed 15 Apr 2020

Zaleznik A (1970) Power and politics in organizational life. Harv Bus Rev 48(3):47–60. Retrieved from https://hbr.org/1970/05/power-and-politics-in-organizational-life. Accessed 17 Dec 2019

Zhao Y, von Delft S, Morgan-Thomas A, Buck T (2019) The evolution of platform business models: exploring competitive battles in the world of platforms. Long Range Plann. https://doi.org/10.1016/j.lrp.2019.101892

Conclusion: Management Theory in Crisis

46

Jean-Etienne Joullié

Contents

The Birth of Management Theory 1049
Theoretical Foundations 1052
    Mainstream Management Research 1054
    Postmodern Management Research 1057
The Collapse of Theory 1058
Conclusion: Management Scholarship for the Twenty-First Century 1063
Cross-References 1066
References 1066

Abstract

The quest for management theory started in earnest at the dawn of the twentieth century. Its goal is to make management a reliable undertaking, leading to predictable results. Disagreement exists about the research framework best suited to this pursuit. However, except for postmodern authors, management researchers assume the existence of stable and causally effective structures underpinning organizational life. Such an existence implies a deterministic picture of human agency. Equivocations, ambiguities, tautologies, and imprecise language obfuscate this implication, hollowing out management theory of its performative quality. A century after its inception, the quest for management theory has failed. Other avenues for management scholarship exist.

This chapter has been in the main extracted from Joullié, J.-E. 2018. Management without theory for the twenty-first century, Journal of Management History, 24(4): 377–395.

J.-E. Joullié (✉)
Gulf University for Science and Technology, Hawally, Kuwait

Université Laval, Québec, QC, Canada
e-mail: joullie.j@gust.edu.kw

© The Author(s), under exclusive licence to Springer Nature Switzerland AG 2020
B. Bowden et al. (eds.), *The Palgrave Handbook of Management History*,
https://doi.org/10.1007/978-3-319-62114-2_2

Keywords

Management theory · Research paradigm · Positivism · Postmodernism · Determinism

As Professor Gould notes in the introduction of the present volume, Fordism underpinned public policy making during much of the twentieth century – and in many ways still does. Starting as an industrial management theory, under the name of scientific management, Fordism evolved into a political regime associated with economic growth and welfare state. Although the social consequences of Fordism in general and scientific management in particular have been widely discussed (including in the preceding chapters and volumes of this *Handbook*), the implications of the idea of management theory have received less scholarly attention. This is unfortunate, because, as this chapter shows, such an exploration sheds new lights on management research. This endeavor starts with an examination of the concept of theory.

In everyday language, a theory is a speculation or hypothesis, a loosely substantiated conjecture about a general or particular aspect of human experience. In scientific and scholarly literature, the term acquires a more precise meaning and stands for a group of statements about the world and their logical consequences (Bogen 2017). Scientific theories range from descriptions of regularities observed in natural or experimental conditions, to laws, like Newton's, that are universally applicable within a field of study. In all cases, the validity of theories goes beyond the phenomena that underwrote their (inductive) formulation, all other things remaining the same. That is, scientific theories express permanence: they describe and codify patterns deemed stable enough to serve as bases for predictions about as yet unobserved phenomena, thus allowing, in principle at least, for control of these phenomena. Lyotard (1984) called "performativity" this predictive, instrumental quality of scientific theoretical knowledge, from which science draws its legitimacy.

Management researchers have embraced the performativity of scientific theories. In management studies, a theory is a testable proposition, or group of propositions, through which scholars describe organizational phenomena with the view of predicting the occurrence and course of similar ones (Shapira 2011: 1313; Sutton and Staw 1995: 378; Gioia and Pitre 1990: 587). If they want to contribute to management theory, researchers must therefore study managers' environment and behavior as well as their consequences, in the hope of identifying regular relationships between them. Once identified, such relationships are codified as management theories, that is, are formalized as expectations that identical consequences will follow should the same behavior be repeated, everything else (environmental conditions especially) remaining equal.

As Locke (1989) notes, donning the mantle of science enabled management to acquire the status of an academic discipline. At university, if students cannot practice management, they can study theory. Theoretical knowledge offsets the lack of experience of future managers by allowing them to predict organizational phenomena, including the consequences of their own behavior. Theory also helps current managers improve their practice (Christensen and Raynor 2003). Expressed differently, theory allows managers to manage like engineers engineer and doctors heal patients: safely, reliably, and on the back of a formal body of theoretical knowledge acquired at university. Such has been in any case management academia's overall promise since its inception (Khurana 2007). This has been a convincing pledge: while business and management programs have established themselves as the most popular ones among US undergraduates (about 20% of current enrolments), faculty in business, management, and related disciplines command the highest salaries, after those of legal studies academics (Snyder et al. 2018; CUPA-HR 2016).

The Birth of Management Theory

If the origins of management thought are multiple and date back to ancient philosophy (Joullié and Spillane 2015), management theory has a much more recent history. Commentators (e.g., Kiechel 2012; Wren and Bedeian 2009) have located its formal birth in the address that Henry Towne, co-founder of the Yale Lock Manufacturing Company, delivered in May 1886 to the American Society of Mechanical Engineers. In his talk, Towne lamented that, whereas engineering was in his day already endowed with a formal body of knowledge, the "management of works," a modern art essential to social welfare, was still a scholarly orphan. In Towne's view, the missing discipline would be rooted in economics (but developed by engineers), since management's ultimate objective is economic gain.

Despite calling for its development, Towne came short of uttering the expression "management theory." He was also seemingly unaware that, over a century before his talk, an economist had laid the first foundation of the notion. In *The Wealth of Nations*, published in 1776, Smith (2007: 603) indeed held that division of labor contributes to economic growth through increased efficiency, if also making workers' "stupid and ignorant" and widening the distance between them and their employer. Empirical confirmation of Smith's insight became available when, in the first decade of the twentieth century, Frederick Taylor argued and Henry Ford showed that manufacturing process simplification and standardization made spectacular productivity gains possible, enabling in turn lower consumer prices and increased wages. Unlike Towne, Taylor (1919: 27) did use the term "theory" to refer to his "principles of scientific management." Although industrialist and social reformer Robert Owen (1771–1858) preceded Taylor when he advanced principles to regulate cooperative work, the latter can justifiably claim the title of first self-conscious management theorist (Besides Owen and Taylor, one must mention Charles Babbage, Henry Gantt, Henri Fayol, as well as Frank and Lillian Gilbreth (among a few others) as pioneers of management theory (Wren 2004; Wren and Greenwood 1998).).

Following Smith, Taylor insisted on the distinction between mental and physical work, that is, between managing (task specification and planning) and executing. With the control of the work, prestige and power went to the production managers.

As Smith feared, however, workers resented such a loss of status and tended to go on strike where industrialists implemented Taylor's ideas. To no avail: once scientific management had proved its mettle in a variety of settings, the idea that management can be systematized and that there are techniques available to managers the implementation of which makes their organization more profitable and society more prosperous (if perhaps less harmonious) proved irresistible. Management theory was no longer a project, but, in some ways at least, a tangible reality.

Early twentieth-century management theorists contemplated a vast research program. In an effort to improve workshop productivity and in the spirit of Taylor's time and motion studies, the US National Academy of Sciences launched in 1924 a series of experiments at Western Electric's Hawthorne Plant in Cicero, Illinois. The results of the Hawthorne studies were puzzling at first: although productivity within a small group of women assembling relay parts improved, no change in environmental conditions, in work schedules, or even in incentives could explain why. This succession of rejected hypotheses led to the studies' abandonment, until Harvard Business School's Elton Mayo revived them. Mayo (2007 [1933]) held that he could explain the otherwise unexplainable by factoring in the relationships that developed between workers, between workers and their supervisor, and between the entire group under analysis and the researchers. Work organizations, extended to those in contact with them, were "social systems" transforming inputs into outputs (Roethlisberger and Dickson 1934).

In 1915, as scientific management consolidated its influence over North American manufacturing, English engineer Frederick Lanchester applied mathematics to warfare (Lanchester 1956). In particular, Lanchester devised a series of mathematical equations to predict the outcome of the confrontation of land forces. During WWII, British and American army engineers extended Lanchester's ideas first to aerial and naval battles and then to the control of resources and logistic processes. After the conflict, their models, enriched with statistical tools and numerical algorithms, proved their usefulness in the private sector. Called today "operations research" or "management science" when specifically applied to business situations, these mathematical techniques and concepts enable the optimization of any situation adequately represented by an objective function, be it crop yield, assembly line performance, or vehicle routing (Beer 1968).

Beyond the control of resources and logistics processes, the quest for a general management theory continued. For instance, Chester Barnard (1968 [1938]) held that work organizations are cooperative systems. If, unlike the Catholic Church, they rarely survive for long, Barnard argued, it is mainly because they do not meet two essential criteria. These, for Barnard, were effectiveness and efficiency, which he defined as attainment of collective purposes and fulfilment of personal motives, respectively. Accepting much of Barnard's analysis, Simon (1997 [1947]) set out to lay down the foundations of an "administrative science." In the management of administrations, Simon argued, efficiency must receive the highest priority, and decision-making is the most important process. This endeavor, which rests on logical and mathematical considerations, requires distinguishing value judgments from factual observations. However, since, as Barnard taught, efficiency involves personal motives, decision-making is never entirely rational. It is bounded by the values of the decision-maker. Not that this individual is beyond scientific study and understanding: intelligence is merely computation, and human beings are simple "behaving systems," complex only insofar as they respond to an environment that is itself complex (Simon 1996 [1969]).

Simon joined what would become the Carnegie School of Industrial Administration (GSIA) in 1949. Working notably with James March and Richard Cyert, he established the bases of the Carnegie School, an intellectual movement known for its emphasis on decision-making based on quantitative methods. Quite naturally, when in 1959 the Carnegie Foundation for the Advancement of Teaching delivered its report railing against the poor academic standards of management programs (the Ford Foundation report of the same year delivered a similar verdict), it considered GSIA's methods and agenda as models to imitate (Khurana and Spender 2012). Thanks to the endorsement of the American Association of Collegiate Schools of Business (AACSB) and to generous grants made available to those institutions that implemented its prescriptions, the 1959 Carnegie Foundation report's recommendations were widely implemented, reshaping management academia first in North American then all over the world.

Igor Ansoff, an engineer who worked for NATO before joining Simon at GSIA, applied quantitative methods to long-term corporate planning. As part of this effort, Ansoff coined the expression "corporate strategy," then an unknown and empty phrase to which an eponymous book (Ansoff 1965) gave substance and popularity. Ansoff was an academic pioneer, but he was neither the first nor the only one to promote strategy as a management concern. In 1963, Bruce Henderson had started what would a few years later be the Boston Consulting Group, a management consultancy hailing "business strategy" as its specialty (BCG 2013). Based on historical data, Henderson found in particular that the evolution of manufacturing costs follows in most industries a predictable pattern, which corporate portfolio managers can use to decide on investments and divestments. Bringing the mathematical rigor of his PhD in economics, Michael Porter (1980, 1985) provided additional theoretical support to his predecessors' work. He notably argued that organizations determine their strategy after in-depth analysis of the "competitive forces" that operate in their industries and markets. Chief executives respond to these forces by following one of three possible generic strategies, which Porter analyzed as chains of value-adding activities and resources. Among these are competitive advantages, the attributes that enable an organization to outperform its competitors.

Lanchester evaluated organizational resources, Mayo observed people working in groups, Simon analyzed decision-making, Ansoff investigated corporate investments, and Henderson delved into manufacturing costs, while Porter probed into corporations' economic environments, processes, and resources. All the same: despite their differences, these endeavors, for successful and influential as they have been on their own, belong to the same tradition. Called by Kiechel (2010: 4) "Greater Taylorism," this tradition is more accurately qualified as structural-functionalist-positivist, for reasons to be exposed shortly. It is a tradition that assumes that management research is a scientific endeavor, because it aims at an objective similar to that of the natural sciences: the production of a performative body of knowledge, that is, theory allowing for prediction and control of particular types of phenomena.

Theoretical Foundations

The quest for management theory has not ended since the days of the pioneers mentioned in the foregoing. More appropriate today is to speak of management theories, for contemporary management studies is a field marked by increasing theoretical multiplicity. Taylor sought to improve the efficiency of physical tasks and based his theory on the view that line workers only execute, not organize, their work. Conversely, Mayo could formulate a theory about the data collected at Hawthorne only after taking account of employees' interpretations of the experiment. Different levels of analysis produce different management theories. On this basis, there seems to be no end to their multiplication (Whitley 1984). Already in 1961, Koontz (1961) lamented a theoretical "jungle" of thickening complexity, identifying first 6, then 11, distinct families of theories less than two decades later (Koontz 1980). The jungle has not receded since: an overarching criterion for article acceptance in a leading management journal today is that the research it reports extends existing theory or builds new theory.

About the phenomena they study, what these phenomena encompass and how to study them, management researchers explicitly or implicitly develop clusters of assumptions. For instance, scholars wanting to develop a theory describing how people behave in organizations must first define what they believe qualifies (or not) as an organization, what kind of behavior is relevant, and what kind is not. As the examples of Taylor and Mayo illustrate, however, such definitions rest themselves on different conceptions about human nature and social reality. Underlying the plethora of management theories lies therefore another profusion, that of ontological, epistemological, and methodological assumptions. Different clusters of assumptions lead to different conclusions about how to conduct management research, about what kind of phenomena should attract researchers' attention and therefore about what counts as a management theory.

In management and organizational studies, an influential study of the assumptions scholars espouse when conducting their research is Burrell and Morgan's (1979). At the time of writing, the work has attracted over 15,597 citations according to Google Scholar; already in 1996, the work's influence was judged "hegemonic" (Deetz 1996: 191) (In 2013, the work attracted over 6000 citations (Hassard and Cox 2013: 1701); this shows that, rather than waning, the influence of Burrell and Morgan's study is growing.). That Burrell and Morgan's study has been influential does not mean it has been consensual, however. For example, disagreements exist about the number of research frameworks, their names, or the research practices they produce. Thus, in place of the four frameworks identified by Burrell and Morgan, authors have proposed three (Locke 2001: 7–12) or two (Lakomski and Evers 2011; Boisot and McKelvey 2010; Clegg and Ross-Smith 2003). In the related field of sociology of work, Watson (2003) has distinguished three sets of methodological assumptions leading to six different research approaches (In a later work, Watson (2017) argues for four different approaches.). What remains certain is that Burrell and Morgan's work has shaped discussions about such matters; its terminology has been retained in the discussion about to unfold.

Burrell and Morgan (1979: 21–25) called "paradigms" the four clusters of assumptions that frame management and organizational research and named them "functionalist," "interpretivist," "radical structuralist," and "radical humanist." In their view, these paradigms are incommensurable, in the sense that they rest on fundamentally incompatible views about social science and social reality, leading to radically different research practices, objectives, and results. For instance, researchers working as per the radical structuralist and functionalist paradigms share an emphasis on objective study of social reality, while those following the radical humanist and the interpretive paradigms believe that social phenomena can only be understood subjectively. That is, it is the perspective and intentions of those individuals the behavior of whom is studied that primarily concern the latter group of scholars, not the actual manifestations or consequences of that behavior (which concern the former group of researchers). However, still according to Burrell and Morgan, adepts of the interpretivist and functionalist paradigms promote social regulation, while those scholars following the radical humanist and the radical structuralist paradigms stimulate research enabling social change.

Burrell and Morgan's (1979: 32–33) radical humanist scholars deserve further exposition, for their conception of research sets them apart on management academia's scene. These researchers believe that ideological constructs dominate human consciousness and estrange human beings from their full potentialities. In particular, they see a science of management as a construct leading to alienation, with the Taylorization of the workplace held as a prime example of such dehumanization. In the radical humanist perspective, the trust invested in management as an applied science is one of these ideological barriers to human fulfilment. Radical humanist scholars thus see their mission as identifying the multifarious manifestations of the management science ideology and help fellow human beings in their attempts to liberate themselves from it.

A critical evaluation of Burrell and Morgan's classification is not immediately relevant to the present argument (Hassard and Cox 2013 and Deetz 1996 are examples of such evaluations). Similarly, whether the paradigms Burrell and Morgan identified are truly incommensurable, thus leading to irreconcilable research practices and incompatible management theories, or can be somehow reconciled within one or more meta-paradigms is a question that can be postponed, at least for now (Clegg and Ross-Smith (2003) answer it by the negative, while Lakomski and Evers (2011) claim that "naturalistic coherentism" can account for the main paradigms that actually exist. Boisot and McKelvey (2010) argue that complexity science provides a bridge between research paradigms, while Wicks and Freeman (1998) believe that pragmatism provides a research ground common to all paradigms.). General comments about management research are in order before a discussion on such matters is possible.

Mainstream Management Research

Beyond their disagreements, authors who have analyzed the assumptions underpinning management research grant a dominant role and influence to the sort of research that Burrell and Morgan called "functionalist," if under a different name. For instance, while Watson (2017), Clegg and Ross-Smith (2003), and Johnson and Duberley (2000) have called such research "positivist," Boisot and McKelvey (2010) and Locke (2001) have preferred to name it "modernist" and Lakomski and Evers (2011) "empiricist." Although connected, these terms deserve to be distinguished.

"Modernism" refers to a period in the history of Western ideas, arts, and culture, with roots in the nineteenth century but culminating in the first decades of the twentieth century. "Empiricism" is the view, developed from the sixteenth century onward, that the exclusive source of knowledge is experience, that is, information conveyed by the senses. Positivism is a philosophy of science first given systematic exposition by Auguste Comte (1798–1957) and further developed in the 1920s and 1930s (Kolakowski 1969). Positivist science accepts the empiricist premise: it studies reality in its phenomenal manifestations. It ignores moral values to focus exclusively on facts, defined as corroborated, intersubjective sense data. Accordingly, positivist scientists strive for objective (value-free) observations of phenomena, from which they inductively infer theories that they confront to new observations by way of predictions and experiments. In the life and physical sciences, positivism is the arch-dominating, not to say quasi exclusive, philosophy.

Functionalism is not a philosophy of science but a conception of social reality. Although often said obsolete, functionalism is still central to sociology (Kingsbury and Scanzoni 2009). Functionalists believe that they can adequately describe any social phenomenon (institution, pattern of behavior, norm, or belief) in the terms of the function (and of the effects of this function) this phenomenon discharges on other phenomena under analysis, irrespective of the intentions of the individuals that animate or harbor it (Gellner 1970). As Radcliffe-Brown (1940) long argued, however, functionalism is intimately associated with another sociological ontology, namely, structuralism (on this theme, see also Lévi-Strauss 1963). Structuralism is the view that phenomena only exist through their relationships with larger, ordering structures (Blackburn 2005: 353). The connection between functionalism and structuralism is a natural one, for the concept of relationship almost invariably leads to that of function. Further, to speak of function is to imply that there is an entity that functions. If phenomena are only observable through relationships seen as functional manifestations and if functions manifest the existence of entities that can be decomposed into sub-entities, the difference between functions and structures is merely lexical. In this sense, dissociating functionalism from structuralism and holding them to be incommensurable views of social reality, as Burrell and Morgan did, are unwarranted moves; many authors understandably speak of structural-functionalism (e.g., Dew 2014).

In social science, the structural-functionalist tradition is perhaps best exemplified in the work of Émile Durkheim (2002 [1897]). For Durkheim, society is the ultimate structure, a determined, complete, coherent, and self-regulating system made of causally interconnected components (structures). Among these are work organizations, which stand for and discharge social functions. Individuals do not exist as autonomous beings but only as components (substructures) of society and its institutions, i.e., as vehicles of the various social functions they simultaneously embody and discharge.

In management studies, the combination of structuralism, functionalism, and positivism has been attractive to scholars. Indeed, the research framework such a combination produces provides immediate ontological, epistemological, and methodological support to the quest for management theory. As per the structural-functionalist view, work organizations, their internal components and attributes (equipment, patents, brands, employees, hierarchies, processes, etc.), and their partners, suppliers, customers, inputs, and outputs are nothing but structures which discharge and embody regular and causally effective functions (relationships) on other structures. Further, as per the positivist research framework, the behavior (function) of these structures is amenable to objective observation, thus ensuring the scientific status and value neutrality of the resulting management theory.

In the structural-functionalist-positivist (SFP) perspective, management research is an endeavor modeled on that of natural science, resting on similar assumptions and aiming at the same overall objective of performativity: prediction and control by way of theories. Management is itself a practice conducted as per a body of theoretical knowledge, expressed in scientific language and grounded on objective observation and quantitative data analysis. As in other applied sciences, there are universal, value-free, and predictive methods available to managers through which they can improve their practice. The SFP conception of management studies is that which Taylor pioneered and to which Simon and his peers at GSIA first gave unassailable academic credentials. It has formed the backbone of management academia to this day (hence the qualifiers "traditional," "orthodox," or again "mainstream" that are also used to denote it). As attested by AACSB's mission statement, it is a conception of management research and practice that, in typical positivist fashion, equates scholarly and scientific progress with social progress and general human welfare ("The vision of AACSB is to transform business education for global prosperity. Business and business schools are a force for good, contributing to the world's economy, and AACSB plays a significant role in making that benefit better known to all stakeholders – serving business schools, students, business, and society" (AACSB n.d.).).

Besides Simon, one can cite Blau (1963), Pfeffer (1982), or Donaldson (1996) as salient representatives of the SFP tradition in management and organization studies. The appearance of game theory, the rise of economics and finance in management schools' curricula, and the preponderance of quantitative studies in management journals are signs that the SFP tradition is not only current but also gaining influence because quantitative analysis is associated with certainty, objectivity, and instrumentality, all notions at the heart of the positivist research program. "Evidence-based management" (Pfeffer and Sutton 2006; Rousscau and McCarthy 2007), insofar as it is conceived as a research agenda and not merely a body of practice, is another outgrowth of the positivist branch of management studies.

Burrell and Morgan's radical structuralist account of management research, as its name indicates, hinges on the view that stable structures underpin social reality. Citing Marx as example, Burrell and Morgan (1979: 34) note that, for radical structuralists, "radical change is built in the very nature and structure of contemporary society" and that such structure "provide[s] explanations of the basic interrelationships within the context of total social formations." Interpretivist social researchers espouse this (structural-functionalist) conception of social reality insofar as they are committed to the position, as Burrell and Morgan (1979: 31) put it, that "the world of human affairs is cohesive, ordered and integrated." When Mayo and Roethlisberger spoke of causally effective "social systems" to account for what happened at Hawthorne, they did not mean differently.

In *The Theory of Social and Economic Organization*, Max Weber (1969 [1915]) argued that social scientists should inquire in the causes of unintended events, but ignore intended ones. If an event occurs as the deliberate result of an individual's action, this particular individual is the cause of that event, and there is no need to engage in scientific inquiry to discover what caused it. However, if the event is unintended, then its real causes are unknown, and it is therefore worthwhile to mobilize scientific means to discover them. Such a discovery will make it possible to judge whether the event in question will occur again or to control its occurrence. In this argument at least, Weber did not deviate from positivist science's overall performative agenda, according to which the ultimate purpose of scientific knowledge is to expand and consolidate control of reality. The interpretive school of social research is thus not an alternative but a complement to the picture provided by the positivist account (Khurana 2007: 394).

The radical humanist management researcher, according to Burrell and Morgan (1979: 32), has much in common with his interpretivist counterpart. Both believe in the existence of stable, superordinate arrangements of organizational reality buried in human consciousness (for instance, in the shape of ideologies or moral constraints), which they strive to discover and codify. Where radical humanists differ from interpretivists is in how to use such knowledge: to regulate organizations for interpretive scholars or to change it for radical humanist researchers. In either case, however, scholars retain the central performative agenda of SFP research.

In summary, although differing in their methods and in some of their assumptions about social reality, the four paradigms of management research identified by Burrell and Morgan (1979) share a central agenda. They are variations on the quest for stable and ordering features underpinning organizational reality, the existence of which is assumed. In making this assumption, management researchers walk in the steps of their illustrious predecessors in social science, be it Marx, Durkheim, or Weber, all of whom took the existence of causal trends or relationships structuring the social phenomena they studied for granted (Giddens 2000: 239). The alleged incommensurability of Burrell and Morgan's research paradigms must therefore be requalified: in a crucial aspect, it is merely superficial. They differ not on the nature of the ultimate substratum of organizational reality (stable, causally effective structures) but on where to locate that substratum and how to study it.

Once suitably identified and codified by management researchers, stable and causally effective structures form bases from which prediction and control of organizational phenomena are possible. For instance, if organizational cultures manifest themselves along fixed dimensions (stable and causally effective structures), then managers must take advantage of these dimensions when restructuring or regulating organizations (management theory; see Buono and Bowditch 2003). The idea that there is such a thing as a management theory to be discovered because there are such things as stable, causally effective features that determine organizational reality is therefore *the* theory underpinning all management theories. However, in this statement, "theory" is not to be understood in the scientific sense (i.e., as lawlike generalization stemming from past observations intended to predict future ones), but, in the everyday sense, as mere speculation. Management researchers accept it a priori, as an axiom, because without it, the performativity of their research cannot be justified.

In its current format, management academia as a whole hinges of the possibility of theory. It is thus unsurprising that, despite their alleged incommensurability, the various approaches to management research that Burrell and Morgan identified have gained momentum within management research. Not that their respective influences are equivalent; for instance, compared to the dominating influence of the functionalist account, that of the radical humanist paradigm appears modest (Gioia and Pitre 1990). Whatever the case, if management academics suffer from "physics envy" (Bygrave 1989: 16), they also labor under a managerial bias, since the ultimate objective of their research is to provide means for organizational regulation or transformation, that is, executive control. Irrespective of their research paradigm, they are all, in Baritz's (1960) apt expression, "servants of power."

Postmodern Management Research

Published in 1979, Burrell and Morgan's work could not include a discussion of a stream of management studies that is embryonic in their analysis but only took shape in earnest in the early 1990s. It is a stream of management studies that appears in later discussions of research paradigms, albeit with a much weaker degree of agreement about what sort of research it consists of and to what sort of theories (if any at all) it leads. This is the research framework called "postmodern" (Hassard 1994), "postpositivist" (Clegg and Ross-Smith 2003), "postmodernist" (Lakomski and Evers 2011; Boisot and McKelvey 2010; Johnson and Duberley 2000), or again "deconstructionist" (Hassard and Cox 2013). Another umbrella term for this body of management research is "critical management studies" (Alvesson and Willmott 1992; Fournier and Grey 2000; Boje et al. 1996; Adler et al. 2007), although other commentators have preferred to speak of the "symbolic perspective" (Sulkowski 2010) or "subversive functionalism" (Koss Hartmann 2014). Supported by dedicated journals, postmodern management research, in its multifarious hues, represents today an active area of scholarship. However, even if many postmodern research themes have found their way in mainstream management research

(Hassard and Cox 2013), postmodern management scholarship has had little influence on the content of current management curricula. There are good reasons for this.

Along the lines followed by Burrell and Morgan's radical humanist scholars, postmodern management researchers seek to distance themselves from the tradition of Taylor and Simon because they are wary of its consequences. They, too, pursue a "political" research agenda insofar as they oppose what they believe are the noxious effects of a science of management. What makes postmodern management researchers' position distinctive, however, is their rejection of stable empirical referents. Following such thinkers as Foucault, Feyerabend, and Derrida, postmodern management authors either reject the notion of "truth," which they see as an element of a discourse seeking domination or, if they accept it, believe it to be inaccessible (Joullié and Spillane 2015: 278–283). As a result, postmodern management authors are not merely suspicious of management science for being an instrument of social oppression; rather, they dismiss it altogether. They deny society a stable, neutral existence and see institutions, symbols, words, and texts not as having fixed meaning or pointing to permanent entities. Rather, postmodernists analyze such components of social experience as repressive processes silencing other institutions, symbols, words, and texts, all the while promoting the agendas of their incumbents or of those who author them. In the postmodern worldview, there cannot be a science of management because the objectivity demanded by SFP research is a delusion, a mirage: what passes for reality is in fact a fabrication, a socially constructed illusion, a lie. In particular, organizational life is politically motivated, a scene on which vested interests constantly play out and collide, in any case an experience escaping passive or neutral recording.

While there are merits to a critical view of organizational life, it is easier to understand what postmodern management researchers oppose than what they propose, if anything. This impotence is mainly the consequence of their radical (anti-)epistemological stance that condemns them to an anti-performative position. Rejecting the idea that organizational reality exists as a permanent object of study, postmodern management scholars find themselves incapable of recommending a course of action, be it to fellow management academics or managers. In the absence of stable, causally effective social structures, there is indeed no ground upon which a theory could develop. If postmodern management authors are correct in their views of social reality, their work itself stems from and embodies an ideology that is politically motivated, that is, oppressive in its intentions. Surprisingly, however, this insurmountable difficulty has not prevented some postmodern management authors from proposing practical advice to managers and academic peers (see Donaldson (2003) for an extended discussion on this theme).

The Collapse of Theory

The ethical, logical, epistemological, and ontological difficulties met by researchers in social science have been long documented (e.g., Giedymin 1975). In fact, it was their progressive articulation (in the hands of Weber, Adorno, Horkheimer, and

Popper, most notably) that spurred the development of the different versions of social research that Burrell and Morgan mapped. Various strategies are available to mitigate the difficulties that each research paradigm generates (see especially Johnson and Duberley 2000; see also Boisot and McKelvey 2010; Wicks and Freeman 1998; Gioia and Pitre 1990). Rather than these well-travelled themes, the following explores an overlooked aspect of management research's difficulties.

The main issues social researchers face in their work stem from the influence that they inevitably exert on the agents the behavior of whom they study, the complexity of social phenomena, the impossibility of studying them in laboratory conditions, and the challenge of identifying control groups before conducting experiments. Considered together, these difficulties rule out explanations of social events similar to those advanced in the natural sciences, which are in terms of causes and effects of these causes. As Andreski (1969: 58) observed, at most, in social sciences, only "possibilistic" explanations can be advanced, that is, explanations why something could happen, not why it happened, let alone why it had to happen. In other words, in social science, explanations do not express sufficient conditions of occurrence of an event (causal explanation), but necessary conditions of occurrence. As such, explanations of social phenomena are not predictive and thus cannot be performative (On this account, there cannot be theory in social science, and "social science" is itself an oxymoronic expression. For an extended discussion on this theme, see Gellner 1986: 101–127); see also Morgenbesser (1970).). Moreover, if one accepts the reality of free will, i.e., if one understands that human behavior is by nature unpredictable, then one must also accept that causal explanations of social events are impossible in all cases where these events are determined by the choices of one or a handful of individuals. Such is typically the case in management situations where decision-making rests with one or a small number of people.

If the indeterminacy of human actions vitiates the possibility of causal explanations, it follows that the possibility of causal explanation requires that human actions are predictable. Expressed differently, the quest for performative (because causal) management theories must assume a degree of psychological determinism, at least on the part of those to whom the theories apply. For example, in *For Positivist Organization Theory*, Donaldson (1996) argues that organizational decisions are entirely contingent on phenomena over which managers and executives have little or no control, such as general economic conditions, competitors' offering, legal constraints, or simply shareholders' expectations. There is therefore no such thing as strategic choice. Managerial free will, if it exists, is of negligible consequence; trying to account for it in management studies is a pointless endeavor. If true, such a deterministic view of organizational reality leaves little room for such widely debated notions as business ethics and corporate social responsibility. Scholars engaged in these latter research agendas are mistaken in their efforts.

Even if they do not share Donaldson's positivist commitment, management theorists, irrespective of their research paradigm, share his view on human agency, knowingly or not. This is the case because if organizational reality is structured along stable and causally effective features (be they buried in the depths of human consciousness), then organizational life is ultimately determined in some aspects.

These aspects are the phenomena that management researchers study, the occurrences of which their theories describe and predict. It is thus possible to determine future occurrences of the phenomena the theories encompass, like the behavior of elementary particles is predictable and controllable by way of the electromagnetic forces theorized by physicists. As discussed, postmodern management scholars escape these comments at the cost of being incapable of proposing any management theory at all.

Being performative, management research, irrespective of its paradigm, requires and implies a degree of psychological determinism. Yet, bar for theorists like Donaldson, most management scholars do not realize this implication, as their concern for managerial and corporate responsibility attests. It thus behooves the present commentator to explain the discrepancy between what management researchers actually do and what most of them profess they do. Although such an argument requires more sustained development than space affords here, I submit in the following paragraphs that management authors do not recognize the psychological determinism implied in their research and conveyed by their theories because they obfuscate it, presumably unwittingly, behind a cloud of equivocations, ambiguities, tautologies, and imprecise language.

Scholarly management and organization studies offer equivocations aplenty. Although a systematic survey of the concerned literature is normally required to substantiate such an assertion, three examples will suffice to provide it credibility and prosecute the present case. They pertain to the use of "authority," "personality," and "motivation," three terms that are pervasive in management literature.

"Authority" is an ambiguous word that management authors generally leave undefined. Dictionaries (e.g., the *Merriam-Webster* online dictionary, accessed on 14 March 2018) acknowledge this ambiguity when they define the term as "the power to influence or command thought, opinion, or behaviour." To influence is not to command, however: the former verb leaves room for subjective interpretation and thus psychological freedom; the latter does not and implies necessary obedience by way of psychological control. Thus, when Rojas (2010: 1264) writes in his study of academic authority "some actors [...] seek the authority to coerce others" and that "connections help individuals acquire the legitimate authority to influence events" (2010: 1265), he equivocates on the two meanings of the term and leaves the practical implications of his theory uncertain. Such an equivocation is doubly convenient. First, should the theory be implemented, the equivocation protects the theorist from the charge that his research does not result in employee coercion. Second and more to the point of the current discussion, the equivocation presumably leaves the same theorist unaware of the deterministic implications of his theory. Had the meaning of "authority" been clarified or a less ambiguous word like "power" or "control" been used, these implications would have been either avoided or made apparent.

"Personality" is a concept central to managerial psychology and to a large component of management and organizational behavior literature. Although there are over 200 different definitions of personality (Spillane and Martin 2005: 71), most of them advance personality as a stable psychological structure or process that confers individual behavior an overall degree of consistency. In this perspective, personality explains (i.e., causes) behavioral regularities (McRae and Costa 1996: 57–58). The concept of personality thus assumes that there are aspects of behavior that remain beyond the volition of the individuals. Notwithstanding claims to the contrary, the psychological determinism of personality theories is particularly evident when personality is viewed as a bundle of stable traits (dispositions) existing within the person and controlling his or her behavior (Clarke 2009). Indeed, behavioral predictions based on the results of personality tests have been a major goal and justification of personality research since its beginnings (Baritz 1960: 21–41).

The psychological determinism implied in personality psychology is not without consequences on personal freedom, intelligence, and creativity. If individuals behave as per fixed psychological structures beyond their control, they are not completely free and thus not entirely responsible for what they do: they behave in ways constrained by their personality. It is illusory to expect from them behavior outside of the range of activities that their personality allows. The narrower the range of activities in which the concerned individuals can engage, the more consistent their behavior remains regardless of environmental conditions. In other words, the stronger the personality, the less intelligent (in the sense of adaptive) and the less creative the individual. Although this argument is of sound logic and in accord with explanations of aberrant or deviant behavior in terms of personality factors or mental illnesses (Spillane and Martin 2005: 72–74), it is not widely recognized by management authors. This confusion is evident in the use of such oxymoronic expressions as "creative personality" (Oldham and Cummings 1996), "imaginative personality" (Kartono et al. 2017), and again "intelligent personality" (Bartone et al. 2009), which are common in management and management-related literature (One influent (about 500 citations) study even mentions the concept of "responsible personality" (Berkowitz and Lutterman 1968).).

Lastly, "motivation" is a concept often found in management and organizational behavior articles and textbooks, if generally left without a clear definition. When a definition is provided, it is typically along the lines provided by Griffin and Moorhead (2012: 90), that is, one which conceives of motivation, in transparently physicist language, as "the set of forces that causes people to engage in one behavior rather than some alternative behaviour." In this reading, motivation is a causally effective factor, the reach of which is inescapable: motivated employees are caused to behave as they do (i.e., they do not act but react). These individuals' choice and free will, should they exist, are of no consequence. In ordinary language, however, motivation has a different meaning. As the *Oxford* online dictionary attests (accessed on 20 February 2018), motivation typically refers to a reason for acting in certain ways, a desire to do something, that is, a volition, a fear, an incentive, or an objective. This second definition makes room for choice and free will: if a motivation is a reason for action and not a cause for reaction, then one can change one's behavior by changing one's motivation. As is the case for "authority" and "personality," the equivocation that surrounds "motivation" is convenient for management authors, for it hides, perhaps even to themselves, the determinism of their motivation theories. It also makes their theories unfalsifiable, thus unscientific in Popper's (2004) sense, since whatever experimental evidence produced will be compatible with the theory. Should "motivated" employees behave as expected, motivation-as-cause will figure centrally in results' interpretation; should these same employees not behave as expected, researchers will call on motivation-as-reason when interpreting the results of their experiment.

The afore-discussed equivocations and conceptual ambiguities allow the concerned management scholars to cloak their theories in a scientific veneer. In strategic management literature, circular reasoning provides the scientific varnish. In two distinct streams of publications, Powell (2001, 2002) and Priem and Butler (2001a, b) have indeed observed that, since competitive advantages and valuable resources are only identified within successful organizations, these competitive advantages and valuable resources cannot, in and of themselves, explain these organizations' successful performance. Implying, as Porter (1985) and countless others after him do, that competitive advantages or valuable resources produce organizational success thus amounts to implying that organizations are successful because they are successful. The proposition is true, but trivially so. It does not state a theory but only a tautology without predictive, let alone performative, quality.

Strategic management literature is not alone in advancing tautologies masquerading as scientific theories. Such propositions also abound in the "implications for practice" sections of management articles. Bartunek and Rynes (2010) reviewed 1738 empirical articles published in 5 leading management and management-related journals in 1992 and 1993 and between 2003 and 2007. Bartunek and Rynes (2010: 105) found that, overall, 74% (up to 89% for some journals, depending on the year considered) of these "implications for practice" sections rely on tentative language, that is, make use of "may," "speculate," "potentially," or other words of similar meaning. Propositions expressed in this sort of language are either tautological or unfalsifiable; in either case, they have no empirical implications.

Although Bartunek and Rynes based their analysis on articles published in 1992–1993 and 2003–2007, more recent exemplars are not difficult to find, showing that the phraseology they identified is still prevalent. For instance, Su and Tsang (2015: 1143) write, as practical implications of their research, that "results suggest that firms may strategically control the scope of the secondary stakeholders in which they are interested." The verb "suggest" signals that the proposed interpretation contains a part of subjectivity and that other researchers could interpret the same results differently; the modal "may" indicate that the opposite result is possible. If the sentence has some appearance of performativity, it has none of its core attributes, namely, objectivity and causality.

Tentative and speculative language, like the equivocations, conceptual ambiguities, and tautologies reviewed earlier, either obfuscates management literature's inherent determinism or hollow it out of practical consequences. In both cases and crucially, such language does not convey theoretical knowledge. Sentences like "X suggests Y," "X may cause Y," and "X potentially triggers Y" imply that Y does necessarily follow from X and that something else, or nothing at all, can possibly follow from X. That such formulation is widespread in management literature shows that scholars, despite their intentions to identify and codify theory, have been incapable of doing so.

If management research is a quest for performativity, this goal has disappeared from its practical conclusions. When engaging in management research, scholars assume that stable, causally effective structures underpin the way organizations operate, yet the language these same scholars use to report the result of their research implicitly but unambiguously betrays the inexistence of such structures. The fact is that management researchers have yet to identify a single theory they can apply in the world of organizations with the same reliability that physicists apply theirs in the world of objects. The limitations, weaknesses, and adverse social consequences of scientific management, the first and perhaps most successful of all management "theories," need no rehearsal here: scientific management is not the panacea, the "one best method" Taylor (1919: 25) insistently claimed it was. The promise of performativity made by management researchers has remained a promise. Except in their intentions and research hypotheses, there is no such a thing as a management theory. The failure of management theorists illustrates Gellner's (1986: 126–127) argument that, if science is characterized by its ability to generate cumulative knowledge capable of improving human existence by way of predictions and controls (i.e., what Lyotard called science's performativity), then the so-called social sciences (to which management studies belong) are not scientific.

Conclusion: Management Scholarship for the Twenty-First Century

The idea of management theory has had a successful run since its inception in the first decade of the twentieth century. From Taylor to Simon to Porter (and countless others), the contention that there exists a theoretical body of knowledge enabling managers reliably and predictably to improve their practice has been widely accepted. Current management education is predicated on this conception, to which tens of thousands of management researchers around the world have given flesh – or so it seems.

In scholarly literature, theory is a performative and deterministic notion. Anyone proposing a theory about natural or experimental phenomena implies that, should the conditions that presided over their initial observation persist, these phenomena will continue to occur as they have occurred and can thus be controlled or at minimum predicted. Proposing a theory about given phenomena thus amounts to claiming that the behavior of these phenomena is predictable, that is, somehow determined. Applying the notion of theory to management and organizational concerns thus requires, implies, and conveys the idea that the phenomena management researchers study are determined in some essential but inescapable ways. Organizations, however, are made of people; management is, ultimately, the management of people. The notion of theory applied to management phenomena involves a deterministic picture of human agency, one in which human beings, in some ways at least, do not act but merely react and do not behave as they wish but as they must.

To escape the psychological determinism that is inherent to the structural-functional-positivist research agenda, management theorists have developed alternative ontological, epistemological, and methodological assumptions upon which to conduct research. Despite incommensurability claims by their advocates, these competing research frameworks come together in one crucial assumption: they all rely on the existence of underlying stable and causally effective features of organizational life upon which it is possible to develop management theories. Scholars for whom this comment does not hold are postmodern management researchers for whom there are no fixed structures in social reality and therefore no basis upon which to ground theory. Postmodern management scholars escape the charge of determinism, only to face that of practical paralysis and empirical irrelevance.

Except for a few hard-core positivists such as Donaldson, management scholars do not openly commit to the idea of psychological determinism – in fact, most of them typically deny such a commitment. Nevertheless, if management theories were not deterministic in at least some of their aspects, there would not be any way to justify their performativity and consequently their teaching in management schools. It is only because management theories are supposedly performative that their knowledge is meant to enable managers to improve their practice and management graduates to pretend to management positions.

Willingly or not, knowingly or not, management scholars obfuscate their commitment to psychological determinism thanks to equivocations, conceptual ambiguities, tautologies, speculative wording, and tentative language when reporting their theories. Constructs such as "personality" and "motivation," common in management literature, demand psychological determinism to be used as support of theories, yet are often employed as if it was not the case, obscuring their meaning. The notion of "authority" and specifically its articulation with the concepts of "power" and "control" is rarely, if ever, elucidated, leaving its practical implication uncertain. Circular reasoning is at the heart of competitive advantage and valuable resource theories, carving them out of practical relevance. As for the sections of articles that spell out the practical implications of research, they rely in their vast majority on a language that denudes them of predictive application. Their theoretical content is only apparent and their performativity inexistent. The quest for management theory has failed.

A handful of scholars have perceived that management studies are facing a crisis of theory (Ghoshal 2005); that current management scholarship is mostly irrelevant to theory, practice (George 2014), and teaching (Pearce and Huang 2012); and that management academia is facing an existential and legitimacy crisis (Khurana 2007). Management academia must reinvent itself if it wants to survive these crises. If this reinvention goes through the abandonment of theory to make room for managerial freedom and responsibility, then so be it. In any case, forfeiting the claim to theoretical knowledge will not be at management studies' cost. If the pursuit of theory cannot be reconciled with a world picture in which managers act, choose, and are responsible for their decisions, then so much the worse for theory. Scholars sensitive to this line of argument will remember, however, that such an abandonment of theory must remain compatible with management academia's claim to instrumentality, if not to its promise of performativity. That is, unless they are ready to embrace critical management authors' practical irrelevance quagmire, scholars must find ways to make their research useful, if not predictive, to managers. The work of Peter Drucker, who never claimed to have a theory of management (and insisted there would never be such a thing; cf. Drucker 1986: 39), shows in the most convincing of ways that such an endeavor is possible.

The time has come for an a-theoretical management scholarship to emerge or, rather, to rise from the structural-functional-positivist grave in which Simon and others buried it. For more than 2000 years, education for community citizenship and leadership was based on *studia humanitatis*, the branches of knowledge that investigate how people document and make sense of human experience. To prepare himself for a senior administrative position, Machiavelli, to take one famous example, studied Latin, rhetoric, logic, diplomacy, history, and moral philosophy (Skinner 1981). Such an education provides analytical and critical methods of inquiry rooted in an appreciation of diverse human values, skills that managers, as decision-makers, require (Tomey 2009).

Further, to the extent that management is a linguistic activity, to learn management is to learn to speak and to think (a form of self-talk) clearly and convincingly about matters at hand. Doing this requires that one appreciates the tenets and conceptions, especially when these concern human nature, implied and conveyed by the terms one uses to frame the problems one is trying to solve. As the present analysis of the concept of management theory shows, such a liberating endeavor is impossible in the obscurity of an imprecise language, in the absence of moral and aesthetic references, or in the chaotic outline of a world grasped outside of its intellectual and historical origins. Mastery of language supports the use of reason, encourages critical argument, and produces mature individuals. The critical evaluation of assumptions brings about the awareness of alternatives: intellectual freedom, citizenship engagement, and moral leadership have no other possible origins.

In human affairs, ambiguity is the norm and necessity of behavior never encountered (one can always choose, if only how to die). If their environment is complex, human beings are even more so, because their decisions always contain an irrational and emotional element that makes them unpredictable. Despite Simon's assertions to the contrary, mathematical models cannot adequately represent human endeavors. Rather than looking for an elusive (and humanly demeaning) management theory, scholars can contribute to management thought. Expressed differently, rather than trying to predict management phenomena by way of theories, management scholars can try to understand them. Instead of searching for causes, researchers have the option to expose and clarify reasons, those that led to executive choices and managerial actions, taking into account objectives, situational constraints, and material contingencies. Elucidating past decisions of managers, their tenets, and their glorious or inglorious outcomes reveals what alternatives these managers could have pursued and what other opportunities were available to them. Defeats are humbling, successes are fleeting, and possibilities are attractive but elusive; all, however, are sources of learning. A vast and fertile research agenda beckons.

Cross-References

▶ A Return to the Good Old Days: Populism, Fake News, Yellow Journalism, and the Unparalleled Virtue of Business People
▶ Introduction: Public Policy Failure, the Demise of Experts, and the Dawn of a New Era
▶ Labor and Employment Practices: The Rise and Fall of the New Managerialism
▶ Management History in the Modern World: An Overview
▶ The New Executive: Interconnected Yet Isolated and Uninformed – Leadership Challenges in the Digital Pandemic Epoch
▶ Trade Union Decline and Transformation: Where to for Employment Relations?
▶ What Is Management?
▶ Why Did the Great Recession Fail to Produce a *New* New Deal in the USA?

References

AACSB (n.d.). http://www.aacsb.edu/about/mission. Accessed 09 Nov 2017
Adler PS, Forbes LC, Willmott H (2007) Critical management studies. Acad Manag Ann 1:119–179
Alvesson M, Willmott H (eds) (1992) Critical management studies. SAGE, London
Andreski S (1969) The uses of comparative sociology. University of California Press, Berkeley
Ansoff I (1965) Corporate strategy. McGraw-Hill, New York
Baritz L (1960) The servants of power. Wesleyan University Press, Middletown
Barnard CI (1968) The functions of the executive (Andrews KR intr.). Harvard University Press, Cambridge
Bartone BT, Eid J, Johnsen BJ, Laberg JC, Snook SA (2009) Big five personality factors, hardiness, and social judgment as predictors of leader performance. Leadersh Org Dev J 30(6):498–521
Bartunek JM, Rynes SR (2010) The construction and contributions of "implications for practice": what's in them and what might they offer? Acad Manag Learn Educ 9(1):100–117
BCG (2013) BCG HISTORY: 1965, www.bcg.com/about_bcg/history/history_1965.aspx. Accessed 01 Feb 2018
Beer S (1968) Management science: the business use of operations research. Doubleday, London
Berkowitz L, Lutterman KG (1968) The traditional social responsible personality. Public Opin Q 32(2):169–185
Blackburn S (2005) The Oxford dictionary of philosophy, 2nd edn. Oxford University Press, Oxford
Blau PM (1963) The dynamics of bureaucracy: study of interpersonal relations in two government agencies. University of Chicago Press, Chicago
Bogen J (2017) Theory and observation in science. In: Zalta EN (ed) The Stanford encyclopedia of philosophy. https://plato.stanford.edu/entries/science-theory-observation/. Accessed 05 Feb 2018
Boisot M, McKelvey B (2010) Integrating modernist and postmodernist perspectives on organizations: a complexity science bridge. Acad Manag Rev 35(3):415–433
Boje DM, Gephart RP, Thatchenkery TJ (eds) (1996) Postmodern management and organization theory. SAGE, Thousand Oaks
Buono AF, Bowditch JL (2003) The human side of mergers and acquisitions: managing collisions between people, culture, and organizations. BeardBooks, Washington
Burrell G, Morgan G (1979) Sociological paradigms and organisational analysis. Ashgate, London
Bygrave W (1989) The entrepreneurship paradigm (I): a philosophical look at its research methodologies. Entrep Theory Pract 14(1):7–26

Christensen CM, Raynor ME (2003) Why hard-nosed executives should care about management theory. Harv Bus Rev 81(9):66–74

Clarke R (2009) Dispositions, abilities to act, and free will: the new dispositionalism. Mind 118(470):323–351

Clegg SR, Ross-Smith A (2003) Revising the boundaries: management education and learning in a postpositivist world. Acad Manag Learn Edu 2(1):85–98

CUPA-HR (2016) Tenured/Tenure-Track Faculty Unweighted Average Salaries by 2-Digit Classification of Instructional Programs (CIP) Discipline, Academic Rank, and Affiliation. https://www.cupahr.org/wp-content/uploads/2017/07/FHE-2016-2-Digit-Average-Salaries-Tenured-and-Tenure-Track.pdf. Accessed on 13-March 2018

Deetz S (1996) Describing differences in approaches to organization science: rethinking Burrell and Morgan and their legacy. Organ Sci 7(2):191–207

Dew K (2014) Structural functionalism. In: Cockerham WC, Dingwall R, Quah S (eds) The Wiley Blackwell encyclopedia of health, illness, behavior, and society. Wiley, London

Donaldson L (1996) For positivist organization theory. SAGE, London

Donaldson L (2003) A critique of postmodernism in organizational studies. Res Sociol Organ 21:169–202

Drucker PF (1986) Management: tasks, responsibilities, practices. Truman Talley Books, New York

Durkheim É (2002) On suicide (ed: Simpson G; trans: Spaulding JA, Simpson G). Routledge Classics, London

Fournier V, Grey C (2000) At the critical moment: conditions and prospects for critical management studies. Hum Relat 53:7–32

Gellner E (1970) Concepts and society. In: Emmet D, MacIntyre A (eds) Sociological theory and philosophical analysis. The Macmillan Company, New York, pp 115–149

Gellner E (1986) Relativism and the social sciences. Cambridge University Press, Cambridge

George G (2014) Rethinking management scholarship. Acad Manag J 57(1):1–6

Ghoshal S (2005) Bad management theories are destroying good management practices. Acad Manag Learn Edu 4(1):75–91

Giddens A (2000) Capitalism and modern social theory. Cambridge University Press, Cambridge

Giedymin J (1975) Antipositivism in contemporary philosophy of social science and humanities. Br J Philos Sci 26(4):275–301. https://www.jstor.org/stable/686676?seq=1#metadata_info_tab_contents

Gioia DA, Pitre E (1990) Multiparadigm perspectives on theory building. Acad Manag Rev 15(4):584–602

Griffin RW, Moorhead G (2012) Organizational behavior: managing people and organizations, 10th edn. South Western, Cengage Learning, Mason

Hassard J (1994) Postmodern organizational analysis: toward a conceptual framework. J Manag Stud 31(3):303–324

Hassard J, Cox JW (2013) Can sociological paradigms still inform organizational analysis? A paradigm model for post-paradigm times. Organ Stud 34(11):1701–1728

Johnson P, Duberley J (2000) Understanding management research: an introduction to epistemology. SAGE, London

Joullié J-E, Spillane R (2015) The philosophical foundations of management thought. Lexington Books, New York

Kartono K, Hilmiana H, Muizu WOZ (2017) Personality and organisational politics on employees performance: studies at local government enterprises of people credit bank in West Java region III. Int J Bus Glob 18(4):524–538

Khurana R (2007) From higher aims to hired hands: the social transformation of American business schools and the unfulfilled promise of management as a profession. Princeton University Press, Princeton

Khurana R, Spender JC (2012) Herbert A. Simon on what ails business schools: more than 'a problem in organizational design'. J Manag Stud 49(3):619–639

Kiechel W (2010) The lords of strategy: the secret intellectual history of the new corporate world. Harvard Business Press, Boston

Kiechel W (2012) The management century. Harv Bus Rev 90(11):62–75

Kingsbury N, Scanzoni J (2009) Structural-functionalism. In: Boss P, Doherty WJ, LaRossa R, Schumm WR, Steinmetz SK (eds) Sourcebook of family theories and methods. Springer, Boston

Kolakowski L (1969) The alienation of reason: a history of positivist thought (trans: Guterman N). Anchor Books, New York

Koontz H (1961) The management theory jungle. J Acad Manag 4(3):174–188

Koontz H (1980) The management theory jungle revisited. Acad Manag Rev 5(2):175–187

Koss Hartmann R (2014) Subversive functionalism: for a less canonical critique in critical management studies. Hum Relat 67(5):611–632

Lakomski G, Evers CW (2011) Analytic philosophy and organization theory: philosophical problems and scientific solutions. In: Tsoukas H, Chia R (eds) Philosophy and organization theory. Res Sociol Organ. Emerald Group Publishing Limited, Bingley. 32:23–54. https://www.emerald.com/insight/content/doi/10.1108/S0733-558X(2011)0000032004/full/html

Lanchester FW (1956) Mathematics in warfare. In: Newman J (ed) The world of mathematics, vol 4. Simon & Chuster, New York

Lévi-Strauss C (1963) Structural anthropology (trans: Jacobson C, Schoepf BG). Basic Books, New York

Locke R (1989) Management and higher education since 1940. Cambridge University Press, Cambridge

Locke KD (2001) Grounded theory in management research. SAGE, London

Lyotard J-F (1984) The postmodern condition: a report on knowledge (trans: Bennington G, Massumi B). The University of Minnesota Press, Minneapolis

Mayo E (2007) The human problems of an industrial civilization. In: Thompson K (ed) The early sociology of management and organizations, vol VI. Routledge, London

McRae RR, Costa PT (1996) Toward a new generation of personality theories: theoretical contexts for the five-factor model. In: Wiggins JS (ed) The five-factor model of personality: theoretical perspectives. Guilford Press, New York, pp 51–87

Morgenbesser S (1970) Is it a science? In: Emmet D, MacIntyre A (eds) Sociological theory and philosophical analysis. The Macmillan Company, New York, pp 20–35

Oldham GR, Anne Cummings A (1996) Employee creativity: personal and contextual factors at work. Acad Manag J 39(3):607–634

Pearce J, Huang L (2012) The decreasing value of our research to management education. Acad Manag Learn Educ 11(2):247–262

Pfeffer J (1982) Organizations and organization theory. Pitman, Boston

Pfeffer J, Sutton RI (2006) Evidence-based management. Harv Bus Rev 84(1):62–75

Popper KR (2004) Conjectures and refutations: the growth of scientific knowledge. Routledge, London

Porter ME (1980) Competitive strategy: techniques for analyzing industries and competitors. The Free Press, New York

Porter ME (1985) Competitive advantage: creating and sustaining superior performance. The Free Press, New York

Powell TC (2001) Competitive advantage: logical and philosophical considerations. Strateg Manag J 22:875–888

Powell TC (2002) The philosophy of strategy. Strateg Manag J 23:873–880

Priem RL, Butler JE (2001a) Is the resource-based theory a useful perspective for strategic management research? Acad Manag Rev 26(1):22–40

Priem RL, Butler JE (2001b) Tautology in the resource-based view and implications of externally determined resource value: further comments. Acad Manag Rev 26(1):57–66

Radcliffe-Brown AR (1940) On social structure. J R Anthropol Inst G B Irel 70(1):1–12

Roethlisberger FJ, Dickson WJ (1934) Management and the worker: an account of a research program conducted by the Western Electric Company, Hawthorne works, Chicago. Harvard University Press, Boston

Rojas F (2010) Power through institutional work: acquiring academic authority in the 1968 third world strike. Acad Manag J 53(6):1263–1280

Rousseau DM, McCarthy S (2007) Educating managers from an evidence-based perspective. Acad Manag Learn Edu 6:84–101

Shapira Z (2011) "I've got a theory paper – do you?": conceptual, empirical, and theoretical contributions to knowledge in the organizational sciences. Organ Sci 22(5):1312–1321

Simon HA (1996) The sciences of the artificial, 3rd edn. The MIT Press, Cambridge

Simon HA (1997) Administrative behavior: a study of decision-making processes in administrative organizations, 4th edn. The Free Press, New York

Skinner Q (1981) Machiavelli. Oxford University Press, Oxford

Smith A (2007) An inquiry into the nature and causes of the wealth of nations. MetaLibri, Amsterdam

Snyder TD, de Brey C, Dillow SA (2018) Digest of education statistics 2016. U.S. Department of Education, Washington

Spillane R, Martin J (2005) Personality and performance. UNSW Press, Sydney

Su W, Tsang EWK (2015) Product diversification and financial performance: the moderating role of secondary stakeholders. Acad Manag J 58(4):1128–1148

Sulkowski L (2010) Two paradigms in management epistemology. J Int Manag 2(1):109–119

Sutton RI, Staw BM (1995) What theory is not. Adm Sci Q 40:371–384

Taylor FW (1919) The principles of scientific management. Harper and Brothers Publishers, New York

Tomey AM (2009) Nursing management and leadership, 8th edn. Elsevier, New York

Watson TJ (2003) Sociology, work and industry, 4th edn. Routledge, London

Watson TJ (2017) Sociology, work and industry, 7th edn. Routledge, London

Weber M (1969) The theory of social and economic organisation (trans: Henderson AM, Parsons T). Oxford University Press, Oxford

Whitley R (1984) The fragmented state of management studies. Reasons and consequences. J Manag Stud 21(3):331–348

Wicks AC, Freeman RE (1998) Organization studies and the new pragmatism: positivism, anti-positivism, and the search for ethics. Organ Sci 9(2):123–140

Wren DA (2004) The evolution of management thought. Wiley, New York

Wren DA, Bedeian AG (2009) The evolution of management thought, 6th edn. Wiley, New York

Wren DA, Greenwood RG (1998) Management innovators. Oxford University Press, New York

Part IX

Different Experiences: Europe, Africa, and the Middle East

Different Experiences: Europe, Africa, and the Middle East – An Introduction

47

Bradley Bowden

Contents
Interlinked Histories 1074
Section Chapters 1076
Cross-References 1079
References 1080

Abstract
Europe, Africa, and the Middle East have long shared a common and intertwined history. Prior to the Muslim conquests of the sixth and seventh century AD, the Mediterranean acted as a source of unity. After the Muslim conquests, however, it increasingly marked a dividing line between the Christian north and the Muslim south. At the same time another distinctive culture emerged in Byzantium, a culture built on loyalty to Greek Orthodoxy that subsequently did much to shape Russian developments. From the sixteenth century, sub-Saharan Africa also found itself increasingly drawn into an emerging global economy. By the twentieth century, the Middle East also experienced a vexed relationship with Western models of capitalism and management. In short, the last millennia and a half have witnessed forces of both convergence and divergence, some emphasizing a common model of capitalism and management and others a contrary course. In this Part of the Handbook, we trace this process of societal and managerial convergence and divergence across three continents.

Keywords
Management · Ethnocentrism · African management · Saudi Arabia · Russia · France · Denmark · Christianity · Islam

B. Bowden (✉)
Griffith Business School, Griffith University, Nathan, QLD, Australia
e-mail: b.bowden@griffith.edu.au

© The Author(s), under exclusive licence to Springer Nature Switzerland AG 2020
B. Bowden et al. (eds.), *The Palgrave Handbook of Management History*,
https://doi.org/10.1007/978-3-319-62114-2_120

Interlinked Histories

In an interview conducted late in his life, Jacques Derrida (2003/2008: 31), reflecting upon his youth in Algeria, declared himself "a child of the Mediterranean, who was not simply French, not simply African." Among French existentialist and postmodernist philosophers, Derrida was hardly alone in being Algerian born. Albert Camus and Michel Foucault were also born in Algeria. The idea that the Mediterranean provided an integral link between Europe and Africa, and between the cultures of Western Europe and those of the Middle East, is one that runs deep in the historical imagination. "The Roman Empire, at the end of the third century," the great Belgian historian, Henri Pirenne (1925/1952: 3) observed, "had one outstanding characteristic: it was an essentially Mediterranean commonwealth...The Mediterranean was, without question, the bulwark of both its political and economic unity." For millennia, the most prosperous and intellectually advanced cultures of the Mediterranean basin – Egypt and Carthage – were found on the inland's seas African rather than its European shores. Of the great Greek cities of antiquity, none had a longer and more glorious existence than Alexandria. During the dying years of the Roman Empire no one exerted a greater intellectual influence that the Tunisian-born St Augustine, a scholar who made Christianity acceptable to the Mediterranean's Greek and Latin-speaking elites by merging Platonist and Neo-Platonist ideas with those of Christianity (Camus 1935/2007). Indeed, it is arguable that the Catholic dogma that prevailed in Western Europe from the fifth century owed as much to St Augustine as it did to the New Testament. Evidence of St Augustine's profound effect on Western intellectual thought is found in the fact that even the revolutionary Protestant theologian, John Calvin, who repudiated most Catholic dogma, framed his thinking in an Augustinian framework, declaring "I am teaching no novel doctrine, but what was long ago advanced by Augustine" (Calvin 1536/2014: 345).

To the extent that the Mediterranean divided rather than united these divisions – prior to c.AD 700 – these manifested themselves in an East-West divide rather than a North-South division. The reason for North-South unity, and East-West division, was found blowing in the winds. For although trade winds that blew in the direction of the Middle East in the spring, and Italy and Spain in the autumn, allowed trans-Mediterranean commerce in spices and foodstuffs, for most of the year it was far easier to island-hop in a north-south direction. Writing of the situation that prevailed in the early modern era, the French historian, Fernand Braudel (1963/1975: 123) observed,

> The two halves of the sea, in spite of their trading links and cultural exchanges, maintained their autonomy and their own spheres of influences. Genuine intermingling of populations was to be found only inside each region ... All links between different ends of the Mediterranean, by contrast, remained an adventure or at least a gamble.

During the Roman Empire, the Mediterranean's east-west division manifested itself in a continuing linguistic and cultural division between the Empire's Latin-speaking west and its Greek-speaking east. With the rise of Christianity, this linguistic and cultural division also became a religious divide as the Latin-speaking popes in Rome gradually asserted their independence from the Church's Metropolitan or Patriarch in Constantinople. The long-term result of this division, which we explore in ▶ Chap. 49, "Work and Society in the Orthodox East: Byzantium and Russia, AD 450–1861," by B. Bowden, was the emergence of what were in effect two distinct civilizations, one centered on the Latin and Germanic-speaking populations of the West who initially looked to Rome for religious leadership and the other centered upon Greek Orthodoxy. In his study, *Clash of Civilizations*, Samuel Huntington argued that the result of this divide was both profound and permanent. As "a society and a culture," Huntington (1996/2003: 140) argued, early modern Russia – with its intellectual roots in Greek Orthodoxy – bore "little resemblance" to the geographical adjacent West.

If, historically, the Mediterranean, divided along an east-west axis and united along a north-south orientation, there emerged with the Muslim conquests of the seventh and eighth centuries a new divide between a Muslim Middle East and North Africa and a largely Christian Europe. In articulating what has become known as the "Pirenne thesis," Henri Pirenne argued that it was the Arab conquests – not the earlier Germanic *Völkerwanderung* of the fifth and sixth centuries – that destroyed the cultural and economic unity of the old Roman world. As Pirenne (1939: 164) expressed it, Islam,

> ... shattered the Mediterranean unity which the Germanic invasions had left intact. This was the most essential event in European history which had occurred since the Punic Wars. It was the end of the classical tradition.

There is no doubt that Pirenne exaggerated the effects of the Muslim conquests. Muslim Spain, in particular, long provided a conduit between the Christian north and the Muslim south. Nevertheless, there is a fundamental truth in Pirenne's observation as the Mediterranean became a dividing line across which the Christian and Muslim worlds regarded each other with suspicion, if not enmity.

Although maritime trade continued to act as a unifying force for the societies of the Old World, by the sixteenth century the Mediterranean was becoming an economically stagnant backwater as the nations of the North Atlantic littoral (Portugal, Spain, France, the Netherlands, and Britain) opened sea-lanes to the Americas and the Indian Ocean. The result was a new and largely exploitative relationship between Europe and Africa as European traders turned to Sub-Saharan Africa in search of a labor force for the plantation economies of the Caribbean and the Americas. Whereas the Baltic remained Western Europe's principal provider of time-honored commodities (i.e., grain and timber), the plantations of the Caribbean and the Americas serviced novel demands for sugar, coffee, and tobacco. It was sugar, in particular, which provided the foundation for the plantation economies of the Americas. In 1773, for example, the value of Britain's trade with the sugar-island of Jamaica was worth five times that of all its North American colonies (Ferguson 2008: 72). In every locality, this sweet, lucrative bounty fed an insatiable demand for slaves. In the Caribbean, where slavery was a comparative rarity prior to 1600, an estimated 450,000 African slaves, most traded by African chiefs intent on acquiring Western weapons and trade goods, were imported during the course of the seventeenth century. Brazil imported another half a million. Across the Americas as a whole an estimated 1,325,000 Africans arrived in chains during the seventeenth century, destined for a life of misery (Curtin 1969: 77). The seventeenth century slave trade, however, remained a comparatively small-scale affair compared to the ensuing century. In a single decade, 1740–1750, British ships carried a record 200,000 slaves to the Americas, a figure that equated to almost half the total Caribbean trade during the previous century (Thomas 1997: 264). It should be noted, became a source of wealth not only for European slavers and plantation owners. It also added to the personal wealth of the African kings and traditional chiefs, such as the Fulani and Mande in Senegal and Gambia, and the king of Dahomey (Wickins 1981: 163–165). An ancient European and African institution that had experienced a long and permanent retreat in Europe, the plantation economies revitalized slavery as an institution not only in the Americas but in Africa itself.

Invariably, the relationships between – and within – Europe, Africa, and the Middle East societies were profoundly altered as an integrated world-economy emerged. As Grietjie Verhoef (▶ Chap. 52, "Pre-colonial Africa: Diversity in Organization and Management of Economy and Society") observes, "The infiltration by Islam into the Sudan or sub-Saharan lands of West Africa had a profound impact on the indigenous kingdoms," bringing in its wake "well-organized administrative structures and introducing sophisticated financial management." Even more profound effects resulted from the process of European conquest in the eighteenth and nineteenth centuries and through the creation of a single integrated global economy in the twentieth century. In Africa, the Middle East and in Europe outside the Anglosphere, new models of management initially built around the industrial experiences of Britain and the United States clashed, informed and transformed indigenous models of business and management. Nowhere did a single model of capitalism and management emerge that was simply a mirror image of British or American experiences. Writing of the French experience, Fernand Braudel (1986/1990: 666) observed that, "France was never consumed by the necessary passions for the capitalist models, by that unbridled thirst for profits without which the capitalist engine cannot get started." In the countries and regions that constitute the focus of this study of management outside the Anglosphere – the Middle East, Africa, South Africa, France, Denmark, and Russia and the Orthodox East – the question to have constantly before us, is: Are we witnessing in this national or regional situation a variety of the model of Western management that emerged from the industrializing economies of the North Atlantic, or are we witnessing something fundamentally different?

Section Chapters

This Section owes a particular debt to the University of Johannesburg's Grietjie Verhoef, one of Africa's leading business historians, who has committed three chapters to this Section, each of which deals with a different aspect of the African experience. In her first ▶ Chap. 52, "Pre-colonial Africa: Diversity in Organization and Management of Economy and Society" Verhoef begins by noting that, "The vast land comprising Africa constitutes the location of dynamic contestation, conquest, and expansion of power." Of the traditional sub-Saharan African societies, Verhoef notes that although they "were essentially communal," they were not characterized by "collective decision-making." Instead, tribal leaders and kings used their political authority to exert a large measure of control over commerce and trade. Over time, however, different indigenous models of management emerged in response to the penetration of both Muslim and European commercial and business interests. In western Africa, for example, the *wari* system saw the emergence of semi-autonomous managers who oversaw the production and trade of goods (and people) under a system of royal permission and protection. In her second chapter ▶ Chap. 53, "Africa and the Firm: Management in Africa Through a Century of Contestation," Verhoef returns to the theme of adaptation and change, exploring the transition from the traditional models of commerce to those centered upon "management styles aligned with modern western management." In doing so, Verhoef pays special heed to the argument that indigenous African society produced a unique system of management, *Ubuntu*, which potentially provides for a moral and commercial reawakening of commerce and production on models different to the West. In her estimation, evidence to support claims as to the strength of business traditions based upon *Ubuntu* is weak. Instead, Africa has witnessed a gradual transference of leadership roles in enterprises and firms based on Western models to people of black African or mixed ancestry. In other words, modern models of business and management have come to prevail in Africa's formal economy. In her final ▶ Chap. 54, "Managing Africa's Strongest Economy: The History of Management in South Africa, 1920–2018" Verhoef explores the South African experience during the twentieth century, noting that, "Management in South Africa developed within the western tradition." During the so-called *apartheid* era, in particular, Afrikaans-language businesses and educational institutions embraced an American model that made a Master's degree in Business Administration the quintessential management qualification. Rather than the post-*apartheid* era opening up a new era of business success, however, Verhoef identifies the emergence of a profound "crisis of management in South Africa," one that has seen the country "fully integrated into the African culture of corruption and ruling party nepotism." This development places at risk well-managed corporations, of which many have relocated their primary listings outside the country. Undoubted, Verhoef's assessments may solicit discourse, but no one can doubt that she brings to her analysis a lifetime of research and deep thought.

In his ▶ Chap. 48, "Management in the Middle East," which opens this Section of the *Handbook*, my co-Editor Anthony Gould explores similar themes to Verhoef. Across the decades since the emergence of national Arab states in the World War II, Gould traces a vexed relationship between an Arab society still wedded to traditional cultural and religious values and a modern global economy. In Gould's estimation, this vexed relationship is most pronounced in Saudi Arabia, where an attempted "Saudization" of private-sector businesses has produced "disappointing" results. In 2012, for example, only 13% of Saudi nationals were employed in privately-run businesses. Where Saudi citizens are employed in senior private sector positions they often play little or no effective role in the running of the business, instead owing their command of their job to government-mandated quotas. To a lesser degree, similar trends are identified in the United Arab Emirates, Gould observing that the functioning of the Emirates economy is largely entrusted to expatriates. As of 2011, Emirati nationals comprised only 4.2% of the workforce, a percentage that is unlikely to have grown significantly in the interim.

In our second chapter in this Section, ▶ Chap. 49, "Work and Society in the Orthodox East: Byzantium and Russia, AD 450–1861," I explore circumstances in Europe's Orthodox East, a region whose historical trajectory has differed significantly from that found in the adjoining West. Often overlooked by Western scholars, the Orthodox East has provided some of the most important societies in the human experience. For a thousand years, Byzantium not only provided a living link to the Greek, Roman, and Judeo-Christian worlds of antiquity, it also acted as the eastern gatekeeper for European Christendom. Among the societies that owed a cultural and religious debt to Byzantium, none was more historically important than Russia. Like Byzantium before it, Russia occupied a precarious geographical position on Europe's eastern flank, exposing it to invasion by nomadic horsemen. Like Byzantium before it, Russian society also possessed a deeply held belief in its own historic destiny, not only as a defender of Orthodox faith but also as the flagbearer of a culture and civilization that it felt to be superior to all others. Confronted with constant invasion and threats to its very survival, Russian society – like Byzantium before it – chose to give a primacy to communal solidarity and defense, organized around a strong centralized state. In both Byzantium and Russia, however, this centralized state proved as much a hindrance as an assistance in providing the resources necessary for societal advance and progress. For, in both Byzantium and Russia the survival and success of the society came to be associated with a social pact between the state and a militarized aristocracy, an alliance that marshalled economic and military resources by bleeding other sections of society. Invariably, social solidarity was prioritized at the expense of individual freedom, entrepreneurship, and private, commercialized endeavor.

The unique experiences of France are the focus of Peter Wirtz's ▶ Chap. 50, "Changing Corporate Governance in France in the Late Twentieth Century." As Wirtz notes, France differs from the free market model that has predominated in the Anglosphere in that the state has traditionally exerted considerable influence, acting as the perceived guardian of "social interest." Since the 1980s, however, France has witnessed a gradual weakening of the state's economic authority. It is the effect of this transition that is the primary focus of Wirtz's study. In Wirtz's account, the procedures that brought about the privatization of large swathes of the French economy "took on a very particular form, which would shape the face of French capitalism." In essence, the French state wanted a model of privatization that would ensure ownership remained in the hands of French, rather than foreign interests. Over time, however, the achievement of this goal proved increasingly difficult as Anglo-Saxon investors gained growing leverage over both individual firms and entire industries. In turn, Wirtz observes, the "massive arrival of foreign capital stimulated an intensifying debate over the efficiency of the French corporate governance system." In short, France has witnessed the progressive erosion of its own distinctive model of capital and management in favor of one that increasingly resembles the Anglo-Saxon norm.

A similar story, albeit with different outcomes, is the focus of Jørgen Burchardt's ▶ Chap. 51, "Flexicurity: The Danish Model." In a word of introduction it should be noted that *flexicurity* is the term used to describe Denmark's unique labor market, built around both employee security and firm flexibility. Initially a society characterized by low levels of employment protection, Denmark moved in a different direction in the early twentieth century as a result of the so-called "September Agreement" between organized labor and employer groups. As Burchardt's account records, across the course of the twentieth century Denmark witnessed a strengthening of employer-labor cooperation, a trend that witnessed not only a strengthening of labor market protections but also of joint management-employee representation bodies in larger workplaces. At the same time, Burchardt observes, "job security in the Danish labour market is low." There is also a high degree of work-time flexibility with work times negotiated locally. In summing up the Danish Model, Burchardt notes that it "provides security for employment, rather than job security." Instead of job security, Danish workers pay into a generous unemployment insurance scheme that provides up to 90% of a worker's previous salary, conditional on 12 months membership in the insurance scheme. Proof of the flexibility of the Danish system is found in the fact that each year around 20% of the workforce is affected by unemployment at some time. In tracing how the Danish system has coped with recent global economic pressures, Burchardt concludes, "The Danish Model is still alive."

If we look across our various chapters, a number of conclusions are evident. First, although France and Denmark have been central participants in the Western model of capitalism and management, they have each varied this model to produce a distinctive national system of corporate governance and/or labor market regulation. Somewhat surprisingly, the Danish system of *flexicurity* has proved more enduring than the French system. The second conclusion that we can come to is that in Africa and the Middle East as well a Western model of capitalism and management has prevailed within the formal economy, albeit a model that has come under increasing pressure in recent decades from interventionist governments, each intent on pursuing a social reform agenda. Our third conclusion stems from the Byzantine and Russian experience. Located on the eastern fringes of Europe, and subject to constant invasions, the Orthodox East has proved infertile soil for Western models of capitalism and management.

Cross-References

▶ Africa and the Firm: Management in Africa Through a Century of Contestation
▶ Changing Corporate Governance in France in the Late Twentieth Century
▶ Flexicurity: The Danish Model

- Management in the Middle East
- Managing Africa's Strongest Economy: The History of Management in South Africa, 1920–2018
- Pre-colonial Africa: Diversity in Organization and Management of Economy and Society
- Work and Society in the Orthodox East: Byzantium and Russia, AD 450–1861

References

Braudel F (1963/1975) The Mediterranean and the Mediterranean world in the age of Philip II, vol 1. Fontana Press, London

Braudel F (1986/1990) The identity of France: people and production, vol 2, 2nd edn. Harper Torchbooks, New York

Calvin J (1536/2014) Institutes of the Christian religion, vol 1. Project Gutenberg eBook. http://www.gutenberg.org/ebooks/45001

Camus A (1935/2007) Christian metaphysics and neoplatonism. University of Missouri Press, Columbia

Curtin PD (1969) The Atlantic slave trade: a census. University of Wisconsin Press, Maddison

Derrida J (2003/2008) To have lived, and to remember, as an Algerian. In: Derrida J (ed) Islam and the West: a conversation with Jacques Derrida (ed: Chérif M and trans: Fagan TL). University of Chicago Press, Chicago, pp 29–35

Ferguson N (2008) Empire: how Britain made the modern world, 2nd edn. Penguin, London

Huntington SP (1996/2003) The clash of civilizations and the remaking of world order. Simon & Schuster, New York

Pirenne H (1925/1952) Medieval cities: their origins and the revival of trade (trans: Halsey FD). Princeton University Press, Princeton

Pirenne H (1939) Mohammed and Charlemagne (trans: Miall B). Barnes & Noble, New York

Thomas H (1997) The slave trade: the history of the Atlantic slave trade 1440–1870. Picador, London

Wickins P (1981) An economic history of Africa, from the earliest times to partition. Oxford University Press, Cape Town

Management in the Middle East

48

Anthony M. Gould

For several years Professor Anthony M. Gould held professional jobs in Middle Eastern countries. Anthony dedicates this chapter to his father, Tony Gould Snr. Tony was a brilliant and extraordinary man. The day before his death he was imporving this text.

Contents

Introduction	1082
The Kingdom of Saudi Arabia (KSA): A Blueprint for Islam, and Islamic Management	1085
Managing in the Arabian Gulf States: The Influence of History	1092
The United Arab Emirates: A Bridge to the Western World	1095
Conclusion: The Influence of Islamic Management in the non-Islamic World	1097
Cross-References	1099
References	1100

Abstract

This chapter is about management philosophy and practice in the Middle East. It argues that, unlike in other multi-country regions such as Europe or Asia, the Middle East does have a unique, distinctively non-Western, governance blueprint. In prosecuting its case, the chapter proposes that geographical conceptions do little to aid understanding the Arab world. Rather, the influence of Islamic history and the circumstance of oil discovery in the twentieth century is pivotal in creating a conception of the Middle East. This view deemphasizes jurisdictions and civic (secular) identity. The chapter examines three partially overlapping instantiations of the Middle Eastern management construct: the Kingdom of

---

A. M. Gould (✉)
Département des relations industrielles, Université Laval, Québec, QC, Canada
e-mail: anthony.gould@rlt.ulaval.ca

© The Author(s), under exclusive licence to Springer Nature Switzerland AG 2020
B. Bowden et al. (eds.), *The Palgrave Handbook of Management History*,
https://doi.org/10.1007/978-3-319-62114-2_119

Saudi Arabia (KSA), the Gulf States generally (GCC), and the United Arab Emirates (UAE). It proposes that the first of these instantiations – which, in key ways, most approximates fidelity to Islam – is where the analyst can best appreciate the philosophical underpinnings of Middle Eastern management.

Keywords

Middle East · Management · Saudi Arabia · Gulf States · United Arab Emirates · Islam · Muslim · Religion · Prophet Muhammad · Oil · Petroleum · Arab Region

Introduction

The term "Middle East," although literally topographical in conventional usage, is not necessarily a reference to geography. Rather, in general parlance, it is common to employ the expression when communicating imprecisely about culture, language, and religious-orientation. Hence, it is unsurprising to find that, unlike for example when speaking of Europe or North America, there are both broad and narrow definitions in play. Broad views tend to be associated with fuzzy boundaries and sometimes invoke expressions such as Middle-East-North-Africa (MENA), South-West Asia, the Arabian Peninsula, or the Arab World. However, more focused conceptions put the emphasis squarely on distinct jurisdictions that obviously do have borders such as the Gulf States (GCC) of Kuwait, Saudi Arabia, Bahrain, Qatar, the United Arab Emirates (UAE), and Oman; the adjoining Islamic nations of Iraq and Iran; and elements of the Levant region, notably Syria, Lebanon, Turkey, and Egypt. Sometimes, geographically orientated definitions are enlarged under the influence of a specific guiding principle. For example, the North African countries of Morocco, Libya, Algeria, Tunisia, and Mauritania are mostly Islamic and therefore often counted as forming "part of the Middle-East." What is notable in each of these cases is that, in spite of its physical location, the nation state of Israel is typically not viewed as being within the region, prompting those in the popular media to sometimes use expressions such as "Israel and the Middle East," etc. (e.g., Musmar 2020).

For analytic purposes, it is noteworthy that the bulk of people living in the Middle East are dedicated adherents to Islam and the Muslim faith. To the extent that spiritual mores are causally prior to manifestations of lifestyle, values, and preferences, as authors such as Al Bahar et al. (1996) have argued, this kind of commitment likely will have workplace consequences, in particular. In the present case, these may include being more loyal to one's family than to an employer, not being especially committed to productivity but nonetheless attaching importance to material success and education and, valuing politeness and respectfulness more than candor and straightforwardness (Abdalla and Al-Homoud 1995; Al Bahar et al. 1996; Klein et al. 2009). There is empirical evidence for such a view of religious faith's pervasive secular influence. Specifically, to gain a comparative perspective on work and employment, Hofstede (1980) examined 53 countries from five continents. He proposed four dimensions of national culture that, taken together, give an overarching profile of individual nations or groups of nations (that share either common history or geography). Hence, depending on an object of analytic interest, the results of such pioneering research can be disaggregated in multiple ways. For present purposes, for his sample of Arab countries (which included Egypt, Iraq, Kuwait, Lebanon, Libya, Saudi Arabia, and the UAE), the following conclusions are germane. First, the Middle Eastern world has a large "power distance" (7th out of 53 countries), indicating that, within the region, there is a relatively high acceptance of wealth and influence inequality. Second, by comparison to other countries and regions, Arab people are ill at ease with uncertainty, a dimension he labelled "uncertainty avoidance." Third, the region has a "masculinity" score only slightly higher than the mean (in rank-order terms, the 23rd – out of 52 – of all countries/regions examined). This result, at least as interpreted by authors such as Waxin and Bateman (2016), suggests that, although much is often made of how Muslim women have limited rights and, in some contexts, restricted access and equity, such comparative disadvantage is principally due to the practice of Islam as opposed to non-religious cultural elements. Fourth, concerning the dimension of "individualism," Arabic society is relatively collectivist in its orientation and thus its citizens reveal especially close allegiance to, for example, their family/tribe. More recent research inquiring into the social and cultural character of the Arabian Gulf States has produced similar findings to those of Hofstede's. For example, Trompenaars and Hampden-Turner (1998) examined Bahrain, Egypt, Kuwait, Oman, Saudi Arabia, and the UAE. Somewhat like Hofstede (1980), these authors concluded that day-to-day Arabic life embraces, to varying degrees, Quranic values. Specifically, Muslim people are relatively universalistic, communitarianist (attach importance to community), affective, embodying of a diffuse view of life, ascriptive, have a synchronic time orientation (past, present, and future are not well differentiated) and substantially controlled, and constrained, by their belief structure (i.e., score highly on "internal control").

Insofar as its history is concerned, the Middle East is the birthplace of the first human civilizations including the Sumerians (now modern Iraq), the Babylonians, the Phoenicians and the Egyptians. It is where each of the world's three Abrahamic religions have their origins and where the last of these in particular, Islam, has become dominant, exerting a pervasive influence over consequential elements of public policy and governance. Aside from being bedeviled by tribal conflict and bloodshed, the long story of the Middle East is also associated with intellectual and technical sophistication, especially during antiquity. For example, archaeologists have recently discovered rock-engraved images in Shumway's (in North Western Saudi Arabia) indicating that, perhaps 8,000 years ago, locals were domesticating (and leashing) dogs and using them for hunting (Grimm 2018). Furthermore, there is compelling evidence that 7,000 years ago arable food production was taking place in the Levant, notably Mesopotamia and Egypt (Main 2013; Bowman and Rogan 1999). From the sixth century until the middle ages, the region was home to civilizations that used modes of mercantilism akin to industrial-age market-economies and had forged trading links with East Asia, Africa and Europe (Crone 1987). Enlightenment of such kind render expressions such as the "dark ages," in some respects, a Eurocentric construct.

In the modern era, economic and social development of subregions of the Middle East have been regulated by discovery of oil, and marred by military and tribal conflict and, since 1947 in particular, an uneasy relationship between Arabs and Jews. In the twenty-first century, these trends have continued with the proclamation of the world caliphate by ISIS (*Islamic State of Iraq and Syria*), the Arab Spring movement and the toppling of dictatorships such as Saddam Hussein's Iraq and the war in Syria. A consequence of such recent turmoil – one with employment relations and human capital implications – has been unprecedented levels of mass migration, especially from Syria, within the Middle East itself and into Europe (Matherly and Al Nahyan 2015; Singh and Sharma 2015). Such phenomena suggest that a fundamental ever-present influence on approaches to management in the region tend to be historical, a proxy term for religious. In this vein, in the current chapter, I argue that the starting point for appreciating the distinctive elements of Middle Eastern workplace governance is to note that it is not the region per se that is important for understanding but rather consideration of cultural affiliation and history. A consequence of such a thesis is that the student gains insight when they give special analytic attention to the Kingdom of Saudi Arabia (KSA), the birthplace of Islam and the quintessential Muslim country. Aside from its distinctive historical significance, Saudi Arabia is the economically largest (according to the IMF in 2018 its GDP was 1.9 trillion dollars and its per capita income 56,817 dollars) and most populated (30 million natives) of the Gulf States (or, what is commonly known as Gulf Cooperation Council, GCC, countries). Within the Kingdom, a patriarchal and conservative hegemony governs key elements of legal, civil, and political life. Since the discovery of oil in the 1930s and its fully-fledged commercialization in the 1970s, Saudi society has experienced structural changes that mirror elements of Western-style industrialization. These include the arrival of multinational corporations and the emergence of a vexing question concerning what to do about those locals who lack necessary skills to take on roles created within sectors of the economy concerned with extracting, refining and exporting petroleum products. In these circumstances, the Saudis have gingerly accepted immigrants; frequently experts from Western countries who have created something of a transient middle class, as well as unskilled workers to do domestic and menial chores. The majority of those in this latter category (the unskilled migrants) have mostly come from the Indian sub-continent, South Asia (e.g., the Philippines), and sub-Saharan Africa. Other Middle Eastern states, such as Kuwait, Bahrain, and Oman have, roughly speaking, typically followed a recent similar developmental trajectory to the Kingdom of Saudi Arabia (KSA). Successive administrations from these countries have not been able to well diversify their industries and thus diminish their economic reliance on oil. Similarly, due to a formalized commitment to Islam, they have been disinclined to act fulsomely on Western-style political and social reform agendas. Indeed, within these jurisdictions, there is mostly no clean separation of the practice of Islam and management of State-sponsored institutions. As such, throughout the Middle East, *Sharia* law undergirds public policy and is implicit – and sometimes formally explicit – in matters of worker superintendence and governance.

This chapter commences with a discussion of the Kingdom of Saudi Arabia (KSA), the Middle East's quintessential Islamic country. Its second section provides a general overview of work, employment, and management in Gulf Cooperation Council (GCC) countries. Its third section addresses these same content areas in the United Arab Emirates (UAE), perhaps the most divergent nation-State in the region.

The Kingdom of Saudi Arabia (KSA): A Blueprint for Islam, and Islamic Management

Little has been written about the theory and practice of management in Saudi Arabia in the modern era (Tlaiss and Elamin 2016). However, there is a measure of scholarly consensus that the subject cannot be understood – and may even be viewed as an outgrowth of – the country's distinctive approach to the practice of Islam (e.g., Mellahi and Wood 2001; Budhwar and Mellahi 2016). The present discussion therefore commences with an overview of the history of religion in Saudi Arabia. It briefly examines how a commitment to the faith's key tenets has become woven into the nation's approach to public administration and integral to certain of its state governance structures and processes, particularly those impacting law and the judiciary and relations between the sexes.

In December of the year 629, the Prophet Muhammad led a march of 10,000 of his converts from the city of Medina (then known as *Yathrib*) in what is now Saudi Arabia to Mecca, his birthplace and from where he had emigrated in 622 following rumors that he was to be assassinated if he stayed (Holland 2012; Serjeant 1964). The Prophet's influence following the *Hijra* (beginning of the Islamic calendar) in that year had been growing. While in exile, he had united disparate tribes under the constitution of Medina (Holland 2012; Serjeant 1964). Furthermore, he had chalked up impressive military conquests. For example, in what was to become the Battle of Badr, in March 624 he had planned a raid on a Meccan merchant caravan that was to commence with an ambush (Armstrong 1992; Rubin 1995). However, somehow the Meccans where tipped-off about the plot and dispatched a force to protect the caravan and then confront the Muslims. Though outnumbered more than three to one, the Prophet defeated his adversaries, killing at least 45 Meccans while limiting the death toll amongst his followers to only 14 (Hodgson 1974; Ramadan 2007). Moreover, he succeeded in massacring key Meccan leaders, including the influential *Abu Jahl* and in taking captives, many of who were later ransomed (Ramadan 2007; Rubin 1995). For an emerging spiritual leader, such spectacular conquests where seen by disciples as confirmation that they had chosen wisely. Indeed, it was becoming clear that Muhammad's earlier time of seclusion in the mountain cave, *Hira*, where the archangel Gabriel had visited him and his subsequent revelations from God that submission to Islam is the only way were now being coupled with superhuman feats (indeed, "Islam" – ‍ا ل س‍ – literally means submission in Arabic). In matters of war and conquest, the invisible group of guiding angels that the Prophet spoke of so eloquently when referring to his destiny were indubitably there to protect him (Rodgers 2012). To the chagrin of pagan non-converts, Islam was on the rise and leaving no room for disbelievers. In this vein, likely with the sanction of the Prophet himself, two of its detractors, *Asma bint Marwan* of the *Aws Manat* tribe and *Abu 'Afak* of the *'Amr b.* who had authored verses taunting and mocking Muslims were ruthlessly slaughtered by members of their own clan who had become new converts to the Islamic faith (Hodgson 1974; Ramadan 2007; Rubin 1995).

In spite of the bloodshed that occurred in the 7 years of intermittent fighting with Meccan tribes before Muhammad's return to the Holy city, most scholars conclude that the return itself went largely without incident (Berg 2003; Cook 1983; Hamidullah 1998; Motzki 2000; Musa 2008; Rubin 1995). Indeed, for reasons that are not fully clear, it appears that Meccan polytheists mostly converted voluntarily to Islam. There is also a measure of scholarly consensus that, following the Prophet's death and ascension to heaven on a winged horse in 632, previously warring tribes where largely united in a single Islamic polity (Berg 2003; Hamidullah 1998; Musa 2008). In the following decades, the Muslim faith spread from the Holy City of Mecca to beyond the Arabian Gulf as far east as modern Pakistan and west to the Iberian Peninsula. In fact, for hundreds of years following such expansion, at least until the early part of the twentieth century, the disparate tribal regions of Arabia were meagre and peripheral elements of the Muslim realm (Hamidullah 1998). During the period, although local Islamic rulers, known as the *Sharif of Mecca*, controlled the area, the world's most important centers of faith were in the empires of Baghdad, Istanbul and Cairo. However, for analytic purposes, it is worth reiterating that, the birthplace of Islam was the modern Kingdom of Saudi Arabia, a fact that has contemporary relevance. Specifically, as of 2015, 98% of the nation's inhabitants are Muslims and engage in practices mandated by the Quran (Budhwar and Mellahi 2016). These protocols are woven into the fabric of key elements of Saudi life, notably for the present discussion, those concerning the world of work and employment.

Abdulaziz (later known as Ibn) Saud, from the House of Saud, founded the modern Kingdom of Saudi Arabia in 1932. In a series of conquests, beginning in 1902 with the capture of Riyadh the ancestral home of Saud's family, the nation was formed through bringing together the regions of *Hejaz, Najd, Al-Ahsa* (Eastern Arabia), and *Asir* (Southern Arabia). As a single entity, henceforth the new nation-state was to be ruled, essentially, as a totalitarian monarchical dictatorship.

Although (and as mentioned) the actual figure is perhaps 98%, officially Saudi Arabia is a 100% Muslim country with approximately 75–78% of the population being Sunni and those remaining being Shia (Al-Rasheed 2010). The bulk of Saudi Sunnis belong to the ultra-conservative and puritanical *Wahhabism*, founded in the eighteenth century by Muhammad ibn *Abd al-Wahhab* (Al-Rasheed 2010). As an absolute monarchy, the nation has no political parties or national-level elections. However, according to Saudi edict adopted by royal decree in 1992, *Sharia* law, as stated in the *Quran* and exemplified by the deeds of the Prophet Muhammad in the *Sunnah*, is the nation's constitution and hence the basis of consequential decision making, especially in the judicial arena. Certainly, there do exist Royal decrees, particularly pertaining to labor management and commerce-related matters. However, these are mere regulations. As such, they are subordinate to *Sharia*

(Al-Rasheed 2010). Insofar as participation in decision-making is concerned, political influence in the Kingdom mostly boils down to consideration of tribal affiliation with a select few sheiks maintaining control over national governance and civic development. The prevailing Saudi system of tribal rule allows for adult males to petition the King through a meeting structure known as *majlis* (Tripp and North 2009). The media is forbidden from reporting about these kinds of deliberations (Tripp and North 2009).

The Economist (2012) rated the Saudi government as the fifth most authoritarian out of 167 rated in its 2012 Democracy Index, and Freedom House gave it its lowest "Not Free" rating, 7.0 ("1=best, 7=worst") for 2019 (FreedomHouse.org 2019). The nation is one of only eight from 56 that did not sign on to the 1948 United Nation's Declaration of Human Rights (it is noteworthy that six of these eight – then – Communist countries did not endorse the declaration because their representatives believed it should have more fulsomely condemned Fascism and Nazism). To provide further context, in 2008 *Human Rights Watch* raised concern that, although Saudi authorities introduced a criminal procedure code in 2002, its tenets are inadequate (at least by Western standards) and, in any case, are routinely ignored by the judiciary (Shoult 2006; Tripp and North 2009). Indeed, under the Influence of *Sunni* Islam, the Kingdom of Saudi Arabia (KSA) has gained a special reputation for its secretiveness, aggressive opposition to counter perspectives, and harshness. For example, since 2001 the country's Ministry of Media has engaged in widespread Internet censorship that focuses on identifying and banning websites with sexual content, those promoting non-Muslim ideology and ones critical of the nation's rulers (Freedomhouse.org 2018; Alisa and Issaev 2018; Albab.com 2001). As the *Quran* is the country's constitution, the primary source of its law is the Islamic *Sharia*. Unlike in other Muslim countries, the *Sharia* is not coded in Saudi Arabia. Moreover, the nation does not have jury trials and judicial precedent does not constrain the scope and severity of sentencing decisions (Human Rights Watch 2008; Shoult 2006; Tripp and North 2009). In criminal matters, defendants are assumed a-priori to be guilty and may be beaten or tortured until they confess (Human Rights Watch 2008; Shoult 2006; Tripp and North 2009). They are typically not given access to legal counsel, not necessarily informed of the crime they are accused of committing, and not given opportunity to examine witnesses or present exculpatory evidence (Human Rights Watch 2008).

Most criminal trials within the Kingdom of Saudi Arabia (KSA) are conducted secretly (Miller 2003; Human Rights Watch 2008). In practice, judges are inclined to follow what is known as the *Hanbali* School of jurisprudence (Hefner 2011). In so doing, they routinely resort to a literal interpretation of the *Quran* and *Hadith*. By Western standards, they are prone to being lenient, for example, in the way they deal with crimes committed against women such as wife beating or sexual assault by men of influence (The Economist 2001, 2007). However, they are often excessively harsh in the penalties they impose for transgressions that have overt religious connotations (beheading for witchcraft for example) (The Economist 2007). In the twenty-first century, punishments meted out by Saudi courts include stoning to death (mostly inflicted on women judged guilty of adultery), amputations (usually of the hand for theft), lashings (often for neglect of mandated prayer and fasting obligations during the holy month of Ramadan), and forms of crucifixion (Miethe and Lu 2004; di Giovanni 2014; Human Rights Report 2007, 2008, 2009, 2010). Homosexual acts are routinely punishable by floggings or execution (Human Rights Report 2007, 2008, 2009, 2010) and Atheism or, more precisely *"calling into question the fundamentals of the Islamic religion on which the country is based"* is viewed by the judiciary as akin to terrorism and dealt with accordingly (The Independent 2014). Similarly, apostasy or conversion from Islam, is forbidden in Saudi Arabia and punishable by death (Miethe and Lu 2004; Human Rights Report 2007, 2008, 2009, 2010). Retaliatory punishments, for example, surgical removal of eyes, or *Qisas*, have occurred within the Kingdom since the year 2000 (Human Rights Report 2007, 2008, 2009, 2010; Miethe and Lu 2004; The Washington Post 2008). Another theme of *Sharia* protocol is strict separation of men and women, and puritanical approaches to relations between the sexes (Miethe and Lu 2004; Tripp and North 2009). For example, public places in Saudi Arabia are gender segregated and non-married men and women are forbidden from dining together. In 2018, a man was taken into custody by Saudi police for the crime of appearing in a film where he was having breakfast with a woman who was not his wife in the hotel where they both worked (CNN 2018a).

Consistent with Saudi-style approaches to the management of civil disobedience and malfeasance, it is perhaps axiomatic that open protest against the government or the country's Royal Family, even if peaceful, is forbidden (The Peninsula 2011). For example, in January 2016, Saudi authorities executed the Shia cleric Sheikh Nimr who, as a proponent of democracy, had called for elections in the country (The Guardian 2016). In a similar vein, although details are sketchy at the time of writing, there is credible evidence that, on 2 October 2018, journalist and Washington Post columnist Jamal Khashoggi was tortured to death inside the Saudi consulate in Istanbul (BBC.com 2018; CNN.com 2018b). However, in spite of such recent incidents, in the last decade, it is noteworthy that the rule of the *Al-Saud* has faced intermittent opposition from circumscribed sources including, *Sunni* Islamic activists, liberal critics concerned mostly with a Western-type construct of human rights, the *Shi'ite* minority (particularly in the Eastern Province), and long-standing tribal and regionalist particularistic opponents (for example in the *Hejaz*). The minority activists have been the most conspicuous threat to the *Al-Saud* regime and, in recent years, perpetrated violence (The Atlantic 2015).

The Saudi Arabian economy – unambiguously a command economy – is heavily dependent on the export of oil and petroleum products with more than 80% of public revenue and 55% of GDP, derived from this source (Jadwa Investment 2017). In the last several decades, successive Saudi administrations have indicated varying degrees of disquiet about the nation's narrow industry base and instituted diversification-related reforms. Much of this emphasis has concerned preparing the Saudi workforce for a labor market that is better integrated into the global economy. In practical terms, educational transformations have been a central part of the agenda. Indeed, since the discovery of oil in the Middle East in the 1930s and its full-scale commercialization in 1941 commencing under the (then) supervision of the US-controlled *Aramco* (Arabian-American Oil Company), vocational training has played a special role in the development of the region. In the case of Saudi Arabia, with the emergence of oil extraction and refinery industries, it became clear that the country's growing demand for specialized skill and expertise could not be met by locals who had mostly come from backgrounds as Bedouin fishermen (Tlaiss and Elamin 2016). Furthermore, throughout the middle decades of the twentieth century, a large public infrastructure, including schools and emergency services facilities, was created. As a consequence of such influences, Saudi Arabia (and the other Gulf States), has come to have something of an imported and ephemeral middle class of professionals while simultaneously wrestling with how best to prepare its own people for more demanding jobs. Moreover, Saudi Arabia has had one of the highest birth rates it the world. As a result, at least 60% of its population is under the age of 21 as of 2013 (Jadwa Investment 2017). Authors such as Ramady (2010) and Tlais and Elamin (2016) have observed that successive administrations have failed to adequately deal with the challenge of providing fulfilling jobs to young people and the youth unemployment rate is, at least, 30%.

In spite of inadequate work opportunities for young Saudi men in particular, it is noteworthy that, due mostly to the influence of Islam, the nation is decidedly stratified, patriarchal, high on power distance and – at least by Western standards – oppressive towards women (Mellahi 2006, 2007). In practice, economic prosperity is largely the preserves of the male population and mediated by access to power (*wasta*) and the kind of work in which one is engaged. As is often the case throughout the Middle East and Central Asia, locals view low status occupations to be those that are technical or manual in nature and typically consign them to immigrants (Achoui 2009; Tlaiss and Elamin 2016). There is evidence that Saudi men often shun the idea of applying for a job, viewing this form of approach as admission that they are not well connected (Harry 2007; Tliass 2013). Hence, within banks, investment firms and a large public sector, it is common for HR departments to avoid incurring the disapproval of family-based power networks. As such, these institutions often devote resources to managing a continuous inflow of unsolicited job applications and to creating superfluous positions for young males (Al-Asfour and Khan 2014). What emerges is often a two-tiered HRM system, one for local men and another for expats. Consequently, expatriates invariably must not only stand second in line to locals when it comes to the plumb jobs but, in a formal sense, are typically employed using a visa permit system that gives their Saudi employers control over key elements of their work including duration of their contract (Elamin 2012). Hence, in practice, they mostly cannot change jobs without their boss's endorsement and have little bargaining power. Such discriminatory conditions have prompted human rights watch groups to speak out on behalf of low-skilled foreign workers in the Kingdom of Saudis Arabia (KSA) (Mellahi 2006, 2007). In recent times, the late King Abdallah responded somewhat to such criticism. Through his "Vision" project, he granted foreign workers and women in particular more rights and freedoms. Even more recently, King Salmon doubled-down on a commitment to such initiatives. He also reiterated that, to avoid civil unrest, it is necessary to continue to focus on the role of education in preparing the national workforce.

Such an emphasis on training is present in his expansionary budgets of 2016 and 2017. Concomitantly, the King has indicated that he views wealth redistribution as a key element of a future reform agenda and signaled, with several recent cabinet changes, increasing interest in the opinions of younger Saudis (Tlaiss and Elamin 2016).

Administrative recognition that within Saudi Arabia there are distinctive labor-related problems has a history that began several decades ago. Indeed, in 1994 the Saudis formally identified national work and employment-related concerns and proposed strategy for their amelioration (Atiyyah 1996; Al-Harbi 1997). As noted, the Kingdom has had a decade's long problem pertaining to high levels of local unemployment, particularly youth unemployment. As a partial remedy, it has created a bloated and inefficient public sector (Ramady 2010; Tlaiss and Elamin 2016). Concomitantly, the nation's private sector has mostly employed foreigners, particularly to carry out high-skilled jobs. In the 1990s, following formal identification of structural imbalances, authorities devised a strategy known as Saudi-nationalization or Saudization (Atiyyah 1996; Al-Harbi 1997). At the time, and ever since, this agenda has been concerned with establishing private-sector quotas for local hires. The quotas system has been implemented in tandem with a long-term development initiative based on tailored vocational training that aims to equip resident job seekers with industry-relevant expertise. Hence, Saudization has been something of a work in progress (Tlaiss and Elamin 2016). For example, in 2007 authorities renewed their commitment to creating a private sector that would reduce, and eventually eradicate, unemployment. Ultimately, Saudization became subsumed in the late King Abdullah's aforementioned progressive "Vision" project which broadly addressed, not just skills shortages, but also economic diversification and expansion of the private sector. As of 2013, 25% of the nation's public expenditure was devoted to education of one kind or another. Another element of the "Vision" project is the *Hafiz* initiative (2011) which has seen the establishment of employment centers, job fairs, job-search websites, etc. (Al-Asfour and Khan 2014; Tliass and Elamin 2016).

Insofar as the success of Saudization is concerned, key indicators are disappointing. For example, by 2012, only 13% of locals were employed in the nation's privately-run industries (Al-Asfour and Khan 2014). In the 5 years prior to 2017, local unemployment never dipped below 10% and, overall, 60% of the country's workforce is made up of expatriates (Jadwa Investment 2017). Ramady (2010) proposes that a key reason why employers favor a strategy of importing labor is purely economic; in essence it is mostly the case that foreign workers receive lower wages than their local counterparts (an issue to be further discussed). Adding to the malaise is the phenomenon of "ghost workers." Specifically, the *Nitaqat* program of 2011 mandated that Saudi employers meet hiring quotas for locals. There is evidence that managers of more profitable firms holding negative stereotypes of young Saudi males, will nonetheless hire them, pay them a salary, and ask them not to come to work (Al-Asfour and Khan 2014). In so doing, they are able to report that they have met their quotas and cultivate relationships with families of influence and key officials.

Saudi Arabian religious conscientiousness and fidelity to Islam, at least as judged by Western standards, is associated with discreetness. This stance, uncompromising commitment to faith as practiced privately (or at least in a way that is not amenable to international scrutiny), creates much of the context for a distinctively Saudi approach to management. The opaque nature of Saudi management has been noted by Afiouni et al. (2013) and Tlaiss and Elamin (2016). These authors observe that, although it is possible to generate a statistical portrait of macro-level features of the nation's economic, cultural, religious and legal circumstances, little of substance is known about, for example, its HRM practices or their philosophical underpinnings. Indeed, they conclude that knowledge about Saudi management was "*almost non-existent until early 2000.*" (Tlaiss and Elamin 2016, p. 148). In this same vein, Afiouni et al. (2013) searched Emerald and Scopus databases using descriptor terms including *human resource management, personnel, Islam, Saudi Arabia, GCC* and *culture*. This effort produced merely 23 articles published between 1996 and 2006. It turned out that these mostly concerned the GCC and Levant regions generally. Such a dearth of knowledge has been addressed, somewhat, in recent decades. For example, in Budhwar and Mellahi 2007, Budhwar and Mellahi guest edited a special edition of the *International Journal of Human Resource Management* (*IJHRM*) that focused on people management practices in Middle Eastern countries. In the same journal, Afiouni et al. (2014) edited a more recent special issue on a similar topic. In 2010, Mellabi and Budhwar oversaw a special issue of *Personnel Review* entitled "Islam and HRM."

Notwithstanding the dearth of scholarship addressing employment relations and management-related phenomena in Saudi Arabia, the aforementioned recent effort (in the form of regionally focused special issues of scholarly journals, etc.) has produced some notable insights. First, concerning compensation, by Western standards Saudi employees have restricted input into the design and implementation of pay and recognition structures (Ramall et al. 2011). Also, somewhat at odds with how things are done in the Western world, at least in recent decades, employee benefits in Saudi Arabia are typically based more on seniority than merit (Mellahi and Wood 2001; Tlaiss and Elamin 2016). Whatever the case, wages and salaries within the Kingdom typically are not regulated by external points of reference such as pay scales or formally sanctioned industry/sector benchmarks (Tlaiss and Elamin 2016). Second, Elamin (2012) found that perception of the nonfinancial elements of organizational justice, once again at least in comparison to the West, have a decisive impact on employee commitment and productivity. In practice, for example, it appears that Saudi employees will have higher productivity if they consider that their employer is treating them "fairly" in matters pertaining to non-pecuniary recognition. Indeed, the psychological contract between employers and employees, broadly conceived, seems more important than financial rewards when it comes to engaging and retaining Saudi local talent (Budhwar and Mellahi 2016). With respect to the Middle East as a whole, Aon-Hewitt (2011) identified the factors of "career growth" and "learning and development" as more consequential than "pay and benefits" when seeking to improve employee engagement and retention.

Insofar as strategic HRM in Saudi Arabia is concerned, Tlaiss and Elamin (2016) undertook a recent exploratory project drawing on 11 semi-structured anonymous interviews with HRM managers of private sector firms operating in Riyadh, Jeddah and Mecca (obtained using a snowball sampling strategy). Not published in one of the aforementioned journal special issues, these authors give unprecedentedly textured insight into matters such as recruitment and selection and training and development. In relation to the former of these elements, recruitment and selection, line managers have divergent views about whether Saudization is a good thing. By way of preamble, there was consensus that two employment regimes applied, one for locals and one for expats. Interviewees were also typically well aware of the associated quota system for Saudis, a system that they mostly viewed as their responsibility to implement. However, in some instances, managers said they viewed two regimes as unduly burdensome whereas others indicated that they saw it as a creative development agenda. Of those who were critical of the bifurcated labor market, some commented negatively on the role *wasta* (roughly translated as "nepotism") plays in Arabic society. These same managers also often indicated that, compared to expats, Saudis are less inclined to use official channels to secure employment. For example, they are often loath to submit their CVs online or write customized letters for specifically identified and advertised jobs. In relation to training and development, Tlaiss and Elamin (2016) found that Saudi firms rarely have in place an integrated long-term strategy. Rather – and perhaps surprising given the emphasis of King Abdullah's "Vision" project – on-the-job training is mostly relegated to low priority status, typically done on an ad-hoc basis and rarely associated with either formal needs analyses or Western-style evaluation protocols. Somewhat controversially, the researchers concluded that expats are more enthusiastic about training opportunities than their Saudi-local counterparts. This latter group, the Saudi workers, were described by the study's participants as possessing a sense of entitlement and as being unduly mindful that, for them, Saudization represents employment and economic security (Tlaiss and Elamin 2016).

Managing in the Arabian Gulf States: The Influence of History

As with Saudi Arabia, within the Gulf Cooperation Council (GCC) region overall there has been high levels of economic growth since approximately the 1970s. Moreover, the population rate of increase amongst GCC member countries in the 50 years since 1950 has been higher than any other region in the world; rising from four million in 1950 to over 40 million in 2000 (Kapiszewski 2000). Insofar as work and employment is concerned, several of the challenges that are present in Saudi also exist elsewhere in the Middle East. Such difficulties arise mostly due to an overreliance on expatriates to do skilled tasks and an associated need to create meaningful job opportunities for locals. To address these problems, two elements have been integral to public policy; substantial investment in vocationally orientated education and the notion of quota setting for locals employed in the private sector. These components are part and parcel of Bahrain's *Vision 2030*, Qatar's *Vison 2030*,

Oman's 5-year strategic plan, Kuwait's development plan, and the UAE's *Strategy 2011–2021*.

Within the GCC, unemployment has been unremittingly high for decades. This has been especially so for the youth labor market, perhaps not surprising in a *milieu* of overall rapid population growth. In GCC region countries in the first decade of the twenty-first century, aggregate unemployment for all nationals has hovered around 10%, and been jammed persistently at around 17% for 15–29-year-olds (Forstenlechner and Rutledge 2010). As is the case with Saudi Arabia, the GCC labor market has two idiosyncratic characteristics. First, locals prefer public to private sector jobs. In this regard, it is common for young males, in particular, to turndown industry opportunities and wait for more lucrative government work (Waxin and Bateman 2016). Second, the participation of women in GCC country labor markets remains low by OECD standards. For example, in 1975 women represented a maximum of 8% of the nonagricultural workforce (Willoughby 2008). Between 2005 and 2008, this figure, which is an aggregate for nationals and expatriates, was generally in the mid-30s (28% in the UAE, 30% in Bahrain, 35% in Qatar, 25% in Oman, and 51% in Kuwait) (Shehadi et al. 2011). Most national women who hold jobs in the GCC are employed in the public sector (Shehadi et al. 2011).

As with Saudization, within other GCC countries, a need to better prepare locals for cutting-edge work within the private sector has shaped public policy as well as management philosophy in recent decades. According to Waxin and Bateman (2016), administrations within the region have implemented localization initiatives of three kinds. First, there has been reform in the education sector. In this regard, until the 1980s Middle-Eastern Secondary schools focused much of their teaching effort on such things as the study of Arabic and Islamic culture, history, and traditions. Hence, vocational training, to the extent that it occurred, was typically carried out on the job. To remedy the "training relevance" problem several strategies have been implemented including: engaging leading international providers in consultancy roles (such as the *Rand* Corporation to update school curricula, etc.), increasing resource allocation (i.e., enhancing education budgets), and permitting leading Western universities to establish local satellite campuses (e.g., Qatar's Education City or Dubai's Academic City) (Waxin and Bateman 2016). Second, there has been an emphasis on economic diversification. In this regard, success has been patchy but has occurred, for example, with State run enterprises created intentionally to employ nationals, particularly in Dubai (Speiss 2010). The finance and banking sectors have also established themselves throughout the GCC as a bastion of employment for locals. Third, there have been forms of direct labor market intervention. As noted, in practice this has mostly boiled down to imposing quotas for local hires. For example, Forstenlechner and Rutledge (2010) point out that, in Kuwait, bank executives must ensure that 50% of their workforce is comprised of locals and Saudi authorities have mandated that certain jobs be made available only to locals.

Somewhat like Saudi Arabia, management practice within other GCC countries has been shaped principally by contextual elements such as commitment to Islam and the aforementioned, perhaps more pressing, challenges arising from mismatch between private sector skills shortages and locally available talent. Employers, at least passively, have often resisted government edicts concerning this matter. For example, Scott-Jackson et al. (2014c) found that, within the United Arab Emirates (UAE), firm executives often view GCC-based job applicants somewhat contemptuously. Specifically, they typically perceive locals as unduly motivated by money. In a survey addressing this matter, Waxin and Bateman (2016) found that less than 10% indicated that they believed Middle-Eastern Muslims want to help society and none of them indicated that such locals want to contribute to the country's development. Forstenlechner (2010) delineates three hurdles concerning the recruitment of UAE nationals which (in order) are: reticence on the part of employers to lower selection standards, creation of applicant pools of sufficient size, and an overabundance of resumes from newly-minted graduates who have never held a job and therefore cannot be well differentiated. Insofar as the practice of training and development-related activities is concerned, authors such as Scott-Jackson et al (2014b, c, d) note that there are two kinds of private firms operating within GCC countries: those that are exclusively quota-focused, and others that go beyond compliance and, for example, use talent management techniques to develop locals for leadership roles. In the same (multi-document) body of research, the authors report mixed results concerning the efficacy of modes of delivery of training, with firms operating in the UAE, for example, generally using ineffective strategies (e.g., classroom-based instruction) as opposed to instruction that is appropriately embedded in a workplace context (e.g., on – the-job delivery techniques).

To combat the problem of employee turnover of qualified locals, and to ensure that progress with state-imposed quotas is not compromised, firm executives operating within GCC countries are inclined to view employee engagement as a more consequential family of strategies than those pertaining to training (Scott-Jackson et al. 2014a). In a comparative study, which used surveys (4,599) to assess the relative difference in workplace commitment among expats, and locals, Singh et al. (2012) scrutinized 40 firms operating in the UAE, Qatar, and Bahrain. Their principal finding was that GCC nationals were less engaged with their job than expats (50.8% vs. 56.9%). They further noted that men were more engaged than women (57.3% vs. 49.7%) and, perhaps axiomatically, that female nationals were the least engaged (48.4%). The same authors also found that, through the middle decades of a lifespan/career (i.e., 25–45-year-olds) engagement drops to its lowest ebb. To appreciate these results some context is necessary; specifically, Aon-Hewitt's worldwide scores on workplace engagement place the Middle-Eastern cohort data as representative of the least impressive in the world. The authors who undertook the research (i.e., Singh et al. 2012) give clues about why this is so, specifically why there is a high differential in levels of engagement between locals and expats. They note that 65% of locals indicated that their national and religious identity "strongly" or "very strongly" influences their approach to work, a result approximately twice that of expats.

Related to employee commitment and engagement is the question of turnover. Within the Middle East, and taking account of international industry norms, this is typically high for both locals and expats. For example, in the UAE private sector, across the board for locals engaged as professionals, turnover is at least 60% (AMEInfo 2007). Forstenlechner (2010) has suggested that this is mostly due to culture. Specifically, many nationals are not interested in occupying non-managerial roles within firms. As such, if they are not engaged initially in a management job, they will soon leave if their status does not change. The problem is exacerbated in circumstances where there is inadequate training and development and in instances where those in authority are not influencing employee expectations (Ali-Ali 2008). Moreover, low levels of workplace commitment and ensuing high degrees of turnover intention (and actual turnover) are also likely due to the possibility that, to develop a career within Middle Eastern firms, one is often required to relocate (Forstenlechner 2010).

When writing about employment relations practices in OECD countries, particularly when approaching the subject matter from an historical perspective, it is conventional to devote attention to the circumstances of women in the labor market and public policy measures aimed at remedying their systemic disadvantage. Insofar as the Middle East is concerned, Al-Lamki (1999, 2000) and Metcalfe (2007) have noted that problems faced by women in the region who aspire to take on management roles are similar (but mostly of greater magnitude) to those faced by their Western counterparts. For example, Metcalfe (2007) scrutinized the experiences of professional women in the Gulf State of Bahrain. In examining both locals and expats, she concluded that the key barriers to their career advancement were (in order of importance), a patriarchal culture (76.5%), few female role models (72.5%), child-related family commitments (62.7%), stereotyped perception of women managers (60.8%), limited training opportunities (56.9%), and other family commitments (37.3%). However, somewhat unlike is the case in the West, Metcalfe (2007) also concluded that these problems are mostly not dealt with through public or organizational-level polices. For example, she observed that GCC firms typically do not have formal strategies addressing equal employment opportunity, mentoring for women, sexual harassment, and work-life balance. She also noted that the aforementioned problem with a paucity of workplace relevant training and development opportunities is especially acute for women. Metcalfe's (2007) overall conclusion concerned the influence of Islam in Middle-Eastern workplaces and, in particular, its "equal but different" view of the sexes and the implications of such a view for equity, inclusion and career advancement.

The United Arab Emirates: A Bridge to the Western World

In 1972 the United Arab Emirates (UAE) was formed as a consequence of a formal agreement struck between seven loosely confederated sheikdoms on the North-East horn of the Arabian Peninsula; Abu Dhabi, Dubai, Sharjah, Ajman, Um Al Quwain, Ras Al Khaimah, and Fujairah. In the decades since, the UAE has established itself as the Middle East's most developed – and Westernized – economy. Driven initially by its substantial oil and gas reserves, mostly around Abu Dhabi, it has achieved relative success in recent years in diversifying its economic base such that, by 2012, it had a per capita gross domestic product that ranked it the 15th largest economy in the world (Waxin and Bateman 2016). Today, the UAE has one of the most sophisticated and high-tech public infrastructure systems on the planet, comprising arguably the world's best sea ports, airports and internal transport facilities (including a flying "drone" taxi service that is being rolled out at the time of writing). Dubai, to the North of Abu Dhabi, has become an international trading hub (bosting two of the largest and most hi-tech shopping malls in the world, *the Dubai Mall* and *the Emirates Mall*). The city is also a global center for financial and banking services and emerging as an iconic Western tourist destination (with world-class theme parks such as *Atlantis* and, soon, *Dubailand*; with a projected cost of more than 65 billion dollars, possibly the most ambitious leisure development ever conceived).

Although Emirati life has identifiable links with Islam and traditional tribal mores, culturally the modern UAE has emerged as more similar to Western countries and, in so doing, diverged somewhat from other Middle-Eastern States (Afiouni et al. 2013; Zhao et al. 2012). Perhaps partly due to such similitude, more has been written about management practice in the Emirates than elsewhere in the region (Afiouni et al. 2013).

As is the case throughout the Middle East, the UAE private sector relies heavily on the contributions of expatriates, particularly professionals from Western countries with management skill and technical expertise (notably the UK, Australia, the USA, and Canada), and has a dual labor market (Fasano-Filho and Goyal 2004). Insofar as unskilled and semiskilled workers are concerned, those from low wage countries, mostly on the Indian sub-continent (India, Pakistan, Bangladesh, Nepal, and Sri Lanka) comprise about 60% of the nation's inhabitants and are engaged in construction and service-related and other trade-based industries (Al Bayan 2008). It is noteworthy that Emirati nationals comprise only 11.6% of the country's total population at any given time and a mere 4.2% of its workforce (Forstenlechner and Rutledge 2010). In both the public and private sectors, local employees typically enjoy more privileged conditions than expats, including, for example, mandated higher wages, shorter working hours, and guaranteed job security. The UAE work visa system unambiguously gives substantial negotiating advantage to the employer. For example, employees may only change employers with a letter of "no-objection" from their prior sponsor (Waxin and Bateman 2016). However, notwithstanding such institutionally based power and negotiating lopsidedness in the employment relationship, the country's heavy reliance on foreigners places special burdens on HRM departments, particularly concerning such matters as diversity management, government liaison, and workforce integration.

As with the region generally (and as noted), public policy in the UAE has emphasized the importance of education and talent development for several decades. Associated with such a focus is a formal government commitment to, so-called, *Emiratization* based on the three pillars of educational enhancement, economic diversification, and labor market regulation. However, once again as elsewhere in the Middle East, there is evidence that training initiatives, in particular, are not effective in preparing Emiratis for working life. For example, authors such as

Randeree (2009) provide data indicating that the nation's high school and college graduates typically lack industry relevant skills, Ali-Ali (2008) and Randeree (2009) conclude that they have sub-standard English, and Rees et al. (2007) and Forstenlechner (2010) observe that, in a relative sense, they mostly lack vocational motivation. Perhaps even more revealingly, Vazquez-Alvarez (2010) found that the relatively few Emirati locals who enter the workforce, typically do so with one to two more years of schooling than that of comparable expatriates but manifest skill and knowledge that is about one to two years behind this reference cohort. Forstenlechner and Rutledge (2010) highlighted that the preamble to the government reform agenda, known formally as "*Strategy 2010–2020*," indicates that 94% of students entering one of the country's national universities require at least one remedial course.

Given the persistence of some of the aforementioned dysfunctional aspects of the nation's labor market, it is perhaps unsurprising to find evidence that, compared to the West, HRM departments in UAE-based firms and within the public sector (or more precisely the executives who administer such units) do not have the status of strategic partners (Yaseen 2013). Indeed, these organizational elements mostly focus on process-related tasks (Yaseen 2013; Scott-Jackson et al. 2014a). Another (related) conclusion from these studies is that managers struggle to establish, and make use of, HRM systems; a problem that appears to be due to something of a chasm concerning what HR executives and those with core operational responsibilities consider to be important. In this vein, Scott-Jackson et al. (2014a) found that when HRM and operationally focused executives within the UAE were each asked to assess performance on orthodox elements of people management, the HRM managers gave consistently higher appraisal ratings than their operationally orientated peers. The authors noted that, although this kind of finding is somewhat universal, its relative magnitude is disproportionately large in the GCC region, including especially, in the UAE. More recently, authors such as Budhwar and Mellahi (2016) have concluded that, comparatively speaking, the UAE private sector has a persistent problem concerning not being able to well align HR strategies with broader organizational goals and priorities. Consistent with this malaise, Scott-Jackson et al. (2014a) has examined data pertaining to the training of HRM professionals and found that within the GCC region generally, and the Emirates in particular, human resource practitioners are often inadequately qualified.

Conclusion: The Influence of Islamic Management in the non-Islamic World

There is a paucity of scholarship concerning the practice of management in the Middle East. Indeed, much of what is known about the topic must be inferred from, in particular, public policy priorities, priorities that are influenced by both Islamic values and the jinx that comes paradoxically with having an abundance of natural resources. In these circumstances, it is perhaps no coincidence that the most socially and culturally shut-off nation-State in the region, the Kingdom of Saudi Arabia

(KSA), is also the one whose work and management philosophies have received the least scholarly scrutiny. In the same vein, the region's most open and outward looking country, the United Arab Emirates (UAE), is the jurisdiction, about which, most has been written. Despite such an analytic differential, Middle Eastern work, employment and people management has discernible generic characteristics. For example, in a contemporary global environment where public policy is increasingly deemphasizing the use of fossil fuels and where, as a finite resource, Arabian Gulf oil supplies are dwindling, nation-States in the region have been mostly unsuccessful in diversifying their economic base. Associated with this problem has been that – aside from being exporters of their product – the same countries have not well integrated themselves into the world economic system (with the partial exception of the UAE). Simultaneously, Middle Eastern public sectors have become bloated bureaucracies; largely acting to abate unemployment amongst locals who are unsuitable for private sector jobs and, in any case, only disposed to accept high-status managerial postings. Furthermore, these same public sectors have played key regulatory roles; in more extreme cases in relation to the uncompromising enforcement of distinctively Quranic tenets however, more typically, to preserve civic decorum and maintain a culture of politeness and respect for Islamic institutions (but – as Ali and Al Kazem 2006 note – not necessarily fully manifesting a commitment to the faith).

In a context of massive population growth over the last 70 years, the Middle East has also had persistently high rates of unemployment, particularly amongst young people. This problem has been met with various nationalization initiatives. These have been based principally on quotas for locals in the private sector, educational reform, and top-down "forced" industry diversification. Overall, such agendas have not been especially successful. However, they have been consequential in creating a distinctive Middle-Eastern approach to work and management. A key element of the approach is that it invariably – and formally – establishes a dual labor market based, not for example on the Western construct of flexibility (core vs. peripheral workers, etc.), but on privilege (locals vs. expats). Furthermore, even among locals, an often-sophisticated workplace pecking order is ensconced in the employment culture. Authors such as Mellahi and Budhwar (2006) have developed a portrait of this archetype. They characterize the typical Middle-Eastern workplace as high on power distance and, thus, as an arena where executives engage in limited delegation. They view the locally based hierarchical system of privilege as one sustained by a distorted, somewhat partial, commitment to Islam. Specifically, they consider that many locals are more loyal to their family and friends than they are to their employer. As such, although those with *wasta* cut bureaucratic corners, they also thrive through relying on inequitable criteria for such things as recruitment, promotion and compensation. Indeed, the word "*wasta*" quickly becomes part of the vocabulary of those who work in the region (as in, *he is being paid more/has more weeks of vacation*, etc., *because he has* "*wasta*"). Another (related) element of working life in Middle Eastern countries is the notion of "*shura*" (Ali 2004; Mellahi 2006). This construct, distinctively Quranic but mostly only partially embraced (e.g., Ali and Al-Kazemi 2006), concerns an ancient Arabic tendency for consensus-style decision-making taking account of respect for authority and age, as well as patriarchal (as opposed to institutional) commitment to employees and society (in countries like Kuwait and Saudi Arabia).

A final point about Middle Eastern work-related stratification concerns women. Specifically, occupational power structures, based on affiliation and wealth, are typically intertwined with a crosscutting dimension of inequality: gender. Indeed, and as noted (e.g., Hofstede 1980), mostly due to the influence of the faith, females in Arabic countries experience some of the same institutional work-related impediments as their Western sisters, albeit often in heightened form. In practice, they are largely excluded from being given a seat at the important tables, whether such tables be in the boardroom or the executive office.

In 1492, Christopher Columbus discovered the new world of the Americas whilst ostensibly *en route* to India. His passage – via the west – was both uncharted and unorthodox. Rumor has it that he proceeded the long way because he wanted to avoid being embroiled in Middle-Eastern conflict. Up until the twentieth century, and indeed into the twenty-first, Columbus's concern – and his apparent perception of the region – has remained widespread. However, aside from its reputation as a place of turmoil and score settling (perhaps a somewhat strawman view), in modern history, the Arab world has seen momentous renovation. Specifically, in the 1930s, it transitioned from being a largely preindustrial arid region marked generally by comparatively low standards of subsistence living and recurrent tribal skirmishes, to being a place of affluence and high income, albeit with associated ramped inequality. In parallel with this shift, the area's population grew more rapidly than anywhere else in the world in the 50 years until 2000. Unambiguously, it was the discovery and commercialization of oil and petroleum-related products that made possible such metamorphosis. However, in the twenty-first century, the good fortune brought by liquid gold has proved to be something of a mixed-blessing for the Arabian Gulf. Obviously, oil brings prosperity (but not necessarily shared prosperity). In the case of the Middle East, particularly recently, it has also come with work-related challenges. Commitment to Islamic values has influenced – but only influenced – the way administrators have coped with these trials. In this regard, it is worth remembering that Islam, like the other Abrahamic religions, survives because it embodies profoundness. However, insofar as its application in the world of work and employment is concerned, the student should remember that ordinary people distil and apply religious doctrine. As mortals, they are by definition, not the Prophet and thus inevitably fall short in applying his wisdom.

Cross-References

- ▶ Africa and the Firm: Management in Africa Through a Century of Contestation
- ▶ Changing Corporate Governance in France in the Late Twentieth Century
- ▶ Different Experiences: Europe, Africa, and the Middle East – An Introduction
- ▶ Flexicurity: The Danish Model
- ▶ Managing Africa's Strongest Economy: The History of Management in South Africa, 1920–2018

- Pre-colonial Africa: Diversity in Organization and Management of Economy and Society
- Why Entrepreneurship Failed to Emerge in "Developing Countries": The Case of Colonial Africa (1952–1972)
- Work and Society in the Orthodox East: Byzantium and Russia, AD 450–1861

References

Abdalla IA, Al-Homoud M (1995) A survey of management training and development practices in the State of Kuwait. J Manag Dev 14(3):14–25

Achoui MM (2009) Human resource development in Gulf countries: an analysis of the trends and challenges facing Saudi Arabia. Hum Resour Dev Int 12(1):35–46

Afiouni F, Karam CM, El-Hajj H (2013) The HR value proposition model in the Arab Middle East: identifying the contours of an Arab Middle-Eastern HR model. Int J Hum Resour Manag 24(10):1895–1932

Afiouni F, Ruël H, Schuler R (2014) HRM in the Middle East: toward a greater understanding. Int J Hum Resour Manag 25(2):133–143

Al Bahar AA, Peterson SE, Taylor WGK (1996) Managing training and development in Bahrain: the influence of culture. J Manag Psychol 11(5):26–32

Al Bayan (2008) www.albayan.ae3servlet/Satelllite?c=Article$cid=1223993414930$pagename=Albayan/Article/FullDetail. Accessed 10 Jan 2020

Al-Asfour A, Khan SA (2014) Workforce localization in the Kingdom of Saudi Arabia. Issues and challenges. Hum Resour Dev Int 17(2):243–253

Al-Harbi K (1997) Markov analysis of Saudization in engineering companies. J Manag Eng 13(2):87–97

Ali A (2004) Islamic perspectives on management and organization. Edward Elgar, Cheltenham/Northampton

Ali A, Al-Kazemi A (2006) Human resource management in Kuwait. In: Budhwar P, Mellahi K (eds) Managing human resources in the Middle East. Routledge, London, pp 79–96

Ali-Ali J (2008) Emiratisation: drawing UAE nationals into their surging economy. Int J Sociol Soc Policy 28(9):365–379

Alisa S, Issaev L (2018) Internet censorship in Arab Countries: religious and moral aspects. Religions 9(11):358–363

Al-Lamki SM (1999) Paradigm shift: a perspective on Omani women in management in the Sultanate of Oman. Adv Women Leadersh J (Spring) 2:1–30

Al-Lamki SM (2000) Women in the labour force in Oman: the case of the Sultanate of Oman. Int J Manag 17(2):166–174

Al-Rasheed M (2010) A History of Saudi Arabia. Cambridge. Cambridge University Press

AMEInfo (2007) Nationalisation taking root in Gulf Region, 26 Sept 2007. www.ameinfo.com/133128.html. Accessed 3 Dec 2019

Aon Hewitt (2011) Qudurat report. www.aon.com/middle-east/thought-leadership/hr/qudurat/default.jsp. Accessed 15 Dec 2019

Armstrong K (1992) Muhammad: biography of the Prophet. HarperCollins, New York

Atiyyah HS (1996) Expatriate acculturation in Arab Gulf countries. J Manag Dev 15(5):37–47

Berg H (2003) Method and theory in the study of Islamic origins. Brill Academic, Toronto

Bowman AK, Rogan E (1999) Agriculture in Egypt: from Pharaonic to modern times. Oxford University Press, London

Budhwar P, Mellahi K (2007) Introduction: human resource management in the Middle East. Int J Hum Resour Manag 19(1):2–10

Budhwar PS, Mellahi K (2016) Handbook of human resource management in the Middle East. Edward Elgar, Cheltenham pp 3–15

CNN.com (2018a) Man arrested in Saudi Arabia for having breakfast with woman, 11 Sept 2018
CNN.com (2018b) Turkey has "shocking" audio and visual evidence of Saudi journalist's killing. Retrieved 12 Nov 2019
Cook M (1983) Muhammad. Oxford University Press, Oxford
Crone P (1987) Meccan trade and the rise of Islam. Blackwell, London
Elamin AM (2012) Perceived organisational justice and work-related attitudes: a study of Saudi employees. World J Entrepr Manag Sustain Dev 9(1):71–88
Fasano-Filho U, Goyal R (2004) Emerging strains in GCC labour markets. Working paper no WP/04/71. International Monetary Fund
Forstenlechner I (2010) Workforce localisation in emerging Gulf economies: the need to fine-tune HRM. Pers Rev 39(1):135–152
Forstenlechner I, Rutledge E (2010) Unemployment in the Gulf: time to update the social contract. Middle East Policy 17(2):38–51
FreedomHouse (2018) Saudi Arabia. https://freedomhouse.org/report/freedom-world/2019/saudi-arabia. Accessed 1 Nov 2019
FreedomHouse (2019) Saudi Arabia. https://freedomhouse.org/report/freedom-world/2019/saudi-arabia. Accessed 9 Nov 2019
Grimm D (2018) These may be the world's first images of dogs and they're wearing leashes. www.sciencemag.org/news/2017/11/these-may-be-the-world-s-first-images-dogs-and-they-re-wearing-leashes. Science magazine. Retrieved 11 June 2019
Hamidullah M (1998) The life and work of the Prophet of Islam. Islamic Research Institute, Islamabad
Harry W (2007) Employment creation and localisation: the crucial human resource issues for the GCC. Int J Hum Resour Manag 18(1):132–146
Hefner RW (2011) Shari'a politics: Islamic law and society in the modern world. Indiana University Press, Bloomington
Hodgson M (1974) The venture of Islam: the classical age of Islam. University of Chicago Press, Chicago
Hofstede G (1980) Culture's consequences: international differences in work-related values. SAGE, Beverly Hills
Holland T (2012) In the shadow of the sword: the battle for global empire and the end of the ancient world. Abacus, London
BBC News (2018) https://www.bbc.com/news/world-europe-45812399. Turkish officials have audio and video evidence that shows missing Saudi journalist Jamal Khashoggi was killed inside the Saudi consulate in Istanbul. Retrieved 12 Oct 2019
Human Rights Report: Saudi Arabia (2007) U.S State Department. 11 Mar 2008
Human Rights Report: Saudi Arabia (2008) U.S State Department. 25 Feb 2009
Human Rights Report: Saudi Arabia (2009) U.S State Department. 11 Mar 2009
Human Rights Report: Saudi Arabia (2010) U.S State Department. 8 Apr 2011
Human Rights Watch (2008) Precarious justice, pp 3–4, 101–102, 108–115
Jadwa Investment (2017) Macroeconomic update. Economic projections for 2017. Jadwa Investment, Riyadh
Kapiszewski A (2000) Population, labour and education dilemmas facing GCC states at the turn of the century. www.crm.hct.ac.ae/events/archive/tend/AndKP.html. Accessed 20 Dec 2019
Klein A, Waxin M-F, Radnell E (2009) The impact of the Arab national culture on the perception ideal organizational culture in the United Arab Emirates: an empirical study of 17 firms. Educ Bus Soc Middle East Issue 2(1):44–56
Main D (2013) Holly land framing began 5000 years earlier than thought. Live Science. https://www.livescience.com/28011-ancient-agriculture-israel.html. Accessed 15 Feb 2020
Matherly L, Al Nahyan SS (2015) Workplace quotas: building competitiveness through effective governance of national expatriate knowledge transfer and development of sustainable human capital. Int J Organ Anal 23(3):456–471

Mellahi K (2006) Human resource management in Saudi Arabia. In: Budhwar P, Mellahi K (eds) Managing human resources in the Middle East. Routledge, London, pp 97–120

Mellahi K (2007) The effect of regulations on HRM: private sector firms in Saudi Arabia. Int J Hum Resour Manag 18(1):85–99

Mellahi K, Budhwar PS (2006) HRM challenges in the Middle East: an agenda for future research and policy. In: Budhwar P, Mellahi K (eds) Managing human resources in the Middle East. Routledge, London, pp 291–301

Mellahi K, Wood G (2001) Human resource management in Saudi Arabia. In: Budhwar PS, Debrah Y (eds) Human resource management in developing countries. Routledge, London, pp 135–152

Metcalfe BD (2007) Gender and human resource management in the Middle East. Int J Hum Resour Manag 18(1):54–74

Miethe TD, Lu H (2004) Punishment: a comparative historical perspective. Cambridge University Press, Cambridge

Miller J (2003) "Open secrets" "Open secrets". D+Z. Deutsche Gesellschaft für Internationale Zusammenarbeit (GIZ) GmbH. Archived from the original on 21 Feb 2011. Retrieved 05 Apr 2011

Motzki H (2000) The biography of Muhammad: the issue of the sources – Islamic history and civilization: studies and texts, vol 32. Brill Academic, Toronto

Musa AY (2008) Hadith as scripture: discussions on the authority of prophetic traditions in Islam. Palgrave, New York

Musmar F (2020) Israel could be key to 2020 geopolitics. The Begin-Sadat Centre for strategic studies. Center perspectives paper no. 1,389, 2 Jan 2020

Newsweek (2014) Janine di Giovanni. When it comes to beheadings, ISIS has nothing over Saudi Arabia. 14 Oct 2014

Ramadan T (2007) In the footsteps of the Prophet. Oxford University Press, New York

Ramady MA (2010) Population and demographics: Saudization and the labor market. In the Saudi Arabian economy: policies, achievements and challenges, 2nd edn. Springer, New York, pp 351–393

Ramall S, Maimani K, Diab A (2011) Compensation practices and plan effectiveness in Saudi Arabia. Compens Benefits Rev 43(1):52–60

Randeree K (2009) Strategic policy and practice in the nationalisation of human capital: "project emiratisation". Res Pract Hum Resour Manag 17(1):71–91

Rees CJ, Mamman A, Bin Braik A (2007) Emiratization as a strategic HRM change initiative: case study evidence from a UAE petroleum company. Int J Hum Resour Manag 18(1):33–53

Rodgers R (2012) The generalship of Muhammad: battles and campaigns of the Prophet of Allah. University of Florida Press, Miami

Rubin U (1995) The eye of the beholder: the life of Muhammad as viewed by the early Muslims. Darwin Press, London

Saudi internet rules (2001) Al-bab.com. https://al-bab.com/country/saudi-arabia. Retrieved 13 Mar 2019

Scott-Jackson W, Owen S, Whitacker D, Kariem R, Druck S (2014a) HRM in the GCC: a new world HRM for the new world economy. Oxford Strategic Consulting, Research Series, Oxford, UK

Scott-Jackson W, Owen S, Whitacker D, Cole M, Druck S, Kariem R, Mogielnicki R, Shuaib A (2014b) Building GCC talent for strategic competitive advantage. Oxford Strategic Consulting, Research Series, Oxford, UK

Scott-Jackson W, Owen S, Whitacker D, Cole M, Kariem R, Mogielnicki R, Shuaib A (2014c) Maximising Emirati talent in engineering. Oxford Strategic Consulting, Research Series, Oxford, UK

Scott-Jackson W, Owen S, Whitacker D, Druck S, Kariem R, Mogielnicki R (2014d) Maximising Qatari Talent. Oxford Strategic Consulting, Research Series, Oxford, UK

Serjeant RB (1964) The constitution of Medina. Islam Q 8:3–16

Shehadi R, Hoteit L, Lamaa A, Tarazi K (2011) Educated, ambitious essential women will drive the GCC's future. Booz and Co. www.strategyand.pwc.com/media/uploads/Strategyand-Educated-Ambitous-Essential.pdf. Accessed 1 Dec 2019

Shoult A (2006) Doing business with Saudi Arabia. GMB Publishing, London

Singh A, Sharma J (2015) Strategies for talent management: a study of select organisations in the UAE. Int J Organ Manag 23(3):337–347

Singh A, Jones DB, Hall N (2012) Talent management: a research based case study in the GCC region. Int J Bus Manag 7(24):94–107

Speiss A (2010) Demographic transitions and imbalances in the GCC: security risks, constraints and policy challenges. Exeter Gulf Studies Conferences. The 21st Century Gulf: The Challenge of Identity

The Atlantic (2015) When beheadings won't do the job, 24 Dec 2015. 014

The Economist (2001) Saudi Arabian justice: cruel or just unusual; Saudi Arabia. 14 June 2001

The Economist (2007) International: law of God versus law of man; Saudi Arabia. 13 Oct 2007

The Economist Intelligence Unit (2012) Democracy index 2012 Democracy at a standstill (PDF)

The Guardian (2016) Saudi execution of Shia Cleric sparks outrage in the Middle East. 2 Jan 2016. P12

The Independent (2014) Saudi Arabia declares all atheists are terrorists in new law to crack down on political dissidents. April 2014

The Peninsula (2011) Dozens detained in Saudi over flood protests. Qatar/Thompson-Reuters. 2. https://www.thepeninsulaqatar.com/middle-east/140720-dozens-detained-in-saudi-over-flood-protests.html. Retrieved 10 Nov 2019

The Washington Post (2008) Saudi face soaring blood-money sums, 27 July 2008

Tliass H (2013) Women managers in the United Arab Emirates. Successful careers or what? Equality Diversity Inclusion 32(8):756–776

Tlaiss H, Elamin A (2016) Employment Relations in Saudi Arabia. In: Budhwar PS, Mellahi K (eds) Handbook of human resource management in the Middle East. Edward Elgar, Cheltenham pp141–161

Tripp H, North P (2009) CultureShock! A survival guide to customs and etiquette. Saudi Arabia, 3rd edn. Marshall Cavendish, London

Trompenaars F, Hampden-Turner C (1998) Riding the waves of culture. Understanding diversity in global business. McGraw-Hill, New York

Vazquez-Alvarez R (2010) The micro-structure of wages and wage determination in the UAE. Dubai Economic Council, Dubai

Waxin M, Bateman RE (2016) Human resource management in the United Arab Emirates. In: Budhwar PS, Mellahi K (eds) Handbook of human resource management in the Middle East. Edward Elgar, Cheltenham

Willoughby J (2008) Segmented feminisation and the decline of neopatriarchy in GCC countries of the Persian Gulf. Comp Stud South Asia Afr Middle East 28(1):184–199

Yaseen ZK (2013) Clarifying the strategic role of the HR managers in the UAE educational institutions. J Manag Sustain 32(2):110–118

Zhao F, Scavarda AJ, Waxin MF (2012) Key issues and challenges in e-government deployment: an integrative case study of the number one eCity in the Arab world. Inf Technol People 25(4):395–422

Work and Society in the Orthodox East: Byzantium and Russia, AD 450–1861

49

Bradley Bowden

Contents

Introduction	1106
The Byzantine Experience and Heritage	1113
From Freedom to Serfdom: The Muscovite Experience	1117
The Limits to Modernization: Russia, 1682–1861	1124
Ideas, Management, and Russian Reality	1132
Conclusion	1136
Cross-References	1137
References	1137

Abstract

Often overlooked by Western scholars, the Orthodox East has provided some of the most important societies in the human experience. For a thousand years, Byzantium provided a living link to the world of antiquity. Over the last 300 years, Russia, in a variety of guises (Muscovy, Imperial Russia, Soviet Russia, the Russian Federation), has always been a major world power. Despite the success of these societies, however, many of the attributes that we have associated with "modern management" – competition, legal protection of person and property, and guaranteed freedom of movement for labor – have often been absent. In exploring the reasons for such outcomes, we argue that blame should not be ascribed to a Byzantine cultural heritage supposedly hostile to individual identity. Nor is it the case that Orthodox societies such as Russia are hostile to concepts such as freedom and individualism. The resonance of the works of Tolstoy, Dostoyevsky, and Solzhenitsyn indicates that such values are deeply ingrained. Rather than being the result of cultural attributes, this chapter argues that the absence (or weak presence) of societal protections for person and

B. Bowden (✉)
Griffith Business School, Griffith University, Nathan, QLD, Australia
e-mail: b.bowden@griffith.edu.au

© The Author(s), under exclusive licence to Springer Nature Switzerland AG 2020
B. Bowden et al. (eds.), *The Palgrave Handbook of Management History*,
https://doi.org/10.1007/978-3-319-62114-2_47

property reflects peculiar historic experiences. Located at Europe's eastern periphery, the security of these societies was always precarious. In both Byzantium and Russia, the state feared that personal and economic freedoms would weaken its capacity to defend the frontiers. However, by denying freedom of movement, and protection of property, to its citizens, imperial Russia – like Muscovy and Byzantium before it – curtailed the entrepreneurship essential to its long-term success.

Keywords

Russia · Byzantium · Moscow · Freedom · Serfdom · Dostoyevsky · Orthodox Christianity

Introduction

Is Russia profoundly different to the societies of Western Europe? Did it experience the managerial revolution of the eighteenth and nineteenth centuries in ways that bear comparison with Britain, France, the United States, and other nations in the West, and if not, why not? This chapter speaks to these questions.

On the eve of World War I, the Czech historian and political theorist, Thomas Masaryk, reflected on the unique "Spirit of Russia." A longtime advocate of a separate Slav identity, Masaryk arguably had a better understanding of Eastern European affairs than most. In 1919, he was elected as Czechoslovakia's first President. Yet, even Masaryk found prerevolutionary Russia mystifying. "Slav as I am," Masaryk (1913/1955: 5) recorded, "a visit to Russia has involved many more surprises than a visit to any other land." In Masaryk opinion, what made Russia different was the cultural and religious heritage of Byzantium, the Greek Orthodox society that emerged from the breakup of the Roman Empire in the fifth century AD. As Masaryk (1913/1955: 24–25) expressed it, "the decisive centralizing force" in Russian society stemmed from "the dependence of the grand princes upon the church... princely absolutism received a religious sanction." The view that Russia's peculiarity stemmed from its Byzantine and Orthodox heritage was one shared by the great Belgium historian, Henri Pirenne. It was from Byzantium, Pirenne (1925/1952: 51) recorded that Russians "received Christianity...it was from her that they borrowed their art, their writing, the use of money and a good part of their administration organization." The French historian, Fernand Braudel (1987/1993), and the American political theorists, Samuel Huntington (1996/2003) and Carroll Quigley (1979), have also argued that Russia's uniqueness is a product of its Byzantine heritage, a heritage that supposedly emphasizes communal and state solidarity at the expense of individual identity. As "a society and a culture," Huntington (1996/2003: 140) noted, early modern Russia bore "little resemblance" to the geographical adjacent West. In consequence, "distinctive feature of Western civilization" that did much to explain the West's historical success – "separation of church and state, rule of law, social pluralism, representative bodies, individualism" – "were almost totally absent from the Russian experience."

For Masaryk, Pirenne, Braudel, Quigley, and Huntington, the historical uniqueness of Russia – which typically manifested itself in an all-powerful state that retarded the emergence of free-market capitalism and associated managerial endeavor – was more a curse than a benefit. "At the end of the seventeenth century," Huntington (1996/2003: 140) explained, "Russia was not only different from Europe it was also backward compared to Europe." For others, however, the unique features of Russia – supposedly built around communal and social solidarity – brought peculiar benefits to both the workplace and the wider society. In articulating this view, the nineteenth-century Russian novelist, Alexander Herzen, suggested that an excessive Western focus on politics and government caused a profound misunderstanding of Russian society. Yes, it was true, Herzen (1855/1956: 13) conceded, that in Russia "the individual has always been crushed...engulfed by the state." The modern, centralized state was, however, in Herzen's opinion, an alien Western import. Despite the best efforts of bureaucratic oppression, true Russian values survived in "the principle of community," in "the village commune" (Herzen 1855/1956: 15; Herzen 1851/1956: 183). Rather than adopt the rampant and destructive individualism of the West, the Russian commune shared wealth according to need in a form of "rural communism" (Herzen 1851/1956: 189). In consequence, so Herzen (1851/1956: 189) argued, Russian communalism offered Western societies – torn apart by the economic and social tensions of industrialization – a beacon in the darkness, "an actual instance of an attempt ... in the direction of the division of the land amongst those who work it." The view that Russian communal values offered Europe a pathway to "prosperity and contentment," built around "harmony and unity," was one Herzen shared with Leo Tolstoy (see Tolstoy 1876/1978: 369). In Tolstoy's (1876/1978: 367) *Anna Karenina*, for example, the central character – the high-minded aristocratic reformer, Kostya Levin – only makes a success of his rural estate when he comes to the realization that the ideas of John Stuart Mill and classical economics do "not apply in Russia." For, "where capital was expended in the European fashion," thereby coming into conflict with "the spirit of the [Russian] people," so it was that "little was produced." In short, any managerial activity in Russia could only succeed when it operated on Russian rather than Western principles.

Whether one views Russian uniqueness positively or negatively, there is no gainsaying the fact that not only Russian but also the Orthodox East as a whole followed a different *historical* trajectory to the Latin West from the mid-fifth century AD onward. Whereas the West retreated into rural barbarism after the great Germanic *Volkerwanderung* of the fifth century, Byzantium maintained a physical connection with the world of classical antiquity for another millennium. The splendors of Constantinople and Byzantium, and its profound impact on early Russian societies, are well recorded in the so-called Russian Primary Chronicle, our main source of evidence on the formative experiences of the Russian and Ukrainian people. In reporting on their visit to Constantinople's *Hagia Sophia* (the Church of Holy Wisdom) in AD 987, a delegation from Kiev is recording as saying:

... the Greeks led us up to the edifices where they worship their God, and we knew not whether we were in heaven or on earth. For on earth there is no such splendour or such beauty, and we were at a loss to describe it ... God dwells there among men. (Russian Primary Chronicle 1337/1953: 111)

So impressed were the Kievan Rus, the most significant of the early Russian societies, that in the ensuing year they converted to the Orthodox faith. Subsequent to his momentous decision, which set Russia on a different *cultural* path to the West, Kiev's Prince Vladimir, so it is reported (Russian Primary Chronicle 1337/1953: 117), "began to found churches and to assign priests throughout the cities...He took the children of the best families, and sent them for instruction in book learning." At a time when the peasantry of medieval Europe suffered the indignity of serfdom, the ordinary Russian enjoyed social freedom, pursuing "slash-and-burn" agriculture in the forest of conifers and deciduous trees that lay to the north of Kiev. In the ninth and tenth centuries, the various Russian principalities also enjoyed a flourishing commerce with both Byzantium and the Muslim Caliphate of Baghdad, Pirenne (1925/1952: 54) observing that "Russia was living by trade at an era when the Carolingian Empire [of Western Europe] knew only the demesnial regime." From the eleventh century, however, these outwardly benign circumstances took a turn for the worse. First, a nomadic people, the Pechenegs, occupied the Ukrainian steppe, destroying trade with the Muslim South and Byzantine. Then, in the thirteenth century, invading Mongol hordes destroyed Kiev, occupying both the Volga basin and the Ukrainian steppe. In 1453, the fall of Constantinople to the Ottoman Turks cut Russia's physical ties to its Byzantium roots. The collective effect of these experiences was to isolate Russia from the wider world, even as Western Europe enjoyed a commercial and cultural Renaissance.

As the "West" looked outward, Russia suffered economic isolation, becoming a "self-contained" society, living "by and upon itself" (Braudel 1977: 83). With the emergence of a new Russian state in the fifteenth century, centered on Moscow rather than Kiev, the society also witnessed a process of gradual enserfment that culminated in the Legal Code (*Sobornoe Ulozhenie*) of 1649, a document described as "the most important written document in all of Russian history before the nineteenth century" (Hellie 2006a: 551). Under its terms, Russian society was subject to a serfdom that was more restrictive and onerous than the earlier Western European variety. Whereas in the medieval West, a peasant who found city employment effectively escaped serfdom, Russian serfs were legally denied the possibility of an urban existence after 1649, becoming instead a closed rural caste. In Russia's towns, the code of 1649 also bound urban dwellers to their existing occupation and place of residence, denying merchants the capacity "to move elsewhere, even if superior commercial opportunities seemed to warrant it" (Shaw 2006a: 587).

The consequences of the *Ulozhenie* of 1649, and Russia's belated embrace of serfdom, were profound. Rural activities and values were emphasized at the expense of commerce, industry, and entrepreneurship. Such problems remained even after the "Westernizing" reforms of Peter the Great (1682–172), which were premised on the assumption that Western technology and military methods could be grafted on to

Russian society without the need for far-reaching social or managerial changes. In consequence, even after the emancipation of Russia's serfs in 1861, Russia lagged other European societies in a host of business-related areas. In describing post-emancipation circumstances, Roger Portal (1966: 803) observed that "Russia was a country where commercial capitalism was scarcely developed, credit economy weak, and banking organization almost non-existent." Although Herzen, Tolstoy, and Ivan Turgenev penned romanticized accounts of peasant life – Herzen (1855/ 1956: 190) declaring that the "future of Russia rested with the *moujik*" [peasant] – the lived experience of the ordinary Russian was abysmal. In describing life inside the typical peasant abode, which normally housed three generations of a single family, Hellie (2006b: 289–290) records how "The smoke was so dense that it left a line around the wall about shoulder height, where the bottom of the smoke cloud hung. The air was so toxic that it disinfected the hut to the extent that not even cockroaches could survive." The industrial backwardness of Russia is perhaps best indicated by its inability to exploit the nation's abundant coal resources. For without coal for heating and cooking, Russia's urban population was restricted to wood fueled fires with accompanying risk of fire, Turgenev (1862/2009: 52) recording in his classic novel, *Fathers and Sons*, that "It's a well-known fact that our provincial towns burn down every five years or so." Without coal, the large-scale production of steel was also impossible, curtailing the growth of heavy machinery, railroads, and shipping. Theoretically, the vast deposits of the Donbas basis should have ensured comparative Russian advantage. Such, however, was not the case. In 1830, the Russian production of 300,000 tons was only 50% above the output that Britain managed in 1560 (Pollard 1980: 216; Portal 1966: 817). In 1890, as Fig. 1 indicates, Russian coal production was still a tiny fraction of that obtained by the industrializing societies of Britain and the United States.

If Fig. 1 points to economic and managerial backwardness, then Fig. 2 – which compares population growth in Muscovy/Russia with the United States – suggests the reverse: a growing and dynamic society. Whereas prior to 1700 the Russian homelands were geographically vast but sparsely populated, a transformation occurred around 1700 (i.e., the era of the Petrine reforms). By 1800, Russia's population (35 million) exceeded that of France (25–26 million), making it Europe's most numerous society. In the course of the nineteenth century, despite the social burdens of serfdom, population growth accelerated, surpassing even that of the United States with its large immigrant populations. Such gains would have been impossible unless the society possessed the wherewithal to feed tens of millions of extra mouths. The much-maligned backwardness of tsarist Russia was also belied by its battlefield performances, where time and again Russian armies shattered those of the West.

What explains the dynamic expansion of Russia's population during the eighteenth and nineteenth centuries, a growth that was to make Russia one of the world's preeminent powers? The most obvious answer is geographical. Like the United States, Russia in the eighteenth and nineteenth centuries was a frontier society, availing itself of the Ukrainian and Kuban steppes as well as the great Siberian wilderness. Agriculturally, the steppes of the Ukraine and the Kuban and, more

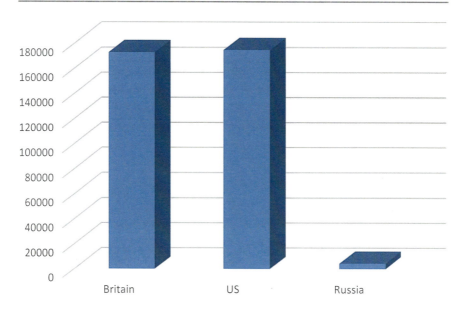

Fig. 1 British, the United States, and Russia coal output, 1890 (in thousands of tons). (Sources: UK Department of Business, Energy & Industrial Strategy, *British Coal Data 1853–2018*; U.S. Department of Commerce, *Historical Statistics of the United States*, Series M 93–103 and Series M 123–137; Portal, "The Industrialization of Russia," 817)

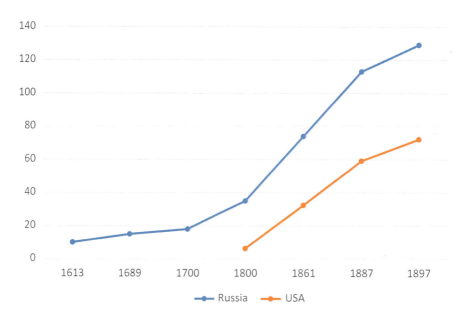

Fig. 2 Population of Russia and the United States, 1613–1897 (in millions)∗. (Sources: Cipolla, *Before the Industrial Revolution*, Table 1.1; Portal, "The Industrialization of Russia," 817; U.S. Department of Commerce, *Historical Statistics of the United States*, Series A 9–22)

particularly, the Central Black Earth region that lay between the Ukrainian steppe and the forested Russian heartlands offered almost unlimited potential. Whereas previously a number of nomadic warrior people had largely confined Russian settlement to the forests north of the Oka River, the victories of Peter the Great opened the southern expanses to agriculture. By 1719, an estimated 43% of the Russian population farmed the Central Black Earth region, a 250–500 kilometer strip of land to the north of the Ukrainian steppe that arguably boasts the world's most fertile soils (Shaw 2006b: 27–28).

As with the opening up of the American frontier, however, the Russian pioneering efforts of the eighteenth and nineteenth centuries could not have occurred in a population devoid of curiosity, inventiveness, and individuality. Certainly, the view that Russia is a society alien to ideas of liberty and freedom is a misnomer, contradicted by the deep resonance that the works of Alexander Pushkin, Tolstoy, and, above all, Fyodor Dostoyevsky obtained in Russian society. Indeed, among the canon of "Western literature," none arguably speaks to the importance of individual conscience and liberty more poignantly than Dostoyevsky does. Sentenced to 10 years in tsarist Russia's "Gulag" during his youth, Dostoyevsky understood that liberty and freedom were threatened not only by the educated agents of Russia's absolutist state but also by its revolutionary foes. As Dostoyevsky (1864/1972: 31–32) expressed it in his *Notes from Underground*, it is "the most civilized," those most prone to "abstract" political theorizing, who are the greatest "shedders of blood," an observation that prefigured Albert Camus's (1951/1978: 297) maxim that the most "homicidal" individuals are those who claim to act in the interest of "pure and unadulterated virtue." The Russian quest for political and economic liberty was reflected in not only poetry and literature. It also found expression in scientifically informed managerial ideas and practices. In 1765, the year before Adam Smith published *The Wealth of Nations*, the newly established Liberal Economic Society began publication of its annual conference proceedings, a work directed toward the formulation of "progressive" ideas for "household management" and the economic development of "the state" (cited, Marshev 2019: 288). By the mid-nineteenth century, interest in new managerial concepts, whether indigenous or imported, was widespread. "If we look at the studies ... in the areas of history, law, management, sociology, political economy and politics," Vadim Marshev (2019: 286) observes, we find "chapters and whole sections containing historical analysis of the development of management thought."

If Russian society by the mid-nineteenth century was one characterized by profound contradictions – in which works of towering literary genius and the pioneering settlement of new lands existed alongside authoritarian rule and primitive living conditions – how then can we effectively gauge its managerial achievements? As is the case in every other society, it comes down to what we mean by the term "management." If we go by the standard textbook definition – that "management" amounts to "planning, organizing, leading and controlling" – then we must conclude that Russia possessed effective systems of "management" capable of feeding its many citizens. However, from the very first chapter in this *Palgrave Handbook* (▶ Chap. 2, "What Is Management?"), I have argued in favor of a broader definition, associating "management" with attention to costs, competitive markets, legal protections of person and property, and the need to motivate legally free workforces. By this definition, the answer as to whether or not the world of mid-nineteenth century Russia can be regarded as a society where the norms and practices of "modern management" were commonplace must be "no." As the central figure in Ivan Turgenev's (1862/2009: 10–11) *Fathers and Sons* observed, Russian society in the late 1850s was one characterized "neither by its prosperity nor by its industriousness," a world where the peasantry "were all in rags" and the "shaggy cows" that they farmed with care were "mere bags of bones." It is difficult to attribute these unfortunate circumstances – as Masaryk, Pirenne, Huntington, and others have done – to Russia's Byzantine cultural and religious heritage. In essence, Greek and Russian Orthodoxy differs only in degree from Roman Catholicism. Both Orthodoxy and Catholicism emphasized individual worth and protection for the poor even as they preached acceptance of the secular power. In the West, Hapsburg and Bourbon Spain exhibited authoritarian tendencies, and a suspicion of capitalism and market forces, that shared much in common with tsarist Russia. Nor is it possible to attribute all the blame to serfdom. In France, Italy, England, and the Low Countries, the historical experience of serfdom led to a diffusion rather than a concentration of power. The same tendencies were evident in Poland, Lithuania, and Hungary in the sixteenth and seventeenth centuries. In all of these societies, a government-mandated enserfment of the rural population led to a weaker rather than a stronger state as magnates accumulated wealth and power at the expense of officialdom. In the case of Poland, the state was so enfeebled that it disintegrated, partitioned among its more powerful neighbors (one of which was Russia).

In the final analysis, Russia's problems, like that of Byzantium before it, were a product of geography and historical experience rather than of religion or culture. Like Byzantium before it, Russia found itself at the eastern edge of Europe, exposed to assault from societies (Arab, Turkish, Mongol, Tartar) that both Latin and Orthodox Christians regarded as mortal foes. Given the historic and geographic circumstances in which they found themselves, the emphasis on security at the expense of personal and economic freedom was understandable, even if the suppression of economic and political freedom came at a long-term cost. Similarly, the xenophobia and paranoia that often characterized Byzantium and Russia reflected more than Eurocentric racism. In 1453, the Ottoman Turks destroyed Byzantium. On repeated occasions, Muslim Tartars drawn from the southern steppes sacked and burned Moscow, the final outrage occurring in 1571. In the seventeenth and eighteenth centuries, Russia also suffered from the depredations of Polish and Swedish invaders. Accordingly, it was not only the peasantry who accepted subjugation at the hands of the state. So too did Russia's aristocrats, Kleimola (1979: 210) accurately noting that it was "the top levels of Russia [which] were the first to suffer subjugation to the service of the state." Unfortunately, the assumption that authoritarian states are better than market economies at allocating resources, thereby ensuring economic growth and greater military and political power, is not one supported by the historical evidence. For, in curtailing markets and individual liberty, authoritarian regimes invariably prove to be inefficient rather than efficient economic mentors. As Stephen Kotkin (2017: 417) notes in reflecting upon the Russian experiences under Joseph Stalin:

Dictatorial power is never efficient, all-knowing, and all-controlling: it shows its strength by violently suppressing any hint of alternatives but is otherwise brutally inefficient.

The Byzantine Experience and Heritage

There is an overwhelming tendency among both historians and the population at large to associate the Roman Empire almost solely with the Latin-speaking West rather than with the Greek-speaking East. In truth, the eastern sections of the Empire were always far more prosperous and populace than the western provinces. In the Late Empire, the population of Egypt (7.5 million), the wealthiest eastern province, far exceeded that of Gaul (2.5 million), the bedrock of imperial power in the West (Jones 1964: 1040–1041). By the sixth century AD, the most populace cities of the Mediterranean basin (Constantinople, Antioch, Alexandria) were all in the east, Constantinople perhaps boasting 750,000 by AD 500. In contrast, Rome, the papal headquarters of the Latin Church, became a shadow of its former self, described by Pope Gregory the Great (c. AD 593/1959: 81) as "buried in its own ruin ... its dilapidated buildings surrounded by their own debris." Across the Late Empire, every region confronted the same basic problem: how to defend the frontiers with the limited (and diminishing) resources of a society that was overwhelmingly rural. This produced an inevitable tension between a desire to maximize the taxes and other imposts required to fund armies and bureaucracies and the need to maintain a viable soldier-peasantry.

In the Latin-speaking West, where large slave-operated *latifundia* had long prevailed, the soldier-peasantry that once provided the backbone for imperial armies was a distant memory by the fourth century AD, forcing Western generals to recruit Germanic barbarians from beyond the frontiers. Even in the East, however, taxes and other imposts became unbearable. During the reign of the Roman Emperor, Diocletian (AD 284 – AD 305), taxes were not only increased but tied to what the state *believed* a given plot of land *should* produce – rather what it *actually* produced. In AD 332, to mitigate the ensuing flight of destitute peasants from the land, the Code of Constantine made the peasant's tillage of their plot a hereditary obligation. In the cities and towns, the craft worker was also denied the possibility of social mobility as their trade was also made a hereditary responsibility (Koerner 1941/1966: 25–26). In addition, taxes were increasingly made a collective responsibility of the village or commune, an outcome that caused neighbor to oversee neighbor in the knowledge that they would have to make up tax shortfalls caused by either peasant flight or subterfuge. The unintended consequence of this extension of state power was the so-called *patrocinium* movement, which saw peasants surrender both their families and their land to a wealthy local patron. In commenting upon the *patrocinium* movement, Ostrogorsky (1941/1966: 206) observed that "it was the government itself, driven by financial and military needs, which ... handed over the peasants to the landowners." Unfortunately for the state, the large landholder who came to dominate much of the East revealed a greater propensity for tax evasion than did the peasant proprietor, leaving the imperial armies and bureaucracies in a perilous state. To remedy this state of affairs, the Byzantine Emperor, Heraclius, who ruled the East from AD 610 to AD 641, came up with a solution that led to the recreation of an independent soldier-peasantry within Byzantium. This entailed the settlement of Slavonic immigrants on abandoned land, where they gained freehold possession and exemption from taxation in return for military service (Ostrogorsky 1941/1966: 207–208). Without Heraclius' reforms, it is probable that Byzantium would not have survived the Arab conquests of the seventh century, a time when Arab military success swept Egypt and much of the Middle East from imperial sovereignty. As the frontiers were stabilized within a shrunken state, however, few Byzantine emperors proved capable of resisting the temptation to increase the tax base at the expense of the soldier-peasant. The result was a cyclical process of renewed tax demands, peasant flight, and a further extension of aristocratic estates at the expense of the peasantry, followed by belated attempts at imperial reform directed toward the reinvigoration of a soldier-peasantry. In the end, it is arguable, the greatest threat to Byzantine survival came not from the Muslim Arabs and Turks beyond the frontier but rather from the semifeudal aristocrats within the borders, who "continually absorbed the land of the peasants and solders and made the owners their serfs" (Ostrogorsky 1941/1966: 221). Put another way, the centralizing tendencies of Byzantium were undermined not only by the excessive burdens placed on the peasantry but also by the state's inability to curtail the growth of aristocratic power at its own expense.

As the power of the Byzantine state slowly disintegrated, the Orthodox Church became an increasingly important buttress for imperial power, both within the frontiers and without. Within the frontiers, imperial oversight of ecclesiastical circumstances dates from AD 325 and the Council of Nicaea. Not only was the Council called at the Emperor Constantine's bequest, the articles of faith that emerged from it – the Nicaean Creed – also owed much to Constantine, who made rejection of the Creed a criminal matter (Davis 1970: 19). As the Church expanded in the East, the appointment of "Metropolitans" (i.e., bishops) occurred under imperial auspices. So extensive was imperial control of the eastern Church that Emperor Constantius II is reporting as saying, "My will is law for the church" (cited, Masaryk 1913/1955: 37). For their part, the Orthodox Patriarchs in Constantinople were anxious to draw on imperial authority to ward off challenges to ecclesiastical supremacy from rival claimants, most particularly those put forward by Rome's bishops and popes. In Orthodox opinion, Constantinople was the "second Rome," eclipsing the authority of the original imperial capital. As one Patriarch asserted in the late fifth century AD, "I hold that the most holy Church of the old and the new Rome to be one" (cited, Davis 1970: 71). From the point of view of the Byzantine state, there was also much benefit in having not only a loyal and faithful Orthodox population within the borders of Byzantium but also a wide circle of Orthodox believers beyond the frontier. Byzantium's most successful missionary efforts were among the Bulgarian and Slavic populations to its north. In the Russian Primary Chronicle (1337/1953: 62), for example, it is recorded how in the ninth century the Byzantine Emperor,

Michael III, sent missionaries (Cyril and Methodius) among the Moravians (Czechs) and that "When they arrived, they undertook to compose a Slavic alphabet." Within a century, the resultant "Cyrillic" script gained wide acceptance among the Slavic populations of Eastern Europe, permanently demarking the literary traditions of this region from the Latin West.

Enthusiasm for Orthodoxy was most pronounced in the Rus (Russian) lands where, as we noted the introduction, the Kievan Prince, Vladimir, converted to the faith in AD 988. Under his successor, Prince Yaroslav, the Russian Primary Chronicle (1337/1953: 137) reports how "new monasteries came into being. Yaroslav loved religious establishments and was devoted to priests, especially to monks ... He assembled many [religious] scribes, and translated from Greek into Slavic." Despite the indigenization of Greek Orthodox faith under Vladimir and Yaroslav, the Byzantine influence remained profound. Of the 23 individuals who served as Metropolitan of Kiev between the ninth and thirteenth centuries, only 3 were Russian with another 3 arriving from Slav lands to the West. All the rest were Greeks (Masaryk 1913/1955:36). So extensive was Byzantine influence on the first, Kiev-based Russian state that Masaryk (1913/1955: 36) declared it, with some degree of exaggeration, to be "no more than a dependency of Byzantium." Russian ecclesiastical subservience to Byzantium continued even the destruction of Kievan Rus by the Mongols in the thirteenth century. Only in the dying days of Byzantium, when Constantinople began making overtures for reconciliation with Rome, did the now Moscow-based Metropolitan assert independence from the Greek Orthodox Patriarch.

In declaring its independence from Constantinople, the Russian Church adopted two beliefs or ideologies that were to have incalculable consequences. First and most importantly, it assumed Byzantium's sense of historic destiny, the belief that Orthodoxy and Russia were predestined for world leadership. For, on hearing of Constantinople's fall to the Turks in 1453, a Russian priest is supposed to have declared:

> Two Romes have fallen and have passed away, the western and the eastern; destiny has prescribed Moscow the position of the third Rome; there will never be a fourth. (cited Masaryk 1913/1955: 41)

This ideology of the "Third Rome," which caused Orthodox Russians to perceive themselves as culturally unique, was combined with what Masaryk (1913/1955: 37) referred to as Byzantine "caesaropapism," whereby the perceived interests of church and state become inextricably intertwined. This church-state partnership culminated in the coronation of Ivan Grozny (the Terrible) as Tsar or Emperor of all Russia in 1547. In taking this step, Moscow's Metropolitan, Iosif Volotskii, articulated a Russian version of the "divine right of kings," declaring that "though an emperor [tsar] in body be like all other men, yet in power he is like God" (cited Flier 2006: 389). This proclamation had profound significance for the future. As Richard Hellie (2006c: 364) observes, "This Russian version of the divine right of kings underpinned Russian law and the monarchy down to its fall in 1917."

If the ties between the Orthodox Church and secular authority were typically closer than was the norm in the Latin West, it is nevertheless a mistake to see Orthodoxy as a mere agent of princely authority. From the outset, the Orthodox Church, like its Latin counterpart, articulated beliefs and practices that set it apart – and often at odds – with prevailing state norms. Nowhere was this more obvious than in attitudes to wealth, poverty, and almsgiving, domains where the preachings of St John Chrysostom were most influential. Serving as Archbishop of his native Antioch from AD 386 to AD 397, Chrysostom became the Metropolitan or Archbishop of Constantinople in AD 397, advocating viewpoints that were to leave an enduring legacy in the Orthodox world. In St John Chrysostom's opinion (c.AD 398/1848: 282), wealth was nothing more than a "vain shadow, dissolving smoke" that delivered little benefit to the human spirit. "True honor," Chrysostom (c.AD 398/1848: 282) argued, lay not in the acquisition of wealth but rather in its surrender through "almsdoing." As Archbishop of Antioch, Chrysostom practiced what he preached. Acquired Church wealth was constantly redistributed, the Antioch diocese providing for the support of 3000 widows and other women in need on a daily basis (Mayer 2009: 91).

This emphasis on almsgiving, of giving to those who had fallen upon hard times, was to become deeply entrenched in the Russian Orthodox psyche. Dostoyevsky (1862/1911: 22), for example, in his account of his long years of convict servitude, criticizes the "upper classes of our Russian society" for not understanding "to what extent merchants, shopkeepers, and our people generally, commiserate the unfortunate. Alms were always forthcoming." The Russian Orthodox emphasis on protection of the poor, or those devoid of normal means of support, is also found in its insistence that "Church people" come under its jurisdiction, rather than that of the state. Included among such "Church people" were not only priests and monks but also "society's helpless ...widows, beggars, wanderers" (Hellie 2006c: 362). Like the Catholic Church in the West, Russian Orthodoxy also accumulated immense wealth and resources held in its own name. By 1600, it is estimated (Miller 2006: 347) that Orthodox monasteries held at least 20 percent of Russia's arable land. One monastery located close to Moscow, the Simonovskii, owned 50 villages, along with the serfs who resided within them. The Church was, in short, a state within a state, an ally of tsarism but distinct from it.

If we are to summarize the importance of Byzantium's Orthodox heritage in Russian history, we can conclude in the first instance that it was sufficiently similar to other varieties of Christianity for Russians to feel a common religious bond with their Western neighbors, yet sufficiently different in that it caused Russians to feel a unique sense of cultural identity. Above all, Orthodoxy – and the belief that Moscow was the "Third Rome" – conveyed to Russian society a sense of historic destiny, pretentions to world leadership that was shared by wealthy and poor alike. Easily overlooked in the Byzantine experience, however, is a cautionary tale as to the dangers of state power. For in seeking to extend the power of the state so as to better defend itself, Byzantium ultimately destroyed itself.

From Freedom to Serfdom: The Muscovite Experience

In the mid-fifteenth century, despite the ongoing construction of new Italian-built walls around the Kremlin, Muscovy was but one of many insignificant principalities located within the central forests of Russia. While Italy and Flanders experienced the glories of the Renaissance, the peasants of Russia continued a time-honored existence. Although most were legally free, life was nevertheless hard and precarious. Long, cold winters restricted agriculture to the growing of oats and, more particularly, rye, along with a few hardy vegetables such as turnips. Planted in autumn and harvested in summer, rye was prone to a fungus (ergot) that caused hallucinations among sufferers. Although fields crops were supplemented by the bounty of the forests during summer (mushrooms, berries, honey, game), the monotonous Russian diet was associated with a variety of health conditions. By late winter, most Russians were suffering from deficiencies in vitamin A, vitamin D, vitamin C, niacin, and calcium (Hellie 2006b: 291). Thin soils, long winters, and a lack of pastures made the draft animals that were commonplace in Western agriculture (oxen, horses) a comparative rarity in Russia. Even in the late nineteenth century, when Russian occupancy of the Ukrainian and Kuban steppes made horse raising a comparatively easy exercises, only 44.1% of peasant households in European Russia owned more than one horse. The horseless households comprised 27.3% of the total (Lenin 1898/1964: 143). Where peasants did own a farm animal (typically a small dairy cow), the long winters required indoor stalling for 6 months of the year. By spring, chronically underfed cows were normally so weak that they had to be carried to the spring pastures (Hellie 2006b: 290). A shortage of farm animals meant there was little manure for fertilizing the thin *podzol* soils of Russian forest heartlands. In consequence, Russian grain yields in the fifteenth century were comparable to those of Western Europe in the eighth century (Hellie 2006b: 287). The Russian forests also boasted few coal, iron, copper, or silver deposits. Accordingly, few Russian peasants owned a metal-tipped plow, most making do with a primitive wooden instrument that did little more than create a "two-pronged scratch in the soil" (Hellie 2006b: 291). In such conditions, food shortages and famine were regular occurrences. In describing one of medieval Russia's all-too-common famines, a chronicler from Novgorod, a prosperous northern town, recorded how "the people ate limes, leaves, birch bark, pounded wood pulp mixed with husks and straw...their corpses were in the streets, in the market place, and on the roads, and everywhere" (cited, Engel and Martin 2015: 12).

In many ways, the transformation of Muscovy from an inconsequential backwater into a preeminent European power under imperial Tsarist rule remains almost inexplicable. Muscovy, and the other historic Russian principalities (Pskov, Novgorod, Vladimir), possessed few resources other than wood, grain, and people, of which only the former was plentiful. As the American economist, Jeremy Sachs (2005: 147) has observed, "during most of Russian history" cities and towns "were few and far between. The division of labor that depends on urban life and international trade were never dominant features of social life." Because land was plentiful, Russian society in the fifteenth century had little understanding of private property, peasants typically moving to new fields when the soil on one plot was exhausted (Dennison 2011: 132). The "fundamental law" of medieval and early modern Russia, the *Russkaya Pravda*, gave ownership to those who tilled the soil after 4 to 5 years. Conversely, those who failed to work the land surrendered the title after 10 years (Hellie 2006c: 366). Even where land was sold, the owner (or their heirs) could repurchase it at the original sale price at any time over the ensuing 40 years, a right that discouraged any would-be buyers (Hellie 2006c: 384). Until the twentieth century, comparatively few Russians could read or write, Dostoyevsky (1862/1911: 12) reporting with amazement that "half" the convicts he was imprisoned with during the 1850s "knew how to read and write." Nowhere else in Russia, "in no matter what population," Dostoyevsky (1862/1911: 12) continued, would you find such a high level of literacy.

To escape from the predicament in which it found itself, Muscovy had only one realistic option: to import technology, people, and material from the West. As was to remain the case in subsequent periods of Russian history – most notably under Peter the Great in the eighteenth century, Joseph Stalin in the twentieth century, and Vladimir Putin in the twenty-first century – Western imports were only purchasable with income derived from primary commodities. Russian eagerness to trade staples for Western manufactured goods, it must be noted, was hardly unique in the sixteenth and seventeenth century. By 1500, the rise of nascent forms of capitalism in Western Europe was creating an insatiable desire for imported grain and timber, driving Eastern Europe toward what Braudel (1979/1982: 267) refers to as "a *colonial* destiny as a producer of raw materials" [emphasis in the original]. In return for imported (largely Dutch) luxury goods, the aristocracy of Central and Eastern Europe organized the felling of vast forest reserves and the growing of huge quantities of grain (principally rye) on new, commercialized estates. Polish rivers became chocked with immense rafts of wood destined for the Baltic ports (Braudel 1979/1982: 269). In Poland, Lithuania, Hungary, and Romania, the society witnessed what Braudel (1979/1982: 267) called "the second serfdom," in which previously free peasants were enserfed with the assistance of state and sent to work on the new commercialized estates. In Poland, where compulsory labor for the local lord rarely occurred in 1500, a century later the peasant was required to work for 6 days per week. Things were little better in Hungary, where peasants were forced to work at the "pleasure of the lord" (Braudel 1979/1982: 267).

Although Russian experienced the "second serfdom" (i.e., the second *European* era of serfdom) at the same time as other Eastern European societies, the dynamic that drove it was fundamentally different. In Poland, Lithuania, and Hungary, an aristocracy desirous of entering into new commercial relationships with the West underpinned the process of enserfment. While the state collaborated in this process, it was also weakened by it, as the local aristocracy strengthened its position vis-à-vis *both* the peasantry *and* the state. In Russia, however, international commerce – freely undertaken by either producers or traders – was insignificant in the fifteenth and sixteenth centuries. A number of hostile states – most notably Poland, Sweden, and the Grand Duchy of Lithuania – blocked Russia's access to the Baltic. To the south, the Crimean Tartars barred the way to the Black Sea. Even during the reign of Ivan

Grozny (1533–1584), when Russian armies reclaimed the Volga basin from the Tartars, the only trade route to the West went via the White Sea and Archangel, and even this was only open for a few summer months.

Rather than reflecting commercial dynamics, both Moscow's relationship with the West *and* the process of Russian enserfment were *both* driven by the state, acting in the interests of the state. For, under the last three representatives of the Rurik dynasty – Ivan III (1662–1505), Vasilii III (1505–1533), and Ivan IV (Grozny) – all sections of Russian society, with the partial exception of the Church, found themselves subject to the power of an increasingly authoritarian regime. This process of state subjugation arguably began with Muscovy's annexation of the commercial center of Novgorod in 1478. Deporting the local aristocracy, Ivan III initiated the first so-called service-class revolution, distributing land in return for service in either the military or the bureaucracy. Unlike the holders of hereditary estates (the *votchinniks*), this new aristocracy of "servitors" (the *pomeschiks*) only occupied their properties while they remained in state service. Finding this system much to their liking, Ivan III and his heirs then proved remarkably successful, as Kleimola (1979: 213) observed, "in developing a system of rewards and punishments that bound servitors every more tightly to the ruler." In the first instance, the system of service estates (*pomest'e*) was extended at the expense of hereditary properties. Under Ivan III and his son, Vasilii, members of high-ranking families were packed off to monasteries so that their estates would pass to the state on their death (Kleimola 1979: 214). At the local level, military governors assumed control of civil administration. Under Ivan Grozny, the campaign to make the aristocracy an agency of the state reached a new level of intensity, Russia entering into one of the darkest periods in its history. The wives and children of aristocrats and officials were held hostage to guarantee allegiance. Whole families were massacred for the supposed transgressions of a single individual. Between 1565 and 1572, Russia entered into a state-driven bloodbath, the *Oprichnina*, which saw some 6000 black-clad *oprichniks* arrest, torture, and massacre any suspected of disloyalty. During the *Oprichnina*, Kleimola (1979: 219) notes, "Almost no elite family was left untouched." In 1570, Novgorod, Russia's gateway to the West, was sacked. Among those massacred, according to one contemporary account, were "2770 Novgorod nobles and wealthy merchants" (Graham 1987: 181). As with the purges of Joseph Stalin in the 1930s, the irrationality and violence of the *Oprichnina* produced a ruthless concentration of power in the hands of the state, the *oprichniks* collecting more tax in 1 year than had previously been raised in 7 (Hellie 2006b: 393).

If the Russian aristocracy suffered grievously at the hands of the state, it also benefited, as the nation's once free peasantry were transformed into serfs. In this retrograde endeavor, the Muscovite autocracy was assisted by all levels of elite society: the aristocracy, the bureaucracy, and the Church. As had been the case in both Byzantium and Western Europe, serfdom in Russia arose through a series of restrictions rather than a single event. From the 1450s, the peasant's right to move freely from place to place was restricted to a single day: St George's Day (26 November). In 1592, even this freedom was denied. At the same time, the period in which a lord could reclaim a runaway serf became longer and longer, extended from 3 years in 1497 to 15 years in 1641. Eventually, under the Code (*Ulozhenie*) of 1649, the statute of limitations was abolished altogether (Dennison 2011; Hellie 2006c). Significantly, the passage to serfdom advanced hand-in-hand with the "service-class revolution," which saw bureaucrats, military officers, and cavalrymen allocated *pomest'e* (estates) in return for state service. By the late sixteenth century, most arable land was under the management of *pomeschiks*, state servants who benefited from the labor of the peasant households allocated to them by the Muscovite state. This peasant workforce not only worked the *pomeschik's* land; it was also obliged to pay "quit-rents" for the plots of land upon which they grew their own meager crops (Hellie 2006c: 382–383). Under the so-called obedience charter (*poslushnaia gramota*) of 1607, serfs were also required "to obey their landholder in everything" (cited, Hellie 2006b: 297).

To add to peasant misery, they also assumed the great bulk of the tax burden, a liability to which the new service aristocracy was exempt. As was the practice in Byzantium, rural taxes were imposed on a collective basis, an outcome that left remaining members of the village or commune with a larger bill in instances of peasant flight. Even the rents and labor obligations imposed by the local lord were collective in nature, the job of collecting rent and taxes falling to the village commune. Because the commune was responsible for collecting feudal dues, it also assumed the tasks of allocating land – including the strips to be worked for the lord as well as those exploited for household use. Because the commune was mindful of meeting its imposed state and feudal financial obligations, there was a universal tendency to allocate land to the most capable and "wealthy" peasant households (i.e., those most likely to meet the imposed demands), rather than to those most in need (Dennison 2011: 133). Herein we find the explanation for the supposed "communal" nature of Russian society. Rather than it being the case, as Herzen (1851/1956: 189) believed, that the Russian commune was an exemplar of "rural communism," it was in truth the agent of the absolutist state and the feudal lord. It was not only the peasantry, however, that found itself subject to the collectively imposed demands of the state. The same circumstances prevailed in Russia's towns, where merchants and traders were confined to special suburbs (*posads*). Such people were declared "black" by the Muscovite state. This meant that they were required to pay a tax, the *tiaglo*, imposed on the entire *posad*. *Posad* members were also liable for a host of other state-imposed obligations: acting as city guards, customs-collectors, and general agents of the state (Shaw 2006c: 305). This put them at a commercial disadvantage to those urban dwellers allowed to trade while remaining "white," i.e., they did not have to pay taxes. Unsurprisingly, the most significant group of tax-exempt competitors were state "servitors," most particularly musketeers and cavalrymen, who supplemented their meager pay through small-scale commerce (Shaw 2006c: 306).

The inevitable result of the extension of state power, as described above, was a replication of many of the same unintended consequences that afflicted the Byzantine state between the fifth and twelfth centuries. Imitating the Byzantine *patrocinium* movement, many peasants fled to the estates of "strong people" (*sil'nye liudi*), where living conditions were generally better than on smallholdings (Hellie 2006b: 296). As was the case in Byzantium, mass flight from the land also occurred, many taking off for a life beyond the frontiers in the Volga basin, Siberia, and the Ukrainian steppe. Others risked their lives by settling in the Central Black Earth region to the south of the Russian forests, even though Tartar raids carried off thousands each year to the slave markets of the Crimea. In commenting upon the lives of these rural fugitives, Robert Smith (1977/2010: 31) observed that although their lives were "hard, at times brutal ... they evidently felt that it was not as hard as the exactions and injustices imposed on them by the state." The most significant manifestation of this process of mass flight was the emergence of a new class of seminomadic cavalrymen along the Dnieper and Don rivers, the "Cossacks." Inevitably, the end result of the Muscovite attempt to create a highly ordered body politic was – in many areas – the reverse of what was intended: the emergence of "a disordered and sometimes chaotic society" (Shaw 2006b: 41). In the regions around Moscow and Novgorod, where state control was most exacting, it is estimated that 85% of the rural population had fled the land by the latter stages of Ivan Grozny's reign (Hellie 2006b: 294). Mass flight also characterized the towns, where the number of taxpaying households fell by 35% between 1550 and the late 1580s. In describing the resultant urban landscape in 1588–1589, an English visitor, Giles Fletcher, recorded how Russia's towns boasted nothing "memorable save many ruins ... which showeth (sic) the decrease of the Russe people under this government." Of the smaller villages, Fletcher observed that many stood "vacant and desolate without an inhabitant" (cited, Shaw 2006a: 303–304).

As is the case with most authoritarian societies, the response of the Muscovite state to the social chaos engendered by its own policies was not social and economic liberalism but the reverse: an ever-tighter battening down of the hatches. Following the Time of Troubles (1598–1613), when the Muscovite state virtually collapsed in the face of popular revolt and foreign invasion, the new Romanov dynasty responded by enacting the Code (*Ulozhenie*) of 1649, entrenching a system of oppression that was to last to 1861 and beyond. To halt the Russian equivalent of the *patrocinium* movement, penalties were imposed on aristocrats who allowed fugitive serfs to work on their estates. Eventually, under this provision, the state confiscated four serfs for each fugitive retrieved from a given property. Under the Code, peasants without a nominal feudal lord became state serfs. Those who worked in cities and towns were forced to return to their home estate, selling up any business venture they had undertaken (Hellie 2006c). Merchants and traders, who belonged to the various urban *posads*, were legally bound to the town in which they resided. "Henceforth," Shaw (2006c: 587) records, "the *posad* dweller was to stay put and share the burden of taxation and service laid upon the *posad* community as a whole." In essence, the Code of 1649 did far more than simply entrench serfdom. It created a rigid caste system that restricted social mobility, individual initiative, and creativity.

If we look to the managerial practices of the Muscovite state, we can ascertain two distinct domains: a higher level associated with the state and its various agents, and a lower level of predominately serf-based production. In the higher domain, associated with the state, we witness management as subjugation, management as secret police, and management as state-sponsored terror. As Marshall Poe (2006: 454) has observed, "the Muscovite elite focused nearly all its energy in ruling others ...Domination was their *raison d'être*." Although, in theory, the Muscovite bureaucracy operated according to principles of aristocratic precedence (*mestnichestvo*) that favored old-established families, in practice the demand for literate and capable people provided one of the few avenues for social advancement. Accordingly, an overwhelming majority of the 3000 officials who staffed the central bureaucracy in the late seventeenth century were people of comparatively humble means (Poe 2006: 454). For this group the *Oprichnina*, which devastated the ranks of the old aristocracy, provided more benefit than threat. Away from the Kremlin, the lives of the middle-level "servitors" – who served as provincial governors and the like – were more precarious. Subject to constant transfers that kept them away from their home estates, the main concern of this group was to transfer their *pomest'e* (service estate) into a hereditary property, a feat which was achieved in practice if not in law by the early eighteenth century (Hellie 2006c: 383). Even more precarious were the lives of those at the bottom of the state hierarchy, the semiprofessional soldiers (the *streltsy*) and cavalrymen who typically commanded a miserable estate worked by half a dozen peasant households. Seldom able to survive on their government-derived income, most were forced to rely on small-scale trading as well as the produce garnered from working land adjacent to their barracks (Hellie 2006a: 549; Shaw 2006c: 587–588).

Among the peoples of Europe, arguably none experienced a worse fate than that of the Russian serf after 1649. Serfs, male and female, young and old, could be sold off at any time, either individually or as a family. Males were regularly packed off for military service, where serfs came to make up the great bulk of Russia's infantry force (Gerschenkron 1965: 714). The greatest failing of the Russian version of serfdom, however, was the attribute that Herzen and Tolstoy hailed as its greatest strength: its emphasis on communalism rather than individualism. This had many unfortunate effects. Because collective taxes were calculated on a household basis between the 1640s and the 1720s, the Russian serf crowded as many people as possible into the one smoke-filled hut so as to minimize their tax liability. Once normalized, this practice continued even after the tsarist state circumvented the ploy by calculating the collective tax liability on the basis of individual "souls" (Dennison 2011). Even more problematic was the communal practice of redistributing land between peasant households on a regular basis. This was unlike the situation that prevailed in the Western version of serfdom, where peasants enjoyed de facto occupation of the same plot of land generation after generation. By custom and practice, the Western peasant family was also guaranteed a fixed share of their crop. Both of these factors incentivized productivity as a bigger crop added to household wealth. The Russian serf, by contrast, had no reason to invest in agricultural improvements. A plot of land allocated to one household for 1 year could be given to another the next. In the Russian commune, any indication of personal wealth was also unwise, typically causing the commune to allot a bigger share of the village's tax burden to the household concerned.

By comparison with the Byzantine state, with which the Muscovite/Russian state shared many similarities, the latter succeeded in one key area that caused constant grief to the former: it subjugated its aristocrats as well as its peasants. The benefits of this achievement – which delivered Muscovy a highly centralized and cohesive state – can be ascertained by the state's military successes in the Volga basin, which secured its access to the Caspian Sea for the first time. By the mid-seventeenth century, the agricultural bounty of the Central Black Earth region was also under the control of the Russian state. In the first half of the seventeenth century, the vast expanse of Siberia was won by force of arms. In 1649, Russian settlements were even appearing along Siberia's Pacific coast, providing bases from which Russian fur traders and explorers pushed on to claim the Alaskan territories of North America. When the Muscovite state turned west, however, its many economic and social frailties were exposed. Despite marshaling all available resources, a long and brutal campaign to gain access to the Baltic ended in a costly Russian defeat in the so-called Livonian war (1558–1583). Yes, it is true, that the Muscovite state boasted state-owned cannon foundries, gunpowder works, brickworks, and even two state-owned paper mills (Shaw 2006a: 59). There was, however, little in the way of private sector entrepreneurship. Muscovy, and the Russia of the early Romanovs, also lacked the deep capital markets, and the class of middling merchants and producers, that allowed Western states a capacity to raise money through the issuance of government bonds. Such circumstances meant that Russia was always reliant on Western imports to make up for its own deficiencies. With regard to "major technology transfer after 1613," Hellie (2006a: 544) observes that "nothing happened without government intervention." A similar comment could be made with regard to almost every other area of economic activity.

In summary, it is evident that the Muscovite state set Russian society upon a path of state intervention and control that suppressed individualism while emphasizing state and communal solidarity. Once set upon this path, it became difficult to move in a fundamentally different direction in ways that emphasized individual initiative and entrepreneurship. This is *not* to say that the Russian *people* lack these qualities. Evidence to the contrary is all too apparent in the settlement of the Russian frontier, a task largely undertaken by runaway serfs and Cossacks acting under their own volition. The individual quest for freedom, however, constantly ran up against the logic of the state; a contest that rarely ended in the victory of individualism over collectivism. The question is, however, could the Muscovite state have chosen a different path and survived, given the geopolitical circumstances in which it operated? The answer is, probably not. As Dominic Lieven (2006: 17) has observed, "On Europe's periphery one paid a high price for both power and powerlessness." If one failed to mobilize the resources of a powerful state, as occurred in Poland, then the partition and destruction of the society was more than probable. If, as occurred in Byzantium, one allowed the resources of a centralized state to dissipate, then a similar outcome was also likely. To create a strong, militarized society in the vast continental areas of Central and Eastern Europe – regions characterized by endless forests and steppes – was also difficult. Muscovy achieved this feat but at great social cost.

The Limits to Modernization: Russia, 1682–1861

As we have previously observed in this *Palgrave Handbook on Management History*, the bedrock of every civilization is located in its command of metals: copper, bronze, and iron. The primacy of metals in the production process is particularly apparent in what we think of as the Industrial Revolution. For, although in the popular imagination, the Industrial Revolution is typically associated with the mechanization of textile production, its success really hinged on the availability of cast iron: iron for steam engines, factory machines, railroad locomotives, railroad running rails, and iron-hulled ships. In reflecting upon the central importance of iron to the human experience, the American historian, Lewis Morgan (1878: 43), had cause to observe:

> The production of iron was the event of events in human experience, without a parallel, and without an equal . . . Out of it came the metallic hammer and anvil, the axe and the chisel, the plough with the iron point, the iron sword; in fine, the basis of civilization.

Backward in many areas of economic and managerial endeavor, the production of cast iron was an area where tsarist Russia appeared to excel during the late eighteenth and early nineteenth centuries. In the late eighteenth century, iron was one of Russia's principal exports, the society exporting 4.64 million kilograms of iron in 1762. As late as the 1820s, Russian production, which drew of the rich iron deposits of the Ural Mountains, far exceeded that of most Western European nations. In most years across the decade, Russia's production of pig iron was 50% higher than that of France. It was also three times higher than that of Belgium, a long-term leader in new industrial techniques (Lenin 1898/1964: 485). Yet, as Fig. 3 indicates, by the end of the nineteenth century, the Russian lead had evaporated. By comparison with the Britain, the United States, France, Germany, and Belgium, Russia remained a primarily agricultural society. Wood, grain, and people were plentiful. Iron, steel, and steam engines remained scarce. In the early 1830s, the total motive power of all Russia's steam engines amounted to the feeble equivalent of 2,200 horses. Prior to the mid-1870s, virtually all of the locomotives that operated on Russia's railroads were imported (Portal 1966: 810). Writing of the situation that prevailed at the end of the nineteenth century, the revolutionary Marxist, Vladimir Lenin (1898/1964: 431), lamented the fact that manufactured goods remained largely the preserve of "hand production," carried out in a "mass of small establishments." Where advanced forms of management and production existed, it typically owed much to Western European firms who opted to establish factories behind Russia's wall of protective tariffs. Writing of the situation that prevailed on the eve of World War I, the Russian anarchist and social theorist, Prince Kropotkin (1912/1968: 41), noted with considerable pride how "English engineers and foreman, have planted within Russia the improved cotton manufacturers . . . they are busy now in improving the woollen industries and the production of machinery." At the same time, Kropotkin (1912/1968: 41) continued, "Belgians have rapidly created a great iron industry in South Russia."

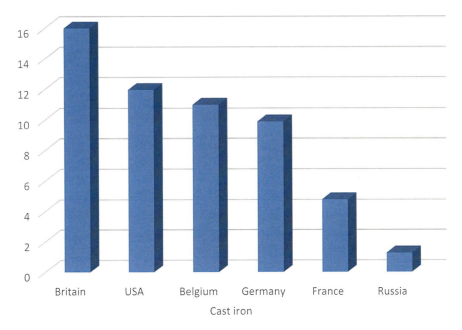

Fig. 3 Per capita cast iron production, 1898: Britain, the United States, Belgium, Germany, France, and Russia (in kilograms). (Source: Calculated from Ananich, "The Russian Economy and Banking System," p. 415)

To understand the success and failure of not only the Russian iron industry but also of Russian management more generally, we need to remind ourselves that, in the wake of the Legal Code (*Ulozhenie*) of 1649, the work activities that one could undertake were largely determined by the social class into which one was born. Accordingly, if one was to undertake any sort of industrial or mining activity, there was only two ways in which this could be legally done. First, one could hire serfs on a wage-labor basis, a feat that could only be undertaken *if* the serf had their lord's permission *and* the serf acquitted their feudal dues by paying a "quit-rent" to their lord. The problems with this "solution" are manifest. Not only was labor supplied at the whim of the feudal lord, the resultant wage had to be high enough to make the exchange attractive to both the serf *and* the lord (Gerschenkron 1965: 715). The second and more reliable method – and the one which was most typically pursued – involved the purchase of a landed estate (serfs included) adjacent to the would-be factory or mine. Such individuals, legally referred to as "possessional serfs," then worked in the mine or factory in return for the right to farm a plot of land (Pipes 1974: 210–211). It was this latter approach that was universally pursued by the iron miners and smelters of the Urals, Lenin (1898/1964: 485) observing how, "serfdom was the basis of the greatest prosperity of the Urals and its dominant position, not only in Russia, but partly also in Europe." Not only were money wages close to zero under this system, the close ties that existed between peasant and land also assured the industrialist a more reliable worker than was normally the case under a system of waged labor. As a certain V.D. Belov testified to an imperial commission of inquiry in 1887:

> Workers in other factories ... have not the interests of their factory at heart: they are here today and gone tomorrow ... They and their employers are permanent enemies ... The position is entirely different in the case of the Ural workers. They are natives of the place; and in the vicinity of the works they have their own land, their farms and their families ... to leave means to wreck their whole world, to abandon the land, farm and family ... And so they are ready to hang on for years, to work at half pay ... they are ready to accept any terms the employers offer, so long as they are allowed to remain. (cited, Lenin 1898/1964: 487)

The situation described by Belov, it should be noted, existed long after Russia's serfs were legally freed in 1861. At the end of the nineteenth century, as at the beginning, the ironworkers of the Urals worked in the knowledge that any complaint could see them evicted not only from their job but also from their farm.

In the mines and furnaces of the Urals, we witness the difference between premodern forms of management and what we have consistently defined as "modern management." For while the semifeudal industrialists of the Urals could not have survived unless they fulfilled the basic activities of management (planning, organizing, leading, and controlling), conspicuous by their absence are other attributes that are essential to dynamic and innovative forms of "modern management": individual freedom, secure property rights, and a legally free workforce that is motivated to work efficiently. Lacking these latter attributes – which *were* a defining characteristic of Western mines and smelters in the nineteenth century – the iron producers of Russia steadily fell behind their competitors. For, with low wage costs and plentiful supplies of wood, the producers of the Urals had little obvious reason to innovate. Whereas English producers began switching to coal-based coke in the eighteenth century, Russian smelters in the Urals still used charcoal well into the nineteenth century. In turn, the use of charcoal constrained furnace size, denying Russian smelters the economies of scale enjoyed in the West. Inevitably, charcoal-based smelters stripped the forests in the areas adjacent to their workings. Confronted with this problem, Russian producers were unable to respond – as their medieval counterparts in Western Europe had done – by relocating to virgin forest reserves. To do so would require the abandonment of their serf labor force. Tied to the spot, Ural producers suffered the expense of transporting wood and charcoal from ever more distant locales. Prior to the 1880s, the Russian iron industry also suffered from the lack of a well-developed railroad system, the construction of which was curtained by a lack of iron and steel. Although it was possible to ship iron to Moscow and the new capital of St Petersburg via a complicated system of rivers and canals, the transport process was slow and labor-intensive. With rivers and canals freezing in winter, it typically took 18 months to ship a barge load of iron from the Urals to St Petersburg, most barges wintering in Tver at the junction of the Volga and Tvertsa rivers (Baykov 1954: 141–142). As the nineteenth century progressed, many businesses found that it was quicker and cheaper to import iron from abroad rather than from the Urals. Accordingly, by the 1870s some 59% of Russia's iron and steel was imported (Baykov 1954: 143).

Russia's long embrace of serfdom not only delayed the adoption of "modern management" practices; it also curtailed the emergence of an economic middle class comprised of entrepreneurs and factory owners. For, in pre-1861 Russia the only way one could operate an industrial undertaking was with serf labor, a workforce that Russia's merchant class was typically prohibited from owning. Given the right to own serfs by Peter the Great in 1721 – who was intent on facilitating Western-style commerce and industry – urban merchants promptly lost this benefit in 1762 under Peter III (Pipes 1974: 210–211). Indeed, rather than Russia witnessing increasing levels of labor mobility under Peter the Great's reforms, labor suffered new restrictions due to the introduction of a system of internal passport controls. This linked serf movement to the express, written approval of their lord (Riasanovsky 1993: 235). In such circumstances, the only viable way in which most merchants could secure their own manufactured products was through the practice of "putting out," whereby the merchant and their agents purchased raw materials and then outsourced processing and assembly to a mass of handicraft workers. For both serf and lord, this system had numerous benefits. In the case of the peasant, commercialized handicraft work provided additional income without a commensurate need to leave the land. Increased cash income also allowed the peasant to substitute labor service on the lord's estate with "quit-rents" that allowed more time for the cultivation of the serf's "home" plot. For the lord, larger "quit-rents" provided an additional (and much sought after) source of cash. As was the case in the iron industry, however, the persistence of the "putting out" system delayed the emergence of "modern management" across broad swatches of the economy. As a result, innovation was typically conspicuous by its absence as peasant handicraft workers continued to work according to time-honored traditions even after the abolishment of serfdom. In 1894–1895, for example, a census of manufacturing workers in the province of Perm – one of Russia's most industrialized regions – found that 80.9% of "artisans" combined industrial activities with traditional agricultural pursuits (Lenin 1898/1964: 333). The feeble advance of mechanized production is also indicated by trends in the woolen industry, historically a dominant sector in Russian textile production. As late 1875–1979, official factory statistics indicated the presence of only 209 steam engines in this sector across the whole of European Russia (Lenin 1898/1964: 470). The association of merchants with "putting out," and backward forms of production, also demeaned their social standing. In his massive study, *The Development of Capitalism in Russia*, Lenin (1898/1964: 383), for example, declared merchants engaged in "putting out" to be "leeches," "usurers," and "kulaks." After the communist seizure of power in 1917, such designations entailed fatal consequences.

If the "managerial revolution" of the nineteenth century made little headway in Russia prior to the century's closing decades, this failing was long disguised by the dynamism that was evident in civil administration, the military, and territorial and demographic expansion. As is the norm in Russian history, the most significant developments related to the state, where the reforms of Peter the Great (reigned 1682–1725), Catherine the Great (1762–1796), and Alexander I (1801–1825) laid the foundations for "an effective military and fiscal state apparatus" (Lieven 2006: 11).

Under Peter, as most readers would be aware, a frantic process of "Westernization" occurred, conducted at a pace that caused Nikolai Karamzin, a leading eighteenth-century writer, to lament how "We became citizens of the world, but ceased in certain respects to be citizens [of Russia]" (cited, Hughes 2006: 88). The key to Peter's reforms involved a social pact with Russia's nobility, whereby they were guaranteed control of their serfs in return for state service. This pact manifested itself in Peter's promulgation in 1722 of the Table of Ranks, which required members of the aristocracy to enter either the bureaucracy or the army at age 16 and to continue in service for the rest of their lives. Although this universal obligation was relaxed in 1762, it continued as an informal social expectation. Unless one had some pressing excuse, the norms of aristocratic service required a lifetime of service at the state's behest (Hartley 2006: 456). Social prestige, in short, was *primarily* associated with where one stood in the state bureaucracy or the army, *rather* than with wealth acquired through entrepreneurial endeavor. This association of social prestige with service was also manifest at the local level. Under Catherine the Great, two new legal codes – the *Statute of Provincial Administration 1755* and the *Charter to the Nobles 1785* – provided for triennial aristocratic assemblies entrusted with the election of local officials. Meanwhile, central administration was coordinated through various "Colleges" (Foreign Affairs, War, Navy, Mining, etc.), reorganized as "Ministries" in 1810 (Shakiba 2006). A determined effort was also made to raise the educational level of Russia's aristocratic "servitors." In 1755, Russia's first university, the Imperial Moscow University (now called Moscow State University), was established under the direction of the scientist philosopher, Mikhail Lomonosov. To facilitate literacy and the spread of Western ideas, Peter also created a simplified Cyrillic script that differed from Slavonic in having fewer letters. In 1710, Russia witnessed the first printed books in the new script (Hughes 2006: 75). The growth of the bureaucracy also provided jobs for ambitious non-aristocrats. Legally designed the *raznochintsy* (literally, "people of diverse origins"), this group of what were effectively lower-level aristocrats was eventually expanded to include university graduates not born into the nobility (Wirschafter 2006: 248–249).

As with most successful reforms, the organizational and social transformations initiated by Peter the Great and Catherine the Great produced positive effects that reinforced the initial benefits. By better marshaling the resources of the state, the Russia of the Romanovs proved a more formidable military foe than its Muscovite predecessor. Following Peter the Great's historic victory against the Swedes at Poltava in 1709, Russia secured access to the Baltic through the annexation of Livonia (modern-day Estonia and Latvia). Under Catherine the Great, Russia also gained access to the Black Sea, occupying the entire northern coastline of this inland waterway. The military weight of imperial Russia also allowed it to participate in the partition of Poland in the closing decades of the eighteenth century. In addition to their strategic benefits, each of these military advances brought with it a basket of human, economic, and organizational resources. Arguably, no ethnic minority provided a greater service to imperial Russia than did the Baltic Germans, an educated elite who were to subsequently make up a disproportionate proportion of the Russian officer corps and senior bureaucracy. So significant was the role of this German elite in the mid-nineteenth century that Herzen (1851/1956: 165, 174, 183–185) complained at length as to the "German" composition of the Russian "government," an administration in which he perceived the swallowing up of the "Slav world" by "the German element." In Poland, the presence of a large Jewish minority also provided Russia with millions of literate, commercially oriented citizens; a group designated as "townspeople" (*meschchane*) so as to fit them within Russia's complex system of social caste. Unlike the highly regarded German population, however, the Russian state always regarded its Jewish members with suspicion. Under a statute enacted in 1804, Russian Jews were confined to the infamous "Pale of Settlement," an area comprising Poland and the Western Ukraine but excluding areas dominated by ethnic Russians (Weeks 2006: 31).

Of all the territorial additions secured by the reformed tsarist state, none was of greater economic and social importance than the Southern Ukraine and the neighboring Kuban steppe, areas that had long acted as the frontier of settlement. As was the case with the American and Canadian frontier, the Ukrainian and Kuban steppes acted as a social safety valve, providing a refuge and a new start as Cossacks for generations of runaway serfs. The closing of Russia's southern frontier, and the "Trans-Volga" frontier to the east of the Volga River, thus entailed immense dangers as well as almost limitless opportunities for imperial Russia. Initially, dangers were more apparent than opportunities as a series of Cossack-led rebellions resisted the enforcement of tsarist control. Of these revolts, the Kondraty Bulavin-led uprising of the Don Cossacks in 1707–1708 and the Pugachev rebellion of 1773–1774 were the most significant, the latter shaking the imperial regime to its core. In the end, tsarist Russia solved its Cossack problem by offering them special status as peasant soldiers, a solution that saw the Cossacks gain free use of their land in return for military service. More problematic for the long-term future of Russia was the incorporation of large numbers of Ukrainians, Byelorussians, Jews, Tartars, and other ethnic groups into the empire as imperial Russia's population rose from 18 million in 1700 to 74 million in 1861. By the late nineteenth century, ethnic Russians (Great Russians) found themselves in a minority, comprising only 44% of the total (Lieven 2006: 22). As security was enforced across the Ukrainian and Kuban steppes, however, the agricultural potential of these regions was realized. Unburdened by the historic legacy of serfdom and its associated agricultural practices, the Ukraine witnessed the emergence of large, commercial estates in the wake of the Napoleonic wars. In his study, *The Development of Capitalism in Russia*, Lenin (1898/1964: 259) records how this "Novorossiya" (New Russia) differed from old Russia in its possession of "huge farms," operating on an "unprecedented" scale and utilizing the most recent forms of agricultural machinery. Increasingly, these new estates were directing toward the growing of wheat for export rather than rye, the traditional Russian staple. Such developments underpinned a doubling of Russia's foreign trade between 1820 and 1840 with agricultural products comprising around three-quarters of Russian exports by value. In this export trade, the most dynamic region was Odessa and the Black Sea littoral rather than St Petersburg and the Baltic, the Black Sea ports being responsible for two-thirds of Russia's grain exports (Ananich 2006: 400).

If the agricultural successes of "Novorossiya" during the nineteenth century were self-evident, it nevertheless remained the case that farm-based exports played the same economic role under the Romanovs as in past periods of Russian history, a role that was to be replicated with devastating and transformative effects in Stalinist Russia. In essence, the agricultural sector was squeezed to fund the lifestyles of a small elite as well as the imported accouterments of a modern state: railroad locomotives, rolling stock, machinery, weapons, etc. The brutal dynamic that lay at the heart of the tsarist economy was revealed in the terrible famine of 1891–1892, when an estimated 500,000 people died even as the port cities of the Black Sea filled foreign freight ships with grain. In describing this tragedy, historians invariably use terms such as "great, disastrous, devastating, and catastrophic" (Simms 1982: 64). In addition to the 500,000 peasants who died, the Russian countryside also witnessed the loss of 3.1 million horses, 6 million sheep, 1.6 million cattle, and 700,000 pigs (Simms 1982: 69). In reflecting upon this tragedy, Sidney Harcave (1968: 275) makes the pertinent point that Russia's peasants always operated "at the margin of existence," without "any reserve of supplies." Despite the immensity of the tragedy, the tsarist state behaved in ways similar to that followed by the Stalinist state in the catastrophic famine of the early 1930s, Simms (1982: 67) observing that "the export of cereals for 1891 was almost as great as that of the previous year." For the tsarist state, the need to import Western machinery and technology, which could only be paid with primary commodities, was more important than peasant lives, Russia's foreign minister infamously declaring that "We will not eat our fill, but we will export" (cited Kotkin 2017: 127).

The famine of the early 1890s points to profound failings in Russian management. Everywhere, the short- and medium-term interests of the state came at the expense of innovation and private sector managerial endeavor. As we have already noted, the Russian state placed heavy demands on its aristocracy in terms of military and governmental service. Even heavier demands were placed on the peasantry. Under the Petrine reforms, annual levies typically took 1.25% of the adult male service for military service. Although the term of military service was reduced to 25 years in 1793 in lieu of the original lifetime requirement, it is likely that few of these conscripts ever returned home (Moon 1999: 87–88; Moon 2006: 371–372). Those most likely to be picked for service were free-spirited and rebellious souls, their removal reinforcing the inherently conservative nature of Russian peasant life (Moon 2006: 385). It is also estimated that collectively imposed taxes and feudal dues typically stripped the peasant household of "around half of the product of their labor" (Moon 2006: 372). Legally enforced restrictions on movement made the transport of goods and people a difficult feat, a problem compounded by the vastness of the Russian landscape and the paucity of transport. The result was a series of disconnected local markets, in which producers in one region remained blissfully ignorant of innovations occurring in an adjacent area. In commenting upon the practices of the peasant artisan and the small, landlord operated factory, Lenin (1898/1964: 382) insightfully observed how:

Their interests do not transcend the bounds of the small area of surrounding villages. . . . they are in mortal terror of 'competition', which ruthlessly destroys the patriarchal paradise of the small handicraftsmen and industrialists, who live lives of stagnant routine undisturbed by anybody or anything.

Tragically, the legal emancipation of Russia's serfs in 1861 failed to alter the working and living conditions of rural peasants and artisans, a failing that had profound consequences for the future of Russian society. For not only did the *Emancipation Act* fail to deliver the peasant ownership of the land they worked, a number of provisions rigged the process of land settlement in favor of the aristocracy. First, only the landlord – not the peasant – could insist on the sale of the plot that the peasant had historically worked. This favored both the landlord who operated in agriculturally fertile areas (e.g., the Black Earth region) who did *not* want to sell, as well as the proprietor of a derelict estate working poor soil who *did* want to sell. In other words, the law forced peasants to buy poor land while denying them a commensurate right to acquire good land. A related provision also denied the peasant the right to concentrate multiple plots into a single, continuous property. Once more, a right denied to the peasant was given to the landlord, who was given the right to concentrate his holdings at the peasant's expense. Where land was sold to the peasant, the estimations as to an appropriate sale price invariably favored the landlord at the peasant's expense. In the Black Earth region, where few landlords were interested in selling, sale prices were set 20% above prevailing market rates. In the Russian forest heartlands, however, where landlords typically did want to sell, prices were set 90% above normal market prices (Gerschenkron 1965: 743, 738). Moreover, although the Russian state did offer the peasants loans to buy land, it did so by charging interest rates that were 25% to 50% above normal bank rates (Gerschenkron 1965: 736–737).

While the *Emancipation Act* did facilitate the growth of large, commercial estates worked by waged labor in "Novorossiya" (i.e., the Ukraine, the Kuban, the Trans-Volga), elsewhere it had two principal effects, both of which were retrograde. In regions where the peasants proved incapable of acquiring land – whether due to the opposition of the gentry or financial reasons – it left a mass of resentful, poverty-stricken, and largely landless peasants. Where land was acquired, it was typically obtained at exorbitant prices, leaving little money for productive investment in machinery or farm animals. The peasant's capacity to move into a new occupation or line of work also remained severely restricted. Whereas before 1861 the peasant needed to obtain the landlord's permission to move elsewhere, after 1861 peasants required approval from the head of the *mir* or village commune. If approval for permanent departure was allowed, it invariably required the express surrender of all land claims as well as the discharge of all central and local taxes (Gerschenkron 1965: 752). Collectively, such outcomes worked to retard progress in not only agriculture but also the wider economy. Across the 1880s and the 1890s, per capita output of wheat and rye – the two principal grain crops – was lower than it had been in the early 1870s (Gerschenkron 1965: 778). Growth in per capita income also lagged that obtained in the industrializing societies of Northwest Europe, barely improving in 20 years between 1860 and 1880. Indeed, according to the estimates of Paul Gregory (1972: 423), the *comparative* situation of the average Russian was worse in 1913 than it had been in 1860 when measured in constant US dollars. Whereas in 1860, Russia's per capita income was 50% of the British-French-German average, by 1913 it had fallen to around one-third of the Western average. In the final analysis, such failings must be attributed to what Marc Raeff (1983: 206) refers to as an "interventionist and coercive state" that "always assumed that it had the power and the obligation to govern all aspects of the lives of citizens." By seeking to control everything, the tsarist state ended up curtailing the innovation and creativity that characterized "modern management" elsewhere, an outcome that worked to its own long-term disadvantage.

Ideas, Management, and Russian Reality

In his *Fathers and Sons*, Turgenev provides an account of how his central character, Arkady Kirsanov, returns home to the family estate in southern Russia during the summer of 1859, i.e., on the eve of emancipation. What Arkady finds is a semiderelict property, in which the grand living conditions of his own family stands in sharp contrast to the abysmal circumstances of the serfs whom he finds living in "low peasant huts under dark roofs often missing half their thatch." Distraught, Arkady declares to himself, "it's impossible, impossible for it to stay like this; reforms are essential ... but how to implement them, where to begin?" (Turgenev 1862/2009: 10–11).

In Arkady Kirsanov's mix of enthusiasm and confusion, Turgenev arguably captures the sentiments of his age, in which wide sections of Russian society agreed as to the need for far-reaching economic and managerial reform while disagreeing as to proposed solutions. Thus, we find in the pages of Turgenev, Herzen, Tolstoy, and Dostoyevsky – as well as in the treatises of revolutionary figures such as Kropotkin and Lenin – a profound and constant interest in rational principles of management. In Tolstoy's (1876/1978: 357) *Anna Karenina*, for example, we read how a leading noble (Sviazhsky) engages "a German expert from Moscow" and pays "him 500 roubles to investigate the management of their property," only to find "that they were losing 3000 roubles odd per year." Similarly, in Turgenev's (1862/2009: 9) *Fathers and Sons*, Arkady's father, Nikolai, employs "a steward who's a townsman," paying "him a salary of two hundred and fifty roubles a year" in the vain hope of returning a profit from his estate. Constantly, however, we read how such reform efforts were obstructed by a peasantry resistant to change. Writing at the end of the nineteenth century, Lenin (1898/1964: 315) lamented how in Russia, "the production of agricultural produce was always carried out in an unchanging, wretchedly small way." Similarly, in *Anna Karenina*, the reform-minded Kostya Levin "struggled with all his might for many years" against the peasant's "everlasting slovenliness" (Tolstoy 1876/1978: 170). Similarly, in *Fathers and Sons*, the revolutionary nihilist, Yevgeny Bazarov, doubts whether "emancipation" would "do any good because our peasants are happy to steal from themselves, as long as they can get stinking drunk at the tavern" (Turgenev 1862/2009: 42).

Concerns as Russia's managerial backwardness, most particularly in the agricultural sector, evoked three main intellectual responses. The first involved doing what most Russian reformers had done across the generations: turn to the West for theoretical and practical guidance. According to Marshev (2019: 286–287), the study of "management" as an intellectual discipline can be effectively dated from 1832 and the publication in Russian of Charles Babbage's *On the Economy of Machinery and Manufactures*. "This treatise," Marshev (2019: 287) observes, "soon became well-known to various professors of Russian universities, as well as statesmen and nineteenth-century entrepreneurs." By the 1840s, the Law Faculties of all four imperial universities were offering courses in public sector management. In the 1860s, German theories of management also gained a following after the publication (in German) of Lorenz von Stein's *Die Verwaltungslehre* (*The Administration*). In this work, von Stein argued that once a student becomes "thoroughly engaged in management" they soon realize "that there is no science that would equal this one in its richness and value" (cited, Marshev 2019: 287). Significantly, von Stein differed from classical economics, with its emphasis on self-interest and markets, in placing the state at the center of effective systems of management. According to von Stein, the state was the personification or "organism of the general will" (cited Mengelberg 1961: 269). Only through the benevolent guidance of the state, von Stein continued, could meaningful social reform occur in ways that avoided destructive conflict (Mengelberg 1961: 272). This emphasis on the state's supposed capacity to foster socially progressive models of management gained wide academic acceptance following the publication of Viktor Goltsev's *The Doctrine of Management* in 1880. The head of the Law School at the Imperial Moscow University, Goltsev had previously studied under von Stein at the University of Vienna. "Like von Stein," Marshev (2019: 287) observes, Goltsev "emphasized the role of the state in fostering an 'improvement of the individual'."

If Western ideas of management – emphasizing alternatively the free-market approach of British classical economics and von Stein's concept of state mentorship – gained an academic following, the idea that Russia should seek solution for its problems by looking to the West was resolutely opposed by "Slavophiles" such as Herzen and Tolstoy and the so-called Narodnik or populist movement. For Tolstoy, the idea that estate managers should be profit-oriented, "fighting for every farthing," was not only an impracticable goal in Russia; it was also "a most unworthy one" (see Tolstoy 1876/1978: 344). Rather than blindly adopting "the European way," the central character in *Anna Karenina* argues, managerial models in Russia only succeed when they accepted "the Russian peasant" as they are, organizing systems of work around them (Tolstoy 1876/1978: 363). For Herzen (1851/1956: 190, 189), as we have previously noted, "the future of Russia" was also identified with "the *moujik*" or peasant, with their supposed aversion to "private ownership." In short, according to Slavophile opinion, the best model for management was one located in Russia's rural and peasant past, rather than in an urban and industrial future.

The view that Russian managerial and work practices should be based on the ethics of the Russian peasant drew criticism from many directions, from both advocates of Western-style liberal democracy such as Turgenev and proponents of far-reaching revolution such as Kropotkin and Lenin. Declaring himself "an inveterate and incorrigible Westerner," Turgenev (1869/2009: 169, 173) accused the Slavophiles – most particularly Tolstoy – of never removing their "rose-tinted glasses even for a moment." Rather than perceiving in the Russian village an idyllic world living in harmony with nature, Turgenev saw a rural society sunk in ignorance, illiteracy, and intellectual backwardness. For Turgenev (1869/2009: 169, 173), no gains were possible without an extension of education and learning to the mass of the Russian population, arguing that "Nothing liberates ... as much as learning." The view that Slavophiles such as Herzen and Tolstoy perceived the world through "rose-tinted glasses" was one that won Lenin's endorsement, Lenin (1898/1964: 211) accusing the Slavophiles and their "Narodnik" allies of "monstrous idealism." For Lenin (1898/1964: 211), as with Turgenev, Russian peasant life was one characterized by "technical and social stagnation" that led to mass misery rather than enlightenment. Along with most modern scholars, Lenin (1898/1964: 211) also made the valid point that the village commune was far from being an independent expression of popular will. Rather it owed its existence primarily to state and landlord support, ensuring the collection of state taxes and "a supply of labor for the landlords." Of Russia's nineteenth century writers, arguably none had a better appreciation of the gulf that existed between the romanticized understanding of the Russian "progressive" elite and the brutal reality of peasant life than Dostoyevsky, a person who spent a decade working alongside peasant convicts in the tsarist Siberian "Gulag." No matter how "kindly, just-minded, intelligent a man of the higher class may be," Dostoyevsky (1862/1911: 308–309) recorded in *The House of the Dead*, "a bottomless abyss separates him from the lower classes." The gulf between Russia's Slavophile elite was amply demonstrated in the 1870s when thousands of well-educated "Narodniks" ventured into the countryside to enlighten the peasantry as to their revolutionary potential. As Turton (2009: 239) observes, when confronted with these strange city folk, "the profoundly conservative peasants did one of two things: they ignored them or turned them over to the Tsarist gendarmes."

One result of the "Narodniks" failed education campaign was that it convinced significant sections of the Russian intelligentsia that social and economic change was only achievable through violence and terror. From among the ranks of the old "Narodnik" movement emerged a new organization, *Narodnaya Volya* (Peoples Will), dedicated to the destruction of the tsarist state through carnage and force. When the assassination of Alexander II in March 1881 failed to bring down the regime, a campaign to murder his successor (Alexander III) was initiated under the leadership of Alexander Ulyanov. Arrested and executed in 1887, Ulyanov's execution spurred the formation of even more virulent and revolutionary opposition, led by his brother Vladimir, who adopted the *nom-du-guerre* of Lenin. In advocating a Marxist-based revolution, however, Lenin had to explain how a proletarian revolution – based on an industrial working class – could occur in a country where overwhelming majority were peasants. Lenin's attempt to circumvent this theoretical and practical problem in his *The Development of Capitalism in Russia* reveals – despite its collation of a mass of useful statistics – a greater level of confused thinking than is typical even among Slavophile writers. Significantly, most of Lenin's study is given over to a discussion of Russia's peasantry rather than capitalism *per se*, his central argument being that Russia had experienced a profound process of "depeasantizing" (Lenin 1898/1964: 181). On one hand, Lenin (1898/1964: 185–186, 339) pointed to the supposed emergence of wealthy rural "kulaks," a class made up of "the peasant industrialist" and the "peasant bourgeoisie." In truth, most of these "kulaks," who were to be murdered in their millions under Stalin, were wealthy only by comparison with their neighbors. At the other end of the rural spectrum, Lenin (1898/1964: 179) discerned a large "rural proletariat," forced to combine work on their farms with agricultural and industrial wage labor. For Lenin, the fact that this "rural proletariat" still lived on the land, farmed the land, and resided in their ancestral farmhouse was immaterial. As revolutionary socialists, Lenin (1898/1964: 324) declared, "we are very indifferent to the question of the form of peasant land tenure." Lenin's analysis represents a particular unfortunate example of bending facts to suit a predetermined conclusion. For, despite Lenin's arguments to the contrary, the fact that a peasant worked part- or full-time as a waged laborer did not necessarily make them either a proletarian or a socialist. As subsequent events under communist rule were to demonstrate, the Russian peasant certainly viewed proposals for collectivization and state ownership with extreme disfavor. Accordingly, the attempt to build a revolutionary new society on the peasant's presumed proletarian instincts was to culminate, under communism, in one of the greatest tragedies in human history.

The revolutionary enthusiasm of both the *Narodnaya Volya* and Lenin's Bolsheviks brings to the fore the most fundamental question in not only management history but the social sciences more generally: to what extent should changes that promise immense long-term advantages be constrained by the possibility – or necessity – of violence in bringing those changes to fruition? Arguably, none confronted this question more ably than Dostoyevsky does in *Crime and Punishment*, which recounts whom a destitute student (Roskolnikov) seeks to better his own circumstances through the murder and robbery of a wealthy widow. In Roskolnikov we witness not only an individual making criminal choices but also a symbolic representation of a whole class of dissatisfied intellectuals. For those favoring economic amelioration through violence, the matter is, as one character observes in *Crime and Punishment*, just a question of "simple arithmetic" with one "crime" or act of violence "wiped out by thousands of good deeds" (Dostoyevsky 1866/1963: 66). Elsewhere in *Crime and Punishment*, Roskolnikov declares that "the man of the future" always has "a sanction for wading through blood" if this leads to historic good (Dostoyevsky 1866/1963: 236–237). In Dostoyevsky's estimation, however, in words conveyed by the words of Roskolnikov's criminal prosecutor, Porfiry Petrovich, crimes committed in the pursuit of a supposed good never end well; the ill-effects shared not only by the victim but also by the perpetrator, who is transformed from well-meaning reformer into murderous killer. Unfortunately for the future of management in Russia, and the society more generally, in the twentieth-century Russian society was to have the viewpoint of Roskolnikov imposed upon it, rather than that of Petrovich.

Conclusion

Often overlooked by Western scholars, the Orthodox East has provided some of the most important societies in the human experience. For a thousand years, Byzantium not only provided a living link to the Greek, Roman, and Judeo-Christian worlds of antiquity; it also acted as the eastern gatekeeper for European Christendom. Among the societies that owed a cultural and religious debt to Byzantium, none was more historically important than Russia. Like Byzantium before it, Russia occupied a precarious geographical position on Europe's eastern flank, exposing it to invasion by nomadic horsemen. Like Byzantium before it, Russian society also possessed a deeply held belief in its own historic destiny, not only as a defender of Orthodox faith but also as the flagbearer of a culture and civilization that it felt to be superior to all others. Confronted with constant invasion and threats to its very survival, Russian society – like Byzantium before it – chose to give a primacy to communal solidarity and defense, organized around a strong centralized state. In both Byzantium and Russia, however, this centralized state proved as much hindrance as help in providing the resources necessary for societal advance and progress. For, in both Byzantium and Russia, the survival and success of the society came to be associated with a social pact between the state and a militarized aristocracy, an alliance that marshaled economic and military resources by bleeding other sections of society. Invariably, social solidarity was prioritized at the expense of individual freedom, entrepreneurship, and private commercialized endeavor. The historical uniqueness of the Orthodox East has also caused scholars such as Huntington to argue that it is profoundly different from Western Europe, Huntington (1996/2003: 141) declaring that even after the Petrine reforms, Russia remained a society in which "Asiatic and Byzantine ways, institutions and beliefs predominated." According to Huntington and likeminded scholars (Masaryk, Pirenne, Quigley), this cultural orientation has resulted in a society that places little value on individual freedom and liberty. This is a viewpoint that this study rejects. Constantly, across the centuries, the battle to maintain values associated with freedom, individual identity, and personal conscience have remained a constant in Russian history, a battle often waged in the most difficult of circumstances. Certainly, no one can read the works of Herzen, Tolstoy, Turgenev, Gogol, Dostoyevsky, and Solzhenitsyn without realizing that their emphasis on human dignity and freedom has a deep resonance within Russian society. Yet, it is also true that in the highly centralized societies that Russia has produced – Muscovy, imperial Russia, Soviet Russia – an inner sense of freedom could only be maintained through shows of outward compliance and obedience. In justifying such behavior in the Russia of the Romanovs, Dostoyevsky (1864/1972: 48) lamented, "Every decent man in this age is and must be a coward, a coward and a slave ... Only donkeys and mules make a show of bravery."

If Russian culture has maintained a belief in individual freedom and personal identity, the state's constant emphasis on outward compliance demands a reconsideration of our understanding of what we mean by the terms "management" and, more specifically, "modern management." Yes, it is true that if we look to the classic definition of "management – i.e., planning, organizing, leading, controlling" – we can assume that "leading" necessarily entails employee "motivation." But how does one motivate a serf to work that little bit harder when they know that the fruits of that additional effort will be taken from them? Similarly, how does one motivate a peasant to make additional investments in their plot of land when they know that their village commune will allocate that land to another family in the ensuing summer? Russian estate owners and managers never found an adequate answer to these fundamental questions. As David Moon (2006: 386) observes in relation to the typical peasant response to managerial control in imperial Russia:

> They worked badly on their landowners' land when performing their labour services, stole estate property, accidently broke new machinery ... paid less than the full amount of their cash dues late, feigned incomprehension of orders, hid in the woods.

Within the confines of imperial Russian society, a host of people sought solutions to the low productivity of the workforce without real success: Peter the Great, Herzen, Tolstoy, Lomonosov, and Goltsev. The reason for this is clear: Russia lacked the supporting social and legal structures that are integral to "modern management" as it is emerged in Western Europe. In the West, such supporting structures not only fostered competition; they also provided labor a genuine freedom to choose their occupation and employer, along with guarantees of individual freedom and protection of property. In looking to the Russian experience, one can understand why these attributes were seldom fostered. By allowing such freedoms and protections, the state feared a weakening of the organizing ability it regarded as essential to national defense and security. However, by denying its citizens freedom of movement and protection of property, the imperial Russian state – like Muscovy and Byzantium before it – curtailed the creativity and entrepreneurship that is the hallmark of a successful society. In the final analysis, this failure proved more damaging to the society than any military defeat inflicted by an invading foe.

Cross-References

▶ What Is Management?

References

Ananich B (2006) The Russian economy and banking system. In: Lieven D (ed) The Cambridge history of Russia, vol 2. Cambridge University Press, Cambridge, UK, pp 394–425
Babbage C (1832) On the economy of machinery and manufactures. Charles Knight, London
Baykov A (1954) The economic development of Russia. Econ Hist Rev 7(2):137–149
Braudel F (1977) Afterthoughts on material civilization and capitalism. John Hopkins University Press, Baltimore
Braudel F (1979/1982) The wheels of commerce: civilization and capitalism, 15th – 18th century, vol 2. Collins, London
Braudel F (1987/1993) A history of civilizations. Penguin Books, London
Camus A (1951/1978) The rebel: an essay on man in revolt. Alfred A Knopf, New Work

Cipolla CM (1981) Before the industrial revolution: European society and economy, 1000–1700, 2nd edn. Cambridge University Press, Cambridge, UK

Davis RHC (1970) A history of medieval Europe: from Constantine to Saint Louis, 2nd edn. Longman, London

Dennison T (2011) The institutional framework of Russian serfdom. Cambridge University Press, Cambridge, UK

Dostoyevsky F (1862/1911) The house of the dead, or prison life in Siberia. J.M. Dent and Sons, London

Dostoyevsky F (1864/1972) Notes from underground. In: Dostoyevsky F (ed) Notes from underground/The double (trans: Coulson J). Penguin, Harmondsworth, pp 15–126

Dostoyevsky F (1866/1963) Crime and punishment. Dodd, Mead & Company, New York

Engel BA, Martin J (2015) Russia in world history. Oxford University Press, Oxford

Flier M S (2006) Political ideas and rituals. In: Pirenne M (ed) The Cambridge history of Russia, vol. 1. Cambridge University Press, Cambridge, UK, pp. 387–408

Gerschenkron A (1965) Agrarian policies and industrialization: Russia 1861–1917. In: Habakkuk HJ, Postan M (eds) The Cambridge economic history of Europe, vol 6. Cambridge University Press, Cambridge, MA, pp 706–800

Graham HF (1987) How do we know what we know about Ivan the terrible. Rus Hist 14(1):179–198

Gregory P (1972) Economic growth and structural change in tsarist Russia: a case of modern economic growth? Sov Stud 23(3):418–434

Harcave S (1968) Years of the golden cockerel. Macmillan, New York

Hartley JM (2006) Provincial and local government. In: Lieven D (ed) The Cambridge history of Russia, vol 2. Cambridge University Press, Cambridge, UK, pp 449–467

Hellie R (2006a) The economy, trade and serfdom. In: Pirenne M (ed) The Cambridge history of Russia, vol 1. Cambridge University Press, Cambridge, UK, pp 539–558

Hellie R (2006b) The peasantry. In: Pirenne M (ed) The Cambridge history of Russia, vol 1. Cambridge University Press, Cambridge, UK, pp 286–297

Hellie R (2006c) The law. In: Pirenne M (ed) The Cambridge history of Russia, vol 1. Cambridge University Press, Cambridge, UK, pp 360–386

Herzen A (1851/1956) The Russian people and socialism: An open letter to Jules Michelet. In: Herzen A (ed) From the other side & The Russian people and socialism (trans: Wolheim E). Weidenfeld and Nicholson, London, pp 164–208

Herzen A (1855/1956) From the other side. In: Herzen A (ed) From the other side & The Russian people and socialism (trans: Wolheim E). Weidenfeld and Nicholson, London, pp 3–162

Hughes L (2006) Russian culture in the eighteenth century. In: Lieven D (ed) The Cambridge history of Russia, vol 2. Cambridge University Press, Cambridge, UK, pp 67–91

Huntington SP (1996/2003) The clash of civilizations and the remaking of world order. Simon & Schuster, New York

Jones AHM (1964) The later Roman empire 284–602: a social, economic and administrative survey, vol 2. Basil Blackwell, Oxford

Kleimola AM (1979) Up through servitude: the changing condition of the Muscovite elite in the sixteenth and seventeenth centuries. Rus Hist 6(2):210–229

Koerner R (1941/1966) The settlement and colonization of Europe. In: Postan MM (ed) The Cambridge economic history of Europe, vol 1. Cambridge University Press, Cambridge, UK, pp 1–91

Kotkin S (2017) Stalin: waiting for Hitler 1929–1941. Penguin Books, London

Kropotkin P (1912/1968) Fields, factories and workshops, 2nd edn. Bejamin Blom, London/New York

Lenin VI (1898/1964) The development of capitalism in Russia. In: Lenin VI (ed) Collected works, vol 3. Progress Publishers, Moscow, pp 21–607

Lieven D (2006) Russia as empire and periphery. In: Lieven D (ed) The Cambridge history of Russia, vol 2. Cambridge University Press, Cambridge, UK, pp 9–26

Marshev V (2019) Formation of management thought in Russia and early USSR from the 1800s to the 1920s. J Manag Hist 25(3):285–303
Masaryk TG (1913/1955) The spirit of Russia. George Allen & Unwin, London
Mayer W (2009) John Chrysostom on poverty. In: Allen P, Bronwen N, Mayer W (eds) Preaching poverty in late antiquity. Evangelische Verlagsnstalt, Leipzig
Mengelberg K (1961) Lorenz Von Stein and his contribution to historical sociology. J Hist Ideas 22(2):267–274
Miller DB (2006) The Orthodox Church. In: Pirenne M (ed) The Cambridge history of Russia, vol 1. Cambridge University Press, Cambridge, UK, pp 338–359
Moon D (1999) The Russian peasantry, 1600–1930: The world the peasants made. Longman, London
Moon D (2006) Peasants and agriculture. In: Lieven D (ed) The Cambridge history of Russia, vol 2. Cambridge University Press, Cambridge, UK, pp 393–369
Morgan LH (1878) Ancient society. Henry Holt and Company, New York
Ostrogorsky G (1941/1966) Agrarian conditions in the Byzantine Empire in the middle ages. In: Postan MM (ed) The Cambridge economic history of Europe, vol 1. Cambridge University Press, Cambridge, UK, pp 205–234
Pipes R (1974) Russia under the old regime. Charles Scribner's Sons, New York
Pirenne H (1925/1952) Medieval cities. Their origins and the revival of trade. Princeton University Press, Princeton
Poe M (2006) The central government and its institutions. In: Pirenne M (ed) The Cambridge history of Russia, vol 1. Cambridge University Press, Cambridge, UK, pp 435–463
Pollard S (1980) A new estimate of British coal production, 1750–1850. Econ Hist Rev 33(2):212–235
Portal R (1966) The industrialization of Russia. In: Habakkuk HJ, Postan M (eds) The Cambridge economic history of Russia, vol 6. Cambridge University Press, Cambridge, UK, pp 801–875
Quigley C (1979) The evolution of civilizations: an introduction to historical analysis, 2nd edn. Indianapolis Library Press, Indianapolis
Raeff M (1983) The well-ordered police state: social and institutional change through law in the Germanies and Russia, 1600–1800. Yale University Press, New Haven
Riasanovsky NV (1993) A history of Russia, 5th edn. Oxford University Press, Oxford, UK
Russian primary chronicle (1337/1953) The Laurentian text. Medieval Academy of America, Cambridge, MA
Sachs J (2005) The end of poverty: economic possibilities for our time. Penguin Press, London
Shakiba ZP (2006) Central government. In: Lieven D (ed) The Cambridge history of Russia, vol 2. Cambridge University Press, Cambridge, UK, pp 429–448
Shaw DJB (2006a) Urban developments. In: Pirenne M (ed) The Cambridge history of Russia, vol 1. Cambridge University Press, Cambridge, UK, pp 579–599
Shaw DJB (2006b) Russia's geographical environment. In: Pirenne M (ed) The Cambridge history of Russia, vol 1. Cambridge University Press, Cambridge, UK, pp 19–43
Shaw DJB (2006c) Towns and commerce. In: Pirenne M (ed) The Cambridge history of Russia, vol 1. Cambridge University Press, Cambridge, UK, pp 298–316
Simms JY (1982) The economic impact of the Russian famine of 1891–92. Slavonic and East European Review 60(1):63–74
Smith R (1977/2010) Peasant farming in Muscovy. Cambridge University Press, Cambridge, UK
St Gregory the Great (c.AD 593/1959) Dialogues: the fathers of the Church. Catholic University of America Press, Washington, DC
St John Chrysostom (c.AD 398/1848) The homilies of St John Chrysostom on the Gospel of St John. John Henry Parker, London
Tolstoy L (1876/1978) Anna Karenina. Penguin Classics, London
Turgenev I (1862/2009) Fathers and children: Norton critical edition. W.W. Norton and Co., New York. [Note: in the interests of political correctness, recent additions have abandoned the original title, Father and sons]

Turgenev I (1869/2009) Apropos of fathers and sons. In: Katz MR (ed) Fathers and children: Norton critical edition. W.W. Norton and Co., New York, pp 167–174

Turton G (2009) The historical context of fathers and sons. In: Katz MR (ed) Fathers and children: Norton critical edition. W.W. Norton and Co., New York, pp 236–240

United States Department of Commerce (1975) Historical statistics of the United States. Colonial times to 1970: bicentennial edition. U.S. Department of Commerce, Washington, DC

Weeks TR (2006) Managing empire: tsarist nationalities policy. In: Lieven D (ed) The Cambridge history of Russia, vol 2. Cambridge University Press, Cambridge, UK, pp 27–44

Wirschafter EK (2006) The groups between: raznochintsy, intelligentsia, professionals. In: Lieven D (ed) The Cambridge history of Russia, vol 2. Cambridge University Press, Cambridge, UK, pp 245–263

Changing Corporate Governance in France in the Late Twentieth Century

50

Peter Wirtz

Contents

Introduction	1142
Historical Evolution of the French Corporate Governance System	1144
The Historical Roots of French Corporate Governance	1144
A Brief Description of the Major Transformations	1147
The Evolution of Corporate Governance and the Economic Theory of Institutional Change	1148
The History of French Corporate Governance in the Light of Institutional Change Theory	1150
The Traditional Mental Pattern Initially Resisted Disruptive Change (1945–1983)	1151
The State as a Platform for Institutional Entrepreneurs (1984–1994)	1153
The Increasing Capital Stakes of International Investors and Their Consequences (1995 and Later)	1156
Conclusions	1159
Cross-References	1160
References	1160

Abstract

France belongs to those highly developed western European countries that belong to the G7, the group of seven countries with the most developed national economies. Its national capital, Paris, is home to the Organization for Economic Co-operation and Development (OECD). OECD is an active promoter of international standards of corporate governance best practice. Historically, governance practices are however highly heterogeneous when comparing different national settings. At present, France shares most of the characteristics of a liberal market economy, and its code of reference for corporate governance was the first of its kind in continental Europe when first published in 1995. France's economic

P. Wirtz (✉)
IAE Lyon School of Management, Magellan Research Center, University of Lyon, Lyon, France
e-mail: peter.wirtz@univ-lyon3.fr; peter.wirtz.fcs@gmail.com

© The Author(s), under exclusive licence to Springer Nature Switzerland AG 2020
B. Bowden et al. (eds.), *The Palgrave Handbook of Management History*,
https://doi.org/10.1007/978-3-319-62114-2_95

history, however, has a longstanding tradition of interventionism by the State, and liberal market mechanisms did not have the favor of the political elite after World War II. Since the middle of the 1980s, the French system of corporate governance has undergone major transformations at a relatively fast pace. The public administration has increasingly retired from its active role in corporate governance matters, increasing the weight of shareholder-oriented market mechanisms. This chapter retraces the history of the French corporate governance system over the second half of the twentieth century. Significant change is shown to have occurred in three stages, whose underlying rationale appears to be broadly consistent with North's theory of institutional change.

Keywords

Corporate governance · France · Institutional change · Mental patterns · Shareholder orientation · Stakeholder orientation

Introduction

Corporate governance is a timely and much studied issue. Its historical dimension is however often neglected (Gomez and Wirtz (2018) are a recent exception). The public debate over governance in different countries has led to the spread of corporate governance codes of best practice worldwide (Aguilera and Cuervo-Cazurra 2004). Those codes are in large part inspired by mainstream-theories of corporate governance (Daily et al. 2003; Wirtz 2008) and focus typically on the single dimension of shareholder interest protection. They strongly resemble each other from one country to another, giving the impression of a certain uniformity. Historically, however, there have been major differences in national corporate governance systems. A corporate governance system can be loosely defined as a set of mechanisms (such as legal systems, financial markets, boards of directors) which restrict managerial discretion of the top executive, that is to say the CEO's latitude of action (Charreaux 1997). In doing so, the instances of governance achieve an alignment of managerial behavior with the interests of different types of stakeholders, such as stockholders, financial intermediaries, employees, suppliers, clients, and the State. Mainstream explanations of corporate governance standing in the tradition of agency theory commonly focus on suppliers of financial capital (Shleifer and Vishny 1997: 737), whereas the more recent institutional literature interested in explaining cross-border differences in corporate governance equally considers other stakeholder categories (Aguilera and Jackson 2003). In fact, when examining the practice of governance in real context, one observes the existence of substantial differences in systems across national borders (Aoki 1994; Hall and Soskice 2001; Porter 1992). The Anglo-Saxon systems are traditionally described as being primarily driven by shareholder interests, whereas the Japanese and German systems are thought of as more stakeholder oriented (Guillén 2000; Schneper and Guillén 2002). Yoshimori (1995) makes an empirical investigation concerning a national philosophy's answer to the following question: "In whose interest should the firm be managed?" (Yoshimori 1995: 33). His study identifies three different concepts of the firm: monistic (Anglo-Saxon), dualistic (German), and pluralistic (Japanese), where monistic means focus on shareholder interests, dualistic includes employees' interests and pluralistic refers to multiple stakeholders.

In a way consistent with this observation concerning the underlying "philosophy," the control instruments at the disposal of different stakeholders that are to achieve the interest alignment are traditionally characterized by the important weight of the financial market in Anglo-Saxon countries and by more relational control instances in Japan and Germany (Berglöf 1997; Franks and Mayer 1990; Hall and Soskice 2001; Moerland 1995; Porter 1992; Schneper and Guillén 2002).

Much of the comparative literature is rich of relatively static descriptions of national corporate governance systems. They somewhat obscure the fact that, as a phenomenon of social interaction, corporate governance systems are dynamic and thus evolve over time (Lazonick and O'Sullivan 1997). It is thus important to consider history when studying corporate governance systems. Jensen (1993) describes the example of the American system, inside of which the weight of the capital market has experienced several changes over a long time horizon (Jensen 1993: 850–852). His study suggests some future research perspectives aiming, among other things, at an improved understanding of "how politics, the press, and public opinion affect the types of governance, financial, and organizational policies that firms adopt" (Jensen 1993: 872). Hence, history is needed to further our understanding of the determinants of the dynamic process constantly reshaping the incentive and control mechanisms to which a CEO is subject.

In this respect, the French corporate governance system is an interesting case to study, because it has experienced major transformations over the second half of the last century. As most continental European countries, France's governance system was initially at a long distance from what OECD considers presently as international best practice, but it has also been a fast mover, being the first continental European country to have adopted a governance code in 1995 inspired by the mainstream (Wirtz 2008).

The present chapter retraces the history of the French governance system over the second half of the last century. In doing so, it distinguishes three main stages of development. In search of an understanding of the rationale underlying the temporal dynamics of French corporate governance, this particular historical evolution appears to be broadly consistent with the theory of institutional change set out by D. North (1990, 1993). The remainder of this chapter is structured as follows. The first section gives a brief descriptive account of the basic features of the French system of corporate governance as well as of its most significant transformations. Section "The Evolution of Corporate Governance and the Economic Theory of Institutional Change" briefly summarizes North's theory of institutional change and its implications for corporate governance systems dynamics. The last section then confronts the institutional change theory with the reality of French history.

Historical Evolution of the French Corporate Governance System

Over the past three decades, the French corporate governance system has undergone several especially strong transformations. To fully appreciate their impact, one should be familiar with the historical origins of French style corporate governance.

The Historical Roots of French Corporate Governance

Traditionally, the French attitude towards business makes room for multiple stakeholders. In 1995, Marc Viénot, a former CEO of one of France's most important banks, published a report on corporate governance which benefited from widespread attention in the French business community. It stipulated the "obligation" of the board of directors "to act in all circumstances in the *social interest* of the firm" (Viénot 1995: 6, our translation, italics added). The report then went on to explicitly distinguish this perspective from an approach purely guided by the maximization of shareholder value (Viénot 1995: 9). According to Peyrelevade (1998: 31), a longtime CEO of formerly state-owned Crédit Lyonnais, the concept of the firm which underlies the Viénot report reflected the opinion of the majority of managers in France. Traditionally, in the French public opinion, "profit has a bad smell" (Lesourne 1998: 103). As a consequence, the dominant ideology favored "the prosperity and the continuity of the firm" (Peyrelevade 1998: 39).

The traditional French business philosophy took into account the interests of multiple stakeholders. The French tradition then designated the State as the best suited actor to assure the alignment of all economic decisions with the previously described philosophy. According to Albert (1991: 266), France has cultivated "social colbertism" for a long time. The same author summarizes this doctrine, referring to Colbert, a very influential minister under France's absolutistic monarch Louis XIV, as follows: "the State [...] commands the economy in the name of a political ambition and of a strive for social progress" (Albert 1991: 266, our translation). From this perspective, the State's role was perceived as one of a referee between the demands of different stakeholders. It "acts in place of the economic and social actors" (Les Echos 11/17/1998, our translation). In doing so, the State was considered to be a "protector who assures redistribution according to the republican principle of *égalité*" (Les Echos 11/17/1998, our translation).

It is important to emphasize that the control instruments of quite different corporate governance systems are theoretically consistent with a pluralist stakeholder approach of the firm. Why, then, did the French tradition assign such a central role to the State in spite of privileging the mechanisms of direct negotiation between different stakeholder categories? One factor which is likely to contribute to an answer is the existence of very polarized interests in France. In fact, French trade unions are traditionally characterized by a "class-fight ideology" (Albert 1991: 268, our translation). Hence, there is a tendency towards adopting extreme opposite positions. According to Peyrelevade (1998: 32), the notion of compromise often has a negative connotation. Consequently, the State plays the role of a referee. In fact, since direct compromise between certain stakeholder groups is problematic, the structuring of mutual relations necessitates the aid of a "superior" instance. The latter's position was traditionally occupied by the State. Unlike the approach of certain other countries, the French State "is not [...] a simple instrument of social administration at the disposal of the citizens. It transcends the individuals and receives of the latter a sort of divine blessing, comparable to the one the monarchs received in the past" (Lesourne 1998: 92, our translation).

France's traditional concept of the firm was thus based on a "profoundly anti-liberal instinct of a large part of the French opinion" (Les Echos 11/16/1998, our translation). This opinion refused to consider a company as a tradable merchandise among others (Albert 1991: 280). Traditionally, free market mechanisms were regarded rather suspiciously, and there was a belief in the benefits resulting from the State's role as an organizer of economic activity. According to this reasoning, the State must intervene in order to eliminate suspicions of private benefits primarily destined to financial investors. As Denis Kessler put it (Les Echos 11/20 and 11/21/1998): "Historically, the two great nationalized sectors were banks and insurance companies; *firms making money business simply had to be state owned*" (our translation, italics added).

Consistent with the philosophy outlined above, the corporate governance system of a substantial fraction of the most important French corporations was characterized by the State's strong influence during a significant lapse of time. In fact, in the past, this influence was exercised at least at four different levels. (1) Industrial politics sometimes led the State to interfere directly with certain important firms' corporate strategies. (2) Its control over the financial circuit was a significant vehicle of influence. (3) The governance structures of the nationalized corporations, which included a certain number of "champions" of the domestic industry, depended directly on government decisions. (4) And, finally, a significant part of the managerial elite owed (and still owe) their education and first professional experience to the public administration.

At the end of the 1940s, a certain number of reforms translated into legal rules the perception according to which the State had the privilege of efficiently organizing economic activity. This exerted a more or less direct influence on the managerial discretion in big corporations. In fact, in sectors considered to be strategic, the State conducted several nationalizations (e.g., energy), or very closely followed the management of firms which had remained in private hands. The latter case concerned, for example, the steel industry. In spite of the fact that it was not officially nationalized until the beginning of the 1980s, the constraints which the State imposed on its strategy were very strong (Lesourne 1998: 96). These constraints' justification was primarily based on the financial resources directed to the development of the sector, which essentially took the form of public funds. The State granted, in fact, loans at a reduced rate of interest. Lesourne (1998: 96) quotes the statement made close to 1970 by a steel manager: "You want to know details concerning our accounts? Ask the public administration. They know them better than we do!" (our translation).

More generally speaking, the State controlled the essential dimensions of the whole financial circuit. Hence, capital export and import were limited because of exchange controls. The stock exchange played but a minor role in corporate finance. In this context, a famous quotation by de Gaulle, former French president and founder of France's "Fifth Republic" (defined by the constitution of 1958), is quite significant: "French politics are not decided at the stock exchange." (our translation). On the contrary, banks and the public treasury and its satellites contributed an essential fraction to financing the economy (Albert 1991: 269). In this context, the State's privileged position appears even more clearly knowing that the large deposit banks were also nationalized after World War II.

The specific governance structures of the nationalized firms depended directly on the government's policy. This concerned notably the composition of their boards of directors. It is, however, important to stress that the force of the State-controlled governance mechanisms varied with the type of firm under study. This force appeared to be most intense in the case of the nationalized firms. But even the private sector felt the (more indirect) influence of the State. In fact, beyond its control of the financial circuit, the public sector was often a major client. In this way, "a close symbiosis takes place between the State and the private groups" (Lesourne 1998: 98).

Close ties between the State and certain corporations, be they nationalized or private, also existed, and still exist, at the level of higher education of the managerial *élite*. In fact, a significant fraction of the biggest French firms' CEOs have received their education at the ENA (*Ecole Nationale de l'Administration*) and/or have started their professional career in the public administration. Bertin-Mourot and Bauer (1996: 22) observe that "it is in France [...] that the transfer of *élites* from the State's to the firms' top positions is greatest" (our translation).

Obviously, the State played traditionally an important role in the French corporate governance system. Albert (1991: 267) describes it as "a *colbertistic* State that has not ceased to dominate the economy: protectionistic and dirigistic on the one hand, but also an investor, [and] entrepreneur [...] on the other" (our translation).

Starting from the mid-eighties, State-control was progressively alleviated. This retreat of the State from corporate control took place gradually. In 1990, Franks and Mayer (1990: 228) still concluded that the public authorities had great discretion in the application of the takeover rules. Hence, in certain cases, the French government had allegedly retarded the takeover of firms by foreigners in order to find a domestic solution (Franks and Mayer 1990: 209). Almost a decade later, the turn-of-century takeover battle opposing BNP to Société Générale and Paribas, three major banks, represented a late attempt of interference by the public administration. But at the same time, it perfectly illustrates the weakening of the effective means of public intervention. In fact, the Minister of Finance and the Governor of the Central Bank would clearly have preferred a privately negotiated solution to an open battle in the market place. In the course of these events, the State's representatives used their right to suspend a revised bid by Société Générale for Paribas to invite the different protagonists to the negotiation (Le Monde 06/27 and 06/28/1999). During the negotiations, the Governor of the Central Bank submitted his own proposals to the conflicting parties. Lacking the power to actually impose his project, the unsuccessful end of the negotiations implied, however, the obligation to wait for the closure of the official stock-exchange procedure. A leading economic newspaper had the following comment. "This frustrating and unfruitful negotiation demonstrates that the public authority lacks the means of actively opposing the fact – in spite of the Finance Minister's publicly expressed wish to the contrary – that the mere 'luck of the market' determines one of the most important movements in banking France has ever known." (Les Echos 07/01/1999, our translation).

A Brief Description of the Major Transformations

The BNP-Société Générale-Paribas case illustrates that the French corporate governance system underwent significant change. In fact, following deregulation, which was initiated by the government in 1984, the evolution of French corporate governance was characterized by the diminishing role of the State (Schmidt 1996). In this context, the 1984 event lay the foundations of a rehabilitation of the capital market. The fact that this step was undertaken under a socialist government may appear as somewhat surprising. French deregulation implied as a consequence that certain companies gained direct access to the financial market to cover their need of capital funds. Hence, the State's control over the financial circuit was alleviated. At first, an important fraction of the major corporations remained, however, under the direct control of the public administration. The government changed in 1986, bringing along a first wave of major privatizations. This further exasperated the State's retreat from direct corporate governance. The impact of the privatization program on the corporate sector in France was significant. In fact, reviewing the literature on privatization worldwide and referring to the aggregate value as well as the number of firms, Alexandre and Charreaux (2004: 467) describe "the French program [as] one of the world's most ambitious privatization programs." The movement was temporarily interrupted due to another change in the political landscape, only to be continued in the form of a second wave of privatizations beginning in 1993. It should be noted, however, that the State's retreat was not complete. In fact, by installing the so-called *noyaux durs* (literally hard cores), the public administration maintained the capacity of at least indirectly influencing the development of the corporate governance structures of the newly privatized companies. *Noyau dur* is the term used to identify the group of major shareholders who were co-opted in the privatization process. Hence, in a first stage, direct control by the State was replaced by control through other companies which held significant capital stakes. The government thus exerted a certain influence by participating in building up these major shareholder groups. What is interesting is the fact that the circle of companies called upon to compose the *noyaux durs* in the context of the different privatizations was rather restrained. As a consequence, the system of corporate governance applying to some of the largest French corporations, formerly subject to the State's direct influence, was characterized by a dense network of cross shareholdings for several years. These cross shareholdings went generally hand in hand with personal ties in the form of an exchange of corporate directors. Finally, around 1995, this network was starting to be undone (Les Echos 12/08/1998), progressively replacing the prevailing system of relational governance by more capital-market related mechanisms. As a result of this process, some of the major companies were henceforth exposed to the pressure of potential takeover.

Significant changes have occurred in the French corporate governance system since the mid-eighties. What were the drivers of this evolution? The following section briefly sketches out the basic rationale of institutional change theory to gain deeper insight into the dynamics of the national corporate governance system.

The Evolution of Corporate Governance and the Economic Theory of Institutional Change

North (1993) defines institutions as "the constraints that human beings impose on human interaction." There is a great variety of such constraints ranging from formal (rules of law) to implicit (ethical conduct). One implication of the existence of institutions is that, if the institutional constraints are properly enforced, their transgression is costly. In this way, the institutional matrix has a very strong influence on the economic opportunities of the agents it constrains. It is however important to stress that even though institutions impose limits on human behavior, they are never capable of closely determining *every single* decision made by the agents who act in their realm (Mayer and Whittington 1999). For this reason, the human actor has discretion over a number of decisions.

In order to gain a better understanding of the drivers of change of existing institutional constraints, North (1990: 17) makes some behavioral assumptions as to the fundamentally procedural nature of human reasoning and action (Simon 1982). This implies that economic agents act along the lines of trial and error (Simon 1983). This type of behavior can be explained by the fact that a human being never has complete knowledge of all parameters characterizing the environment he acts in, nor does he perfectly understand all factors that affect the outcome of his actions. What helps the economic agent to make decisions in the context of such uncertainty is a theory he holds on the functioning of the world in which he lives. In North's work on institutional change, such theories are referred to as "mental patterns" or "mental models." They are the starting block for concrete action within – or on the limits of – a given institutional framework. North (1993) expresses this in the following way. "The key to the choices that individuals make is their perceptions, which are a function of the way the mind interprets the information it receives." The mental pattern shapes these interpretations and hence influences an actor's perception of the opportunities implied by the institutional matrix. The latter is the "incarnation" of the dominant ideology, that is to say a mental pattern which is shared by several (influential) individuals. Hence, a given institutional framework can be looked upon as the translation of a shared mental pattern into real institutions. This is somewhat close to Aoki's (2001) conceptualization of institutions as "a self-sustaining system of shared beliefs." To understand institutional dynamics, an understanding of changing mental patterns is thus required. As Denzau and North (1994) put it, "institutions clearly are a reflection of the evolving mental models."

In the theory of institutional change, ideologies and the institutions they shape are modified by the action of so-called "organizational entrepreneurs." According to North (1993), "the entrepreneurs of organizations induce institutional change as they perceive new or altered opportunities." This statement can be translated into the terminology of mental patterns, because the latter help explain the perception of opportunities. In fact, an actor must weigh the costs and benefits he anticipates from action inside the existing institutional framework against the costs and benefits he hopes to derive from a change in the rules of the game. In this sense, an individual mental pattern is "entrepreneurial" to the degree that it diverges from traditional ideology, leading to the perception of better opportunities resulting from institutional innovations when compared to a strategy inside an unchanged environment. In spite of its appeal to a (boundedly) rational economic tradeoff, this perspective should not be confounded with accounts depicting man as over-rational and under-socialized. According to economic institutionalism, individuals do not choose their course of action as a function of some set of supposedly objective "real" parameters, but on the basis of their subjective representation of relevant parameters. According to Denzau and North (1994), "people act in part upon the basis of [...] 'half-baked' theories." The formation of these theories or mental patterns is partly dependent on the specific socio-cultural context and the personal experience of organizational entrepreneurs. "History matters" to speak with Aoki (2001).

The foregoing discussion highlights the organizational entrepreneur as the driving force behind institutional change. In this context, two general traits characterize the typical entrepreneur. The first has already been presented, namely, the holding of a mental pattern capable of transgressing the limits of dominant ideology. But an innovative approach to institutional matters alone is insufficient to translate one's philosophy into real action. For this to be possible, the potential entrepreneur also has to dispose of effective means of action. This explains why, in North's theory, it is not the individual that interacts directly with the institutional matrix. What brings about real change is, in fact, supposed to be the "continuous interaction between institutions and organizations" (North 1993). Thus, the organization can be seen as an enabling device making real action possible. Hence, institutional entrepreneurs are typically the leaders of organizations. It should be noted, however, that the organizations that potentially serve entrepreneurs in an effort to influence institutions of corporate governance are not restricted to the corporate sector alone. The leaders of such diverse organizations as the national government, trade unions, professional associations, and firms may use their organizational infrastructure and resources as a vehicle to initiate institutional change.

The foregoing developments can briefly be summarized as follows. Human individuals act in response to opportunities that are perceived as such through the lens of mental patterns. To the extent that an actor perceives better opportunities in an altered institutional environment than in the existing one, he has incentives to become an entrepreneur. He may initiate real change if he disposes of sufficient

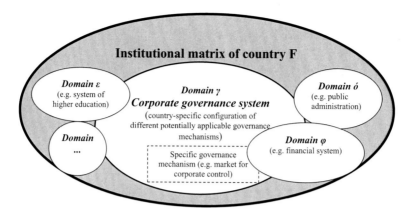

Fig. 1 Different levels of analysis – the relation between a country's institutional framework and its system of corporate governance

resources. The availability of the latter is typically conditioned on the support of an organizational infrastructure.

It should be noted that according to North (1993) the nature of the evolutionary process is supposed to be "overwhelmingly incremental and path dependent." This is consistent with Bebchuk and Roe (1999) demonstrating the relevance of path dependence for an analysis concerning more specifically the institutions of corporate governance.

Restrictions on managerial discretion, as corporate governance was defined earlier, are a special case of "the constraints that human beings impose on human interaction," which corresponds to North's definition of institutions. As a consequence, the system of corporate governance consists of a subset of the entire set of rules composing the institutional matrix of a given country. Figure 1 represents this relationship between institutions and corporate governance, where corporate governance is one specific institutional domain among others, the different domains typically being complementary (Aguilera and Jackson 2003; Hall and Soskice 2001).

The History of French Corporate Governance in the Light of Institutional Change Theory

The following account is mainly based on French sources. The latter range from accounts by academic observers (Albouy and Schatt 2004; Hirigoyen 1994; Lesourne 1998) and by well-informed managers of large corporations having occupied major positions in the French business landscape (Albert 1991; Fauroux 1998; Peyrelevade 1998; Riboud 1999; Viénot 1995) to articles and special inquiries published in the economic and general press (Les Echos; Le Monde). Figure 2 recalls some of the most significant milestones in the process transforming the French corporate governance system.

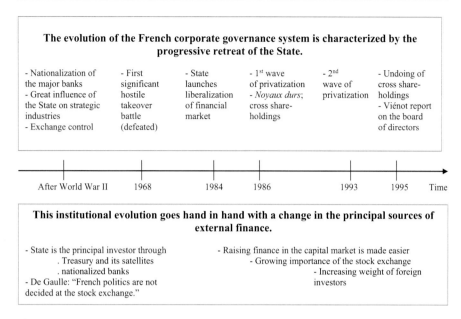

Fig. 2 Significant milestones in French corporate governance

The following analysis systematically examines these changes in the light of institutional change theory. This reading of the evolution of corporate governance in France since the end of the Second World War suggests that it is possible to roughly subdivide the total period into three distinct stages. In fact, a first subsection illustrates how the dominant ideology contributed to effectively counteract the initiative of an individual (isolated) organizational entrepreneur. In spite of such transitory resistance, however, institutional entrepreneurs located at the very heart of traditional French-style capitalism – that is to say the State – eventually succeeded in triggering deep reaching transformations, as will be shown in the second sub-section. Among other things, these transformations brought about a liberalization of capital transfers on a deregulated financial market. In the following years, this made it possible for foreign investors to increase their influence on major French corporations, which is the central theme of the third subsection. In this context, the activism of certain institutional investors, especially from the Anglo-Saxon sphere, appears to have contributed to the promotion and the increasing acceptance of new standards of corporate governance.

The Traditional Mental Pattern Initially Resisted Disruptive Change (1945–1983)

The traditional French concept of the firm was rather hostile towards governance mechanisms that enhance private benefits which can easily be appropriated by shareholders. According to this point of view, the interests of different stakeholder categories were thought to be properly represented by the State's predominant role in corporate governance. On the technical side, this representation was coupled with a preference for relational control mechanisms working through a network of personal ties over anonymous mechanisms of the market. Such an economic "philosophy" was not necessarily shared by every single individual, however, which means that entrepreneurial initiative could not be excluded. This assessment is well illustrated by the conditions surrounding the first important control fight in the French capital market since the end of World War II.

In fact, in December 1968, Antoine Riboud, then CEO of B.S.N. (Boussois-Souchon-Neuvesel), an important glass manufacturer which later took on the name of Danone, one of its better known brand names, launched a hostile raid on his major French competitor, Saint-Gobain. The latter company had been founded in 1665 by Colbert (prime minister to King Louis XIV), and its trajectory has been an integral part of France's industrial history. In his own words, Riboud described the strategic motives of his initiative as follows.

> We [A. Riboud and A. de Vogüé, CEO of Saint-Gobain] had two opposite strategic visions. Our own strategy was to rapidly gain strength in our [main] activities, to concentrate our investments and to specialize our factories in order to ameliorate productivity. [...] On the other side, at Saint-Gobain, management was based on a *'colbertistic'* conception of enhancing the value of assets in the long run. 'Immediate profits and short-term return on investment must in certain circumstances be limited to assure long-term security and growth', Arnaud de Vogüé had said. These to strategies had led to results which were translated into the share prices. The 200,000 Saint-Gobain shareholders had seen the value of their shares decline between 1958 and 1968, whereas the BSN share had tripled. (Riboud 1999: 82–83, our translation, italics added).

Perceiving an important potential to create value through the merger of the two groups and in the face of his counterpart's refusal, A. Riboud decided to launch a hostile tender offer. The latter was, at that time, a very unusual strategy in the French context. It thus appears that in Riboud's perception only a radical departure from traditional corporate governance routines, which his active sponsorship of hostile takeover clearly implied, would help to realize the anticipated wealth gains. This observation qualifies Riboud as an organizational entrepreneur in the terms of institutional change theory, for he perceived the opportunities of a change of particular features of country-specific corporate governance where hostile takeovers favoring shareholder value had been absent as a function of his individual mental pattern. The CEO of B.S.N. appears to have lent relatively more attention to shareholders as a stakeholder category than did his counterpart at Saint-Gobain. The latter actually promoted a more traditional *colbertistic* approach. In a manner consistent with his emphasis on shareholder value, Riboud had recourse to a governance mechanism of the capital market, that is to say a hostile tender offer.

The defense of the incumbent Saint-Gobain management was to a large extent based on a campaign mobilizing many stereotypical perceptions that were shaped by the traditional ideology. Thus, Hirigoyen (1994: 377) holds "cultural inertia" responsible for "the impossible success" of the takeover attempt. He shows that different stakeholder categories, such as the employees at different hierarchical levels, members of the board of directors, and even the shareholders, were very attached to continuity. In fact, Saint-Gobain's capital was characterized by weak mobility, hence corresponding to a system of "dedicated capital" (Porter 1992). As Hirigoyen (1994: 378) puts it, "one inherits Saint-Gobain shares, one does not buy them." Hence, in a manner consistent with the traditional shared mental pattern of France, the shareholders' mentality refused to look at Saint-Gobain as a tradable merchandise.

When defending his position, A. de Vogüé, the incumbent CEO, explicitly linked his approach to the public opinion. In fact, he called B.S.N.'s takeover attempt a maneuver "stimulating *instinctive* opposition in the public" (quoted in Hirigoyen 1994: 379, our translation, italics added). By integrating aspects of the dominant ideology into his rhetoric, Saint Gobain's incumbent CEO was able to rally the different stakeholders to his cause. The support given to de Vogüé's defense as a response to perceptions shaped by the shared mental pattern appears hence as a significant cause of the outcome of the takeover battle. Roger Fauroux, who became Saint-Gobain's president in 1980, gives his version of the takeover fight. "[...] in order to defeat the financial offers of its adversary, Saint-Gobain had established secret relationships with friendly firms which were to acquire a significant stake of its shares for a high price. Today, these things may seem surprising, but *when honor was at stake, ethical conduct forbade that one counts his money.*" (Fauroux 1998: 42–43, our translation, italics added). The "friendly" companies' support appears thus to have been motivated by shared moral standards. Further contributing to our evaluation of B.S.N.'s strategy as having been opposed to dominant ideology, Fauroux (1998: 43) describes the public opinion's image of the aggressor as "really poorly educated." Riboud (1999: 91) also states that in traditional business circles he had a rather bad image. So everything indicates that in the institutional context of his time, B.S.N.'s CEO transgressed a major taboo.

B.S.N.'s tender offer was eventually defeated, largely because of resistance which was mainly justified by elements of the shared mental pattern. The latter thus contributed to keeping the French system of corporate governance on its historical path. As a matter of fact, France did not develop a relatively active market for corporate control until the 1990s. The turn-of-century takeover-fight (1999) opposing three major banks (BNP, Paribas, Société Générale) indicates the great distance French capitalism has traveled since B.S.N.'s defeat. The following section delves deeper into the events that subsequently influenced the gradual change of French-style corporate governance.

The State as a Platform for Institutional Entrepreneurs (1984–1994)

According to Lesourne (1998: 132), the traditional representation of French business relations was at its highest in the 1960s. In fact, at that time, economic growth increased people's confidence with respect to the predominant ideology, which seems consistent with the idea of a positive feedback loop linking supposedly efficient outcomes to a perpetration of the dominant ideology. Subsequently, the French mental pattern however underwent certain transformations. In this context, some well-informed observers speak of "a forceful penetration of American values into France" (Albert 1991: 274, our translation). This evolution was made possible by the State itself. The latter appeared to be the central instance of governance according to the shared mental pattern. Interestingly, it is precisely the initiative of the public administration which triggered a vast transformation of the French financial market. In fact, in the middle of the 1980s, the government "heals France's inhibitions and rehabilitates the fundamental values of the market economy" (Albert 1991: 269, our translation). The increasing role of the capital market in corporate finance progressively induced a change in the attitude towards certain governance mechanisms. Hence, ideas spread, which were traditionally more readily associated with the Anglo-Saxon referential. The increasingly internationalized capital market thus appears to have been one important vector pushing a change in dominant ideology. As a matter of fact, a significant proportion of the largest French firms is presently in the hands of foreign investors. The most active among them, as it is the case of certain American pension funds, promoted – and still do – a mental pattern which emphasizes shareholder demands and governance mechanisms supposed to maximize shareholder value. Accordingly, the pressure coming from the capital market came to be perceived by French managers as a challenge to the established system of corporate governance. The following quotation from the Viénot report is a typical example of the influence the perception of the demands from the market exerted on French thinking about corporate governance: "the Committee notes that the participation of independent directors complies with a *demand from the market*" (Viénot 1995: 15, our translation, italics added). According to Peyrelevade (1998: 43), who is even more radical in his conclusions, the need to have recourse to finance of foreign origin forces compliance with the "ideas of the *Financial Times*."

To summarize the preceding developments, one can say that the State, which was at the very heart of the traditional shared mental pattern, was also at the origin of an important move to liberalize the French financial market. In this way, the public administration contributed to legitimize a concept of the firm, which diverged from traditional ideology. Following this initial move, the financial market became an important vector for the diffusion of a "philosophy" of corporate governance, which gradually started moving away from the traditional French representation of efficacious control and incentive mechanisms. The public debate concerning the rules of "good governance," which put increasing emphasis on shareholder interests (Peyrelevade 1998), was far from being neutral with respect to the actual institutions of governance. The shared mental pattern (or dominant business philosophy) in France hence made increasing room for the market.

It was in 1984 that the State created the basis for its progressive retreat from the control of large corporations. What is interesting is the fact that this major reorientation took place under a socialist government. A priori, this may strike as rather surprising, but it eventually facilitated the legitimization of the increased importance of the market by other political currents. In the middle of the 1980s, the role of the entrepreneur with an innovative approach to the conditions of corporate governance was thus played by leading members of the French national government. Financial deregulation, which was initiated in this way, has been a significant cause of the long-term development of the market's role in corporate control. The COB (later re-baptized AMF, which is Frances's equivalent to the SEC) received strong authority (Albert 1991: 271) in order to ascertain the proper functioning of the capital market mechanisms. Conceived to assure the security of operations and to guarantee investor interests, the new rules contributed to extract the stock exchange from its formerly marginal position in the French economy. Hence, for certain firms, the State facilitated the direct access to market finance.

But at a first stage, in spite of the impulse given to a liberalization of the financial market, not all firms were free to procure themselves finance at the stock exchange. In fact, the nationalized sector, being composed of some of the biggest companies, continued to play a very significant role. In this context, a second major change took place in 1986. The Chirac government launched the first important wave of privatizations. The following account helps appreciate the far reaching implications of this event.

> [...] eight large groups, the majority of which are of enormous importance (e.g. Saint-Gobain, Paribas, CGE, Havas, Société Générale, and Suez), were transferred from the national to the private sector. The initial motivations of this new French policy can make one think of a target such as approaching the Anglo-Saxon model, in that increasing the dimension of the stock exchange by creating several million new stockholders had priority. (Prodi 1991 'Entre les deux modèles'. *Il Molino*, quoted in Albert 1991: 265, our translation).

The privatization procedure, however, took on a very particular form, which should shape the face of French capitalism for several years to come. In fact, the French State did not want the newly privatized firms to become easy takeover targets for foreign interests. Because of this, the so-called *noyaux durs* (hard cores) were installed. These were groups of permanent shareholders, controlling significant capital stakes. In this way, even though it retired from direct control of privatized firms, the public administration still maintained some influence on the future evolution of their control structure. One important peculiarity of the *noyaux durs* system was that a relatively restrained circle of companies was called upon to compose the groups of permanent shareholders (Les Echos 12/08/1998 'Le Planisphère'). Consequently, a very dense network of cross shareholdings was created. "Hence, most of the big French companies, be they private or privatized between 1986 and 1987 or between 1993 and 1994, were often shareholders of their own principal shareholders" (Les Echos 12/08/1998, our translation). It is also interesting to note that the exchange of capital stakes generally went hand in hand with an exchange of corporate directors. Consequently, the corporate governance system was characterized by a relational network which was relatively well shielded off against outsiders.

The privatizations of 1986 clearly decreased the State's direct control. However, the initiative was temporarily interrupted as a result of the election of a new government. Hence, an analysis of the evolution of financial relations concerning the biggest French firms shows that, in 1991, the nationalized companies were still quite numerous and of considerable weight (Les Echos 12/07/1998). Later, a new change of governments took place in 1993 leading to a second wave of privatizations. The latter still operated by installing groups of permanent shareholders and thus reinforced the previously described network of mutual relations.

It is interesting to note that these major institutional changes were launched as initiatives by the State. The organizational entrepreneurs, who were at the origin of this process, must hence be located at the level of the public administration. With respect to this issue, it is useful to recall the assumption that an entrepreneur has to comply with two conditions. First, he should have a perception of opportunities that partially diverges from traditional ideas. Second, he should dispose of some sort of enabling device to realize his strategy. In this context, it seems probable that liberalization gained legitimacy by the fact that the representatives of the State, central player in the shared mental pattern, were themselves the initiators. This may explain why, in this case and quite to the opposite of Riboud's earlier isolated initiative, the traditional ideology was not a serious obstacle to institutional change any more. The first *noyaux durs*, which were in part composed of still nationalized firms, featured a clear preference for a French solution. In this way, the State indicated its wish to transform the system, without stimulating too violent a departure from national routines.

The growing importance of capital market mechanisms for the governance of French firms at the end of the 1980s is also illustrated by Franks and Mayer's (1990: 198) observation, according to which only recently "a number of hostile bids have been launched in France and [...] these are set to increase in the future." In fact, simultaneously with the State's first major draw-back from direct corporate control, the disciplining force of a potential hostile-takeover risk was kept small for certain companies, as a consequence of the abovementioned network of cross shareholdings. Hence, the evolution of the governance system since 1984 really was double. It was characterized by two distinct forms of control substituting for the traditional State-dominated governance mechanisms. In fact, direct control by the State was progressively replaced, either by a system of cross shareholdings or, in the rare cases of widely held firms, by the pressure stemming from a potential hostile tender offer.

The Increasing Capital Stakes of International Investors and Their Consequences (1995 and Later)

In the context of globalization, French firms have increasingly been exposed to international competition. But on a global scale, the big French companies not always played in the major league. A strategy oriented towards internationalization, as explicitly promoted by some CEOs, such as those of French steel producer Usinor (Wirtz 2001), later renamed Arcelor-Mittal, for a relevant example, led to important demands for external capital funding. In this context, one possible solution for firms was to call on the liberalized financial market to supply the necessary financial resources. Recall that certain companies had gained direct access to the capital market due to the various initiatives of deregulation and privatization conducted during the 1980s. As a consequence of the growing international integration of capital markets, transaction costs were constantly reduced. This facilitated the implementation of those investors' strategy wishing to (geographically) diversify their financial investment portfolios. Hence, a major proportion of the biggest French firms came to be characterized by a capital structure where foreign investors gained increasing weight. In fact, a study conducted by the *Conseil National du Crédit et du Titre* on corporate finance in France considered that, "during recent years, finance from nonresidents has been amplified because of their wish to diversify their placements" (CNCT 1999: 181, our translation). In only 10 years, the proportion of the French stock exchange's capitalization held by foreign investors increased from originally 10% to 36% (statistics from *Banque de France*, quoted in Les Echos 12/09/1998). Hence, CEOs wishing to issue new equity increasingly came under the influence of actual and potential foreign stockholders. In this context, especially the Anglo-Saxon pension funds, very attached to shareholder value, were quite active in defending their own stockholder-centered "philosophy" of corporate governance. Aguilera and Cuervo-Cazurra (2004) have recently put significant emphasis on Anglo-Saxon institutional investors' activism as one important driver of the diffusion of codes of "best practice" in corporate governance on a global scale. The following account highlights institutional investors' potential role as organizational entrepreneurs relating to issues of corporate governance: "Activism represented a shift [...] to institutions challenging managers and directors on a variety of issues, such as urging firms to make structural changes in their boards of directors and redesign firm voting procedures. Leading institutional investors, such as CalPERS in the USA, believe that 'good governance is good business', and hence will by default create shareholder value. The fact that in 1996 CalPERS established a corporate governance office to pressure domestic and international firms to adopt shareholder-friendly proposals and other measures designed to improve stock performance is an example of growing shareholder activism." (Aguilera and Cuervo-Cazurra 2004: 428).

Anglo-Saxon institutional investors of this sort typically disliked the opaque network of cross shareholdings and interlocking directorships pervasive in the French economy up to the mid-1990s. Consequently, the growing importance of foreign investors in big French companies' ownership structures coincided with successively disentangling the capital links established in the middle of the 1980s and at the beginning of the 1990s. Les Echos (12/08/1998), comparing data for 1991 and 1998, observed a "historical decline of cross shareholdings." This phenomenon appears to have been accelerated since 1995. Consequently, some of the largest French firms acquired more diffuse ownership than in the past, exposing them to disciplinary mechanisms historically absent from French-style corporate governance, such as hostile tender offers. Capital structure statistics concerning the biggest French firms and published by Les Echos (12/08/1998) show that ten of the corporations composing the CAC 40 stock market index had attained a proportion of permanent shareholders inferior to 15%. To be sure, when compared to Anglo-American ownership patterns, the capital structure of French corporations remained relatively concentrated on average (La Porta et al. 1999). However, the present chapter's emphasis lies on the historical transformation of a given national corporate governance system, and France experienced real change in the form of a significant decrease in the density of cross shareholdings (Les Echos 12/07–12/10/1998), in spite of persisting international differences. So, what continued relative concentration of ownership really teaches us about patterns of corporate control in France is not that they were static, but that their past evolution was highly path-dependent. In certain cases, the real influence exerted by active Anglo-Saxon investors on the governance mechanisms of (even family controlled) listed firms became especially strong. This can be demonstrated by the analysis of the successful proxy contest over Groupe André, initiated in early 2000 by the Franco-American investor Guy Wyser-Pratte and supported by another Anglo-Saxon investment fund, NR Atticus (Albouy and Schatt 2004). After having acquired a significant foothold through the stock market in Groupe André's capital structure, initially 25% family-controlled, the professional Anglo-Saxon investors defeated incumbent management and successfully imposed significant changes in the composition of the supervisory board. This precedent casts, as a matter of fact, serious doubt on the continuing relevance of a representation of French capitalism as being efficiently shielded off against the interests of shareholders acting in the stock market. The fact that the André proxy contest was quite unique in the French setting when it occurred made it an entrepreneurial initiative in the above-defined sense. Quite interestingly, the protagonist of this move to actively curb managerial discretion, Guy Wyser-Pratte, explicitly stated his desire to push French practice of corporate governance toward "American principles" (Albouy and Schatt 2004: 60).

The increasing weight of foreign investors may be explained, at least partially, by the conditions surrounding the supply of and the demand for foreign capital funds in the French economy. On the supply side, big institutional investors wished to geographically diversify. They were and are, above all, interested in firms (French or other) that offer *from their point of view* the best perspectives with respect to return on equity. The latter is conditioned by a company's approach to the creation and the redistribution of value. The investors' appreciation of a firm's capacity to create value and to distribute it in a supposedly "appropriate" way, thus enhancing return on equity, depends on their mental pattern. Hence, it appears to be plausible that at least those French corporations which came to be characterized by very large capital stakes held by Anglo-Saxon institutional investors gave an image of themselves as being managed according to shareholder-oriented standards of governance.

When examining the demand for foreign capital funds emanating from French companies, one may observe that it was to a great extent stimulated by certain structural features of national savings. In fact, "[French] households have a strong preference for the liquidity and the security of their investments" (CNCT 1999: 182, our translation). Thus, even though the study of the CNCT (1999: 183) clearly indicated national savings in excess of domestic needs, households invested only an insignificant part of their savings in corporate shares. In addition, those of the French financial institutions traditionally specialized in the management of a significant proportion of national savings also invested very little of the funds under their control in corporate equity. The CNCT (1999: 184) concluded from figures from the *Comité Européen des Assurances* (European Insurance Committee) that, "in a group of seven European countries [Germany included], France is the one where insurance companies invest the weakest part of their funds in corporate shares [approximately 15%]." Consequently, it seems plausible to suppose that French firms issuing equity in the financial market, probably more so than their counterparts in other national economies, underwent increasing pressure to comply with demands from foreign investors. This was at least partially a consequence of the weak propensity of domestic investors to put their money into corporate shares and of the simultaneous supply of excess funds from nonresidents. Hence, the CNCT (1999: 194) stated that "the portfolio investments of nonresidents in the French market progress strongly and have attained 414 billion French Francs in 1997 [, against 257 billion Francs of portfolio investments made by residents in foreign countries]" (our translation).

As far as corporate governance is concerned, the massive arrival of foreign capital stimulated an intensifying debate over the efficiency of the French corporate governance system. Hence, the recommendations of the Viénot report were mainly justified by the perception held by French CEOs concerning the demands from investors acting in the financial market. Marc Viénot expressed this in the following way: "[...] the strongest pressure in favor of transparency and of better shareholder information has come from Anglo-Saxon pension funds, the latter being very determined on this issue. The weight of their capital stakes also gives much weight to their recommendations." (quoted in Les Echos 12/09/1998, our translation). As a matter of fact, the fundraising activity of several significant corporations exposed French firms to entrepreneurial action emanating from institutional investor activists aiming at a transformation of particular features of the historical French configuration of corporate governance mechanisms.

Conclusions

This chapter proposes an analytical account of the major historical transformations of the French corporate governance system over the second half of the twentieth century. Two main objectives guided this investigation. Historically, there was a gap in the comparative international literature on corporate governance systems, which much neglected the French case. The latter is of special interest because of several major changes that took place over a relatively short time span. It is thus a particularly relevant case to study the underlying rationale of institutional change. The stylized facts concerning the transformation of corporate France over the last decades seem roughly consistent with D. North's theory of institutional change. Different initiatives to introduce new governance mechanisms into the French setting emanated from so-called organizational entrepreneurs. These entrepreneurs disposed of mental patterns that diverged more or less from traditional business culture and ideology. The latter represented however a serious obstacle to disruptive changes in traditional routines of corporate governance in certain circumstances. So the evolution of the French national corporate governance system, though real it may be, was shown to be highly path dependent.

The analysis indicates that the State was, for a long time, the primary platform for institutional entrepreneurs in France. Private initiative played a relatively less important role. In fact, an institutional innovation was attempted by the CEO of B.S.N., in 1968, but ran into fierce opposition and was consequently abandoned. One of the interesting aspects of the transformation of French capitalism is that the State was at the origin of its own progressive retreat. Hence, the traditionally strong institutional support for the entrepreneurial initiative by members of the State executive having diminished, the field was left open to potentially new types of entrepreneurs. Recently, institutional investors have proved very active on this front, promoting a "philosophy" of corporate governance which aims at enhancing shareholder interests.

Cross-References

▶ Keynesianism: Origins, Principles, and Keynes's Debate with Hayek

References

Aguilera R, Cuervo-Cazurra A (2004) Codes of good governance world-wide: what is the trigger? Organ Stud 25(3):415–443

Aguilera R, Jackson G (2003) The cross-national diversity of corporate governance: dimensions and determinants. Acad Manag Rev 28(3):447–465

Albert M (1991) Capitalisme contre capitalisme. Seuil Points, Paris

Albouy M, Schatt A (2004) Les prises de contrôle par les actionnaires contestataires: le cas André'. Finan Contrôle Strat 7(2):33–65

Alexandre H, Charreaux G (2004) Efficiency of French privatizations: a dynamic vision. J Corp Finan 10:467–494

Aoki M (1994) The Japanese firm as a system of attributes: a survey and research agenda. In: Aoki M, Dore R (eds) The Japanese firm: sources of competitive strength. Oxford University Press, Oxford

Aoki M (2001) Toward a comparative institutional analysis. MIT Press, Boston

Bebchuk L, Roe M (1999) A theory of path dependence in corporate ownership and governance. Stanford Law Rev 52(1):127–170

Berglöf E (1997) Reforming corporate governance: redirecting the European agenda. Econ Policy 12(24):92–123

Bertin-Mourot B, Bauer M (1996) Vers un modèle européen de dirigeants? Une comparaison Allemagne/France/Grande-Bretagne. Probl Écon 2482:18–26

Charreaux G (1997) Vers une théorie du gouvernement des entreprises. In: Charreaux G (ed) Le gouvernement des entreprises. Economica, Paris, pp 421–469

Conseil National du Crédit et du Titre (1999) Le financement de l'entreprise. CNCT, Paris

Daily C, Dalton D, Cannella A (2003) Corporate governance: decades of dialogue and data. Acad Manag Rev 28(3):371–382

Denzau A, North D (1994) Shared mental models: ideologies and institutions. Kyklos 47:3–31

Fauroux R (1998) Etats de service. Hachette Littératures, Paris

Franks J, Mayer C (1990) Capital markets and corporate control: a study of France, Germany and the UK. Econ Policy 10:191–231

Gomez P-Y, Wirtz P (2018) Successfully mobilizing for employee board representation: lessons to be learned from post-war Germany. J Manag Hist 24(3):262–281. https://doi.org/10.1108/JMH-08-2017-0039

Guillén M (2000) Corporate governance and globalization: is there convergence across countries? Adv Comp Int Manag 13:175–204

Hall P, Soskice D (2001) Varieties of capitalism: the institutional foundations of comparative advantage. Oxford University Press, Oxford

Hirigoyen G (1994) Brève histoire de l'O.P.A. de B.S.N. sur Saint-Gobain (décembre 1968- janvier 1969). In: De Jacques Coeur à Renault. Gestionnaires et organisations, 3ème rencontres des 25 et 26 novembre 1994. Collection Histoire, Gestion, Organisations 3. Presses de l'Université des Sciences Sociales, Toulouse, pp 369–391

Jensen M (1993) The modern industrial revolution, exit, and the failure of internal control systems. J Financ XLVIII(3):831–880

La Porta R, Lopez-de-Silanes F, Shleifer A (1999) Corporate ownership around the world. J Financ LIV(2):471–517

Lazonick W, O'Sullivan M (1997) Finance and industrial development. Part I: the United States and the United Kingdom. Finan Hist Rev 4:7–29

Le Monde (06/27 and 06/28/1999) Forcing de la Banque de France pour un accord entre la BNP, SG et Paribas

Les Echos (11/16–11/21/1998) L'exception française. special inquiry

Les Echos (12/07–12/10/1998) Le planisphère. special inquiry on cross-shareholdings

Les Echos (07/01/1999) Une nouvelle époque

Lesourne J (1998) Le modèle français, grandeur et décadence. Odile Jacob, Paris

Mayer M, Whittington R (1999) Strategy, structure and 'systemness': national institutions and corporate change in France, Germany and the UK, 1950–1993. Organ Stud 20(6):933–959

Moerland P (1995) Alternative disciplinary mechanisms in different corporate systems. J Econ Behav Organ 26:17–34

North D (1990) Institutions, institutional change and economic performance. Cambridge University Press, Cambridge

North D (1993) Five propositions about institutional change. Working paper. Center for the Study of Political Economy, Washington University, St. Louis

Peyrelevade J (1998) Le corporate governance ou les fondements incertains d'un nouveau pouvoir. Notes de la Fondation Saint-Simon, Paris

Porter M (1992) Capital disadvantage: America's failing capital investment system. Harv Bus Rev 70:65–82

Riboud A (1999) Le dernier de la classe. Grasset, Paris

Schmidt V (1996) From state to market? The transformation of French business and government. Cambridge University Press, Cambridge

Schneper W, Guillén M (2002) Stakeholder rights and corporate governance: a cross-national study of hostile takeovers. Working paper. The Wharton School, Philadelphia

Shleifer A, Vishny R (1997) A survey of corporate governance. J Financ 52:737–783

Simon H (1982) From substantive to procedural rationality. In: Simon HA (ed) Models of bounded rationality, vol. 2: Behavioral economics and business organization. MIT Press, Cambridge, MA, pp 129–148

Simon H (1983) Reason in human affairs. Stanford University Press, Stanford

Viénot M (1995) Le conseil d'administration des sociétés cotées. CNPF-AFEP, Paris

Wirtz P (2001) Financial policy, managerial discretion and corporate governance: the example of Usinor. Glob Focus 13(1):127–141

Wirtz P (2008) Les meilleures pratiques de gouvernance d'entreprise. La Découverte, Paris

Yoshimori M (1995) Whose company is it? The concept of the corporation in Japan and the west. Long Range Plan 28(4):33–44

Flexicurity: The Danish Model

51

Jørgen Burchardt

Contents

Introduction	1164
The History of the Danish Model	1164
The Flexible Labor Market	1169
Income Security	1170
The Third Leg: Active Labor Market Policy	1171
Three Meanings of the Word *Flexicurity*	1172
Flexicurity in Different Countries	1173
Flexicurity Became EU Policy	1175
Is the Danish Model Under Liquidation?	1177
Summary	1180
References	1181

Abstract

The Danish labor market system is often referred to as the Danish Model. It is an example of *flexicurity*, a term that combines the words security and flexibility.

This system boasts of more than 100 years of history, and it is one of the preconditions for the rich Danish welfare state, which has a generally high income based on rather small but adaptable firms. The basis for this system is the collective agreements established through negotiation with a "balance of compromise" accepted by both employers and employees. The state normally does not interfere in the negotiations.

The well-functioning Danish Model has many similarities with the systems in the other Nordic countries. The word *flexicurity* was first used in the Netherlands

---

J. Burchardt (✉)
Museum Vestfyn, Assens, Denmark
e-mail: jorgen.burchardt@mail.dk

in the mid-1990s to refer to political initiatives. Flexicurity inspired by the Danish Model became official EU policy incorporated into the European Employment Strategy in 2007, and it has since become a political initiative promoted in different plans and closely monitored.

Policy is probably not transferable from one country to another. The Danish society is a sizeable welfare state with high taxes and social benefits, but the Danish Model is itself under pressure from both internal and external forces during a time of rapid globalization and international competition. Regardless, the Danish labor market and government policy still effectively balance both employers' and employees' interests. The Danish Model is still alive.

Keywords

Flexicurity · Denmark · Labor market · Danish Model · Income security · Active labor market policy

Introduction

The Danish labor market system is considered a well-functioning arrangement and is often referred to as the Danish Model. It is often cited in the literature as an exemplary model of flexibility plus security, or flexicurity. The Organisation for Economic Co-operation and Development (OECD) highlighted the model in 2004, and the European Commission officially made it a part of the European Employment Strategy in 2007.

The basis for this system is the collective agreements established through negotiation with a "balance of compromise" that is accepted by both employers and employees. This article discusses the formation of this long-lived relationship and the recent state. It is compared to the situation in other countries and to political efforts to export the system to other countries. The system itself is under pressure, and its future development concludes the discussion.

The History of the Danish Model

The young American economist Walter Galenson worked as a labor attaché at the American embassy in Denmark just after World War II. He was fascinated by the Nordic method of handling the labor market, which led him to research how it functioned. His study was published in 1952 in the book "The Danish System of Labor Relations. A Study in Industrial Peace" (Galenson 1952). He observed a relatively harmonious relationship between the trade unions and employer associations. Both parties handled most labor market regulations without governmental regulation. The few conflicts that did occur were small and resolved in a controlled way.

Research on the Danish system (or the Danish Model as it later was called) was still a rather understudied field until the publication of "The survival of the Danish Model. A historical sociological analysis of the Danish system of collective bargaining" (Due et al. 1994), which was one of the many studies performed by the Employment Relations Research Centre (FAOS) in the Department of Sociology at the University of Copenhagen. A similarly productive national center was established to study the Danish Model at Aalborg University in the CARMA (Centre for Labor Market Research).

The Danish Model was the outcome of numerous historical developments (Due et al. 1994; Jensen 2017a, b; Knudsen and Lind 2018; Kristiansen 2015a, b; Larsen and Ilsøe 2016; Madsen 2008; Scheuer 2007). It was not a result of a preconceived overall plan but was instead the product of different political elements established in different situations over time. Once implemented, an element had a strong aspect of path dependency during later development. Over the years, the parties have cultivated mutual trust and respect such that the bargaining model has been solidified as a joint ideology for more than 100 years (Dunlop 1959). All Danish governments on the left and right have accepted this ideology.

A low level of employment protection was established in 1899 after a long period of worker strikes. It ended in negotiations between the two main organizations – the Confederation of Danish Employers (Dansk Arbejdsgiverforening – DA) and the Danish Confederation of Trade Unions (De samvirkende Fagforbund – later LO, now FH). After a rather peaceful process, the Danish workers' unions accepted the employers' right to freely hire and fire in the so-called September Agreement. Employers had the right to manage and distribute work. In return, the employers recognized the unions' right to organize and to be the representative counterpart in collective agreements on behalf of the unions' members. With this compromise, the Danish employers were among the first to accept trade unions and negotiations for collective agreements. This step was important for workers. Previously, employees could be criminally liable for taking part in collective actions. However, with this new agreement, collective actions were allowed in certain situations.

The Danish labor market is characterized by a high level of self-management by social partners. The government followed the September Agreement with legislation (Kristiansen 2015b). A joint commission consisting of representatives from the two areas of industry was established in 1908 on an initiative from the government. Two years later, the government decided to establish the Labor Court Act and Mediation Act. Both instruments enable the labor market to solve problems themselves. Through the rules of the Mediation Act, "neutral" mediators can take care of compromises in collective bargaining rounds. "Conflicts of rights" can be solved by the labor court by judges appointed by the organizations themselves and with a legal judge appointed by the government. It has become a special court with high decision-making authority and without the possibility of appeal.

The development has experienced a periodization based on the degree of centralization in negotiations after the current rules for collective bargaining were introduced in 1934. Until 1950, national bargaining was decentralized by trade through the next period in 1979 by national agreements between the two national organizations for employers and employees. A third period from 1981 to 1991 shifted back to a trade-by-trade bargaining, while the structure of both national organizations progressed. Within a few years, the number of bargaining agreements fell from 650 to 20–25. Currently, most negotiations are local and are performed under a national frame called an *organized/centralized decentralization.*

To help make agreements, a state mediation body was established 1910 called the Conciliation Board, which has extended competencies that enable the parties to renew collective agreements. Through this approach, a rather strong centralized system of collective bargaining was established. An arbitrator was allowed to intervene in conflicts if he or she judged a conflict to have negative consequences nationwide. The arbitrator could send suggestions for a ballot. It has become possible to send suggestions in packets with several areas of the labor market together, and the majority can decide and overrule single areas.

This framework established the labor market's basic structure. In many ways, it is an unusually and internationally unknown system with its detailed rules for intervening in the parties' actions. As a result, the Danish state expanded legal control of the labor market at a time when the general attitude was that a state should not interfere in economic and social life. Relatively few areas of working life were covered by law compared to other countries. Even many International Labour Organization (ILO) conventions concerning working life issues were not ratified as, for example, the 1919 convention regarding the 48-hour work week.

The September Compromise existed until 1960 when it was replaced by a new compromise, the Main Agreement. One new element was a rule pertaining to the dismissal of an employee. The agreement established that a dismissal should be reasonably justified either by the circumstances associated with the employee or the employer.

The pragmatic solution was now a "mirror image" of the dominant political situation in the Social Democratic labor movement in which the political party in parliament accepted the market economy and capitalism (Jensen 2017b). Politics concerned "politics along the market" to secure better living conditions by improving market function. The trade union movement was very closely connected to the dominant Social Democratic party. Except in the years after each of the two World Wars was the ideological rivalry very weak, and the labor movement performed to a large degree as a unified whole. The majority of unions in 1898 joined the national labor organization. This organization had representatives in the Social Democratic party, and the party had representatives in the labor organization executive committee.

The trade unions have traditionally displayed a high degree of unionization. Most trade unions have been organized along craft principles together with two unions for unskilled workers. Craft unionism can position union members in the labor market better than trade unions based on principles of geography to be general or divided after industrial area. In particular, over their history, crafts have developed traditions in the guild-based production system to help unemployed peers and prevent them from experiencing decreasing wage levels. The craft unions became forerunners in the formation of union-run unemployment funds. The first funds emerged in the

1880s, and in 1905, 32% of all union members were covered by union-run unemployment funds. Since 1907, the state supported those funds. The voluntary system was chosen because it was cheaper for the state to have income from insured persons. The system, which was called a "Ghent system" after the Belgian city, has only been established in a few countries. Besides Denmark and Belgium, the system is only operating in Sweden and Finland (Lind 2009).

The trade unions have, in general, been pragmatic and cooperative (Knudsen and Lind 2012b). In reality, the important unions have never been split into religious or political parties. In 2018, the union of Christians (KRIFA) had only 135,000 members out of almost 3 million workers, and it had never influenced collective agreements. In 1995, the tight connection between the Labor Organization and the Social Democratic party was formally halted. During those years, new non-political, or "yellow," unions came on the scene. The majority of workers were still members of trade unions, which gave them the ability to be a powerful negotiating body against employers.

In the 1960s and 1970s, the unemployment insurance system was improved. During years of increased unemployment, the government raised the benefits to 90% of former wages up to a maximum. This improvement was paid by the state. A number of conditions must have been satisfied for the workers to get unemployment benefits, but since 1979, they have gradually tightened. The length of the period receiving benefits was gradually shortened from 9 years in 1994 to 2 years in 2011.

Workers have received a high level of representation and participation in decision-making in the workplace. Shop stewards as the representatives of the local trade union appeared in 1900 in agreements for the iron industry, and they later spread to all other sectors (Knudsen 1995). Their role is to represent the interests of the employees and the union locally and to "do his best to further good and smooth co-operation in the shop."

Another institution involved in decision-making is cooperation committees. They are joint management-employee bodies established in larger workplaces to discuss "management issues." In the seats are shop stewards and representatives of employees without a shop steward. This institution has existed since 1947 after an agreement between the Labor Organization and the Danish Employers' organization. Since then, the rest of the labor market has followed suit, including the public sector.

A third institution in the local cooperation is the health and safety committees for workplaces. They are organized under the auspices of governmental laws made after intense negotiations with the members of the labor market. They play a role in discussing and monitoring conditions relating to safety and health. The representative from the employees is a type of shop steward and has job security.

The company boards are the first institution permitting employees' involvement. In public limited companies, they elect representatives to one-third of the seats on the boards according an act established in 1973.

There has never been an official minimum wage enacted by the government. A wage level is negotiated between the labor markets themselves. In general, the government is neutral with regard to wage negotiations except in cases of unsolved conflicts that threaten the economy.

An active labor market policy was a new issue for the Danish Model as a result of major reforms during the 1960s. Inspired by the Swedish Rehn-Meidner model (Hedborg and Meidner 1984), reforms were implemented with a slightly lighter touch. The aim was to improve qualification flexibility, especially for reforms relating to the education and training of workers (Fig. 1).

The previously mentioned advantages of the labor market need to be viewed in connection with the development of the welfare state, which is thanks to "welfare capitalism" as a result of an efficient economy and an equity outcome (Esping-Andersen 1989). However, the welfare state is not only the result of the labor market, but it emerges in parallel with the rise of a modern state bureaucracy.

Another reform was the move of the Labor Exchange away from the municipalities and trade union-controlled unemployment funds to the hands of a central governmental body in the middle of the 1970s. The unions lost their control of the local labor market, but the reform was combined with increased financing of the unemployment funds by the state. In the 2000s, the Labor Exchange was returned to the municipalities.

The policy around 1970 touted full employment as an official goal, and macroeconomic policies inspired by Keynes to regulate the market economy were believed to be responsible for unemployment. Training and retraining became an instrument during the 1980s. This scheme became a duty in the 1990s, and since 2000, this has become a means to encourage the unemployed to find jobs.

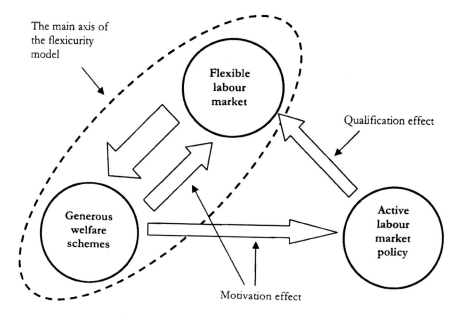

Fig. 1 The Danish flexicurity model. The two most important axles in the model are at the left, but a third leg at right is added to shape the "golden" triangle with the active labor market policy (Madsen 2007, 66)

As with all models, the reality is more complex. This is the case with the Danish Model. Some researchers have discussed whether there is more than one Danish Model. The mostly researched model is a blue-collar flexicurity model for primary skilled and unskilled workers. Another model could be considered a white-collar flexicurity model covering the primarily employees with midrange or high-range education and qualifications (Jensen 2011).

The Flexible Labor Market

The employment flexibility index for EU and OECD countries ranks Denmark first in flexibility with an overall score of 96.9% (Table 1; Lithuanian Free Market Institute (pub) 2018). The United States and Japan are the closest competitors in the overall ranking with a score on 92.4% and 91%, respectively. The index constitutes four subindexes: hiring received a score of 100 because of the lack of restrictions or limits on the duration of fixed-term contracts, in addition to the existence of no governmental rules regarding a mandatory minimum wage. The subindex for redundancy rules likewise provided a score of 100 because redundancy dismissals are allowed by law and there are no restrictions on redundancies. The redundancy costs also gave a score of 100 because of the lack of a statutory notice period or statutory severance pay in cases of redundancies for normal workers. Only the subindex for working hours scored 87.5. Despite a mandatory 25 working days paid annual leave, the score reduction was the result of no restrictions and no

Table 1 Employment Flexibility Index 2019. Selected countries from the index. (Lithuanian Free Market Institute 2018, 6).

Denmark	96.9
United States	92.4
Japan	91.0
United Kingdom	83.2
Canada	82.6
Switzerland	79.0
Italy	74.3
Australia	71.6
Belgium	68.2
Germany	63.5
Spain	60.8
Sweden	57.7
Poland	57.5
Netherlands	56.5
Greece	50.6
Korea. Rep.	46.2
Mexico	45.1
France	38.4

premiums for night work, overtime, or work on a weekly holiday (at least not regulated by the state).

Such indices need to be considered with healthy skepticism, although the data have been collected by the World Bank with a case assumption to ensure comparability across economies over time. Flexibility is assessed in light of an assumption regarding the situation for a typical worker who is 19 years old, has 1 year of work experience, is employed full time, and the business is a supermarket with 60 employees.

In general, job security in the Danish labor market is low (Knudsen and Lind 2018). The research literature refers to this as "numerical flexibility." Legislation pertaining to job security only exists for salaried employees ("white collar workers"). Since 1937, these workers have benefited for a period of up to 6 months in cases of dismissal after the first month of employment. Otherwise, other workers' job security is entirely regulated through collective bargaining.

At the end of 2010, an agreement on notice periods was established that sets a protection after 6 months of employment for 14 days. The notice period goes up to 90 days after 9 years of employment. Only workers older than 50 years get a longer notification period of up to 120 days after 12 years of employment.

In spite of the general trend for employers to hire and fire, most workers have a local agreement for relatively long termination notice. Around 64% of employees are covered for a rather long notice of 3–6 months (Andersen et al. 2011; Scheuer 2009).

Work time flexibility is significant, too. This has been the case since the 1990s, and work time flexibility is often negotiated at the local workplace. The typical 37-hour work week can be adjusted over a year.

The costs for employers when they reduce their workforce are rather low. When workers are dismissed and unemployed after 3 years of service (and have right to unemployment benefits), they receive severance pay. The amount is doubled after 6 years of employment and tripled after 8 years of employment. However, severance pay will never exceed 3 months of wages. In the case of an unfair dismissal, the employer must pay compensation during the notice period equal to the wage that should have been paid.

The most flexible agreements on notices are in sectors often hit by cyclical declines, such as in the construction business. In contrast, the industry often does not want to dismiss employees, but instead keep them through reduced working time or other solutions. Thus, the employers do not risk giving new employees expensive training.

Income Security

The Danish Model provides security for employment, rather than job security. As mentioned, there is little employment protection at specific workplaces, but income security eases job changes.

The majorities of workers are member of an unemployment fund (around 70% in 2019) and pay around €67 per month for the insurance. In the event of unemployment, the central government administers the system as later explained in the chapter on active labor market policy (Beyer et al. 2017). After a membership period of

12 months and with employment of 1924 hours within the last 3 years, a member can obtain up to 90% of his or her previous wage with a maximum of around €30,000 per year after 2 years of employment.

Higher paid workers have a lower rate of benefit because of the maximum benefit. An engineer may receive compensation of less than 40% of his or her previous wage, and a male skilled worker may receive only 55% (Andersen et al. 2011). This is not higher than that in the rest of Europe. Nevertheless, when Danish wage earners generally have not been nervous about losing their jobs, it is less about the amount of unemployment benefits, but rather that Denmark has had very low unemployment over a number of years. The ability to get into new employment quickly has encouraged employees' acceptance of the Danish Model.

For noninsured persons, municipalities are administering active programs and can provide cash benefits in some circumstances. A receiver must have been living in Denmark for 7 of the last 8 years and must be willing to accept a job. The duration of the cash benefit is not limited, but the receiver has to accept offers from the municipality to participate in active programs. The amount is calculated based on the individual's family situation with no help in case of equity in a house or if the spouse has a high income. For a single person over 30 years of age, the benefit is around €67 per day.

The Third Leg: Active Labor Market Policy

According to the OECD (2018), Denmark has the largest spending in the world on active labor market policy (Table 2). Although the publisher mentions uncertainty of this statistic, Denmark is certainly ranked among the countries that have the largest expenditure, if not the largest.

The structure of the labor market in the new millennium is at a high level of transition, and there are four key challenges (Andersen et al. 2015). There are changes related to the international division of labor, the introduction of new technologies with their new organizations of work, demographic changes, and the climate agenda. Thus, there is a risk of the future labor market lacking skilled labor while at the same time over-exploiting labor with limited competencies. Structural changes have created new challenges with regard to education and employment policies. High labor mobility and a flexible educational system directly supported by government policies may be crucial for both competitiveness and future prosperity.

The Employment Service is central to this policy. From the first day of unemployment, a worker must be registered at the local job center to obtain the benefit (Nordic Council of Ministers 2010). To receive benefits, the person needs to be actively job seeking. A curriculum vitae must be entered into a nationwide job bank on the Internet operated by the National Labour Market Authority, and active support in job seeking is offered.

The main programs include job training with a wage subsidy, implying that the unemployed person is paid a normal wage from a public or private employer for a limited time period up to 1 year. Less technically specialized groups of unemployed

Table 2 Public expenditure and participant stocks in labor market programmes 2016. Selected OECD countries. Percentage of GDP. (Source: OECD 2018, 293).

	Total	Active programmes
Denmark	3.22	2.07
Sweden	1.73	1.17
Finland	2.84	0.99
Hungary	1.18	0.94
Austria	2.29	0.77
Belgium	2.31	0.73
Netherlands	2.40	0.72
Germany	1.45	0.63
Switzerland	1.33	0.62
OECD	1.31	0.54
Norway	1.06	0.53
Portugal	1.68	0.48
Poland	0.69	0.45
Canada	0.90	0.25
Australia	0.89	0.24
Japan	0.30	0.14
United States	0.27	0.11
Mexico	0.01	0.01

people receive special job training, which typically include special projects in the public sector. A wide range of educational and labor market training for up to 1 year is offered. Special groups, such as immigrants or older workers, are targeted through special programs. All unemployed individuals are offered mandatory counselling, including assistance with job search activities.

The active programs benefit about 70,000 people per year in a workforce of about 3 million. In addition, around 63,000 participants have the so-called flexi-jobs (2015), which are jobs with a permanent wage subsidy for persons with persistently reduced work capacity.

In a business cycle downturn, the unemployment insurance system will stabilize domestic demand (Madsen 2005; Jørgensen and Klindt 2018). In business cycle upturns, employers hire new employees. In a normal liberal economy, companies can hire and fire at low cost and have no incentives to improve wage earners' skills. This behavior risks inefficiencies, skills shortages, and inflation. The job of improving skills has been taken over by the state through various active labor market initiatives. As a result, a bottleneck in the labor market is prevented.

Three Meanings of the Word *Flexicurity*

The word *flexicurity* is a rather new and commonly used concept. The word has at least three different meanings.

The word was coined in the Netherlands where a system had developed based on corporatist principles (Visser and Hemerijck 1997). Flexicurity was first used by the Dutch sociologist Hans Adriaansen in the mid-1990s in speeches and interviews to address a phenomenon in which political parties discuss policy issues relating to reforms of the labor market (Oorschot 2004; Wilthagen 1998). The word was simultaneously used at the political level by the Danish social democratic Prime Minister Poul Nyrup Rasmussen in the 1990s (Flaschel and Greiner 2012).

One common definition of flexicurity is as follows:

> a policy strategy that attempts, synchronically and in a deliberate way, to enhance the flexibility of labor markets, the work organization, and labor relations on the one hand, and to enhance security – employment security and social security – notably for weaker groups in and outside the labor market on the other hand. (Wilthagen and Tros 2004, 4)

Thus, flexicurity is defined here as a coordinated policy strategy.

The OECD deemed the Danish Model to be a flexicurity system. After many years with the critique of high Danish unemployment compensation, the OECD changed its opinion. The low unemployment rate in Denmark compared to most other European countries was remarkable. "Overall, the Danish model of 'flexicurity' has proved to be rather effective in guaranteeing sufficient dynamism in the labor market," and the report praised the Danish flexicurity system as a "result of a long series of reforms started in 1994" (OECD 2004, 98).

The definition does not fit with the Danish Model because the Danish labor market developed over the years without any overarching strategy. It only describes the situation relating to the labor market. For this, the following definition is more appropriate:

> Flexibility is understood here in economic terms as the degree to which the labor market is capable of creating opportunities for employers and employees to meet their demands for qualified workers and jobs. (Muffels and Luijkx 2008, 223)

For many researchers, flexicurity has become a useful analytical tool in the discussion of labor market issues. As such, flexicurity can also be defined as follows:

> An analytical frame that can be used to analyze developments in flexibility and security and compare national labor market systems. (Madsen 2007, 60)

Flexicurity in Different Countries

The labor market models the world differently in numerous aspects. As shown in Fig. 2, European nations can be placed on a graph showing the location of welfare regimes in the theoretical relationship between flexibility and income/employment security. Muffels and Luijkx (2008) conclude: "Europe demonstrates 'unity in diversity,' showing that there is not one world of welfare, but many." To illustrate

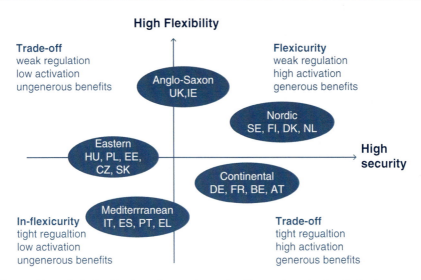

Fig. 2 Theoretical classification of countries and policy regimes in the flexicurity context. European countries. (From Nardo and Rossetti 2013, 21; modified version from Muffels and Luijkx 2008, 225)

some of the dimensions, they have mapped four different archetypes. Later, Nardo and Rossetti (2013, 239) expanded the figure to include the extra regime type from Eastern Europe. According to this graph, the Nordic countries, Denmark, Sweden, and Finland, together with the Netherlands, are characterized by high flexibility and security, but with some differences. Norway and Sweden differ in terms of their strict employment protection legislation, while Finland and Norway have less generous unemployment benefits. In fact, Finland spends the least on active labor market programs.

Is the placement of the Netherlands among the Nordic flexicurity countries correct? Compared to the Danish Model, the Dutch flexicurity model has a narrower focus on normalizing atypical work (Bekker and Mailand 2018). It is a different situation for Denmark versus the Netherlands. While the temporary employees as a percentage of the total employees has experienced a slight decline between 2007 and 2014 in Denmark to 8.6%, the percentage of the total employees in the Netherlands has increased to 21.1%.

The Dutch labor law did not consider temporary agency workers or people with a contract for a definite period. This was the background for reforms where persons with a permanent contract should be more flexible, and those already flexible should have more security (Pennings 2018).

A supplemental model to describe the combination of flexibility and security in different flexicurity regimes suggests "distinguishing between internal and external dimensions of flexibility and security, and arriv[ing] at two ideal models of either internal or external flexicurity" (Bredgaard et al. 2008). According to this model, the Danish Model is close to the external archetype, while the Japanese system with an internal flexibility and security is close to the other type. In the Japanese system, dismissals are the last solution after relocation, wage reduction, and reduction in working hours have been implemented. The German system is similar to the internal model, and Sweden is similar to the external model.

Flexicurity Became EU Policy

The concept of flexicurity slowly took hold in the EU. In 1997, the Commission's Green Paper, "Partnership for a new Organization of Work" stated that "the key issue for employees, management,...social partners, and policy-makers alike is to strike the right balance between flexibility and security...It is the achievement of this balance between flexibility and security [that] is at the heart of the partnership for a new organization of work" (European Commission 1997, 12).

Eight years later, the concept became official policy. The Council of Ministers approved a suggestion in the "Integrated guidelines for growth and jobs (2005–2008)" in which point 20 under "Employment guidelines" was "Promote flexibility combined with employment security and reduce labour market segmentation" (Press release 12 April 2005, MEMO/05/123). This principle came into the revised version of the Lisbon Agenda, and the principles were reaffirmed within the EU 2020 strategy (Nardo and Rossetti 2013; Tangian 2011). The plan was described as being modern, likely because of its emphasis on a broad array of social protections and helps to combine work with private life and family responsibilities.

In the same way, it is a political target for EU to create more and better jobs, modernize labor markets, and promote good work. Even flexicurity is a principle of employment policy, and the EU looks at flexicurity as having a scope far beyond the strict confines of employment policy and the labor market, arguing in a commission report that "[i]f we wish to encourage flexicure transitions in the broadest sense of the word, we will need to investigate other economic and social effects" (Rodriguez et al. 2010, 21).

This kind of policy is generally only implemented as a recommendation by the EU. The institution has no power to force a policy at a national level, but the EU follows up with the member states and suggests some ways to implement the concept. A one-size-fits-all approach is not possible for all countries. One recommendation from the EU has been a minimum wage system. In 2019, six of the 28 member states did not have a minimum wage regulated through national legislation, which included Denmark.

The EU policy with regard to the Danish Model has been criticized as well. It is called "a Political Celebrity" (Jørgensen and Madsen 2007, 8) and described as follows:

> There is something in it for everybody. We will have a world inhabited of wage earners, who feel economically secure, and of satisfied employers with a high degree of flexibility in hiring, firing, and allocating their workforce. For society as a whole, growth and prosperity will be the expected outcome of a more dynamic and flexible labour market. The politician

who is able to put forward and implement such a win-win strategy should be up for a guaranteed re-election.

The European rules address conflicting considerations. For instance, in a conflict, do the three European courts necessarily take the same approach? In 2015, a report from the Nordic Council of Ministers provided an analysis of the complex interaction between Nordic and European labor laws. The EU had, through the consequence of a steadily more complicated legislation system, regulated wages in the financial sector and influenced wage conditions (e.g., for migrating workers, posted workers, part-time workers, and fixed-term workers) (Kristensen 2015).

In a comprehensive book published the same year, Kristensen deepens the discussion of the European challenge to the Danish Model. He finds it paradoxical that the Danish state plays a very active role in adopting, implementing, and applying labor law directives in contradiction to its historically less prominent role (Kristensen 2015a).

For the multidimensional flexicurity concept, the Flexicurity Matrix developed by Wilthagen and Tros (2004) (Fig. 3) has been widely used in EU publications and research. Policy is monitored through indicators collected mainly by the OECD and Eurostat in order to understand the ongoing transition of the area.

According to this monitoring, there are considered to be four types of flexibility. The *external numerical flexibility* refers to the management's possibility to vary the amount of labor even in response to short-term changes in demand (Pacelli et al. 2008). The *internal numerical flexibility* relates to the possibility of changing the number of workers by varying the patterns of working hours. *Functional flexibility* concerns the possibility of quickly redeploying employees to other tasks and

Flexibility/Security	Job security	Employment security	Income security	Combination security
External numerical flexibility	- Types of employment contracts - Employment protection legislation (EPL) - Early retirement	- Employment services / active labour market policies (ALMP) - Training / lifelong learning	- Unemployment compensation - Other social benefits - Minimum wages	- Protection against dismissal during various leave schemes
Internal numerical flexibility	- Shortened work weeks / part-time working arrangements	- EPL - Training / lifelong learning	- Part-time supplementary benefit - Study grants - Sickness benefit	- Different types of leave schemes - Part-time pension
Functional flexibility	- Job enrichment - Training - Labour leasing - Subcontracting - Outsourcing	- Training / lifelong learning - Job rotation - Teamwork - Multiskilling	- Performance-related pay systems	- Voluntary working time arrangements
Labour cost/wage flexibility	- Local adjustments in labour costs - Scaling or reductions in social security payments	- Changes in social security payments - Employment subsidies - In-work benefits	- Collective wage agreements - Adjusted benefit for shortened working week	- Voluntary working time arrangements

Fig. 3 Flexicurity matrix. Four types of flexibility and four different forms of security are combined in a matrix in order to illustrate the broad range of policy tools available to policymakers. (Wilthagen and Tros 2004; source: Pacelli et al. 2008, 7)

activities, while *financial flexibility* enables employers to alter standardized pay structures, including reward systems

Four forms of security can be classified. *Job security* concerns the expectation of high job tenure in relation to a specific job, while *employment security* takes the degree of certainty of a worker to remain in work into account. *Income security* relates to the protection of income in case of such occurrences as unemployment or maternity, and *combination security* is associated with the possibility of combining paid work with an employee's private life and social responsibilities.

Policy is probably not transferable from one country to another. The Danish society is a sizeable welfare state with high taxes and social benefits (Madsen 2007). The dynamic and well-functioning labor market is indirectly supported by a well-developed childcare system, a well-functioning and publicly financed health-care system, and so on. The employment of women is 73% in 2018 compared to the OECD average of 61% (OECD data). Transferring elements of labor market policy to a low-tax country has no guarantee of success. As emphasized in a central article about the Danish Model (Madsen 2005, 35), "[t]he model is thus a prime example of the specific Danish version of the negotiated economy. Therefore, it should be taken as a source of inspiration for new ideas about alternative configurations of flexible labour markets and economic security for the individual – not as a simple scheme, which is ready for immediate export."

The economic crisis of 2008 influenced the political process associated with the implementation of the European flexicurity policy, and a "farewell to flexicurity" was announced with a reduction in the security component of flexicurity (Hastings and Heyes 2016). Some weakening happened from the initially strong focus on the transition from job security to employment security, in addition to the divisions between insiders and outsiders in the labor market (Mailand 2010). Recent research has resulted in a revitalization of the policy (Bekker 2018), and although the EU-level concept changes every year, it still encompasses a growing number of flexicurity issues (Bekker and Mailand 2018).

Is the Danish Model Under Liquidation?

One researcher found it paradoxical that the Danish Model was recognized in the 1990s and became conceptualized and discursivated as a flexicurity policy when many of the individual building blocks of the Danish Model had deteriorated over the previous years (Jensen 2017a). Jensen explains it by the "employment miracle" from 1993 to 2001 in which unemployment declined from more than 12% to about 5% in parallel with low inflation, low levels of inequality, and a well-developed social dialogue. Most people looked at the flexicurity system, and the system became famous as "an export article." In reality he mentions other factors contributed to the decline of unemployment, for example, the substantial income from the North Sea oil fields.

The Danish system is affected by both internal and external forces. Some researchers argue that the system is under pressure (Lind and Knudsen 2018).

Internally, collective bargaining is more decentralized than ever. Therefore, a solidarity principle cannot be proposed using the same rules and standards nationwide, and the wage levels are more dependent on the market and business cycle. Decentralization started in the early 1980s and was radically changed in the early 1990s to allow more bargaining at the individual's workplace. Wages negotiated at the national level have since become minimum standards, and they are supplemented by agreements from local negotiations.

In the past two decades, decentralization has been introduced to deliver good employment performance, better productivity outcomes, and higher wages for the covered workers. Such local agreements could erode general agreements without coordination within and across sectors. This is not the case, at least for now. A recent study showed that in comparison to the decentralization of collective bargaining in Germany, the Netherlands, and Denmark, the Danish system leaves scope for local bargaining even when the minimum wage levels are generally observed and bargaining coverage has not suffered (Ibsen and Keune 2018; OECD 2018).

A central issue is how employer and employee interests are balanced within the system. As Knudsen and Lind (2018) emphasize, how are rights, privileges, and financial gains distributed between the parties, and how does the balance change over time? Many variables have influenced the distribution of power between employers and workers under changing business cycles.

Trade unions have lost power because the membership rate decreases, which is caused by several factors. One is governmental initiatives through a weakening of the unemployment insurance system. Trade unions have lost their monopoly on insurance funds, and private actors subsequently entered the market. This erodes membership share in trade unions (Lind 2009).

There have always been job sectors without a high level of union organization, such as hotels, restaurants, and shops. Central areas still have a high percentage of organization in both unions and organizations for employers (Larsen and Ilsøe 2016). In 2012, around 53% of employers were members of an employers' association (almost all the large companies). However, 84% of the labor market should be covered by a contract with 74% for the private market alone.

Another variable is the decline of benefits related to unemployment compensation. Since the 1980s, the system has been weakened several times. Coverage is not as high as it once was. Moreover, the time permitted for financial support has been shortened. When union-administered funds are reduced, the unions themselves are weakened. The compensation rate has, as mentioned, dropped from 80% in the 1970s to around 50% in the 2010s.

Active labor market policy has changed in another way in relation to the unemployed. Since a reform in 1993, the focus has shifted from the demand side to supply side such that unemployment benefits have been reduced to increase the interest for the unemployed to seek jobs.

The increasing internationalization placed pressure on the system for the internationalization of firms, resulting in foreign firms coming to Denmark with another culture and background for handling agreements. At the same time, many foreign workers have gone to Denmark from other EU countries and from abroad. For instance, IBM has never made agreements with unions. Many of these firms do not have the same attitude toward the traditions related to the labor market of native Danish workers (Larsen and Ilsøe 2016).

The Danish system is under pressure as a result of interference by foreign policy-makers. Since the EU system declared the "Community Charter of the Fundamental Social Rights of Workers," a platform for political initiatives was established. An EU policy for helping countries with a low organization share of the labor is necessary because of the weak labor unions in many countries. The strong unions in Denmark are indirectly affected by this interference (Kristiansen 2015a; Sørensen 2006).

Concurrently, there is pressure from ILO, which has established conventions for freedom related to organization and agreements, and the European Convention on Human Rights to demand judicial decisions by public courts.

The development could make the flexicurity system dramatically less relevant due to changes in class (Jensen 2017a). Because the unemployment benefit is a flat-rate system primarily for blue-collar workers, and with a decline in the number of workers in this group, flexicurity is far from an all-encompassing model. In addition, the system does not secure low-educated people suffering from longstanding illness (Heggebø 2016).

Since 1980s, there has been a change in the dominant political ideology relating to welfare and market ideology in Denmark (Jørgensen and Klindt 2018; Knudsen and Lind 2018; Larsen and Ilsøe 2016; Lind and Knudsen 2018). The interests of employers have been favored, while the interests of labor have been neglected. The last issue is "social dumping," which is thanks to a strengthening of market forces and EU regulations that favor the free movement of labor. Although Lind and Knudsen (2018, 598) conclude:

> [i]n spite of the changes in the favor of capital, the Danish development has also been one of the continuities. The national institutions regulating [the] labor market and working life are still strong and encompassing. The class compromise founded in 1899, although reformed and changed in many respects over the years, is still in force. Strong corporatist features are still present, although increasingly encroached by market forces. Danish industrial relations are still distinctly different from liberalist as well as legalistic models.

While impairment in the active labor market polity related to reducing the corporatist elements occurred in the 2000s, the parts on the labor market themselves have taken over. For instance, many social chapters in the collective agreements were made and, in a way, compensated for the loss of security in the flexicurity system and re-established the balance between flexibility and security (Jørgensen and Klindt 2018). These kinds of solutions could shift the labor market toward more inequalities between labor market insiders and outsiders as is seen in other countries, most notably in Germany.

The conclusion from most researchers is "that institutional complementarities between flexibility and security are fragile and liable to disintegrate if the institutions providing flexicurity are not maintained and supported" (Bredgaard and Madsen 2018, 375).

After the political changes of the last decade of the Danish Model, researchers have asked whether the balance between flexibility and security has changed significantly toward more flexibility and less security (Knudsen and Lind 2018). Yet in comparison with other European countries, the labor market policy in Denmark probably still deserves the term flexicurity. The Danish system is still alive.

Summary

The Danish labor market system, which is often referred to as the Danish Model, is an exemplary model of *flexicurity* (a term that combines the words security and flexibility). The OECD highlighted the Danish Model in 2004, and the European Commission officially incorporated it into the European Employment Strategy in 2007.

The Danish labor market system has more than 100 years of history, and it is one of the preconditions for the rich Danish welfare state, which has a generally high income based on rather small but adaptable firms. The basis for this system is the collective agreements established through negotiation with a "balance of compromise" that is accepted by both sides: employers and employees. The state normally does not interfere in labor negotiations and has established some institutions to help both parties in case of disagreements and for nationwide negotiations. It is only in cases where a conflict has nationwide interest that the state can interfere.

The Danish labor market system has two important characteristics. The first is benefit to employers through limited employment protection. Employers are allowed to easily change their business in shifting economic conditions when it is easy to dismiss employees. The employees accept this behavior because of the second factor: the employees receive generous economic support when unemployed. Employees do not lose much money during the time they are seeking their next job. Each year, around 20% of the workforce is affected by unemployment, but mobility in the labor market is high and is measured by job creation, job loss, and average tenure.

A country's capacity to maintain high employment depends on its ability to restructure and adapt production. This has become especially important in recent decades because Denmark, like other countries, has been influenced by a new international division of labor, the continuous introduction of new technology to this demographic (including a new organization of work), and climate change. Since the 1980s, a new "leg" has been added to the two dimensions of flexicurity. One leg is an active labor market policy, which aims to ensure a well-functioning labor market through initiatives like education, training, etc. Expenditures on the active labor market policy have been substantial. In 2016, the cost of the active labor market policy was more than 2% of gross domestic product in top of all countries.

The well-functioning Danish Model was deemed to be a flexicurity system due to its flexibility for the employers and security for the employees. It has many similarities to the systems in the other Nordic countries, including the Dutch model. The

Nordic Model is different from the flexicurity systems of Mediterranean countries, with limited benefits in the Anglo-Saxon countries and tight regulation in the mainland countries.

The word *flexicurity* was first used in the Netherlands to refer to political initiatives in the mid-1990s. Since then, the term not only became a useful analytical tool in the discussion of labor market issues or an economic term to describe labor market capabilities that create opportunities for employers and employees, but it also came to signify a coordinated political strategy.

Since flexicurity inspired by the Danish Model became official EU policy, it has become a political initiative promoted in different plans and closely monitored.

Policy is probably not transferable from one country to another. The Danish society is a sizeable welfare state with high taxes and social benefits, but the Danish system is itself under pressure from both internal and external forces. Internally, collective bargaining is more decentralized than ever. Therefore, a solidarity principle cannot be proposed using the same rules and standards nationwide. The increasing internationalization has placed pressure on the system to internationalize firms, resulting in foreign firms coming to Denmark and bringing with them another culture and method for handling agreements. Foreign workers are coming to Denmark with other traditions as well.

As results of this increasing pressure, initiatives from international organizations have been instituted, the foremost being the EU. Regardless, the Danish labor market and governmental policy still have the necessary balance between employers' and employees' interests. The Danish Model is still alive.

References

Andersen SK, Lubanski N, Pedersen OK (2011) De nordiske landes konkurrencedygtighed – fra flexicurity til mobication. TemaNord. Nordic Council of Ministers, København

Bekker S (2018) Flexicurity in the European semester: still a relevant policy concept? J Eur Publ Policy 25:175–192. https://doi.org/10.1080/13501763.2017.1363272

Bekker S, Mailand M (2018) The European flexicurity concept and the Dutch and Danish flexicurity models: how have they managed the great recession? Soc Policy Admin 53:142–155. https://doi.org/10.1111/spol.12441

Beyer M, Frederiksen CL, Kureer H (2017) Samfundsfag C. Systime iBog. Systime, Aarhus

Bredgaard T, Madsen PK (2018) Farewell flexicurity? Danish flexicurity and the crisis. Trans Eur Rev Labour Res 24:375–386. https://doi.org/10.1177/1024258918768613

Bredgaard T, Larsen F, Madsen PK (2008) Flexicurity: in pursuit of a moving target. Eur J Soc Secur 10:305–323. https://doi.org/10.1177/138826270801000401

Due J, Madsen JS, Strøby Jensen C (1994) The survival of the Danish model: a historical sociological analysis of the Danish system of collective bargaining. Jurist- og Økonomforbundet, København

Dunlop JT (1959) Industrial relations systems. Henry Holt & Co, New York

Esping-Andersen G (1989) The three political economies of the welfare state. Can Rev Sociol 26:10–36

European Commission (1997) Partnership for a new organization of work: green paper: document drawn up on the basis of COM(97)128 final. Bulletin of the European Union. Supplement, 1997/04. EUR-OP, Luxembourg

Flaschel P, Greiner A (2012) Flexicurity capitalism: foundations, problems and perspectives. Oxford University Press, New York

Galenson W (1952) The Danish system of labor relations: a study in industrial peace. Harvard University Press, Cambridge

Hastings T, Heyes J (2016) Farewell to flexicurity? Austerity and labour policies in the European Union. Econ Ind Democr 39:458–480. https://doi.org/10.1177/0143831X16633756

Hedborg A, Meidner R (1984) Folkhemsmodellen. Tema nova. Rabén & Sjögren, Stockholm

Heggebø K (2016) Hiring, employment, and health in Scandinavia: the Danish 'flexicurity' model in comparative perspective. Eur Soc 18:460–486. https://doi.org/10.1080/14616696.2016.1207794

Ibsen CL, Keune M (2018) Organised decentralisation of collective bargaining. OECD, Paris. https://doi.org/10.1787/1815199X

Jensen CS (2011) The flexibility of flexicurity: the Danish model reconsidered. Econ Ind Democr 32:721–737. https://doi.org/10.1177/0143831X11401928

Jensen PH (2017a) Danish flexicurity: preconditions and future prospects. Ind Relat J 48:218–230. https://doi.org/10.1111/irj.12176

Jensen PH (2017b) Origins of Danish flexicurity. In: Olofsson G, Hort SEO, Therborn G (eds) Class, sex and revolutions: Göran Therborn-a critical appraisal. Arkiv förlag, Lund, pp 97–114

Jørgensen H, Klindt MP (2018) Revisiting Danish Flexicurity after a decade of reform: does the labour market still work for everyone? In: Fabian M, Breunig R (eds) Hybrid public policy innovations: contemporary policy beyond ideology. Routledge, New York, pp 134–151

Jørgensen H, Madsen PK (2007) Flexicurity and beyond: reflections on the nature and future of a political celebrity. In: Jørgensen H, Kongshøj Madsen P (eds) Flexicurity and beyond: finding a new agenda for the European social model. DJØF Publishing, Copenhagen, pp 7–35

Knudsen H (1995) Employee participation in Europe, SAGE London/Thousand Oaks/New Delhi

Knudsen H, Lind J (2012a) De danske modeller – Plus ca change, plus c'est la même chose? Tidsskrift for Arbejdsliv 14:9–30. https://doi.org/10.7146/tfa.v14i2.108904

Knudsen H, Lind J (2012b) Is the Danish model still a sacred cow? Danish trade unions and European integration. Trans Eur Rev Labour Res 18:381–395. https://doi.org/10.1177/1024258912458863

Knudsen H, Lind J (2018) Danish Flexicurity: not the same today as yesterday. In: Sander GG, Tomljenović V, Bodiroga-Vukobrat N (eds) Transnational, European, and National Labour Relations: Flexicurity and new economy. Springer International Publishing, Cham, pp 197–211

Kristiansen J (2015a) The growing conflict between European uniformity and national flexibility: the case of Danish flexicurity and European harmonisation of working condition. DJØF, Copenhagen

Kristiansen J (ed) (2015b) Europe and the Nordic collective-bargaining model: The complex interaction between Nordic and European labour law. TemaNord, vol 541. Nordisk Ministerråd; Nordisk Råd, København

Larsen TP, Ilsøe A (2016) Introduktion til den danske model. In: Larsen TP, Ilsøe A (eds) Den danske model set udefra. Jurist- og Økonomforbundets Forlag, København, pp 21–49

Lind J (2009) The end of the Ghent system as trade union recruitment machinery? Ind Relat J 40:510–523. https://doi.org/10.1111/j.1468-2338.2009.00543.x

Lind J, Knudsen H (2018) Denmark: the long-lasting class compromise. Empl Relat 40:580–599. https://doi.org/10.1108/ER-01-2017-0012

Lithuanian Free Market Institute (pub) (2018) Employment flexibility index 2019: EU and OECD countries. Lithuanian Free Market Institute, Vilnius

Madsen PK (2005) How can it possibly fly? The paradox of a dynamic labour market in a Scandinavian welfare state. Carma Research Papers, 2:2005. Center for Arbejdsmarkedsforskning, Carma, Aalborg

Madsen PK (2007) Flexicurity: a new perspective on labour markets and welfare states in Europe. Tilburg Law Rev 14:57

Madsen PK (2008) The Danish road to 'Flexicurity': where are we compared to others? And how did we get there? In: Muffels RJA (ed) Flexibility and employment security in Europe: labour markets in transition. Edward Elgar, Cheltenham/Northampton, pp 341–362

Mailand M (2010) The common European flexicurity principles: how a fragile consensus was reached. Eur J Ind Relat 16:241–257. https://doi.org/10.1177/0959680110375134

Muffels R, Luijkx R (2008) Labour market mobility and employment security of male employees in Europe: 'trade-off' or 'flexicurity'? Work Employ Soc 22:221–242. https://doi.org/10.1177/0950017008089102

Nardo M, Rossetti F (2013) Flexicurity in Europe. European Union, Brussels

Nordic Council of Ministers (2010) Labour market mobility in Nordic welfare states. Labour market & working environment. Nordic Council of Ministers, København

OECD (pub) (2004) OECD employment outlook 2004. OECD, Paris

OECD (pub) (2018) OECD employment outlook 2018. OECD, Paris

Pacelli L et al (2008) Employment security and employability: a contribution to the Flexicurity debate. Eurofound, Dublin

Pennings F (2018) Dilemmas in Organising the labour market, experiences with Flexicurity in the Netherlands. In: Sander GG, Tomljenović V, Bodiroga-Vukobrat N (eds) Transnational, European, and national labour relations: flexicurity and new economy. Springer International Publishing, Cham, pp 213–222

Rodriguez R, Warmerdam J, Triomphe CE (2010) The Lisbon strategy 2000–2010: an analysis and evaluation of the methods used and results achieved. EU, Brussels

Scheuer S (2007) Dilemmas of collectivism: Danish trade unions in the twenty-first century. J Lab Res 28:233–254. https://doi.org/10.1007/BF03380044

Scheuer S (2009) Funktionær eller ej? Funktionæransættelsens omfang og betydning i den danske aftalemodel. HK/Privat, København

Sørensen C (2006) Arbejdsmarkedet og den danske flexicurity-model. Økonomisk samfundsbeskrivelse. Academica, Aarhus

Tangian A (2011) Flexicurity and political philosophy: towards a majority-friendly Europe. European political, economic, and security issues. Nova Science Publishers, Inc, Hauppauge

van Oorschot W (2004) Flexible work and flexicurity policies in the Netherlands. Trends and experiences. Trans Eur Rev Labour Res 10:208–225. https://doi.org/10.1177/102425890401000206

Visser J, Hemerijck A (1997) A Dutch miracle: job growth, welfare reform and corporatism in the Netherlands. Amsterdam University Press, Amsterdam

Wilthagen T (1998) Flexicurity: a new paradigm for labour market policy reform? WZB discussion paper, Berlin

Wilthagen T, Tros F (2004) The concept of 'flexicurity': a new approach to regulating employment and labour markets. Trans European Rev Labour Res 10:166–186. https://doi.org/10.1177/102425890401000204

Pre-colonial Africa: Diversity in Organization and Management of Economy and Society

52

Grietjie Verhoef

Contents

Early Egyptian Civilization in North Africa	1187
Indigenous Bantu-Speaking Peoples and Islam	1190
African Societies in the East and Southern Africa	1195
Management and Organization	1196
Conclusion	1203
Pre-colonial Management in Africa	1203
References	1204

Abstract

Management was integral to state organization, traditional hierarchical stratification of authority, and ownership of resources in Africa. The history of dynamic state formation, challenge of authority and conquest in Africa. Limited separation existed between state and commercial activity. Islam expanded and conquered indigenous empires, while some indigenous peoples converted to Islam. Traditional management was integral to state management. In some geographical locations, the monarch allowed private enterprise and decentralized management of commerce. In West Africa, more decentralized commercial management occurred, while in East Africa Muslim traders controlled trade routes. This chapter shows how state formation and business management developed in parallel trajectories before colonial intervention. Limited organizational structures emerged as distinctly managerial in origin. This chapter illustrates diversity of management culture and sophistication before the late nineteenth century.

G. Verhoef (✉)
College of Business and Economics, University of Johannesburg, Johannesburg, South Africa

College of Global Business, Monash University, Melbourne, VIC, Australia
e-mail: gverhoef@uj.ac.za; grietjie.verhoef@monash.edu

© The Author(s), under exclusive licence to Springer Nature Switzerland AG 2020
B. Bowden et al. (eds.), *The Palgrave Handbook of Management History*,
https://doi.org/10.1007/978-3-319-62114-2_85

Keywords

Sacred king · Hierarchy · Middlemen · Commerce · Kinship · Owner-managed · Centralized state · Trade routes · Chief · Trader

The vast land comprising Africa constitutes the location of dynamic contestation, conquest, and expansion of power. Africa comprises around 30 million square kilometers, the second largest continent. Africa is therefore the size of China, India, the USA, and most of the European countries combined. It is home to a rich diversity of indigenous cultures and linguistic entities engaged in sustaining the livelihood of sprawling communities. The people of Africa speak more than 1000 different ethnic languages, belonging to around 100 language groups. The history of Africa is testimony to consistent flux or movement of peoples in ever-changing social formations. This dynamic demographic configuration displayed a constant movement as populations expanded and sought to secure their existence. History begins with geography. Confronted by typographical and climatic extremes, societies settled where they could sustain a livelihood. With high mountains, long rivers, a series of lakes in the Great Rift Valley (approximately 6000 km, stretching from Lebanon's Beqaa Valley to Southeastern Africa, around modern Tanzania and Mozambique – July 1998: 5), desert and fertile soil, and rich vegetation in equatorial jungles and sweeping grasslands/savannahs human survival depended on management thereof. The population is unevenly distributed. The fertile soils attracted the highest density of people. Concentrations of settlements developed on the North African coastline, in West Africa, along the Nile River valley, and finally southward to the Witwatersrand highlands in the south. In this vast geography, societies organized themselves for sustainability. The history of Africa reflects the complex discontinuities and change as societies responded to climatic, social, and political developments similar to the experiences of the people of Europe, Asia, Latin America, North America, and Australasia. As civilizations expanded across the world, contestation followed and led to new social formations, new sociopolitical configurations, and ultimately socioeconomic organization. How societies survived or failed to survive and resulted in new social formations paved the way for the modern global configuration of people, states, and economy.

In this chapter the underlying principles of social and economic management in Africa emerge as a function of social formation. From the Latin *civilis*, which means "political" or "civic," the word civilization refers to the emergence of an entity of humans, a civic entity, in a formation called a *state*. The *state* takes on a variety of forms, but remains the core of societies considered to be "civilized." As civilization spreads across Africa, the unfolding of state formation becomes the dynamic of emerging sovereign public power. The power of the sovereign supersedes the social bindings of families and ethnic tribe's local communities. The sovereign power organizes the subject to serve the interests of the state as a collective, but the interests of the rulers are not necessarily representative of the entire population. The early history of the peoples of Africa exhibits a tendency toward centralized state authority, with a small ruling class or bureaucratic officialdom. Institutional diversification was limited, since state power did not distinguish different dimensions of social autonomy. In the early state, rulers claimed some form of religious or spiritual authority. In the history of Africa religion or pagan ancestry devotion was a significant dimension of all power. The underlying principles of management, namely, planning, organizing, leading, and controlling, rise vividly in the sociopolitical organization of societies since earliest times, albeit in a social configuration prior to the emergence of the institutions fundamental to western management theory.

The meaning of the concept "management," as Peter Drucker phrased it, justifies consideration. Drucker defines management as "a discipline – that is an organized body of knowledge and as such applicable everywhere – it is also a "culture." It is not value-free science. Management is a social function and embedded in a culture – a society – a tradition of values, customs, and beliefs, and governmental and political systems. Management is – and should be – culture-conditioned; but, in turn, management and managers shape culture and society" (Drucker 1974). The manifestation of pre-colonial African management practices displays the traditional culture embeddedness of emerging management practices. The distinct culture of traditional African societies in their vast diversity, constitute the basis of social capital formation and community networks underlying business activities. As the dynamic dispersion of peoples progressed since more than two million years ago, (Fage and Tordoff 2002; July 1998; Oliver 1977), social organization delivered the ecosystem of the development of African management. The ecosystem of management in Africa is the political history of Africa. The history of the management of all social activities, political, social, and economic, unfolds with the slow adoption of the market and market-reinforcing institutions in protracted fashion (George et al. 2016). The historical succession of state formation and social organization of states offer an insight into the organization of economic and commercial activity. In this context practices evolved for the management of society, political power, and economic activities.

Early Egyptian Civilization in North Africa

From the earliest civilizations of Mesopotamia around 3500 B.C., the Sumerian city-states emerged. The civilization spread to the northern part of Africa. From 3200 B.C., the Egyptian civilization developed around the Nile River. The powerful Egyptian civilization spread southward along the Nile Valley. The ruler presented himself as a god-king, or *pharaoh*, who unified the peoples along the Nile into a single state in 3100 B.C. The settlement in the north, known as Lower Egypt, and the settlement in the south, known as Upper Egypt, henceforth functioned as a centralized state for 2000 years. Egypt had periods of internal instability and international challenge to its power. The power of the unified Egyptian state crumbled toward the tenth century B.C. This allowed the Kush kingdom in the south to return itself to independence from Egyptian domination, only to be reconquered later in the seventh century B.C., and by 591 the Kushite kings were again defeated, allowing Egypt to reoccupy the Upper and Lower parts of the empire. These developments underlined the mutual dependence of the divine king, the military forces, the scribes and the elites in sustaining the state. As Egypt reestablished its political power over the southern Kush kingdom, bidirectional cultural assimilation characterized coexistence, but not shared power. State power returned to the Egyptian king (Wickins 1981: 2–6; Van Aswegen 1980: 26–30; July 1998: 27–37). The culturally rich and powerful empire of Axum developed to the southeast of Egypt on the Ethiopian highlands. Axum was a wealthy state, but was finally succumbed by Islamic Arab conquest. Between 814 B.C. and the first century after Christ, North Africa and Egypt fell to the colonization by the Phoenicians, the Greek, and Roman civilizations (Andrea and Overfield 2001a: 16–18; Wickins 1981: 7–9; Van Aswegen 1980: 13–61). Despite these latter developments, the "sacred king" phenomenon spread to African societies neighboring the Egyptian civilization. As far south as current-day Uganda, the southwestern Ethiopian highlands and the Great Zimbabwe-Monomotapa similar powers of deity in state authority existed by the twelfth century. The divine kingship phenomenon later came to be considered "more or less (a) natural evolution from the development of agriculture." Since societies' sustainability and prosperity were inextricably linked to "the spirits of the water and the land," the king as descendant of the ancestors became the mediator with the other world and thereby increasingly the personification of supernatural powers of the ancestors (Fage and Tordoff 2002: 37–41; Andrea and Overfield 2001a: 23).

The Egyptian pharaoh ruled the state with unlimited powers, but priests, officials, and nobles assisted in executing duties delegated to them. As the sole owner of all the land, all economic activities and exchange occurred at his will and to his benefit. Africa became integrated into European economic and trade activities across the Mediterranean through the colonization of the Phoenicians, Greeks, and Romans during the century before the birth of Christ. These conquests did not penetrate deep into Africa, but affected primarily the northern seaboard lands. Trade routes with Europe and Asia developed as colonies of the Roman Empire until the third century B.C. By the first century before Christ, the dominant civilizations of North Africa were loosely linked through a series of trade networks and imperialist expansions. Under direct control of the Egyptian pharaoh and European civilizations, ships traded across the Mediterranean Sea and in the southeast region across the Red Sea with Arab settlements.

Before the unification of the Egyptian state during the fourth millennium before Christ, well before 3000 B.C., peasants cultivated the fertile lands and exchanged their produce. This stimulated the successful expansion of agricultural production in the Egyptian kingdom. People had domesticated animals, cattle, sheep, or goats and cultivated flax for textile production and grain for food. The fertile Nile lands delivered considerable wealth. Surpluses in production, supplemented with craft production, supplied the comparative advantage leading to specialization and trade with civilizations outside Egypt. Specialized craftsmen and traders created wealth, which gave rise to a wealthy class and growing inequality in society. After unification the organization of commercial exchange was a direct function of divine state power. Individual merchants were the entrepreneurial agents seeking markets, supplying goods, and engaging in commercial agreement, always sanctioned by the authoritarian ruler. Trading fleets crossed the oceans under the authority of the monarch. The Egyptian civilization was prosperous, but grew more prosperous under state-induced specialization in agricultural production. Specialization in grain and textile production, although not exclusively, led to the emergence of a class structure of increasing complexity. Capable artisans and craftsmen produced goods for exchange. The latter and agricultural surpluses thus oiled the wheels of trade and delivered the tax adding to the wealth of the state. The king employed priests, an administrative class of bureaucrats, and a professional army to secure his position and future prosperity.

Following colonization by societies from elsewhere in the Mediterranean, the first trade was conducted across the Sahara desert, operating from trading posts on the coast. These trading routes only developed into established trading routes after the Islamic invasions. The most frequent exchange was to the northeast with Arab settlements and across the Indian Ocean with people of Asia. In the Egyptian civilization, merchants traveled up and down the Nile to connect suppliers and "him who wants," while tax was collected in the form of gold. The "scribe," who recorded the transactions, was not physically a strong person in society, but a person occupying "a fine profession" (Andrea and Overfield 2001a: 23–24; July 1998: 18–22). Officials in the state bureaucracy, scribes, and tax collectors thus assumed an important function in administering commercial exchange, as well as managing subjects on behalf of the divine ruler. The scribes played a vital role in developing the art of writing, pictographic, and later cursive script. The Egyptian civilization was therefore able to accumulate knowledge systematically, develop a sun calendar, and predict cyclical climatic patterns. Calculating time improved agricultural production and wealth creating. The nexus between land, agriculture, and the divine ruler witnessed in the Egyptian civilization was not unique in Africa. In other African kingdoms, this nexus also constituted the essence of state authority and centralized power of the king. The significance of this nexus became accentuated through the turbulent history of Africa, as protracted introduction of modernizing technology from western civilizations in most parts of Africa perpetuated the dependence on agriculture as organized in centralized state formations.

The sophisticated Egyptian civilization developed in North Africa at the same time as civilizations developed in the Americas and China. Limited contact, if any, can be traced between the Americas and Africa during the earliest centuries of human settlement in Africa. Traces of Chinese coins and porcelain were found in East Africa pointing to exchanges between the peoples of East Africa and China during the fifth century B.C. Trading activities on the East African coast established connections with the Greek and later Roman civilization, as well as the Indian and Chinese civilizations. The commercial contacts facilitated exchange. These did not change sociopolitical organization but cultural enrichment and the ability to accumulate wealth. The powerful divine king encouraged commercial exchange, under his auspices, to grow the revenue of the state. Economic specialization based on comparative advantages (as explained by David Ricardo) stimulated trade, growing wealth accumulation, and social stratification. Whether in a centralized unified state or in smaller seats of political power, the king was the sole authority. He determined social organization; he planned, led the state, and controlled all functions of the state.

No independent business management function transpired, but the outcome of planning, organization, leadership, and control is witnessed in the scientific, architectural, and engineering achievements of the Egyptian civilization. Constructing the pyramids, aqueducts, and roads and raising agricultural production by calculating a calendar to predict the cycles of flooding of the Nile River are all achievements testifying to state capacity to plan, manage, and execute state projects. In the absence of sources explaining systematically the process of planning, managing, and execution (Bartol and Martin 1991), the student of management is left to interpret the sociopolitical trajectory of the civilizations or societies as evidence of the sustainability of management in early African history. Architectural wonders, such as the pyramids, display advanced intellectual capabilities, applied managerial skills, and the ability to mobilize labor to execute the plans. From the nature of state management, as was vividly illustrated in the development of the Egyptian civilization, underlying dimensions of management in Africa may transpire.

Indigenous Bantu-Speaking Peoples and Islam

The hunter-gatherers in indigenous Africa were primarily located in the southern parts of Africa. These were the Khoi-Khoin and San peoples. Indigenous black people were agriculturalists and pastoralists. They settled in the lands to the southwest of the Sahara desert, on the Southeastern highlands of East Africa, and in Central and Southern Africa. The peoples of the southwestern region of Africa were called *Bilhad-al*-Sudan – an Arabic reference meaning "the land of the black people." Early climatic transformation of the once water-rich Sahara lands caused massive catastrophe to the inhabitants, but came to an end around 2000 B.C. The subsequent desert conditions mandated a survival response. The Bantu-speaking peoples gradually migrated to lands in the west and central parts of Africa where better rainfall and rivers offered enhanced survival opportunities. This migration resulted in the movement of Bantu-speakers across the Cameroon Gabon area to East Africa around the Lake Victoria by 300 B.C. Small groups formed small states in what is today known as Hausaland and Yorubaland in modern-day Nigeria, as well as in the forest belt of the Volta River. Long-distance trade developed in gold and kola nuts. In West Africa the kingdom of Ghana was founded around 400 but was later succeeded by the kingdom of Mali around the eleventh century and the Kanem-Bornu Empire in the region of Lake Chad, after the thirteenth century. The next massive Bantu migration occurred from around 400 from the Shaba in the central part of Africa, to the south and southeast regions as far south as the Kei River in current South Africa. This massive migration drove the dispersion of Bantu culture, iron-manufacturing skills and agricultural knowledge across sub-Saharan Africa. Ultimately the Bantu migration continued for almost a thousand years and ended with the settlement of the Bantu-speaking peoples through Central, East, and

Southern Africa (Wickins 1981; Fage and Tordoff 2002; Andrea and Overfield 2001a).

The significance of the Bantu migration is that their sociopolitical organization was transferred to the largest geographies of the continent. Economic activities were performed through a social organization around a central authority, a king, as the core of social organization and management. It is significant that the sociopolitical organization and economic functions displayed stability. In the ancient kingdom of Ghana, the king exercised control over smaller kingdoms, permitted smaller tribes to control trade routes across the Sahara, but extracted gold from the different smaller sociopolitical entities under its control. The king succeeded his predecessor as the son of his predecessor's sister, thus not the son on the predecessor became king, but the son of the sister of the former king, succeeded as the next king. He sometimes presented himself as a woman, wearing necklaces, bracelets, and turban headgear. He ruled as an autocrat. This king, as in the Egyptian empire, was served with divine honors as the center of the indigenous cult. The king used priests and an army (of around 200,000 soldiers on command) to secure his position. State power centralized in the state, personified in the king, who simultaneously controlled economic activities: permitting cultivation, pastoralism, trade, and exchange. Control of trans-Saharan merchant routs meant commercial control, strengthening the power of the king. It was only late during the twelfth century that an environmental crisis rendered the kingdom of Ghana to disintegrate, paving the way for the rise of other empires in the Sudan. The kingdom of Ghana was originally a non-Muslim kingdom, but the king once accepted the Islamic faith when a Muslim preacher prayed, and it suddenly started to rain at a time when the kingdom suffered severe drought. The entire kingdom was not converted to Islam, but subsequent kings accepted the title *al-usulmani*, depicting a title of a leader in the Muslim faith. Muslims were allowed to settle in the kingdom alongside non-Muslims (Fage and Tordoff 2002: 59, 67; Andrea and Overfield 2001a: 382–386).

To the east of Ghana was the Kanem Empire, known for the worship of their king, who they believed to be the source of "life and death, sickness and health." Kanem later formed part of the Bornu-Kanem Empire. With the demise of the kingdom of Ghana and Muslim invasions, the thirteenth century witnessed the rise of the kingdom of Mali to include all of the territories of the former kingdom of Ghana. Mali became a powerful kingdom, with wealthy caravans crossing the Sahara up to Cairo, but was succeeded by the Songhai Empire during the fifteenth century. This empire was closely aligned to Islam, but also disintegrated to pave the way for the nomadic Negroid hunting and fishing societies of the Kanem-Bornu and Hausa states.

Successive raids by nomadic pastoralist groups could be withstood through the military power of the state/king. The incoming pastoralist groups swelled the size of the kingdom and contributed to the revenue stream of the kingdom. The political institutions of the state were flexible enough to retain internal stability in the wake of adjusting and incorporating adjoining populations. African kingdoms also went through different stages of internal stability and turmoil. A dispersion of power between contesting chiefs could undermine internal stability. Few indigenous black kingdoms remained stable, centralized, and strong for very long. Kingdoms rose to power, but were challenged, either by migrating pastoralists or by internal strife. Strong centralized government was the exception in sub-Saharan Africa (Wickins 1981: 228), and July (1998) called them "ephemeral political entities without great intrinsic unity" (July 1998: 63). It was the king who succeeded with varying degrees of success, to stabilize his position through a personal allegiance of priests, soldiers, and other subjects. The personal agency of the ruler was decisive. Generally African kingdoms did not constitute a strong centralized state, but rather a sociopolitical organization aligned to the king. The absence of a strong centralized state administration, an effective executive function, and fragmented public functions undermined the emergence of strong states. These limitations impacted on longevity, stability, and sustainability.

The Muslim Arab invasion of Africa from the seventh century established Arab domination and Islam as religious-political power in Africa exposing the vulnerability of the indigenous African kingdoms. The Muslim invasions revealed the existence of the ancient indigenous kingdoms of the Sudan, as educated Arab persons documented their experiences and findings in the unknown parts of the continent they penetrated. A dynamic period of complex challenges to power, realignment of authority, and new and intensified networks of exchange put Africa on a trajectory of rapid transformation. The Islamic invasions perhaps had the most profound long-term impact on the history of Africa. More than European colonial control that lasted only for around 60–70 years (1885 to between 1950 and 1960), Islamic Arab invasions transformed Africa permanently. The Islamic conquests since the eighth century resulted in longer and more persistent conquest of indigenous African empires and the development of Islamic states as people of Africa were converted to Islam. Conversion to the Muslim faith seemed popular. Relatively small Arab armies conquered vast parts of Africa. The conquered were subjected to pay poll tax, since they were non-Muslims. Accepting the Muslim faith ruled out the payment of the tax and therefore Islam spread relatively smoothly across sub-Saharan Africa.

A major new chapter in the history of Africa commenced with the Arab Muslim invasions of the seventh century. Systematically Muslim armies invaded and conquered Africa. Starting in the mid-seventh century with the conquest of Egypt, Muslim armies advanced along the Mediterranean coastline to Gibraltar and Cordoba by 711, thereby controlling *al-Maghrib*, or North Africa. Islamic expansion also proceeded south across the Sahara into the Sudanese black indigenous kingdoms. The success of the Islamic invasions was grounded in the religious and therefore non-secular calling to submit themselves to the will of "God" of whom they believed, Mohammed was the Prophet. Strict adherence to the principles of submission to the teachings of the Prophet translated into a disciplined religious army driven with the calling to make all humanity subordinate to the will of one God. The concept of the universal submission (*Islam*) of all mankind to one God served to encourage the Arab tribes to unite if they wanted to succeed in achieving the calling of the Prophet. This conviction also served to motivate the conquest and submission of non-Muslim believers, as well as the organization of conquered societies according to the rules of the Islam faith (Fage and Tordoff 2002). After the Muslim conquest began in the seventh century, the penetration of Muslim beliefs and Arab culture followed new waves of Arab out-movement. The Fatimids' conquest of Egypt, in 969 particular, consolidated Arab control over the fertile lands and resulted in massive trade expansion, across the northern African coastline, but also internationally. Merchants accumulated impressive wealth, despite the high taxes extracted by the new rulers (Oliver 1977). In North Africa the Islamic invasions resulted in several Muslim states – the Merinid kingdom (1248), the ABD Al-Wahid kingdom (1248), the Hafsid kingdom (1229), and Egypt. The conquest of the *al-Maghrib* took a lengthy period of time, because of resistance by the Berber tribes. From the initial expansion across the *al-Maghrib*, the conquests proceeded across the Sahara into the Sudan.

The infiltration by Islam into the Sudan or sub-Saharan lands of West Africa had a profound impact on the indigenous kingdoms, but did not usurp them entirely. Internal struggles for power undermined Islamic expansion. It was only in 1076 that a Muslim army under Abu Bakr conquered Ghana. From the kingdom of Ghana, Islam domination penetrated into the kingdom of Mali, which resulted in King Mansa Musa accepting the Muslim faith. When Mali fell to the rising Songhai kingdom during the sixteenth century, the Songhai king had already been converted to Islam. Also in the kingdom of Kanem-Bornu the indigenous ruler, mai Umme (mai is the title of the king) converted to Islam in 1086. The kingdom was thus not conquered by Islam, but accepted aspects of the faith in public and private life. The loosely constituted Hausa states to the east of the Sudan, accepted aspects of the Muslim faith and implemented administrative systems inherited from the Songhai Empire. These were closely molded to Islamic directives.

The North African Muslim states were strictly organized along Islamic principles. The governor of the state or province occupied the central state power, supported by a military and civil administration. Finances were managed by a separate Department of Finance, responsible for the extraction and management of revenue from the conquered territory. The Islamic bureaucracy was characterized by professional officials/bureaucrats each assigned specific specialized duties of state administration. All conquered land came under the ownership of the Islamic state. Indigenous peoples were permitted to work their lands and work as artisans or craftsmen but were incapable of taking administrative office. Social stratification developed. The Arab Muslims were the aristocracy or highest class; the indigenous people who had converted to Islam were subordinate to the Arab Muslims. They were exempt from poll tax, but had to pay land and poor taxes, and shared in the material benefits of all Muslims. The third class, or lowest social stratum, was the non-Muslims. These indigenous peoples were heavily taxed and had to support the military. A fourth category was the Jews and Christians, who maintained cultural and religious autonomy, but were subject to Muslims in society (Baulin 1962; Trimmingham 1968; Holt et al. 1970).

Even though the Muslim conquests were associated with the setting up of well-organized administrative structures and introducing sophisticated financial management, including mathematical calculation of taxes and other revenue, Islam had a limited influence on the source of state power or the execution of power. Despite conversion to the Muslim faith, most of the indigenous African kings crafted a unique blend of pagan religion, from which they derived their authority, and Islam.

This was very obvious among the Berber tribes – they were conquered by the Islamic armies, but essentially remained loyal to their tribes, tribal traditions, and tribal dialects. Fage and Tordoff observed, "Kings and their machineries of government might seem to be Islamised, but the principles of Sudanic royal power remained pagan" (Fage and Tordoff 2002: 188). In the last resort, the authority and legitimacy of the king originated from the acceptance by his subjects that he was the descendant of the ancestors of the people. Islam was nevertheless often used to strengthen the authority of the king, to improve state organization, to enhance his legitimacy through association with a specialized educated merchant class, and to promote education through Islamic schools. It is important to remember that the monarch determined the degree to which Islam was put to use in his kingdom.

The organization of the state in North Africa before the invasion of Islam, and in indigenous kingdoms in the Sudan, during the period up to around the first two centuries after Christ, was fairly simple. The king or monarch was the sole ruler, assisted by persons of his selection, from designated social categories. As the primary owner of factors of production, such as land and other natural resources, he determined the scope and scale of agricultural production. The monarch also controlled trade and revenue collection. The history of successive kingdoms since earliest Neolithic times to the Iron Age and thereafter tells of the centralization of all management functions in the ruling monarch. This monarch may have been reigning a large and strong empire. He may have been reigning a small state, sometimes a single city-state, or a group of weakly integrated states, such as the Hausa states in the eastern Sudan region. The degree of undisputed authority fluctuated – some states operated under strong central authority of the king, such as the united Egyptian kingdom after 400 B.C. Other states experienced different factors contributing to weakening central authority, the demise of the power of the kingdom and the succession of either a new ruler or another kingdom. The sole underlying principle of management was power – derived through descent or conquest.

Individual merchants and traders exercised their entrepreneurial capacities within the confines of the permission of the absolute monarch, who controlled all economic activities. On the macrolevel he gave permission for commercial activities and collected the taxes from such profitable transactions. Business was not an autonomous enterprise, but an extension of state authority. The Islamic rulers exercised strict control over trading caravan routes and merchant activities in ports and markets at intersecting caravan routes. Depending on the strength of the centralized authority of the indigenous monarch, commercial operations were organized by individual businessmen, working with members of his/her family or community. As central authority collapsed, contesting tribes competed for trade routes and markets. The disintegration of the Songhai kingdom, for example, enabled the formation of a confederation of pastoralist tribes, themselves causing instability as they competed for trading routes, markets, and grazing fields (Fage and Tordoff 2002: 191). Where Islam penetrated the indigenous society, it also caused profound ethnic shifts. An example of this occurred when Fulani pastoralists began to gradually join Muslim towns in sub-Saharan Africa during the sixteenth century. Many joined in the rights and privileges of Muslims. Much later the Fulani used the Islam *jihad* to extend power in the region.

African Societies in the East and Southern Africa

The Christian peoples of the Kush kingdom and later the Aksum Empire (current state of Ethiopia) experienced constantly changing dynamics in their relationships with the Egyptian kingdom and, subsequent to Muslim conquest of Egypt, successive Islamic sultans. The peoples of the Horn of Africa lived in a dynamic coexistence of Christians, Muslims, and pagan indigenous African communities. The eastern coastline and the Red Sea were the location of extensive trade between Asia and Africa, but as the Bantu-speaking migration from the western regions gained momentum just before the Christian era, a new period of agriculture and pastoralism started in East Africa. The Bantu-speaking peoples took with them their knowledge of agriculture and animal husbandry. They had also acquired the skills to manufacture iron tools. These indigenous African black people's migration from the western Sudan, proceeded across the Congo Basin toward the south and eastern coast of Africa. These pastoralists pushed the hunter-gatherers south, and by the sixteenth century, the Bantu-speaking peoples had arrived from the Shaba/Katanga region of the current Democratic Republic of the Congo (DRC), in the region of the Kei River in what is currently known as the Eastern Cape province of South Africa. The ethnic changes resulting from the migration included the settlement of the Lund and Luba kingdoms in the Shaba and Kasai regions of the DRC, and the Shona/Mbire kingdom to the south in the Great Zimbabwe. Further migration of Nilotes (people from the Upper Nile region) and Muslim Arabs into the region gave rise to economic competition, cultural integration, and political contestation. Muslim traders from Asia met with fierce indigenous defense, resulting in the appearance of permanent inland Muslim city-states, such as the city-state of Harar (located in modern-day Ethiopia). Muslim traders used Harar to source ivory, gold, and slaves to distribute through the cross Indian Ocean trade routes to Asia and beyond. Along the Eritrean coastline, colonies of Arab merchants and settlers were converted to Islam after the Islamic invasions commenced. By the twelfth century, Kilwa (located in modern-day Tanzania) was the most prosperous east-coast trading city and firmly under Muslim control. Kilwa emerged as the center from which Indian Ocean trade routes were reestablished after the Greek control was unseated. Regular upheavals of conquests and resistance between Islam, Christian, and pagan indigenous communities occurred. The Christian kingdom of Ethiopia succeeded in sustaining its sovereignty and between the fifteenth and sixteenth centuries expanded its territory (Fage and Tordoff 2002; Wickins 1986; Oliver and Atmore 2001).

The organizational structures of the dispersed African societies in East and Southern Africa differed greatly. The kingdom of the Great Zimbabwe displayed strong central authority in the hands of the king, supported by a bureaucracy and kinship support. The royal power of the king controlled all trade, exchange of gold and ivory. The ruling elite lived in an enclosed compound, served by ordinary people loyal to the king. As in other indigenous kingdoms, land ownership was with the king, and he determined usage. He also owned the crops and distributed food. The most significant achievement of the Great Zimbabwe was the building of the large "houses of stone" (*dzimba*), using crafted stone and iron, to secure safe living to the Shona people. The king, just as had been the case with the construction of the Egyptian pyramids, provided leadership in planning, organizing, and executing the massive stone construction of walls at some places 30 ft high and at base 15 ft thick. A similar strong and powerful king reigned the Bakongo people in current-day DRC. The *Manikongo* (king for the Kongo people) headed up a hierarchy of provincial and sub-provincial chiefs, appointed by the king, and on their part ruled over traditional villages with traditional headmen. The king depended on his "lords," which was not much more than a bodyguard of soldiers, to appoint him from members of the royal family. Social stratification entrenched a class structure. The king used the social organization to accumulate wealth through trading and taxation (Fage and Tordoff 2002).

The same strong inward-looking power structure was not present among the indigenous black African peoples of what today is known as Tanzania and Kenya. In Tanzania the organization of the monarchy was on a lower and more limited scale. The organization of the kingdom was much smaller and less centralized. The land was less suitable to agriculture and therefore fewer people settled there to sustain themselves. There were simply far less people in Tanzania than in the kingdom of the Great Zimbabwe. Further the region of what is today known as Kenya emerged almost "stateless." Smaller chieftainships defended the livelihood of smaller groups of black African peoples. A less powerful central tribal structure allowed the extensive network of Muslim Arab trading settlements to gain relative permanency. By the middle of the fifteenth century, these traders had penetrated deep into the central parts of the region, but indigenous societies, despite being less organized than the kingdoms of West Africa, resisted permanent Arab settlement into the interior. The relations among the Arab Muslim traders, the indigenous black African tribes, and Christian societies in Ethiopia between the Islamic invasions and European penetration in East Africa were dynamic, volatile, sometimes collaborative, and coexistent, but did not afford any single entity permanent domination. During the fourteenth century, the Christian empire of Ethiopia was superior to the Arab Muslims. The Christian army of Ethiopia was better organized and had better manpower, which secured them the upper hand against the Muslims. The Christian empire expanded during the late fourteenth and early fifteenth century, but then Islamic expansion to Mogadishu halted the Christians. The arrival of the Portuguese fleet during the fifteenth century supported the indigenous Christian societies in Ethiopia in the wake of existential threats by advancing Islamic forces (Oliver 1977). This contributed to the coexistence in the region.

Management and Organization

The unfolding of the history of statehood, power, and economy is a prerequisite to the understanding of the foundation of management and organization in the diverse African contexts. Before the onset of scientific management, the organization of society, polity, and economy developed within the realm of traditional culture. African societies were no different from other ancient societies in Asia, the Americas, or Europe. Society was organized according to a hierarchical social system involving distinct classes of royal and ordinary people, an elite or aristocracy/ nobles, free persons, occupational casts, or classes (such as jewelers, blacksmiths, tanners, tailors, workers, and unfree persons/slaves) (Andrea and Overfield 2001a). The history of management in Africa is an extension of the sociopolitical trajectory of its people. The earliest management of society was, as in the rest of the world, in the hands of a chief. This position depended on wealth, which evolved from the ability to organize, manage, and control resources and ultimately lead her/his subjects to sustain and improve their existence under her/his authority. As illustrated vividly in the early history of the Egyptian and subsequent indigenous black African societies, centralized sociopolitical power was directly linked to the mobilization of resources, natural and human. In different form and substance, power resided in a single person, irrespective of the title. Various succession paradigms existed – hereditary, paternal ancestor, and maternal ancestry. In all societies kinship relations determined social position, either in political management, economic management, or military or bureaucratic management. The history of Africa shows the inherent stratified nature of society and the prolonged perpetuation of privilege, inequality, and power. The inherent instability caused by military power to defend authority meant repeated challenges to power, succession insecurity, and, as described in the history, succession of kingdoms or empires.

While societies were organized around a social kinship nucleus, the leader managed society, polity, and economy. Management is concentrated centrally and functions delegated according to the prerogative of the individual leader. African societies were essentially communal, which does not imply collective decision-making. The undisputed authority of the ruler translated into the management decisions of the entity. In the absence of codified law, both domestically and internationally, the ruler's power was curtailed only by the degree of adherence to tribal customs.

The organization of the polity was integrated with the mobilization of economic resources. At no stage in the history of Africa can be contended that there were no markets. Market always existed. Exchange was in the form of barter and was actively pursued with neighboring regions in the Arab world, the Greek civilization, and the Phoenicians. The Arab Islamic invasions opened up trading routes, as explained. Extended markets existed for natural resources, such as salt, gold, iron, copper, kola nuts, food, etc. The merchant exchanges were planned, organized, and controlled by the political authority sanctioning trade. Macroeconomic management was part of the central state function, and micromanagement of merchants, traders, or producers was simply the extension of the authority of the king or emperor. In the Muslim states, the Muslim ruler exercised oversight control over the caravans. Literate Muslim merchants from the urban centers, however, organized the collection of commodities for exchange, the routes of travel, the conditions of exchange, and control over the finances by systematic bookkeeping. In some cases the merchant appointed an agent, or employee of the merchant, to accompany the caravan on behalf of the owner. These caravans were sometimes organized in a firm-like business structure, with owner of the assets, and employees engaged in the actual business of exchange or barter. Islamic law recognized "partnerships" between merchants, as well as the extension of credit between merchants, which reflects collaborative management. The management paradigm was centralized direct owner-managed business control of entities, sanctioned by the state (Oliver 1977; Wickins 1981; Oliver and Atmore 2001; Fage and Tordoff 2002; Verhoef 2017).

In the indigenous black African kingdoms of the Sudan, the king exercised direct control over the core economic activities – production and trade – but private individual merchants were allowed to compete with the large state enterprises. Authorized by the king, private businessmen operated as middlemen between producers and the state. Management of economic activities therefore operated on three levels: overall macro-management on the state level by the ruler, intermediation as middlemen by strategically thinking entrepreneurial merchants, and on the lowest level of kinship and the tribe, where the chief manages peasant production and delivery. The management of the production function fell within the responsibility of the chiefs. They also organized localized market exchange or the so-called petty trading in communities. Local merchants organized the trade expeditions (similar to the Muslim traders' organization of caravans) in urban centers as well as between urban centers and states/kingdoms. These merchants appointed transport agents to accompany the trade expedition in return for commission. The merchants were typically rich, influential members from respected families, private owners of the trading business, operating under state sanction in ways that complemented state business/trading operations. The merchants also depended on the military protection of the state to engage successfully in the trans-Saharan trade. In these Sudanese kingdoms, state formation and trade development were mutually reinforcing and not competing processes (Austin 1996; Austin and Cordell 2002; Verhoef 2017). Despite central state authority, albeit sometimes weak, multilayer management of commercial activities existed.

The organization of the lucrative salt trade offered a case in point of state management of a key economic activity. Salt production was a family enterprise, but the trade depended on state permission. Again, the merchants facilitated the acquisition of the salt, organized the trade on routes they managed, and earned commission on their endeavors, and the state collected the taxes on the salt production (Lovejoy 1986). The extensive organization of trade in humans (slaves) in Africa, especially in Sudan during the eighteenth century, illustrates the importance of strategic management of trade by indigenous kings. The permission of the king was required for the selling of slaves. He also determined the numbers of slaves to be offered on exchange, and thereby he could manipulate the price. Slaves were sourced from both inland and coastal kingdoms, but the king had preemptive rights on offering the sale of his slaves. During the heyday of the transatlantic slave trade, kings and their military structures dominated that specific trade (Law 1977). A significant dynamic in management appears at this juncture in Africa's history. The king/state's unchallenged power to plan the state economy, that is, to decide on organizational goals and devise a strategy to achieve the plan, remained her/his sole right. That right was exercised in collaboration with lower levels of management – i.e., the merchants and chiefs. The organization of the task (manufacturing salt, extracting, selling, or extract slaves, determine price, exchange the slaves), constituted her/his sole authority but was again exercised through mutual input. The king depended on the lower levels of management for success in realizing organizational goals. Leadership in execution was not limited to the king, but actually in most cases more dependent on the skills, professionalism and competency of the merchants. The final dimension of management, namely, control, was primarily exercised by lower levels of management – merchants, the military, and bureaucracy. Despite changes in the political authority, be that Muslim caliphate of indigenous African kingdom, the relation between producers and merchants remained the same (Lovejoy 1986).

A significant phenomenon in the management of African economic activity is the hierarchy of management. The ruler, irrespective of her/his source of power, managed with varying degrees of intensity on the macrolevel. On the operational level, a middle order of management exercised managerial control. As the massively lucrative slave trade came to an end (with Britain's abolition of slave trade in 1833, slave ownership remained legal), an interest developed in the exchange of other commodities. While the kings and Muslim rulers exercised almost monopoly control over the slave trade, the trade in other goods was open (Hopkins 1973; Coquery-Vidrovitch 1972; Law 1977). An interesting example was the development in palm oil in Dahomey. The demand for other raw materials from Africa after the period of active slave trade offered an opportunity for trade in palm oil. This developed into a successful enterprise and finally the Dahomey king declared a royal monopoly on palm oil. The king appointed the private merchants in that market as his agents. The royal monopoly secured the king control over the trade as well as the proceeds, but private business was still permitted alongside the royal operations. The private entrepreneurs were more successful, since they had experience and skills acquired through their development and organization of the industry. The royal appointment of experienced merchants as agents and permission to other merchants to operate independently resulted in a dynamic coexistence between the royal monopoly and independent merchants. It was apparent that the king acknowledged the efficient and successful managerial expertise that had developed on the operational level of business (Law 1977).

A fine example of the evolving hierarchy of management in West African societies is the organization of management by the Asante in Ghana. King Osei Kwadwo (1764–1777) organized the bureaucratic administrative system of state management. Trade in the Asante kingdom was organized as delegated authority to the middle level of management, to officials of the king. The king selected officials on the basis of skills, merit, and performance. These bureaucrats derived their authority directly from the king. They developed into a managerial officialdom with systematically evolving duties. These duties evolved around specific "departments" of administrative offices (*dampans* in Asante), but were also allowed to have their own independent business activities. These officials were therefore remunerated by the king, but could also establish their own private fortunes. The officials performed explicitly defined administrative duties to organize trade. Systematic records of transactions were kept according to the traditional accounting method using cowries. In this respect the king used educated Muslims and members of his own household, trained in the Muslim schools, to maintain the records. The extension of this system of administrative management spread across the kingdom as a display of royal authority. The decentralized "offices" of administration served as locations of further training of new officials. These positions were nevertheless not hereditary – a successful father could not count on his son inheriting his position. An extensive administrative class developed. Some were diplomats, who had to engage with neighboring kingdoms and cities. This position as an appointed official of the king gave these bureaucrats the opportunity to earn state remuneration and permission to accumulate personal wealth. Royal sanction thus created and perpetuated hierarchy and class formation (Wilks 1966, 1967, 1975; Andrea and Overfiled 2001b; Austin 2002; Wariboko 1997, 2002).

The reality of ethnic differences played out in another distinct form of management. In the eastern region of the Niger delta, a federal system of collaborative management developed. The management of business during the eighteenth and nineteenth centuries was a joint enterprise between managers and employees. Independent business people engaged in transatlantic trade along the western African coast. The business entities were organized in so-called trading houses (*war*), which constituted the control centers of trade and warfare. The leader of a business unit, or *wari,* was the manager who was responsible for the performance of the house. This manager was an indigenous chief, but he could not rely on the chieftainship to become or remain a manager of the *wari.* Success in the managerial position depended on the performance of the house. Promotion depended on performance and failure to perform could result in removal of office. Different houses competed with one another and failure to perform could bring an end to the managerial position of the leader. Individual ambition, intelligence, and responsibility toward the interests of the entire house were the traits which secured successful leadership of the house and a prolonged career to the manager. Since performance determined sustained leadership, both in business and warfare, the *wari* brought together like-minded, equally ambitious and dedicated persons working for their own prosperity. None of the positions in *the wari* was hereditary, but clearly conceptualized in indigenous law and customs. Merchants surveyed markets for the commodities in demand, sourced the goods they could trade and transacted in the most efficient way so as to manage transaction costs for the *wari*. *M*erchants invested in transaction-specific assets on the basis of the successful transaction conducted across various boundaries (each *wari* operated in a specific region, but was not confined to that operational space). These transaction-specific assets included human capital assets for trading and security protection, links to other trading partners, and transport equipment (Jones 1963; Horton 1969; Alagoa 1964; Wariboko 1998, 2002).

The *wari* operated in a federal form or association. A single *wari* operated under the management of a chief or manager, while a group of *wari* formed a *polo* for the purposes of collaboration in bigger trade enterprises. A number of *polo's* combined to make up a "corporation" (Wariboko 1998), which functioned loosely, but in a coordinated fashion in the interest of all the polo's. Each wari strove for optimal performance, thus motivating employees to work hard for the common prosperity.

Employees operated semiautonomously, since their functions were outlined only broadly as the objectives of the *wari*. Employees enjoyed a high degree of discretion on operational strategy, but the benchmark of conduct was optimal performance. If the *wari* underperformed, employees were at risk, since weaker performance could lead to the absorption by better performing *wari's* of underperforming ones. The employee is driven by the potential adverse effects of underperformance. The employee is managed by the manager but also afforded semiautonomous room to act according to her/his assessment of the context. The fundamental underpinning of trust – among employees mutually, between employee and manager – constituted the strength of the management "coalition" (Jones 1963; Wariboko 1998, 2002). Wariboko (2002) considered the wari (or canoe house system) not to constitute a systematic management strategy, but rather a collective assessment of context and decision-making toward realizing mutual goals. There was no doubt about the leadership role of the manager, but rigid hierarchies did not characterize this approach to management. He concludes: "Management was not a planned process of 'analysis and logic, but of emotion an intuition', and *ad hoc* responses to immediate needs" (Wariboko 2002: 245).

This case of the *wari* approach to management in western Africa illustrates the middle layer of management in Africa, where royal permission allows relative autonomy at the lower levels, both formal and informal, of management. The risk posed by this approach is the intuitiveness and lack of exact or precise boundaries to discretion. Under conditions of mutual trust and integrity, the *wari* succeeded, but once the underlying trust was broken, the entire system was at risk. More personalized individual "firms" also emerged as the indigenous African population responded successfully to the opportunities of coastal trade with European merchants passing the shores. Several interesting studies on successful entrepreneurs have been recorded. Such Ghanaian coastal merchant entrepreneurs were John Sarbah, John Kabes, and John Konny, who built prosperous family trading enterprises (Dummett 1973; Daaku 1970; Verhoef 2017). These developed into family enterprises trading with European firms on the coast. These indigenous black African enterprises functioned as the "middlemen" between suppliers in the interior and the European traders on the coast. The form of organization borrowed from the European firms as the entrepreneur operated as the private owner, the risk taker, and the beneficiary of profit. Extensive businesses developed under these conditions, but when European firms and chartered companies penetrated the African interior after colonization, the frailty of these businesses were exposed by international competition. Dummett held the following reasons responsible for the demise of many a West African trading firm: excessive competition, overextension of credit, ineffective accounting, natural disasters, lack of succession planning and death of the owner, fragmentation of business and property, oligopolistic price fixing by European traders, and finally the extensive rate-fixing and rebate policies of the West African shipping companies (Dummett 1973: 687). Many of these factors lay outside the control of the African entrepreneurs. Nevertheless, they exposed the shortcomings of the indigenous management system. Wariboko put the demise of the family trading firms down to the "...the non-European strands were short-circuited in their development. The European trading firms in the face of competition from African middlemen called in their governments to protect their trade" (Wariboko 2002: 249). In the colonial and postcolonial eras, Africa's entrepreneurs experienced a different form of managerial hierarchy. The newly independent state intended to achieve economies of scale and scope. The state intervened to coordinate and monitor the flow of business activities and to plan for the future allocation of resources (Drucker 1964). This exposed entrepreneurs to a new world of management.

The smaller African kingdoms, the strong presence of Muslim Arab and Indian traders from the seventeenth century, and the Portuguese presence gave rise to a more contested, dynamic business environment in East Africa. Zanzibar was the center of complex trading networks between the indigenous African kingdoms, the Omani Arab Indian Ocean traders of Zanzibar, other Indian trading families, and the Portuguese. The Omani traders established trading posts on the coast, from where exchanges were made with the indigenous African kingdoms (Austen 1987; Andrea and Overfield, 2001b; Abu-Lughod 1991; Seligman 2015). The African kingdoms managed trade as explained. Direct authority was with the king, who allowed his subjects, officials, or military men, to operate on his behalf. Ultimately, however, it was the king who collected the taxes. The Arab and Indian Muslim traders all operated in the family firm paradigm, led by a father, or manager. The managerial structure of the Arab and Indian Muslim family firms was simple: centralized control by the founding father and collaboration and execution by family members. The indigenous African people were less inclined to commercial trading, but intermarriage between them and the immigrant Indian trading families assisted in the transfer of some business acumen. The Indian families did not travel in caravans as the Muslim traders in North and West Africa, but lived in closed family communities where sociopolitical organization overlapped with the family enterprise. The Indian trading firms controlled the export trade from East Africa across the Indian Ocean and therefore exercised strict control over credit and the sourcing of commodities for export. These family enterprises had access to capital either through accumulated savings or credit lines from families in India. They also extended credit to Arab-Swahili traders in the region (Oonk 2011, 2015; Brown and Brown 1976). Similar Indian family enterprises develop on the Natal east coast during the nineteenth century. The Natal Indian family firms were also closely knit enterprises, managed by the founding father, employing family members and living in relatively secluded family compounds (Pachai 1971; Hiralal 2000a, b; Padayachee and Morrel 1991; Guest and Sellers 1985). Indian entrepreneurs also moved to the Transvaal after the discovery of gold to take advantage of new markets and the rapidly exploding population (Collier 1965; Huttenback 1971). Indian family firms emerged in nineteenth-century Transvaal and are today still operating under the fourth-generation family control. Similar family enterprises were started in East Africa (current Tanzania) during the late nineteenth century by Kanji Jeraj Manek, Subrash M. Patel, and Manu Chandaria (Sutton 2012) and by the Madhvani brothers in current-day Uganda and Mohan Kothari in modern-day Ethiopia (Sutton and Kellow 2010; Verhoef 2017). The management structures of East African trading firms, primarily in the hands of Arab Muslim or Indian families, offered no unique form of management in Africa. These were basically small and centrally controlled family enterprises. The longevity of these firms is testimony to the capable leadership, strategic planning, organization (succession planning and execution), and control by family members. This characterized management of family firms along the entire East African coast.

Conclusion

Pre-colonial Management in Africa

When Frederick Taylor developed his theory of the scientific management of business during the late 1890s, indigenous African managers generally considered their managerial function as an extension of the political system. Management was centralized and authoritarian, an outcome that reflected traditional African cultures, as well as Muslim perceptions of authority at the time. That was the "culture" of the time. European powers decided at the Conference of Berlin in 1884 on a framework for the division of Africa. From the last decade of the nineteenth century, European colonial powers systematically "scrambled" for control over parts of Africa which were considered in the interest of the metropolitan nation. Prior to this, international commercial enterprises commenced a new era of global expansion during the seventeenth century. The Dutch East India Company was the world's first "multinational" enterprise. The British East India Company operated in the East India region. Several other chartered companies received royal sanctioning to operate outside Britain. These internationally operating companies were managed by experienced businessmen, capable of directing operations across vast geographical areas. By contrast, management theory was in its infancy during the pre-colonial era in Africa. As the theory of scientific management theory introduced the concept of "thinkers" and "doers," or the distinction between managers and workers (Senge 1990; Schachter 2010), in Africa the ecosystem of diverse traditional indigenous cultures shaped the historical trajectories, capabilities, and cultural nuances giving rise to the African management sociopsychological norms (Honig 2016). The trends in African management emerging during the long pre-colonial era are twofold. First blurred boundaries between state power and economic power typified the sociopsychological integrated conception of power. Centralized and authoritarian power manifested on three levels – national or macro-state political level; intermediary ruler-appointed middlemen, bureaucrats, and military officials; and on the lowest level of primary producers and small traders. In the absence of the institution of property rights, decision-making and, therefore, original managerial decisions were only taken on the basis of delegated authority. The second trend is found in the ways that the nature of power led to social hierarchies and was perpetuated by Muslim penetration and expansion. The only evidence of collective social capital formation on the grounds of traditional culture is in the *wari* and family business contexts.

The distinction between state and enterprise management in western society emerged from the transition from mercantilism into laissez-faire during the nineteenth century. European nations, the Netherlands, Portugal, Britain, and France, encouraged extensive international voyages of discovery and establishment of trade connections. Up to the late nineteenth century Africa, both under indigenous African and Muslim Arab control, the management function was integral to sociopolitical power. As explained through the unfolding of the history of Africa before colonial penetration, managing the state implied managing the economy as an extension of royal power – either indigenous kingdoms or Muslim religious authority. In the sphere of business management in Africa, the separation of state power from the sphere of business was comparatively rare, since market-oriented policies were not implemented. Operational freedom depended on the political authority. Societies were highly hierarchical, thus hampering entrepreneurial freedom and the development of business-facing management. This culture of centralization and authoritarianism is still prevalent today (Jackson 2004; Mapunda 2013; Honig 2016).

In the case of the West African *wari* and in the Muslim-dominated family enterprises of East Africa, performance-driven collective culture contributed to the adoption of management practices supporting successful enterprise. The longevity of enterprise is supported by capable management. Business-facing management in Africa was seriously handicapped by the ecosystem, which is the concentration of state and economic power. This was prevalent during its history and persisted deep into the independence era. This chapter outlined the historical development explaining the failure to implement strong management in business under the "omnipotent" god-like king, religious ruler, or traditional indigenous all-powerful chief. In the wake of colonial control and subsequent authoritarian post-independence state systems, the dichotomy between collective culture and authoritarian sociopolitical power exercises a profound impact on the development of management practices in Africa.

References

Abu-Lughod JL (1991) Before European hegemony: the world system AD 1250–1350. Oxford University Press, Oxford
Alagoa EJ (1964) The small brave city-states: a history of Nembe(Brass) in the Niger Delta. University of Ibadan Press, Ibadan
Andrea AJ, Overfield JH (2001a) The human record. Sources of global history. Volume 1: to 1700, 4th edn. Houghton Mifflin Company, New York
Andrea AJ, Overfield JH (2001b) The human record. Sources of global history. Volume 2: since 1500, 4th edn. Houghton Mifflin Company, New York
Austen RA (1987) African economic history. Heinemann, London
Austen R, Cordell DD (2002) Trade, transportation and expanding economic networks: Saharan caravan commerce in the Era of European expansion, 1500–1900. In: Jalloh A, Falola T (eds) Black business and economic power. University of Rochester Press, New York, pp 80–113
Austin G (1996) No elders were present: commoners and private ownership in Asante, 1807–1896. J Afr Hist 37(1):1–30

Austin G (2002) African business in nineteenth century West Africa. In: Jalloh A, Falola T (eds) Black business and economic power. University of Rochester Press, New York, pp 114–144

Bartol KM, Martin DC (1991) Management. McGraw-Hill, New York

Baulin J (1962) The Arab role in Africa. Penguin African Library, Harmondsworth

Brown B, Brown W (1976) East African towns: a shared growth. In: Arens W (ed) A century of change in Eastern Africa. Mouton, The Hague, pp 183–200

Collier J (1965) The purple and the gold. The story of Pretoria and Johannesburg. Longman, Cape Town

Coquery-Vidrovitch C (1972) Le "Congo Francais" au Temps des Grandes Compagnies Concessionaires, 1898–1930. Mouton, Paris

Daaku KY (1970) Trade and politics on the Gold Coast, 16—11720: a study in the reaction to European trade. Oxford University Press, Oxford

Drucker P (1964) Managing for results. Harper and Row Publishers, New York

Drucker P (1974) Management: tasks responsibilities practices. Heinemann, London

Dummett RE (1973) John Sarbah, the elder and African mercantile entrepreneurship in the Gold Coast in the late nineteenth century. J Afr Hist 14(4):653–679

Fage JD, Tordoff W (2002) A history of Africa. Routledge, London

George G, Cornishley C, Khanyesi JN, Haas MR, Tihanyi L (2016) Bringing Africa in: promising directions for management research. Acad Manag J 59(2):377–393

Guest B, Sellers JM (1985) Enterprise and exploitation in a Victorian Colony. Aspects of the economic and social history of colonial Natal. University of Natal Press, Pietermaritzburg

Hiralal K (2000a) Indian family business in the Natal economy 1890–1950. Unpublished D.Phil thesis, University of Natal

Hiralal K (2000b) Impact of World War 1 on the Indian commercial class in Natal. Historia 46(1):418–432

Holt PM, Lambton AKS, Lewis B (1970) The Cambridge history of Islam, vol 2. Cambridge University Press, Cambridge, UK

Honig B (2016) Entrepreneurship and SME management across Africa: a perspective and short review. In: Achtenhagen L, Brundin E (eds) Frontiers in African business research, pp. 213–218. Springer

Hopkins AG (1973) An economic history of West Africa. Longman, London

Horton R (1969) From fishing village to city state: a social history of CALABAR. In: Douglas M, Kaberry PM (eds) Man in Africa. Tavistock Publishers, London

Huttenback RA (1971) Ghandi in South Africa. British imperialism and the Indian question, 1860–1914. Cornell University Press, Ithaca

Jackson T (2004) Management and change in Africa. A cross-cultural perspective. Routledge, London

Jones GI (1963) Trading states of the oil rivers. Oxford University Press, London

July RW (1998) A history of the African people, 5th edn. Waveland Press, Prospect Heights

Law R (1977) Royal monopoly and private enterprise in the Atlantic trade: the case of Dahomey. J Afr Hist 4:555–577

Lovejoy PE (1986) Salt of the desert sun: a history of salt production and trade in the central Sudan. University of Wisconsin Press, Madison

Mapunda G (2013) African philosophy of management in the context of African traditional cultures and organisational culture: the case of Kenya and Tanzania. Philos Manag 12(2):9–22

Oliver R (ed) (1977) The Cambridge history of Africa. Vol 3, from 1050 to c.1600. Cambridge University Press, Cambridge, UK

Oliver R, Atmore A (2001) Medieval Africa, 1250–1800. Cambridge University Press, Cambridge, UK

Oonk G (2011) Clothing matters: Asian-African businessmen in European suits, 18801–1980. Comp Sociol 10:528–547

Oonk G (2015) Gujarati Asians in East Africa, 1880–2000: colonization, de-colonization and complex citizenship issues. Diaspora Stud 8(1):66–79

Pachai B (1971) The international aspects of the South African Indian question, 1860–1971. Struik, Cape Town

Padayachee V, Morrel R (1991) Indian merchants and Dukawallas in the Natal economy, c 1875–1914. J South Afr Stud 17(1):73–102

Schachter HL (2010) The role played by Frederick Taylor in the rise of the academic management fields. J Manag Hist 16(4):437–448

Seligman AF (2015) Wealth not by any other name: inland African material aesthetics in expanding commercial times, ca. 16th – 20-th centuries. Int J Afr Hist Stud 48(3):449–469

Senge PM (1990) The fifth discipline: the art and practice of the learning organisation. Doubleday, New York

Sutton J (2012) An Enterprise map of Tanzania. International Growth Centre, London

Sutton J, Kellow N (2010) An enterprise map of Ethiopia. International Growth Centre, London

Trimmingham J (1968) The influence of Islam upon Africa. Longmans, London

Van Aswegen HJ (1980) Die Geskiedenis van Afrika. Van die vroegste oorsponge tot Onafhanklikheid. Academica, Pretoria

Verhoef G (2017) The history of business in Africa. Complex discontinuities to emerging markets. Springer International, Cham

Wariboko N (1997) Mind of African strategists: a study of Kalabari management practice. Fairley Dickinson University Press, New York

Wariboko N (1998) A theory of the canoe house corporation. Afr Econ Hist 26:141–172

Wariboko N (2002) Management in post-colonial Africa: historical and contemporary perspective. In: Jalloh A, Falola T (eds) Black business and economic power. Univerity of Rochester Press, Rochester, pp 238–276

Wickins PL (1981) An economic history of Africa from the earliest times to partition. Oxford University Press, Cape Town

Wickins PL (1986) Africa 1880–1980. An Economic History. Cape Town: Oxford University Press

Wilks I (1966) Aspects of bureaucratization in Ashanti in the nineteenth century. J Afr Hist 7:216–231

Wilks I (1967) Ashanti government. In: Forde D, Kaberry P (eds) West African kingdoms in the nineteenth century. Oxford University Press, Oxford

Wilks I (1975) Asante in the nineteenth century: the structure and evolution of political order. Cambridge University Press, New York

Africa and the Firm: Management in Africa Through a Century of Contestation

53

Grietjie Verhoef

Contents

Introduction	1208
Introducing the Firm: African Management Complexity and Diversity	1209
Scramble and Control	1210
Distorted Markets	1212
Into Its Own: African Management in Independent Africa	1217
State and Firm: African Renaissance	1219
The Management Discourse: Collective or Strategic Performance Drive?	1222
Distinct African?	1223
Concept and Ideology	1226
Conclusion: Organization and Business in Africa	1229
References	1232

Abstract

As the contours of exchange between African merchants and external agents changed, so did management practices develop in Africa. Three stages of global interaction developed to connect African business with the rest of the world. From pre-colonial to post-colonial interaction emerged managerial practices as African entrepreneurs negotiated the changing context of business. Management slowly adapted to the transition from traditional control to individual enterprise. In the late twentieth century, market liberalization supported the rise of individual entrepreneurs. This gave rise to management styles aligned with modern western management. A complex management dynamics was perpetuated through the sustained state intervention in post-independence economies. A claim to a distinct African management style raised a discourse on the essence of how firms are

---

G. Verhoef (✉)
College of Business and Economics, University of Johannesburg, Johannesburg, South Africa

College of Global Business, Monash University, Melbourne, VIC, Australia
e-mail: gverhoef@uj.ac.za; grietjie.verhoef@monash.edu

© The Author(s), under exclusive licence to Springer Nature Switzerland AG 2020
B. Bowden et al. (eds.), *The Palgrave Handbook of Management History*,
https://doi.org/10.1007/978-3-319-62114-2_98

managed in Africa, especially in the context of growing globalization of African business. The dynamics of management in Africa in the twenty-first century is the fusion between modernity and tradition.

Keywords

Middlemen · Technology · Institutions · Decentralise · State-owned enterprise · Family firm · Conglomerate · Indigenous knowledge

Introduction

The dynamic processes of historical change follow human agency. The question about why some nations are wealthy and other nations poor has taken on a "great divergence" discourse. The key to understand the development paths of peoples is understanding exchange. It concerns the action of human agency to extend beyond isolation and gain from human ingenuity in other distant geographies. Adam Smith argued in his 1776 *Wealth of Nations* that exchange between markets promotes accumulation and wealth. It is the ability of societies to overcome the "diffusion barriers" (Day 1998) that allowed for exchange. This exchange was not only trade in commodities but also exchange in capabilities – the ability to write and technology to master environmental challenges and social organization (institutions) – enhancing progress from subsistence to wealth. It was essentially the voyages of discovery by Vasco da Gama and Christopher Columbus since the fifteenth century that paved the way for the division between rich and poor (Madison 2007; Allen 2011). Geography facilitated the early diffusion of civilization across Eurasia and North Africa, while the Sahara desert posed a barrier to the diffusion of the progressive technologies of civilization to spread to sub-Saharan Africa. Some technology (pottery and iron metallurgy) arrived in Africa at almost the same time as in Western Europe, but only found its way to the southern tip of Africa 1000 AD. Once the geographical barrier was overcome, the dominance of the advanced European technology and social organization had a profound influence on African societies. The first globalization of the fifteenth and sixteenth centuries took European nations by ships to distant part of the globe, enabling extensive exchange and physical penetration or colonization. Between 1500 and 1800, the foundations for progress and prosperity were laid in societies currently considered to be rich nations – the Low Countries and Britain (and societies of British settlement – Australia, Canada, New Zealand, and the USA). The difference in wealth between these countries and all of Africa did not commence in 1500, but was exacerbated by subsequent developments. In 1500 Africa was already poor by international comparison – the poorest region in the world. Reflecting on the fundamentals underlying the prosperity of the wealthy nations, the factors are geography, institutions, culture, and "accidents of history." The human agency contributing to successful wealth creation in countries that outcompeted most other countries of the world, Western European countries, Britain, and the USA, are the following: developing an integrated internal market through the removal of internal tariffs and transport infrastructure, external protective tariffs to secure the domestic market, mass education to strengthen literacy and numeracy, and chartering of banks to stabilize the currency and finance industrial development (Hellriegel and Slocum 1985; Pritchett 1997; Day 1998; Fogel 2004; Milanovic 2005; Madison 2007; Allen 2011).

Africa's development since colonization brings the intersection of Africa with the nations of the world that succeeded in building wealthy societies. This is the context of a distant tapestry of societies engaging with the western "firm" – a unit of entrepreneurial organization that shaped the integration into the global community. The path dependence on authoritarian political rule and limited human agency by indigenous black Africans in expanding exchange outside of the continent meant that the benefits of Smithian trade fell to the early Arab and Asian Indian merchants who crossed the Indian Ocean. Extensive intra-African trade soon linked to European interest in African commodities. The transmission barriers between technologically advanced societies were gradually overcome as European penetration delivered exchange between Africa and Europe. It also introduced the peoples of Africa to western institutions, sociopolitical organization, and economic systems. This chapter explores how management developed its economy and society in Africa in the era of colonial penetration and postcolonial independent Africa.

Introducing the Firm: African Management Complexity and Diversity

An overview of the history of African interaction with European organization of trade, enterprise, and society since the first wave of globalization through to the second wave of globalization unpacks the complexity of management in Africa. African history can be distinguished in three phases of global interaction. The first phase is trade exchanges and European colonization from the 1820s to the post-1945 World War II era. Africa then entered the postcolonial period of independence. The third phase emerged from crisis and restructuring. The last decade of the twentieth century ushered in a fundamental reconceptualization of firms, business, and society in Africa. Throughout these phases, dynamic interaction between social organization, political power, and economic activity influenced the degree of convergence between the western nations that had taken a lead in making their societies prosperous and progressive (the so-called Atlantic economy – O'Rourke 1997) and the African peoples. A brief outline of the African experience with globalization follows, thereby setting the context to understand management in Africa. Management in Africa does not reflect simply on the management philosophy and practices of indigenous black African people but to management of enterprises in Africa. This includes the management philosophy and practices of business owned by people of Asian and European descent. Africa has a multiethnic, multiracial, and multilingual population claiming Africa to be home (Verhoef 2017).

Scramble and Control

The fifteenth-century Portuguese colonization of Mozambique represented the first European establishment of political control over the indigenous African population on the east coast of Africa. However, competition and contestation over access to trading routes and trading posts – generally sponsored by the European dynastic or nation state – intensified during the seventeenth and eighteenth centuries. Prior to the actual colonization, European nations established trading settlements around the West African coast. When the Dutch East India Company (DEIC) usurped Portuguese power in the Indian Ocean during the first decade of the seventeenth century – the Dutch West India Company having previously evicted the Portuguese from their trading establishments on the West African coast between 1637 and 1642 – it followed this action up by establishing a refreshment station at the Cape of Good Hope in 1652, a station that became the main transit point for first Dutch and then English-speaking peoples into the Southern African interior. Other northern European societies to establish trading settlements in this era included Denmark, Sweden, France, and Brandenburg. In most cases, European trading companies operating on the West African coast initially focused on the highly profitable slave trade to the Americas (Lovejoy 2000). After the abolition of slave trade in the British Empire in 1834, however, commercial exchange in other commodities underlined the entrepreneurial nature of African societies. Through the existing trade networks under the auspices of the king or ruler, well-organized middlemen secured the flow of goods between suppliers and the market. European demand for palm oil, cocoa, rubber, cotton, gold, ivory, kola nuts, and salt witnessed the exchange of these products in return for European manufacturing goods (Austen and Cordell 2002; Ayittey 1991). Africa was therefore fully integrated into the global trade network, in humans as well as other commodities. The trade with sovereign indigenous black African rulers (chiefs, kings) depended on the establishment of a relationship of trust and goodwill between trading company and ruler. European merchants engaged with the independent political authority of the region from where goods were sourced. The organization and management of exchange with Africa did not change, but European trading companies restructured operations. Private business enterprises consolidated into larger businesses and sought British Royal Charters to sanction operations. Examples of such companies were the Royal Niger Company, which secured a Royal Charter in 1886, the Imperial British East Africa Company in 1888, and the British South Africa Company in Southern Africa in 1888. Apart from royal sanctioning of the companies' business activities, the companies were also granted the responsibility to administer the regions of operation on behalf of the British Monarch. Although this constituted the roots of British colonial conquest, it did not deliver the chartered company undisputed authority. That belonged to the indigenous king, to whom taxes were paid. The same applied to the Portuguese companies the *Companhia de Mocambique* (1888), the *Companhia da Zambezia* (1890), and the *Companhia do Nyassa* (1891) operating in Portuguese territories (Verhoef 2017; Fage and Tordoff 2002; Swainson 1980; Van Aswegen 1980; Hopkins 1976a, b; Smith 1974; Vail 1975).

The "Scramble for Africa" entered a complex juncture in the 1880s and 1890s. Britain had established small colonies in Sierra Leone, France in Senegal, and the Belgian King in Congo de Brazza. In each case, these representatives of European civilization were distinctly different from the African societies they encountered through trade. Intra-African exchange and conflict between very diverse African societies prevailed. But Africa engagement with the Europeans was not only with people of a distinctly different civilization. It was also qualitatively different in terms of technology and resources (Austin 2002; Austen and Cordell 2002). The European peoples commanded considerable wealth and superior military technology (arms and ammunition). Moreover, a highly contested situation in Africa among competing European nations resulted in an agreement on the rules governing the future partitioning of Africa into spheres of influence. Accordingly, effective occupation of colonies occurred only after the Conference in Berlin 1884–1885, with systematic European colonization occurring between 1885 and the first decade of the twentieth century, decades that saw the introduction and consolidation of European state administration. As colonial administration became more firmly established, chartered companies relinquished their charters and entered into concession agreements with the new colonial authorities. This was the beginning of colonial control, albeit gradually, over sovereign African states/kingdoms and Muslim trading positions. Increasingly, British, French, German, Italian, and Belgian colonial administrations subjected most of sub-Saharan Africa to their bureaucratic administration. The only two non-colonized territories at that time were Liberia (which became home to a repatriated population of African-American freedmen after the US Civil War) and Ethiopia. Management of the colonies was direct: central administration extended over all aspects of colonial subjects' existence. Since colonies were managed to render revenue to the mother country, or at least pay for its own administration, the managerial structures differed notably from the centralized state administration of the indigenous kingdoms/Muslim states. Although colonial expansion typically met with fierce opposition, by the close of the nineteenth century, the last pockets of resistance to direct European rule were being extinguished. By 1898, British authority was forcefully exerted over the Fashoda around the Upper White Nile River. In Southern Africa, in 1902, Britain exerted its authority by force of arms over the independent Boer Republics, the *Oranje Vrijstaat* and the *Zuid-Afrikaansche Republiek*. The solitary exception to this pattern of domination was Ethiopia, which successfully defeated attempted Italian conquest at the Battle of Adwa in 1891. The sole beacon of African independence, Ethiopia was subsequently conquered by Mussolini's Italy in 1935 to occupy Ethiopia, only to reassert its independence after World War II (Wickins 1986).

Political control allowed colonial powers centralized management of the economy. This in turn resulted in preferential treatment of national concession companies and policies that monopolized access to trade goods. Colonial control, until systematic decolonization since the 1950s and 1960s, sustained the managerial dichotomy between European state and enterprise and indigenous black African state and enterprise. Once contestation over markets, access to commodities, and control of transport routes, prices, and labor swung in favor of the imperialists, local business was confined to an adjunct function of European enterprise. Nevertheless, distinct features of African management practices remained fundamental to the organization of society and enterprise. The new colonial masters did not seek to replicate the mother country in Africa but govern the African possessions to supplement the dominant European market. This constitutes a fundamental difference between the colonial settlements in the New World of Australia, Canada, and New Zealand. In each of these latter mentioned geographies of European settlement, the majority of the emerging settler community originated in European societies, established institutions and organizations resembling those of the societies of origin, and soon established populations consisting primarily of a majority of European settlers. These locations of new settlement inherited settlers from "advanced agrarian civilizations," who took with them "productive agriculture, diversified manufacturing, and the institutional and cultural resources necessary for 'modern economic growth.' These vital elements included private property in land and landless labour, the cultural correlates required to organise property and commerce – 'writing, land surveying, geometry, arithmetic, standardized weights and measures, coins and a legal system based on written documents and officials who could manage those texts'" (Allen 2011: 92). The settlers dispersed those advanced technologies and institutions in the societies of their new settlement. In Africa the ratio of settlers to indigenous peoples was always the reverse. European colonial powers did not implement the full scope of the nineteenth-century development model in its African colonies. Three aspects were crucial: transportation networks (infrastructure), education, and financial institutions to facilitate investment. Colonial authorities did build transportation links, but did not implement mass education or transfer financial services expertise to the African population during colonial control. Suboptimal institutions developed as the colonial population was first subjected to direct authoritarian government and then in certain areas (especially West Africa) granted "indirect rule." This was a system of recognition of traditional chiefs, which resulted in the transfer of government functions to them by the colonial bureaucracy, allowed the perpetuation of practices not considered supportive of modern economic development, such as the right of chiefs to extract unpaid labor from his subjects (Allen 2011).

Distorted Markets

In Africa, colonial administrations governed their subjects without representation for more than a half century. After World War II, Britain led the way in implementing phased in degrees of self-government, a process that typically led to the granting of independence in the late 1950s or early 1960s. In West Africa, the former British colony of Ghana became the first nation to become independent in 1957. The postindependence economic development of such nations was, however, mitigated by many of their colonial experiences. Neither Britain nor France, the dominant African colonial powers, did much to foster the industrial development of their colonies. Instead, they were managed primarily with an eye to the supply of commodities which they could provide so as to augment metropolitan manufacturing. Under colonial administration, bureaucratic management of economic activity is manifested in macroeconomic management. Colonial administrations managed access to land, encouraged the production of cash crops, organized purchasing monopolies, arranged access to credit, and introduced marketing boards to control supply and prices (Nwabughuogu 1982; Austen 1987, 2016; Olukoju 2002b). The marginalization of indigenous business through colonial market intervention thus hampered convergence between the imported form of business organization, most notably the "firm" – associated with management practices drawn from European societies – and those in Africa. Moreover, under colonial control, African business had to operate within distorted markets. Consistently, the colonial state, be it British, French, Belgian, German, or Italian, manipulated markets through policies and institutions that favored metropolitan commercial interests. By the 1920s commercial business in West Africa was dominated by three companies: the CFAO (*Compagnie Francaise de l'Afrique Occidentale*), the SCOA (*Société Commerciale del'Ouest Africain*), and the United African Company. European-based merchants even organized themselves into a cartel, the West African Merchants (WAM), to offset any challenge from local entrepreneurs (Austen 1987; Wickins 1982; Hopkins 1976a, b; Jones 2000; Van den Bersselaar 2011; Murillo 2011). Such companies enjoyed guaranteed access to capital, new technology, and markets that the local African businesses did not. By contrast to the globally oriented European monopolies, African businesses rested on the agricultural operations of peasants and subsistence farmers, each of whom was seeking to secure the best price for their produce, a task made difficult by the colonial state sanctioned price-fixing by European buyer pools for commodities such as cocoa, palm oil, etc. Consistently, colonial authorities managed the state to the benefit of the "enterprises of the mother country." This constituted an exercise tied to imperial power and prestige.

In form, colonial administrations were organized to accord with Weberian ideas of bureaucratic scientific management. This involved a systematic approach to each aspect of economic life, careful training of each official to ensure that acted in accordance with the objectives of the colonial administration, and appropriate divisions of work and responsibilities between managers and officials. The colonial "enterprise" also operated on the basis of standardized tasks, reward for bureaucratic excellence, and routine tasks (Bateman and Snell 2009: 43). The management paradigm of the colonial state was thus bureaucratic. It did not encourage or allow opposition, integration of "worker" inputs (in the colonial context, the inputs of colonial subjects), or socioeconomic convergence. Through the different stages of colonial administration (from simple British protectorate status to representative government and finally responsible government in the case of British colonies, direct central administration from Paris in the case of French colonies, direct control from Lisbon in Portuguese colonies, and in a similar centralized authoritarian style by Germany, Italy, and Belgium (see Fage and Tordoff 2002; Collins and Burns 2007), a classic bureaucratic management style characterized the administration of state, economy, and enterprise.

Alongside the dominant colonial system of management, there existed an indigenous black African and Muslim business environment. Almost always, operations in this sector were conducted by the small owner-manager. African business had a strong agricultural base around small farmers or peasants and communal cultivation under chieftainship. Operating in a competitive market with indigenous African farmers were local entrepreneurs and merchant middlemen, the so-called "expatriate" businessmen of Arab Muslims, Levantines, and Jews (i.e., people were not indigenous black Africans nor agents of the dominant colonial society; see Olukoju 2000a: 192). This local class of business people helped with the planning of indigenous production, sourcing of commodities, and organizing the supply of indigenous market demand. In other words, these middlemen adjusted their activities so as to fill the business space that existed outside of colonial control with its concession agents and concession companies. On the small scale of localized production or exchange, management of indigenous black African and Muslim trading enterprises was simple. Basic functional diversification existed. Some produced foodstuffs as farmers. Others sourced ivory, gold, and other commodities for exchange. Others organized transport. The success of this entrepreneurial adaptation to European-induced market distortion is apparent in the overall strong economic growth in Africa during the colonial era (Killick 1981; Austen 1987, 2016; Collins and Burns 2007; Heldring and Robinson 2012; Prados de la Escosura 2011). Under conditions of economic growth, entrepreneurs built business entities that showcased efficient managerial capabilities: assessing market conditions, diversifying operations, and securing access to labor (primarily family) and capital (through accumulated savings). There is no shortage of cases of successful indigenous black African entrepreneurs under colonial rule. In Nigeria, the family-owned Dawodu automobile importing business was a notable entrepreneurial success by the 1920s. James George and Son established a general trading business in Nigeria. Another Nigerian success was the tailoring enterprise of Salami Agbaje, which diversified from clothing to transport, food, and entertainment. This outcome facilitated the second generation of Agbaje siblings to diversify further after 1950 (Olukoju 2002a, 2015; Oladipo 2012; Verhoef 2017). In East Africa, most notably Kenya, similar local businesses were typically smaller and largely confined to agricultural production and marketing. Coffee, tea, wattle bark, meat, tobacco, and sisal were supplied to the manufacturing enterprises of the BEAC. Meanwhile, Asian Indian Muslim trading families controlled both the export trade across the Indian Ocean and the wholesale trade, an outcome that caused animosity between local traders and the Asian Muslim traders from Gujarat who had been in that market for two to three generations. As an enduring feature of East African commercial life, this animosity continued to fester until the establishment of an independent Kenyan state (Kennedy 1988; Swainson 1980; Cowen 1972; Marris and Somerset 1971).

The colonial period closed without any fundamental digression from the centralized bureaucratic management paradigms in Africa, paradigms whose broad principles were accepted both by the colonial state and traditional enterprise. Irrespective of the adverse or positive assessment of colonial rule, African people from all the different ethnic, religious, or language groups did not have any meaningful participation in the government of their states/colonies. Nor did they have much say in the rules that governed economic life. Centralized management perpetuated a dualism – European rulers and accompanying society and diverse African social entities operating separate and relatively distinct socioeconomic institutions. This was clearly reflected in the management practices of small African business enterprises. Business organization was primarily built around the founder and his/her family or kinship. The "house" system (*wari*) of businessmen trading on behalf of the king/state was closer to a modern "firm" since business transactions were mainly concluded between such units rather than between individual buyers and sellers. This form of business organization fed into small firms during the colonial era, since the political power of the indigenous king was replaced by that of the colonial authority. The use of kinship networks to secure market access, gain knowledge about demand and supply, and reduce costs through information flows account for much of the success of such enterprises (Curtin 1984). In East Africa family enterprises constituted the backbone of private enterprise, a pattern that remained constant during the pre-colonial, colonial, and postcolonial eras. Despite being small entities, these local businesses displayed traits of the modern firm through their organization of information flows, market knowledge, sourcing of supplies, price levels, and costs. The size of these enterprises, however, limited the scope and sophistication of management capabilities acquired, compared to those of large cross-continental trading businesses. Consequently, during the decolonization period of the 1960s, there were comparatively few African enterprises which had expanded beyond the small business unit. Perhaps unsurprisingly, the expectation that prosperity would accompany political freedom after independence failed to materialize. Instead, the newly emerging political elites undertook what amounted to state capture of the commanding heights of the economy. As Mbaku observed: "They failed to constrain the state, providing ruling elites with opportunities to abuse their public mandates and engage in corruption, rent seeking and other forms of opportunism to enrich themselves at the expense of the rest of society" (Mbaku 2002: 213). In doing so, they undermined the institutional and organizational infrastructure of the indigenous black African entrepreneurial activities, limiting the potentially positive impact that organizations and institutions could have on future economic growth (Lamoreaux and Wallis 2017).

Indigenous black African and Indian entrepreneurs in South Africa also experienced similar restrictions to those experienced in other colonies on the continent. With the formation of the Union of South Africa in 1910, the new state introduced formalized racial separation. This restricted open market competition by confining people of color to designated geographical areas. Even prior to independence, this pattern of segregation was emphasized with the discovery of diamonds and gold in the last quarter of the nineteenth century, discoveries that effectively heralded an era of African development. In the mining towns, black African survival strategies gave rise to informal enterprises: trading in basic consumer goods, sewing, blacksmithing, transport with horse-drawn carts, domestic work, beadwork and basketmaking, etc. (Verhoef 2001; Copland 1982; Mayer 1961; Cobley 1990). Such activities grew in scale as urbanization gained momentum during the 1920s and 1930s. As wage labor expanded, women often took to informal entrepreneurial opportunities to sustain themselves outside the traditional sector. Opportunities were, however, limited by statutory racial segregation from the mid-1920s, a segregation that limited free access to markets. Similarly, access to land ownership was confined to the traditional communal land of the ethnic tribes (Native Land Act, No 27 of 1913). Residence in urban areas was confined to designated "native locations" (Native (Urban Areas) Act, No 2 of 1920) (South African Institute of Race Relations (SAIRR: n.d.). After World War II, restrictions became even more pronounced. Africans in urban areas were only permitted to engage in business activities in their designated areas (Native (Urban Areas) Consolidation Act, 1945). In economic terms, racial segregation constituted market intervention. Although this segregation restricted non-white business opportunities in the "European" sector, state policies also protected African entrepreneurs in their designated areas from competition by European and Indian businesses. As one official pronouncement declared, such protections were depicted as "one of the most important steps of economic development which goes hand in hand with the government's scheme of Native development" (SAIRR, B4/2: 1930). State policies in South Africa therefore facilitated business development, but in segregated geographies – a policy strongly opposed by urban African businessmen. From the 1930s, these businessmen organized themselves in African trading associations and in the 1960s established the National African Federated Chamber of Commerce and Industry (NAFCOC). Significantly, the state permitted such African business activism and indeed encouraged entrepreneurial conduct as fostering self-development. Certainly, the confined "township" (name of the urban locations of the African people) environment "nurtured" early entrepreneurs by prohibiting European or Indian businesses from operation in the African townships. African entrepreneurs engaged in milk and beverage trade, laundry services, transport, bicycle repairs, general trading, eating houses, etc. These businesses were small, owner-managed, and community-based. The difference between the South African context and the other African countries was that the state provided specialist assistance and funding to the entrepreneurs in designated African areas. Barred from operation in so-called white areas, black businesses competed both in urban and rural settings. In Johannesburg alone, the number of black businesses who were licensed to operate in its townships rose from 1137 to 11,460 between 1959 and 1969 (Mogotsi 1977). Many African businessmen accumulated great wealth and business acumen. When, finally, racial segregation was scrapped in the 1980s, they used this acumen to acquire powerful business empires. The Kunene family, the Maponya family, and the Tshabalala family are all examples of successful African business families who operated within the limitations of South Africa's system of racial segregation. The same was the case with Indian families such as the Mia family and the Dockrat family, both of whom successfully conducted their enterprises within the confines of designated Indian areas (Verhoef 2017).

Their power seemingly entrenched during the 1930s, the colonial administrations became an anachronism after World War II. The signing of the Atlantic Charter in 1942 toward the end of World War II not only signified the liberation of subjected peoples in Europe; it was similarly interpreted as the beginning of liberation for subjected African peoples from colonial control. For among the fundamental human rights which the Charter endorsed was the right to self-determination of peoples (Roberts 1998; Collins and Burns 2007; Van Aswegen 1980; Cooper 2002). Although colonialism did not grind to an abrupt halt in 1945, most British and French colonies were independent by the late 1960s. Where a colonial power attempted to defy the movement toward independence – as Portugal did in the case of Angola and Mozambique until a revolution in the metropolitan homeland in 1974 drew a close on the colonial era – it faced increasingly costly armed struggles. The reality of the new freedom, however, was the choice about the future: What political and constitutional models would be selected? What kind of economic system would be pursued? What must the institutional and organizational paradigm be?

At this conjecture in time developments in organizational and management thinking progressed beyond the scientific and bureaucratic management theories. The initial focus on the manager as decision-maker, the authority, and almost undisputed leader was supplemented by the growing perspective from the collective, the organization, or a wider stakeholder community in management. With decolonization and the dawning of independence and the complex intersection of centralized bureaucratic management by European colonial officials and expatriate businessmen, with rising African nationalist leaders in politics, economy, and society, Africans extended a challenge to existing management paradigms applied in Africa to colonies.

Into Its Own: African Management in Independent Africa

The expectation of independence was prosperity. The vision of independence was the modern state, the modern society with its modern quality of life (Cooper 2002). With a few exceptions, economic growth and improved standards of living evaded Africa. By the mid-1980s, Africa was caught in widespread poverty, crippling debt, and political instability. A complex convergence of factors contributed to this outcome. These factors include the previous economic policies of most colonial administrations, policies directed toward the extraction of commodities rather than the development of a diversified, inclusive economy. The colonial state also "managed" the colonies without integrating the colonized into an active, democratic citizenry. It was only toward the end of colonial rule that representative models of government found their way into the colonies. Many newly independent states fell into autocratic military dictatorships or one-party rule governments. After independence, the new political elite also insisted on centralized state control, but then in their hands. As the colonial state monopolized resource allocation and labor supplies, so did the newly independent states. Two macroeconomic models emerged, state capitalism and state socialism, or "Afro-Marxism," as Mbaka termed it (Mabaka 2002: 219). African states did not implement fully fledged socialism, except for Tanzania, where Nyerere enforced *ujamaa* in a one-party autocratic state. Neither was the Kenyan state capitalism a free market, but a state-captured capitalist market benefitting the ruling Kikuyu elite. Postindependence economic policy was described as "African socialism," but it was actually "managed capitalism." The state did not redistribute economic assets and opportunities through nationalization but through *Kenyanization.* That was local indigenization, favoring the ruling Kenya African National Union (KANU) political elite. The KANU-controlled state established SOEs, such as the Kenya Tea Development Authority, which controlled tea planation and distribution. The state controlled the "commanding heights" of the Kenyan economy – the power industry, the Kenya Commercial Bank, the Industrial Development Bank, the East African Oil Refinery, and the East African Portland Cement Company. By means of the Industrial and Commercial Development Commission (ICDC) and the Treasury directly, the Kenyan state secured participation in all major industries in the country (Leys 1975; Illife 1983; Killick 1981; Himbara 1994). Mbaka called these reforms "institutional reforms to 'decolonize' their economies..." which unfortunately "failed to enhance the development of indigenous capitalism" and which "stunted" indigenous entrepreneurship (Mbaka 2000: 218, 219). In both models the new independent African states resorted to nationalization of property, enterprise, and opportunity, which marginalized all capitalist business (Taylor 1992; Blunt and Jones 1992; Jackson 2004).

In the ideologically most committed socialist states, such as Ethiopia, Sudan, Tanzania, and Zambia, there was extensive expropriation (nationalization) in key sectors of the economy. The rationale of the Tanzanian state was "to ensure the proper management of the commanding heights of the economy: 'to transform the economy by articulating the principles of socialism and self-reliance'" (Msamichaka and Bagachwa 1984: 384). Autocratic political leaders were not accountable. Corruption spread, and social stratification widened the gap between rich and poor (World Bank 1991, 2000; Guest 2004; Verhoef 2017). Since the 1980s, the International Monetary Fund and the World Bank's international institutions' structural adjustment programs (SAP) have tried to overcome such endemic problems by tying loans and other forms of financial aid to the introduction of macroeconomic policies based on market-friendly policies. The demise of the Soviet Union in 1989, and the ending of its ideological (and often its financial and military) support for socialist economies in Africa, increased the vulnerability of many regimes. Any fundamental overhaul of state-controlled economies, however, required political leaders relinquishing power and allowing a private enterprise market conducive to business, something that many were loath to do. As liberal market reforms swept across global markets during the Thatcher and Reagan eras of the 1980s, many African states introduced market-friendly reforms, politically, economically, and socially. It is during this poststructural adjustment era of the last decade of the twentieth century and dawn of the twenty-first century that state policies increasingly incentivized private enterprise. The return to the market included privatization of the dominant postindependence state-owned sector. The postindependence era in Africa is therefore divided between the predominantly centrally planned state-controlled economic models and subsequent market reforms since the 1980s.

State and Firm: African Renaissance

Within the scope of two decades (1960s and 1970s), state-owned enterprises (SOEs) accounted for 17% of total GDP of African states. This is compared to a world average of around 10% and 5% in OECD countries. Some African countries were well below that level, such as Botswana, Liberia, and Sierra Leone. In Algeria net state flows to the SOEs amounted to 25% of GDP (Nellis 2005a; Hertog 2010). SOEs dominated economic activity: they accounted for 25% of all formal sector employment in all reporting African countries and more than 18% of nonagricultural employment, compared to 4% in OECD, 15% in Asia, 5.5% in Latin America, and 10% in North African countries reporting on SOE employment. It was estimated that SOEs in Africa contributed more than 20% to gross domestic investment in their economies, more than 14% of foreign debt, and more than 33% of domestic credit. In more than 75% of the francophone countries, SOEs dominated domestic sales (Nellis 2005b). The massive expansion of SOEs after independence contributed to the economic woes of Africa. General economic freedom was curtailed, entrepreneurship discouraged, and property rights undermined (Mbaku 2002). SOEs had a track record of persistent underperformance. From the 12 West African states, 62% of surveyed SOEs showed net losses, and 36% were in a financial state of negative worth (Bovet 1985; Nellis 1986). A 1985 survey of SOEs in 18 francophone countries showed that only 20% generated sufficient revenue to cover operating, depreciation, and financing costs. Another 20% of SOEs could only cover variable, depreciation, and finance costs. A further 20% could only cover operational costs. The bottom 20% failed to get close to covering any of its core costs (World Bank 1985). Generally poor performance of SOEs went hand in hand with inadequate governance practices (Nellis 1986; World Bank 2006; Bouri et al. 2010). The SOEs in the infrastructure sector were the worst performing SOEs. These malfunctioning SOEs had a spillover effect on the rest of the services sector, such a telephone line delivery, water supply, etc. Peter Drucker argued that the task of business is to create a customer, to innovate, and then to enhance productivity (Pearson 2012), but SOEs were not customer-facing. They were instruments of state power. These enterprises generally ran losses of a significant magnitude, secured low earnings, and thus delivered a heavy burden on already strained national budgets. SOEs were generally heavily overstaffed and suffered from consistent political interference, a weak human resource base, and an incompatibility of civil service bureaucratic procedures with commercial operations. A lack of experience in markets manifested in poor investment decisions by SOEs, under capitalization, below cost pricing, deficiencies in collection practices, poor reporting systems, and deficiencies in the composition and functioning of Boards of Directors. These deficiencies were management capability deficiencies. Put simply, "many African PEs (public enterprises) should simply never have been created" (Nellis 1986).

The development of enterprise management during the postindependence era suffered from the dominant state role and an associated distrust of private enterprise. Entrepreneurs soon realized that they could reduce risk and grow their business through aligning their business with the source of political power. The entrepreneur concentrated on exploiting economic opportunities and acquiring business opportunity (often through quasi-political means), not on running the organization efficiently. By prioritizing profit stream rather than profit margin, management directed resources toward optimizing business opportunities, volumes of deal flows, and expanding operations through "cultivating good relations and potential customers, creditors, and bureaucrats who control access to key resources" (Wariboko 2002). This client relationship between private enterprise and the independent African state encouraged firm expansion, not efficient firm performance.

The distrust of private enterprise and its ability to deliver on the promise of economic prosperity gave rise to a context of business unfriendly economic and industrial policies, systematically marginalizing private entrepreneurs or tying them in a clientele relationship to the state (Wariboko 2002; Verhoef 2017). In Ghana, President Nkrumah expanded the state sector in capital-intensive industries and state plantations in rubber, cotton, and sugar production. The surviving small privately owned enterprises built on capabilities in the general trading market. These businesses remained small, operated in exchange of agricultural crops, small-scale craft manufacturing (not industrial manufacturing of significance), and transport and construction sectors. In Nigeria the indigenization programs secured the transfer of ownership of enterprises to Nigerians. A lack of managerial capacity and capital finally convinced the state to allow foreign investment back into the country in the late 1970s. By 1986 Nigeria also undertook market reforms with the assistance of the international institutions' structural adjustment facilities. Latent entrepreneurial capabilities suppressed by a centralized corrupt postindependence state could take advantage of market-friendly opportunities. Big Nigerian-owned corporations, such as the Dangote cement conglomerate, succeeded in weathering the storms of political instability by maintained close ties to the sources of power in the Nigerian state. In contrast, the successful Ibru Organization sustained itself through the managerial and entrepreneurial capabilities acquired in the United African Company (UAC) and a legacy of a maternal trading family. The founder of the Ibru Organization, Michael Ibru, first worked for the British concession company UAC and subsequently invested his business skills acquired from UAC into the family trading company. This business diversified its activities to emerge as a multidivisional corporation by the 1990s – without alignment to the state. The Ibru family also had a tradition of women engaged in trade. This strengthened family entrepreneurial traits and supported business expansion independent of state alignment. In other West African postindependence markets, both Francophone and Anglophone, private enterprise, remained small scale. In East Africa, indigenization programs secured the transfer of enterprise to Kenyans and Ugandans. Once more, the significant state sector failed to secure economic growth and national prosperity. In Kenya, corporate capitalism thrived, but these businessmen were close to the ethnic seat of power. This sector was not protected from mismanagement. The small and informal sector still dominated business activities. Across East Africa, ethnic discrimination against Asian Indian citizens resulted in expulsions and business destruction. All the East African countries filed for assistance under the IMF and World Bank's international institutions' restructuring scheme at some stage during the 1980s. Central Africa was no different. Unlike many other states, Botswana followed an inclusive nonracial economic development policy. The state monopolized the mining, beef, and textile industries. By the 1980s, organized private business owners, labor, and the Botswana state arrived at a negotiated state-business relationship fostering state market-friendly policies. Mining and beef remained state monopolies, but in all other sectors, an open market was implemented. Botswana never needed structural adjustment, but sustained moderate growth (Verhoef 2017).

The "Africa Rising" paradigm emerged from the glimmer of hope as African economies commenced recovery from the deep and prolonged slump of the 1980s and 1990s. By the first decade of the twenty-first century, the NEPAD (New Partnership for Africa's Development) charter was accepted at the inaugural meeting of the African Union in Durban, December 2001. African leaders realized that Africa needed collaboration with the international community to address Africa's poverty. Suddenly African statesmen wanted to sponsor partnership between government and the private sector, a partnership in which the private sector would act as the "veritable engine of economic growth" and government as the provider of "infrastructure" and a favorable "macroeconomic environment" (NEPAD/AHG/ 235; Sec 23; Ojieda 2005; NEPAD 2015). African leaders admitted with growing frequency that, although the state retained an important role in socioeconomic development, it was also the case that the private sector had a funsdamental role in restoring Africa to "a place of dignity." All the elements of the institutional context underlying successful economic growth – institutions of individual freedom, property rights, rule of law, and security of democracy – found their way into the new discourse on reviving Africa's economy. Postindependence blaming of colonialism and a hostile world economic environment (Killick 1992) found another dimension of explanation in clientelism of the neo-patrimonialism discourse. According to this narrative, highly bureaucratic state apparatuses after independence facilitated the entrenchment of a patron-client relationship in Africa, favoring resource allocation to the loyal "clients" of state power. "Patrons" of the state developed a position of privilege, power, and protection which undermined governance and fostered corruption (Clapham 1985, 2002; Migdal 1998; Englebert 2000; Van de Walle 2005). The awakening of a sense of responsibility by African leaders for the economic and social destiny of the continent mandated the destruction of this system of neo-clientelism.

As the discourse shifted away from the postindependence "underdevelopment" paradigm, the "African Renaissance" dialogue assisted African leaders in admitting to the lack of state capacity and institutional quality. An important policy reform was privatization. The NEPAD Charter propagated a partnership between private enterprise and the state. Two models emerged: PPPs (Public-Private Partnerships) or full privatization. Privatization was managed with varying degrees of success (Nellis and Kikeri 1989). Nevertheless, by 2007, foreign direct investment into Africa rendered outstanding returns and oiled the wheels of privatization. Together with FDI went conditions: substantially improved governance of state and enterprise, market-friendly policies, security of property rights and democratic societies. These reforms mandated the systematic destruction of the neo-patrimonial state and the opening of society and the market to the dynamic energies of individual freedom and an associated drive to succeed (Englebert 2000).

The full impact of enterprise performance on the economic growth of African states became the stark reality of "Africa Rising." Having argued that slavery was the root cause of Africa's plight of poverty and slow economic growth, then placing it at the door of colonial exploitation, and subsequently pinning it down to the underdevelopment conspiracy, African leaders began in halting fashion to recognize their own agency in unlocking the full potential of entrepreneurial capacity in Africa. The evidence of entrepreneurial agency in capitalist economic activities in agriculture and trade in West Africa, and the smaller scale trading operations of generations of indigenous black African and Asian Muslim traders in East Africa, provided an adequate foundation for the confidence in Africa's capability to succeed in a market economy. There is no dearth of cases of successful African businessmen. There is also ample evidence of contextual constraints to the growth of small enterprises – through centralizing state monopolies, insufficient access to funding, lack of simultaneous industrial development policies, entrepreneurial incentives, and market protection to foster business development. Nevertheless, African business was not unprepared for the market. Small and medium enterprises have populated African markets since pre-colonial times. A smaller number of big corporations, having survived close to the source of political power, were able and prepared to take advantage of the market (Verhoef 2017). Illiffe (1983) had identified the deep-seated roots of African capitalism, soon to be supplemented by a new generation of African businessmen.

The Management Discourse: Collective or Strategic Performance Drive?

The dilemma of Africa is one of identity. Who are Africans? What is African? How does the continent account for its diverse people, cultures, and languages? Can a systematic inquiry into African management and business in all its diversity – emerging management philosophies, professional management strategies, western-style firms, informal business, and small- and medium-sized enterprises, – realistically have a single answer? The extensive literature on what "African management" may be, whether it exists as a coherent phenomenon and whether it encompasses management in Africa, present fundamental questions not addressed adequately in this literature. The current surge in the interest of what "African management" might be (Nzelibe 1986; Goldman 2013; Jackson 2004, 2013; Nkomo 2011; Van Rinsum and Boessenkool 2013; Mapunda 2013; Corbishley et al. 2013; Kan et al. 2015; George 2015; Achtenhagen and Brundin 2017) is motivated by the "unprecedented growth" in Africa since the early 2000s (Kan et al. 2015). Two considerations are prevalent. First, Africa needs sustained economic growth and therefore needs to follow international best practice in management of society and the economy (Marsden 1991; Perry 1997; Kuada 2006), a process that places emphasis on the business enterprise as a means of securing the sustained growth required to deliver on the NEPAD aim of alleviating poverty. Second, the multicultural diverse ethnic and linguistic nature of its population mandates managerial strategies harnessing the power of cross-cultural diversity in management. As a revisiting of the opportunity of markets dawned in Africa, the diversity of entrepreneurs and their enterprise is part of the new reality in Africa.

Distinct African?

Despite the increasing importance of corporate Africa – South Africa in particular being a base for well-known global firms such as Anglo-American, De Beers, BHP Billiton, and Woolworths – the informal sector and small- and medium-sized enterprises still dominate the business landscape in Africa (World Bank 2000). In Africa, entering the market in competition with entrepreneurs of diverse ethnic, linguistic, and cultural origins exposed business people to the cultures of conducting, organizing, and engaging with business competition. However, the discourse as to what is African management, what is the African philosophy of management, and what is indigenous management tends to be one-sided, focusing on the dominant ethnic groups to the exclusion of others. There is thus no literature on what Indian, Asian, Muslim, and Afrikaner management models, all integral to Africa for generations, might be. These constituent peoples of Africa all contribute to the rich diversity of management cultures of Africa, as vividly described by Gomes et al. (2013; Nkomo 2011; Honig 2016). This omission is more surprising considering the persistent emphasis on Africa's cultural diversity and complexity (Nyambegera 2002; Nkomo 2011; Kiggundu 1991; Kan et al. 2015). The discourse tends to reflect an "exclusion and expulsion" of something that is "not-African." The concept "African" was used as a metaphor, which, in the philosophy of Paul Ricoeur, acquired the power of "redescribing." In the postcolonial drive for establishing African authenticity, "African" served as a metaphor for "liberation." This "liberation" was from hegemonic Eurocentric science and technology, from hegemonic rationalist and instrumentalist organization theory, and from neoliberal market theory and commercial interests of global business – in any case, liberation from "Empire" and its global reach. This was an essentialist act to "create" an identity, an "authentic moment" which easily becomes an "invention of tradition" (Van Rinsum and Boessenkool 2013; Kan et al. 2015). In fact, as illustrated in the previous chapter, African merchants engaged extensively in capitalist markets, used acquired technology from European traders, developed their own international business networks, and organized their business in units resembling European firms. In East Africa, the Indian Muslim business communities have been instrumental in developing trade and commerce in the different independent states. In North Africa, Muslim entrepreneurs dominate commerce, and in Southern Africa, Indian businessmen and Afrikaners and different European cultural communities contribute to the economy of the region. A one-dimensional conceptualization of the people of Africa as indigenous black Africans adds to the poverty of the discourse on management in Africa. This is a fundamental flaw in management research. The question should be as follows: What are the diversity of management cultures in Africa and what are the dynamics of their interaction? How does the multicultural diversity of African entrepreneurs explain the development of Africa's economy?

What sparked the interest in the specific nature of indigenous black African entrepreneurs and management is the lack of systematic research into the nature and application of management approaches by indigenous black African entrepreneurs (Jackson 2004, 2013; Goldman 2013; George 2015; George et al. 2016; Kan et al. 2015). As international development agencies and multinational corporations engage more with business partners in Africa, a certain type of disconnect emerged. Africa needed institution building, leadership empowerment, and business development, but it assumed an understanding of how indigenous black African businesses were organized and managed. An understanding of so-called indigenous management factors was a prerequisite for successful business integration and international exchange (Dia 1990, 1996; Wohlgemuth et al. 1998).

As post-adjustment indigenous black African-owned enterprises entered into business with non-African business in the domestic market, with other enterprises in neighboring markets in Africa, or in the global environment with multinational corporations, it became apparent that the nature and culture of "African management" was vague or not understood. A literature emerged on what constitutes "African management." The context was indigenous black Africans repositioning themselves in the global environment. The awakening of and mobilization of opposition against colonial control early in the twentieth century, black intellectuals such as Edward Blyden and William du Bois, propagated Pan-Africanism. As the rejection of western intellectual domination mounted after World War II, African leaders propagated the concept of *Negritude*, a conscious movement to reevaluate African cultural values. When *Negritude* failed to solicit all-African support for being too closely articulated in a western conceptual framework, new ideologies developed around *Uhuru* (liberation and nation-building), *ujamaa* (African socialism) and *ubuntu* (African humanism), and the *African Renaissance*, popularized during the 1990s. Although not a new concept, *Ubuntu* was revived by Bishop Desmond Tutu, to give new theological content to the concept. The resurgence of the African mobilization concepts since the 1990s coincided with the structural adjustment of weak African economies and the rise of private enterprise. This was the context of the indigenous black African reappraisal of African identity as mobilizing dynamism toward economic reconstruction. As African leaders accepted their responsibility to grow Africa's economy, as articulated in the NEPAD Charter, the redemption of the concept of a distinct "African management" identity, underpinned by a distinct "African thought" and inherent African values embedded in *ubuntu*, proved to be a strategic tool to revive entrepreneurial agency so profoundly marginalized under colonial and postindependence heavy statism. A fundamental paradigm shift in policy and organizational change often met with opposition, since it was perceived as a threat to the influence and power of the new ruling class (Blunt and Jones 1992). Effecting organizational change within African organizations (state and private) was premised on defining what "African" is – African thought, organizations, culture, etc. Kan et al. describe "African management" as "an object of ideological posture of which ideal types of management styles can be distinguished... (which) is purposely mobilised in the literature on 'African management' as an essential tool for emancipation and resistance attitude" (Kan et al. 2015: 268). The systematic literature on "African management" as a distinct model of management has well-articulated agendas of positioning "African management" beyond the previously legitimized universal management knowledge (Nkomo 2015) and reveals the denied identity of the management of African organizations. This literature does not seek to place management research in Africa in the new context of Africa but to develop an "African management theory" of African organization, an Afrocentric knowledge of African organizations (Bamberger 2008; Lutz 2009; Holtbrügge 2013). No sufficiently coherent scholarly academic research on "African management" has yet been produced (Nkomo 2015).

The reinvention of "African management" resulted in extensive literature on the nature, underlying values, and complex diversity of the phenomenon. Central to "African management" were concepts such as ethnocentrism, traditionalism, communalism, and cooperative teamwork. The discourse positioned these elements as opposites to "western management," which was purported to promote Eurocentrism, individualism, and modernity (Nzelibe 1986). Embeddedness in African customs, beliefs, and practices is assumed to regulate every individual's conduct. Management practices are presented as recognizing the family as the "basic unit of socialization." An integrated existence between members of the family and nature exists, which brings the connection to the ancestry. This integrated nature of family is considered to underpin human communication in African organizations. For management in Africa, this means unity between the spiritual and material, of which the unified phenomenon moves in grand unity. This delivers the notion of "communalism" or communal sociability, which is the communality between the family as fundamental socializing unit and the tribe/clan, as the basic socializing unit. Communal sociability is the harmonization between different institutional levels in African society. This notion brought to African management thought the idea of the communality of persons' culture outside the organization with their position inside the organization (Kan et al. 2015). The notion of consultation is deemed to evolve from the tribal chief's decision-making process: "decisions were not made but they seemed to emerge. Elders did not take unilateral decision without informally consulting with other members in the society..." (Mbaku 2002). A strong emphasis is placed on the nexus between societal values and the operation of the organization, which suggests adherence to collective and communal conduct. These traits are also identified in informal mutual self-help social entities. The reference to "insider knowledge" as one dimension of the meaning of "indigenous" (Marsden 1991), the analysis of "African management" as a distinct concept, integrates the specific cultural elements outlined above (Nzelibe 1986; Kiggundu 1988; Barrat Brown 1995; Wild 1997; Safavi and Tweddell 2007; Jackson et al. 2008).

What transpires is an extensive literature on African thought and social organization, which has been extended into the organizational context as essentially part of the African renaissance paradigm of revitalizing Africa. Kan et al. (2015) interpret the main body of literature on "African management" as essentially "an act of resistance to the dominant literature in management. The African system of thought is mobilised as a means of (re) appropriation of African authenticity" (p. 260). This interpretation dovetails with Tony O Elumelu, the Nigerian banker's idea of an African capitalism, called *Africapitalism*. *Africapitalism* is advocated to promote African economic development through investment that generates prosperity and social wealth (Amaeshi 2013a, b; Elumelo 2015; Akinyoade et al. 2017). The explanation for the limited success of African business organizations concerned African scholars, who expressed discontent with the rationalist and functionalist conceptions of business in Africa. It was argued that the western conceptions of African business organizations fail to understand the indigenousness of such organization. Jackson (2013) unpacked "indigenousness and endogenous" as concepts explaining the knowledge from within the specific society, "a function of place and context, of collective values" (p. 22) – in this case the African society. The alternative conception considered to be better suited to the nature of African society and business is the humanist and cultural conception, which considers a distinctive African culture or identity underpinning African organizations (Jackson 2013; Mapunda 2013; Walsh 2015; Zoogah et al. 2015). The discourse on "African management" is essentially about the nature of African culture, society, and organizations from within the "indigenous" knowledge base, which Kane et al. describe as "part of a general reasoning having a dual objective: emancipation and resistance to domination of the Western world through Western management precepts" (Kan et al. 2015: 264). Promoting a fundamental understanding of the nature of African culture, as manifested in society and organization, and resembling the antithesis between "South" and "North," African renaissance management wants to place more emphasis on the human dimension of the organization, the "stakeholders," thus reconnecting with African culture. Culture emanates from outside the organization, but the people working in the organization bring that culture into the organization, and therefore in Africa, the management model is expected to reflect that "culture." A cognitive dilemma is that Africa is ethnically diverse and harbors multiple cultures and more than 1000 languages (Verhoef 2017).

Concept and Ideology

The recent engagement with conceptualizing "African management" gave rise to a reappraisal of concepts considered to be at the core of "African culture." The one concept central to the African renaissance is "Ubuntu." The extensive engagement with conceptualizing *ubuntu* as an Afrocentric concept has been part of the postcolonial search for African identity (Bernstein 2002; Lutz 2009; West 2014; Kan et al. 2015). *Ubuntu* is presented as a specific form of African humanism, which emphasizes the individual as a moral being, an African world view or a collective consciousness of the people of Africa. *Ubuntu* was presented as unique authentic African values of humanness, respect, caring, sharing, social justice, righteousness, care, empathy for others, and compassion. Most scholars explain *Ubuntu* as a communitarian ethic, articulated as *umuntu ngumuntu ngabantu* (*Nguni indigenous language*) – which can be translated as "I am, because we are; and since we are, therefore I am." This communitarian ethic is inclusive and expressed in solidarity, compassion, and sacrifice. These "values" are presented to constitute the essence of the African community, expressed in reciprocity, dignity, harmony, and humanity in building and maintaining community (Mbiti 1989; Mbigi 1997; Kamwangamalu 1999; Karsten and Illa 2005; Prinsloo 2000; Mbigi and Maree 2005; Schutte 2001; Broodryk 2005, 2006; Nussbaum 2009; Lutz 2009; West 2014). These notions are presented as characteristic of sub-Saharan societies as distinct from underlying western values and business philosophy. The constituent Ubuntu concepts are submitted to offer a unique African concept of behavior, applied to different spheres of human conduct, such as the legal sphere, education, nursing, government, and business management. The notion of communalism holds a potential contradiction with individualism and self-preservation, which has implications for entrepreneurial self-driven ambition and vision, but Mbigi (1997) considers *ubuntu* a dynamic spiritual/religious experience or spirituality, which does not rule out "an individual existence of the self and the simultaneous existence for others" (Schutte 2001). Thus the hallmark of *Ubuntu* is submitted to "be a good community member. It is also about living and enjoying life rather than the acquisition of the material creature comfort of life" (Mbigi and Maree 2005).

Despite the widespread acceptance of *ubuntu* as a distinctly African concept, it lacks systematic scientifically reconstructed content, based on systematic empirical research (Bernstein 2002; Metz 2007, 2009; Luts 2009; West 2014; Kan et al. 2015). No research confirms actual universality or consensus in Africa on analytical content or application of a preference for collectivism as opposed to individualism. In actual fact, Hofstede found in his systematic international cross-cultural survey of employees of the computer company, IBM, in 53 countries, a distinct lack of preference for collective conduct in Africa. Hofstede revealed an affinity among his African participants for a loosely knit social framework and a higher degree of interdependence. Choosing individualism (or "I") on a scale of 1–100, with 100 being highly individualistic, as opposed to interdependence (or "we") being rated close to naught, employees in East Africa and West Africa scored 27 and 20 (with the mean of the study lying at 43) and employees in the USA at 91 and Australia at 90. This outcome seemed to refute the inherent alignment of African people to communalism (Hofstede 2001; West 2014). The results for South Africa were 65, but West (2014) considered them to be unreliable, since the study was conducted while South Africa was still under a white-controlled national government applying policies of racial segregation. Accordingly, Thomas and Bendixen repeated the Hofstede investigation by surveying 586 South African middle managers a decade after the nation's holding of its first democratic elections in 1990. The result was a score of 81 by South African middle managers on the Individualism-Collectivism scale used by the Thomas and Bendixen study, a result that confirmed a stronger alignment to individualism in South Africa by both white and African people. White Afrikaans-speaking managers scored 77, Sotho managers 79, Xhosa managers 78, Zulu managers 83 [the last three categories are African managers], and English-speaking managers 88. These results revealed the notion of African people being less individualistic and white people more individualistic, as an unfounded simplistic generalization (Thomas and Bendixen 2000). This conclusion was substantiated by the Trompenaars and Hampden (1997) survey of company managers. On a wider geographical scale, Noorderhaven and Tidjani (2001) confirmed the complexity of cultural notions of communalism, social responsibility, human goodness, and sharing among African peoples in 12 sub-Saharan countries, compared to the UK and the USA. On these four dimensions of culture, aligned to elements of *ubuntu*, African countries (Ghana, Cameroon, Senegal, Tanzania, and Zimbabwe) scored less than 50 on the scale of "human goodness," while South Africa, the UK, and the USA scored higher than 76. On the notion of "sharing," the USA and Zimbabwe scored 45, as opposed to higher score of 62 and above by managers in Ghana, Cameroon, Senegal, and Tanzania. On collectivism the highest scores were achieved by managers in Cameroon, Ghana, Tanzania, Zimbabwe, and the UK, while Senegal and the USA had the lowest scores. Finally on the notion of societal responsibility, the lowest score was achieved by managers from Tanzania and Zimbabwe, while the highest scores were posted by managers from Cameroon, Ghana, Senegal, South Africa, the UK, and the USA (Noorderhaven and Tidjani 2001). These studies confirm the complexity and diversity of alignment with notions of collectivism, social responsibility, and other notions aligned to key elements of *ubuntu*. These studies refute the notion of an exclusive African concern for the collective or a lack of individualism among African managers. The fluidity of managerial traits seems to align more to the nature of the business context in which they operate than to ethnic cultural distinctions.

The most extensive body of literature on the concept *ubuntu* emerged from South Africa, as a supposed tool toward demographic transformation in the economy, specifically in business management. Van Binsbergen (2001) describes *ubuntu* as a utopian and prophetic philosophy, an "exhortative instrument," and a "tool for transformation in the context of globalisation" (Van Binsbergen 2001: 73). He argues: "Ubuntu offers the appearance of an ancestral model to (those who fought to attain majority rule) that is credible and with which they can identify, regardless of whether these urban, globalised people still observe ancestral codes of conduct- of course in most respects they do not, regardless of whether the ancestral codes are rendered correctly (often they are not)." Bernstein (2002) also argues that "the rediscovery of African values and culture is largely an elite reinterpretation of residues of what used to be... the fashionable celebration of Ubuntu is intended more for white consumption or to display a badge of (Africanist?) honour than as sincere moral reconstruction" (Bernstein 2002: 210). The skepticism is echoed by Chen (2014) and Kragh (2012), who question the idealism with which the concept is presented as only the positive aspects of African social norms. The dilemma for management research is that the literature on *ubuntu* remains anecdotal. In the absence of any systematic empirical research, the utility as a distinctive concept in African management is seriously constrained. Scholars have refuted the attempt to present *ubuntu* as a uniquely African idea of "humanness," a sense of social connectedness of individuals to society and fellow humans, exclusive to African societies. The notion of interpersonal relationships embedded in a moral philosophy,

Metz (2007, 2009) argued, has its foundations in traditional European normative theories. Aristotle developed the idea of self-realization and of interpersonal relationships as supplementary and noncontradictory. Applying the ancient and medieval moral philosophy of "the common good is my good" allows a wider understanding of human universalism which confirms shared rather than contradictory normative values in western civilization (Lutz 2009; Kan et al. 2014; West 2014). The studies on *ubuntu* outside South Africa illustrated that the concept was not widely held, thus undermining the claim to its general depiction of a typical African value and therefore fundamental element of a distinct "African management" model.

Conclusion: Organization and Business in Africa

The reality of management in Africa is that western management thought penetrated business practice systematically as scholars joined business schools in the UK and the USA (Kamoche 2011; Perry 1997; Kuada 2006). Since the IMF's structural adjustment programs opened market opportunities to entrepreneurs, private business has expanded. Although privatization programs were slow and often incomplete, they nevertheless offered the "dormant" African entrepreneur access to business opportunities – for which some were remarkably well prepared. In East Africa well-capitalized and well-managed family businesses, often with generations of entrepreneurial experience, were able to acquire loss-making SOEs. In a short period of time, such businesses were restructured, business operations diversified, and operations extended into neighboring markets (White and Bhatia 1998; Sutton and Kelow 2010; Suttton and Kapenty 2012; Sutton and Olomi 2012; Sutton and Langmead 2013; Sutton 2014). Within a short time, business organizations resembling the western firm, or corporation, characterized the emerging African economies. Two elements marked these enterprises: firm bureaucratic control from the center by the patriarch or head of the family (or by the new entrepreneur) and individual ownership. Many emerging poststructural adjustment businesses perpetuated firm structures built around patterns of pre-colonial kinship or family connections. Although the family structure epitomizes the *ubuntu* principle of collective benefit, it was nevertheless the case that sustainability of enterprises mandated adherence to market requirements, such as capital efficiency, productivity, operational efficiency, and profitability. Not one of the diversified conglomerates in Africa (excluding South Africa) is a public-listed company. In each conglomerate, the first- and/or second-generation family managers benefit from the next generation being educated in the USA or the UK, plowing back western management principles and expertise into the firm. A number of these conglomerates now dominate their chosen markets not only within their own country but across entire African regions. Here consideration can be given to the Trade Kings, a Zambian conglomerate owned by the Patel family, a firm, which during the 1990s merged its cotton ginnery operations with those of the Kenyan-based cotton businesses of Munir Zaveri, whose grandfather had settled in Kenya during the nineteenth century. The Unity Group of companies, owned by Manu Shah, also developed from humble trading operations, having been started by the current owner's Gujarat-born grandfather, an entrepreneur who arrived in Kenya in the late 1890s. Originally confined to Kenya, the Shah family business interests have recently extended into Tanzania. In each family enterprise, the second or third generation acquired business education outside Africa to benefit the business. Similar examples of firms that have witnessed a restructuring of long-established family business along modern management and business principles are found in the Mohan Kothari Group of companies in Ethiopia, the Azam Group of companies owned by the Bakhresa family in Tanzania, the MeTL Group owned by the Dewji family (operating in Tanzania as well as in most other SADC countries), the Madhvani Group in Uganda, the Sawiris family of the Egyptian Orascom Group (some of the companies in the Orascom Group are listed on the Egyptian Stock exchange), the Comcraft Group in Kenya owned by the Chadaria family, and the Dangote Group in Nigeria (Verhoef 2017). New African global conglomerates (operating outside Africa) include the Craft Silicon Group and the Mara Group.

The successful operation of conglomerates such as those mentioned above, as well as the dominant small- and medium-sized enterprises across the continent, occurs typically within the paradigm of modern management thought. The *ubuntu* discourse, by contrast, is an ideologically motivated "rewriting of Africa" discourse, which only impacts on modern management through the existing organizational development (OD) thinking in management theory (Hellriegel and Slocum 1985; Wren 2005; Wren and Bedian 2009; Shafitz et al. 2005). In truth, private enterprise in Africa has benefitted from more market-friendly business policies as well as from the example of successful businesses across the African continent. The management model was not something distinctly African but aligned to the development in international management theory. Indeed, management thought in Africa has progressed systematically since the mid-1950s. The only contribution of the concept of *ubuntu* to this development is through its emphasis on African cultural diversity. As Kamoche noted, "Any scholarly quest for a distinctive 'African' management style is almost always going to be futile." The cultural, linguistic, and leadership styles are simply too diverse across the continent (Kamoche 2011). The *ubuntu* discourse highlights the dimension of African culture, but cannot offer a single comprehensive view of "African culture," since it does not exist. African culture is diverse, complex, and contextually determined. The contribution to OD theory is therefore to sensitize management to contextual complexity.

The literature on *ubuntu* is essentially propagating a frame of thought, but, as argued, fails to present a concrete and distinct system of management. Nkomo (2015) admits to the inability of the proponents of "African management" to construct a coherent body of knowledge on the subject. Elumelu's *Africapitalism* and Eze's call for the revitalization or reinterpretation of "*Ubuntu* as a moral ideal for a new age" (Eze 2010) are similar expressions of a desire for a future dispensation. Zoogah et al. (2015) propose a framework to explain the effectiveness of African organizations, but unfortunately there is no case of an *ubuntu*-managed enterprise in Africa that can be tested against the performance of non-*ubuntu*-managed enterprises. Nkomo also appeals for an assessment of the impact of "indigenous African knowledge transfer" on operations of multinational corporations in Africa. She nevertheless admits that there is an illusion of cultural uniqueness in the rhetoric on "African management" (Nkomo 2011). Again, what this "indigenous knowledge" is and how it is transferred is still to be established. How then can this system of management be identified and studied systematically? The tentative nature of the "African management" model remains vague, thus inhibiting systematic scrutiny, assessment, and comparison. This literature seeks to achieve a form of "Africanization" of management to enhance organizational efficiency. In a multicultural context, this appeal is directed at achieving four outcomes: greater equity among employees, higher productivity, strong loyalty to the organization, and improved organizational citizenship (Kan et al. 2015). These outcomes (proposed in the study of McFarlin et al. 1999) are all encompassed in the Hawthorne effect in management enabling people to achieve their full potential as fulfilled employees, by considering the human side of the enterprise of equal strategic importance.

The dilemma of the "African management" narrative lies in the ideological nature of the discourse. Kan et al. (2015) offer a concise position. They argue that the research on "African management" can be separated into three different intellectual postures: "convergence, divergence, and crossvergence." On the one hand, the proponents resist convergence of cultural values that may be affected through managerial action. The insistence on a distinct "African management" model based on the "unique" concept of *ubuntu* leaves a point between divergence and crossvergence. By insisting on the filter of "African thought systems" to conceptualize organizations, the proponents admit to the contextual nature of organizational processes. This is clearly a "rewriting" exercise, pursuing an "ideal type of the African renaissance management" – albeit it being "not sufficiently abundant to form a coherent body of knowledge" (Kan et al. 2015: 272; Kamoche 2011). In seeking to "rewrite" or revitalize "African management" in practice, this work is tentative – the "hybridization" of management systems and the development of concepts of crossvergence have been developed in management research in Hong Kong, but not yet to any significant degree in Africa (Jackson 2004: 30; Kuada 2006). The "African management"/*ubuntu* discourse fails to contribute to the identification of an authentic African management model. It has rather become an aspect of OD's focus on cross-cultural perspectives on management (Bendixen and Burger 1998).

The rise of indigenous black African persons to positions of leadership and management, e.g., under conditions of indigenization programs (such as statutory enforced Black Economic Empowerment (BEE) in South Africa – Verhoef 2017; Taylor 2002), or through entrepreneurial ingenuity, as displayed in the rise of African-owned conglomerates mentioned above, occurred in the form of the modern firm. Emerging from business schools in South Africa, the UK, and the USA, the new managers and leaders run enterprises to achieve optimal efficiency and profitability as socially responsible enterprises, having to report on the triple bottom line: financial sustainability, environmental sustainability, and social sustainability/responsibility (Witzel 2012). Indigenization policies were implemented widely across Africa in the postindependence states, but with checkered success. These policies must not be confused with the discourse on "African management." These policies were about the transfer of ownership of private business assets from so-called expatriates to the indigenous population, irrespective of the business acumen or management capability of the recipient. In South Africa, the state intervened in the market on the justification of correcting "historical" legacies of discrimination. The BEE program encompasses extensive statutory sanctioned transfer of ownership and control of sectors of the economy, and thus of individual businesses within the sectors, to black people (black people are defined as indigenous African black persons, colored persons, and Indian persons). The state mandated the "negotiation" of so-called Sectoral Charters between white owners and black persons, for the transfer of ownership and control of specified portions of the sector within a specified timeframe. To supplement ownership and control, employment of persons of the dedicated demographic groups is statutorily mandated. Furthermore, non-compliance with the BEE requirements excluded enterprises from doing business with the state. Statutorily sanctioned procurement policies are BEE aligned (Verhoef 2017; DTI 2003; Empowerdex 2012). The visible profile of black persons in management, ownership, and control of business across the board in South Africa, as well as in the composition of the employee profile, impacted primarily on human resource management thinking. In the context of the organization, in South Africa, as well as in all other African business contexts, OD is deeply grounded in cross-cultural dynamics. In South Africa, statutory sanctioning forced business enterprise to address those dynamics over a very short period of time, while the experience in other African countries was more delayed and linked to the dynamics in multinational corporations. MNCs were largely expelled from independent Africa, with few exceptions, but returned to the African market after structural adjustment and the dawn of market-oriented state policies. The phenomenon of multiculturalism poses complex challenges to management. These challenges are not addressed by perpetuating the earlier "colonial/indigenous" binary divide of the colonial era through insisting on a distinct "African management" model. Bendixen and Burger (1998) found that the market-oriented management model is the only management model positively correlated to organizational effectiveness (Bendixen and Burger 1998). The emerging management model in Africa is indeed aligned to those of successful western corporations, but must consciously address organizational diversity. Fundamental dissimilarity in value priorities of the societies encapsulating them is not limited to Africa but is a universal phenomenon. The resource-based perspective on management, which is fundamental to organization theory, mandates dealing with diversity, irrespective of the source of the diversity – race, creed, culture, or language. This is the constructive discourse on management in Africa.

References

Achtenhagen L, Brundin E (2017) Entrepreneurship and SME Management across Africa. Springer, Singapore

Akinyoade A, Dietz T, Uche C (2017) Entrepreneurship in Africa. Brill, Leiden

Allen RC (2011) Global economic history. A very short introduction. Oxford University Press, Oxford

Amaeshi K (2013a) Africapitalism: a philosophy for sustainable business in Africa? Guardian. www.theguardian.com/sustainable-business/africcapitalism-philosophy-sustainable-business-africa. Accessed 24 Oct 2018

Amaeshi K (2013b) Africapitalism: unleashing the power of emotions for Africa's development? African Arguments of Royal African Society. http://africanargument.org/2013/10/02/africaptails-unleashing-the-power-of-emotions-for-africas-developemnt-by-kenneth-ameshi. Accessed 24 Oct 2018

Austen R (1987) African economic history. James Currey, London

Austen RA, Cordell DD (2002) Trade, transport and expanding economic networks: Sahara caravan commerce in the era of European expansion, 1500–1900. In: Jalloh A, Falola T (eds) Black business and economic power. Rochester University Press, Rochester, pp 80–112

Austin, G (2002) African business in nineteenth century West Africa Jalloh, A, Falola, T Black business and economic power. Rochester: University of Rochester Press: 114–144

Austin G (2016) The state and business in Ghana: precolonial colonial and post-colonial (1807–2000). Unpublished paper to African economic History Network, Sussex, October 2016

Ayittey GBN (1991) Indigenous African institutions. Transnational Publishers, New York

Bamberger P (2008) From the editors beyond contextualization: using context theories to narrow the micro-macro gap in management research'. Acad Manage J 51(5):839–846

Barratt Brown M (1995) Africa's choices: after thirty years of the world bank. Penguin, London

Bateman TS, Snell SA (2009) Management: leading and collaborating in a competitive world, 8th edn. Boston, McGraw-Hill Irwin

Bendixen M, Burger B (1998) Cross-cultural management philosophies. J Bus Res 42(2):107–114

Bernstein A (2002) Globalization, culture and development: can South African be more than an offshoot of the West? In: Berger PL, Huntington SP (eds) Many globalizations: cultural diversity in the contemporary world. Oxford University Press, New York, pp 185–249

Blunt P, Jones MI (1992) Managing organizations in Africa. Walker de Guyter, Berlin

Bouri M, Nankobogo F, Frederick R (2010) Synthesis of review of corporate governance of state-owned enterprises in Burkina Faso, Mali, and Mauritania, African Region Working paper Series, No 131. World Bank, Washington, DC

Bovet D (1985) Financial aspects of public enterprises in Sub-Saharan Africa. Unpublished paper submitted to the World Bank

Broodryk J (2005) Ubuntu management philosophy. Knowledge Productions, Randburg

Broodryk J (2006) The philosophy of ubuntu: some management guidelines. Manage Today, August: 52–56

Chen MJ (2014) Presidential address- becoming ambicultural: a personal quest, ad aspiration for organisations. Acad Manag Rev 39(2):119–137

Clapham C (1985) The third world state. Third world politics: an introduction. Croom Helm, London

Clapham C (2002) Third world politics: an introduction. Routledge, London

Cobley AG (1990) Class and consciousness: the black petty-bourgeoisie in South Africa, 1924–1950. Greehiod Press, London

Collins RO, Burns JM (2007) A history of Sub-Saharan Africa. Cambridge University Press, Cambridge, UK

Coplan D (1982) The emergence of an African working-class. In: Marks S, Atmore A (eds) Economy and society in pre-industrial South Africa. Longman, London, pp 358–375

Cowen MP (1972) Differentiation in a Kenya location. Unpublished paper to the East African Social Science Conference, Nairobi, Kenya

Cooper F (2002) Africa since 1940. The past of the present. Cambridge University Press, Cambridge, UK

Curtin PD (1984) African traders and trade communities. In: Curtin P (ed) Cross-cultural trade in world history. Cambridge University Press, Cambridge, UK

de la Escosura LP (2011) Human development in Africa: a long-run perspective. University Carlos III, Working Papers in Economic History, WP 11-09

Department of Trade and Industry (DTI) (2003) South Africa's economic transformation: a strategy for broad-based black economic empowerment. DTI, Pretoria
Dia M (1990) Le management Africain: mythe ou réalité? Afr Dev 15(1):61–78
Dia M (1996) Africa's management in the 1990s and beyond. World Bank, Washington, DC
Elumelo TO (2015) The rise of Africapitalism. The World in 2015. The Economist, London
Empowerdex (2012) BEE cannot be the only aspect of transformation. Empowerdex, Johannesburg
Englebert P (2000) Pre-colonial institutions, post-colonial states, and economic development in Tropical Africa. Polit Res Q 53(1):1–36
Eze MO (2010) Intellectual history in South Africa. Palgrave Macmillan, New York
Fage JD, Tordoffm W (2002) A history of Africa, 4th edn. Routledge, London
Fogel R (2004) The escape from hunger and premature death, 1700–2100. Cambridge University Press, Cambridge, UK
George G (2015) Expanding context to redefine theories: Africa in management research. Manag Organ Rev 11(1):5–10
George G, Corbishley C, Khayesi JN, Haas MR, Tihanyi L (2016) Bringing Africa in: promising directions for management research. Acad Manag J 59(2):377–393
Goldman GA (2013) On the development of uniquely African management theory. Indilinga Afr J Indigenous Knowl Syst 12(2):217–230
Gomes E, Cohen M, Mellahi K (2013) When two African cultures collide: a study of interactions between managers in a strategic alliance between two African organizations. J World Bus 46(1):5–12
Guest R (2004) The shackled continent: power, corruption and African lives. Macmillan, London
Heldinger L, Robinson JA (2012) Colonialism and economic development in Africa. NBER Working Paper Series, Working Paper 18566. http://www.nber.org/papers/w18566
Hellriegel D, Slocum J (1985) Management. Oxford University Press, Cape Town
Hertog S (2010) Defying the resource curse: explaining successful state-owned enterprises in rentier states. World Polit 62(2):261–301
Himbara T (1994) Domestic capitalists and the state in Kenya. In: Berman B, Leys C (eds) African capitalists in African development. Lynne Rienner, London, pp 69–94
Hofstede G (2001) Culture's consequences: comparing values, behaviors, institutions and organizations across nations, 2nd edn. Sage Publications, London
Holtbrügge D (2013) Indigenous management research. Manag Int Rev 53(1):1–11
Honig B (2016) Entrepreneurship and SME maqnagement acroiss Africa: a perspective and a short review. In: Achtenhagen L, Brundin E (eds) Entrepreneurship and SME management across Africa. Springer, Heidelberg, pp 213–218
Hopkins AG (1976a) Imperial business in Africa. Part 1: sources. J Afr Hist 17(1):29–48
Hopkins AG (1976b) Imperial business in Africa, part 11: interpretation. J Afr Hist 17(2):267–290
Iliffe J (1983) The emergence of African capitalism. Macmillan Press, London/Basingstoke
Jackson T (2004) Management and change in Africa. Routledge, London
Jackson T (2013) Reconstructing the indigenous in African management research. Manag Int Rev 53(1):13–38
Jackson T, Amaeshi K, Yavuz S (2008) Untangling African indigenous management: multiple influences on the success of SMEs in Kenya. J World Bus 43(4):400–416
Jones G (2000) Merchants to multinationals: British trading companies in the nineteenth and twentieth centuries. Oxford University Press, Oxford
Kamoche K (2011) Contemporary developments in the management of human resources in Africa. J World Bus 46:1–4
Kamwangamalu N (1999) Ubuntu in South Africa: a socio-linguistic perspective to a pan-African concept. Crit Arts 13(2):24–41
Kan KA, Apitsa SM, Adegbite E (2015) "African management": concept, content and usability. Soc Bus Rev 10(3):258–279
Karsten L, Illa H (2005) Ubuntu as a key African management concept: contextual background and practical insights for knowledge application. J Manag Psychol 20(7):607–620

Kennedy P (1988) African capitalism. The struggle for ascendency. Cambridge University Press, Cambridge, UK

Kiggundu MN (1988) Africa. In: Nath R (ed) Comparative management: a regional view. Ballinger, Cambridge, MA

Kiggundu MN (1991) The challenges of management development in Sub-Saharan Africa. In J Manag Dev 10(6):32–47

Killick T (1981) Papers on the Kenyan economy: performance, problems and policies. Heinemann Education, London

Killick T (1992) Explaining Africa's post-independence development experiences. Working Paper 60. Overseas Development Institute, London

Kragh SU (2012) The anthropology of nepotism social distance and reciprocity in organisation in developing countries. Int J Cross Cult Manag 12(2):247–265

Kuada J (2006) Cross-cultural interactions and change management practices in Africa: a hybrid management perspective. Afr J Bus Econ Res 1(1):96–112

Lamoreaux NR, Wallis JJ (2017) Organizations, civil society and the roots of development. Chicago University Press, Chicago

Leys C (1975) Underdevelopment in Kenya. The political economy of neo-colonialism. Heinemann, London

Lovejoy P (2000) Tansformations in slavery. A history of slavery in Africa. Cambridge University Press, Cambridge

Lutz DW (2009) African "Ubuntu: philosophy and global management". J Bus Ethics 84(3):313–328

Maddison A (2007) Contours of the world economy 1–2030 AD. Essays in macro-economic history. Oxford University Press, Oxford

Mapunda G (2013) African philosophy of management in the context of African traditional cultures and organisational culture: the case of Kenya and Tanzania. Philos Manag 12(2):9–22

Marris P, Somerset A (1971) African businessmen. A study of entrepreneurship and development in Kenya. Routledge & Kegan Paul, London

Marsden D (1991) Indigenous management. Int J Hum Resour Manag 2(1):21–38

Mayer P (1961) Tribesmen and townsmen. Conservatism and the process of urbanisation in a South African city. Oxford University Press, Cape Town

Mbaku JM (2002) The state and indigenous entrepreneurship in post-independence Africa. In: Jalloh A, Falola T (eds) Black business and economic power. Rochester University Press, Rochester, pp 212–236

Mbigi L (1997) Ubuntu: the African dream in management. Knowledge Resources Publications, Randburg

Mbigi L, Maree J (2005) Ubuntu: the spirit of African transformation management. Knowledge Resources, Randburg

Mbiti JS (1989) African religions and philosophy, 2nd edn. Heinemann, Oxford

McFarlin DB, Coster EA, Mogale-Pretorius C (1999) South African management development in the twenty-first century: moving toward an Africanized model. J Manag Dev 18(1):63–78

Metz T (2007) Towards an African moral theory. J Polit Philos 15(3):321–341

Metz T (2009) African moral theory and public governance: nepotism, preferential hiring and other partiality. In: Murove MF (ed) African ethics: an anthology of comparative and applied ethics. University of KwaZulu Natal Press, Pietermaritzburg, pp 335–356

Migdal JS (1998) Strong societies and weak states: sate-society relations and state capabilities in the third world. Princeton University Press, Princeton

Milanovic B (2005) Worlds apart: measuring international and global inequality. Princeton, Princeton

Mogotsi STT (1977) Black urban entrepreneurship. Southern African Freedom Foundation, August

Msamnichaka L, Bagachwa MSD (1984) Public sector enterprises in Tanzania: problems and constraints. Viertel Jahres Berichten [J Friedrich Ebert Found] December. University Press

Murillo A (2011) The devil we know: Gold Coast consumers, local employees, and the united African company, 1940–1960. Enterp Soc 12(2):317–355
Nellis J (1986) Public Enterprises in Sub-Saharan Africa. WDP-1. World Bank, Washington, DC
Nellis J (2005a) Privatization in Africa: what has happened? What is to be done? Nota Di Avoro 127.2005. Fondazione Eni Enrico Matthei, Milan. www.feem.it
Nellis J (2005b) The evolution of enterprise reform in Africa: from state-owned enterprise to private participation in infrastructure- and back? World Bank, Washington, DC
Nellis J, Kikeri S (1989) Public enterprise reform: privatization and the World Bank. World Dev 17(5):659–672
NEPAD (2015) Strengthening the institutional capacity of the Communatué des Sahhélo-Sahariens (CEN_SAD). African union capacity development support programme to RECs (M0CDP). NEPAD, Midrand
New Partnership for Africa's Development (NEPAD) (2001) AHG/235 (XXXVlll): annex 1: declaration on democracy, political, economic and corporate governance. Durban, December
Nkomo SM (2011) A post-colonial and anticolonial reading of 'African' leadership and management in organisation studies: tensions, contradictions and possibilities. Organization 18(3):365–386
Nkomo S (2015) Challenges for management and business education in a 'developmental' stat: the case of South Africa. Acad Manag Learn Educ 14(2):242–258
Noorderhaven NG, Tidjani B (2001) Culture, governance, and economic performance: an exploratory study with a special focus on Africa. J Cross Cult Manag 1(1):31–52
Nussbaum B (2009) Ubuntu: Reflections of a South African on our common humanity. In: Murove MF (ed) African ethics: an anthology of comparative and applied ethics. University of KwaZulu Natal Press, Pietermaritzburg, pp 100–110
Nwabughuogu AI (1982) From wealthy entrepreneurs to petty traders: the decline of African middlemen in Eastern Nigeria, 900–1950. J Afr Hist 23(3):365–379
Nyambegera SM (2002) Ethnicity and human resource management practice in sub-Saharan Africa: the relevance of managing diversity discourse. Int J Hum Resour Manag 13(7):1077–1090
Nzelibe CO (1986) The evolution of African management thought. Int Stud Manag Organ 16(2):06–16
O'Rourke KH (1997) Globalization and history: the evolution of a 19th century Atlantic economy. MIT University Press, Cambridge, MA
Ojieda TO (2005) Implementing the new partnership for African development. NEPAD, South Africa
Oladipo O (2012) The Nigerian motor transporters since the 1920s. Int J Humanit Soc Sci 2(12):230–237
Olukujo A (2002a) 'Buy British, sell foreign': external trade control policies in Nigeria during World War II and its aftermath. Int J Afr Hist Stud 35(2–3):363–384
Olukoju A (2002b) The impact of colonialism on the development of African business in colonial Nigeria. In: Jalloh A, Falola T (eds) Black business and economic power. University of Rochester Press, Rochester, pp 176–198
Olukoju A (2015) Family firms: inter-generational succession and business strategies in colonial Western Nigeria. Unpublished paper presented to World Economic History Congress. Kyoto, August 2015
Pearson G (2012) The rise and fall of management. A brief history of practice, theory and context. Gower, Farnham
Perry C (1997) Total quality management and reconceptualising management in Africa. Int Bus Rev 6(3):233–243
Prinsloo ED (2000) The African view of participatory business management. J Bus Ethics 25:275–286
Pritchett L (1997) Divergence, big time. J Econ Perspect 11:3–17
Roberts A (1998) Towards a world community? The United Nations and international law. In: Howard M, Loouis WR (eds) The Oxford History of the twentieth century. Oxford University Press, Oxford, pp 128–138

Safavi F, Tweddell CE (2007) Attributes of success in African management development programmes: concepts and applications. J Manag Dev 9(6):50–63
Schutte A (2001) Ubuntu: an ethic for a new South Africa. Cluster Publications, Pietermaritzburg
Shafitz JM, Ott JS, Jang YS (2005) Classics of organization theory, 6th edn. Thompson, Wadsworth
Smith AK (1974) Antonio Salazar and the reversal of Portuguese colonial policy. J Afr Hist 15(4):654–668
South African Institute of Race Relations (SAIRR) (n.d.) Rheinalt Jones papers: – B4/2: Memorandum of the Location Advisory Board Congress (LABC) on the Proposed Amendment to the Urban Areas Act, No 21 of 1923
Sutton J (2014) An enterprise map of Mozambique. International Growth Centre, London. www.londonpublishingpartnership.co.uk
Sutton J, Kapenty B (2012) An enterprise map of Ghana. International Growth Centre, London. www.londonpublishingpartnership.co.uk
Sutton J, Kellow N (2010) An enterprise map of Ethiopia. International Growth Centre, London. www.londonpublishingpartnership.co.uk
Sutton J, Langmead G (2013) An enterprise map of Zambia. International Growth Centre, London. www.londonpublishingpartnership.co.uk
Sutton J, Olomi D (2012) An enterprise map of Tanzania. International Growth Centre, London. www.londonpublishingpartnership.co.uk
Swainson N (1980) The development of corporate capitalism in Kenya. Heinemann, London
Taylor H (1992) Public sector personnel management in three Africa countries: current problems and possibilities. Public Adm Dev 12:193–207
Taylor S (2002) The challenge of indigenization, affirmative action and black empowerment in Zimbabwe and South Africa. In: Jalloh A, Falola T (eds) Black business and economic power. Rochester University Press, Rochester, pp 347–380
Thomas A, Blendixen M (2000) The management implications of ethnicity in South Africa. J Int Bus Stud 31(3):507–519.i
Trompenaars F, Hampden-Turner C (1997) Riding the waves of culture: understanding cultural diversity in business. Nicholas Brealey Publications, London
Vail L (1975) The making of an imperial slum: Nyassaland and its railways, 1895–1935. J Afr Hist 16(1):89–112
Van Aswegen HJ (1980) Die Geskiedenis van Afrika. Pretoria, Academica
Van Binsbergen W (2001) Ubuntu and the globalisation of Southern African thought and society. Quest: Afr J Philos 15(2):53–89
Van de Walle N (2005) Democratic reform in Africa. Lynne Rienner Publishers, Washington, DC
Van den Bersselaar D (2011) Doorway to success. Reconstructing African careers in European business from company house magazines and oral history interviews. History in Africa 38:257–294
Van Rinsum HJ, Boessenkool J (2013) Decolonising African management: Okot p'Bitek and the paradoxes of African management. Philos Manag 12(2):41–55
Verhoef G (2001) Stokvels and economic empowerment: the case of African women in South Africa, c. 1930–1998. In: Lemire B, Pearce R, Campbell G (eds) Women and credit. Researching the past, refiguring the future. Berg Publishers, Oxford, pp 91–116
Verhoef G (2017) The history of business in Africa. Complex discontinuities and emerging markets. Springer, Cham
Walsh JP (2015) Organisation and management scholarship in and for Africa [...] and the world. Acad Manag Perspect 29(1):1–6
Wariboko N (2002) Management in postcolonial Africa historical and comparative perspectives. In: Jalloh A, Falola T (eds) Black business and economic power. Rochester University Press, Rochester, pp 238–276
West A (2014) *Ubuntu* and business ethics: problems, perspectives and prospects. J Bus Ethics 121(1):47–61
White OC, Bhatia A (1998) Privatization in Africa. World Bank, Washington, DC

Wickins P (1982) Agriculture. In: Coleman FL (ed) Economic history of South Africa. HAUM, Pretoria, pp 37–88
Wickins PL (1986) Africa 1880–1980. An economic history. Oxford University Press, Cape Town
Wild V (1997) Profit for profit sake: history and business culture of African entrepreneurs in Zimbabwe. Baobab Books, Harare
Witzel M (2012) A history of management thought. Routledge, Oxford
Wohlgemuth L, Carlsson J, Kifle H (1998) Introduction. In: Wohlgemuth L, Carlsson J, Kifle H (eds) Institution building and leadership in Africa. Nordikska Afrikainstitutet, Uppsala, pp 5–11
World Bank (1985) Les politiques de transport en Afrique francophone au Sud du Sahara: Problèmes et Choix. Economic Development Institute, World Bank, Washington, DC
World Bank (1991) World development report. The challenge of development. World Bank, Washington, DC
World Bank (2000) Can Africa claim the 21st century? World Bank, Washington, DC
World Bank (2006) Held by the visible hand. The challenge of SOE corporate governance for emerging markets. World Bank, Washington
Wren DA (2005) The history of management thought, 5th edn. Wiley, Hoboken
Wren DA, Bedeian AG (2009) The evolution of management thought, 6th edn. Wiley, Hoboken
Zoogah D, Peng M, Habte W (2015) Linking management research and African organisations: institutions, cultures and resources. Acad Manag Perspect 29(1)

Managing Africa's Strongest Economy: The History of Management in South Africa, 1920–2018

54

Grietjie Verhoef

Contents

Periphery at the Center	1240
Entrepreneurial Opportunity: Family, Nationalism, and Global Networks	1241
Nurturing Business Leadership Through Formal Education	1246
Delivering on the Political Agenda	1253
Management *quo vadis*?	1260
Conclusion	1264
Cross-References	1265
References	1266

Abstract

Business development follows successful entrepreneurs and managers. This chapter explains the trajectory of management development in South Africa as it supported the growth of the only modern industrial economy in Africa. Education in commerce and accounting branched out to dedicated management education after the Second World War. The symbiosis between business and institutions of education developed along the domestic sociopolitical contours of racial segregation. The basis of management development was and still is grounded in sustained alignment with European and American scientific models of best practice in management. The history of management in South Africa is explored to account for the distinct position of internationally recognised leadership of the locally trained management corps and executive leadership.

G. Verhoef (✉)
College of Business and Economics, University of Johannesburg, Johannesburg, South Africa

College of Global Business, Monash University, Melbourne, VIC, Australia
e-mail: gverhoef@uj.ac.za; grietjie.verhoef@monash.edu

© The Author(s), under exclusive licence to Springer Nature Switzerland AG 2020
B. Bowden et al. (eds.), *The Palgrave Handbook of Management History*,
https://doi.org/10.1007/978-3-319-62114-2_115

Keywords

Economy · Transformation agenda · Capital · Management · Primary industry · Diversification · Executive · Political economy

Periphery at the Center

The territories at the southern tip of Africa were inextricably linked to the British Empire by the 1800s, through both enterprise and conquest. The modern business organisation came to Africa through capitalist enterprises developing commerce, mining, and manufacturing in the last half of the seventeenth century. The first global multinational enterprise, the Dutch East India Company, established the refreshment station at the Cape of Good Hope in 1652. Subsequently, Dutch and British colonial rule opened opportunities for extensive commercial exchange between the colonial economies and the European metropolis. Small owner-managed firms in food processing, clothing manufacturing, transport, and general retail trade soon expanded into well-capitalized companies able to operate in the large-scale mining and manufacturing sectors. The mineral discoveries of the late nineteenth century transformed the primarily agricultural and small mining operations in the Cape and Natal colonies and the *Zuid-Afrikaansche Republiek (ZAR)* and the *Oranje Vrijstaat (OVS)* into capital-intensive enterprises capable of supporting the rapidly growing economies. Big well-capitalized, imperial banks entered the colonies of southern Africa during the last half of the nineteenth century to replace the small unit banks scattered across the colonial landscape. The capital needs of the mining-driven economy mandated access to substantial capital resources. The imperial banks, the Standard Bank, the African Banking Corporation, the Oriental Banking Corporation, and, after 1926, Barclays Bank DCO (which acquired the National Bank, which had operated in the ZAR since 1888) and the Dutch *Nederlandsche Bank voor Zuid-Afrika* (later Nedbank), laid the foundation of the financial spine of the South African economy. Together with an extensive network of long-term and short-term insurance companies, building societies and savings banks, South Africa benefitted from the depth of the western management tradition at the heart of capital provision for a modern economy (Solomon 1982; Webb 1992; Verhoef 2013b; Hagedorn-Hansen 2017). Mining houses soon organised their own finance houses, adding to the emergence of a sophisticated financial services industry. By the time of the establishment of the Johannesburg Stock Exchange in 1887, three other equity exchanges had already entered the equity exchange business to capitalize new enterprise (Lukasiewicz 2018). Business and finance almost immediately attracted accountants, who added to the knowledge base establishing the foundation of business management in South Africa (Verhoef and Van Vuuren 2012; Verhoef 2013a, 2014).

Firmly grounded in the western tradition of market exchanges and enterprise, the South African economy developed as an industrial economy from the late nineteenth century. It relied on the managerial expertise of internationally linked businesses, investing in the local market, and local entrepreneurs linked to foreign capital markets. Business operated on the periphery of western capitalist economies of Britain, America, and Europe. From the seventeenth century, market integration remained the life blood of the most diversified industrial economy in Africa. The "periphery" sustained direct connections to the western center, from where managerial knowledge flowed (Kipping et al. 2008). A primary economy embedded in agriculture and mining by the eighteenth century, the consolidated South African economy since 1910 displayed remarkable resilience in sustaining levels of growth and diversification surpassing that found anywhere else in the entire African continent. This chapter explores the development of management in South Africa, as the settler economy transitioned from a primary economy to a diversified industrial economy. The central argument is that management in South Africa was moulded by embeddedness of business in western market relations. This accounts for the nation's successful economic modernization and industrialization. In 1912 agriculture contributed 17% to national income, mining 27%, manufacturing 7%, and commerce 13.5%. Structural change occurred slowly as the domestic industrialization policies of the 1930s supported the development of domestic industries. By 1990, however, agriculture contributed less than 6% to gross domestic product, mining 12%, manufacturing 25%, commerce 13%, and finance 13% (SARB Quarterly Statistical Bulletins 1920–1990). The most advanced modern economy in Africa developed in a liberal open market, directed by state policies of inward-looking industrialization and export promotion. Private enterprise and entrepreneurial opportunity were rooted in the notion of the firm, the entrepreneur, and the market. As the economy diversified, the domestic market developed specialist professional and managerial capabilities, or imported expertise from shareholder markets. These capabilities developed the capacity to support and direct the growth of the local economy. Despite international political adversity, the South African economy maintained business and managerial networks linked to the international economy (Verhoef 2011).

The purpose of the chapter is to develop the first systematic historical explanation of the development of management in South Africa. Management is a function of business, enterprise, society, and economic agency. This development in South Africa constitutes the contours of building managerial capabilities to support business and industry in the making of a modern economy in Africa. This chapter will show how management evolved in the political economy of South Africa.

Entrepreneurial Opportunity: Family, Nationalism, and Global Networks

Long before management education entered the academic education sphere during the mid-twentieth century (Amdam 1996: 2; Brown et al. 1996: 155; Byrkjeflot 2000), successful enterprises in the southern territories of what later became South Africa operated business endeavours in agriculture, finance, trade, mining, and general commerce. The multicultural heritage of the society, in which it drew people and ideas from Britain, the Netherlands, Germany, France, and other British colonies such as Australia, New Zealand, and India, fostered powerful traditions of entrepreneurship. The source of entrepreneurship, management knowledge, and business culture was ethnic, cultural, and personal (Casson 2003: 224). Black African participation in commerce and formal business activity in the organisational form of individual enterprise was nonexistent. Where market exchanges did occur in traditional African communities, the activity required the sanction of an authoritarian monarch, ruling a centralized inherited kingdom. Such exchanges occurred primarily through barter, mostly in the form of natural resources and animal products such as ivory, hides, and skins and, to a very limited extent, surplus food. This barter-based exchange secured access to manufactured goods from European traders. Monetary revenue was also extracted from migrant labour (Wilson and Thompson 1971; Muller 1977). Among the various European ethnic groups, Jewish and English-speaking businessmen were prominent in creating a culture of business, enabling them to forge a dominant place in the commerce and trade of South Africa by the early twentieth century. There was thus no singular business culture, but rather one moulded through the ethnic cultural diversity of the immigrant population. Nevertheless, the migration of Jewish immigrants from central Europe at the end of the nineteenth century, as well as British and European immigrants, injected an entrepreneurial gene pool into the predominantly rural and agricultural Dutch communities. Grooming of management occurred in the family, at the dinner table, through more distant family ties linked through long-standing business relationships. In the South African society of settlers, nationalists, and capitalists, the emerging traditions of nineteenth-century business management relied heavily on the personal traits of the entrepreneur, his connections to family and/or friends, and state policies. In the Cape Colony, the first organised business association was formed in 1822, followed in 1881 by the Cape Chamber of Commerce and subsequently by similar chambers of commerce in Port Elizabeth, Graaff-Reinet, and East London (Davenport and Saunders 2000: 101–103, 104–113, 273, 294; Giliomee and Mbenga 2007: 118–119; Houghton 1976: 4–7; Robinson et al. 1961: 8–9). Statutory regulation of limited liability enterprise also found its first manifestation in the British colonies – in the Natal Colony by means of the *Natal Joint Stock Companies Limited Liability Law of 1864* and the *Cape Colony in the Cape Companies' and Trustees Act of 1973* and the *Cape Companies Act 1892* (Verhoef 2014). The regulation of private business followed the pattern of British joint stock company laws, on which the Cape statute was modelled. This was the model until the first South African Companies Act was passed in 1926. Subsequently, English mercantile law formed the basis of company law in South Africa. An environment favouring business development was further stimulated by the strong presence of accountants of British origin, who organised themselves into societies of professional closure (Verhoef 2013a, 2014).

It was ultimately businessmen of British origin, who dominated, but not exclusively controlled, the corporate landscape of the early twentieth century. The founding fathers of the Johannesburg Exchange and Chambers Company Limited in February 1887 were London-born Benjamin Minors Woollan as chairman, Dr. T.-G. Lawrence, James Lang, Frederick Gray, James B. Taylor, J.L. Bussey, and

T.P. O'Meara (Rosenthal 1912: 71). A number of German Jews and Afrikaners also joined as members of the exchange, but British domination remained a feature of its membership for most of the first half of the twentieth century. It was also the English-dominated manufacturing lobby that called for tariff protection to support domestic industrial development. By the 1930s, English and Jewish capital dominated mining, secondary manufacturing, trade, and finance. The grooming of managerial expertise occurred internally in the family or the organisation – from the dinner table, through the *shul*, to the shareholders' meeting and the board room. As has been the history of the emerging of management in Europe and the United States, managers came from within. "Within" refers to the family or kin network of the enterprise where a position of leadership was earned through experience and the acquisition of the core knowledge base of the enterprise and the industry (Byrkjeflot 2000: 5–7, 40–42; Baba 2018). Firmly within the English tradition of grooming the business elite, young successors to business leadership either went through the school of the former generation or studied toward a professional career as accountant, engineer, or lawyer, before joining the corporation. The British education system, from which many South African English-speaking business families came, was still based on the notion of the "gentlemanly ideal" sculptured on the preference for the liberal arts in educating their elite (Locke 1989: 58–99). When, therefore, mining corporations such as the Anglo American Corporation, Gold Fields of South Africa, Anglo Vaal Corporation, and Barlow Rand developed into diversified mining enterprises – operating in gold, coal, other minerals and metals, and the secondary processing of ores – their managerial elites were invariably educated in this British tradition. The financial sector was also under foreign control. The dominant banks, the Standard Bank and Barclays Bank, were incorporated in Britain, while the Netherlands Bank of South Africa was majority owned in the Netherlands.

After the First World War, the Union of South Africa witnessed a new wave of immigration. Initially on a small scale, it gained strength as Nazi German expansion pushed across Europe, leading to a wave of Dutch and German immigration to South Africa during the 1930s. Smaller Italian, Portuguese, and Greek communities had already established themselves as small business owners in retail services, food production, and manufacturing on the fringes of urban areas. By the end of the first decade of the twentieth century, Afrikaners' participation in the mainstream South African economy was limited to agriculture. Some wealthy Afrikaner families had established themselves as wheat, wine, and sheep farmers in the Cape Colony and escaped the devastation of the South African War of 1899–1902. In contrast to significant wealth among Cape Afrikaner farmers (Nash 1997), Afrikaners in the former Boer Republics experienced poverty and marginalisation. As a combination of wartime destruction, droughts, weak personal ambition, and work ethic caused massive white impoverishment by the 1920s, Afrikaner nationalist leaders urged self-redemption to address marginalisation. Afrikaners sought to refute the public statement by the Vice-Chancellor of the University of Cape Town, Sir Carruthers Beattie, that poor whites were "intellectually backward" and that there was something inherent in the Afrikaners that resulted in the phenomenon of [poor whiteism] assuming such alarming proportions in their case (Giliomee 2005: 384). Afrikaner initiative mobilised their own capital to establish their own newspaper and subsequently a publishing house, *De Burger* newspaper and *De Nationale Pers* (currently known as Naspers) in 1915, and then followed by the establishment of an Afrikaner-controlled short-term insurance company, *De Suid-Afrikaanse Trust en Versekeringsmaatskappy (Santam)*, and the life assurance company, *De Suid-Afrikaanse Nasionale Lewens Assuransie Maatskappy (Sanlam)* in 1918. In 1934 Afrikaners formed their own bank, *Volkskas Bank*, to render banking services to Afrikaner people excluded from such credit facilities by the imperial banks. The systematic rise of Afrikaner business received a major boost from the *Ekonomiese Volkskongres* (Economic People's Congress). Organised by an Afrikaner cultural organisation in 1939, the congress was guided by the explicit aim of devising a strategy of economic upliftment of fellow Afrikaners and ascendancy into the mainstream South African economy (Du Toit 1939). These efforts fed into the establishment of social welfare organisations (*Reddingsdaadbond – RDB*), small business and manufacturing industry initiatives funded by Afrikaner savings (*Federale Volksbeleggings – FVB*), a foothold in the mining industry (*Federale Mynbou* – FM), a massive education drive, and a chamber of Afrikaner business (the *Afrikaanse Handelsinstituut* – AHI) to mentor the young Afrikaner entrepreneur. In following the English example, aspiring Afrikaners were sent to universities to study toward professional careers in accounting, business, law, engineering, and medicine. Ambitions to succeed were further spurned on by the public claim by Professor W H Hutt, from the University of Cape Town, that Afrikaners had serious deficiencies in engaging successfully in business (Cape Argus, 15/8/1946). By the early 1960s, Afrikaner business had established itself in financial services, manufacturing, mining, and commercial agriculture, securing around 25% effective Afrikaner control of the mainstream economy (Verhoef 2018; Giliomee 2005; Sadie 2002).

The business culture introduced by immigrant European settlers gave rise to the varied landscape of business in South Africa. Business culture was diverse in origin and developed a confluence of ethnic culture and context. Formal management education did not exist. In the home British market, industry and the public frowned upon business education (Wilson 1992, 1996; Byrkjeflot 2000: 5, 32), giving rise to what Coleman described as "a cult of amateurism" (Coleman 1973: 101). In South Africa, therefore, the managerial class emerged from the convergence of personal family or enterprise grounded business culture and experience, combined with a critical intellectual and educational grounding in professional education as engineers or lawyers. There remained, however, a preference for business leaders who had emerged through the schooling of the firm. It was this tradition of managerial expertise handed down through generational transfer, which infused the corporate sector in South Africa, however, during the first half of the twentieth century. The emerging Afrikaner business elite was not considered part of the business elite. Theirs was a consciously constructed nationalist project, as described above. It was not surprising, therefore, that in higher education it would be inspired Afrikaners who would take the first steps toward the introduction of formal management education in South Africa. Lacking long-standing generational human capital resources from family businesses – as had characterised British and

European businesses – the emerging Afrikaner business elite was motivated to acquire that knowledge base from the successful international business elites. There is in this a degree of comparison with the Japanese model of acquiring managerial experience and expertise from the west so as to transform their economy (Nishizawa 1996). In South Africa, it was not state policy, however, that drove this acquisitive orientation but rather a conscious decision by Afrikaners to learn from international best practice.

The management paradigm in the western world was all but homogenous prior to the Second World War, displaying even greater diversity in the years following the postwar reconstruction. By the 1950s American business schools had established themselves as the source of managerial training for business. However, as European nations also began to develop programmes for management education, they did not simply copy the so-called American model of management education. Instead, the restoration of international trade, fast-growing national economies, and growing internationalisation of business operations in the postwar world shaped national demands for business growth, as well as capacity to expand business into international markets. The keystone to successful business expansion is managerial capabilities. These developed both nationally and internationally. While the successful reconstruction of both the German and Japanese economies was achieved without imprinting an American model of management education (see Amdam 1996: 19; Byrt 1992; Lawrnece 1989; Locke 1988: 93; 1989: Chap. 5), historical experience also points to the existence of distinct variations in social, cultural, and ethnic frameworks in nurturing strategic leadership, business elites, and innovative entrepreneurs.

Central to the eventual (and belated) British and European ventures into formal management education were two characteristic features. First, managers were part of the elite, either the upper middle class, which seemed the overwhelming case in the United States, or from the upper class, which was predominantly the case in Europe (Byrkjeflot 2000: 40–42; Wilson 1996: 135). Second, management education was to ensure wealth creation and economic growth. At the onset of the second wave of globalisation, the American management education paradigm was the powerful sender agent (Kipping et al. 2008). This process was driven by different agents, such as the Ford Foundation and the leading business schools, such as the Harvard Business School. This dominance, nevertheless, did not completely overshadow the emergence of national systems of leadership and business management suited to the culture of the nation. Amdam (1996) noted that the successful economic recovery and emerging international competitiveness of the Japanese and German economies in the postwar era highlighted the fact that the American model of management education proved, indeed, not to be a blueprint for every society. The transfer of the American MBA degree to many countries "has been an expression of weakness; and that the MBA degree has been imported in a major way only by those European countries that lack a strong tradition of training future elites in which their corporations have confidence" (Amdam 1996: 1; see also Nioche 1992: 23). Consequently, British and European university systems grappled with the notion of management as a "science," which required a reconfiguration of management as disciplinary construct, able to offer solutions to managerial problems through the application of science.

Nurturing Business Leadership Through Formal Education

Preparing management for the world of business only entered the realm of disciplinary formalisation during the late nineteenth century, when Frederick Taylor proposed that management must be explored as a science. Moving beyond experience-based transferred managerial techniques mandated empirical backing. To achieve business goals and objectives, management education was formalised to encompass scholarship that can deliver systematic information to facilitate successful management operations. In a similar way as the Industrial Revolution in Britain and the second Industrial Revolution in Europe gave rise to the demand for more systematic knowledge about business and management, Taylor's *The Principles of Scientific Management* (1909) formulated a set of scientific principles underlying business and management able to respond to changing business conditions. These scientific principles, to be identified through scholarly inquiry, tested empirically and applied across the spectrum of business operations, were dynamic and subject to contextual substantiation. In South Africa, the former practice of preparing business elites through training as accountants, lawyers, or engineers – or as intellectuals equipped with PhDs in politics, philosophy, and economics (PPE) – gradually gave way to experiential preparation in management and, eventually, systematic management education (Locke 1989: 58–61).

The University of Pretoria established the first business school outside the United States. This was a remarkable development, since Britain and Europe were not at all enthused by the concept of formal business education before 1960. At the University of Pretoria, an institution of Afrikaans tuition, Mr. Piet W Hoek initiated the process to establish a dedicated institution for advanced education in management (The Transvaal University College (TUC) was established in 1909 as an English tuition institution for tertiary education. The college became a full university in October 1930. It remained an English tuition institution until 1932, after which it changed to the Afrikaans tuition institution, the University of Pretoria). As the first chartered accountant in South Africa to insist on writing his final qualifying examination to become a chartered accountant, in his mother tongue, Afrikaans, Piet Hoek qualified as a chartered accountant in 1938. He then established an accounting firm with Arthur Cross and Barry Wiehahn (Hoek, Wiehahn and Cross) in 1946. Hoek, as the junior partner, identified management, as the core dimension in business, that suffered from a lack of systematic scholarly inquiry in South Africa. Previously, the Transvaal University College (TUC) had offered the first Bachelor of Commerce degree in 1919. The degree included subjects such as business organisation and Business Economics as entry-level courses. In the College's Faculty of Trade and Business Administration, the first Master of Commerce degree in Trade was awarded in 1931. Professor W A Macfayden also lectured banking and accounting to bank clerks and candidates studying toward the qualifying examinations of the Transvaal

Society of Accountants. In Pretoria, the city of civil servants, TUC formalised education in commerce, banking, trade, and Business Economics. In 1944, a separate Department of Trade and Business Economics was also formed, the first at a South African university. In 1946, Hoek visited the United States and attended the Annual Meeting of the Academy of Management. As a guest of Dr. Lillian Gilbreth, the "mother of modern management," Hoek participated in a 2-week summer school, taught by Gilbreth and her husband, Frank Bunker Gilbreth. Hoek experienced firsthand the so-called Gilbreth system of teaching scientific management. He also visited Columbia University and the Harvard Business School, familiarizing himself with advanced management education in the United States. On the basis of his assessment of several MBA programmes, Hoek prepared a strong case for the introduction of an MBA programme at the University of Pretoria. The Harvard Business School supplied extensive material to strengthen Hoek's case, but he preferred to model his proposal on the Columbia management programme. Hoek was appointed lecturer in Accountancy at the University of Pretoria in 1948. In November 1948, the accounting firm Hoek, Wiehahn & Cross submitted a formal proposal to the University of Pretoria for the establishment of an Institute for Management and Administration. In March 1949 the university authorised the first postgraduate master's programmes in management at a South African university. However, university management refused to confer a Master's Degree in Business Administration (MBA), since UP did not offer an undergraduate degree in business administration. The university agreed to confer a Master's of Commerce degree in Management and Administration. This South African discourse was similar to the aversion in Germany to master's qualifications in business administration, where preference was given to the disciplinary foundation of Economics and Business Economics (Byrkjeflot 2002: 13). Finally, in 1955 the UP changed the name of the degree to that of an MBA (Adendorff 2012: 53–58).

The UP MBA established a nexus between the university and industry. The Iron and Steel Corporation (ISCOR; established in 1928 as a state-owned iron and steel manufacturing enterprise) made a grant to UP in 1948 toward the introduction of an MBA qualification. The context of the establishment of the first business school offering an MBA qualification was significant. The initiative came from an Afrikaans tuition university, driven by a chartered accountant following the American example of teaching scientific management. During this period, the South African economy also experienced strong growth, especially in manufacturing. In addition, the state supported extensive industrial development through the Industrial Development Corporation (state-owned entity formed in 1940 to promote industrial development through expertise, business mentorship, and financial support) and ISCOR. After the National Party came to power in 1948, and commenced systematic implementation of a policy of separate development, an additional injection into domestic manufacturing came from the groundbreaking chemical technology developed by the South African Oil and Gas Corporation (Sasol), a firm that from 1950 onward played a central role in the establishment capable of serving the needs of both mining and manufacturing. As international markets surged, the South African economy was perfectly positioned to take advantage of growing demand and rising incomes, except for sufficiently skilled human capital, especially managers. It was into this nexus of growth and demand for higher end human capital that the UP MBA was positioned. The MBA was a postgraduate qualification, aiming to establish systematic education in the knowledge of management by replacing the former emphasis on disciplinary education (Economics, Accountancy, Politics) with a focus on empirical enterprise and organisation management. The language of tuition was Afrikaans, but lecturers had to be bilingual. The MBA was a part-time programme offered over a period of 2 years. Accounting, Business Economics, Economics, and Trade, Money and Banking were compulsory subjects. The teaching method was the Harvard Business School case study method. Only 30 students were admitted to the first degree, 25 graduated in 1951, including 1 woman, Frances Mercia Lombard (Adendorff 2012: 58–60).

It is important to note that the MBA programmes in South Africa evolved in parallel to faculties of commerce, where students completed first and second degrees. Management training in the MBA programmes was "post-experience," that is, it was assumed that students had already obtained a first degree, acquired some experience in that market, and then enrolled for dedicated industry-based management education. The postgraduate business school phenomenon of South Africa is therefore different from the international experience of undergraduate programmes in management schools leading up to MBA qualifications.

By the early 1950s, it was clear that a new era had arrived in management education in South Africa. Whereas managers traditionally entered business leadership from the professions, such as engineering, accountancy, or law, the American business school concept now infused tertiary education in South Africa. This educational shift also aligned with the Afrikaner nationalist ambition to develop local business leaders, especially young Afrikaners, for the corporate world. The UP initiative was, however, not exclusive. English-speaking students were welcomed. A manager at the Anglo American Corporation enrolled in 1963. UP also offered an advanced business management degree, capturing the domestic market while aligning it to international best practice.

Management in South Africa developed within the western tradition. Strong influences from both the American model and European tradition were present. The UP Institute of Business and Administration solicited the services of renowned international academics during its formative years. At UP, Professor Jan Goudriaan, an eminent Dutch academic (he graduated in Economics at the Delft Technische Hogeschool), established Business Economics as a discipline. Significantly, Goudriaan came from the European tradition that saw a disciplinary grounding in Business Economics as the best route into management. He was convinced that the HBS case study method was the optimal way to teach on the integrated nature of industry issues, since it harmoniously facilitated a perspective on a seemingly contradictory position of different operational functions in business and industry. Goudriaan, however, was also critical of the HBS case study method. He insisted that the HBS case study method must be integrated into the European tradition that emphasized the need for a firm theoretical foundation as a basis for critical thinking. Dr. Gerhard de Kock, who later joined the International Monetary Fund as economist, taught Economics. Professor H W J Wijnholds, from Tilburg in the Netherlands, lectured on Trade, Money, and Banking. Dr. Bared de Loor, born in the Netherlands, laid the foundation for the Department of Statistics and Business Mathematics at UP (Adendorff 2012: 67–68). By 1952, the content of management and business administration courses at UP reflected alignment to American business school best practice. The course content included the following: Administrative Policy, Administrative Practice, Public and Labor Relations, Financial Management, Statistics, Issues of Marketing Distribution, Finance, and Production (Adendorff 2012: 69–70).

First-mover advantage did not last long. Between 1949 and 1968, another six South African universities established business schools and offered MBA qualifications. In 1964 the University of Stellenbosch (USB) and the University of Cape Town (UCT) GSB (Graduate School of Business) both introduced business schools offering postgraduate MBA degrees and then followed by the Potchefstroom University and, the distance education/correspondence university, the University of South Africa and in 1968 the University of the Witwatersrand (Wits). In 1970 the University of Durban-Westville, dedicated to the Indian community of South Africa, opened its business school and offered the MBA qualification. The fact that the business school at Wits was much later than institutions outside the main business center of South Africa can be ascribed to the established and long-standing position of the university in delivering engineers and other accounting professionals to business and mining in South Africa. In 1960, however, the Council of Wits resolved to establish a Graduate School of Business Administration. The Principal-Professor I D MacCrone visited Harvard Business School to solicit support for the initiative. Subsequently, in 1963 Wits created a chair in Business Administration. The person appointed to the position was Professor Leonard Harold Samuels, an economist, Head of the Department of Commerce and Applied Economics. In 1964 businessman John Schlesinger donated R400 000 (worth around R33 million in 2019) to Wits for the establishment of a Graduate School of Business. MacCrone commented that "This University is the only English medium university in the Republic situated north of the Orange River, and if we can fully utilise the opportunity... we shall be in a position to make quite a unique contribution of a fundamental kind to the welfare of our country, particularly in this phase of its economic development" (UW Gazette 1964: 16; Financial Mail, 4/9/1964). Following internal indecisiveness about course content and appointments (Financial Mail, 3/9/1967), Wits finally inaugurated the first short 8-week executive management course in August 1968 and the first 2-year MBA in September 1969 (UW Gazette, December 1968; Wits Convocation Commentary, March 1969). Wits therefore forfeited a first-mover advantage among the English tuition universities, an opportunity the Principal had hoped the university could take advantage of. It was only in 1968, 4 years after USB and UCT GSB, that Wits got its short Executive Development Programmes of 8 weeks underway. By comparison, UP enrolled its first full MBA programme in 1950, followed by short courses for managers in different sectors of the economy, such as managers in agricultural cooperatives.

The University of the Witwatersrand established international links from the outset. This positioned Wits firmly within the western university management education paradigm. Professor Gottfried Haberler from HBS visited the university in July 1965, during the preparation for the introduction of its MBA (*Die Transvaler*, 23/7/1965), and by 1968 Wits had appointed three American professors to the school. They were H E Dougall, professor at the Stanford Graduate School of Business in Finance; Professor G E Germane, professor in logistics at Stanford Graduate School of Business; and Professor F L Webster, Jr, professor of Business Administration of the Amos Tuck School of Business Administration, Dartmouth College. Also appointed were Professor Harold J Leavitt, professor of Organisational Behaviour and Psychology at the Stanford Graduate School of Business; Professor Henry Eyring, specialising in business management, also from Stanford; and Professor Harold B Rose, professor in Finance from London's Graduate School of Business Studies (UW Gazette 1968: 180; Convocation Commentary, March 1969: 18–19).

These links to HBS were indicative of the early integration of South African management education into the leading American model of business schools. UP also maintained close links with the European scientific community through the appointment of academics to its teaching staff. Nevertheless, management theory followed the leading American business schools. At a time of high economic growth, associated with a surge in industrial production, demand for managerial expertise rose exponentially. Afrikaner industrial and financial enterprise entered a strong growth trajectory, mandating increased access to skilled human capital. Sanlam contributed handsomely to tertiary education, especially at Afrikaans tuition universities such as UP and US (Verhoef 1995, 1999, 2016, 2018). Sanlam thus supported professional and managerial capacity building for emerging Afrikaner conglomerates, para-state institutions such as marketing councils, agricultural cooperatives, and state-owned enterprises (ISCOR, Sasol, Escom, IDC). The Afrikaner's rise to power, its own economic empowerment ambitions, and the growth trajectory of the inward-looking industrial economy certainly served as impetus to the emergence of business schools in South Africa. The scholarly endeavour in management science owed much to the new Afrikaner business elite's desire to measure up with the international leaders in business. Hoek's American exposure paved the way for the future HBS connection. Whereas English and Jewish business in South Africa sustained the legacy of capital and kin links to the "city" and the "home" market in London, Afrikaners ventured out to America. The confluence of Afrikaner nationalist business ambitions and strong post-1950 growth positioned management education in South Africa squarely within the western model.

Business attracted its leaders from two sources at this time in South Africa: either through family or kin networks, as characterised the English elite in the mining industry, or university qualified professionals, which was the route pursued by emerging Afrikaner businessmen. Since the universities were subsidised by the state in South Africa, it necessarily followed that they operated broadly within state policy. The symbiosis between universities and business is fundamental to the understanding of what business education was expected to deliver. The key and overriding role of business is to create wealth for its shareholders and thereby generate economic growth for all. Business education thus targets the enterprise because – in the broad context of society – that benefit ultimately brings massive advantages to the entire population. Social responsibility is, therefore, not the aim of business education. Instead, the wider societal benefit flows to society through employment and access to commodities, thereby enhancing the standard of living, while the reciprocal benefit to business is growing demand for its product and, hence, profits. This interconnectedness of value creation, value exchange, value optimization, and value allocation in creating wealth is the essence of what business managers must learn, understand, and apply (Baba 2016: 270–272, 2018: 140–142). Universities facilitated the rollout of formal management education, not to serve a political agenda, but to deliver to business an operational enhancing service, that is, to support better business through systematic management education. American business success and global leadership were seminal to South Africa following this approach. The UP was the first in South Africa to do so, acting in advance of many institutions in Britain and Europe.

What the business schools offered as formal advanced business education was, in fact, advanced education premised on a bachelor's degree. The target market was business managers, an elite cohort meant to deliver on the efficiency of enterprise for profit. By the time of the establishment of the business schools, white students outnumbered those of colour. Black students studied at English tuition institutions because of their better proficiency in English. Students of colour were never denied access to tertiary education. At the time the National Party assumed power, only 41% of black African children, between the ages of 7 and 16 years, actually attended school. The National Party introduced compulsory education for black African children, and by 1968 the number of black African children in grade 12 (matriculation) had risen from 146 in 1961 to 33,236. Between the late 1960s and 1990, this number rose to 255,669. The number of black African children passing at a level that allowed university entry rose from 15.9% of black matriculants passing grade 12 in 1961 to 35.5% (a total of 3404 successful grade 12 s) in 1976 and 43% (a total of 109,936) in 1990. Both Arithmetic and Mathematics were subjects taught in black schools, thus refuting the popular myth (see Clark and Worger 2014) that black African children were not supposed to be taught mathematics at school (This selective quote was taken out of context from a speech by Dr. H F Verwoerd, on 7 June 1954, before the Senate. Verwoerd argued that Bantu (Black African) education must serve the needs of the community. Schools should ideally deliver educated young people able to work toward the development of their own communities, not as labour tailored to the needs of the white economy. In no sense did Verwoerd ever say or imply that black African education may never prepare its children for professions or careers in business. There is not a single reference in his speech to the alleged view that black children should not be taught Mathematics. See Pelser 1963: 59–79.). The first black African students were permitted to the University of Natal in 1932, and subsequently also to the other English tuition universities, as well as the University of Fort Hare. A medical school for black students opened in Durban at the University of Natal in 1950. Admittedly, the number of black African,

Indian, or Coloured students at South African universities was limited by 1950. In 1953, only 526 scholars out of a total of 7877 matriculants who achieved scores allowing university admission were black African, Indian, and Coloured. The total number of black African, Indian, and Coloured students enrolled at South African universities was 2957 out of a total student population of 27,336. However, the national distance education university, the University of South Africa, enrolled black students from 1951, totalling 2236 in 1969 (Annual Reports, Department of Bantu Education, 1953–1970). When the government introduced Bantu Education for black African children in 1952 under the auspices of the Department of Bantu Education (DBE), there was an outcry from the liberal English opposition. This constituency wanted one single education system for all children. Similarly, when the state introduced separate universities for the different black ethnic groups in 1959, the same outcry rang out. The government argued that education within own communities held the greatest benefit for community development, an enhancement of performance and ultimately the broad-based development of black African young people. Of course this was an integral part of the policy of separate development, criticized by the left and the international community. The promulgation of the *Extension of University Education, Act 45, of 1959*, nevertheless, paved the way for the development of ethnic black African universities as well as universities for the Indian community and the Coloured community. B.Com degrees with Accounting, Business Economics, and Applied Mathematics, and a BA degree in municipal and rural management, were offered at Fort Hare University from 1964. A full LLB degree, which is the postgraduate professional law degree, commenced at the University of KwaZuluNatal at KwaDlangezwa, near Empangeni, in 1966. Persistent opposition to separate development finally led in 1994 to the first universal democratic election in South Africa – and the introduction of black African majority rule. All the former black universities were merged with former white universities, except for the University of Fort Hare. What is nevertheless clear is that, despite South Africa's troubled politics, people of colour enjoyed access to a world-class business education in ever growing numbers.

At the time of the ascendancy of business schools at former so-called white universities (never exclusively so, as demonstrated above), students of colour were permitted entry into the programmes, provided they complied with admission requirements. Wits boasts to have enrolled "a person of colour in WBS's inaugural MBA" (UW 2018: 3). There was no "restriction of management education opportunities to Black South Africans," as alleged by Ruggunan and Sooryamoorthy (2019). Nor is it correct that they did not receive a quality education, denying them aspirations to hold positions the political system of the time did not allow (Arnold 2017). As students could enroll for tertiary business and commerce education, both at former white universities and at the ethnic universities, the numbers were, not surprisingly, limited, given the school performance statistics quoted. Black African students wanting to enroll for degrees not offered at their designated institutions were granted permission by the state to enroll for such degrees at institutions willing to accept them on the basis of compliance with access requirements. Statutory job reservation never excluded black African people from taking up positions in business, or the right to manage their own enterprises. As illustrated, by the 1960s Indian and black African people established and managed successful enterprises in urban townships and rural areas. They also organised their own business associations. In 1966, the National African Federation of Chambers of Commerce (Nafcoc) was formed, seceding from the Johannesburg-based African and Indian Trading Association (established 1927) and the Orlando Traders' Association. These successful businessmen in 1958 also established the *Ikageng Finance Corporation*, which provided loans, guarantees, trained personnel, and business advice to their members. It also negotiated access to bank services. On the Witwatersrand the *Bantoe Winkeliers se Helpmekaar* (Bantu shop owners' Mutual Assistance Association) and the Johannesburg and District Traders' Association, established in 1959, performed similar credit operations by advancing cash loans to their members (Verhoef 2017: 111–112). As a growing number of African scholars qualified as lawyers (of whom Nelson Mandela was an example, completing his BA through Fort Hare and UNISA in 1943 and LLB in 1952 at the University of the Witwatersrand), they emerged as the champions of African business in disputes with municipal authorities. It was from this active business context that Wits enrolled a student of colour right from its first MBA course. By the 1970s, the University of Durban-Westville offered an MBA at its own business school. In short, at the time when the MBA was becoming the qualification of choice in the world of South African business and management, students of colour had access to the qualification from the outset (CHE 2004: 17).

Delivering on the Political Agenda

South Africa's business schools expanded slowly. By the mid-1980s, when the policy of separate development was effectively dismantled, only seven institutions from the early 1970s still offered MBAs. The political agenda of the post-1994 ruling party, Communist Party, and trade union tripartite alliance to "redistribute wealth" gave rise to policies of statutory enforced affirmative action. These policies were justified on "redressing the legacy of Apartheid" (http://www.anc.org.za/ancdocs/history/charter.html). The initial Reconstruction and Development Programme (RDP) soon made way for an extensive network of statutes enforcing the transfer of ownership and control of business to black persons. The South African example of the so-called indigenisation is called Black Economic Empowerment (BEE). Cyril Ramaphosa defined Black Economic Empowerment as "economic empowerment for all South Africans – [it] is a very deliberate programme to achieve meaningful participation of disadvantaged South Africans in the mainstream South African economy" (Ramaphosa 1997: 12). The actual transfer of ownership and control to black Africans did not, however, occur to the satisfaction of the ruling party (Jack 2003, 2007). This gave rise to more comprehensive statutes administered by the Department of Trade and Industry (DTI). In 2003, the DTI issued a summary of the statutory landscape. To justify a faster and more comprehensive transformation of the South African economy, a report entitled *A Strategy for Broad-based Black Economic Empowerment* (DTI 2003) introduced the principle of economic, sector-based charters to manage the transfer of ownership, managerial control, and skills to the broad black community in South Africa. This was mapped out sector by sector. If a sector failed to sign such a "charter," business in those sectors was either severely fined or completely marginalised, effectively excluded from doing any business with the state. These transfers occurred by means of a DTI *Code of Good Conduct* assessing the degree of black ownership of enterprises, the number of black directors of corporations, blacks in executive management, skills transfer to enable black managers to take control, the number of black employees, as well as the effective empowerment of the broad black community through compulsory procurement of goods and services from black enterprises. Non-compliance thus excluded private enterprise from participating in any business with the state. Compliance secured accreditation in the form of a "prize" or score – Code of Good Conduct (scorecards) – ranging from 1 to 4. Under this scorecard, 4 indicated full compliance, securing such enterprises public contracts, preferential procurement by government, and a general positive image as a business concern contributing to the economic transformation of the country (DTI 2003: 11–14; Jack 2007: 108–109; Andrews 2008: 33–36).

The synchronised enforcement of BEE occurred through several other statutes. First there was the *Employment Equity Act No 55 of 1998*. This act mandated the employment of persons on the basis of race, justified as "restitution of the legacies of Apartheid" to reflect the demographic composition of the country, as per quota of population group. The *B-BBEE Code of Good Conduct*, it should be noted, had a significant impact on the operation of the liberal open market in the South African economy: only companies with a B-BBEE score were eligible to do business with the state through preferential procurement by state departments, provinces, and municipalities. The *Public Finance Management Act No 3 of 1998* tasked the treasury to prepare a framework for public procurement. The *Public Procurement Policy Framework Act No 5 of 2000* finally excluded all non-B-BBEE companies from any public business (Bolton 2008; Smit 2016). The *Skills Development Act No 97 of 1998* also mandated racial quotas in skills development programmes at all levels of training and industry skills development, thus enforcing new-style "job reservation" or race-based employment reservation and training. In higher education similar politically sanctioned racism in the name of reversing so-called injustices of the past resulted in preferred access to universities by dedicated demographic categories of the population. The expected outcome of the reinstitution of statutory discrimination is that institutions of higher learning were flooded by students insisting on admission on the basis of statutory justified entitlement. White employees in the civil service were retrenched and replaced by party loyalists. This created an implosion of capacity, leading the Minister of Public Services to issue a directive to public services employees at the middle and senior level, asking them to enroll in MBA degree programmes (CHE 2004: 6). It is not surprising then that higher education institutions experienced a crisis of admission and an assault on scientific integrity, academic freedom, and standards.

The political economy of the transformation agenda distorts the purpose of advanced management education, turning it into a tool to take control of business. Where advanced business education is intended to advance capacity of experienced business leaders – the knowledge base and capacity in business to grow profit and wealth – the South African agenda burdens business with an entitled cohort, having to deliver on a political agenda rather than sound business. State intervention through the directive of the Minister of Public Services confused business private sector and wealth creation with public sector management education and policy implementation. This contributed to tension and a loss of focus for both business and public management education, as the boundaries between the two have become blurred. Master's degrees in public administration lost its appeal as public servants chose to enroll for an MBA qualification instead. Business schools gradually began focussing more on qualifications in policy than business management.

Business schools experienced the tension between the public sphere and business. It no longer was the best managers who entered business schools to enhance managerial capabilities but the politically sanctioned candidates. Between 1990 and 2004, the number of private and public (university-linked) business schools in South Africa mushroomed from 7 to 27, of which 18 were public higher education institutions (13 universities and 5 technikons) and 9 were private institutions (5 local and 4 foreign service providers). As could be anticipated from the high expectations created by the new ruling party in terms of economic redistribution through statutory sanctioning, the number of students in MBA programmes rose rapidly. In 2000, 4868 students enrolled for MBA degrees at the different business schools. By 2002, numbers had risen to 5081. At this point, the Council for Higher Education (CHE) conducted an assessment of the quality of MBA programmes, a review undertaken between November 2002 and March 2004. What was becoming evident even before the review, however, was that an opportunistic entry into the market for MBAs, driven by the BEE agenda, was compromising quality. The transformation agenda opened the door to a proliferation of MBA offerings of questionable quality. This development contributed to a growing disconnect between business and the business schools. Very public criticism of MBA graduate's employability (CHE 2004; Financial Mail 2003), and outright refusal by some business corporations to employ MBA graduates, impacted negatively on the existing business schools' standing.

The CHE inquiry into the MBA qualification in South Africa implied, ultimately, an assessment of business schools as institutions of higher learning. The HEQC was tasked to assess all MBA programmes. This assessment commenced with an assessment of governance of the business schools. The question was to what extent did the existing business schools dovetail with the official CHE policy and the entire BEE policy framework? Were these institutions' mission statements aligned to the "broader developmental and societal objectives of the state" In principle, this implied alignment with the political transformation agenda of the state. The second set of assessment criteria investigated the course content, pedagogy, assessment, and weight of research content in the assessment toward a master's qualification. The last category of the MBA programme assessment was directed toward ascertaining how the programme interacted with its "stakeholders" or context. The key question here was whether business schools were responsive to their immediate environment? (CHE 2004). The assessment was conducted on the basis of three criteria: governance, learning programmes, and context. Apart thus from purely academic content and management governance, the CHE mandated compliance with BEE statutes (Arnold 2017). Faculty and students had to comply with reintroduced statutory racial discrimination. "Context" is the concept used to justify race-based faculty composition and student enrollment, as well as geographical location. Ultimately, business schools are also BEE accredited (FM 2018: 14).

As a result of the review, 15 business schools were assessed fit to continue their operations. Another 15 had to reapply for accreditation. (See Table 1, displaying the CHE-accredited business schools between 2009 and 2018.) In 2018, 17 business schools have HEQC (Higher Education Quality Council) accreditation. By recalling accreditation of 15 business schools in 2004, the CHE introduced state regulation of business schools as part of the ideological manipulated university education system. In 2019 there are 18 accredited business schools in South Africa, 13 at universities and 5 private. State intervention in the business school landscape was a function of the political economy of the race-based ideological reform agenda (euphemistically referred to as the "transformation" agenda) of the post-1994 state. The ultimate intention of the HEQC assessment, therefore, was not only the quality of

Table 1 CHE accreditation

Gordon Institute of Business Science	MBA
Henley Management College of South Africa	MBA
Management College of South Africa (MANCOSA)	MBA GeneralMBA Tourism Management and Development
Milpark Business School	MBA
Nelson Mandela Metropolitan University of Technology, MBA Unit	MBA
North-West University, Mafikeng Campus	MBA
Potchefstroom Business SchoolNorth-West University: Potchefstroom CampusVaal Triangle Campus	MBA (Contact)
Regenesys Management (Pty) Ltd	MBA
Regent Business School	MBA
Rhodes Investec Business School (RIBS)	MBA
Tshwane university of technology business school	MBA
Turfloop Graduate School of Leadership (TGSL)	MBA
University of Cape Town Graduate School of Business (GSB)	MBAEMBA
University of the Free State School of Management	MBA General
University of KwaZulu-Natal (Westville Campus), Graduate School of Business	MBA
UNISA Graduate School of Leadership (SBL)	MBAMBL
University of Stellenbosch Business School (USB)	MBA
Wits Business School	MBA

Source: SABSA MBA 2009 to 2018. Business School Information, June 2019.

management education but also the alignment of business schools with the transformation agenda of the state – i.e., the responsiveness to the BEE transformation agenda. Significantly, the CHE posed a concluding question in the 2004 assessment: "Are business schools conservative or subversive? Are they simply a vehicle for changing the racial composition of business in South Africa, or can they redefine the relationship between business and society?" (CHE 2004: 124). The problem with such ideological interference in scholarly endeavour is the inevitable contradictory outcome. Quality becomes conditional to the political economy of the state.

In essence, the South African state reconfigured the business school environment to deliver what the state mandated – a growing number of black African MBA holders. By 2019, the core of business school excellence remained with those schools who had pioneered international alignment in faculty, curriculum, and didactics. In these institutions, the transformation noise is subdued due to the presence of a core of faculty committed to the maintenance of historic standards. In an attempt to coordinate delivery on the state's transformation agenda, and to assist business schools accredited for the sole purpose of delivering the state's transformation agenda, a collective association, the South African Business Schools Association, was established in 2004.

As the South African state pursued its transformation agenda, the leading South African business schools – in following the American business school model – looked toward international accreditation to support the standing of the programmes offered, for, in the United States, the demand for MBA-qualified managers caused American business schools to develop a domestic standards body, the AACSB (American Assembly of Collegiate Schools of Business) (Aaronson 1996: 213). This development influenced local business school strategies to enhance the quality of programmes and, thereby, demand by business for its programmes. By 2000, however, only the UCT Graduate School of Business was successful in gaining European Foundation of Management Development (EQUIS accreditation). In 2001, the USB gained a similar status. By 2009, Wits Business School and the Gordon Institute of Business Science (GIBS) were awarded AMBA (the British Association of MBAs) accreditation. More local business schools received international accreditation after the HEQC accreditation exercise. In 2009, the *Financial Times* rankings of international business schools placed the UCT's MBA in the top 100 (at 71); GIBS (49) and USB (55) were in the top 100 for open executive education; and for customised executive education, GIBS was positioned at 41, WBS at 62, and USB at 63. By 2018, only 8 of the 18 accredited business schools in South Africa managed to receive accreditation from the AMBA in the United Kingdom. Four gained AACSB (Association to Advance Collegiate Schools of Business in the United States (note: this body changed its name in the interim)) accreditation. Three business schools received EQUIS accreditation. By contrast, the majority of the South African business schools had CHE and AABS (African Association of Business Schools) accreditation in 2018 (SABSA 2019: 5). In 2019 the *Financial Times* included two South African business schools in its top 100 executive MBA ranking list: the UCT GSB is ranked 47th in the world and is the best in Africa. This is specifically for the executive MBA, which is a part-time programme for persons more established in their careers. The Gordon Institute of Business Science (GIBS) is ranked 87th for its executive MBA. This is the successor business school to the UP business school (https://businesstech.co.za, 21/11/2019) (The Gordon Institute of Business Science was established in 2000, when the University of Pretoria's business school merged with a newly established business school in Johannesburg. Professor N A Binedell, former director of the Wits Business School, was the founder and director of GIBS. Sir Donald Gordon, after whom the institution was named, [Gordon was the founder of Liberty Life, in 1957] donated capital for the establishment of GIBS. By 2010 GIBS was ranked 40th in the top 50 *Financial Times* business school ranking (Adendorff 2012: 276–294).).

The three EQUIS-accredited business schools, UCT GSB, USB, and Henley Business School, have the most significant share of international faculty, both full-time and part-time. The Henley Business School is the only foreign business school that was prepared to negotiate the political "transformation" agenda of South Africa to establish operations in South Africa. Apart from Henley, only two South African business schools can be considered internationally competitive (Arnold 2017: 271–273). The CHE and AASB accreditation is nothing more than self-styled justification of the politically driven transformation agenda. It does not enhance international competitiveness. It does, however, encourage African scholars from outside South Africa to enroll, bringing in much needed foreign exchange. By contrast, the globally oriented business corporations in South Africa still send their senior executives to the Harvard Business School and the INSEAD advanced management programmes.

The CHE succeeded in transforming the business schools in South Africa. All the management programmes are graduate programmes – applicants must have a 3-year baccalaureus degree or hold a postgraduate diploma. The business schools were always graduate institutions. The evolution of the MBA programmes was from part-time offerings, initially, then to full-time programmes. At present many business schools have closed their full-time programmes altogether. The general trend is for only part-time MBA programmes. This aligns with the shift toward public administration and the focus on policy. There is a significant shift toward executive education, which follows from the preoccupation with the transformation agenda. This sees people placed in executive positions without a previous career in business management where they would have gained both practical and theoretical understanding as to the operation of an enterprise. Consequently, executive education through short courses has overtaken academic programmes as the primary source of revenue for many domestic business schools. This development is contextually determined. A cohort of executives have landed themselves positions without the growth in the family enterprise, or the systematic buildup of experience in the corporate business environment. As a growing wave of skepticism about the MBA management education mounts internationally (*The Economist*, 2/11/2019; Moyo 2019), there is a significant shift toward short executive programmes, designed to the needs of the sponsoring business community.

The composition of faculty and student bodies has changed to comply with the transformation agenda. The proportion of black South African citizen faculty rose from 23% in 2009 to 29% in 2018, and black faculty from outside South Africa declined from 10% in 2009 to 8% in 2018. International faculty (both African and other international origins) declined from 30% to 19% in 2018. Meanwhile, the proportion of black students rose from 46% in 2009 to 60% in 2018. The number of graduations rose from 1439 in 2009 to 2424 in 2018 – an increase of 58%. The overall success rate of MBA/MBL graduates, however, was unimpressive. In 2011, only 33.9% of the total student body completed the qualification. In 2018, the success rate was only marginally better with only 38.8% graduating. Significantly, SABSA does not reveal the racial composition of the *graduandi* (SABSA 2019: 3–27). Emphasis is placed instead on enrollments. The *Financial Mail* annual MBA survey of 2019, for example, afforded much publicity to the fact that 61.12% of the student body is made up of black South African students. Women comprise 40.1% of the total student body. But when reflecting on the number of successful students graduating (2711 students), there was no demographic breakdown (FM 2019: 16, 124). In other words, we know the race and gender of those who are studying, but not those completing.

One of the changes introduced after the 2004 HEQC accreditation exercise was to require a research component as prerequisite for the awarding of a master's degree. This meant that the accreditation of the MBA as a master's degree be conditional on candidates completing a dedicated research component. An added research focus implied that faculty also had to be research active. This requirement thus mandated business schools' academic research to focus more in line with the academic research requirements of university faculty. The compliance with this requirement varied. In 2015, 17 business schools published 171 articles in ISI international-accredited journals. By 2018, however, 14 business schools published only 71 articles in ISI-accredited journals. A similar trend occurred with respect to IBSS international-accredited journals: 17 South African business schools published 122 articles in IBSS-accredited journals, but this declined to 61 articles by 14 business schools in 2018 (Research published in accredited peer-reviewed scholarly journals originated from both the MBA research projects and independent research activity of business school faculty). The dismal research output in Scopus-accredited journals in 2018 was 32 out of a total of 630 publications listed (5% of the total publications).

Following an investigation into who published with whom and from which institutions, it was reported that the all-white publication profile prior to 1993 had changed to fit the transformation agenda. By 2015 the racist analytical paradigm used to classify authors according to their race displayed a shift from an all-white authorship before 1993 to 72.2% white authors, 19.8% black African authors, 4.1% Indian authors, and 3% publications by "others" – no explanation of who constituted this "new race" depicted as "others" was provided (Ruggunan and Sooryamoorthy 2019: 54). This research is an exercise in quantitative insignificance, since to know what the race of an author is has no bearing on the scientific scholarly contribution to disciplinary discourses or developments. The transformation agenda is, nevertheless, clearly served. However, this self-serving outcome failed to enhance the scientific scholarly standing of research output of South African business schools. The number of ISI-, IBSS-, and Scopus-accredited outputs continues what has become a sustained declining trend since 2004. Significantly, the GSB at UCT opted for a reversal of this trend, by formulating the school's mission to establish a coherent research identity and focus and by developing a strong research culture. This enabled the GSB to increase ISI-accredited publications from 5 in 2012 to 33 in 2018. At the same time, the GSB delivered six PhDs between 2015 and 2019. This scholarly inclination has placed the GSB ahead of the Faculty of Management at the University of Cape Town in terms of research output (Hamann 2019).

Reputable international accreditation of local business schools remains limited to three institutions, of which one is an international institution operating in South Africa. A distinct question mark seems to have appeared over the quality of management education in South Africa, except for at the three triple internationally accredited business schools.

Management *quo vadis*?

When the perspective shifts from the domestic South African context to the wider context of Africa as an emerging business hub, there is a dearth of research and publications on African business and management (Kolk and Rivera-Santos 2018; Verhoef 2017). There is a steady stream of enthusiastic calls for research on Africa (George 2015; Nkomo 2017; Nkomo et al. 2015; Baba 2018; Amankwah-Amoah 2018). However, conceptual consensus on management in Africa is yet to emerge. No distinct African management framework exists. Africa is no monolithic entity (Baba 2018). Management in South Africa emerged from a core knowledge base, grounded in western management theories and practices. Its purpose was to strengthen business and create wealth. Despite the political economy of the transformation agenda, a core of the discipline of Management was preserved. In the subject offerings toward an MBA qualification, finance and accounting, strategy, leadership, human resources, and marketing make up the top six core subjects offered in all programmes (apart from research, which became compulsory since 2004). The second set of six subjects consists of Economics, International Business, Operations, Change Management, Statistics, and Management. Ethics, information systems, entrepreneurship, sustainable development, and social responsibility make up the third batch of six subjects. It is significant that business law, business communication, and innovation are at the bottom end of core MBA subjects (FM 2019: 21; SABSA 2019: 33). In the core subject content, it is therefore evident that management education in South Africa offers students a curriculum in tandem with business schools in the leading western geographies. The CHE acknowledged in 2004 that there was no such qualification as a "South African MBA" or a French MBA or a Mexican MBA, but only a management education that explores functional areas of management. The prevalence of this model points toward a worldwide demand. What carries the distinction of quality in this pattern of global offering is the scholarly standing of faculty and the internationally recognised research output feeding into the teaching programmes. In this respect, the South African business schools fail dismally (CHE 2004: Chap. 5; Arnold 2017: 262). The CHE assessment report in 2004 alluded very clearly to the fact that business management is driven by motivations of efficiency and profit, but that the goals of the state and non-governmental organisations (NGOs) were welfare and socially driven development. The inherent difference between the political economy of the transformation agenda and the orientation of business toward efficiency creates a tension within both business schools and the business community. In order to deliver on the BEE targets in the transformation agenda, the primary aim of enhanced business efficiency (wealth creation, profit, international expansion) is secondary to the political agenda. State regulatory intervention to align the MBA programmes to the transformation agenda also gave rise to the clear division between business schools with credible international accreditation and the majority of business schools aligned to the AASB. Whereas advanced business education should enhance the best minds and the capabilities of the business enterprise, in South Africa MBA education has become highly politicized. The absorption of business school graduates (or lack thereof) indicates that the corporate entities in South Africa do not recruit their leaders or their elite from this environment. A recent survey indicated that only 16% of the top 100 companies listed on the JSE employ MBA graduates as CEOs/top executives (Moyo 2019). The *Financial Mail* 2019 survey showed that 24% of graduates (the largest component) of MBA programmes ended up in positions of general management, 10% in strategic planning, 11% in financial management, and 9% into project management (FM 2019: 62).

This dilemma caused the SABSA to meet late in 2017 to consider the threats to its core function. In a document entitled *Alternative Futures for Business Schools in South Africa*, SABSA acknowledged the high level of diversity between business schools, as well as the persistent decline in the number of South African business schools with international accreditation. The transformation agenda also resulted in staff still in need of so-called academic development. At the same time, business schools grappled with the practical function of the MBA qualification, given the demographic change in the student body and the western grounding of business schools' core function. Growing state intervention in public universities also concerned delegates, suggesting strategies to seek private funding that may facilitate business models less dependent on research. Meanwhile, a slowing demand for MBA degrees was evident as formal employment opportunities diminished amid persistent problems in the South African economy. On the other hand, the demand for global competitiveness highlighted the need for a business education directed toward a globally relevant and competitive experience. As the economic situation became more acute, business schools also experienced growing competition from specialised consulting service providers. This reduced demand for local MBAs. Among the innovative offerings by the various international consultancies are those delivered by firms such as Google, Apple, and Pearson which were prominent. International competition also syphoned potential students from the South African business schools. The latter's survival was increasingly linked to a revival of economic growth based on domestic consensus and human capital development. To achieve desired targets, business schools needed to improve international competitiveness, apply advanced technology in their curricula, and bypass the stifling regulatory environment through private stakeholder alliances. SABSA acknowledged that the "mineralization" of the research component of the MBA prepared candidates only for a *cognate* doctorate, not a PhD. This compromised the quality and standing of the programmes in the business schools.

In the end, the ability of the SABSA members to navigate the landscape of regulatory and institutional intervention was deemed fundamental to their ability to succeed internationally and locally in the medium term. This scenario was put forward as a "strategy for the future." But it was also recognised that "pockets of excellence" existed among those business schools successful in negotiating the social, institutional, technological, and financial landscape of South Africa. Such schools maintained a globally competitive foothold. It remained, however, almost impossible to reconcile the contradictions inherent in the situation. On the one hand, SABSA noted that academic staff development was vital. The question was: could the young staff deliver on what business schools required? Transformation imperatives meant that staff had to be developed. There are, however, insufficient numbers of PhD-qualified black staff who can be employed. Newly trained business academics are, therefore, not delivered at the required rate from the restricted transformation mandated pool. On the other hand, in the name of "transformation and decolonisation of curricula," the political experience was that "sound practice and theories are discarded in favour of politically motivated offerings" without consultation with business and employers. Then, off course, globalisation, the new catchphrase of international business, made it far easier for students to study business and management outside South Africa (Moyo 2019). This global accessibility simply heaped up pressures on South African business schools to convince aspiring executives that they have an offering able to deliver "globally relevant and competitive" training (SABSA 2017).

The political economy of the transformation agenda incapacitated management education in South African business schools. One manifestation of the context is the leadership crisis in business schools. It has become increasingly difficult to identify leaders for the business schools complying with the transformation agenda. The WBS is one such institution suffering from frequent leadership changes, which impacted on strategic leadership and continuity. The complexities of the social and political context of South Africa widened the gulf between the globally aligned models characteristic of the established business schools, such as UCT GSB and USB, and the political subservient models of later entrants. A strategy for the future, built around a vision for business, embedded in the science of management, innovative application of advanced technology, and scholarly responsiveness to industry, is compromised. To address financial viability, business schools engaged in two other educational activities. One of these is executive education. The other is government, civil corps education. The first of these, executive education, has always comprised part of business school education. However, since business schools were absorbed by the transformation agenda – and the capabilities of loyalist civil servant appointments fell short of the needs of a professional civil service – quick fixes such as short executive programmes at business schools seemed the solution (Arnold 2017: 272–273). For the executive short courses, no minimum academic qualification is required. Since 1949 UP offered short courses for civil servants. By 2018, however, separate schools of government were no longer a rarity. Prominent among these were the WBS (the Wits School of Governance, established in 1993 as the Wits School of Public and Development Management) and the School of Business and Governance at North-West University (created through a restructuring of their business school). In addition, the Turfloop (University of the North) and UNISA business schools also incorporated government management training. It is also interesting to note that part-time faculty increased by more than 53% between 2009 and 2018. However, only 49% of these held doctoral degrees. The component of black African faculty grew to 35% in 2018 – of which 11% were recruited from outside South Africa (SABSAa 2019: 9).

The nature of the course offerings shows how business schools operated in support of the transformation agenda. The bulk of executive programmes was now customised to the needs of the client. Between 2009 and 2018, the number of students enrolled in the customised executive programmes rose from 12,198 to 20,844 – a 52% increase (SABSAa 2019: 12). In open executive courses, by contrast, the number of students declined from 15,743 in 2009 to 12,647 in 2018 (SABSAa 2019: 13). The courses attracting the highest number of students (commissioned by the employer) were those associated with the middle management programme, followed by senior management programme, then the business management programme, and, in the fourth position, the executive management programmes (SABSAa 2019: 24). South African business schools also commenced an African export initiative. By 2018, around 43 short executive programmes were rolled out in other parts of Africa. In some cases, corporations from other African markets sent executives to attend short programmes in South Africa. These executive programmes now comprise a substantial contribution to the revenue flows of business schools.

The crisis of management in South Africa is closely associated with the delivery on the political economy of the transformation agenda. South Africa has become fully integrated into the African culture of corruption and ruling party nepotism. The trajectory of management education moved from a university/business stakeholder relationship to a political economy of transformation, based around statutory sanctioned racism. Although Wits claims to be the preferred business school of choice for engineers seeking business acumen (UW 2018: 11, 14), South African business executives attend international executive management programmes in the United States, the United Kingdom, and Europe in preparation for the global world of business. As attendance of executive management programmes of the local business schools indicates, actual executive education for the corporate sector occurs with increasing rarity at these local institutions. The greater attention to socially responsible business is, however, not specific to South Africa. The 2007 UN-initiated Principles for Responsible Management Education (PRME), for example, claims to address responsible corporate conduct, a programme in which management is directed toward goals of inclusive global economic and business development (Alcatraz and Thiruvattal 2010; Singhal et al. 2017). The PRME principles seek to develop business school students' capabilities to become agents of a sustainable, responsible, and inclusive global economy. Business schools must inculcate those values. They must align the teaching didactics to transfer those values and skills. Research agendas must reflect a commitment toward achieving those goals. In South Africa, only 8 of the 18 business schools signed the PRME charter (GIBS, UCT GSB, MANCOSA, Milpark Business School, Nelson Mandela University Business School, Regenesys Business School, Rhodes Business School, USB). The signatories' sharing of information on progress (SIP) reports shows a commitment to implementing the six PRME principles in curriculum, teaching didactics, and research. It also shows in outward communication and partnerships. A fine example is the UCT GSB partnership with health providers to achieve crucial improvements in southern African public health systems and hospitals. The GSB's Embedding Project received the Academy of Management International Impactful Collaboration Award in 2018 and the AACSB's "Innovations That Inspire" award in 2019. The GSB assists companies in embedding sustainability across the full scope of operations and decision-making via the Embedding Project (Hamann 2019). UCT GSB has thereby positioned itself in alignment with international best practice. The voluntary PRME participation has the potential of strengthening the strategic repositioning of management education in South Africa with international best practice (Oosthuizen et al. 2018). These strategies point to a gradual realignment by the leading business schools in South Africa with their international western roots. It challenges state intervention and politicization of management education. It also makes a crucial move to refocus on business management as opposed to politically induced public management.

Conclusion

The South African corporate landscape nurtured many global business leaders. Many South Africans – Sir Ernest Oppenheimer of the De Beers Corporation, Dr P E Rossouw of Sasol, Dr H J van der Bijl from ISCOR, Dr F J du Toit of the IDC, Sir Donald Gordon of Liberty Life Assurance, Dr M H de Kock President of the South African Reserve Bank, B E Hersov of Anglovaal Mining Corporation, Dr W de Villiers of Gencor, C S (Punch) Barlow of Barlow Rand Mining Ltd, A E Rupert of Rembrandt Corporation, W H Hofmeyer of Sanlam, Graham Mackay of SA Breweries, Sydney Press of Edgars, and many other business leaders in the country – had no formal management training. Their education prepared them – either as professionals or as engineers, lawyers, or economists – for a life in business built around social engagement, responsibility, and leadership. Across their careers, they patiently learnt the art of management in the business corridors. As Indian and African businesspeople entered commerce, they used either family acumen or a broad education, to prepare them for the discipline of dedication and hard work. These traits are vital to grow their enterprise and develop society. The careers of Richard and Marina Maponya of Maponya Enterprises; Ephraim Tshabalala of

Tshabalala General Trading, Fuel and Real Estate; S J J Lesolang of Black Chain Supermarket; Habakuk Shikwane of Habakuk Cane (Pty) Ltd; Fortune Kunene and his sons Keith (lawyer), Dudu (medical doctor), and Zanossi of Kunene Enterprises; and Herman Mashaba of Black Like Me, Rajen Pillay of the Coastal Group, A M Moolah of the AM Moola Group in entertainment and shipping, and Sayed H Mia of the SHM Group all testify to the gradual building of business enterprise and managerial expertise through patience, risk, and diligence. Accordingly, professional management in South Africa emerged systematically from both the small enterprise and the large corporation. It developed through the scientific development of a specialised knowledge base, grounded inevitably in research. Leading business schools over the world distinguish them from others through research as the differentiating factor. The intellectual foundation of business training constitutes the indispensable dimension of management as a science. Jeffrey Pfeffer (2011: 38) argues: "The most important actors, however, are the public and private organisations where management gets done. They must cultivate in their people the belief that good decisions depend on relevant evidence and data. They should compel managers to draw on sound research and learn deliberately from experience."

It is the scientific basis of management as a discipline – as it developed since the mid-twentieth century – which gave rise to a profession combining expertise from other professionals in the world of business. In South Africa, the scientific development of the discipline delivered a core of world-class corporate executives, taking small mining and industrial enterprise into the global market. The political economy of the post-1990 transformation agenda, however, has eroded the scientific and research grounding of management education in business schools. Unsurprisingly, corporate South Africa has responded with initiatives to bypass this development: globalise the business to avoid the effects of South African mandates, list on international bourses, and grow management expertise in the business' foreign locations. Such developments indicate that if management education no longer seeks to enhance the creation of wealth, but to allocate ownership to a political agenda, business will depart from this market.

Cross-References

- ▶ Africa and the Firm: Management in Africa Through a Century of Contestation
- ▶ British Management 1950–1980
- ▶ Kurt Lewin: Organizational Change
- ▶ Pre-Colonial Africa: Diversity in Organization and Management of Economy and Society
- ▶ The Age of Strategy: From Drucker and Design to Planning and Porter
- ▶ The Origins of Robust Supply Chain Management and Logistics in the Caribbean: Spanish Silver and Gold in the New World (1492–1700)
- ▶ Think Big and Privatize Every Thing That Moves: The Impact of Political Reform on the Practice of Management in New Zealand

References

Aaronson S (1996) Dinosaurs in the global economy? American graduate business school in the 1980s and 1990s. In: Amdam RPS (ed) Management education and competitiveness. Europe, Japan and the United States. Routledge, London, pp 212–226

Adendorff SA (ed) (2012) Pioneering the MBA in South Africa. The University of Pretoria: innovation from the Graduate School of Management to the Gordon Institute of Business Science, 1949–2011. University of Pretoria, Pretoria

Alcatraz J, Thiruvattal E (2010) An interview with Manuel Escudero 'The United Nations' principles for responsible management: a global call for sustainability. Acad Manag Learn Edu 9(3):542–550

Amankwah-Amoah J (2018) Creating greater confidence in African management research. Thunderbird Int Bus Rev 60:511–522

Amdam RPS (ed) (1996) Management education and competitiveness. Europe, Japan and the United States. Routledge, London

Andrews M (2008) Is Black Economic Empowerment South Africa's growth catalyst? (...or could it be?) J F Kennedy School of Government, Harvard University. Working paper RWP, pp 8–33

Arnold MW (2017) Higher education in management: the case of South Africa. In: Damperon S, Durand T (eds) The future of management education challenges facing business schools around the world, vol 1. Palgrave Macmillan, London, pp 255–264

Baba VV (2016) Editorial essay on business theory and influential scholarship: what makes research interesting? Can J Adm Sci/Revue Canadienne des Sciences de l'Administration 33(4):268–276

Baba V (2018) On globalizing business training in Africa: toward a theory of business education and managerial competence. Afr J Manag 4(2):137–157

Bolton P (2008) The public procurement system in South Africa: main characteristics. Public Contract Law J 37(4):781–802

Brown R, McCartney S, Clowes J (1996) Do they mean business? An investigation of the purpose of the 'new university' business schools in Britain. In: Amdam RPS (ed) Management education and competitiveness. Europe, Japan and the United States. Routledge, London, pp 150–170

Byrkjeflot H (2000) Management education and selection of top managers in Europe and the United States. Norwegian Research Centre in Management and Organisation, Bergen

Byrkjeflot H (2002) Management models and technical education systems: Germany and the United States 1870–1930. The Expansion of Management Knowledge: Careers, Ideas and Sources, Palo Alto: Stanford University Press, pp 212–245

Byrt W (1992) Management education: an international survey. Routledge, London

Cape Argus, 15 /8/1946: Developing business in South Africa: 2

Casson M (2003) Entrepreneurship, business culture and the theory of the firm. In: Handbook of entrepreneurship research. Springer, Boston, pp 223–246

Clark NL, Worger WH (2014) South Africa: The rise and fall of apartheid. New York: Routledge

Coleman DC (1973) Gentlemen and players. Econ Hist Rev 26(1):92–116

Council for Higher education (CHE) (2004) The state of the provision of the MBA in South Africa, vol 2. Higher Education Monitor, CHE, Pretoria

Davenport T, Saunders C (2000) South Africa: A modern history. Springer

Department of Trade and Industry (DTI) (2003) South Africa's economic transformation: A strategy for broad-based Black Economic Empowerment. DTI, Pretoria

Du Toit SJ (1939) Van die Breë Beleid van die Volkskongres (1934) tot die Ekonomiese Selfstandigmaking as Kernvraagstuk. In: Ekonomiese Volkskongres Referate, Besluite en Presensielys. 3–5 October 1939. Federasie van Afrikaanse Kultuurverenigings, Johannesburg, pp 20–29

Financial Mail (South Africa), 27/9/1967: WITS Business School Depressing Delay

Financial Mail, 4/9/1964: Wits appointment

Financial Mail (South Africa) Survey of MBA's in South Africa. Business Day, 2003

Financial Mail (South Africa) MBA survey. Tiso Blackstar Group, 2017

Financial Mail (South Africa) MBA survey. Tiso Blackstar Group, 2018
Financial Mail (South Africa) MBA survey. Tiso Blackstar Group, 2019
George G (2015) Expanding context to redefine theories: Africa in management research. Manag Organ Rev 11(1):5–10
Giliomee HB (2005) The Afrikaners. A biography of a people. Tafelberg, Cape Town
Giliomee HB, Mbenga B (2007) New History of South Africa. Nasionale Boekhandel Limited
Hagedorn-Hansen Y (2017) Transformation of the South-African short-term insurance industry: the case of Santam, 1918–2011. Unpublished PhD thesis, University of Johannesburg
Hamann R (2019) Note on GSB Research strategy. Internal GSB memorandum, 25/4/2019. (Supplied by R Hamann)
Houghton DH (1976) The South African Economy. Cape Town; New York: Oxford University Press
Jack V (2003) From the starting bloc: a decade of black economic empowerment. EmpowerDEX, Johannesburg
Jack V (2007) Unpacking the different waves of black economic empowerment. In: Mangcu X, Marcus G, Shubane K, Hadland A (eds) Visions of black empowerment. Jacana Press, Johannesburg, pp 105–117
Jones FS, Müller AL (1992) The South African economy, 1910–1990. Macmillan, London
Kipping M, Engwall L, Üsdiken B (2008) Preface: the transfer of management knowledge to peripheral countries. Int Stud Manag Organ 38(4):3–16
Kolk A, Rivera-Santos M (2018) The state of research on Africa in business and management. Bus Soc 57(3):415–436
Lawrnece P (1989) Management education in West Germany. In: Byrt W (ed) Management education: an international survey. Routledge, London
Locke RR (1988) Educational traditions and the development of business studies after 1945 (Anglo-French-German comparison). Bus Hist 30(1):84–115
Locke RR (1989) Management and higher education since 1940: the influence of America and Japan on West Germany, Great Britain and France. Cambridge University Press, Cambridge
Lukasiewicz M (2018) From diamonds to gold. The making of the Johannesburg stock exchange, 1880–1890. J South Afr Stud 43(4):715–732
Moyo B (2019) Is an MBA still worth the effort? Financial Mail. https://businessmediamags.co.za/category/xfeature. Accessed 29 Nov 2019
Müller AL (1977) Die ekonomiese geskiedenis van Suid-Afrika. Academica, Pretoria
Nash A (1997) Wine-farmers, heresy trials and the 'whole personality': the emergence of the Stellenbosch philosophical tradition, 1916–1940. S Afr J Philos 16(2):56–75
Nioche JP (1992) The war of degrees in European management education. EFMD, Forum 1:21–24
Nishizawa T (1996) Business studies and management education in Japan's economic development – an institutional perspective. In: Amdam RPS (ed) Management education and competitiveness. Europe, Japan and the United States. Routledge, London, pp 96–109
Nkomo SM (2017) Time to look in the mirror: producing management theory and knowledge for Africa. Afr J Manag 3(1):7–16
Nkomo SM, Zoogah D, Acqaah M (2015) Why *Africa Journal of Management* and why now? Afr J Manag 1(1):4–26
Oosthuizen JH, Usher JV, Tankou Epse Nukunah CN (2018) Principles of responsible management education: an assessment of South African business schools. J Contemp Manag 15:37–56
Pelser AN (1963) Verwoerd aan die Woord. Speeches 1948–1962. Afrikaanse Pers Boekhandel, Johannesburg
Pfeffer J (2011) Management a profession? Where's the proof? Harv Bus Rev 38
Ramaphosa C (1997) Black economic empowerment. Financial Mail 4 Apr 1997: 6
Robinson R, Gallagher J, Denny A (1961) Africa and the Victorians. New York
Rosenthal E (1912) On change. South African Mining Journal. Potter SR (ed) vol 21, p 71
Ruggunan S, Sooryamoorthy R (2019) Management studies in South Africa. Exploring the trajectory in the apartheid era and beyond. Palgrave Macmillan, London

Sadie JL (2002) The fall and rise of the Afrikaner in the South African economy. University Annals, Department of Economics, Stellenbosch
SABSA (2019) MBA 2009 to 2019. Business School Information. Johannesburg: Lodestar
SARB Quarterly statistical bulletins, 1920–1990
Singhal N, Suryawanshi P, Mittal G (2017) Crafting responsible management practices in business school learning outcomes: an Indian case study. SAGE 21(2):46–62
Smit AH (2016) The public procurement process in South Africa and the law of contract. Unpublished LLM mini-dissertation, University of Pretoria
Solomon V (1982) Banking. In: Coleman FL (ed) Economic history of South Africa. HAUM, Pretoria
South African Business Schools' Association (SABSA) (2017)
The Economist, 2/11/2019: Management education. The next business revolution, pp 56–57
Transvaler, Die, 23/7/1965: Professoressor verwelkom
University of the Witwatersrand (UW) Gazette, vol 6, 1964
University of the Witwatersrand Gazette, vol 10, 1968
University of the Witwatersrand Gazette, Convocation Commentary, December 1968
University of the Witwatersrand (2018) 50 faces of Wits Business School, 1968–2018. Wits, Johannesburg
Verhoef G (1995) Nationalism and free enterprise in mining: the case of Federale Mynbou, 1952–1965. South Afr J Econ Hist 10(1):89–107
Verhoef G (1999) The development of diversified conglomerates: Federale Volksbeleggings – a case study. J Contemp Hist 24(2):55–78
Verhoef G (2011) The globalisation of South African conglomerates, 1990–2009. Econ Hist Dev Regions 26(2):83–106
Verhoef G (2013a) Reluctant ally: the development of statutory regulation of the accountancy profession in South Africa, 1904–1951. Account Hist 18(2):163–191
Verhoef G (2013b) South Africa: leading African Insurance. In: Borscheid P, Haueter NV (eds) World insurance. The evolution of a global risk network. Oxford University Press, Oxford, pp 325–348. ISBN 978-19657964
Verhoef G (2014) Globalisation of knowledge but not opportunity: closure strategies in the making of the South African accounting market, 1890s to 1958. Account Hist 19(1–2):193–226
Verhoef G (2016) Innovation and expansion: the product innovation and expansion in insurance in South Africa. The case of Sanlam, 1920–2000. Historia 61(1):69–91
Verhoef G (2017) The history of business in Africa. Complex discontinuity to emerging markets. Studies in economic history. Springer, Cham
Verhoef G (2018) The power of your life. The Sanlam century of insurance empowerment, 1918–2018. Oxford University Press, Oxford
Verhoef G, Van Vuuren LJ (2012) South Africa. In: Previts GJ, Walton P, Wolnitzer P (eds) A global history of accounting, financial reporting and public policy. Eurasia, the Middle East and Africa. Studies in the development of accounting thought, vol 14D. Emerald Books, Bingley, pp 135–182
Webb AC (1992) The roots of the tree: a study in early South African banking: the predecessors of First National Bank, 1838–1926. First National Bank of Southern Africa, Cape Town
Wilson JF (1992) 'The Manchester experiment': a history of Manchester Business School, 1965–1990. Paul Chapman, London
Wilson JF (1996) Management education in Britain. A compromise between culture and necessity. In: Amdam RPS (ed) Management education and competitiveness. Europe, Japan and the United States. Routledge, London, pp 133–149
Wilson M, Thompson LM (eds) (1971) The Oxford History of South Africa: South Africa. 2 from 1870–1966. Clarendon Press, Oxford
Here are the best executive MBAs in the world – including 2 from South Africa. https://businesstech.co.za.news/business/354751/here-are-the-best-executive-mbsa-in-the-world. Accessed 21 Nov 2019

Why Entrepreneurship Failed to Emerge in "Developing Countries": The Case of Colonial Africa (1952–1972)

55

Michele Akoorie, Jonathan M. Scott, Paresha Sinha, and Jenny Gibb

Contents

Introduction	1270
Why Entrepreneurship Failed to Emerge in Former Colonies	1271
Periodization as an Historical Method	1272
Unique Explanatory Factors Inhibiting the Rise of Entrepreneurship in Underdeveloped Countries	1275
Summary: Developing an Explanatory Framework	1282
References	1284

Abstract

This chapter builds on historical approaches to entrepreneurship (e.g., Wadhwani D, Entrepreneurship in historical context: using history to develop theory and understand process. In: Welter F, Gartner W (eds) A research Agenda for entrepreneurship and contexts. Edward Elgar, Cheltenham, 2016) to review and synthesize this literature from 1952 to 1972 into three contextually driven interrelated factors to explain why entrepreneurship failed to emerge in colonial Africa during the early period of decolonization. This chapter argues that the temporal, economic, and spatial contexts presented by extant theories are not appropriate to explain why entrepreneurship failed to emerge and discusses how

M. Akoorie (✉)
ICL Graduate Business School, Auckland, New Zealand
e-mail: micheleakoorie@icl.ac.nz

J. M. Scott
School of Management and Marketing, University of Waikato Tauranga CBD Campus, Tauranga, New Zealand
e-mail: j.scott@waikato.ac.nz

P. Sinha · J. Gibb
School of Management and Marketing, University of Waikato, Hamilton, New Zealand
e-mail: psinha@waikato.ac.nz; jenny.gibb@waikato.ac.nz

© The Author(s), under exclusive licence to Springer Nature Switzerland AG 2020
B. Bowden et al. (eds.), *The Palgrave Handbook of Management History*,
https://doi.org/10.1007/978-3-319-62114-2_103

these insights can advance understanding of how entrepreneurship contributes to the economic development of emerging economies. First, there was the political situation in African countries of this time: the liquidation of European colonial power in the former colonies in Africa which happened over two decades from the 1950s to the 1970s. Second, the economic conditions which prevailed as Africa, as a resource-rich country, continued to rely on the wealth of resource extraction. Third, rationalism in Europe in the seventeenth Century had paved the way for an industrial revolution, but Africa had not even been explored by Europeans at this time. This chapter offers new objective insights based on historical analysis and synthesis from the contemporary literature of the selected time period, rather than drawing on post hoc subjective and ahistorical literature that lacks the explanatory power of this chapter's historical approach. The explanatory framework and narrative historical synthesis analysis of why entrepreneurship failed to emerge in the former colonies of Africa hopefully goes some way towards addressing critical research gaps.

Keywords

Entrepreneur · Entrepreneurial failure · Entrepreneurship · Ownership · Small business · Start-up structure

Introduction

Entrepreneurs have generally been treated as uniform and universal actors in economic theory, regardless of the stage of economic development of their host countries (Kilby 2011). The origins of the "classic" entrepreneurial theories offered by Cantillon, Say, and Knight (for a review of their contributions see Van Praag 1999), Schumpeter and later Kirzner (see Hébert and Link 1989) were largely (with the exception of Kirzner) constructed by surveying Western sites at the time of the industrial revolution or pre- or post-World War II. The relevant contemporary literature on the historical context of small firms has been explored and reviewed in the postindustrial Western context (e.g., Cassis and Minoglou 2005; Casson 1982, 1997, 2011; Casson and Casson 2013a, b, 2014; Casson and Godley 2005, 2007; da Silva Lopes and Casson 2007; Harris 1967; Hébert and Link 1989, 2006, 2009; Kirzner 1997; Murphy et al. 2006; Popp and Holt 2013). However, these insights cannot be applied to build knowledge of entrepreneurial history in emerging economies. Entrepreneurship is not the same all over the world.

Nevertheless, there has been an undeniable tendency to apply entrepreneurial theories grounded in the Western canon to emerging economies, without taking account of the context in which business activity occurs. This has particularly been the case in Africa. Although there has been an explosion of recent scholarly interest in entrepreneurship in Africa, the main frameworks used are those grounded in frameworks dating from the postindustrial Western context. In other words, the current studies are a-contextual. This finding leads to two issues. The first is the absence of context. The renewed interest in context and entrepreneurship led by Baker and Welter (2018) suggests that studies on entrepreneurship are deficient in that they focus exclusively on the behavior of entrepreneurs and treats the social, economic, and political infrastructure as externalities in which these activities take place. The second issue is that if the social, economic, and political structure is unfavorable towards the development of an entrepreneurial culture, could this explain why entrepreneurship failed to emerge in some countries, while in other countries where the climate was favorably structured towards entrepreneurship, it flourished? If that is the case, then Wadhwani's (2016) approach suggests that a historical perspective explaining the process and theory of entrepreneurship could be a most useful way forward. Hence, the chapter examines the development of entrepreneurship (or lack of) in colonial Africa during 1952–1972 by reviewing and synthesizing literature to derive contextual (Welter 2011; Zahra 2007; Zahra et al. 2014) insights from this period that explain entrepreneurship's failure to emerge in emerging economies. This chapter argues that the temporal, economic, and spatial contexts presented by these theories are not appropriate to explain why entrepreneurship failed to emerge in the early postcolonial period (1952–1972). The chapter discusses how these insights can advance understanding of the contribution of entrepreneurship to the economic development of emerging economies: lacking from ahistorical and a-contextual approaches to the topic. Therefore, an historical analysis – as proposed by Wadhwani (2016) – that is highly contextualized can offer insights that "sterile" (Zahra 2007), noncontextual contemporary academic studies neglect (Zahra et al. 2014).

The chapter is organized as follows. The first part of the chapter explains why entrepreneurship failed to emerge in the newly independent formerly British African colonies between 1952 and 1972, why this period was chosen, and of the newly independent former colonies, why these countries were selected. The next part of the chapter examines, using the historical method of counterfactual analysis, what were the perceived barriers to the growth of entrepreneurial activity, in this group of countries at this time. A conclusion is offered in the final section.

Why Entrepreneurship Failed to Emerge in Former Colonies

While a postwar Europe (apart from Britain) was concerned with reconstruction and the re-building of business activity, politically, the major concerns were between the pre-war hegemony of the West versus the postwar concerns of the expansion of Communist power. The concerns were about the vacuum of world leadership which both the United States and the Union of Soviet Socialist Republics (USSR) were contending for, and in particular whether the essentially bankrupt European economies could continue to tend the Colonial Empires which they had built in Sub-Saharan Africa from the 1860s to 1870s. If they were not able to continue what or who would fill the space?

Concerns were expressed at the newly formed United Nations that the USSR would try to form alliances and influence the direction of the colonies of Africa.

Another concern was how to deal with persistent underdevelopment in countries which had been exploited for their resources and peoples in the less developed areas of the world and were politically and economically dependent. Until the Second World War each of the British colonies was supposed to subsist on their own; so there was nothing whatever to spend on development. With the passing of the first Colonial Development and Welfare Act during the war, the word "development" entered the Colonial lexicon (Allen 1980). Development was a relatively new proposition. Its currency was promoted by development economists (none, except Harris 1967, had ever been to Africa) but they were called on to give their advice on how underdeveloped economies could improve their position.

Periodization as an Historical Method

Buckley (2016) suggests four categories for historical method which can be usefully applied to the study of business history. The first is source criticism (covering the provenance of documents and using triangulation of evidence to avoid bias). Historical analysis of documentary evidence involves analyzing what is not present in archives, not what is. Records of a period contained in Colonial Office documents may not be representative of what a District Officer in the field (the colony in question) quite thought of the same situation, which is why oral histories from the ranks of the Colonial Administrative Service in Africa as recorded by Charles Allen in 1980, represent a rich narrative of what it what it was like for them. The second approach is the analysis of sequences using time series analysis and process theorizing. This approach is called "periodization" by Decker (2013) taking a selected period of time and using thick contextualization in time and space to develop a historical narrative of the sequenced period. The comparative approach or method is where a comparison is drawn between say, a firm operating in different geographic locations, or, as for colonial histories what differentiated the experience of one colony from another in the same period of time. The final approach is counterfactual analysis – the "what if" question, which enables the researcher to pose the question, what would have happened had some crucial turning point of history had turned out differently? (Buckley 2016, p. 890). However, Buckley warns that hindsight occurs if the counterfactual is contaminated by ex post knowledge of the outcome. For this chapter, two methods were used. The first was periodization (taking a particular period in time in the history of former colonies in British controlled sub-Saharan Africa) as they transitioned from British rule to full independence over a remarkably short period of time (1952–1972). The second method, counterfactual analysis, poses the question "Why did entrepreneurship fail to emerge in British Colonial Africa?" Entrepreneurship was being promoted by development economists as a way for emerging economies who were then mired in poverty, to break out of this morass.

To understand the perspective that development economists were using, a literature search using the term "entrep∗" and "small∗" (as in small firms) was undertaken. This initial literature search uncovered articles from 1952 onwards. Perhaps not surprisingly, as Table 1 shows, the literature search uncovered that the majority of articles were written between 2000–2009 (35.2%) and 2010–2014 (45.2%) compared with the previous decades, apart from the 1950s where only one article was identified, had relatively similar proportions of reviewed articles. This growing trend of writing about entrepreneurship in emerging economies suggests a burgeoning interest in the broad subject area.

Myrdal (1968), as an ardent proponent of institutional approaches, could see that the problems of underdevelopment could not be tackled in isolation. Consequently, he questioned economists who applied Western approaches to the problems of underdevelopment and did not consider the institutional framework in which these solutions had to be applied. Thus, he advocated consideration of shortages of skilled labor, a result of low education levels, rigidities of attitudes, class, and religion which would hamper developmental efforts.

Apart from Myrdal (1968), the authors found few other contemporary writers concerned with the impact of the political situation on the future of underdeveloped countries. This scarcity may tentatively ascribe this to the increasing demarcation of lines of scholarship in Western thought. Whereas the writings of Smith, Ricardo, John Stuart Mill, and Keynes were aware of the political background of their contributions, the expanding literature on development problems constituted a major re-direction of economic science, indeed of all social science. Hence, the focus by other contemporary writers (Leibenstein 1968; Silberman 1956; Shetty 1964) on the problems of underdevelopment tended only to look at the economic problems facing the underdeveloped countries. The post-Second World War period 1952–1972 saw vast political change in underdeveloped countries. Prior to the war, the most intensive work had been done by Western cultural anthropologists who studied the static structure of institutions and attitudes of people living and working in these countries and their survival plight. As Myrdal (1968, p. 9) pointed out, the re-direction of the work of social scientists was not "an autonomous and spontaneous development of social science but a result of vast political changes." Silberman (1956, p. 41) was no less convinced than Myrdal (1968) that entrepreneurs, due to specific differences in these "underdeveloped countries" would be able to act as engines for growth, would be manifested in the same way that they had done in the Western economies. He describes the tensions between the "United Nations School"

Table 1 Temporal analysis of meta-analysis articles

Year category	Count	Percent (%)
1950–59	1	0.5
1960–69	7	3.5
1970–79	7	3.5
1980–89	10	5
1990–99	14	7
2000–09	70	35.2
2010–14	90	45.2
Grand total	**199**	**100**

Source: the authors

or the "New-Welfare Economics" as he calls it who believed in industrialization for the underdeveloped countries, "favoring policies which change the ratios of rural to urban population...concentrate attention on large-scale investments and measurable indexes of progress" over the "New Laissez Faire" school who were convinced that induced mechanization was the answer for countries which have a high abundance of labor. In this sense, he refers to Knight's (1921) caution that such an approach would mean that "man's energies are devoted to doing things automatically" (Knight, p. 21). It would destroy the creative impulse, of entrepreneurship which depends on ingenuity and shrewdness, judgment, and heterodoxy. Such enterprise as Silberman (1956) could find in the underdeveloped economies were all related to local production for the building industries, repair and maintenance, wood-milling garment making, and exploiting cultural traits fused with a developing tourism industry.

This nascent form of entrepreneurship, tested by Harris (1967) in Nigeria, suggests that growth begins with a small cadre of local entrepreneurs and would only proceed if they were drawn into the nexus of the international economy, going overseas to obtain the requisite skills. Harris (1967) commented that the local education system emphasized literary skills, rather than technical and managerial skills, so he saw no future of the development of entrepreneurship. This argument focuses on differences in education systems. Leibenstein (1968) claimed that routine entrepreneurs, who coordinated and managed a well-established going concern where there were opportunities in established markets, were distinctive from nascent entrepreneurs who carry out an enterprise where not all markets are clearly defined and/or where parts of the production function are not completely known.

Leibenstein (1968) saw that the rigidities of institutions were part of the problem. Developmental economists need to focus on studying the gaps, obstructions, and impediments in the market network and assist potential entrepreneurs in these economies to be trained to spot opportunities. This theme pervades in other studies such as Shetty (1964, p. 917) who was less than sanguine about the potential of private entrepreneurs to promote economic growth in underdeveloped economies. "In fact, in most developing countries of Asia and Africa, entrepreneurship has been found to be the most important limiting factor in their economic development." Spengler (1958), also pointed at the expansion of the public sector at the expense of the private sector which "slows down the aggregate number of entrepreneurs" (p. 472), curiously suggesting that a solution to this problem would be either to bring into the bureaucracy individuals who could have been or who currently are entrepreneurs, thus displacing people in over-manned or inefficient bureaucracies. This approach Spengler (1958) ascribes to the continuing presence of the politico-legal frameworks established by colonial administrators. Bonné (1956, p. 10) also referred to this dominance of public and semi-public bodies, stating that: "Occidentals in their socio-economic credo are not aware of the potential for growth in underdeveloped economies."

This recurrent theme of underdeveloped countries adhering to the customs and traditions of public administrations which prevailed since colonial expansion over generations dominates the scholarly literature on entrepreneurship in undeveloped countries during this period 1952–1972. The legacy of these administrations was perceived as being actively hostile to measures required for transformation, even to the point of suggesting the creative destruction of such enterprises. Governments should work on a neutral plane and promote the interests of the community at large, irrespective of the changing political conditions. It was entirely possible that this group of commentators on the position of underdeveloped countries would have been influenced by the views of a collective group of 150 political and social scientists (the Group convened by Colonel House, a Presidential advisor) who contributed the material contained in the text of the speech given by President Woodrow Wilson, on 8 January 1918 (Wilson 1918). This text subsequently became the inspiration for the mandate of the League of Nations.

Wilson's viewpoint would have become widely known among political and social scientists and no doubt forms the basis for the critical stance on colonialism taken by Western scholars, especially those educated in the United States. However, even when nationalist movements were ongoing, they never perceived what impact "the rising tide of nationalism" would have on the economies of underdeveloped countries? They were overtly critical of the "colonial system" of administration, order, and judicial systems; they were concerned with what the effect of these systems was – especially regarding administration. Public administration engendered "institutional rigidities," the answer to which was to remove the blockages in the system, replace them with other systems, or develop a rudimentary form of developmental planning. That would free the way up for the establishment of an entrepreneurial economy. Few scholars, unlike Myrdal (1968) who, though focusing his work entirely on Asia, were prepared to consider institutional rigidities as encompassing political, economic, and sociocultural factors and to consider that this complex interrelationship of factors might be able to explain why entrepreneurship failed to emerge in underdeveloped countries.

A counterfactual approach considers the question "what if" the underdeveloped countries of Sub-Saharan Africa had not experienced the institutional rigidities comprising political, economic, and sociocultural factors during the period 1952–1972? Would that then have been the explanation for the absence of entrepreneurialism? Several examples from a select group of British colonial territories (East Africa, Ghana, and Nigeria) were chosen for the sake of parsimony, although experiences in non-British colonies were certainly similar in so far as their own experiences on the path to independence were concerned. Table 2 shows the contextual factors which contributed to the infrastructural void.

Unique Explanatory Factors Inhibiting the Rise of Entrepreneurship in Underdeveloped Countries

Factor 1: Colonization of Africa and the Corrosion of Tribal Communities

The Scramble for Africa started from the 1860s to 1870s when the French and the British begin exploring Western Africa systematically and signed bilateral agreements assigning respective spheres of influence. The Berlin Conference in 1885 laid down the principles that would be used among Europeans to divide the continent. In the next 30 years, European powers signed hundreds of treaties that partitioned the largely unexplored continent into protectorates, free-trade-areas, and colonies. What

Table 2 Key factors inhibiting the rise of entrepreneurship in underdeveloped countries

Contextual factors	Description	Area studied
Contextual factor #1:	Politics, institutions and uncertainty in explaining the emerging economies	Example: "Colonial" and "postcolonial" African nations
Contextual factor #2:	Economic structure and economic direction in emerging economies	Example: "Colonial" and "postcolonial" African nations
Contextual factor #3	The role of religion/culture and education in entrepreneurship in emerging economies	Example: "Colonial and "postcolonial" African nations

Source: the authors

were the consequences of this arbitrary division? European powers were stimulated by the prospect of access to hitherto undiscovered resources – such as the prospect of minerals, agricultural production, land, and labor to fuel the continuous process of industrialization in developed economies. However, the Scramble for Africa had created new nations, with more communication and economic interchange within borders, and a common administration, legal system and common political institutions, the "new" nations symbolized territorial individuality (Coleman 1954). The imposition of Western technology, socio-political institutions, and ideology were disruptive in the introduction of new techniques and symbols for the acquisition of wealth, status, and prestige. However, the new system had no place for these techniques and symbols. Nevertheless, new administrations felt that it was their duty and in their interest to develop parts of Africa but it was not in the direction of the development of entrepreneurship as the development economists (referred to earlier) had suggested were necessary to promote economic development. For British Colonial Administrators, the objective was to maintain law and order or encourage economic and social development. It could not be either/or; it had to be first/then (Kirk-Greene 1980). If anything could typify the Victorian liberal colonial administrator, it would be that their code of conduct was based around the three "G's," that is, God, Good Governance, and Gratuitous Behavior. It was benevolent paternalism, with an initial assumption of racial superiority. As the keeper of the King's peace, a Colonial Governor was seen as "Mother and Father of the People" (Allen 1980, p. 77). However, as a result of colonial empire building, the structure of traditional society was changing.

Perham (1963) describes two "acids" that corroded the traditional structure of tribal communities. The first of these was the introduction of the Western exchange economy. As a consequence of this economy, young men were drawn away from villages to live in labor camps and towns which disrupted the traditional subsistence economy and the cumulative effect of living in dual worlds, halfway between primitive agriculture to disciplined wage labor and back again. This effect occurred rapidly, and disruptively. As a source of discontent, this disaffection from traditional ways could be harnessed as a potent force by newly educated leaders. British administrators focused more on the "happy and progressive development of rural agricultural communities and too little on what was happening under our noses in the big urban centres" (Allen 1980, p. 179).

The second "acid" was the introduction of a Western education system. Although largely begun by missionaries even before annexation, governments left education in religious hands.

Schools were teaching English history and literacy with governments taking over the more advanced and expensive activities in the form of higher education where young men would go to England for advanced education (as the Indian graduates had done before them). Here they would learn about civil liberties and observe a free political life. The Western education system provided tools of scientific education with which to attack alien rule and colonialism and to develop an awareness and conviction that they could shape their own destiny (Coleman 1954). However, on their return to their African homelands, the racial discrimination that they might have experienced in England and the USA was also present in their inability to find positions for which, by their own academic achievements, they considered themselves fit for. The Pan-African trans-territorial movements were led by Western elites who had, through their educational experience both in the United States and Britain, been stimulated by the ideas of West Indians of African descent living abroad (Marcus Garvey (Cronon 1955), W.E.B du Bois and George Podmore) and the emancipation movement of African Americans in 1922.

Factor 2: The Case of Nationalism in Colonial Africa (1952–1972)

The colonial countries of the empires of Britain, Belgium, the Netherlands, and Germany were preoccupied with gaining independence from colonial rule in the postwar period. The purpose of this movement was to "achieve absolute, social and political equality and local autonomy within a broader European-African grouping (French and Portuguese Africa) within what is a manifestly plural society" (Coleman 1954, p. 407). Coleman (1954) was referring to the African continent in this context. Empires were more trouble than they were worth during the period 1957–1965. In terms of costs of administration, particularly in postwar Britain, which was preoccupied with reconstruction and nationalization of key industries; the costs of administration born by the Colonial Office were progressively burdensome. Some 27 former colonies in Asia, African, and the Caribbean became independent during this period (Coleman 1954). It is here suggested that the preoccupation with nationalist movements both from the perspective of the pro-national independence movements and that of the colonial powers meant that little attention was paid to economic development. The rise of nationalism in tropical Africa needs to be understood in light of the (in historic terms) somewhat brief tenure of the colonial European powers in the continent. Whereas developed economies in the West had gone through a process of commercialization, industrialization, social mobility, and the establishment of democracies which spanned several centuries, the history of the colonization, de-colonization, and subsequent establishment of weakly-held democracies endured for merely a century. A British administrator (Allen 1980) equated the single party state with military dictatorships, both being as distinctly distasteful. These dictatorships (with their later attendant inter-tribal atrocities) were too much like the fascism which troubled Europe in the 1930s.

Anti-imperialism sentiments expressed by Roosevelt and Willkie and Africans living in the United States also played a part in the awakening nationalism movement (Coleman 1954). The goal of influential leaders such as Nkrumah (Gold Coast) Aggrey, Eyo Ita, and Azikiwe in Nigeria was to create a global consciousness and unity to agitate for advancement of the welfare of the members of the African race, wherever they may be and devising plans for future nationalistic activity in specific regions. This development sowed the seeds of incipient nationalism whereby individuals such as Nkrumah in Ghana (which became independent in 1957) could mobilize the masses and organize the new discontents into a movement for self-government, turning against Britain her own political and judicial weapons (Hodgkin 1956). Uncompromising demands, mobilizing parties, by appealing to the people in the towns and villages, the growing threat of force, and attempts by the British government to contain the negotiations came to naught. Even when imprisoned, Nkrumah was allowed to stand for election and, being elected, immediately assumed power.

In West Africa, a policy of identity was carried out by representatives of the British colonial service. For humanitarian reasons, in the aftermath of the antislavery movement, the policy was to regard all men as the same. Here, while British citizenship was given, English law established, and incipient legislative and municipal councils were established in coastal footholds, it did not overcome the problem of governance of the large population in the interior. Here, F.D Lugard, later Lord Lugard (1926; Perham 1963), applied an indirect rule or the dual mandate policy to Nigeria, which had ruled the protectorates in British India (North-West Frontier). Lugard linked native systems closely with British administration, adjusted to all sizes and types of African society, "defining the exact measure of administration and judicial authority to each" (Perham 1963, p. 41). As a bottom-up approach, indirect rule reflected an understanding of the limits of English power to control indigenous populations directly. Indirect rule, however, drew individuals out of their societies into central government, to wage labor, to work in offices, and to the growing towns – in effect, the urbanization of labor. For educated Africans, it led nowhere and the Colonial Service had no place for them. "'Africanization' provided the main stumbling block in every territory's progress towards self-government" (Allen 1980, p. 160). The failure to build up an indigenous executive cadre was widely recognized as perhaps the greatest error of colonial rule. This failure was largely due, in one of the former Governor's view (Sir James Robertson, a former Governor General of Nigeria (1955–1960), to not so much a lack of will, but a lack of imagination (Allen 1980). Promoting local officials to higher administrative posts was hampered by views that they would be unable to offer as good a service and as good administration as they had from British Officers. Despite attempts at further inclusiveness by nominating or elected African members to legislative Councils – a gradual move in the direction of the English local government model – it was insufficient to offer a solution to the ambitions of the educated elite, with future political hopes for their territories: ultimately independence.

On the one hand, the British administrators were trying to preserve and control tribal societies and on the other hand, it was opening it up to economic forces which would eventually undermine it (Perham 1963). However, it would be naïve to think that the British had not already thought of decolonization as a part of their colonial policy. The Durham formula had been developed in 1838 to reconcile the differences between English speaking settlers in Upper Canada and French speakers in Quebec. In the nineteenth century, the Durham formula emerged as a solution to the demands for home rule posed by various extensions of the home country. It was a response the potential failure of policy (Coleman 1954).

The French move towards independence for its former colonies was moderated by the notion of faith in universal human reason and unity through government, law, and culture, offering citizenship to the assimilated, and the same chances of political inclusion and education, in effect becoming citizens of France. France with her ideas of centralization, and her belief in equality, had little respect for tribal hierarchy and custom (Hodgkin 1956; Perham 1963). The colonies (even after independence) were described as the Rassemblement Démocratique Africain and benefitted from continuing and considerable financial assistance, economic and staff privileges. The Portuguese favored the "spiritual assimilation of the Africans" (Hodgkin 1956, p. 50).

The outcome for the former Belgian economies was less happy. Vast areas were taken over in the name of King Leopold of Belgium for whom it was originally a private estate (Coleman 1954). The imposition of European power over it did not even "provide that fragile basis for the future co-operation of disparate tribes which a Western elite, native representation at the centre and the freedom to create a native press and parties, had given to the British territories" (Perham 1963, p. 113). While Belgium had followed policies of assimilation and identity (in part due to the presence of a settled white population (Coleman 1954)), it had not prepared its territory adequately for independence and the speed and nationalist assertion created a foundation-less movement which appeared in a matter of months (fuelled by nationalist assertions in a wave of liberation in nearby states). The crisis in 1959–1960 engineered by the intransigence of Patrice Lumumba led to the demotion, dispossession, ill-treatment, and expulsion of former officials and colonials associated with the former regime.

Lumumba called for United Nations aid to no avail and turned to the Soviet Union for military intervention, with the Congo thus caught in Cold War politics, and Lumumba being perceived by the USA as having communist ties. The country then fell under military leadership led by Joseph Motubu, and Lumumba was taken to Katanga (a Belgian fortified secession under military rule) and subsequently tortured and assassinated. Motubu Seko became the military dictator of the Democratic Republic of the Congo from 1965 to 1977, renaming it Zaire in 1977. His brutal legacy epitomized the broken framework of a colonial state, ending in corruption and chaos (Clark 2002). Political ambitions rather than a political future led to political authoritarianism and patrimonial predatory practices. Kenya (the former East Africa) from the brutal Mau Mau rebellion in 1952 where land was the initiating issue, made Administrators such as Sir Frank Lloyd (cited in Allen 1980) realize that the Africans had enormous power should they wish to use it. The same issues appeared in Rhodesia (later renamed Zimbabwe), where settlers wanted independence on their own terms, leading to their Unilateral Declaration of Independence (UDI) in 1965 after a protracted war between the European settlers and the local people (supported by insurgents). Zimbabwe achieved independence in 1980 led by Robert Mugabe who was to retain the Presidency for three decades. In this mix was the position of European settlers who could be described in these colonial quasi-segments of society. They were totally dependent on the official sanctions and support from imperial powers and had to contend with religious authorities such as missionary groups and a relatively mobile indigenous population whom they came to rely on as sources of labor.

Factor 3: Economic Factors in Africa (1952–1972)

Why did entrepreneurship, which could have, as it did in developed economies in the eighteenth century, fail to provide a catalyst for economic growth in former colonies? A retrospective review of the main events and trends affecting food and agriculture, over the last 50 years, drawing on the annual series of *The State of Food and Agriculture*, first published in 1947 by the Food and Agriculture Organization (FAO), provides clues (www.fao.org). WW2 had a profound effect on agriculture – world agricultural production was 5% below prewar levels.

However, regional disparities in these impacts were particularly evident in the case of Asia and Africa. Indeed, Africa was perceived to be a comparatively empty continent with potential for increased production. Demand was strong for many of its agricultural commodities and minerals and many territories were able to expand economic activity and agricultural production. The production of industrial crops, notably cotton and sisal, expanded faster than food crops. Although it was an economically less advanced region, economic and social development was only a matter of time. Indeed, hopes were expressed that Africa would become to Europe what the West was to the United States in the latter half of the nineteenth century. This view was the conventional one of the time and, when compared with the food situation in Asia in the post war period, not surprisingly the term "African hope-Asian drama" summed up the situation at the time (The State of Food and Agriculture 2000, p. 2). As reports for the late 1950s showed, Africa, under increasing urbanization, had areas of population density which were too high for the maintenance of soil fertility under shifting cultivation. Its forest cover was being destroyed, with serious consequences for its soil and water resources (ibid., p. 27). In the late 1960s the "alleviation of poverty" became the central concern of economic development with rural areas of agricultural production being the lagging sector relative to industry. Various institutional studies during the 1960s highlighted the problems of poverty and inequalities of distribution in the international arena (such as the World Food Program in 1961 and the World Food Congress in 1962 (The State of Food and Agriculture 1962). This "basic needs" approach became the subject of debate in the economics and development arena. Neo-classical economists claimed to have rediscovered agriculture and claimed that freer markets, a more liberal trade regime, and a growing agricultural economy would be conducive to economic growth. Agricultural growth and exports would and did respond to incentives (or disincentives). Despite these views, agriculture never appeared on the agenda of the Kennedy Round of tariff negotiations under the auspices of the General Agreement on Tariffs and Trade (GATT), concluded in 1967.

The neo-classical agenda was opposed by structuralists – strong supporters of the import-substitution industrialization – including social scientists from the United Nations Economic Commission for Latin America (ECLA). Having long opposed the theory of comparative advantage, they argued that emerging economies were not advantaged by specializing and exporting primary and agricultural products when industrialized nations were exporting manufactured goods with greater value added. Although not directly entering into the debate, the FAO remained faithful to agriculture's potential contribution to overall economic development. The United Nations Conference on Trade and Development (UNCTAD) established in 1964 was to serve as an agent of accelerated development and aimed to raise the export earnings of emerging economies (UNCTAD 1968). In its second session in 1968, UNCTAD focused on the issues of access of primary commodities to markets in industrialized countries, volume, terms, and conditions for development aid, and economic integration and cooperation among emerging economies. UNCTAD was also instrumental in negotiating international commodity agreements, such as the extension of the International Sugar Agreement for a period of 5 years from 1969. It had lapsed since 1961.

Other food and nonfood commodity agreements were negotiated with varying degrees of success. FAO favored commodity-by-commodity approaches as being more practical rather than UNCTAD's plan of having world commodity agreements. For resource-rich countries in Africa, emphasis was placed on extractive industries, such as coffee and cocoa, rice, sugar, and cotton, so they became monoculture (commodity or mineral) exporters. On a continent of household-based agrarian economies with very limited long-distance trade, colonialism imposed cash-crop production for export, and mineral extraction, with manufacturing supposed to come later (Saul and Leys 1999). Seventy-five percent of the land of the Gold Coast (subsequently Ghana) was used for commercial production between 1947 and 1950. Africa changed from a subsistence to a money economy promoting the cash nexus of economic individualism – weakening the communal and lineage responsibility of traditional ties. As the economies became more urbanized, the pool of wage labor grew (Coleman 1954), leading to the rise of a new middle class, with opportunities for western education and social mobility. However, educational gains were directed to farmers employing labor, individual traders, lorry drivers and middlemen, and for the elite, the desiderata was a career as a doctor or a lawyer. The conditions for the development of an entrepreneurial ecosystem were simply not in place in these newly independent countries. They either stayed with the economic systems set in place by colonists, or they took the route of state-led industrialization. Bonné (1956, p. 6) exhibited remarkable prescience stating that "development in colonial or dependent areas is a special case of capitalist expansion." By this remark, he would have been referring to capital required from developed countries to invest in plantations, provide managerial skills, and access to markets, or in the case of mineral exploitation the technological capabilities to needed for extraction of resources and development of supply chains. But Bonné (1956, p. 10) believed that that entrepreneurship in the underdeveloped countries could be promoted by "semi-public or public bodies." He was never apparently aware of the British Colonial Development Corporation (CDC), established by the Colonial Office in 1948, as a "pump primer" for colonial investment (either private or public) (Wicker 1955). The CDC raised capital by way of loans and fixed interest rates. They then made equity investments which carried no obligation to return proceeds to the CDC.

Failed ventures such as the Gambian egg producing project (begun in 1948 and abandoned in 1950) owed not a little to the propensity of the CDC not to undertake pilot studies or test markets to prove commercial viability. Investments in tea and fish farming in Zambia and sugar in Swaziland yielded a return on capital of 8–9%, not the 20% return which private investor consortia such as Barclays Overseas Development Corporation would expect. They, Barclays, were more profitable and had less staff whereas the CDC was burdened with by bureaucracy, having to both satisfy the Colonial Office as to the effectiveness of their administration as well as to manage the investments locally. Development goals sat uneasily with bureaucratic tendencies. "The CDC had no inclination to pursue industrialization" (Cowen 1984, p. 64). After decolonization in the African states, the CDC continued to provide finance for African governments for the nationalization of large agricultural estates (formerly privately owned by foreign investors) and promoted small holding schemes (such as tea planting in East Africa). However, although farmers' incomes increased, the liabilities assumed by newly nationalized governments contributed to the crises of public finances of many African countries. Routine or low-level entrepreneurship such as wood processing, metal working, or handicrafts did not develop beyond the level whereby innovation in products and processes by the individual entrepreneur would have a transformative effect on the local economy. The resources in mining, tobacco, chromium, asbestos, and coal deposits were based on British and American capital, without which neither the technological expertise to extract the resources nor the access to markets to sell the resources would have been possible, as the nationalization of the copper mines in Zambia in 1969 was to prove. Myrdal (1968) criticized the "soft state," but his critique has been misunderstood. Their softness lies in their unwillingness to coerce in order to implement declared policy goals, and to resist the hard local power of caste, land, and culture. It is not the result of gentleness or weakness, but reflects the power structure and a gap between real and professed intentions.

Summary: Developing an Explanatory Framework

Entrepreneurship failed to emerge in colonial Africa during the period 1952–1972 because of three interrelated explanatory factors. First, the political situation in African countries of this time: the liquidation of European colonial power in the former colonies in Africa and South East Asia, which happened over the relatively short decade from the 1950s to the 1970s. Second, the economic conditions which prevailed as Africa, as a resource-rich country, continued to rely on the wealth of resource extraction. Third, rationalism in Europe paved the way for an industrial revolution, but did not do so in Africa. The countries are marked by heterogeneity but these factors have the same degree of interrelatedness. Nevertheless, it is the first factor, the political conditions in Africa, which is a factor which has been largely overlooked by developmental economists writing in this period have been shown helps explain the entrepreneurial void in former colonies at this time. Figure 1 summarizes this point by showing how these factors contributed to the entrepreneurial void.

Thus, the historical analysis has synthesized, integrated, and explained the events that happened in the past. The extant development economists exhibited largely prescriptive views during the chapter's study period and said what should happen in emerging economies but largely ignored the ongoing political situation regarding the liquidation of colonial empires. This chapter offers new objective insights based on historical analysis and synthesis from the contemporary literature of the selected time period, rather than drawing on post hoc subjective and ahistorical literature that lacks the explanatory power of this chapter's historical approach. The explanatory framework and narrative historical synthesis analysis of why entrepreneurship failed

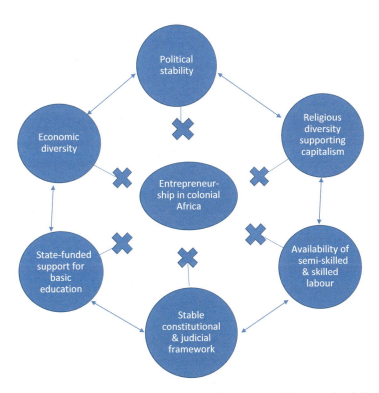

Fig. 1 Institutional Factors required for entrepreneurship to emerge. (Source: authors). **Note:** The interrelated institutional factors which are necessary for the development of entrepreneurship are shown below. In the absence of these factors (shown by the truncated lines), entrepreneurship in "colonial" Africa (1952–1972) simply could not emerge. Without these truncations, the framework can be used to describe the emergence of entrepreneurship in developed economies

to emerge in colonial Africa at this time hopefully goes some way towards addressing critical research gaps.

References

Allen C (1980) Tales from the dark continent. Macdonald Futura Publishers, London
Baker T, Welter F (2018) Contextual entrepreneurship: an interdisciplinary perspective. Found Trends® Int Entrepr 14:357–426
Bonné A (1956) Towards a theory of implanted development in underdeveloped countries. Kyklos 9:1–26
Buckley PJ (2016) Historical research approaches to the analysis of internationalization. Manag Int Rev 56:879–900
Cassis Y, Minoglou IP (2005) Entrepreneurship in theory and history: state of the art and new perspectives. In: Cassis Y, Minoglou IP (eds) Entrepreneurship in theory and history. Palgrave Macmillan, Basingstoke, pp 3–21
Casson M (1982) The entrepreneur: an economic theory. Rowman and Littlefield, London
Casson M (1997) Entrepreneurial networks in international business. Bus Econ Hist 26(2):811–823
Casson M (2011) Historical context of entrepreneurship. In: Dana LP (ed) World encyclopedia of entrepreneurship. Edward Elgar, Cheltenham, pp 211–226
Casson M, Casson C (2013a) The entrepreneur in history: from medieval merchant to modern business leader. Palgrave Pivot, Basingstoke
Casson M, Casson C (eds) (2013b) History of entrepreneurship: innovation and risk-taking 1200–2000 and industry case studies. Edward Elgar, Cheltenham
Casson M, Casson C (2014) The history of entrepreneurship: medieval origins of a modern phenomenon. Bus Hist 56:1223–1242
Casson M, Godley A (2005) Entrepreneurship and historical explanation. In: Cassis Y, Minoglou IP (eds) Entrepreneurship in theory and history. Palgrave Macmillan, Basingstoke, pp 25–60
Casson M, Godley A (2007) Revisiting the emergence of the modern business enterprise: entrepreneurship and the Singer global distribution system. J Manag Stud 44:1064–1077
Clark DA (2002) The capability approach: its development, critiques and recent advances. Working paper, GPRG-WPS-032. The University of Manchester, Manchester. http://www.gprg.org/pubs/workingpapers/pdfs/gprg-wps-032.pdf. Accessed 24 Feb 2020
Coleman J (1954) Nationalism in tropical Africa. Am Polit Sci Rev 48:404–426
Cowen M (1984) Early years of the Colonial Development Corporation: British state enterprise overseas during late colonialism. Afr Aff 83:63–75
Cronon E (1955) Black Moses and the story of Marcus Garvey and the universal Negro improvement association. The University of Wisconsin Press, Madison
da Silva Lopes T, Casson M (2007) Entrepreneurship and the development of global brands. Bus Hist Rev 81:651–680
Decker S (2013) The silence of the archives: business history post-colonialism and archival ethnography. Manag Org 8(2):155–173
FAO of the United Nations (1962) The state of food and agriculture. Rome: 1–308
FAO (2002) http://www.fao.org/state-of-food-agriculture/2018/en/. Accessed 24 Feb 2020
Harris J (1967) Some problems in identifying the role of entrepreneurship: the case of Nigeria. PhD dissertation, Northwestern University, Evanston
Hébert RF, Link AN (1989) In search of the meaning of entrepreneurship. Small Bus Econ 1:39–49
Hébert RF, Link AN (2006) The entrepreneur as innovator. J Technol Transf 31:589–597
Hébert RF, Link AN (2009) A history of entrepreneurship. Routledge, London
Hodgkin T (1956) Nationalism in colonial Africa. Frederick Muller, London
Kilby P (2011) Third world entrepreneurship. In: Dana LP (ed) World encyclopedia of entrepreneurship. Edward Elgar, Cheltenham, pp 463–474

Kirk-Greene A (1980) Introduction. In: Allen C (ed) Tales from the dark continent. Macdonald Futura Publishers, London

Kirzner IM (1997) Entrepreneurial discovery and the competitive market process: an Austrian approach. J Econ Lit 35:60–85

Knight F (1921) Risk uncertainty and profit. Houghton Mifflin, Boston

Leibenstein H (1968) Entrepreneurship and development. Am Econ Rev 58:72–83

Lugard FD (1926) The dual mandate in British tropical Africa. W. Blackwood and Sons, London/Edinburgh

Murphy PJ, Liao J, Welsch HP (2006) A conceptual history of entrepreneurial thought. J Manag Hist 12:12–35

Myrdal G (1968) Asian drama. Allen Lane, London

Perham M (1963) The colonial reckoning: the Reith lectures. Collins, London

Popp A, Holt R (2013) The presence of entrepreneurial opportunity. Bus Hist 55:9–28

Saul JP, Leys C (1999) Sub-Saharan Africa in global capitalism. The Monthly Review 51. https://monthlyreview.org/1999/07/01/sub-saharan-africa-in-global-capitalism/. Accessed 24 Feb 2020

Shetty MC (1964) Entrepreneurship in small industry. The Economic Weekly, 6 June, 917–920

Silberman L (1956) The evolution of entrepreneurship in the process of economic development. Ann Am Acad Pol Soc Sci 305:32–44

Spengler JJ (1958) Public bureaucracy, resource structure and economic development: a note. Kyklos 11:459–489

The State of Food and Agriculture (2000) Half a century of food and agriculture. FAO Document Repository Economic and Social Development Department. http://www.fao.org/3/x4400e/x4400e.pdf. Accessed 24 Feb 2020

UNCTAD (1968) Proceedings of the United Nations conference on trade and development: report and annexes. http://unctad.org/en/Docs/td97vol1_en.pdf. Accessed 24 Feb 2020

van Praag M (1999) Some classic views of entrepreneurship. De Economist 147:311–334

Wadhwani D (2016) Entrepreneurship in historical context: using history to develop theory and understand process. In: Welter F, Gartner W (eds) A research Agenda for entrepreneurship and contexts. Edward Elgar, Cheltenham

Welter F (2011) Contextualizing entrepreneurship: conceptual challenges and ways forward. Entrep Theory Pract 35:165–184

Wicker E (1955) The Colonial Development Corporation. Rev Econ Stud 23:213–228

Wilson W (1918) President Wilson's message to Congress, 8 Jan 1918. Records of the United States Senate Record Group 46 National Archives

Zahra S (2007) Contextualizing theory building in entrepreneurship research. J Bus Ventur 22:443–452

Zahra S, Wright M, Abdelgawad S (2014) Contextualization and the advancement of entrepreneurship research. Int Small Bus J 32:479–500

Part X

Different Experiences: Asia, Latin America, and the Pacific

Introduction: Management Heterogeneity in Asia

56

Anthony M. Gould

Contents

Introduction: The Quest to Understand Asian Heterogeneity	1290
A Recent History of Management in Each of Asia's Subregions	1293
The Western Liberal-Democratic Regulated Market Economies of Australia and New Zealand	1293
Japan	1296
The Asian Tigers (or "Four Little Dragon Countries") of Hong Kong, Singapore, Taiwan, and South Korea	1301
China	1306
Indonesia	1311
Conclusion: Inescapable Diversity but Perplexing Recent Similarity	1314
Cross-References	1314
References	1315

Abstract

This chapter introduces the concept of diversity as it applies to Asia. It argues that, throughout the twentieth century, Asia was best thought of as a mix of jurisdictions with little in common other than shared geography. In prosecuting its case, the chapter implicitly proposes, insofar as approaches to management and governance are concerned, a thesis of partial regional convergence in the digital-age era. However, the bulk of the chapter's narrative is about distinct jurisdictions. As such, the work does not devote substantial analytic attention to convergence but rather gives a thumbnail sketch of the management blueprints of exemplar countries as a means of creating context for this volume's other more focused chapters, the next of which does pertain to convergence. Another key objective is to introduce subsequent chapters in this volume that, following

---

A. M. Gould (✉)
Département des relations industrielles, Université Laval, Québec, QC, Canada
e-mail: anthony.gould@rlt.ulaval.ca

© The Author(s), under exclusive licence to Springer Nature Switzerland AG 2020
B. Bowden et al. (eds.), *The Palgrave Handbook of Management History*,
https://doi.org/10.1007/978-3-319-62114-2_112

▶ Chap. 57, "The Perfect Natural Experiment: Asia and the Convergence Debate," address in detail management philosophy and practice in individual Asian countries.

Keywords

Demming · Asian Tigers · Australian management · Japanese management · Korean management · New Zealand · Indian management · China

Introduction: The Quest to Understand Asian Heterogeneity

The region of Asia, however defined, is the most culturally, economically, and socially heterogeneous swathe of the world. Much of the reason for the area's multi-dimensional diversity concerns history. Specifically, Asia is a collection of countries/jurisdictions that, despite sharing geography, developed under largely nonoverlapping influences. In the face of this kind of miscellany, it is unsurprising that various taxonomies have been created that wrestle with the problem of how best to group the region's subareas/countries for purposes of characterizing the Asian construct (e.g., Thelan 2014; Katz and Darbishire 2000; Hofstede 1980/2003). In light of this context, classificatory schemes tend to be conceptually inadequate, or at least not robust. Indeed, to be applied, they often require the making of multiple assumptions and qualifications. Such malaise is exacerbated when proposed schemes categorize countries based on an unduly narrow object of analytic interest, or (relatedly) when it is difficult to reach consensus concerning an appropriate investigative focus. For example, when inquiring into management or employment relations-related content, the region is often conceptualized as encompassing the following five categories (e.g., Bamber and Leggett 2001; Bamber and Davis 2001)[1].

(i) The Western liberal-democratic regulated market economies of Australia and New Zealand
(ii) Japan
(iii) The Asian Tigers (or "four little dragon countries") of Hong Kong, Singapore, Taiwan and South Korea
(iv) China
(v) Indonesia

As noted, the aforementioned five-category view of Asian diversity establishes management or employment relations-related concerns as the basis for national classification. However, when the object of scholarly interest is broadened in its

---

[1] For exposition purposes, these categories are somewhat cut-down in nature and thus exclude from consideration important countries on the edge of the region such as India – and Indian subcontinent countries such as Bangladesh, Pakistan, and Sri Lanka – and economically smaller countries within Asia – such as Malaysia, Myanmar (formerly Burma), Laos, the Philippines, and Vietnam.

scope – for example, when the analyst is considering, say, economic development status – another regional grouping option suggests itself as well reflecting reality (e.g., Thelan 2014; Bamber et al. 2016). In this regard, in the digital age era,

- Countries such as China, India, and Indonesia are sometimes lumped together as either industrializing or "recently industrialized."
- The Asian Tigers remain an identifiable subset because they are viewed as having entered the industrial age in lockstep during the 1960s, and as each having had parallel good financial fortune until East Asia's economic crisis of 1997.
- Japan retains its single-country category status due to it being the first nation to industrialize in a distinctively Asian way, during the 1950s; thus being separated (in time) from the Tigers.
- The Western country category comprising Australia and New Zealand remains intact on the basis that its constituent jurisdictions have had steady economic and social development throughout the twentieth century.

While still on the question of how best to make sense of diversity in the Asian region (and the associated categorization problem), in circumstances where dimensions such as religious orientation, degree of embrace of a Western-style construct of human rights, or cultural/social elements are instituted as classificatory criteria, other analytic categories seem germane (e.g., Hofstede 1980/2003; Jackson 2002; Gerhart 2008). For example, when the pervasive lifestyle influences of faith/religion is established as consequential, the comparative analyst can confidently defend juxtaposing Indonesia (the largest exemplar Muslim country in the world) with China (until relatively recently, the largest unambiguously Communist-regime country in the world). However, when the criteria used for sorting is embrace of human rights *à la* the enlightenment, it is perhaps appropriate to place China and Indonesia together on the basis that they are polar opposites to, say, Australia and New Zealand.

This chapter largely sets the stage for subsequent chapters in the present *tome*. It argues that, insofar as the problem of management is concerned, although Asia remains an exemplar of postindustrial diversity, as is the case elsewhere in the world, its constituent countries are yielding to globalization's homogenizing influences. In this sense, nations are largely jettisoning twentieth-century ideological orientations that came to characterize their cultures generally and their approaches to labor and capital superintendence, in particular. Hence, whether it be in the work-arena or society more broadly, some overarching conclusions about Asian jurisdictions during the industrial age provide context for what follows. In particular, Australia was the irreverent place of subsidized affluence and the fair go (and, as will be shown by Andrew Cardow and William Wilson in ▶ Chap. 62, "Think Big and Privatize Every Thing That Moves: The Impact of Political Reform on the Practice of Management in New Zealand" of this volume, ditto for New Zealand). By contrast, Japan is the place where postwar recovery was achieved through forbearance, conscientiousness, and self-improvement was established in a *milieu* of according respect through allowing participation in consequential decision making. As "second-order" imitators, Asian tiger countries experienced something of an identity crisis. In the 1960s – and 1970s – they changed their orientation from militaristic command and control-style authoritarian regimes to being clever, single-minded, and outwardly looking liberal market economies, trailing somewhat in the wake of Japan that had made a similar transition 10 years earlier. Very dissimilarly, late twentieth-century Red China was locked-down, inward looking and controlling of its citizenry (qualities of the country comprehensively analyzed by Leung in ▶ Chaps. 59, "The Making of a Docile Working Class in Pre-reform China," and ▶ 60, "Governmentality and the Chinese Workers in China's Contemporary Thought Management System" of this volume), whereas Indonesia during the same period was, bellicose, austere and with limited instantiation of a western human rights construct, and simultaneously the largest Muslim country in the world.

It is noteworthy that this chapter does not dwell extensively on the convergence issue: a mission left for the next, which is essentially an exposition of relevant theory examined using an historical lens (accompanied by some discussion of how such theory illuminates understanding of Asia). Rather, in its five key sections, the present chapter is principally jurisdictional. As such, it addresses the practice of management and its undergirding philosophy in exemplar Asian nations, mostly during the twentieth century. Somewhat frustratingly, the chapter cannot be comprehensive, in terms of either the nations it covers or the depth it devotes to each. Instead, it has the twin objectives of: (i) revealing the nature and character of idiosyncratic management blueprints for identified countries and (ii) providing a liberal education as prelude for the more specialized chapters that will follow. Insofar as these subsequent chapters are concerned, one – Carlos Davila's contribution addressing Latin American history during the last 150 years – is not about Asia in a strict geographic sense. Rather, his discussion of a cluster of unambiguously non-Western countries on the other side of the Pacific is intended to enlarge the construct of Asia and, more particularly, allow the analyst to test Chap. 2's theory which, as will be discussed, was mostly intended to be generic.

The next chapters in this volume are:

- ▶ Chapter 57, "The Perfect Natural Experiment: Asia and the Convergence Debate," authored by myself, Anthony M Gould from Laval University in Quebec City Canada, addressing the convergence debate generally and as it pertains to the Asian case specifically.
- ▶ Chapter 58, "Indian Management (?): A Modernization Experiment," by Nimruji Jammulamadaka from the Indian Institute of Management in Kolkata that addresses India, a large emerging liberal market economy and one not dealt with (in resume form) in this chapter. In this work, Jammulamadaka makes a compelling case concerning the emergence of an Indian management blueprint under the influence of distinctively Western elements that were, initially a colonialist British stimulus and, after 1947, a postcolonial American stimulus.
- ▶ Chapters 59, "The Making of a Docile Working Class in Pre-reform China," and ▶ 60, "Governmentality and the Chinese Workers in China's Contemporary Thought Management System," by Elly Leung from the University of Western Australia are each focused examinations of China's circumstances. In these

essays, Leung argues that the twentieth-century blueprint philosophy of Chinese management is one of control and coercion. In making her case, she gives a nuanced view of relevant history. In so doing, she fleshes out the overview of China given in this chapter.

- ▶ Chapter 61, "In Search of the Traces of the History of Management in Latin America, 1870–2020," by Carlos Davila from *Univeridada de los Andes* in Bogata Colombia is about the Latin American blueprint for management. As noted, although not strictly part of Asia's geography, the theoretical contribution of this work, and in particular, its discussion of three regional approaches, enlarges the Asian construct.
- ▶ Chapter 62, "Think Big and Privatize Every Thing That Moves: The Impact of Political Reform on the Practice of Management in New Zealand," by Andrew Cardow and William Wilson, is about the evolving New Zealand blueprint. In reflecting on this essay, the reader will see synergy between the material being discussed and the more truncated discussion of the region's other Western liberal market economy, Australia, which is dealt with (in summary form) in this chapter.
- ▶ Chapter 63, "Management in Australia – The Case of Australia's Wealthiest Valley: The Hunter," is by Bradley Bowden from Griffith University in Queensland, Australia. This essay is essentially a case study of the wealthy Hunter Valley to the North of Sydney. The piece's insights are instructive for the student of management history. They pertain to themes of forced transition and letting-go of affluence. As such, they illuminate understanding of the broader Australian context and, ultimately, have wide-ranging theoretical implications.

The remainder of the substantive part of this chapter is an overview of the recent historical circumstances of subregions of Asia. The five countries briefly examined are Australia, Japan, South Korea, China, and Indonesia. Because the focus of the book series is management, the first aforementioned taxonomic scheme – that which classifies mostly on the basis of how this issue, in particular, is dealt with in sub-regions – is used to structure these discussions. As noted, for practical reasons, it has not been possible to cover all relevant countries in this chapter or to address selected countries in appropriate depth. Hence, consistent with the eight-chapter structure described above, material has been selected because it has been judged representative and contextualizing for the rest of this volume.

A Recent History of Management in Each of Asia's Subregions

The Western Liberal-Democratic Regulated Market Economies of Australia and New Zealand

Throughout the twentieth century and until the 1980s, Asia's liberal democratic countries of Australia and New Zealand introduced, incrementally, management and employment-relations polices and established institutions that, almost without exception, conferred, rights and benefits on employees. During this reference period, such advantage mostly accrued under the influence of employee protest activity (and progressively elaborated public policy allowing for its expression), an active and broadly based union movement that controlled electorally successful labor political parties, migration policies instituted to sustain and enhance employment conditions for locals, and the early establishment of independent arbitration systems (Gould 2010, 2014). Each country's approach arose in a context of: relative affluence; industry tariff protection and subsidies; a distinctively Western construct of human rights; and, rejection of European-style class structures. However, under the influence of conservative and labor federal governments, from the 1980s onwards both Australia and New Zealand dismantled much of their worker-friendly regulatory and institutional apparatus. From approximately this time, each has embraced, relatively quickly, a culture of decentralized and somewhat more individualised workplace bargaining over terms and conditions of employment including pay, edged-out union influence and weakened the regulatory authority of labor-related state-based institutions (particularly quasi-judicial institutions such as employment tribunals and arbitration commissions). The purported benefits of such a metamorphosis are frequently touted as being increased flexibility for parties to the employment relationship and productivity enhancement. More broadly, in the digital era, both Australia and New Zealand have brazenly pursued as public policy priorities international commercial competitive objectives and sought to better integrate their economies into the global system (Katz and Darbishire 2000). In practice, this mostly entailed a strategy of national regional integration, thus privileging geography (i.e., alliances with other Asian countries) over history (i.e., each nation's European colonial heritages).

For exposition purposes, in this section, key elements of Australia's approach to management are described and discussed. As noted, much of the philosophy underpinning Australia's twentieth-century national management and employment relations system also existed in New Zealand (Gould 2014).

Since Australia's Federation in 1901 and until the latter part of the Hawke/Keating Labor-government administrations of the mid 1990s, key facets of the nation's public policy progressively but conspicuously embraced welfare and support for the disadvantaged and a distinctively non-European form of egalitarianism. Indeed, in a context where the majority of Australia's first immigrants were Irish and had often been deported following conviction for petty crimes, the fair-go philosophy that came to epitomize the Australian way of resolving problems is perhaps best interpreted as a reaction against Britain's class system. Insofar as the workplace management problem is concerned, it is likely also that union and strike activity of the 1890s left an enduring legacy. Largely due to these influences, despite long periods of conservative government in the twentieth century, a pluralist view of the relationship between capital and labor became the basis for the Australian philosophy, a philosophy that was incrementally instantiated with the creation of a system based on labor market and workplace regulation (Gould 2010). In these circumstances, early in the piece, a view emerged that a "living wage" should form the basis of an enlightened approach to worker remuneration. This construct was defined in 1907 by Justice Higgins in the Harvester case as *"the amount a family needs to live in frugal comfort"* (Martyn 2005).

Aside from the impact of the living wage, four specific influences shaped the character of Australian management and employment relations in the twentieth century (Gould 2014). First, the 1904 Conciliation and Arbitration Act made third party arbitration compulsory and the orthodoxy for resolving conflict between capital and labor. This statute established the Conciliation and Arbitration Court (later the Industrial Relations Commission) as independent of executive government and with power to create industrial awards that prescribed minimum employment terms and conditions, including pay-rates, and intervene in employment disputes. In practice, tribunal decisions, although technically arbitrated solutions, often had the hallmarks of collectively negotiated agreements in that they met with the consent of employers and union officials (Chin 2005; Gould 2010, 2014). Second, the federal government pursued a racially discriminatory immigration policy as a means of limiting supply of labor. Part of the intent here was to maintain low unemployment. Indeed, between 1901 and the end of the Vietnam war in 1973, successive Australian governments adopted the conspicuously anti-Asian and Pro-European *White Australia Policy* (Bamber and Davis 2001). Third, manufacturing was protected by tariffs and trade embargos. This arrangement effectively established the nation's lucrative agricultural and mining sectors as cash cows to be used for subsidizing less competitive industries that were concerned with manufacturing consumer goods for the domestic market. In such a context of relative affluence, using a process known as centralized wage fixation, the Conciliation and Arbitration Court (later the Industrial Relations Commission) mostly embraced the principle of comparative wage justice when tinkering with award remuneration provisions (Gould 2010). In this process, consideration of employer capacity to pay and firm commercial performance was theoretically a relevant input. However, in practice, these concerns were largely irrelevant, or at least of a much lower priority status than the imperative of across the board wage parity. Fourth, Australia's trade union movement was sophisticated and benefited from high levels of institutional legitimacy. Specifically, the nation's organized labor has always differed from, for example, that of the United States because it has a centralized corporate structure and an active and successful political arm, the Australian Labor Party (Gould 2010). Union density in the Australian workforce was mostly over 50% throughout the first half of the twentieth century, reaching a peak of 65% in 1953 (Bamber and Davis 2001). In the years between 1970 and 1980, 25% of Australia's workforce took industrial protest action (Briggs 2005). In the twentieth century, the Australian Labor Party (ALP) formed governments in the federal parliament during the periods 1929–1931, 1941–1949, 1972–1975, and 1983–1996 and had been successful in winning control of the legislatures of each Australian State.

A key watershed in the Australian management blueprint came with the election of the conservative John Howard Liberal/National party coalition administration in 1996 (and, in particular, its subsequent re-election in 2005). Although, as noted, some of the substance of the altered course in fact originated in the years immediately preceding Howard's election, it was really as a result of the priorities of the incoming government that the nation began to embrace earnestly a philosophy of workplace deregulation and decentralized wage negotiations (Gould 2010). Specific changes made during the era include a jettisoning (or at least deemphasizing) of minimum (award) wage provisions, unfair dismissal laws, compulsory arbitration, the "no disadvantage test" in employment negotiations, and a central role for unions and collective bargaining.

Japan

Unlike Australia and New Zealand, Japan has not had a history of import tariffs, government industry subsidies, or large agricultural and commodities sectors. Rather, following its widespread devastation during the Second World War, it cultivated manufacturing as a seminal element of reconstruction. From the outset, the notion of national industry subsidies and institutional support was not part of the Japanese recovery blueprint. Instead, to foster prosperity, the nation developed distinctive human resource management principles such as jobs for life, and team and committee systems that blur boundaries between management and non-management work. Insofar as globalization is concerned, Japan – as part of its postwar explicit emphasis on being economically self-sustaining – has the special status of being the first Asian country to be ruthless in adopting an export focus. In this vein, as part of its industrial culture, it embraced a national second-mover advantage strategy as a means of expanding into international markets (essentially copying, but having learnt from competitors' mistakes). In this sense, management theorists typically conceive of Japan's approach to employment relations as something of a reference-point (e.g., Barry and Wilkinson 2011). Thus, in several contexts but particularly insofar as employment relations is concerned, its single country status category is often orthodoxy.

Commencing soon after the Second World War, and continuing until 2006, the business-oriented Liberal Democratic Party mostly governed Japan. In contrast to other Asian countries, the national Japanese approach to management and employment relations was established early during this era and has not substantially altered (Katz and Darbishire 2000). Indeed, the defining elements of the nation's system identified in this section continue to operate, albeit, as will be described, somewhat modulated by globalization-related influences, including in particular a less prominent state regulatory role. In this regard, in the twenty-first century as Japan's industries transitioned incrementally into a new era of restructure and renaissance and emerged from their period of creation and growth during the years of the Japanese Economic Miracle, the new management imperative became to privilege labor flexibility over the inculcation of workforce commitment.

As noted, the history of modern Japanese management unambiguously begins soon after the Second World War. Specifically, in the late 1940s and early 1950s during the aftermath period of Japan's physical and psychological devastation, the nation's products were of poor-quality and often the butt of jokes. As part of the reconstruction effort, the United States assisted its former adversary's war-ravaged commercial-sector to promote corporate and national cultures of product enhancement (Inkster 2001). William Edwards Deming was a prominent theorist and consultant in this effort. He used *statistical process control* to identify product variation as a means of bettering quality. Along the way, he may also have influenced broader issues of people management and, in particular despite being American, unwittingly become a seminal figure in establishing a distinctively Japanese approach to inculcating employee commitment and loyalty. Specifically, he proposed "14 key principles for improving management practice" including to: *"remove barriers that stand between the hourly worker and his right to pride of workmanship"* (principle 12) and *"institute a vigorous program of education and retraining"* (principle 13) (Deming 2000). In the wake of Deming's influence, the Japanese management approach came to have several characteristics. This section delineates and describes the four most consequential of these.

First – and most frequently noted – in postwar Japan there existed the principle of a job for life or the understanding that an employee can commence with a firm and receive employment continuity until their retirement. The extent to which such a prescription was ever adopted is a somewhat contested subject. Specifically, recent conjecture about Japanese workforce participation indicates that long-term employment guarantees were rarely offered to women, minorities, workers in small firms, or those who failed in education or in their first job (Hanami 2004, p. 10). However, regardless of whether such a benefit is – or ever was – universal, the phenomenon itself has been bolstered since 1961 by at least 100 case law decisions as well as the custom and practice of high-profile Japanese industries including those in the auto-manufacturing, telecommunications, and electronics sectors (Tackney 2000; Suzuki et al. 2016). Promotion on the basis of seniority is an element of the philosophy of lifetime employment.

Another controversy concerning jobs for life in Japan concerns how best to interpret the meaning of the construct and/or expose its underpinning philosophy. In the debate on these matters, one distinction is between institutionalists and those who emphasis strategy, pragmatism, and commercial competitive advantage. Abegglen (1959), who first used the term "lifetime employment," is a proponent of the former of these theses. Writing soon after the war, he argued that loyalty is an especially conspicuous element of Japanese culture. Insofar as the world of management and employment is concerned, work-related institutions (including often those that are state-sponsored) instantiate the value of devotion through promoting and sustaining job continuity, irrespective of whether an enterprise is commercially competitive. Another early advocate of this general idea is Gordon (1985) who, possibly because he entered the debate later, argued that during Japan's postwar reconstruction effort, the nation's culture, state-sponsored structures and agencies, and employment patterns changed to embrace new values. Whatever the case, as one of their defining characteristics, institutionalist arguments about lifetime employment depict the phenomena as a distinctively Japanese resolution to the problem of conflict between capital and labor (Tackney 2000; Suzuki et al. 2016).

In contrast to institutionalists, some management history scholars examining the case of Japan depict strategic competitive advantage as a critical cause of lifetime employment. This *genre* emphasizes a contingency perspective. Specifically, it portrays successful Japanese firms as being especially good at adapting – often more rapidly than their Western counterparts – in response to broader economic circumstances. For example, Aoki (1987, 1988) used the term *J-firm* to describe major postwar companies such as JVC (Japan Victor Corporation), Sony, and Toyota that embraced an HRM-perspective of the employment relationship. He thus drew attention to the possibility that the nation's corporate culture is one of team-work, creation, and application of methods for promoting employee commitment and, ultimately in a more overarching sense, a focus on aspects of the employment relationship where the interests of each party are aligned[2]. Another strategy perspective on jobs for life has come to be known as *White-Collarisation* (e.g., Kaoki 1991, 1995). This view portrays the phenomenon as an integral part of employee inclusion. Specifically, it suggests that to gain commercial advantage, Japanese managers create structures for shop-floor workers to participate in decision-making, a characteristic that is identified as the country's second defining element of its national approach to employee superintendence.

A second feature of Japan's approach to management and employment relations is participatory decision-making and embrace of employee inclusion in matters of firm governance. This aspect of postwar Japanese corporate life was transplanted from the German system that uses works councils and co-determination schemes (Keller and Kirsch 2016). To implement the strategy, since 1946 collective agreements in Japan have typically provided a formal means for employees to become part of consequential firm decision making (Tackney 2000; Gould 2014; Suzuki et al. 2016). In practice, such input mostly occurs through a "joint-committee" system. For example, there are often "on-line"[3] forums, known as quality-circles, which exist to improve performance within a workgroup as well as "offline" committees which may span teams and typically operate on an ad hoc basis (Katz and Darbishire 2000). It is noteworthy that, for several decades, some Japanese firms have instituted structures allowing participation and inclusion opportunities for non unionized employees.

A third element of the Japanese management blueprint concerns organized labor and, by Western standards, the narrow role played by unions. Specifically, Japanese unions exist mostly to promote and sustain lifetime employment and worker participation arrangements (Suzuki et al. 2016). Unlike in the West, they are thus somewhat elitist institutions (Gould 2014). To fulfill their nationally distinctive function, they are typically enterprise based. As such, most unionized Japanese employees are long-term personnel working in larger firms. For example, Hanami (2004) found that the unionization rate at firms with fewer than 100 employees is less than 1.3% compared with 20% overall. In recent years, similar results have been reported (Suzuki et al. 2016). In 2002, the country's main labor federation, *Rengo*, (Japanese Trade Union Confederation) established an evaluation team to review critically union philosophy and practice. The committee concluded that organized labor in Japan unduly emphasizes the interests of privileged male employees and

---

[2]As distinct from its national culture, which as noted, is the analytic preoccupation of institutionalists.

[3]This term does not refer to use of the Internet.

inadequately assists the disadvantaged, including those without lifetime employment assurances (Hanami 2004).

The fourth noteworthy feature of Japanese employment relations is its distinctive legal framework. Specifically, the country's approach uses a civil legal system. As such, it relies on case law rather than the national legislature (Diet) to create employment and work-related norms (Suzuki et al. 2016; Gould 2014). One consequence of this system is that the country's anti-discrimination and equal opportunity protections have been weaker than those instituted elsewhere in the western hemisphere. In this regard, although Japan does have legislation addressing discriminatory treatment of women, the relevant act is inadequate because it does not cover the critical area of bias in recruitment and promotion (Suzuki et al. 2016; Tackney 2000). More broadly, it may be that reliance on judicial rulings to improve the lot of employees has perpetuated employment-related inequality and created a workplace underclass based on a distinction between those with safeguarded employment surety who have union representation and better working conditions and others (Hanami 2004, pp. 10–11). The former of these cohorts, those with lifetime employment, have substantial protection against employer abuse of their dismissal perogative due to an accumulation of Local, Regional and Supreme Court rulings.

During the 1990s, Japan experienced rising unemployment, falling domestic demand for consumer goods, and a growing services sector (Gould 2014; Suzuki et al. 2016). These factors prompted some revision of the nation's approach to employment relations and hastened certain labor market trends. In the latter part of the decade, despite an 18-month long national flirtation with the pro-union Socialist Party government, Japan became increasingly hard-edged in maintaining its international competiveness at the dawn of the digital age.[4] Indeed, since the 1990s aside from there being a trend towards a somewhat tougher stance against employer abusive dismissal, changes to the Japanese industry people management agenda boiled down to two related elements: labor market deregulation and greater diversity in employment contract arrangements and an associated diminished emphasis on unions and collective bargaining.

In the digital age, a conspicuous trend in Japanese management concerns the modern fete of lifetime employment. Specifically, irrespective of the extent to which such a phenomenon ever existed, there is evidence that the nation's employers are becoming less inclined to provide open-ended job assurances. For example, in the 10 years between 1992 and 2002, there was a 110% increase in the number of people employed on sunset clause contracts (Labor Force Survey 2002). The proportion of the part-time workforce increased from 10% in 1980 to 23% in 2001 (Hanami 2004). During the same reference period, the percentage of women workers has doubled and is now close to 40% (Hanami 2004). A consequence of these trends is that, by 2004, those employed on nonregular employment contracts

---

[4]Recall, that for most of the pro-war years, the Liberal Democratic government was aggressively pro-business in its orientation.

in Japan accounted for approximately one third of the entire workforce (Hanami 2004). Also during the digital age, unionization rates in Japan declined precipitously. For example, national density rates dropped from 28.9% to 20.7% between 1985 and 2001 (Hanami 2004). By 2005, the country's workforce union density had slipped further, to 18%. In the following 10 years, this edging-out trend has unambiguously continued (Suzuki et al. 2016). As has been the experience in other developed market economies, Japan's union leaders have had difficulty recruiting new members in the services and high-tech sectors. However, somewhat distinctive to the case of Japan, in the contemporary era officials from enterprise-based unions have been disinclined to sign-up members from new firms, largely for cultural reasons. Specifically, unlike their western counterparts, union delegates working in traditional J-firms view their affiliation with organized labor as a source of privilege and exclusivity (Gould 2014; Suzuki et al. 2016). The Japanese word for this construct – a word which has no Western equivalent – is "sei-sha-in" (Suzuki et al. 2016). As such, they (the union delegates) often attach little priority to increasing membership and may even resist the idea.

Aside from a patently lessened emphasis on lifetime employment, within modern Japan the twentieth-century management blueprint is evolving under the ubiquitous influence of international economic deregulation. In this regard, insofar as the labor market is concerned, two phenomena are conspicuous. First, there is a trend towards greater employment contract diversity. Specifically, unlike during the Japanese Economic Miracle years during which permanent employees mostly had a monopoly on overtime and shift arrangements, the current tendency is for labor demand surges to be managed using nonstandard workers. For example, Nekkei (2003) reported in 2003 that Japan's top 1000 companies, especially those operating in the nation's electronics industry (the third largest sector of the economy), were planning to recruit 7% fewer new graduates and increase by 9.3% limited-tenure and contract-based workers (Nekkei 2003). These labor market trends have intensified in recent years (Suzuki et al. 2016). Second, in the late 1990s, Japanese employers were increasingly augmenting seniority-based pay arrangements through embracing other approaches such as dividend apportionment for employees and individual merit evaluations (Katz and Darbishire 2000; Suzuki et al. 2016). Changes to pecuniary recognition strategies of these kinds, as a matter of orthodoxy hallmarks of a move towards individualism in the management of the employment relationship (e.g., Kaufman 2011), are an unambiguous influence on a widening salary gap within and across wage sectors.

In keeping with the institutional refurbishment experienced by most Western countries at the dawn of the digital age, in 1998, Japan updated its centerpiece work and employment legislation, the Labor Standards Act (1947). Following consultation with – and opposition from – unions, the national parliament (Diet) sanctioned an amendment bill that set the stage for workplace deregulation. In practice, this revision gave employers an option to offer certain worker classes 3 year rather than standard employment contracts. Another, somewhat cosmetic, adjustment was that employers would henceforth be required to provide explanation certificates to employees receiving severance. In theory, such an onus was an employee concession in the wage-effort exchange and would likely aid judges who may subsequently be obliged to make decisions about whether employers acted justly. Alternatively, the formalized giving of reasons for employment termination may be interpreted as a means of placating unions engaged in defending the remnants of the lifetime tenure system. In 2003, in the wake of Japan's emergence from a 12 year recession, another amendment to the nation's Labor Standards Act was enshrinement of just-cause dismissal provisions. In the postindustrial neo-liberal *milieu* that contextualized this change, ensuing debate has focused mostly on how such a change will influence job creation rather than whether it will increase protection for those already employed.[5]

The Asian Tigers (or "Four Little Dragon Countries") of Hong Kong, Singapore, Taiwan, and South Korea

In the "Asian Miracle," from the 1960s until the East-Asian financial crisis of 1997, the Tigers each achieved average annual rates of economic growth of at least 7%. During their periods of rapid expansion – particularly the initial years of these eras – they had low levels of democratic participation. Inspired by Japan's emergence during the 1950s – and thus adapting much of the Japanese blueprint – their generic formula for success has nonetheless been the subject of debate. At one extreme, a World Bank report of 1993 says it was largely attributable to neoliberal-inspired policies of export orientation, limited welfare, and low taxation (e.g., Gregory et al. 2009). However, more institutionally orientated perspectives typically view State intervention as salient (e.g., Rodrik 1997). Whatever the case, there is consensus that the Tigers, from early-on, aggressively pursued an export orientated trade policy and each established cutting-edge transport-related infrastructure (e.g., ports, rail systems) to support a single-minded focus on GDP growth. Insofar as their people management practices are concerned, the Tiger strategy was influenced by the culture of Confucianism; a view of employment, similar to the Protestant Work Ethic, which attaches importance to stability and forbearance, respect for organizational hierarchies, discipline, loyalty, and conscientiousness. Much of this orientation commences with childrearing practices, and in particular, education. Indeed, part of the Tiger ideology is to emphasize scholarly excellence, at all levels.

As an exemplar Tiger, the management blueprint of South Korea (mostly put in place in the late twentieth century) will be further scrutinized in this section. This nation has an employment relations system that arose under the influence of military dictatorships that existed for several decades following the Korean War. Indeed, for at least 10 years after the ceasefire in 1953, South Korea had an agrarian economy

---

[5]Indications are that unemployment is diminishing in spite of it being more difficult to dismiss employees. For example, in the immediate aftermath of the change, in January 2004, the nation's official unemployment rate dipped below 5% for the first time in 3 years (Mizushima 2004, p. 6).

and poverty-level per capita incomes. During this period, the nation was dependent on United States aide.

South Korea's industrialization agenda resulted from a series of 5-year development plans which were formulated and implemented from 1961 when General Park Chung-hee installed himself as the nation's president following a military coupe. During the Park regime – which lasted until the leader's death in 1979 – national economic development was accompanied by authoritarian leadership, political repression including restrictions on freedom of speech and association, human rights violations, and abuses of key state institutions. Although progress had been conspicuous since the 1960s, it was from the 1980s onwards that South Korea came of age as an economic powerhouse. The nation's main industrial sectors are automobile manufacturing, steel production, and shipbuilding. It also is one of the world's leading producers and exporters of digital monitors, mobile phones, and semiconductors. In 2006, the country's economy ranked in the top 15 largest in the world (nominal value) and was the third largest in Asia, behind Japan and China (Labor Statistics Team, South Korea Ministry of Labor 2006, pp. 38–39). By 2016, it had further consolidated this status, with a GDP of US 1198 Billion (in that year) and remaining within the 15 largest economies in the world (Lee 2016).

Although Western-style democratic principles were notionally adopted when South Korea entered its third republic era in 1960, it was not until 1987 – when the nation's president Chun Doo-hwan bowed to popular pressure – that direct and representative presidential elections were held and a multiparty parliamentary system was allowed to flourish[6]. Hence, contemporary South Korea is a republic with relatively independent legislative, executive, and judicial branches of government. Its 1948 constitution has been substantially revised nine times; the latest being in 1987 when, in its June 29 declaration, the nation began the aforementioned process of democratization. As of 2016, it has a population of more than 50 million.

Until 1987, the South Korean government tightly regulated employment relations. During this formative period, the State: controlled organized labor, allowing only one union to exist per industry; monitored national wages; and generally dictated terms and conditions of work. Between 1960 and 1987, the Federation of Korean Trade Unions (FKTUs) operated as an umbrella group for the nation's 17 industry-based worker associations (Lee 2016). Hence, in contrast to what was occurring throughout the West, during the era, South Korea's unions were largely docile and compliant state-controlled institutions. Moreover, collective bargaining and thus overt expression of conflictual relations between capital and labor was generally not on the employer agenda throughout the 1960s and 1970s. Indeed, during the period, because economic growth was mostly achieved through increasing workforce size (i.e., employing more people) rather than workforce efficiency (compelling the same number of people to be more productive), a hard-line employer

---

[6]Since South Korea became a republic in 1948, its various administrations have been described in chronological order. Park Chung-hee was the third president since Federation and therefore led the third republic.

stance concerning the perennially contested wage-effort bargain was mostly not a high priority. Also during the predemocracy era, South Korean industry leaders typically welcomed state intervention in the management process; typically viewing it as intended to keep workers in check and therefore as being employer-friendly (Lee 2016).

From 1987 onwards, as part of the process of achieving political democracy, the government of South Korea changed its stance on employment relations and, as a consequence, the substance of the nation's blueprint was altered somewhat in three respects. First, there was introduction of, what was known as, the principle of labor-management autonomy. In practice, this reform meant less state intervention in governance of the private sector. Second, in 1988 the nation began a phased introduction of a minimum wage regime. Third, there was a focus on bringing labor law in line with international standards. This latter agenda embraced more recognition of – and participation by – unions, influencing, at a shop-floor level, enhanced management emphasis on European-style joint-regulation. Another consequence of the new pluralism was less ephemeral. Specifically, between mid-1987 and mid-1988, South Korea experienced a 70% increase in the union density of its workforce and a 125% increase in the number of its registered unions (Lee 2016). In tandem, there was the growth of large independent trade union peak bodies including the Federation of Korean Trade Unions (FKTUS) and the Cheonnohyup (Korean Council of Trade Unions) (KCTU) (Park and Park 2000). A surge in collective bargaining in the following years resulted in wages increasing and a spike in inflation in 1991 (Korea International Labor Foundation 2006). In 1992, the government of the day intervened through setting a cross-sector 5% growth cap on salaries (Korea International Labor Foundation 2006, p. 12). However, in something of a display of how egalitarian the nation had become since its days of authoritarian rule, in 1992 the State attempted to undo some of its post-1987 union recognition legislation but was unsuccessful due to worker opposition and, as part of the new order, greater worker authority.

In the years since 1987, an influence on South Korea's embrace of organized labor and collective bargaining has been its growing international ties. The country joined the International Labor Organisation (ILO) in 1991, thus affording the nation's workers an option to have their grievances dealt with outside the national arena. Where such external measures of redress have occurred, the ILO has typically castigated the South Korean regime because of its limited embrace of the principle of freedom of association. In 1996, the nation joined the Organisation for Economic Co-operation and Development (OECD). In the years beforehand – and even despite the post 1987 reforms – other member countries had been disinclined to allow South Korea to join until worker rights were elaborated to a threshold standard and, in particular, employees could form and join unions without impediment (Park and Park 2000; Lee 2016).

In the wake of lingering international criticism, in 1996 the South Korean government re-examined its nation's employment relations strategy. To undertake the review task, a team comprised of union representatives, known as the Tripartite Committee, was formed. The group recommended reforms including: reducing restrictions on union recognition; third parties being allowed to participate in union activities; and unions being permitted to be active politically. At that time, employer groups were focusing their agenda on streamlining the worker dismissal process and enhancing labor flexibility options. In such circumstances, they were uneasy with the Tripartite Commission's recommendations. Consequently, the government sent a hollowed-out version of the proposals to the National Assembly. Eventually, following still further concessions to employers, the New Korea Party (ruling party) passed the reform bill. The ensuing legislation, being a substantially watered-down iteration of what had been recommended – and what the labor movement was seeking – prompted multisector strikes. To broker a final deal, the government made still further changes. Ultimately, new laws of the late 1990s limited the number of unions that were allowed to exist in a workplace but sanctioned the presence of multiple national and industry-level unions. However, the comprise legislation also authorized an employer's perogative to undertake collective redundancy but postponed activation of this option.

In the immediate wake of the East-Asia economic crisis of 1997, with fewer viable businesses to support the labor force, there was a large increase in unemployment in South Korea. In the early part of 1997 the rate had been 2.7% but by 1999 it was 8.5% (Park and Park 2000). The IMF provided financial relief to aide national recovery. As one of the conditions of this support, the government had to implement reforms, including labor market flexibility initiatives, across the economy. The new Kim-Dae Jung government reacted by embarking on restructuring the financial, banking, and public sectors and labor market.

In 1998, a Second Tripartite Committee, represented by organized labor[7], employers, and the government, was established to push further South Korea's management blueprint reform agenda. The ensuing recommendations ultimately proved broadly beneficial in assisting the nation to repay its IMF loans faster than other Asian nations effected by the era's foreign exchange crisis. The revamped approach facilitated a resurgence of economic growth which was somewhat reflected in improved unemployment statistics. For example, South Korea's jobless rate fell to a postcrisis low of 3.1% in 2002 and mostly remained between 3.5 and 4.0% from 2003 until 2005 (Korea International Labor Foundation 2006). In terms of substance, the second committee recommended giving employers the option of dismissing workers if they could show that this was unavoidable or in cases of mergers and acquisitions. Its somewhat controversial other resolutions included allowing firms to use: temporary workers where there is a short-term surge in demand as well as a broader range of employment contracts generally; more flexible roster systems; performance-based remuneration; an annualized salary system which rolled worker benefits into a base-pay structure; and employee dismissal provisions in cases of diminished performance (Korea International Labor Foundation 2006). To accompany these changes, the *chaebols* (industry clusters) were restructured to make them leaner and more internationally competitive.

---

[7]Although – according to Lee – 2016 – not necessarily – the views of individual union members.

The economic and labor management-related changes implemented in South Korea's postcrisis era assisted the country to recover from the crisis. Indeed, in the first decade of the twenty-first century South Korean economic growth generally outstripped the OECD average. For example, it was 8.5% in 2000, 7.0% in 2002, 4.8% in 2004, and 5.2% in 2005 (Labor Statistics Team, South Korea Ministry of Labor 2006). However, the process of recovery brought with it strained labor-management relations and labor-government relations. Indeed, unions and sections of the workforce had something of a case of buyer's remorse over concessions they made after the financial crisis. A lot of their angst concerned the employment rights – or lack thereof – of nonregular workers and the proliferation of industry-wide pattern-bargaining (Korea International Labor Foundation 2006). To address such disquiet, the government expanded employment insurance provisions for workers and provided subsidies for medical and living costs for the low paid (Korea International Labor Foundation 2006). In another compromise, the legislature passed a new Minimum Wage Act in 2005 that provided slightly broader coverage than had existed previously and streamlined payment regulations (Korea International Labor Foundation 2006). In 2006, Lee Sang Soo, South Korea's Labour Minister outlined objectives for the forthcoming years. In acknowledging that his nation's approach to employment relations was a work in progress, he indicated that his priorities did not necessarily pertain to better employment conditions but:

"....*creating an environment favourable to dialogue (involving unions, management and government) is as important as dialogue itself*...." (Korean International Labor Foundation 2006, p. 13) and

".... *such dialogue should not focus too much on worker agendas but should include topics such as job creation and workplace innovation*...." (Korea International Labor Foundation 2006, p. 13)

In the same speech, Lee Sang-Soo indicated that the South Korean labor market was still not sufficiently flexible. He highlighted that one sector of the workforce in particular – that involving regular employees including those engaged by large firms – remained unduly nonresponsive to the realities of commercial life. His solution was sliding wage scales for affected employees (Korea International Labor Foundation 2006, p. 13).

At the time of writing, South Korea's unions must be registered with the department of Labor. The State's guidelines for such registration are broad, possibly reflecting a bedding-down of the pluralist orthodoxy that was initially embraced in the post-1987 years of inclusion. What is striking about this development is that it is somewhat at odds with the experience of much of the postindustrial west. It is also noteworthy that, compared to the West, South Korean unions (as exemplars of those in other Tiger countries) are young and finding their way. In this sense, unlike in most other OECD nations, they have not had a 100-year odd history of experience with self-correction or a sustained opportunity to market their message. Rather, in the post-East Asia financial crisis era – and the post-2008 GFC era – organized labor in South Korea has been on a steep-learning curve as it faces the challenge of protecting employment standards won throughout the 1990s and pushing ahead on advancing members' interests in a context of digital age economic restructure. Hence, despite the aforementioned differences between the circumstances of Tiger unions in the twenty-first century and their Western counterparts, there are also some similarities. Specifically, like other countries in the region and elsewhere, organized labor faces the prospect of a workforce with fewer permanent employees, higher levels of job turnover, and an expanding services sector. From a management perspective, more specifically from the perspective of delineating the emerging Korean management blueprint, in practice something of a neo-liberal orientation towards markets and productivity is largely the *ordre du jour*. In the last decade, employers have regained the upper hand in advancing a hard-edged agenda, perhaps not so much with institutional support but more in response to the aforementioned fact the unions have been largely illprepared to take advantage of the opportunities that came with democratization three decades ago.

China

Since 1949, China's twentieth-century communist philosophy has manifested through an unambiguous totalitarian dictatorship regime that has no compelling parallel with other Asian countries, at least for purposes of understanding its national approach to management. Hence, as is the case with Japan (but for entirely different reasons) China exists as a single-nation category.

By Western standards mainland China's leaders have had a preoccupation with directing and controlling production. In the second half of the twentieth century, the nation's distinctive command economy structure gave rise to a workforce management strategy that is well characterized as the embodiment of shop floor communism. China still has the hallmarks of this approach. For example, it remains a one-party state, exerting substantial control over the lives of its citizens, including imposing freedom of association restrictions. In the twenty-first century, the nation has not transitioned easily into a liberal market economy. Likewise, in spite of some consequential changes that will be briefly examined below, its communist-era approach to employment relations and management remains, in some respects, the default blueprint for national worker superintendence.

Until recently, workplace management in China was often considered to be undergirded by a philosophy that changed when Mao Zedong died and the Cultural Revolution ended in 1976 (Zhu and Warner 2000; Cooke 2016). Perhaps however it is more appropriate to discern three, somewhat indistinct, recent epochs. These correspond approximately to the time of the Cultural Revolution (1967–1976) and, more broadly, to the Maoist era (1949–1976); the initial period of Deng Xiaoping's administration (1976–1990s), and from the 1990s onwards. For purposes of understanding management in China, delineation of this last epoch makes sense for several reasons. First, it establishes a point where the nation began economic deregulation such as restructuring state-owned industry to give local administrators greater decision making autonomy and productive enterprises a pseudo-commercial orientation. This change was accompanied by partial embrace of Western-style HRM practices and the founding of US and UK business schools within the country. Second, under the influences of laws passed in 1992, 1993, and 1995, China's single trade union entity, the All-China Federation of Trade Unions (ACFTU) began an arduous transition. In the twenty-first century, this evolution continued, creating the semblance of a market-based system of labor management that now has some features of Western-style approaches (Cooke 2016). In this regard, even though there have been discernable, somewhat step-wise, changes in China's employment relations philosophy, the actual practice of people management has altered more incrementally. In the remainder of this section, a more detailed examination of these eras is undertaken.

After 1949, the Chinese government began uncompromisingly implementing Maoist communist principles. The new regime pursued its revolutionary class struggle agenda through pugnaciously opposing the remnants of Chiang Kai-shek's former administration. In a practice that became known as "politics on demand" (e.g., Zhu and Warner 2000; Cooke 2016), throughout the era, China's central press and broadcasting agency promulgated Mao's philosophy using public speakers which were installed by the regime in schools, army units, and other state-run institutions. In this environment, iconoclasts, the bourgeois and/or perceived intellectuals, were designated as China's enemies and dispatched to labor camps. A key aspect of the new communist message concerned management and work organization, in particular, the benefits of the Soviet-style iron rice-bowl/lifetime employment system (Kaple 1994; Cooke 2016; Chan 2010). The imposed blueprint was austere but came with a degree of certainty for each actor. It entailed job continuity within exclusively state-owned and operated enterprises, a standardized and non-discriminatory wage system (introduced in 1956) and industry-sponsored welfare (Zhu and Warner 2000; Cooke 2016; Chan 2010). Essentially, it legitimized publicly owned enterprises as monopolistic providers of, on the one hand, consumer and military goods and services and, on the other, worker benefits. Insofar as the latter of these functions was concerned, as part of such domination, they (the publicly owned enterprises) were to also have an all-inclusive role in providing subsidized housing, cultural and leisure activities, and sickness and old-age support.

Management of China's state owned enterprises during the Maoist era was tailored to suit the ruling regime's, decidedly ideological, objectives. The overriding goal was to meet domestic demand through producing a limited range of no-frills products. The "new industrial management mechanism" fused Taylorist principles for efficiency attainment with the Soviet-imported communist prescription of egalitarianism, seniority-based workplace advancement and restrictions on Western-style freedoms of expression (Kaple 1994). To maintain central control, party officials were mostly responsible for the management of productive units (Zhu and Warner 2000). Administrative arrangements were undertaken through an institutionalized regulatory structure that typically included a party committee, a workers' congress, and the union[8]. In these circumstances, it is perhaps axiomatic that during the Maoist

---

[8] As will be explained, during the Maoist era, unions in China did not fulfill the same role as those in the West.

era, notions of workplace oversight and worker surveillance did not embrace application of western-style human resource management, particularly insofar as planning and strategy is concerned. Rather, state bureaucratic personnel departments maintained worker files and undertook recruitment, training, and work group allocation functions (Ng and Warner 1998).

From 1949, the All-China Federation of Trade Unions (ACFTU) was created through consolidating "red unions," which had operated illegally as underground movements. Consequently, henceforth, and until the Cultural Revolution, a single state sponsored labor organization communicated party propaganda to the nation's workers (Zhu and Warner 2000). The elements of this function were typically to: promote party policy; market enterprise economic reforms; regulate welfare benefits; and, in some cases, undertake training (Ng and Warner 1998). As the antithesis of capitalist systems with their tradition of voluntarism and the ever-present influence of the profit motive, communist regimes are often conceived of as churning-out their gross national product in circumstances of forced alignment of manager and worker interests (Chang-Hee 2006; Cooke 2016). In China, this characteristic influenced the construct of unionism to develop in a distinctively non-Western way. For example, during the Maoist era, the ACFTU had an organizational structure with formal accountability linkages to the management committees of work units and the communist party leadership (Zhu and Warner 2000). In practice, factory administrators were often also party officials and responsible for appointing union delegates. Furthermore, ACFTU units were comprised of members from each level of enterprise organizational hierarchies including executives and supervisors. Hence, and explicitly at odds with Western orthodoxy, the Chinese union movement does not have a history of exclusively – or even mostly – representing worker interests.

From 1966 and the commencement of the Cultural Revolution, union activity in China and the continued operation of the ACFTU was banned (Zhu and Warner 2000). The State's rationale for disallowing organized labor was somewhat ambiguous. Specifically, such an influence was alleged to be distracting the party from its revolutionary class-struggle activities and encouraging bourgeoisie thinking. However, in recent times, the change in emphasis is sometimes interpreted as Mao attempting to regain control over the Communist party following the failure of his flamboyant but ill-conceived and ultimately poorly executed "great leap forward experiment" which had begun in 1958 (Zhu and Warner 2000; Cooke 2016). In concocting this initiative, the supreme leader was preoccupied with coordinating better his nation's agricultural and industrial sectors. He believed that a lack of such synchronization, and (relatedly) the fact that he was finding it difficult to rally China's rural peasant population, were key obstacles in the quest to ramp-up grain and steel production. In undertaking postmortem analyses of the Great Leap Forward, it is instructive to note that Mao was disdainful of intellectuals (Cooke 2016). As a consequence, he mostly did not seek advice from experts such as, metallurgists, engineers, and economists when formulating or implementing his policy agendas.

After Mao's death in 1976 and the end of the Cultural Revolution, China was reeling from the results of years of failed social and economic policy. At the time, the nation had a stockpile of military hardware but an undersupply of food and clothing.

Adding to the urgency of the shortages, from 1966 to 1976, China's population had grown from 740 million to over 950 million (Zhu and Warner 2000). Furthermore, within workplaces, there was low morale. Throughout the entirety of the Cultural Revolution period, there had been no increase in wages. Also, during the epoque leaders of the defunct ACTFU as well as those articulating counter-perspectives had been imprisoned. Adding to the malaise was the state of the country's education system. Indeed, by the 1970s China's national school and university sectors had almost ceased operating and illiteracy was widespread (Chan 2010).

In the power vacuum that ensued after Mao's death, Deng Xiaoping became chairman of the Communist Party. Deng's ascendancy marked an end to what Yuan (1990) referred to as the "cult-of-personality" approach to China's administration. The new leader gave mere tacit commendation to Mao. In damning his predecessor with faint praise, he judged the ratio of Mao's mistakes to contribution as three to seven (Zhu and Warner 2000) and committed his nation to a decidedly different theoretical orientation. Zhu and Warner (2000) interpret the new regime's altered priorities as being founded on two principles: "seeking truth from facts" and "the liberation of thought." This more critical and less ideologically driven approach was a watershed for China. Henceforth, the nation began tolerating, albeit slowly and at times unenthusiastically, a pluralist and more broadly accommodative stance on public policy, economic reform, and relations with the West (Zhu and Warner 2000, p. 120).

During the Deng administration, Mao's inflexible "three irons" view of production oversight was partially replaced by an approach influenced by the, conspicuously Western, constructs of labor contracts, floating wage rates, and management engagement strategies (Yuan 1990). With aid from the International Labor Organisation, by the 1990s this new tripartite system was well ensconced and being augmented by collective bargaining, established and then championed by the ILO (Zhu and Warner 2000). It is likely that this latter reform, collective bargaining, was responsible for increased union membership and participation in China (e.g., Zhang 2005; Cooke 2016). For example, by December 2003, there were 35.79 million Chinese workers covered by wage-agreements, a rate of coverage that had risen at least 40% since the mid-1990s (Zhang 2005). The refurbished approach legitimized, and in some respects leveled, the roles of three national stakeholders: the Chinese Enterprise Directors Association (CEDA), representing employers; the Labor Ministry, representing the State; and the ACFTU, representing workers. In subsequent years, responsibility for employment relations practice was somewhat devolved, providing for enhanced local autonomy and flexibility (Chang-Hee 2006).

In the twenty-first century, China's management and governance-related institutions remained largely similar to those reformulated during the Deng administration. For example, the ACFTU continues to be the only officially sanctioned union, effectively remaining as part of the State's top-down bureaucratic apparatus. However, the collective bargaining and dispute settlement provisions of Deng's tripartite system have supported an expanded role for organized labor including representative and advocacy functions (Chang-Hee 2006). In 2001, this reform was augmented by legislation allowing the ACFTU more independence and an enlarged role so that it can participate in social and labor policy development. The substance of this change has been implemented using a Tripartite Consultation Committee (TCC) structure, the mission of which is to improve workplace relations through enhanced coordination among the key labor management actors, specifically: the State, employers, and workers (Chang-Hee 2006).

In the early digital age, a trend in Chinese employment relations was the rising number of employee disputes, both individual and collective. Chang-Hee (2006) suggests that this has little or nothing to do with the increase in collective bargaining. Rather, he points out that in modern China, new employee/employer disputes may be expressions of the ACFTU's inability to adequately discharge its full range of responsibilities in changing circumstances. For example, it may be that union sub-units are unable to assist individual workers redress their grievances because they are focusing their efforts and resources on wage bargaining. Chang-Hee (2006) at the time suggested that this phenomenon is evidence of a growing informal or unofficial sphere of Chinese employment relations in the early twenty-first century (Chang-Hee 2006, p. 126). It is noteworthy also that, within China, penalties for labor-related expressions of dissent occurring outside the formal legal system are still, by ILO standards, particularly harsh.

Notwithstanding an upsurge in industrial disputation in China, by 2016 there were still practical and psychological impediments to the expression of worker voice. Each such hindrance is unambiguously a legacy of the Maoist era blueprint and largely a result of the workplace relations context (Cooke 2016). Perhaps the most notably of these contextual elements is the presence of a pervasive climate of fear about the consequences of engaging in illegal strike activity. However, also in the twenty-first century, it is noteworthy that enterprises continue to provide dormitory housing, thus limiting easy and regular interaction and information exchange with workers and their comrades in other factories. Furthermore, in the modern era in China, a registration system exists that impedes migrant workers from, in particular, leaving their job or applying for another if management confiscates relevant documents.

There is diverse opinion concerning how to interpret China's changing management agenda[9]. Those who emphasize the "forced local-cloning" of the tripartite structure have described the 21st century's emerging approach as "*a preemptive corporatist strategy applied in a top-down manner*" (Chang-Hee 2006). This view depicts the nation as moving towards embrace of a Western industrial-age model where conflicting employer and employee interests are acknowledged and managed within a regulatory framework. Others stress the nation's range of different employment relations systems that came to exist in the early 2000s. For example, one survey suggested that China simultaneously has several disparate philosophies. In the early digital era, these included: "the traditional," "internationally orientated HRM," and "HRM with Chinese features" (Benson and Zhu 1999). Another view of the current approach emphasizes a unique and culturally distinctive course of change. Such reasoning became associated with the term "*third way of gradualism*" (e.g., Zhu and

---

[9]Perhaps the word "administration" is more appropriate than "management" in the case of China.

Warner 2000). This perspective is that China has moved from being a State-run economy based on Stalinist principles of bureaucracy and Taylorism to an economic system embracing "market-socialism" with "Chinese characteristics" (Zhu and Warner 2000; Cooke 2016). Advocates of the third way perspective argue that China is different from the West because its approach does not involve adversarial relations between employers and their workforce, but nonetheless, is internationally competitive. Despite a certain lack of clarity and detail, this view suggests that the nation retains some of the ideals of communism whilst, at the same time, finding legitimacy in a globalized trading economy. Hence, in summary, although there is a plurality of opinion about the best way to characterize China's management philosophy trajectory, scholars appear to consider that, broadly speaking, the nation is in transition. Where it has come from is somewhat easy to characterize. Where it is going, more challenging.

Indonesia

Among Asian countries Indonesia is idiosyncratic because: the vast majority of its citizens are Islamic; its industrial base has emerged from an abundance of natural resources such as, oil, gas, bauxite, tin, copper, gold, and coal; and it has a history of government ownership and control of commercial enterprise. This latter feature of Indonesia's economy is a legacy of the nation's 1945 constitution that says: "...*branches of production which affect the life of most people will be controlled by the state*." Specifically, in 2003, the Indonesian national government had stewardship of 158 commercial enterprises and utilities and controlled prices on vital goods including commodities such as fuel, rice, and electricity (Drakeley 2005, p. 30).

In some respects, since 2004, Indonesia has come to resemble a liberal democratic country, in particular holding direct elections for its President. In the prior era, members of a single legislature elected an executive branch of government. In this former period, a specified number of parliamentary seats were set aside for leaders of the armed forces, an arrangement which self-evidently curtailed representative participation and effectively established the country as a militaristic one-party state. Indonesia has a population of 224 million, of whom 87% are Muslim (US Department of State 2017). Although these statistics represent the largest Islamic population in the world, unlike for example in Middle Eastern countries, Indonesia is officially secular, thus managing its activities in such a way as to make a clean distinction between the practice of faith and affairs of State. In 2017, the nation derived at least 16% of its Gross Domestic Product from natural resources and employed the majority of its workforce in the public sector.

Insofar as its national blueprint for workforce management is concerned, modern Indonesia has been through three identifiable stages since gaining independence from the Dutch in 1945. These correspond approximately to the period before the Suharto era (prior to 1967); the time of the Suharto regime, sometimes known as the *new order* (1967–1998); and thereafter, the *Reformasi* (Reformation). During the first of these periods – the transition to sovereignty era – trade unionists largely neglected workplace concerns but rather dedicated themselves to the goal of achieving full independence, often acting in a paramilitary role in circumstance of protracted violent protest activity. By 1949, they had played a seminal part in forcing out of the country the last of the remaining Dutch colonialists who had been exerting influence over the agriculture sector, in particular.

Throughout the twentieth century (approximately the first two of the three identified eras), labor management in Indonesian was routinely a matter of coercion in circumstances where local supervisors were largely inconsequential. As such, it entailed regular overt displays of power and authority by the State and periodic resistance by nonrecognized unions, in particular. In this respect, historically the nation's approach was dominated by government intervention in the form of heavy-handed regulation of the employment relationship and a consequent marginalization of employers, intimidation, confrontation, and in some cases, human rights abuses. Until the end of the Suharto era, the Indonesian Ministry of Manpower (Depnaker) regulated the labor market and management practice. Specifically, it set terms and conditions of employment, intervened in disputes and – the most consequential of its priorities – created national strategy for improving productivity. On advice from a committee with regional and district representation, the Ministry established the minimum wage for each of Indonesia's 27 provinces (Suwarno and Elliott 2000).

As noted, the construct of organized labor in Indonesia has different intellectual and historical origins to its Western equivalent. However, having played a key role in liberating the country from its colonialist shackles, from around 1950 unions began concerning themselves with a Western-style notion of work-life betterment, albeit in a largely short-term, informal, and paternalist manner. For example, mostly on an ad hoc basis, a key part of their role became to advocate for individual employees concerning their specific grievances rather than addressing collective bargaining or scoping out development agendas (Suwarno and Elliott 2000). Furthermore, prior to the Suharto era (commencing in 1967), Indonesia did not have an arbitration system or regime of labor market regulation (Suwarno and Elliott 2000).

Throughout the Suharto period (1967–1998), forced national economic development was a key priority in Indonesia. However, despite high levels of growth in the 1980s and 90s, the nation's working conditions were harsh, inequitable and discriminatory, particularly for women (Ford 2013). To support the regime's hard-edged agenda, the Indonesian management philosophy came to embody three features. First, the state curtailed trade union activities using an inflexible recognition process and through denying workers opportunity to strike or indicate dissent. Second, government employees, including those working for publicly owned enterprises, were forbidden from forming or joining trade unions. As something of a token gesture, in 1972 the State established the Indonesian Civil Servants' Corps (KORPRI) to represent public sector workers in grievance matters. (Suwarno and Elliott 2000, p. 134). Third, unions – and union officials – were monitored, often in a heavy-handed way, by the State (Suwarno and Elliott 2000; Gould 2014). In such a climate, leaders and organizers of nonrecognized labor alliances were frequently imprisoned or harassed by the police and military (Bamber and Leggett 2001; Gould 2014).

The three aforementioned characteristics of Suharto-era employment relations philosophy had their formal origins in the PIR, *Pancasila Industrial Relations* system that began in 1974. This strategy was officially established following a seminar sponsored by the Indonesian government in collaboration with *Friedrich Ebert Stiftung,* a German labor studies research institute. It was intended to inculcate partnership and cooperation between employees, managers, and the State through (in the stated order of importance): *"peace and stability, discipline, a dedicated workforce, increasing productivity, and a commitment to improve workers' welfare and human dignity"* (Suwarno and Elliott 2000). However, somehow this blueprint was never really implemented. Instead, what emerged in late twentieth-century Indonesia under the auspices of the PIR approach was a harsh and militaristic government stance in the regulation of industrial disruption and strike activity. Moreover, PIR established Indonesia as a comparatively low-wage country (Schwarz 1997).

President Suharto resigned in 1998 following revelations that his government was corrupt. Another influence on the change of administration was Indonesia's strained relations with Western countries because of its human rights abuses in East Timor (Gould 2014). Habibe, the incoming president, softened aspects of the nation's approach to organized labor and brought his country somewhat more in line with international employment standards. In this vein, in 1999 Indonesia released some of its political prisoners, several of whom had been incarcerated because of their union affiliations. Also in 1999, President Habibe ratified the key ILO conventions on Freedom of Association and protection of the right to organize (Suwarno and Elliott 2000) and lessened controls on press reporting and the activities of rival political parties. In 1999, the Indonesian military was given a reduced role in public administration and, in particular, of monitoring unions. As part of these reforms, the police and military functions were separated.

In the twenty-first century, the mechanism for wage-setting in Indonesia has been developed in the wake of a government reform agenda explicitly concerned with elements such as: commitment to employee participation and inclusion, greater tolerance for industrial disputation and employee dissent, and a renewed focus on commercial competitiveness. In 2000, Indonesia ceded some of the Ministry for Manpower's authority, including responsibility for setting a minimum wage, to a more independent employment tribunal service. This reform has formed one element of the nation's transition to a liberal democracy. However, aside from this change, the recent trajectory of Indonesian development has resembled that of Western liberal market economies; in particular, it has had a decidedly neoliberal character (Gould 2014). For example, the recently embraced philosophy emphasizes notions such as flexible employment, particularly in the manufacturing sector. Hence, in one sense, the refurbished approach echoes sentiments of PSI, re-establishing commercial success and economic development as more important objectives than pay equity and extending to employees the right to organize or engage in industrial disruption. It has been suggested also that the twenty-first-century approach will likely ensconce Indonesia as a low wage country (Gould 2014). In particular, the nation had stagnant wage growth in the first 15 years of the twenty-first century.

Since 2004, Indonesian employment relations-related changes have been planned without, by western standards, substantial consultation. However, these same changes have more legitimized unions and reduced the State's role in enforcement and compliance matters. Specifically, they have mostly come from a top-down influence. Indeed, in light of the fact that changes that were intended prior to 2010 were being held-up due to union resistance, it now seems that the nation's workers have the semblance of a voice.

Conclusion: Inescapable Diversity but Perplexing Recent Similarity

When speaking about human beings and their personality, it is somewhat tautological to point out that the twin circumstances of experience and innate constitution are 100% defining. It follows that where each of these elements are – in a relative sense – different for, say, two individuals one should expect to observe, in each case, unalike temperaments. Although there are dangers in reasoning by analogy, the binary nature of the aforementioned template (the idea that only two element clusters create personality) mitigates such hazards when talking about the case of countries. Specifically, nations inevitably – and certainly true for Asia – have ubiquitous cultures, their innateness[10]. They also have their recent histories, their experiences. Thus, it follows that where more than one country occupy shared space but do not have meaningful interaction, it is inevitable that each's approach will be different, irrespective of whether an object of analytic interest concerns management philosophical orientation or other human endeavor. This is the unwieldy and disjointed story of Asia, a difficult story to tell.

Up until about 30 years ago, a patent intra-regional isolationism existed in Asia. For example, Australia's most proximal neighbor was Indonesia. Japan's was China. These nations had little of cultural consequence in common and decidedly different histories. It is somewhat axiomatic that their respective national management blueprints turned-out to be different. The five cases presented in this chapter laid bare other such contrasts. However, the selected national case studies also hinted at, in an overall sense, how in the Internet era – the digital age – countries within the region are becoming, at least partially, similar. In an effort to keep the spotlight on the nations themselves, the chapter sidestepped discussing theory about why this may be. However, chapter 2 of this volume takes up the challenge. It addresses the so-called convergence debate and, in so doing, gives to the reader some new analytic tools to think about what is happening in Asia. It is noteworthy that, compared to any other of the world's geographic regions, it is within Asia that these analytic tools are best put to the test. Indeed, Asia is the perfect natural experiment for assessing conjecture about whether and how nations influence each other.

Cross-References

- ▶ Governmentality and the Chinese Workers in China's Contemporary Thought Management System
- ▶ In Search of the Traces of the History of Management in Latin America, 1870–2020
- ▶ Indian Management (?): A Modernization Experiment
- ▶ Management History in the Modern World: An Overview
- ▶ Management in Australia – The Case of Australia's Wealthiest Valley: The Hunter

---

[10]Not, of course, literally because of DNA but nonetheless often inculcated over hundreds or thousands of years.

- The Making of a Docile Working Class in Pre-reform China
- The Perfect Natural Experiment: Asia and the Convergence Debate
- Think Big and Privatize Every Thing That Moves: The Impact of Political Reform on the Practice of Management in New Zealand
- What Is Management?

References

Abegglen JC (1959) The Japanese factory. Aspects of its social organisation. Free Press, Glenco

Aoki M (1987) The Japanese firm in transition. In: Yamamura K, Yasuba Y (eds) The political economy of Japan. Vol. 1: The domestic transformation. Stanford University Press, Stanford

Aoki M (1988) Information incentives and bargaining in the Japanese Economy. Cambridge University Press, Cambridge

Bamber GJ, Davis EM (2001) In: Bamber GJ, Park F, Lee C, Ross PK, Broadbent K (eds) (2001) Employment relations in the Asia Pacific: changing approaches. Allen and Unwin, Sydney

Bamber G, Leggett C (2001) Changing employment relations in the Asia-Pacific region. Int J Manpow 22(4):300–317

Bamber GJ, Lansbury RD, Wailes N, Wright C (2016) International and Comparative Employment Relations National Regulation, Global Changes Sixth Edition. Sage Books. London

Barry M, Wilkinson A (2011) Research handbook of comparative employment relations. Edward Elgar, Cheltenham

Benson J, Zhu Y (1999) Markets, firms and workers: the transformation of human resource management in Chinese state owned enterprises. Hum Resour Manag J 9(4):58–74

Briggs C (2005) Strikes and lockouts in the antipodes: neo-liberal convergence in Australia and New Zealand. N Z J Employ Relat 30(3)18–33

Chan CKC (2010) The challenge of labour in China. Strikes and the changing regime in global factories. Routledge, London

Chang-Hee L (2006) In: Hall R (ed) Industrial relations: a current review. SAGE, London

Chin D (2005) The encroaching federal industrial relations system. http://www.australianreview.net/digest/2005/09/chin.html

Cooke FL (2016) Employment relations in China. In: Bamber J, Lansbury R, Wailes N, Wright C (eds) International and comparative employment relations, 6th edn. Allen and Unwin, Sydney

Deming WE (2000) The new economics for industry, government, education, 2nd edn. MIT Centre for Advanced Educational Services, Cambridge

Drakeley S (2005) The history of Indonesia. Greenwood, Westport

Ford M (2013) Violent Industrial Protest in Indonesia: Cultural Phenomenon or Legacy of an Authoritarian Past?. In: Gall G. (eds) New Forms and Expressions of Conflict at Work 171–189. Palgrave Macmillan, London

Gerhart B (2008) Cross-cultural managerial research. Assumptions, evidence, and suggested directions. Int J Cross-cult Manag 8(3):259–274

Gordon A (1985) The evolution of labor relations in Japan: heavy industry. 1853–1955. Harvard University Press, Cambridge

Gould AM (2010) Americanisation of Australian Workplaces. Labor History, 51(3):363–388

Gould A (2014) Les relations d'emploi et le marché du travail: similarité apparaissant dans six pays asiatiques (Employment relations and labor markets: emerging similarity in six Asian countries). In: Thwaites JD (ed) La Mondialisation: origines, développement et effets. Les Presses de l'Université Laval, Québec

Gregory D, Johnson R, Pratt G, Watts MJ, Whatmore S (2009) Asian miracle: the tigers. The Dictionary of human geography, 5th edn. Blackwell, Malden

Hanami T (2004) The changing labor market, industrial relations and labor policy. Japan Labor Rev 1(1):10–11

Hofstede G (1980/2003) Cultures consequences, 1st edn/2nd edn. Sage Publishing, Thousand Oaks

Inkster I (2001) Japanese Industrialization – Historical and Cultural Perspectives. Routledge, London

http://faostat.fao.org/faostat/help-copyright/copyright-e.htm

http://www.economist.com/world/asia/displaystory.cfm?story_id=7925064

Jackson T (2002) International management of people across cultures: valuing people differently. Hum Resour Manag 41(4):45–75

Kaoki K (1991) Shigoto no keizaigaku (the economics of work). Toyo Keizai, Tokyo

Kaoki K (1995) The economics of work in Japan. LTCB International Library Foundation, Tokyo, English translation of Koike (1991b)

Kaple D (1994) Dream of a red factory: the legacy of high Stalinism in China. Oxford University Press, Oxford

Katz HC, Darbishire O (2000) Converging divergences: worldwide changes in employment relations. Cornell University Press, Ithaca

Kaufman B (2011) Comparative employment relations: institutional and neo institutional theories. In: Barry, Wilkinson (eds) Research handbook of comparative employment relations. Edward Elgar, Cheltenham

Keller B, Kirsch A (2016) Employment relations in Germany. In: Bamber J, Lansbury R, Wailes N, Wright C (eds) International and comparative employment relations, 6th edn. Allen and Unwin, Sydney

Korea International Labor Foundation 2006: https://www.business-humanrights.org/en/koilaf-korea-international-labour-foundation

Labor Force Survey (2002) Japanese Ministry of Public Management, home affairs, posts and telecommunications. Report on the Special Survey of the Labor Force

Labor Statistics Team, South Korea Ministry of Labor (2006) Korea Labor Rev 2(9), July–Aug

Lee BH (2016) Employment relations in South Korea. In: Bamber J, Lansbury R, Wailes N, Wright C (eds) International and comparative employment relations, 6th edn. Allen and Unwin, Sydney

Martyn T (2005) Industrial relations: reform or vandalism? www.jss.org.au/documents/IRCritique2.pdf

Ng SH, Warner M (1998) China's trade unions and management. Macmillan, London

Nikkei Asian review. https://asia.nikkei.com/ Accessed on 16 January, 2020

Park F, Park YB (2000) In: Bamber GJ, Park F, Lee C, Ross PK, Broadbent K (eds) Employment relations in the Asia Pacific: changing approaches. Allen and Unwin, Sydney

Rodrik D (1997) The paradoxes of the successful state. Eur Econ Rev 41(3/4):411–442

Schwarz A (1997) Indonesia after Suharto. Foreign Affairs 76, July/August

Suwarno S, Elliott J (2000) In: Bamber GJ, Park F, Lee C, Ross PK, Broadbent K (eds) Employment relations in the Asia Pacific: changing approaches. Allen and Unwin, Sydney

Suzuki H, Kubo K, Kazuya O (2016) Employment relations in Japan. In: Bamber J, Lansbury R, Wailes N, Wright C (eds) International and comparative employment relations, 6th edn. Allen and Unwin, Sydney

Tackney CT (2000) In: Bamber GJ, Park F, Lee C, Ross PK, Broadbent K (eds) Employment relations in the Asia Pacific: changing approaches. Allen and Unwin, Sydney

Takafusa N, Konosuke O (eds) (1999) Economic History of Japan 1914–1955 – A Dual Structure. Oxford University Press, Takafusa Nakamura

Thelan KA (2014) Varieties of liberalisation and the new politics of social solidarity. Cambridge University Press, New York

US Department of State (2017) http://www.state.gov/Bureauofeastasiaandpacificaffairs

Yuan LQ (1990) Zhongguo Laodong Jingji Shi (The history of Chinese Labor Economy). Beijing Economic Press, Beijing

Zhang JG (2005) Institutional achievements and future prospects of collective bargaining in China. Unpublished paper

Zhu Y, Warner M (2000) In: Bamber G, Park F, Chanwon L, Ross P, Broadbent K (eds) Employment relations in Asia Pacific: changing approaches. Allen and Unwin, Sydney

The Perfect Natural Experiment: Asia and the Convergence Debate

57

Anthony M. Gould

Contents

Introduction	1318
Asian Approaches to Management in Historical Perspective: The Convergence Debate	1319
Varieties of Capitalism	1325
Katz and Darbishire's Four Pattern Formulation	1326
Conclusion: Management Convergence in Asia	1327
Cross-References	1328
References	1328

Abstract

This chapter is about international approaches to management and the convergence debate. It interprets convergence as a manifestation of the comparative problem, the second most consequential big-picture dilemma in management studies, the first being concerned with the how-to question. On the one hand it argues that "the how-to" dilemma has largely been viewed as a problem for the West in the twentieth century. On the other hand, the comparative problem became of interest after World War 2. Two questions expose its nature: Which, of various nationally distinctive approaches to management, is most effective? Will internationally distinctive approaches to management converge? The chapter contends that progress on the comparative question has been impeded because, with the exception of Japan, theory has mostly not been built on a base of data that embraces non-Western Asian countries. It further argues that such a lack of inclusion of Asia has rendered theory about convergence, in particular, limited in its scope.

A. M. Gould (✉)
Département des relations industrielles, Université Laval, Québec, QC, Canada
e-mail: anthony.gould@rlt.ulaval.ca

© The Author(s), under exclusive licence to Springer Nature Switzerland AG 2020
B. Bowden et al. (eds.), *The Palgrave Handbook of Management History*,
https://doi.org/10.1007/978-3-319-62114-2_121

> **Keywords**
>
> Asia · Convergence · Industrialisation · Management theory · Industrial age · Japan · Western management · Post-war · Asian tigers · Digital-age · American exceptionalism · Ideology · Emile durkheim · Max weber · Thomas dunlop · Clark kerr · Karl marx · Adam smith · Alexander hamilton · Henri fayol · Frank and lillian gilbreth · Henry ford · Frederick taylor

Introduction

Asia's bewildering cultural, social and economic heterogeneity renders the region the ideal testing ground for determining what works in management. In reflecting on such diversity, two points – implicitly exposed in ▶ Chap. 56, "Introduction: Management Heterogeneity in Asia" of this volume – are noteworthy. First, when looked at in cross-section, Asia, however defined, consists of different kinds of jurisdictions. Second, its constituent countries have changed to varying degrees and thus at varying rates since the mid-twentieth century. For example, on the one hand, the closed-off dynastic totalitarian regime of North Korea has remained essentially the same across most consequential societal and economic dimensions since United States Lieutenant-General William Harrison Jnr and North-Korean General Nam II each signed the Korean armistice agreement on July 27, 1953, effectively ending the Korean War with a "temporary" truce. On the other hand, South Korea's near neighbor, Japan, entirely supplanted its national management blueprint in the 1950s and made substantial, albeit more incremental, macro-level change in the digital age. Likewise, South Korea, an even closer neighbor to its Northern namesake became an aggressively export-orientated Asian tiger in the 1960s, thus joining the ranks of Western-style industrialized economies and soon taking a healthy share of their key product markets. In the post-1987 period of its democratization, South Korea embarked on further governance-related reforms, and did so again following the East-Asian financial crisis of 1997 (Gould et al. 2015). Such reflections suggest that, for a circumscribed period of analysis (say the 70 years until 2020), in just one relatively small corner of the Asian region, there is simultaneously difference and similarity at the commencement of the reference period and an altered mix of these elements at its ending. In light of such temporal and spatial multi-facetedness, making sense of what is going on overall is daunting. Certainly, it calls for theory. The mission of this chapter is to respond to this call or at least survey some of what others have done to push the agenda.

Using history to contextualize discussion of key ideas, this short chapter presents, interprets – and reveals the limitations of – theory addressing regional similarity and difference in management philosophy and practice. It will be argued that, in the wake of the industrial revolution, the new problem of management was in fact two problems. First, there is the "how to" conundrum, a dilemma about which, in the West, progress was slow in the nineteenth century but accelerated in the twentieth. Second, there is a more recent dilemma, the comparative problem, a concern about whether there are better ways – notably ways outside the West – and, if so, whether the West is influenced by – or influences – these. The chapter will further argue that, when compared to other global regions, Asia, the place of diversity and changing identities, holds the most latent potential to make progress on the second of these issues, henceforth referred to as the comparative problem. In prosecuting the case, it will be noted that conjecture about matters such as convergence and macro-economic taxonomy has mostly been a Western-hemisphere enterprise. Thus, it is common to find mainstream ideas about these topics being tested mostly within Europe and North America. As such, theory addressing change in management philosophy and practice is not typically invoked to understand Asia, sometimes with the exception of the decontextualized case of Japan. There are two reasons for such distorted application. The first concerns parochialism. The second pertains to the fact that theory is not sufficiently developed to cope with the multidimensional complexity that exists when Asia is established as an object of analytic interest. Simply put, Asia is a tough case.

This chapter has a straightforward, two-part structure. In the next section, an overview is given of the convergence debate. The objectives of this section are threefold. First, it will place conjecture about convergence in its historical context. Second, it will indicate that the issue itself is a manifestation of the comparative question, arguably the second most important big-picture concern for management theorists in the postindustrial revolution era. Third, it will illustrate how – other than in the case of Japan – non-Western parts of Asia have largely been excluded from consideration in formulating relevant theory. The conclusion offers general further commentary about the circumstances of Asia and calls for twenty-first century management theorists to create their conceptual frameworks based on a broader data set than exists in the West, in particular to consider previously neglected Asian countries.

Asian Approaches to Management in Historical Perspective: The Convergence Debate

In the digital age, a key message that could be being sent from Asia concerns convergence. The important words here are "could be." Precisely, the West, notably Western theorists, is either largely unreceptive to the missive or ill-equipped theoretically to receive and interpret it. The reasons for such tone deafness are explored at the end of this section. In the meantime, insofar as convergence is concerned, the issue at hand is whether different approaches to management – approaches emanating from dissimilar contextual starting points – become alike (Kaufman 2011; Gould et al. 2015). Of equal importance is delineation and defense of a relevant explanatory mechanism. It is noteworthy that theory about convergence is intended to be – but in fact is not – robust. In this regard, it will be argued that robustness is unattainable when frameworks are created exclusively from examination of an arbitrarily delimited data set, in this case mostly only through considering the cases of Western countries.

A cursory glance at pertinent literature reveals the convergence controversy as a central concern for modern management theorists, notably North American and European comparative political economists and their colleagues seeking to enumerate comprehensively ways of managing (Gould et al. 2015; Kaufman 2011; Katz and Darbishire 2000). Indeed, since the industrial revolution, convergence (however articulated) is arguably the second most consequential big-picture issue on the scholarly agenda, the first being what is the best/most effective/most appropriate method for undertaking the mission. Reflection on Western history's long arc reveals why each of these preoccupations creates the lion's share of impetus for management scholars. Thus, before returning to the case of Asia, consideration will be given to the long-arc issue.

Following the late eighteenth century's industrial revolution, the construct of the nation-State came of age as the feudalist production mode gave way to capitalism and jurisdictionally regulated market economies (Gould et al. 2017; Joullié and Spillane 2015). Throughout the nineteenth century, the century of the modern emergence of the middle class, the question of how to combine capital and labor in factories – the archetypal unit of production – was left largely unaddressed (Park and Gould 2017). Indeed, although steam technology had brought new benefits and the allure of enhanced prosperity, finding a means for fully realizing such potential (the management problem) remained elusive. Two characteristics are notably about early progress in this area. The first concerns its piecemeal nature. For example, the Scottish industrialist, Robert Owen (1771–1858), in establishing himself as the first management theorist, used his textile mill in Lanark to experiment with methods for employee motivation (Joullié and Spillane 2015; Gould et al. 2017). In so doing, he created a specific sense of what worked on a case-by-case basis but provided no general theory. The second notable feature of initial commentary on management is its ideological bent. For example, early in the piece, Alexander Hamilton in his *Report on the Subject of Manufactures* (1791) extolled the transformative potential of a destabilizing new management middle class (Joullié and Spillane 2015). However, he was deafeningly silent on what the agents of capital should actually do within – and to – the workplace. Similarly, at first glance, Adam Smith's *Inquiry into the Nature and Causes of the Wealth of Nations* (1776) obliquely touches on the management problem but did so merely incidentally. Specifically, Smith portrayed his division of labor construct as an adaptive response to the virtues of market-based capital allocation (the invisible hand) rather than as having anything to do with the craft of governance. As such, a careful reading of Smith on this issue reveals that he was merely identifying job specialization as an emergent property of capitalist market economies. Indeed, he was mostly silent on the question of what management should or will do.

To reiterate, mainly because the West was the initial key beneficiary of steam technology, early exploration of the modern management challenge was typically a Western hemisphere concern. Whatever the case, the problem was largely solved – or at least well addressed – in the twentieth century. Scientific management (Taylorism and Fordism, etc.) provided initial generic insight and gave birth to the so-called "classical solution" (Robbins et al. 2015). Ultimately such a view of enterprise governance became large enough in scope to embrace, not just Frank and Lillian Gilbreth's fine-tunings vis-à-vis time and motion and appropriate use of tools (Robbins et al. 2015), but the more philosophically orientated contributions from Henri Fayol (1916) and Max Weber (Swedberg 1999). These latter theorists were not technicians with engineering or psychology backgrounds. Rather, they were industrial sociologists who concerned themselves with the rational nature of organizational life and how such nature can be tamed to achieve optimization. Subsequent solutions to the "how to" problem were often in conflict with the classical (or first) view. The most notable of these commenced with insights provided by the Hawthorne studies and the ensuing rise of the human relations movement emphasizing the roles played by psychological influences, particularly worker social-perception and attitudinal elements. Even more recently, for example, in the 1960s, systems and contingency theory has provided competing perspectives (Robbins et al. 2015). For present purposes, it is noteworthy that this entire corpus of scholarship (in other words all twentieth century consequential effort on the "how-to" question) established Western workplaces as its object of analytic interest. Furthermore, the aforementioned effort came from Western scholars influenced by the transformations that occurred in the wake of the industrial revolution and the parallel European enlightenment movement with its emphasis on sensory-informed reason. As such, key mainstream influences on how to manage were decidedly non-Asian.

Whilst those in Western management schools were making headway on the how-to problem, in the aftermath of the Second World War, another dilemma was looming. Indeed, commencing most explicitly with Durkheim's optimistic perspective of modernity (Durkheim 1893), but also having its theoretical roots in John T. Dunlop's systems view of industrial relations (Dunlop 1958), the research agenda was being forced to shift (or at least be augmented). The emerging conundrum no longer only concerned the question of the best way (or ways) as defined and debated by Western intellectuals but was now a matter of cultural comparison. Japan had been decimated at the end of the conflict that culminated in the allies dropping atomic bombs on its cities of Hiroshima and Nagasaki. Curiously, however, by the 1950s, the Rising Sun empire was well on the way to becoming an export-orientated economic powerhouse. Equally intriguingly, Russia was ravaged by Hitler's military adventurism on the Eastern front but was still able to beat the Americans in the space-race, launching "Sputnik," the first satellite, in 1957. Such impressively rapid reconstruction efforts, gave rise to two questions. Is it possible that non-Western cultures find superior ways of doing things? If so, would such better ways ultimately become universal? At this point, Japan, became – and has remained – of special relevance to the management research agenda. Hence, in asking about convergence, the theorist is really asking about the extent to which clever cultures vicariously learn from – and teach – each other. Given that a cursory reflection on Asia provides much support for the view that the region is replete with clever cultures, the more focused questions are: Does the West learn from Asia? If so, what does Asia teach the West? Setting aside the case of Japan, beguilingly and, as noted, these questions have never really been asked, let alone answered. They have certainly not been a central concern for those caught-up in debate about convergence, and, for example, the relative merits of institutionalism versus globalization. This matter will be further explored, however, in the meantime, it is appropriate to provide a defense of the proposition that historians of management generally and comparative employment relations scholars, more specially, are just not that interested in Asia. This task is now tackled.

Cummings et al. (2017) recently surveyed the world's most important journals of management and business history including the *Journal of Management History* (whose chief editor, Bowden, is one of the editors of this book series), *Business History*, and *the Business History Review*. Their objective was to establish the geographic focus of articles published in each journal since its first edition. Their conclusions were as follows. First, about 80% of the 2068 published articles did in fact have a geographic focus. Second, when they sent data on this matter to Worldmapper.org to create an image of relativities (Worldmapper.org specializes in distorting cartographic images to represent data), the regions of North America and Western Europe became massively bloated. Hence, they concluded that the United Kingdom and the United States attract the vast majority of scholarly attention; and, Japan, Australia, New Zealand, and South Africa are represented at a frequency that is roughly equivalent to their economic and demographic influence. However, the bulk of the non-Western parts of Asia, and the majority of Africa and South America are almost entirely off the analytic radar screen. Insofar as this chapter's scholarly preoccupation is concerned – the case of the region of Asia – such a circumstance raises the specter that Western-developed theory was created from an unduly narrow database and, hence, is not robust (i.e., fails to live up to its pretentions of being generic).

A distinctively Western scholarly preoccupation has been the issue of convergence. As noted, a key initial contributor to speculation about the subject was Emile Durkheim. Durkheim asserted that capitalist market economies are self-correcting and thus inclined to move their participants towards optimization and, in so doing, lift general living standards (Durkheim 1893; Godard 2017). He interpreted a key tenet of the Marxist view – that class-conflict is endemic to capitalism – to be largely ill-conceived (Godard 2017). Rather, his sanguine industrialization thesis was that such malaise, to the extent that it occurs, is an ephemeral teething pain; one that will vanish when preindustrial mechanistic solidarity (the collective consciousness possessed by those in feudal society) is replaced by organic solidarity (the interdependence that emerges among consumers and producers who are bound together through market-mediated relationships). In the mid-twentieth century, this genre of view of the trajectory of the industrial world was unambiguously being borne out by empirical evidence. For example, in the West, albeit under regimes of regulated state capitalism *a la* the New-Dealist prescription, the general population's material circumstances were improving (Thelan and Kume 2006). In such a *milieu*, later thinkers such as Clark Kerr considered how management and employment relations fit into the bigger picture. It is in the work of Kerr et al. (1960) that the convergence debate has its formal genesis.

Kerr et al.'s (1960) *magnum opus, Industrialism and Industrial Man* (Kerr et al. 1960) has two patently identifiable influences. The first of these is the (aforementioned) work of Durkheim who created much of the intellectual scaffolding for the argument that the capitalist production mode was not as disconsolate a prospect as had been predicted by Marx, or even Weber who proposed the necessity for a stultifying bureaucracy as a means of sustaining postindustrial revolution organizational existence (Weber 1961/1922). The second notable influence on Kerr et al. (1960) more directly pertained to management, specifically the industrial relations perspective of labor espoused two years earlier by John T. Dunlop. Dunlop wrote "Industrial Relations Systems" (1958) wherein he presented a view that interconnected elements give rise to what ends-up being recognized as a nation's distinctive approach to the reconciliation of capital and labor's discordant interests. These elements are the system's: actors (employers and their representatives, employees and their representatives, and government and its agencies); structural components (budget constraints, technology, power relations, and status of the actors and their respective labor management ideology), and the labor management ideology of the aforementioned actors. In proposing such an account, Dunlop was concerned to explain why certain rules are established within a given system and possibly even predict their establishment. His view was decidedly jurisdictional in nature. Hence, although aptly designated as systems-based, it is more precisely described as adopting a closed-system perspective of its subject matter. These shortcomings provided impetus for Kerr et al. (1960) whose contribution was, in a sense, to propose a more generalized perspective, imbuing Dunlop's original conception with both dynamic and international comparative elements.

Kerr et al.'s (1960) derivative (Durkheimian and Dunlopian) industrialization thesis was based on the proposition that – in a universal sense – management patterns can be viewed as embracing both unity and diversity components (Kaufman 2011). In Western capitalist market economies, the first of these, the unity element, ultimately emerges from industrialization's homogenizing influence, notably the establishment of large firms, bureaucratic employment regimes and organized labor movements. The second, the diversity element, comes from country-specific stimuli that may include such things as the priorities of ruling elites, as well as cultural, social, and ideological dissimilarity. It is noteworthy that the unity/diversity formulation establishes the Western construct of industrialization as of central causal importance. Thus, in a sense, it potentially excludes *a-priori* from consideration countries where such a construct does not apply or applies differently.

Implicit in the Kerr et al. industrialization thesis – at least as they originally formulated it – is that jurisdictionally distinctive features of labor management contribute to national economic development. More specifically, they argued that science and technology are consequential drivers of societal development and, as such, impose a homogenizing influence on global heterodoxy. To support this contention, they argued that there are five industrializing elite groups which each, in various ways, seek to install and elaborate technology (Gould et al. 2017). Eventually, these elites fleetingly amalgamate into two larger groups, a middle class and another cohort they identified as revolutionary intellectuals. Ultimately, there is a concluding fusion of such assemblages and the emergence of a new and enriched middle class. According to Kerr et al.'s (1960) derivative thesis, this "final" and enhanced middle class will be the same in all important respects for each country impacted by postindustrial revolution technology, no matter how dissimilar that country's national starting point.

Debate about convergence *à la* Kerr et al. (1960), and more broadly about industrialization, *à la* Durkheim and Dunlop influenced the emergence of the aforementioned enduring controversy about whether an ultimate international homogenization is inevitable. For example, at the dawn of the digital age, authors such as Fukuyama (1992) with his "End of History" thesis pushed the envelope on convergence, extending the construct to include elements other than those concerning management and employment relations. At a more practical level, Kerr et al.'s (1960) view has provided much of the rationale for the doctrine of best practice (Wood et al. 2014). Indeed, despite conjecture that convergence is at best partial (see, for example, Katz and Wailes 2014; Wailes et al. 2008; Djelic 2010; Katz and Darbishire's 2000, influential book, *Converging Divergences*), the – inherently Western – construct of economic development is ever-present in deliberation about emerging similarity in management philosophy and practice (Barry and Wilkinson 2011; Wilkinson et al. 2014). In the twenty-first century, two perspectives have come to represent the sides in this debate. On the one hand, there are globalizationists who contend that societies inevitably become more similar in how they do business. This view depicts national governments as increasingly boxed-in by forces that compel them to bid-down regulatory oversight in circumstances where capital searches out jurisdiction where it will yield the best return (Sewell 2008; Barry and Wilkinson 2011). Those pushing such a line typically cite as evidence for their position an international tendency to reduce labor costs, increase workforce flexibility, and find alternatives to labor unions. On the other hand, there are institutionalists who originally concerned themselves with economic phenomena in the immediate post-World War 2 years, went into hibernation for approximately four decades and, remerged as new-Institutionalists in the digital age. Insofar as management and employment relations are concerned, institutionalists eke out a middle ground between radical-Marxists and neo-liberalists (Kaufman 2011). For example, their recent proponents such as Kathleen Thelan (2004) and Richard Locke (1992) argue that the apparatus of the State is effective at absorbing, countering, or refracting technological and globalization-related homogenizing pressures. Somewhat incongruously, much of the early modern impetus for the renaissance of such a view came from Kerr himself who reentered the convergence debate. Specifically, in the wake of the charge of undue "technological determinism" (e.g., Doeringer 1981; Piore 1981), Kerr (1983) revised his industrialization thesis to account for the modulating role of institutional elements.

Aside from consideration of degree, another strand of debate about convergence – one with direct consequences for understanding Asia – concerns which jurisdiction will become the template. Conjecture about this matter has a special historical connotation because it puts the spotlight on one of Kerr et al.'s (1960) key implicit original assumptions, apparently influenced by a hegemonic cold war view that has come to be known in the modern era as American exceptionalism. This perspective is explicit in monographs published in the 1960s such as Daniel Bell's (1962) "The

End of Ideology" and W.W. Rostow's (1960) "The Stages of Economic Growth." These works propose that observed averaging effects and/or regression towards the mean are misleading and gloss-over the fact that other nations will embrace the United States' political economy blueprint (Goldthorpe 1984). Theorists such as Dore (1973) were not impressed with this thesis. His argument was that Japan, a nation that had instituted an idiosyncratic manufacturing production paradigm at least 100 years after Great Britain, would learn from mistakes made by Western countries and therefore emerge as the archetype for how to manage. Indeed, such a view seems reasonable in light of the fact that so much of the post-war Japanese economic renaissance was based on second mover advantage (essentially copying) (Gould 2014). For present purposes, in reflecting on Dore's contribution, it is instructive to note that, it is really only because of the case of Japan that non-Western Asian countries are included in debate about convergence.

Up to now, this chapter's discussion has focused on whether convergence is likely to happen and, if so, whether it will be partial or more comprehensive. The point was made that such discussion was largely oblivious to the non-Western experience. In recent years, aspects of the debate have become more sophisticated. Specifically, to reconcile data, some theorists have proposed and defended models of partial-convergence. Two of these that came at approximately the same time will be briefly examined below (e.g., Hall and Soskice's – 2001 – Varieties of Capitalism Theory and Katz and Darbishire's – 2000 – four pattern formulation). It is noteworthy that, in each of these cases, the object of scholarly interest is Western countries, thus excluding from analysis non-Western parts of Asia other than Japan.

Varieties of Capitalism

The Hall and Soskice's (2001) Varieties of Capitalism conception, as originally formulated, is a two-category taxonomy which establishes a distinction between liberal and coordinated market economies. According to the perspective, liberal market economies have well developed capital markets, "outsider" forms of corporate governance and use the market solution and contractual arrangements to regulate relations within value-chains as well as across sectors and industries. With respect to their management blueprints, they typically have high levels of labor flexibility concerning – in particular – hiring, firing, and remuneration. This arrangement creates relatively ephemeral employer-employee associations. Examples of liberal market economies include, most notably, the United States, Australia, New Zealand, Canada, Ireland, and the United Kingdom. By contrast, coordinated market economies (CMEs) have more "patient" forms of capital, "insider" approaches to corporate governance, nonmarket mechanisms for managing value chains (often industry-based regulatory regimes), and centrally managed horizontal connections within and across economic sectors. The governance blueprints for these kinds of countries are characterized by lessened scope for labor flexibility, widespread use of collective bargaining, comparatively more uniformity of wage outcome (including often seniority-based systems of promotion and appointment), and greater employment security or, at least, longer-term employment contracts. Germany, Japan, and Northern European countries are often touted as quintessential coordinated market economies (Dore 2000; Hall and Soskice 2001).

Varieties of Capitalism, as its title suggests, makes an initial delimiting assumption: that to be subject to classification, a country must be conspicuously capitalist, or at least use a market-mediated system for capital allocation. Perhaps partly as result of such initial implicit bias in how the framework was originally conceived, some Asian countries, such as Maoist China or North Korea, are not dealt with and indeed are excluded *a-priori* from consideration by definition (as noted, Japan is an exception). In this vein, despite attempts to expand its coverage – such as Waile's et al. (2008) conception of an Asian market economy which differentiates Japan in particular from nations such as twenty-first century China and South Korea – efforts to validate Hall and Soskice's original conception mostly examine the West (Walter and Zhang 2012; Wood and Frynas 2006). Sometimes the defense against such a near exclusive focus is that the Varieties of Capitalism typology is not designed for Asia (e.g., Witt and Redding 2014). This kind of justification may exonerate the framework from the charge that it is conceptually inadequate but is also tacit acknowledgement that, overall the view is not well adapted for interpreting post-industrial organizational and commercial life (Gould et al. 2015). A similar point has been made by Hay (2005) who portray Hall and Soskice's (2001) characterization as pertaining to varieties of two regional capitalisms rather than of world capitalism.

Katz and Darbishire's Four Pattern Formulation

Katz and Darbishire (2000) proposed a nuanced view about the nature of convergence that is influenced by precipitous union decline in the late twentieth century as well as two other elements. First, the view they propose attaches importance to the fact that, in spite of a Western implicit tendency towards parochialism and xenophobia, evidence suggests that the post-war Japanese management blueprint is unambiguously superior to the West's with respect to its capacity to inculcate quality, its labor flexibility provisions, and its emphasis on cost containment. Such advantages are especially pertinent to the all-important manufacturing sector. The second conspicuous influence on Katz and Darbishire's view comes from Richard Locke (1992) who, in looking at the case of Italy, concluded that there is no international tendency towards convergence on a common template. Indeed, Locke (1992) argued that even the construct of national-level blueprints is illconceived. Hence, in light of the possibility of underestimation of intranational variation, industries themselves should mostly be the elemental analytic focus. Given such phenomena, the compromise solution proposed by Katz and Darbishire (2000) was a partial convergence view based on the global emergence of four patterns: low wage, human resource management, Japanese oriented, and joint-team based. For present purposes, such a framework is relevant for two reasons. First, it is mostly inspired by the Western experience. Second, to the extent that it embraces the Japanese blueprint, it only does so because Japan has been impressive in outperforming Western countries simultaneously on several key industry benchmarks. In other words, whereas Western nations were included for analysis by default, Japan became part of the focus because of its patently superior economic performance.

Conclusion: Management Convergence in Asia

It was argued in this chapter that studying the philosophy and practice of management in Asia – broadly conceived – is an undertaking that holds the most promise for making progress on the convergence problem. The region's aforementioned diversity and the myriad comparisons that such variance allows will be the key to progress. Furthermore, it should not escape attention that, in the twentieth century, Asian countries experienced serious setbacks and, in some cases, near annihilation; mostly due to military conflict during the Second World War, and the wars in Korea, Vietnam, and Cambodia's (Kampuchea's) civil war. In each of these cases, national recovery efforts were astonishing, both in terms of their rapidity and sophistication. Such revitalization provides the prospect of outlier data for theorists interested in comparison and contrast. Hence, and to reiterate, when it comes to learning about convergence, Asia is – or should be – the new region of interest. Along the way, it is likely to also be where scholars get to fine-tune their understanding of the twentieth century's aforementioned "how-to" problem.

It was argued in this chapter that, despite Asia's latent educative potential, such prospect indeed remains merely latent. Rather, theory has emerged in the West in the postindustrial revolution/post-enlightenment period to deal, initially with the "how-to" problem and subsequently with the comparative dilemma. Although Japan and Western-style Asian countries have been included in theorizing about the comparative question, other parts of Asia have not. Such an oversight leaves open the door for future research opportunities – and makes imperative the reading of the next chapters of this volume. Indeed, the task now is to learn as much as possible about Asian countries that have been left off the research agenda. The goal is to determine what the individual and collective experiences of these countries may add to theory about convergence so that such theory really does become generic.

In concluding, this volume summarizes key trends in management for selected Asian countries in the latter half of the twentieth century. The reader is encouraged to reflect on ideas presented in this chapter when considering the experience of individual countries. In the case of Australia and New Zealand, there has been a shift away from an emphasis on employee welfare and a concomitant move towards decentralized and individual bargaining. In the case of Japan, there has been perpetuation of an approach that was largely put in place after the Second World War. In the case of South Korea, there has been augmentation of an export-oriented industrial growth strategy with a capacity to change in response to evolving international circumstances. In the case of China and Indonesia, there has been a commitment to embrace basic standards of employee welfare and Western-style work-related institutions. Hence, in summary, for countries that have come from an employee-centered approach to labor management, the Nation-State now has less influence. Whereas, for those countries emerging from a background of military dictatorship or suppression of human rights, the changes that have so-far occurred are transitional. Nonetheless, they appear to be oriented towards establishing management strategies based on a commitment to global trade and an international commercial focus.

Cross-References

- ▶ Governmentality and the Chinese Workers in China's Contemporary Thought Management System
- ▶ In Search of the Traces of the History of Management in Latin America, 1870–2020
- ▶ Indian Management (?): A Modernization Experiment
- ▶ Introduction: Management Heterogeneity in Asia
- ▶ Management History in the Modern World: An Overview
- ▶ Management in Australia – The Case of Australia's Wealthiest Valley: The Hunter
- ▶ The Making of a Docile Working Class in Pre-reform China
- ▶ Think Big and Privatize Every Thing That Moves: The Impact of Political Reform on the Practice of Management in New Zealand
- ▶ What Is Management?

References

Barry M, Wilkinson A (eds) (2011) Research handbook of comparative employment relations. Edward Elgar, Cheltenham

Bell D (1962) The end of ideology. On the exhaustion of political ideas in the fifties. The Free Press, New York

Cummings S, Bridgman T, Hassard J, Rowlinson M (2017) A new history of management. Cambridge University Press, New York

Djelic M-L (2010) Institutional perspectives – working towards coherence or irreconcilable diversity? In: Morgan G, Campbell J, Crouch C, Pedersen OK, Whitey R (eds) The Oxford handbook of comparative institutional analysis. Oxford University Press, Oxford/New York

Doeringer PB (1981) Industrial relations research in international perspective. In: Doeringer PB, Gourevitch P, Lang P, Martin A (eds) Industrial relations in international perspective: essays on research and policy. McMillan, London, pp 1–21

Dore R (1973) British factory, Japanese factory: the origins of national diversity in industrial relations. Allen and Unwin, London

Dore R (2000) Stock market capitalism. Welfare capitalism. Cambridge University Press, Cambridge

Dunlop J (1958) Industrial relations systems. Holt, New York

Durkheim E (1893) The division of labour in society (trans: Halls WD; intro: Coser LA). The Free Press, New York, 1997

Fukuyama F (1992) The end of history and the last man. Hamish Hamilton, London

Godard J (2017) Industrial relations, the economy and society, 5th edn. Captus Press, Ontario

Goldthorpe JH (1984) The end of convergence: corporatist and dualist tendencies in modern Western societies. In: Goldthorpe JH (ed) Order and conflict in contemporary capitalism: studies in the political economy of Western European nations. Clarendon, Oxford, pp 315–343

Gould A (2014) Le travail et l'emploi après la crise globale financière: émergence d'un nouveau agenda de recherche dans un monde en état de choc. In: Thwaites JD (ed) La Mondialisation: origines, développement et effets. Les Presses de l'Université Laval, Québec

Gould AM, Barry M, Wilkinson A (2015) Varieties of capitalism revisited current debates and possible controversies. Ind Relat 70(4):603–621

Gould AM, Bourk MJ, Joullié JE (2017) From the industrial revolution to trump: six periods of changing perceptions of American business managers. J Manag Hist 23(4):471–488

Hall P, Soskice D (2001) An introduction to the varieties of capitalism. In: Hall P, Soskice D (eds) Varieties of capitalism: the institutional basis of competitive advantage. Oxford University Press, Oxford, pp 1–68

Hay C (2005) Two can play at that game …. can they? Varieties of capitalism, varieties of institutionalism. In: Coates D (ed) Varieties of capitalism, varieties of approaches. Palgrave Macmillan, Basingstoke, pp 106–121

Joullié JE, Spillane R (2015) The philosophical foundations of management thought. Lexington Books, Sydney

Katz H, Darbishire O (2000) Converging divergences: worldwide changes in employment systems. Cornell University Press, New York

Katz H, Wailes N (2014) Convergence and divergence in employment relations. In Wilkinson A, Wood G, Deeg R (ed) The Oxford handbook of Employment Relations. Oxford University Press, Oxford

Kaufman B (2011) Comparative employment relations: institutional and neo-institutional theories. In: Barry M, Wilkinson A (eds) Research handbook of comparative employment relations. Edward Elgar, Cheltenham

Kerr C (1983) The future of industrial societies: Convergence or continuing diversity? Harvard University Press, Cambridge Mass

Kerr C, Dunlop JT, Harbison FH, Myers CA (1960) Industrialism and industrial man: the problems of labour and management in economic growth. Penguin, London

Locke RM (1992) The decline of the national union in Italy. Lessons for comparative industrial relations theory. Ind Labor Relat Rev 45(1):229–249

Park KM, Gould AM (2017) The overlooked influence of personality, idiosyncrasy and eccentricity in corporate mergers and acquisitions: 120 years and six distinct waves. J Manag Hist 23(1):7–31

Piore M. (1981) Convergence in industrial relations? The case of France and the United States. Working paper no 286. Massachusetts Institute of Technology, Department of Economics, Cambridge, MA

Robbins SP, Coulter M, Sidani Y, Jamali D (2015) Management, 2nd edn. Pearson Educatioon Limited, London

Rostow WW (1960) The stages of economic growth: a non-Communist Manifesto. Cambridge University Press, Cambridge

Sewell W (2008) The temporalities of capitalism. Soc Econ Rev 6(3):517–537

Swedberg R (1999) Max Weber as an economist and as a sociologist. Am J Econ Sociol 58(4):561–582

Thelan K (2004) How institutions evolve: the political economy of skills in Germany, Britain, the United States and Japan. Cambridge University Press, New York

Thelan K, Kume I (2006) Coordination as a political problem in coordinated market economies. Governance 19(1):11–42

Wailes N, Kitay J, Lansbury R (2008) Varieties of capitalism, corporate governance and employment relations under globalization. In: Marshall S, Ramsay I (eds) Varieties of capitalism, corporate governance and employees. Melbourne University Press, Melbourne, pp 19–38

Walter A, Zhang X (2012) Understanding variations and changes in East Asian capitalism. In: Walter A, Zhang X (eds) East Asian capitalism: diversity continuity and change. Oxford University Press, Oxford, pp 247–280

Weber M (1961/1922) General economic history (trans: Knight FH). Collier McMillan, New York

Wilkinson A, Wood G, Deeg R (2014) Comparative employment systems. In: Wilkinson A, Wood G, Deeg R (eds) The Oxford handbook of employment relations: comparative employment systems. Oxford University Press, Oxford

Witt MA, Redding G (2014) The spirits of corporate social responsibility. The Head Foundation working paper

Wood G, Frynas G (2006) The institutional basis of economic failure: anatomy of the segmented business system. Soc Econ Rev 4:239–277

Wood G, Dibben P, Ogden S (2014) Comparative capitalism without capitalism and production without workers: the limits and possibilities of contemporary institutional analysis. Int J Manag Rev 16:384–396

Indian Management (?): A Modernization Experiment

58

Nimruji Jammulamadaka

Contents

Introduction	1332
Questions, Hypotheses, and the Course of Indian Management Development	1333
Illegalization of Traditional Work Organization	1334
State-Driven Institutionalization of Management Education	1340
Indianizing Management Education	1344
Developing Instruments and Concepts for India	1345
Self-criticism of Management in India	1345
Conclusion	1348
Cross-References	1348
References	1349

Abstract

This chapter explores the history of the emergence of management as a discipline and professional practice in India. By tracing the history of commerce education into the British period, the chapter argues that modern management in India emerged with a strong association with English language in the midst of the colonial encounter. Postindependence in 1947, this English emphasis continued. It grew through the import of a discipline from United States of America, under the modernizing aspirations of a newly independent country struggling with inferiority and developmental challenges. And in order to meet India's development challenges, Indianizing management was attempted by invoking ancient Indian texts, or adapting models and techniques to India's socio-economic and cultural context. Nevertheless, management in India has remained tethered to core Western management theories and concepts.

N. Jammulamadaka (✉)
Indian Institute of Management Calcutta, Kolkata, India
e-mail: nimruji@iimcal.ac.in

© The Author(s), under exclusive licence to Springer Nature Switzerland AG 2020
B. Bowden et al. (eds.), *The Palgrave Handbook of Management History*,
https://doi.org/10.1007/978-3-319-62114-2_66

Keywords

Indian · British colonialism · Management practice · Bombay textile mills · Traditional work organization · IIMs · Ford Foundation

Introduction

Modern management as a body of knowledge and practices is generally understood to have emerged in tandem with modern industrialization and technological developments in the West in the late eighteenth and early nineteenth centuries, subsequently spreading to the various European colonies and to other parts of the globe. Following the World Wars, it has had an accelerated exportation and/or diffusion into the rest of the world. In such narrations of *history* of management, it is possible to ignore the intricate relationship of developments in *modern* West such as industrialization, with colonization (Bhambra 2014). However, in attempting a narration of history of management in an ex-colony such as India, it is close to impossible to disentangle the emergence of management as an occupation, institution, and academic discipline from colonization. Modern management in India emerged in the midst of the colonial encounter and it grew under the modernizing aspirations of a newly independent country struggling with inferiority and developmental challenges. Contemporary discussions on management in India, even after seven decades of independence, still bear the imprint of colonial modernizing experience. Indian management is yet to figure out what is Indian in its management.

The present chapter elaborates upon this idea. Often essays on management education in India take the setting up of Indian Institutes of Management in the late 1950s and early 1960s as the starting point. But this essay goes further back and closely examines the colonial encounter and the tryst with western modernity in the creation of the occupation and discipline of management. The chapter is organized into four sections. The first section provides an overview of Indian context of work organization and industry. The second section provides an overview of the situation during the colonial encounter. While British made their presence felt in India much before 1860, the discussion here generally looks at the period after 1860, when the British crown took over the administration of India from the British East India Company after the "Indian Mutiny," an alteration in circumstance that created new institutional contexts for work organization and production such as legal and educational systems. This continued till 1947 when India became independent. This was the period during which not only were many modern industries set up in India, but management and manager entered the Indian vocabulary (Birla 2009; Morris 1965). The third section describes the scenario during the dawn of independence which articulated a felt need for "management" as a discipline and occupation. The fourth section explores issues encountered by management as a full-fledged established discipline in India and the attempts made for Indianizing it. The chapter ends with a few conclusions.

Questions, Hypotheses, and the Course of Indian Management Development

India had had quite a productive system of work organization within its largely home-based cottage enterprise agrarian economy. It was a system that was personalized, with the household as the locus and based on traditional occupational groups and communities (along with dependent labor), rather than slave labor of the kind found elsewhere in the world. This informal system was supported by a guild like corporate arrangement known as *srenis* in which producers and traders of specific products/occupations participated (Coomaraswamy 1908, 1909; Ghoshal 1930; Majumdar 1920; Mookerji 1919) as well as a unique social organization known as *jajmani* system (a symbiotic relationship within the Indian social structure) that did not necessitate the emergence of a market-mediated exchange transactions (Seth 2015). With the rise of the Mughal Empire in 1500s, such household production was accompanied by the gradual development of a "traditional flexible manufacturing system" in which artisanal producers had limited independence and depended more on merchants and traders (Seth 2015). These systems of work organization managed to generate enough surplus to support India's thriving international trade. Trade and other production activity – excluding agriculture – contributed to 37% of the national income around 1600, a date when the British had not yet entered India (Maddison 2007: 123). High quality wootz steel, for instance, was made from sixth century B.C. in home furnaces, and exported to various parts of the world. It was even used by Egyptians (Srinivasan and Ranganathan 1997).

In the early eighteenth century, it is estimated that India had a 22.6% share of world GDP (Das 2006) suggesting that the systems of work organization and production that India had been following were working for it. It is into this household and community-based flexible work organization that modern western industry and modern western bureaucratic organization entered under British colonial rule, which began in the 1700s. At this juncture, several lines of questioning are possible. Had India not been colonized, would it still have beaten the path to such industrialization? If yes, what could have been its course? A second line of questioning could be whether India would have appropriated modern western management knowledge and practice (as a part of broader education efforts), the way it has had, had it not been colonized, but had it retained its autonomy and sovereignty (Basu 1974). One response has been to simply associate British colonialism with modern technological advancements and argue that but for British, India could never have entered industrialization and modern management. Another view has been to point to native attempts at technological development as evidence of India's own attempts at industrialization and contend that the nation's industry, work organization, and management might have evolved differently, more in line with its ethos. However, passionate such debates, they are mostly in the realm of the counterfactual. This chapter therefore does not engage in any debate about what might have occurred. Instead, it focuses solely on the turn of events and the course of management thought and practice as it occurred in India during the British period and in the early years after independence. By the time of independence in 1947, India was an impoverished nation and a laggard in modern industrialization.

Central to the modern economic and managerial transformation of India were the railways, one of the earliest modern industries to be set up in India. Established in 1830s and managed by the British, it followed a western bureaucratic style of management. Indians were employed at the shopfloor level as wage laborers and as jobbers who coordinated gangs of workmen. Just like railways, many other industries such as mining, jute mills, water ways were also owned and managed by British (Morris 1965). Since the ownership was far away, in England, a system of managing agent firms based in India was developed to manage operations in India (Prasad and Negandhi 1968). Managers were almost always British or Scottish. A British bureaucratic model of management and administration was adopted for most business organization and administration, a model which also aimed at extracting the most surplus from workers. However, the usual Indian workers combined industrial wage labor with other occupations such as agriculture which had a seasonal character to it and took regular and long absences from work (in keeping with the traditional flexible production system, there were exceptions of industries like tea plantations where workers suffered inhumanly) (Varma 2014). In order to induce workers to come back to the enterprise on a regular basis, British resorted to several interventions such as setting up of liquor shops at the gates of enterprises so that workmen spent all their wages, thereby being forced to seek more work (see Simeon 1999 for examples of strategies proposed by the British to induce workers to come back to work). The general trade and commercial environment and policy such as business law, labor laws, tariffs favored the interests of the empire more than the colony (Chandavarkar 1994; Jammulamadaka 2016). Domestic industry suffered serious setbacks (Chandavarkar 1994). Consequently, in the period between 1600 and 1947, Indian per capita income rose a meager 12%. By comparison, British per capita income rose nearly seven fold during the same period (Maddison 2007: 120). The next section discusses the gradual process of illegalization of the Indian work organization and the way in which the need for western managerial practices and education was created within the country.

Illegalization of Traditional Work Organization

During the British period, most production and commercial activity came under British control and industry. Mining, railways, jute mills, water works, and other major industries were owned and managed through British firms. In most cases, the managers were British or Scottish (IIC 1916–18). The management style not only had the imprint of industrial Britain but also a markedly civilizing flavor to it. Views such as "Labour, in its **ignorance,** is certain to make **unreasonable** demands which could not be granted without destroying industry" (Sir Alexander Murray, Report of the Committee on Industrial Unrest, 1920-1, cited in Chakrabarty 1983, emphasis in Chakrabarty) were common. In such industries, it is therefore unlikely that we can explore the workings of native organizing practices, since Indians did not have managerial authority in those places. To the extent Indians participated in these industries, they were confined to the shop floor, although some jobbers – who recruited local workers and subcontracted tasks – performed some lower-level supervisory functions (especially arranging labor supply since they belonged to the same communities).

Under British rule, there was only one industry, the textile industry of Bombay, which was dominated by Indians (Morris 1965). Bombay's textile industry, therefore, provides the opportunity to examine the colonial encounter in styles of work organization and management more closely, given that Indian owners and managers actually had the scope to do things their way and the flash points between Indian work organization and the Western approach can be observed.

The first spinning mill to be set up in Bombay was the work of an Indian in 1854, the machinery having been imported from England. Also imported into this pioneer mill were the managerial and technical staff, all of whom were drawn from Britain. Despite this initial British managerial domination, by 1895 Indians formed half the staff of managerial levels. Indians thus not only owned, managed (as both managing agent firms and managers) but also supervised as jobbers and worked on the shop floor. Here the mill had substituted the household as the locus of production. Other features of traditional flexible production systems (Seth 2015), such as relationships of communities, kinship, geographies, which sustained and organized production (or transactions in the parlance of transaction cost economics) in the household-communitarian form, continued into the mills. An informal, personalized network that spanned both within the mill and outside into the neighborhood existed. Similar to an autonomous household form, this network sustained individual autonomy of various levels of employees including workers, jobbers, managers, and owners. Even individual mill owners valued their autonomy and resisted collusion or employer collective action (Chandavarkar 1994; Morris 1965). Similar to the traditional communitarian model, the networks in the mills had reputations as an integral governing and risk managing mechanism in which the autonomy of the various members of the work organization became the basis for regular conflict both within and outside the mill. Such conflict instead of leading to breakdowns, however, more often than not formed the basis for co-operation. Conflict and resistance triggered the pursuit of dialogue and eventually cooperation (Chandavarkar 1994; Jammulamadaka 2016). Such outcomes acted to mediate intense economic competition which was a regular feature of this industry, as any perusal of the annual reports of the mill owners' association will show.

The system that applied in the Indian-owned and managed mills markedly differed from the British approach of administrative fiat as the basis of organization. Even though on paper, a similar managerial hierarchy was described, in practice, it was anything but a British work organization (Morris 1965). Organizational hierarchy and reporting relationships of a bureaucracy were not followed. Family and other traditional ties of kinship, caste, and village formed the basis for negotiating employment and job performance. This was a reflection of Indian societal character, where the public and private are not treated as "distinct, a priori spheres" (Birla 2009). Thus, work in the mill and personal life overlapped and influenced each other as a matter of routine. Workers combined industrial wage labor with other occupations such as agriculture which had a seasonal character to it. The first generation of industrial workers were mostly peasants, Indians drawn from tribal regions, and other traditional occupational communities. An individual worker's seasonal absence was managed at the mill and industry level by having a surplus of labor who worked in the mills. Decentralized authority, work sharing, and flexible labor deployment allowed management of surplus labor, tolerable working conditions, and ongoing skill development. Even though mill level labor productivity was low in contrast to other countries, it allowed workers to pursue their other, more personal and community-oriented objects. It allowed mills to manage their risk of sustaining a higher level of employment than was suggested by normal managerial dictates, a level that allowed businesses to adjust comfortably to business and economic fluctuations. Contrast this with the approach followed by British-based practices. To induce labor to continue in the enterprise, managerial practice sought to make workers dependent on the mill (Simeon 1999), restricting waged employment to the minimum number of hands necessary as per the Tariff Board's rationalization measures (Chandavarkar 1994, 2008).

Within the Bombay mills, employees and owners maintained personal networks of information which enabled decision making (Jammulamadaka 2016). Decision making and management was not a "scientific approach" to production. Instead, it was driven by trust, contingency, pragmatism, proprietary and embodied job knowledge and insights, social network capitals, and flexible and "excess" labor deployment (Chandavarkar 1994). Power and authority was diffused within the organization and provided enough autonomy at all levels to safeguard personal interests even as organizational interests were satisfied (Jammulamadaka 2016). These systems operated even in large mills employing over a 1000 people (Morris 1965).

Bombay mills, even though a modern industry that was technically imported from Britain (in terms of machinery, early managers, and technicians), survived great competition and highly adverse policy environment through its native work organization and managerial practices. It continued to be competitive in the global context of the time (Jammulamadaka 2016). The success of these mills elicited British interventions both for retaining imperial control and subordinating Indian economic interest to British manufacture. Slowly over a period of several decades, a range of laws such as the *Factories Act, Payment of Wages Act, Industrial Disputes Act, Trade Union Act* were enacted between 1881 and 1945 and applied to Indian industry (Chandavarkar 1994; Kydd 1920; Jammulamadaka 2016, 2018). Combined with the fervor of nationalist freedom struggle (for instance, the Civil Disobedience Movement of 1930, Quit India Movement in 1942), the debilitating strikes which hit the textile mills (between 1921and 1938, there were 430 strikes in Bombay, see Wolcott (2008)) provided a perfect opportunity for such British legal interventions (Chandavarkar 1994; Jammulamadaka 2016). These interventions consistently illegalized and forbid traditional managerial practices of coordinating production such as jobber system, informal employment systems, flexible labor use, use of temporary *(badli)* workers, shopfloor or neighborhood based conflict resolution, personal dialogue, and intervention for conflict resolution (Jammulamadaka 2016, 2018). "*...colonial officialdom interpreted the characteristic use of informality,* *discretion and protest in Bombay mills as evidence of cavalierness, whimsicality, exploitation, indiscipline and inefficiency, thereby denigrating mill practices in public and official discourse*" (Jammulamadaka 2016: 463).

In lieu of the traditional Indian systems, the British legal and Tariff Board interventions enforced a bureaucratic and impersonal system that ostensibly pursued profits and efficiency, onto the mill organization. Mill owners resisted such imposition tooth and nail, as their practices supported profits, efficiency, risk sharing, and autonomy. However, mill owners had to bow to the colonial authority and accept the "law" of the land, even though it not only violated the ethos of the land but also interfered with those features that enabled the industry to be competitive.

The Indian managing-agent firm itself posed a contrast to British managing-agent firms. Indian firms were defined by family-based patriarchal ownership and succession within the family network in contrast to a firm partner succession in British firms (Prasad and Negandhi 1968). The Indian practice emerged in the context of a tradition of nonseparation between the firm and the family (Birla 2009) and continuity of occupations within the community structure. However, these practices came under the continuous onslaught of modern bureaucratic organization propagated by British both in public discourse and in law. They acquired a pejorative and illegitimate patina (Jammulamadaka 2018; Prasad and Negandhi 1968) over time. Under colonial rule, these communitarian and informal production systems were perceived as a less modern or primitive form, rather than a different system of production. It was anticipated that this "primitive form" would be replaced by modern industrial organization. Newer and western systems of accounting and book keeping were also introduced rendering traditional forms of book keeping illegitimate. Such silencing, illegitimization, and destruction of native work practices occurred in spite of the fact that India's work practices and the ensuing performance were helping the country stay relevant in the scheme of the Empire. In a speech, in 1898 the Viceroy Lord Curzon said,

> *...whereas if we lost India, I maintain that our sun would sink to its setting...I find that the total sea borne trade for India for 1896–97 which was an unprosperous year...constituted nearly one-tenth of the trade of the whole British empire and was more than one-third of the trade of the whole empire outside of the United Kingdom...* (Speeches of Lord Curzon, GOI 1900: xxiv–xxv).

He further adds about the "*extraordinary recuperative power of the country*" "*...there has quite recently been a devastating famine in the country, and yet after the complete disappearance of the famine, India exported by sea more produce than in any previous half year...*" (p. xxv). By 1914, India had the world's third largest railway network in the world, largest jute industry, fourth largest cotton textile industry, and largest canal system and still retained 2.5% of world trade (Das 2006). However, the imprint of British industrial organization and a bureaucratic management style had come to stay.

The combined effect of continuous illegalization of traditional work organizing practices and an "orientalist" view on India was to create within the governing classes, a sense that Indians lacked the necessary "managerial skills and knowledge" required for modern industrial organization, i.e., managerial knowledge that was possessed only in the west. Even though Indians formed almost 70% of the managerial class in India by 1921 (Prasad and Negandhi 1968, citing Buchanan 1934), the lament was about lack of managerial skills and knowledge since they had not got adequate opportunities for training (IIC 1916–18).

The orientalist view – propounded and propagated by the likes of William Jones and Colebridge – located the performative greatness of Indian practices in a distant unknown past and in ancient texts and painted extant practices and society as a quagmire of decay and poverty. Under this view, it was also the solemn responsibility of the British to help India rediscover its past (through interpretation of texts) and marry it with the present. Such British intervention and recasting of India was presented as the only way out of the decay and into a reinvigorated sense of Indian greatness, a greatness that would see India secure its place in modernity (Niranjana 1992). This ideology made its way into the country's psyche through the British education system that was introduced in 1835. Though the British system initially emphasized higher education, by 1868, Lord Curzon had recognized that primary education was necessary to ensure a successful British administration and neutralize the opposition of educated Indian elite to British rule. British education system and policy thereby emphasized both primary and higher education. In the 5 year period from 1868 to 1873, primary school enrolment had increased by 25% (Basu 1974). This expansion of modern English education occurred even as traditional educational systems were being destroyed (Coomaraswamy 1908; Dharampal 1983). These interventions deemed most Indian cultural and social practices as inferior just as the Indian industrial organization itself was posited as inferior and inefficient. These led to the development of a sense of "inferiority" within the Indian psyche (Das 2006; Nandy 1994; Niranjana 1992). So deep was this sense of inferiority that even several nationalist leaders such as Nehru, India's first prime minister, began looking up to British and Western education as the means through which India could redeem itself and claim its "rightful" place it had had in global history (Jammulamadaka 2018; Nandy 1994). In subsequent years, pre- and post-independence, India's status as an underdeveloped, Third World, developing country was entrenched (Sauvy 1952, in Economist 2010), adding to the national sense of inferiority.

Together, orientalism and illegalization of traditional practice helped create a context in which Indian demand for Western education in management became an entrenched feature of national life. In highlighting the supposed need for Western management education, the Indian Industrial Commission of 1916–18, for example, declared, *"To create an industrial organisation in this country comparable to that of western nations, to build up an industrial community capable of working such an organisation, certain positive measures were required, including the provision of industrial and technical education ..."* (IIC 1916–18: 92). The first formal training in commerce education in Asia was started in October 1913 at the Sydenham College in Bombay (www.sydenham.ac.in). In terms of content, this new management education differed from the traditional jobber system (and even contemporary management) in that there was little emphasis on developing capabilities in managing people. Instead, as the Industrial Commission's report observed about Sydenham's training, the education's focus was directed towards understanding the bureaucratic norms of British firms, it being reported that:

> It is obviously-beneficial to any Indian about to engage in commerce, who desires to rise above the rank of a clerk...[that education] should provide teaching in shorthand, typewriting, the methods of book-keeping and precis writing and, **above all, in modern English**. These subjects may be regarded as essential for the routine working of an office, but to them should **be added instruction** in the mechanism of banking, exchange, and foreign trade, together with such subjects as commercial geography and **a detailed study of the economic resources of India**. (p.116, emphasis added).

Governing classes both within Britain and India were acutely aware of the paucity of such modern commercial business training for Indians. The IIC report drew attention to this several times. It stated, "... *The opportunities for gaining experience were not easy for Indians to come by, and there was no attempt at technical training for industries until nearly the turn of the century, and then only on an inadequate scale.*" (p. 92). In critiquing existing government educational provisioning for business, the report stated,

> ... the system of education introduced by Government was, at the outset, mainly intended to provide for the administrative needs of the country and encouraged literary and philosophic studies to the neglect of those of a more practical character. **In the result it created a disproportionate number of persons possessing a purely literary education, at a time when there was hardly any form of practical education in existence** (p. 92, emphasis added).

Management training was already being understood as a "practical" education similar to technical and engineering training. Such "practical education" was positioned in stark contrast to "not-so-practical" literary/philosophical education. Such dichotomizing of education on the practical/impractical divide was a significant departure from traditional Indian artisanal systems of occupational training. In these household-based artisanal systems, aesthetic-technical-commercial logics were combined in a wholistic way. It was during this period in Indian history that a material division between practical and not-so-practical education emerged and practical education became privileged – a perception which continues even today in India.

By the 1920s, as the Indian independence movement began to gain momentum, Indian industrialists began asserting themselves much more. Private philanthropy also helped foster an expansion of commercial education (Jammulamadaka 2018). Much of this training was of the kind offered by Sydenham College, with a particular emphasis on the conventions of British business organization and English language. Commercial education, however, also occurred alongside an expansion of nascent engineering and technical education institutions whose educational efforts were explicitly focused on supporting industry (IIC 1916–18). By 1947–1948, there were 38 technical institutes offering degree-level courses. Collectively, these degree-level institutions had the capacity to train 2940 students. Another 3960 students were being trained annually in 53 diploma-level institutions (Phillip and Narayan 1989).

State-Driven Institutionalization of Management Education

Preparatory to India's independence in 1947, a group of eight leading Indian industrialists issued what came to be known as the Bombay Plan of 1944, a plan that sought to overcome Indian lack of private capital and capability through a socialistic pattern of development that emphasized state-intervention. To overcome continual shortfalls in terms of managerial education and training, in 1945 the All India Council for Technical Education was set up. The need for such a body was evident because, when India became independent in 1947, there was not a single postgraduate course in engineering or commerce (Phillip and Narayan 1989).

With the inauguration of an independent Indian nation in 1947, much of the legal framework laid down by the British with regards to business continued as it was. Even though Companies Act was amended to account for problems of managing agency system, labor and other laws stayed the same (Kennedy 1958, 1965). Consequently, the illegal status of "traditional ways of managing" that began during British times continued even in independent India. Further, modernizing aspirations of national elite provided the impetus for the next phase of growth in management education in the country. The first Prime Minister, Nehru, placed an emphasis on heavy industry, science, and technology as the mantra for Indian modernization. Whether it was large hydel power projects, research institutes, or core engineering and industries, all of them were set up as government entities and designed along the lines of Western industrial bureaucracies.

Reflecting the broad support for state intervention in the economy, post-independence economic policy hinged in a series of 5 Year Plans, Plans whose implementation was accompanied by the formation of a large number of state owned enterprises. These enterprises were typically headed by civil servants, who neither had the traditional knowhow of indigenous business organizations nor the entrepreneurial courage of innovative Western firms. Prime Minister Nehru's assessment of Indian managerial acumen was not flattering. At the Annual Meeting of the Federation of the Indian Chamber of Commerce and Industry in 1949 he said, *"Generally the idea is spreading that their [senior management] stature is rather small and that they get frightened at the slightest upset and start complaining and retiring into their shells and asking others to help them."* (cited in Dasgupta 1968: 7). Unlike Gandhi, he also did not hold industrialists and capitalists in much regard (Sundar 2000). Such beliefs bolster the desire for a formal training in modern western management for existing captains of industry. It was expected that such training would help overcome traditional business "inefficiencies" and enable educated risk-taking and contribute to India's growth.

Echoing earlier views of Indian Industrial Commission (1916–1918), trained management was seen as arguably India's scarcest natural resource, a scarcity that was holding back the country's industrial growth. However, by this time commerce education or the Bachelor of Commerce degree had fallen out of grace. By contrast, "scientific management" and an MBA degree was catching up, it being held true that the utilization of modern management techniques was of particular importance in industrial engineering and associated operations.

During the first Plan period of 1951–1956, the All India Council for Technical Education (AICTE) was tasked with ensuring a trained workforce for achieving India's planned industrialization. In 1951–1952, a special committee of AICTE examined the need for specialized management courses. Based on the Committee's recommendations, a Board of Management Studies was set up in 1953 under the Education Ministry. Pursuant to the Board's recommendations, part-time, postgraduate level management courses for junior executives were started in four universities in Calcutta, Delhi, Madras, and Bombay. These management courses were positioned differently from the commerce courses of the previous era. Two tracks were envisaged. The first track provided training in business administration for arts and commerce graduates. The second track instructed engineering students in industrial administration (Chandrakant 1973; Dasgupta 1968; Hill et al. 1973). Part-time courses were preferred as universities had no prior experience in teaching management courses. The Board of Management Studies – anxious that the MBA should not "*degenerate... to the level of the much-criticised B.Com degree*" – exercised considerable oversight, even providing specific recommendations as to course content (Chandrakant 1973: 17). Despite such interventions, the "management" courses taught at the universities overseen by the Board were typically designed based on foreign text books and practices that were in vogue in advanced countries of the time. Indian adaptation was carried out by "*including appropriate topics in different subjects in order to make the participants aware of the country's industrial and other characteristics and their impact on management*" (Dasgupta 1968: 65). Eventually, the first full time MBA program patterned on a Harvard style MBA was initiated in Andhra University in 1957 by Professor Das who had returned from Harvard (www.andhrauniversity.edu.in), an outcome that indicated the primacy given to Western-based models in general and the United States-based educational models in particular.

To meet the specific management training needs of senior executives, the Administrative Staff College of India (ASCI) was set up in 1957 under joint business and government oversight (Chandrakant 1973; Dasgupta 1968, Hill et al. 1973; Sinha 2004). Patterned on London's Henley College, the Staff College offered 12-week general management courses. Not a single faculty member was an academic. Faculty were instead drawn from distinguished industry practitioners and a syndicate method was followed for imparting training (Sinha 2004). The syndicate method involved facilitating experience sharing and problem-solving in groups with participants drawn from the same organization. The success of the ASCI initiative in building the capacity of senior management in Indian industry and bureaucracy can be ascertained in the fact that the Government increasingly looked towards ASCI for building managerial capacity in state-owned enterprises.

Another important change was heralded in 1952 when the Ford Foundation established offices in India under the direction of Douglas Ensminger, the organization's head in India. Ensminger was a man who believed that India would have developed differently if it had thrown out the British pattern of liberal education with the same intensity with which it threw out British (Staples 1992: 32). Ensminger was aware of India's deficit in "managerial capacity" and responded by establishing a long-term institution building program under the Foundation's umbrella. Ensminger's plans for institution building found ready resonance within the Indian elite establishment including the likes of Prime Minister Nehru, Minister for Scientific Research and Cultural Affairs Prof. Humanyun Kabir, Vikram Sarabhai, and other industrialists who shared modernist aspirations and believed in the superior capabilities of the West and United States. Ensminger cultivated the view that India's economic growth would be more effectively fostered if the nation abandoned British-style training in commerce and adopted instead the United States' system of managerial education, a system that gave a preeminent place to Masters in Business Administration (MBA) programs. To foster support for American-style management education, the Ford Foundation, over many years, systematically sponsored awareness visits to American business schools of chosen members of India's elite, visits that helped impress the benefits of American management education and scientific techniques over educational systems that focused on the liberal arts. The Ford Foundation was also seminal in the creation of an All India Management Association, funding senior management training programs both through ASCI and outside of it. All this served to create a market in the country for American management education (Taylor 1976; Jammulamadaka 2017; Sancheti 1986; Staples 1992). The post-War shift in the global balance of economic and military power also had an effect on education as India increasingly looked towards United States for exemplars in its pursuit of industrial growth directed towards the establishment of a modern industrial economy (Jammulamadaka 2017). Summing up the general view, Professor Dasgupta (1968: 169) – who served as head of the Department of Business Management and Industrial Administration at University of Delhi, one of the places that imparted the earlier form of Board-approved MBAs – said *"the only country which has the appropriate resources for giving aid to India for the development of Management education ...is the USA. Its superiority in respect of organisation ... and their success has been acknowledged all the world over."*

The size of the task of management education in India is indicated by the fact that in 1960 a Government committee estimated that by the end of the decade India would need a further 4000 personnel trained in technical management, and 7200 trained in general and commercial management, to meet its industrial goals (Chandrakant 1973). Another estimate indicated that during the years between 1961 and 1976 over 145,000 managerial personnel would need to be trained (Chandrakant 1973). Few companies placed a premium on firm-specific training. Only a few enterprises, located mainly in the banking and railway sectors, had introduced in-house staff training facilities. Among foreign-owned companies, the situation was even more dire with less than 3% of the 560 foreign companies present in India at that time having comprehensive training programs for staff. The consequence of this was that Indians were being chosen for managerial roles without the expected training and knowledge. This aggravated perceptions of lack of managerial capabilities within the country, perceptions that reinforced the view that India's progress was being held back by a lack of managerial talent and that urgent action was required to shore up this vital resource for industrial growth. The Ford Foundation sponsored team that visited America in 1959 concluded that a "*state has now been reached when whole-time programmes, catering for a limited number of students in the initial stages, should also be started at the centres which, at the instance of the Government of India, are already conducting management courses*" (cited in Dasgupta 1968).

Between 1959 and 1962, the Ford Foundation also sponsored a series of visits to India by Professor George Robbins, a business Dean at the University of California at Los Angeles. His subsequent consultancy report provided the blue print for the setting up of two Indian Institutes of Management (IIM) in Ahmedabad and Calcutta, respectively, as state supported institutions. These IIMs were set up as autonomous institutions outside the university system (which followed the British model) in 1961–1962, being designed so as to effect a clean break with commerce and management teaching as it had previously been conducted in India. The Ahmedabad IIM was mentored by Harvard and the Calcutta IIM by MIT. Faculty from Harvard and MIT stayed in India, setting up academic protocols and procedures, course pedagogy, admission procedures, and administrative norms and practices. Indian faculty were trained in the respective institutions, and a long period of transition was worked out so that fidelity to American pedagogical and academic contents could be maintained even when the institutes were run completely by Indian faculty. The authority of the American mentors was almost absolute. For instance, Indian concerns that an admissions test in English would entrench educational elitism were set aside. Subsequently, an English-language admission test patterned on the American Graduate Management Aptitude Test was adopted, a test that continues to be used today (Sancheti 1986). Courses were offered in various functional areas such as marketing, organizational behavior, economics, finance and accounting, business policy, etc., an outcome that led to the creation of disciplinary silos that began displacing traditional views of wholistic interconnectedness in business. The Indian adaptation of MBA was carried out by adding specific content on Indian business history and social structure as special courses, in a manner similar to the first Bachelor of Commerce degree course. Harvard even supported the preparation of several hundred Indian teaching cases that could illustrate the same western theories and models!

Thus, management was imported and absorbed into India from America as a set of universally valid techniques and body of truths. The India in this education was only a contextual factor, a context in which the insights on social structure and business history (much of which was written from "orientalist" and/or western perspectives) held India's tradition responsible for its state of underdevelopment. Indian here only meant descriptions of Indian organizations. Hardly any western theories were tested for their validity in the Indian context, even though there were constant refrains questioning the validity of such extensions, especially within the organization behavior discipline. This education contributed significantly to silencing the wisdom and practices of traditional work organization which – in spite of an adverse public opinion – continued to survive in a subterranean and often illegal fashion. The assertions of the American mentors that they had not found any suitable model of management in India were unquestioned (Jammulamadaka 2017).

Indianizing Management Education

By the time of the third 5 Year Plan (1961–1965), discussions of higher technical and managerial education had given way to specific delineation of the issues management education had to cover: secure adequate return on capital employed; increase contribution to national resources; make organization more efficient and effective, *"how best to manage, not just set up establishments,"* i.e., careful planning, good management, cordial worker and management relationship, prompt operational decisions, greater delegation of authority, flexibility in operation, identification of remedial areas (GOI Third 5 Year Plan). The Third Plan document stated:

> Lack of delegation within the enterprise is another common failure... usually accompanied by a failure to define responsibilities and duties. ....Luck (sic) of quality of managerial personnel is another factor prejudicing the success of an enterprise....often the key positions are held by people who do not have the requisite training ...The consciousness of profit and cost is also not as widespread as is necessary. The purpose of management should be to secure economic efficiency; cost consciousness is necessary to achieve the desired results.

These articulations of the challenges of managing public enterprises defined the early mandate for Indianizing management education in the country post-independence. Meanwhile, the early graduates of IIMs mostly found employment within the foreign multinationals operating in India (Sancheti 1986), receiving lucrative pay checks in comparison to others. The rising salaries and social status of the graduates led to increasing demand for such education. The success of these graduates was read as direct evidence of the ability of management education to offer growth for the country. The first Indian chairman of the Indian subsidiary of Unilever, Prakash Tandon, observed, *"That a developing economy needs management even more than resources is now becoming abundantly clear to all students of growth."* (foreword to Prasad and Negandhi 1968). However, with the graduates opting to serve multinationals, the needs of India's diverse sectors continued to be unmet. In this context, the first form of Indianizing management education occurred through the setting up of targeted, sector-focused management schools. IIM Bangalore, for example, was set up in 1973 to meet the specific needs of state-owned enterprises. The Institute of Rural Management was set up for serving the needs of rural, agricultural, and dairy sectors. These schools taught the same management theories and models and added additional courses and contents that dealt with their sectoral focus. *Managerialism*, an *"acknowledged Western concept"* was translated as the *"...effective deployment of human and material resources...a whole spectrum of those activities which are imperative to augment industrialization in a country.*" (Prasad and Negandhi 1968: 4).

Developing Instruments and Concepts for India

A second mode of Indianizing occurred as a response to perceived foreignness of management knowledge and practice. Located firmly within the Western social science traditions, some scholars took to the task of examining foreign theories, especially those relating to human behavior in the Indian context and sought to adapt them to India. The development of the human resource function by TV Rao and Udai Pareek echoed some of these sentiments. A recent reminiscence of that period states,

> At a time when India was still an underdeveloped country and the importance of human factor in organisations was not adequately recognised, Pareek's work focussing on human processes, OD, and institution building in some sense raised the level of thinking of emerging management profession and HR professionals....His pioneering work with TV Rao ... led to an effective and integrated framework of HRD, which was far more comprehensive than the understanding of HRD by the West at that time." T V Rao and Khandelwal 2016: preface).

Despite their focus on Indian-specific issues and understandings in adapting organizational behavior concepts such as motivation and role efficacy, the reference point for such theories remained rooted in Western management education. It was argued, for example, that since an employee spent significant period in the organization, it was the moral responsibility of the employer to provide for the growth and capacity development of the employee, viewpoints that were instrumental in stimulating companies to set up human resource departments rather than just focus – as most previously had – on reactive industrial relations strategies (Rao and Khandelwal 2016; Rao 2010; Sullivan n.d.). For most of those operating within this genre, India's cultural difference and social structure was seen as an important influence on management practice (Jammulamadaka 2017). Research was carried out into developing and adapting psychometric instruments that were culturally attuned to India.

Self-criticism of Management in India

Although often embraced by foreign-owned firms, the graduates of the two early IIMs found lukewarm receptions within Indian firms and public enterprises. Accordingly, their faculty spent much time and many resources persuading captains of Indian industry about the suitability of the graduates (Paul 2012). Many "*wondered how these youngsters would add value to their operations....Indian companies and, in particular family enterprises, were more negative in their responses than foreign firms...*" (Paul 2012: 87). Despite such tepid initial receptions, the demand for management education within the country grew exponentially during the 1970s. By the late 1980s, management education was being provided by 60 university departments, four IIMs, and 35 other institutions (usually sectorally focused), each offering a variety of management education programs (Phillip and Narayan 1989: v) with vast differences in quality. In this increasingly crowded market, IIMs not only retained the quality crown but were also accused of elitism, of being only open to an urban, English speaking elite (Rao 1989 and Tandon 1989 in Phillip and Narayan 1989).

The success of managerial education in terms of the social status of its graduates ensured that the relevance of such education to the country remained constantly under scrutiny. Some questioned the appropriateness of government subsidizing such education given that the graduates hardly served the nation's needs (Nanda Committee on reviewing IIMs), Shankar Narayan (1989), Professor at IIM Bangalore remarked,

> It is no secret that most of the output of MBAs are absorbed by western-oriented Private and Public Sectors leaving high and dry other sectors which are in real need of management. To entertain any expectations contrary to the obtaining situation would have been naïve, since the purpose of setting up IIMs, ... their curricula, their value systems, their program orientation, ...create" such outcomes. (1989: 29).

Others questioned the content and curriculum of management education. During the 1970s, management education and practice was dominated by various techniques of scientific management. A survey of Indian industry by one school NITIE found that techniques such as method study, work study, work sampling, production planning, and inventory control were being followed by over 50% of the industry. Even within course curricula, ergonomics was an important part of behavioral sciences courses just as procedure analysis was in operations courses. (Chandrakant 1973). Such emphasis on techniques and methods began to elicit criticism. A joint educational advisor to Government of India opined in 1973,

> ... the need to do away with traditional concepts is very great ... the most difficult part of management education is to retain those parts of the traditional systems which are both appropriate and effective ... One of the important parts of management education is to build in the student of business management, precisely this discrimination. (Chandrakant 1973; 10).

While views questioning the relevance of western management education continued all through the 1970s, they gathered momentum in the 1980s. By this time, India as a nation had had experience both with management education (for close to two decades) and with modern Western state, governance, and institutions for almost four decades. The young independent nation had had its share of disillusionments with modernity and western institutional structures. The hopes that after independence India's many problems such as poverty would be resolved were crashed. The famines in the 1970s shook the country's faith in the capability of its government. The rise of Naxalite (neo-Marxist) insurgency was one symptom of this condition. This disillusionment was reflected categorically in the concerns of several speakers at the first ever national conference on "policy implications in management education" held at IIM Bangalore in 1988 which questioned the contents of MBA programs that were widely taught. While prima facie a case of educated elite talking to itself, this was also the first opportunity the Indian management academics had to engage in an interrogation of the knowledge that had been transferred from the United States in previous decades, knowledge which had found ready market in India. These academics while part of the system they were critiquing were different from the modernist elite who had been instrumental in bringing in management education into the country. It was also a case of self-reflexivity and was in keeping with the ethos of India where the educated were expected to be more conscious of their wider social and moral responsibility. At this conference, Kamala Choudhary, an IIM professor and key note speaker, stated,

> What we have today in terms of Indian education and therefore of the attitudes, orientation and values, of the educated class are, to use Macaulay's language ....Indian in blood and colour, but English in taste, in opinions, in morals and in intellect....Management education... has built an edifice of learning but has deprived it of its foundations- foundations which are rooted in the social, economic, political and cultural life of the people.... Management education should be not merely leaning technocratic calculations but understanding the milieu in which decision making is effective" (Chowdhry 1989; Phillip and Narayan 1989: 17–18)

The Chairman of IIM Bangalore Prof. Abad Ahmed who was also a member of the Planning Commission added in the same conference, *"presently apparent disorientation in values, concentration on a few sectors, methodologies and narrow syllabi will have to be corrected by providing for both value orientation, broad-based education as well as technique orientation."* (Ahmed 1989; Phillip and Narayan 1989: ix). Yet others dismissed management education and schools totally, *"Management education may be good but it does not serve our needs ...Management schools are totally irrelevant. You give us only American education. You have not produced any Indian education."* (Phillip and Narayan 1989: x).

Such criticisms created pressure for further Indianizing of management education. Kamla Chowdhry opined in her address, *"If management education in India has to have an identity (sic) of its own, it must have its own views and ways of thinking about progress, development, responsibility, authority, commitment, etc."* This "own view" took the form of a re-engagement with Indian values. In keeping with the "orientalist" approach that still permeated India's education system (which continued more or less as is from 1835), Indian values and tradition were understood as a fixed, frozen body of knowledge and philosophy that was locked in sacred and revered texts. Indianizing thus occurred through recourse to invocation of revered and sacred texts such as the Bhagavad Gita. Such texts were invoked to provide evidence of an Indian's spiritual orientation to work. Strategies of meditation, karma ethic discussed in these were invoked to improve employee's stress management abilities and motivation levels. The Management Center for Human Values set up at IIM Calcutta in the 1990s is one instance of this. Unfortunately though, this remained a strategy of cherry picking. Generally only those aspects that contributed to making a worker docile and apolitical were invoked. All other critiques of human behavior implicit in those texts were ignored.

Conclusion

The history of management in India is not a story of pursuit of technological efficiencies or profits. Instead, it has been fashioned out of power, the colonizer's power. Sometimes, this has happened by the direct visible invocation of authority to create laws defining the course of management. At other times, power has operated in more subtle and enduring ways by influencing perceptions of what counts as "management" or even "Indian" and simultaneously illegitimizing existing native practices and/or valourising a few ancient texts. Emerging as a part of the imperial efforts of managing a colony, English as a language has remained integral to defining the character of modern western management in India, its contents and constituents.

Consequently, the Indian in all the above attempts at Indianizing management outlined above are accessorized to a core western management theory in vogue. Even though it is common knowledge that traditional practices such as use of jobbers and personal networks continued to be practiced even in contemporary India, modern management in India in its quest to overcome inferiority and become a developed nation has continued to ignore such living traditions! Hardly any conversation has occurred between traditional business practice and modern management.

> The fact is that the main stay of Indian industrial business is managed through indigenous talents, processes and know-how, though surprisingly, researches and publications in the field of management in India so far tend to give a lower order priority to them. (Tandon in Phillip and Narayan 1989: 77)

So, the question what is Indian in Indian management remains open. The colonizers have left, but colonization of knowledge and thinking has not. Tracing the course of management in India in more recent times, in the era of globalization and neo-liberalization, business schools' pursuit of internationalization and accreditation would be equally fascinating and equally revealing of the colonial imprint. However, such an enterprise has to be set aside for another time.

Cross-References

Governmentality and the Chinese Workers in China's Contemporary Thought Management System
In Search of the Traces of the History of Management in Latin America, 1870–2020
Introduction: Management Heterogeneity in Asia
Management History in the Modern World: An Overview
Management in Australia – The Case of Australia's Wealthiest Valley: The Hunter
The Making of a Docile Working Class in Pre-reform China
The Perfect Natural Experiment: Asia and the Convergence Debate
Think Big and Privatize Every Thing That Moves: The Impact of Political Reform on the Practice of Management in New Zealand
What Is Management?

References

Ahmed A (1989) Management education curricula: present status and new directions. In: Phillip J, Narayan DS (eds) Management education in India. Indian Institute of Management Bangalore, Bangalore, pp 43–51

Basu A (1974) The growth of education and political development in India, 1898–1920. Oxford University Press, New Delhi

Bhambra G (2014) Connected sociologies. Bloomsbury Publishing, London

Birla R (2009) Stages of capital: law, culture, and market governance in late colonial India. Duke University Press, Durham

Buchanan DH (1934) The development of capitalistic enterprise in India. MacMillan & Co, New York

Chakrabarty D (1983) On deifying and defying authority: managers and workers in the jute mills of Bengal, circa 1890–1940. Past and Present 100(1):124–146

Chandavarkar R (1994) The origins of industrial capitalism in India. Cambridge University Press, Cambridge

Chandavarkar R (2008) The decline and fall of the jobber system in the Bombay cotton textile industry, 1870–1955. Mod Asian Stud 42:117–210

Chandrakant LS (1973) Management education and training in India. D B Taraporevala Sons and Co, Bombay

Chowdhry K (1989) Keynote address: management for development: search for relevance. In: Phillip J, Narayan DS (eds) Management education in India. Indian Institute of Management Bangalore, Bangalore, pp 11–19

Coomaraswamy AK (1908) The village community and modern progress. Colombo Apothecaries Company, Limited, Colombo

Coomaraswamy AK (1909) The Indian craftsman. Probsthain & Company, London

Das G (2006) India: how a rich nation became poor and will be rich again. In: Harrison LE, Berger P (eds) Developing cultures: case studies. Routledge, New York, pp 141–162

Dasgupta A (1968) Management education in India. University of Delhi, New Delhi

Dharampal (1983) The beautiful tree: indigenous Indian education in the eighteenth century. the Other India Press, Mapusa

Ghoshal UN (1930) The agrarian system in ancient India. University of Calcutta, Calcutta

GoI (1900) Speeches of Lord Curzon of Keddleston, viceroy and governor general of India, 1898–1900, vol I. Office of the Superintendent of Government Printing, Calcutta

GOI Third Five Year Plan Organisation of Public Enterprises at http://planningcommission.nic.in/plans/planrel/fiveyr/3rd/3planch16.html. Accessed 1 Apr 2018

Hill TM, Haynes WW, Baumgartel HJ (1973) Institution building in India. Harvard University Press, Boston

Jammulamadaka N (2016) Bombay textile mills: exploring CSR roots in colonial India. J Manag Hist 22(4):450–472

Jammulamadaka N (2017) A post-colonial critique of management education scene in India. In: Thakur M, Babu R (eds) Management education in India: trends and pathways. Springer, Singapore

Jammulamadaka N (2018) Indian business: notions and practices of responsibility. Routledge, Oxon

Kennedy VD (1958) The conceptual and legislative framework of labor relations in India. Ind Labor Relat Rev 11(4):487–505

Kennedy VD (1965) The sources and evolution of Indian labour relations policy. Indian J Ind Relat 1(1):15–40

Kydd JC (1920) History of factory legislation in India. University of Calcutta, Calcutta

Maddison A (2007) Contours of the world economy, 1-2030 AD. Oxford University Press, Clarendon

Majumdar RC (1920) Corporate life in ancient India. Calcutta University, Calcutta

Mookerji R (1919) Local government in ancient India. Clarendon Press, Oxford

Morris MD (1965) The emergence of an industrial labour force in India: a study of the Bombay cotton mills, 1854–1947. University of California Press, Berkeley
Nandy A (1994) The illegitimacy of nationalism. Oxford University Press, New Delhi
Niranjana T (1992) Siting translation: history, post-structuralism and the colonial context. University of California Press, Berkeley
Paul S (2012) Samuel Paul: a life and its lessons. Public Affairs Centre, Bangalore
Phillip J, Narayan DS (1989) Management education in India. Indian Institute of Management Bangalore, Bangalore
Prasad SB, Negandhi AR (1968) Managerialism for economic development: essays on India. MartinusNijhoff, The Hague
Rao GP (1989) Management education in India: a proposal. In: Phillip J, Narayan DS (eds) Management education in India. Indian Institute of Management Bangalore, Bangalore
Rao TV (2010) Beyond management: some conceptual contributions of Udai Pareek to the modern world. Indore Manag J 2(2):9–26
Rao TV, Khandelwal AK (2016) HRD, OD and institution building: essays in memory of Udai Pareek. Sage, New Delhi
Report of the Indian industrial commission (1916–18) London, His Majesty's Stationery Office
Sancheti N (1986) Educational dependency: an Indian case study in comparative perspective. Unpublished doctoral thesis, University of London, Institute of Education. http://eprints.ioe.ac.uk/7430/. Accessed 25 Mar 2015
Sauvy A (1952) Trois Mondus, une Planete, L Observateur (no.18), 14
Seth VK (2015) A story of Indian manufacturing: encounters with Mughal and British empires (1500–1947). Athena Academic, London
Simeon D (1999) Work and resistance in the Jharia coalfield. In: Parry PJ, Breman J, Kapadia K (eds) The worlds of Indian industrial labour. Sage, New Delhi, pp 43–75
Sinha DP (2004) Management education in India: perspectives and challenges. ICFAI University Press, Hyderabad
Srinivasan S, Ranganathan S (1997) Wootz steel: an advanced material of the ancient world. http://materials.iisc.ernet.in/~wootz/heritage/WOOTZ.htm. Accessed 4 Apr 2018
Staples (1992) Forty years: a learning curve: Ford foundation programs in India, 1952–1992
Sullivan R (n.d.) History of OD in India by Dr.UdaiPareek an interview by Roland Sullivan at https://www.nationalhrd.org/file/13992. Accessed 12 Apr 2018
Sundar P (2000) Beyond Business: From Merchant Charity to Corporate Citizenship: Indian Business Philanthropy Through the Ages. Tata McGraw-Hill Publishing Company, New Delhi
Tandon BB (1989) Management education: some policy issues. In: Phillip J, Narayan DS (eds) Management education in India. Indian Institute of Management Bangalore, Bangalore, p 37
Taylor HS (1976) Oral History Interview with Douglas Ensminger. https://www.trumanlibrary.org/oralhist/esmingr.htm. Accessed 10 Apr 2018
The Economist (2010) Seeing the world differently. https://www.economist.com/node/16329442. Accessed 14 Apr 2018
Varma N (2014) Unpopular Assam: notions of migrating and working for tea gardens in. In: Bhattacharya S (ed) Towards a new history of work. Tulika, New Delhi, pp 227–244
Wolcott S (2008) Strikes in colonial India, 1921–1938. Ind Labour Relat Rev 61(4):460–484
Yolland Z (1994) Boxwallahs: the British in Cawnpore, 1857–1901. M. Russell, Norwich

The Making of a Docile Working Class in Pre-reform China

59

Elly Leung

Contents

Introduction	1352
Genealogy and the Uses of History	1353
Confucian (*li*) Rules: A Genealogy of Chinese Workers	1354
The "Demise" of Confucianism Under Mao Zedong	1357
The *Making* of a Chinese Working Class	1357
Conclusion	1363
Cross-References	1363
References	1364

Abstract

The aim of this chapter is to analyze how the Chinese Communist Party (CCP) Chairman Mao Zedong attained his status of rightful ruler by embedding the Confucian values in his concept of mass participation to create docile bodies and minds among the Chinese workers. In so doing, this chapter draws on Michel Foucault's (ed. Rabinow P, The Foucault reader: an introduction to Foucault's thought. Penguin, Harmondsworth, 1984/1991) genealogical (or historicalization) account to trace the key historical events that spiritually and bodily made a docile working class in Mao's period. The chapter argues that this mindset was a central component in maintaining Chinese workers' subordination to the Chinese rulers in the past and even in today's China.

I am indebted to my PhD supervisor Dr. Donella Caspersz in the Business School at the University of Western Australia for her unfailing support, encouragement, and constructive feedback to my work.

E. Leung (✉)
Business School, University of Western Australia, Perth, WA, Australia
e-mail: elly.leung@uwa.edu.au

© The Author(s), under exclusive licence to Springer Nature Switzerland AG 2020
B. Bowden et al. (eds.), *The Palgrave Handbook of Management History*,
https://doi.org/10.1007/978-3-319-62114-2_113

Keywords

Genealogy · Chinese history · Chinese working class · Mao Zedong · Confucianism · Thought control · Docility

Introduction

As a supposedly socialist society, the legitimacy of the Chinese Communist Party (CCP) has long rested on its claim to represent the interest of the Chinese industrial working class – the proletariat. In broad brush, the founding principles of the Chinese State were spelled out by the CCP Chairman Mao Zedong with a speech that was subsequently published *On the People's Democratic Dictatorship*. In this speech, delivered a few months prior to the formal establishment of the People's Republic of China (PRC or China) on 1 October 1949, Mao (1949/2013: 4) defined the "people" as "the workers, the peasants, the urban petty bourgeoisie and the national bourgeoisie." By categorizing "the people" into different classes, Mao further declared that "the people" were "led" by the "working class" – an alliance of workers and peasants (proletariats or masses) – and the CCP. From these principles, Mao proclaimed his theory of "New Democracy" as the basis of the CCP policies, a form of "democracy" that associated communism with the direct and active role of "the people" in Chinese politics to resist the class domination characteristic of "imperialism, feudalism and bureaucratic capitalism" (Mao 1949/2013: 5–7). Explicit in Mao's outlining of the principles of the Chinese State was a very different understanding of civil society to that found in Western liberal democracies. Where Western liberal democracies perceive the "State" as a neutral force, and class conflict as something that needs to be alleviated, Mao's understanding of "People's Democracy" was theoretically built on the reverse: on the constant mobilization of the "people" and the "working class" in an ever-present class struggle. Implicit in Mao's understandings of ever-present class conflict and popular mobilization was the elimination of the traditional Confucian link between the ruler and the ruled. Instead of being built on mass conformity, the new Marxist doctrine spoke of equality through political integration of the masses. As Weatherley (2006) has suggested, Mao's revolutionary concepts built around ever-present mobilizations became the backbone of the socialist policies for "New Democratic China." In the mid-1960s, commitment to these policies was manifest in the mass mobilizations associated with the Cultural Revolution (Bridgham 1967). Subsequently, these phenomena were framed by the Marxist exponents as evidence of continuous working class struggles, emerging from below, directed in a class struggle against lurking "capitalist movements" (Chen 2006; Hurst 2008, 2009; Lee 2000, 2002; Walder 1991; Walder and Gong 1993). Over the years, a plethora of studies have taken up this theme, producing an academic narrative built around the centrality of the Chinese proletariat as the de facto "masters of the State," a discourse that perceives a continuing collective class consciousness among workers in the socialist China (Chen 2006; Lee 2000; Walder 1991; Walder and Gong 1993).

Against this background, this chapter suggests that the concept of mass participation in Chinese politics was used as a discourse in enabling Mao to monopolize his political power and to establish himself as a legitimate ruler of China. The chapter argues that Mao's political legitimacy was drawn on the Confucian elements to internalize *Mao Zedong Thought* (or *Maoism*) (Mao 1949/1966) – a blend of Marx and Mao's revolutionary ideology associated with his charismatic authority (Chai 2003; Fu 1974) – in the minds of Chinese workers through the symbolic mass participation in politics. The aim of this chapter is to analyze how Mao attained his status of rightful ruler by embedding the Confucian values in his concept of mass participation to create docile bodies and minds among the Chinese workers. In so doing, this chapter draws on Michel Foucault's (1984/1991) genealogical (or historicalization) account to trace the key historical events that spiritually and bodily made a docile working class in Mao's period. The chapter argues that this mindset was a central component in maintaining Chinese workers' subordination to the CCP. This chapter begins with a brief discussion of the purposes and methods of Foucault's genealogy and his uses of this tool to question the development of thought, before applying the tool of genealogy to analyze how "Chinese workers" were historically constituted into "docile bodies and minds" in successive historical periods through to Mao's China. The chapter concludes with considering the implications of this "thought construction" for the Chinese working class in the present day.

Genealogy and the Uses of History

> The process writer would thus be interested in how the particular *now* generates its context, as well as how the context makes the particular achieve being in a specific way. If there is a guide, supplementing Nietzsche's urge that we build our own way in our study, it would be Foucault's (no doubt Nietzsche-inspired) genealogical tracing of how the particular has become what it is today, and, focusing on the particular, in the context of its emergence, studying how it generates its context where we presently find it. (Helin et al. 2014: 13)

Mao Zedong, as a Marxist, perceived history as a process of class struggle, driven by a constant dynamic for change. By contrast, the French philosopher-historian Michel Foucault (1976/1978: 100) declares in *History of Sexuality* – originally published in French under the more apt title of *La Volonté de Savoir* ("The Will to Know") – that "it is in discourse that power and knowledge are joined together." In the same work, Foucault (1976/1978: 86) also accurately observes that "power is tolerable on the condition that it masks a substantial part of itself. Its success is proportional to its ability to hide its own mechanism." In other words, in any society the survival of those in a position of domination primarily depends not on coercion, but rather in those who are ruled sharing the acceptance discourse, a discourse that masks the reality of power imbalances and inequality. In his essay *Nietzsche, Genealogy, History*, Foucault (1971/1977: 150) also notes that accepted accounts of "history" – of what is historically "true" – always exist in the present as "the endlessly repeated play of dominations," of accepted rules and "rituals" that "permits the perpetual instigation of new dominations." As such, Foucault (1971/1977: 150) accounts of what is accepted as historically "true" have not so much a history, as a "genealogy," a process in which certain groups and individuals construct a "history" that is popularly held to be true. In other words, "history" is socially constructed, a superior form of discourse, a discourse whose "genealogy" cannot only be traced and understood but also combated, resisted, and overturned. Arguably, nowhere in the world today does Foucault's concept of "genealogy" of greater applicability than in China, a place where understandings of what is historically "true" have been meticulously crafted.

One of the essential characteristics of Foucault's genealogical approach is his rejection of the notion of continuity that underpins much in traditional historiography (Gutting 2003; O'Farrell 1989, 2005). While history, by definition, is about the past, Foucault perceives it as a form of knowledge and at the same time a form of power that constitutes the "truth" about "how things are" in establishing the basis for modern *episteme* (or knowledge) (Poster 1982) to form the foundations of human perceptions and ways of thinking (O'Farrell 1989). In this respect, Foucault's (1970/2002) critique of knowledge (or episteme) is that traditional historians' efforts to write history in a way that maintains and reinforces a continuous status of knowledge, such as "sexuality" and "madness," to reflect "where we are," "who we are," and "what we do" are inevitably resulting from cumulative knowledge of causes and effects (Gutting 2003; Hook 2005). As a result, Foucault calls for a suspension of the notion of continuous progression alongside the intellectual landscapes of necessary forms of thinking to instead develop an "effective history" (a genealogical study or "history of the present") by focusing upon the fragmentary nature of histories (Nicholls 2009) to free our thought "from what it silently thinks, and enable it to think differently" in our present day (Foucault 1978/1990: 9).

Confucian (*li*) Rules: A Genealogy of Chinese Workers

Foucault's genealogical approach has informed the interpretation of key events in Chinese histories that are drawn on in this chapter to explore the constitutive methods exercised by the Chinese Communist Party (CCP) Chairman Mao Zedong (1949–1976) (Teiwes 1997) and his followers (the Maoists) to create a docile working class as a technique to legitimate his authority. Although much has noted the imperial order associated with the Confucian values were substituted by orthodox Marxism since 1949 (Mathur 1987; Goldman 1975; Tsou 1986), it is argued that the "Chinese Marxism" was used to reshape the thoughts and behaviors of the working class according to the CCP and Mao's purposes through the so-called mass politics that were frequently, albeit selective, referenced to the Confucian past. Thus, the Confucian-related events are selected for the exploration of the making of a working class in Mao's period by investigating how Confucianism produced important – but hidden – rules to continuously constituted filial practices to maintain docility among workers and the hierarchical power of rulers in Chinese histories (Grasso et al. 2009).

Originating in the pre-Confucian primitive society as early as 2070 B.C.E., *li* 禮 rules were predominately associated with the concept of *tian* 天 (heaven) and *di* 地 (earth) (Zhou c. 1100 B.C.E./1930: 168) to make it mandatory for the Chinese on earth (the low) to naturally worship the spirits of the heaven (the high) (Zhang 2014). Based on this utmost filial practice toward the spirits, *li* rules were transformed into mandatory rules of conduct by various emperors to standardize Chinese thinking and behaviors to maintain the monarchical power of the rulers from the Zhou Dynasty (13th B.C.E.) onward (Grasso et al. 2009). Zhou Gong (922 B.C.E.–900 B.C.E.), who was the sixth king of the Western Zhou Dynasty (1040 B.C.E.–771 B.C.E.) (Melton 2014), modified *li* rules to facilitate the making of a social hierarchy to differentiate the social ranks of the noble (the high) and the peasants (the low) in a feudalistic social system (Zhou c. 1100 B.C.E./1930). To fortify the dominant position of the royal ruling classes and maintain the status quo, *li* rules were subsequently linked to a code of capital punishment (or death penalties – *sihsing*) to forbid certain speech, thoughts, and actions among the masses under the laws of the ancient Zhou.

The criminal code enacted by the Zhou Dynasty exemplified *li* rules that focused on the true values of filial piety (*xiao* 孝) (Zhou c.1100 B.C.E./1930), through which the violations of the stated prohibitions and restrictions were subject to forms of torturous capital punishments. Methods of torture and execution ranged from being boiled in oil or water to being stoned or crushed or "death by a thousand cuts" (or *Lingchi* 凌遲 in Qing criminal code) by slicing the body of a confessed criminal with a maximum of 3600 cuts, in a public space (Brook et al. 2008; Miethe and Lu 2005). The punitive logic of these public punishments was directed toward the protection of the truth of the *li*, that is, the conduct of filial piety through a political ritual of judicial torture by producing pain in the body of a convicted criminal to demonstrate the sovereign's power for all to see. By vislizing the supreme power of the sovereign, the torturous public executions served to suppress the thoughts and actions of the masses in order to secure the hegemony of the ruling classes in the feudal society (Lu 1998).

Using Zhou *li* as a template, Confucius (c. 475 B.C.E./2003) sought to legitimize dynastic *li* rules by rectifying social ranks and names to establish an orderly set of social relations of the high and low positions, such as the father and the son, the older and the younger brother, and the husband and the wife, under a truth of the "Mandate of Heaven" (*tianming* 天命). In the Confucius discourse (c. 475 B.C.E./2003), the "Mandate of Heaven" articulated the individuals' true positions that then identified their life tasks and responsibilities in their *ming* 命 (fate or destiny). These were predetermined by *tian* 天 (or heaven) from birth:

> The relation between superiors and inferiors is like that between the wind and the grass. When the wind blows across it, the grass must bend. (Confucius c. 475 B.C.E./2010: 111)

The Confucius truth (c. 475 B.C.E/2003) of the "oneness of nature-human" (*tianren tongxing*天人同行) order in the doctrine of the "Mandate of Heaven" codes of *li* moral conduct emphasized as paramount the need to accept and obey the "natural" ruling order and the power of superiors imposed on *ming* by *tian*. Superiors, such as the emperors, were regarded by Confucius as the "Sons of Heaven" (*tianzi*天子), with divine mandates to rule and control the lower classes (or inferiors) (Confucius c. 475 B.C.E./2003; Grasso et al. 2009). A challenge to the "Mandate of Heaven" of the ruling classes (or superiors) by inferiors was to disobey or deviate from the *li* codes of conduct (Confucius c. 475 B.C.E/2003). These codes of proper conduct of filial piety and obedience to superiors were central to Confucius thought to regulate the social behavior of the inferiors, such as son, wife, and pupil, by reaffirming their given status imposed by their *ming* (Confucius c. 475 B.C.E./2003).

By connecting the truth of *ming* with individuals' status (or positions), the followers of Confucius (or the Confucians) sought to inculcate a morality of obedience (or a mentality of respect for authority) into their mindsets in order to create an orderly society (Fouts and Chan 1995; Rojek 1989). In this context, the Confucian *li* rules prioritized the moral teaching of proper conduct from the moment of birth (Fouts and Chan 1995). One example was the teaching of filial piety to children (Rojek 1989), which contributed to influencing and correcting individuals' actions by their given status in broader contexts, such as community schools and extended family networks. By socializing an individual in the practices of education and culture, one's behavior became observable to others (Fairbank and Goldman 2006; Rojek 1989). In this way, individuals' behavior became increasingly regulated by others based on a collective moral judgment of others and the self (Fairbank and Goldman 2006; Rojek 1989). The creation and maintenance of the culture of obedience had thus enabled the royal ruling classes continued to produce docile bodies and minds to serve their interests until the Qing Dynasty – the last imperial dynasty – in China (Grasso et al. 2009; Rojek 1989).

Toward the final years of the Qing Dynasty, Western moral values that challenged the Confucian tradition were introduced into China (Chen 2002; Dreyer 1993). The inability of the Qing emperors to stop the imposition of Western influences through foreign trade relations, diplomatic missions, and ideas of democracy made it difficult for the Chinese State to exert the control they would have liked over people's lives (Whyte 1988). Social conflicts, such as the Boxer Rebellion by peasants to oppose the European and Japanese power in 1900, and particularly after the fall of the Qing Dynasty in 1911, became apparent as the nation came to be characterized by cultural diversity (Grasso et al. 2009). In the period after 1919 (the "May Fourth Movement"), Chinese pro-Western intellectuals asserted that the "backwardness" of Confucian culture was the cause of individual passivity, and it accounted for the restriction of individual freedoms (Mao 1967/1986). The May Fourth Movement (1915–1922) was brought about by the complete rejection of Confucian values by advocating a substitution of Western values, such as democracy, egalitarianism, republicanism, and Marxism. See Grasso et al. 2009) Subsequently, new Western cultural and political values, ranging from socialism to liberalism (Mao 1949/1966), were advocated as alternative moral frameworks to guide Chinese society.

The "Demise" of Confucianism Under Mao Zedong

With the formal establishment of the People's Republic of China (PRC or China) following the victory over the anti-Japanese War (1937–1945) and Kuomintang (KMT or the Nationalist) Party in the Chinese Civil War (1946–1949) (MacFarquhar 1997), the Chinese Communist Party (CCP) – as a product of the "May Fourth Movement" between 1915 and 1922 – deplored the "intolerable elements" of Confucian values, exalting instead the socialist ideology (or Stalinism) of the Union of Soviet Socialist Republics (USSR or Soviet Union) (Leung 2016; Whyte 1988). By embracing Stalinism as a base, the CCP Chairman Mao Zedong (1949/1966) (1949–1976) – who was perceived as the charismatic leader with his prolonged character of his revolutionary struggle for the "New China" – subsequently developed Marxism-Leninism into the *Thought of Mao Zedong* (or Maoism) to impose revolutionary ideologies, that is, to destroy the system of private property ownership, for Chinese model of socialism. However, post-1949 Chinese society was characterized by a relatively small middle-class population dominating a much larger urban proletariat in the cities. Despite this, Chinese society was also characterized by a relatively small number of landowners dominating a greater number of peasants in rural areas (Chen 2013). Over 80% of the entire Chinese population resided in the rural areas, while less than 20% resided in the cities (Chen 2013). For this reason, Mao emphasized the important role of peasants, rather than the proletariat as identified by Marx and Lenin, in the success of the Chinese revolution (1949/1966). Mao contended that the virtues of the peasants, such as purity and simplicity, were the strengths of the Chinese people because they could be taught, educated, indoctrinated, and "proletarianized" by the CCP to transform society (1949/1966).

The *Making* of a Chinese Working Class

Hence, while denouncing a range of Confucian values, Mao initiated the Confucian-inspired thought reform program *zhengfeng* 整風 (or "Rectification Campaign") (Mao 1949/1966: 2) to impose his revolutionary ideologies on the Chinese masses in the already poor China (Chen 2013). In contrast to the models of Marx and Lenin, who believed a revolutionary consciousness was derived from one's economic and class conditions, Mao insisted that reforming one's consciousness to alter norms and behavior was a more effective way to accomplish a socialist society (1949/1966). To achieve this purpose, Mao sought to revolutionize the peasants to get them to adhere to the truth of Maoism (Guo 2013). In this context, the Confucian inner control technique was once again manipulated to define the destiny (*ming*) of the Chinese inferior masses by facilitating their internalization of the correct Maoist truth (Rojek 1989; Pye 1999).

Manipulating the Chinese *ming* was exercised through Confucian thought control methods by turning the masses into a total obedient instrument of Mao (Schram 1969; Pye 1986; Teiwes 2000; Landsberger 2002). To begin with, the CCP sought to align the correctness of Mao's ultimate truth and leadership with Marx and Lenin to legitimize his hierarchically superior position:

> In our Party, there are no special privileges for individuals; any leadership which is not exercised in the name of the organization cannot be tolerated [...] We obey the Party, we obey the Central Committee, we obey the truth; we do not obey individuals. No individual merits our obedience. Marx, Lenin and Mao [Zedong] have done their work well; they represent the truth, and it is only for this reason that we obey them [...]. (Mao 1966/2013: 154–155)

The validity of the new "mandate" of Mao's ruling legacy was further reinforced through all possible means of propaganda, including newspapers and public broadcasts, to transmit principles of obedience to his sole authority (Weatherley 2006). This Confucian-inspired thought control method was adopted to persuade prospective supporters to form the Red Army (or the People's Liberation Army) to combat the Nationalists in the civil war in the late 1920s (Lu 2004). While discrediting the Confucian culture, a large-scale thought reform program, Rectification Campaign (*zhengfeng*), commenced in the early 1940s to control the behavior of the CCP members (Mao 1949/1966). This was extended further after 1949 to control nonparty members by eradicating negative thoughts about Maoism (Grasso et al. 2009; Lu 2004). A more personalized method of compulsory study groups (Mao 1949/1966), conducted by CCP authority figures, was also used to inculcate correct thought into the masses. Either willingly or under duress, the masses had to self-criticize and confess any incorrect personal thoughts that ran counter to Maoism (Mao 1949/1966). Party cadres had to report the political thought of the masses to the CCP leaders (Dittmer 1973). These strategies enabled the CCP leaders to evaluate the thoughts of the masses and then implement the most appropriate techniques to continuously cultivate docile bodies and minds to Mao.

To demonstrate a high level of loyalty to Mao, the docile bodies had to translate their political ideas into revolutionary practice (Schram 1969; Barlow 1981). In the early 1950s, Mao launched nationwide land reform campaigns aimed at transferring land ownership (Chen and Goodman 2013) from "feudal" landlords (middle class or bourgeoisie) to the peasantry (Mao 1949/1966). Following Mao's order of "criticizing the seizure of land" in a series of "mini-revolutions," peasants denounced their "feudal" landlords under the slogan "spitting bitter water" (*tukushui*吐苦水) (Lu 2004). This provocative slogan aimed to raise the revolutionary consciousness of the peasantry such that they were reminded of the suffering caused by landlord exploitation over the centuries (Weatherley 2006). Many landlords were forced to publicly confess their own so-called crimes, while others were executed or stoned to death, as in the "empire system" (Grasso et al. 2009; Lu 2004). Exposing and publicly criticizing other people's wrongdoings was thought to be a way to demonstrate loyalty to Mao and the CCP (Lu 2004).

In proclaiming themselves the advocates of social justice, the CCP massacred approximately 15 million "feudal exploiters" to dismantle the traditional hierarchical landlord-tenant relationship in the rural areas (Grasso et al. 2009: 139; Lu 2004). Despite transferring land ownership to the peasantry, however, rural poverty continued and was exacerbated by a rapidly expanding population and a scarcity of farmland, which led to the next stage of agricultural development – the collectivization of farmland (Mao 1967/1986).

The assault on the disobedient "feudal exploiters" had subsequently pushed the rural masses to engage in Mao's (1967/1986) program of collectivization of farmland (Weatherley 2006). In this program, Mao sought to reshape public life through the creation of a collective economy by introducing work units (*danwei*單位) in urban areas and the Chinese commune in rural areas within the State-owned enterprises (SOEs) (Mao 1967/1986). (The significance of the work units (*danwei*單位) was that, beginning from 1951, all SOE workers were guaranteed pensions of approximately 80–90% of their salaries at the retirement age of 55 (women) and 60 (men) (Hurst and O'Brien 2002). This was followed in 1952 by the release of the important document "Decisions on the Problems of Employment," the effect of which was to guarantee job security and welfare benefits, known as the *iron rice bowl* (*tie fanwan*鐵飯碗), and which secured the livelihood of the SOE workers (Fung 2001) The establishment of the latter was by forcing the rural masses to participate in agricultural cooperative planting and harvesting through the scheme of agricultural producers' cooperatives (APCs) (Dikotter 2010). Under this arrangement, approximately 20–40 peasant households (Lin et al. 1996: 56) were formed into production teams by consolidating their farmland into collective agricultural units (Mao 1967/1986). To coerce peasant families to join APCs, the CCP made it illegal to sell or purchase anything not produced through the APCs in the countryside (Grasso et al. 2009), while unwilling peasants who wanted to survive were forced to join the APCs in order to participate in agricultural development in the rural areas (Dikotter 2010).

While it was assumed that the APCs would enable the peasants to farm more efficiently by achieving economies of scale, the APC collectivization experiment resulted in poor harvests in both 1953 and 1954 (Grasso et al. 2009: 148). Food shortages occurred because of poor weather conditions and inadequate agricultural production outputs combined with stable consumption and a rapidly growing population (Breslin 2014). Yet rather than denouncing the collectivization project, Mao attempted to reinvigorate the APC structures by transforming them into people's communes for agriculture and steel productions (Mao 1967/1986). This decision was part of a more far-reaching program called the Great Leap Forward (1958–1961) (Mao 1967/1986) for China's industrialization.

Despite food shortages, the deterioration of USSR-Sino relations that was due to different interpretations of Marxism as well as the anti-communist movements arose around the world after 1956 was another element causing Mao to launch the Great Leap Forward programs to generate self-sufficiency for Chinese socialism

(Fung 2001; Oi 1995; Teiwes 1997). In 1958, Mao mobilized the masses to transform China into an industrialized socialist country under the Great Leap slogan of "overtaking Britain's steel production in less than 15 years" (Breslin 2014: 5). To accelerate industrial productivity, the masses were forced to labor in both the agricultural and industrial sectors on collective farms (Withington 2008). In this program, Mao converted the APCs into large-scale labor armies by combining 750,000 collective farmlands, containing over 500 million people, into 26,000 small people's communes (Ahn 1975: 632). Each "small" commune contained small-scale manufacturing facilities (or backyard steel furnaces), and individuals were forced to labor day and night to achieve Mao's daily production quotas and targets to surpass Britain's steel industry (Breslin 2014; Grasso et al. 2009). They were later forced to melt personal items such as cooking pots and pans to achieve Mao's objective of the Great Leap Forward (Li and Yang 2005; Weatherley 2006). This policy led to the reduction of peasants harvesting the fields and caused the subsequent nationwide famine in 1959 and 1960 (Grasso et al. 2009).

During the Great Famine of 1959 and 1960, Mao further tightened the *hukou* 戶 □(or household registration) system to restrict peasant mobility (Wu and Treiman 2004). In 1955, the *hukou* system was introduced to register all households and categorize them as either agricultural or nonagricultural (Mao 1967/1986: 752). In the early period, Chinese people were guaranteed the right to move into and out of urban cities and throughout the countryside in China (Chan and Li 1999). Between 1953 and 1957, millions of rural peasants sought employment in exchange for the guaranteed job security and welfare benefits of *iron rice bowl* (*tie fanwan*鐵飯碗) within SOEs in the urban cities (Chan and Li 1999). Yet in the aftermath of the Great Leap Forward, there was an influx of an additional 25 million rural workers into the cities in search of work (Fung 2001: 261). The demands that were placed on the State by this rapid shift triggered an "overheating" of the *iron rice bowl* program and economic disaster, as the Chinese State struggled to meet the demands of the populace (Fung 2001).

The State's response was to force the return of thousands of former SOE *danwei* workers to their original rural villages with only minimal resources to help their survival. This confinement of the greater portion of population to the rural environment was reinforced by introducing the household registration or *hukou* system, which regulated rural-urban migration (Mallee 2000). Those who secured an urban *hukou* were entitled to food, housing, education, work, and other social services, whereas those tied to a rural *hukou* had to fend for themselves (Cheung and Selden 1994; Fan 2004). Through this system, Mao secured a permanent supply of low-cost agricultural products, because thousands of workers were confined to rural areas (Fan 2004), while State-enforced policies demanded that these rural cadres continue to supply grain to the State, even though they had minimal or no grain for their own consumption which caused 30 million Chinese died of starvation between 1958 and 1961 (Mitter 2004: 3–6). Yet in the aftermath of the Great Leap Forward, the *hukou* system was further used to restrict rural-urban migration more stringently and to effectively remove approximately 18 million peasant workers from the urban cities (Chan and Li 1999). As a result, the restriction of peasant mobility in the wake of the famine conditions contributed to another 45 million deaths in the rural areas (Dikotter 2010).

Concern about the Maoist policies that had led to these effects triggered another revolutionary movement within the CCP itself. CCP Vice Chairman Liu Shaoqi (1961–1968), who until then had been publicly acknowledged as Mao's successor and had supported the Great Leap Forward (Dittmer 1981), voiced concerns about the deleterious effects of Mao's policies and, along with others such as Deng Xiaoping, who became the leader of the CCP following Mao's death in 1976, introduced a system of contract employment and other economic reforms to address the effects of the Great Leap Forward (Fung 2001). With Liu and Deng's post-Great Leap success, Mao was pushed to the CCP sidelines. In order to retain his mandate to rule the CCP and the country, Mao sought to regain political power by removing his CCP opponents, particularly Liu and Deng, through a program of mass criticism (later the Cultural Revolution) to "criticize bourgeois reactionary thinking" in 1965 (McCormick 2010: 3–16; Tsou 1969). To gain support for the Cultural Revolution, Mao exploited the fear that he had created in the populace against those who became known as "capitalist roaders" (Dittmer 1981) by asserting that their initiatives would see the return of capitalism to China. In this context, Mao sought to legitimize his Cultural Revolution by mobilizing the masses against not only his CCP opponents but also educators (or teachers), "intellectuals," and Confucian sympathizers, who were "enthusiastic" in their support of capitalism (McCormick 2010; Tsou 1969). Mao (1966/2013) argued that Confucianism and its associated economic philosophy had historically been maintained in China through education, literature, and the arts. He proclaimed that educators, intellectuals, writers, and artists perpetuated the "Confucian standards" that inherently harbored the economic values of the dominant capitalist class that were established in traditional China (Mao 1966/2013). Although the capitalist means of production had largely been removed, Mao contended that a dominant proletarian culture of the peasantry was still unrealized in socialist China (Grasso et al. 2009). He insisted that China's socialist revolution could be realized only if the feudalistic (or capitalistic) consciousness deeply rooted in Confucian culture was destroyed and replaced by his own idea of working-class values to establish a proletarian culture in China (2013). Mao thus sought to mobilize the masses through a Cultural Revolution, which he hoped would defeat his free market opponents (MacFarquhar and Schoenhals 2006).

Immediately before the Cultural Revolution, Mao's followers (the Maoists) promoted knowledge of *Mao's Thought* to new heights (Tsou 1969). From 1964, the Maoist Lin Biao, commander of the People's Liberation Army (PLA), promoted "Mao Zedong Thought" by circulating the publication *Quotations from Chairman Mao* (or *Little Red Book*) to every Chinese citizen (Grasso et al. 2009). Later, Lin turned *Mao's Quotations* into PLA policy. He further politicized the PLA through the establishment of several compulsory political classes for soldiers (Weatherley 2006). The purpose of repositioning Mao as a "supreme leader" was to enable him to gain a new sense of legitimacy and correctness. Through this newfound legitimacy, the disobedient CCP leaders, such as Deng and Liu, who turned against Mao, were subject to criticism (Tsou 1969).

To ensure that the inferior masses were thinking and feeling what he wanted them to think and feel, the apotheosis of Mao and his Cultural Revolution was promoted through art and literature in China's cultural sphere (Grasso et al. 2009). Jiang Qing, Mao's wife and a former actress and later a member of the Gang of Four, was appointed to take charge of China's cultural and artistic affairs (Weatherley 2006).[1] Subsequently, Jiang and her allies began to establish Mao's values about revolution and the working class in the Beijing opera (Grasso et al. 2009; Weatherley 2006). In this context, traditional performances of "Confucian-feudal style" plays, which featured characters such as emperors and princes, were outlawed (Grasso et al. 2009). Writers, directors, and performers were forced to write and act scenes that portrayed the masses as destined to "master the country" (Tsou 1969; Lippit 1982). This revolutionary type of theatrical production was further extended to schools, factories, and neighborhoods to mobilize young people throughout the country to join the Red Guards (*hongweibing*紅衛兵) (Mao 1949/1966) in order to "save China" (Grasso et al. 2009). Bewitched by the Maoist propaganda that was pushed by PLA commander Lin and Jiang's committees, millions of Chinese joined the ranks to participate in the Cultural Revolution (Grasso et al. 2009).

In 1966, the Red Guards and the PLA were ordered to repudiate the traditional Confucian culture of feudalism and capitalism under the slogan "eliminate the Four Olds: old ideas, old culture, old customs and old habits" (Grasso et al. 2009; Weatherley 2006). As well as destroying items of traditional Chinese culture, such as books and paintings, the masses were instructed to capture and seize control of labor organizations, including the Ministry of Labour and All-China Federation of Trade Unions (ACFTU), as bases to promote the socialist vision of Mao (Bridgham 1968). This involved further brutal attacks on members of the Chinese populace. Approximately 142,000 teachers, 53,000 scientists, and 2600 writers and artists, who had been identified as "capitalist supporters," were assaulted and murdered, while the disobedient CCP "capitalist roader" Liu was repeatedly beaten to death by Mao's supporters, and Deng was imprisoned in solitary confinement when the revolution was abandoned by 1969 (Dillon 2015; Grasso et al. 2009; Weatherley 2006).

In summary, the turmoil of the Cultural Revolution alongside a series of mass campaigns revealed the Maoists were concerned with generating loyalty of the Chinese masses to Mao being as a legitimate ruler. The use of the old social system to complement and bolster the "new Chinese Marxism" to build a fierce repudiation of the old feudal order was designed to reinforce the Confucian concept of "mandate" to the "virtuous" Mao and the pro-Mao CCP leaders. While Mao's discourse "mass participation in Chinese politics" appeared to show a "genuine concern" for the needs of the masses, our genealogical analysis has illustrated that "mass politics" were linked with the "truth" of Maoism. In other words, "mass participation" was intended as a series of thought reform programs to reshape the consciousness of those labelled as a class of workers (or proletariats) to legitimize Mao's

---

[1]Gang of Four was coined by Mao to describe Jiang Qing and her allies Wang Hongwen, Zhang Chunqiao, and Yao Wenyaun, who supported the Cultural Revolution. (Grasso et al. 2009)

hierarchically superior position. This point was reflected in the active participation of the docile working class in what Mao defined as "anti-capitalist movements" under the "class" discourse. Rather than bringing benefits to the masses by "liberalizing" China, the success of the Maoist thought control programs had created a working class of hundreds of millions of docile bodies and minds to automatically respond to Mao's revolutionary ideologies and practices in deteriorating the already poor country into chaos.

Conclusion

The application of Foucault's genealogical method to the exploration of the making of a working class in this chapter has illustrated how the Confucius thought had historically created docile bodies and minds among the Chinese workers since the Zhou Dynasty (13th B.C.E.) (Grasso et al. 2009). While the traditional imperial order associated with the Confucius values was reportedly replaced by Marxism with the formal establishment of the People's Republic of China (PRC or China) since 1949, the chapter has showed how the Chinese Communist Party (CCP) Chairman Mao Zedong had selectively modified Confucianism and Marxism into *Mao Zedong Thought* (or *Maoism*) and detailed the internalization processes of these values into the minds of the masses (workers or proletariats). In contrast to the workers' experiences in England (Thompson 1966) where the *making* of the English working class was a self-activity among the workers who articulated their feelings and experiences toward their material conditions through which they came to think and struggle as a class of workers, the Chinese working class was spiritually and bodily *made* docile to actively engage in a series of pre-organized revolutionary events through the CCP's Confucian-inspired thought control programs. It is argued that these traditional constitutive elements are retained and updated by the post-Mao CCP leaders to maintain their monopoly on political power while at the same time creating an abundance of cheap and docile workers for China's export-oriented industrialization after Mao's death in 1976. The next chapter will analyze how the post-Mao CCP continues the centuries-long Confucian values to reshape the thoughts and behaviors of the Chinese working class for China's ongoing economic development in the present day.

Cross-References

- ▶ Governmentality and the Chinese Workers in China's Contemporary Thought Management System
- ▶ In Search of the Traces of the History of Management in Latin America, 1870–2020
- ▶ Indian Management (?): A Modernization Experiment
- ▶ Introduction: Management Heterogeneity in Asia
- ▶ Management History in the Modern World: An Overview

- Management in Australia – The Case of Australia's Wealthiest Valley: The Hunter
- The Perfect Natural Experiment: Asia and the Convergence Debate
- Think Big and Privatize Every Thing That Moves: The Impact of Political Reform on the Practice of Management in New Zealand
- What Is Management?

References

Ahn B-J (1975) The political economy of the people's commune in China: changes and continuities. J Asian Stud 34(3):631–658
Barlow J (1981) Mass line leadership and thought reform in China. Am Psychol 36(3):300–309
Breslin S (1998/2014) Mao: profiles in power. Routledge, New York/London
Bridgham P (1967) Mao's "Cultural revolution": origin and development. China Q 29:1–35
Bridgham P (1968) Mao's cultural revolution in 1967: the struggle to seize power. China Q 34:6–37
Brook T, Bourgon J, Blue G (2008) Death by a thousand cuts. Harvard University Press, Cambridge, MA/London
Chai W (2003) The ideological paradigm shifts of China's world views: from Marxism-Leninism-Maoism to the pragmatism-multilateralism of the Deng-Jiang-Hu era. Asian Aff Am Rev 30(3):163–175
Chan KW, Li Z (1999) The hukou system and rural-urban migration in China: processes and changes. China J 160:818–855
Chen X (2002) Social control in China: applications of the labeling theory and the reintegrative shaming theory. Int J Offender Ther Comp Criminol 46(45):45–62
Chen F (2006) Privatization and its discontents in Chinese factories. China Q 185:42–60
Chen J (2013) A middle class without democracy: economic growth and the prospects for democratization in China. Oxford University Press, Oxford
Chen M, Goodman D (2013) Introduction: middle class China – discourse, structure and practice. In: Chen M, Goodman D (eds) Middle class China: identity and behaviour. Edward Elgar, Cheltenham, pp 1–11
Cheung T, Selden M (1994) The origins and social consequences of China's hukou system. China Q 139:644–668
Confucius (c. 475 B.C.E./2003) The analects of Confucius. Beijing Book Co, Beijing
Confucius (c. 475 B.C.E./2010) The analects of Confucius (trans: Legge J). The Floating Press, Auckland
Dikotter F (2010) Mao's great famine: the history of China's most devastating catastrophe, 1958 – 1962. Bloomsbury Publishing Plc, New York/London
Dillon M (2015) Deng Xiaoping: the man who made modern China. I.B. Tauris & Co, New York/London
Dittmer L (1973) Mass line and "mass criticism" in China: an analysis of the fall of Liu Shao-Ch'i. Asian Surv 13(8):772–792
Dittmer L (1981) China in 1980: modernization and its discontents. Asian Surv 21(1):31–50
Dreyer J (1993) China's political system: modernization and tradition. Paragon House Publishers, New York
Fairbank J, Goldman M (2006) China: a new history, 2nd edn. The Belknap Press of Harvard University Press, Cambridge
Fan C (2004) The state, the migrant labor regime, and maiden workers in China. Polit Geogr 23:283–305
Foucault M (1970/2002) The order of things: an archaeology of the human sciences (trans: Tavistock/Routledge). Routledge, London/New York

Foucault M (1971/1977) Nietzsche, genealogy, history. In: Bouchard D (ed) Language, counter-memory, practice: selected essays and interviews. Cornell University Press, Ithaca, pp 139–164

Foucault M (1976/1978) The history of sexuality. Penguin Books, New York

Foucault M (1978/1990) The use of pleasure (trans: Hurley R). Vintage Books, New York

Foucault M (1984/1991) The Foucault reader: an introduction to Foucault's thought (ed: Rabinow P). Penguin, Harmondsworth

Fouts J, Chan J (1995) Confucius, Mao and modernization: social studies education in the People's Republic of China. J Curric Stud 27(5):523–543

Fu C (1974) Confucianism, Marxism-Leninism and Mao: a critical study. J Chin Philos 1:339–371

Fung H-l (2001) The making and melting of the "iron rice bowl" in China 1949 to 1995. Soc Policy Adm 35(3):258–273

Goldman M (1975) China's anti-Confucian campaign, 1973–74. China Q 63:435–462

Grasso J, Corrin J, Kort M (2009) Modernization and revolution: from the opium wars to the olympics, 4th edn. M.E. Sharpe, New York

Guo S (2013) Chinese politics and government: power, ideology and organization. Routledge, London/New York

Gutting G (2003) Michel Foucault: a user's manual. In: Gutting G (ed) The Cambridge companion, 2nd edn. Cambridge University Press, Cambridge, pp 1–28

Helin J, Hernes T, Hjorth D, Holt R (2014) Process is how process does. In: Helin J, Hernes T, Hjorth D, Holt R (eds) The Oxford handbook of process philosophy and organization studies. Oxford University Press, Oxford, pp 1–16

Hook D (2005) Genealogy, discourse, 'effective history': Foucault and the work of critique. Qual Res Psychol 2(1):3–31

Hurst W (2008) Mass frames and worker protest. In: O'Brien K (ed) Popular protest in China. Harvard University Press, Cambridge, MA, pp 71–87

Hurst W (2009) The Chinese worker after socialism. Cambridge University Press, Cambridge

Hurst W, O'Brien K (2002) China's contentious pensioners. China Q 170:345–360

Landsberger S (2002) The deification of Mao: religious imagery and practices during the cultural revolution and beyond. In: Chong WL (ed) China's great proletarian cultural revolution. Rowman & Littlefield Publishers, Oxford, pp 139–184

Lee CK (2000) The 'revenge of history': collective memories and labor protests in north-eastern China. Ethnography 1(2):217–237

Lee CK (2002) From the specter of Mao to the spirit of the law: labor insurgency in China. Theory Soc 31:189–228

Leung E (2016) Docile bodies and minds: a genealogy of Chinese workers in China. In: Chou M (ed) TASA 2016 conference proceeding. The Australian Catholic University, Fitzroy, pp 215–221

Li W, Yang DT (2005) The Great Leap Forward: anatomy of a central planning disaster. J Polit Econ 113(4):840–877

Lin J, Cai F, Li Z (1996) The China miracle: development strategy and economic reform. The Chinese University of Hong Kong, Hong Kong

Lippit V (1982) China's socialist development. In: Selden M, Lippit V (eds) The transition to socialism in China. M.E. Sharpe, New York

Lu X (1998) Rhetoric in ancient China, fifth to third century B.C.E: a comparison with classical greek rhetoric. University of South Carolina Press, Columbia

Lu X (2004) Rhetoric of the Chinese cultural revolution: the impact on Chinese thought, culture, and communication. University of South Carolina Press, Columbia

MacFarquhar R (1997) Introduction. In: MacFarquhar R (ed) The politics of China: the eras of Mao and Deng. Cambridge University Press, Cambridge, pp 1–4

MacFarquhar R, Schoenhals M (2006) Mao's last revolution. Harvard University Press, Cambridge

Mallee H (2000) Migration, hukou, resistance in reform China. In: Perry E, Selden M (eds) Chinese society, change, conflict and resistance. Routledge, London/New York

Mao Z (1949/1966) Mao Zedong thought. People's Publishing House, Beijing
Mao Z (1966/2013) Quotations from chairman Mao Tse-Tung. Read Books Ltd, Beijing
Mao Z (1967/1986) The writings of Mao Zedong: 1949 – 1976. M.E. Sharpe, New York
Mao Z (1949/2013) On the people's democratic dictatorship. Green Apple Data Center, Hunan
Mathur P (1987) The Chinese enlightenment movement. China Report 23(4):457–463
McCormick J (2010) Comparative politics in transition. Cengage Learning, Boston
Melton G (2014) Faiths across time: 5,000 years of religious history. ABC-CLIO, Oxford
Miethe TD, Lu H (2005) Punishment: a comparative historical perspective. Cambridge University Press, Cambridge
Mitter R (2004) A bitter revolution: China's struggle with the modern world. Oxford University Press, New York
Nicholls D (2009) Putting Foucault to work: an approach to the practical application of Foucault's methodological imperatives. Aporia 1(1):30–40
O'Farrell C (1989) Foucault: historian or philosopher? The Macmillan Press Ltd, London
O'Farrell C (2005) Michel Foucault. SAGE, California
Oi J (1995) The role of the local state in China's transitional economy. China Q 144:1132–1149
Poster M (1982) Foucault and history. Soc Res 49(1):116–142
Pye L (1986) Reassessing the cultural revolution. China Q 108:597–612
Pye L (1999) An overview of 50 years of the People's Republic of China: some progress, but big problems remain. China Q 159:569–579
Rojek D (1989) Social control in the People's Republic of China. Crim Justice Rev 14:141–153
Schram S (1969) The party in Chinese communist ideology. China Q 38:1–28
Teiwes F (1997) The establishment and consolidation of the new regime, 1949 – 57. In: MacFarquhar R (ed) The politics of China: the eras of Mao and Deng, 2nd edn. Cambridge University Press, Cambridge, pp 5–86
Teiwes F (2000) The Chinese state during the Maoist Era. In: Shambaugh D (ed) The modern Chinese state. Cambridge University Press, Cambridge, pp 105–160
Thompson EP (1966) The making of the English working class. Vintage Books, New York
Tsou T (1969) The cultural revolution and the Chinese political system. China Q 38:63–91
Tsou T (1986) The cultural revolution and post-Mao reforms: a historical perspective. The University of Chicago Press, Chicago
Walder A (1991) Workers, managers and the state: the reform era and the political crisis of 1989. China Q 127:467–492
Walder A, Gong X (1993) Workers in the Tiananmen protests: the politics of the Beijing workers' autonomous. Aust J Chin Aff 29:1–29
Weatherley R (2006) Politics in China since 1949: legitimizing authoritarian rule. Routledge, New York
Whyte M (1988) Evolutionary changes in Chinese culture. Transformations 14:1–22
Withington J (2008) A disastrous history of the world: chronicles of war, earthquake, plague and famine. Hachette Digital, London
Wu X, Treiman D (2004) The household registration system and social stratification in China: 1955 – 1996. Demography 41(2):363–384
Zhang J (2014) The tradition and modern transition of Chinese law. Springer, Heidelberg
Zhou G (c. 1100 B.C.E./1930) In: Li Z (ed) Zhou Li compilation: vol 108–114. Harvard University, Harvard

Governmentality and the Chinese Workers in China's Contemporary Thought Management System

60

Elly Leung

Contents

Introduction	1368
Foucault's Concept of Governmentality	1369
Reinterpretation of a Chinese History of the Present	1371
Governmental Technologies and Thought Management in Post-Mao China	1373
Chinese Habits of Making Docile Bodies and Minds within Social Hierarchy	1375
The Destiny (*ming* 命) of Low-Quality (or Low-Educated) Workers in the Chinese Occupational Hierarchy	1379
Conclusion	1380
Cross-References	1380
References	1381

Abstract

The aim of this chapter is to understand how the Chinese Communist Party (CCP) creates an abundantly cheap and docile worker to meet the labor market needs required for economic development in present-day China. Drawing on the genealogical analysis of the Chinese historical events from the previous chapter, this chapter engages with Michel Foucault's (1982) work of governmentality (*government of mentalities*) to argue that workers' docility is maintained by the CCP's ability to retain, update, and incorporate Confucian values into its thought management system to regulate the ways of thinking and acting among workers in a social hierarchy as in the time of Imperial and Mao's China.

Keywords

Governmentality · Power-knowledge · Quality · Docility · Discourses · Confucian hierarchy · Thought management

E. Leung (✉)
Business School, University of Western Australia, Perth, WA, Australia
e-mail: elly.leung@uwa.edu.au

Introduction

The success of economic reform in transforming China from a rural, revolutionary-based economy into a modern, industrialized socialist market economy (Leung and Caspersz 2016) following the death of Mao Zedong in 1976 (see ▶ Chap. 59, "The Making of a Docile Working Class in Pre-reform China") has repositioned the country as the world's factory and export leader (Leung and Pun 2009) with the largest and cheapest workforce of a minimum of 769 million workers (The World Bank 2019). Much has noted that this abundantly cheap labor force is developed by converting millions of peasants into urban industrial and service workers and by dismantling the lifetime employment (or *iron rice bowl*) that was developed in the Maoist State (see ▶ Chap. 59, "The Making of a Docile Working Class in Pre-reform China") for millions of laid-off workers across Chinese State-owned enterprises (SOEs) (Chan 2001; Fan 2003, 2004; Hurst and O'Brien 2002; Leung and Pun 2009; Li and O'Brien 1996; O'Brien 1996; Pun 2007; Pun et al. 2009; Pun and Lu 2010a, b). It is suggested that workers' past experience of Mao's socialism (Lee 2000; Walder 1991; Walder and Gong 1993) or their brutal work-based experiences (Chan and Pun 2009; Chan 2010; Chan and Hui 2012, 2016; Leung and Pun 2009; Pringle 2011; Pun and Lu 2010a, b; Pun et al. 2009, 2016; Smith and Pun 2006) have progressively stimulated their class consciousness to spark a rising number of "mass incidents," including environmental and work protests and other strikes, from 74,000 in 2004 and to 87,000 in 2005 (Leung and Pun 2009) in advancing their collective work rights and benefits to improve their overall conditions. Despite the view that this increased volume of protest activities in China depicts a "rising class consciousness" (Chan 2010; Chan and Hui 2016; Chan and Selden 2016; Chan and Pun 2009), alternative studies (Blecher 2002; Chan 2011; Chan and Siu 2012; Chen 2000, 2006; 2016a; Cooke et al. 2016; Franceschini et al. 2016; Lee 1999, 2007) spotlight the quiescence of labor as a factor constraining workers to against their exploitative conditions. For example, Lee (1999) claims that disorganized despotism has produced labor subordination through the flexible recruitment and dismissal of workers from a disposable labor market. Chan and Siu (2012) find that the absence of collective rights to organize independent unions and the lack of knowledge about trade unionism led to workers' disunity that consequently destabilized their protest actions. It is further argued that the outbreaks of worker protests are mainly triggered by workers' desperation to defend their "rights to subsistence" (Chen 2006). For instance, the wages that workers demand in their protests were "lower than the amount they are legally entitled to" (Franceschini et al. 2016: 440), and therefore, their actions "can be easily defused by a government promise of a couple of yuan as compensation" to secure their subsistence level (Chen 2016b: 4). These phenomena are arguably directed by workers' self-values that they believe their given conditions are inevitable (Blecher 2002), hence dissuading them from speaking up for themselves and others (Cooke et al. 2016) or from engaging in sustained labor movements that focus on issues beyond their individual needs (Chan 2011; Chan and Siu 2012; Franceschini et al. 2016).

Aligned with this body of literature, the aim of this chapter is to understand how the post-Mao CCP continues to monopolize its political power while at the same time creating an abundance of cheap and docile workers to meet the labor market needs required for China's economic development. The chapter argues that workers' docility is indelibly influenced by the "old" forms of consciousness and interactions that existed in Imperial and Mao's periods (see ▶ Chap. 59, "The Making of a Docile Working Class in Pre-reform China"). Drawing on the genealogical analysis of the Chinese historical events from the previous chapter, the chapter further engages with Michel Foucault's (1982) work of governmentality (*government of mentalities* or conduct of conduct) to argue that workers' docility is maintained by the CCP's ability to retain, update, and incorporate Confucian values of filial piety (*xiao*孝); "Mandate of Heaven" (*tianming*天命); and destiny (or *ming*命) (see ▶ Chap. 59, "The Making of a Docile Working Class in Pre-reform China") into its thought management system to regulate the ways of thinking and acting among workers in a social hierarchy as in the time of Imperial and Mao's China.

The chapter begins with an overview of Foucault's concept of governmentality before discussing the techniques used by the CCP in pursuing a contemporary thought management system to consolidate their "mandate" to rule. The chapter concludes that the CCP's thought management as a means for the continuation of the (re-) production of docile minds and bodies in serving its interests has been the key strategy that strengthens its political power with little violence in China.

Foucault's Concept of Governmentality

Under the rubric of genealogy (or History of the Present) (see ▶ Chap. 59, "The Making of a Docile Working Class in Pre-reform China"), Michel Foucault (1980a, b) proposes the concept of governmentality to investigate the technologies (techniques or strategies) that govern individuals. Defined as the "conduct of conduct," Foucault's genealogical work of governmentality describes how certain knowledge emerged as a social "truth" (see ▶ Chap. 59, "The Making of a Docile Working Class in Pre-reform China") to shape thought and behavior (conducts or practices) according to a *given* "truth" in particular society (1980b; 1982). Foucault's genealogical analysis of madness (1961/2006), medical knowledge (1963/2003, 1969/2002), imprisonment (1977), and sexuality (1976/1978) demonstrates that social practices at a specific historical moment resulted from the construction of knowledge (truth or reality) that informed their experiences of their existence according to the particular cultural values and criteria. On this basis, Foucault (1980a) notes that all histories contain thoughts from particular cultures that are inseparable from individuals' actions (practices or behaviors) and from their experiences of existence.

In *The History of Sexuality* (1976/1978, 1978/1990, 1984/1986), for example, Foucault analyzes how individuals' experiences of "homosexuality" were objectified and influenced by the medical knowledge (discourse or truth) that had emerged since the nineteenth century. Hence those categorized as "homosexuals" were viewed according to that knowledge which became the dominant thought in Western societies. Foucault contends that these forms of knowledge created culturally specific views and practices that eventually came to constitute (or affirm certain practices as inimitable) the conditions that lead to the categorization of people as – for instance – "homosexuals." Foucault argues that our "knowing" of how these conditions became linked to this categorization cannot be solely revealed by studying the experience of a person or historical moment but by analyzing the knowledge that is embedded in the relevant society (Foucault 1976/1978, 1978/1990, 1984/1986).

Foucault crafts the concept of power-knowledge to describe how we come to know the "rules of right" or the *pouvoir-savoir* (discourse) that shape, form, and hence constitute our social identities (statuses or positions) (Foucault 1991). That is, an individuals' understanding of identity, such as in the case of homosexuality, emerges because of the relations of power that confirm this as "knowledge" (or objectify) in webs of beliefs (Foucault 1954/2001, 1984/1991). In this context, Foucault conceptualizes knowledge as a specific technique of power which is exercised to internalize disciplinary power (or "microphysics of power" or "biopower") by the individuals so that they discipline their own bodies, minds, and souls in their social relationships (or power-knowledge relations) (1977: 26). Thus, unlike the juridical view that power is exercised by the State and its apparatuses (see Crowther and Green 2004; Giddens and Dallmayr 1982; Musto 2012; Noon et al. 2013), Foucault focuses on the capillary nature and the dispersed character of micro-power that is exercised through the networks of productive, individual relations which produces reality by co-constructing the discourses ("truth" or knowledge) of rituals and identities, such as "criminals" and "madmen," in guiding individuals to shape and correct their minds as well as their behaviors in society (1984/1991). Foucault's view of power draws upon Jeremy Bentham's (1843: 39) nineteenth century drawings of the interior design of the Panopticon (or prison) that consists of a circular structure with an inspection house at the center of the tower. The concept of this design is to guide the prisoners to believe the watchmen in the tower are observing them as they cannot see into the tower, and hence they self-regulate their behaviors as if they are being watched. This form of self-government (or self-regulation) creates a "new mode of obtaining power of mind over mind [governmentality or 'conduct of conduct' in Foucault's terminology], in a quantity..." (Bentham 1843: 39) to effectively control and reform the criminals (Magill 1997; Oksala 2007: 57). This is because the truth of *being watched* under constant surveillance in the panoptic system facilitates the automatic functioning of a disciplinary power within the minds and bodies of the criminals without external authority being imposed (Ransom 1997).

Using the metaphor of the Panopticon, Foucault (1977) notes that a disciplinary power is embedded in all levels of social relations in smaller elements like the hospitals, the schools, the factories, the prisons, and even in individuals' families. Together these social relations exercise a *regime* of a disciplinary power among the masses of people to produce a norm (truth or rule) of behaviors, all the while ensuring that deviant behaviors from this norm are identified as needing to be corrected according to their identities such as "homosexuals" or even "criminals."

For example, schools and families constitute minute social "observatories" and surveillance systems to train and correct children's behavior – their piety and morals – toward their teachers and parents (Foucault 1977). Foucault (1977) suggests that these domains subsequently resemble a carceral (or prison) system that creates a dominant class of managed, controlled, and useful bodies who serve as the judges of normality in society – the teacher-judge, the doctor-judge, and the social worker-judge – and ensure that everyone acts to the discourses of truth that are embedded in a particular society (Foucault 1980a, b, 1991).

The extensions of the panoptic system to various unofficial settings in exercising forms of indirect supervision have thus made individuals subject to their bodies, soul, gestures, behaviors, and practices to the given discourses of truth within their relations of power-knowledge (Foucault 1977). It is in this context that Foucault (1980a, b) argues that a disciplinary society emerges, not by the making of laws but by the internalization of norms that have conjoined the mind, body, and movement of individuals. This effect is referred to as governmentality (or conduct of conduct) that guides the individuals to self-regulate their own (and others') behavior, to achieve the status of truths (or norms) of their society within their power-knowledge network of their culture without engaging in critical thinking (Foucault 1980b). Foucault thus describes the outcome of this government of mentalities as the effective operations of both direct (the State or institutions per se) and indirect (the social network) forms of disciplinary power in guiding people's behaviors to the *desired end* of others (1978/2008).

Reinterpretation of a Chinese History of the Present

Drawing on the genealogical analysis from the Previous Chapter, this chapter argues that China's thought management epitomizes the trend of blending the centuries-long Confucian methods of persuasion (see ▶ Chap. 59, "The Making of a Docile Working Class in Pre-reform China") with new governmental discourses (truths or technologies) (Foucault 1979/2014) and rationalities to maintain workers' docility for ongoing economic development. Beginning with dismantling and privatizing both the State-owned enterprises (SOEs) and the people's communes (see ▶ Chap. 59, "The Making of a Docile Working Class in Pre-reform China"), peasants along with SOE workers are pushed to participate in low-rate wages and a high-rate of capitalist exploitation in the coastal areas (Gabriel 2006). Despite poor working conditions that led to their first major protest involvement in the 1989 Tiananmen movement (Howell 1993; Warner 1991; Walder and Gong 1993), workers remain working in appalling conditions enduring 12 hours a day or longer for 7 days a week, in the labor-intensive export-led manufacturing sector (Mah 2011). Although the All-China Federation of Trade Unions (ACFTU) – the only legal, State-owned trade unions – has a "mandate" to defend workers' rights and interests under the *Labour Law* (1995) and the subsequent *Labour Contract Law* (2008), the capacity of the ACFTU to provide workers with assistance is constrained by a set of other laws, including the *Trade Union Laws* (1992 & 2001), *Assembly Law* (1989), and the

Criminal Law (1987) (Pringle 2011). The failure of the Chinese Communist Party (CCP) to eliminate the abuse of its labor force has thus progressively incited workers to turn to nonlegal methods, such as collective protests, to voice their dissatisfaction with their employment conditions (Chan 2010).

The dual concern of the CCP with the increased protest activities and the need to secure a cheap and docile labor force for economic growth are highlighted in the Eleventh Five-Year Plan (2006–2010) with the governmental discourse of maintenance of social stability (*weiwen* 維穩) (*China Daily* 2006). *Weiwen*, therefore, indicates not only the shift in emphasis away from coercive administrative measures and control of workers but also a new strategy of the CCP to "connect to the global track" (Xu 2009: 38). Xu (2009) uses the phrase "connecting to the global track" to describe China's role in participating in the global supply chain production and ensuring administrative practices comply with international norms, including business and labor regulations. Given the rights of workers are fundamentally grounded in their labor contracts, the CCP, for instance, promulgated the 2008 *Labour Contract Law* to emphasize workers' responsibility of ensuring their employers sign a labor contract with them in order to protect their legal rights (Pringle 2011). While the CCP appears to be concerned with the labor rights, it is argued that the CCP seeks to guide the willingness of workers to subject themselves to the exploitative conditions to reinforce the *weiwen* project under the governmental discourses of the development of a well-off (*xiaokang* 小康) and harmonious society (*hexie shehui* 和諧社會) (Brady 2012a; Benney 2016; Xu 2009).

A key component of building a *xiaokang* and harmonious society under *weiwen* discourse is linked with the CCP's "zero target" (Benney and Marolt 2015) project, aiming to eliminate visible forms of protest actions, through the horizontal coordination with government agencies and private entrepreneurs (Benney 2016; Chen 2015). Since the last decade, private entrepreneurs are encouraged to become members of the People's Political Consultative Conference (PPCC) to participate in the governing activities at the national and local levels (Chen 2015). Together with the PPCC, the CCP, the Chinese People's Government, and the People's Congress are referred to as *the four sets of leadership* (*si tao banzi* 四套班子), which constitute a "multi-party co-operation and political consultation" system (Chen 2015: 616–617). The PPCC in this system serves as a channel for entrepreneurs to express opinions and thus influence State policies and regulations to protect their particular interests as a group (Chen 2015). For example, the concern with the protection of private property rights raised by the members at the PPCC annual meeting in 2001 was passed into the *Property Law* in 2007 (Chen 2015: 627). The privilege status of the PPCC membership further prevents the entrepreneurs from legal responsibilities even when enterprises had violated the provincial laws and regulations (Chen 2015). By turning private entrepreneurs into the State's "allies" by raising protection for the PPCC members beyond laws and regulations, it is suggested that the CCP leaders seek to "buy stability" by marginalizing the notions of laws and rights (Benney and Marolt 2015).

"Buying stability" in the context of the "retreat from law" is thus extended to China's social system to facilitate the work of *weiwen* (Benney and Marolt 2015). The establishment of local *stability maintenance offices* (*weiwenban* 維穩辦) which draws officials from the legal profession, the police, quasi-government organizations, and local government has been the mechanism to prevent protest and acts of resistance from formalizing (Benney 2013; Benney and Marolt 2015). Despite exercising physical force occasionally, *weiwenban* tends to use informal negotiation and renegotiation associated with financial compensation or small "coordination fees" to "encourage" workers to discontinue their disputes (Benney 2013). Subsequently, worker protests are reportedly easily defused by a couple of yuan as compensation (Chen 2016a: 4). While shifting away from using military forces for social control, the ability of the CCP to exercise *weiwen* strategies to continue to manage and dominate workers through the ongoing historical cycles of "coercive authoritarianism" (Benney 2013) is because workers' psyche has been embedded with a truth about their inferior status (or position) and those considered superior through these cycles.

It is argued that China's *weiwen* project is grounded on the expansion and development of productive forces by guiding "the Chinese," particularly the "dissident groups," to engage in a market economy (Xu 2009). Drawing on Mao's thought control methods, the post-Mao leaders from Deng to current President Xi Jinping seek to revitalize the Confucian ideologies of filial piety and obey the superiors to continue their "mandate" to rule under the control of the CCP (Dillon 2015). Already in 1982, the Confucian values of filial piety and obey the superiors have been indicated in the *Four Cardinal Principles*, that is, *Marxist-Leninism, Socialism, Party Leadership, and People's Democratic Dictatorship*, to demonstrate the CCP's commitment to Mao's idea of embracing absolute political control of the masses (Zhang and Li 2011). This insistence is further announced in the *Five Nos* (*wugebugao* 五個不搞) policy for the modernization process:

> We have made a solemn declaration that we will not employ a system of multiple parties holding office in rotation; diversify our guiding thought; separate executive, legislative and judicial powers; use a bicameral or federal system, or carry out privatization (Wu 2011b, p. 9). (The word "privatization" in China was replaced by numerous terms, such as reorganization, cooperatives, incorporation, leasing contract, and shareholding cooperatives. See Guo 2013)

Combining with the *Four Cardinal Principles*, the *Five Nos* policy which emphasizes Deng's message on economic reform with limited political change is circulated to legitimize his absolute power through the CCP's Central Propaganda Department (Weatherley 2006).

Governmental Technologies and Thought Management in Post-Mao China

As in the Maoist period (see ▶ Chap. 59, "The Making of a Docile Working Class in Pre-reform China"), the manipulation and utilization of the Propaganda Department have been an important tool to initiate thought management for complementing and supporting the CCP policies (Brady 2012a; Benney 2013). Using the logic of laws and legal system that is developed since the 1980s, the CCP develops the "law popularization campaign" (*pufa yundong*普法運動) or "disseminating legal knowledge" (*pufa changshi*普法常識) to herald new policies in activating the masses to engage in the State's defined "good socialist behaviors" (Gallagher 2005, 2006):

> In the interest of developing socialist democracy and improving the socialist legal system, it is necessary to place the law in the hands of the masses of people so that they will know what the law is, abide by the law, acquire a sense of legality and learn to use the law as a weapon against all acts committed in violation of the Constitution and the law [...]. (Thirteen Meeting of the Standing Committee of the Sixth National People's Congress, November 22, 1985)

Rather than focusing on legal resolution of grievances, the dissemination or *pufa* movement enacted in 1991 aiming at acquainting the masses with basic knowledge of the laws by inculcating them with a wide variety of State's propaganda or ideologies to shape their legal consciousness (Benney 2013). These legal educational campaigns are implemented by the CCP cadres through workplaces, mass media, and educational systems (Gallagher 2005). For example, the "thought emancipation movement" (1979–1981) is regularly used to transmit the truth about *Deng Xiaoping Theory* of economic reform and modernization to cultivate them with correct thoughts and practices – filial piety and hard work – through the Chinese media (Jeffreys and Su 2016). Other ideological campaigns "anti-spiritual pollution" (1983–1984) and the "socialist spiritual civilization campaign" (1987–1998) are launched against the influx of Western democratic values and habits (Leung 2017). These campaigns are eventually a call for CCP members to promote *Deng Xiaoping Theory* of economic reform and modernization in order to command support from the workers over whom they were to rule (Grasso et al. 2009).

As the *pufa* campaign progressed, a wide range of compulsory reeducation programs of the "party rectification campaigns" and "theoretical study movements" (1989–2000) of *Marxism-Leninism, Mao Zedong Thought*, and *Deng Xiaoping Theory* are implemented to penetrate the socialist ideologies and moralities (Li 2015) into the minds of workers. For instance, at the national conference on the "party rectification campaigns" and "theoretical study movements" in 1998, the philosophical absolutism of the CCP in command of the absolute "truth" and correctness in building a "socialist market economy" is emphasized:

> Taking the socialist road is the inevitable outcome of Chinese history and the correct choice of the Chinese people [...] Any attempt to abandon socialism or take the capitalist road is completely wrong and fundamentally infeasible [...] Our reform is absolutely not to engage in capitalism, but is the self-perfection of the socialist system and the need of consolidating and developing socialism. Anything that might jeopardise socialism and the fundamental interest of our people must not be tolerated and must not be allowed to spread unchecked at any time and under any circumstances. (Jiang Zemin cited in Guo 2013: 118)

The above message is further transmitted via the implementation of "scientific development" and "harmonious society campaigns" (2010) through the national education system, mass media, residential areas, and workplaces to stress the important role of "patriotism as a unifying force" by emphasizing "[...] China's [workers] is a matter of concern for China's destiny" (Brady 2008: 51) in order to mobilize "the whole party and the whole people of the nation" to work for economic modernization (Guo 2013:119). All of these political campaigns for economic modernization have indicated that many of the Maoist mobilization mechanisms and practices are retained by the post-Mao leaders to indoctrinate the general population daily with the "correct" CCP "truth" and the *Four Cardinal Principles* to construct a "socialist market economy" under the legal discourses (Guo 2013).

Chinese Habits of Making Docile Bodies and Minds within Social Hierarchy

Henceforth, while dissociating from Mao's revolutionary orthodoxy, the Maoist past "habits" of ideological indoctrination and techniques of propaganda have been repeatedly employed by different generations of post-Mao leaders to shape workers' consciousness align with the vague ideas of the laws (*pufa*) to constitute them as docile bodies and minds for sustainable socioeconomic development (*kechixuxing de shehui jingjin fazhan*可持續性的社會經濟發展) (Jeffreys and Su 2016). With rapid economic development associated with the growth of poverty, the third and the fourth generations of the CCP leaders Jiang Zemin and Hu Jintao seek to minimize social discontent and instability by upgrading the control methods (Xu 2009). From 2001 onward, the Hu administration incorporated new governmental discourses into the Confucian values to promote awareness of "proper behavior," such as respect for authorities, between the positions (or status) of workers and work superiors, to meet the needs of economic modernization in a well-off (*xiaokang*) and harmonious society (*hexie shehui*) (Brady 2012b). The new sets of values that are guiding the behavior of workers begin with the creation of numerous identities through the mass media through which the CCP aims to change social images of both peasant migrant and SOE workers by referring to the latter as *gongren*工人 (SOE workers or government slaves 宫人in Imperial China) (Wagner 1998) and the former as *non-mingong* 農民工 (peasant workers), as well as *mangliu* 盲流 (blind floats), *wailaigong* 外來工 (outside workers), and *dagong* 打工 (working for bosses). Unlike their former status as "masters of the State" (see ▶ Chap. 59, "The Making of a Docile Working Class in Pre-reform China") under Mao's period, workers' new identities are now accorded a subservient status, which is programmed to be at a lower social position. This status degradation, according to Xu (2009), is linked to the new discourse of "low personal quality" (*suzhi* 素質or human capital) aiming at creating a self-value to serve as a rational justification among workers for accepting social inequalities in the market economy. This effort is an attempt to mold workers into "low personal quality" subjects to become active participants in capitalist exploitation in the updated hierarchy of social relationships.

In making China's economy globally competitive, the value of education has become a priority to constitute "low personal quality" workers to ensure the supply of a mass of cheap labor for production (Wang 2008). This objective is achieved through the rapid expansion of educational opportunities by popularizing secondary and tertiary vocational-technical education that teaches employment skills to enable graduates to work in the cities (Postiglione 2011). The admission criterion is subject completion of the 9-year education program under the *Compulsory Education Law* (Wang 2008). While the national population is "guaranteed" 9 years of compulsory schooling by law, access to education is determined by the *hukou* (or household) status (see ▶ Chap. 59, "The Making of a Docile Working Class in Pre-reform China") the person held (Rong and Shi 2001). The difference in the educational arrangements between rural and urban populations is that the latter is entitled to a set of social rights associated with the provision of medical care, housing, childcare, and access to local schools with very low fees (Wang 2008). These basic entitlements are denied to the rural peasants – which accounted for more than half of the national population – both in their village hometowns and the cities (Wu 2011a).

Children of migrant peasants are thus either left behind (*liushou ertong*留守兒童) with relatives in the villages or brought into the cities for education (Zhang et al. 2015). In the former case, rural children began a 2- to 3-year education in the villages when they turned 8 years old, because rural schools are far from home and the roads were generally unsafe for small children (Postiglione 2011). In the latter case, migrant children, formally referred to as *jiedu* 借讀 students (students from outside the community that borrowed a place to study), have to pay *jiedu* fee ranging from 4,000 yuan to 15,000 yuan (Jia et al. 2019) to the public schools in the cities. Given the monthly household income of most migrant parents is between 1,000 and 2,000 yuan which is around the local poverty line in most localities (Leung and Caspersz 2016), a large proportion of the children of migrants are either educated in migrant schools (*minban xuexiao*民辦學校) in the cities or in rural schools in the villages. Due to financial issues, these schools have low-quality teaching staff and poor facilities (Postiglione 2011; Wang 2008).

By creating this rural-urban divide – that is historically defined by birth – the structure of the Chinese educational system provides a specific means of producing and reproducing "low personal quality" workers for the CCP's market socialism. Thus, rather than focusing on ideas of "Marxism" in the education provision, the making of a socialist market in the CCP's economic modernization concerns with the ability of the population to pay for a quality education that might gain them employment (Postiglione 2011). Compared to their urban counterparts, the majority of poor rural households are excluded from the mainstream norm of access to public schools that offer quality education, both in the cities and in their villages (Wang 2008). This deliberate exclusion of the rural groups from access to educational resources and opportunities beyond a limited circle of eligibilities thus led to high dropout rates from the low-quality, rural, and migrant primary schools:

> [...] dropout rates [...] were between 3.66% and 54.05% [...] beyond food and clothing, dropping out is caused by a lack of confidence and interest in continuing their education, difficult textbooks, a monotonous school life, tense relationships between students and

teachers, poor food and lodging, inconvenient transportation and rising costs of school lodgings. (Postiglione 2011: 90)

By confining rural and migrant populations to the category of low-quality education, the CCP leaders thus implicitly encouraged children to discontinue education, through which a minimum of 300 million illiterate and semi-illiterate people are created in China (Mao 2004). The intentional education inequality thus ensured that a large proportion of people could not get a higher education in order to produce and reproduce "low personal quality" workers for the marketplace.

Images of "low personal quality" workers are further portrayed as a specific segment of the population that prevent China's progress toward civilization (*wenming*文明) (Gabriel 2006; Xu 2009). In an editorial comment in a prestigious State-owned newspaper, "low-quality" population is described as lacking discipline and modern civility because "they behav[e] like barbarians [...] forgetting [...] civility demands [...]" (China Daily 2014). As a result of widespread indoctrination, this official "truth" becomes an everyday discourse that appeared in various cultural mechanisms, such as television and magazines. For example, in a national newspaper *Nanfang Zhoumo* 南方週末 (*Southern Weekend*), a reader complained to the editor that "the low-quality people are the reason for many things not getting done or not getting done well" (Xiaoyong 1999: 11). In his book, *China's Two Pillars in the Twenty-First Century*, Yi (2001: 748) suggests a more pessimistic view of the large numbers of so-called "low-quality" citizens by making the point that it is these people that "made it so difficult to advance our country [...] we must get rid of the illiterate people [...] particularly those illiterate young people."

Social recognition of the "low-quality" population is applied predominantly to workers and is central to the production of "new city people" (*xin shimin*新市民) as the subjects of Chinese "development" (Yan 2003; Xu 2009). This "development" centers on the "rectification" of population quality, in terms of which workers are identified by the CCP from the 1980s, as the major focus for "improvement": "The national strength and the stamina of economic development is highly dependent on the quality of the labourers" (Zeng 1989: 165). Embedded in this invocation of "quality improvement" (or development) is the CCP's interest to continue poverty by recoding such "problem" as "quality poverty relief" (*suzhi fupin*素質扶貧) and "cultural poverty relief" (*wenhua fupin*文化扶貧) in the labor market (Yan 2003). In this context, "poverty-relief" discourses are functioned as a "motivating force" to cultivate a desire within the "low personal quality" workers' to escape from poverty (*tuopin*脫貧) (Yan 2008). Thus, the introduction of this new discourse by the State marks a shift from projecting workers as being an object to becoming a subject for "poverty-relief" actions (Yan 2003). The project of producing these desiring subjects is appositely a subtle task of producing "new city people" for Chinese "development" (or improvement).

It is argued that the production of the *desiring* subjects is conditioned by the production of a market consciousness among workers for "development" through cultural processes (Yan 2008). In these processes, images of the outcomes of "poverty relief" that resulted from "improvement," for example, with the increased affordability of mobile phones and cars, are promoted in the Chinese media (Gabriel 2006). These commercial activities are used to promote the idea that "the future belongs to those who succeed in the capitalist labor power markets" to turn workers into customers (Gabriel 2006: 58). By inculcating consumerism into the popular consciousness, instruments of mass media are again mobilized as a form of "social education" (*shehui jiaoyu*社會教育) to publicize the benefits of "improvement" to inspire the subjects' "intentionality" toward the "development" of the labor market (Yan 2003). This vision produces a positive demonstration of "poverty relief" being gifted through the opportunities afforded by "development," because "low-quality" workers could "improve themselves by learning from their "high-quality" superiors at work in the cities" (Yan 2008).

By introducing a self-perception of workers as the subjects of "development," the discourse of "quality improvement" further constituted a "status consciousness" (Koo 2001) or "older rules consciousness" (Perry 2009) that is connected to an updated Confucian status ideology framework of a "quality hierarchy" within social relationships (Chen and Goodman 2012; Yan 2003). This "hierarchal relationship" is defined in terms of the deterministic identities with which the "lower-quality" workers are shaped and "programmed" to see themselves as inferior to their "higher-quality" superiors in the labor market (Gabriel 2006). The perception of a fundamental difference of "quality" that comprised distinct "races" of human beings is thereby notionally created:

> [...] "white" workers gaining status as a consequence of racism. To the extent that certain workers gain status within the workplace as a consequence of racism, these workers may be willing to work for less material compensation. This is one way in which racism may reduce the value of labour power. It may also do so by creating self-doubt, self-hatred and low self-esteem in those excluded from the transcendental race. The "black" [...] worker [...] for instance, believe[s] herself lucky to have any job and to be worthless [...]. (Gabriel and Todorova 2003: 34–35)

By substituting "high quality" for white and "low quality" for black, the racialized interactions of the perceived inferiority (the low) and the perceived superiority (the high) in China served to lower the value of workers in a quality hierarchy (Gabriel 2006; Yan 2008). Rather than a "quality improvement," the discourse of "development" hence imposed the notion of destiny (*ming*命) on inferiority (see ▶ Chap. 59, "The Making of a Docile Working Class in Pre-reform China") so that it would then function as a "truth" of the "low personal quality" workers to think of themselves as low within their subjectivities concerning their given positions in the current labor market system (Yan 2003). The CCP's strategies of keeping the "low personal quality" workers to think and act within their prescribed *ming* by restricting their educational opportunities are the foundation of thought management established since the Zhou dynasty (13th B.C.E.) via *li* rules (later Confucian rules) (see ▶ Chap. 59, "The Making of a Docile Working Class in Pre-reform China") to maintain social status for producing and reproducing docile bodies and minds to meet the political, ideological, and economic needs in different historical periods.

The Destiny (*ming* 命) of Low-Quality (or Low-Educated) Workers in the Chinese Occupational Hierarchy

The intention of indoctrinating workers to accept their positions as their *ming* and the discourse of "quality development" is to subject the perceived "inferiors" to continual readjustment and retraining (*zhongsheng xuexi*終生學習) in order to integrate them into the market economy (Yan 2008). To achieve this goal, the workers are taught to "love labor" and "respect regulations" to behave "properly" according to the everyday behavioral norms (*richang xingweu judong*日常行為舉動) of the workplaces (Efthymiou-Egleton 2016). For example, they are taught to respect authority to ensure the maintenance of social order (Xu 2009). In this context, compliance with the social order is highlighted by the Chinese media as a way for workers to protect their rights. For example, even today the Chinese popular press publishes cautionary tales about workers trying to find work in their own way outside the norms. These narratives typically end with the victims either being cheated by "black" labor market brokers (*hei zhongjie*黑中介) (Zhengzhou Wǎnbào 2016) or sold into prostitution (Ma 2013). To reduce social disruptions, services are provided to workers by the "carceral network" (Foucault 1980a) of governmental and nongovernmental organizations, such as job seeking and educational training regarding laws and regulations to highlight the importance of signing labor contracts (Xu 2009). By exposing themselves to these forms of knowledge, the inferior subjects are supposedly guided to "improve" their understanding of labor rights and conditions throughout the process of "development." While the "low-quality" workers are offered new training opportunities for continuous "self-improvement," these "opportunities" are arguably designed to engage them as potential agents in their own governance (Jeffreys and Sigley 2009).

This social management goal is embodied in the knowledge in which an array of CCP's conceived standards of modernized behavior is promoted through service activities (or programs) (Cartier 2016). Cooperating with the CCP's interest in developing "population quality" (*renkou suzhi*人口素質) in the discourse of modernization, social programs run by the everyday "carceral network" (Foucault 1980a) focus on the Chinese cultural economy and industry and standards for social conduct (National Civilised City Evaluation System 2011). These cultural standards are evident in large-format advertising slogans, including *Be a Civilized Person, Build a Civilized City* (*Zheng zuo wenming ren, gong chuang wenming cheng*爭做文明人共創文明城) and *Speak Civilly, Act Civilly* (*Shuo wenming hua, ban wenming shi...*說文明話辦文明事) (Cartier 2016). These civilizing perspectives are extensively reinforced by "quality training" (*suzhi peixun*) and "quality programs" (*suzhi jiemu* 素質節目) throughout cultural institutions such as the mass media, within schools, and on the streets (Cartier 2016) and are printed in the form of "self-help" manuals to encourage workers to act according to sanctioned behavioral standards. In one "self-help" manual (MDGIF 2011), for example, "low-quality" workers are encouraged to be satisfied with low-wage employment, relinquish excessive consumption behavior, obey traffic lights, adopt good hygiene habits, and exhibit "proper" manners. Constructing these official and standardized "civilized behaviors" (or cultural norms) highlights the CCP's desire to "improve" self-constraint and self-control (or "self-governance") of workers to ensure that they constitute appropriate subjects in the context of "development" programs.

In this manner, the discourse of "development" confines the "low-quality" population to a specific status. The discourse of "development" is aimed at conditioning the self-attitude and conduct of the workers so that they will behave (Davidson 2003) in accordance with cultural norms and the "quality-based" occupational hierarchy in China. The governmental knowledge that has been facilitated by the everyday "carceral network" to continuously inculcate forms of discourses of *truth* in the minds of workers is inherent to this normative Chinese cultural behavior (Clifford 2001). This then enables the ongoing production and reproduction of docile minds and bodies by co-opting workers' thoughts, bodies, and movements to serve the will of the CCP within the power-knowledge networks in China.

Conclusion

This chapter has engaged with Foucault's (1980a, b) genealogical work of governmentality to explore the governmental technologies that are exercised by the post-Mao CCP leaders both to maintain their monopoly on political power and secure an abundantly cheap and docile labor force for ongoing economic development. Drawing on historical cycles since the Zhou dynasty (13th B.C.E.) (see ▶ Chap. 59, "The Making of a Docile Working Class in Pre-reform China"), the chapter has argued that the CCP continues to consolidate their "mandate" to rule by continuing the (re-) production of docile bodies and minds among Chinese workers through the internalization of the Confucian concepts of filial piety and social status. These concepts are updated and embedded in the new governmental discourses of "quality" (*suzhi* 素質), stability maintenance (*weiwen* 維穩), well-off (*xiaokang* 小康), and harmonious society (*hexie shehui* 和諧社會) through their power-knowledge networks to guide the "low personal quality" workers to think of themselves as destined for marginal positions (or governmentality) in their everyday lives in China's thought management programs. Because of this, it is debatable whether Chinese workers can overcome the centuries-old cultivation of docile bodies and minds among themselves to engage in activism that will lead to the formation of an active working class to improve their living and working conditions for themselves and others in China.

Cross-References

- ▶ In Search of the Traces of the History of Management in Latin America, 1870–2020
- ▶ Indian Management (?): A Modernization Experiment
- ▶ Introduction: Management Heterogeneity in Asia
- ▶ Management History in the Modern World: An Overview

- Management in Australia – The Case of Australia's Wealthiest Valley: The Hunter
- The Making of a Docile Working Class in Pre-reform China
- The Perfect Natural Experiment: Asia and the Convergence Debate
- Think Big and Privatize Every Thing That Moves: The Impact of Political Reform on the Practice of Management in New Zealand
- What Is Management?

References

Benney J (2013) Defending rights in contemporary China: reserving the right. Routledge, London/New York

Benney J (2016) Weiwen at the grassroots: China's stability maintenance apparatus as a means of conflict resolution. J Contemp China 25(99):389–405

Benney J, Marolt P (2015) Modes of activism and engagement in the Chinese public sphere. Asian Stud Rev 39(1):88–89

Bentham J (1843) The works of Jeremy Bentham. William Tait, Edinburgh

Blecher M (2002) Hegemony and workers' politics in China. China Q 170:283–303

Brady A-M (2008) Marketing dictatorship: propaganda and thought work in contemporary China. Rowman & Littlefield Publishers, Maryland

Brady A-M (2012a) Introduction: market-friendly, scientific, high tech, and politics-lite: China's new approach to propaganda. In: Brady A-M (ed) China's thought management. Routledge, London/New York, pp 1–10

Brady A-M (2012b) State Confucianism, Chineseness, and tradition in CCP propaganda. In: Brady A-M (ed) China's thought management. Routledge, London/New York, pp 57–75

Cartier C (2016) Governmentality and the urban economy: consumption, excess, and the 'civilised city' in China. In: Bray D, Jeffreys E (eds) New mentalities of government in China. Routledge, London/New York

Chan A (2001) China's workers under assault: the exploitation of labour in a globalizing economy. An East Gate Book, New York

Chan C (2010) Class struggle in China: case studies of migrant worker strikes in the pearl river delta. S Afr Rev Sociol 41(3):61–80

Chan A (2011) Strikes in China's export industries in comparative perspective. China J 65:27–51

Chan C, Hui E (2012) The dynamics and dilemma of workplace trade union reform in China: the case of the Honda workers' strike. J Ind Relat 54(5):653–668

Chan C, Hui E (2016) Bringing class struggles back: a Marxian analysis of the state and class relations in China. Globalizations 1–13

Chan C, Pun N (2009) The making of a new working class? A study of collective actions of migrant workers in South China. China Q 198:287–303

Chan J, Selden M (2016) The labour politics of China's rural migrant. Globalizations 1–13

Chan A, Siu K (2012) Chinese migrant workers: factors constraining the emergence of class consciousness. In: Carrillo B, Goodman D (eds) China's peasants and workers: changing class identities. Edward Elgar Publishing Ltd, Massachusetts, pp 79–101

Chen F (2000) Subsistence crises, managerial corruption and labour protests in China. China J 44:41–63

Chen F (2006) Privatization and its discontents in Chinese factories. China Q 185:42–60

Chen M (2015) From economic elites to political elites: private entrepreneurs in the people's political consultative conference. J Contemp China 24(94):613–627

Chen F (2016a) China's road to the construction of labour rights. J Sociol 52(1):24–38

Chen X (2016b) Elitism and exclusion in mass protest: privatization, resistance, and state domination in China. Comp Pol Stud 1–27

Chen M, Goodman D (2012) The Asia Pacific, regionalism and the global system. In: Dent C, Dosch J (eds) The Asia-Pacific, regionalism and the global system. Edward Elgar Publishing Limited, Massachusetts, pp 185–200

China Daily (2006) Key points of the 11th five-year plan. http://www.chinadaily.com.cn/bizchina/2006-03/07/content_585089.htm. Accessed 9 January 2020

China Daily (2014) Editorial: tourists, behave yourselves. http://www.chinadaily.com.cn/opinion/2014-12/15/content_19084867.htm. Accessed 23 July, 2016

Clifford M (2001) Political genealogy after Foucault: savage identities. Routledge, London/New York

Cooke F-L, Xie Y, Duan H (2016) Workers' grievances and resolution mechanisms in Chinese manufacturing firms: key characteristics and the influence of contextual factors. Int J Hum Resour Manag 27(18):2119–2141

Crowther D, Green M (2004) Organisational theory. Chartered Institute of Personnel and Development, London

Davidson A (2003) Ethics as ascetics: Foucault, the history of ethics, and ancient thought. In: Gutting G (ed) The Cambridge companion to Foucault, 2nd edn. Cambridge University Press, New York, pp 123–148

Dillon M (2015) Deng Xiaoping: the man who made modern China. I.B. Tauris & Co. Ltd, London

Efthymiou-Egleton I (2016) Do we really know China?: an outsiders view. Xlibris Corporation, Bloomington

Fan C (2003) Rural-urban migration and gender division of labor in transitional China. Int J Urban Reg Res 27(1):24–47

Fan C (2004) The state, the migrant labor regime, and maiden workers in China. Polit Geogr 23:283–305

Foucault M (1954/2001) Power: the essential works of Foucault 1954–1984. (trans: Hurley R). Penguin Books, London

Foucault M (1961/2006) History of madness. (trans: Murphy J, Khalfa J). Routledge, London/New York

Foucault M (1963/2003) The birth of the clinic: an archaeology of medical perception. (trans: Sheridan A). Psychology Press, East Sussex

Foucault M (1969/2002) Foucault: archaeology of knowledge. (trans: Smith S). Routledge, London/New York

Foucault M (1976/1978) The history of sexuality. Penguin Books, New York

Foucault M (1977) Discipline and punish: the birth of the prison. (trans: Sheridan A). Vintage Books, New York

Foucault M (1978/1990) The use of pleasure. (trans: Hurley R). Vintage Books, New York

Foucault M (1978/2008) The birth of biopolitics: lectures at the collège de France, 1978–1979. (trans: Burchell G). Palgrave Macmillan, New York

Foucault M (1979/2014) On the government of the living: lectures at the college de France 1979–1980. (trans: Burchell G). Palgrave Macmillan, New York

Foucault M (1980a) Power/knowledge: selected interviews and other writings 1972–1977. (trans: Gordon C, Marshall L, Mepham J, Soper K). Vintage Books, New York

Foucault M (1980b) Truth and subjectivity. University of California, Berkely

Foucault M (1982) The subject and power. In: Dreyfus H, Rabinow P (eds) Michel Foucault: beyond structuralism and hermeneutics. University of Chicago Press, Chicago, pp 208–226

Foucault M (1984/1986) The care of the self. (trans: Hurley R). Pantheon Books, New York

Foucault M (1984/1991) The Foucault reader: an introduction to Foucault's thought. Penguin Books, London

Foucault M (1991) Politics and the study of discourse. In: Burchell G, Gordon C, Miller P (eds) The Foucault effect: studies in governmentality: with two lectures by and an interview with Michel Foucault. The University of Chicago Press, Chicago, pp 53–72

Franceschini I, Siu K, Chan A (2016) The "rights awakening" of Chinese migrant workers: beyond the generational perspective. Crit Asian Stud 48(3):422–442

Gabriel S (2006) Chinese capitalism and the modernist vision. Routledge, London/New York

Gabriel S, Todorova E (2003) Racism and capitalist accumulation: an overdetermined nexus. Crit Sociol 29:29–46

Gallagher M (2005) "Use the law as your weapon!": institutional change and legal mobilization in China. In: Diamant N, Lubman S, O'Brien K (eds) Engaging the law in China: state, society, and possibilities for justice. Stanford University Press, Stanford, pp 54–83

Gallagher M (2006) Mobilizing the law in China: "informed disenchantment" and the development of legal consciousness. Law & Society Review 40(4):783–816

Giddens A, Dallmayr F (1982) Profiles and critiques in social theory. University of California Press, Los Angeles

Grasso J, Corrin J, Kort M (2009) Modernization and revolution: from the opium wars to the Olympics, 4th edn. M.E. Sharpe, Inc., New York

Guo S (2013) Chinese politics and government: power, ideology and organization. Routledge, London/New York

Howell J (1993) China opens its doors: the politics of economic transition. Lynne Rienner Publishers, Boulder

Hurst W, O'Brien K (2002) China's contentious pensioners. China Q 170:345–360

Jeffreys E, Sigley G (2009) Governmentality, governance and China. In: Jeffreys E (ed) China's governmentalities: governing change, changing government. Routledge, London/New York, pp 1–23

Jeffreys E, Su X (2016) Governing through Lei Feng: a Mao-era role model in reform-era China. In: Bray D, Jeffreys E (eds) New mentalities of government in China. Routledge, London/New York

Jia N, Jiang A, Han X (2019) Analyzing the status of compulsory education for children of migrant workers (Nóngmín gōng zǐnǚ yìwù jiàoyù xiànzhuàng fēnxī). https://m.xzbu.com/4/view-2288841.htm. Accessed 15 Jan 2020

Koo H (2001) Korean workers: the culture and politics of class formation. Cornell University Press, London

Lee CK (1999) From organized dependence to disorganized despotism: changing labour regimes in Chinese factories. China Q 45:44–71

Lee CK (2000) The 'revenge of history': collective memories and labor protests in North-Eastern China. Ethnography 1(2):217–237

Lee CK (2007) Against the law: labor protests in China's rustbelt and sunbelt. University of California Press, Berkeley

Leung L (2017) Contemporary Chinese fiction writers: biography, bibliography, and critical assessment. Routledge, London/New York

Leung E, Caspersz D (2016) Exploring worker consciousness in China. Labour Ind 26(3):237–250

Leung P, Pun N (2009) The radicalisation of the new Chinese working class: a case study of collective action in the gemstone industry. Third World Q 30(3):551–565

Li H (2015) Political thought and china's transformation: ideas shaping reform in post-Mao China. Palgrave Macmillan, New York

Li L, O'Brien K (1996) Villagers and popular resistance in contemporary China. Modern China 22(1):28–61

Ma X (2013) 14-year-old girl forced into prostitution (14 suì shàonǚ zhǎo gōngzuò shàngdàng bèi bī màiyín 20 tiān jiēkè 200 cì). http://news.sina.com.cn/s/2013-09-27/112128316363.shtml. Accessed 4 Dec 2019

Magill K (1997) Surveillance-free-subjects. In: Lloyd M, Thacker A (eds) The impact of Michel Foucault on the social sciences and humanities. Macmillan Press Ltd, New York

Mah B (2011) China and the world: global crisis of capitalism. iUniverse, Bloomington

Mao X (2004) China: views of a medical geneticist. In: Wertz D, Fletcher J (eds) Genetics and ethics in global perspective. Kluwer Academic Publishers, London, pp 208–222

MDGIF (2011) Life skill manual (Shenghuo jineng shouce). MDG Achievement Fund in China, Beijing

Musto M (2012) Revisiting Marx's concept of alienation. In: Musto M (ed) Marx for today. Routledge, London/New York, pp 92–116

National Civilised City Evaluation System (2011) Spiritual civilisation commission (Quanguo wenming chengshi ceping tixi). http://www.hzwh.gov.cn/wmcs/201103/120110325_247842.html. Accessed 22 Dec 2019

Noon M, Blyton P, Morrell K (2013) The realities of work: experiencing work and employment in contemporary society, 4th edn. Palgrave Macmillan, New York

O'Brien K (1996) Rightful resistance. World Polit 49:31–55

Oksala J (2007) How to read Foucault. Granta Books, London

Perry E (2009) A new rights consciousness? J Democr 20(3):17–20

Postiglione G (2011) Education. In: Zang X (ed) Understanding Chinese society. Routledge, London/New York, pp 80–95

Pringle T (2011) Trade unions in China: the challenge of labour unrest. Routledge, London/New York

Pun N (2007) Gendering the dormitory labor system: production, reproduction, and migrant labor in South China. Fem Econ 13(3–4):239–258

Pun N, Lu H (2010a) A culture of violence: the labor subcontracting system and collective action by construction workers in post-socialist China. China J 64:143–158

Pun N, Lu H (2010b) Unfinished proletarianization: self, anger, and class action among the second generation of peasant-workers in present-day China. Modern China 36(5):493–519

Pun N, Chan C, Chan J (2009) The role of the state, labour policy and migrant workers' struggles in globalized China. Global Labour Journal 1(1):132–151

Pun N, Shen Y, Guo Y, Lu H, Chan J, Selden M (2016) Apple, Foxconn, and Chinese workers' struggles from a global labor perspective. Inter-Asia Cult Stud 17(2):166–185

Ransom J (1997) Foucault's discipline. Duke University Press, London

Rong X, Shi T (2001) Inequality in Chinese education. J Contemp China 10(26):107–124

Smith C, Pun N (2006) The dormitory labour regime in China as a site for control and resistance. Int J Hum Resour Manag 17(8):1456–1470

The World Bank (2019) Overview – China. https://www.worldbank.org/en/country/china/overview. Accessed 10 Oct 2019

Wagner D (1998) A classical Chinese reader: the Han Shu biography of Huo Guang. Routledge, London/New York

Walder A (1991) Workers, managers and the state: the reform era and the political crisis of 1989. China Q 127:467–492

Walder A, Gong X (1993) Workers in the Tiananmen protests: the politics of the Beijing workers' autonomous. Aust J Chin Aff 29:1–29

Wǎnbào Z (2016) 8000 yuan cheated, migrant workers hanged himself (Bèi piàn 8000 yuán nóngmíngōng shàngdiào zìshā). http://zzwb.zynews.com/html/2016-02/03/content_716552.htm. Accessed 14 Dec 2019

Wang L (2008) The marginality of migrant children in the urban Chinese educational system. Br J Sociol Educ 29(6):691–703

Warner M (1991) Labour-management relations in the People's Republic of China: the role of the trade unions. Int J Hum Resour Manag 2(2):205–220

Weatherley R (2006) Politics in China since 1949: legitimizing authoritarian rule. Routledge, London/New York

Wu B (2011a) Improving socialist legal system with Chinese characteristics on a new starting point. The People's Congress Journal, Beijing

Wu X (2011b) The household registration system and rural-urban education inequality in contemporary China. Chin Sociol Rev 44(2):31–51

Xiaoyong (1999) Not allowing to improve quality (Burang tigao suzhi). Nanfang Zhoumo (Southern Weekend), p 11

Xu F (2009) Governing China's peasant migrants: building xiaokang socialism and harmonious society. In: Jeffreys E (ed) China's governmentalities: governing change, changing government. Routledge, London/New York, pp 38–62

Yan H (2003) Neoliberal governmentality and neohumanism: organizing suzhi/value flow through labor recruitment networks. Cult Anthropol 18(4):493–523

Yan H (2008) New masters, new servants: migration, development, and women workers in China. Duke University Press, London

Zeng M (1989) The relationship between the cultural quality of guangxi's population and commodity production (Guangxi renkou de wenhua suzhi yu shangpin shengchan de guanxi). In: Yunnan provincial census office and Yunnan provincial research Centre for Population Development Strategies (ed) studies of the present situation of china's southwestern population (Zhongguo Xinnanbu Renkou Xianzhuan Yanjiu). Yunnan Renmin Chubanshe, Kunming, pp 165–172

Zhang R, Li J (2011) Practical training materials for joining the party (Rudang Peixun Shiyong Jiaocai). People's Publishing House, Beijing

Zhang D, Li X, Xue J (2015) Education inequality between rural and urban areas of the People's Republic of China: migrants' children education, and some implications. Asian Dev Rev 32(1):196–224

Zhou Y (2001) China's two pillars in the twenty-first century: science and technological education (Shìjì zhōngguó liǎng dà zhīzhù: kējì jiàoyù huà yǔ jiàoyù kējì huà). Fujian Education Press, Fuzhou

In Search of the Traces of the History of Management in Latin America, 1870–2020

61

Carlos Dávila

Contents

Introduction	1388
Management: A Missing Link in the Development Ideology?	1390
Modernization Theory: The Transition from "Traditional" Toward "Modern" Societies	1391
Dependency Theory's Disregard for Management	1392
Business History's Potential to Pursue the Traces of Management	1393
Entrepreneurs, Entrepreneurial Families, and Business Groups: Key Actors	1395
Gold Mining: A "Practical" Entrepreneurship and Management School	1399
Management as a Profession and Management Education, 1900–1970	1401
Conclusion	1405
Cross-References	1406
References	1407

Abstract

Little is known about the history of management in Latin America and other emerging markets. Nor notice of interest on its existence is to be found in recent debates on the need of a "new," or "radical," or "critical" history of management. This chapter explores the possibility of doing research on this field and proposes a research agenda for "a" history of management in Latin America. For that purpose, it examines the impact of three management approaches in the region, during the period of 1870–2020. The approaches considered are management as part of the development ideology, as a practice, and as knowledge diffused through management education. The core is the traces left by the ideas and practices (strategies and techniques) by which economic actors in specific settings responded to dynamic, historical contextual realities in some of the countries in the region. The findings and lessons, both theoretical and methodological, that

C. Dávila (✉)
School of Management, Universidad de los Andes, Bogotá, Colombia
e-mail: cdavila@uniandes.edu.co

have emerged from the flourishing Latin American business historiography – an illustration of the alternative business history (ABH) – are used to identify some of the traces of management and to assess their research potential. A research agenda for further discussion in proposed.

Keywords

Emerging markets · Development ideologies · Alternative business history · Management education

Introduction

This chapter approaches its subject matter from two geopolitical standpoints: first, from the fact that, as part of the South Atlantic littoral, Latin America has been and still is an underdeveloped region, an "emerging market," in twenty-first century terms and, secondly, from the notion that management knowledge has historically been Anglophone and, more distinctively, US-centric. Latin America consists of South America (ten countries), Central America (six countries), Mexico, and two Spanish-speaking Caribbean countries (Cuba and Dominican Republic). For some citizens of the Anglosphere, this region keeps being sort of a black box: a vast land whose main feature would seem to be the "backyard" of the United States. Spanish is the official language of 18 of these 19 countries; Portuguese is Brazil's lingua franca. For over three centuries and up to the early decades of the nineteenth century, these countries were colonies ruled by the Spanish crown, except for Brazil, which was a Portuguese colony. The role played by the colonial rule and its institutions was long-lasting: administering the Spanish and Portuguese empires, along with their trade, maritime transportation, mining, and plantations operation, was no minor enterprise (Stein and Stein 1970). With the purpose of providing an overview of the history of management in the region, this chapter is circumscribed to the post-Independence period. More precisely, it starts off when Latin America becomes part of the world economic system of the first global economy (1870–1929), which brought about "extraordinary transformations" (Jones 2007: 161). This is known as Latin America's commodity export-led growth stage (Bulmer-Thomas 1994; Bértola and Ocampo 2012). The chapter goes up to the present.

The chapter puts together sparse information from varied sources regarding Argentina, Brazil, Chile, and Mexico, but it focuses deeper and more broadly on the case of an Andean country, Colombia. It must be said that, in the landscape of management, Latin America's role has usually been stereotyped as a merely passive consumer in the transfer process of modern management knowledge and technology. This ill-informed, reductionist view denies the State, the business systems, and other actors any agency in the above process. Latin America's economic, social, and business reality, as far as management is concerned, is complex, diverse, and dynamic. Therefore, the study of the evolution of management in the region should be approached without ignoring a context wherein inequality, social and political unrest, turbulence, and instability have been a perennial rule. There is a need to search for the management ideas and practices that Latin American economic actors, among others, have developed to deal with evolving contextual realities. The intent is not to go after a folkloric, exotic sort of indigenous management. Instead, it is to point out the areas in which traces of management ideas and practices associated with the development of the region's economy can be observed. This chapter is just an attempt in that direction. Given the sparsity of research on this field, to explore its potential is a much-needed step. Purposedly, it may stimulate further research on the history of management in this part of the world, one that may converse with colleagues in the North Atlantic and other regions of the world. To entail in such a conversation, it is necessary that the ongoing debates in the field of management history encompass a global vision of the *past*, not circumscribed to the North Atlantic nor the Anglosphere.

In approaching the history of management in Latin America, it is relevant to point out that, in the international academic community, the history of management and business history are two different scholarly fields, with their own distinctive paths and evolution. Business history is epitomized by the *Business History Review* (BHR), a journal established at Harvard Business School (HBS) in 1926. On the other hand, the study of the evolution of management is identified with two publication venues, the *Journal of Management History*, launched in 1995, and *Management & Organizational History* released in 2006.

In Latin America, business history is a young academic field with noticeable growth since the 1980s (Barbero 2003; 2008; Barbero and Dávila 2009; Dávila 2003b, 2013; Austin et al. 2017). On the other hand, research and publications on the history of management are rather scarce and scattered. Hardly somebody who portrays him/herself as "management historian" is to be found across the region to the south of the (US) Río Grande. Furthermore, Latin American scholarship in business history (as in other fields) experiences the toll of being outside the Anglosphere, as well as strives to enter it, as the sole way of existing in the monolingual management international academic community.

In this context, the present chapter approaches the historical development of management in the Latin American emerging markets by exploring the ways in which a few currents of thought and practice on the subject have exerted an impact on the region. They are not necessarily identified nor categorized as such in conventional textbooks management histories and current surveys of the literature. These, by the way, are plenty of flaws that made them the target of a recent book aimed at the indispensable pledge of "rethinking the map of management history" (Cummings et al. 2017). The currents of management thought chosen represent a "reading" of the management academic literature pondered from a scholarly standpoint located in a peripheral emerging market. Such a "reading" is grounded on teaching and research conducted at a private university located in a Latin American country (Colombia) over the past half century (Dávila 1985/2001). In this view, management theory is not a science, but an interdisciplinary field still in pursuit of conformation. Characteristically, it has been highly dynamic and growing since First World War and, to a great extent, led by the American corporate world and business schools. Its iconic product of export, the Master in Business Administration (MBA), was keenly referred to by British magazine, *The Economist*, as one that "amounts to 'Mastering Being in America'" (The Economist 1991: 23).

In its conformation as a field of inquiry, teaching, and "application," an ample, often disparate, variety of approaches have emerged. Over time, to expect their "integration" into an all-encompassing theory would seem naïve, if not pretentious and/or futile. All this notwithstanding, management has played a key role in the development of capitalism given that, at its core, it deals with and tackles two key phenomena: productivity and competitiveness.

A non-exhaustive arrangement or list of conceptualizations of management that have been influential in Latin America over the last century and a half would include the following: management as practice and technology; as the quest for efficiency (Taylor 1912); a process guided by "principles" (Fayol 1916/1930); as rational form of domination (Weber 1922/1944); as control of labor force (Braverman 1974; Edwards 1979); as a profession (Fayol 1916; Follet 1927/1970; McGregor 1967); as leadership (Barnard 1938; Selznick 1957; Likert 1961); as decision-making (Simon 1945); as a capitalist institution (Drucker 1954); as a managerial ideology (Bendix 1956); as entrepreneurship (Drucker 1985); as the visible hand of market (Chandler 1977); and as a mystique (Zaleznik 1990). Needless to say, they are not mutually exclusive. Several overlaps coexist and interplay in the empirical reality; none is to be found in its pure, ideal form. To achieve the goal of this chapter, only three of these conceptualizations will be addressed: management as an ideology, as practice and technology, and as a profession.

Management: A Missing Link in the Development Ideology?

Bearing in mind that the theme of this chapter is the history of management in Latin America, not the history of economic development theories, it must be mentioned that the ideals of "material progress" and "civilization" throughout the region were part of the transition across the nineteenth century, from colonial economies to the post-Independence era. By the mid-century, these ideals were key elements of liberal ideology, anchored on ideas of free-trade, free initiative, private enterprise, and non-State intervention. At the turn of the nineteenth century, and throughout most of the twentieth century, industrialization became the aegis of progress. The impact of the Industrial Revolution in this part of the South Atlantic littoral implied a shift from the monopoly of trade, plantation, colonial mining, and handicraft to manufacture. The transition, from an agrarian (hacienda and plantation-based) to a modern economy dominated by industry and machine manufactures, took place in the context of Latin America's role in the international division of labor, more to the point, its position within the first global economy (1870–1929), the ensuing disintegration phase (1930–1950), the origins of a second wave of globalization (1950–1979), and the new global economy (1979-the present).

In the aftermath of the Second World War (WW2), "progress" became synonymous for *economic development*, a term championed for geopolitical reasons, mostly by the United States. Likewise, *underdevelopment, third world, poor countries, backward nations*, and *developing countries* have become coined terms widely used by academics, multilateral organizations, and political and public policy quarters. They refer to countries where the real income per capita is lower than that of the United States, Canada, Australia, New Zealand, and Western Europe. Latin America served as a showcase to illustrate what the new terms meant.

Modernization Theory: The Transition from "Traditional" Toward "Modern" Societies

Concurrently, in the midst of the Cold War, the decade of the 1960s was officially named "the United Nations Development Decade of Development." The academic underpinnings of the international cooperation program that followed were provided by some of top American universities: MIT, Harvard, and Berkeley. They contributed "modernization theory," which stressed the importance of the "noneconomic factors" of economic development (Finkle and Gable 1968; Prezeworski and Limongi 1997). The vicinity of the Cuban Revolution (1959) being a key geopolitical concern, Latin America served as a "testing ground" for some of the psychological, sociological, and cultural conceptual frameworks that ensued. More precisely, President Kennedy's Alliance for Progress was the icon of a US-government program to further the region's development (Taffet 2007).

It should be mentioned that, in "modernization theories," themes such as efficiency, entrepreneurship, elites, decision-making, and education were considered key issues to understand underdevelopment. For instance, an alleged lack of entrepreneurship in the region was bluntly aired without proper research to support it. At the same time, armchair generalizations on the region's elites obliterated their role in agricultural exports and, more generally, in foreign trade. Rigorous empirical research was missing. Yet, the novel theory enjoyed some glamourous flavor and circulated amply in the United States, perhaps due to the prestige of some of their pioneer scholars (Dávila 2010): MIT economist, Everett Hagen, and his "withdrawal of status" psychocultural theory (Hagen 1962); Berkeley's Seymour Lipset and his sociological concept of the entrepreneur as a "deviant" in traditional societies (Lipset and Solari 1967); and, Harvard's psychology professor, David McClelland and his n-achievement theory (McClelland 1961). Yet, early serious criticism pointed out the danger of ill-supported generalization and the need for empirically based research that would shed light on economic development in a long-term historical perspective. Interestingly, the scarce empirical research based on these theories dealt with Colombia, Brazil, and Argentina and was mostly carried out by American scholars (Horowitz 1966; Bendix 1967; Frank 1967; Lipman 1969; Bodenheimer 1970). For the most part, they did not leave any major follow-up or imprint in the landscape of Latin American social sciences, which were moving on to other intellectual paradigms. The title of a book reuniting Latin American social scientists critical stance was eloquent, *Sociología Subdesarrollante* (Frank et al. 1969), that is, a sociology and, more generally, modernization theory that fosters underdevelopment.

Dependency Theory's Disregard for Management

Dependency theory was Latin America's intellectual contribution to the field of economic development, which saw the emergence of abundant intellectual production by region scholars, mainly from Argentina, Brazil, and Chile during the 1960s and 1970s. Its origins may be traced back to the work by the United Nations Economic Commission for Latin America (ECLA; CEPAL for its acronym in Spanish) on "central-peripheral" relationships in the 1950s, known as ECLA's structuralism. Dependency theory outcome was "an extensive but unbalanced literature" (Miller 2010: 7). Interestingly, some of its major works and authors were translated into English and read in American and British universities (Cardoso and Faletto 1979; Frank 1974); a handful of Latin American Centers, specialists in the region ("Latin Americanists"), and area programs were created in top British, American, and German universities. The central theoretical concept is that of the economic, cultural, and technological dependency that Latin America has experienced vis-à-vis the urban hegemonic centers since its conquest by Spain and Portugal (Cardoso and Faletto 1979; Frank 1974; Evans 1979). It offers a harsh critique of modernization theory and its concept of development as an evolutionary, linear process that forms part of a passage from a traditional to a dual society and, subsequently, to a modern one. It also rejects the idea that underdeveloped nations exhibit an anomalous development, along with the associated assumption that they must repeat the history of developed nations, in disregard of historical phases and different contexts (Kay 1989).

Although dependency theory was indeed nourished by Marxism, it was also the subject of critiques by some orthodox Marxist currents. Drawing on theory of imperialism, some authors criticized dependency theory for remaining silent on the matter of the contemporary characteristics of imperialism and for its careless application of Marxist theory (Fernández and Ocampo 1974). Others considered that the theory of economic imperialism was the "missing link" of dependency theory (Bodenheimer 1970), while some British academic quarters acerbically dubbed it a "theology" (Platt 1980).

The dependentistas' radical views on the political role of intellectuals germinated in a complex context that was entirely different from that of the industrialized North. The political context in Latin America during the 1960s and 1970s was one of dictatorial military regimes that seized power, violated human rights, and brushed aside civil resistance in major Latin American economies (Argentine, Brazil, Chile), smaller South Cone countries (Paraguay, Uruguay), as well as several Central American "banana republics" (Guatemala, Nicaragua, Panama). As a counterpart, those decades witnessed the rise of leftist guerrilla warfare (Bolivia, Colombia, Venezuela), growing social conflict, and triumphant leftist revolutions in Central America (Nicaragua and Salvador).

Inspired on the Gramscian perspective of the "organic intellectual" (Gramsci 1971), academic rigor and research standards were not a major concern for *dependentistas*' writers. This is reflected in the "characterizations" of specific countries' economic, political, and social situation that, instead, were fine-tuned to specific leftist ideological currents views. They were the basis to orient political action programs and reflected heated debates within the left. To be coherent and aligned either with the Soviet or the Mao's doctrine was more important than to conform to standards for publication and the like. The all-time "publish or perish" syndrome proper of the academic world, the field of management included, would have seemed as an incomprehensible issue that could not be compared to the dilemma many Latin American *dependentista* scholars faced. In their setting, political activism, "action-oriented" research with guerrilla and protest movements (Simposio Mundial de Cartagena 1978), imprisonment, and "life or death" were real options.

Dependency theory did not pay specific attention to management issues even though management education expanded across Latin America since the 1960s, as attested in a further section. A major concern was power relations between international hegemonic centers and domestic governments and perennial uneven, unfair conditions in foreign trade, as well as rampant poverty, exploitation, and inequality in the periphery. The tenets of dependency theory harshly denounced the economic imperialism embodied in multinationals operating in the region, which controlled the sectors of oil, mining (gold, silver, copper), railroads, and banana. Emerging nationalism and anti-imperialism, labor conflict, relations with local government, and economic and social policies were issues of major concern in a large body of dependency theory literature. Intriguingly, its *principal enemy* did not seem to be management itself nor its theories or techniques. The unit of analysis of dependency theory focused on the macro and meso levels and social and structural, rather than on the micro (specific business, entrepreneurs, workers unions) and individual levels.

Business History's Potential to Pursue the Traces of Management

In contrast to the scarce research on the history of management, business history has flourished in Latin America since the 1980s. Interestingly, it has departed from the two abovementioned intellectual traditions that emerged from opposite ideological stances: American-based modernization theory and Latin American-rooted dependency theory.

In the case of modernization theory, business history flourished, to a fair extent, to redress its overriding oversimplifications and generalizations. Conceptual and empirical flaws of noted works carried out under the modernization paradigm made evident the need to get beyond criticizing them. A way to do it was to resort to advances in social science research during the 1970s anchored in alternative approaches to what in the case of sociology was aptly labelled "the coming crisis of western sociology" (Gouldner 1970). Nascent Latin American (qualitative) economic history and business history paved the way to undertake serious study of development issues in specific geographical and sectoral spaces and from a temporal, dynamic perspective and with focus on units of analysis (e.g., economic actors, specific economic sectors) amenable to empirical inquiry (Cerutti 2004; Barbero and Jacob 2008).

A showcase is what occurred in Colombia wherein the application of Hagen's elegant withdrawal-of-status theory to a region (Antioquia) moved others to carry out a series of historical studies on *Antioqueños'* entrepreneurship in mining, commerce, finance, coffee, etc. that would constitute a rebuttal of his theory. Whereas Hagen's determination to discern the factors contributing to economic growth was high-minded, he failed, however, because he refused to focus on the questions that guide the historian's work: "who, where, when, how, and why." Hagen rather preferred "to adopt a kind of determinism that historians abhor" (Dávila 2006: 134).

Also paradoxical is the relationship of historical studies with the foregoing dependency theory whose antibusiness ethos was evident. It demonized both foreign and local business actors. Domestic entrepreneurs, in particular, were criticized for being either second-to or allies of international, monopoly capital rather than striving to become a "national bourgeoise." And foreign capital and multinationals were at center stage of its denounces, as agents of economic imperialism. Yet, as it was mentioned, for some versions of Marxist-Leninism, dependency theory did not fulfill their orthodox canons (Frank 1972; Miller 1999, 2010).

It was not until *dependentistas'* paradigm progressive decay, and the parallel upsurge of neoliberalism, market reforms, and globalization, at the late 1980s, that the study of business, firms, entrepreneurship, State monopolies, and the like gained legitimation and acceptance as an object of scholarly endeavor. Business historians being different from macroeconomic historians and historical economists "offers a depth in terms of time perspective that specialist in business and management schools often lack" (Miller 2010: 37). And, certainly, they are not condemned to be "apologists of the bourgeoisie."

Surveys of Latin American business historiography, conducted at the dawn of the twenty-first century, revealed that Mexico, Argentina, Colombia, and Brazil (in this order) were the leading producers, in terms of quantity and quality of works, followed by Uruguay, Peru, Chile, and Venezuela (Dávila and Miller 1999; Barbero 2003; Dávila 2003b). Recent state-of-the-art works (Dávila 2013; Miller 2017; Lluch et al. 2018), as well as institutionalization advances, attest to the emergence of the field of business history in other Andean countries such as Perú and leave no doubt that, although a diversity of political, economic, and academic reasons accrued for the late development of the field in Chile, it has much to offer to the understanding of the different organizational, management, and institutional features of business development in the region as a whole (Lorca-Jana et al. 2019); Central America, Costa Rica, and Honduras have also appeared into the field during the present decade (Bull et al. 2014; Fernández Pérez and Lluch 2015/2016). It must be added that this historiography has come out more in the form of books and book chapters published in Spanish than as journal articles in the international monolingual venues of this discipline. These two features constitute a barrier that has slowed down the dissemination of the research produced in the region.

It should be said that, with the exception of Colombia, Latin American business history research and teaching has been developed away from the grounds of management and organizational studies. The intellectual points of reference of Latin American business historians stem, more readily, from economic and social history and economic development. This is a key reason for history of management in Latin America to be an academic challenge yet to be undertaken. Interestingly, until recent decades, the lack of interaction between the camps of management scholars and historians has not been exclusively of the emerging world, but rather a global phenomenon. There have been exceptions, however, like the Harvard Business School's seat of the *Business History Review*, for over nine decades, and other less-aged vintage cases in North Europe (United Kingdom, Scandinavia), South Europe (Italy), Japan, and India. It is only as recently as the first decade of the new century that business historians began to be employed by business schools and exposed to different management and related disciplines' approaches and paradigms (Bucheli and Wadhwani 2013). And publication venues opened up, such as the aforementioned *Journal of Management History* (JMH) and the youngest *Management & Organizational History* (MOH).

It is noteworthy that Latin American business history has become part of the recently coined "alternative business history" (ABH) of emerging markets. ABH represents a more intellectually challenging venture than one that just provides data on new settings or an enlarged scope to replicate mainstream frameworks. Among commonalities of the history of business across Latin America, Asia, and Africa, ABH also focuses on the response of business systems to the institutional context, a response that differs from that of the West. In the scholarly world, the history of business "should not be ignored, nor relegated to the margins of mainstream journals and conferences, but rather be studied as equally central as the business history of Western Europe, the United States and Japan" (Austin et al. 2017: 568).

Several findings and research directions entailed in ABH are useful to trail traces of the history of management in the region. A selection of two of them may serve for illustrative purposes. First, business organizational structures and actors, different from those in advanced capitalist countries, have had a leading role in economic development. Second, since the beginnings of the period under consideration (1870–2010), sectorial developments in oil, mining, foreign trade, and industrial development required management practices for the profit-oriented handling of scarce resources (capital, labor, technology). The latter were either indigenous, brought in by foreign capital and multinationals, or adapted from varied agents involved in the diffusion and transfer of management concepts and tools. And, irrespective of the way in which they were registered or identified, several management functions (finance, production, marketing, industrial relations, and personnel) were deployed in varied size and scale. What follows provides a sample of each of this couple of traces of management history.

Entrepreneurs, Entrepreneurial Families, and Business Groups: Key Actors

ABH has pointed out that the leading business actors of economic development in emerging markets have not been the same as in the West. Capitalism in America and Western Europe cannot be understood without focusing on the firm, especially on the big business enterprise. By contrast, in the present case – the Latin American business landscape as of the post-Independence period – entrepreneurs, managers, entrepreneurial families, and business groups constitute forms of business organization indispensable to grasp the evolution of emerging markets. This is not to deny that foreign capital and multinationals of American or European origin have played an important role and have been key players in several sectors of Latin American countries. But to focus only on them or to suppose that other ways of organizing business are backward, anomalous, or relics of the past is misleading. In spite of this being a deeply flawed approach, it is embedded in management literature and, more generally, in management education and consulting. Cases in point include management textbooks, whose context, examples, illustrations, exercises, cases, bibliographic references, etc. are, almost without exception, based on big businesses and large business firms.

Departing from this, ABH has revealed organizational structures as well as leadership and managerial patterns that differ significantly from those seen in Chandlerian, large multidivisional companies in the United States and Europe.

In Latin America, entrepreneurial histories have roused more attention than company histories. Since the 1990s, there have been conceptual and analytical advances that have furthered the study of entrepreneurship. These advances came together with changes in legitimacy of entrepreneurial history. As a result, the scholarly biographical works of the last two decades do not fit with the "great men" image conventionally associated with entrepreneurial history. They are not hagiographies nor denunciatory works: entrepreneurs are neither heroes nor villains. It is fair to say that evolving management practices and ideas in this part of the globe could have hardly been identified if attention had not been given to entrepreneurs, entrepreneurial families, and business groups. That is, if studies had been just limited to firms.

The past few decades have witnessed an increase in number and quality of this production in Argentina, Brazil, Chile, Colombia, Mexico, and Peru. They contain a wealth of information featuring the function of entrepreneurs in economic development. It must be made clear that their role was not just circumscribed within the industrialization period that started off at the turn of the nineteenth century. In fact, entrepreneurs had been decisive players in agriculture, commerce, finance, mining, and communication, in their respective countries, since the second half of the nineteenth century (Austin et al. 2017; Lluch et al. 2018).

Alertness to business opportunities has been a distinctive feature of Latin American entrepreneurship throughout the past century and a half (Meisel and Viloria 2003; Molina 2006). Nowadays, in Brazil and the Andean countries (Bolivia, Colombia, Ecuador, Peru) there still exist large, unexploited rural areas with plenty of agribusiness opportunities (Villegas 2014). Furthermore, entrepreneurial activity in Latin America has always been highly diversified, in terms of investment, not only across countries in the region but also among economic sectors within a given country. The degree, rhythm, and type of diversification may vary along the life span of an individual and are indicative of particular risk management strategies, ways of dealing with uncertainty, and willingness to associate capital in different countries, for instance, in Argentina (Reguera 2006; Cochran and Reina 1962/2011), Chile (Herrero 2014), Colombia (Ripoll 2007), México (Cerutti 1995, 2018), and Perú (Portocarrero 2007). Certainly, after 1930, industrial entrepreneurs properly became distinguishable actors that needed specialized capabilities in the management of capital, technology, and workforce, for example, in Argentina (Cochran and Reina 1962), Colombia (Londoño 2016), and Mexico (Recio 2016). It is interesting, however, that in face of the second wave of globalization and the ensuing business restructuring, by the end of the twentieth century, the diversification imprint revived as a valuable entrepreneurial asset. At the same time, this is related to what strategy management and business policy specialists call vertical and horizontal and backward or forward integration (Davila 2003a, b, 2013, 2015).

The role of entrepreneurs as innovators has been explored in ongoing works. In Latin America, entrepreneurs' innovations were not often in new methods of production and new products, but, rather, in other forms of Schumpeterian innovations, such as opening new markets, exploiting new sources of supply, and crafting new ways to organize business (Dávila 2013; Londoño 2016). Research has also clearly established that there was no uniformity across Latin America.

In addition, the increasing research output on business history in Latin America points out a number of topics that could serve to complement management development programs. These topics include the differentiation between entrepreneurial and managerial functions; the importance of the local and regional base of many entrepreneurial ventures; their role within local and regional elites; the importance of land ownership, which was not limited to providing original capital accumulation; the development of capabilities to deal with recurring crisis and instability; and the capability to learn and adapt best practices of large business firms based in the developed West, in which varied forms of entrepreneurship are present.

In general, the activities of individual entrepreneurs have been inextricably interwoven with family ties over time; there is a wealth of empirical evidence of this. Historical research, for its part, based on the notion that Latin America's economy has been supported by family businesses along the last two decades and has also contributed to an important conceptual and methodological reorientation of current debates and research agendas, more precisely, by taking the entrepreneurial family as a unit of analysis. This may constitute a twofold step forward in the academic study of family firms, a subfield of academic and consulting management. In the first place, it redirects the object of inquiry from family firm to entrepreneurial family (Fernández Pérez and Lluch 2015/2016). Secondly, it points out the advantages of a long-term approach so as to understand the dynamics of change and evolution of this particular management model, whose endurance, across different, not just emerging, markets, cultures, political, and institutional frameworks, is noteworthy (Fernández Pérez and Colli 2013). The last of these two purposes is perhaps more difficult to achieve. Indeed, mainstream business and management literature are full of archetypal prejudices against family-owned businesses. The list of ideological imaginaries about family business is long and illustrative of the ethnocentric, deeply flawed supremacist views that are not uncommon in the field of management. Family firms are often depicted as another vestige of the past:

obsolete, inefficient, and reluctant to relinquish power and control. Supposedly, they are non-innovative and maintain autocratic management structures. These inaccurate characterizations are epitomized by the notion that family-run businesses are a phase to be superseded along the evolution from *traditional* to *modern* societies and are not a few who, more blatantly, consider it an anomaly of capitalist development.

Against this ideological backdrop, research from the Latin American Southern Cone has resorted to a theoretical category, *family capitalism*, which makes it possible to examine research questions related to the relevance of family business during the last century, its dominant forms of organization, and longevity. The study covers 100 of the largest businesses for 10 benchmark years, from 1923 to 2010 (1923, 1937, 1944, 1954/1956, 1970, 1980, 1990, 2004, and 2010); it makes use of quantitative and qualitative analysis based on a rich variety of data. The main conclusion is definite: "Argentinean capitalism is and has been based on family-owned business" (Barbero and Lluch 2015/2016: 148).

Beyond the Argentinean case, it should be remarked that many of the entrepreneurial families across Latin America has organized as business groups (BG) whose role in the region has, and continues to be, prominent. To the point that without taking them into account, the contemporary functioning of the Latin American economy cannot be understood. A pioneer, nine-country (Spain and eight Latin American countries) comparative research project on BGs carried out in the present decade carried out by business historians is a good exemplar of the subdiscipline advances (Fernández Pérez and Lluch 2015/2016). Centered on Mexico, a recent book includes six studies on the generational transitions in entrepreneurial families (Almaraz and Ramírez 2016). It should be said that contrary to conventional wisdom, the role of BGs in developed economies has recently began to be revisited (Colpan et al. 2010; Colpan and Hikino 2018). Another visible pattern of the last quarter of century is the internationalization strategies of several of these largest Latin American BGs that have been conducive to their transformation into multinationals, the so-called multilatinas (Casanova 2009; Barbero 2014).

Another conclusion highlights an issue of interest in the international business and management literature: the relationship between immigration and entrepreneurship. In the case of Argentina, immigration was large and extensive to the point that, by 1914, one third of the country's population was constituted by immigrants: Italian, for the most part, followed mainly by Spaniards, Germans, and Britons. They brought technical expertise, maintained close linkages with their countries of origin, and created a strong Italian-Argentinean business community. As a result of this, "corporate networks created at the end of the nineteenth century lasted well into the twentieth century" (Barbero and Lluch 2015/2016: 149). In terms of scale, longevity, and diversification, entrepreneurial families of immigrant origin have played an important role all across Latin America since the second half of nineteenth century (Fernández Pérez and Lluch 2015/2016). The distinctively turbulent economic, political, and social context, and the ensuing inherent uncertainty, led business actors, whether native or of immigrant descent, to develop a strategic managerial competence that helped to deal with uncertainty, in both the contextual and the institutional frameworks. A key component of said competence pertains to the relationships with politics and the State, as documented in the nine-country studies (Argentina, Brazil, Chile, Colombia, Costa Rica, Honduras, México, Peru, and Spain) included in the mentioned comparative research project (Fernández Pérez and Lluch 2015/2016). As well as analyzed in a book that covers seven Mexican entrepreneurs during the nineteenth and twentieth centuries (Palacios 2015).

On this regard, a research group (GHE, for its acronym in Spanish) from the abovementioned Colombian management school developed an analytical framework to conduct biographical entrepreneurial research. One of its six categories deals with business-politics relations, which are part of the political capital of entrepreneurs and managers. It is broken down into almost ten variables, which include political affiliation, voting in elections, funding electoral campaigns, contracting with the State, public sector positions by election or appointment, participation in political parties, membership and participation in business associations, leadership in private foundations, support to NGOs, and civil society organizations (Dávila 2012, Chap. 9).

Gold Mining: A "Practical" Entrepreneurship and Management School

The second instance to illustrate business history potential contribution to the history of management in the Latin American region refers to the history of mining. Gold and silver mining was important, especially in Mexico, Peru, and Bolivia since colonial times. As for silver, the region still holds the third place among the largest silver-producing mines in the world. On the other hand, Chilean economic development in the twentieth century could not overshadow the continuing importance of copper mining to the overall society. In the case of gold, this mineral has played an important role in Mexico, Colombia, and Peru. Colombia's case is interesting, particularly with respect to an isolated mountainous region named Antioquia. Gold was Colombia's chief export product during the nineteenth century, before coffee turned this Andean nation into a *país cafetero* (a country with a coffee-based economy) in the early 1900s. Antioquia's gold mining experience has entailed a wealth of expertise and practices that have been documented in Colombian business history bibliography, more specifically, those historical studies that, during the last decades of the twentieth century, stemmed from the academic debate on Antioquia's entrepreneurship and its so-called exceptionalism (Dávila 2012, Chap. 2).

The research on the history of mining companies, regional elites, and biographical studies of entrepreneurs, whose original capital accumulation started off with mining, in combination with high diversification in commerce, finance and banking, railroad and river steam navigation, pack mule transportation, and land colonization enterprises (Brew 1977; Molina 2003; Botero 2007), makes possible to learn about a number of entrepreneurship and management topics.

The list includes institutional change (e.g., a mining code on mines ownership, exploitation, and gold trade that replaced the Colonial Law) and role of foreign capital and of the British engineers who, acting both as technicians and managers, ventured into a "non-immigrant land," technical expertise and adaptation to technological change, labor relations, alertness to opportunities, risk management, capital association, technical innovation, and investment diversification through internal and export commercial networks. To this it should be added the financial issues related to the role of gold in international trade as a financial instrument in a "free banking" economy.

An example helps to ascertain homegrown management practices in the mining sector. By the 1870s, one of the largest Colombian mining companies (*El Zancudo*) already used economic incentives for their workers. One of these was to further the retention of scarce labor, for which other mines, railroad companies, and seasonal coffee harvesting competed. Another incentive aimed at motivating workers to increase productivity, especially in the processing of gold ore. The first incentive consisted in granting married workers the property of small plots of land in rural areas near the lode mines – which allowed them to be close to their families and help out in land cultivation during their spare time – and single workers received housing and board and lodging. On the other hand, increasing productivity was tied to a monetary incentive. The whole scheme was designed in the early 1860 by one of the company's female owners. These practices were put into operation three decades before Frederick W. Taylor's classic book, *The Principles of Scientific Management* (Taylor 1912), came out. The scheme also included money penalties (fines), which fueled a fund for the purchase of clothing and personal utensils that were later raffled among the workers (Molina 2003).

Taylorism and, years later, Henri Fayol's general management theory were eagerly studied during the first decades of the twentieth century at the *Escuela Nacional de Minas* [National School of Mines], located in Medellin, Antioquia's capital city. A cadre of engineers was trained on Taylorism, which would be applied in railroad operations, local and regional public administration, and some of the pioneering local manufacturing firms. One of these engineers, Alejandro López, head of the mining company El Zancudo, made a keen use of Taylor's scientific management theory to improve the existing incentive scheme. He later became president of the mentioned engineering school and exceled by taking advantage of the company's *practical* management legacy, combined with leading-edge academic knowledge (Mayor 1984; Orozco and Anzola-Morales 2019). Overall, cases like these were not uncommon: Antioquia's mining sector, in conjunction with the commercial sector, became a "practical entrepreneurship and management school" since the mid-nineteenth century.

Behind these and other related management practices and techniques, an entrepreneurial and managerial way of thinking began to develop, one that is part of the "capitalist ethos" that took decades of individual, group, and organizational learning, a kind of learning that, by struggling with material, geographical, and economic potentials and limitations – not through cultural, religious or ethnic deviance – "forced *Antioqueños* along enterprising pathways." They excelled "not only as the miners and merchants, but also as the colonizers, bankers, tobacco growers, railroad builders, coffee producers, and industrialist of Colombia" (Twinam 1982: 149–150).

The use of business historiography on the mining sector as well as of other branches of the Colombian economy (agroexport products – coffee, banana, oil, manufacturing industry, banking and finance, transportation) in teaching at the aforementioned Universidad de los Andes' Management School for half a century has been an experience plenty of learnings on the interaction between research on the country's reality and teaching management. Hundreds of undergraduates; managers-to-be, who enrolled in the ample portfolio of MBA programs; and seasoned managers and businesspersons, who participated in executive education seminars, have passed as part of their education through the analysis and discussion of some of these topics since the mid-1970s. The corresponding teaching chores have been in the hands of a business history research group (GHE for its acronym in Spanish) established in 1974 (Dávila 2015; GHE 2019).

Management as a Profession and Management Education, 1900–1970

The bulk of this chapter has focused on (i) the diffusion throughout Latin America of the ideology of development and the ensuing academic debates, and the marginal space for management within them, and (ii) the traces of the evolution of management practices resulting from research on the "alternative business history" (ABH) of emerging markets. The last part of the present chapter provides an outline of the traces of management professionalization in the region. It is undertaken from the perspective of the pathway of formal management education along the 1900–1970 period.

In Latin America, the origins of management education are intertwined with the development of the liberal professions. The legal profession is the oldest and, for a long time, the most prestigious. It was taught at universities since colonial times, mostly from a definite Roman Catholic stance, by religious orders such as the Jesuits, who ruled their own universities and educated the local elites in several countries (Dávila 1991). In the case of Colombia, by the mid-nineteenth century, the "ideal of the practical" moved elite members to send their sons to universities abroad, especially to England and the United States, for them to become familiar with a technical culture (commerce, engineering, and medicine). The impact of this was varied (Safford 1976). The abovementioned *Escuela Nacional de Minas* was established in 1886 and played a key role in exposing cadres of mining and civil engineers to the new field of management. This school gave the new discipline the name of *industrial economics*, which encompassed not only Taylor and Fayol's theories but also the French positivist sociology of work (Mayor 1984, 2001). The latter pertained to an intellectual tradition, different from that of the human relations school, which sprouted by those same years in the United States. Counting on its prestige and trajectory, the school became incorporated into a public university and began to offer a program since the early 1960s, whose name *ingeniería administrativa* (management engineering) better reflected what it had accomplished during the first half of the twentieth century.

During the first global economy (1870–1929), the export-led model reached its peak (1870–1914) and industrialization furthered its course, especially in Mexico, Brazil, Argentina, and Chile. Law schools did not go unchallenged as recruitment sites for top managerial positions. In fact, top engineering schools began to play a role in the training and development of a new type of engineer, who would combine technical skills with the basics of the emerging field of business management. Two noted cases are the Commercial Engineering undergraduate program, established at the University of Chile in 1935, and the Instituto Tecnológico de Monterrey [Monterrey Institute of Technology], founded in 1943 by a group of leading industrialists of this Mexican pioneering industrial city, located close to the United States' southern border. The Monterrey Tech was modelled after MIT, where several generations of Mexican elite members had studied. The founder of Monterrey Tech, Eugenio Garza Sada (1892–1973), did not agree with the idea of having a School of Law nor one of Philosophy and Letters. Instead, the new educational institution established two new management-related undergraduate programs: one in the School of Industrial Engineering, which would award the degree of Administrator; the other, based on the Escuela Contable (School of Accounting), awarded the degree of *Administrador de Negocios* (Business Administration) (Recio 2016, Chap. 7).

In the case of Colombia, the scope of the influence of the engineers from *Escuela Nacional de Minas*'s was not circumscribed to a region (Antioquia) but reached other major cities, the capital of the country included, and went beyond occupying top positions in industrial companies to have some impact in the public sector and in the organization of collective action, chiefly that of the coffee growers association (*Fedecafe)* which since its foundation in 1927 became a major center of power regarding Colombia's economic policy. Alejandro López the abovementioned former president of the *Escuela* became head of *Fedecafe* in the 1930s as well as minister of education. Another graduate (Mariano Ospina-Pérez, member of a Colombian "presidential family" as were the founders of the *Escuela*) who taught at the Escuela during the 1920s became general manager of Fedecafé in 1930. During the 1930s Ospina-Pérez taught "industrial economics" at the Jesuit's *Universidad Javeriana* Law School in Bogotá. He published an abridged translation into Spanish of Fayol's book (in French) as a textbook for his course (Ospina-Pérez 1938). A section of the textbook was aimed to explain the idea that the country's development could be enhanced by combining the coffee economy culture with industrialization. To be remarked, Ospina-Pérez became President of the country between 1946 and 1950.

Interestingly, Fayol's *Administration Industrielle et Générale* (1961) only reached the anglophone audience in a translation published in 1930 in Geneva by the International Management Institute (Fayol 1930), just 8 years before its Spanish translation (1938). The industrial economics course was taught in the school of Law at Jesuit's Universidad Javeriana together with courses on accounting and statistics. The degree conferred was one on "juridical, economic, and social sciences" which lasted until the mid-1970s when the school of *Ciencias, Económicas, y Administrativas* (economic and administrative sciences) was launched. It signified the differentiation between law, management, and economics. The new school was organized into three departments and remains so to the present (economics, management, and accounting), each one conferring a different professional degree after 5 years of study. Ospina-Pérez also taught the novel subject at Colombia's leading public university (*Universidad Nacional de Colombia*) since the late 1930s (Mayor 1984, 2001). An Economics Sciences Institute was set up there as part of the School of Law and Political Sciences in 1945. The Institute became the School of Economics in 1952 that by 1960 was composed by three units: public economics, private economics, and economic statistics. As can be seen, from a disciplinary view management was in the realm of economics, a discipline dealing not only with the market/private sphere but also with economic policy and the State. The importance of data and measurement was reflected by the space given to statistics within the curriculum. By signaling a wider phenomenon taking place in the largest urban centers of this "country of cities," an undergraduate, 5-year degree in business administration and another one in public accounting were established in 1965; they came after the degree in economics launched in the early 1960. http://www.fce.unal.edu.co/facultad/mision-y-vision#historia

Having risen as a new theme for teaching at established professional schools (Engineering, Law) during the first decades of the twentieth century, the process of professionalization of management made important advancements in cases like those mentioned in Chile, Colombia, and Mexico during the 1940–1970 period. To them it should be added the foundation of Sao Paulo School of Business Administration (FGV EASP) in 1954, sponsored by the joint effort of the business community, through a private foundation (FGV), and the Brazilian government. The academic support was provided by Michigan State University.

The creation of specific undergraduate programs in management conferring a professional degree whose duration was the same than of other professions like engineering was a step ahead in the legitimation of the new profession. It came parallel to the surge of economics and the ensuing differentiation among economics, management, and accounting.

In some countries, the influence of the legal profession was also reflected in the role that played in the idea of applying nascent management concepts, techniques, and tools to the public sector via the establishment of schools of public administration. Fayol's principles and his administrative process were conceived by the French author as useful both to business enterprises and the public sector – an administrative theory of the State. His theory provided a basis for teaching management, and he was an untiring advocate of the need and possibility of formal teaching of management. This could be seen in the founding in Rio de Janeiro in 1952 of the Brazilian School of Public Administration (EBAPE), the first institution dedicated to studies of administration in Latin America. This school was promoted both by the Brazilian government and the already mentioned private foundation (FGV). In México the *Instituto Nacional de Administración Pública* (INAP) was established in 1955 followed in 1958 by Argentina's *Instituto Superior de Administración Pública* (ISAP) (Kliskberg 1984). In the same year in Colombia, the School of Public Administration (ESAP) was founded under the auspices of an experts' mission sponsored by the United Nations. From its beginnings ESAP orientation closely followed Fayol's administrative doctrine reflected in the school's curriculum. Its normative approach left an imprint in the hundreds of public officials who attended it and in the organization of the country's civil service (Dávila 1985/2001, 1991). The ideas of public management would came throughout Latin America in the 1990s concurrent with the liberal reforms that included a minor role of the State in economic development, privatization of public enterprises, and the like (Cabrero and Nava 1999).

The origins of a leading private management school (Universidad de los Andes' School of Management (UASM)) in the country's capital (Bogotá) can be traced to *Escuela Industrial y Comercial del Gimnasio Moderno* (EICGM) created in 1943 as annex to a private high school. Harvard Business School provided some support through a member of its faculty and the HBS case method was used in some courses; in its initial years another novelty was a course on work psychology taught by a Spaniard mining engineer. By the end of that decade, it was incorporated into the School of Economics of Universidad de los Andes, a private, independent, non-denominational university founded by a group of local elite members in 1948. This school offered a 5-year undergraduate program in ("pure") economics and one in "industrial economics," the name coined for management studies in the mentioned Escuela de Minas de Medellín. Courses in economic theory, accounting, finance, and marketing were at the core of the curriculum. Some faculty members went to Stanford for graduate training during the mid-1960s yet none followed the PhD track. This contrasted with the economics department whose early interest in research was fueled by the establishment of a center for economic development (CEDE by its acronym in Spanish) in 1958; later on a handful of its graduates went to undertake doctoral training at American universities. By the end of the 1960s, CEDE has already reached an international reputation as one of the top research centers in economic development in Latin America (Ospina et al. 2008).

To some extent management, as an academic discipline was sidelined vis-a-vis the "pure" economists housed at the same school. By the mid-1960, an industrial engineering department was established within the renowned School of Engineering of that university (Uniandes). From its beginnings offered courses in management theory, including authors like Douglas McGregor (1960) and Rensis Likert (1961) and on planned change approach, coined as organizational development – OD – approach (Margulies and Raia 1972; French et al. 1978). Those and related courses on industrial sociology and business and society represented an early critical standpoint in management education in that country. In fact, it departed from sole resilience on Taylor (the father of industrial engineering) and especially in Fayol's administrative doctrine after which most of management education in the country would be modeled. This was reflected in the prevalent curriculum structure patterned along the administrative process and the underlying faith in administrative principles and their ensuing prescriptions on administrative and managerial action (Dávila 1985/2001, Chap. 3).

By 1973 *La Facultad de Administración de la Universidad de los Andes* (UASM by its acronym in English) was chartered as a new school, separated from the School of Economics. At its bottom was the industrial economics department and the potential that represented the existing close relationship with the industrial engineering department. In returning from graduate training in research at American and British universities (Northwestern, Oxford, MIT, Harvard, NYU, Pittsburgh, Pennsylvania), a handful of former industrial engineering faculty members either joined UASM or stayed at the School of Engineering whose courses could be taken by UASM students. At the same time, five of them started pioneering empirical research on Colombian business and managerial reality on novel themes related to business history, labor unions history, organizational change, and development and management of technology. A quest for innovation in research and teaching as complementary activities, long-term research agendas, multidisciplinary composition of faculty, a curriculum that departed from conventional management functions and introduced courses on organization theory, business history, public management, social enterprise, and the like have been a distinctive UASM signature over almost half a century of existence. The MBA was established in 1974 and the Ph.D. in management came three decades later (2007). Suffice to say, this school that self-portrays as a *school of management not a (private) business school* by the mid-2000s received the triple international accreditation ("triple crown") by American (AACSB), European (EQUIS), and British (AMBA). By 2019, 90 business schools around the world hold this distinction: 68.2% of them are European, 10.6% Latin American, 7.6% from Oceania, 6% from Asia, 4.5% from Africa, and 3% from North America. Among the ten Latin American "triple crown" schools, Mexico and Brazil each have two, and one is located, respectively, in Argentina, Chile, Colombia, Costa Rica, Perú, and Venezuela. https://www.mba.today/guide/triple-accreditation-business-schools UASM 45-year history, as well as these other top management and business schools, is one of the topics of a bulky research agenda on the history of management in Latin America in whose traces the present chapter has started to make inroads.

Conclusion

The initial search for the traces of the history of management in Latin America attempted in this chapter leaves a note of optimism. Indeed, it seems meaningful to develop a research agenda on the history of management in this region. The three approaches to management utilized to examine a sample of management ideas, practices, and tools that Latin American actors have developed over the period of 1870–2020 rendered some interesting results. First of all, one of them refers to the debates around development and underdevelopment that emerged during the 1960s and the 1970s between adherents of the American modernization theory and those of the Latin American dependency theory. For a variety of theoretical and methodological reasons, management issues were not at the central stage at the time, neither for the *dependentistas nor* for modernization theory followers. This notwithstanding, the debates left no doubt about the pressing need for rigorous research to counteract the overriding generalizations that emanated from both opposite ideological stances. Secondly, business history provides a trail of traces in this quest for specific issues in management history. The few instances described about the mining sector, both as a source and a "practical school" of entrepreneurship and management, are encouraging. Also promising are the scores of management topics found in existing historical studies on entrepreneurs, entrepreneurial families, business groups (BGs), and *multilatinas*. Thirdly, the short profiles of the origins and evolution of management education institutions in a few countries, from 1900 to 2020, suggest issues that allow for a comparative research on top management schools in the region.

Finally, there are a series of topics that could have been addressed, but that for reasons of space could not be dealt with in this chapter; they may be included in a research agenda on the history of management in Latin America, in addition to those explored herein. In short, the historical trajectory of the following topics in the capitalist development in this region of the world needs to be object of scholarly inquiry: management and business practice; management education; public management; Latin American management thought (thinkers, publications, academic journals); management innovations; sustainable development management; multilateral agencies' role in management development; regional management academic associations and networks; labor relations and workers' organizations; managerial fashions, panaceas, gurus, and missionaries; evolution of specific management techniques in the functional areas (strategy, organizations, marketing, finance, operations, and logistics); and management consulting. Obviously, to further an umbrella sort of research agenda like this is a complex, long-term endeavor to be discussed across the Latin American management and related disciplines environment. Experience indicates that for specific settings (university departments, management schools, research groups) in a given country, to undertake one or a pair of this long list of research themes is a fascinating intellectual challenge. In decades ahead it could contribute to the present (and future) debates for management history to have a genuine global scope.

Cross-References

▶ Governmentality and the Chinese Workers in China's Contemporary Thought Management System
▶ Indian Management (?): A Modernization Experiment
▶ Introduction: Management Heterogeneity in Asia
▶ Management History in the Modern World: An Overview
▶ Management in Australia – The Case of Australia's Wealthiest Valley: The Hunter
▶ The Making of a Docile Working Class in Pre-reform China
▶ The Perfect Natural Experiment: Asia and the Convergence Debate
▶ Think Big and Privatize Every Thing That Moves: The Impact of Political Reform on the Practice of Management in New Zealand
▶ What Is Management?

References

Almaraz A, Ramírez LA (eds) (2016) Familias empresariales en México. Sucesión generacional y continuidad en el siglo XX. El Colegio de la Frontera Norte, Tijua

Austin G, Dávila C, Jones G (2017) The alternative business history: business in emerging markets. Bus Hist Rev 91(3):537–569

Barbero MI (2003) Business history in Latin America – issues and debates. In: Amatori F, Jones G (eds) Business history around the world. Cambridge University Press, Cambridge, pp 317–338

Barbero MI (2008) Business history in Latin America: a historiographical perspective. Bus Hist Rev 82(3):555–575

Barbero MI (2014) Multinacionales latinoamericanas en perspectiva comparada: teoría e historia. Cátedra Corona 23. Universidad de los Andes, Facultad de Administración, Bogotá

Barbero MI, Dávila C (2009) Introduction: a view from Latin America. Entrep Hist 54:6–15

Barbero MI, Jacob R (eds) (2008) La nueva historia de empresas en América Latina y España. Temas Grupo Editorial, Buenos Aires

Barbero MI, Lluch A (2015/2016) Family capitalism in Argentina: changes and continuity over the course of a century. In: Fernández Pérez P, Lluch A (eds) Evolution of family business. Continuity and change in Latin America and Spain. Edward Elgar, Cheltenham, pp 123–153

Barnard C (1938) The functions of the executive. Harvard University Press, Cambridge, MA

Bendix R (1956) Work and authority in industry. Harper & Row, New York

Bendix R (1967) Tradition and modernity reconsidered. Comp Stud Soc Hist 9(3):292–346

Bértola L, Ocampo JA (2012) The economic development of Latin America since independence. Oxford University Press, Oxford

Bodenheimer S (1970) The ideology of developmentalism: American political science's paradigm-surrogate for Latin American studies. Berkeley J Sociol XV:95–173

Botero MM (2007) La ruta del oro: una economía primaria exportadora, Antioquia 1850–1890. Ediciones Eafit, Medellín

Braverman H (1974) Labor and monopoly capital. The degradation of work in the twentieth century. Monthly Review Press, New York

Brew R (1977) El desarrollo económico de Antioquia desde la independencia hasta 1920. Publicaciones del Banco de la República, Bogotá

Bucheli M, Wadhwani RD (eds) (2013) Organizations in time: history, theory, methods. Oxford University Press, Oxford

Bull B, Castellacci F, Kasahara Y (eds) (2014) Business groups and transnational capitalism in Central America. Economic and political strategies. Palgrave Macmillan, London

Bulmer-Thomas V (1994) The economic history of Latin America since independence. Cambridge University Press, Cambridge, MA

Cabrero E, Nava G eds (1999) Gerencia municipal. Conceptos básicos y estudios de caso. Centro de Investigación y Docencia Económicas (CIDE), México, D.F

Cardoso FH, Faletto E (1979) Dependency and development in Latin America. University of California Press, Berkeley

Casanova L (2009) Global Latinas: Latin America's emerging multinationals. Palgrave Macmillan, London

Cerutti M (1995) Empresarios españoles y sociedad capitalista en México (1840–1920). Fundación Archivo de Indianos, Colombres

Cerutti M (2004) Los estudios empresariales en América Latina ¿El debate interminable? In: Grupo de historia empresarial, Universidad Eafit (eds) Las regiones y la historia empresarial. Universidad Eafit, Medellín, pp 11–25

Cerutti M (2018) Problemas, conceptos, actores y autores. La historia económica y empresarial en el norte de México (y en otras latitudes). El Colegio de San Luis, San Luis Potosí

Chandler AD (1977) The visible hand: the managerial revolution in American business. Harvard University Press, Cambridge, MA

Cochran T, Reina RE (1962) Entrepreneurship in argentine culture. Torcuato Di Tella and S. I. A. M. University of Pennsylvania Press, Philadelphia

Colpan AM, Hikino T (eds) (2018) Business groups in the west: the evolutionary dynamics of big business. Oxford University Press, Oxford

Colpan AM, Hikino T, Lincoln JR (eds) (2010) The Oxford handbook of business groups. Oxford University Press, Oxford

Cummings S, Bridgman T, Hassard J, Rowlinson M (2017) A new history of management. Cambridge University Press, Cambridge

Dávila C (1985/2001) Teorías organizacionales y administración. Enfoque crítico. Interamericana, Revised ed. McGraw Hill, Bogotá

Dávila C (1991) The evolution of management education and development in Latin America. J Manag Dev 10(6):22–31

Dávila C (ed) (2003a) Empresas y empresarios en la historia de Colombia, Siglos XIX-XX, 2 vols. Ediciones Uniandes, Editorial Norma, Cepal, Bogotá

Dávila C (2003b) La historia empresarial en América Latina. In: Erro C (ed) Historia empresarial: pasado, presente y retos. Ariel, Barcelona, pp 349–381

Dávila C (2006) Books that made a difference. On the theory of social change: how economic growth begins. By Everett Hagen. Bus Hist Rev 80(1):131–134

Dávila C (2010) Entrepreneurship and cultural values in Latin America, 1850–2000: from modernization, national values and dependency theory towards a business history perspective. In: García-Ruiz JL, Toninelli PA (eds) The determinants of entrepreneurship. Pickerig & Chatto, London, pp 143–160

Dávila C (2012) Empresariado en Colombia. Perspectiva histórica y regional. Ediciones Uniandes, Bogotá

Dávila C (2013) The current state of business history in Latin America. Aust Econ Hist Rev 53(2):109–120

Dávila C (2015) Docencia e investigación en Historia Empresarial en América Latina: El caso de la Universidad de los Andes, Colombia, 1974–2015. Contribuciones Científicas y Tecnológicas 140. Universidad Santiago de Chile, Santiago de Chile, pp 18–30

Dávila C, Miller R (eds) (1999) Business history in Latin America. The experience of seven countries. Liverpool University Press, Liverpool

Drucker P (1954) The practice of management. Harper & Row, New York

Drucker P (1985) Innovation and entrepreneurship. Practice and principles. Butterworth-Heinemann, London

Edwards R (1979) Contested terrain. The transformation of the workplace in the twentieth century. Basic Books, New York

Evans P (1979) Dependent development: the alliance of multinational, state, and local capital in Brazil. Princeton University Press, Princeton

Fayol H (1916/1930) Industrial and general administration. International Management Institute, Geneve. (Original 1916 French version: Administration industrielle et genérale; translation into English by J.A. Coubrough)

Fernández R, Ocampo JF (1974) The Latin American revolution: a theory of imperialism, not dependence. Lat Am Perspect 1(1):30–61

Fernández Pérez P, Colli A (eds) (2013) The endurance of family business. A global overview. Cambridge University Press, New York

Fernández Pérez P, Lluch A (eds) (2015/2016) Familias empresarias y grandes empresas familiares en América Latina y España. Una visión de largo plazo. Bilbao, Fundación BBVA. English version: Evolution of family business. Continuity and change in Latin America and Spain. Edward Elgar, Cheltenham

Finkle JL, Gable RW (eds) (1968) Political development and social change. Wiley, New York

Follet MP (1927/1971) La administración como profesión. In: Merrill HF (ed) Clásicos en administración. Trillas, México, pp 265–277. (Original version: (1927) Management as a profession. In: Metcalff HC (ed) Business management as a profession. A.W. Shaw Company, Chicago, Chap. IV, pp 73–87). Translation: Aurelio Romeo del Valle

Frank AG (1967) Capitalism and underdevelopment in Latin America: historical studies of Chile and Brazil. Monthly Review Press, New York

Frank AG (1972) Lumpen bourgeoise, Lumpen development: dependence, class and politics in Latin America (trans: Marion Davis Bordewcio). Monthly Review Press, New York

Frank AG (1974) Dependence is dead, long live dependence and the class struggle: an answer to critics. Latin Am Perspect 1(1):87–106

Frank AG, Real de Azúa C, González-Casanova P (1969) La sociología subdesarrollante. Aportes, Montevideo

French W, Bell C, Zawacki R (1978) Organization development: theory, practice and research. Business Publications, Dallas

GHE (2019) Business history at a Latin American University, 1974–2019. Leaflet. Universidad de los Andes, Facultad de Administración

Gouldner AW (1970) The coming crisis of western sociology. Basic Books, New York

Gramsci A (1971) Prison's book: selections. International Publisher, Moscow

Hagen EE (1962) On the theory of social change. How economic growth begins. The Dorsey Press, Homewood

Herrero V (2014) Agustín Edwards Eastman. Una biografía desclasificada del dueño de El Mercurio. Penguin House Random House Grupo Editorial, Santiago de Chile

Horowitz IL (1966) Three worlds of development: the theory and practice of international stratification. Oxford University Press, New York

Jones G (2007) Globalization. In: Jones G, Zeitlin J (eds) The Oxford handbook of business history. Oxford University Press, Oxford, pp 141–170

Kay C (1989) Latin American theories of development and underdevelopment. Routledge, London

Kliskberg B (1984) Para investigar la administración pública. Instituto Nacional de Administración, Alcalá de Henares

Likert R (1961) New patterns of management. McGraw Hill, New York

Lipman A (1969) The Colombian entrepreneur. University of Miami Press, Coral Gables

Lipset S, Solari A (eds) (1967) Elites in Latin America. Oxford University Press, Oxford

Llorca-Jaña et al (eds) (2019) Capitalists, business and state-building in Chile. Palgrave Macmillan, London

Londoño JC (2016) Manuel Carvajal Sinisterra. Una vida dedicada a generar progreso con equidad. Universidad Icesi, Cali

Lluch A et al (2018) Empresas y empresarios en la Argentina desde una perspectiva histórica: una breve síntesis. In: Cortes R, della Paolera G (eds) Nueva historia económica de la Argentina. Edhasa, Buenos Aires, pp 223–242

Margulies N, Raia AP (1972) Organizational development: values, processes and technology. McGraw Hill, New York

Mayor A (1984) Etica, trabajo y productividad. Una interpretación sociológica sobre la influencia de la Escuela Nacional de Minas en la vida, costumbres e industrialización regionales. Tercer Mundo, Bogotá

Mayor A (2001) Técnica y utopía. Biografía intelectual y política de Alejandro López, 1876–1940. Fondo Editorial Universidad Eafit, Medellín

McClelland DC (1961) The achieving society. D. Van Nostrand Company, Princeton

McGregor D (1960) The human side of enterprise. McGraw Hill, New York

McGregor D (1967) The professional manager. McGraw Hill, New York

Meisel A, Viloria J (2003) Barranquilla hanseática. El caso de un empresario alemán. In: Dávila C (ed) Empresas y empresarios en la historia de Colombia. Siglos XIX y XX. Una colección de estudios recientes. Ediciones Uniandes, Editorial Norma, Cepal, Bogotá, pp 513–548

Miller R (1999) Business history in Latin America: an introduction. In: Dávila C, Miller R (eds) Business history in Latin America. The experience of seven countries. University of Liverpool Press, Liverpool, pp 1–16

Miller R (2010) Foreign firms and business history. Cátedra Corona 18. Universidad de los Andes, Facultad de Administración, Bogotá

Miller R (2017) The history of business in Latin America. In: Wilson JF, Toms S, de Jong A, Buchnea E (eds) The Routledge companion to business history. Routldege, London, pp 187–201

Molina LF (2003) La Empresa Minera del Zancudo (1848–1920). In: Dávila C (ed) Empresas y empresarios en la historia de Colombia. Siglos XIX-XX. Una colección de estudios recientes. Ediciones Uniandes, Editorial Norma, Cepal, Bogotá, pp 633–676

Molina LF (2006) Empresarios colombianos del siglo XIX. Ediciones Uniandes, Facultad de Administración, Bogotá

Orozco LA, Anzola-Morales O (2019) A Colombian classic management thinker: Alejandro López Restrepo. J Manag Hist 25(2):221–236

Ospina MJ, Fajardo M, Bonilla JA, Sánchez F (2008) Historia del Cede 50 años de investigación en economía 1958–2008. Universidad de los Andes, Facultad de Economía, Centro de Estudios sobre Desarrollo Económico, Bogotá

Ospina-Pérez M (1938) Economía industrial y administración. Minerva, Bogotá

Palacios M (ed) (2015) Negocios, empresarios y entornos políticos en México, 1827–1958. El Colegio de México, Centro de Estudios Históricos, México

Platt DC (1980) Dependency in nineteenth-century Latin America: an historian objects. Lat Am Res Rev 15(1):113–130

Portocarrero F (2007) El imperio Prado 1890–1970. Universidad del Pacífico, Lima

Przeworski A, Limongi F (1997) Modernization. Theories and facts. World Polit 49(2):155–183

Recio G (2016) Don Eugenio Garza Sada. Ideas, acción, legado. Editorial Font, Monterrey

Reguera A (2006) Patrón de estancias. Ramón Santamarina: una biografia de fortuna y poder en La Pampa. Eudeba, Buenos Aires

Ripoll MT (2007) Empresarios centenaristas en Cartagena: cuatro estudios de caso. Ediciones Unitecnológica, Cartagena de Indias

Safford F (1976) The ideal of the practical: Colombia's struggle to form a technical elite. University of Texas Press, Austin

Selznick P (1957) Leadership in administration: a sociological interpretation. Harper & Row, New York

Simon H (1945) Administrative behavior. A study of decision-making processes in administrative organizations. The Free Press, New York

Simposio Mundial de Cartagena (1978) Crítica y política en ciencias sociales. El debate sobre teoría y práctica. Punta de Lanza, Bogotá

Stein SJ, Stein BH (1970) The colonial heritage of Latin America. Essays on economic dependence in perspective. Oxford University Press, Oxford

Taffet JF (2007) Foreign aid as foreign policy: the Alliance for progress in Latin America. Routledge, New York

Taylor F (1912) The principles of scientific management. Harper & Row, New York

The Economist (1991) A job for life. A survey of management education 1–26

Twinam A (1982) Miners, merchants and farmers in colonial Colombia. University of Texas Press, Austin

Villegas B (2014) Una gesta admirable. Vida y obra de Don Hernando Caicedo. Villegas Editores, Bogotá

Weber M (1922/1944) Economía y sociedad. Esbozo de sociología comprensiva. Fondo de Cultura Económica, México. (Original versión in German: Wirtschaft und Gesselchaft, Grundriss der Verstehenden Soziologie, C.B. Mohr (Paul Siebeck), Tubinga, 2 vols. Translation into Spanish: José Medina Echavarría, Juan Roura Parella, Eduardo Gaercía Máynez, Eugenio Imaz y José Ferrater Mora)

Zaleznik A (1990) The managerial mystique. Harper & Row, New York

Think Big and Privatize Every Thing That Moves: The Impact of Political Reform on the Practice of Management in New Zealand

62

Andrew Cardow and William Wilson

Contents

Introduction: The New Zealand Frontier, 1790–1900	1412
Home Ownership and the Creation of a Welfare State	1414
The Unraveling of a Century of State Intervention	1417
Privatization and Reinvention of Public Service	1418
Impact of Political Reforms on the Practice of Management in New Zealand	1423
Conclusion	1426
Cross-References	1427
References	1427

Abstract

With the change of government in 1984, there was a perceived need by the incoming government to undertake a fundamental change in the way New Zealand was governed. This in turn saw a change how business managers and those in high government office approached their jobs. This change coincided with a western trend toward the embracement of the neo-liberal agenda. In the case of New Zealand, the reforms put in place by the incoming Labor government and continued through successive administrations on the left and right, manifested in a paradigm shift in the perception and role of management and managers within New Zealand. The chapter does not take a stand on whether such changes were beneficial or otherwise but rather traces the developments that lead to a change in management theory and motivation in New Zealand.

A. Cardow (✉)
School of Management, Massey University, Albany, New Zealand
e-mail: A.Cardow@massey.ac.nz

W. Wilson
School of Economics and Finance, Massey University, Albany, New Zealand

© The Author(s), under exclusive licence to Springer Nature Switzerland AG 2020
B. Bowden et al. (eds.), *The Palgrave Handbook of Management History*,
https://doi.org/10.1007/978-3-319-62114-2_59

Keywords

New Zealand · Political history · Management reform · Managerialism

Introduction: The New Zealand Frontier, 1790–1900

A study of management history is in effect a study of the organization of commercial activity. Initially like many "frontier" societies, European commercial activity in New Zealand was based entirely around the need for Europeans to secure natural resources. Michael King, in his well-regarded History of New Zealand, places the start of such activity in the decade beginning 1790 (2003, p. 118). New Zealand's flora and fauna was unique and abundant, wood and flax were easily harvested from virgin forests and lowlands while abundant sea mammals around the coast, who were largely unafraid of man, provided fur, oil, and blubber. All products were much in demand in the capitals of Europe and formed the basis of many European fortunes. A pattern of exploitation undertaken by private businesspersons set the template for early New Zealand industry. Volume 1 of the Dictionary of New Zealand Biography is replete with such people. One such person is Ranulph Dacre, a trader and exploiter of whale and timber products in precolonial New Zealand (Rogers 1990). Although not a "major" player, he is indicative of the type of business person that was active in precolonial New Zealand. A self-made man who entered service in the British navy at the age of 13, Dacre subsequently became a merchant's ship captain, making and losing fortunes with some regularity over the course of an Australasian business career built around trading and land speculation that covered the years 1824 to 1872, years that eventually saw Dacre return to Britain with modest wealth. New Zealand was, in short, until the late twentieth century, a country built upon biological resource exploitation and farming. Consequently, it was land, most particularly for agriculture, which was the primary driver of commercial and managerial activity in early New Zealand. Yes, the entrepreneurial exploits of the early traders cannot be overlooked. But it must be emphasized that it was with ecological exploitation that New Zealand experienced something close to organized management.

As King (2003) notes, the pattern of ecological exploitation that has characterized New Zealand history predated European settlement, commencing in the 13th CE with Maori colonization of what they called *Aotearoa* ("Land of the Long White Cloud"). From the start, human relationships with the natural world were troubled, the Māori, upon their arrival, driving to extinction the large, flightless Moa that stood at the top of the ecological pecking order. Relationships with the natural world became even troubled in the 19th CE with the arrival of Europeans in search of fuel, land, and "the exotic" (furs, whale oil, gold, etc.). While European settlers to New Zealand in the 1800s viewed the country as a new frontier, the indigenous people of New Zealand, collectively known as Māori, were initially supportive of European settlers. Some but not all Maori also saw some advantage in adopting the methods of the Europeans. Again, the Dictionary of New Zealand Biography details how Hone Tuhawaiki – a Māori leader of the Ngai Tahu people who dominated

New Zealand's South Island – was adept at selling land in order to buy goods from traders and sealers, goods that included a ship on one occasion. He also adopted many of the "trappings" of the European, living in a weatherboard house and wearing a full Naval Uniform. By 1840 when he signed the Treaty of Waitangi, he was the acknowledged leader of the Ngai Tahu (Anderson 1990). While the first generation of European traders, whalers, and sealers posed little threat to Māori land occupancy, this changed when in the early 1820s they were joined by flax exporters, Kauri loggers, and shipbuilders; the latter group being initially concentrated in and around the settlement at Kororāreka (now known as Russell) in the north of the country (Sinclair 1991, p. 39). However, it was not until the third decade of the nineteenth century that systematic European colonization of the country was considered by the British government (King 2003, p. 156; Temple 2002).

By 1840 the increasing number of European, North American, Australian, and Asian settlers was causing tension, not only between the Māori and the newcomers, but also among the settlers themselves. This prompted a call for the British Crown (King 2003, p. 152) to provide certainty of security. Subsequently, British authority was formalized when, on 6 February 1840 at Waitangi, a treaty between Governor Hobson, as the Representative of the British Monarchy, and several Māori chiefs, ostensibly representing all Māori, essentially ceded sovereignty of New Zealand to Britain. The Treaty of Waitangi is now taken by many to be the founding document of New Zealand.

The signing of the Treaty of Waitangi may have given many a sense of increased security. For those entrepreneurs, however, who were actively organizing the colonization of the country, it threatened to undermine their entire business model, a model premised on their ability to buy land from the Māori to sell to colonists. As Burns (1989, p. 154) notes, when William Wakefield, leader of the New Zealand Company in Wellington, was given a copy of the treaty by the Reverend Williams, he swore at him. Wakefield and the New Zealand Company relied on selling land to investors in UK. It is likely that his anger was caused by a (genuine) fear that he would no longer be the sole arbiter of land exploitation in the Wellington region. Nevertheless, from 1840 there was an increase in settlers arriving, mainly from the United Kingdom. In part, this upsurge reflected the efforts by the New Zealand Company to consolidate its position *vis-a-vis* the Crown. However, ongoing disagreement over the meaning of the Treaty, along with a growing reluctance by Māori to sell land suitable for settlement to the government, eventually brought to head the steadily building tensions, tensions that resulted in a series of armed conflicts from 1842 to 1872 (Ministry for Culture and Heritage 2014).

By 1845 the New Zealand government was in a difficult position. With an estimated European population of 12,744 (Statistics New Zealand 2015), necessary infrastructure was lacking. There was a feeling of disquiet that in some circles the Maori, no longer had sovereignty over their own land. This fundamental confusion within the meaning of Rangatiratanga (governance or sovereignty) continues to be a source of tension between Maori and the Crown. In the mid-nineteenth century, the tensions led to warfare which lasted until the early 1870s. What came to be known as the New Zealand Wars devastated the Māori population, which went from 80,000 in 1845 to 56,000 by 1851 (NZ Government Staff 1893 to 2010; Statistics New Zealand 2015).

With the Māori more or less defeated by 1872, with holdouts confined to the rugged fastness of the "King Country" of New Zealand's North Island, New Zealand in the latter half of the nineteenth century went through a number of boom and bust cycles. As was the case previously, these were driven by land hunger and the demand for natural resources. Behind this new boom, however, was a fundamental alteration in the New Zealand landscape. After the Treaty was signed, the Crown gained control of vast native kauri forests covering much of the North Island. Subsequently, these forests were felled and the lumber shipped to Australia and the UK. Forest land, once cleared, became available for settlement. Increasing numbers of settlers spread out across the country, establishing towns and farms. Mining also attracted immigrants. With gold rushes occurring in California (1848) and Australia (1851), New Zealand also attracted prospectors (La Croix 1992, pp. 204–227; Umbeck 1977, pp. 197–226). These bonanza seekers were rewarded with gold finds in the Coromandel peninsula in 1841, Central Otago in 1861, and West Otago in the late 1860s (King 2003, p. 208). Fuelled by such new found sources of wealth, the New Zealand population rose to 668,652 in 1891. By this stage, the Māori component was outnumbered by almost eight to one, having stabilized around the 42,000–44,000 mark. Increasing European population dominance, however, did solve the question of land ownership. Never fully defeated, and never accepting the Crown's interpretation of the Treaty of Waiangi, Māori discontent and opposition was never resolved. The unresolved nature of this conflict can be ascertained by the fact that in 1975 – when the Māori numbered some 360,000 in a population of 3.2 million – a Hikoi (land march) from the Hokianga in Northland culminated in thousands of marchers and their supporters descending on Parliament, demanding that not one more acre of Maori land should be alienated. In response, the Government established the Waitangi Tribunal to hear Maori grievances. The Tribunal's power was limited to make findings of fact and recommendations, progress was slow, and in 1977 there was a 506 day occupation of land at Bastion point in Auckland. Eventually, in the face of continuing Māori opposition, the Crown entered into direct negotiations with the Māori in 1988, bypassing the Waitangi tribunal. Even this measure, however, failed to resolve the situation. Even today, with individual claimants (iwi and hapū) and a number of multimillion dollar settlements, countless disputes over land ownership are still outstanding.

Home Ownership and the Creation of a Welfare State

As noted in the previous section, the issue of land ownership has long been central to patterns of commercial activity in New Zealand. From the 1890s onwards, however, problems relating to land ownership increasingly assumed an urban hue. As Gibson (1973) indicates, by 1891 some 45.4% of the New Zealand population were town dwellers with 28.4% of the total found in the four main urban centers, namely, Auckland and Wellington (both North Island) and Christchurch and Dunedin (both South Island). By 1936, the comparable figures were 60% and 36.4%, respectively. As the twentieth century progressed, this trend became more and more manifest, making matters relating to urban circumstance the central factors in the New Zealand experience. By 1971, almost half the nation's total population (47%) was found in the four large metropolitan centers. Another 31.8% lived in smaller towns, leaving only 21.2% living in rural settings (Gibson 1973, pp. 71–84). At the time of writing (2018), approximately a third of New Zealand's population of 4.7 million lived in Auckland. By comparison with Auckland's outsized growth, the preeminent South Island cities – Christchurch and Dunedin – remain modest in size, the former boasting 360,000 inhabitants and the latter 120,000. Among North Island cities, only Wellington, with 412,000 citizens, remotely rivals Auckland in size.

As early as the 1890s, the then Liberal Government in New Zealand recognized that growing urban areas was starting to affect the quality of city life and began to encourage the better off working class buy their own house in the quickly growing suburbs (Fergusson 1994). They provided low interest loans; however, there was a very poor uptake, mainly because the transport cost outweighed the shift from low quality city accommodation. In 1905–1906, as a way of building upon the work done by previous administration, the reforming administration of Richard Seddon (Prime Minister, 1983–1906) passed two pieces of legislation that both indicated the growing importance of the urban population and the willingness of New Zealand governments to override market forces in the pursuit of social objectives. The first of these two pieces of legislation, the *Workers Dwelling Act 1905*, made provision for the construction of houses in suburbia designed for inner city workers. The second, the *Advances to Workers Act 1906*, encouraged the purchase of a single level standalone house on a plot of land in suburbia, houses which the government itself intended to construct. Like the administration before them, however, Seddon's government discovered they could not build the houses cheaply enough for their intended market (Schrader 2005). By 1910 only 126 of an anticipated 5000 had been built. Despite this practical failure, the government intervention in housing supply and purchase, helped spell out an interventionist strategy by government that was to persist for most of the twentieth Century, had been cast. The State would, when it became involved in the market, build high quality buildings that would help working people afford to purchase their part of the New Zealand dream. In expressing the continuing importance of this social objective, in 1950 Sidney Holland, the then Prime Minister Holland, is reported as saying: "the Government has great faith in the social value of home ownership ... it promotes imitative, self-reliance, thrift and other good qualities which go to make up the strength of the nation" (Schrader 2005). It is this first approach towards "self-help" that in turn lay the foundations that would lead to a change in the way management was practiced in New Zealand during the 1980s.

It was not only in terms of housing policy that the New Zealand governments of the late nineteenth and early twentieth centuries showed themselves to be receptive to reforming measures. Particularly prominent among these measures was the

Industrial Conciliation and Arbitration Act 1894, a piece of legislation introduced by one of the great reforming figures in New Zealand history, William Pember-Reeves, who served as a Liberal Party Minister for Labor between 1892 and 1896. Under this piece of legislation, the first of its type to apply to a national economy, trade unions gained official recognition as representations of workers. Wages and other working conditions became subject to de facto state regulation as the "awards" of the Arbitration Court were legally binding on all parties. In reflecting on New Zealand's system of compulsory conciliation and arbitration system – which was to endure in a largely unchanged forms until 1991 – Pember-Reeves (1903) accurately observed in his book, *State Experiments in Australia and New Zealand,* that "to a large extent" it was "the Labor Laws" of Australia and New Zealand "which helped to distinguish the spirit of these democracies from that of countries like Canada and parts of the United States." In both their "boldness and stringency," Pember-Reeves added, "they are not matched elsewhere." Other reforming legislation that characterized the Liberal governments of the late nineteenth and early twentieth centuries included female suffrage, introduced in 1893, and old age pensions, introduced in 1898.

Significantly, the great industrial and social welfare reforms of the late nineteenth and early nineteenth centuries were due to the actions of middle-class based Liberal Governments, not working-class or trade union based Labor Governments. After a generation of relatively inaction, however, the interventionist creed was given new force with the articulation and legislation of a "cradle to grave" welfare state under the administration of Labor's Joseph Savage (Prime Minister 1935–1940) and Peter Fraser (1940 to 1949). Subsequently, the social policies of full employment and the provision of a *"social welfare safety net"* for all New Zealanders were adopted by both National and Labor governments. In the 1950s and 1960s, the economic cost of these welfare initiatives was comparatively modest. These decades were prosperous times for all New Zealanders with the country ranked towards the top of the OECD league tables; a position based almost entirely upon the bounty of its agricultural produce, most of which was sold to the United Kingdom. However, by the mid-1970s the wheels started to come off the interventionist model that had long characterized New Zealand society. New Zealand found itself without a major purchaser of agricultural product when the UK entered the EEC in 1973. At home, the advent of Supplementary Minimum prices and the OPEC price increases lead to some major financial issues. In an attempt to redress these issues and in part an attempt to "future proof" the New Zealand economy, the National government under Prime Minister Muldoon put in place a number of initiatives. They closed down and redistributed the national superannuation fund, fixed the exchange rate, and embarked on a number of large scale infrastructural programs colloquially known as Think Big. Finally in the last few years of their tenure, the National government presided over a wage and price freeze. When a snap election was called the government fell, it was a first part of the post landslide victory for Labor. However, the Labor government did not inherit a "star." Rather the economy was very close to collapse. Reform was required; the scale of such reform and the method of such reform contributed to a change in the way management was see and practiced with New Zealand to this day.

The Unraveling of a Century of State Intervention

The previous sections have been provided as background, for what is the real context of this chapter; New Zealand in the 1970s and 1980s – when New Zealand came of age and the practice of management in New Zealand changed forever. The 1950s and 1960s were our teenage years, life was easy, and New Zealanders were prosperous. A Treasury working paper by Mawson (2002) ranks the country either third or fourth place among OECD countries at this time. Unemployment in the 1950s was extremely low, with a popular joke of the time being, *"they were personally known to the Minister of Labour."* Socially the population of three million people also found its voice, demonstrating, against New Zealand's involvement in the Vietnam War, sporting contact with South Africa and nuclear testing in the Pacific. Domestically, New Zealand land rights and the women's movement were inciting passion. New Zealand was truly the land of milk and honey; however, events outside New Zealand were soon to end the good times. For example, Britain joined the European Economic Community in 1973, limiting access to what had been our primary export market. In 1973 and again in 1979, Arab OPEC countries substantially increased oil prices, as a result, New Zealand plunged down the OECD league tables. The response of a newly elected Prime Minster, Robert Muldoon in 1975, was to invest heavily in *"Think Big"* projects designed to make New Zealand self-sufficient in energy while creating employment opportunities. However, while waiting for these projects to come online New Zealand faced rising inflation, Muldoon's response in 1982 was to freeze prices, wages, and interest rates while at the same time, to earn much-needed foreign currencies he offered farmers subsidies and minimum prices. Muldoon's wage and price freeze were unpopular and by 1984, his majority in Parliament had shrunk to one. When faced with the dissenting voice of National MP Marilyn Waring threatening to vote for an opposition sponsored nuclear-free legislation; Muldoon called a snap general election. National lost the 1984 winning only 37 seats in a 95-seat parliament, thus effectively ending the political career of one of New Zealand's most powerful and polarizing prime ministers and minister of finance.

With power suddenly thrust upon them Labor immediately faced a crisis, as prior to the election Muldoon had been receiving advice from the Reserve Bank to devalue the New Zealand dollar. Muldoon steadfastly refused, resulting in the New Zealand dollar coming under pressure from speculators. Following the election, the New Zealand dollar faced increased pressure and New Zealand faced a constitutional crisis as Muldoon refused the convention to take advice from the incoming government. Eventually Muldoon acceded the dollar was devalued 20% and funds flowed back into the country. The newly sworn in Labor government, following advice from Treasury, the Reserve Bank and others immediately set about reforming New Zealand constitutionally, economically, and socially. They followed a "neoliberal" ideology being promulgated by the major players within Bretton Woods institutions and which was fast gaining ground in the UK and the USA. The remainder of this chapter examines the policies of the fourth Labor Government and the legacy left by its three main actors, Prime Minister Lange (the great debater), Roger Douglas (Minister of Finance whom the term Rogernomics was coined), and

Richard Prebble (Minister of Railways). Following a brief literature review, illustrative examples are provided demonstrating how the management reforms impacted on management practice and the country as a whole. These are followed by brief discussion and conclusion.

The 4th Labor Government, over the 6 years from 1984, became one of the most aggressive proponents on neoliberalism in the OECD. Christopher Pollitt (2000, p. 185) writing about rise of neoliberalism in the west went as far to say, although New Zealand was in the vanguard of reform, it is certainly not recognized as a model to imitate. This then is the story of how a Labor Government enacted and institutionalized the ideology of neoliberalism in New Zealand, changing the way New Zealanders saw management and business, forever. This chapter necessarily relies on contemporaneous government publications and management commentary. This is to illustrate the change in management practice in New Zealand because of the Government's adoption of neoliberalism. Granted, the country was not the first to dabble in this paradigm; it was however seen at the time and continues to be seen in hindsight as the most neoliberally "progressive" of the western democracies (Boston and Eichbaum 2014; Eichbaum 2006; Pollitt 2000).

The neoliberal agenda was set by the Lange administration and it was not until the second term of the Labor government the "reforms" which were to have such an impact on management practice in New Zealand began to bite. The Lange administration had signaled far-reaching changes. Since 1984 they had been actively putting in place foundational reform, after another victory in 1987 the mooted changes began to be entrenched. It was an institutional desire to be seen as responsible and business like, that led to the "*success*" of the reforms firstly within the public sector then the wider management arena in New Zealand. This is based on the theory that individual managers within government controlled business organizations are more influenced by their need to achieve identity and legitimacy from "business" practitioners than their in their desire to better serve the public (Litvin 2002). Thus, managers may wish to be seen by their peers, and by society in general, as owners and managers of a "business" and so will adapt their behavior to reflect what they believe are the appropriate and commonly held assumptions surrounding the concept of management. Because individual actors choose to adopt behavior patterns that clearly identify them as belonging to a collective, the literature of institutional theory accommodates both collectivist and individual approaches to the subject. These oppositional elements – individualism versus collectivism – inherent in institutional theory can be used to build a theory for government managers, since management is perceived as being at once an individual and a collective construct (Haugh and Pardy 1999; Pfeffer 1982; Weber 1947, p. 360).

Privatization and Reinvention of Public Service

Following from the above and outlined below are the main ideas promoted by the movement for the "re-invention of government" which themselves were not new. Well before the publication of the book by Osborne and Gaebler, *Reinventing*

Government (1993), much had been written regarding the benefits, or otherwise, of encouraging government managers to adopt the techniques of private-sector business managers. One of the more significant authors in this field was Selznick (1947/1966) who in his book, *The TVA and the Grass Roots*, clearly described how government workers clothed themselves as private businesspeople. At the time, the phrase privatization was not used. However, by the time Considine and Painter (1997) published their book on managerialism, the concept had become not only entrenched but colonized within both the public and private sector in New Zealand. In the latter part of the twentieth century, the ideas first raised by Weber became enmeshed in the reinvention of government movement and gained support from a mixture of neo-liberal contributions. These inputs ranged from the sociological through to the economic and political and helped lay the foundation for what was variously known as Thatcherism in the United Kingdom, Reganomics in the United States, and Rogernomics in New Zealand. These neo-liberal political/economic adjustments to macropolicy occurred close enough in time to be seen as a western trend; they all emphasized privatization of government commercial operations, together with a belief that private enterprises were more efficient, beneficial, and equitable than state-owned and staffed operations.

The ideology gathered support throughout the 1980s and was, by the 1990s, sufficiently established for academic and industry papers to appear chronicling the push for privatization. Most of these stories were ones of acceptance and encouragement (OECD Staff 1993; Osborne and Gaebler 1993; Prokopenko and Pavlin 1991; Schneider and Teske 1992). The OECD had interpreted economic rationalism to mean pursuing Market-Type Mechanisms. However, it would be erroneous to suggest that the path was universally approved. Concurrently, there was gathering critique. Many critics, in New Zealand and overseas, were far from convinced of the economic and social benefits promised by the Market-Type Mechanisms or the new efficiencies suggested by the "*New Public Management*" (Kelsey 1993, 1994, 1997, 1999; Pollitt 2000, 2001; Sharp 1994). Such a focus on central government management reform is important within the context of New Zealand. In New Zealand, the managerilaist reforms undertaken in the public sector had a large influence on the private sector. In some ways, they assisted in shaping the way managers saw their job. In New Zealand managerialism, usually a term of derision, had become entrenched – to the point that the term itself was colonized by its practitioners. For example, a State Services publication, Current problems in Public Management (State Services Commission 2002), suggests that government policy advisors were not only aware of the term "managerialism" but saw it as a laudable rather than a derogatory term. It states:

- *Before 1984 (dominated by bureaucracy and process), it took 6 weeks to get an initial benefit payment.*
- *Now (with the development of managerialism and an output focus), assessment and payment are much quicker, and emergency benefits for food and shelter are available on the day (p. 3). Parenthesis in original.*

Of all the seeds for New Zealand's adoption of managerialism sown in the reforming legislation of the Labor government (1984–1990), the most important legislation was the State-owned Enterprises Act (1986), the State Sector Act (1988), and the Public Finance Act (1989). No matter how necessary the reforms were seen to be; one international commentator has written the New Zealand government was deluding itself that the reforms would be universally viewed in a positive light (Pollitt 2000, p. 185). The power of legitimacy and identity influenced by Treasury and the Business Round table led the government to believe their reforms were desirable, supported, and the only possible way to act.

The belief held by individual managers that they were acting in accordance with accepted business definitions and the normative isomorphic identification with the institutional norms of the private sector manager was another strong influence in New Zealand. For example, Considine and Painter (1997), Enteman (1993), Pollitt (2000), and Gregory (1999) provide a contemporaneous critique of the concept of managerialism and the adoption by government actors of the language and techniques associated with it. Managerialism is seen as a politically rationalist and therefore "correct" approach to public business organization in that emotions should not be part of the business equation. It has been argued that from time to time public servants undertake activities that resemble those of a private company, then that activity must be organized in accordance with accepted business practice. The New Zealand Treasury supported this line of reasoning, urging that "corporatisation would achieve considerable efficiency gains" (1987, p. 119). This advice from Treasury was heeded, and the legislation to enable the privatization and commercialization of activities previously undertaken by government was passed through Parliament.

However, there was some contemporaneous dissent, professor Michael Peters of Auckland University, in a 2001 article, was especially critical of these developments. He suggested that New Zealand had not only successfully enacted neo-liberalist policy but restructured the way New Zealand governments relate to the public domain. In Peters' opinion, New Zealand was close to an almost religious devotion to the market concept. Such an emphasis, he suggested, has elevated the market from a contrived to a natural construct. In other words, the market-driven approach as practiced in New Zealand is now almost beyond question. In New Zealand, government policy has placed such importance on privatization of services and the free-market paradigm associated with it that the rationalist private sector model is the only business model to be considered within a business framework. Peters argues that these policies had the effect of placing the state, democracy, and the community in a subservient role with respect to the market. Finally, Peters views the free-market paradigm expounded by the government, and the free trade philosophy of the WTO, IMF, and World Bank, as evidence that New Zealand has abandoned its historical ties to the community and embraced the market (Peters 2001, p. 209). It is this paradigm of free trade and market forces that has allowed the structures of managerialism to find legitimacy with managers government business operations.

The major proponents of this prescriptive path believed that a public business is no different from a private business and therefore needs the same sort of management structure (Osborne and Gaebler 1993; Pinchot 1985; Prebble 1996; Schneider and Teske 1992). This argument, however, fails to take into account the cultural differences that exist between a publicly owned business organization and a private organization. In addition, the argument does not accommodate the way power is exerted within a public service environment, or the individual motivators for success that influence a public manager as opposed to a private businessperson (Schneider and Teske 1992).

This theoretical model has involved an almost rigid adherence to the principles of market-type mechanisms outlined above (Peters 2001; Schick 1996; Wilson and Doig 2000). Central to the philosophy of government reform in New Zealand was the importance placed on the need for government agencies to be financially and economically accountable. The authors of the Treasury briefing paper Government Management, essentially the briefing paper for the incoming Labor government, envisaged that the reforms be extended even into "noncommercial areas" (New Zealand Treasury Staff 1987) of government and local government activity. This aspect of accountability is met through contractual arrangements which clearly and specifically lay down outputs against which the particular operation will be measured. For example, the State-Owned Enterprises Act (1986) Part1 s 4 reads in part: "The principal objective of every State enterprise shall be to operate as a successful business and to this end be as profitable and efficient as comparable businesses that are not owned by the Crown." The State Sector Act (1988) s 51(6) reinforces these managerialist expectations by requiring senior management to "promote efficiency" as part of their duties. Managers need only refer to the Public Finance Act (1989) for guidance as to how efficiency should be interpreted. Further, even when conducting noncommercial activities, the Act requires the enterprise to exact a fee from the receiver of the goods or services (State-owned Enterprises Act (1986) S7).

Central government's emphasis on financial efficiency is overt in the objectives of the Public Finance Act (1989):

> An Act to amend the law governing the use of public financial resources and to that end to (a) Provide a framework for Parliamentary scrutiny of the Government's management of the Crown's assets and liabilities, including expenditure proposals; and (b) Establish lines of responsibility for the use of public financial resources; and (c) Establish financial management incentives to encourage effective and efficient use of financial resources in departments and [Crown entities]; and (d) Specify the minimum financial reporting obligations of the Crown, departments, and [Crown entities]; and e) Safeguard public assets by providing statutory authority and control for the raising of loans, issuing of securities, giving of guarantees, operation of bank accounts, and investment of funds.

Such demands have an inevitable effect on those charged with managing services offered to the public. The penetration of market-driven notions within both central and local government can be demonstrated by a document published by the Hillary

Commission for Sport and Recreation in 1994. Rather than suggest ways in which the public could benefit from improved access to sporting and cultural opportunities, the Hillary Commission for Sport, in their desire to be effective and efficient, attempted to entrench the ideals of managerialism. For example, the Commission advocated user charges for leisure services provided by local government, going as far as reporting that "if people want it [the service] then they will pay for it" (1994, p. 7) and "by introducing user charges, lower income groups have the option of whether they wish to use a service instead of paying for a service they don't use"(1994, p. 10).

The advocacy of such measures revealed the making for institutional identity. Managers working within a public organization were openly advocating economic efficiency in line with the institutional management norms of the private sector. This should have raised questions regarding the very existence of the Hillary Commission. Influenced by the neo-liberal paradigm, an organization designed to encourage leisure activity, motivated by legitimating elements, looked to the market for reasons for nonparticipation rather than for the cause of low participation. Such efforts would have been applauded by the Business Roundtable which in 1995 advocated blanket user charges on library services on the basis that only a small section of the community utilized these facilities (Zohrab et al. 1995). The Hillary Commission's attitude was indicative of how deeply entrenched the rationalist paradigm had become within the service provision arm of local government in a very short time. In 1994, the acceptance of such neo-liberal practices appeared to be strong.

It is unlikely that the Hillary Commission would have acted in this way if it were not for the passing of the Public Finance Act (1989), which had a major impact on the development of business operations in government. Through the introduction of the Act, the government sought to ensure that government departments, and other Crown agencies, adopted a financial emphasis in their reporting. This is made clear in Section 34(A) of the Act. In so doing, the government attempted to hold government departments to the same "generally accepted accounting practices" (Public Finance Act, (1989)) as private business operations. The government's action could be interpreted as looking beyond a financial return; it was also interested in ensuring that the organizational structures and management procedures of public companies and departments were a mirror of their counterparts in private industry. For example, by 1994 the requirement for government-owned operations, be they local or central government concerns, to be run as successful businesses, introduced in the State Owned Enterprise Act 1986, had also been incorporated into the Local Government Act 1974, the Port Companies Act 1988, the Energy Companies Act 1993, the Housing Restructuring Act 1992, Southland Electricity Act 1993, and the Crown Research Act 1992 (Petrey 1994). Such an attitude failed to recognize that government business operations were, and in some cases still are, the sole provider of social services or, indeed, of essential goods and services such as water reticulation. Historically, it had never been envisaged that in New Zealand such entities would need to make profits.

Impact of Political Reforms on the Practice of Management in New Zealand

The fourth Labor Government, elected in 1984, made a philosophical change to the management and the provision of government services. This philosophical change was implemented when Labor was re-elected in 1987 and was also adopted and further extended by the National government of Prime Minister Bolger and Finance Minister Richardson, elected in 1990. Presented below are examples of Government actions, which resulted in change to the practice of management throughout the entire country. First is the corporatization of government business units into standalone State Owned Enterprises (SOEs) and their subsequent conversion to limited liability companies, which could be sold as trade sales or listed on the New Zealand Stock Exchange (NZX). The remainder of this section provides three examples of how this change in government philosophy played out, with the sale of Air NZ, the sale of the telephone section of the NZ Post Office, and lastly the supply of water in the Auckland region by local councils. We demonstrate that although privatization/corporatization provided funds for the State it was also about it was more about government philosophy.

In the nineteenth century, evidence of a countries success was the provision of an efficient rail service, while in the twentieth century it was a national airline. In the New Zealand, the flag bearer was Air New Zealand (Air NZ). Air NZ developed in 1965 out of Tasman Empire Airways Ltd. (TEAL) a trans-Tasman flying boat service and in 1978 New Zealand's domestic carrier was merged into Air NZ. One-year later tragedy struck Air NZ and the entire country when one of its DC1 0 s on a sightseeing flight over Antarctica crashed on Mt. Erebus with the loss of 257 lives. In April 1989, while still a government owned airline, Air NZ was sold for $660 million to Brierley Investment, Qantas, Japan Airlines, and American Airlines. The first public sale of Air New Zealand (AIR) was an offering of 30% (5% reserved for airline staff and 25% for the NZ public) of the shares in October 1989 at a price of $2.40 (Reuters News Official 1989).

In 1996 Air New Zealand purchased Ansett Australia, for A$475 million, and moved to full ownership of Ansett in February 2000, when they purchased the remainder from News Corporation Ltd. for A$580 million. Ansett was solely a domestic carrier and the board of Air NZ saw opportunities to enhance Air NZ's trans-Tasman service by linking into the Australian domestic network. As well as these synergies, they also expected to be able to increase profitability at Ansett by applying some of their experience in running a profitable Air NZ. This did not happen and in September 2001 Ansett into administration on behalf of its creditors. In NZ, the media lay blame for the collapse at the feet of the Australian unions who were considerably more powerful and militant than NZ unions. In Australia, the consequence of bad management by Air NZ, Leiper (2002) in his analysis of the Ansett collapse, identifies the original decision of the Board of Air NZ to purchase Ansett as being flawed and compounded by paying too much for what was in reality a struggling domestic airline. A decision repeated in 2000 when they again paid too much to achieve complete ownership, a classic case of hubris by an overconfident board. Regardless of the causes of the Ansett collapse, Air NZ was in breach of its existing borrowing covenants and required a substantial capital injection by the New Zealand Government if it was not suffer the same fate as its subsidiary Ansett.

The privatization of the Bank of New Zealand (BNZ) is interesting because its history is markedly different from other assets privatized in New Zealand. In 1861 the BNZ was established, and although it is banker for the government.

It was privately owned by three well-respected New Zealanders, politicians Thomas Henderson and Thomas Russell as well as the "Father of Auckland" John Logan Campbell. The driver for the BNZ was to compete against the foreign owned Union Bank and Bank of New South Wales. The BNZ's early history was as turbulent as the countries were with the NZ wars and the boom and bust cycles of gold mining and property speculation. The BNZ made a number of bad loans in the 1880s requiring them to sell down their London investments and build up cash reserves while transferring £125,000 from reserves to a debt suspension account in anticipation of loan write-downs (Colgate et al. 1990). Despite assurances by directors in June 1894 all was well, they were forced to inform the Colonial Treasure the bank would be forced to close if it did not receive state support (Colgate et al. 1990). The Bank of New Zealand Act 1895 allowed the BNZ to write off £900,000 of capital and £450,000 of the proceeds of the previous call. The Government then subscribed for £500,000 of six year 3.5% preference shares, while shareholders were required to subscribe anther £3/6/8 per share, bearing 5% interest. The government then became a BNZ shareholder in 1904 before a Labor Government nationalized the bank in 1945 (Wilson 2010).

The fourth Labor Government in 1987 allowed the bank to recapitalize itself by way of an issue of 15% equity capital and in 1988 the government announced it would sell all its shares. However, this was delayed when a conflict of interest was revealed, with preferred bidder Brierley Investments, as Ron Brierley was on the BNZ board at the time (Wilson 2010). In 1989 a further rights issue was made and the Government not wanting to invest further funds in the BNZ gave their rights to Capital Markets Ltd., after which the resulting share structure was the Government 51.6%, Capital Markets 30.5%, and the public 19.9% (Singleton et al. 2006). Despite everyone believing capital the bank was adequately capitalized the incoming, National Government was required to deal with problems from the bank's aggressive lending in Australia. After the government provided $620 million and Capital markets provided $100 million, the government sold its remaining shares in the BNZ to National Australia Bank (Wilson 2010).

A clear indication the neoliberal business model did not always pay dividends is given by the privatizations of Air NZ and the BNZ. Both State Owned Enterprises faced immanent collapse after the Government allowed them free reign. Both required substantial additional funding after being cut lose from Government control. It is not possible to say if under Government control, they would have required this additional funding, but clearly both pursued high-risk business strategies after privatization. The privatization push for efficiency and introduction of managerialism was not limited to central government operations. It was also seen most markedly in local government with privatization program extended to local body business units, such electricity lines companies, ports, and airports, enabled by amendments to the Local Government Act (1974), which established Local Authority Trading Enterprises (LATE), now known as a Council Controlled Organisations. A LATE, like an SOE, was required to make a profit and follow recognized business practice. In addition the amendments, mentioned below, organized the employment relationship for local government employees. This followed the separation of operations and policy which was in vogue in central government at the time.

Through the Local Government Amendment Act (1989, No 1) and the Local Government Amendment Act (1989, No2), local government business operations such as water, power, waste collection were encouraged to be set up along the same lines as a State Owned Enterprise. In essence these reforms separated the "rowing from steering, and established new administrative structures. Like the SOE they were reorganized" so that the general manager of the individual units became a CEO and in turn the CEO was the employer for the council workers who were employed within the LATE. These organizations (LATE) were required under the legislation to make a profit. Richard Prebble ex Labour Minister of Transport, writing about reforming the local government businesses retells a story "... I've already put in place some reforms from when I was Minister of Transport that is going to force the ARA [Auckland Regional Authority] to be more efficient" (Prebble 1996, p. 46). A legacy of the 1984–1990 reforms is the Land Transport Amendment Act 2013, which makes it clear that local authorities can only provide public transport under contract. Simply put, they must use private sector operators to provide public transport.

An example of the way these organizations changed their management practice can be seen in the story of Water Care. This bulk and waste-water operator owned by the Auckland Regional Council and supplier of water to Metrowater, the water reticulation organization for Auckland City and wholly owned by Auckland City. Water Care embodies both the institutional language and attitude of a private company. Managerialist phraseology is peppered throughout its 2002 Asset Management Plan – expressions that may show identification with the wider institution of the management profession but mean little to customers. Water Care assures the people of Auckland that it will "ensure negotiated customer service levels are achieved at minimum prices following rigorous risk assessment processes which meet best industry practice" (Water Care Staff 2002). The company's "customers" are Auckland citizens who have no alternative supplier. The use of the term shows how Water Care's managers see the ratepayers – not as owners in a collective sense, but as individual purchasers of a product.

This attitude is in contrast to the stance of the Auckland Regional Authority (ARA), which performed Water Care's duties prior to the establishment of the Water Care, as reflected in its (ARA) annual reports. In the annual report for 1982, for example, the chairman noted "that Auckland simply could not work adequately as a metropolitan area ... without the basic services the Authority provides" (Auckland Regional Authority Staff 1982). On the question of bulk water delivery, the annual report for 1982 notes only that bulk water is delivered to local authorities connected to the ARA dams. There is no mention of customers or consumers. It is not until 1987 that the annual reports specifically mention "consumers" in regard to water, and even then it is only the recipient councils that are termed as such. However, by 1991 the Auckland Regional Authority was referring to both the councils it supplied, and the citizens using the water, as "customers." In addition, in 1991 the ARA first used the term "market," registering its intent to conduct "market surveys" of its newly perceived customers (Auckland Regional Authority Staff 1990–1991, pp. 67–68). Finally, in 2002, in a flourish of managerialist language, Water Care concludes its 2002 Asset Management Plan with the intent of producing "A triple bottom line Annual Sustainable Development report as defined by the Global Reporting Initiative." (p. 55). Since this document is found on Water Care's web site, it seems to have been intended for external, as well as internal, consumption. That Water Care management believed such a sentence was meaningful to the citizens of Auckland demonstrates the distance between the two groups. More revealingly, the use of accepted business language shows it to be an open appeal for legitimization from the external management profession.

In presenting the above three examples of privatization, we have illustrated how the reforms initiated in 1984 changed not only the employment relationship of public servants but also the way government managers related to their jobs. The above illustrations also demonstrate how the use of "management" language and acceptance of private sector management technique became seen as the only way to conduct "business." The neoliberal paradigm embraced by the reforms and subsequent governments has led to establishment of a New Zealand paradigm of management based on rationality and efficiency.

Conclusion

The Treasury authors of Government Management (1987) suggested that not only are markets efficient and ensure maximization (p. 15), but that they also provide a check on wastage (p. 38). Such views – that appear to be widely accepted within the New Zealand business community – are again indicative of how deeply entrenched in the New Zealand economic psyche is the notion that private sector models of business can be applied to public organizations without modification.

The move towards the market-type mechanism for government operations was seen as a way to encourage innovation and entrepreneurship by holding managers and government controllers accountable for outputs (Treasury, 1987; Public Finance Act, 1989; State-owned Enterprises Act 1986). The manager in turn is prompted by career imperatives – job security – to either adopt or adapt to the new regime, thus ensuring that the manager will see that following the neo-liberal pathway is in his or her best interests. It was argued that, in order to achieve the desired change in direction, new management personnel were needed (Prebble 1996, pp. 75–78) managers who could lead by example, who could operate within the rationalist mold and help form a new culture to replace the "staid" business organizations of both local and central government. In response, there was increased recruitment of private sector management into the upper echelons of both central and local government organizations (Boston et al. 1996).

The introduction of private sector managers did not see an increase in business innovation within either central or local government business operations. For example, Gregory (1999) quotes a 1997 report which explained the lack of internal innovation within government departments as a reaction to the need for managers to fulfill output obligations. By embracing economic accountability as a management tool, the manager is in danger of becoming focused on the current objective and is less inclined to consider the long-term holistic implications of his or her actions lest they interfere with meeting the agreed output. It would appear that the reforms themselves, rather than the activities of the management within them, were seen as the prime example of innovation. Considine and Lewis (1999) have suggested that the application of management theory within the entities created by the reforms has placed too much emphasis on accountability and monitoring of outputs. This has resulted in a lack of entrepreneurial innovation and, in practice, reproducing traditional features of private-sector management which, in the long term, may not be the best or beneficial form of management. Nevertheless in New Zealand, thanks in no small part to the Labor government of 1984–1990 it is the form of management that became entrenched within both the public and private sector.

Cross-References

Governmentality and the Chinese Workers in China's Contemporary Thought Management System
In Search of the Traces of the History of Management in Latin America, 1870–2020
Indian Management (?): A Modernization Experiment
Introduction: Management Heterogeneity in Asia
Management History in the Modern World: An Overview
Management in Australia – The Case of Australia's Wealthiest Valley: The Hunter
The Making of a Docile Working Class in Pre-reform China
The Perfect Natural Experiment: Asia and the Convergence Debate
What Is Management?

References

Anderson AJ (1990) Tuhawaiki, Hone. Retrieved 27 Aug 2018. https://teara.govt.nz/en/biographies/1t110/tuhawaiki-hone
Auckland Regional Authority Staff (1982) Annual report Auckland Regional Authority. Auckland Regional Authority, Auckland, New Zealand
Auckland Regional Authority Staff (1990–1991) Auckland Regional Authority annual report. Auckland Regional Authority, Auckland
Boston J, Eichbaum C (2014) New Zealand's neoliberal reforms: half a revolution. Gov: An Int J Policy, Adm Inst 27(3):373–376

Boston J, Martin J, Pallot J, Walsh P (1996) Public management: the NZ model. Oxford University Press, Oxford

Burns P (1989) Fatal success: a history of the New Zealand company. Heinemann Reed, Auckland

Colgate P, Sheppard DK, Guerin K, Hawke GR (1990) A history of the Bank of New Zealand, 1862–1982. Part I, 1862–1934. Victoria University of Wellington. Money and Finance Group, Wellington

Considine M, Lewis JM (1999) Governance at ground level: the frontline bureaucrat in the age of markets and networks. Public Adm Rev 59(6):467–480. https://doi.org/10.2307/3110295

Considine M, Painter M (1997) Managerialism. Carlton South, Melbourne

Eichbaum C (ed) (2006) The third way. Oxford University Press, Melbourne

Enteman W (1993) Managerialism; the emergence of a new ideology. In. The University of Wisconsin Press, Madison

Fergusson G (1994) Building the New Zealand dream, Dunmore press Palmerston North. Dunmore Press, Palmerston North

Gibson C (1973) Urbanization in New Zealand: a comparative analysis. Demography 10(1):71–84. https://doi.org/10.2307/2060751

Gregory R (1999) Social and administrative reform; maintaining ethical probity in public services. Public Adm Rev 59(1):63–75

Haugh HM, Pardy W (1999) Community entrepreneurship in north east Scotland. Int J Entrep Behav Res 5(4):163–172. https://doi.org/10.1108/13552559910293119

Hillary Commission for Sport, F. a. L. S (1994) User pays and the pricing of leisure services: discussion paper for local government. Wellington, Hillary Commission

Kelsey J (1993) Rolling back the state. Bridget Williams Books, Wellington

Kelsey J (1994) Aotearoa. A state in crisis. In: Sharp A (ed) A leap into the dark. Auckland University Press, Auckland

Kelsey J (1997) The New Zealand experiment: a world model for structural adjustment. In. Auckland University Press, Auckland

Kelsey J (1999) Reclaiming the future. Bridget Williams Books, Wellington

King M (2003) The Penguin history of New Zealand. Penguin Books, Auckland

La Croix SJ (1992) Property rights and institutional change during Australia's gold rush. Explor Econ Hist

Leiper N (2002) Why Ansett Airlines failed and how to prevent it happening again. Curr Issue Tour 5(2):134–148. https://doi.org/10.1080/13683500208667912

Litvin D (ed) (2002) The business case for diversity and the iron cage. Routledge, London

Mawson P (2002) Measuring economic growth in New Zealand. The Treasury, Wellington

Ministry for Culture and Heritage (2014, 20 June) End of the New Zealand Wars. Retrieved 26 Sept 2014 from http://www.nzhistory.net.nz/war/new-zealand-wars/end

New Zealand Treasury Staff (1987) Government Management: brief to the incoming Government. Government Print, Wellington

NZ Government Staff (1893 to 2010) The New Zealand official year-book. Retrieved Sept 2014 from http://www3.stats.govt.nz/New_Zealand_Official_Yearbooks/1893/NZOYB_1893.html

OECD Staff (1993) Managing with Market type Mechanisms. Organisation for Economic Co-operation and Development, Paris

Osborne D, Gaebler T (1993) Reinventing Government: how the entrepreneurial spirit is transforming the public sector. Plume, New York

Pember-Reeves W (1903) State experiments in Australia and New Zealand, vol 1. E.P. Dutton & Co, New York

Peters M (2001) Environmental education; Neo-liberalism and globalism: the New Zealand experiment. Educ Philos Theory 33(2):203–217

Petrey A (1994) The public sector in the year 2000, Building on reforms. Wellington, New Zealand Institute of Public Administration

Pfeffer J (1982) Organisations and organisational behaviour. Pitman, Boston

Pinchot G (1985) Intrapreneuring: why you don't have to leave the corporation to become an entrepreneur. Harper Row, New York

Pollitt C (2000) Is the emperor in his underwear? Public Manag: Int J Res Theory 2(2):181–200. https://doi.org/10.1080/14719030000000009

Pollitt C (2001) Clarifying convergence; striking similarities and durable differences in public management reform. Public Manag Rev 3(4):471–491

Prebble R (1996) I've been thinking. Seaview, Auckland

Prokopenko J, Pavlin I (1991) Entrepreneurship development in public enterprises. International Labour Office, Geneva

Reuters News Official (1989, 8 September) Air NZ Shares Floated at $2.40

Rogers F (1990) Dacre, Ranulph. Retrieved 27 Aug 2018. https://teara.govt.nz/en/biographies/1d1/dacre-ranulph

Schick A (1996) The spirit of reform. State Services Commission, Wellington

Schneider M, Teske P (1992) Toward a theory of the political entrepreneur. Evidence from local government. Am Polit Sci Rev 86(3):737–748

Schrader B (2005) We call it home: a history of state housing in New Zealand. Reed, Auckland

Selznick P (1947/1966) TVA and the grass roots. Harper Torchbooks, New York

Sharp A (ed) (1994) The changing role of the state in NZ since 1984. Auckland University Press, Auckland

Sinclair K (1991) A history of New Zealand. Penguin, Auckland

Singleton J, Grimes A, Hawke G, Holmes F (2006) Innovation and independence: the Reserve Bank of New Zealand 1973–2002. Auckland University Press in association with the Ministry for Culture and Heritage, Wellington

State Services Commission (2002) Current problems in public sector management. State Services Commission, Wellington

Statistics New Zealand (2015) History of the census in New Zealand. Retrieved from http://www.stats.govt.nz/Census/about-2006-census/introduction-to-the-census/history-of-the-census-in-nz.aspx

Temple P (2002) A sort of conscience: the Wakefields. Auckland University Press, Auckland

Umbeck J (1977) The California gold rush: A study of emerging property rights. Explorations in economic history. Academic Press Inc, 14:197–226

Water Care Staff (2002) Water care asset management plan. WaterCare, Auckland

Weber M (ed) (1947) Theory of social and economic organisation. Free Press, New York

Wilson J (2010) Short history of post-privatisation in New Zealand. Retrieved 12 Sept 2012 from http://www.comu.govt.nz/resources/pdfs/mixed-ownership-model/mom-shppnz-wilson-dec10.pdf

Wilson J, Doig A (2000) Local government management; a model for the future? Public Manag 2(1):57–84

Zohrab J, Dyer P, Dwyer G (1995) Local government in New Zealand: an overview of economic and financial issues. New Zealand Business Roundtable, Wellington

Management in Australia – The Case of Australia's Wealthiest Valley: The Hunter

63

Bradley Bowden

Contents

Introduction	1432
A Transplanted Society: The Hunter in the Nineteenth Century	1438
The Hunter in the Twentieth Century: The Rise and Fall of Heavy Manufacturing	1445
Wealth and Poverty: The Hunter in the Twenty-First Century	1454
Conclusion	1457
Cross-References	1460
References	1460

Abstract

The Hunter Valley, a 287-mile long dale to the north of Sydney, encapsulates the peculiarities and problems of Australian management. In an overwhelmingly urban society, the prosperity of the Hunter – as is the case with the wider society – rests on a resource-based economy. In a society characterized by a strongly democratic and egalitarian ethos, the region's prosperity has been built on a small number of wealthy families and firms. In a society increasingly concerned with the problems of climate change, the wealth of the Hunter still rests on the exploitation of fossil fuels, resources used for both export and the energy-intensive smelting of aluminum. In microcosm, therefore, the Hunter provides insight into both the history of management in Australia and its profound contemporary problems. The paradoxes of the Hunter also speak to the very purpose of modern management. Is the purpose of management still primarily associated with wealth creation and the efficient allocation of resources? Or is it the case that environmental concerns should be given pride of place? If the latter is accepted, does this necessarily entail the destruction of the resource-based industries upon which not only the prosperity of the Hunter but of Australia more generally has been premised?

B. Bowden (✉)
Griffith Business School, Griffith University, Nathan, QLD, Australia
e-mail: b.bowden@griffith.edu.au

© The Author(s), under exclusive licence to Springer Nature Switzerland AG 2020
B. Bowden et al. (eds.), *The Palgrave Handbook of Management History*,
https://doi.org/10.1007/978-3-319-62114-2_86

Keywords

Australia · Hunter Valley · Newcastle · Climate change · Coal mining · Horse-breeding · Pastoralism · Trade unions

Introduction

Australia has always been a land of paradoxes. Boasting a land area almost exactly the same as that of the continental United States, its population (25.55 million) in January 2019 was only a third larger than that of the Netherlands. One of the world's most urbanized societies, with more than two-thirds of the population living in the nation's mainland capitals (Melbourne, Sydney, Brisbane, Adelaide, Perth), the society's extraordinary wealth has always rested on the highly productive export-driven industries in the interior. In the nineteenth century, and in the first half of the twentieth century, the export of wool was the key to prosperity, it being often said that "Australia was a nation that road on the sheep's back." In 1886–1890, for example, Australia's pastoral sector was responsible for 12.8% of national Gross Domestic Product (GDP). By comparison, the manufacturing and agricultural sectors provided only 11.8% and 5.8% of GDP, respectively (Butlin 1964/1972: 22). In the twenty-first century, it is mineral exports that underpin Australian prosperity. In 2018, of the top ten exports by value – which in order were coal (AUD$66.9 billion), iron (AUD$63.6 billion), natural gas (AUD$43.3 billion), education (AUD$35.2 billion), tourism (AUD$22.2 billion), gold (AUD$19.2 billion), aluminum and alumina (AUD$11.3 billion), beef (AUD$8.7 billion), oil ($8.1 billion), and copper (AUD$6 billion) – six were minerals (Department of Foreign Affairs and Trade 2019). A seventh, aluminum and alumina, was a de facto mineral, involving as it does the processing of bauxite with the benefit of Australia's (once) cheap electricity, the product of the nation's plentiful coal supplies.

If Australia's wealth has always rested on resource-based industries in the interior, one does not necessarily have to travel that far from the coast to find evidence of this highly productive economy. In Queensland, my native state, the coalfields of the Bowen Basin – which supply the bulk of the world's seaborne trade in metallurgical or coking coal – are found within a three to four hour drive of the coast. In the Hunter Valley, some 110 miles (180 km) to the north of the great metropolis of Sydney, Australia's principal source of thermal coal is located only 43 miles (70 km) upstream from the port city of Newcastle. From the vast open-cut pits and underground mines of the central and lower Hunter – discretely hidden from passing motorist view by raised embankments – the large mining companies who dominate production enjoy a huge transport advantage over international competitors, given the short flat rail journey to Newcastle. Accordingly, in 2018 Newcastle was the world's busiest and most prosperous coal port, exporting 158.6 million tons of coal worth $23.6 billion to the coal-fired power-stations of East Asia (Kirkwood 2019). For generations of Hunter Valley residents, the bountiful wealth of the region's coalfields manifested itself not only in mining jobs but also in a large heavy-manufacturing sector. Opened in 1915, BHP's Newcastle steelworks provided 5,739 direct jobs by 1921 (Mauldon 1927: 87). Although employment in the steelworks was in decline by the 1970s, this decline was offset by new industries associated with coal-fired power generation. Between 1963 and 1993 the state-owned Electricity Commission built six coal-fired power-stations: Vales Point A, Vales Point B, Munmorah, Bayswater, Liddell, Eraring (Longworth 1968: 2). By 2001, the Hunter's power stations provided 80% of the electricity needed by New South Wales (NSW), Australia's most populous state. In the footsteps of the power-stations followed new aluminum smelters at Kurri Kurri (lower Hunter) and Tomago (Newcastle) that were soon responsible for 40% of Australia's aluminum production (Bowden 2006a: 50).

As with the Australian interior more generally, the resource-based riches of the Hunter Valley have also long been associated with the pastoral sector and agriculture. In the early-to-mid-nineteenth century the fact that the Hunter Valley was navigable upstream to Morpeth, adjacent to regional centers of Maitland and East Maitland, made the well-watered pastures and fields of the lower Hunter the principal source of farm produce for Sydney's growing population, a steam-powered ship able to make the journey from Morpeth to Sydney in 12 h. As a local history of Maitland records, this "cost-advantage made the demand for Hunter Valley produce so strong that it practically eliminated any competition" (Maitland City Council 1983: 16). By the 1860s, the lower Hunter also boasted a wine industry, an area of endeavor for which the region is now famed. Indeed, if one goes to the Tourism Australia (2019) website for the Hunter region, one would scarcely understand that the Hunter was responsible for any other activity other than wine production, the subtitle for the Hunter webpage being: *Give your tastebuds a serious thrill in Australia's oldest wine growing region*. Although most of the wine grown in the Hunter today comes from irrigated fields in the upper Hunter, where product is destined for cheap bulk wine, the old-established vines of the lower Hunter abutting the Wollemi forest are in a different class. Along a ridge of limestone and clay not dissimilar to Burgundy's famed Cote d'Or, iconic family businesses such as Tyrrell's and Mount Pleasant produce sublime Shiraz and Semillon. Whereas agriculture, wine-growing, and dairying dominated in the lower Hunter – fields often abutting the district's coal mines – in the Hunter's middle and upper reaches pastoralism has long prevailed, a correspondent for the *Pastoral Review* recording in 1899 that nowhere had he seen "such country, such good water, such all-round stock, such management and such method" (cited Eldred-Grigg 1978: 9). Prime sheep-raising country in the nineteenth and early twentieth centuries, the upper Hunter is today home to many of the world's leading horse-breeding estates, businesses often owned by Gulf sheikhs and princelings. In summing up the global status of the upper Hunter, the website of the Hunter Thoroughbred Breeders Association (2019a) declares:

> The Upper Hunter country is home to more than 200 thoroughbred stud businesses and the centre of Australia's multi-billion dollar thoroughbred breeding industry ... The origins of the Hunter Valley's stud industry date back more than 200 years, and it is the second largest concentration of thoroughbred studs in the world – alongside Kentucky in the USA.

Without doubt the richest and most historically significant valley in the Australian experience, the Hunter's capacity to provide insight into wider national problems of managerial endeavor and economic development has long been appreciated. Writing in 1927, the Australian economic historian F. R. E. Mauldon (1927: 158) reflected that although the "Valley of the Hunter is but a small portion of the whole national field ... it can be claimed to represent almost a microcosm of national industry." In large part, the Hunter's peculiar research value is found in three interrelated factors: its comparatively small and well-defined dimensions, the diversity of activities that have occurred within its geographical borders, and the tensions and deep social divisions that have resulted from the exploitation of the region's natural bounty.

Running in a northwest direction, the 287 mile (462 km) long valley of the Hunter is easily escaped at its northwest extremity, where the low peaks of the Liverpool Ranges give way to the deep volcanic soils of the Liverpool Plains and the high pastureland of the New England Tableland. By comparison, passage to Sydney and the south is restricted by the sandstone fastness of the Wollemi forest and the expanses of Lake Macquarie, an outcome that forced road and rail routes to follow either the sand isthmus that lay between the lake and the Pacific Ocean or the sandy western shores of Lake Macquarie. To the north a similar situation prevailed, the forested ridges of the Barrington Tops forcing road and rail traffic along a narrow coastal corridor. Within the Valley itself, three distinct geographical and economic zones (Newcastle, lower Hunter, and upper Hunter) can be discerned. Around the mouth of the Hunter, the land was, in the words of an early clerical visitor, the Rev. John Dunmore Lang (1852: 190–191), "sterile and uninteresting," a place of "sandhills and swamps" that ruled out agriculture. In this region, in what became Newcastle, surface outcroppings of coal made it apparent that wealth was, as Lang (1852: 191) advised, best "obtained from underground." Initially, this swampy coastal area was bypassed by would-be settlers, intent on disembarking at Morpeth, 21 miles (34 km) upstream, a town that acted as gateway to the lush lands of the lower Hunter and its adjacent tributaries, the Williams and the Patterson. Dominated by large estates and their tenant farmers, by the 1850s the lower Hunter was responsible for one-third of NSW's agricultural produce (Hirst 1988: 89). Almost purely rural in orientation in 1900, the lower Hunter was transformed by the discovery of the immeasurable riches of the Greta coal seams. Far thicker and deeper than those exploited at Newcastle, the mining of the Greta seams caused Cessnock – located on the doorstep of the Hunter's historic vineyards – to supplant Newcastle as Australia's leading coalmining locality. Boasting only 150 people in 1903, by 1933 Cessnock was NSW's third largest city. Totally given over to the pursuit of coal, Cessnock was, as a student of the town's sociology observed in 1945, "an isolated, parochial community ... It lives apart from the rest of Australia, thinking little of problems beyond mining" (Walker 1945: 133). As one moved further up the Hunter towards Singleton, Muswellbrook, and, above all, Scone, one transitioned to land that was – and still is – pastoral country *par excellence*. With half the rainfall of the lower Hunter, and ideally suited for the raising of sheep and horses, the upper Hunter has long been the domain of Australia's landed gentry, sheep-lords boasting vast estates.

In 1885, 88 members of this social elite, representing 1.4% of Hunter Valley's landholders, owned 54% of the useable land, 73% of the regional sheep flock, and 35% of the Hunter's cattle herd (Eldred-Grigg 1978: 38). In describing the nineteenth-century existence of one of the great pastoral families of the upper Hunter, the Dangar's, Manning Clark (1973a: 249) describes how they "spent the summer on the estate, and went down to Sydney in the autumn to sell the wool clip, and enjoy race week, the agricultural show, the ball for the Queen's birthday, and dinners at Government House." By the late 1960s, however, to the chagrin of the sheep-lords and horse-breeders, historic estates found themselves living cheek-by-jowl with enormous open-cut coal pits as miners chased seams up the Valley in the direction of Singleton and Muswellbrook.

In pursuing entrepreneurial and managerial success in the Hunter (as elsewhere in Australia), there has always been one golden rule: arrive with an existing fortune, wealth that is fortified by well-established political connections. If one is unable to follow this golden rule then one must pursue with all vigor a subsidiary rule: to acquire a fortune as quickly as one can, transitioning from the ranks of small business to large enterprise before one is ruined by a well-established and well-connected competitor.

Proof of the golden rule was evident from the dawn of European settlement in the Hunter. In 1822 the military governor of NSW instructed the government's Assistant Surveyor, Henry Dangar, to divide pastoral land into 1 square mile "selections," which were then allocated to men of financial substance, many of whom were military officers or government officials. Under the terms of the land grants, pastoralists were offered a 100 acres of land for each convict they offered to support, a solution that gave them not only land but also an unpaid labor force. In 1825, during the first year of the scheme's operation, some 20 well-connected individuals secured vast estates along the upper reaches of the Hunter (Wood 1972: 20–21, 49). Among the beneficiaries of this government largess was the Assistant Surveyor himself, who by 1842 had six vast estates in the Hunter and its environs. Dangar's brothers also obtained substantial properties, including the main hotels in both Muswellbrook and Scone. The Dangar brothers also controlled a string a stores along the Valley as well as a distillery that enabled them to sell alcohol to their workers and others at inflated prices (Clark 1973a: 249–250). In 1848, the Dangar brothers also opened the Newcastle Meat Preserving works in Newcastle, a business that enabled them to export their excess stock in tinned form. Once again political connections proved important as the British Admiralty stepped in to buy their stock (Turner 1980: 34). Even more obvious proof of the golden rule is found in the experiences of the Australian Agricultural Company (AA Co.). Granted vast estates to the Hunter Valley's immediate north, the AA Co. included among its founding shareholders 28 members of the British parliament, the Governor of the Bank of England, and a number of directors from the British East India Company. In 1828, the AA Co. was also granted a 500 acre coal lease in Newcastle as well as "such a proportion of the frontage to the [river] water" as the company "may liberally require" (Twiss 1828/1982: 133). The company was also promised a "monopoly ... for the next thirty-one years" (Twiss 1828/1982: 134). Although the AA Co.'s monopoly was ended prematurely in 1847, the company remained the Hunter's largest coal producer throughout the nineteenth century (Turner 1982). In manufacturing, proof of the golden rule is found in the history of BHP's steel-works. An incorporated company that made its initial fortune mining silver and lead at Broken Hill as the Broken Hill Proprietary Co. by the early twentieth century BHP had also acquired a mountain of iron ore at Iron Knob on the South Australian coast. Wishing to turn this latter resource into manufactured product, BHP benefited from an Act of the NSW Parliament in 1912, which provided the company with land grants and a range of concessions and subsidies (Hughes 1964: 63–67). Early profits were guaranteed by the sale of the bulk of its output to Australia's government-owned railways at inflated prices (Mauldon 1927: 91). When BHP's profitability was threatened by international competition the federal government came to the rescue, imposing prohibitive tariffs on steel imports in both the early 1920s and early 1930s. In a similar fashion, the establishment in the 1970s of a large-scale aluminum smelting industry, as a local journalist remarked, "just did not happen" (Haslam 1976: 8). Rather it followed the time-honored Valley tradition, in which various self-interested parties – led by the Miners Federation, intent on finding more customers for the region's coal-fired power stations – sought and obtained a range of government grants and subsidies, (Haslam 1976). Under the interventionist policies of the Wran Labor government in NSW (1976–1986), the historic mining and manufacturing sectors of the Hunter Valley received a particular boost. Splurging money on new coal loaders, railroad infrastructure, and subsidies for the aluminum industry, Wran spoke of transforming the Hunter into an Australian version of Germany's Ruhr Valley (Steketee and Cockburn 1986: 202).

If an overlap of economic and political power underpinned the operation of the golden rule in the Hunter, it also contributed to a constant undercurrent of social divisions that periodically erupted into open conflict. From the outset, the displacement of the original Aboriginal population involved acts of unspeakable violence that were either ignored or condoned by officialdom. When 11 shepherds were tried for the massacre of 31 Aboriginal men, women, and children on a Dangar estate outside the Hunter, there was an outpouring of public anger, directed not against the perpetrators but the officials who brought them to trial, an anger that intensified when seven of the accused were subsequently hanged (Clark 1973b: 107). By the 1850s, conflict revolved around land reform as – following the granting of self-government to NSW in 1856 – the tenant farmers of the lower Hunter elected "liberal" candidates to parliament so as to "unlock" the land. While the passage of land reform *did* secure freehold ownership for the small farmers of the lower Hunter, it never threatened the local gentry's control of the best land. Of the 530 rural landowners who lived between Maitland and Newcastle in 1885, 429 owned less than 100 acres. By contrast, 21 occupied grand estates that boasted more than 1000 acres (NSW Parliament 1887: 612–613). A more constant, and more violent, pattern of relations characterized the Hunter's coalfields. Living in isolated communities adjacent to the mines at which they worked, the coal miners of the Hunter were among Australia's fiercest advocates of trade unionism. Outsiders unwilling to be bound by community values seldom survived long. Recounting his experiences as a strike-breaker in 1879, a Mr. H. V. Higgs (1880: 778) testified before a parliamentary inquiry that on arrival at the mine-site he and his fellow strike-breakers were met by "hundreds of miners and their wives...Some (young men chiefly) had guns, others pistols." After being advised by the miners that "if we dared to sleep in the cottages they would burn them over our heads, or blow them up," Mr. Higgs wisely opted to seek employment elsewhere. More tragic outcomes ensued in the "Great Lockout" of 1929–1930, when police at Cessnock's Rothbury mine fired into a crowd of miners, killing one, Norman Brown, and wounding 49 others, an event that remains the most violent experience in Australian labor relations history.

Prior to the 1970s the Hunter's pattern of social conflict invariably involved discord *within* the various sectors of the resource-based economy, disputation that saw small landholders at loggerheads with the landed gentry, miners in conflict with mine-owners, and steel-workers at odds with BHP management. Since the 1970s, however, a fundamentally new pattern of conflict has emerged, one that threatens the very survival of the Hunter's historic economy built around coal mining, power generation, and metal smelting, a conflict that sees adherents to the old economy at odds with a new educated, professional class for whom coal mining is an abomination, an existential threat to the environment.

Discord between the "old" and "new" economies was first heralded in the 1981 NSW election, when Dr. Levitch, a local dentist, attracted 8% of the vote running in declared opposition to new aluminum smelters (Bowden 2006a: 61). In the 1995 state election the Green Party candidate for Newcastle attracted 13.5% of the vote, a higher total than that found anywhere else in the state. At the same time the region witnessed a hollowing out of Newcastle's traditional "blue-collar" workforce. Whereas the Commonwealth census of 1971 recorded 20,923 factory workers in the Newcastle City area – a group that represented 34.6% of the workforce – by 2016 the city's 4,017 manufacturing employees made up only 5.5% of the labor force. By comparison, in the Newcastle City area in 2016 those employed in health care and social assistance made up 18.4% of the workforce. Another 10% were employed in education and training. A greater percentage were employed in public administration and defense (7%) than manufacturing (ABS 1971, 2019a). Outside Newcastle, amid the coal mines, coal-fired power-stations and vineyards of the wider Hunter Valley, members of the "old" economy also find themselves in a minority, albeit by significantly smaller margins (ABS 2019b). To believe, however, that the Hunter Valley is now a bastion of a new "knowledge economy" would be a total misnomer. According to the 2016 Australian census, the largest "occupational group" in the Newcastle area were those of working age who were *not* in the workforce: a cohort that comprised 43.5% of the working age population. Of those of working age, 49.5% had not completed high school (ABS 2019a). Support for the Green Party remains a distinctly minority persuasion, the party winning 15.6% of the vote in Newcastle in the May 2019 federal election (Australian Electoral Commission 2019a).

If the economic alternative to the old resource-based economy remains weak, outside Newcastle, in the wider stretches of the Hunter, the highly unionized workforce is nevertheless increasingly concerned that environmental activism threatens their livelihoods. Long a Labor Party stronghold, in the 2019 election almost a quarter of the Hunter electorate voted for the conservative and nationalistic Pauline Hanson's One Nation Party. Significantly, One Nation's candidate, Stuart Bonds, was not only a working miner but also a workplace official for Australia's most militant union: the Construction Forestry Mining & Energy Union (Australian Electoral Commission 2019b). Certainly, hostility to the "old" economy in general, and coal mining in particularly, is now evident on many fronts. Whereas the pastoral sector lived cheek-by-jowl with coal mining for more than a century, the Hunter Valley's landed gentry and horse-breeders now declare their interests to be incompatible with coal mining, the Hunter Thoroughbred Breeders Association (2019b) website advising readers "that open cut coal mining and international scale thoroughbred breeding operations cannot co-exist in close proximity." The future of coal mining in the Valley is now also imperiled by legal challenges to every mine extension. In the most significant development to date, in February 2019 the Chief Judge of the NSW Land and Environment Court, Brian Preston, dismissed an appeal by Gloucester Resources for a new mine to the immediate north of the Hunter Valley. In doing so, Preston (2019a: sections 440, 556, 436) ruled that to allow the new mine would be a breach of the Paris Climate Agreement, and that increased carbon emissions posed a direct threat to Australia in terms of flooding, heat-waves, bushfires, and increased rainfall.

The deep divisions that now characterize the Hunter reflect, in miniature, wider conflicts in not only Australia but the world as a whole as to the fundamental purpose of management. Is the prime purpose of management still that delineated by Dan Wren and Art Bedeian (1972/2017: 3), namely one of wealth creation "through the efficient allocation and utilization of human and material resources"? Or is it the case that environmental and social concerns should be given pride of place? If the latter is accepted, does this necessarily entail the destruction of the resource-based industries upon which not only the prosperity of the Hunter but of Australia more generally has long been premised? If the highly productive, export-driven industries in the Hunter's upper reaches are destroyed, then where is it that governments will find the taxable income to fund employment and services in education, health, and defense?

A Transplanted Society: The Hunter in the Nineteenth Century

In most societies, even in the New World, the state and its agencies emerge from the fundamental needs of civil society. Australia is an exception to this rule. For, as most readers would be aware, the first European settlement in Australia stemmed not from mercantile or agricultural endeavors, but rather from a penal colony, transplanted to Sydney Cove in January 1788. Accordingly, for the next half century and beyond, effective power rested with the British military governor and, more particularly, the officers and associates of the military detachments sent to protect the infant colony. As the so-called Rum Rebellion of 1808 demonstrated, when the military deposed the Governor, William Bligh (of mutiny on the Bounty fame), when he interfered with their illegal sale of alcohol, the interests of the "state" and the military elite overlapped but were never identical. The Governor, as an agent of the Crown, wanted to run the new settlement at minimal cost to the taxpayer. By contrast, the military elite and their associates saw opportunities for great riches, both through control of mercantile trade in and out of the colony, and in running various rural pursuits in the Sydney hinterland. Where the interests of the two overlapped was in the official belief that the cost of the penal colony could be much reduced by "assigning" convicts to private estates, whereby the private provider was granted land and convict labor in accordance with the number of convicts they opted to feed and clothe. What turned the elite's opportunistic pursuit of short-term wealth into the basis for long-term national prosperity was the realization that one particular endeavor – sheep-raising – was more profitable than any other. Significantly, this chance discovery corresponded to a pressing need in the British textile industry, where the production of woolen textiles was constrained by the limited volume of available fleece from Germany and Spain, the traditional sources of imported wool. As we have previously noted in ▶ Chap. 12, "Transformation: The First Global Economy, 1750–1914," and as indicated in Fig. 1, by 1845 Australia and New Zealand had become the principal source of British wool imports. For the next 45 years, the demand of the British mills appeared insatiable, an outcome that made wool the backbone of the Australian economy.

Historically, Australia's pastoral employers and managers have been ill-regarded by the wider society with its democratic and egalitarian ethos, readily dismissed as "bunyip aristocrats" and "squatters," a privileged elite who obtained their land by dubious means. Building a prosperous export business in the Australian interior – even in a comparatively well-watered region as the upper Hunter – was, however, not one for the faint hearted. Exposed to climatic perils (flood, drought, bush-fire, frost) and the vagaries of distant markets, the rewards often appeared disproportionate to the risks. The Australian economic historian, R. V. Jackson (1977: 56) calculates the cost of establishing a medium-sized pastoral property (20,000 sheep) in the 1840s at £7,932. Annual expenses would have amounted to £3,063 with the most expensive items being labor (£1,360), interest at 8% (£633), and freight and commissions (£433). The income from the sale of both wool and meat products would have amounted to £3,250, leaving a paltry profit of £187 – little more than what a skilled city tradesperson in Sydney would have earned.

As Fig. 1 indicates, as early as the 1840s Australasia was already the primary source of wool imports into Britain with the bulk of production subsequently coming from the three eastern Australian colonies – NSW, Victoria, and Queensland. Despite this success, however, the Australian pastoral sector remained in a primitive state prior to the 1860s. Many pastoralists lacked legal title to their land, simply squatting on land with their flocks – a practice that caused pastoralists to be derided, then as now, as "squatters." In managing their flocks, pastoralists also simply transplanted European practices to Australia. Invariably, sheep were overseen by a shepherd, who brought his small flock into the safety of a wooden hurdle at night, sleeping alongside them in a primitive hut. In describing pastoral life in the late 1840s, Roberts (1935: 347) observed that, "Even a prosperous squatter would be content to live in a collection of slab hovels, with hurdles moving from place to place as each

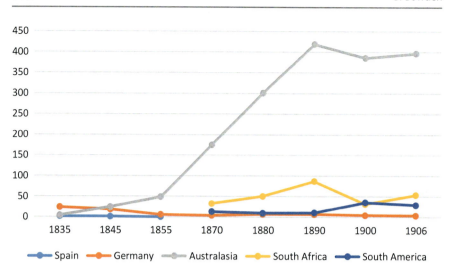

Fig. 1 British Wool Imports, 1835 – 1906 (in millions of lbs). (Sources: Clapham (1932/1967): 6; Ville (2005): Table 3; Knibbs 1909: 293)

became filthy with the inevitable heaps of sheep dung and sheep bones piled everywhere. It was a sordid, filthy existence." This "nomadic" existence, characterized by constant movement to new pasture, even characterized much of the upper Hunter, an area where freehold ownership was commonplace by the 1840s. As Eldred-Grigg (1978: 380) noted in his doctoral thesis on the Hunter's pastoral industry, most members of this well-to-do elite "were rather nomadic" with few owning their properties outright. Instead, estates were operated on large "overdrafts and mortgages," the Hunter's sheep-lords constantly up-sizing and down-sizing their holdings in accordance with the vagaries of their shifting fortunes.

In essence, the successful management of a nineteenth-century pastoral property in the upper Hunter (as elsewhere in Australia) required expertise in 4 distinct areas: finance and a capacity to borrow and service the debt; land and livestock acquisition; property and labor management; marketing and logistics. Significantly, each of these activities solicited a specialized response in form of mortgage brokers, stock and station agents, fencers and shearing contractors, and wool brokers.

In terms of finance, two types of institutions specialized in pastoral investment: commercial banks and mortgage finance houses. In both cases, lenders harnessed British investment funds, providing overdrafts and loans on mortgages of both land and livestock. In the case of pastoral mortgage brokers, funds were obtained from the sale of fixed-term debentures. Commercial banks, in contrast, obtained money from deposits. In both cases, funds were obtained through the use of agents, typically legal firms, who encouraged small-scale investors with assurances of high returns and capital safety. Certainly, the interest rates paid on both debentures and deposits – typically around 8% – were much higher than what could be obtained in Britain, where government consols (bonds) paid less than 3% by the 1880s (Butlin 1964/ 1972: 150–158). By the 1880s, 10 financial institutions (Australian Mortgage Land

& Finance Company, New Zealand Land & Mortgage Agency, South Australian Land Mortgage & Agency Co., Australasian Mortgage and Agency Co., British and Australasian Trust & Agency Co., Queensland Investment Land Mortgage & Agency Co., Australasian Agency & Banking Corporation, Trust and Agency Co., Dalgety & Co., Union Mortgage & Agency Co.) dominated pastoral finance alongside a number of commercial banks: the Bank of NSW, Commercial Banking Company of Sydney, Australian Joint Stock Bank, the Union Bank of Australia, and the Queensland National Bank. Together, these companies accounted for more than 90% of pastoral mortgages by the late 1880s (Butlin 1964/1972: 142). Over time these institutions gradually increased their exposure to the pastoral industry, undertaking a range of services that facilitated the sale and transport of the wool. As Simon Ville (2005) has shown, Australian-based companies went from firms that facilitated sales in the London market to enterprises that organized sales on their own behalf, often by-passing London and selling directly into European markets. By the early decades of the twentieth century, Ville (2005: 85) concludes, wool sales were dominated by the five leading pastoral agencies (Dalgety, New Zealand Loan and Mercantile Agency, Australian Mortgage Land & Finance, Elder Smith, Goldsborough Mort), companies that "were among the largest businesses operating in Australia." Mortgage brokers and other financial institutions also found themselves operating pastoral properties in their own right. Most commonly, this outcome resulted from "squatters" defaulting on their mortgages. The Trust and Agency Co., for example, was operating 10 vast properties in Queensland by 1891, estates that ran 1.2 million sheep. Alongside such reluctant owners, there also existed investment companies that were created for the specific purposes of stock-raising. In 1891, the largest of these was the English-owned Australian Pastoral Company, which ran 750,000 sheep across southern Queensland (Svensen 1989: 14, 24).

If the natural advantages of the upper Hunter – ease of access to permanent water, reliable rainfall, and vicinity to a deep-water port – meant that comparatively few of the Valley's pastoralists suffered the indignity of foreclosure, it was also the case that finance and trade was heavily reliant on another Australian financial institution: the stock and station agent. Typically based in the larger regional towns, the stock and station agent was responsible for a myriad of mercantile activities: the buying and selling of local livestock, the forwarding of wool at the behest of either the pastoralist or a wool broker, the sale of station supplies, general merchant activities. In the Hunter, many of these regional merchants were Jewish, the success of this group finding its most obvious expression in the Maitland-based firm of Cohen & Co. Owned by David Cohen and his cousin, Lewis Levy, Cohen & Co. was by far the most successful mercantile business in the lower Hunter in the late nineteenth century. Regularly returned as members of the NSW parliament between 1874 and 1885, the prestige and wealth of Cohen and Levy rivaled that of any of the Hunter's sheep-lords (Bowden 2006b: 56–57).

Initially, pastoralism in the Hunter as elsewhere in Australia was based on transplanted English ideas and techniques: the use of shepherds and sheep hurdles, a large permanent workforce, and a semi-feudal relationship between master and servant. From the 1860s, however, this situation was transformed as the sheep-lords utilized a revolutionary new invention: barbed wire. Realizing that sheep could be left unattended overnight in the mild Australian climate, the pastoralists' use of barbed wire allowed sheep to be confined within definable limits with few permanent workers. The scale of this pastoral endeavor can be ascertained from the NSW experience, where some 1.625 million miles (2.6 million kilometers) of fencing was built between the 1870s and the 1890s (Glover 2008: 32). Whereas a typical Hunter pastoral property may have employed 100 or more prior to fencing, after the installation of barbed wire the average estate employed only 10 permanent hands (Eldred-Grigg 1978: 288). As employment fell, sheep numbers soared, the national herd growing from 16 million in 1861 to 90 million in 1892 (Butlin 1964/1972: 62).

By dispensing with most of their permanent workforce, the typical sheep-lord inadvertently traded one problem for another. On the one hand, labor costs were dramatically reduced, turning the Australian wool industry into the most efficient in the world. On the other hand, the pastoral industry became reliant on a huge, seasonal labor force of shearers that typically had no bonds of loyalty to their employer. In most cases, pastoral employers outsourced their shearing to "gangers," who then put together a "gang" of shearers who moved from property to property, being paid according to the number of sheep that were shorn. Enjoying considerable bargaining power, by the late 1880s the shearing workforce provided the largest and most militant body of unionized workers in Australia. Created in 1886, the Amalgamated Shearers Union (ASU) claimed 20,000 members by 1890. Another 10,000 belonged to a separate and even more militant union: the Queensland Shearers Union (Merritt 1987: 136).

The ability of this unionized workforce to cripple the pastoral sector was amply demonstrated in the Queensland shearers' strike of 1891 and the national shearers' strike of 1894, disputes that remain arguably the most significant in Australian history. Unlike their counterparts elsewhere in Australia, however, the pastoralists of the upper Hunter largely avoided the labor relations problems experienced by the wider industry. Reason for this is found in the fact that Hunter pastoralists rarely hired from the professional shearing workforce for whom seasonal work was their main source of income. Instead, they recruited from the small "selectors" of the Valley. Typically, these selectors and their families operated small wheat and/or dairy farms, occupying marginal land that was seldom commercially viable. For this rural population, seasonal work on their local sheep-lord's estate often meant the difference between modest prosperity and bankruptcy. Accordingly, when the great strikes occurred the shearers of the Hunter Valley stood aside, proving to be "domestic and even docile" in their behavior (Eldred-Grigg 1978: 290). This is not to say that the small farmers of the upper Hunter had any great love for their wealthier neighbors. In the 1891 general election, they voted in favor of the Labor Party candidate, Thomas Williams, who also served as the full-time Secretary of the local branch of the ASU, rejecting the candidacy of two leading pastoralists in the process (Bowden 2006b: 60). As brave as they were in the secrecy of the ballot booth, however, the Hunter's small-scale farmers were proven cowards when it came to open industrial conflict.

Whereas the operation of the golden rule left the sheep-lords in largely untrammelled control of the upper Hunter, a more complex set of arrangements prevailed in Newcastle, where the growth of coal mining created both wealth and social division. As noted in the introduction to this chapter, from 1828 to 1847 the mining of coal in the Hunter was legally the preserve of the AA Co., a monopoly position that should have guaranteed the company a highly profitable business. The large expected profit, however, failed to materialize, even though AA Co. increased output from 5000 t in 1831 to 41,000 t in 1847 (Turner 1982: 33). Instead, during the first 22 years of operation, the total dividend paid to shareholders was 37%, a lower annual return than could have been obtained by investing in government bonds (Turner 1982: 51). The AA Co.'s fundamental problem – one which was to subsequently blight other Newcastle coal miners – was labor relations. When, for example, the AA Co. imported a large workforce of Welsh miners in the early 1840s, they immediately went on strike, the company's manager, Captain Phillip King, lamenting the fact that the Welsh had "brought with them a spirit of insubordination that will be difficult to subdue" (cited Turner 1982: 41). When the industry was thrown open to competition in 1847, both the economic potential and labor relations perils of the industry were brought into even clearer focus. Benefiting from the demand from both steam-powered shipping and railways, output rose from 41,000 t in 1847 to 3.5 million tons in 1900 (Turner 1982: 33, 100). Between 1861 and 1890, employment grew from 852 to 8,874 (Bowden 2006b: 57). Constantly, however, production and even firm survival was imperiled by industrial disputes waged by the Coal Miners Association of Newcastle and its successor, the Hunter District Miners Protective Association. In 1885, for example, the operations of Newcastle's second largest mining company, the Scottish Australian Mining Company, were crippled by a 6 month long dispute. At other mines, strikes of 1 to 2 months in duration were commonplace (Turner 1982: 104).

One effect of the labor relations difficulties that characterized Newcastle and its environs in the second half of the nineteenth-century was that it allowed space for local entrepreneurs, possessing modest capital, to transition from the ranks of small business to large enterprise in proof of the Hunter Valley's subsidiary rule.

The clearest proof of the Hunter's subsidiary rule is found in the success of the firm of A & J Brown, a partnership established by two brothers, Alexander and James Brown, during the 1850s. The key to the brothers' success was flexibility. At various times they were supporters of regulated employment, at other times they aggressively fought union influence and wage rates. Similarly, in their dealings with other employers the Brown brothers were at various times supporters of a selling cartel – the Vend – and at other times a major factor in the Vend's demise as they undercut the coal prices charged by their competitors. Significantly, James Brown was the first to challenge the AA Co.'s monopoly of coal production in the Hunter, negotiating a contract in 1844 to sell 4,000 t a year to the Hunter River Steamship Navigation Company at its Morpeth port facility. When sued by the AA Co. for a breach of its monopoly rights, Brown turned a nominal legal defeat into an operational victory as – in a bizarre decision – the court ruled that Brown could continue to mine coal even as it reaffirmed the AA Co.'s monopoly (Turner 1982: 46). Even with the benefit of this ruling, however, the expansion of the Brown brothers' endeavors seemed improbable. Unlike AA Co., which mined Newcastle's best seams, in the

1850s the Brown brothers worked inferior deposits at Minmi near Maitland, a mine that could only be accessed "after crossing six miles of undeveloped swamp and bush land" (Turner 1964: 3). To compensate for this disadvantage, the Brown brothers worked their mine at lower cost than AA Co.'s more highly capitalized operation. They also aggressively targeted new markets, most particularly the steamer trade with South America and the other Australian colonies, even establishing selling agents in London (Turner 1982: 65, 110). By 1859 the ingenuity of the brothers was publicly recognized, a rival mine manager observing that, "although labouring under considerable disadvantages at such a distance up the Hunter...the two brothers" had revealed themselves to be "practical men" and fierce "competitors" (cited Turner 1982: 65). From their initial base at Minmi, the two brothers engaged in a risky expansion, buying a better located mine at New Lambton in Newcastle, which by 1867 was producing 131,000 t per year compared to the 69,000 t extracted from the Minmi deposit (Turner 1982: 76). As A & J Brown expanded, the firm's pursuit of overseas markets became increasingly aggressive. By 1890, the Brown brothers were undercutting their Newcastle rivals, destroying the Vend created in 1881. The ruthlessness of the Brown brothers was indicated by their willingness to attack the well-established trade union influence in the Hunter coalfields. In locking out their workforce in December 1894 the Brown brothers not only sacked their unionized workforce, they also evicted miners and their families from their company homes. Despite considerable violence, which including the dynamiting of nonunion homes, the Brown brothers succeeded where others failed, operating their mines on a nonunion basis from April 1895 (Turner 1964: 6). Having reduced their operating costs, A & J Brown proceeded to drive their rivals out of the flourishing trade with South America (Turner 1982: 114). At century's end, A & J Brown was the largest family-owned business in the Hunter, operating four mines and employing 2000 workers (Mauldon 1927: 58).

If the success of A & J Brown proved that, even in the Hunter, entrepreneurs of modest means could establish highly profitable businesses, their need to aggressively target overseas markets pointed to a fundamental business problem: the constraining effects of small local markets. Despite the wealth of the Hunter Valley coal seams, the region's mines were piddling affairs when compared to the highly capitalized mines of Britain, Germany, and the United States. In 1900, the Hunter's entire production (3.5 million tons) amounted to only 1.7% of the tonnage mined in Great Britain (207 million tons). With a population of only 3.8 million people in 1900, Australia as a whole also lacked the consumer markets that were a prerequisite for unaided large-scale manufacturing ventures. Lacking any steel-making facilities prior to 1915, industrial demand for coal remained modest, an outcome that made the Hunter coal industry heavily reliant on sales to the state-owned railways and coastal shipping ventures.

The constraining effects of markets were even more obvious in manufacturing, where Newcastle failed to sustain any large-scale ventures during the nineteenth century, despite the city and its suburbs providing a home to 50,000 residents in the 1890s. In this, once more, the Hunter reflected in miniature the wider Australian experience, an editorial in the *Newcastle Morning Herald* (1889: 4) lamenting how colonial society was "utterly dependent upon other countries for many of the necessities and almost all the luxuries of life." Where factories of any sort of scale were attempted in Newcastle they were characterized by two essential features: they were family-owned and short-lived. Even the Newcastle Meat Preserving factory established by the Dangar brothers in 1848 only lasted for 7 years before closing its doors (Turner 1980: 34). A. W. Scott, a local politician and entrepreneur who established Newcastle's first metal foundry in 1842, was also bankrupt by 1866 (Turner 1980: 29). In the 1880s another family-owned venture, Hudson's Wickham Rolling Stock Works, appeared to be on the verge of long-term success. Employing 200 workers, Hudson's benefited from a large order from the NSW Railways Department. When, however, the railways reduced their order, the viability of the business was fatally compromised (Turner 1980: 53–54). Even the Valley's most successful nineteenth-century manufacturer, William Arnott – who turned Arnott's biscuits into an iconic Australian brand that still dominates the supermarket shelves in the twenty-first century – found the small Hunter Valley market a constraining factor. In 1894, Arnott began closing down his Newcastle operation in favor of one located in western Sydney, closer to its principal market (Turner 1980: 67).

Newcastle's manufacturing difficulties highlighted the fact that the very factor that favored development of the region's resource-based industries – ease of transport along a flat valley to a deep-water port – curtailed factory expansion by making imports readily available. On this front, the establishment of a railway connection to Sydney in 1889 exacerbated rather than alleviated the plight of local manufacturers. For the coal mining population of the lower Hunter, the lack of a significant manufacturing sector was their central political concern by the late 1870s. Believing that political intervention was needed if manufacturing was to succeed, the coal mining electorate of Northumberland returned nothing other "protectionist" candidates belonging to the Working Men's Defence Association between 1880 and 1894, continuing to vote for protectionist politicians even after the formation of the Labor Party in 1891 (Bowden 2006b: 57, 59). At the end of the nineteenth century, however, the Hunter remained what it had been 100 years earlier: a resource-based economy. In recording their impressions of Newcastle in May 1900, a "Visitor" (1900: 3) noted that the city was "practically kept alive by the great coaling industry," adding: "The whole city ...appears to be practically hidden from view by the continuous cloud of smoke ...the density of the smoke renders it impossible to even get a glimpse of several outlying suburbs."

The Hunter in the Twentieth Century: The Rise and Fall of Heavy Manufacturing

In 1900 it appeared that calls for government action to facilitate large-scale manufacturing in the Hunter had fallen on deaf ears. A few years later, however, things looked very different. In two separate terms in office (1903–1904, 1905–1908), the Protectionist Party government of Alfred Deakin, acting with

Labor Party support, introduced some of the most far-reaching political and economic changes in Australian history: the compulsory conciliation and arbitration of industrial disputes, restricted immigration under the terms of the "White Australia" policy, old age pensions, and tariff protection to encourage a substantial manufacturing sector. Generally referred to as the "Deakinite Compromise" or the "Historic Compromise," Deakin's legislation did more than provide material assistance to would-be manufacturers. It also legitimated heavy state intervention in the economy at the expense of market forces.

In the lower Hunter, the effects of protectionist policies, pursued with vigor by both state and federal governments, were clearly evident by 1921, when a third of Newcastle's 33,372 male workforce was employed in manufacturing. The largest number (5,739) was employed at the BHP steel-works. Another 2,200 were employed at five heavy manufacturing firms operating close by: the Walsh Island Docks, Ryland Brothers, Goninan & Co., Commonwealth Steel Products, and the Sulphide Corporation. Of these establishments, only the Sulphide Corporation was in operation at the dawn of the century (Mauldon 1927: 87, 105–106). Newcastle's burgeoning manufacturing sector received another major boost when the British-based firm, John Lysaght, agreed to relocate its operations to Newcastle in return for government protection and a guaranteed de facto monopoly status. A major producer of galvanized iron sheeting – the preferred roofing material for Australian homes, then as now – John Lysaght had exported 85,000 t of galvanized iron to Australia on an annual basis prior to World War I, a tonnage that represented 70% of national consumption (Hughes 1964: 85). In reflecting upon these developments, Mauldon (1927: 93) described it as evidence of the positive effects of "localization," whereby the location of one large producer (i.e., BHP steel) led to the relocation of other firms that serviced its needs and utilized its output. The Commonwealth Steel Works, for example, used BHP's iron ingots to produce steel automobile wheels. Similarly, the government-owned docks and shipyards at Walsh Island used BHP's steel in ship repair and manufacture (Mauldon 1927: 95–97). By the mid-1920s, BHP was also operating its own coal mines – as well as a company shipping fleet – to service the steel-work's needs (Hughes 1964: 99–100).

At many different levels, the development of a heavy manufacturing sector brought with it managerial practices and problems that were new not only to Hunter but Australia as a whole. Historically, employment in the Hunter had revolved around stable workforces, in which families often lived on their employer's estate, be it a mine or a pastoral property. By contrast, labor turnover in the new manufacturing plants was extraordinarily high. At Ryland Brothers, for example, labor turnover stood at 300% in 1920 – a rate similar to that experienced at the Ford Motor Co. in 1913. Seven years later the company was still recruiting up to 3,000 workers a year in order to maintain a workforce of 1,000 employees. At John Lysaght in 1927 the company was forced to recruit 400 men so as to keep 100 workers at their tools (Mauldon 1927: 121). It was not only the boring and monotonous nature of the work which alienated workers. Shift work, and round-the-clock operation, was also detested, Mauldon (1927: 125) recording that the effect of shift-work "on the home life of the district is undeniably bad."

The arrival of large industrial corporations also brought with it new skills, new ways of looking at problems, and new types of managers. On occasion these practices fitted into the existing practices and values of the region without undue difficulty. When John Lysaght's relocated to Newcastle in 1921, for example, it sent over not only many of the firm's managers but also 75 mill workers and 28 galvanizers, along with their families. Transplanted from a highly unionized environment in Bristol, the John Lysaght managers and workers found the Newcastle labor relations environment to be little different to that which they had left behind (Murray and White 1982: 57). By contrast, the employment ethos at the BHP steel-works was totally alien to the collectivist values of the typical Hunter Valley worker. Many of the steelworkers initially employed by BHP – and most of the middle managers and nearly all the senior managers – were recruited directly from the United States. Virtually all of these new arrivals were opposed to unionism on principle. The propensity of BHP managers to build mansions for themselves on a hill overlooking the steel-works also did little to endear them to the workforce, most of whom lived in crude weatherboard cottages at Carrington, adjacent to the mill. At these Carrington properties, home life – like working life – was "dominated by the heat, fumes, and dirt of iron and steel working" (Hughes 1964: 76). Even the Australian or British-born managers of BHP tended to be vehemently antiunion in their attitudes, having engaged in grueling conflicts with their unionized mining workforce at Broken Hill in both 1909 and 1919–1920, the latter dispute lasting from May 1919 to November 1920. To mitigate the influence of unionism, BHP management promoted those workers perceived to be company loyalists to "staff" positions that excluded them from union membership; an outcome that allowed the mill's operation during any strike. The company also experimented in 1921 with a "company union," the short-lived Iron and Steel Workers' Association (Hughes 1964: 95–97).

Despite the antagonism with which it was viewed by much of the workforce, BHP proved a flexible and dynamic producer during the 1920s and 1930s, the company taking over a second steel-works at Port Kembla to the south of Sydney in 1935. With the assistance of a new round of tariff protection and concessional railroad freight charges, BHP modernized in the late 1920s, shifting the focus of production from heavy plate to the lighter rolled sheets required by new consumer-driven needs (automobiles, fridges, stoves, canned food). As a result, Australia's imports of rolled steel fell from 275,000 t in 1929–1930 to 90,000 t in 1930–1931 (Hughes 1964: 110). Overall, BHP's steel production rose from 284,669 t in 1923–1924 to 1.65 million tons in 1940–1941 (Hughes 1964: 101, 132–133). Writing in 1970, the economic historian, Colin Forster (1970: 158) advised his readers that, "The development of the steel industry by BHP is regarded as one of the outstanding success stories in Australian industrialization," its production symbolizing "the maturity of Australian manufacturing."

The transformative effects of BHP's success were evident on many fronts. Despite the devastating effects of the Great Depression, which at its peak saw almost a third of the Australian workforce unemployed, overall factory employment rose from 450,000 in 1928–1929 to 656,000 in 1938–1939 (Hughes 1964: 130). Whereas only 15% of the Australian workforce were employed in manufacturing in

1900–1901, by the 1940s an estimated 26.3% of the labor force worked in a factory, a percentage that rose to 28.1% in the 1950s (Butlin 1970: 291). Manufacturing's contributing to GDP – which averaged 12.8% in 1886–1890 and 14.4% between 1911 and 1920 – rose to an average of 28.4% in the 1950s, before peaking at 29.5% in the early 1960s (Butlin 1970: 290). Where workers were employed in a factory, this was by the 1940s likely to be in a large, well-capitalized operation rather than the small-scale affairs of yesteryear. In 1906, for example, only 35.5% of factory workers were employed in firms with 100 workers or more. By 1938–1939, however, almost half the factory workforce were engaged by this type of business (Forster 1970: 141). The improved efficiency of the manufacturing factor was arguably most evident in steel-making. Whereas the existence of BHP's steel-works had long depended on tariff protection, by the mid-1930s it was selling its iron and steel at lower prices than the duty-free price of imports (Forster 1970: 158).

As the Hunter's miners had long hoped, Newcastle's burgeoning steel industry underpinned a large-scale increase in coal production. By the late 1930s, BHP's Newcastle steel-works was using 1.5 million tons of coal per year, a tonnage equivalent to one-eighth of the entire national production. Most of this coal came from BHP's own mines, the BHP mine at Lambton in Newcastle being the first to be fully mechanized (Hughes 1964: 121–122). Significantly, the growing demands of the Hunter's manufacturing sector supported the development of the Cessnock field, which rapidly overtook the Newcastle region as Australia's principal source of black coal. Whereas only 2,776 coal miners were employed in Newcastle mines in 1921, there were 6,266 coal miners in Cessnock, where the town population rose from 150 in 1903 to 14,385 in 1933 with another 25,000 living in the surrounding hamlets and villages (Bowden 2006b: 62: Walker 1945: 3, 151). By 1925, the Hunter region was producing a record 7.67 million tons of coal per year, more than double that produced at the beginning of the century (Walker 1945: 37). Most of this production was from a small number of large producers, a concentration of ownership that became more pronounced in 1932 when BHP acquired the Burwood and Lambton mines from the Scottish-owned Scottish Australian Company (Lewis 1948/2009: 598). Shipping companies also increased their exposure to coal mining, the Howard Smith Shipping Company taking over the mines of another Scottish company, Caledonian Collieries, a firm that had pioneered the extraction of coal from the Cessnock field (Walker 1945: 3; Ross 1970: 153). By the early 1930, 60% of Cessnock's production came from mines fully or partially owned by shipping companies (Ross 1970: 326).

If both manufacturing and coal mining experienced boom conditions in the first quarter of the twentieth century, in the Hunter Valley's pastoral sector – as with the Australian pastoral industry more generally – things were more subdued. Following a collapse in wool prices in the 1890s, and the terrible Federation Drought (1895–1903), sheep numbers declined markedly, only returning to 1890 levels during the early 1950s. This is not to say that sheep-raising lost its preeminent role as an export leader. In 1924–1925, pastoral products still provided 55.1% of Australia's merchandise exports (Cain 1970: 77). However, pastoral exports lost their oversized role as a contributor to national wealth and employment. Overall, the contribution of exports to national income declined from 26% of the total in the first decade of the twentieth century to 17% in the 1930s (Cain 1970: 118). In terms of employment, the rural sector's share fell from 25.3% in 1900–1901 to 13.9% in the 1950s. Similarly, the rural sector's addition to GDP declined from 28.1% in 1900–1901 to 13.1% in the early 1960s (Butlin 1970: 290–291).

Within the Hunter the most significant changes to pastoral production occurred not in the upper Hunter – the domain of the sheep-lords – but in the lower Hunter, where dairying flourished. The rise of the dairy industry in the Hunter was integral to what Hagan and Turner (1991: 53) referred to as the Australian "Dairy Revolution," in which the spread of refrigerated transport allowed for a massive increase in both fresh milk production and manufactured milk products (i.e., butter, cheese, etc.). As was the case with the earlier expansion of agriculture, dairying in the lower Hunter benefited from ease of transport and its vicinity to Sydney's metropolitan population. Accordingly, by 1914–1915 the Hunter and the adjacent Manning district were producing one-quarter of NSW's milk output (NSW Parliament 1915: 1203). As is the norm in Australian business circumstances, politics and state regulatory practices also played a significant role in the success of dairying in the lower Hunter. Whereas milk producers in more remote regions produced for the butter and cheese industries, where most production was exported, Hunter Valley growers in 1914 were officially deemed to be part of the "Sydney Milk Zone." This meant that Hunter Valley milk was sold fresh to the household, delivering per gallon returns that were often double those obtained by farmers outside the "Milk Zone" (Bowden 2006b: 71). Despite this happy circumstance, the typical Hunter dairy farmer and their family eked out a grueling, hand-to-mouth existence. Reason for this is found in the fact that by the early twentieth century the best pastoral land had long been claimed, either by a sheep-lord or by some other early settler. As a result, the great bulk of dairy farmers worked as sharecroppers, obtaining land and cattle, and a share of the milk cheque, from the "owner" in return for their unrelenting labor. As one dairyman, Mr. McKitchie, complained in 1922: "Women and children had to assist or the farmer could not make a living. It was impossible to earn the minimum wage without working 80 hours" (Dungog Chronicle 1922: 3). Despite the prevalence of such work practices, dairying grew in importance. By the late 1960s, it was responsible for 40% of the Hunter's rural production, measured by value (Farrelly 1968: 2).

Built on apparently sold foundations, the hard-earned prosperity of the Hunter – as with the Australian nation as a whole – was always vulnerable. The fundamental problem, in the twentieth as in the nineteenth century, was the constraining effects of small local markets. Astutely, this problem was recognized by the General Manager of BHP, Essington Lewis, in 1938, at a time when the profitability and competiveness of the company's steel-works appeared unassailable. Writing for his company's own journal, *BHP Review*, Lewis advised his staff that the steel-works was struggling to achieve proper economies of scale due to "the smallness of the home market." Lewis went on to note that, whereas the "most economical unit of iron and steel production is normally very large – the Australian demand is relatively small" (cited, Forster 1970: 158). Compounding the inevitable problems that stemmed from a small home market, BHP was slow to accept new ideas and technologies during the 1940s and 1950s, a time when steel technology developed at a faster pace "than it had at any time in the previous hundred years" (Hughes 1964: 161). By the late 1950s the deficiencies of BHP were exposed by the rise of innovative Japanese exporters who – despite the strength of Australia's tariff barriers – began to capture an ever larger share of the local iron and steel market. For a time the lackluster development of BHP was disguised by its propensity to sell much of its iron and steel production to its various subsidiaries – which by the 1940s included Ryland's and John Lysaght – who then on-sold finished product as tin-plate, pressed sheeting, or galvanized iron (Hughes 1964: 179). By 1970, however, when BHP closed its ageing plate mill, the increasingly obsolete nature of the Hunter's manufacturing base could no longer be disguised. Despite various state and federal government rescue efforts, employment at the steel-works fell away sharply, dropping from 11,500 in 1981 to 6500 in 1983 before closing in 1999 (Bowden 2006a: 61).

In the domestically oriented Hunter coal industry, the prosperity of the early 1920s evaporated even more rapidly. Despite the increased demand provided by BHP's steel-works, NSW's state-owned railways remained the industry's principal customer. When the railway's freight and passenger business collapsed in the mid-1920s due to competition from road transport, the well-being of the coal trade collapsed with it, the production of the Hunter Valley falling from a record 7.6 million tons in 1925 to 3.7 million tons in 1930 (Walker 1945: 37). Although the collectivized ethos of the miners curtailed unemployment, with workers sharing available work, the average number of days worked fell from 200 in 1922 to 169 in 1929 (Ross 1970: 325). Constant industrial disputes also curtailed not only production but orders as customers rebelled over poor delivery times, a problem that became even more pronounced during the "Great Lockout," a dispute that shutdown the Hunter coalfields between February 1929 and June 1930 amidst an undercurrent of violence. When the miners returned to work, the union fought a long and – for a time – successful campaign against mechanization, mistakenly believing that such action was the best guarantor of future employment.

Declaring mechanization to be "an uncontrollable monster," the Central Council of the Miners Federation resolved in 1935 that, "The time has arrived for organized resistance to further mechanization, which threatens to render destitute and desolate whole districts and communities." As a result, despite the efforts of companies such as BHP, production continued to revolve around "pick and shovel mining" (Dingsdag 1988: 179). Indeed, as Donald Dingsdag's (1988) doctoral thesis reveals, levels of mechanization were actually lower in the 1930s that they were in the immediate aftermath of World War I. Even after another crushing union defeat in the 1949 general coal strike – primarily fought over the issue of mechanization – manual labor remained the norm in most mines (Dingsdag 1988: 296). The inevitable result of this Luddite-like opposition to mechanization was an antiquated industry, ill-equipped to deal with a collapse in coal demand associated with the railway's transition away from coal-fired locomotives to diesel engines. Across the Cessnock field, coal mining employment fell from 6,700 in 1954 to 1,400 a decade later (Holmes 1965: 108).

Throughout the Hunter, the decline in coal mining and steel-making was associated with a hollowing out of the "blue-collar" workforce that had previously characterized regional employment. Between 1971 and 1986, the population of

Newcastle City fell from 146,009 to 129,956 (Bowden 2006a: 59). On the Cessnock coalfields, a study by the urban geographer, J. H. Holmes (1965: 111) revealed that 39% of the nonrural workforce was commuting outside of the Cessnock area so as to obtain work. In most cases, Holmes (1965: 109) observed, "They have been obliged to accept ... unskilled, less remunerative labouring jobs."

If the Hunter's resource-based economy appeared to be on its knees in the early 1960s, in the last third of the twentieth century it staged a remarkable recovery, albeit one that was more pronounced in terms of wealth produced than jobs created. As in earlier periods of economic growth, the post-1960 expansion was attributable to four factors: the Valley's natural wealth, politics, external demand, and the arrival of well-financed firms that had made their fortune elsewhere.

The first pointer to the eventual recovery of the Hunter's resource-based economy came on the political front, when in February 1956 the NSW Premier, Joe Cahill, promised to "place orders for a huge coal-fired power station on the Northern [i.e., Hunter] coalfield." Cahill also promised the voters of the lower Hunter that "every possible step would be taken to safeguard the interests of all engaged in the coal mining industry" (cited, Newcastle Morning Herald 1956: 1). When construction of the promised Vales Point power-station began in 1959, up to 1,600 former coal miners were employed in its construction, many of whom eventually found permanent work in the Newvale colliery built to service its needs. When construction began on a second, even larger power-point at nearby Munmorah in January 1962, the local press declared, somewhat optimistically, that, "The future of the [coal] industry is assured" (Newcastle Morning Herald 1962: 2). The importance of electricity generation for the Hunter coal industry can be ascertained from the fact that of the 8.1 million tons produced in 1967 – a tonnage slightly above the prewar peak obtained in 1925 – 48.1% went to the Hunter's coal-fired power generators (Longworth 1968: 2). By itself, however, the needs of the power industry would have merely slowed the coal sector's decline, reducing it to the status of a small ancillary economic activity. Instead, it was the export industry, fuelled by the power-generation needs of South Korea, Taiwan, and, above all, Japan that proved the real salvation of the Hunter's coal mines. In terms of both the speed at which it occurred, and the scale it assumed, the growth of the Hunter's export coal industry was truly extraordinary. Where exports provided markets for only 6.2% of the Hunter's coal in 1967, by 1970–71 an estimated 33.35% of a much expanded production was exported (Longworth 1968: 2; Dingsdag 1988: 321). Whereas the Hunter exported 0.5 million tons in 1967, by 1991–1992 exports through Newcastle amounted to 56.1 million tons (Longworth 1968: 2; NSW Department of Mineral Resources 1998: 3).

The revival of the Hunter coal industry's fortunes was associated with a geographical, technological, and managerial transformation. Whereas historically, the Hunter's coal had come from underground pits adjacent to either Newcastle or Cessnock, by the mid-1990s most of the region's coal – and the great bulk of exports – was coming from open-cut mines in the mid-Hunter flanking either Singleton or Muswellbrook. Admittedly, open-cut mining was not new to the Hunter's upper reaches. To offset war-time and postwar coal shortages the government-owned Joint Coal Board (JCB) effectively pioneered open-cut mining in the Hunter, operating 7 mines by 1950. However, the JCB mines were so poorly run that all had closed by 1954 (Dingsdag 1988: 287–289). For its part, the private-sector was loath to venture where government had failed, given that a single dragline – the key piece of technology in open-cut technology – cost tens of millions of dollars in the 1970s. As a result, the development of the open-cut sector required a different type of company to that which had traditionally operated in the Hunter, namely a multinational with very deep pockets. In providing continuing evidence of the Hunter's golden rule, the first such venture was Clutha Development, a subsidiary of the oil giant, BP. Soon joined by Rio Tinto and another oil giant, Shell, these mining behemoths engaged in an investment spree of staggering dimensions. Between 1973–1974 and 1981–1982, investment in the open-cut sector rose from AUD$1.83 million to AUD$512.58 million (Dingsdag, 313). Amid a constant process of rationalization, Rio Tinto eventually emerged as the Hunter's largest producer through its subsidiary, Coal & Allied. By 1997, Rio Tinto's 6 mines, which included 2 in Queensland, were producing an annual total of 29.5 million tons – 4 times the tonnage produced by all the Hunter Valley's miners 20 years before (Carrington Coal Company 1998:41). In the vast open-cut pits of the Hunter, the traditional skills of underground mining were largely redundant. Instead, mining came to resemble a large civil construction project, in which heavy earth-moving equipment was used to create roadways, move enormous quantities of overburden, and haul huge tonnages of both earth and coal as the mines reshaped the physical landscape. By utilizing capital-intense mining techniques to the full, the Hunter Valley miners also made their industry one of the world's most efficient, dominating the Pacific Basin trade in thermal coal. Whereas, for example, a Cessnock miner had typically produced around 917 t per year in 1939, by 1997 a Hunter miner extracted 6,920 t on average (Walker 1945: 38; NSW Department of Mineral Resources 1998: 3).

In reflecting upon the political economy of the Hunter at the close of the twentieth century, Macdonald and Burgess (1998: 10) concluded that coal mining "remained the single most important industry" in the region. A year later a government survey estimated that coal mining provided the region with 7,700 direct jobs and 50,000 indirect jobs (Agnew 1999: viii). Elsewhere in the Hunter the region's resource-based economy also assumed a new appearance. Traditional forms of pastoral activity, which had revolved around sheep-raising in the upper Valley and dairying in the lower Valley, fell into abeyance. In the case of dairying the fatal blow was delivered by the NSW Parliament when it abolished the "Sydney Milk Zone" in 1976, allowing larger and more efficient producers from further afield access to this lucrative market. In the upper Hunter, more of the district's 5,424 primary producers were running beef than sheep in 2001, focusing on high-value product for the restaurant and export trade (Bowden 2006a: 50). As noted in the introduction, the upper Hunter also emerged as one of the world's principal horse-breeding regions as old-established pastoral families sold out to overseas interests. In the lower Hunter the most significant rural activity by the early 1990s was the raising and processing of chickens on an industrial scale, the Steggles' processing plant at Beresford killing and packaging 30 million chickens in 1991 (Newcastle Herald 1991: 15). The success of Steggles was proof of the continued relevance of the Hunter's subsidiary rule, which associates managerial success with a rapid transition from small to large business. A long established family of produce merchants, who had specialized in the supply of their home-made chicken feed to local growers, the dynasty's fortunes were transformed when Bruce Steggle hit upon the idea of supplying supermarkets with precut packaged chicken. Transforming an old grain mill at Beresford into a processing plant, by the late 1980s Steggles was part of a duopoly – along with its great rival, Ingham's – that dominated the Australian market (Insch 2005: 116). By 1991, Steggles was responsible for 1,500 direct and indirect jobs, in both processing and supply, the latter including 196 chicken-breeding farms (Newcastle Herald 1991: 15). As with previous rural ventures in the lower Hunter, much of Steggles' success is attributable to geography and vicinity to the large Sydney market.

In the lower Hunter, adjacent to Cessnock, wine-growing also grew in economic significance, a success that was in many ways paradoxical given the fact that the Hunter region remained an insignificant wine-growing region. In the early twenty-first century, for example, the Hunter crushed only 35,000 tons of grape per year, a tiny fraction of national production of 1.5 million tons. Despite this fact, however, wine-growing in the Hunter at this time was worth $350 million on an annual basis, employing 1,720 full-time workers and a small army of casuals at harvest time (Henderson et al. 2009: 267). Explanation for the disproportionate economic impact of the Hunter wine industry is found in two factors. First, producers often garnered a reputational advantage by bottling wine grown elsewhere in the Hunter, a ploy that caused an association with the lower Hunter's old vines. Secondly, and far more significantly, the typical Hunter vineyard operated as a de facto tourist venture, benefiting from the vicinity of vineyards to Sydney, a two to three hour freeway drive away to the south. By 2005, an estimated 2.3 million tourists were visiting the Hunter's wine districts each year (Henderson et al. 2009: 266). In explaining the principles upon which they ran their business, one well-established vigneron noted, "when I first came here [in 1985] my comment to my shareholders was that we are almost first a tourist business and [only] then in the business of growing good grapes" (cited, Henderson et al. 2009: 266).

For all the wealth created by the Hunter's resource-based industries, the employment effect of these endeavors was far less at the end of the twentieth century than it was at the beginning. Indeed, the very conditions upon which the success of the resource-based economy came to be premised – high levels of capital-intensity and labor productivity – curtailed large-scale employment increases. Outside the shrinking opportunities of the resource-based sector, an increasing number found work in part-time jobs in retail, hospitality, and community service. As a result, by 2001 only 60.2% of the jobs in Newcastle, and the adjoining cities of Lake Macquarie and Port Stephens, were full-time. At the other end of the employment spectrum, 31.7% of the Newcastle workforce were professionals by 2001. Unlike the situation that prevailed in the 1930s and 1940s, when professional employment tended to be associated with BHP or another large private-sector employer, the professional jobs at the close of the twentieth-century were typically associated with public sector employment or with work that was tax-payer funded (i.e., education, health, defense). At the same time, however, Newcastle City had more unemployed workers, and more single-parent families, than any other area in the Hunter (Bowden 2006a: 64). In short, the Hunter labor market had fractured, leaving four distinct groups with little in common: blue-collar workers in the resource-based sector, urban professionals, part-time service-sector workers, and those who boasted little or no connection with the paid workforce.

Wealth and Poverty: The Hunter in the Twenty-First Century

In 2020 the Hunter was still Australia's wealthiest valley, a claim that the region could have argued with equal justification in 1820 and 1920. More than ever, the material wealth of the Valley is associated with the primary sector. By comparison with the situation which prevailed in the mid-twentieth century, comparatively little of the Valley's natural wealth is now subject to processing or manufacture. Outside of the former steel-making city of Newcastle, the percentage of the workforce engaged in manufacturing (6.7%) in 2016 was less than half that employed in primary pursuits, namely mining (9%), and agriculture, fishing, and forestry (3.4%) (ABS 2019b). In the city of Newcastle, the percentage of the workforce recorded as working in manufacture (5.5%) in the 2016 census was even lower (ABS 2019a). Nowhere is there evidence of a successful transition to a high-tech, "knowledge-based" economy. Outside of Newcastle, the percentage of the workforce engaged in information technology and media services stood at a derisory 1% in 2016. The percentage of the workforce engaged in education and training (6.7%) was identical to that found in the shrunken manufacturing sector. Despite the much spruiked success of wine-based tourism, the percentage of Hunter Valley (excluding Newcastle) workers engaged in accommodation and food services (8.1%) was less than that found in mining (9%) in 2016 (ABS 2019b). Even in Newcastle, the percentage of workers employed as managers or professionals (37.2%) was only modestly superior to that recorded in 2001 (31.7%), an outcome that leaves the educated professional a distinctly minority breed in the Hunter Valley.

If the broad structure of the Hunter's economy in the second decade of the twenty-first century was little different from that found when BHP closed its steel-works in 1999, there is one cohort that has grown in significance: those with little or no engagement with the workforce. Whereas in 2001 the Hunter's labor force participation rate outside of Newcastle City stood at 70.4%, by 2011 it was down to 58.4%, reaching a new low-point of 56.4% in 2016 (ABS 2001: Table B25; ABS 2019b). If we exclude the 7.5% of the labor force who were unemployed from our calculations, it is evident that in 2016 barely half (52.6%) the Hunter Valley's (outside Newcastle) working age population had any gainful employment. At the time of the 2016 Australian census, it was also the case that barely half (56.9%) the working age population had any postsecondary school qualification. In 2016, moreover, only one-third (33.3%) of the working age population outside Newcastle had completed high school (i.e., grade 12) (ABS 2019b). Even in Newcastle, only 56.5% of the working age population was employed in 2016. Barely half (50.5%) had completed high school (ABS 2019a).

The problems that now bedevil the Hunter speak to the very purpose of management in the modern world, in not only this region but in every industrial society. As we noted in the introduction to this chapter, "management" has historically been associated with what Wren and Bedeian (1972/2017: 3) refer to as wealth creation "through the efficient allocation and utilization of human and material resources." In his defining study, *The Genesis of Modern Management*, Pollard (1965: 2) similarly declared the purpose of management to be "the efficient use of resources within the firm," a task which he associated with "the creation of a proper institutional and human framework to make this possible." What made management such a socially progressive force, Pollard (1965: 7) continued, was the fact that the pursuit of efficiencies forced a constant struggle against those forces – unfree labor markets, "a hostile State," "unsympathetic legal systems," barriers to the movement of people and goods.

Arguably, it was the self-serving pursuit of such principles that drove the extraordinary economic successes of Hunter businesses throughout the nineteenth and twentieth centuries, whether those endeavors were directed towards securing pastoral land for wool exports, tariff protection for steel production, or the construction of coal-fired power-stations to foster aluminum smelting and job creation. Admittedly, the pursuit of these self-interested objectives often brought Hunter managers into conflict with their workers, the most savage struggles in the Valley's history being those associated with opposition to the mechanization of coal mining. Opposed as they were when it came to short-term objectives, there was little difference between workers, managers, and unions when it came to long-term aspirations for the region. All wanted successful, wealth producing industries. Even communists supported wealth creating industries, hoping to inherit prosperous industries rather than moribund ones come the revolution. Such unanimity is now a thing of the past.

Nowhere is the divisions between the exponents and opponents of the Hunter's (and Australia's) resource-based industries more evident than in the use of coal-fired power-stations to drive lower electricity prices and, hence, both lower costs and the relocation of energy-intensive industries such as aluminum smelting. Between the 1950s and 1980s, as we have observed, the pursuit of such of such objectives was central to successive NSW governments, who saw in cheap electricity a pathway to greater prosperity in not only the Hunter but the society more generally. As Graham et al. (2015) indicate, across Australia the real price of electricity halved between 1955 and 1975. Between 2007 and 2013, however, the inflation-adjusted price of electricity charged to manufacturing businesses grew by 60%. During the same period, household electricity prices rose by 72% in real terms (Graham et al. 2015; Swoboda 2013). Since then prices have continued to increase at a similar rate. Although there are many factors behind these price increases – which have turned Australia from a low-cost to high-cost energy producer – a central factor has clearly been the propensity of recent Australian governments to shift generating capacity from coal-fired units to renewables (i.e., solar, wind). In describing the economic effects of this change, the Australian Aluminium Council (2018: 1) – the peak council representing Australia's seventh largest export industry – formally warned the Commonwealth Government's Energy Security Board in July 2018 that,

"Australia no longer has internationally competitive energy costs and this has halted investment ... and is imperilling the viability of existing [smelter] assets." The Council went on to advise that "nonthermal options" (i.e., renewables) "are not yet cost competitive at scale" and that as a result, "In the short- to medium-term at least, thermal generation will be required" (Australian Aluminium Council 2018: 1–2). There is, of course, an argument that we can maintain energy-intensive industries such as aluminum smelting *and* abandon the use of fossil fuels at the same time. In the so-called "New Green Deal," introduced by Rep. Alexandrina Ocasio-Cortez (2019: 3, 7) into the United States House of Representatives in February 2019, we are told that the rapid transition to a system where "100 percent" of "power demand" will come from "clean renewable, and zero emission energy sources" will actually reverse a process of "deindustrialization" that is now "4-decade" (sic) old. However, while Ocasio-Cortez believes this feat is possible, the Australian Aluminium Council clearly disagrees. Objectively, the evidence appears to support the Australian Aluminium Council's more pessimistic conclusion. In the Hunter, the Kurri Kurri smelter near Cessnock has already closed. Another, at Portland in Victoria, is facing imminent closure. Despite efforts by all levels of Australian government to expand the use of renewables, the Australian Government's Department of Energy and the Environment (2019) official "Energy" website indicates that in 2018 fossil fuels provided 81% of Australia's electricity, whereas wind and solar contributed 11%. In other words, the focus on renewables has driven the cost of electricity up without fundamentally altering the nation's dependence on fossil fuel.

Given that there appears little realistic prospect that the aluminum industry's needs can be met by renewables, it is evident that some (if not many) are happy to condone the closure of Australia's smelting industry as part of the transition to a more environmentally friendly society. In 2014, for example, the federal parliamentary leader of Australia's Green Party, Christine Milne, vehemently opposed efforts to support aluminum smelting, declaring the industry to be "big polluters" (cited, McCulloch 2014). Easy in principle, allowing the aluminum industry to close would have devastating effects for the Australian economy, causing the loss of export income equivalent to half of all the nation's tourist income. Nowhere would the effects be felt more severely than in Newcastle and the Hunter, a region where disengagement with the paid workforce is becoming almost the norm. It is, of course, not only the smelting industry that is under threat. The coal industry, long the bedrock of the regional economy – and of the Australian economy more widely – has even more vocal and influential foes. Some oppose the industry's expansion because it interferes with the peace and quiet of a bucolic existence. In opposing the proposed Rocky Hill coal mine, for example, Brad Bowden (no relation) declared that, "Like many of my fellow tree-changer residents, I can now see my vision for peaceful country living crumbling before my eyes" (Bowden 2017: 1). More significant opposition is found in senior legal circles. In a paper given to the Dundee Climate Conference in Scotland in September 2019, for example, Chief Judge Brian Preston (2019b: 19) declared that the severity of climate change – and the mandates of the Paris Climate Agreement – meant that it was "increasingly difficult for courts to accept that the individual emissions of an entity are inconsequential," a "drop in the bucket" that would allow a business to legally proceed where its activities contributed to climate change even in a modest way. In reflecting on his own decision to block a new mine to the Hunter's immediate north, Preston (2019b: 22) observed, "Australia had a responsibility as a developed country to take the lead" in opposing projects that might lead to increased emissions. There is no doubt that Preston's comments would be endorsed by many Australians. However, the closure of the Australian coal industry would be far more consequential that the loss of the nation's smelting industry. In terms of export income, it would cause a loss equivalent to that associated with the placement of a permanent ban on the arrival of all international tourists and international students into the country. In the Hunter, it would cause what many already fear: a large-scale loss of employment in not only mining but also in transport, the railways, the Newcastle port, and a host of service providers (i.e., vehicular maintenance, business services, finance, etc.).

Whether one supports or opposes the continuation of the Hunter's resource-based economy, built around the mining and the use of fossil fuel, there is no gainsaying the fact that it is today the most divisive issue in the region, overshadowing other social and economic concerns: unemployment, falling labor force participation, increasing levels of poverty among those excluded from the workforce.

Conclusion

As we have noted continually throughout this chapter, the golden rule for business and managerial success in the Hunter has been to arrive with a preexisting fortune and well-established political connections. This is another way of saying that in the Hunter, as with Australia more generally, politics and state intervention have played a disproportionate role in the success of any industry or venture. When the Hunter was first settled by Europeans, the fact that all land was regarded as belonging to the British Crown, rather than the original Aboriginal inhabitants, meant that political connections were useful, if not essential, to the acquisition of good quality land with river frontages. Among those who benefited from official largesse in the initial subdivision of the Valley was the man entrusted with the land survey, Henry Dangar, a man whom Manning Clark (1973a: 250), describes as someone "consumed by the passion to acquire land" who "ended up laying up for himself large landed treasures." When commercial coal mining commenced in the Hunter in the 1830s it did so in the form of a government-mandated monopoly granted to the AA Co., a company that boasted many British parliamentarians and the Governor of the Bank of England among its directors. The establishment of BHP's steel-works in the early twentieth century followed the passage of the "Iron and Steel Works Bill" by the NSW parliament on 2 October 1912, in which the parliament pledged to take "all necessary steps" to assist BHP, measures that included land grants, the dredging of harbors, and the resumption of waterfronts (NSW Parliament 1912a: 1705). The coal-fired power-stations constructed in the Valley between the late 1950s and early 1990s were not only state-funded they were also government-owned, built in part to alleviate the then-depressed state of the local coal industry. The development of a large-scale aluminum industry in the lower Hunter in the 1970s and 1980s was also facilitated by government subsidies and support, the then Premier, Neville Wran, driven by the "dream of creating a Ruhr Valley in NSW" (Steketee and Cockburn 1986: 202).

The state's constant favoring of self-interested business endeavors appears to suggest that the Hunter, and Australia more widely, is a place where nepotism, corruption and illicit government-business relationships operate at the expense of normal market forces, favoring certain well-connected parties at the expense of others. There is some measure of truth in this. Nevertheless, to see government-business relations in the Hunter as activities driven by self-serving interests at odds with the needs of the wider community is to engage in fundamental error. Australia is a fiercely democratic society. In NSW, politicians have been exposed to popular election since 1856. Even before this date the strongly democratic and egalitarian values of the society brought any ill-favored government action before the court of public opinion, where a free and vocal press quickly exposed any activities contrary to the commonweal. Of the great pastoral families who dominated the upper Hunter during the nineteenth-century, Eldred-Grigg (1978: 230) observes that they "were by no means in a position of dominant political power," and that "for years at a time" the district was represented "by men who were the antithesis of landed gentlemen." Although the sheep-lords were typically ill-regarded by their poorer neighbors, there was never any serious attempt to evict them from their estates. Instead, most recognized that only well-connected and well-financed individuals and firms possessed the wherewithal to run a pastoral property. Accordingly, the pastoralists – for all their narrow, self-serving behavior – served a beneficial societal role, marshaling resources and demonstrating a level of managerial expertise that was beyond the abilities of the small wheat-farmer. Indeed, it was only the existence of the pastoral estates that made neighboring small-scale farming possible, allowing the wheat farmer – and his sons and daughters – the capacity to supplement their farm income with waged-labor on the sheep-lord's property (Eldred-Grigg 1978: 289).

If we consider the circumstances of the parliamentary bill that provided BHP with an array of tax-payer funded benefits in 1912, it is evident that this was also done in accordance with – rather than contrary to – public opinion. The Labor Party minister who steered the "Iron and Steel Works Bill" through parliament, Arthur Griffith, was no corrupt business lackey. Instead, the university-educated Griffith was one of the leading socialists of his generation. A person of privileged personal circumstance, Griffith was constantly returned by the working-class voters of Newcastle between 1894 and 1901 before transferring to the electorate of Broken Hill, where support for socialism was even more pronounced among Labor voters (Bowden 2006b: 60–63). In neither Newcastle nor Broken Hill was BHP much loved, given the company's propensity to engage in industrial conflict with its unionized workforce. Once more, however, pragmatism – and the recognition that BHP alone had the physical and financial resources to develop a steel industry – overcame voter dislike. As Griffith informed parliament, "Any Government in power would welcome the establishment of a great iron industry, which after all is the basis of every other industry" (NSW Parliament 1912a: 1706). If pragmatism overrode sentiment in the case of BHP, it is also wrong to see this decision as in anyway unusual. On 1 October 1912, for example, the day before the passage of the "Iron and Steel Works Bill," the NSW parliament passed another bill, the "Newcastle District Abattoir Bill," which provided government funding for a Newcastle abattoir. In describing the government's rationale in introducing the bill, the Premier, Jack McGowen, declared, "It is the outcome of representations that have been made to the Government for the last twenty years by the local governing bodies interested, which represent a population of 60,000 or 70,000" (NSW Parliament 1912b: 1579).

A propensity to constantly seek government assistance and protection in the Hunter, as in Australia more generally, points to the constraining effects of small markets, a problem historically associated with a small population. In 1900, Australia's entire population (3.8 million) was not much more than 40% of that found in the greater London metropolitan area. While small businesses could provide for many of the basic household needs of the population (carpentry, bootmaking, baking, retailing, etc.), large-scale business activity typically required external sources of finance, technology, personnel, and managerial expertise. This tendency was most pronounced in the interior, where the export-oriented ventures that underpinned national prosperity – wool-growing and mining – typically required both deep pockets and a knowledge of international markets and logistics. Given the smallness of the population and the vastness of the Australian landscape, the risks involved in such ventures were always high. In such circumstances, it is hardly surprising that business would seek some sort of government support or guarantee before venturing their capital. It is also hardly surprising that the most common support offered by government was the provision of something that Australia had in abundance: land.

If business in the Hunter, and Australia more generally, has long sought and obtained the protective support of the state, it is also the case that national prosperity has always heavily relied upon the exploitation of the natural world in the form of sheep and cattle-raising, farming, forestry, and mining. This was true in the nineteenth and twentieth centuries, and it is equally true in the twenty-first. As noted in the introduction, in 2018 minerals comprised 6 of the nation's top 10 exports. The nation earns far more from fossil fuels such as coal (AUD$66.9 billion) and natural gas (AUD$43.3) than it does from either education (AUD$35.3 billion) or tourism (AUD$22.2 billion). The only manufacturing sector of export note – aluminum and alumina smelting – is also fossil-fuel reliant. As Australia's wealthiest valley, the Hunter is a notable contributor to this export wealth, most particularly in relation to coal and aluminum. Until 20 years or so ago, the businesses and managers associated with this export wealth were held in considerable esteem. Increasingly, however, at least in metropolitan Australia – where the sources of the nation's export wealth and prosperity often seem distant and inconsequential in terms of their positive economic effects – those associated with resource-based industries are regarded with opprobrium, condemned for despoiling the climate and environment. The result is a society increasingly torn asunder. As urban professionals look on their regional cousins with ill-disguised scorn, those in regional areas such as the Hunter show a greater willingness to follow the same path as that pursued by the Trump-voting and

Brexit-voting blue-collar workers in America and Britain, putting their hopes in populist politicians. Amid this turmoil, the very purpose of managerial endeavor appears more uncertain than at any other time in the nation's history.

Cross-References

- ▶ Governmentality and the Chinese Workers in China's Contemporary Thought Management System
- ▶ In Search of the Traces of the History of Management in Latin America, 1870–2020
- ▶ Indian Management (?): A Modernization Experiment
- ▶ Introduction: Management Heterogeneity in Asia
- ▶ Management History in the Modern World: An Overview
- ▶ The Making of a Docile Working Class in Pre-reform China
- ▶ The Perfect Natural Experiment: Asia and the Convergence Debate
- ▶ Think Big and Privatize Every Thing That Moves: The Impact of Political Reform on the Practice of Management in New Zealand
- ▶ Transformation: The First Global Economy, 1750–1914
- ▶ Trade Union Decline and Transformation: Where to for Employment Relations?
- ▶ What Is Management?

References

Agnew D (1999) Strategic study of the northern NSW coalfields. NSW Department of Mineral Resources, Sydney

Australian Aluminium Council (2018) Correspondence to the Energy Security Board: National energy guarantee – draft detailed design consultation paper, 14 July. Australian Aluminium Council, Canberra. https://aluminium.org.au/news/aac-submission-on-the-consultation-paper-national-energy-guarantee-draft-detailed-design-consultation-paper/

Australian Bureau of Statistics (1971) Commonwealth census of 1971: characteristics of the population and dwellings of local government areas, New South Wales – Hunter statistical division. Australian Government Printing Office, Canberra, pp 145–201

Australian Bureau of Statistics (2001) Commonwealth Census of 2001: characteristics of the population and dwellings of local government areas, New South Wales – Hunter statistical division: balance. Australian Government Printing Office, Canberra

Australian Bureau of Statistics (2019a) Regional statistical summary – Newcastle. Australian Bureau of Statistics, Canberra. https://itt.abs.gov.au/itt/r.jsp?RegionSummary&region=15900&dataset=ABS_REGIONAL_LGA2018&maplayerid=LGA2018&geoconcept=LGA_2018&datasetASGS=ABS_REGIONAL_ASGS2016&datasetLGA=ABS_REGIONAL_LGA2018&regionLGA=LGA_2018&regionASGS=ASGS_2016

Australian Bureau of Statistics (2019b) Regional statistical summary – Hunter. Australian Bureau of Statistics, Canberra. https://itt.abs.gov.au/itt/r.jsp?RegionSummary&region=106&dataset=ABS_REGIONAL_ASGS2016&geoconcept=ASGS_2016&measure=MEASURE&datasetASGS=ABS_REGIONAL_ASGS2016&datasetLGA=ABS_REGIONAL_LGA2018&regionLGA=LGA_2018&regionASGS=ASGS_2016

Australian Electoral Commission (2019a) 2019 federal election – Newcastle City division. Australian Electoral Commission, Canberra. https://results.aec.gov.au/24310/Website/HouseDivisionPage-24310-136.htm

Australian Electoral Commission (2019b) 2019 federal election – Hunter division. Australian Electoral Commission, Canberra. https://results.aec.gov.au/24310/Website/HouseDivisionPage-24310-126.htm

Australian Government Department of the Environment and Energy (2019) Electricity generation. Department of the Environment and Energy, Canberra. https://www.energy.gov.au/data/electricity-generation

Bowden B (2006a) The Hunter. In: Hagan J (ed) People and politics in regional New South Wales: the 1950s to 2006. Federation Press, Sydney, pp 49–72

Bowden B (2006b) The Hunter. In: Hagan J (ed) People and politics in regional New South Wales: 1856 to the 1950s. Federation Press, Sydney, pp 53–77

Bowden B (2017) Correspondence to NSW Planning Assessment Commission: Rocky Hill Coal Project. 13 November. NSW Planning Assessment Commission, Sydney. https://www.ipcn.nsw.gov.au/resources/pac/media/files/pac/projects/2017/10/rocky-hill-coal-project/comments-and-presentations/comments/brad-bowden.pdf

Butlin NG (1964/1972) Investment in Australian economic development 1861–1900. Australian National University Press, Canberra

Butlin NG (1970) Some perspectives of Australian economic development, 1890–1965. In: Forster C (ed) Australian economic development in the twentieth century. George Allen & Unwin, Sydney, pp 266–327

Cain N (1970) Trade and economic structure at the periphery: the Australian balance of payments, 1890–1965. In: Forster C (ed) Australian economic development in the twentieth century. George Allen & Unwin, Sydney, pp 66–122

Carrington Coal Company (1998) Coal 1998. Carrington Coal Company, Carrington

Clapham JH (1932/1967) Economic history of modern Britain: free trade and steel 1850–1886. Cambridge University Press, Cambridge, UK

Clark CMH (1973a) A history of Australia, vol 2. Melbourne University Press, Melbourne

Clark CMH (1973b) A history of Australia, vol 3. Melbourne University Press, Melbourne

Department of Foreign Affairs and Trade (2019) Australia's top 10 goods & services exports and imports. Department of Foreign Affairs and Trade, Canberra. https://dfat.gov.au/trade/resources/trade-at-a-glance/Pages/top-goods-services.aspx

Dingsdag DP (1988) The restructuring of the NSW coalmining industry. PhD Thesis, University of Wollongong, Wollongong, pp 1903–1982

Dungog Chronicle (1922) 21 March, pp 3–3

Eldred-Grigg ST (1978) The pastoral families of the Hunter valley, 1880–1914. PhD thesis, Australian National University, Canberra

Farrelly A (1968) Crying over the milk industry. Newcastle Morning Herald, 13 January, pp 2–2

Forster C (1970) Economies of scale and Australian manufacturing. In: Forster C (ed) Australian economic development in the twentieth century. George Allen & Unwin Limited, Sydney, pp 123–168

Glover I (2008) Fence me in. Outback 62:28–45

Graham PW, Brinsmead T, Hatfield-Dodds S (2015) Australian retail electricity prices: can we avoid repeating the rising trend of the past? Energy Policy 86:456–469

Hagan J, Turner K (1991) A history of the labor Party in New South Wales 1891 – 1991. Longman Cheshire, Melbourne

Haslam PA (1976) ALCAN: a symbol of community. Newcastle Morning Herald, 4 May, pp 8–8

Henderson L, Waterhouse J, Mitchell R, Burgess J (2009) Key features of the Hunter Valley wine cluster. In: Wine Business Research Symposium Proceedings. University of Newcastle, Newcastle, pp 264–283

Higgs HV (1880) Testimony to the parliamentary inquiry into assisted immigration to New South Wales. In: New South Wales Votes & Proceedings, vol 5. New South Wales Parliament, Sydney, pp 776–783

Hirst JB (1988) The strange birth of colonial democracy: New South Wales 1848–1884. Allen & Unwin, Sydney
Holmes JH (1965) The suburbanization of Cessnock coalfield towns, 1954–1964. Aust Geogr Stud 3(1):105–128
Hughes H (1964) The Australian iron and steel industry 1848 – 1962. Melbourne University Press, Melbourne
Hunter Thoroughbred Breeders Association (2019a) Stud tours. Hunter Thoroughbred Breeders Association, Scone. https://www.htba.com.au/stud-tours
Hunter Thoroughbred Breeders Association (2019b) What is it all about? Hunter Thoroughbred Breeders Association, Scone. https://www.htba.com.au/drayton-south
Insch A (2005) The effects of marketing organisation on the delivery of added value: a historical comparison of Australia's beef and chicken meat marketing systems. PhD thesis, Griffith University, Brisbane
Jackson RV (1977) Australian economic development in the nineteenth century. Australian National University Press, Canberra
Kirkwood I (2019) After decades of growth Newcastle coal exports appear to have levelled off. Newcastle Herald, 30 January. https://www.newcastleherald.com.au/story/5876889/newcastle-coal-exports-dip-slightly-but-growth-expected/
Knibbs CH (1909) Commonwealth of Australia yearbook, 1908. Commonwealth of Australia Printer, Melbourne
Lang JD (1852) An historical and statistical account of New South Wales, vol 2, 3rd edn. Longman, Brown and Green/London
Lewis E (1948/2009) 1948: the importance of the iron and steel industry. In: Anderson K (ed) The Joseph Fisher lectures, 1904–1954. University of Adelaide Press, Adelaide, pp 589–619
Longworth K (1968) The great battle for coal gets underway. Newcastle Morning Herald, 20 February, pp 2–2
Macdonald D, Burgess J (1998) Globalization and industrial relations in the Hunter. J Ind Relat 40 (1):3–24
Maitland City Council (1983) A new history of Maitland. Maitland City Council, Maitland
Mauldon FRE (1927) A study in social economics: the Hunter river valley. Workers Educational Association, Melbourne
McCulloch D (2014) Greens leader stands against aluminium sector, Examiner, 8 October. https://www.examiner.com.au/story/2610761/greens-leader-stands-against-aluminium-sector/
Merritt J (1987) The making of the AWU. Oxford University Press, Melbourne
Murray R, White K (1982) The ironworkers: a history of the Federated Ironworkers' Association of Australia. Hale & Iremonger, Sydney
New South Wales Department of Mineral Resources (1998) 1998 NSW coal industry profile. NSW Department of Mineral Resources, Sydney
New South Wales Parliament (1887) New South Wales statistics for 1886. In: New South Wales Votes & Proceedings, vol 5. New South Wales Parliament, Sydney, pp 612–613
New South Wales Parliament (1912a) Hansard of the New South Wales Legislative Assembly, 2 October. New South Wales Parliament, Sydney. https://www.parliament.nsw.gov.au/hansard/Pages/home.aspx?s=1
New South Wales Parliament (1912b) Hansard of the New South Wales Legislative Assembly, 1 October. New South Wales Parliament, Sydney. https://www.parliament.nsw.gov.au/hansard/Pages/home.aspx?s=1
New South Wales Parliament (1915) New South Wales statistical register, 1914–1915. New South Wales Parliament, Sydney
Newcastle Herald (1991) Supplement, 14 May
Newcastle Morning Herald (1889) Editorial. 12 October, pp 4–4
Newcastle Morning Herald (1956) 14 February, pp 1–1
Newcastle Morning Herald (1962) 3 January, pp 2–2

Ocasio-Cortez A (2019) A new green deal: house of representatives resolution 109. United States House of Representatives, Washington, DC. https://www.congress.gov/116/bills/hres109/BILLS-116hres109ih.pdf

Pollard S (1965) The genesis of modern management: a study of the Industrial Revolution in Great Britain. Edward Arnold, London

Preston B (2019a) Gloucester Resources Limited v Minister for Planning. Land and Environment Court of New South Wales. https://www.caselaw.nsw.gov.au/decision/5c59012ce4b02a5a800be47f

Preston B (2019b) The impact of the Paris agreement on climate change litigation and law. Dundee Climate Conference, 27–28 September. University of Dundee, Dundee. http://www.lec.justice.nsw.gov.au/Documents/Speeches%20and%20Papers/PrestonCJ/Preston%20CJ%20-%20The%20Impact%20of%20the%20Paris%20Agreement%20on%20Climate%20Change%20Litigation%20and%20Law.pdf

Roberts SH (1935) The squatting age in Australia, 1835–47. Melbourne University Press, Melbourne

Ross E (1970) A history of the Miners Federation of Australia. Australasian Coal and Shale Employee's Federation, Sydney

Steketee M, Cockburn M (1986) Wran: an unauthorised biography. Allen & Unwin, Sydney

Svensen S (1989) The shearers' war: the story of the 1891 shearers' strike. University of Queensland Press, St Lucia

Swoboda K (2013) Energy prices – the story behind rising costs. Parliament of Australia, Canberra. https://www.aph.gov.au/About_Parliament/Parliamentary_Departments/Parliamentary_Library/pubs/BriefingBook44p/EnergyPrices

Tourism Australia (2019) Guide to the Hunter valley: give your tastebuds a serious thrill in Australia's oldest wine growing region, Tourism Australia. https://www.australia.com/en/places/sydney-and-surrounds/guide-to-the-hunter-valley.html

Turner JW (1964) An incident at Minmi, 1895. Labour Hist 6:3–9

Turner JW (1980) Manufacturing in Newcastle, 1801–1900. Newcastle City Council, Newcastle

Turner JW (1982) Coal mining in Newcastle 1801–1900. Newcastle City Council, Newcastle

Twiss H (1828/1982) The terms of the 1828 agreement between the secretary of the state for the colonies and the Australian Agricultural Company. In: Turner JW (ed) Coal mining in Newcastle 1801–1900. Newcastle City Council, Newcastle

Ville S (2005) The relocation of the international market for Australian wool. Aust Econ Hist Rev 45(1):73–95

Visitor (1900) A glimpse of Newcastle. Newcastle Morning Herald, 2 May, pp 3–3

Walker A (1945) Coaltown: a social survey of Cessnock, NSW. Melbourne University Press, Melbourne

Wood WA (1972) Dawn in the valley: the story of settlement in the Hunter river valley to 1833. Wentworth Books, Sydney

Wren DA, Bedeian AG (1972/2017) The evolution of management thought. Wiley, New York

Index

A
Aboriginal inhabitants, 1457
Academy of Management (AOM), 4
Action research technique, 867
Action theory, 622
Active labour, 418
　market policy, 1171–1172
Actor-network theory (ANT), 947
A Discourse on the Arts and Sciences, 661
Adriaansen, H., 1173
Advances to Workers Act 1906, 1415
Aesthetics, 844
Africa
　Bantu-speaking people and Islam, 1190–1194
　Egyptian civilisation, 1187–1190
　management and organisation, 1196–1203
　pre-colonial management, 1203–1204
　societies in East and Southern, 1195–1196
African management, three phases of global interaction, 1209
Africapitalism, 1226
A History of Management, 26
Air New Zealand, 1423
Allen, R.C., 451
All India Council for Technical Education (AICTE), 1340, 1341
Alternative business history (ABH), 1395, 1401
Althusser, Louis, 655
Aluminium smelting, 1455, 1456, 1459
Amalgamated Shearers Union (ASU), 1442
Ancient Egypt
　Athenian democracy, 116
　capital intensity, 116
　farmer's market, 114
　Great Pyramids, 115
　legal attributes, 117
　legally free workers, 116
　machine power, 116

Andrews, C.M., 75
Andrews model, 791
An Essay on Economic Theory, 347, 349, 353
A New History of Management, 654, 655
Anglo-Saxon systems, 1142
Anglosphere, 1076, 1078
Ankersmit, Frank, 647
Anna Karenina, 1107
Ansoff, H.I., 791–793
Antagonism, 1447
Antibiotics, 751
Anti-Hawthorne movement, 556
ANTi-history approach, 98–99, 405
Anti-imperialism sentiments, 1278
Antiquity
　agricultural wealth, 141
　architectural marvels, 133
　civilizations, 154
　dry-land farming, 142–144
　entrepreneurial business pathways, 135
　failure of empire, 171–174
　geographic and economic diversity, 141
　Germanic cultures, 148
　Hellenic Mediterranean, 156–162
　managerial and economic performance in, 137–140
　maritime powers, 145
　nomadic horse people, 146–147
　Roman legacy, 174–177
　Roman Republic, 162–171
　Roman society, 133–137
　wheat trade, 139
Anti-semitism, 625
Anti-union activism, 833
Anti-union politics, 832
Aquinas, St. Thomas, 220
Aphorism, 1029
Arab Spring movement, 1084
Archaeological approach, 674

Aristotelian philosophy, 220
Asia
   jurisdictions, 1318
   management convergence in, 1319–1327
Asian Tigers, 1301–1306
Athenian democracy, 135
Atlantic economy, 1209
Atomistic and individualistic transactions, 368
A Treatise on Human Nature, 328, 346, 357
Attraction-selection-attrition model, 629
Auckland Regional Authority (ARA), 1425
Australia
   paradoxes, 1432
   resource-based industries, 1432
   urbanized societies, 1432
   See also Hunter Valley
Australian Agricultural Company
   (AA Co.), 1435
Australian Aluminium Council, 1455
Australian Council of Trade Union
   (ACTU), 983
Australian Dairy Revolution, 1449
Australian financial institution, 1441
Australian industrialization, 1447
Australian management, 1294–1296
Australian union density, 990–994
Australian workforce
   in blue-collar and low-wage service
      industries, 974
   high-paid, medium-paid and low-paid
      workers, 977
   union density and blue-collar
      workforce, 980
   in white-collar and scientific industries, 975
Australia's gross domestic product, 278
Australia union membership, 992–993
Authority, 1060
Automobile industry, 1014–1017

B
Babbage, Charles, 482
   computer and management, work on, 483
   economic principles of manufacturing, 484
   education, 483
   innovations, 484
   narcissism, 484
Bank of New Zealand (BNZ), 1424
Barack Obama, 952, 961, 962
Barnard, Chester, 578, 581–584, 784–785
Barthes, Roland, 651
Bedeian, A.G., 5, 8, 13, 14, 17, 19, 587
Behavior, 629
Belgium, 1167

Belnaves, M., 908
Bentham's principle of utility, 369
Berkeley, George, 323, 656
Bilhad-al-Sudan, 1190
Bill of exchange, 203–204
Bingham, Walter Van Dyke, 573, 575
Bio-politics, 675, 684, 687
Bio-power, 685, 693
Black Economic Empowerment (BEE), 1253,
   1257, 1261
Blake, William, 661
Bombay's textile industry, 1335
Branding, 843, 846
Brands, 843
Braudel, Fernand, 31, 332, 451, 1076
Britain
   agricultural advantage, 34
   canals and seaborne coal trade, 36
   factory managers, 29
   industrial revolution in, 34, 273
   textile industry, 27
British and US coal output, 276
British bureaucratic model, 1334
British coal production, 125, 126
British education system and policy, 1338
British empiricism, 327, 330, 336
British management
   Churchill, 599
   education and culture, 600–605
   enterprise calculation, 876
   Georgian period, 599
   managerial capacity in UK companies,
      883–885
   Marlborough, 599
   piecework systems, 874
   retail price maintenance, 877
   structure and performance, 879–883
   Tavistock group, 608–609
   Taylorism, Fordism, and human relations in,
      605–608
   from 1870 to 1940, 596–599
   Urwick, L., 605
British military, 863, 865, 869
British wool imports, 274, 1439, 1440
British workplaces, 916
Bunge, Mario, 653
Burke, Edmund, 329, 330
Burnham, James, 507
Burrell & Morgan study, 1052–1053,
   1055–1057
Business, epistemological foundations
   empiricist tradition, 326–333
   idealist tradition, 333–339
   logic, 339–342

Business education, 847, 849
Business knowledge, 847
Business leadership, 1027
Business models, 1027
Business policy, 783, 788–789
Business power, 837
Byzantium, 1112
  independent soldier-peasantry, 1114
  Orthodox population, 1114
  rural tax, 1120

C
Calculative mentality, 227–234
Calvinism, 31, 445
Camus, Albert, 641, 642, 674, 676, 683, 692, 694, 700, 718
Canadian union membership, 995–998
Canoe house system, 1201
Cantillon, Richard, 347, 349, 352, 355, 363
Capital-intense mining techniques, 1452
Capitalism, 27, 30, 36, 40, 388–391, 412, 423, 688, 1076, 1079, 1325–1326
  benefits and drawbacks, 414
  commercial, 31
  impersonal production processes, 428
  in India, 422
  industrial, 31
  labour, 414
  profits, 416
  proletariat and the bourgeois, 426
Capitalist enterprises, 1240
Capitalist roaders, 1361
Capital theory, 775
Caribbean trade, 1076
Carthaginian peace, 763
Catholic legacy, 222–227
  Catholic Church, 222
  Christian denominations, 222
  Church theologian, 223
  dogma, 223
  ethical rules, 222
  faith, 224
  monasteries, 225
  monastic movement, 226
  puritan work, 225
  Western European culture, 225
Centralised wage fixation, 1295
Centre for Labor Market Research (CARMA), 1165
Ceteris paribus, 380
Chandler Jr., Alfred D., 29, 290–294
  academic career, 803
  books, 804, 805

business history field knowledge, 804
career, 802
cooperative capitalism, 808
critiques, 809–817
enterprise as dynamic process, 807
intellectual influence, 803
personal capitalism, 808
Scale and Scope, 802, 809
strategic management concepts, 806
Strategy and Structure, 802
The Visible Hand, 802
works, 802
Child labor, 33
Chinese Communist Party (CCP)
  docile bodies and minds for socioeconomic development, 1375–1378
  low-quality workers, 1379–1380
  thought management and governmental policies, 1373–1375
Chinese histories, 1354, 1355
Chinese management, 1306
  All-China Federation of Trade Unions (ACFTU), 1308
  cult-of-personality approach, 1309
  cultural revolution, 1306
  Deng's tripartite system, 1309
  employment relations, 1310
  Maoist communist principles, 1307
Chinese Working Class, 1357–1363
Christianity, 1074
Chucknorris facts site, 942
Cipolla, C.M., 451
Civilisation, 1186
Civilization and Capitalism, 31
Civil society, 1438
Civil War, 567
Clapham, J., 452–455
Clarke, Roger, 938
Classical economics
  gross domestic product, 353
  intrinsic value and market price, 353, 354
  productive and unproductive labor, 351, 352
  productive capacity, 352
  wealth and productive capital, 352
Climate change, 1456
Clutha development, 1452
Coal-fired power-stations, 1433, 1457
Coal mining, 1437, 1438, 1443, 1445, 1448, 1450, 1452, 1455, 1457
Colbertistic approach, 1152
Collapse of theory, 1058–1063
Collective bargaining model, 1002
Columbus syndrome, 62

Combination Act 1799, 283
Commercial capitalism, 31
Commodity, 373
Common Rule, 300
Communist Manifesto, 27, 413, 419–420
Competitive advantage, 795
Competitive strategy, 794
Compulsory Competitive Tendering (CCT), 849
Computing technology, 846
Conciliation and Arbitration Act, 1295
Conciliation Board, 1166
Condition of the Working-Class in England, 38
Confectionary, 844
Confederation of Danish Employers, 1165
Confucianism, 1357
Confucian rules, 1354–1357
Confucian values, 1373, 1375
Conseil National du Crédit et du Titre, 1157
Conspiracy theories, 540
Consumer markets, 1444
Consumer's direct demand, 382
Consumer surplus, 379
Context, 77–81
Contingency theory, 1321
Cooke's approach, 54
Cooperation, 559
Co-opetition, 851
Copernicus, Nicholas, 322, 339
Corporate governance, 1142
  evolution of, 1148–1150
  French, 1144–1147 (*see also* French corporate governance)
  institutional change theory, French, 1150–1159
Corruption, 1458
Council for Higher Education (CHE), 1255, 1258, 1260
Council of Ministers, 1175
Counterfactual analysis, 1272
COVID-19, 1017, 1020, 1021, 1023, 1024
Creative destruction, 289
Critical management, 7
Critique of Practical Reason, 324
Critique of Pure Reason, 32
Croce, B., 729–731
Cultural inertia, 1152
Cunningham, Hugh, 33, 484
Customer-centricity, 843, 853
Customer control, 845
Customer-perceived quality, 852
Cyber communicator, 1014

D

Daily grain wage, 448
Danish Confederation of Trade Unions, 1165
Danish Model
  active labor market policy, 1171–1172
  flexible labor market, 1169–1170
  history of, 1164–1169
  income security, 1170
  liquidation, 1177–1180
Danish system, 1079
Dansk Arbejdsgiverforening (DA), 1165
Dark Ages, 218
Darnton's work, 77
Darwin, Charles, 568
Dasein (being-in-the-world), 678
Data-driven marketing, 845
Data kept scientific management theory, 895
Data mining, 845
Deakinite Compromise, 1446
Deconstructionism, 653, 654, 711, 712
Deindustrialization, 827, 828, 1456
Deming, W.E., 1296
Demobilization, 864–866
Democracy, 676
Deng Xiaoping Theory, 1374
Denmark, 1076, 1079
Department of Bantu Education (DBE), 1252
Department of Trade and Industry (DTI), 1253
Dependency theory, 1392
Derrida, Jacques, 8, 315, 636, 638, 641, 642, 646, 648, 652, 653, 672, 674, 678, 679, 681, 683, 692, 725, 741, 1074
  deconstructionist methodology, 658, 703–704
  and Foucault, M., 701
  knowledge, 706
  language, 708–710
  philosophy, 701
  radical arguments, 649
  social and political critic, 714–717
  spirit concept, 705–706
  western intellectual heritage, 710–713
De samvirkende Fagforbund, 1165
de Saussure, Ferdinand, 648, 651
Descartes, Rene, 335
Detroit Automobile Company, 524
Development ideology, 1390–1391
Development of Capitalism in Russia, 1127
Dewey, John, 568, 576
Digital business strategy, 1028
Digital divide, 1023
Digital economy, 1013, 1016, 1019, 1021, 1026, 1028, 1029

Digital epoch
  disrupting practice, 1028
  ethical perspectives, 1026, 1027
  landscape, 1027, 1028
  technology, power and organizational context, 1029, 1030
  virtual worlds and organizational directions, 1025, 1026
Digital interconnections, 1012
Digital personae, 938
  active, 938
  passive, 939
Digital revolution, 1022, 1026
Diplomacy, 851
Disciplinary power, 684
Disciplinary society, 686, 687
Discourses, 1370
  of development, 1380
  governmental, 1375
  poverty-relief, 1377
  quality development, 1379
  weiwen, 1372
Discrimination, 685
Diversification, 1241
Divine kingship phenomenon, 1188
Division of labor, 348, 359
Division of labour, 414, 416, 428
Docility, 1355, 1371, 1375–1378
Driving forces, 621
Drucker, Peter, 662, 786–788
Dry-land farming, 142–144
Durepos, G., 8, 9, 15, 17
Durham formula, 1279
Dutch East India Company, 1240

E
Eastern Cape province of South Africa, 1195
East India company, 205
Economic liberalism, 918
Economics
  classical economics, 350–356
  economic outcomes, 347
  French economy, 347
  political economy, 347
  society and markets, 356–362
Economy, 1240, 1241, 1244, 1245, 1247, 1249, 1250, 1253, 1255, 1256, 1260, 1265
Electricity generation, 1451
Emerging markets
  "Alternative Business History" (ABH) of, 1395

  economic development in, 1395
  Latin American, 1389
Emiratisation, 1096
Empiricism, 314, 317
Employee savings plan, 530
Employee security, 1079
Employment Relations Research Centre, 1165
Engels, Frederick, 27, 34, 38, 349, 443
English cast-iron production, 440
English-language admission test, 1343
Ensminger's plans, 1342
Entrepreneurial failure, 1271–1272
Entrepreneurs, 1270, 1274
Entrepreneurship in colonial Africa, 1271
  colonization of Africa and corrosion of tribal communities, 1275–1277
  counterfactual analysis, 1272
  economic factors, 1280–1282
  factors inhibiting the rise in underdeveloped countries, 1275–1282
  literature search, 1272
  nationalism, 1277–1280
  periodization, 1272
  politico-legal frameworks, 1274
  problems of underdevelopment, 1273
  source criticism, 1272
Environmental consciousnesses, 1014–1017
Environs, 1435
Episteme, 681
Epistemology, 398, 401, 406
Ethnocentrism, 8
European commercial capitalism, 31
European Commission, 1164
European Convention on Human Rights, 1179
European economy
  evolution of, 247–248
  quest for gold, 248–249
European Enlightenment, 32, 323, 326, 330, 346
European population, 192–194
European Working Conditions Survey, 925
Europe's Classical Age, 680
Eurostat, 1176
Evidence and knowledge, 398
Exchange value, 370
  of home bread, 373
  milk, 375
  Mill's concept, 375
Executive education, 1257, 1258, 1262, 1263
Existentialism, 678, 679, 692
Expatriate businessmen, 1214

F

Facebook, 940, 1017–1021
Factory Act 1833, 36
Facts, example of, 68
Factual evidence, 69
False news, 936
Fascism, 546
Fayol, Henri, 488
Fechner, G.T., 567
Female workforce participation, 10
Feudalism
   historical experience, 187–190
   modernity, 184–187
   Western feudalism, 190–192
   world of production (*see* Medieval and early modern life)
Financialization, 918
Financial systems, 203–206
Finland, 1167, 1174
First global economy
   Chandler, railroads, management and markets, 291–295
   immigration to United States, 286
   industrial/managerial revolution, 279–285
   management, slavery and colonial subjugation, 295–297
   Victorian and Chicago benchmark wheat prices, 288
   workers and problems, 297–301
First World War, 576–578
Five forces, 794
Flexicurity, 1079
   definition, 1172–1173
   EU policy, 1175–1177
   in Nordic countries, 1174
Follett, Mary Parker, 579–581
Forced labour, 40
Force field analysis, 621
Ford, Henry, 522, 906
   anti-semitic comments, 540
   biography, 523–526
   black employees, 530–531
   business practices, 522
   contribution to management thought, 528
   corporate governance, 534–536
   five-dollar day, 528–529
   hatred of Jews, 539
   Jacksonian viewpoint and ideology, 526–527
   management talent, 536
   narcissism, 539
   sociological department and savings plan, 529–530
   Taylorism, 532–534
   unions and politics, 531–532
Ford Foundation, 1342, 1343
Fordism, 528, 533–534, 894–896
Fordist work method, 983
Ford Motor Company, 526
Foreign capital markets, 1241
Foucault, Michel, 8, 9, 16, 28, 32, 313, 315, 325, 337, 349, 362, 636, 637, 639, 640, 646, 649, 657, 700–702, 704, 709, 717, 725, 734–736, 946
   analysis, 655
   archaeological/genealogical approach, 674
   governmentality, 1369–1371
   history, 672, 673
   language and culture, discussions of, 655
   1945-1970, 677–682
   1970-1978, 682–687
   1978-1984, 687–692
   the rebel, 675
   power and uses, 655
   thinking, 664
Fourth Labour Government, 1418, 1423, 1424
France, 1076, 1078, 1079
Frankenstein, 661
French corporate governance
   capital stakes of international investors and consequences, 1156–1159
   historical roots, 1144–1147
   institutional entrepreneurs, 1153–1156
   traditional mental pattern, 1151–1153
French economy, 347
French Revolution, 331
Full time marketers (FTMs), 850

G

Galenson, W., 1164
Galton, Frances, 577
#Gamergate, 942
Gaps model, 853
Genealogical approach, 674, 684, 686
Genealogy, 1353–1354
General and Industrial Management, 488, 491
General Motors, 535, 538, 539
General Theory of Employment, Interest and Money, 361
George-Wren-Greenwood-Bedeian tradition, 739
German totalitarianism, 678
German vocational skill system, 917
German workplaces, 917
Germany, 1179

Ghent system, 1167
Gig economy, 973
Gilbreth, Frank Bunker, 570, 572
Gilbreth, Lillian Moller, 570, 572
Glacier Project, 867
Global economy, 1076, 1077
Global Financial Crisis, 359
Globalization, 919
Global sporting events, 846
Godard, J., 908
Golden age
   demise of, 917–919
   economy, 825–829
   and industrial pluralism, 914–917
   society, 829–833
   workplaces, 833–836
Good neighbour' policy, 784
Gordon, A., 1297
Gove, M., 906
Governmentality, 674, 687, 1369–1371
Grain wages, 194–195
Great Britain, 596
   industrial state, 597
   Taylorism, Fordism, and human relations in, 605–608
Great Depression, 1447
   elections, 965
   inequality, 954
   Laissez-Faire ideology, 953, 959
   opposite reactions, 957
   public policy mistakes, 959
   Ronald Reagan, 960
   severe crises, 956
   Wall street, 961
Great Inflation, 124
Great recession, *see* Great Depression
Greek culture, 158–162
Greenwood, Ronald, 5, 7, 13
Green workers, 828
Grenznutzen, 377
Gross domestic product (GDP), 10, 352, 1432
Group dynamics, 622
Growth Share Matrix, 846
Growth vector components' matrix, 791
Grumpy Cat, 940
Grunwick strike, 832
Gulf Cooperation Council (GCC), 1092–1095
Gutman, Herbert, 513

H
Hargadon, Andrew, 506
Harvard Business School, 789
Hawthorne and human relations, 547

Hawthorne studies, 56–58, 71, 79
Hayek, Friedrich, 360
   articles, 758
   debate with Keynes, 773–776
   supporter of laissez-fair economics, 758
Hearst, William Randolph, 936
Heavy manufacturing
   capital-intensity and labor productivity, 1453
   coal production, 1448
   consumer-driven needs, 1447
   economic growth, 1451
   galvanized iron sheeting, 1446
   Hunter Valley's pastoral sector, 1448
   iron and steel production, 1450
   JCB mines, 1452
   local markets, 1449
   managerial practices and problems, 1446
   mechanization, 1450
   milk production and products, 1449
   national wealth and employment, 1448
   political and economic changes, 1446
   power industry, 1451
   protectionist policies, 1446
   steel-making, 1448
   unionized environment, 1447
   wine-growing, 1453
Hegel, Georg, 323, 335, 337, 656
Heidegger, Martin, 636, 640, 650, 652, 705–707
Herbert, J.F., 567
Herschel, John, 483
H-4 Hercules concept, 904
Higgling of the market, 999
Hindess, Barry, 937
Historical context, 61
Historic Compromise, 1446
Historicism, 732
Historic turn, 638
History of the Peloponnesian War, 326, 327
Hobbes, Thomas, 30, 323, 326, 327, 356, 357
Homo œconomicus, 690
Horse-breeding, 1433, 1452
Human capital, 256–257, 1248
Human intentionality, 848
Humanities, 847
Human reality, 672
Human relations movement, 461
Human relations programs, 554
Human resource management (HRM), 566, 914, 920, 921, 923, 925, 927
   emergence of, 569
   in Europe, 567

Human resource management (HRM) (*cont.*)
  function, 927
  and high performance paradigm, 921
  practitioners, 926
  professional, 924
  total quality management systems, 921
Hume, David, 328, 329, 346
Hunter District Miners Protective Association, 1443
Hunter Thoroughbred Breeders Association, 1433, 1438
Hunter Valley
  agriculture, 1434
  economic and political power, 1436
  entrepreneurial and managerial success, 1435
  knowledge economy, 1437
  nineteenth century, 1438–1445
  political connections, 1435
  power stations, 1433
  research value factors, 1434
  residents, 1432
  resource-based riches, 1433
  thermal coal, 1432
  time-honoured Valley tradition, 1436
  twentieth century, 1445–1454
  twenty-first century, 1454–1457
  wealth creation, 1438
  wine industry, 1433
Husserl, E., 652, 701, 705–708
Hypercompetition, 795

I

Iberian Peninsula, 266
Idealism, 314–317
Idealist philosophy, 656
Ideological bent, 1320
Ideological State Apparatus, 679, 680
Illicit government-business relationships, 1458
Income compression, 1030
Income security, 1170
India, 414, 422–423
Indian independence movement, 1339
Indian Industrial Commission, 1340
Indian Institutes of Management (IIM), 1343
Indian management, 1292
  Bombay's textile industry, 1335
  British colonialism, 1333
  illegalisation of traditional work organisation, 1334
  instruments and concepts for, 1345
  railways, 1334
  self-criticism, 1345
  spinning mill, 1335
  state driven institutionalisation of education, 1340
  traditional flexible manufacturing system, 1333
Indian managing-agent firm, 1337
Indigenous management factors, 1224
Indonesia, 1311–1313
Industrial capitalism, 8, 16, 17, 31, 36, 349, 914
Industrial Conciliation and Arbitration Act 1894, 1416
Industrial Development Corporation, 1247
Industrialization, 388, 397, 405
  thesis, 1322–1325
Industrial Marketing and Purchasing (IMP), 851
Industrial-organizational (I-O) psychology, 573, 576
Industrial psychology, 576
Industrial relations, 914
  affluent worker, 835
  business roundtable, 832, 833
  car plant, 835
  class and community, 830
  declinism, 827
  deindustrialization, 827, 828
  distribution of employment, 827
  earthmoving equipment factory, 834
  female union membership, 829
  gender, 831
  green workers, 828
  Grunwick strike, 832
  labour government, 826
  legal environment, 831
  racism, 829
  RCA, 828
  real wages, 825, 826
  right-to work laws, 828
  social authority, 834
  social justice, 830
  Trico strike, 832
  UAW, 829, 833
  union-channel worker directors, 833
Industrial relations systems, 1323
Industrial Revolution, 27, 29, 31, 32, 34, 35, 37, 38, 41, 184, 322, 346, 350
  Clapham, J., 452–455
  Nef, J., learning and public life, 447–452
  Pollard, S. and modern management, 462–467

Index 1473

prehistory in the sixteenth and seventeenth century, 440
Thompson, E.P., capitalism and management, 455–459
Toynbee, A. and Tawney, R.H. on, 441–446
Webbs, B., capitalism and management, 459–462
Industrial smelting, 133
Industrial sociology., 554
Inequality, 954–956
Information age
  financial implications, 1020
  image rehabilitation and redemption, 1020
  innovation, 1019
  personally identifiable user information, 1018
  philanthropic allocations, 1019
  privacy controls and buying competitors, 1018
  revenue-producing insights, 1021
  risk factors, 1019
  social media revolution, 1017
Innovation ecosystems, 1027
Institutional change
  economic theory of, 1148–1150
  French corporate governance, 1150–1159
  theory, 1152
Institutional reforms, 1218
Institutional statesmanship, 786
Interconnectedness, 1013, 1014, 1016
Intercontinental trade, 264
International Labour Organization (ILO), 1166, 1179
International Trade Union Confederation (ITUC), 40
Internet era, 1017
Intra-organizational relationship magnitude, 257–258
Investment, 767–769, 771
Iron and Steel Corporation, 1247
ISIS Twitter, 943
Islam, 1075

J
Jackson's policies, 74
Jacques, R., 8, 15, 17
Jajmani system, 1333
James, William, 568
Japan, 1169, 1296–1301
Japanese management
  jobs for life, 1297–1298
  Labor Standards Act, 1300

legal framework, 1299
organised labor, 1298
participatory decision-making, 1298
trend in, 1299
Johannesburg Stock Exchange, 1240
Joint Coal Board (JCB), 1451
Joullié, J-E., 909

K
Kahn, R.
  and Keynes' ideas, 766–767
  multiplier theory, 765
Kanem Empire, 1191
Kant, Immanuel, 32, 314, 324, 335, 340, 566, 568
Katz and Darbishire's four pattern formulation, 1326–1327
Kellner, Hans, 660
Kennedy, David, 576
Keynes, John Maynard, 38, 272, 361, 756
  debate with Hayek, 773–776
  economist, 756
  employment, 758
  factors influencing investment, 771–772
  free market, 773
  and Henderson, 768
  with Kahn, 757
  multiplier, 768
  peace, economic consequences of, 759–765
  real classical model, 771
  revolutionary solution, 769
  unemployment fund, 767
  wages and price, 772–773
Keynesian economics, 770
Keynesian thinking, 751
King, Michael, 1412
Kingdom of Ghana, 1191
Kingdom of Saudi Arabia (KSA), 1084
  Al-Saud rule, 1088
  capture of Riyadh, 1086
  command economy, 1088
  criminal trials, 1087
  opaque nature of management, 1091
  Saudization, 1090
  with Meccan tribes, 1086
Kloppenberg, J.T., 568, 569
Knowledge, 672
Knowledge-based economy, 1454
Knudsen, W., 535
Kolb's learning cycle, 626
Korean management, 1306

L

Labour, 368, 375
  Exchange, 1168
  force, 928
  force survey, 974
  government, 826
  market, 1079
  movement, 982
  resistance, 914
  stability, 916
Labour and employment practices
  British workplaces, 916
  bureaucratic work organization, 917
  bureaucratic workplace practices, 914
  employee selection, 915
  flexible firm thesis, 921, 922
  German vocational skill system, 917
  ideology *vs.* practice, 922–926
  industrial relations, 914
  Japanese management practices, 919
  job stability, 923
  labour-capital accords, 914
  labour markets, 930
  labour stability and acquiescence, 916
  non-union employers, 916
  performance appraisals, 920
  personnel management and industrial relations, 917
  post-war model of management, 919
  seniority-based benefits, 915
  state social and labour market programs, 915
  team-based work systems, 921
  total quality management systems, 921
  training and development, 920
  unemployment, 914, 915
  union recognition, 916
  union substitution strategy, 916
  US employers, 915
  US-style internal labour markets, 917
Labour-capital accords, 914
Labor Court Act and Mediation Act, 1165
Laissez-Faire ideology, 953–954
Laissez-faire leadership, 624
Lake Macquarie, 1434
Latour, Bruno, 8
Law of diminishing marginal utility, 378
Law popularisation campaign, 1374
Leadership, 864, 869
  challenges, 1017
  connecting, disconnecting and reconnecting crises, 1030, 1031
  digital pandemic epoch, 1012, 1025–1030
  global digital economy, 1012

Levinas, Emmanuel, 652
Lewin, K.
  and Agryis, C., 626
  biography, 617–620
  contribution to management, 620–624
  criticism, 627–630
  criticism of Taylor, 625
  and Mayo, E., 625
  Milgram, S. and Zimbardo, P., 627
  and Minor, 625
  as psychologist, 616
Liberal Government in New Zealand, 1415
Liberalism, 688, 691
Liberation historiography, 726
Lifetime employment, 1297
Lincoln heritage, 77
Linguistic system, 708–710
Linguistic turn, 732
LinkedIn, 1027
Liquidation approach, 878
Literary de-constructionism, 651
Local Authority Trading Enterprises (LATE), 1425
Local Government Act, 1425
Local Government Amendment Act, 1425
Localisation, 1446
Locke, Edwin, 324, 501
Locke, John, 30, 325, 327
Logic of Discovery, 341
Logistics
  definition, 252
  Spaniards process of, 252–253
  supply chain management, 252
Logocentrism, 648
Long-distance trade, 264–266
Lyotard, Jean-François, 349, 655, 660

M

Machavellianism, 629
Madison, James, 476
Madness, 680
Magazine, 844
Main Agreement, 1166
Mainstream management research, 1054–1057
Malcomson, A., 524
Management, 1076, 1077, 1079, 1187
  capital intensity and productivity, 33
  characteristics of, 27
  development, South Africa (*see* South African management)
  division of labour, 29
  estimating costs, 29
  Fayol, Henri, 488

features of, 28
  management-related disciplines, 28
  managerial revolution, 29
  Owen, Robert (*see* Owen, Robert)
  Ure, Andrew, 485
Management education, 847, 849
  dependency theory, 1393
  management as profession and, 1401–1405
Management heterogeneity
  Australia, 1294–1296
  China, 1306–1311
  Indonesia, 1311–1313
  Japan, 1296–1301
  New Zealand, 1293–1294
Management history, 4–13, 19, 73, 89, 310
  ANTi-history, 98–99
  chronological periods, 90
  context, 77–81
  economics, 310–312
  foundations, 94
  historians and creativity, 75–77
  and labor relations, 973
  Mayo's work, 72
  positivist factual truth-claims, 94
  problems, 96–98
  problems of epistemology, 312–318
  theory and quantification, 81–83
  traditional narrative of, 89–91
Management theory, 1048
  birth of, 1049–1052
  idea of, 1063
  theoretical foundations, 1052–1053
Management thinkers, 60–62
Managerial capitalism, 359
Managerialism, 751, 753, 783, 1025
Managerial revolution, 463, 467
Manufacturing sector, Canada, 996
Mao, Z., 1353, 1357
Maori colonisation, 1412
Marian reforms, 168
Maritime people, 155
Market capitalization, 1016
Market economy, 6, 14, 18, 31
Marketers, 851
Marketing, 752
  academic interpretations, 842
  balanced and interdependent relationship, 851
  business education, 847, 849
  business management thinking, 845
  CCT, 849
  consumer-goods sector, 851
  cultures, 843
  definition, 842
  entrepreneurs, 843
  geopolitical environment, 844
  history, 842
  long-term interactive relationships, 851
  management education, 847, 849
  national governments, 849
  operational capabilities, 850
  performance measure, 852
  professional and industry bodies, 843
  scientific management, 843
  service customers, 853
Marketization, 689
Market-method, 14, 19
Marshall, A.
  and neo-classical economics and, 376–382
  Principles of Economics, 368
Marx, Karl, 27, 34, 325, 347, 348, 355, 362, 412
  The British Rule in India, 422–423
  Communist Manifesto, 419–420
  economist, 423–426
  labour-power, 418
  management history, 426–429
  and Proudhon, P.-J., 415–419
  significance of work, 413
  theory of value, 414
  wage labour and capital, 420–422
Marxism, 388, 619, 655, 674, 679
Master of Business Administration (MBA), 848
Matthew effect, 63, 72
Mayo, E., 56–60, 625–626
  findings, 548–550
  in *Fortune* magazine, 555
  Great Depression, 551–553
  humanistic management, 554
  inchoate movement, 556–558
  mayoism, 554
  as therapist, 558–560
MBA program, 1341
Medieval church, 219
Medieval and early modern Europe
  culture and market institutions, 195
  divergence of living standards, 195
  European population, 192–194
  grain wages, 194
Medieval and early modern life
  capital investment, 201
  financial systems, 203–206
  industrialization, 198–201
  manufacture, 202
  Roman antiquity, 196–197
  rural productivity, 197–198
  trade and commerce, 206–209
Mercantilist police state, 688

Merchandising, 846
Metahistory, 658
Middle East, management philosophy and practice
  in Arabian Gulf states, 1092–1095
  in Kingdom of Saudi Arabia, 1085–1092
  in United Arab Emirates, 1095–1097
Middle Eastern oil shock, 691
Miller, P., 75
Mintzberg, H., 782, 792
Model T, 525
Modern industrial enterprise, 751, 782, 786, 791
Modernity and postmodernism, 660
Modern management, 7, 9, 18, 19, 42, 462–463
  characteristics of, 27
  features of, 28
  market-based democracies, 29
  mass markets and production systems, 30
Modern marketing, 843
Monetary revenue, 1242
Money, 379
Moral creativeness, 785
Morse, Samuel, 476
Muldoon, Robert, 1417
Multiunit enterprise, 293
Munsterberg, Hugo, 573–574
Muslim Arab invasion of Africa, 1192

N
Narcissism, 1022
Nascent entrepreneurs, 1274
Nation, State and the Industrial Revolution: The Visible Hand, 31
National African Federation of Chambers of Commerce (Nafcoc), 1253
National Association of Marketing Teachers (NATM), 844
National Association of Teachers of Advertising (NATA), 844
National economic development, 1027
National Labour Market Authority, 1171
National Recovery Administration (NRA), 532
Natural price, 354
Nedbank, 1240
Nef, J., 447–455
Negotiation, 851
Neo-liberalism, 687, 689, 691, 848, 849, 898–903, 918, 920, 979
  advantages, 901
  and age of crisis, 903
  Chilean dalliance, 900
  global economic effects, 902
  tax reduction, 899
Nepotism, 1458
Netherland, 1173, 1174
  economy, 124
Newcastle, 1432, 1434, 1437, 1443, 1448, 1451, 1453, 1454, 1456, 1458
Newcastle District Abattoir Bill, 1459
Newcomen engine, 125
New Criticism, 653
New Deal, 576, 579, 584–586, 952, 953
New Jerusalem, 608
New managerialism, 928–930
New Public Management (NPM), 849
Newshole, 936
Newtonian models, 567
New Zealand, 1291, 1293–1294
  adoption of managerialism, 1420
  European commercial activity in, 1412
  European settlers to, 1412
  4th Labour Government, 1418
  home ownership and creation of welfare state, 1414–1416
  land rights, 1417
  political reforms, impact of, 1423–1426
  privatisation and re-invention of public service, 1418–1422
  "Think Big" projects, 1417
  Treaty of Waitangi, 1413
  women's movement, 1417
Nietzsche, Friedrich, 315, 324, 636, 641, 642, 648, 656
  contribution to postmodernism, 657
Nietzschean philosophy, 393
Non-governmental organisations (NGOs), 1261
Non-human digital personae, 943
Nordic Council of Ministers, 1176
Normalization, 693
North's theory, 1149
Noyau dur, 1147
Numidian, 145
Nurses Professional Association of Queensland (NPAQ), 987–988

O
Obama, Barack, 936
Objectivity in Social Science and Social Policy, 326
Object's utility, 373
Omani traders, 1202

On the Economy of Machinery and Manufactures, 483
OPEC crisis, 897
Oppression, 675, 676
Optimisation, 1321, 1322
Ordoliberalism, 752
Organizational behaviour, 916
Organizational entrepreneurs, 1149
Organizational history, 738
Organizational identities, 1029
Organizational psychology, 750
    definition, 860
    histories of, 861–862
    patronage and professionalization of, 866–868
    planning for demobilization, 864–866
    selection in services, 863–864
    at war, 862–863
Organization for Economic Co-operation and Development (OECD), 1164, 1173, 1176
Organizing model, 984–986
Owen, Robert, 477
    contribution, 481
    failure, 481–482
    ideas and biography, 478–481
    radical reactionary, 477–478
Ownership, 1282
Oxford History of the United States, 69

P
Pain, 372
Paine, Thomas, 483
Pan-African trans-territorial movements, 1277
Pancasila Industrial Relations (PIR), 1312
Panopticon, 684, 693
Paris Peace conference, 757
Part time marketers (PTMs), 850
Pastoralism, 1433, 1441
Peacock, George, 483
People's Republic of China, 41
Performativity, 1048
Periodization approach, 1272
Personal capitalism, 802
Personal data, 845
Personal identity, 683, 691
Pettigrew, A., 628
Phaedrus, 664
Phelan, C., 909
Phillips, U.B., 80
Philosophic idealism
    and empiricism, 398
    German, 402

Philosophy of objectivism, 898
Phoncentrism, 648
Picard, Raymond, 653
Pirenne, Henri, 1075
Pirenne thesis, 1075
Plantation economies, 39
Plato, 334, 340
    knowledge, views about, 651
    Phaedrus, 651
    The Republic, 650
    thesis, 651
Pleasure, 372
Plutocracy, 1025
Political connections, 1457
Political economy, 347, 1241, 1255, 1257, 1260, 1263, 1265, 1452
Political science, 849
Pollard, Sidney, 6, 7, 17, 19, 462–467
Pooled interdependent tasks, 261
Popper, Karl, 313, 324, 325, 332, 333, 341
Porter, M., 793–796
Porter's generic strategies, 852
    of cost leadership, 526
Possessional serfs, 1125
Postan, M., 453
Postmodernism, 9, 68, 95–98, 314, 315, 337, 338, 388, 392, 400, 404, 406, 672, 673, 716
    in business and management studies, 393
    Foucauldian strand, 392
    management research, 1057–1058
    and nature of freedom, 640–642
    Nietzsche to Foucault and White, 655–660
    origins and principles, 636–640
    Plato to Derrida, 650–655
    postmodernist influence, 647
    Rousseau to Lyotard, 660–663
Post-structuralism, 651, 653
Post-war accord, 917, 918
Post-World War II model, 917
Potter, D.M., 83–84
Poverty, 360, 1454–1457
Power, 672, 673, 677, 685, 688
Power-knowledge, 1370, 1371
Pre-modern management
    ancient Egyptians, 114–118
    characteristics, 126
    economy of Netherlands, 124–125
    England mines, 125
    European population, 119
    iron and steel production, 120
    non-agricultural workforce, 118
    production and logistical, 127

Pre-modern management (*cont.*)
  real consumption wages, 122–125
  Roman society, 119
  working class, 118
Prime cost, 354, 380
Principal-agent conflicts, 1025
Principles in Responsible Management Education (PRME), 1263, 1264
Principles of Economics, 348
Principles of Human Knowledge, 335, 656
Principles of Political Economy, 374
Principles of Scientific Management, 500
Private-sector business management, 849
Processuality, 790
Productive and unproductive labor, 351, 352
Professionalization, 844
Professional training, 847
Progressive Era, 577
Progressivism, 502
Protestantism, 31, 221
Proudhon, P.-J., 413, 415–419
Psychology
  Bingham, Walter Van Dyke, 575
  Darwin, Charles, 568
  Dewey, John, 568
  Fechner, G.T., 567
  historical psychology studies, 566
  Kant, Immanuel, 567
  Kloppenberg, J.T., 568
  laboratory, 568
  Munsterberg, Hugo, 573–574
  Scott, Walter Dill, 574–575
  "transformation of psychology", 567
  Viteles, Morris, 575
Public administration, 849
Public Finance Act, 1421, 1422
Public opinion, 1458
Public policy, 890
  and social commentary, 907
  teachers, 892
  Western-style, 903
Public sector, 849
  unions in Canada, 997
Public social expenditure, 10
Pufa movement, 1374
Pullman Boycott, 299
Punch-card technology, 845
Purchasing power, 369, 381

Q
Quality, 1379–1380
Queensland Nurses Union (QNU), 987
Queensland Shearers Union, 1442
Quesnay, Francois, 351, 352

R
Racism, 829
Radical history, 94
Radio Corporation of America (RCA), 828
Rasmussen, P.N., 1173
Rationalism, 848
Real wage, 825, 826
  index, 297
  of skilled building worker, 11
  of unskilled building labourers, 12
Reciprocal interdependent tasks, 262
Reconstruction and Development Programme (RDP), 1253
Reconstruction policies, 80
Rectification campaign, 1357
Red flag law, 526
Reform Darwinism, 569
Refreezing/freezing framework, 620
Rehn-Meidner model, 1168
Relational working, 753
Rengo, 1298
Research Center for Group Dynamics, 620
Research Paradigms, 1053
Resource-based economy, 1437, 1445, 1451, 1453
Respiratory infection, 1017
Restrictive Trade Practices Act 1956, 877
Revolutionary effects, 199
Rhetorical attitude, 739
Riboud's perception, 1152
Ricardo, David, 361, 414, 416, 423, 424, 431
Ricoeur, Paul, 646
Right-to work laws, 828
Robust supply chain
  bargaining power, 261–262
  complexity, 263
  human capital, 256–257
  intra-organizational relationship magnitude, 257–258
  leadership commitment, 255–256
  node criticality, 260–261
  risk management, 258–260
  visibility, 262–263
Rodgers, Daniel, 567
Roman antiquity, 196–197
Roman economic model, 172
Roman empire, economic distribution in, 120
Romanticism, 314, 315, 317, 390, 396, 402
Rousseau, Jean-Jacques, 28, 330, 331, 661, 663, 665, 666
Routine entrepreneurs, 1274
Rowlinson, Michael, 647
Rum Rebellion of 1808, 1438
Russia, 1075, 1076, 1078

and Britain and US, coal production of, 1109
Byzantine experience and heritage, 1113–1116
cast-iron production, 1124–1125
communal values, 1107
Cossack problem, 1129
Emancipation Act, 1131–1132
features of, 1107
formative experiences of people, 1107
historical uniqueness, 1107
ideas, management and Russian reality, 1132–1135
industrial backwardness, 1109
managerial achievements, 1111
military service, 1128–1130
modern management, 1126
Muscovite experience, 1116–1123
population, 1109
putting-out system, 1127
slash-and-burn agriculture, 1108
social prestige, 1128
Russian peasantry, 731
Russian Primary Chronicle, 1107

S

'Sacred king' phenomenon, 1188
Sales, 843, 848, 851, 853
Sartre, J.-P., 672, 674, 676, 678, 682, 683, 692, 693, 700, 712, 718
Saudi Arabia, 1077
Saudization, 1090, 1092
Schneider's framework, 629
Schumpeterian phenomenon, 899
Schutz, Alfred, 945
Scientific management, 533, 605, 751, 843
Scott, Walter Dill, 573–575
Sectoral Charters, 1232
Seddon, Richard, 1415
Self-employment, 975
Self-government, 1436
Self-interest, 788
Self-limitation, 688
Selznick, P., 785–786
September Agreement, 1165
Sequentially interdependent tasks, 261
Servicing model, 984
SERVQUAL, 853
Severe crises, 956–957
Sexuality, 683, 691
Shareholder-orientation, 1158
Sharia law, 1086
Sharif of Mecca, 1086

Sharing of information on progress (SIP), 1264
Shelley, Mary, 661
Shipping tonnages, United States, 276
Shop, Distributive and Allied Trades Association (SDA), 993
Silver and gold deposits in Mexico, 250
Skilled human capital, 1248, 1250
Slavery
　American, 53
　anti-slavery movements, 54
　issue, 51
　treatment, 54
Sloan, A., 537–539
Small business, 1270
Smith, Adam, 35, 329, 346, 348, 351, 353, 355, 357, 363, 414, 416, 424, 431
Social colbertism, 1144
Social conflict, 1437
Social control, 845
Social engineering, 325
Social enlightenment, 618
Social exchange theory, 72
Social identity theory, 1015
Social immobility, 1030
Social institution, 708
Socialism, 1458
Social justice, 830
Social media
　acquisitions, 1018
　connectivity, 1018
　hyper-wealthy, 1019
　MySpace, 1018
　network node, 1013
Social movement unionism, 987–988
Social participation, 676
Social presence, 944
Social proof, 944
Social responsibility, 1012
Social segmentation, 845
Social unionism, 980
Societal and managerial models, 388
Society and scientific revolution, 234–238
　Aristotelian dogma, 237
　Aristotelian mechanics, 238
　electrical apparatus, 235
　French philosopher, 235
　industrial revolution, 235
　nascent scientific revolution, 236
　political philosophy, 236
　politics and civic philosophy, 234
Socioeconomic status, 1023
Songs of Innocence and Experience, 661
South African management, 1260
　business leadership, formal education, 1246–1253

South African management (*cont.*)
  crisis of, 1263
  family, nationalism and global networks, 1241–1246
  market exchanges and enterprise, 1240
  political agenda, 1253–1260
  primary economy, 1241
  PRME, 1264
  SABSA, 1261, 1262
South African Oil and Gas Corporation, 1247
Spanish gold and silver, 251
Spartan's constitution, 157
Spearman, Charles, 577
Spinning jenny, 281
SPIN selling method, 853
Spontaneity, 552
Spontaneous cooperation, 58
Srenis, 1333
Stakeholder management, 790
Stakeholder orientation, 1142
Stampp, K., 80
State Experiments in Australia and New Zealand, 1416
State intervention, 1255, 1256
State-Owned Enterprises Act, 1421
Stealth transmission, 1017
Steam technology, 1320
Stigler's conjecture, 63, 72
Stock exchange finance, 878
Stonewall riots, 683
Strategic actions, 1029
Strategic management, 751, 847
  golden age of design and planning schools, 788–793
  positioning strategy, 793–796
  proto-strategy, 784–788
Strategic planning, 752
Strengths, weaknesses, opportunities and threats (SWOT), 789, 852
Structural analysis, 681
Structural-functionalist-positivist (SFP) research, 1055
Stumpf, C., 618
Supplementary costs, 380
Supply chain management
  and Spanish logistics, 252–253
  Spanish supply chain practices, 254–255
Surplus value, 349, 352, 355, 418–419, 423, 425
  creation, 425
  by labour, 431
Sweden, 1167, 1174

Sydenham's training, 1339
Sydney Milk Zone, 1449, 1452
Syndicate method, 1341

T
Tadpole principle, 442
Tanzania, 1196
Tavistock Institute of Human Relations, 866
Taylor, Frederick Winslow, 55–56, 58–60, 476, 487, 662, 1246
  assumptions, 517
  contribution, 501–502
  criticisms, 507–509
  and peasant culture, 513–515
  Progressivism, relationship to, 502–506
  role, 506–507
  and unions, 509–513
Taylorism, 55–56, 78, 91, 93, 502, 504, 505, 510, 516, 532, 560, 572, 573, 587, 895, 1051
  emergence of, 566
Taylorist work method, 983
Taylor Rule, 901
Technological determinism, 278
Technology strategy, 1028
Textbooks, 847, 853
Thatcherism, 1419
19th century management
  Babbage, Charles, 482–487
  Fayol, Henri, 487–494
  Owen, Robert (*see* Owen, Robert)
  Ure, Andrew, 485–487
The 1908 Companies Act, 874
The Archaeology of Knowledge, 648, 681
The Commonwealth Steel Works, 1446
The Communist Manifesto, 349
The Development of Capitalism in Russia, 1129
The European Grain Invasion, 34
The Fatigue Study, 572
The Genesis of Management, 322
The Genesis of Modern Management, 27, 283, 1455
The Logic of Scientific Discovery, 333
The Making of the English Working Class, 33
The Order of Discourse, 683
The Postmodern Condition, 349
The Practice of Management, 26
The Principles of Scientific Management, 300, 663
The Republic, 334, 650
The Spirit of the Laws, 346, 357

The Visible Hand: The Managerial Revolution in American Business, 291
The Visible Hand, 29
The Wealth of Nations, 29, 35
The Wealth of Nations, 329, 347, 348, 351, 357, 358, 363, 486, 1111
The Wealth of Nations in 1776, 369
Thompson, E.P., 17, 33, 455–459
Thought control, 1358, 1363
Thought management, 1373–1375
Thucydides, 326, 327
Tiberius' program, 168
Time and Being, 650
Towne, Henry, 476
Trade and commerce, 206–209
Trade policies, 919
Trade unionism, 1436
Trade Unionism and the Labor Problem, 300
Trade unions, 829
    decline and academic explanations, 981–988
    and employment relations, 998–1003
    occupational distribution in US, Australia and Canada, 978
    productivity and economic growth, 1000
    real wage growth, 1000, 1001
    sociological transformation, 979
    in United States, Australia, Canada, 988–998
Tradition, 70
Traditional history, 89–91
Trait activation theory, 629
Trans-Atlantic slave trade, 1198
Transformation agenda, 1255, 1257, 1263, 1265
Transplanted society
    bunyip aristocrats and squatters, 1439
    commercial banks, 1441
    English ideas and techniques, 1441
    family-owned and short-lived, 1445
    fundamental business problem, 1444
    Hunter's subsidiary rule, 1443
    labor costs, 1442
    military detachments, 1438
    overdrafts and mortgages, 1440
    pastoral agencies, 1441
    pastoral investment, 1440
    resource-based industries, 1445
    risky expansion, 1444
Transport and General Workers' Union (TGWU), 830
Transvaal University College (TUC), 1246

Treatise on Human Nature, 324
Treaty of Versailles, 761–763
Treaty of Waitangi, 1413
Trico strike, 832
Trump, Donald, 904–909, 936
    economic isolation, 1022
    Facebook leadership privacy violations, 1021
    global economic shocks, 1023
    psychological isolation, 1022
    scientific and intellectual isolationism, 1023
    strategic isolation, 1024
    tax incentives and policies, 1023
Two Treatises on Government, 30
Tyranny, 229

U
Uber phenomenon, 973
Ubuntu, 1077
UK
    affluent worker, 835
    culture clash, 834
    deindustrialization, 827
    distribution of employment, 827
    employers of pluralism, 833
    Ford car plant, 831
    Ford strike, 831
    Grunwick strike, 832
    labour government, 826
    Margaret Thatcher, 827
    racism, 829
    real wages, 825
    social movements, 829
    trade unions, 829
    Trico strike, 832
Unemployment, 914, 915
Unilateral Declaration of Independence (UDI), 1280
Unionism, 1447
Union of Christians (KRIFA), 1167
Union substitution strategy, 916
United Arab Emirates (UAE), 1095–1097
United Automobile Workers (UAW), 829
United Nations Conference on Trade and Development (UNCTAD), 1281
United States, 1169
    cotton exports, 274
United States of American Assembly of Collegiate Schools of Business (AACSB), 1257
United States of American democracy, 76

United States of American Federation of State, County and Municipal Employees (AFSCME), 830
United States of American union membership, 989–992
United States of American union strength, 992
United Steel Companies, 880
Universal theory of management, 605
University of Cape Town (UCT), 1249
University of Pretoria, 1246
University of Stellenbosch (USB), 1249
University of the Witwatersrand, 1250
Urbanization, 132
Ure, Andrew
  birth, 485
  capitalism, 487
  contributions of, 486
  factory system, 485, 486
  management philosophy, 486
  manufacturing, book on, 486
  radical improvements to workers conditions, 487
  role of specialization and division of labor, 487
Urwick, L., 605, 607
USA
  booster-ism, 828
  Business Roundtable, 832
  declinism, 827
  multinational Caterpillar, 834
  RCA, 828
  trade unions, 829
  UAW, 829
  workplace contractualism, 826
Use value, 373
Utility
  Bentham to Mill, 371–376
  Marshall, A. and neo-classical economics and, 376–382

V

Value in exchange, 369, 373
Value in use, 369, 373
Values-centered leadership, 1021
Variable capital, 425
Veblen, Thorstein, 505
Verhoef, Grietjie, 1076, 1077
Vico, Giambattista, 337, 649, 650, 659, 729, 741
Vietnam War, 917
Viteles, Morris, 575

W

Wakefield, William, 1413
Wari system, 1077
Washington Consensus, 919
Water Care management, 1426
Wealth, 1454–1457
Wealth creation, 765
Webbs, B., 459–462
Weber, Max, 30, 32, 36, 325, 341
Weiwen project, 1373
Welfare capitalism, 71, 552, 584–586
Western commerce, 206
Western education system, 1277
Western European
  Aristotelian philosophy, 232, 233
  Calvinism and capitalism, 231
  Catholic dogma, 232
  Catholic faith, 229
  new knowledge elite, 227
  renaissance Italy, 234
  renaissance religious faith, 228
  secular humanism, 228
  tyranny, 229
  Weber-Tawney thesis, 230
Western exchange economy, 1276
Western feudalism, 190–192
Western industrial capitalism, 36
Whig interpretation, 78
Whig tradition, 522
White, Hayden, 9, 636, 641, 656, 658, 659, 673, 674
  Croce, B. and Vico, G., 729
  employment modes, 734
  Foucault Decoded, 735
  graduation, 728
  historical writing, 724
  Holocaust controversy, 736–738
  influence in management history, 738–740
  methodology, 726
  progressive history, 726
  publication, 728
  Romanticism, 733
  strategy by historians, 734
White Australia policy, 1446
White-Collarisation, 1298
Will to power, 675, 687
Wirtz, Peter, 1078
Wisconsin school, 981
Wisman, J.D., 909
Witzel's approach, 102
Woodward, J., 609
Workers Dwelling Act 1905, 1415

Workforce, 1454
Workplace automation, 1029
Workplace employment, 36
Workplace relations, 926
World Bank, 359
Wrege, C., 76
Wren, D., 76
Wren, Dan, 4, 7, 13, 14, 17, 19, 501
Wren's approach, 91
Wulff, Bettina, 936
Wulff, Christian, 936
Wundt, Wilhelm, 568

X
Xenophobia, 1023

Y
Yellow journalism, 941
Yerkes, Robert M., 578